Introductory Econometrics

A MODERN APPROACH

SIXTH EDITION

Jeffrey M. Wooldridge

Michigan State University

CENGAGE
Learning·

Australia · Brazil · Mexico · Singapore · United Kingdom · United States

CENGAGE
Learning®

Introductory Econometrics, 6e
Jeffrey M. Wooldridge

Vice President, General Manager, Social Science & Qualitative Business: Erin Joyner

Product Director: Mike Worls

Associate Product Manager: Tara Singer

Content Developer: Chris Rader

Marketing Director: Kristen Hurd

Marketing Manager: Katie Jergens

Marketing Coordinator: Chris Walz

Art and Cover Direction, Production Management, and Composition: Lumina Datamatics, Inc.

Intellectual Property Analyst: Jennifer Nonenmacher

Project Manager: Sarah Shainwald

Manufacturing Planner: Kevin Kluck

Cover Image: ©kentoh/Shutterstock

Unless otherwise noted, all items © Cengage Learning

For product information and technology assistance, contact us at **Cengage Learning Customer & Sales Support, 1-800-354-9706**

For permission to use material from this text or product, submit all requests online at www.cengage.com/permissions
Further permissions questions can be emailed to permissionrequest@cengage.com

Library of Congress Control Number: 2015944828

Student Edition:
ISBN: 978-1-305-27010-7

Cengage Learning
20 Channel Center Street
Boston, MA 02210
USA

Cengage Learning is a leading provider of customized learning solutions with employees residing in nearly 40 different countries and sales in more than 125 countries around the world. Find your local representative at **www.cengage.com**.

Cengage Learning products are represented in Canada by Nelson Education, Ltd.

To learn more about Cengage Learning Solutions, visit **www.cengage.com**

Purchase any of our products at your local college store or at our preferred online store **www.cengagebrain.com**

Printed in the United States of America
Print Number: 05 Print Year: 2018

Brief Contents

Contents

Preface

My motivation for writing the first edition of *Introductory Econometrics: A Modern Approach* was that I saw a fairly wide gap between how econometrics is taught to undergraduates and how empirical researchers think about and apply econometric methods. I became convinced that teaching introductory econometrics from the perspective of professional users of econometrics would actually simplify the presentation, in addition to making the subject much more interesting.

Based on the positive reactions to earlier editions, it appears that my hunch was correct. Many instructors, having a variety of backgrounds and interests and teaching students with different levels of preparation, have embraced the modern approach to econometrics espoused in this text. The emphasis in this edition is still on applying econometrics to real-world problems. Each econometric method is motivated by a particular issue facing researchers analyzing nonexperimental data. The focus in the main text is on understanding and interpreting the assumptions in light of actual empirical applications: the mathematics required is no more than college algebra and basic probability and statistics.

Organized for Today's Econometrics Instructor

The sixth edition preserves the overall organization of the fifth. The most noticeable feature that distinguishes this text from most others is the separation of topics by the kind of data being analyzed. This is a clear departure from the traditional approach, which presents a linear model, lists all assumptions that may be needed at some future point in the analysis, and then proves or asserts results without clearly connecting them to the assumptions. My approach is first to treat, in Part 1, multiple regression analysis with cross-sectional data, under the assumption of random sampling. This setting is natural to students because they are familiar with random sampling from a population in their introductory statistics courses. Importantly, it allows us to distinguish assumptions made about the underlying population regression model—assumptions that can be given economic or behavioral content—from assumptions about how the data were sampled. Discussions about the consequences of nonrandom sampling can be treated in an intuitive fashion after the students have a good grasp of the multiple regression model estimated using random samples.

An important feature of a modern approach is that the explanatory variables—along with the dependent variable—are treated as outcomes of random variables. For the social sciences, allowing random explanatory variables is much more realistic than the traditional assumption of nonrandom explanatory variables. As a nontrivial benefit, the population model/random sampling approach reduces the number of assumptions that students must absorb and understand. Ironically, the classical approach to regression analysis, which treats the explanatory variables as fixed in repeated samples and is still pervasive in introductory texts, literally applies to data collected in an experimental setting. In addition, the contortions required to state and explain assumptions can be confusing to students.

My focus on the population model emphasizes that the fundamental assumptions underlying regression analysis, such as the zero mean assumption on the unobservable error term, are properly stated conditional on the explanatory variables. This leads to a clear understanding of the kinds of problems, such as heteroskedasticity (nonconstant variance), that can invalidate standard inference procedures. By focusing on the population, I am also able to dispel several misconceptions that arise in econometrics texts at all levels. For example, I explain why the usual R-squared is still valid as a goodness-of-fit measure in the presence of heteroskedasticity (Chapter 8) or serially correlated errors (Chapter 12); I provide a simple demonstration that tests for functional form should not be viewed as general tests of omitted variables (Chapter 9); and I explain why one should always include in a regression model extra control variables that are uncorrelated with the explanatory variable of interest, which is often a key policy variable (Chapter 6).

Because the assumptions for cross-sectional analysis are relatively straightforward yet realistic, students can get involved early with serious cross-sectional applications without having to worry about the thorny issues of trends, seasonality, serial correlation, high persistence, and spurious regression that are ubiquitous in time series regression models. Initially, I figured that my treatment of regression with cross-sectional data followed by regression with time series data would find favor with instructors whose own research interests are in applied microeconomics, and that appears to be the case. It has been gratifying that adopters of the text with an applied time series bent have been equally enthusiastic about the structure of the text. By postponing the econometric analysis of time series data, I am able to put proper focus on the potential pitfalls in analyzing time series data that do not arise with cross-sectional data. In effect, time series econometrics finally gets the serious treatment it deserves in an introductory text.

As in the earlier editions, I have consciously chosen topics that are important for reading journal articles and for conducting basic empirical research. Within each topic, I have deliberately omitted many tests and estimation procedures that, while traditionally included in textbooks, have not withstood the empirical test of time. Likewise, I have emphasized more recent topics that have clearly demonstrated their usefulness, such as obtaining test statistics that are robust to heteroskedasticity (or serial correlation) of unknown form, using multiple years of data for policy analysis, or solving the omitted variable problem by instrumental variables methods. I appear to have made fairly good choices, as I have received only a handful of suggestions for adding or deleting material.

I take a systematic approach throughout the text, by which I mean that each topic is presented by building on the previous material in a logical fashion, and assumptions are introduced only as they are needed to obtain a conclusion. For example, empirical researchers who use econometrics in their research understand that not all of the Gauss-Markov assumptions are needed to show that the ordinary least squares (OLS) estimators are unbiased. Yet the vast majority of econometrics texts introduce a complete set of assumptions (many of which are redundant or in some cases even logically conflicting) before proving the unbiasedness of OLS. Similarly, the normality assumption is often included among the assumptions that are needed for the Gauss-Markov Theorem, even though it is fairly well known that normality plays no role in showing that the OLS estimators are the best linear unbiased estimators.

My systematic approach is illustrated by the order of assumptions that I use for multiple regression in Part 1. This structure results in a natural progression for briefly summarizing the role of each assumption:

MLR.1: Introduce the population model and interpret the population parameters (which we hope to estimate).

MLR.2: Introduce random sampling from the population and describe the data that we use to estimate the population parameters.

MLR.3: Add the assumption on the explanatory variables that allows us to compute the estimates from our sample; this is the so-called no perfect collinearity assumption.

MLR.4: Assume that, in the population, the mean of the unobservable error does not depend on the values of the explanatory variables; this is the "mean independence" assumption combined with a zero population mean for the error, and it is the key assumption that delivers unbiasedness of OLS.

After introducing Assumptions MLR.1 to MLR.3, one can discuss the algebraic properties of ordinary least squares—that is, the properties of OLS for a particular set of data. By adding Assumption MLR.4, we can show that OLS is unbiased (and consistent). Assumption MLR.5 (homoskedasticity) is added for the Gauss-Markov Theorem and for the usual OLS variance formulas to be valid. Assumption MLR.6 (normality), which is not introduced until Chapter 4, is added to round out the classical linear model assumptions. The six assumptions are used to obtain exact statistical inference and to conclude that the OLS estimators have the smallest variances among all unbiased estimators.

I use parallel approaches when I turn to the study of large-sample properties and when I treat regression for time series data in Part 2. The careful presentation and discussion of assumptions makes it relatively easy to transition to Part 3, which covers advanced topics that include using pooled cross-sectional data, exploiting panel data structures, and applying instrumental variables methods. Generally, I have strived to provide a unified view of econometrics, where all estimators and test statistics are obtained using just a few intuitively reasonable principles of estimation and testing (which, of course, also have rigorous justification). For example, regression-based tests for heteroskedasticity and serial correlation are easy for students to grasp because they already have a solid understanding of regression. This is in contrast to treatments that give a set of disjointed recipes for outdated econometric testing procedures.

Throughout the text, I emphasize ceteris paribus relationships, which is why, after one chapter on the simple regression model, I move to multiple regression analysis. The multiple regression setting motivates students to think about serious applications early. I also give prominence to policy analysis with all kinds of data structures. Practical topics, such as using proxy variables to obtain ceteris paribus effects and interpreting partial effects in models with interaction terms, are covered in a simple fashion.

New to This Edition

I have added new exercises to almost every chapter, including the appendices. Most of the new computer exercises use new data sets, including a data set on student performance and attending a Catholic high school and a time series data set on presidential approval ratings and gasoline prices. I have also added some harder problems that require derivations.

There are several changes to the text worth noting. Chapter 2 contains a more extensive discussion about the relationship between the simple regression coefficient and the correlation coefficient. Chapter 3 clarifies issues with comparing R-squareds from models when data are missing on some variables (thereby reducing sample sizes available for regressions with more explanatory variables).

Chapter 6 introduces the notion of an average partial effect (APE) for models linear in the parameters but including nonlinear functions, primarily quadratics and interaction terms. The notion of an APE, which was implicit in previous editions, has become an important concept in empirical work; understanding how to compute and interpret APEs in the context of OLS is a valuable skill. For more advanced classes, the introduction in Chapter 6 eases the way to the discussion of APEs in the nonlinear models studied in Chapter 17, which also includes an expanded discussion of APEs—including now showing APEs in tables alongside coefficients in logit, probit, and Tobit applications.

In Chapter 8, I refine some of the discussion involving the issue of heteroskedasticity, including an expanded discussion of Chow tests and a more precise description of weighted least squares when the weights must be estimated. Chapter 9, which contains some optional, slightly more advanced topics, defines terms that appear often in the large literature on missing data. A common practice in empirical work is to create indicator variables for missing data, and to include them in a multiple regression analysis. Chapter 9 discusses how this method can be implemented and when it will produce unbiased and consistent estimators.

The treatment of unobserved effects panel data models in chapter 14 has been expanded to include more of a discussion of unbalanced panel data sets, including how the fixed effects, random effects, and correlated random effects approaches still can be applied. Another important addition is a much more detailed discussion on applying fixed effects and random effects methods to cluster samples. I also include discussion of some subtle issues that can arise in using clustered standard errors when the data have been obtained from a random sampling scheme.

Chapter 15 now has a more detailed discussion of the problem of weak instrumental variables so that students can access the basics without having to track down more advanced sources.

Targeted at Undergraduates, Adaptable for Master's Students

The text is designed for undergraduate economics majors who have taken college algebra and one semester of introductory probability and statistics. (Appendices A, B, and C contain the requisite background material.) A one-semester or one-quarter econometrics course would not be expected to cover all, or even any, of the more advanced material in Part 3. A typical introductory course includes Chapters 1 through 8, which cover the basics of simple and multiple regression for cross-sectional data. Provided the emphasis is on intuition and interpreting the empirical examples, the material from the first eight chapters should be accessible to undergraduates in most economics departments. Most instructors will also want to cover at least parts of the chapters on regression analysis with time series data, Chapters 10 and 12, in varying degrees of depth. In the one-semester course that I teach at Michigan State, I cover Chapter 10 fairly carefully, give an overview of the material in Chapter 11, and cover the material on serial correlation in Chapter 12. I find that this basic one-semester course puts students on a solid footing to write empirical papers, such as a term paper, a senior seminar paper, or a senior thesis. Chapter 9 contains more specialized topics that arise in analyzing cross-sectional data, including data problems such as outliers and nonrandom sampling; for a one-semester course, it can be skipped without loss of continuity.

The structure of the text makes it ideal for a course with a cross-sectional or policy analysis focus: the time series chapters can be skipped in lieu of topics from Chapters 9 or 15. Chapter 13 is advanced only in the sense that it treats two new data structures: independently pooled cross sections and two-period panel data analysis. Such data structures are especially useful for policy analysis, and the chapter provides several examples. Students with a good grasp of Chapters 1 through 8 will have little difficulty with Chapter 13. Chapter 14 covers more advanced panel data methods and would probably be covered only in a second course. A good way to end a course on cross-sectional methods is to cover the rudiments of instrumental variables estimation in Chapter 15.

I have used selected material in Part 3, including Chapters 13 and 17, in a senior seminar geared to producing a serious research paper. Along with the basic one-semester course, students who have been exposed to basic panel data analysis, instrumental variables estimation, and limited dependent variable models are in a position to read large segments of the applied social sciences literature. Chapter 17 provides an introduction to the most common limited dependent variable models.

The text is also well suited for an introductory master's level course, where the emphasis is on applications rather than on derivations using matrix algebra. Several instructors have used the text to teach policy analysis at the master's level. For instructors wanting to present the material in matrix form, Appendices D and E are self-contained treatments of the matrix algebra and the multiple regression model in matrix form.

At Michigan State, PhD students in many fields that require data analysis—including accounting, agricultural economics, development economics, economics of education, finance, international economics, labor economics, macroeconomics, political science, and public finance—have found the text to be a useful bridge between the empirical work that they read and the more theoretical econometrics they learn at the PhD level.

Design Features

Numerous in-text questions are scattered throughout, with answers supplied in Appendix F. These questions are intended to provide students with immediate feedback. Each chapter contains many numbered examples. Several of these are case studies drawn from recently published papers, but where I have used my judgment to simplify the analysis, hopefully without sacrificing the main point. The end-of-chapter problems and computer exercises are heavily oriented toward empirical work, rather than complicated derivations. The students are asked to reason carefully based on what they have learned. The computer exercises often expand on the in-text examples. Several exercises use data sets from published works or similar data sets that are motivated by published research in economics and other fields.

A pioneering feature of this introductory econometrics text is the extensive glossary. The short definitions and descriptions are a helpful refresher for students studying for exams or reading empirical research that uses econometric methods. I have added and updated several entries for the fifth edition.

Data Sets—Available in Six Formats

This edition adds R data set as an additional format for viewing and analyzing data. In response to popular demand, this edition also provides the Minitab® format. With more than 100 data sets in six different formats, including Stata®, EViews®, Minitab®, Microsoft® Excel, and R, the instructor has many options for problem sets, examples, and term projects. Because most of the data sets come from actual research, some are very large. Except for partial lists of data sets to illustrate the various data structures, the data sets are not reported in the text. This book is geared to a course where computer work plays an integral role.

Updated Data Sets Handbook

An extensive data description manual is also available online. This manual contains a list of data sources along with suggestions for ways to use the data sets that are not described in the text. This unique handbook, created by author Jeffrey M. Wooldridge, lists the source of all data sets for quick reference and how each might be used. Because the data book contains page numbers, it is easy to see how the author used the data in the text. Students may want to view the descriptions of each data set and it can help guide instructors in generating new homework exercises, exam problems, or term projects. The author also provides suggestions on improving the data sets in this detailed resource that is available on the book's companion website at http://login.cengage.com and students can access it free at www.cengagebrain.com.

Instructor Supplements

Instructor's Manual with Solutions

The *Instructor's Manual with Solutions* contains answers to all problems and exercises, as well as teaching tips on how to present the material in each chapter. The instructor's manual also contains sources for each of the data files, with many suggestions for how to use them on problem sets, exams, and term papers. This supplement is available online only to instructors at http://login.cengage.com.

PowerPoint Slides

Exceptional PowerPoint® presentation slides help you create engaging, memorable lectures. You will find teaching slides for each chapter in this edition, including the advanced chapters in Part 3. You can modify or customize the slides for your specific course. PowerPoint® slides are available for convenient download on the instructor-only, password-protected portion of the book's companion website at http://login.cengage.com.

Scientific Word Slides

Developed by the author, Scientific Word® slides offer an alternative format for instructors who prefer the Scientific Word® platform, the word processor created by MacKichan Software, Inc. for composing mathematical and technical documents using LaTeX typesetting. These slides are based on the author's actual lectures and are available in PDF and TeX formats for convenient download on the instructor-only, password-protected section of the book's companion website at http://login.cengage.com.

Test Bank

Cengage Learning Testing, powered by Cognero® is a flexible, online system that allows you to import, edit, and manipulate content from the text's test bank or elsewhere. You have the flexibility to include your own favorite test questions, create multiple test versions in an instant, and deliver tests from your LMS, your classroom, or wherever you want. In the test bank for INTRODUCTORY ECONOMETRICS, 6E you will find a wealth and variety of problems, ranging from multiple-choice to questions that require simple statistical derivations to questions that require interpreting computer output.

Student Supplements

MindTap

MindTap® for INTRODUCTORY ECONOMETRICS, 6E provides you with the tools you need to better manage your limited time—you can complete assignments whenever and wherever you are ready to learn with course material specially customized by your instructor and streamlined in one proven, easy-to-use interface. With an array of tools and apps—from note taking to flashcards—you will get a true understanding of course concepts, helping you to achieve better grades and setting the groundwork for your future courses.

Aplia

Millions of students use Aplia™ to better prepare for class and for their exams. Aplia assignments mean "no surprises"—with an at-a-glance view of current assignments organized by due date. You always know what's due, and when. Aplia ties your lessons into real-world applications so you get a bigger, better picture of how you'll use your education in your future workplace. Automatic grading and immediate feedback helps you master content the right way the first time.

Student Solutions Manual

Now you can maximize your study time and further your course success with this dynamic online resource. This helpful Solutions Manual includes detailed steps and solutions to odd-numbered problems as well as computer exercises in the text. This supplement is available as a free resource at www.cengagebrain.com.

Suggestions for Designing Your Course

I have already commented on the contents of most of the chapters as well as possible outlines for courses. Here I provide more specific comments about material in chapters that might be covered or skipped:

Chapter 9 has some interesting examples (such as a wage regression that includes IQ score as an explanatory variable). The rubric of proxy variables does not have to be formally introduced to present these kinds of examples, and I typically do so when finishing up cross-sectional analysis. In Chapter 12, for a one-semester course, I skip the material on serial correlation robust inference for ordinary least squares as well as dynamic models of heteroskedasticity.

Even in a second course I tend to spend only a little time on Chapter 16, which covers simultaneous equations analysis. I have found that instructors differ widely in their opinions on the importance of teaching simultaneous equations models to undergraduates. Some think this material is fundamental; others think it is rarely applicable. My own view is that simultaneous equations models are overused (see Chapter 16 for a discussion). If one reads applications carefully, omitted variables and measurement error are much more likely to be the reason one adopts instrumental variables estimation, and this is why I use omitted variables to motivate instrumental variables estimation in Chapter 15. Still, simultaneous equations models are indispensable for estimating demand and supply functions, and they apply in some other important cases as well.

Chapter 17 is the only chapter that considers models inherently nonlinear in their parameters, and this puts an extra burden on the student. The first material one should cover in this chapter is on probit and logit models for binary response. My presentation of Tobit models and censored regression still appears to be novel in introductory texts. I explicitly recognize that the Tobit model is applied to corner solution outcomes on random samples, while censored regression is applied when the data collection process censors the dependent variable at essentially arbitrary thresholds.

Chapter 18 covers some recent important topics from time series econometrics, including testing for unit roots and cointegration. I cover this material only in a second-semester course at either the undergraduate or master's level. A fairly detailed introduction to forecasting is also included in Chapter 18.

Chapter 19, which would be added to the syllabus for a course that requires a term paper, is much more extensive than similar chapters in other texts. It summarizes some of the methods appropriate for various kinds of problems and data structures, points out potential pitfalls, explains in some detail how to write a term paper in empirical economics, and includes suggestions for possible projects.

Acknowledgments

I would like to thank those who reviewed and provided helpful comments for this and previous editions of the text:

Erica Johnson, *Gonzaga University*

Mary Ellen Benedict, *Bowling Green State University*

Yan Li, *Temple University*

Melissa Tartari, *Yale University*

Michael Allgrunn, *University of South Dakota*

Gregory Colman, *Pace University*

Yoo-Mi Chin, *Missouri University of Science and Technology*

Arsen Melkumian, *Western Illinois University*

Kevin J. Murphy, *Oakland University*

Kristine Grimsrud, *University of New Mexico*

Will Melick, *Kenyon College*

Philip H. Brown, *Colby College*

Argun Saatcioglu, *University of Kansas*

Ken Brown, *University of Northern Iowa*

Michael R. Jonas, *University of San Francisco*

Melissa Yeoh, *Berry College*

Nikolaos Papanikolaou, *SUNY at New Paltz*

Konstantin Golyaev, *University of Minnesota*

Soren Hauge, *Ripon College*

Kevin Williams, *University of Minnesota*

Hailong Qian, *Saint Louis University*

Rod Hissong, *University of Texas at Arlington*

Steven Cuellar, *Sonoma State University*

Yanan Di, *Wagner College*

John Fitzgerald, *Bowdoin College*

Philip N. Jefferson, *Swarthmore College*

Yongsheng Wang, *Washington and Jefferson College*

Sheng-Kai Chang, *National Taiwan University*

Damayanti Ghosh, *Binghamton University*

Susan Averett, *Lafayette College*

Kevin J. Mumford, *Purdue University*

Nicolai V. Kuminoff, *Arizona State University*

Subarna K. Samanta, *The College of New Jersey*

Jing Li, *South Dakota State University*

Gary Wagner, *University of Arkansas–Little Rock*

Kelly Cobourn, *Boise State University*

Timothy Dittmer, *Central Washington University*

Daniel Fischmar, *Westminster College*

Subha Mani, *Fordham University*

John Maluccio, *Middlebury College*

James Warner, *College of Wooster*

Christopher Magee, *Bucknell University*

Andrew Ewing, *Eckerd College*

Debra Israel, *Indiana State University*

Jay Goodliffe, *Brigham Young University*

Stanley R. Thompson, *The Ohio State University*

Michael Robinson, *Mount Holyoke College*

Ivan Jeliazkov, *University of California, Irvine*

Heather O'Neill, *Ursinus College*

Leslie Papke, *Michigan State University*

Timothy Vogelsang, *Michigan State University*

Stephen Woodbury, *Michigan State University*

Some of the changes I discussed earlier were driven by comments I received from people on this list, and I continue to mull over other specific suggestions made by one or more reviewers.

Many students and teaching assistants, too numerous to list, have caught mistakes in earlier editions or have suggested rewording some paragraphs. I am grateful to them.

As always, it was a pleasure working with the team at Cengage Learning. Mike Worls, my long-time Product Director, has learned very well how to guide me with a firm yet gentle hand. Chris Rader has quickly mastered the difficult challenges of being the developmental editor of a dense, technical textbook. His careful reading of the manuscript and fine eye for detail have improved this sixth edition considerably.

This book is dedicated to my wife, Leslie Papke, who contributed materially to this edition by writing the initial versions of the Scientific Word slides for the chapters in Part 3; she then used the slides in her public policy course. Our children have contributed, too: Edmund has helped me keep the data handbook current, and Gwenyth keeps us entertained with her artistic talents.

Jeffrey M. Wooldridge

About the Author

Jeffrey M. Wooldridge is University Distinguished Professor of Economics at Michigan State University, where he has taught since 1991. From 1986 to 1991, he was an assistant professor of economics at the Massachusetts Institute of Technology. He received his bachelor of arts, with majors in computer science and economics, from the University of California, Berkeley, in 1982, and received his doctorate in economics in 1986 from the University of California, San Diego. He has published more than 60 articles in internationally recognized journals, as well as several book chapters. He is also the author of *Econometric Analysis of Cross Section and Panel Data*, second edition. His awards include an Alfred P. Sloan Research Fellowship, the Plura Scripsit award from *Econometric Theory*, the Sir Richard Stone prize from the *Journal of Applied Econometrics*, and three graduate teacher-of-the-year awards from MIT. He is a fellow of the Econometric Society and of the *Journal of Econometrics*. He is past editor of the *Journal of Business and Economic Statistics*, and past econometrics coeditor of *Economics Letters*. He has served on the editorial boards of *Econometric Theory*, the *Journal of Economic Literature*, the *Journal of Econometrics*, the *Review of Economics and Statistics*, and the *Stata Journal*. He has also acted as an occasional econometrics consultant for Arthur Andersen, Charles River Associates, the Washington State Institute for Public Policy, Stratus Consulting, and Industrial Economics, Incorporated.

CHAPTER 1

The Nature of Econometrics and Economic Data

C hapter 1 discusses the scope of econometrics and raises general issues that arise in the application of econometric methods. Section 1-1 provides a brief discussion about the purpose and scope of econometrics and how it fits into economic analysis. Section 1-2 provides examples of how one can start with an economic theory and build a model that can be estimated using data. Section 1-3 examines the kinds of data sets that are used in business, economics, and other social sciences. Section 1-4 provides an intuitive discussion of the difficulties associated with the inference of causality in the social sciences.

1-1 What Is Econometrics?

Imagine that you are hired by your state government to evaluate the effectiveness of a publicly funded job training program. Suppose this program teaches workers various ways to use computers in the manufacturing process. The 20-week program offers courses during nonworking hours. Any hourly manufacturing worker may participate, and enrollment in all or part of the program is voluntary. You are to determine what, if any, effect the training program has on each worker's subsequent hourly wage.

Now, suppose you work for an investment bank. You are to study the returns on different investment strategies involving short-term U.S. treasury bills to decide whether they comply with implied economic theories.

The task of answering such questions may seem daunting at first. At this point, you may only have a vague idea of the kind of data you would need to collect. By the end of this introductory econometrics course, you should know how to use econometric methods to formally evaluate a job training program or to test a simple economic theory.

Econometrics is based upon the development of statistical methods for estimating economic relationships, testing economic theories, and evaluating and implementing government and business policy. The most common application of econometrics is the forecasting of such important macroeconomic variables as interest rates, inflation rates, and gross domestic product (GDP). Whereas forecasts of economic indicators are highly visible and often widely published, econometric methods can be used in economic areas that have nothing to do with macroeconomic forecasting. For example, we will study the effects of political campaign expenditures on voting outcomes. We will consider the effect of school spending on student performance in the field of education. In addition, we will learn how to use econometric methods for forecasting economic time series.

Econometrics has evolved as a separate discipline from mathematical statistics because the former focuses on the problems inherent in collecting and analyzing nonexperimental economic data. **Nonexperimental data** are not accumulated through controlled experiments on individuals, firms, or segments of the economy. (Nonexperimental data are sometimes called **observational data**, or **retrospective data**, to emphasize the fact that the researcher is a passive collector of the data.) **Experimental data** are often collected in laboratory environments in the natural sciences, but they are much more difficult to obtain in the social sciences. Although some social experiments can be devised, it is often impossible, prohibitively expensive, or morally repugnant to conduct the kinds of controlled experiments that would be needed to address economic issues. We give some specific examples of the differences between experimental and nonexperimental data in Section 1-4.

Naturally, econometricians have borrowed from mathematical statisticians whenever possible. The method of multiple regression analysis is the mainstay in both fields, but its focus and interpretation can differ markedly. In addition, economists have devised new techniques to deal with the complexities of economic data and to test the predictions of economic theories.

1-2 Steps in Empirical Economic Analysis

Econometric methods are relevant in virtually every branch of applied economics. They come into play either when we have an economic theory to test or when we have a relationship in mind that has some importance for business decisions or policy analysis. An **empirical analysis** uses data to test a theory or to estimate a relationship.

How does one go about structuring an empirical economic analysis? It may seem obvious, but it is worth emphasizing that the first step in any empirical analysis is the careful formulation of the question of interest. The question might deal with testing a certain aspect of an economic theory, or it might pertain to testing the effects of a government policy. In principle, econometric methods can be used to answer a wide range of questions.

In some cases, especially those that involve the testing of economic theories, a formal **economic model** is constructed. An economic model consists of mathematical equations that describe various relationships. Economists are well known for their building of models to describe a vast array of behaviors. For example, in intermediate microeconomics, individual consumption decisions, subject to a budget constraint, are described by mathematical models. The basic premise underlying these models is *utility maximization*. The assumption that individuals make choices to maximize their well-being, subject to resource constraints, gives us a very powerful framework for creating tractable economic models and making clear predictions. In the context of consumption decisions, utility maximization leads to a set of *demand equations*. In a demand equation, the quantity demanded of each commodity depends on the price of the goods, the price of substitute and complementary goods, the consumer's income, and the individual's characteristics that affect taste. These equations can form the basis of an econometric analysis of consumer demand.

Economists have used basic economic tools, such as the utility maximization framework, to explain behaviors that at first glance may appear to be noneconomic in nature. A classic example is Becker's (1968) economic model of criminal behavior.

EXAMPLE 1.1	**Economic Model of Crime**

In a seminal article, Nobel Prize winner Gary Becker postulated a utility maximization framework to describe an individual's participation in crime. Certain crimes have clear economic rewards, but most criminal behaviors have costs. The opportunity costs of crime prevent the criminal from participating in other activities such as legal employment. In addition, there are costs associated with the possibility of being caught and then, if convicted, the costs associated with incarceration. From Becker's perspective, the decision to undertake illegal activity is one of resource allocation, with the benefits and costs of competing activities taken into account.

Under general assumptions, we can derive an equation describing the amount of time spent in criminal activity as a function of various factors. We might represent such a function as

$$y = f(x_1, x_2, x_3, x_4, x_5, x_6, x_7), \qquad [1.1]$$

where

y = hours spent in criminal activities,
x_1 = "wage" for an hour spent in criminal activity,
x_2 = hourly wage in legal employment,
x_3 = income other than from crime or employment,
x_4 = probability of getting caught,
x_5 = probability of being convicted if caught,
x_6 = expected sentence if convicted, and
x_7 = age.

Other factors generally affect a person's decision to participate in crime, but the list above is representative of what might result from a formal economic analysis. As is common in economic theory, we have not been specific about the function $f(\cdot)$ in (1.1). This function depends on an underlying utility function, which is rarely known. Nevertheless, we can use economic theory—or introspection—to predict the effect that each variable would have on criminal activity. This is the basis for an econometric analysis of individual criminal activity.

Formal economic modeling is sometimes the starting point for empirical analysis, but it is more common to use economic theory less formally, or even to rely entirely on intuition. You may agree that the determinants of criminal behavior appearing in equation (1.1) are reasonable based on common sense; we might arrive at such an equation directly, without starting from utility maximization. This view has some merit, although there are cases in which formal derivations provide insights that intuition can overlook.

Next is an example of an equation that we can derive through somewhat informal reasoning.

EXAMPLE 1.2	**Job Training and Worker Productivity**

Consider the problem posed at the beginning of Section 1-1. A labor economist would like to examine the effects of job training on worker productivity. In this case, there is little need for formal economic theory. Basic economic understanding is sufficient for realizing that factors such as education, experience, and training affect worker productivity. Also, economists are well aware that workers are paid commensurate with their productivity. This simple reasoning leads to a model such as

$$wage = f(educ, exper, training), \qquad [1.2]$$

where

$wage$	= hourly wage,
$educ$	= years of formal education,
$exper$	= years of workforce experience, and
$training$	= weeks spent in job training.

Again, other factors generally affect the wage rate, but equation (1.2) captures the essence of the problem.

After we specify an economic model, we need to turn it into what we call an **econometric model**. Because we will deal with econometric models throughout this text, it is important to know how an econometric model relates to an economic model. Take equation (1.1) as an example. The form of the function $f(\cdot)$ must be specified before we can undertake an econometric analysis. A second issue concerning (1.1) is how to deal with variables that cannot reasonably be observed. For example, consider the wage that a person can earn in criminal activity. In principle, such a quantity is well defined, but it would be difficult if not impossible to observe this wage for a given individual. Even variables such as the probability of being arrested cannot realistically be obtained for a given individual, but at least we can observe relevant arrest statistics and derive a variable that approximates the probability of arrest. Many other factors affect criminal behavior that we cannot even list, let alone observe, but we must somehow account for them.

The ambiguities inherent in the economic model of crime are resolved by specifying a particular econometric model:

$$crime = \beta_0 + \beta_1 wage_m + \beta_2 othinc + \beta_3 freqarr + \beta_4 freqconv$$
$$+ \beta_5 avgsen + \beta_6 age + u, \quad\quad [1.3]$$

where

$crime$ = some measure of the frequency of criminal activity,
$wage_m$ = the wage that can be earned in legal employment,
$othinc$ = the income from other sources (assets, inheritance, and so on),
$freqarr$ = the frequency of arrests for prior infractions (to approximate the probability of arrest),
$freqconv$ = the frequency of conviction, and
$avgsen$ = the average sentence length after conviction.

The choice of these variables is determined by the economic theory as well as data considerations. The term u contains unobserved factors, such as the wage for criminal activity, moral character, family background, and errors in measuring things like criminal activity and the probability of arrest. We could add family background variables to the model, such as number of siblings, parents' education, and so on, but we can never eliminate u entirely. In fact, dealing with this *error term* or *disturbance term* is perhaps the most important component of any econometric analysis.

The constants $\beta_0, \beta_1, \ldots, \beta_6$ are the *parameters* of the econometric model, and they describe the directions and strengths of the relationship between *crime* and the factors used to determine *crime* in the model.

A complete econometric model for Example 1.2 might be

$$wage = \beta_0 + \beta_1 educ + \beta_2 exper + \beta_3 training + u, \quad\quad [1.4]$$

where the term u contains factors such as "innate ability," quality of education, family background, and the myriad other factors that can influence a person's wage. If we are specifically concerned about the effects of job training, then β_3 is the parameter of interest.

For the most part, econometric analysis begins by specifying an econometric model, without consideration of the details of the model's creation. We generally follow this approach, largely because careful derivation of something like the economic model of crime is time consuming and can take us into some specialized and often difficult areas of economic theory. Economic reasoning will play a role in our examples, and we will merge any underlying economic theory into the econometric model specification. In the economic model of crime example, we would start with an econometric model such as (1.3) and use economic reasoning and common sense as guides for choosing the variables. Although this approach loses some of the richness of economic analysis, it is commonly and effectively applied by careful researchers.

Once an econometric model such as (1.3) or (1.4) has been specified, various *hypotheses* of interest can be stated in terms of the unknown parameters. For example, in equation (1.3), we might hypothesize that $wage_m$, the wage that can be earned in legal employment, has no effect on criminal behavior. In the context of this particular econometric model, the hypothesis is equivalent to $\beta_1 = 0$.

An empirical analysis, by definition, requires data. After data on the relevant variables have been collected, econometric methods are used to estimate the parameters in the econometric model and to formally test hypotheses of interest. In some cases, the econometric model is used to make predictions in either the testing of a theory or the study of a policy's impact.

Because data collection is so important in empirical work, Section 1-3 will describe the kinds of data that we are likely to encounter.

1-3 The Structure of Economic Data

Economic data sets come in a variety of types. Whereas some econometric methods can be applied with little or no modification to many different kinds of data sets, the special features of some data sets must be accounted for or should be exploited. We next describe the most important data structures encountered in applied work.

1-3a Cross-Sectional Data

A **cross-sectional data set** consists of a sample of individuals, households, firms, cities, states, countries, or a variety of other units, taken at a given point in time. Sometimes, the data on all units do not correspond to precisely the same time period. For example, several families may be surveyed during different weeks within a year. In a pure cross-sectional analysis, we would ignore any minor timing differences in collecting the data. If a set of families was surveyed during different weeks of the same year, we would still view this as a cross-sectional data set.

An important feature of cross-sectional data is that we can often assume that they have been obtained by **random sampling** from the underlying population. For example, if we obtain information on wages, education, experience, and other characteristics by randomly drawing 500 people from the working population, then we have a random sample from the population of all working people. Random sampling is the sampling scheme covered in introductory statistics courses, and it simplifies the analysis of cross-sectional data. A review of random sampling is contained in Appendix C.

Sometimes, random sampling is not appropriate as an assumption for analyzing cross-sectional data. For example, suppose we are interested in studying factors that influence the accumulation of family wealth. We could survey a random sample of families, but some families might refuse to report their wealth. If, for example, wealthier families are less likely to disclose their wealth, then the resulting sample on wealth is not a random sample from the population of all families. This is an illustration of a sample selection problem, an advanced topic that we will discuss in Chapter 17.

Another violation of random sampling occurs when we sample from units that are large relative to the population, particularly geographical units. The potential problem in such cases is that the population is not large enough to reasonably assume the observations are independent draws. For example, if we want to explain new business activity across states as a function of wage rates, energy prices, corporate and property tax rates, services provided, quality of the workforce, and other state characteristics, it is unlikely that business activities in states near one another are independent. It turns out that the econometric methods that we discuss do work in such situations, but they sometimes need to be refined. For the most part, we will ignore the intricacies that arise in analyzing such situations and treat these problems in a random sampling framework, even when it is not technically correct to do so.

Cross-sectional data are widely used in economics and other social sciences. In economics, the analysis of cross-sectional data is closely aligned with the applied microeconomics fields, such as labor economics, state and local public finance, industrial organization, urban economics, demography, and health economics. Data on individuals, households, firms, and cities at a given point in time are important for testing microeconomic hypotheses and evaluating economic policies.

The cross-sectional data used for econometric analysis can be represented and stored in computers. Table 1.1 contains, in abbreviated form, a cross-sectional data set on 526 working individuals

TABLE 1.1 A Cross-Sectional Data Set on Wages and Other Individual Characteristics

obsno	wage	educ	exper	female	married
1	3.10	11	2	1	0
2	3.24	12	22	1	1
3	3.00	11	2	0	0
4	6.00	8	44	0	1
5	5.30	12	7	0	1
.	.	.	.	.	.
.	.	.	.	.	.
.	.	.	.	.	.
525	11.56	16	5	0	1
526	3.50	14	5	1	0

for the year 1976. (This is a subset of the data in the file WAGE1.) The variables include *wage* (in dollars per hour), *educ* (years of education), *exper* (years of potential labor force experience), *female* (an indicator for gender), and *married* (marital status). These last two variables are binary (zero-one) in nature and serve to indicate qualitative features of the individual (the person is female or not; the person is married or not). We will have much to say about binary variables in Chapter 7 and beyond.

The variable *obsno* in Table 1.1 is the observation number assigned to each person in the sample. Unlike the other variables, it is not a characteristic of the individual. All econometrics and statistics software packages assign an observation number to each data unit. Intuition should tell you that, for data such as that in Table 1.1, it does not matter which person is labeled as observation 1, which person is called observation 2, and so on. The fact that the ordering of the data does not matter for econometric analysis is a key feature of cross-sectional data sets obtained from random sampling.

Different variables sometimes correspond to different time periods in cross-sectional data sets. For example, to determine the effects of government policies on long-term economic growth, economists have studied the relationship between growth in real per capita GDP over a certain period (say, 1960 to 1985) and variables determined in part by government policy in 1960 (government consumption as a percentage of GDP and adult secondary education rates). Such a data set might be represented as in Table 1.2, which constitutes part of the data set used in the study of cross-country growth rates by De Long and Summers (1991).

The variable *gpcrgdp* represents average growth in real per capita GDP over the period 1960 to 1985. The fact that *govcons60* (government consumption as a percentage of GDP) and *second60*

TABLE 1.2 A Data Set on Economic Growth Rates and Country Characteristics

obsno	country	gpcrgdp	govcons60	second60
1	Argentina	0.89	9	32
2	Austria	3.32	16	50
3	Belgium	2.56	13	69
4	Bolivia	1.24	18	12
.	.	.	.	.
.	.	.	.	.
.	.	.	.	.
61	Zimbabwe	2.30	17	6

(percentage of adult population with a secondary education) correspond to the year 1960, while *gpcrgdp* is the average growth over the period from 1960 to 1985, does not lead to any special problems in treating this information as a cross-sectional data set. The observations are listed alphabetically by country, but nothing about this ordering affects any subsequent analysis.

1-3b Time Series Data

A **time series data** set consists of observations on a variable or several variables over time. Examples of time series data include stock prices, money supply, consumer price index, GDP, annual homicide rates, and automobile sales figures. Because past events can influence future events and lags in behavior are prevalent in the social sciences, time is an important dimension in a time series data set. Unlike the arrangement of cross-sectional data, the chronological ordering of observations in a time series conveys potentially important information.

A key feature of time series data that makes them more difficult to analyze than cross-sectional data is that economic observations can rarely, if ever, be assumed to be independent across time. Most economic and other time series are related, often strongly related, to their recent histories. For example, knowing something about the GDP from last quarter tells us quite a bit about the likely range of the GDP during this quarter, because GDP tends to remain fairly stable from one quarter to the next. Although most econometric procedures can be used with both cross-sectional and time series data, more needs to be done in specifying econometric models for time series data before standard econometric methods can be justified. In addition, modifications and embellishments to standard econometric techniques have been developed to account for and exploit the dependent nature of economic time series and to address other issues, such as the fact that some economic variables tend to display clear trends over time.

Another feature of time series data that can require special attention is the **data frequency** at which the data are collected. In economics, the most common frequencies are daily, weekly, monthly, quarterly, and annually. Stock prices are recorded at daily intervals (excluding Saturday and Sunday). The money supply in the U.S. economy is reported weekly. Many macroeconomic series are tabulated monthly, including inflation and unemployment rates. Other macro series are recorded less frequently, such as every three months (every quarter). GDP is an important example of a quarterly series. Other time series, such as infant mortality rates for states in the United States, are available only on an annual basis.

Many weekly, monthly, and quarterly economic time series display a strong seasonal pattern, which can be an important factor in a time series analysis. For example, monthly data on housing starts differ across the months simply due to changing weather conditions. We will learn how to deal with seasonal time series in Chapter 10.

Table 1.3 contains a time series data set obtained from an article by Castillo-Freeman and Freeman (1992) on minimum wage effects in Puerto Rico. The earliest year in the data set is the first

TABLE 1.3 Minimum Wage, Unemployment, and Related Data for Puerto Rico					
obsno	year	avgmin	avgcov	prunemp	prgnp
1	1950	0.20	20.1	15.4	878.7
2	1951	0.21	20.7	16.0	925.0
3	1952	0.23	22.6	14.8	1015.9
.	.	.	.	.	.
.	.	.	.	.	.
.	.	.	.	.	.
37	1986	3.35	58.1	18.9	4281.6
38	1987	3.35	58.2	16.8	4496.7

observation, and the most recent year available is the last observation. When econometric methods are used to analyze time series data, the data should be stored in chronological order.

The variable *avgmin* refers to the average minimum wage for the year, *avgcov* is the average coverage rate (the percentage of workers covered by the minimum wage law), *prunemp* is the unemployment rate, and *prgnp* is the gross national product, in millions of 1954 dollars. We will use these data later in a time series analysis of the effect of the minimum wage on employment.

1-3c Pooled Cross Sections

Some data sets have both cross-sectional and time series features. For example, suppose that two cross-sectional household surveys are taken in the United States, one in 1985 and one in 1990. In 1985, a random sample of households is surveyed for variables such as income, savings, family size, and so on. In 1990, a *new* random sample of households is taken using the same survey questions. To increase our sample size, we can form a **pooled cross section** by combining the two years.

Pooling cross sections from different years is often an effective way of analyzing the effects of a new government policy. The idea is to collect data from the years before and after a key policy change. As an example, consider the following data set on housing prices taken in 1993 and 1995, before and after a reduction in property taxes in 1994. Suppose we have data on 250 houses for 1993 and on 270 houses for 1995. One way to store such a data set is given in Table 1.4.

Observations 1 through 250 correspond to the houses sold in 1993, and observations 251 through 520 correspond to the 270 houses sold in 1995. Although the order in which we store the data turns out not to be crucial, keeping track of the year for each observation is usually very important. This is why we enter *year* as a separate variable.

A pooled cross section is analyzed much like a standard cross section, except that we often need to account for secular differences in the variables across the time. In fact, in addition to increasing the sample size, the point of a pooled cross-sectional analysis is often to see how a key relationship has changed over time.

TABLE 1.4 Pooled Cross Sections: Two Years of Housing Prices						
obsno	year	hprice	proptax	sqrft	bdrms	bthrms
1	1993	85,500	42	1600	3	2.0
2	1993	67,300	36	1440	3	2.5
3	1993	134,000	38	2000	4	2.5
.	.	.	.	.	.	.
.	.	.	.	.	.	.
.	.	.	.	.	.	.
250	1993	243,600	41	2600	4	3.0
251	1995	65,000	16	1250	2	1.0
252	1995	182,400	20	2200	4	2.0
253	1995	97,500	15	1540	3	2.0
.	.	.	.	.	.	.
.	.	.	.	.	.	.
						.
520	1995	57,200	16	1100	2	1.5

1-3d Panel or Longitudinal Data

A **panel data** (or *longitudinal data*) set consists of a time series for *each* cross-sectional member in the data set. As an example, suppose we have wage, education, and employment history for a set of individuals followed over a 10-year period. Or we might collect information, such as investment and financial data, about the same set of firms over a five-year time period. Panel data can also be collected on geographical units. For example, we can collect data for the same set of counties in the United States on immigration flows, tax rates, wage rates, government expenditures, and so on, for the years 1980, 1985, and 1990.

The key feature of panel data that distinguishes them from a pooled cross section is that the *same* cross-sectional units (individuals, firms, or counties in the preceding examples) are followed over a given time period. The data in Table 1.4 are not considered a panel data set because the houses sold are likely to be different in 1993 and 1995; if there are any duplicates, the number is likely to be so small as to be unimportant. In contrast, Table 1.5 contains a two-year panel data set on crime and related statistics for 150 cities in the United States.

There are several interesting features in Table 1.5. First, each city has been given a number from 1 through 150. Which city we decide to call city 1, city 2, and so on, is irrelevant. As with a pure cross section, the ordering in the cross section of a panel data set does not matter. We could use the city name in place of a number, but it is often useful to have both.

A second point is that the two years of data for city 1 fill the first two rows or observations. Observations 3 and 4 correspond to city 2, and so on. Because each of the 150 cities has two rows of data, any econometrics package will view this as 300 observations. This data set can be treated as a pooled cross section, where the same cities happen to show up in each year. But, as we will see in Chapters 13 and 14, we can also use the panel structure to analyze questions that cannot be answered by simply viewing this as a pooled cross section.

In organizing the observations in Table 1.5, we place the two years of data for each city adjacent to one another, with the first year coming before the second in all cases. For just about every practical purpose, this is the preferred way for ordering panel data sets. Contrast this organization with the way the pooled cross sections are stored in Table 1.4. In short, the reason for ordering panel data as in Table 1.5 is that we will need to perform data transformations for each city across the two years.

Because panel data require replication of the same units over time, panel data sets, especially those on individuals, households, and firms, are more difficult to obtain than pooled cross sections. Not surprisingly, observing the same units over time leads to several advantages over cross-sectional data or even pooled cross-sectional data. The benefit that we will focus on in this text is that having

obsno	city	year	murders	population	unem	police
\multicolumn{7}{l}{**TABLE 1.5 A Two-Year Panel Data Set on City Crime Statistics**}
1	1	1986	5	350,000	8.7	440
2	1	1990	8	359,200	7.2	471
3	2	1986	2	64,300	5.4	75
4	2	1990	1	65,100	5.5	75
.	.	.	.	.	.	.
.	.	.	.	.	.	.
.	.	.	.	.	.	.
297	149	1986	10	260,700	9.6	286
298	149	1990	6	245,000	9.8	334
299	150	1986	25	543,000	4.3	520
300	150	1990	32	546,200	5.2	493

multiple observations on the same units allows us to control for certain unobserved characteristics of individuals, firms, and so on. As we will see, the use of more than one observation can facilitate causal inference in situations where inferring causality would be very difficult if only a single cross section were available. A second advantage of panel data is that they often allow us to study the importance of lags in behavior or the result of decision making. This information can be significant because many economic policies can be expected to have an impact only after some time has passed.

Most books at the undergraduate level do not contain a discussion of econometric methods for panel data. However, economists now recognize that some questions are difficult, if not impossible, to answer satisfactorily without panel data. As you will see, we can make considerable progress with simple panel data analysis, a method that is not much more difficult than dealing with a standard cross-sectional data set.

1-3e A Comment on Data Structures

Part 1 of this text is concerned with the analysis of cross-sectional data, because this poses the fewest conceptual and technical difficulties. At the same time, it illustrates most of the key themes of econometric analysis. We will use the methods and insights from cross-sectional analysis in the remainder of the text.

Although the econometric analysis of time series uses many of the same tools as cross-sectional analysis, it is more complicated because of the trending, highly persistent nature of many economic time series. Examples that have been traditionally used to illustrate the manner in which econometric methods can be applied to time series data are now widely believed to be flawed. It makes little sense to use such examples initially, since this practice will only reinforce poor econometric practice. Therefore, we will postpone the treatment of time series econometrics until Part 2, when the important issues concerning trends, persistence, dynamics, and seasonality will be introduced.

In Part 3, we will treat pooled cross sections and panel data explicitly. The analysis of independently pooled cross sections and simple panel data analysis are fairly straightforward extensions of pure cross-sectional analysis. Nevertheless, we will wait until Chapter 13 to deal with these topics.

1-4 Causality and the Notion of Ceteris Paribus in Econometric Analysis

In most tests of economic theory, and certainly for evaluating public policy, the economist's goal is to infer that one variable (such as education) has a **causal effect** on another variable (such as worker productivity). Simply finding an association between two or more variables might be suggestive, but unless causality can be established, it is rarely compelling.

The notion of **ceteris paribus**—which means "other (relevant) factors being equal"—plays an important role in causal analysis. This idea has been implicit in some of our earlier discussion, particularly Examples 1.1 and 1.2, but thus far we have not explicitly mentioned it.

You probably remember from introductory economics that most economic questions are ceteris paribus by nature. For example, in analyzing consumer demand, we are interested in knowing the effect of changing the price of a good on its quantity demanded, while holding all other factors—such as income, prices of other goods, and individual tastes—fixed. If other factors are not held fixed, then we cannot know the causal effect of a price change on quantity demanded.

Holding other factors fixed is critical for policy analysis as well. In the job training example (Example 1.2), we might be interested in the effect of another week of job training on wages, with all other components being equal (in particular, education and experience). If we succeed in holding all other relevant factors fixed and then find a link between job training and wages, we can conclude that job training has a causal effect on worker productivity. Although this may seem pretty simple, even at this early stage it should be clear that, except in very special cases, it will not be possible to literally hold all else equal. The key question in most empirical studies is: Have enough other factors been held fixed to make a case for causality? Rarely is an econometric study evaluated without raising this issue.

In most serious applications, the number of factors that can affect the variable of interest—such as criminal activity or wages—is immense, and the isolation of any particular variable may seem like a hopeless effort. However, we will eventually see that, when carefully applied, econometric methods can simulate a ceteris paribus experiment.

At this point, we cannot yet explain how econometric methods can be used to estimate ceteris paribus effects, so we will consider some problems that can arise in trying to infer causality in economics. We do not use any equations in this discussion. For each example, the problem of inferring causality disappears if an appropriate experiment can be carried out. Thus, it is useful to describe how such an experiment might be structured, and to observe that, in most cases, obtaining experimental data is impractical. It is also helpful to think about why the available data fail to have the important features of an experimental data set.

We rely for now on your intuitive understanding of such terms as *random*, *independence*, and *correlation*, all of which should be familiar from an introductory probability and statistics course. (These concepts are reviewed in Appendix B.) We begin with an example that illustrates some of these important issues.

EXAMPLE 1.3	**Effects of Fertilizer on Crop Yield**

Some early econometric studies [for example, Griliches (1957)] considered the effects of new fertilizers on crop yields. Suppose the crop under consideration is soybeans. Since fertilizer amount is only one factor affecting yields—some others include rainfall, quality of land, and presence of parasites—this issue must be posed as a ceteris paribus question. One way to determine the causal effect of fertilizer amount on soybean yield is to conduct an experiment, which might include the following steps. Choose several one-acre plots of land. Apply different amounts of fertilizer to each plot and subsequently measure the yields; this gives us cross-sectional data set. Then, use statistical methods (to be introduced in Chapter 2) to measure the association between yields and fertilizer amounts.

As described earlier, this may not seem like a very good experiment because we have said nothing about choosing plots of land that are identical in all respects except for the amount of fertilizer. In fact, choosing plots of land with this feature is not feasible: some of the factors, such as land quality, cannot even be fully observed. How do we know the results of this experiment can be used to measure the ceteris paribus effect of fertilizer? The answer depends on the specifics of how fertilizer amounts are chosen. If the levels of fertilizer are assigned to plots independently of other plot features that affect yield—that is, other characteristics of plots are completely ignored when deciding on fertilizer amounts—then we are in business. We will justify this statement in Chapter 2.

The next example is more representative of the difficulties that arise when inferring causality in applied economics.

EXAMPLE 1.4	**Measuring the Return to Education**

Labor economists and policy makers have long been interested in the "return to education." Somewhat informally, the question is posed as follows: If a person is chosen from the population and given another year of education, by how much will his or her wage increase? As with the previous examples, this is a ceteris paribus question, which implies that all other factors are held fixed while another year of education is given to the person.

We can imagine a social planner designing an experiment to get at this issue, much as the agricultural researcher can design an experiment to estimate fertilizer effects. Assume, for the moment, that the social planner has the ability to assign any level of education to any person. How would this planner emulate the fertilizer experiment in Example 1.3? The planner would choose a group of people and randomly assign each person an amount of education; some people are given an eighth-grade education, some are given a high school education, some are given two years of college, and so on. Subsequently, the planner measures wages for this group of people (where we assume that each person then works in a job). The people here are like the plots in the fertilizer example, where education plays the role of fertilizer and wage rate plays the role of soybean yield. As with Example 1.3, if levels of education are assigned independently of other characteristics that affect productivity (such as experience and innate ability), then an analysis that ignores these other factors will yield useful results. Again, it will take some effort in Chapter 2 to justify this claim; for now, we state it without support.

Unlike the fertilizer-yield example, the experiment described in Example 1.4 is unfeasible. The ethical issues, not to mention the economic costs, associated with randomly determining education levels for a group of individuals are obvious. As a logistical matter, we could not give someone only an eighth-grade education if he or she already has a college degree.

Even though experimental data cannot be obtained for measuring the return to education, we can certainly collect nonexperimental data on education levels and wages for a large group by sampling randomly from the population of working people. Such data are available from a variety of surveys used in labor economics, but these data sets have a feature that makes it difficult to estimate the ceteris paribus return to education. People *choose* their own levels of education; therefore, education levels are probably not determined independently of all other factors affecting wage. This problem is a feature shared by most nonexperimental data sets.

One factor that affects wage is experience in the workforce. Since pursuing more education generally requires postponing entering the workforce, those with more education usually have less experience. Thus, in a nonexperimental data set on wages and education, education is likely to be negatively associated with a key variable that also affects wage. It is also believed that people with more innate ability often choose higher levels of education. Since higher ability leads to higher wages, we again have a correlation between education and a critical factor that affects wage.

The omitted factors of experience and ability in the wage example have analogs in the fertilizer example. Experience is generally easy to measure and therefore is similar to a variable such as rainfall. Ability, on the other hand, is nebulous and difficult to quantify; it is similar to land quality in the fertilizer example. As we will see throughout this text, accounting for other observed factors, such as experience, when estimating the ceteris paribus effect of another variable, such as education, is relatively straightforward. We will also find that accounting for inherently unobservable factors, such as ability, is much more problematic. It is fair to say that many of the advances in econometric methods have tried to deal with unobserved factors in econometric models.

One final parallel can be drawn between Examples 1.3 and 1.4. Suppose that in the fertilizer example, the fertilizer amounts were not entirely determined at random. Instead, the assistant who chose the fertilizer levels thought it would be better to put more fertilizer on the higher-quality plots of land. (Agricultural researchers should have a rough idea about which plots of land are of better quality, even though they may not be able to fully quantify the differences.) This situation is completely analogous to the level of schooling being related to unobserved ability in Example 1.4. Because better land leads to higher yields, and more fertilizer was used on the better plots, any observed relationship between yield and fertilizer might be spurious.

Difficulty in inferring causality can also arise when studying data at fairly high levels of aggregation, as the next example on city crime rates shows.

EXAMPLE 1.5   ## The Effect of Law Enforcement on City Crime Levels

The issue of how best to prevent crime has been, and will probably continue to be, with us for some time. One especially important question in this regard is: Does the presence of more police officers on the street deter crime?

The ceteris paribus question is easy to state: If a city is randomly chosen and given, say, ten additional police officers, by how much would its crime rates fall? Another way to state the question is: If two cities are the same in all respects, except that city A has ten more police officers than city B, by how much would the two cities' crime rates differ?

It would be virtually impossible to find pairs of communities identical in all respects except for the size of their police force. Fortunately, econometric analysis does not require this. What we do need to know is whether the data we can collect on community crime levels and the size of the police force can be viewed as experimental. We can certainly imagine a true experiment involving a large collection of cities where we dictate how many police officers each city will use for the upcoming year.

Although policies can be used to affect the size of police forces, we clearly cannot tell each city how many police officers it can hire. If, as is likely, a city's decision on how many police officers to hire is correlated with other city factors that affect crime, then the data must be viewed as nonexperimental. In fact, one way to view this problem is to see that a city's choice of police force size and the amount of crime are *simultaneously determined*. We will explicitly address such problems in Chapter 16.

The first three examples we have discussed have dealt with cross-sectional data at various levels of aggregation (for example, at the individual or city levels). The same hurdles arise when inferring causality in time series problems.

EXAMPLE 1.6   ## The Effect of the Minimum Wage on Unemployment

An important, and perhaps contentious, policy issue concerns the effect of the minimum wage on unemployment rates for various groups of workers. Although this problem can be studied in a variety of data settings (cross-sectional, time series, or panel data), time series data are often used to look at aggregate effects. An example of a time series data set on unemployment rates and minimum wages was given in Table 1.3.

Standard supply and demand analysis implies that, as the minimum wage is increased above the market clearing wage, we slide up the demand curve for labor and total employment decreases. (Labor supply exceeds labor demand.) To quantify this effect, we can study the relationship between employment and the minimum wage over time. In addition to some special difficulties that can arise in dealing with time series data, there are possible problems with inferring causality. The minimum wage in the United States is not determined in a vacuum. Various economic and political forces impinge on the final minimum wage for any given year. (The minimum wage, once determined, is usually in place for several years, unless it is indexed for inflation.) Thus, it is probable that the amount of the minimum wage is related to other factors that have an effect on employment levels.

We can imagine the U.S. government conducting an experiment to determine the employment effects of the minimum wage (as opposed to worrying about the welfare of low-wage workers). The minimum wage could be randomly set by the government each year, and then the employment outcomes could be tabulated. The resulting experimental time series data could then be analyzed using fairly simple econometric methods. But this scenario hardly describes how minimum wages are set.

If we can control enough other factors relating to employment, then we can still hope to estimate the ceteris paribus effect of the minimum wage on employment. In this sense, the problem is very similar to the previous cross-sectional examples.

Even when economic theories are not most naturally described in terms of causality, they often have predictions that can be tested using econometric methods. The following example demonstrates this approach.

EXAMPLE 1.7 **The Expectations Hypothesis**

The *expectations hypothesis* from financial economics states that, given all information available to investors at the time of investing, the *expected* return on any two investments is the same. For example, consider two possible investments with a three-month investment horizon, purchased at the same time: (1) Buy a three-month T-bill with a face value of $10,000, for a price below $10,000; in three months, you receive $10,000. (2) Buy a six-month T-bill (at a price below $10,000) and, in three months, sell it as a three-month T-bill. Each investment requires roughly the same amount of initial capital, but there is an important difference. For the first investment, you know exactly what the return is at the time of purchase because you know the initial price of the three-month T-bill, along with its face value. This is not true for the second investment: although you know the price of a six-month T-bill when you purchase it, you do not know the price you can sell it for in three months. Therefore, there is uncertainty in this investment for someone who has a three-month investment horizon.

The actual returns on these two investments will usually be different. According to the expectations hypothesis, the expected return from the second investment, given all information at the time of investment, should equal the return from purchasing a three-month T-bill. This theory turns out to be fairly easy to test, as we will see in Chapter 11.

Summary

In this introductory chapter, we have discussed the purpose and scope of econometric analysis. Econometrics is used in all applied economics fields to test economic theories, to inform government and private policy makers, and to predict economic time series. Sometimes, an econometric model is derived from a formal economic model, but in other cases, econometric models are based on informal economic reasoning and intuition. The goals of any econometric analysis are to estimate the parameters in the model and to test hypotheses about these parameters; the values and signs of the parameters determine the validity of an economic theory and the effects of certain policies.

Cross-sectional, time series, pooled cross-sectional, and panel data are the most common types of data structures that are used in applied econometrics. Data sets involving a time dimension, such as time series and panel data, require special treatment because of the correlation across time of most economic time series. Other issues, such as trends and seasonality, arise in the analysis of time series data but not cross-sectional data.

In Section 1-4, we discussed the notions of ceteris paribus and causal inference. In most cases, hypotheses in the social sciences are ceteris paribus in nature: all other relevant factors must be fixed when studying the relationship between two variables. Because of the nonexperimental nature of most data collected in the social sciences, uncovering causal relationships is very challenging.

Key Terms

Causal Effect	Economic Model	Panel Data
Ceteris Paribus	Empirical Analysis	Pooled Cross Section
Cross-Sectional Data Set	Experimental Data	Random Sampling
Data Frequency	Nonexperimental Data	Retrospective Data
Econometric Model	Observational Data	Time Series Data

Problems

1 Suppose that you are asked to conduct a study to determine whether smaller class sizes lead to improved student performance of fourth graders.
   (i)   If you could conduct any experiment you want, what would you do? Be specific.
   (ii) More realistically, suppose you can collect observational data on several thousand fourth graders in a given state. You can obtain the size of their fourth-grade class and a standardized test score taken at the end of fourth grade. Why might you expect a negative correlation between class size and test score?
   (iii) Would a negative correlation necessarily show that smaller class sizes cause better performance? Explain.

2 A justification for job training programs is that they improve worker productivity. Suppose that you are asked to evaluate whether more job training makes workers more productive. However, rather than having data on individual workers, you have access to data on manufacturing firms in Ohio. In particular, for each firm, you have information on hours of job training per worker (*training*) and number of nondefective items produced per worker hour (*output*).
   (i)   Carefully state the ceteris paribus thought experiment underlying this policy question.
   (ii) Does it seem likely that a firm's decision to train its workers will be independent of worker characteristics? What are some of those measurable and unmeasurable worker characteristics?
   (iii) Name a factor other than worker characteristics that can affect worker productivity.
   (iv) If you find a positive correlation between *output* and *training*, would you have convincingly established that job training makes workers more productive? Explain.

3 Suppose at your university you are asked to find the relationship between weekly hours spent studying (*study*) and weekly hours spent working (*work*). Does it make sense to characterize the problem as inferring whether *study* "causes" *work* or *work* "causes" *study*? Explain.

4 States (and provinces) that have control over taxation sometimes reduce taxes in an attempt to spur economic growth. Suppose that you are hired by a state to estimate the effect of corporate tax rates on, say, the growth in per capita gross state product (GSP).
   (i)   What kind of data would you need to collect to undertake a statistical analysis?
   (ii) Is it feasible to do a controlled experiment? What would be required?
   (iii) Is a correlation analysis between GSP growth and tax rates likely to be convincing? Explain.

Computer Exercises

C1 Use the data in WAGE1 for this exercise.
   (i)   Find the average education level in the sample. What are the lowest and highest years of education?
   (ii) Find the average hourly wage in the sample. Does it seem high or low?
   (iii) The wage data are reported in 1976 dollars. Using the Internet or a printed source, find the Consumer Price Index (CPI) for the years 1976 and 2013.
   (iv) Use the CPI values from part (iii) to find the average hourly wage in 2013 dollars. Now does the average hourly wage seem reasonable?
   (v)   How many women are in the sample? How many men?

C2 Use the data in BWGHT to answer this question.
   (i)   How many women are in the sample, and how many report smoking during pregnancy?
   (ii) What is the average number of cigarettes smoked per day? Is the average a good measure of the "typical" woman in this case? Explain.
   (iii) Among women who smoked during pregnancy, what is the average number of cigarettes smoked per day? How does this compare with your answer from part (ii), and why?

(iv) Find the average of *fatheduc* in the sample. Why are only 1,192 observations used to compute this average?

(v) Report the average family income and its standard deviation in dollars.

C3 The data in MEAP01 are for the state of Michigan in the year 2001. Use these data to answer the following questions.

(i) Find the largest and smallest values of *math4*. Does the range make sense? Explain.

(ii) How many schools have a perfect pass rate on the math test? What percentage is this of the total sample?

(iii) How many schools have math pass rates of exactly 50%?

(iv) Compare the average pass rates for the math and reading scores. Which test is harder to pass?

(v) Find the correlation between *math4* and *read4*. What do you conclude?

(vi) The variable *exppp* is expenditure per pupil. Find the average of *exppp* along with its standard deviation. Would you say there is wide variation in per pupil spending?

(vii) Suppose School A spends $6,000 per student and School B spends $5,500 per student. By what percentage does School A's spending exceed School B's? Compare this to $100 \cdot [\log(6{,}000) - \log(5{,}500)]$, which is the approximation percentage difference based on the difference in the natural logs. (See Section A.4 in Appendix A.)

C4 The data in JTRAIN2 come from a job training experiment conducted for low-income men during 1976–1977; see Lalonde (1986).

(i) Use the indicator variable *train* to determine the fraction of men receiving job training.

(ii) The variable *re78* is earnings from 1978, measured in thousands of 1982 dollars. Find the averages of *re78* for the sample of men receiving job training and the sample not receiving job training. Is the difference economically large?

(iii) The variable *unem78* is an indicator of whether a man is unemployed or not in 1978. What fraction of the men who received job training are unemployed? What about for men who did not receive job training? Comment on the difference.

(iv) From parts (ii) and (iii), does it appear that the job training program was effective? What would make our conclusions more convincing?

C5 The data in FERTIL2 were collected on women living in the Republic of Botswana in 1988. The variable *children* refers to the number of living children. The variable *electric* is a binary indicator equal to one if the woman's home has electricity, and zero if not.

(i) Find the smallest and largest values of *children* in the sample. What is the average of *children*?

(ii) What percentage of women have electricity in the home?

(iii) Compute the average of *children* for those without electricity and do the same for those with electricity. Comment on what you find.

(iv) From part (iii), can you infer that having electricity "causes" women to have fewer children? Explain.

C6 Use the data in COUNTYMURDERS to answer this question. Use only the year 1996. The variable *murders* is the number of murders reported in the county. The variable *execs* is the number of executions that took place of people sentenced to death in the given county. Most states in the United States have the death penalty, but several do not.

(i) How many counties are there in the data set? Of these, how many have zero murders? What percentage of counties have zero executions? (Remember, use only the 1996 data.)

(ii) What is the largest number of murders? What is the largest number of executions? Why is the average number of executions so small?

(iii) Compute the correlation coefficient between *murders* and *execs* and describe what you find.

(iv) You should have computed a positive correlation in part (iii). Do you think that more executions *cause* more murders to occur? What might explain the positive correlation?

C7 The data set in ALCOHOL contains information on a sample of men in the United States. Two key variables are self-reported employment status and alcohol abuse (along with many other variables). The variables *employ* and *abuse* are both binary, or indicator, variables: they take on only the values zero and one.

   (i)   What is percentage of the men in the sample report abusing alcohol? What is the employment rate?
   (ii)   Consider the group of men who abuse alcohol. What is the employment rate?
   (iii)   What is the employment rate for the group of men who do not abuse alcohol?
   (iv)   Discuss the difference in your answers to parts (ii) and (iii). Does this allow you to conclude that alcohol abuse causes unemployment?

PART 1

Regression Analysis with Cross-Sectional Data

P art 1 of the text covers regression analysis with cross-sectional data. It builds upon a solid base of college algebra and basic concepts in probability and statistics. Appendices A, B, and C contain complete reviews of these topics.

Chapter 2 begins with the simple linear regression model, where we explain one variable in terms of another variable. Although simple regression is not widely used in applied econometrics, it is used occasionally and serves as a natural starting point because the algebra and interpretations are relatively straightforward.

Chapters 3 and 4 cover the fundamentals of multiple regression analysis, where we allow more than one variable to affect the variable we are trying to explain. Multiple regression is still the most commonly used method in empirical research, and so these chapters deserve careful attention. Chapter 3 focuses on the algebra of the method of ordinary least squares (OLS), while also establishing conditions under which the OLS estimator is unbiased and best linear unbiased. Chapter 4 covers the important topic of statistical inference.

Chapter 5 discusses the large sample, or asymptotic, properties of the OLS estimators. This provides justification of the inference procedures in Chapter 4 when the errors in a regression model are not normally distributed. Chapter 6 covers some additional topics in regression analysis, including advanced functional form issues, data scaling, prediction, and goodness-of-fit. Chapter 7 explains how qualitative information can be incorporated into multiple regression models.

Chapter 8 illustrates how to test for and correct the problem of heteroskedasticity, or nonconstant variance, in the error terms. We show how the usual OLS statistics can be adjusted, and we also present an extension of OLS, known as *weighted least squares*, which explicitly accounts for different variances in the errors. Chapter 9 delves further into the very important problem of correlation between the error term and one or more of the explanatory variables. We demonstrate how the availability of a proxy variable can solve the omitted variables problem. In addition, we establish the bias and inconsistency in the OLS estimators in the presence of certain kinds of measurement errors in the variables. Various data problems are also discussed, including the problem of outliers.

The Simple Regression Model

The simple regression model can be used to study the relationship between two variables. For reasons we will see, the simple regression model has limitations as a general tool for empirical analysis. Nevertheless, it is sometimes appropriate as an empirical tool. Learning how to interpret the simple regression model is good practice for studying multiple regression, which we will do in subsequent chapters.

2-1 Definition of the Simple Regression Model

Much of applied econometric analysis begins with the following premise: y and x are two variables, representing some population, and we are interested in "explaining y in terms of x," or in "studying how y varies with changes in x." We discussed some examples in Chapter 1, including: y is soybean crop yield and x is amount of fertilizer; y is hourly wage and x is years of education; and y is a community crime rate and x is number of police officers.

In writing down a model that will "explain y in terms of x," we must confront three issues. First, since there is never an exact relationship between two variables, how do we allow for other factors to affect y? Second, what is the functional relationship between y and x? And third, how can we be sure we are capturing a ceteris paribus relationship between y and x (if that is a desired goal)?

We can resolve these ambiguities by writing down an equation relating y to x. A simple equation is

$$y = \beta_0 + \beta_1 x + u. \qquad [2.1]$$

Equation (2.1), which is assumed to hold in the population of interest, defines the **simple linear regression model**. It is also called the *two-variable linear regression model* or *bivariate linear*

TABLE 2.1 Terminology for Simple Regression

Y	X
Dependent variable	Independent variable
Explained variable	Explanatory variable
Response variable	Control variable
Predicted variable	Predictor variable
Regressand	Regressor

regression model because it relates the two variables x and y. We now discuss the meaning of each of the quantities in equation (2.1). [Incidentally, the term "regression" has origins that are not especially important for most modern econometric applications, so we will not explain it here. See Stigler (1986) for an engaging history of regression analysis.]

When related by equation (2.1), the variables y and x have several different names used interchangeably, as follows: y is called the **dependent variable**, the **explained variable**, the **response variable**, the **predicted variable**, or the **regressand**; x is called the **independent variable**, the **explanatory variable**, the **control variable**, the **predictor variable**, or the **regressor**. (The term **covariate** is also used for x.) The terms "dependent variable" and "independent variable" are frequently used in econometrics. But be aware that the label "independent" here does not refer to the statistical notion of independence between random variables (see Appendix B).

The terms "explained" and "explanatory" variables are probably the most descriptive. "Response" and "control" are used mostly in the experimental sciences, where the variable x is under the experimenter's control. We will not use the terms "predicted variable" and "predictor," although you sometimes see these in applications that are purely about prediction and not causality. Our terminology for simple regression is summarized in Table 2.1.

The variable u, called the **error term** or **disturbance** in the relationship, represents factors other than x that affect y. A simple regression analysis effectively treats all factors affecting y other than x as being unobserved. You can usefully think of u as standing for "unobserved."

Equation (2.1) also addresses the issue of the functional relationship between y and x. If the other factors in u are held fixed, so that the change in u is zero, $\Delta u = 0$, then x has a *linear* effect on y:

$$\Delta y = \beta_1 \Delta x \ \text{ if } \Delta u = 0. \tag{2.2}$$

Thus, the change in y is simply β_1 multiplied by the change in x. This means that β_1 is the **slope parameter** in the relationship between y and x, holding the other factors in u fixed; it is of primary interest in applied economics. The **intercept parameter** β_0, sometimes called the *constant term*, also has its uses, although it is rarely central to an analysis.

EXAMPLE 2.1 **Soybean Yield and Fertilizer**

Suppose that soybean yield is determined by the model

$$yield = \beta_0 + \beta_1 fertilizer + u, \tag{2.3}$$

so that $y = yield$ and $x = fertilizer$. The agricultural researcher is interested in the effect of fertilizer on yield, holding other factors fixed. This effect is given by β_1. The error term u contains factors such as land quality, rainfall, and so on. The coefficient β_1 measures the effect of fertilizer on yield, holding other factors fixed: $\Delta yield = \beta_1 \Delta \ fertilizer$.

EXAMPLE 2.2   **A Simple Wage Equation**

A model relating a person's wage to observed education and other unobserved factors is

$$wage = \beta_0 + \beta_1 educ + u. \qquad [2.4]$$

If *wage* is measured in dollars per hour and *educ* is years of education, then β_1 measures the change in hourly wage given another year of education, holding all other factors fixed. Some of those factors include labor force experience, innate ability, tenure with current employer, work ethic, and numerous other things.

The linearity of equation (2.1) implies that a one-unit change in x has the *same* effect on y, regardless of the initial value of x. This is unrealistic for many economic applications. For example, in the wage-education example, we might want to allow for *increasing* returns: the next year of education has a *larger* effect on wages than did the previous year. We will see how to allow for such possibilities in Section 2-4.

The most difficult issue to address is whether model (2.1) really allows us to draw ceteris paribus conclusions about how x affects y. We just saw in equation (2.2) that β_1 *does* measure the effect of x on y, holding all other factors (in u) fixed. Is this the end of the causality issue? Unfortunately, no. How can we hope to learn in general about the ceteris paribus effect of x on y, holding other factors fixed, when we are ignoring all those other factors?

Section 2-5 will show that we are only able to get reliable estimators of β_0 and β_1 from a random sample of data when we make an assumption restricting how the unobservable u is related to the explanatory variable x. Without such a restriction, we will not be able to estimate the ceteris paribus effect, β_1. Because u and x are random variables, we need a concept grounded in probability.

Before we state the key assumption about how x and u are related, we can always make one assumption about u. As long as the intercept β_0 is included in the equation, nothing is lost by assuming that the average value of u in the population is zero. Mathematically,

$$E(u) = 0. \qquad [2.5]$$

Assumption (2.5) says nothing about the relationship between u and x, but simply makes a statement about the distribution of the unobserved factors in the population. Using the previous examples for illustration, we can see that assumption (2.5) is not very restrictive. In Example 2.1, we lose nothing by normalizing the unobserved factors affecting soybean yield, such as land quality, to have an average of zero in the population of all cultivated plots. The same is true of the unobserved factors in Example 2.2. Without loss of generality, we can assume that things such as average ability are zero in the population of all working people. If you are not convinced, you should work through Problem 2 to see that we can always redefine the intercept in equation (2.1) to make equation (2.5) true.

We now turn to the crucial assumption regarding how u and x are related. A natural measure of the association between two random variables is the *correlation coefficient*. (See Appendix B for definition and properties.) If u and x are *uncorrelated*, then, as random variables, they are not *linearly* related. Assuming that u and x are uncorrelated goes a long way toward defining the sense in which u and x should be unrelated in equation (2.1). But it does not go far enough, because correlation measures only linear dependence between u and x. Correlation has a somewhat counterintuitive feature: it is possible for u to be uncorrelated with x while being correlated with functions of x, such as x^2. (See Section B.4 for further discussion.) This possibility is not acceptable for most regression purposes, as it causes problems for interpreting the model and for deriving statistical properties. A better assumption involves the *expected value of u given x*.

Because u and x are random variables, we can define the conditional distribution of u given any value of x. In particular, for any x, we can obtain the expected (or average) value of u for that slice of the population described by the value of x. The crucial assumption is that the average value of u does *not* depend on the value of x. We can write this assumption as

$$\mathrm{E}(u|x) = \mathrm{E}(u).$$ [2.6]

Equation (2.6) says that the average value of the unobservables is the same across all slices of the population determined by the value of x and that the common average is necessarily equal to the average of u over the entire population. When assumption (2.6) holds, we say that u is **mean independent** of x. (Of course, mean independence is implied by full independence between u and x, an assumption often used in basic probability and statistics.) When we combine mean independence with assumption (2.5), we obtain the **zero conditional mean assumption**, $\mathrm{E}(u|x) = 0$. It is critical to remember that equation (2.6) is the assumption with impact; assumption (2.5) essentially defines the intercept, β_0.

Let us see what equation (2.6) entails in the wage example. To simplify the discussion, assume that u is the same as innate ability. Then equation (2.6) requires that the average level of ability is the same, regardless of years of education. For example, if $\mathrm{E}(abil|8)$ denotes the average ability for the group of all people with eight years of education, and $\mathrm{E}(abil|16)$ denotes the average ability among people in the population with sixteen years of education, then equation (2.6) implies that these must be the same. In fact, the average ability level must be the same for *all* education levels. If, for example, we think that average ability increases with years of education, then equation (2.6) is false. (This would happen if, on average, people with more ability choose to become more educated.) As we cannot observe innate ability, we have no way of knowing whether or not average ability is the same for all education levels. But this is an issue that we must address before relying on simple regression analysis.

In the fertilizer example, if fertilizer amounts are chosen independently of other features of the plots, then equation (2.6) will hold: the average land quality will not depend on the amount of fertilizer. However, if more fertilizer is put on the higher-quality plots of land, then the expected value of u changes with the level of fertilizer, and equation (2.6) fails.

> ## EXPLORING FURTHER 2.1
>
> Suppose that a score on a final exam, *score*, depends on classes attended (*attend*) and unobserved factors that affect exam performance (such as student ability). Then
>
> $$score = \beta_0 + \beta_1 attend + u.$$ [2.7]
>
> When would you expect this model to satisfy equation (2.6)?

The zero conditional mean assumption gives β_1 another interpretation that is often useful. Taking the expected value of equation (2.1) conditional on x and using $\mathrm{E}(u|x) = 0$ gives

$$\mathrm{E}(y|x) = \beta_0 + \beta_1 x.$$ [2.8]

Equation (2.8) shows that the **population regression function (PRF)**, $\mathrm{E}(y|x)$, is a linear function of x. The linearity means that a one-unit increase in x changes the *expected value* of y by the amount β_1. For any given value of x, the distribution of y is centered about $\mathrm{E}(y|x)$, as illustrated in Figure 2.1.

It is important to understand that equation (2.8) tells us how the *average* value of y changes with x; it does not say that y equals $\beta_0 + \beta_1 x$ for all units in the population. For example, suppose that x is the high school grade point average and y is the college GPA, and we happen to know that $\mathrm{E}(colGPA|hsGPA) = 1.5 + 0.5\,hsGPA$. [Of course, in practice, we never know the population intercept and slope, but it is useful to pretend momentarily that we do to understand the nature of equation (2.8).] This GPA equation tells us the *average* college GPA among all students who have a given high school GPA. So suppose that $hsGPA = 3.6$. Then the average *colGPA* for all high school graduates who attend college with $hsGPA = 3.6$ is $1.5 + 0.5(3.6) = 3.3$. We are certainly *not* saying that every student with $hsGPA = 3.6$ will have a 3.3 college GPA; this is clearly false. The PRF gives us a relationship between the average level of y at different levels of x. Some students with $hsGPA = 3.6$ will have a college GPA higher than 3.3, and some will have a lower college GPA. Whether the actual *colGPA* is above or below 3.3 depends on the unobserved factors in u, and those differ among students even within the slice of the population with $hsGPA = 3.6$.

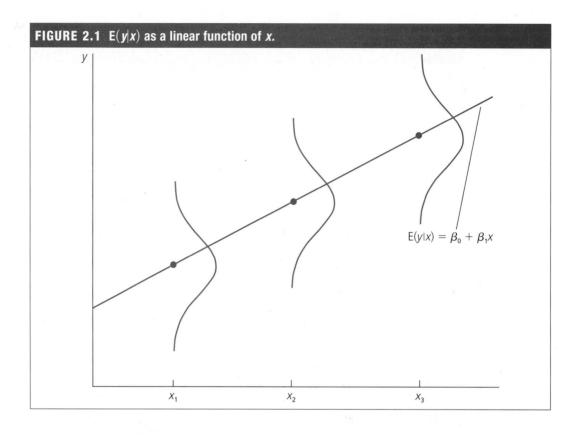

FIGURE 2.1 $E(y|x)$ as a linear function of x.

$$E(y|x) = \beta_0 + \beta_1 x$$

$x_1 \qquad x_2 \qquad x_3$

Given the zero conditional mean assumption $E(u|x) = 0$, it is useful to view equation (2.1) as breaking y into two components. The piece $\beta_0 + \beta_1 x$, which represents $E(y|x)$, is called the *systematic part* of y—that is, the part of y explained by x—and u is called the *unsystematic part*, or the part of y not explained by x. In Chapter 3, when we introduce more than one explanatory variable, we will discuss how to determine how large the systematic part is relative to the unsystematic part.

In the next section, we will use assumptions (2.5) and (2.6) to motivate estimators of β_0 and β_1 given a random sample of data. The zero conditional mean assumption also plays a crucial role in the statistical analysis in Section 2-5.

2-2 Deriving the Ordinary Least Squares Estimates

Now that we have discussed the basic ingredients of the simple regression model, we will address the important issue of how to estimate the parameters β_0 and β_1 in equation (2.1). To do this, we need a sample from the population. Let $\{(x_i, y_i): i = 1, \ldots, n\}$ denote a random sample of size n from the population. Because these data come from equation (2.1), we can write

$$y_i = \beta_0 + \beta_1 x_i + u_i \qquad [2.9]$$

for each i. Here, u_i is the error term for observation i because it contains all factors affecting y_i other than x_i.

As an example, x_i might be the annual income and y_i the annual savings for family i during a particular year. If we have collected data on 15 families, then $n = 15$. A scatterplot of such a data set is given in Figure 2.2, along with the (necessarily fictitious) population regression function.

We must decide how to use these data to obtain estimates of the intercept and slope in the population regression of savings on income.

FIGURE 2.2 Scatterplot of savings and income for 15 families, and the population regression $E(savings|income) = \beta_0 + \beta_1 income$.

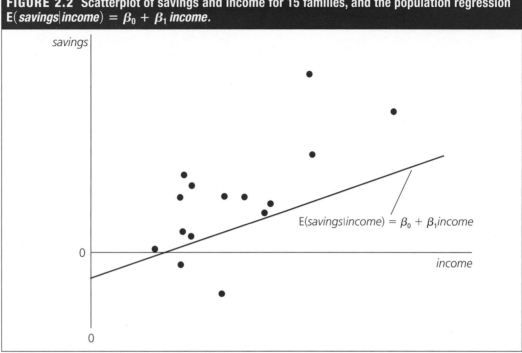

There are several ways to motivate the following estimation procedure. We will use equation (2.5) and an important implication of assumption (2.6): in the population, u is uncorrelated with x. Therefore, we see that u has zero expected value and that the *covariance* between x and u is zero:

$$E(u) = 0 \qquad \text{[2.10]}$$

and

$$Cov(x,u) = E(xu) = 0, \qquad \text{[2.11]}$$

where the first equality in equation (2.11) follows from (2.10). (See Section B.4 for the definition and properties of covariance.) In terms of the observable variables x and y and the unknown parameters β_0 and β_1, equations (2.10) and (2.11) can be written as

$$E(y - \beta_0 - \beta_1 x) = 0 \qquad \text{[2.12]}$$

and

$$E[x(y - \beta_0 - \beta_1 x)] = 0, \qquad \text{[2.13]}$$

respectively. Equations (2.12) and (2.13) imply two restrictions on the joint probability distribution of (x,y) in the population. Since there are two unknown parameters to estimate, we might hope that equations (2.12) and (2.13) can be used to obtain good estimators of β_0 and β_1. In fact, they can be. Given a sample of data, we choose estimates $\hat{\beta}_0$ and $\hat{\beta}_1$ to solve the *sample* counterparts of equations (2.12) and (2.13):

$$n^{-1}\sum_{i=1}^{n}(y_i - \hat{\beta}_0 - \hat{\beta}_1 x_i) = 0 \qquad \text{[2.14]}$$

and

$$n^{-1}\sum_{i=1}^{n}x_i(y_i - \hat{\beta}_0 - \hat{\beta}_1 x_i) = 0. \qquad \text{[2.15]}$$

This is an example of the *method of moments* approach to estimation. (See Section C.4 for a discussion of different estimation approaches.) These equations can be solved for $\hat{\beta}_0$ and $\hat{\beta}_1$.

Using the basic properties of the summation operator from Appendix A, equation (2.14) can be rewritten as

$$\bar{y} = \hat{\beta}_0 + \hat{\beta}_1 \bar{x}, \qquad\qquad [2.16]$$

where $\bar{y} = n^{-1}\sum_{i=1}^{n} y_i$ is the sample average of the y_i and likewise for $\bar{x}$. This equation allows us to write $\hat{\beta}_0$ in terms of $\hat{\beta}_1$, $\bar{y}$, and $\bar{x}$:

$$\hat{\beta}_0 = \bar{y} - \hat{\beta}_1 \bar{x}. \qquad\qquad [2.17]$$

Therefore, once we have the slope estimate $\hat{\beta}_1$, it is straightforward to obtain the intercept estimate $\hat{\beta}_0$, given $\bar{y}$ and $\bar{x}$.

Dropping the n^{-1} in (2.15) (since it does not affect the solution) and plugging (2.17) into (2.15) yields

$$\sum_{i=1}^{n} x_i[y_i - (\bar{y} - \hat{\beta}_1 \bar{x}) - \hat{\beta}_1 x_i] = 0,$$

which, upon rearrangement, gives

$$\sum_{i=1}^{n} x_i(y_i - \bar{y}) = \hat{\beta}_1 \sum_{i=1}^{n} x_i(x_i - \bar{x}).$$

From basic properties of the summation operator [see (A.7) and (A.8)],

$$\sum_{i=1}^{n} x_i(x_i - \bar{x}) = \sum_{i=1}^{n} (x_i - \bar{x})^2 \quad \text{and} \quad \sum_{i=1}^{n} x_i(y_i - \bar{y}) = \sum_{i=1}^{n} (x_i - \bar{x})(y_i - \bar{y}).$$

Therefore, provided that

$$\sum_{i=1}^{n} (x_i - \bar{x})^2 > 0, \qquad\qquad [2.18]$$

the estimated slope is

$$\hat{\beta}_1 = \frac{\sum_{i=1}^{n} (x_i - \bar{x})(y_i - \bar{y})}{\sum_{i=1}^{n} (x_i - \bar{x})^2}. \qquad\qquad [2.19]$$

Equation (2.19) is simply the sample covariance between x_i and y_i divided by the sample variance of x_i. Using simple algebra we can also write $\hat{\beta}_1$ as

$$\hat{\beta}_1 = \hat{\rho}_{xy} \cdot \left(\frac{\hat{\sigma}_y}{\hat{\sigma}_x}\right),$$

where $\hat{\rho}_{xy}$ is the sample correlation between x_i and y_i and $\hat{\sigma}_x$, $\hat{\sigma}_y$ denote the sample standard deviations. (See Appendix C for definitions of correlation and standard deviation. Dividing all sums by $n-1$ does not affect the formulas.) An immediate implication is that if x_i and y_i are positively correlated in the sample then $\hat{\beta}_1 > 0$; if x_i and y_i are negatively correlated then $\hat{\beta}_1 < 0$.

Not surprisingly, the formula for $\hat{\beta}_1$ in terms of the sample correlation and sample standard deviations is the sample analog of the population relationship

$$\beta_1 = \rho_{xy} \cdot \left(\frac{\sigma_y}{\sigma_x}\right),$$

where all quantities are defined for the entire population. Recognition that β_1 is just a scaled version, ρ_{xy} highlights an important limitation of simple regression when we do not have experimental data: In effect, simple regression is an analysis of correlation between two variables, and so one must be careful in inferring causality.

Although the method for obtaining (2.17) and (2.19) is motivated by (2.6), the only assumption needed to compute the estimates for a particular sample is (2.18). This is hardly an assumption at all: (2.18) is true, provided the x_i in the sample are not all equal to the same value. If (2.18) fails, then

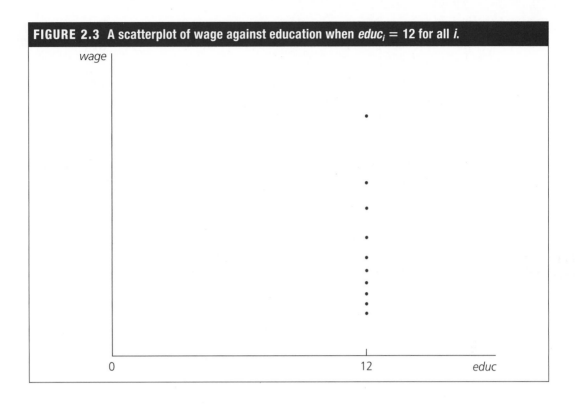

FIGURE 2.3 A scatterplot of wage against education when $educ_i = 12$ for all i.

we have either been unlucky in obtaining our sample from the population or we have not specified an interesting problem (x does not vary in the population). For example, if $y = wage$ and $x = educ$, then (2.18) fails only if everyone in the sample has the same amount of education (for example, if everyone is a high school graduate; see Figure 2.3). If just one person has a different amount of education, then (2.18) holds, and the estimates can be computed.

The estimates given in (2.17) and (2.19) are called the **ordinary least squares (OLS)** estimates of β_0 and β_1. To justify this name, for any $\hat{\beta}_0$ and $\hat{\beta}_1$ define a **fitted value** for y when $x = x_i$ as

$$\hat{y}_i = \hat{\beta}_0 + \hat{\beta}_1 x_i. \qquad [2.20]$$

This is the value we predict for y when $x = x_i$ for the given intercept and slope. There is a fitted value for each observation in the sample. The **residual** for observation i is the difference between the actual y_i and its fitted value:

$$\hat{u}_i = y_i - \hat{y}_i = y_i - \hat{\beta}_0 - \hat{\beta}_1 x_i. \qquad [2.21]$$

Again, there are n such residuals. [These are *not* the same as the errors in (2.9), a point we return to in Section 2-5.] The fitted values and residuals are indicated in Figure 2.4.

Now, suppose we choose $\hat{\beta}_0$ and $\hat{\beta}_1$ to make the **sum of squared residuals**,

$$\sum_{i=1}^{n} \hat{u}_i^2 = \sum_{i=1}^{n} (y_i - \hat{\beta}_0 - \hat{\beta}_1 x_i)^2, \qquad [2.22]$$

as small as possible. The appendix to this chapter shows that the conditions necessary for $(\hat{\beta}_0, \hat{\beta}_1)$ to minimize (2.22) are given exactly by equations (2.14) and (2.15), without n^{-1}. Equations (2.14) and (2.15) are often called the **first order conditions** for the OLS estimates, a term that comes from optimization using calculus (see Appendix A). From our previous calculations, we know that the solutions to the OLS first order conditions are given by (2.17) and (2.19). The name "ordinary least squares" comes from the fact that these estimates minimize the sum of squared residuals.

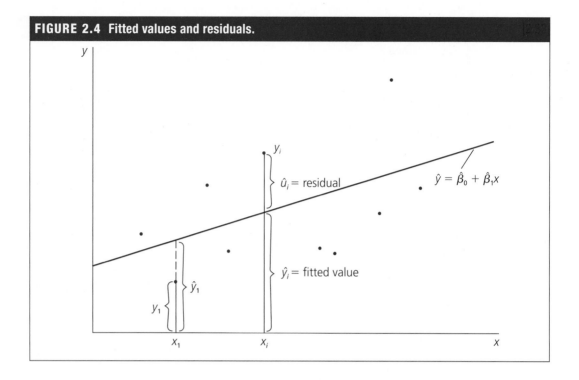

FIGURE 2.4 Fitted values and residuals.

When we view ordinary least squares as minimizing the sum of squared residuals, it is natural to ask: Why not minimize some other function of the residuals, such as the absolute values of the residuals? In fact, as we will discuss in the more advanced Section 9-4, minimizing the sum of the absolute values of the residuals is sometimes very useful. But it does have some drawbacks. First, we cannot obtain formulas for the resulting estimators; given a data set, the estimates must be obtained by numerical optimization routines. As a consequence, the statistical theory for estimators that minimize the sum of the absolute residuals is very complicated. Minimizing other functions of the residuals, say, the sum of the residuals each raised to the fourth power, has similar drawbacks. (We would never choose our estimates to minimize, say, the sum of the residuals themselves, as residuals large in magnitude but with opposite signs would tend to cancel out.) With OLS, we will be able to derive unbiasedness, consistency, and other important statistical properties relatively easily. Plus, as the motivation in equations (2.12) and (2.13) suggests, and as we will see in Section 2-5, OLS is suited for estimating the parameters appearing in the conditional mean function (2.8).

Once we have determined the OLS intercept and slope estimates, we form the **OLS regression line**:

$$\hat{y} = \hat{\beta}_0 + \hat{\beta}_1 x, \qquad [2.23]$$

where it is understood that $\hat{\beta}_0$ and $\hat{\beta}_1$ have been obtained using equations (2.17) and (2.19). The notation $\hat{y}$, read as "y hat," emphasizes that the predicted values from equation (2.23) are estimates. The intercept, $\hat{\beta}_0$, is the predicted value of y when $x = 0$, although in some cases it will not make sense to set $x = 0$. In those situations, $\hat{\beta}_0$ is not, in itself, very interesting. When using (2.23) to compute predicted values of y for various values of x, we must account for the intercept in the calculations. Equation (2.23) is also called the **sample regression function (SRF)** because it is the estimated version of the population regression function $E(y|x) = \beta_0 + \beta_1 x$. It is important to remember that the PRF is something fixed, but unknown, in the population. Because the SRF is obtained for a given sample of data, a new sample will generate a different slope and intercept in equation (2.23).

In most cases, the slope estimate, which we can write as

$$\hat{\beta}_1 = \Delta\hat{y}/\Delta x, \qquad [2.24]$$

is of primary interest. It tells us the amount by which $\hat{y}$ changes when x increases by one unit. Equivalently,

$$\Delta\hat{y} = \hat{\beta}_1\Delta x, \qquad [2.25]$$

so that given any change in x (whether positive or negative), we can compute the predicted change in y.

We now present several examples of simple regression obtained by using real data. In other words, we find the intercept and slope estimates with equations (2.17) and (2.19). Since these examples involve many observations, the calculations were done using an econometrics software package. At this point, you should be careful not to read too much into these regressions; they are not necessarily uncovering a causal relationship. We have said nothing so far about the statistical properties of OLS. In Section 2-5, we consider statistical properties after we explicitly impose assumptions on the population model equation (2.1).

EXAMPLE 2.3   **CEO Salary and Return on Equity**

For the population of chief executive officers, let y be annual salary (*salary*) in thousands of dollars. Thus, $y = 856.3$ indicates an annual salary of $856,300, and $y = 1,452.6$ indicates a salary of $1,452,600. Let x be the average return on equity (*roe*) for the CEO's firm for the previous three years. (Return on equity is defined in terms of net income as a percentage of common equity.) For example, if $roe = 10$, then average return on equity is 10%.

To study the relationship between this measure of firm performance and CEO compensation, we postulate the simple model

$$salary = \beta_0 + \beta_1 roe + u.$$

The slope parameter β_1 measures the change in annual salary, in thousands of dollars, when return on equity increases by one percentage point. Because a higher *roe* is good for the company, we think $\beta_1 > 0$.

The data set CEOSAL1 contains information on 209 CEOs for the year 1990; these data were obtained from *Business Week* (5/6/91). In this sample, the average annual salary is $1,281,120, with the smallest and largest being $223,000 and $14,822,000, respectively. The average return on equity for the years 1988, 1989, and 1990 is 17.18%, with the smallest and largest values being 0.5% and 56.3%, respectively.

Using the data in CEOSAL1, the OLS regression line relating *salary* to *roe* is

$$\widehat{salary} = 963.191 + 18.501\,roe \qquad [2.26]$$

$$n = 209,$$

where the intercept and slope estimates have been rounded to three decimal places; we use "*salary* hat" to indicate that this is an estimated equation. How do we interpret the equation? First, if the return on equity is zero, $roe = 0$, then the predicted *salary* is the intercept, 963.191, which equals $963,191 since *salary* is measured in thousands. Next, we can write the predicted change in salary as a function of the change in *roe*: $\widehat{\Delta salary} = 18.501\,(\Delta roe)$. This means that if the return on equity increases by one percentage point, $\Delta roe = 1$, then *salary* is predicted to change by about 18.5, or $18,500. Because (2.26) is a linear equation, this is the estimated change regardless of the initial salary.

We can easily use (2.26) to compare predicted salaries at different values of *roe*. Suppose $roe = 30$. Then $\widehat{salary} = 963.191 + 18.501(30) = 1,518,221$, which is just over $1.5 million. However, this does *not* mean that a particular CEO whose firm had a $roe = 30$ earns $1,518,221. Many other factors affect salary. This is just our prediction from the OLS regression line (2.26). The estimated line is graphed in Figure 2.5, along with the population regression function E(*salary*|*roe*). We will never know the PRF, so we cannot tell how close the SRF is to the PRF. Another sample of data will give a different regression line, which may or may not be closer to the population regression line.

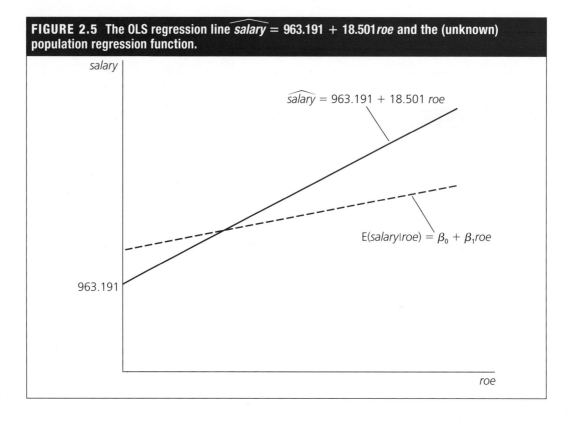

FIGURE 2.5 The OLS regression line $\widehat{salary} = 963.191 + 18.501\,roe$ and the (unknown) population regression function.

$\widehat{salary} = 963.191 + 18.501\ roe$

$E(salary|roe) = \beta_0 + \beta_1 roe$

963.191

salary

roe

EXAMPLE 2.4   **Wage and Education**

For the population of people in the workforce in 1976, let $y = wage$, where *wage* is measured in dollars per hour. Thus, for a particular person, if $wage = 6.75$, the hourly *wage* is \$6.75. Let $x = educ$ denote years of schooling; for example, $educ = 12$ corresponds to a complete high school education. Since the average wage in the sample is \$5.90, the Consumer Price Index indicates that this amount is equivalent to \$19.06 in 2003 dollars.

Using the data in WAGE1 where $n = 526$ individuals, we obtain the following OLS regression line (or sample regression function):

$$\widehat{wage} = -0.90 + 0.54\,educ \qquad\qquad [2.27]$$

$$n = 526.$$

We must interpret this equation with caution. The intercept of −0.90 literally means that a person with no education has a predicted hourly wage of −90¢ an hour. This, of course, is silly. It turns out that only 18 people in the sample of 526 have less than eight years of education. Consequently, it is not surprising that the regression line does poorly at very low levels of education. For a person with eight years of education, the predicted wage is $\widehat{wage} = -0.90 + 0.54(8) = 3.42$, or \$3.42 per hour (in 1976 dollars).

The slope estimate in (2.27) implies that one more year of education increases hourly wage by 54¢ an hour. Therefore, four more years of education increase the predicted wage by $4(0.54) = 2.16$, or \$2.16 per hour. These are fairly large effects.

> **EXPLORING FURTHER 2.2**
>
> The estimated wage from (2.27), when $educ = 8$, is \$3.42 in 1976 dollars. What is this value in 2003 dollars? (*Hint*: You have enough information in Example 2.4 to answer this question.)

Because of the linear nature of (2.27), another year of education increases the wage by the same amount, regardless of the initial level of education. In Section 2.4, we discuss some methods that allow for nonconstant marginal effects of our explanatory variables.

EXAMPLE 2.5   **Voting Outcomes and Campaign Expenditures**

The file VOTE1 contains data on election outcomes and campaign expenditures for 173 two-party races for the U.S. House of Representatives in 1988. There are two candidates in each race, A and B. Let *voteA* be the percentage of the vote received by Candidate A and *shareA* be the percentage of total campaign expenditures accounted for by Candidate A. Many factors other than *shareA* affect the election outcome (including the quality of the candidates and possibly the dollar amounts spent by A and B). Nevertheless, we can estimate a simple regression model to find out whether spending more relative to one's challenger implies a higher percentage of the vote.

The estimated equation using the 173 observations is

$$\widehat{voteA} = 26.81 + 0.464\ shareA \qquad\qquad [2.28]$$

$$n = 173.$$

This means that if Candidate A's share of spending increases by one percentage point, Candidate A receives almost one-half a percentage point (0.464) more of the total vote. Whether or not this is a causal effect is unclear, but it is not unbelievable. If *shareA* = 50, *voteA* is predicted to be about 50, or half the vote.

> **EXPLORING FURTHER 2.3**
>
> In Example 2.5, what is the predicted vote for Candidate A if *shareA* = 60 (which means 60%)? Does this answer seem reasonable?

In some cases, regression analysis is not used to determine causality but to simply look at whether two variables are positively or negatively related, much like a standard correlation analysis. An example of this occurs in Computer Exercise C3, where you are asked to use data from Biddle and Hamermesh (1990) on time spent sleeping and working to investigate the tradeoff between these two factors.

2-2a A Note on Terminology

In most cases, we will indicate the estimation of a relationship through OLS by writing an equation such as (2.26), (2.27), or (2.28). Sometimes, for the sake of brevity, it is useful to indicate that an OLS regression has been run without actually writing out the equation. We will often indicate that equation (2.23) has been obtained by OLS in saying that we *run the regression of*

$$y \text{ on } x, \qquad\qquad [2.29]$$

or simply that we *regress y on x*. The positions of *y* and *x* in (2.29) indicate which is the dependent variable and which is the independent variable: we always regress the dependent variable on the independent variable. For specific applications, we replace *y* and *x* with their names. Thus, to obtain (2.26), we regress *salary* on *roe*, or to obtain (2.28), we regress *voteA* on *shareA*.

When we use such terminology in (2.29), we will always mean that we plan to estimate the intercept, $\hat{\beta}_0$, along with the slope, $\hat{\beta}_1$. This case is appropriate for the vast majority of applications.

Occasionally, we may want to estimate the relationship between y and x *assuming* that the intercept is zero (so that $x = 0$ implies that $\hat{y} = 0$); we cover this case briefly in Section 2.6. Unless explicitly stated otherwise, we always estimate an intercept along with a slope.

2-3 Properties of OLS on Any Sample of Data

In the previous section, we went through the algebra of deriving the formulas for the OLS intercept and slope estimates. In this section, we cover some further algebraic properties of the fitted OLS regression line. The best way to think about these properties is to remember that they hold, by construction, for *any* sample of data. The harder task—considering the properties of OLS across all possible random samples of data—is postponed until Section 2-5.

Several of the algebraic properties we are going to derive will appear mundane. Nevertheless, having a grasp of these properties helps us to figure out what happens to the OLS estimates and related statistics when the data are manipulated in certain ways, such as when the measurement units of the dependent and independent variables change.

2-3a Fitted Values and Residuals

We assume that the intercept and slope estimates, $\hat{\beta}_0$ and $\hat{\beta}_1$, have been obtained for the given sample of data. Given $\hat{\beta}_0$ and $\hat{\beta}_1$, we can obtain the fitted value $\hat{y}_i$ for each observation. [This is given by equation (2.20).] By definition, each fitted value of $\hat{y}_i$ is on the OLS regression line. The OLS residual associated with observation i, $\hat{u}_i$, is the difference between y_i and its fitted value, as given in equation (2.21). If $\hat{u}_i$ is positive, the line underpredicts y_i; if $\hat{u}_i$ is negative, the line overpredicts y_i. The ideal case for observation i is when $\hat{u}_i = 0$, but in most cases, *every* residual is not equal to zero. In other words, none of the data points must actually lie on the OLS line.

EXAMPLE 2.6 **CEO Salary and Return on Equity**

Table 2.2 contains a listing of the first 15 observations in the CEO data set, along with the fitted values, called *salaryhat*, and the residuals, called *uhat*.

The first four CEOs have lower salaries than what we predicted from the OLS regression line (2.26); in other words, given only the firm's *roe*, these CEOs make less than what we predicted. As can be seen from the positive *uhat*, the fifth CEO makes more than predicted from the OLS regression line.

2-3b Algebraic Properties of OLS Statistics

There are several useful algebraic properties of OLS estimates and their associated statistics. We now cover the three most important of these.

(1) The sum, and therefore the sample average of the OLS residuals, is zero. Mathematically,

$$\sum_{i=1}^{n} \hat{u}_i = 0. \qquad [2.30]$$

This property needs no proof; it follows immediately from the OLS first order condition (2.14), when we remember that the residuals are defined by $\hat{u}_i = y_i - \hat{\beta}_0 - \hat{\beta}_1 x_i$. In other words, the OLS estimates

TABLE 2.2 Fitted Values and Residuals for the First 15 CEOs				
obsno	roe	salary	salaryhat	uhat
1	14.1	1095	1224.058	−129.0581
2	10.9	1001	1164.854	−163.8542
3	23.5	1122	1397.969	−275.9692
4	5.9	578	1072.348	−494.3484
5	13.8	1368	1218.508	149.4923
6	20.0	1145	1333.215	−188.2151
7	16.4	1078	1266.611	−188.6108
8	16.3	1094	1264.761	−170.7606
9	10.5	1237	1157.454	79.54626
10	26.3	833	1449.773	−616.7726
11	25.9	567	1442.372	−875.3721
12	26.8	933	1459.023	−526.0231
13	14.8	1339	1237.009	101.9911
14	22.3	937	1375.768	−438.7678
15	56.3	2011	2004.808	6.191895

$\hat{\beta}_0$ and $\hat{\beta}_1$ are *chosen* to make the residuals add up to zero (for any data set). This says nothing about the residual for any particular observation i.

(2) The sample covariance between the regressors and the OLS residuals is zero. This follows from the first order condition (2.15), which can be written in terms of the residuals as

$$\sum_{i=1}^{n} x_i \hat{u}_i = 0. \tag{2.31}$$

The sample average of the OLS residuals is zero, so the left-hand side of (2.31) is proportional to the sample covariance between x_i and $\hat{u}_i$.

(3) The point $(\bar{x}, \bar{y})$ is always on the OLS regression line. In other words, if we take equation (2.23) and plug in $\bar{x}$ for x, then the predicted value is $\bar{y}$. This is exactly what equation (2.16) showed us.

EXAMPLE 2.7	**Wage and Education**

For the data in WAGE1, the average hourly wage in the sample is 5.90, rounded to two decimal places, and the average education is 12.56. If we plug $educ = 12.56$ into the OLS regression line (2.27), we get $\widehat{wage} = -0.90 + 0.54(12.56) = 5.8824$, which equals 5.9 when rounded to the first decimal place. These figures do not exactly agree because we have rounded the average wage and education, as well as the intercept and slope estimates. If we did not initially round any of the values, we would get the answers to agree more closely, but to little useful effect.

Writing each y_i as its fitted value, plus its residual, provides another way to interpret an OLS regression. For each i, write

$$y_i = \hat{y}_i + \hat{u}_i. \tag{2.32}$$

From property (1), the average of the residuals is zero; equivalently, the sample average of the fitted values, $\hat{y}_i$, is the same as the sample average of the y_i, or $\bar{\hat{y}} = \bar{y}$. Further, properties (1) and (2) can be used to show that the sample covariance between $\hat{y}_i$ and $\hat{u}_i$ is zero. Thus, we can view OLS as decomposing each y_i into two parts, a fitted value and a residual. The fitted values and residuals are uncorrelated in the sample.

Define the **total sum of squares (SST)**, the **explained sum of squares (SSE)**, and the **residual sum of squares (SSR)** (also known as the sum of squared residuals), as follows:

$$SST \equiv \sum_{i=1}^{n} (y_i - \bar{y})^2. \tag{2.33}$$

$$SSE \equiv \sum_{i=1}^{n} (\hat{y}_i - \bar{y})^2. \tag{2.34}$$

$$SSR \equiv \sum_{i=1}^{n} \hat{u}_i^2. \tag{2.35}$$

SST is a measure of the total sample variation in the y_i; that is, it measures how spread out the y_i are in the sample. If we divide SST by $n - 1$, we obtain the sample variance of y, as discussed in Appendix C. Similarly, SSE measures the sample variation in the $\hat{y}_i$ (where we use the fact that $\bar{\hat{y}} = \bar{y}$), and SSR measures the sample variation in the $\hat{u}_i$. The total variation in y can always be expressed as the sum of the explained variation and the unexplained variation SSR. Thus,

$$SST = SSE + SSR. \tag{2.36}$$

Proving (2.36) is not difficult, but it requires us to use all of the properties of the summation operator covered in Appendix A. Write

$$\sum_{i=1}^{n} (y_i - \bar{y})^2 = \sum_{i=1}^{n} [(y_i - \hat{y}_i) + (\hat{y}_i - \bar{y})]^2$$

$$= \sum_{i=1}^{n} [\hat{u}_i + (\hat{y}_i - \bar{y})]^2$$

$$= \sum_{i=1}^{n} \hat{u}_i^2 + 2 \sum_{i=1}^{n} \hat{u}_i (\hat{y}_i - \bar{y}) + \sum_{i=1}^{n} (\hat{y}_i - \bar{y})^2$$

$$= SSR + 2 \sum_{i=1}^{n} \hat{u}_i (\hat{y}_i - \bar{y}) + SSE.$$

Now, (2.36) holds if we show that

$$\sum_{i=1}^{n} \hat{u}_i (\hat{y}_i - \bar{y}) = 0. \tag{2.37}$$

But we have already claimed that the sample covariance between the residuals and the fitted values is zero, and this covariance is just (2.37) divided by $n - 1$. Thus, we have established (2.36).

Some words of caution about SST, SSE, and SSR are in order. There is no uniform agreement on the names or abbreviations for the three quantities defined in equations (2.33), (2.34), and (2.35). The total sum of squares is called either SST or TSS, so there is little confusion here. Unfortunately, the explained sum of squares is sometimes called the "regression sum of squares." If this term is given its natural abbreviation, it can easily be confused with the term "residual sum of squares." Some regression packages refer to the explained sum of squares as the "model sum of squares."

To make matters even worse, the residual sum of squares is often called the "error sum of squares." This is especially unfortunate because, as we will see in Section 2-5, the errors and the residuals are different quantities. Thus, we will always call (2.35) the residual sum of squares or the sum of squared residuals. We prefer to use the abbreviation SSR to denote the sum of squared residuals, because it is more common in econometric packages.

2-3c Goodness-of-Fit

So far, we have no way of measuring how well the explanatory or independent variable, x, explains the dependent variable, y. It is often useful to compute a number that summarizes how well the OLS regression line fits the data. In the following discussion, be sure to remember that we assume that an intercept is estimated along with the slope.

Assuming that the total sum of squares, SST, is not equal to zero—which is true except in the very unlikely event that all the y_i equal the same value—we can divide (2.36) by SST to get $1 = \text{SSE/SST} + \text{SSR/SST}$. The **R-squared** of the regression, sometimes called the **coefficient of determination**, is defined as

$$R^2 \equiv \text{SSE/SST} = 1 - \text{SSR/SST}. \tag{2.38}$$

R^2 is the ratio of the explained variation compared to the total variation; thus, it is interpreted as the *fraction of the sample variation in y that is explained by x*. The second equality in (2.38) provides another way for computing R^2.

From (2.36), the value of R^2 is always between zero and one, because SSE can be no greater than SST. When interpreting R^2, we usually multiply it by 100 to change it into a percent: $100 \cdot R^2$ is the *percentage of the sample variation in y that is explained by x*.

If the data points all lie on the same line, OLS provides a perfect fit to the data. In this case, $R^2 = 1$. A value of R^2 that is nearly equal to zero indicates a poor fit of the OLS line: very little of the variation in the y_i is captured by the variation in the $\hat{y}_i$ (which all lie on the OLS regression line). In fact, it can be shown that R^2 is equal to the *square* of the sample correlation coefficient between y_i and $\hat{y}_i$. This is where the term "R-squared" came from. (The letter R was traditionally used to denote an estimate of a population correlation coefficient, and its usage has survived in regression analysis.)

EXAMPLE 2.8 **CEO Salary and Return on Equity**

In the CEO salary regression, we obtain the following:

$$\widehat{salary} = 963.191 + 18.501\ roe \tag{2.39}$$

$$n = 209, R^2 = 0.0132.$$

We have reproduced the OLS regression line and the number of observations for clarity. Using the R-squared (rounded to four decimal places) reported for this equation, we can see how much of the variation in salary is actually explained by the return on equity. The answer is: not much. The firm's return on equity explains only about 1.3% of the variation in salaries for this sample of 209 CEOs. That means that 98.7% of the salary variations for these CEOs is left unexplained! This lack of explanatory power may not be too surprising because many other characteristics of both the firm and the individual CEO should influence salary; these factors are necessarily included in the errors in a simple regression analysis.

In the social sciences, low R-squareds in regression equations are not uncommon, especially for cross-sectional analysis. We will discuss this issue more generally under multiple regression analysis, but it is worth emphasizing now that a seemingly low R-squared does not necessarily mean that an OLS regression equation is useless. It is still possible that (2.39) is a good estimate of the ceteris paribus relationship between *salary* and *roe*; whether or not this is true does *not* depend directly on the size of R-squared. Students who are first learning econometrics tend to put too much weight on the size of the R-squared in evaluating regression equations. For now, be aware that using R-squared as the main gauge of success for an econometric analysis can lead to trouble.

Sometimes, the explanatory variable explains a substantial part of the sample variation in the dependent variable.

EXAMPLE 2.9 | **Voting Outcomes and Campaign Expenditures**

In the voting outcome equation in (2.28), $R^2 = 0.856$. Thus, the share of campaign expenditures explains over 85% of the variation in the election outcomes for this sample. This is a sizable portion.

2-4 Units of Measurement and Functional Form

Two important issues in applied economics are (1) understanding how changing the units of measurement of the dependent and/or independent variables affects OLS estimates and (2) knowing how to incorporate popular functional forms used in economics into regression analysis. The mathematics needed for a full understanding of functional form issues is reviewed in Appendix A.

2-4a The Effects of Changing Units of Measurement on OLS Statistics

In Example 2.3, we chose to measure annual salary in thousands of dollars, and the return on equity was measured as a percentage (rather than as a decimal). It is crucial to know how *salary* and *roe* are measured in this example in order to make sense of the estimates in equation (2.39).

We must also know that OLS estimates change in entirely expected ways when the units of measurement of the dependent and independent variables change. In Example 2.3, suppose that, rather than measuring salary in thousands of dollars, we measure it in dollars. Let *salardol* be salary in dollars (*salardol* = 845,761 would be interpreted as $845,761). Of course, *salardol* has a simple relationship to the salary measured in thousands of dollars: *salardol* = 1,000 · *salary*. We do not need to actually run the regression of *salardol* on *roe* to know that the estimated equation is:

$$\widehat{salardol} = 963,191 + 18,501\ roe. \tag{2.40}$$

We obtain the intercept and slope in (2.40) simply by multiplying the intercept and the slope in (2.39) by 1,000. This gives equations (2.39) and (2.40) the *same* interpretation. Looking at (2.40), if *roe* = 0, then $\widehat{salardol}$ = 963,191, so the predicted salary is $963,191 [the same value we obtained from equation (2.39)]. Furthermore, if *roe* increases by one, then the predicted salary increases by $18,501; again, this is what we concluded from our earlier analysis of equation (2.39).

Generally, it is easy to figure out what happens to the intercept and slope estimates when the dependent variable changes units of measurement. If the dependent variable is multiplied by the constant c—which means each value in the sample is multiplied by c—then the OLS intercept and slope estimates are also multiplied by c. (This assumes nothing has changed about the independent variable.) In the CEO salary example, $c = 1,000$ in moving from *salary* to *salardol*.

We can also use the CEO salary example to see what happens when we change the units of measurement of the independent variable. Define *roedec* = *roe*/100 to be the decimal equivalent of *roe*; thus, *roedec* = 0.23 means a return on equity of 23%. To focus on changing the units of measurement

---

EXPLORING FURTHER 2.4

Suppose that salary is measured in hundreds of dollars, rather than in thousands of dollars, say, *salarhun*. What will be the OLS intercept and slope estimates in the regression of *salarhun* on *roe*?

of the independent variable, we return to our original dependent variable, *salary*, which is measured in thousands of dollars. When we regress *salary* on *roedec*, we obtain

$$\widehat{salary} = 963.191 + 1{,}850.1 \; roedec. \tag{2.41}$$

The coefficient on *roedec* is 100 times the coefficient on *roe* in (2.39). This is as it should be. Changing *roe* by one percentage point is equivalent to $\Delta roedec = 0.01$. From (2.41), if $\Delta roedec = 0.01$, then $\widehat{\Delta salary} = 1{,}850.1(0.01) = 18.501$, which is what is obtained by using (2.39). Note that, in moving from (2.39) to (2.41), the independent variable was divided by 100, and so the OLS slope estimate was multiplied by 100, preserving the interpretation of the equation. Generally, if the independent variable is divided or multiplied by some nonzero constant, c, then the OLS slope coefficient is multiplied or divided by c, respectively.

The intercept has not changed in (2.41) because *roedec* $= 0$ still corresponds to a zero return on equity. In general, changing the units of measurement of only the independent variable does not affect the intercept.

In the previous section, we defined *R*-squared as a goodness-of-fit measure for OLS regression. We can also ask what happens to R^2 when the unit of measurement of either the independent or the dependent variable changes. Without doing any algebra, we should know the result: the goodness of fit of the model should not depend on the units of measurement of our variables. For example, the amount of variation in salary explained by the return on equity should not depend on whether salary is measured in dollars or in thousands of dollars or on whether return on equity is a percentage or a decimal. This intuition can be verified mathematically: using the definition of R^2, it can be shown that R^2 is, in fact, invariant to changes in the units of y or x.

2-4b Incorporating Nonlinearities in Simple Regression

So far, we have focused on *linear* relationships between the dependent and independent variables. As we mentioned in Chapter 1, linear relationships are not nearly general enough for all economic applications. Fortunately, it is rather easy to incorporate many nonlinearities into simple regression analysis by appropriately defining the dependent and independent variables. Here, we will cover two possibilities that often appear in applied work.

In reading applied work in the social sciences, you will often encounter regression equations where the dependent variable appears in logarithmic form. Why is this done? Recall the wage-education example, where we regressed hourly wage on years of education. We obtained a slope estimate of 0.54 [see equation (2.27)], which means that each additional year of education is predicted to increase hourly wage by 54 cents. Because of the linear nature of (2.27), 54 cents is the increase for either the first year of education or the twentieth year; this may not be reasonable.

Probably a better characterization of how wage changes with education is that each year of education increases wage by a constant *percentage*. For example, an increase in education from 5 years to 6 years increases wage by, say, 8% (ceteris paribus), and an increase in education from 11 to 12 years also increases wage by 8%. A model that gives (approximately) a constant percentage effect is

$$\log(wage) = \beta_0 + \beta_1 educ + u, \tag{2.42}$$

where $\log(\cdot)$ denotes the *natural* logarithm. (See Appendix A for a review of logarithms.) In particular, if $\Delta u = 0$, then

$$\%\Delta wage \approx (100 \cdot \beta_1)\Delta educ. \tag{2.43}$$

Notice how we multiply β_1 by 100 to get the percentage change in *wage* given one additional year of education. Since the percentage change in *wage* is the same for each additional year of education, the change in *wage* for an extra year of education *increases* as education increases; in other words, (2.42) implies an *increasing* return to education. By exponentiating (2.42), we can write $wage = \exp(\beta_0 + \beta_1 educ + u)$. This equation is graphed in Figure 2.6, with $u = 0$.

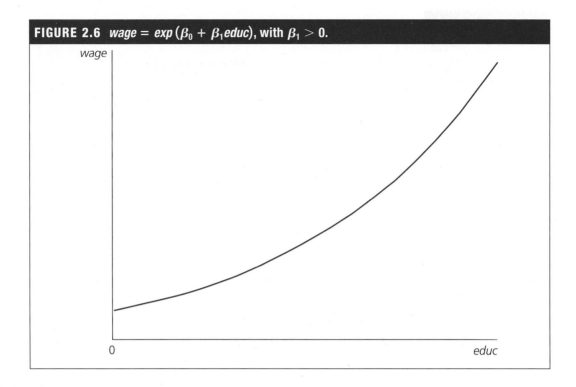

FIGURE 2.6 $wage = exp\,(\beta_0 + \beta_1 educ)$, with $\beta_1 > 0$.

EXAMPLE 2.10   **A Log Wage Equation**

Using the same data as in Example 2.4, but using log($wage$) as the dependent variable, we obtain the following relationship:

$$\widehat{\log(wage)} = 0.584 + 0.083\,educ \qquad\qquad \text{[2.44]}$$

$$n = 526,\ R^2 = 0.186.$$

The coefficient on $educ$ has a percentage interpretation when it is multiplied by 100: $\widehat{wage}$ increases by 8.3% for every additional year of education. This is what economists mean when they refer to the "return to another year of education."

It is important to remember that the main reason for using the log of $wage$ in (2.42) is to impose a constant percentage effect of education on $wage$. Once equation (2.44) is obtained, the natural log of $wage$ is rarely mentioned. In particular, it is *not* correct to say that another year of education increases log($wage$) by 8.3%.

The intercept in (2.44) is not very meaningful, because it gives the predicted log($wage$), when $educ = 0$. The R-squared shows that $educ$ explains about 18.6% of the variation in log($wage$) (*not* $wage$). Finally, equation (2.44) might not capture all of the nonlinearity in the relationship between wage and schooling. If there are "diploma effects," then the twelfth year of education—graduation from high school—could be worth much more than the eleventh year. We will learn how to allow for this kind of nonlinearity in Chapter 7.

Estimating a model such as (2.42) is straightforward when using simple regression. Just define the dependent variable, y, to be $y = \log(wage)$. The independent variable is represented by $x = educ$. The mechanics of OLS are the same as before: the intercept and slope estimates are given by the formulas (2.17) and (2.19). In other words, we obtain $\hat{\beta}_0$ and $\hat{\beta}_1$ from the OLS regression of log($wage$) on $educ$.

Another important use of the natural log is in obtaining a **constant elasticity model**.

EXAMPLE 2.11	**CEO Salary and Firm Sales**

We can estimate a constant elasticity model relating CEO salary to firm sales. The data set is the same one used in Example 2.3, except we now relate *salary* to *sales*. Let *sales* be annual firm sales, measured in millions of dollars. A constant elasticity model is

$$\log(salary) = \beta_0 + \beta_1 \log(sales) + u, \tag{2.45}$$

where β_1 is the elasticity of *salary* with respect to *sales*. This model falls under the simple regression model by defining the dependent variable to be $y = \log(salary)$ and the independent variable to be $x = \log(sales)$. Estimating this equation by OLS gives

$$\widehat{\log(salary)} = 4.822 + 0.257 \log(sales) \tag{2.46}$$

$$n = 209, R^2 = 0.211.$$

The coefficient of log(*sales*) is the estimated elasticity of *salary* with respect to *sales*. It implies that a 1% increase in firm sales increases CEO salary by about 0.257%—the usual interpretation of an elasticity.

The two functional forms covered in this section will often arise in the remainder of this text. We have covered models containing natural logarithms here because they appear so frequently in applied work. The interpretation of such models will not be much different in the multiple regression case.

It is also useful to note what happens to the intercept and slope estimates if we change the units of measurement of the dependent variable when it appears in logarithmic form. Because the change to logarithmic form approximates a proportionate change, it makes sense that *nothing* happens to the slope. We can see this by writing the rescaled variable as $c_1 y_i$ for each observation i. The original equation is $\log(y_i) = \beta_0 + \beta_1 x_i + u_i$. If we add $\log(c_1)$ to both sides, we get $\log(c_1) + \log(y_i) = [\log(c_1) + \beta_0] + \beta_1 x_i + u_i$, or $\log(c_1 y_i) = [\log(c_1) + \beta_0] + \beta_1 x_i + u_i$. (Remember that the sum of the logs is equal to the log of their product, as shown in Appendix A.) Therefore, the slope is still β_1, but the intercept is now $\log(c_1) + \beta_0$. Similarly, if the independent variable is $\log(x)$, and we change the units of measurement of x before taking the log, the slope remains the same, but the intercept changes. You will be asked to verify these claims in Problem 9.

We end this subsection by summarizing four combinations of functional forms available from using either the original variable or its natural log. In Table 2.3, x and y stand for the variables in their original form. The model with y as the dependent variable and x as the independent variable is called the *level-level* model because each variable appears in its level form. The model with $\log(y)$ as the dependent variable and x as the independent variable is called the *log-level* model. We will not explicitly discuss the *level-log* model here, because it arises less often in practice. In any case, we will see examples of this model in later chapters.

The last column in Table 2.3 gives the interpretation of β_1. In the log-level model, $100 \cdot \beta_1$ is sometimes called the **semi-elasticity** of y with respect to x. As we mentioned in Example 2.11, in the log-log model, β_1 is the **elasticity** of y with respect to x. Table 2.3 warrants careful study, as we will refer to it often in the remainder of the text.

TABLE 2.3 Summary of Functional Forms Involving Logarithms

Model	Dependent Variable	Independent Variable	Interpretation of β_1
Level-level	y	x	$\Delta y = \beta_1 \Delta x$
Level-log	y	$\log(x)$	$\Delta y = (\beta_1/100)\%\Delta x$
Log-level	$\log(y)$	x	$\%\Delta y = (100\beta_1)\Delta x$
Log-log	$\log(y)$	$\log(x)$	$\%\Delta y = \beta_1 \%\Delta x$

2-4c The Meaning of "Linear" Regression

The simple regression model that we have studied in this chapter is also called the simple *linear* regression model. Yet, as we have just seen, the general model also allows for certain *nonlinear* relationships. So what does "linear" mean here? You can see by looking at equation (2.1) that $y = \beta_0 + \beta_1 x + u$. The key is that this equation is linear in the *parameters* β_0 and β_1. There are no restrictions on how y and x relate to the original explained and explanatory variables of interest. As we saw in Examples 2.10 and 2.11, y and x can be natural logs of variables, and this is quite common in applications. But we need not stop there. For example, nothing prevents us from using simple regression to estimate a model such as $cons = \beta_0 + \beta_1 \sqrt{inc} + u$, where *cons* is annual consumption and *inc* is annual income.

Whereas the mechanics of simple regression do not depend on how y and x are defined, the interpretation of the coefficients does depend on their definitions. For successful empirical work, it is much more important to become proficient at interpreting coefficients than to become efficient at computing formulas such as (2.19). We will get much more practice with interpreting the estimates in OLS regression lines when we study multiple regression.

Plenty of models *cannot* be cast as a linear regression model because they are not linear in their parameters; an example is $cons = 1/(\beta_0 + \beta_1 inc) + u$. Estimation of such models takes us into the realm of the *nonlinear regression model*, which is beyond the scope of this text. For most applications, choosing a model that can be put into the linear regression framework is sufficient.

2-5 Expected Values and Variances of the OLS Estimators

In Section 2-1, we defined the population model $y = \beta_0 + \beta_1 x + u$, and we claimed that the key assumption for simple regression analysis to be useful is that the expected value of u given any value of x is zero. In Sections 2-2, 2-3, and 2-4, we discussed the algebraic properties of OLS estimation. We now return to the population model and study the *statistical* properties of OLS. In other words, we now view $\hat{\beta}_0$ and $\hat{\beta}_1$ as *estimators* for the parameters β_0 and β_1 that appear in the population model. This means that we will study properties of the distributions of $\hat{\beta}_0$ and $\hat{\beta}_1$ over different random samples from the population. (Appendix C contains definitions of estimators and reviews some of their important properties.)

2-5a Unbiasedness of OLS

We begin by establishing the unbiasedness of OLS under a simple set of assumptions. For future reference, it is useful to number these assumptions using the prefix "SLR" for simple linear regression. The first assumption defines the population model.

Assumption SLR.1   **Linear in Parameters**

In the population model, the dependent variable, y, is related to the independent variable, x, and the error (or disturbance), u, as

$$y = \beta_0 + \beta_1 x + u, \qquad\qquad [2.47]$$

where β_0 and β_1 are the population intercept and slope parameters, respectively.

To be realistic, y, x, and u are all viewed as random variables in stating the population model. We discussed the interpretation of this model at some length in Section 2.1 and gave several examples. In the previous section, we learned that equation (2.47) is not as restrictive as it initially seems; by choosing

y and x appropriately, we can obtain interesting nonlinear relationships (such as constant elasticity models).

We are interested in using data on y and x to estimate the parameters β_0 and, especially, β_1. We assume that our data were obtained as a random sample. (See Appendix C for a review of random sampling.)

Assumption SLR.2   Random Sampling

We have a random sample of size n, $\{(x_i, y_i): i = 1, 2, \ldots, n\}$, following the population model in equation (2.47).

We will have to address failure of the random sampling assumption in later chapters that deal with time series analysis and sample selection problems. Not all cross-sectional samples can be viewed as outcomes of random samples, but many can be.

We can write (2.47) in terms of the random sample as

$$y_i = \beta_0 + \beta_1 x_i + u_i, \quad i = 1, 2, \ldots, n, \qquad [2.48]$$

where u_i is the error or disturbance for observation i (for example, person i, firm i, city i, and so on). Thus, u_i contains the unobservables for observation i that affect y_i. The u_i should not be confused with the residuals, $\hat{u}_i$, that we defined in Section 2.3. Later on, we will explore the relationship between the errors and the residuals. For interpreting β_0 and β_1 in a particular application, (2.47) is most informative, but (2.48) is also needed for some of the statistical derivations.

The relationship (2.48) can be plotted for a particular outcome of data as shown in Figure 2.7.

As we already saw in Section 2.2, the OLS slope and intercept estimates are not defined unless we have some sample variation in the explanatory variable. We now add variation in the x_i to our list of assumptions.

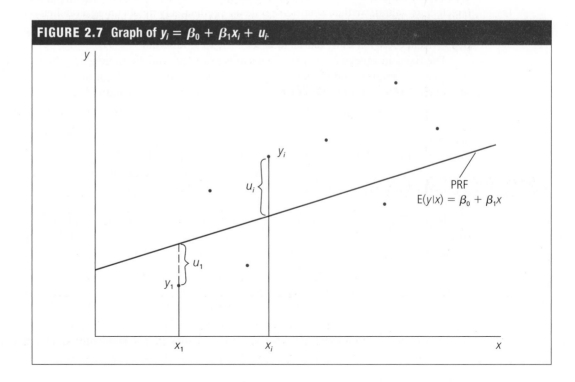

FIGURE 2.7 Graph of $y_i = \beta_0 + \beta_1 x_i + u_i$.

Assumption SLR.3	**Sample Variation in the Explanatory Variable**

The sample outcomes on x, namely, $\{x_i, i = 1, \ldots, n\}$, are not all the same value.

This is a very weak assumption—certainly not worth emphasizing, but needed nevertheless. If x varies in the population, random samples on x will typically contain variation, unless the population variation is minimal or the sample size is small. Simple inspection of summary statistics on x_i reveals whether Assumption SLR.3 fails: if the sample standard deviation of x_i is zero, then Assumption SLR.3 fails; otherwise, it holds.

Finally, in order to obtain unbiased estimators of β_0 and β_1, we need to impose the zero conditional mean assumption that we discussed in some detail in Section 2.1. We now explicitly add it to our list of assumptions.

Assumption SLR.4	**Zero Conditional Mean**

The error u has an expected value of zero given any value of the explanatory variable. In other words,

$$E(u|x) = 0.$$

For a random sample, this assumption implies that $E(u_i|x_i) = 0$, for all $i = 1, 2, \ldots, n$.

In addition to restricting the relationship between u and x in the population, the zero conditional mean assumption—coupled with the random sampling assumption—allows for a convenient technical simplification. In particular, we can derive the statistical properties of the OLS estimators as *conditional* on the values of the x_i in our sample. Technically, in statistical derivations, conditioning on the sample values of the independent variable is the same as treating the x_i as *fixed in repeated samples*, which we think of as follows. We first choose n sample values for $x_1, x_2, \ldots, x_n$. (These can be repeated.) Given these values, we then obtain a sample on y (effectively by obtaining a random sample of the u_i). Next, another sample of y is obtained, using the *same* values for $x_1, x_2, \ldots, x_n$. Then another sample of y is obtained, again using the same $x_1, x_2, \ldots, x_n$. And so on.

The fixed-in-repeated-samples scenario is not very realistic in nonexperimental contexts. For instance, in sampling individuals for the wage-education example, it makes little sense to think of choosing the values of *educ* ahead of time and then sampling individuals with those particular levels of education. Random sampling, where individuals are chosen randomly and their wage and education are both recorded, is representative of how most data sets are obtained for empirical analysis in the social sciences. Once we *assume* that $E(u|x) = 0$, and we have random sampling, nothing is lost in derivations by treating the x_i as nonrandom. The danger is that the fixed-in-repeated-samples assumption *always* implies that u_i and x_i are independent. In deciding when simple regression analysis is going to produce unbiased estimators, it is critical to think in terms of Assumption SLR.4.

Now, we are ready to show that the OLS estimators are unbiased. To this end, we use the fact that $\sum_{i=1}^{n}(x_i - \bar{x})(y_i - \bar{y}) = \sum_{i=1}^{n}(x_i - \bar{x})y_i$ (see Appendix A) to write the OLS slope estimator in equation (2.19) as

$$\hat{\beta}_1 = \frac{\sum_{i=1}^{n}(x_i - \bar{x})y_i}{\sum_{i=1}^{n}(x_i - \bar{x})^2}. \qquad [2.49]$$

Because we are now interested in the behavior of $\hat{\beta}_1$ across all possible samples, $\hat{\beta}_1$ is properly viewed as a random variable.

We can write $\hat{\beta}_1$ in terms of the population coefficient and errors by substituting the right-hand side of (2.48) into (2.49). We have

$$\hat{\beta}_1 = \frac{\sum_{i=1}^{n}(x_i - \bar{x})y_i}{\text{SST}_x} = \frac{\sum_{i=1}^{n}(x_i - \bar{x})(\beta_0 + \beta_1 x_i + u_i)}{\text{SST}_x}, \qquad [2.50]$$

where we have defined the total variation in x_i as $\text{SST}_x = \sum_{i=1}^{n}(x_i - \bar{x})^2$ to simplify the notation. (This is not quite the sample variance of the x_i because we do not divide by $n - 1$.) Using the algebra of the summation operator, write the numerator of $\hat{\beta}_1$ as

$$\sum_{i=1}^{n}(x_i - \bar{x})\beta_0 + \sum_{i=1}^{n}(x_i - \bar{x})\beta_1 x_i + \sum_{i=1}^{n}(x_i - \bar{x})u_i$$

$$= \beta_0 \sum_{i=1}^{n}(x_i - \bar{x}) + \beta_1 \sum_{i=1}^{n}(x_i - \bar{x})x_i + \sum_{i=1}^{n}(x_i - \bar{x})u_i. \qquad [2.51]$$

As shown in Appendix A, $\sum_{i=1}^{n}(x_i - \bar{x}) = 0$ and $\sum_{i=1}^{n}(x_i - \bar{x})x_i = \sum_{i=1}^{n}(x_i - \bar{x})^2 = \text{SST}_x$. Therefore, we can write the numerator of $\hat{\beta}_1$ as $\beta_1 \text{SST}_x + \sum_{i=1}^{n}(x_i - \bar{x})u_i$. Putting this over the denominator gives

$$\hat{\beta}_1 = \beta_1 + \frac{\sum_{i=1}^{n}(x_i - \bar{x})u_i}{\text{SST}_x} = \beta_1 + (1/\text{SST}_x)\sum_{i=1}^{n}d_i u_i, \qquad [2.52]$$

where $d_i = x_i - \bar{x}$. We now see that the estimator $\hat{\beta}_1$ equals the population slope, β_1, plus a term that is a linear combination in the errors $[u_1, u_2, \ldots, u_n]$. Conditional on the values of x_i, the randomness in $\hat{\beta}_1$ is due entirely to the errors in the sample. The fact that these errors are generally different from zero is what causes $\hat{\beta}_1$ to differ from β_1.

Using the representation in (2.52), we can prove the first important statistical property of OLS.

THEOREM 2.1

UNBIASEDNESS OF OLS:

Using Assumptions SLR.1 through SLR.4,

$$E(\hat{\beta}_0) = \beta_0 \text{ and } E(\hat{\beta}_1) = \beta_1, \qquad [2.53]$$

for any values of β_0 and β_1. In other words, $\hat{\beta}_0$ is unbiased for β_0, and $\hat{\beta}_1$ is unbiased for β_1.

PROOF: In this proof, the expected values are conditional on the sample values of the independent variable. Because SST_x and d_i are functions only of the x_i, they are nonrandom in the conditioning. Therefore, from (2.52), and keeping the conditioning on $\{x_1, x_2, \ldots, x_n\}$ implicit, we have

$$E(\hat{\beta}_1) = \beta_1 + E[(1/\text{SST}_x)\sum_{i=1}^{n}d_i u_i] = \beta_1 + (1/\text{SST}_x)\sum_{i=1}^{n}E(d_i u_i)$$

$$= \beta_1 + (1/\text{SST}_x)\sum_{i=1}^{n}d_i E(u_i) = \beta_1 + (1/\text{SST}_x)\sum_{i=1}^{n}d_i \cdot 0 = \beta_1,$$

where we have used the fact that the expected value of each u_i (conditional on $\{x_1, x_2, \ldots, x_n\}$) is zero under Assumptions SLR.2 and SLR.4. Since unbiasedness holds for any outcome on $\{x_1, x_2, \ldots, x_n\}$, unbiasedness also holds without conditioning on $\{x_1, x_2, \ldots, x_n\}$.

The proof for $\hat{\beta}_0$ is now straightforward. Average (2.48) across i to get $\bar{y} = \beta_0 + \beta_1 \bar{x} + \bar{u}$, and plug this into the formula for $\hat{\beta}_0$:

$$\hat{\beta}_0 = \bar{y} - \hat{\beta}_1 \bar{x} = \beta_0 + \beta_1 \bar{x} + \bar{u} - \hat{\beta}_1 \bar{x} = \beta_0 + (\beta_1 - \hat{\beta}_1)\bar{x} + \bar{u}.$$

Then, conditional on the values of the x_i,

$$E(\hat{\beta}_0) = \beta_0 + E[(\beta_1 - \hat{\beta}_1)\bar{x}] + E(\bar{u}) = \beta_0 + E[(\beta_1 - \hat{\beta}_1)]\bar{x},$$

since $E(\bar{u}) = 0$ by Assumptions SLR.2 and SLR.4. But, we showed that $E(\hat{\beta}_1) = \beta_1$, which implies that $E[(\hat{\beta}_1 - \beta_1)] = 0$. Thus, $E(\hat{\beta}_0) = \beta_0$. Both of these arguments are valid for any values of β_0 and β_1, and so we have established unbiasedness.

Remember that unbiasedness is a feature of the sampling distributions of $\hat{\beta}_1$ and $\hat{\beta}_0$, which says nothing about the estimate that we obtain for a given sample. We hope that, if the sample we obtain is somehow "typical," then our estimate should be "near" the population value. Unfortunately, it is always possible that we could obtain an unlucky sample that would give us a point estimate far from β_1, and we can *never* know for sure whether this is the case. You may want to review the material on unbiased estimators in Appendix C, especially the simulation exercise in Table C.1 that illustrates the concept of unbiasedness.

Unbiasedness generally fails if any of our four assumptions fail. This means that it is important to think about the veracity of each assumption for a particular application. Assumption SLR.1 requires that y and x be linearly related, with an additive disturbance. This can certainly fail. But we also know that y and x can be chosen to yield interesting nonlinear relationships. Dealing with the failure of (2.47) requires more advanced methods that are beyond the scope of this text.

Later, we will have to relax Assumption SLR.2, the random sampling assumption, for time series analysis. But what about using it for cross-sectional analysis? Random sampling can fail in a cross section when samples are not representative of the underlying population; in fact, some data sets are constructed by intentionally oversampling different parts of the population. We will discuss problems of nonrandom sampling in Chapters 9 and 17.

As we have already discussed, Assumption SLR.3 almost always holds in interesting regression applications. Without it, we cannot even obtain the OLS estimates.

The assumption we should concentrate on for now is SLR.4. If SLR.4 holds, the OLS estimators are unbiased. Likewise, if SLR.4 fails, the OLS estimators generally will be *biased*. There are ways to determine the likely direction and size of the bias, which we will study in Chapter 3.

The possibility that x is correlated with u is almost always a concern in simple regression analysis with nonexperimental data, as we indicated with several examples in Section 2.1. Using simple regression when u contains factors affecting y that are also correlated with x can result in *spurious correlation*: that is, we find a relationship between y and x that is really due to other unobserved factors that affect y and also happen to be correlated with x.

EXAMPLE 2.12   Student Math Performance and the School Lunch Program

Let *math10* denote the percentage of tenth graders at a high school receiving a passing score on a standardized mathematics exam. Suppose we wish to estimate the effect of the federally funded school lunch program on student performance. If anything, we expect the lunch program to have a positive ceteris paribus effect on performance: all other factors being equal, if a student who is too poor to eat regular meals becomes eligible for the school lunch program, his or her performance should improve. Let *lnchprg* denote the percentage of students who are eligible for the lunch program. Then, a simple regression model is

$$math10 = \beta_0 + \beta_1 \, lnchprg + u, \tag{2.54}$$

where u contains school and student characteristics that affect overall school performance. Using the data in MEAP93 on 408 Michigan high schools for the 1992–1993 school year, we obtain

$$\widehat{math10} = 32.14 - 0.319 \, lnchprg$$
$$n = 408, R^2 = 0.171.$$

This equation predicts that if student eligibility in the lunch program increases by 10 percentage points, the percentage of students passing the math exam *falls* by about 3.2 percentage points. Do we really believe that higher participation in the lunch program actually *causes* worse performance? Almost certainly not. A better explanation is that the error term u in equation (2.54) is correlated with *lnchprg*. In fact, u contains factors such as the poverty rate of children attending school, which affects student performance and is highly correlated with eligibility in the lunch program. Variables such as school quality and resources are also contained in u, and these are likely correlated with *lnchprg*. It is important to remember that the estimate −0.319 is only for this particular sample, but its sign and magnitude make us suspect that u and x are correlated, so that simple regression is biased.

In addition to omitted variables, there are other reasons for x to be correlated with u in the simple regression model. Because the same issues arise in multiple regression analysis, we will postpone a systematic treatment of the problem until then.

2-5b Variances of the OLS Estimators

In addition to knowing that the sampling distribution of $\hat{\beta}_1$ is centered about β_1 ($\hat{\beta}_1$ is unbiased), it is important to know how far we can expect $\hat{\beta}_1$ to be away from β_1 on average. Among other things, this allows us to choose the best estimator among all, or at least a broad class of, unbiased estimators. The measure of spread in the distribution of $\hat{\beta}_1$ (and $\hat{\beta}_0$) that is easiest to work with is the variance or its square root, the standard deviation. (See Appendix C for a more detailed discussion.)

It turns out that the variance of the OLS estimators can be computed under Assumptions SLR.1 through SLR.4. However, these expressions would be somewhat complicated. Instead, we add an assumption that is traditional for cross-sectional analysis. This assumption states that the variance of the unobservable, u, conditional on x, is constant. This is known as the **homoskedasticity** or "constant variance" assumption.

Assumption SLR.5   **Homoskedasticity**

The error u has the same variance given any value of the explanatory variable. In other words,

$$\text{Var}(u|x) = \sigma^2.$$

We must emphasize that the homoskedasticity assumption is quite distinct from the zero conditional mean assumption, $\text{E}(u|x) = 0$. Assumption SLR.4 involves the *expected value* of u, while Assumption SLR.5 concerns the *variance* of u (both conditional on x). Recall that we established the unbiasedness of OLS without Assumption SLR.5: the homoskedasticity assumption plays *no* role in showing that $\hat{\beta}_0$ and $\hat{\beta}_1$ are unbiased. We add Assumption SLR.5 because it simplifies the variance calculations for $\hat{\beta}_0$ and $\hat{\beta}_1$ and because it implies that ordinary least squares has certain efficiency properties, which we will see in Chapter 3. If we were to assume that u and x are *independent*, then the distribution of u given x does not depend on x, and so $\text{E}(u|x) = \text{E}(u) = 0$ and $\text{Var}(u|x) = \sigma^2$. But independence is sometimes too strong of an assumption.

Because $\text{Var}(u|x) = \text{E}(u^2|x) - [\text{E}(u|x)]^2$ and $\text{E}(u|x) = 0$, $\sigma^2 = \text{E}(u^2|x)$, which means σ^2 is also the *unconditional* expectation of u^2. Therefore, $\sigma^2 = \text{E}(u^2) = \text{Var}(u)$, because $\text{E}(u) = 0$. In other words, σ^2 is the *unconditional* variance of u, and so σ^2 is often called the **error variance** or disturbance variance. The square root of σ^2, σ, is the standard deviation of the error. A larger σ means that the distribution of the unobservables affecting y is more spread out.

FIGURE 2.8 The simple regression model under homoskedasticity.

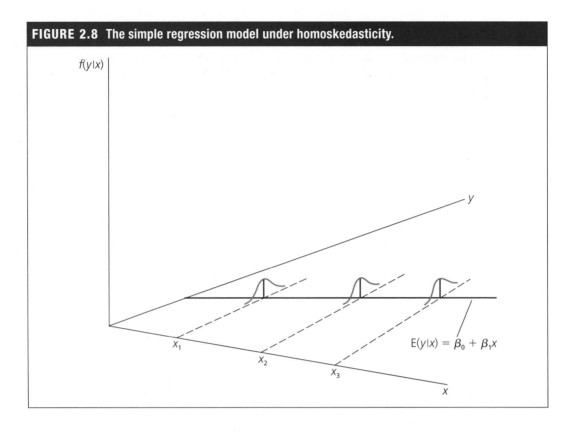

It is often useful to write Assumptions SLR.4 and SLR.5 in terms of the conditional mean and conditional variance of y:

$$E(y|x) = \beta_0 + \beta_1 x. \qquad [2.55]$$

$$\text{Var}(y|x) = \sigma^2. \qquad [2.56]$$

In other words, the conditional expectation of y given x is linear in x, but the variance of y given x is constant. This situation is graphed in Figure 2.8 where $\beta_0 > 0$ and $\beta_1 > 0$.

When $\text{Var}(u|x)$ depends on x, the error term is said to exhibit **heteroskedasticity** (or nonconstant variance). Because $\text{Var}(u|x) = \text{Var}(y|x)$, heteroskedasticity is present whenever $\text{Var}(y|x)$ is a function of x.

EXAMPLE 2.13   **Heteroskedasticity in a Wage Equation**

In order to get an unbiased estimator of the ceteris paribus effect of *educ* on *wage*, we must assume that $E(u|educ) = 0$, and this implies $E(wage|educ) = \beta_0 + \beta_1 educ$. If we also make the homoskedasticity assumption, then $\text{Var}(u|educ) = \sigma^2$ does not depend on the level of education, which is the same as assuming $\text{Var}(wage|educ) = \sigma^2$. Thus, while average wage is allowed to increase with education level—it is this rate of increase that we are interested in estimating—the *variability* in wage about its mean is assumed to be constant across all education levels. This may not be realistic. It is likely that people with more education have a wider variety of interests and job opportunities, which could lead to more wage variability at higher levels of education. People with very low levels of education have fewer opportunities and often must work at the minimum wage; this serves to reduce wage variability at low education levels. This situation is shown in Figure 2.9. Ultimately, whether Assumption SLR.5 holds is an empirical issue, and in Chapter 8 we will show how to test Assumption SLR.5.

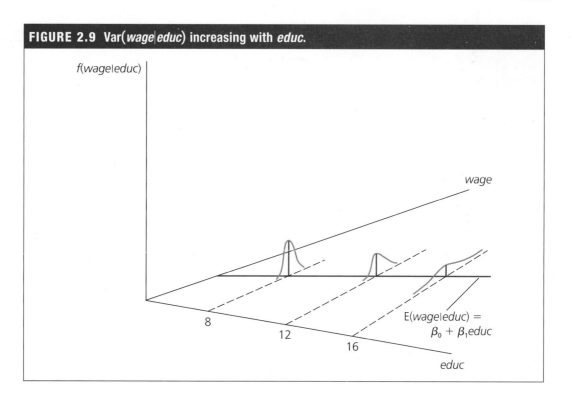

FIGURE 2.9 Var(*wage*|*educ*) increasing with *educ*.

With the homoskedasticity assumption in place, we are ready to prove the following:

THEOREM 2.2

SAMPLING VARIANCES OF THE OLS ESTIMATORS

Under Assumptions SLR.1 through SLR.5,

$$\text{Var}(\hat{\beta}_1) = \frac{\sigma^2}{\sum_{i=1}^{n}(x_i - \bar{x})^2} = \sigma^2/\text{SST}_x, \qquad [2.57]$$

and

$$\text{Var}(\hat{\beta}_0) = \frac{\sigma^2 n^{-1}\sum_{i=1}^{n}x_i^2}{\sum_{i=1}^{n}(x_i - \bar{x})^2}, \qquad [2.58]$$

where these are conditional on the sample values $\{x_1, \ldots, x_n\}$.

PROOF: We derive the formula for $\text{Var}(\hat{\beta}_1)$, leaving the other derivation as Problem 10. The starting point is equation (2.52): $\hat{\beta}_1 = \beta_1 + (1/\text{SST}_x)\sum_{i=1}^{n}d_i u_i$. Because β_1 is just a constant, and we are conditioning on the x_i, SST_x and $d_i = x_i - \bar{x}$ are also nonrandom. Furthermore, because the u_i are independent random variables across i (by random sampling), the variance of the sum is the sum of the variances. Using these facts, we have

$$\text{Var}(\hat{\beta}_1) = (1/\text{SST}_x)^2 \text{Var}\left(\sum_{i=1}^{n} d_i u_i\right) = (1/\text{SST}_x)^2\left(\sum_{i=1}^{n} d_i^2 \text{Var}(u_i)\right)$$

$$= (1/\text{SST}_x)^2\left(\sum_{i=1}^{n} d_i^2 \sigma^2\right) \quad [\text{since Var}(u_i) = \sigma^2 \text{ for all } i]$$

$$= \sigma^2 (1/\text{SST}_x)^2\left(\sum_{i=1}^{n} d_i^2\right) = \sigma^2 (1/\text{SST}_x)^2 \text{SST}_x = \sigma^2/\text{SST}_x,$$

which is what we wanted to show.

Equations (2.57) and (2.58) are the "standard" formulas for simple regression analysis, which are invalid in the presence of heteroskedasticity. This will be important when we turn to confidence intervals and hypothesis testing in multiple regression analysis.

For most purposes, we are interested in $\text{Var}(\hat{\beta}_1)$. It is easy to summarize how this variance depends on the error variance, σ^2, and the total variation in $\{x_1, x_2, \ldots, x_n\}$, SST_x. First, the larger the error variance, the larger is $\text{Var}(\hat{\beta}_1)$. This makes sense since more variation in the unobservables affecting y makes it more difficult to precisely estimate β_1. On the other hand, more variability in the independent variable is preferred: as the variability in the x_i increases, the variance of $\hat{\beta}_1$ decreases. This also makes intuitive sense since the more spread out is the sample of independent variables, the easier it is to trace out the relationship between $\text{E}(y|x)$ and x. That is, the easier it is to estimate β_1. If there is little variation in the x_i, then it can be hard to pinpoint how $\text{E}(y|x)$ varies with x. As the sample size increases, so does the total variation in the x_i. Therefore, a larger sample size results in a smaller variance for $\hat{\beta}_1$.

EXPLORING FURTHER 2.5

Show that, when estimating β_0, it is best to have $\bar{x} = 0$. What is $\text{Var}(\hat{\beta}_0)$ in this case? [*Hint:* For any sample of numbers, $\sum_{i=1}^{n} x_i^2 \geq \sum_{i=1}^{n} (x_i - \bar{x})^2$, with equality only if $\bar{x} = 0$.]

This analysis shows that, if we are interested in β_1 and we have a choice, then we should choose the x_i to be as spread out as possible. This is sometimes possible with experimental data, but rarely do we have this luxury in the social sciences: usually, we must take the x_i that we obtain via random sampling. Sometimes, we have an opportunity to obtain larger sample sizes, although this can be costly.

For the purposes of constructing confidence intervals and deriving test statistics, we will need to work with the standard deviations of $\hat{\beta}_1$ and $\hat{\beta}_0$, $\text{sd}(\hat{\beta}_1)$ and $\text{sd}(\hat{\beta}_0)$. Recall that these are obtained by taking the square roots of the variances in (2.57) and (2.58). In particular, $\text{sd}(\hat{\beta}_1) = \sigma/\sqrt{\text{SST}_x}$, where σ is the square root of σ^2, and $\sqrt{\text{SST}_x}$ is the square root of SST_x.

2-5c Estimating the Error Variance

The formulas in (2.57) and (2.58) allow us to isolate the factors that contribute to $\text{Var}(\hat{\beta}_1)$ and $\text{Var}(\hat{\beta}_0)$. But these formulas are unknown, except in the extremely rare case that σ^2 is known. Nevertheless, we can use the data to estimate σ^2, which then allows us to estimate $\text{Var}(\hat{\beta}_1)$ and $\text{Var}(\hat{\beta}_0)$.

This is a good place to emphasize the difference between the *errors* (or disturbances) and the *residuals*, since this distinction is crucial for constructing an estimator of σ^2. Equation (2.48) shows how to write the population model in terms of a randomly sampled observation as $y_i = \beta_0 + \beta_1 x_i + u_i$, where u_i is the error for observation i. We can also express y_i in terms of its fitted value and residual as in equation (2.32): $y_i = \hat{\beta}_0 + \hat{\beta}_1 x_i + \hat{u}_i$. Comparing these two equations, we see that the error shows up in the equation containing the *population* parameters, β_0 and β_1. On the other hand, the residuals show up in the *estimated* equation with $\hat{\beta}_0$ and $\hat{\beta}_1$. The errors are never observed, while the residuals are computed from the data.

We can use equations (2.32) and (2.48) to write the residuals as a function of the errors:

$$\hat{u}_i = y_i - \hat{\beta}_0 - \hat{\beta}_1 x_i = (\beta_0 + \beta_1 x_i + u_i) - \hat{\beta}_0 - \hat{\beta}_1 x_i,$$

or

$$\hat{u}_i = u_i - (\hat{\beta}_0 - \beta_0) - (\hat{\beta}_1 - \beta_1)x_i. \qquad [2.59]$$

Although the expected value of $\hat{\beta}_0$ equals β_0, and similarly for $\hat{\beta}_1$, $\hat{u}_i$ is not the same as u_i. The difference between them does have an *expected value* of zero.

Now that we understand the difference between the errors and the residuals, we can return to estimating σ^2. First, $\sigma^2 = E(u^2)$, so an unbiased "estimator" of σ^2 is $n^{-1}\sum_{i=1}^{n} u_i^2$. Unfortunately, this is not a true estimator, because we do not observe the errors u_i. But, we do have estimates of the u_i, namely, the OLS residuals $\hat{u}_i$. If we replace the errors with the OLS residuals, we have $n^{-1}\sum_{i=1}^{n} \hat{u}_i^2 = SSR/n$. This *is* a true estimator, because it gives a computable rule for any sample of data on x and y. One slight drawback to this estimator is that it turns out to be biased (although for large n the bias is small). Because it is easy to compute an unbiased estimator, we use that instead.

The estimator SSR/n is biased essentially because it does not account for two restrictions that must be satisfied by the OLS residuals. These restrictions are given by the two OLS first order conditions:

$$\sum_{i=1}^{n} \hat{u}_i = 0, \quad \sum_{i=1}^{n} x_i \hat{u}_i = 0. \qquad [2.60]$$

One way to view these restrictions is this: if we know $n - 2$ of the residuals, we can always get the other two residuals by using the restrictions implied by the first order conditions in (2.60). Thus, there are only $n - 2$ **degrees of freedom** in the OLS residuals, as opposed to n degrees of freedom in the errors. It is important to understand that if we replace $\hat{u}_i$ with u_i in (2.60), the restrictions would no longer hold.

The unbiased estimator of σ^2 that we will use makes a degrees of freedom adjustment:

$$\hat{\sigma}^2 = \frac{1}{(n-2)}\sum_{i=1}^{n} \hat{u}_i^2 = SSR/(n-2). \qquad [2.61]$$

(This estimator is sometimes denoted as S^2, but we continue to use the convention of putting "hats" over estimators.)

THEOREM 2.3

UNBIASED ESTIMATION OF σ^2

Under Assumptions SLR.1 through SLR.5,

$$E(\hat{\sigma}^2) = \sigma^2.$$

PROOF: If we average equation (2.59) across all i and use the fact that the OLS residuals average out to zero, we have $0 = \bar{u} - (\hat{\beta}_0 - \beta_0) - (\hat{\beta}_1 - \beta_1)\bar{x}$; subtracting this from (2.59) gives $\hat{u}_i = (u_i - \bar{u}) - (\hat{\beta}_1 - \beta_1)(x_i - \bar{x})$. Therefore, $\hat{u}_i^2 = (u_i - \bar{u})^2 + (\hat{\beta}_1 - \beta_1)^2(x_i - \bar{x})^2 - 2(u_i - \bar{u})(\hat{\beta}_1 - \beta_1)(x_i - \bar{x})$. Summing across all i gives $\sum_{i=1}^{n}\hat{u}_i^2 = \sum_{i=1}^{n}(u_i - \bar{u})^2 + (\hat{\beta}_1 - \beta_1)^2 \sum_{i=1}^{n}(x_i - \bar{x})^2 - 2(\hat{\beta}_1 - \beta_1)\sum_{i=1}^{n}u_i(x_i - \bar{x})$. Now, the expected value of the first term is $(n-1)\sigma^2$, something that is shown in Appendix C. The expected value of the second term is simply σ^2 because $E[(\hat{\beta}_1 - \beta_1)^2] = Var(\hat{\beta}_1) = \sigma^2/SST_x$. Finally, the third term can be written as $-2(\hat{\beta}_1 - \beta_1)^2 SST_x$; taking expectations gives $-2\sigma^2$. Putting these three terms together gives $E(\sum_{i=1}^{n}\hat{u}_i^2) = (n-1)\sigma^2 + \sigma^2 - 2\sigma^2 = (n-2)\sigma^2$, so that $E[SSR/(n-2)] = \sigma^2$.

If $\hat{\sigma}^2$ is plugged into the variance formulas (2.57) and (2.58), then we have unbiased estimators of $\text{Var}(\hat{\beta}_1)$ and $\text{Var}(\hat{\beta}_0)$. Later on, we will need estimators of the standard deviations of $\hat{\beta}_1$ and $\hat{\beta}_0$, and this requires estimating σ. The natural estimator of σ is

$$\hat{\sigma} = \sqrt{\hat{\sigma}^2} \tag{2.62}$$

and is called the **standard error of the regression (SER)**. (Other names for $\hat{\sigma}$ are the *standard error of the estimate* and the *root mean squared error*, but we will not use these.) Although $\hat{\sigma}$ is not an unbiased estimator of σ, we can show that it is a *consistent* estimator of σ (see Appendix C), and it will serve our purposes well.

The estimate $\hat{\sigma}$ is interesting because it is an estimate of the standard deviation in the unobservables affecting y; equivalently, it estimates the standard deviation in y after the effect of x has been taken out. Most regression packages report the value of $\hat{\sigma}$ along with the R-squared, intercept, slope, and other OLS statistics (under one of the several names listed above). For now, our primary interest is in using $\hat{\sigma}$ to estimate the standard deviations of $\hat{\beta}_0$ and $\hat{\beta}_1$. Since $\text{sd}(\hat{\beta}_1) = \sigma/\sqrt{\text{SST}_x}$, the natural estimator of $\text{sd}(\hat{\beta}_1)$ is

$$\text{se}(\hat{\beta}_1) = \hat{\sigma}/\sqrt{\text{SST}_x} = \hat{\sigma}/\left(\sum_{i=1}^{n}(x_i - \bar{x})^2\right)^{1/2};$$

this is called the **standard error of $\hat{\beta}_1$.** Note that $\text{se}(\hat{\beta}_1)$ is viewed as a random variable when we think of running OLS over different samples of y; this is true because $\hat{\sigma}$ varies with different samples. For a given sample, $\text{se}(\hat{\beta}_1)$ is a number, just as $\hat{\beta}_1$ is simply a number when we compute it from the given data.

Similarly, $\text{se}(\hat{\beta}_0)$ is obtained from $\text{sd}(\hat{\beta}_0)$ by replacing σ with $\hat{\sigma}$. The standard error of any estimate gives us an idea of how precise the estimator is. Standard errors play a central role throughout this text; we will use them to construct test statistics and confidence intervals for every econometric procedure we cover, starting in Chapter 4.

2-6 Regression through the Origin and Regression on a Constant

In rare cases, we wish to impose the restriction that, when $x = 0$, the expected value of y is zero. There are certain relationships for which this is reasonable. For example, if income (x) is zero, then income tax revenues (y) must also be zero. In addition, there are settings where a model that originally has a nonzero intercept is transformed into a model without an intercept.

Formally, we now choose a slope estimator, which we call $\tilde{\beta}_1$, and a line of the form

$$\tilde{y} = \tilde{\beta}_1 x, \tag{2.63}$$

where the tildes over $\tilde{\beta}_1$ and $\tilde{y}$ are used to distinguish this problem from the much more common problem of estimating an intercept along with a slope. Obtaining (2.63) is called **regression through the origin** because the line (2.63) passes through the point $x = 0$, $\tilde{y} = 0$. To obtain the slope estimate in (2.63), we still rely on the method of ordinary least squares, which in this case minimizes the sum of squared residuals:

$$\sum_{i=1}^{n}(y_i - \tilde{\beta}_1 x_i)^2. \tag{2.64}$$

Using one-variable calculus, it can be shown that $\tilde{\beta}_1$ must solve the first order condition:

$$\sum_{i=1}^{n} x_i(y_i - \tilde{\beta}_1 x_i) = 0. \tag{2.65}$$

From this, we can solve for $\tilde{\beta}_1$:

$$\tilde{\beta}_1 = \frac{\sum_{i=1}^{n} x_i y_i}{\sum_{i=1}^{n} x_i^2}, \tag{2.66}$$

provided that not all the x_i are zero, a case we rule out.

Note how $\tilde{\beta}_1$ compares with the slope estimate when we also estimate the intercept (rather than set it equal to zero). These two estimates are the same if, and only if, $\bar{x} = 0$. [See equation (2.49) for $\hat{\beta}_1$.] Obtaining an estimate of β_1 using regression through the origin is not done very often in applied work, and for good reason: if the intercept $\beta_0 \neq 0$, then $\tilde{\beta}_1$ is a biased estimator of β_1. You will be asked to prove this in Problem 8.

In cases where regression through the origin is deemed appropriate, one must be careful in interpreting the R-squared that is typically reported with such regressions. Usually, unless stated otherwise, the R-squared is obtained without removing the sample average of $\{y_i: i = 1, \ldots, n\}$ in obtaining SST. In other words, the R-squared is computed as

$$1 - \frac{\sum_{i=1}^{n} (y_i - \tilde{\beta}_1 x_i)^2}{\sum_{i=1}^{n} y_i^2}. \qquad [2.67]$$

The numerator here makes sense because it is the sum of squared residuals, but the denominator acts as if we know the average value of y in the population is zero. One reason this version of the R-squared is used is that if we use the usual total sum of squares, that is, we compute R-squared as

$$1 - \frac{\sum_{i=1}^{n} (y_i - \tilde{\beta}_1 x_i)^2}{\sum_{i=1}^{n} (y_i - \bar{y})^2}, \qquad [2.68]$$

it can actually be negative. If expression (2.68) is negative then it means that using the sample average $\bar{y}$ to predict y_i provides a better fit than using x_i in a regression through the origin. Therefore, (2.68) is actually more attractive than equation (2.67) because equation (2.68) tells us whether using x is better than ignoring x altogether.

This discussion about regression through the origin, and different ways to measure goodness-of-fit, prompts another question: what happens if we only regress on a constant? That is, we set the slope to zero (which means we need not even have an x) and estimate an intercept only? The answer is simple: the intercept is $\bar{y}$. This fact is usually shown in basic statistics, where it is shown that the constant that produces the smallest sum of squared deviations is always the sample average. In this light, equation (2.68) can be seen as comparing regression on x through the origin with regression only on a constant.

Summary

We have introduced the simple linear regression model in this chapter, and we have covered its basic properties. Given a random sample, the method of ordinary least squares is used to estimate the slope and intercept parameters in the population model. We have demonstrated the algebra of the OLS regression line, including computation of fitted values and residuals, and the obtaining of predicted changes in the dependent variable for a given change in the independent variable. In Section 2.4, we discussed two issues of practical importance: (1) the behavior of the OLS estimates when we change the units of measurement of the dependent variable or the independent variable and (2) the use of the natural log to allow for constant elasticity and constant semi-elasticity models.

In Section 2.5, we showed that, under the four Assumptions SLR.1 through SLR.4, the OLS estimators are unbiased. The key assumption is that the error term u has zero mean given any value of the independent variable x. Unfortunately, there are reasons to think this is false in many social science applications of simple regression, where the omitted factors in u are often correlated with x. When we add the assumption that the variance of the error given x is constant, we get simple formulas for the sampling variances of the OLS estimators. As we saw, the variance of the slope estimator $\hat{\beta}_1$ increases as the error variance increases, and it decreases when there is more sample variation in the independent variable. We also derived an unbiased estimator for $\sigma^2 = \text{Var}(u)$.

In Section 2.6, we briefly discussed regression through the origin, where the slope estimator is obtained under the assumption that the intercept is zero. Sometimes, this is useful, but it appears infrequently in applied work.

Much work is left to be done. For example, we still do not know how to test hypotheses about the population parameters, β_0 and β_1. Thus, although we know that OLS is unbiased for the population parameters under Assumptions SLR.1 through SLR.4, we have no way of drawing inferences about the population. Other topics, such as the efficiency of OLS relative to other possible procedures, have also been omitted.

The issues of confidence intervals, hypothesis testing, and efficiency are central to multiple regression analysis as well. Since the way we construct confidence intervals and test statistics is very similar for multiple regression—and because simple regression is a special case of multiple regression—our time is better spent moving on to multiple regression, which is much more widely applicable than simple regression. Our purpose in Chapter 2 was to get you thinking about the issues that arise in econometric analysis in a fairly simple setting.

THE GAUSS-MARKOV ASSUMPTIONS FOR SIMPLE REGRESSION

For convenience, we summarize the **Gauss-Markov assumptions** that we used in this chapter. It is important to remember that only SLR.1 through SLR.4 are needed to show $\hat{\beta}_0$ and $\hat{\beta}_1$ are unbiased. We added the homoskedasticity assumption, SLR.5, to obtain the usual OLS variance formulas (2.57) and (2.58).

Assumption SLR.1 (Linear in Parameters)
In the population model, the dependent variable, y, is related to the independent variable, x, and the error (or disturbance), u, as

$$y = \beta_0 + \beta_1 x + u,$$

where β_0 and β_1 are the population intercept and slope parameters, respectively.

Assumption SLR.2 (Random Sampling)
We have a random sample of size n, $\{(x_i, y_i): i = 1, 2, \ldots, n\}$, following the population model in Assumption SLR.1.

Assumption SLR.3 (Sample Variation in the Explanatory Variable)
The sample outcomes on x, namely, $\{x_i, i = 1, \ldots, n\}$, are not all the same value.

Assumption SLR.4 (Zero Conditional Mean)
The error u has an expected value of zero given any value of the explanatory variable. In other words,

$$E(u|x) = 0.$$

Assumption SLR.5 (Homoskedasticity)
The error u has the same variance given any value of the explanatory variable. In other words,

$$\text{Var}(u|x) = \sigma^2.$$

Key Terms

Coefficient of Determination	Covariate	Elasticity
Constant Elasticity Model	Degrees of Freedom	Error Term (Disturbance)
Control Variable	Dependent Variable	Error Variance

Explained Sum of Squares (SSE)	OLS Regression Line	R-squared
Explained Variable	Ordinary Least Squares (OLS)	Sample Regression Function (SRF)
Explanatory Variable	Population Regression Function (PRF)	Semi-elasticity
First Order Conditions	Predicted Variable	Simple Linear Regression Model
Fitted Value	Predictor Variable	Slope Parameter
Gauss-Markov Assumptions	Regressand	Standard Error of $\hat{\beta}_1$
Heteroskedasticity	Regression through the Origin	Standard Error of the Regression (SER)
Homoskedasticity	Regressor	Sum of Squared Residuals (SSR)
Independent Variable	Residual	Total Sum of Squares (SST)
Intercept Parameter	Residual Sum of Squares (SSR)	Zero Conditional Mean
Mean Independent	Response Variable	Assumption

Problems

1 Let *kids* denote the number of children ever born to a woman, and let *educ* denote years of education for the woman. A simple model relating fertility to years of education is

$$kids = \beta_0 + \beta_1 educ + u,$$

where u is the unobserved error.

(i)   What kinds of factors are contained in u? Are these likely to be correlated with level of education?

(ii)   Will a simple regression analysis uncover the ceteris paribus effect of education on fertility? Explain.

2 In the simple linear regression model $y = \beta_0 + \beta_1 x + u$, suppose that $E(u) \neq 0$. Letting $\alpha_0 = E(u)$, show that the model can always be rewritten with the same slope, but a new intercept and error, where the new error has a zero expected value.

3 The following table contains the *ACT* scores and the *GPA* (grade point average) for eight college students. Grade point average is based on a four-point scale and has been rounded to one digit after the decimal.

Student	GPA	ACT
1	2.8	21
2	3.4	24
3	3.0	26
4	3.5	27
5	3.6	29
6	3.0	25
7	2.7	25
8	3.7	30

(i)   Estimate the relationship between *GPA* and *ACT* using OLS; that is, obtain the intercept and slope estimates in the equation

$$\widehat{GPA} = \hat{\beta}_0 + \hat{\beta}_1 ACT.$$

Comment on the direction of the relationship. Does the intercept have a useful interpretation here? Explain. How much higher is the *GPA* predicted to be if the *ACT* score is increased by five points?

(ii)   Compute the fitted values and residuals for each observation, and verify that the residuals (approximately) sum to zero.

(iii) What is the predicted value of *GPA* when $ACT = 20$?

(iv) How much of the variation in *GPA* for these eight students is explained by *ACT*? Explain.

4 The data set BWGHT contains data on births to women in the United States. Two variables of interest are the dependent variable, infant birth weight in ounces (*bwght*), and an explanatory variable, average number of cigarettes the mother smoked per day during pregnancy (*cigs*). The following simple regression was estimated using data on $n = 1,388$ *births*:

$$\widehat{bwght} = 119.77 - 0.514 \, cigs$$

(i) What is the predicted birth weight when $cigs = 0$? What about when $cigs = 20$ (one pack per day)? Comment on the difference.

(ii) Does this simple regression necessarily capture a causal relationship between the child's birth weight and the mother's smoking habits? Explain.

(iii) To predict a birth weight of 125 ounces, what would *cigs* have to be? Comment.

(iv) The proportion of women in the sample who do not smoke while pregnant is about .85. Does this help reconcile your finding from part (iii)?

5 In the linear consumption function

$$\widehat{cons} = \hat{\beta}_0 + \hat{\beta}_1 inc,$$

the (estimated) *marginal propensity to consume* (MPC) out of income is simply the slope, $\hat{\beta}_1$, while the *average propensity to consume* (APC) is $\widehat{cons}/inc = \hat{\beta}_0/inc + \hat{\beta}_1$. Using observations for 100 families on annual income and consumption (both measured in dollars), the following equation is obtained:

$$\widehat{cons} = -124.84 + 0.853 \, inc$$

$$n = 100, R^2 = 0.692.$$

(i) Interpret the intercept in this equation, and comment on its sign and magnitude.

(ii) What is the predicted consumption when family income is $30,000?

(iii) With *inc* on the *x*-axis, draw a graph of the estimated MPC and APC.

6 Using data from 1988 for houses sold in Andover, Massachusetts, from Kiel and McClain (1995), the following equation relates housing price (*price*) to the distance from a recently built garbage incinerator (*dist*):

$$\widehat{\log(price)} = 9.40 + 0.312 \log(dist)$$

$$n = 135, R^2 = 0.162.$$

(i) Interpret the coefficient on log(*dist*). Is the sign of this estimate what you expect it to be?

(ii) Do you think simple regression provides an unbiased estimator of the ceteris paribus elasticity of *price* with respect to *dist*? (Think about the city's decision on where to put the incinerator.)

(iii) What other factors about a house affect its price? Might these be correlated with distance from the incinerator?

7 Consider the savings function

$$sav = \beta_0 + \beta_1 inc + u, \, u = \sqrt{inc} \cdot e,$$

where *e* is a random variable with $E(e) = 0$ and $Var(e) = \sigma_e^2$. Assume that *e* is independent of *inc*.

(i) Show that $E(u|inc) = 0$, so that the key zero conditional mean assumption (Assumption SLR.4) is satisfied. [*Hint:* If *e* is independent of *inc*, then $E(e|inc) = E(e)$.]

(ii)   Show that $\text{Var}(u|inc) = \sigma_e^2 inc$, so that the homoskedasticity Assumption SLR.5 is violated. In particular, the variance of *sav* increases with *inc*. [*Hint:* $\text{Var}(e|inc) = \text{Var}(e)$ if *e* and *inc* are independent.]

(iii)   Provide a discussion that supports the assumption that the variance of savings increases with family income.

8 Consider the standard simple regression model $y = \beta_0 + \beta_1 x + u$ under the Gauss-Markov Assumptions SLR.1 through SLR.5. The usual OLS estimators $\hat{\beta}_0$ and $\hat{\beta}_1$ are unbiased for their respective population parameters. Let $\tilde{\beta}_1$ be the estimator of β_1 obtained by assuming the intercept is zero (see Section 2.6).

(i)   Find $\text{E}(\tilde{\beta}_1)$ in terms of the x_i, β_0, and β_1. Verify that $\tilde{\beta}_1$ is unbiased for β_1 when the population intercept (β_0) is zero. Are there other cases where $\tilde{\beta}_1$ is unbiased?

(ii)   Find the variance of $\tilde{\beta}_1$. (*Hint:* The variance does not depend on β_0.)

(iii)   Show that $\text{Var}(\tilde{\beta}_1) \le \text{Var}(\hat{\beta}_1)$. [*Hint:* For any sample of data, $\sum_{i=1}^{n} x_i^2 \ge \sum_{i=1}^{n}(x_i - \bar{x})^2$, with strict inequality unless $\bar{x} = 0$.]

(iv)   Comment on the tradeoff between bias and variance when choosing between $\hat{\beta}_1$ and $\tilde{\beta}_1$.

9 (i)   Let $\hat{\beta}_0$ and $\hat{\beta}_1$ be the intercept and slope from the regression of y_i on x_i, using *n* observations. Let c_1 and c_2, with $c_2 \ne 0$, be constants. Let $\tilde{\beta}_0$ and $\tilde{\beta}_1$ be the intercept and slope from the regression of $c_1 y_i$ on $c_2 x_i$. Show that $\tilde{\beta}_1 = (c_1/c_2)\hat{\beta}_1$ and $\tilde{\beta}_0 = c_1\hat{\beta}_0$, thereby verifying the claims on units of measurement in Section 2.4. [*Hint:* To obtain $\tilde{\beta}_1$, plug the scaled versions of *x* and *y* into (2.19). Then, use (2.17) for $\tilde{\beta}_0$, being sure to plug in the scaled *x* and *y* *and* the correct slope.]

(ii)   Now, let $\tilde{\beta}_0$ and $\tilde{\beta}_1$ be from the regression of $(c_1 + y_i)$ on $(c_2 + x_i)$ (with no restriction on c_1 or c_2). Show that $\tilde{\beta}_1 = \hat{\beta}_1$ and $\tilde{\beta}_0 = \hat{\beta}_0 + c_1 - c_2\hat{\beta}_1$.

(iii)   Now, let $\hat{\beta}_0$ and $\hat{\beta}_1$ be the OLS estimates from the regression $\log(y_i)$ on x_i, where we must assume $y_i > 0$ for all *i*. For $c_1 > 0$, let $\tilde{\beta}_0$ and $\tilde{\beta}_1$ be the intercept and slope from the regression of $\log(c_1 y_i)$ on x_i. Show that $\tilde{\beta}_1 = \hat{\beta}_1$ and $\tilde{\beta}_0 = \log(c_1) + \hat{\beta}_0$.

(iv)   Now, assuming that $x_i > 0$ for all *i*, let $\tilde{\beta}_0$ and $\tilde{\beta}_1$ be the intercept and slope from the regression of y_i on $\log(c_2 x_i)$. How do $\tilde{\beta}_0$ and $\tilde{\beta}_1$ compare with the intercept and slope from the regression of y_i on $\log(x_i)$?

10 Let $\hat{\beta}_0$ and $\hat{\beta}_1$ be the OLS intercept and slope estimators, respectively, and let $\bar{u}$ be the sample average of the errors (not the residuals!).

(i)   Show that $\hat{\beta}_1$ can be written as $\hat{\beta}_1 = \beta_1 + \sum_{i=1}^{n} w_i u_i$, where $w_i = d_i/\text{SST}_x$ and $d_i = x_i - \bar{x}$.

(ii)   Use part (i), along with $\sum_{i=1}^{n} w_i = 0$, to show that $\hat{\beta}_1$ and $\bar{u}$ are uncorrelated. [*Hint:* You are being asked to show that $\text{E}[(\hat{\beta}_1 - \beta_1) \cdot \bar{u}] = 0$.]

(iii)   Show that $\hat{\beta}_0$ can be written as $\hat{\beta}_0 = \beta_0 + \bar{u} - (\hat{\beta}_1 - \beta_1)\bar{x}$.

(iv)   Use parts (ii) and (iii) to show that $\text{Var}(\hat{\beta}_0) = \sigma^2/n + \sigma^2(\bar{x})^2/\text{SST}_x$.

(v)   Do the algebra to simplify the expression in part (iv) to equation (2.58). [*Hint:* $\text{SST}_x/n = n^{-1}\sum_{i=1}^{n} x_i^2 - (\bar{x})^2$.]

11 Suppose you are interested in estimating the effect of hours spent in an SAT preparation course (*hours*) on total SAT score (*sat*). The population is all college-bound high school seniors for a particular year.

(i)   Suppose you are given a grant to run a controlled experiment. Explain how you would structure the experiment in order to estimate the causal effect of *hours* on *sat*.

(ii)   Consider the more realistic case where students choose how much time to spend in a preparation course, and you can only randomly sample *sat* and *hours* from the population. Write the population model as

$$sat = \beta_0 + \beta_1 hours = u$$

where, as usual in a model with an intercept, we can assume $\text{E}(u) = 0$. List at least two factors contained in *u*. Are these likely to have positive or negative correlation with *hours*?

(iii)   In the equation from part (ii), what should be the sign of β_1 if the preparation course is effective?

(iv)   In the equation from part (ii), what is the interpretation of β_0?

12 Consider the problem described at the end of Section 2.6: running a regression and only estimating an intercept.

(i)   Given a sample $\{y_i: i = 1, 2, \ldots, n\}$, let $\tilde{\beta}_0$ be the solution to

$$\min_{b_0} \sum_{i=1}^{n} (y_i - b_0)^2.$$

Show that $\tilde{\beta}_0 = \bar{y}$, that is, the sample average minimizes the sum of squared residuals. (*Hint:* You may use one-variable calculus or you can show the result directly by adding and subtracting $\bar{y}$ inside the squared residual and then doing a little algebra.)

(ii)   Define residuals $\tilde{u}_i = y_i - \bar{y}$. Argue that these residuals always sum to zero.

Computer Exercises

C1 The data in 401K are a subset of data analyzed by Papke (1995) to study the relationship between participation in a 401(k) pension plan and the generosity of the plan. The variable *prate* is the percentage of eligible workers with an active account; this is the variable we would like to explain. The measure of generosity is the plan match rate, *mrate*. This variable gives the average amount the firm contributes to each worker's plan for each $1 contribution by the worker. For example, if *mrate* = 0.50, then a $1 contribution by the worker is matched by a 50¢ contribution by the firm.

(i)   Find the average participation rate and the average match rate in the sample of plans.

(ii)   Now, estimate the simple regression equation

$$\widehat{prate} = \hat{\beta}_0 + \hat{\beta}_1 mrate,$$

and report the results along with the sample size and *R*-squared.

(iii)   Interpret the intercept in your equation. Interpret the coefficient on *mrate*.

(iv)   Find the predicted *prate* when *mrate* = 3.5. Is this a reasonable prediction? Explain what is happening here.

(v)   How much of the variation in *prate* is explained by *mrate*? Is this a lot in your opinion?

C2 The data set in CEOSAL2 contains information on chief executive officers for U.S. corporations. The variable *salary* is annual compensation, in thousands of dollars, and *ceoten* is prior number of years as company CEO.

(i)   Find the average salary and the average tenure in the sample.

(ii)   How many CEOs are in their first year as CEO (that is, *ceoten* = 0)? What is the longest tenure as a CEO?

(iii)   Estimate the simple regression model

$$\log(salary) = \beta_0 + \beta_1 ceoten + u,$$

and report your results in the usual form. What is the (approximate) predicted percentage increase in salary given one more year as a CEO?

C3 Use the data in SLEEP75 from Biddle and Hamermesh (1990) to study whether there is a tradeoff between the time spent sleeping per week and the time spent in paid work. We could use either variable as the dependent variable. For concreteness, estimate the model

$$sleep = \beta_0 + \beta_1 totwrk + u,$$

where *sleep* is minutes spent sleeping at night per week and *totwrk* is total minutes worked during the week.

(i)   Report your results in equation form along with the number of observations and R^2. What does the intercept in this equation mean?

(ii)   If *totwrk* increases by 2 hours, by how much is *sleep* estimated to fall? Do you find this to be a large effect?

C4 Use the data in WAGE2 to estimate a simple regression explaining monthly salary (*wage*) in terms of IQ score (*IQ*).

(i)   Find the average salary and average IQ in the sample. What is the sample standard deviation of IQ? (IQ scores are standardized so that the average in the population is 100 with a standard deviation equal to 15.)

(ii)   Estimate a simple regression model where a one-point increase in *IQ* changes *wage* by a constant dollar amount. Use this model to find the predicted increase in wage for an increase in *IQ* of 15 points. Does *IQ* explain most of the variation in *wage*?

(iii)   Now, estimate a model where each one-point increase in *IQ* has the same percentage effect on *wage*. If *IQ* increases by 15 points, what is the approximate percentage increase in predicted *wage*?

C5 For the population of firms in the chemical industry, let *rd* denote annual expenditures on research and development, and let *sales* denote annual sales (both are in millions of dollars).

(i)   Write down a model (not an estimated equation) that implies a constant elasticity between *rd* and *sales*. Which parameter is the elasticity?

(ii)   Now, estimate the model using the data in RDCHEM. Write out the estimated equation in the usual form. What is the estimated elasticity of *rd* with respect to *sales*? Explain in words what this elasticity means.

C6 We used the data in MEAP93 for Example 2.12. Now we want to explore the relationship between the math pass rate (*math10*) and spending per student (*expend*).

(i)   Do you think each additional dollar spent has the same effect on the pass rate, or does a diminishing effect seem more appropriate? Explain.

(ii)   In the population model

$$math10 = \beta_0 + \beta_1 \log(expend) + u,$$

argue that $\beta_1/10$ is the percentage point change in *math10* given a 10% increase in *expend*.

(iii)   Use the data in MEAP93 to estimate the model from part (ii). Report the estimated equation in the usual way, including the sample size and *R*-squared.

(iv)   How big is the estimated spending effect? Namely, if spending increases by 10%, what is the estimated percentage point increase in *math10*?

(v)   One might worry that regression analysis can produce fitted values for *math10* that are greater than 100. Why is this not much of a worry in this data set?

C7 Use the data in CHARITY [obtained from Franses and Paap (2001)] to answer the following questions:

(i)   What is the average gift in the sample of 4,268 people (in Dutch guilders)? What percentage of people gave no gift?

(ii)   What is the average mailings per year? What are the minimum and maximum values?

(iii)   Estimate the model

$$gift = \beta_0 + \beta_1 mailsyear + u$$

by OLS and report the results in the usual way, including the sample size and *R*-squared.

(iv)   Interpret the slope coefficient. If each mailing costs one guilder, is the charity expected to make a net gain on each mailing? Does this mean the charity makes a net gain on every mailing? Explain.

(v)   What is the smallest predicted charitable contribution in the sample? Using this simple regression analysis, can you ever predict zero for *gift*?

C8 To complete this exercise you need a software package that allows you to generate data from the uniform and normal distributions.

(i)   Start by generating 500 observations on x_i—the explanatory variable—from the uniform distribution with range [0,10]. (Most statistical packages have a command for the Uniform(0,1) distribution; just multiply those observations by 10.) What are the sample mean and sample standard deviation of the x_i?

(ii)   Randomly generate 500 errors, u_i, from the Normal(0,36) distribution. (If you generate a Normal(0,1), as is commonly available, simply multiply the outcomes by six.) Is the sample average of the u_i exactly zero? Why or why not? What is the sample standard deviation of the u_i?

(iii)   Now generate the y_i as

$$y_i = 1 + 2x_i + u_i \equiv \beta_0 + \beta_1 x_i + u_i;$$

that is, the population intercept is one and the population slope is two. Use the data to run the regression of y_i on x_i. What are your estimates of the intercept and slope? Are they equal to the population values in the above equation? Explain.

(iv)   Obtain the OLS residuals, $\hat{u}_i$, and verify that equation (2.60) holds (subject to rounding error).

(v)   Compute the same quantities in equation (2.60) but use the errors u_i in place of the residuals. Now what do you conclude?

(vi)   Repeat parts (i), (ii), and (iii) with a new sample of data, starting with generating the x_i. Now what do you obtain for $\hat{\beta}_0$ and $\hat{\beta}_1$? Why are these different from what you obtained in part (iii)?

C9 Use the data in COUNTYMURDERS to answer this questions. Use only the data for 1996.

(i)   How many counties had zero murders in 1996? How many counties had at least one execution? What is the largest number of executions?

(ii)   Estimate the equation

$$murders = \beta_0 + \beta_1 execs + u$$

by OLS and report the results in the usual way, including sample size and R-squared.

(iii)   Interpret the slope coefficient reported in part (ii). Does the estimated equation suggest a deterrent effect of capital punishment?

(iv)   What is the smallest number of murders that can be predicted by the equation? What is the residual for a county with zero executions and zero murders?

(v)   Explain why a simple regression analysis is not well suited for determining whether capital punishment has a deterrent effect on murders.

C10 The data set in CATHOLIC includes test score information on over 7,000 students in the United States who were in eighth grade in 1988. The variables $math12$ and $read12$ are scores on twelfth grade standardized math and reading tests, respectively.

(i)   How many students are in the sample? Find the means and standard deviations of $math12$ and $read12$.

(ii)   Run the simple regression of $math12$ on $read12$ to obtain the OLS intercept and slope estimates. Report the results in the form

$$\widehat{math12} = \hat{\beta}_0 + \hat{\beta}_1 read12$$

$$n = ?, R^2 = ?$$

where you fill in the values for $\hat{\beta}_0$ and $\hat{\beta}_1$ and also replace the question marks.

(iii)   Does the intercept reported in part (ii) have a meaningful interpretation? Explain.

(iv)   Are you surprised by the $\hat{\beta}_1$ that you found? What about R^2?

(v)   Suppose that you present your findings to a superintendent of a school district, and the superintendent says, "Your findings show that to improve math scores we just need to improve reading scores, so we should hire more reading tutors." How would you respond to this comment? (Hint: If you instead run the regression of $read12$ on $math12$, what would you expect to find?)

APPENDIX 2A

Minimizing the Sum of Squared Residuals

We show that the OLS estimates $\hat{\beta}_0$ and $\hat{\beta}_1$ do minimize the sum of squared residuals, as asserted in Section 2.2. Formally, the problem is to characterize the solutions $\hat{\beta}_0$ and $\hat{\beta}_1$ to the minimization problem

$$\min_{b_0, b_1} \sum_{i=1}^{n} (y_i - b_0 - b_1 x_i)^2,$$

where b_0 and b_1 are the dummy arguments for the optimization problem; for simplicity, call this function $Q(b_0, b_1)$. By a fundamental result from multivariable calculus (see Appendix A), a necessary condition for $\hat{\beta}_0$ and $\hat{\beta}_1$ to solve the minimization problem is that the partial derivatives of $Q(b_0, b_1)$ with respect to b_0 and b_1 must be zero when evaluated at $\hat{\beta}_0, \hat{\beta}_1$: $\partial Q(\hat{\beta}_0, \hat{\beta}_1)/\partial b_0 = 0$ and $\partial Q(\hat{\beta}_0, \hat{\beta}_1)/\partial b_1 = 0$. Using the chain rule from calculus, these two equations become

$$-2 \sum_{i=1}^{n} (y_i - \hat{\beta}_0 - \hat{\beta}_1 x_i) = 0$$

$$-2 \sum_{i=1}^{n} x_i (y_i - \hat{\beta}_0 - \hat{\beta}_1 x_i) = 0.$$

These two equations are just (2.14) and (2.15) multiplied by $-2n$ and, therefore, are solved by the same $\hat{\beta}_0$ and $\hat{\beta}_1$.

How do we know that we have actually minimized the sum of squared residuals? The first order conditions are necessary but not sufficient conditions. One way to verify that we have minimized the sum of squared residuals is to write, for any b_0 and b_1,

$$Q(b_0, b_1) = \sum_{i=1}^{n} [y_i - \hat{\beta}_0 - \hat{\beta}_1 x_i + (\hat{\beta}_0 - b_0) + (\hat{\beta}_1 - b_1) x_i]^2$$

$$= \sum_{i=1}^{n} (\hat{u}_i + (\hat{\beta}_0 - b_0) + (\hat{\beta}_1 - b_1) x_i)^2$$

$$= \sum_{i=1}^{n} \hat{u}_i^2 + n(\hat{\beta}_0 - b_0)^2 + (\hat{\beta}_1 - b_1)^2 \sum_{i=1}^{n} x_i^2 + 2(\hat{\beta}_0 - b_0)(\hat{\beta}_1 - b_1) \sum_{i=1}^{n} x_i,$$

where we have used equations (2.30) and (2.31). The first term does not depend on b_0 or b_1, while the sum of the last three terms can be written as

$$\sum_{i=1}^{n} [(\hat{\beta}_0 - b_0) + (\hat{\beta}_1 - b_1) x_i]^2,$$

as can be verified by straightforward algebra. Because this is a sum of squared terms, the smallest it can be is zero. Therefore, it is smallest when $b_0 = \hat{\beta}_0$ and $b_1 = \hat{\beta}_1$.

CHAPTER 3

Multiple Regression Analysis: Estimation

I n Chapter 2, we learned how to use simple regression analysis to explain a dependent variable, y, as a function of a single independent variable, x. The primary drawback in using simple regression analysis for empirical work is that it is very difficult to draw ceteris paribus conclusions about how x affects y: the key assumption, SLR.4—that all other factors affecting y are uncorrelated with x—is often unrealistic.

Multiple regression analysis is more amenable to ceteris paribus analysis because it allows us to *explicitly* control for many other factors that simultaneously affect the dependent variable. This is important both for testing economic theories and for evaluating policy effects when we must rely on nonexperimental data. Because multiple regression models can accommodate many explanatory variables that may be correlated, we can hope to infer causality in cases where simple regression analysis would be misleading.

Naturally, if we add more factors to our model that are useful for explaining y, then more of the variation in y can be explained. Thus, multiple regression analysis can be used to build better models for predicting the dependent variable.

An additional advantage of multiple regression analysis is that it can incorporate fairly general functional form relationships. In the simple regression model, only one function of a single explanatory variable can appear in the equation. As we will see, the multiple regression model allows for much more flexibility.

Section 3-1 formally introduces the multiple regression model and further discusses the advantages of multiple regression over simple regression. In Section 3-2, we demonstrate how to estimate the parameters in the multiple regression model using the method of ordinary least squares.

In Sections 3-3, 3-4, and 3-5, we describe various statistical properties of the OLS estimators, including unbiasedness and efficiency.

The multiple regression model is still the most widely used vehicle for empirical analysis in economics and other social sciences. Likewise, the method of ordinary least squares is popularly used for estimating the parameters of the multiple regression model.

3-1 Motivation for Multiple Regression

3-1a The Model with Two Independent Variables

We begin with some simple examples to show how multiple regression analysis can be used to solve problems that cannot be solved by simple regression.

The first example is a simple variation of the wage equation introduced in Chapter 2 for obtaining the effect of education on hourly wage:

$$wage = \beta_0 + \beta_1 educ + \beta_2 exper + u, \tag{3.1}$$

where *exper* is years of labor market experience. Thus, *wage* is determined by the two explanatory or independent variables, education and experience, and by other unobserved factors, which are contained in u. We are still primarily interested in the effect of *educ* on *wage*, holding fixed all other factors affecting *wage*; that is, we are interested in the parameter β_1.

Compared with a simple regression analysis relating *wage* to *educ*, equation (3.1) effectively takes *exper* out of the error term and puts it explicitly in the equation. Because *exper* appears in the equation, its coefficient, β_2, measures the ceteris paribus effect of *exper* on *wage*, which is also of some interest.

Not surprisingly, just as with simple regression, we will have to make assumptions about how u in (3.1) is related to the independent variables, *educ* and *exper*. However, as we will see in Section 3-2, there is one thing of which we can be confident: because (3.1) contains experience explicitly, we will be able to measure the effect of education on wage, holding experience fixed. In a simple regression analysis—which puts *exper* in the error term—we would have to assume that experience is uncorrelated with education, a tenuous assumption.

As a second example, consider the problem of explaining the effect of per-student spending (*expend*) on the average standardized test score (*avgscore*) at the high school level. Suppose that the average test score depends on funding, average family income (*avginc*), and other unobserved factors:

$$avgscore = \beta_0 + \beta_1 expend + \beta_2 avginc + u. \tag{3.2}$$

The coefficient of interest for policy purposes is β_1, the ceteris paribus effect of *expend* on *avgscore*. By including *avginc* explicitly in the model, we are able to control for its effect on *avgscore*. This is likely to be important because average family income tends to be correlated with per-student spending: spending levels are often determined by both property and local income taxes. In simple regression analysis, *avginc* would be included in the error term, which would likely be correlated with *expend*, causing the OLS estimator of β_1 in the two-variable model to be biased.

In the two previous similar examples, we have shown how observable factors other than the variable of primary interest [*educ* in equation (3.1) and *expend* in equation (3.2)] can be included in a regression model. Generally, we can write a model with two independent variables as

$$y = \beta_0 + \beta_1 x_1 + \beta_2 x_2 + u, \tag{3.3}$$

where

β_0 is the intercept.
β_1 measures the change in y with respect to x_1, holding other factors fixed.
β_2 measures the change in y with respect to x_2, holding other factors fixed.

Multiple regression analysis is also useful for generalizing functional relationships between variables. As an example, suppose family consumption (*cons*) is a quadratic function of family income (*inc*):

$$cons = \beta_0 + \beta_1 inc + \beta_2 inc^2 + u, \qquad [3.4]$$

where u contains other factors affecting consumption. In this model, consumption depends on only one observed factor, income; so it might seem that it can be handled in a simple regression framework. But the model falls outside simple regression because it contains two functions of income, *inc* and inc^2 (and therefore three parameters, β_0, β_1, and β_2). Nevertheless, the consumption function is easily written as a regression model with two independent variables by letting $x_1 = inc$ and $x_2 = inc^2$.

Mechanically, there will be *no* difference in using the method of ordinary least squares (introduced in Section 3-2) to estimate equations as different as (3.1) and (3.4). Each equation can be written as (3.3), which is all that matters for computation. There is, however, an important difference in how one *interprets* the parameters. In equation (3.1), β_1 is the ceteris paribus effect of *educ* on *wage*. The parameter β_1 has no such interpretation in (3.4). In other words, it makes no sense to measure the effect of *inc* on *cons* while holding inc^2 fixed, because if *inc* changes, then so must inc^2! Instead, the change in consumption with respect to the change in income—the marginal propensity to consume—is approximated by

$$\frac{\Delta cons}{\Delta inc} \approx \beta_1 + 2\beta_2 inc.$$

See Appendix A for the calculus needed to derive this equation. In other words, the marginal effect of income on consumption depends on β_2 as well as on β_1 and the level of income. This example shows that, in any particular application, the definitions of the independent variables are crucial. But for the theoretical development of multiple regression, we can be vague about such details. We will study examples like this more completely in Chapter 6.

In the model with two independent variables, the key assumption about how u is related to x_1 and x_2 is

$$E(u|x_1, x_2) = 0. \qquad [3.5]$$

The interpretation of condition (3.5) is similar to the interpretation of Assumption SLR.4 for simple regression analysis. It means that, for any values of x_1 and x_2 in the population, the average of the unobserved factors is equal to zero. As with simple regression, the important part of the assumption is that the expected value of u is the same for all combinations of x_1 and x_2; that this common value is zero is no assumption at all as long as the intercept β_0 is included in the model (see Section 2-1).

How can we interpret the zero conditional mean assumption in the previous examples? In equation (3.1), the assumption is $E(u|educ,exper) = 0$. This implies that other factors affecting *wage* are not related on average to *educ* and *exper*. Therefore, if we think innate ability is part of u, then we will need average ability levels to be the same across all combinations of education and experience in the working population. This may or may not be true, but, as we will see in Section 3-3, this is the question we need to ask in order to determine whether the method of ordinary least squares produces unbiased estimators.

The example measuring student performance [equation (3.2)] is similar to the wage equation. The zero conditional mean assumption is $E(u|expend, avginc) = 0$, which means that other

---

EXPLORING FURTHER 3.1

A simple model to explain city murder rates (*murdrate*) in terms of the probability of conviction (*prbconv*) and average sentence length (*avgsen*) is

$$murdrate = \beta_0 + \beta_1 prbconv + \beta_2 avgsen + u.$$

What are some factors contained in u? Do you think the key assumption (3.5) is likely to hold?

factors affecting test scores—school or student characteristics—are, on average, unrelated to per-student funding and average family income.

When applied to the quadratic consumption function in (3.4), the zero conditional mean assumption has a slightly different interpretation. Written literally, equation (3.5) becomes $E(u|inc,inc^2) = 0$. Since inc^2 is known when inc is known, including inc^2 in the expectation is redundant: $E(u|inc,inc^2) = 0$ is the same as $E(u|inc) = 0$. Nothing is wrong with putting inc^2 along with inc in the expectation when stating the assumption, but $E(u|inc) = 0$ is more concise.

3-1b The Model with *k* Independent Variables

Once we are in the context of multiple regression, there is no need to stop with two independent variables. Multiple regression analysis allows many observed factors to affect y. In the wage example, we might also include amount of job training, years of tenure with the current employer, measures of ability, and even demographic variables like the number of siblings or mother's education. In the school funding example, additional variables might include measures of teacher quality and school size.

The general **multiple linear regression (MLR) model** (also called the *multiple regression model*) can be written in the population as

$$y = \beta_0 + \beta_1 x_1 + \beta_2 x_2 + \beta_3 x_3 + \ldots + \beta_k x_k + u, \qquad [3.6]$$

where

β_0 is the **intercept**.
β_1 is the parameter associated with x_1.
β_2 is the parameter associated with x_2, and so on.

Since there are k independent variables and an intercept, equation (3.6) contains $k + 1$ (unknown) population parameters. For shorthand purposes, we will sometimes refer to the parameters other than the intercept as **slope parameters**, even though this is not always literally what they are. [See equation (3.4), where neither β_1 nor β_2 is itself a slope, but together they determine the slope of the relationship between consumption and income.]

The terminology for multiple regression is similar to that for simple regression and is given in Table 3.1. Just as in simple regression, the variable u is the **error term** or **disturbance**. It contains factors other than $x_1, x_2, \ldots, x_k$ that affect y. No matter how many explanatory variables we include in our model, there will always be factors we cannot include, and these are collectively contained in u.

When applying the general multiple regression model, we must know how to interpret the parameters. We will get plenty of practice now and in subsequent chapters, but it is useful at this point to be reminded of some things we already know. Suppose that CEO salary (*salary*) is related to firm sales (*sales*) and CEO tenure (*ceoten*) with the firm by

$$\log(salary) = \beta_0 + \beta_1 \log(sales) + \beta_2 ceoten + \beta_3 ceoten^2 + u. \qquad [3.7]$$

This fits into the multiple regression model (with $k = 3$) by defining $y = \log(salary)$, $x_1 = \log(sales)$, $x_2 = ceoten$, and $x_3 = ceoten^2$. As we know from Chapter 2, the parameter β_1 is the ceteris paribus

TABLE 3.1 Terminology for Multiple Regression	
Y	**$x_1, x_2, \ldots, x_k$**
Dependent variable	Independent variables
Explained variable	Explanatory variables
Response variable	Control variables
Predicted variable	Predictor variables
Regressand	Regressors

elasticity of *salary* with respect to *sales*. If $\beta_3 = 0$, then $100\beta_2$ is approximately the ceteris paribus percentage increase in *salary* when *ceoten* increases by one year. When $\beta_3 \neq 0$, the effect of *ceoten* on *salary* is more complicated. We will postpone a detailed treatment of general models with quadratics until Chapter 6.

Equation (3.7) provides an important reminder about multiple regression analysis. The term "linear" in a multiple linear regression model means that equation (3.6) is linear in the *parameters*, β_j. Equation (3.7) is an example of a multiple regression model that, while linear in the β_j, is a nonlinear relationship between *salary* and the variables *sales* and *ceoten*. Many applications of multiple linear regression involve nonlinear relationships among the underlying variables.

The key assumption for the general multiple regression model is easy to state in terms of a conditional expectation:

$$E(u|x_1, x_2, ..., x_k) = 0. \tag{3.8}$$

At a minimum, equation (3.8) requires that all factors in the unobserved error term be uncorrelated with the explanatory variables. It also means that we have correctly accounted for the functional relationships between the explained and explanatory variables. Any problem that causes u to be correlated with any of the independent variables causes (3.8) to fail. In Section 3-3, we will show that assumption (3.8) implies that OLS is unbiased and will derive the bias that arises when a key variable has been omitted from the equation. In Chapters 15 and 16, we will study other reasons that might cause (3.8) to fail and show what can be done in cases where it does fail.

3-2 Mechanics and Interpretation of Ordinary Least Squares

We now summarize some computational and algebraic features of the method of ordinary least squares as it applies to a particular set of data. We also discuss how to interpret the estimated equation.

3-2a Obtaining the OLS Estimates

We first consider estimating the model with two independent variables. The estimated OLS equation is written in a form similar to the simple regression case:

$$\hat{y} = \hat{\beta}_0 + \hat{\beta}_1 x_1 + \hat{\beta}_2 x_2, \tag{3.9}$$

where

$\hat{\beta}_0$ = the estimate of β_0.
$\hat{\beta}_1$ = the estimate of β_1.
$\hat{\beta}_2$ = the estimate of β_2.

But how do we obtain $\hat{\beta}_0$, $\hat{\beta}_1$, and $\hat{\beta}_2$? The method of **ordinary least squares** chooses the estimates to minimize the sum of squared residuals. That is, given n observations on y, x_1, and x_2, $\{(x_{i1}, x_{i2}, y_i): i = 1, 2, ..., n\}$, the estimates $\hat{\beta}_0$, $\hat{\beta}_1$, and $\hat{\beta}_2$ are chosen simultaneously to make

$$\sum_{i=1}^{n} (y_i - \hat{\beta}_0 - \hat{\beta}_1 x_{i1} - \hat{\beta}_2 x_{i2})^2 \tag{3.10}$$

as small as possible.

To understand what OLS is doing, it is important to master the meaning of the indexing of the independent variables in (3.10). The independent variables have two subscripts here, i followed by either 1 or 2. The i subscript refers to the observation number. Thus, the sum in (3.10) is over all $i = 1$ to n observations. The second index is simply a method of distinguishing between different independent variables. In the example relating *wage* to *educ* and *exper*, $x_{i1} = educ_i$ is education for person i in the sample and $x_{i2} = exper_i$ is experience for person i. The sum of squared residuals in equation (3.10) is $\sum_{i=1}^{n} (wage_i - \hat{\beta}_0 - \hat{\beta}_1 educ_i - \hat{\beta}_2 exper_i)^2$. In what follows, the i subscript is reserved for indexing the observation number. If we write x_{ij}, then this means the ith observation on the jth independent variable. (Some authors prefer to switch the order of the observation number and the variable number, so that x_{1i} is observation i on variable one. But this is just a matter of notational taste.)

In the general case with k independent variables, we seek estimates, $\hat{\beta}_0, \hat{\beta}_1, ..., \hat{\beta}_k$ in the equation

$$\hat{y} = \hat{\beta}_0 + \hat{\beta}_1 x_1 + \hat{\beta}_2 x_2 + \cdots + \hat{\beta}_k x_k. \quad [3.11]$$

The OLS estimates, $k + 1$ of them, are chosen to minimize the sum of squared residuals:

$$\sum_{i=1}^{n}(y_i - \hat{\beta}_0 - \hat{\beta}_1 x_{i1} - \cdots - \hat{\beta}_k x_{ik})^2. \quad [3.12]$$

This minimization problem can be solved using multivariable calculus (see Appendix 3A). This leads to $k + 1$ linear equations in $k + 1$ unknowns $\hat{\beta}_0, \hat{\beta}_1, ..., \hat{\beta}_k$:

$$\sum_{i=1}^{n}(y_i - \hat{\beta}_0 - \hat{\beta}_1 x_{i1} - ... - \hat{\beta}_k x_{ik}) = 0$$

$$\sum_{i=1}^{n}x_{i1}(y_i - \hat{\beta}_0 - \hat{\beta}_1 x_{i1} - ... - \hat{\beta}_k x_{ik}) = 0$$

$$\sum_{i=1}^{n}x_{i2}(y_i - \hat{\beta}_0 - \hat{\beta}_1 x_{i1} - ... - \hat{\beta}_k x_{ik}) = 0 \quad [3.13]$$

$$\vdots$$

$$\sum_{i=1}^{n}x_{ik}(y_i - \hat{\beta}_0 - \hat{\beta}_1 x_{i1} - ... - \hat{\beta}_k x_{ik}) = 0.$$

These are often called the OLS **first order conditions**. As with the simple regression model in Section 2-2, the OLS first order conditions can be obtained by the method of moments: under assumption (3.8), $E(u) = 0$ and $E(x_j u) = 0$, where $j = 1, 2, ..., k$. The equations in (3.13) are the sample counterparts of these population moments, although we have omitted the division by the sample size n.

For even moderately sized n and k, solving the equations in (3.13) by hand calculations is tedious. Nevertheless, modern computers running standard statistics and econometrics software can solve these equations with large n and k very quickly.

There is only one slight caveat: we must assume that the equations in (3.13) can be solved *uniquely* for the $\hat{\beta}_j$. For now, we just assume this, as it is usually the case in well-specified models. In Section 3-3, we state the assumption needed for unique OLS estimates to exist (see Assumption MLR.3).

As in simple regression analysis, equation (3.11) is called the **OLS regression line** or the **sample regression function (SRF)**. We will call $\hat{\beta}_0$ the **OLS intercept estimate** and $\hat{\beta}_1, ..., \hat{\beta}_k$ the **OLS slope estimates** (corresponding to the independent variables $x_1, x_2, ..., x_k$).

To indicate that an OLS regression has been run, we will either write out equation (3.11) with y and $x_1, ..., x_k$ replaced by their variable names (such as *wage*, *educ*, and *exper*), or we will say that "we ran an OLS regression of y on $x_1, x_2, ..., x_k$" or that "we regressed y on $x_1, x_2, ..., x_k$." These are shorthand for saying that the method of ordinary least squares was used to obtain the OLS equation (3.11). Unless explicitly stated otherwise, we always estimate an intercept along with the slopes.

3-2b Interpreting the OLS Regression Equation

More important than the details underlying the computation of the $\hat{\beta}_j$ is the *interpretation* of the estimated equation. We begin with the case of two independent variables:

$$\hat{y} = \hat{\beta}_0 + \hat{\beta}_1 x_1 + \hat{\beta}_2 x_2. \quad [3.14]$$

The intercept $\hat{\beta}_0$ in equation (3.14) is the predicted value of y when $x_1 = 0$ and $x_2 = 0$. Sometimes, setting x_1 and x_2 both equal to zero is an interesting scenario; in other cases, it will not make sense. Nevertheless, the intercept is always needed to obtain a prediction of y from the OLS regression line, as (3.14) makes clear.

The estimates $\hat{\beta}_1$ and $\hat{\beta}_2$ have **partial effect**, or **ceteris paribus**, interpretations. From equation (3.14), we have

$$\Delta\hat{y} = \hat{\beta}_1\Delta x_1 + \hat{\beta}_2\Delta x_2,$$

so we can obtain the predicted change in y given the changes in x_1 and x_2. (Note how the intercept has nothing to do with the changes in y.) In particular, when x_2 is held fixed, so that $\Delta x_2 = 0$, then

$$\Delta\hat{y} = \hat{\beta}_1\Delta x_1,$$

holding x_2 fixed. The key point is that, by including x_2 in our model, we obtain a coefficient on x_1 with a ceteris paribus interpretation. This is why multiple regression analysis is so useful. Similarly,

$$\Delta\hat{y} = \hat{\beta}_2\Delta x_2,$$

holding x_1 fixed.

EXAMPLE 3.1   ## Determinants of College GPA

The variables in GPA1 include the college grade point average (*colGPA*), high school GPA (*hsGPA*), and achievement test score (*ACT*) for a sample of 141 students from a large university; both college and high school GPAs are on a four-point scale. We obtain the following OLS regression line to predict college GPA from high school GPA and achievement test score:

$$\widehat{colGPA} = 1.29 + .453\,hsGPA + .0094\,ACT$$

$$n = 141.$$

[3.15]

How do we interpret this equation? First, the intercept 1.29 is the predicted college GPA if *hsGPA* and *ACT* are both set as zero. Since no one who attends college has either a zero high school GPA or a zero on the achievement test, the intercept in this equation is not, by itself, meaningful.

More interesting estimates are the slope coefficients on *hsGPA* and *ACT*. As expected, there is a positive partial relationship between *colGPA* and *hsGPA*: Holding *ACT* fixed, another point on *hsGPA* is associated with .453 of a point on the college GPA, or almost half a point. In other words, if we choose two students, A and B, and these students have the same ACT score, but the high school GPA of Student A is one point higher than the high school GPA of Student B, then we predict Student A to have a college GPA .453 higher than that of Student B. (This says nothing about any two actual people, but it is our best prediction.)

The sign on *ACT* implies that, while holding *hsGPA* fixed, a change in the ACT score of 10 points—a very large change, since the maximum ACT score is 36 and the average score in the sample is about 24 with a standard deviation less than three—affects *colGPA* by less than one-tenth of a point. This is a small effect, and it suggests that, once high school GPA is accounted for, the ACT score is not a strong predictor of college GPA. (Naturally, there are many other factors that contribute to GPA, but here we focus on statistics available for high school students.) Later, after we discuss statistical inference, we will show that not only is the coefficient on ACT practically small, it is also statistically insignificant.

If we focus on a simple regression analysis relating *colGPA* to *ACT* only, we obtain

$$\widehat{colGPA} = 2.40 + .0271\,ACT$$

$$n = 141;$$

thus, the coefficient on *ACT* is almost three times as large as the estimate in (3.15). But this equation does *not* allow us to compare two people with the same high school GPA; it corresponds to a different experiment. We say more about the differences between multiple and simple regression later.

The case with more than two independent variables is similar. The OLS regression line is

$$\hat{y} = \hat{\beta}_0 + \hat{\beta}_1 x_1 + \hat{\beta}_2 x_2 + \ldots + \hat{\beta}_k x_k.$$ [3.16]

Written in terms of changes,

$$\Delta\hat{y} = \hat{\beta}_1 \Delta x_1 + \hat{\beta}_2 \Delta x_2 + \ldots + \hat{\beta}_k \Delta x_k.$$ [3.17]

The coefficient on x_1 measures the change in $\hat{y}$ due to a one-unit increase in x_1, holding all other independent variables fixed. That is,

$$\Delta\hat{y} = \hat{\beta}_1 \Delta x_1,$$ [3.18]

holding $x_2, x_3, \ldots, x_k$ fixed. Thus, we have *controlled for* the variables $x_2, x_3, \ldots, x_k$ when estimating the effect of x_1 on y. The other coefficients have a similar interpretation.

The following is an example with three independent variables.

EXAMPLE 3.2 **Hourly Wage Equation**

Using the 526 observations on workers in WAGE1, we include *educ* (years of education), *exper* (years of labor market experience), and *tenure* (years with the current employer) in an equation explaining log(*wage*). The estimated equation is

$$\widehat{\log(wage)} = .284 + .092 \, educ + .0041 \, exper + .022 \, tenure$$

$$n = 526.$$ [3.19]

As in the simple regression case, the coefficients have a percentage interpretation. The only difference here is that they also have a ceteris paribus interpretation. The coefficient .092 means that, holding *exper* and *tenure* fixed, another year of education is predicted to increase log(*wage*) by .092, which translates into an approximate 9.2% [100(.092)] increase in *wage*. Alternatively, if we take two people with the same levels of experience and job tenure, the coefficient on *educ* is the proportionate difference in predicted wage when their education levels differ by one year. This measure of the return to education at least keeps two important productivity factors fixed; whether it is a good estimate of the ceteris paribus return to another year of education requires us to study the statistical properties of OLS (see Section 3-3).

3-2c On the Meaning of "Holding Other Factors Fixed" in Multiple Regression

The partial effect interpretation of slope coefficients in multiple regression analysis can cause some confusion, so we provide a further discussion now.

In Example 3.1, we observed that the coefficient on *ACT* measures the predicted difference in *colGPA*, holding *hsGPA* fixed. The power of multiple regression analysis is that it provides this ceteris paribus interpretation even though the data have *not* been collected in a ceteris paribus fashion. In giving the coefficient on *ACT* a partial effect interpretation, it may seem that we actually went out and sampled people with the same high school GPA but possibly with different ACT scores. This is not the case. The data are a random sample from a large university: there were no restrictions placed on the sample values of *hsGPA* or *ACT* in obtaining the data. Rarely do we have the luxury of holding certain variables fixed in obtaining our sample. *If* we could collect a sample of individuals with the same high school GPA, then we could perform a simple regression analysis relating *colGPA* to *ACT*. Multiple regression effectively allows us to mimic this situation without restricting the values of any independent variables.

The power of multiple regression analysis is that it allows us to do in nonexperimental environments what natural scientists are able to do in a controlled laboratory setting: keep other factors fixed.

3-2d Changing More Than One Independent Variable Simultaneously

Sometimes, we want to change more than one independent variable at the same time to find the resulting effect on the dependent variable. This is easily done using equation (3.17). For example, in equation (3.19), we can obtain the estimated effect on *wage* when an individual stays at the same firm for another year: *exper* (general workforce experience) and *tenure* both increase by one year. The total effect (holding *educ* fixed) is

$$\Delta \widehat{\log(wage)} = .0041 \, \Delta exper + .022 \, \Delta tenure = .0041 + .022 = .0261,$$

or about 2.6%. Since *exper* and *tenure* each increase by one year, we just add the coefficients on *exper* and *tenure* and multiply by 100 to turn the effect into a percentage.

3-2e OLS Fitted Values and Residuals

After obtaining the OLS regression line (3.11), we can obtain a *fitted* or *predicted value* for each observation. For observation i, the fitted value is simply

$$\hat{y}_i = \hat{\beta}_0 + \hat{\beta}_1 x_{i1} + \hat{\beta}_2 x_{i2} + \ldots + \hat{\beta}_k x_{ik}, \qquad [3.20]$$

which is just the predicted value obtained by plugging the values of the independent variables for observation i into equation (3.11). We should not forget about the intercept in obtaining the fitted values; otherwise, the answer can be very misleading. As an example, if in (3.15), $hsGPA_i = 3.5$ and $ACT_i = 24$, $\widehat{colGPA}_i = 1.29 + .453(3.5) + .0094(24) = 3.101$ (rounded to three places after the decimal).

Normally, the actual value y_i for any observation i will not equal the predicted value, $\hat{y}_i$: OLS minimizes the *average* squared prediction error, which says nothing about the prediction error for any particular observation. The **residual** for observation i is defined just as in the simple regression case,

$$\hat{u}_i = y_i - \hat{y}_i. \qquad [3.21]$$

There is a residual for each observation. If $\hat{u}_i > 0$, then $\hat{y}_i$ is below y_i, which means that, for this observation, y_i is underpredicted. If $\hat{u}_i < 0$, then $y_i < \hat{y}_i$, and y_i is overpredicted.

The OLS fitted values and residuals have some important properties that are immediate extensions from the single variable case:

1. The sample average of the residuals is zero and so $\bar{y} = \bar{\hat{y}}$.

2. The sample covariance between each independent variable and the OLS residuals is zero. Consequently, the sample covariance between the OLS fitted values and the OLS residuals is zero.

3. The point $(\bar{x}_1, \bar{x}_2, \ldots, \bar{x}_k, \bar{y})$ is always on the OLS regression line: $\bar{y} = \hat{\beta}_0 + \hat{\beta}_1 \bar{x}_1 + \hat{\beta}_2 \bar{x}_2 + \ldots + \hat{\beta}_k \bar{x}_k$.

The first two properties are immediate consequences of the set of equations used to obtain the OLS estimates. The first equation in (3.13) says that the sum of the residuals is zero. The remaining equations are of the form $\sum_{i=1}^{n} x_{ij} \hat{u}_i = 0$, which implies that each independent variable has zero sample covariance with $\hat{u}_i$. Property (3) follows immediately from property (1).

EXPLORING FURTHER 3.2

In Example 3.1, the OLS fitted line explaining college GPA in terms of high school GPA and ACT score is

$$\widehat{colGPA} = 1.29 + .453 \, hsGPA + .0094 \, ACT.$$

If the average high school GPA is about 3.4 and the average ACT score is about 24.2, what is the average college GPA in the sample?

3-2f A "Partialling Out" Interpretation of Multiple Regression

When applying OLS, we do not need to know explicit formulas for the $\hat{\beta}_j$ that solve the system of equations in (3.13). Nevertheless, for certain derivations, we do need explicit formulas for the $\hat{\beta}_j$. These formulas also shed further light on the workings of OLS.

Consider again the case with $k = 2$ independent variables, $\hat{y} = \hat{\beta}_0 + \hat{\beta}_1 x_1 + \hat{\beta}_2 x_2$. For concreteness, we focus on $\hat{\beta}_1$. One way to express $\hat{\beta}_1$ is

$$\hat{\beta}_1 = \left(\sum_{i=1}^{n} \hat{r}_{i1} y_i \right) \Big/ \left(\sum_{i=1}^{n} \hat{r}_{i1}^2 \right), \qquad [3.22]$$

where the $\hat{r}_{i1}$ are the OLS residuals from a simple regression of x_1 on x_2, using the sample at hand. We regress our first independent variable, x_1, on our second independent variable, x_2, and then obtain the residuals (y plays no role here). Equation (3.22) shows that we can then do a simple regression of y on $\hat{r}_1$ to obtain $\hat{\beta}_1$. (Note that the residuals $\hat{r}_{i1}$ have a zero sample average, and so $\hat{\beta}_1$ is the usual slope estimate from simple regression.)

The representation in equation (3.22) gives another demonstration of $\hat{\beta}_1$'s partial effect interpretation. The residuals $\hat{r}_{i1}$ are the part of x_{i1} that is uncorrelated with x_{i2}. Another way of saying this is that $\hat{r}_{i1}$ is x_{i1} after the effects of x_{i2} have been *partialled out*, or *netted out*. Thus, $\hat{\beta}_1$ measures the sample relationship between y and x_1 after x_2 has been partialled out.

In simple regression analysis, there is no partialling out of other variables because no other variables are included in the regression. Computer Exercise C5 steps you through the partialling out process using the wage data from Example 3.2. For practical purposes, the important thing is that $\hat{\beta}_1$ in the equation $\hat{y} = \hat{\beta}_0 + \hat{\beta}_1 x_1 + \hat{\beta}_2 x_2$ measures the change in y given a one-unit increase in x_1, holding x_2 fixed.

In the general model with k explanatory variables, $\hat{\beta}_1$ can still be written as in equation (3.22), but the residuals $\hat{r}_{i1}$ come from the regression of x_1 on $x_2, \ldots, x_k$. Thus, $\hat{\beta}_1$ measures the effect of x_1 on y after $x_2, \ldots, x_k$ have been partialled or netted out. In econometrics, the general partialling out result is usually called the **Frisch-Waugh theorem**. It has many uses in theoretical and applied econometrics. We will see applications to time series regressions in Chapter 10.

3-2g Comparison of Simple and Multiple Regression Estimates

Two special cases exist in which the simple regression of y on x_1 will produce the *same* OLS estimate on x_1 as the regression of y on x_1 and x_2. To be more precise, write the simple regression of y on x_1 as $\tilde{y} = \tilde{\beta}_0 + \tilde{\beta}_1 x_1$, and write the multiple regression as $\hat{y} = \hat{\beta}_0 + \hat{\beta}_1 x_1 + \hat{\beta}_2 x_2$. We know that the simple regression coefficient $\tilde{\beta}_1$ does not usually equal the multiple regression coefficient $\hat{\beta}_1$. It turns out there is a simple relationship between $\tilde{\beta}_1$ and $\hat{\beta}_1$, which allows for interesting comparisons between simple and multiple regression:

$$\tilde{\beta}_1 = \hat{\beta}_1 + \hat{\beta}_2 \tilde{\delta}_1, \qquad [3.23]$$

where $\tilde{\delta}_1$ is the slope coefficient from the simple regression of x_{i2} on x_{i1}, $i = 1, \ldots, n$. This equation shows how $\tilde{\beta}_1$ differs from the partial effect of x_1 on $\hat{y}$. The confounding term is the partial effect of x_2 on $\hat{y}$ times the slope in the sample regression of x_2 on x_1. (See Section 3A-4 in the chapter appendix for a more general verification.)

The relationship between $\tilde{\beta}_1$ and $\hat{\beta}_1$ also shows there are two distinct cases where they are equal:

1. The partial effect of x_2 on $\hat{y}$ is zero in the sample. That is, $\hat{\beta}_2 = 0$.

2. x_1 and x_2 are uncorrelated in the sample. That is, $\tilde{\delta}_1 = 0$.

Even though simple and multiple regression estimates are almost never identical, we can use the above formula to characterize why they might be either very different or quite similar. For example, if $\hat{\beta}_2$ is small, we might expect the multiple and simple regression estimates of β_1 to be similar.

In Example 3.1, the sample correlation between *hsGPA* and *ACT* is about 0.346, which is a nontrivial correlation. But the coefficient on *ACT* is fairly little. It is not surprising to find that the simple regression of *colGPA* on *hsGPA* produces a slope estimate of .482, which is not much different from the estimate .453 in (3.15).

EXAMPLE 3.3	**Participation in 401(k) Pension Plans**

We use the data in 401K to estimate the effect of a plan's match rate (*mrate*) on the participation rate (*prate*) in its 401(k) pension plan. The match rate is the amount the firm contributes to a worker's fund for each dollar the worker contributes (up to some limit); thus, *mrate* = .75 means that the firm contributes 75¢ for each dollar contributed by the worker. The participation rate is the percentage of eligible workers having a 401(k) account. The variable *age* is the age of the 401(k) plan. There are 1,534 plans in the data set, the average *prate* is 87.36, the average *mrate* is .732, and the average *age* is 13.2.

Regressing *prate* on *mrate*, *age* gives

$$\widehat{prate} = 80.12 + 5.52\,mrate + .243\,age$$

$$n = 1,534.$$

Thus, both *mrate* and *age* have the expected effects. What happens if we do not control for *age*? The estimated effect of *age* is not trivial, and so we might expect a large change in the estimated effect of *mrate* if *age* is dropped from the regression. However, the simple regression of *prate* on *mrate* yields $\widehat{prate} = 83.08 + 5.86\,mrate$. The simple regression estimate of the effect of *mrate* on *prate* is clearly different from the multiple regression estimate, but the difference is not very big. (The simple regression estimate is only about 6.2% larger than the multiple regression estimate.) This can be explained by the fact that the sample correlation between *mrate* and *age* is only .12.

In the case with k independent variables, the simple regression of y on x_1 and the multiple regression of y on $x_1, x_2, \ldots, x_k$ produce an identical estimate of x_1 only if (1) the OLS coefficients on x_2 through x_k are all zero *or* (2) x_1 is uncorrelated with *each of* $x_2, \ldots, x_k$. Neither of these is very likely in practice. But if the coefficients on x_2 through x_k are small, or the sample correlations between x_1 and the other independent variables are insubstantial, then the simple and multiple regression estimates of the effect of x_1 on y can be similar.

3-2h Goodness-of-Fit

As with simple regression, we can define the **total sum of squares (SST)**, the **explained sum of squares (SSE)**, and the **residual sum of squares** or **sum of squared residuals (SSR)** as

$$\text{SST} \equiv \sum_{i=1}^{n}(y_i - \bar{y})^2 \tag{3.24}$$

$$\text{SSE} \equiv \sum_{i=1}^{n}(\hat{y}_i - \bar{y})^2 \tag{3.25}$$

$$\text{SSR} \equiv \sum_{i=1}^{n}\hat{u}_i^2. \tag{3.26}$$

Using the same argument as in the simple regression case, we can show that

$$\text{SST} = \text{SSE} + \text{SSR}. \tag{3.27}$$

In other words, the total variation in $\{y_i\}$ is the sum of the total variations in $\{\hat{y}_i\}$ and in $\{\hat{u}_i\}$.

Assuming that the total variation in y is nonzero, as is the case unless y_i is constant in the sample, we can divide (3.27) by SST to get

$$SSR/SST + SSE/SST = 1.$$

Just as in the simple regression case, the R-squared is defined to be

$$R^2 \equiv SSE/SST = 1 - SSR/SST, \hspace{2cm} [3.28]$$

and it is interpreted as the proportion of the sample variation in y_i that is explained by the OLS regression line. By definition, R^2 is a number between zero and one.

R^2 can also be shown to equal the squared correlation coefficient between the actual y_i and the fitted values $\hat{y}_i$. That is,

$$R^2 = \frac{\left(\sum_{i=1}^{n}(y_i - \bar{y})(\hat{y}_i - \bar{\hat{y}}) \right)^2}{\left(\sum_{i=1}^{n}(y_i - \bar{y})^2 \right)\left(\sum_{i=1}^{n}(\hat{y}_i - \bar{\hat{y}})^2 \right)}. \hspace{2cm} [3.29]$$

[We have put the average of the $\hat{y}_i$ in (3.29) to be true to the formula for a correlation coefficient; we know that this average equals $\bar{y}$ because the sample average of the residuals is zero and $y_i = \hat{y}_i + \hat{u}_i$.]

EXAMPLE 3.4   **Determinants of College GPA**

From the grade point average regression that we did earlier, the equation with R^2 is

$$\widehat{colGPA} = 1.29 + .453\,hsGPA + .0094\,ACT$$

$$n = 141, R^2 = .176.$$

This means that $hsGPA$ and ACT together explain about 17.6% of the variation in college GPA for this sample of students. This may not seem like a high percentage, but we must remember that there are many other factors—including family background, personality, quality of high school education, affinity for college—that contribute to a student's college performance. If $hsGPA$ and ACT explained almost all of the variation in $colGPA$, then performance in college would be preordained by high school performance!

An important fact about R^2 is that it never decreases, and it usually increases, when another independent variable is added to a regression and the same set of observations is used for both regressions. This algebraic fact follows because, by definition, the sum of squared residuals never increases when additional regressors are added to the model. For example, the last digit of one's social security number has nothing to do with one's hourly wage, but adding this digit to a wage equation will increase the R^2 (by a little, at least).

An important caveat to the previous assertion about R-squared is that it assumes we do not have missing data on the explanatory variables. If two regressions use different sets of observations, then, in general, we cannot tell how the R-squareds will compare, even if one regression uses a subset of regressors. For example, suppose we have a full set of data on the variables y, x_1, and x_2, but for some units in our sample data are missing on x_3. Then we cannot say that the R-squared from regressing y on x_1, x_2 will be less than that from regressing y on x_1, x_2, and x_3: it could go either way. Missing data can be an important practical issue, and we will return to it in Chapter 9.

The fact that R^2 never decreases when *any* variable is added to a regression makes it a poor tool for deciding whether one variable or several variables should be added to a model. The factor that should determine whether an explanatory variable belongs in a model is whether the explanatory variable has a nonzero partial effect on y in the *population*. We will show how to test this hypothesis in Chapter 4 when we cover statistical inference. We will also see that, when used properly, R^2 allows us to *test* a group of variables to see if it is important for explaining y. For now, we use it as a goodness-of-fit measure for a given model.

| **EXAMPLE 3.5** | **Explaining Arrest Records** |

CRIME1 contains data on arrests during the year 1986 and other information on 2,725 men born in either 1960 or 1961 in California. Each man in the sample was arrested at least once prior to 1986. The variable *narr86* is the number of times the man was arrested during 1986: it is zero for most men in the sample (72.29%), and it varies from 0 to 12. (The percentage of men arrested once during 1986 was 20.51.) The variable *pcnv* is the proportion (not percentage) of arrests prior to 1986 that led to conviction, *avgsen* is average sentence length served for prior convictions (zero for most people), *ptime86* is months spent in prison in 1986, and *qemp86* is the number of quarters during which the man was employed in 1986 (from zero to four).

A linear model explaining arrests is

$$narr86 = \beta_0 + \beta_1 pcnv + \beta_2 avgsen + \beta_3 ptime86 + \beta_4 qemp86 + u,$$

where *pcnv* is a proxy for the likelihood for being convicted of a crime and *avgsen* is a measure of expected severity of punishment, if convicted. The variable *ptime86* captures the incarcerative effects of crime: if an individual is in prison, he cannot be arrested for a crime outside of prison. Labor market opportunities are crudely captured by *qemp86*.

First, we estimate the model without the variable *avgsen*. We obtain

$$\widehat{narr86} = .712 - .150\, pcnv - .034\, ptime86 - .104\, qemp86$$

$$n = 2,725, R^2 = .0413.$$

This equation says that, as a group, the three variables *pcnv*, *ptime86*, and *qemp86* explain about 4.1% of the variation in *narr86*.

Each of the OLS slope coefficients has the anticipated sign. An increase in the proportion of convictions lowers the predicted number of arrests. If we increase *pcnv* by .50 (a large increase in the probability of conviction), then, holding the other factors fixed, $\widehat{\Delta narr86} = -.150(.50) = -.075$. This may seem unusual because an arrest cannot change by a fraction. But we can use this value to obtain the predicted change in expected arrests for a large group of men. For example, among 100 men, the predicted fall in arrests when *pcnv* increases by .50 is -7.5.

Similarly, a longer prison term leads to a lower predicted number of arrests. In fact, if *ptime86* increases from 0 to 12, predicted arrests for a particular man fall by $.034(12) = .408$. Another quarter in which legal employment is reported lowers predicted arrests by .104, which would be 10.4 arrests among 100 men.

If *avgsen* is added to the model, we know that R^2 will increase. The estimated equation is

$$\widehat{narr86} = .707 - .151\, pcnv + .0074\, avgsen - .037\, ptime86 - .103\, qemp86$$

$$n = 2,725, R^2 = .0422.$$

Thus, adding the average sentence variable increases R^2 from .0413 to .0422, a practically small effect. The sign of the coefficient on *avgsen* is also unexpected: it says that a longer average sentence length increases criminal activity.

Example 3.5 deserves a final word of caution. The fact that the four explanatory variables included in the second regression explain only about 4.2% of the variation in *narr86* does not necessarily mean that the equation is useless. Even though these variables collectively do not explain much of the variation in arrests, it is still possible that the OLS estimates are reliable estimates of the ceteris paribus effects of each independent variable on *narr86*. As we will see, whether this is the case does not directly depend on the size of R^2. Generally, a low R^2 indicates that it is hard to predict individual outcomes on *y* with much accuracy, something we study in more detail in Chapter 6. In the arrest example, the small R^2 reflects what we already suspect in the social sciences: it is generally very difficult to predict individual behavior.

3-2i Regression through the Origin

Sometimes, an economic theory or common sense suggests that β_0 should be zero, and so we should briefly mention OLS estimation when the intercept is zero. Specifically, we now seek an equation of the form

$$\tilde{y} = \tilde{\beta}_1 x_1 + \tilde{\beta}_2 x_2 + \ldots + \tilde{\beta}_k x_k, \qquad [3.30]$$

where the symbol "~" over the estimates is used to distinguish them from the OLS estimates obtained along with the intercept [as in (3.11)]. In (3.30), when $x_1 = 0, x_2 = 0, \ldots, x_k = 0$, the predicted value is zero. In this case, $\tilde{\beta}_1, \ldots, \tilde{\beta}_k$ are said to be the OLS estimates from the regression of *y* on $x_1, x_2, \ldots, x_k$ *through the origin*.

The OLS estimates in (3.30), as always, minimize the sum of squared residuals, but with the intercept set at zero. You should be warned that the properties of OLS that we derived earlier no longer hold for regression through the origin. In particular, the OLS residuals no longer have a zero sample average. Further, if R^2 is defined as $1 - \text{SSR/SST}$, where SST is given in (3.24) and SSR is now $\sum_{i=1}^{n}(y_i - \tilde{\beta}_1 x_{i1} - \ldots - \tilde{\beta}_k x_{ik})^2$, then R^2 can actually be negative. This means that the sample average, $\bar{y}$, "explains" more of the variation in the y_i than the explanatory variables. Either we should include an intercept in the regression or conclude that the explanatory variables poorly explain *y*. To always have a nonnegative R-squared, some economists prefer to calculate R^2 as the squared correlation coefficient between the actual and fitted values of *y*, as in (3.29). (In this case, the average fitted value must be computed directly since it no longer equals $\bar{y}$.) However, there is no set rule on computing R-squared for regression through the origin.

One serious drawback with regression through the origin is that, if the intercept β_0 in the population model is different from zero, then the OLS estimators of the slope parameters will be biased. The bias can be severe in some cases. The cost of estimating an intercept when β_0 is truly zero is that the variances of the OLS slope estimators are larger.

3-3 The Expected Value of the OLS Estimators

We now turn to the statistical properties of OLS for estimating the parameters in an underlying population model. In this section, we derive the expected value of the OLS estimators. In particular, we state and discuss four assumptions, which are direct extensions of the simple regression model assumptions, under which the OLS estimators are unbiased for the population parameters. We also explicitly obtain the bias in OLS when an important variable has been omitted from the regression.

You should remember that statistical properties have nothing to do with a particular sample, but rather with the property of estimators when random sampling is done repeatedly. Thus, Sections 3-3, 3-4, and 3-5 are somewhat abstract. Although we give examples of deriving bias for particular models, it is not meaningful to talk about the statistical properties of a set of estimates obtained from a single sample.

The first assumption we make simply defines the multiple linear regression (MLR) model.

Assumption MLR.1   Linear in Parameters

The model in the population can be written as

$$y = \beta_0 + \beta_1 x_1 + \beta_2 x_2 + \ldots + \beta_k x_k + u, \qquad [3.31]$$

where $\beta_0, \beta_1, \ldots, \beta_k$ are the unknown parameters (constants) of interest and u is an unobserved random error or disturbance term.

Equation (3.31) formally states the **population model**, sometimes called the **true model**, to allow for the possibility that we might estimate a model that differs from (3.31). The key feature is that the model is linear in the parameters $\beta_0, \beta_1, \ldots, \beta_k$. As we know, (3.31) is quite flexible because y and the independent variables can be arbitrary functions of the underlying variables of interest, such as natural logarithms and squares [see, for example, equation (3.7)].

Assumption MLR.2   Random Sampling

We have a random sample of n observations, $\{(x_{i1}, x_{i2}, \ldots, x_{ik}, y_i): i = 1, 2, \ldots, n\}$, following the population model in Assumption MLR.1.

Sometimes, we need to write the equation for a particular observation i: for a randomly drawn observation from the population, we have

$$y_i = \beta_0 + \beta_1 x_{i1} + \beta_2 x_{i2} + \ldots + \beta_k x_{ik} + u_i. \qquad [3.32]$$

Remember that i refers to the observation, and the second subscript on x is the variable number. For example, we can write a CEO salary equation for a particular CEO i as

$$\log(salary_i) = \beta_0 + \beta_1 \log(sales_i) + \beta_2 ceoten_i + \beta_3 ceoten_i^2 + u_i. \qquad [3.33]$$

The term u_i contains the unobserved factors for CEO i that affect his or her salary. For applications, it is usually easiest to write the model in population form, as in (3.31). It contains less clutter and emphasizes the fact that we are interested in estimating a population relationship.

In light of model (3.31), the OLS estimators $\hat{\beta}_0, \hat{\beta}_1, \hat{\beta}_2, \ldots, \hat{\beta}_k$ from the regression of y on $x_1, \ldots, x_k$ are now considered to be estimators of $\beta_0, \beta_1, \ldots, \beta_k$. In Section 3-2, we saw that OLS chooses the intercept and slope estimates for a particular sample so that the residuals average to zero and the sample correlation between each independent variable and the residuals is zero. Still, we did not include conditions under which the OLS estimates are well defined for a given sample. The next assumption fills that gap.

Assumption MLR.3   No Perfect Collinearity

In the sample (and therefore in the population), none of the independent variables is constant, and there are no *exact linear* relationships among the independent variables.

Assumption MLR.3 is more complicated than its counterpart for simple regression because we must now look at relationships between all independent variables. If an independent variable in (3.31) is an exact linear combination of the other independent variables, then we say the model suffers from **perfect collinearity**, and it cannot be estimated by OLS.

It is important to note that Assumption MLR.3 *does* allow the independent variables to be correlated; they just cannot be *perfectly* correlated. If we did not allow for any correlation among the independent variables, then multiple regression would be of very limited use for econometric analysis. For example, in the model relating test scores to educational expenditures and average family income,

$$avgscore = \beta_0 + \beta_1 expend + \beta_2 avginc + u,$$

we fully expect *expend* and *avginc* to be correlated: school districts with high average family incomes tend to spend more perstudent on education. In fact, the primary motivation for including *avginc* in the equation is that we suspect it is correlated with *expend*, and so we would like to hold it fixed in the analysis. Assumption MLR.3 only rules out *perfect* correlation between *expend* and *avginc* in our sample. We would be very unlucky to obtain a sample where per-student expenditures are perfectly correlated with average family income. But some correlation, perhaps a substantial amount, is expected and certainly allowed.

The simplest way that two independent variables can be perfectly correlated is when one variable is a constant multiple of another. This can happen when a researcher inadvertently puts the same variable measured in different units into a regression equation. For example, in estimating a relationship between consumption and income, it makes no sense to include as independent variables income measured in dollars as well as income measured in thousands of dollars. One of these is redundant. What sense would it make to hold income measured in dollars fixed while changing income measured in thousands of dollars?

We already know that different nonlinear functions of the same variable *can* appear among the regressors. For example, the model $cons = \beta_0 + \beta_1 inc + \beta_2 inc^2 + u$ does not violate Assumption MLR.3: even though $x_2 = inc^2$ is an exact function of $x_1 = inc$, inc^2 is not an exact *linear* function of *inc*. Including inc^2 in the model is a useful way to generalize functional form, unlike including income measured in dollars and in thousands of dollars.

Common sense tells us not to include the same explanatory variable measured in different units in the same regression equation. There are also more subtle ways that one independent variable can be a multiple of another. Suppose we would like to estimate an extension of a constant elasticity consumption function. It might seem natural to specify a model such as

$$\log(cons) = \beta_0 + \beta_1 \log(inc) + \beta_2 \log(inc^2) + u, \qquad [3.34]$$

where $x_1 = \log(inc)$ and $x_2 = \log(inc^2)$. Using the basic properties of the natural log (see Appendix A), $\log(inc^2) = 2 \cdot \log(inc)$. That is, $x_2 = 2x_1$, and naturally this holds for all observations in the sample. This violates Assumption MLR.3. What we should do instead is include $[\log(inc)]^2$, not $\log(inc^2)$, along with $\log(inc)$. This is a sensible extension of the constant elasticity model, and we will see how to interpret such models in Chapter 6.

Another way that independent variables can be perfectly collinear is when one independent variable can be expressed as an exact linear function of two or more of the other independent variables. For example, suppose we want to estimate the effect of campaign spending on campaign outcomes. For simplicity, assume that each election has two candidates. Let *voteA* be the percentage of the vote for Candidate A, let *expendA* be campaign expenditures by Candidate A, let *expendB* be campaign expenditures by Candidate B, and let *totexpend* be total campaign expenditures; the latter three variables are all measured in dollars. It may seem natural to specify the model as

$$voteA = \beta_0 + \beta_1 expendA + \beta_2 expendB + \beta_3 totexpend + u, \qquad [3.35]$$

in order to isolate the effects of spending by each candidate and the total amount of spending. But this model violates Assumption MLR.3 because $x_3 = x_1 + x_2$ by definition. Trying to interpret this equation in a ceteris paribus fashion reveals the problem. The parameter of β_1 in equation (3.35) is supposed to measure the effect of increasing expenditures by Candidate A by one dollar on Candidate A's vote, holding Candidate B's spending *and* total spending fixed. This is nonsense, because if *expendB* and *totexpend* are held fixed, then we cannot increase *expendA*.

The solution to the perfect collinearity in (3.35) is simple: drop any one of the three variables from the model. We would probably drop *totexpend*, and then the coefficient on *expendA* would measure the effect of increasing expenditures by A on the percentage of the vote received by A, holding the spending by B fixed.

The prior examples show that Assumption MLR.3 can fail if we are not careful in specifying our model. Assumption MLR.3 also fails if the sample size, n, is too small in relation to the number of parameters being estimated. In the general regression model in equation (3.31), there are $k + 1$ parameters, and MLR.3 fails if $n < k + 1$. Intuitively, this makes sense: to estimate $k + 1$ parameters, we need at least $k + 1$ observations. Not surprisingly, it is better to have as many observations as possible, something we will see with our variance calculations in Section 3-4.

> ### EXPLORING FURTHER 3.3
>
> In the previous example, if we use as explanatory variables *expendA*, *expendB*, and *shareA*, where *shareA* = 100·(*expendA/ totexpend*) is the percentage share of total campaign expenditures made by Candidate A, does this violate Assumption MLR.3?

If the model is carefully specified and $n \geq k + 1$, Assumption MLR.3 can fail in rare cases due to bad luck in collecting the sample. For example, in a wage equation with education and experience as variables, it is possible that we could obtain a random sample where each individual has exactly twice as much education as years of experience. This scenario would cause Assumption MLR.3 to fail, but it can be considered very unlikely unless we have an extremely small sample size.

The final, and most important, assumption needed for unbiasedness is a direct extension of Assumption SLR.4.

Assumption MLR.4   Zero Conditional Mean

The error u has an expected value of zero given any values of the independent variables. In other words,

$$E(u|x_1, x_2, \ldots, x_k) = 0. \tag{3.36}$$

One way that Assumption MLR.4 can fail is if the functional relationship between the explained and explanatory variables is misspecified in equation (3.31): for example, if we forget to include the quadratic term inc^2 in the consumption function $cons = \beta_0 + \beta_1 inc + \beta_2 inc^2 + u$ when we estimate the model. Another functional form misspecification occurs when we use the level of a variable when the log of the variable is what actually shows up in the population model, or vice versa. For example, if the true model has log(*wage*) as the dependent variable but we use *wage* as the dependent variable in our regression analysis, then the estimators will be biased. Intuitively, this should be pretty clear. We will discuss ways of detecting functional form misspecification in Chapter 9.

Omitting an important factor that is correlated with any of $x_1, x_2, \ldots, x_k$ causes Assumption MLR.4 to fail also. With multiple regression analysis, we are able to include many factors among the explanatory variables, and omitted variables are less likely to be a problem in multiple regression analysis than in simple regression analysis. Nevertheless, in any application, there are always factors that, due to data limitations or ignorance, we will not be able to include. If we think these factors should be controlled for and they are correlated with one or more of the independent variables, then Assumption MLR.4 will be violated. We will derive this bias later.

There are other ways that u can be correlated with an explanatory variable. In Chapters 9 and 15, we will discuss the problem of measurement error in an explanatory variable. In Chapter 16, we cover the conceptually more difficult problem in which one or more of the explanatory variables is determined jointly with y—as occurs when we view quantities and prices as being determined by the intersection of supply and demand curves. We must postpone our study of these problems until we have a firm grasp of multiple regression analysis under an ideal set of assumptions.

When Assumption MLR.4 holds, we often say that we have **exogenous explanatory variables**. If x_j is correlated with u for any reason, then x_j is said to be an **endogenous explanatory variable**. The terms "exogenous" and "endogenous" originated in simultaneous equations analysis (see Chapter 16), but the term "endogenous explanatory variable" has evolved to cover any case in which an explanatory variable may be correlated with the error term.

Before we show the unbiasedness of the OLS estimators under MLR.1 to MLR.4, a word of caution. Beginning students of econometrics sometimes confuse Assumptions MLR.3 and MLR.4, but they are quite different. Assumption MLR.3 rules out certain relationships among the independent or explanatory variables and has *nothing* to do with the error, u. You will know immediately when carrying out OLS estimation whether or not Assumption MLR.3 holds. On the other hand, Assumption MLR.4—the much more important of the two—restricts the relationship between the unobserved factors in u and the explanatory variables. Unfortunately, we will never know for sure whether the average value of the unobserved factors is unrelated to the explanatory variables. But this is the critical assumption.

We are now ready to show unbiasedness of OLS under the first four multiple regression assumptions. As in the simple regression case, the expectations are conditional on the values of the explanatory variables in the sample, something we show explicitly in Appendix 3A but not in the text.

THEOREM 3.1	**UNBIASEDNESS OF OLS**

Under Assumptions MLR.1 through MLR.4,

$$E(\hat{\beta}_j) = \beta_j, j = 0, 1, ..., k, \qquad [3.37]$$

for any values of the population parameter β_j. In other words, the OLS estimators are unbiased estimators of the population parameters.

In our previous empirical examples, Assumption MLR.3 has been satisfied (because we have been able to compute the OLS estimates). Furthermore, for the most part, the samples are randomly chosen from a well-defined population. If we believe that the specified models are correct under the key Assumption MLR.4, then we can conclude that OLS is unbiased in these examples.

Since we are approaching the point where we can use multiple regression in serious empirical work, it is useful to remember the meaning of unbiasedness. It is tempting, in examples such as the wage equation in (3.19), to say something like "9.2% is an unbiased estimate of the return to education." As we know, an estimate cannot be unbiased: an estimate is a fixed number, obtained from a particular sample, which usually is not equal to the population parameter. When we say that OLS is unbiased under Assumptions MLR.1 through MLR.4, we mean that the *procedure* by which the OLS estimates are obtained is unbiased when we view the procedure as being applied across all possible random samples. We hope that we have obtained a sample that gives us an estimate close to the population value, but, unfortunately, this cannot be assured. What is assured is that we have no reason to believe our estimate is more likely to be too big or more likely to be too small.

3-3a Including Irrelevant Variables in a Regression Model

One issue that we can dispense with fairly quickly is that of **inclusion of an irrelevant variable** or **overspecifying the model** in multiple regression analysis. This means that one (or more) of the independent variables is included in the model even though it has no partial effect on y in the population. (That is, its population coefficient is zero.)

To illustrate the issue, suppose we specify the model as

$$y = \beta_0 + \beta_1 x_1 + \beta_2 x_2 + \beta_3 x_3 + u, \qquad [3.38]$$

and this model satisfies Assumptions MLR.1 through MLR.4. However, x_3 has no effect on y after x_1 and x_2 have been controlled for, which means that $\beta_3 = 0$. The variable x_3 may or may not be correlated with x_1 or x_2; all that matters is that, once x_1 and x_2 are controlled for, x_3 has no effect on y. In terms of conditional expectations, $E(y|x_1, x_2, x_3) = E(y|x_1, x_2) = \beta_0 + \beta_1 x_1 + \beta_2 x_2$.

Because we do not know that $\beta_3 = 0$, we are inclined to estimate the equation including x_3:

$$\hat{y} = \hat{\beta}_0 + \hat{\beta}_1 x_1 + \hat{\beta}_2 x_2 + \hat{\beta}_3 x_3. \qquad [3.39]$$

We have included the irrelevant variable, x_3, in our regression. What is the effect of including x_3 in (3.39) when its coefficient in the population model (3.38) is zero? In terms of the unbiasedness of $\hat{\beta}_1$ and $\hat{\beta}_2$, there is *no effect*. This conclusion requires no special derivation, as it follows immediately from Theorem 3.1. Remember, unbiasedness means $E(\hat{\beta}_j) = \beta_j$ for *any* value of β_j, including $\beta_j = 0$. Thus, we can conclude that $E(\hat{\beta}_0) = \beta_0, E(\hat{\beta}_1) = \beta_1, E(\hat{\beta}_2) = \beta_2, E(\hat{\beta}_3) = 0$ (for any values of β_0, β_1, and β_2). Even though $\hat{\beta}_3$ itself will never be exactly zero, its average value across all random samples will be zero.

The conclusion of the preceding example is much more general: including one or more irrelevant variables in a multiple regression model, or overspecifying the model, does not affect the unbiasedness of the OLS estimators. Does this mean it is harmless to include irrelevant variables? No. As we will see in Section 3-4, including irrelevant variables can have undesirable effects on the *variances* of the OLS estimators.

3-3b Omitted Variable Bias: The Simple Case

Now suppose that, rather than including an irrelevant variable, we omit a variable that actually belongs in the true (or population) model. This is often called the problem of **excluding a relevant variable** or **underspecifying the model**. We claimed in Chapter 2 and earlier in this chapter that this problem generally causes the OLS estimators to be biased. It is time to show this explicitly and, just as importantly, to derive the direction and size of the bias.

Deriving the bias caused by omitting an important variable is an example of **misspecification analysis**. We begin with the case where the true population model has two explanatory variables and an error term:

$$y = \beta_0 + \beta_1 x_1 + \beta_2 x_2 + u, \qquad [3.40]$$

and we assume that this model satisfies Assumptions MLR.1 through MLR.4.

Suppose that our primary interest is in β_1, the partial effect of x_1 on y. For example, y is hourly wage (or log of hourly wage), x_1 is education, and x_2 is a measure of innate ability. In order to get an unbiased estimator of β_1, we *should* run a regression of y on x_1 and x_2 (which gives unbiased estimators of β_0, β_1, and β_2). However, due to our ignorance or data unavailability, we estimate the model by *excluding* x_2. In other words, we perform a simple regression of y on x_1 only, obtaining the equation

$$\tilde{y} = \tilde{\beta}_0 + \tilde{\beta}_1 x_1. \qquad [3.41]$$

We use the symbol "~" rather than "^" to emphasize that $\tilde{\beta}_1$ comes from an underspecified model.

When first learning about the omitted variable problem, it can be difficult to distinguish between the underlying true model, (3.40) in this case, and the model that we actually estimate, which is captured by the regression in (3.41). It may seem silly to omit the variable x_2 if it belongs in the model, but often we have no choice. For example, suppose that *wage* is determined by

$$wage = \beta_0 + \beta_1 educ + \beta_2 abil + u. \qquad [3.42]$$

Since ability is not observed, we instead estimate the model

$$wage = \beta_0 + \beta_1 educ + v,$$

where $v = \beta_2 abil + u$. The estimator of β_1 from the simple regression of *wage* on *educ* is what we are calling $\tilde{\beta}_1$.

We derive the expected value of $\tilde{\beta}_1$ conditional on the sample values of x_1 and x_2. Deriving this expectation is not difficult because $\tilde{\beta}_1$ is just the OLS slope estimator from a simple regression, and we have already studied this estimator extensively in Chapter 2. The difference here is that we must analyze its properties when the simple regression model is misspecified due to an omitted variable.

As it turns out, we have done almost all of the work to derive the bias in the simple regression estimator of $\tilde{\beta}_1$. From equation (3.23) we have the algebraic relationship $\tilde{\beta}_1 = \hat{\beta}_1 + \hat{\beta}_2\tilde{\delta}_1$, where $\hat{\beta}_1$ and $\hat{\beta}_2$ are the slope estimators (if we could have them) from the multiple regression

$$y_i \text{ on } x_{i1}, x_{i2}, i = 1, \ldots, n \qquad [3.43]$$

and $\tilde{\delta}_1$ is the slope from the simple regression

$$x_{i2} \text{ on } x_{i1}, i = 1, \ldots, n. \qquad [3.44]$$

Because $\tilde{\delta}_1$ depends only on the independent variables in the sample, we treat it as fixed (nonrandom) when computing $E(\tilde{\beta}_1)$. Further, since the model in (3.40) satisfies Assumptions MLR.1 through MLR.4, we know that $\hat{\beta}_1$ and $\hat{\beta}_2$ would be unbiased for β_1 and β_2, respectively. Therefore,

$$E(\tilde{\beta}_1) = E(\hat{\beta}_1 + \hat{\beta}_2\tilde{\delta}_1) = E(\hat{\beta}_1) + E(\hat{\beta}_2)\tilde{\delta}_1$$
$$= \beta_1 + \beta_2\tilde{\delta}_1, \qquad [3.45]$$

which implies the bias in $\tilde{\beta}_1$ is

$$\text{Bias}(\tilde{\beta}_1) = E(\tilde{\beta}_1) - \beta_1 = \beta_2\tilde{\delta}_1. \qquad [3.46]$$

Because the bias in this case arises from omitting the explanatory variable x_2, the term on the right-hand side of equation (3.46) is often called the **omitted variable bias**.

From equation (3.46), we see that there are two cases where $\tilde{\beta}_1$ is unbiased. The first is pretty obvious: if $\beta_2 = 0$—so that x_2 does not appear in the true model (3.40)—then $\tilde{\beta}_1$ is unbiased. We already know this from the simple regression analysis in Chapter 2. The second case is more interesting. If $\tilde{\delta}_1 = 0$, then $\tilde{\beta}_1$ is unbiased for β_1, even if $\beta_2 \neq 0$.

Because $\tilde{\delta}_1$ is the sample covariance between x_1 and x_2 over the sample variance of x_1, $\tilde{\delta}_1 = 0$ if, and only if, x_1 and x_2 are uncorrelated in the sample. Thus, we have the important conclusion that, if x_1 and x_2 are uncorrelated in the sample, then $\tilde{\beta}_1$ is unbiased. This is not surprising: in Section 3-2, we showed that the simple regression estimator $\tilde{\beta}_1$ and the multiple regression estimator $\tilde{\beta}_1$ are the same when x_1 and x_2 are uncorrelated in the sample. [We can also show that $\tilde{\beta}_1$ is unbiased without conditioning on the x_{i2} if $E(x_2|x_1) = E(x_2)$; then, for estimating β_1, leaving x_2 in the error term does not violate the zero conditional mean assumption for the error, once we adjust the intercept.]

When x_1 and x_2 are correlated, $\tilde{\delta}_1$ has the same sign as the correlation between x_1 and x_2: $\tilde{\delta}_1 > 0$ if x_1 and x_2 are positively correlated and $\tilde{\delta}_1 < 0$ if x_1 and x_2 are negatively correlated. The sign of the bias in $\tilde{\beta}_1$ depends on the signs of both β_2 and $\tilde{\delta}_1$ and is summarized in Table 3.2 for the four possible cases when there is bias. Table 3.2 warrants careful study. For example, the bias in $\tilde{\beta}_1$ is positive if $\beta_2 > 0$ (x_2 has a positive effect on y) and x_1 and x_2 are positively correlated, the bias is negative if $\beta_2 > 0$ and x_1 and x_2 are negatively correlated, and so on.

Table 3.2 summarizes the direction of the bias, but the size of the bias is also very important. A small bias of either sign need not be a cause for concern. For example, if the return to education in the population is 8.6% and the bias in the OLS estimator is 0.1% (a tenth of one percentage point), then

TABLE 3.2 Summary of Bias in $\tilde{\beta}_1$ When x_2 Is Omitted in Estimating Equation (3.40)		
	Corr(x_1, x_2) > 0	**Corr(x_1, x_2) < 0**
$\beta_2 > 0$	Positive bias	Negative bias
$\beta_2 < 0$	Negative bias	Positive bias

we would not be very concerned. On the other hand, a bias on the order of three percentage points would be much more serious. The size of the bias is determined by the sizes of β_2 and $\tilde{\delta}_1$.

In practice, since β_2 is an unknown population parameter, we cannot be certain whether β_2 is positive or negative. Nevertheless, we usually have a pretty good idea about the direction of the partial effect of x_2 on y. Further, even though the sign of the correlation between x_1 and x_2 cannot be known if x_2 is not observed, in many cases, we can make an educated guess about whether x_1 and x_2 are positively or negatively correlated.

In the wage equation (3.42), by definition, more ability leads to higher productivity and therefore higher wages: $\beta_2 > 0$. Also, there are reasons to believe that *educ* and *abil* are positively correlated: on average, individuals with more innate ability choose higher levels of education. Thus, the OLS estimates from the simple regression equation $wage = \beta_0 + \beta_1 educ + v$ are *on average* too large. This does not mean that the estimate obtained from our sample is too big. We can only say that if we collect many random samples and obtain the simple regression estimates each time, then the average of these estimates will be greater than β_1.

EXAMPLE 3.6   **Hourly Wage Equation**

Suppose the model $\log(wage) = \beta_0 + \beta_1 educ + \beta_2 abil + u$ satisfies Assumptions MLR.1 through MLR.4. The data set in WAGE1 does not contain data on ability, so we estimate β_1 from the simple regression

$$\widehat{\log(wage)} = .584 + .083\ educ$$

$$n = 526, R^2 = .186. \tag{3.47}$$

This is the result from only a single sample, so we cannot say that .083 is greater than β_1; the true return to education could be lower or higher than 8.3% (and we will never know for sure). Nevertheless, we know that the average of the estimates across all random samples would be too large.

As a second example, suppose that, at the elementary school level, the average score for students on a standardized exam is determined by

$$avgscore = \beta_0 + \beta_1 expend + \beta_2 povrate + u, \tag{3.48}$$

where *expend* is expenditure perstudent and *povrate* is the poverty rate of the children in the school. Using school district data, we only have observations on the percentage of students with a passing grade and per-student expenditures; we do not have information on poverty rates. Thus, we estimate β_1 from the simple regression of *avgscore* on *expend*.

We can again obtain the likely bias in $\tilde{\beta}_1$. First, β_2 is probably negative: there is ample evidence that children living in poverty score lower, on average, on standardized tests. Second, the average expenditure per-student is probably negatively correlated with the poverty rate: The higher the poverty rate, the lower the average per-student spending, so that $\text{Corr}(x_1, x_2) < 0$. From Table 3.2, $\tilde{\beta}_1$ will have a positive bias. This observation has important implications. It could be that the true effect of spending is zero; that is, $\beta_1 = 0$. However, the simple regression estimate of β_1 will usually be greater than zero, and this could lead us to conclude that expenditures are important when they are not.

When reading and performing empirical work in economics, it is important to master the terminology associated with biased estimators. In the context of omitting a variable from model (3.40), if $\text{E}(\tilde{\beta}_1) > \beta_1$, then we say that $\tilde{\beta}_1$ has an **upward bias**. When $\text{E}(\tilde{\beta}_1) < \beta_1$, $\tilde{\beta}_1$ has a **downward bias**. These definitions are the same whether β_1 is positive or negative. The phrase **biased toward zero** refers to cases where $\text{E}(\tilde{\beta}_1)$ is closer to zero than is β_1. Therefore, if β_1 is positive, then $\tilde{\beta}_1$ is biased toward zero if it has a downward bias. On the other hand, if $\beta_1 < 0$, then $\tilde{\beta}_1$ is biased toward zero if it has an upward bias.

3-3c Omitted Variable Bias: More General Cases

Deriving the sign of omitted variable bias when there are multiple regressors in the estimated model is more difficult. We must remember that correlation between a single explanatory variable and the error generally results in *all* OLS estimators being biased. For example, suppose the population model

$$y = \beta_0 + \beta_1 x_1 + \beta_2 x_2 + \beta_3 x_3 + u \qquad [3.49]$$

satisfies Assumptions MLR.1 through MLR.4. But we omit x_3 and estimate the model as

$$\tilde{y} = \tilde{\beta}_0 + \tilde{\beta}_1 x_1 + \tilde{\beta}_2 x_2. \qquad [3.50]$$

Now, suppose that x_2 and x_3 are uncorrelated, but that x_1 is correlated with x_3. In other words, x_1 is correlated with the omitted variable, but x_2 is not. It is tempting to think that, while $\tilde{\beta}_1$ is probably biased based on the derivation in the previous subsection, $\tilde{\beta}_2$ is unbiased because x_2 is uncorrelated with x_3. Unfortunately, this is *not* generally the case: both $\tilde{\beta}_1$ and $\tilde{\beta}_2$ will normally be biased. The only exception to this is when x_1 and x_2 are also uncorrelated.

Even in the fairly simple model above, it can be difficult to obtain the direction of bias in $\tilde{\beta}_1$ and $\tilde{\beta}_2$. This is because x_1, x_2, and x_3 can all be pairwise correlated. Nevertheless, an approximation is often practically useful. If we assume that x_1 and x_2 are uncorrelated, then we can study the bias in $\tilde{\beta}_1$ as if x_2 were absent from both the population and the estimated models. In fact, when x_1 and x_2 are uncorrelated, it can be shown that

$$\mathrm{E}(\tilde{\beta}_1) = \beta_1 + \beta_3 \frac{\sum_{i=1}^{n}(x_{i1} - \bar{x}_1)x_{i3}}{\sum_{i=1}^{n}(x_{i1} - \bar{x}_1)^2}.$$

This is just like equation (3.45), but β_3 replaces β_2, and x_3 replaces x_2 in regression (3.44). Therefore, the bias in $\tilde{\beta}_1$ is obtained by replacing β_2 with β_3 and x_2 with x_3 in Table 3.2. If $\beta_3 > 0$ and Corr $(x_1, x_3) > 0$, the bias in $\tilde{\beta}_1$ is positive, and so on.

As an example, suppose we add *exper* to the wage model:

$$wage = \beta_0 + \beta_1 educ + \beta_2 exper + \beta_3 abil + u.$$

If *abil* is omitted from the model, the estimators of both β_1 and β_2 are biased, even if we assume *exper* is uncorrelated with *abil*. We are mostly interested in the return to education, so it would be nice if we could conclude that $\tilde{\beta}_1$ has an upward or a downward bias due to omitted ability. This conclusion is not possible without further assumptions. As an *approximation*, let us suppose that, in addition to *exper* and *abil* being uncorrelated, *educ* and *exper* are also uncorrelated. (In reality, they are somewhat negatively correlated.) Since $\beta_3 > 0$ and *educ* and *abil* are positively correlated, $\tilde{\beta}_1$ would have an upward bias, just as if *exper* were not in the model.

The reasoning used in the previous example is often followed as a rough guide for obtaining the likely bias in estimators in more complicated models. Usually, the focus is on the relationship between a particular explanatory variable, say, x_1, and the key omitted factor. Strictly speaking, ignoring all other explanatory variables is a valid practice only when each one is uncorrelated with x_1, but it is still a useful guide. Appendix 3A contains a more careful analysis of omitted variable bias with multiple explanatory variables.

3-4 The Variance of the OLS Estimators

We now obtain the variance of the OLS estimators so that, in addition to knowing the central tendencies of the $\hat{\beta}_j$, we also have a measure of the spread in its sampling distribution. Before finding the variances, we add a homoskedasticity assumption, as in Chapter 2. We do this for two reasons.

First, the formulas are simplified by imposing the constant error variance assumption. Second, in Section 3-5, we will see that OLS has an important efficiency property if we add the homoskedasticity assumption.

In the multiple regression framework, homoskedasticity is stated as follows:

Assumption MLR.5 — Homoskedasticity

The error u has the same variance given any value of the explanatory variables. In other words, $Var(u|x_1, ..., x_k) = \sigma^2$.

Assumption MLR.5 means that the variance in the error term, u, conditional on the explanatory variables, is the *same* for all combinations of outcomes of the explanatory variables. If this assumption fails, then the model exhibits heteroskedasticity, just as in the two-variable case.

In the equation

$$wage = \beta_0 + \beta_1 educ + \beta_2 exper + \beta_3 tenure + u,$$

homoskedasticity requires that the variance of the unobserved error u does not depend on the levels of education, experience, or tenure. That is,

$$Var(u|educ, exper, tenure) = \sigma^2.$$

If this variance changes with any of the three explanatory variables, then heteroskedasticity is present.

Assumptions MLR.1 through MLR.5 are collectively known as the **Gauss-Markov assumptions** (for cross-sectional regression). So far, our statements of the assumptions are suitable only when applied to cross-sectional analysis with random sampling. As we will see, the Gauss-Markov assumptions for time series analysis, and for other situations such as panel data analysis, are more difficult to state, although there are many similarities.

In the discussion that follows, we will use the symbol $\mathbf{x}$ to denote the set of all independent variables, $(x_1, ..., x_k)$. Thus, in the wage regression with *educ*, *exper*, and *tenure* as independent variables, $\mathbf{x} = (educ, exper, tenure)$. Then we can write Assumptions MLR.1 and MLR.4 as

$$E(y|\mathbf{x}) = \beta_0 + \beta_1 x_1 + \beta_2 x_2 + ... + \beta_k x_k,$$

and Assumption MLR.5 is the same as $Var(y|\mathbf{x}) = \sigma^2$. Stating the assumptions in this way clearly illustrates how Assumption MLR.5 differs greatly from Assumption MLR.4. Assumption MLR.4 says that the expected value of y, given $\mathbf{x}$, is linear in the parameters, but it certainly depends on $x_1, x_2, \ldots, x_k$. Assumption MLR.5 says that the variance of y, given $\mathbf{x}$, does *not* depend on the values of the independent variables.

We can now obtain the variances of the $\hat{\beta}_j$, where we again condition on the sample values of the independent variables. The proof is in the appendix to this chapter.

THEOREM 3.2 — SAMPLING VARIANCES OF THE OLS SLOPE ESTIMATORS

Under Assumptions MLR.1 through MLR.5, conditional on the sample values of the independent variables,

$$Var(\hat{\beta}_j) = \frac{\sigma^2}{SST_j(1 - R_j^2)}, \qquad [3.51]$$

for $j = 1, 2, ..., k$, where $SST_j = \sum_{i=1}^{n}(x_{ij} - \bar{x}_j)^2$ is the total sample variation in x_j, and R_j^2 is the R-squared from regressing x_j on all other independent variables (and including an intercept).

The careful reader may be wondering whether there is a simple formula for the variance of $\hat{\beta}_j$ where we do not condition on the sample outcomes of the explanatory variables. The answer is: none that is useful. The formula in (3.51) is a highly nonlinear function of the x_{ij}, making averaging out across the population distribution of the explanatory variables virtually impossible. Fortunately, for any practical purpose equation (3.51) is what we want. Even when we turn to approximate, large-sample properties of OLS in Chapter 5 it turns out that (3.51) estimates the quantity we need for large-sample analysis, provided Assumptions MLR.1 through MLR.5 hold.

Before we study equation (3.51) in more detail, it is important to know that all of the Gauss-Markov assumptions are used in obtaining this formula. Whereas we did not need the homoskedasticity assumption to conclude that OLS is unbiased, we do need it to justify equation (3.51).

The size of $\text{Var}(\hat{\beta}_j)$ is practically important. A larger variance means a less precise estimator, and this translates into larger confidence intervals and less accurate hypotheses tests (as we will see in Chapter 4). In the next subsection, we discuss the elements comprising (3.51).

3-4a The Components of the OLS Variances. Multicollinearity

Equation (3.51) shows that the variance of $\hat{\beta}_j$ depends on three factors: σ^2, SST_j, and R_j^2. Remember that the index j simply denotes any one of the independent variables (such as education or poverty rate). We now consider each of the factors affecting $\text{Var}(\hat{\beta}_j)$ in turn.

The Error Variance, σ^2. From equation (3.51), a larger σ^2 means larger sampling variances for the OLS estimators. This is not at all surprising: more "noise" in the equation (a larger σ^2) makes it more difficult to estimate the partial effect of any of the independent variables on y, and this is reflected in higher variances for the OLS slope estimators. Because σ^2 is a feature of the population, it has nothing to do with the sample size. It is the one component of (3.51) that is unknown. We will see later how to obtain an unbiased estimator of σ^2.

For a given dependent variable y, there is really only one way to reduce the error variance, and that is to add more explanatory variables to the equation (take some factors out of the error term). Unfortunately, it is not always possible to find additional legitimate factors that affect y.

The Total Sample Variation in x_j, SST_j. From equation (3.51), we see that the larger the total variation in x_j is, the smaller is $\text{Var}(\hat{\beta}_j)$. Thus, everything else being equal, for estimating β_j we prefer to have as much sample variation in x_j as possible. We already discovered this in the simple regression case in Chapter 2. Although it is rarely possible for us to choose the sample values of the independent variables, there *is* a way to increase the sample variation in each of the independent variables: increase the sample size. In fact, when one randomly samples from a population, SST_j increases without bound as the sample size increases—roughly as a linear function of n. This is the component of the variance that systematically depends on the sample size.

When SST_j is small, $\text{Var}(\hat{\beta}_j)$ can get very large, but a small SST_j is not a violation of Assumption MLR.3. Technically, as SST_j goes to zero, $\text{Var}(\hat{\beta}_j)$ approaches infinity. The extreme case of no sample variation in x_j, $\text{SST}_j = 0$, is not allowed by Assumption MLR.3.

The Linear Relationships among the Independent Variables, R_j^2. The term R_j^2 in equation (3.51) is the most difficult of the three components to understand. This term does not appear in simple regression analysis because there is only one independent variable in such cases. It is important to see that this R-squared is distinct from the R-squared in the regression of y on $x_1, x_2, \ldots, x_k$: R_j^2 is obtained from a regression involving only the independent variables in the original model, where x_j plays the role of a dependent variable.

Consider first the $k = 2$ case: $y = \beta_0 + \beta_1 x_1 + \beta_2 x_2 + u$. Then, $\text{Var}(\hat{\beta}_1) = \sigma^2/[\text{SST}_1(1 - R_1^2)]$, where R_1^2 is the R-squared from the simple regression of x_1 on x_2 (and an intercept, as always). Because

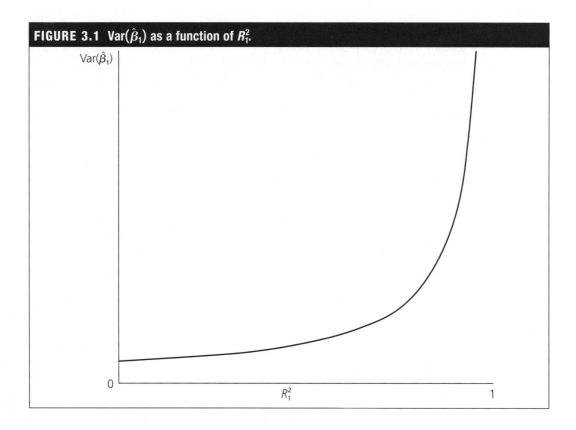

FIGURE 3.1 $\mathrm{Var}(\hat{\beta}_1)$ as a function of R_1^2.

the R-squared measures goodness-of-fit, a value of R_1^2 close to one indicates that x_2 explains much of the variation in x_1 in the sample. This means that x_1 and x_2 are highly correlated.

As R_1^2 increases to one, $\mathrm{Var}(\hat{\beta}_1)$ gets larger and larger. Thus, a high degree of linear relationship between x_1 and x_2 can lead to large variances for the OLS slope estimators. (A similar argument applies to $\hat{\beta}_2$.) See Figure 3.1 for the relationship between $\mathrm{Var}(\hat{\beta}_1)$ and the R-squared from the regression of x_1 on x_2.

In the general case, R_j^2 is the proportion of the total variation in x_j that can be explained by the *other* independent variables appearing in the equation. For a given σ^2 and SST_j, the smallest $\mathrm{Var}(\hat{\beta}_j)$ is obtained when $R_j^2 = 0$, which happens if, and only if, x_j has zero sample correlation with *every other* independent variable. This is the best case for estimating β_j, but it is rarely encountered.

The other extreme case, $R_j^2 = 1$, is ruled out by Assumption MLR.3, because $R_j^2 = 1$ means that, in the sample, x_j is a *perfect* linear combination of some of the other independent variables in the regression. A more relevant case is when R_j^2 is "close" to one. From equation (3.51) and Figure 3.1, we see that this can cause $\mathrm{Var}(\hat{\beta}_j)$ to be large: $\mathrm{Var}(\hat{\beta}_j) \to \infty$ as $R_j^2 \to 1$. High (but not perfect) correlation between two or more independent variables is called **multicollinearity**.

Before we discuss the multicollinearity issue further, it is important to be very clear on one thing: A case where R_j^2 is close to one is *not* a violation of Assumption MLR.3.

Since multicollinearity violates none of our assumptions, the "problem" of multicollinearity is not really well defined. When we say that multicollinearity arises for estimating β_j when R_j^2 is "close" to one, we put "close" in quotation marks because there is no absolute number that we can cite to conclude that multicollinearity is a problem. For example, $R_j^2 = .9$ means that 90% of the sample variation in x_j can be explained by the other independent variables in the regression model. Unquestionably, this means that x_j has a strong linear relationship to the other independent variables. But whether this translates into a $\mathrm{Var}(\hat{\beta}_j)$ that is too large to be useful depends on the sizes of σ^2 and SST_j. As we will see in Chapter 4, for statistical inference, what ultimately matters is how big $\hat{\beta}_j$ is in relation to its standard deviation.

Just as a large value of R_j^2 can cause a large $\text{Var}(\hat{\beta}_j)$, so can a small value of SST_j. Therefore, a small sample size can lead to large sampling variances, too. Worrying about high degrees of correlation among the independent variables in the sample is really no different from worrying about a small sample size: both work to increase $\text{Var}(\hat{\beta}_j)$. The famous University of Wisconsin econometrician Arthur Goldberger, reacting to econometricians' obsession with multicollinearity, has (tongue in cheek) coined the term **micronumerosity**, which he defines as the "problem of small sample size." [For an engaging discussion of multicollinearity and micronumerosity, see Goldberger (1991).]

Although the problem of multicollinearity cannot be clearly defined, one thing is clear: everything else being equal, for estimating β_j, it is better to have less correlation between x_j and the other independent variables. This observation often leads to a discussion of how to "solve" the multicollinearity problem. In the social sciences, where we are usually passive collectors of data, there is no good way to reduce variances of unbiased estimators other than to collect more data. For a given data set, we can try dropping other independent variables from the model in an effort to reduce multicollinearity. Unfortunately, dropping a variable that belongs in the population model can lead to bias, as we saw in Section 3-3.

Perhaps an example at this point will help clarify some of the issues raised concerning multicollinearity. Suppose we are interested in estimating the effect of various school expenditure categories on student performance. It is likely that expenditures on teacher salaries, instructional materials, athletics, and so on are highly correlated: wealthier schools tend to spend more on everything, and poorer schools spend less on everything. Not surprisingly, it can be difficult to estimate the effect of any particular expenditure category on student performance when there is little variation in one category that cannot largely be explained by variations in the other expenditure categories (this leads to high R_j^2 for each of the expenditure variables). Such multicollinearity problems can be mitigated by collecting more data, but in a sense we have imposed the problem on ourselves: we are asking questions that may be too subtle for the available data to answer with any precision. We can probably do much better by changing the scope of the analysis and lumping all expenditure categories together, since we would no longer be trying to estimate the partial effect of each separate category.

Another important point is that a high degree of correlation between certain independent variables can be irrelevant as to how well we can estimate other parameters in the model. For example, consider a model with three independent variables:

$$y = \beta_0 + \beta_1 x_1 + \beta_2 x_2 + \beta_3 x_3 + u,$$

where x_2 and x_3 are highly correlated. Then $\text{Var}(\hat{\beta}_2)$ and $\text{Var}(\hat{\beta}_3)$ may be large. But the amount of correlation between x_2 and x_3 has no direct effect on $\text{Var}(\hat{\beta}_1)$. In fact, if x_1 is uncorrelated with x_2 and x_3, then $R_1^2 = 0$ and $\text{Var}(\hat{\beta}_1) = \sigma^2/\text{SST}_1$, regardless of how much correlation there is between x_2 and x_3. If β_1 is the parameter of interest, we do not really care about the amount of correlation between x_2 and x_3.

The previous observation is important because economists often include many control variables in order to isolate the causal effect of a particular variable. For example, in looking at the relationship between loan approval rates and percentage of minorities in a neighborhood, we might include variables like average income, average housing value, measures of creditworthiness, and so on, because these factors need to be accounted for in order to draw causal conclusions about discrimination. Income, housing prices, and creditworthiness are generally highly correlated with each other.

> ### EXPLORING FURTHER 3.4
>
> Suppose you postulate a model explaining final exam score in terms of class attendance. Thus, the dependent variable is final exam score, and the key explanatory variable is number of classes attended. To control for student abilities and efforts outside the classroom, you include among the explanatory variables cumulative GPA, SAT score, and measures of high school performance. Someone says, "You cannot hope to learn anything from this exercise because cumulative GPA, SAT score, and high school performance are likely to be highly collinear." What should be your response?

But high correlations among these controls do not make it more difficult to determine the effects of discrimination.

Some researchers find it useful to compute statistics intended to determine the severity of multicollinearity in a given application. Unfortunately, it is easy to misuse such statistics because, as we have discussed, we cannot specify how much correlation among explanatory variables is "too much." Some multicollinearity "diagnostics" are omnibus statistics in the sense that they detect a strong linear relationship among any subset of explanatory variables. For reasons that we just saw, such statistics are of questionable value because they might reveal a "problem" simply because two control variables, whose coefficients we do not care about, are highly correlated. [Probably the most common omnibus multicollinearity statistic is the so-called *condition number*, which is defined in terms of the full data matrix and is beyond the scope of this text. See, for example, Belsley, Kuh, and Welsh (1980).]

Somewhat more useful, but still prone to misuse, are statistics for individual coefficients. The most common of these is the **variance inflation factor (VIF)**, which is obtained directly from equation (3.51). The VIF for slope coefficient j is simply $\text{VIF}_j = 1/(1 - R_j^2)$, precisely the term in $\text{Var}(\hat{\beta}_j)$ that is determined by correlation between x_j and the other explanatory variables. We can write $\text{Var}(\hat{\beta}_j)$ in equation (3.51) as

$$\text{Var}(\hat{\beta}_j) = \frac{\sigma^2}{\text{SST}_j} \cdot \text{VIF}_j,$$

which shows that VIF_j is the factor by which $\text{Var}(\hat{\beta}_j)$ is higher because x_j is not uncorrelated with the other explanatory variables. Because VIF_j is a function of R_j^2—indeed, Figure 3.1 is essentially a graph of VIF_1—our previous discussion can be cast entirely in terms of the VIF. For example, if we had the choice, we would like VIF_j to be smaller (other things equal). But we rarely have the choice. If we think certain explanatory variables need to be included in a regression to infer causality of x_j, then we are hesitant to drop them, and whether we think VIF_j is "too high" cannot really affect that decision. If, say, our main interest is in the causal effect of x_1 on y, then we should ignore entirely the VIFs of other coefficients. Finally, setting a cutoff value for VIF above which we conclude multicollinearity is a "problem" is arbitrary and not especially helpful. Sometimes the value 10 is chosen: if VIF_j is above 10 (equivalently, R_j^2 is above .9), then we conclude that multicollinearity is a "problem" for estimating β_j. But a VIF_j above 10 does not mean that the standard deviation of $\hat{\beta}_j$ is too large to be useful because the standard deviation also depends on σ and SST_j, and the latter can be increased by increasing the sample size. Therefore, just as with looking at the size of R_j^2 directly, looking at the size of VIF_j is of limited use, although one might want to do so out of curiosity.

3-4b Variances in Misspecified Models

The choice of whether to include a particular variable in a regression model can be made by analyzing the tradeoff between bias and variance. In Section 3-3, we derived the bias induced by leaving out a relevant variable when the true model contains two explanatory variables. We continue the analysis of this model by comparing the variances of the OLS estimators.

Write the true population model, which satisfies the Gauss-Markov assumptions, as

$$y = \beta_0 + \beta_1 x_1 + \beta_2 x_2 + u.$$

We consider two estimators of β_1. The estimator $\hat{\beta}_1$ comes from the multiple regression

$$\hat{y} = \hat{\beta}_0 + \hat{\beta}_1 x_1 + \hat{\beta}_2 x_2. \tag{3.52}$$

In other words, we include x_2, along with x_1, in the regression model. The estimator $\tilde{\beta}_1$ is obtained by omitting x_2 from the model and running a simple regression of y on x_1:

$$\tilde{y} = \tilde{\beta}_0 + \tilde{\beta}_1 x_1. \tag{3.53}$$

When $\beta_2 \neq 0$, equation (3.53) excludes a relevant variable from the model and, as we saw in Section 3-3, this induces a bias in $\tilde{\beta}_1$ unless x_1 and x_2 are uncorrelated. On the other hand, $\hat{\beta}_1$ is unbiased for β_1 for any value of β_2, including $\beta_2 = 0$. It follows that, if bias is used as the only criterion, $\hat{\beta}_1$ is preferred to $\tilde{\beta}_1$.

The conclusion that $\hat{\beta}_1$ is always preferred to $\tilde{\beta}_1$ does not carry over when we bring variance into the picture. Conditioning on the values of x_1 and x_2 in the sample, we have, from (3.51),

$$\text{Var}(\hat{\beta}_1) = \sigma^2/[\text{SST}_1(1 - R_1^2)], \qquad [3.54]$$

where SST_1 is the total variation in x_1, and R_1^2 is the R-squared from the regression of x_1 on x_2. Further, a simple modification of the proof in Chapter 2 for two-variable regression shows that

$$\text{Var}(\tilde{\beta}_1) = \sigma^2/\text{SST}_1. \qquad [3.55]$$

Comparing (3.55) to (3.54) shows that $\text{Var}(\tilde{\beta}_1)$ is always *smaller* than $\text{Var}(\hat{\beta}_1)$, unless x_1 and x_2 are uncorrelated in the sample, in which case the two estimators $\tilde{\beta}_1$ and $\hat{\beta}_1$ are the same. Assuming that x_1 and x_2 are not uncorrelated, we can draw the following conclusions:

1. When $\beta_2 \neq 0$, $\tilde{\beta}_1$ is biased, $\hat{\beta}_1$ is unbiased, and $\text{Var}(\tilde{\beta}_1) < \text{Var}(\hat{\beta}_1)$.
2. When $\beta_2 = 0$, $\tilde{\beta}_1$ and $\hat{\beta}_1$ are both unbiased, and $\text{Var}(\tilde{\beta}_1) < \text{Var}(\hat{\beta}_1)$.

From the second conclusion, it is clear that $\tilde{\beta}_1$ is preferred if $\beta_2 = 0$. Intuitively, if x_2 does not have a partial effect on y, then including it in the model can only exacerbate the multicollinearity problem, which leads to a less efficient estimator of β_1. A higher variance for the estimator of β_1 is the cost of including an irrelevant variable in a model.

The case where $\beta_2 \neq 0$ is more difficult. Leaving x_2 out of the model results in a biased estimator of β_1. Traditionally, econometricians have suggested comparing the likely size of the bias due to omitting x_2 with the reduction in the variance—summarized in the size of R_1^2—to decide whether x_2 should be included. However, when $\beta_2 \neq 0$, there are two favorable reasons for including x_2 in the model. The most important of these is that any bias in $\tilde{\beta}_1$ does not shrink as the sample size grows; in fact, the bias does not necessarily follow any pattern. Therefore, we can usefully think of the bias as being roughly the same for any sample size. On the other hand, $\text{Var}(\tilde{\beta}_1)$ and $\text{Var}(\hat{\beta}_1)$ both shrink to zero as n gets large, which means that the multicollinearity induced by adding x_2 becomes less important as the sample size grows. In large samples, we would prefer $\hat{\beta}_1$.

The other reason for favoring $\hat{\beta}_1$ is more subtle. The variance formula in (3.55) is conditional on the values of x_{i1} and x_{i2} in the sample, which provides the best scenario for $\tilde{\beta}_1$. When $\beta_2 \neq 0$, the variance of $\tilde{\beta}_1$ conditional only on x_1 is larger than that presented in (3.55). Intuitively, when $\beta_2 \neq 0$ and x_2 is excluded from the model, the error variance increases because the error effectively contains part of x_2. But the expression in equation (3.55) ignores the increase in the error variance because it will treat both regressors as nonrandom. For practical purposes, the σ^2 term in equation (3.55) increases when x_2 is dropped from the equation. A full discussion of the proper conditioning argument when computing the OLS variances would lead us too far astray. Suffice it to say that equation (3.55) is too generous when it comes to measuring the precision of $\tilde{\beta}_1$. Fortunately, statistical packages report the proper variance estimator, and so we need not worry about the subtleties in the theoretical formulas. After reading the next subsection, you might want to study Problems 14 and 15 for further insight.

3-4c Estimating σ^2: Standard Errors of the OLS Estimators

We now show how to choose an unbiased estimator of σ^2, which then allows us to obtain unbiased estimators of $\text{Var}(\hat{\beta}_j)$.

Because $\sigma^2 = \text{E}(u^2)$, an unbiased "estimator" of σ^2 is the sample average of the squared errors: $n^{-1}\sum_{i=1}^{n} u_i^2$. Unfortunately, this is not a true estimator because we do not observe the u_i. Nevertheless, recall that the errors can be written as $u_i = y_i - \beta_0 - \beta_1 x_{i1} - \beta_2 x_{i2} - \ldots - \beta_k x_{ik}$, and so the reason we do not observe the u_i is that we do not know the β_j. When we replace each β_j with its OLS estimator, we get the OLS residuals:

$$\hat{u}_i = y_i - \hat{\beta}_0 - \hat{\beta}_1 x_{i1} - \hat{\beta}_2 x_{i2} - \ldots - \hat{\beta}_k x_{ik}.$$

It seems natural to estimate σ^2 by replacing u_i with the $\hat{u}_i$. In the simple regression case, we saw that this leads to a biased estimator. The unbiased estimator of σ^2 in the general multiple regression case is

$$\hat{\sigma}^2 = \left(\sum_{i=1}^{n} \hat{u}_i^2 \right) \bigg/ (n - k - 1) = \text{SSR}/(n - k - 1). \qquad [3.56]$$

We already encountered this estimator in the $k = 1$ case in simple regression.

The term $n - k - 1$ in (3.56) is the **degrees of freedom (df)** for the general OLS problem with n observations and k independent variables. Since there are $k + 1$ parameters in a regression model with k independent variables and an intercept, we can write

$$df = n - (k + 1)$$
$$= (\text{number of observations}) - (\text{number of estimated parameters}). \qquad [3.57]$$

This is the easiest way to compute the degrees of freedom in a particular application: count the number of parameters, including the intercept, and subtract this amount from the number of observations. (In the rare case that an intercept is not estimated, the number of parameters decreases by one.)

Technically, the division by $n - k - 1$ in (3.56) comes from the fact that the expected value of the sum of squared residuals is $\text{E(SSR)} = (n - k - 1)\sigma^2$. Intuitively, we can figure out why the degrees of freedom adjustment is necessary by returning to the first order conditions for the OLS estimators. These can be written $\sum_{i=1}^{n} \hat{u}_i = 0$ and $\sum_{i=1}^{n} x_{ij}\hat{u}_i = 0$, where $j = 1, 2, \ldots, k$. Thus, in obtaining the OLS estimates, $k + 1$ restrictions are imposed on the OLS residuals. This means that, given $n - (k + 1)$ of the residuals, the remaining $k + 1$ residuals are known: there are only $n - (k + 1)$ degrees of freedom in the residuals. (This can be contrasted with the *errors* u_i, which have n degrees of freedom in the sample.)

For reference, we summarize this discussion with Theorem 3.3. We proved this theorem for the case of simple regression analysis in Chapter 2 (see Theorem 2.3). (A general proof that requires matrix algebra is provided in Appendix E.)

THEOREM 3.3

UNBIASED ESTIMATION OF σ^2

Under the Gauss-Markov assumptions MLR.1 through MLR.5, $\text{E}(\hat{\sigma}^2) = \sigma^2$.

The positive square root of $\hat{\sigma}^2$, denoted $\hat{\sigma}$, is called the **standard error of the regression (SER)**. The SER is an estimator of the standard deviation of the error term. This estimate is usually reported by regression packages, although it is called different things by different packages. (In addition to SER, $\hat{\sigma}$ is also called the *standard error of the estimate* and the *root mean squared error*.)

Note that $\hat{\sigma}$ can either decrease or increase when another independent variable is added to a regression (for a given sample). This is because, although SSR must fall when another explanatory variable is added, the degrees of freedom also falls by one. Because SSR is in the numerator and *df* is in the denominator, we cannot tell beforehand which effect will dominate.

For constructing confidence intervals and conducting tests in Chapter 4, we will need to estimate the **standard deviation of $\hat{\beta}_j$**, which is just the square root of the variance:

$$\text{sd}(\hat{\beta}_j) = \sigma / [\text{SST}_j(1 - R_j^2)]^{1/2}.$$

Since σ is unknown, we replace it with its estimator, $\hat{\sigma}$. This gives us the **standard error of $\hat{\beta}_j$**:

$$\text{se}(\hat{\beta}_j) = \hat{\sigma} / [\text{SST}_j(1 - R_j^2)]^{1/2}. \qquad [3.58]$$

Just as the OLS estimates can be obtained for any given sample, so can the standard errors. Since $\text{se}(\hat{\beta}_j)$ depends on $\hat{\sigma}$, the standard error has a sampling distribution, which will play a role in Chapter 4.

We should emphasize one thing about standard errors. Because (3.58) is obtained directly from the variance formula in (3.51), and because (3.51) relies on the homoskedasticity Assumption MLR.5, it follows that the standard error formula in (3.58) is *not* a valid estimator of $\text{sd}(\hat{\beta}_j)$ if the errors exhibit heteroskedasticity. Thus, while the presence of heteroskedasticity does not cause bias in the $\hat{\beta}_j$, it does lead to bias in the usual formula for $\text{Var}(\hat{\beta}_j)$, which then invalidates the standard errors. This is important because any regression package computes (3.58) as the default standard error for each coefficient (with a somewhat different representation for the intercept). If we suspect heteroskedasticity, then the "usual" OLS standard errors are invalid, and some corrective action should be taken. We will see in Chapter 8 what methods are available for dealing with heteroskedasticity.

For some purposes it is helpful to write

$$\text{se}(\hat{\beta}_j) = \frac{\hat{\sigma}}{\sqrt{n}\,\text{sd}(x_j)\sqrt{1 - R_j^2}},$$

[3.59]

in which we take $\text{sd}(x_j) = \sqrt{n^{-1}\sum_{i=1}^{n}(x_{ij} - \bar{x}_j)^2}$ to be the sample standard deviation where the total sum of squares is divided by n rather than $n - 1$. The importance of equation (3.59) is that it shows how the sample size, n, directly affects the standard errors. The other three terms in the formula—$\hat{\sigma}$, $\text{sd}(x_j)$, and R_j^2—will change with different samples, but as n gets large they settle down to constants. Therefore, we can see from equation (3.59) that the standard errors shrink to zero at the rate $1/\sqrt{n}$. This formula demonstrates the value of getting more data: the precision of the $\hat{\beta}_j$ increases as n increases. (By contrast, recall that unbiasedness holds for any sample size subject to being able to compute the estimators.) We will talk more about large sample properties of OLS in Chapter 5.

3-5 Efficiency of OLS: The Gauss-Markov Theorem

In this section, we state and discuss the important **Gauss-Markov Theorem**, which justifies the use of the OLS method rather than using a variety of competing estimators. We know one justification for OLS already: under Assumptions MLR.1 through MLR.4, OLS is unbiased. However, there are *many* unbiased estimators of the β_j under these assumptions (for example, see Problem 13). Might there be other unbiased estimators with variances smaller than the OLS estimators?

If we limit the class of competing estimators appropriately, then we can show that OLS *is* best within this class. Specifically, we will argue that, under Assumptions MLR.1 through MLR.5, the OLS estimator $\hat{\beta}_j$ for β_j is the **best linear unbiased estimator (BLUE)**. To state the theorem, we need to understand each component of the acronym "BLUE." First, we know what an estimator is: it is a rule that can be applied to any sample of data to produce an estimate. We also know what an unbiased estimator is: in the current context, an estimator, say, $\tilde{\beta}_1$, of β_j is an unbiased estimator of β_j if $\text{E}(\tilde{\beta}_j) = \beta_j$ for any $\beta_0, \beta_1, \ldots, \beta_k$.

What about the meaning of the term "linear"? In the current context, an estimator $\tilde{\beta}_j$ of β_j is linear if, and only if, it can be expressed as a linear function of the data on the dependent variable:

$$\tilde{\beta}_j = \sum_{i=1}^{n} w_{ij}y_i,$$

[3.60]

where each w_{ij} can be a function of the sample values of all the independent variables. The OLS estimators are linear, as can be seen from equation (3.22).

Finally, how do we define "best"? For the current theorem, best is defined as *having the smallest variance*. Given two unbiased estimators, it is logical to prefer the one with the smallest variance (see Appendix C).

Now, let $\hat{\beta}_0, \hat{\beta}_1, \ldots, \hat{\beta}_k$, denote the OLS estimators in model (3.31) under Assumptions MLR.1 through MLR.5. The Gauss-Markov Theorem says that, for any estimator $\tilde{\beta}_j$ that is *linear* and *unbiased*, $\mathrm{Var}(\hat{\beta}_j) \leq \mathrm{Var}(\tilde{\beta}_j)$, and the inequality is usually strict. In other words, in the class of linear unbiased estimators, OLS has the smallest variance (under the five Gauss-Markov assumptions). Actually, the theorem says more than this. If we want to estimate any linear function of the β_j, then the corresponding linear combination of the OLS estimators achieves the smallest variance among all linear unbiased estimators. We conclude with a theorem, which is proven in Appendix 3A.

THEOREM 3.4	**GAUSS-MARKOV THEOREM** Under Assumptions MLR.1 through MLR.5, $\hat{\beta}_0, \hat{\beta}_1, \ldots, \hat{\beta}_k$ are the best linear unbiased estimators (BLUEs) of $\beta_0, \beta_1, \ldots, \beta_k$, respectively.

It is because of this theorem that Assumptions MLR.1 through MLR.5 are known as the Gauss-Markov assumptions (for cross-sectional analysis).

The importance of the Gauss-Markov Theorem is that, when the standard set of assumptions holds, we need not look for alternative unbiased estimators of the form in (3.60): none will be better than OLS. Equivalently, if we are presented with an estimator that is both linear and unbiased, then we know that the variance of this estimator is at least as large as the OLS variance; no additional calculation is needed to show this.

For our purposes, Theorem 3.4 justifies the use of OLS to estimate multiple regression models. If any of the Gauss-Markov assumptions fail, then this theorem no longer holds. We already know that failure of the zero conditional mean assumption (Assumption MLR.4) causes OLS to be biased, so Theorem 3.4 also fails. We also know that heteroskedasticity (failure of Assumption MLR.5) does not cause OLS to be biased. However, OLS no longer has the smallest variance among linear unbiased estimators in the presence of heteroskedasticity. In Chapter 8, we analyze an estimator that improves upon OLS when we know the brand of heteroskedasticity.

3-6 Some Comments on the Language of Multiple Regression Analysis

It is common for beginners, and not unheard of for experienced empirical researchers, to report that they "estimated an OLS model." While we can usually figure out what someone means by this statement, it is important to understand that it is wrong—on more than just an aesthetic level—and reflects a misunderstanding about the components of a multiple regression analysis.

The first thing to remember is that ordinary least squares (OLS) is an estimation method, not a model. A model describes an underlying population and depends on unknown parameters. The *linear model* that we have been studying in this chapter can be written—in the population—as

$$y = \beta_0 + \beta_1 x_1 + \ldots + \beta_k x_k + u, \tag{3.61}$$

where the parameters are the β_j. Importantly, we can talk about the meaning of the β_j without ever looking at data. It is true we cannot hope to learn much about the β_j without data, but the interpretation of the β_j is obtained from the linear model in equation (3.61).

Once we have a sample of data we can estimate the parameters. While it is true that we have so far only discussed OLS as a possibility, there are actually many more ways to use the data than we can even list. We have focused on OLS due to its widespread use, which is justified by using the statistical considerations we covered previously in this chapter. But the various justifications for OLS rely on the assumptions we have made (MLR.1 through MLR.5). As we will see in later chapters, under different assumptions different estimation methods are preferred—even though our model can still be represented by equation (3.61). Just a few examples include weighted least squares in Chapter 8, least absolute deviations in Chapter 9, and instrumental variables in Chapter 15.

One might argue that the discussion here is overlay pedantic, and that the phrase "estimating an OLS model" should be taken as a useful shorthand for "I estimated a linear model by OLS." This stance has some merit, but we must remember that we have studied the properties of the OLS estimators under different assumptions. For example, we know OLS is unbiased under the first four Gauss-Markov assumptions, but it has no special efficiency properties without Assumption MLR.5. We have also seen, through the study of the omitted variables problem, that OLS is biased if we do not have Assumption MLR.4. The problem with using imprecise language is that it leads to vagueness on the most important considerations: what assumptions are being made on the underlying linear model? The issue of the assumptions we are using is conceptually different from the estimator we wind up applying.

Ideally, one writes down an equation like (3.61), with variable names that are easy to decipher, such as

$$math4 = \beta_0 + \beta_1 classize4 + \beta_2 math3 + \beta_3 \log(income) \\ + \beta_4 motheduc + \beta_5 fatheduc + u \tag{3.62}$$

if we are trying to explain outcomes on a fourth-grade math test. Then, in the context of equation (3.62), one includes a discussion of whether it is reasonable to maintain Assumption MLR.4, focusing on the factors that might still be in u and whether more complicated functional relationships are needed (a topic we study in detail in Chapter 6). Next, one describes the data source (which ideally is obtained via random sampling) as well as the OLS estimates obtained from the sample. A proper way to introduce a discussion of the estimates is to say "I estimated equation (3.62) by ordinary least squares. Under the assumption that no important variables have been omitted from the equation, and assuming random sampling, the OLS estimator of the class size effect, β_1, is unbiased. If the error term u has constant variance, the OLS estimator is actually best linear unbiased." As we will see in Chapters 4 and 5, we can often say even more about OLS. Of course, one might want to admit that while controlling for third-grade math score, family income, and parents' education might account for important differences across students, it might not be enough—for example, u can include motivation of the student or parents—in which case OLS might be biased.

A more subtle reason for being careful in distinguishing between an underlying population model and an estimation method used to estimate a model is that estimation methods such as OLS can be used essentially as an exercise in curve fitting or prediction, without explicitly worrying about an underlying model and the usual statistical properties of unbiasedness and efficiency. For example, we might just want to use OLS to estimate a line that allows us to predict future college GPA for a set of high school students with given characteristics.

Summary

1. The multiple regression model allows us to effectively hold other factors fixed while examining the effects of a particular independent variable on the dependent variable. It explicitly allows the independent variables to be correlated.

2. Although the model is linear in its *parameters*, it can be used to model nonlinear relationships by appropriately choosing the dependent and independent variables.

3. The method of ordinary least squares is easily applied to estimate the multiple regression model. Each slope estimate measures the partial effect of the corresponding independent variable on the dependent variable, holding all other independent variables fixed.

4. R^2 is the proportion of the sample variation in the dependent variable explained by the independent variables, and it serves as a goodness-of-fit measure. It is important not to put too much weight on the value of R^2 when evaluating econometric models.

5. Under the first four Gauss-Markov assumptions (MLR.1 through MLR.4), the OLS estimators are unbiased. This implies that including an irrelevant variable in a model has no effect on the unbiasedness of the intercept and other slope estimators. On the other hand, omitting a relevant variable causes OLS to be biased. In many circumstances, the direction of the bias can be determined.

6. Under the five Gauss-Markov assumptions, the variance of an OLS slope estimator is given by $\text{Var}(\hat{\beta}_j) = \sigma^2/[\text{SST}_j(1 - R_j^2)]$. As the error variance σ^2 increases, so does $\text{Var}(\hat{\beta}_j)$, while $\text{Var}(\hat{\beta}_j)$ decreases as the sample variation in x_j, SST_j, increases. The term R_j^2 measures the amount of collinearity between x_j and the other explanatory variables. As R_j^2 approaches one, $\text{Var}(\hat{\beta}_j)$ is unbounded.

7. Adding an irrelevant variable to an equation generally increases the variances of the remaining OLS estimators because of multicollinearity.

8. Under the Gauss-Markov assumptions (MLR.1 through MLR.5), the OLS estimators are the best linear unbiased estimators (BLUEs).

9. Beginning in Chapter 4, we will use the standard errors of the OLS coefficients to compute confidence intervals for the population parameters and to obtain test statistics for testing hypotheses about the population parameters. Therefore, in reporting regression results we now include the standard errors along with the associated OLS estimates. In equation form, standard errors are usually put in parentheses below the OLS estimates, and the same convention is often used in tables of OLS output.

THE GAUSS-MARKOV ASSUMPTIONS

The following is a summary of the five Gauss-Markov assumptions that we used in this chapter. Remember, the first four were used to establish unbiasedness of OLS, whereas the fifth was added to derive the usual variance formulas and to conclude that OLS is best linear unbiased.

Assumption MLR.1 (Linear in Parameters)
The model in the population can be written as

$$y = \beta_0 + \beta_1 x_1 + \beta_2 x_2 + \dots + \beta_k x_k + u,$$

where $\beta_0, \beta_1, \dots, \beta_k$ are the unknown parameters (constants) of interest and u is an unobserved random error or disturbance term.

Assumption MLR.2 (Random Sampling)
We have a random sample of n observations, $\{(x_{i1}, x_{i2}, \dots, x_{ik}, y_i): i = 1, 2, \dots, n\}$, following the population model in Assumption MLR.1.

Assumption MLR.3 (No Perfect Collinearity)
In the sample (and therefore in the population), none of the independent variables is constant, and there are no *exact linear* relationships among the independent variables.

Assumption MLR.4 (Zero Conditional Mean)
The error u has an expected value of zero given any values of the independent variables. In other words,

$$\text{E}(u|x_1, x_2, \dots, x_k) = 0.$$

Assumption MLR.5 (Homoskedasticity)
The error u has the same variance given any value of the explanatory variables. In other words,

$$\text{Var}(u|x_1, \dots, x_k) = \sigma^2.$$

Key Terms

Best Linear Unbiased Estimator
  (BLUE)
Biased Toward Zero
Ceteris Paribus
Degrees of Freedom (*df*)
Disturbance
Downward Bias
Endogenous Explanatory Variable
Error Term
Excluding a Relevant Variable
Exogenous Explanatory Variable
Explained Sum of Squares (SSE)
First Order Conditions
Frisch-Waugh Theorem
Gauss-Markov Assumptions
Gauss-Markov Theorem

Inclusion of an Irrelevant Variable
Intercept
Micronumerosity
Misspecification Analysis
Multicollinearity
Multiple Linear Regression (MLR)
  Model
Multiple Regression Analysis
OLS Intercept Estimate
OLS Regression Line
OLS Slope Estimate
Omitted Variable Bias
Ordinary Least Squares
Overspecifying the Model
Partial Effect
Perfect Collinearity

Population Model
Residual
Residual Sum of Squares
Sample Regression
  Function (SRF)
Slope Parameter
Standard Deviation of $\hat{\beta}_j$
Standard Error of $\hat{\beta}_j$
Standard Error of the
  Regression (SER)
Sum of Squared Residuals (SSR)
Total Sum of Squares (SST)
True Model
Underspecifying the Model
Upward Bias
Variance Inflation Factor (VIF)

Problems

1 Using the data in GPA2 on 4,137 college students, the following equation was estimated by OLS:

$$\widehat{colgpa} = 1.392 - .0135\,hsperc + .00148\,sat$$
$$n = 4{,}137, R^2 = .273,$$

where *colgpa* is measured on a four-point scale, *hsperc* is the percentile in the high school graduating class (defined so that, for example, *hsperc* = 5 means the *top* 5% of the class), and *sat* is the combined math and verbal scores on the student achievement test.

(i)   Why does it make sense for the coefficient on *hsperc* to be negative?

(ii)   What is the predicted college GPA when *hsperc* = 20 and *sat* = 1,050?

(iii) Suppose that two high school graduates, A and B, graduated in the same percentile from high school, but Student A's SAT score was 140 points higher (about one standard deviation in the sample). What is the predicted difference in college GPA for these two students? Is the difference large?

(iv) Holding *hsperc* fixed, what difference in SAT scores leads to a predicted *colgpa* difference of .50, or one-half of a grade point? Comment on your answer.

2 The data in WAGE2 on working men was used to estimate the following equation:

$$\widehat{educ} = 10.36 - .094\,sibs + .131\,meduc + .210\,feduc$$
$$n = 722, R^2 = .214,$$

where *educ* is years of schooling, *sibs* is number of siblings, *meduc* is mother's years of schooling, and *feduc* is father's years of schooling.

(i)   Does *sibs* have the expected effect? Explain. Holding *meduc* and *feduc* fixed, by how much does *sibs* have to increase to reduce predicted years of education by one year? (A noninteger answer is acceptable here.)

(ii)   Discuss the interpretation of the coefficient on *meduc*.

(iii) Suppose that Man A has no siblings, and his mother and father each have 12 years of education. Man B has no siblings, and his mother and father each have 16 years of education. What is the predicted difference in years of education between B and A?

3 The following model is a simplified version of the multiple regression model used by Biddle and Hamermesh (1990) to study the tradeoff between time spent sleeping and working and to look at other factors affecting sleep:

$$sleep = \beta_0 + \beta_1 totwrk + \beta_2 educ + \beta_3 age + u,$$

where *sleep* and *totwrk* (total work) are measured in minutes per week and *educ* and *age* are measured in years. (See also Computer Exercise C3 in Chapter 2.)

(i)   If adults trade off sleep for work, what is the sign of β_1?

(ii)   What signs do you think β_2 and β_3 will have?

(iii)   Using the data in SLEEP75, the estimated equation is

$$\widehat{sleep} = 3{,}638.25 - .148\ totwrk - 11.13\ educ + 2.20\ age$$
$$n = 706, R^2 = .113.$$

If someone works five more hours per week, by how many minutes is *sleep* predicted to fall? Is this a large tradeoff?

(iv)   Discuss the sign and magnitude of the estimated coefficient on *educ*.

(v)   Would you say *totwrk*, *educ*, and *age* explain much of the variation in *sleep*? What other factors might affect the time spent sleeping? Are these likely to be correlated with *totwrk*?

4 The median starting salary for new law school graduates is determined by

$$\log(salary) = \beta_0 + \beta_1 LSAT + \beta_2 GPA + \beta_3 \log(libvol) + \beta_4 \log(cost)$$
$$+ \beta_5 rank + u,$$

where *LSAT* is the median LSAT score for the graduating class, *GPA* is the median college GPA for the class, *libvol* is the number of volumes in the law school library, *cost* is the annual cost of attending law school, and *rank* is a law school ranking (with *rank* = 1 being the best).

(i)   Explain why we expect $\beta_5 \leq 0$.

(ii)   What signs do you expect for the other slope parameters? Justify your answers.

(iii)   Using the data in LAWSCH85, the estimated equation is

$$\widehat{\log(salary)} = 8.34 + .0047\ LAST + .248\ GPA + .095\ \log(libvol)$$
$$+ .038\ \log(cost) - .0033\ rank$$

$$n = 136, R^2 = .842.$$

What is the predicted ceteris paribus difference in salary for schools with a median GPA different by one point? (Report your answer as a percentage.)

(iv)   Interpret the coefficient on the variable $\log(libvol)$.

(v)   Would you say it is better to attend a higher ranked law school? How much is a difference in ranking of 20 worth in terms of predicted starting salary?

5 In a study relating college grade point average to time spent in various activities, you distribute a survey to several students. The students are asked how many hours they spend each week in four activities: studying, sleeping, working, and leisure. Any activity is put into one of the four categories, so that for each student, the sum of hours in the four activities must be 168.

(i)   In the model

$$GPA = \beta_0 + \beta_1 study + \beta_2 sleep + \beta_3 work + \beta_4 leisure + u,$$

does it make sense to hold *sleep*, *work*, and *leisure* fixed, while changing *study*?

(ii)   Explain why this model violates Assumption MLR.3.

(iii)   How could you reformulate the model so that its parameters have a useful interpretation and it satisfies Assumption MLR.3?

6 Consider the multiple regression model containing three independent variables, under Assumptions MLR.1 through MLR.4:

$$y = \beta_0 + \beta_1 x_1 + \beta_2 x_2 + \beta_3 x_3 + u.$$

You are interested in estimating the sum of the parameters on x_1 and x_2; call this $\theta_1 = \beta_1 + \beta_2$.

(i)   Show that $\hat{\theta}_1 = \hat{\beta}_1 + \hat{\beta}_2$ is an unbiased estimator of θ_1.

(ii)   Find $\text{Var}(\hat{\theta}_1)$ in terms of $\text{Var}(\hat{\beta}_1), \text{Var}(\hat{\beta}_2)$, and $\text{Corr}(\hat{\beta}_1, \hat{\beta}_2)$.

7 Which of the following can cause OLS estimators to be biased?

(i)   Heteroskedasticity.

(ii)   Omitting an important variable.

(iii) A sample correlation coefficient of .95 between two independent variables both included in the model.

8 Suppose that average worker productivity at manufacturing firms (*avgprod*) depends on two factors, average hours of training (*avgtrain*) and average worker ability (*avgabil*):

$$avgprod = \beta_0 + \beta_1 avgtrain + \beta_2 avgabil + u.$$

Assume that this equation satisfies the Gauss-Markov assumptions. If grants have been given to firms whose workers have less than average ability, so that *avgtrain* and *avgabil* are negatively correlated, what is the likely bias in $\tilde{\beta}_1$ obtained from the simple regression of *avgprod* on *avgtrain*?

9 The following equation describes the median housing price in a community in terms of amount of pollution (*nox* for nitrous oxide) and the average number of rooms in houses in the community (*rooms*):

$$\log(price) = \beta_0 + \beta_1 \log(nox) + \beta_2 rooms + u.$$

(i)   What are the probable signs of β_1 and β_2? What is the interpretation of β_1? Explain.

(ii)   Why might *nox* [or more precisely, $\log(nox)$] and *rooms* be negatively correlated? If this is the case, does the simple regression of $\log(price)$ on $\log(nox)$ produce an upward or a downward biased estimator of β_1?

(iii) Using the data in HPRICE2, the following equations were estimated:

$$\widehat{\log(price)} = 11.71 - 1.043 \log(nox), n = 506, R^2 = .264.$$

$$\widehat{\log(price)} = 9.23 - .718 \log(nox) + .306\ rooms, n = 506, R^2 = .514.$$

Is the relationship between the simple and multiple regression estimates of the elasticity of *price* with respect to *nox* what you would have predicted, given your answer in part (ii)? Does this mean that $-.718$ is definitely closer to the true elasticity than -1.043?

10 Suppose that you are interested in estimating the ceteris paribus relationship between y and x_1. For this purpose, you can collect data on two control variables, x_2 and x_3. (For concreteness, you might think of y as final exam score, x_1 as class attendance, x_2 as GPA up through the previous semester, and x_3 as SAT or ACT score.) Let $\tilde{\beta}_1$ be the simple regression estimate from y on x_1 and let $\hat{\beta}_1$ be the multiple regression estimate from y on x_1, x_2, x_3.

(i)   If x_1 is highly correlated with x_2 and x_3 in the sample, and x_2 and x_3 have large partial effects on y, would you expect $\tilde{\beta}_1$ and $\hat{\beta}_1$ to be similar or very different? Explain.

(ii)   If x_1 is almost uncorrelated with x_2 and x_3, but x_2 and x_3 are highly correlated, will $\tilde{\beta}_1$ and $\hat{\beta}_1$ tend to be similar or very different? Explain.

(iii) If x_1 is highly correlated with x_2 and x_3, and x_2 and x_3 have small partial effects on y, would you expect $\text{se}(\tilde{\beta}_1)$ or $\text{se}(\hat{\beta}_1)$ to be smaller? Explain.

(iv)   If x_1 is almost uncorrelated with x_2 and x_3, x_2 and x_3 have large partial effects on y, and x_2 and x_3 are highly correlated, would you expect $\text{se}(\tilde{\beta}_1)$ or $\text{se}(\hat{\beta}_1)$ to be smaller? Explain.

11 Suppose that the population model determining y is

$$y = \beta_0 + \beta_1 x_1 + \beta_2 x_2 + \beta_3 x_3 + u,$$

and this model satisfies Assumptions MLR.1 through MLR.4. However, we estimate the model that omits x_3. Let $\tilde{\beta}_0$, $\tilde{\beta}_1$, and $\tilde{\beta}_2$ be the OLS estimators from the regression of y on x_1 and x_2. Show that the expected value of $\tilde{\beta}_1$ (given the values of the independent variables in the sample) is

$$E(\tilde{\beta}_1) = \beta_1 + \beta_3 \frac{\sum_{i=1}^{n} \hat{r}_{i1} x_{i3}}{\sum_{i=1}^{n} \hat{r}_{i1}^2},$$

where the $\hat{r}_{i1}$ are the OLS residuals from the regression of x_1 on x_2. [*Hint:* The formula for $\tilde{\beta}_1$ comes from equation (3.22). Plug $y_i = \beta_0 + \beta_1 x_{i1} + \beta_2 x_{i2} + \beta_3 x_{i3} + u_i$ into this equation. After some algebra, take the expectation treating x_{i3} and $\hat{r}_{i1}$ as nonrandom.]

12 The following equation represents the effects of tax revenue mix on subsequent employment growth for the population of counties in the United States:

$$growth = \beta_0 + \beta_1 share_P + \beta_2 share_I + \beta_3 share_S + other\ factors,$$

where *growth* is the percentage change in employment from 1980 to 1990, $share_P$ is the share of property taxes in total tax revenue, $share_I$ is the share of income tax revenues, and $share_S$ is the share of sales tax revenues. All of these variables are measured in 1980. The omitted share, $share_F$, includes fees and miscellaneous taxes. By definition, the four shares add up to one. Other factors would include expenditures on education, infrastructure, and so on (all measured in 1980).
  (i)   Why must we omit one of the tax share variables from the equation?
  (ii) Give a careful interpretation of β_1.

13 (i)   Consider the simple regression model $y = \beta_0 + \beta_1 x + u$ under the first four Gauss-Markov assumptions. For some function $g(x)$, for example $g(x) = x^2$ or $g(x) = \log(1 + x^2)$, define $z_i = g(x_i)$. Define a slope estimator as

$$\tilde{\beta}_1 = \left(\sum_{i=1}^{n} (z_i - \bar{z}) y_i \right) \Big/ \left(\sum_{i=1}^{n} (z_i - \bar{z}) x_i \right).$$

Show that $\tilde{\beta}_1$ is linear and unbiased. Remember, because $E(u|x) = 0$, you can treat both x_i and z_i as nonrandom in your derivation.

  (ii) Add the homoskedasticity assumption, MLR.5. Show that

$$Var(\tilde{\beta}_1) = \sigma^2 \left(\sum_{i=1}^{n} (z_i - \bar{z})^2 \right) \Big/ \left(\sum_{i=1}^{n} (z_i - \bar{z}) x_i \right)^2.$$

  (iii) Show directly that, under the Gauss-Markov assumptions, $Var(\hat{\beta}_1) \leq Var(\tilde{\beta}_1)$, where $\hat{\beta}_1$ is the OLS estimator. [*Hint:* The Cauchy-Schwartz inequality in Appendix B implies that

$$\left(n^{-1} \sum_{i=1}^{n} (z_i - \bar{z})(x_i - \bar{x}) \right)^2 \leq \left(n^{-1} \sum_{i=1}^{n} (z_i - \bar{z})^2 \right) \left(n^{-1} \sum_{i=1}^{n} (x_i - \bar{x})^2 \right);$$

notice that we can drop $\bar{x}$ from the sample covariance.]

14 Suppose you have a sample of size n on three variables, y, x_1, and x_2, and you are primarily interested in the effect of x_1 on y. Let $\tilde{\beta}_1$ be the coefficient on x_1 from the simple regression and $\hat{\beta}_1$ the coefficient on x_1 from the regression y on x_1, x_2. The standard errors reported by any regression package are

$$se(\tilde{\beta}_1) = \frac{\tilde{\sigma}}{\sqrt{SST_1}}$$

$$se(\hat{\beta}_1) = \frac{\hat{\sigma}}{\sqrt{SST_1}} \cdot \sqrt{VIF_1},$$

where $\tilde{\sigma}$ is the SER from the simple regression, $\hat{\sigma}$ is the SER from the multiple regression, $VIF_1 = 1/(1 - R_1^2)$, and R_1^2 is the R-squared from the regression of x_1 on x_2. Explain why $se(\hat{\beta}_1)$ can be smaller or larger than $se(\tilde{\beta}_1)$.

15 The following estimated equations use the data in MLB1, which contains information on major league baseball salaries. The dependent variable, *lsalary*, is the log of salary. The two explanatory variables are years in the major leagues (*years*) and runs batted in per year (*rbisyr*):

$$\widehat{lsalary} = 12.373 + .1770 \; years$$
$$(.098) \; (.0132)$$

$$n = 353, \; SSR = 326.196, \; SER = .964, \; R^2 = .337$$

$$\widehat{lsalary} = 11.861 + .0904 \; years + .0302 \; rbisyr$$
$$(.084) \; (.0118) \qquad (.0020)$$

$$n = 353, \; SSR = 198.475, \; SER = .753, \; R^2 = .597$$

(i)   How many degrees of freedom are in each regression? How come the SER is smaller in the second regression than the first?

(ii)   The sample correlation coefficient between *years* and *rbisyr* is about 0.487. Does this make sense? What is the variance inflation factor (there is only one) for the slope coefficients in the multiple regression? Would you say there is little, moderate, or strong collinearity between *years* and *rbisyr*?

(iii)   How come the standard error for the coefficient on *years* in the multiple regression is lower than its counterpart in the simple regression?

16 The following equations were estimated using the data in LAWSCH85:

$$\widehat{lsalary} = 9.90 - .0041 \; rank + .294 \; GPA$$
$$(.24) \; (.0003) \qquad (.069)$$

$$n = 142, \; R^2 = .8238$$

$$\widehat{lsalary} = 9.86 - .0038 \; rank + .295 \; GPA + .00017 \; age$$
$$(.29) \; (.0004) \qquad (.083) \qquad (.00036)$$

$$n = 99, \; R^2 = .8036$$

How can it be that the R-squared is smaller when the variable *age* is added to the equation?

Computer Exercises

C1 A problem of interest to health officials (and others) is to determine the effects of smoking during pregnancy on infant health. One measure of infant health is birth weight; a birth weight that is too low can put an infant at risk for contracting various illnesses. Since factors other than cigarette smoking that affect birth weight are likely to be correlated with smoking, we should take those factors into account. For example, higher income generally results in access to better prenatal care, as well as better nutrition for the mother. An equation that recognizes this is

$$bwght = \beta_0 + \beta_1 cigs + \beta_2 faminc + u.$$

(i)   What is the most likely sign for β_2?

(ii)   Do you think *cigs* and *faminc* are likely to be correlated? Explain why the correlation might be positive or negative.

(iii)   Now, estimate the equation with and without *faminc*, using the data in BWGHT. Report the results in equation form, including the sample size and *R*-squared. Discuss your results, focusing on whether adding *faminc* substantially changes the estimated effect of *cigs* on *bwght*.

C2 Use the data in HPRICE1 to estimate the model

$$price = \beta_0 + \beta_1 sqrft + \beta_2 bdrms + u,$$

where *price* is the house price measured in thousands of dollars.
(i)   Write out the results in equation form.
(ii)   What is the estimated increase in price for a house with one more bedroom, holding square footage constant?
(iii)   What is the estimated increase in price for a house with an additional bedroom that is 140 square feet in size? Compare this to your answer in part (ii).
(iv)   What percentage of the variation in price is explained by square footage and number of bedrooms?
(v)   The first house in the sample has *sqrft* = 2,438 and *bdrms* = 4. Find the predicted selling price for this house from the OLS regression line.
(vi)   The actual selling price of the first house in the sample was $300,000 (so *price* = 300). Find the residual for this house. Does it suggest that the buyer underpaid or overpaid for the house?

C3 The file CEOSAL2 contains data on 177 chief executive officers and can be used to examine the effects of firm performance on CEO salary.
(i)   Estimate a model relating annual salary to firm sales and market value. Make the model of the constant elasticity variety for both independent variables. Write the results out in equation form.
(ii)   Add *profits* to the model from part (i). Why can this variable not be included in logarithmic form? Would you say that these firm performance variables explain most of the variation in CEO salaries?
(iii)   Add the variable *ceoten* to the model in part (ii). What is the estimated percentage return for another year of CEO tenure, holding other factors fixed?
(iv)   Find the sample correlation coefficient between the variables log(*mktval*) and *profits*. Are these variables highly correlated? What does this say about the OLS estimators?

C4 Use the data in ATTEND for this exercise.
(i)   Obtain the minimum, maximum, and average values for the variables *atndrte*, *priGPA*, and *ACT*.
(ii)   Estimate the model

$$atndrte = \beta_0 + \beta_1 priGPA + \beta_2 ACT + u,$$

and write the results in equation form. Interpret the intercept. Does it have a useful meaning?
(iii)   Discuss the estimated slope coefficients. Are there any surprises?
(iv)   What is the predicted *atndrte* if *priGPA* = 3.65 and *ACT* = 20? What do you make of this result? Are there any students in the sample with these values of the explanatory variables?
(v)   If Student A has *priGPA* = 3.1 and *ACT* = 21 and Student B has *priGPA* = 2.1 and *ACT* = 26, what is the predicted difference in their attendance rates?

C5 Confirm the partialling out interpretation of the OLS estimates by explicitly doing the partialling out for Example 3.2. This first requires regressing *educ* on *exper* and *tenure* and saving the residuals, $\hat{r}_1$. Then, regress log(*wage*) on $\hat{r}_1$. Compare the coefficient on $\hat{r}_1$ with the coefficient on *educ* in the regression of log(*wage*) on *educ*, *exper*, and *tenure*.

C6 Use the data set in WAGE2 for this problem. As usual, be sure all of the following regressions contain an intercept.
(i)   Run a simple regression of *IQ* on *educ* to obtain the slope coefficient, say, $\tilde{\delta}_1$.
(ii)   Run the simple regression of log(*wage*) on *educ*, and obtain the slope coefficient, $\tilde{\beta}_1$.

(iii) Run the multiple regression of log(*wage*) on *educ* and *IQ,* and obtain the slope coefficients, $\hat{\beta}_1$ and $\hat{\beta}_2$, respectively.

(iv) Verify that $\tilde{\beta}_1 = \hat{\beta}_1 + \hat{\beta}_2\tilde{\delta}_1$.

C7 Use the data in MEAP93 to answer this question.

(i) Estimate the model

$$math10 = \beta_0 + \beta_1\log(expend) + \beta_2lnchprg + u,$$

and report the results in the usual form, including the sample size and *R*-squared. Are the signs of the slope coefficients what you expected? Explain.

(ii) What do you make of the intercept you estimated in part (i)? In particular, does it make sense to set the two explanatory variables to zero? [*Hint*: Recall that $\log(1) = 0$.]

(iii) Now run the simple regression of *math10* on log(*expend*), and compare the slope coefficient with the estimate obtained in part (i). Is the estimated spending effect now larger or smaller than in part (i)?

(iv) Find the correlation between *lexpend* = log(*expend*) and *lnchprg*. Does its sign make sense to you?

(v) Use part (iv) to explain your findings in part (iii).

C8 Use the data in DISCRIM to answer this question. These are ZIP code–level data on prices for various items at fast-food restaurants, along with characteristics of the zip code population, in New Jersey and Pennsylvania. The idea is to see whether fast-food restaurants charge higher prices in areas with a larger concentration of blacks.

(i) Find the average values of *prpblck* and *income* in the sample, along with their standard deviations. What are the units of measurement of *prpblck* and *income*?

(ii) Consider a model to explain the price of soda, *psoda*, in terms of the proportion of the population that is black and median income:

$$psoda = \beta_0 + \beta_1prpblck + \beta_2income + u.$$

Estimate this model by OLS and report the results in equation form, including the sample size and *R*-squared. (Do not use scientific notation when reporting the estimates.) Interpret the coefficient on *prpblck*. Do you think it is economically large?

(iii) Compare the estimate from part (ii) with the simple regression estimate from *psoda* on *prpblck*. Is the discrimination effect larger or smaller when you control for income?

(iv) A model with a constant price elasticity with respect to income may be more appropriate. Report estimates of the model

$$\log(psoda) = \beta_0 + \beta_1prpblck + \beta_2\log(income) + u.$$

If *prpblck* increases by .20 (20 percentage points), what is the estimated percentage change in *psoda*? (*Hint*: The answer is 2.*xx*, where you fill in the "*xx*.")

(v) Now add the variable *prppov* to the regression in part (iv). What happens to $\hat{\beta}_{prpblck}$?

(vi) Find the correlation between log(*income*) and *prppov*. Is it roughly what you expected?

(vii) Evaluate the following statement: "Because log(*income*) and *prppov* are so highly correlated, they have no business being in the same regression."

C9 Use the data in CHARITY to answer the following questions:

(i) Estimate the equation

$$gift = \beta_0 + \beta_1mailsyear + \beta_2giftlast + \beta_3propresp + u$$

by OLS and report the results in the usual way, including the sample size and *R*-squared. How does the *R*-squared compare with that from the simple regression that omits *giftlast* and *propresp*?

    (ii)   Interpret the coefficient on *mailsyear*. Is it bigger or smaller than the corresponding simple regression coefficient?

    (iii)   Interpret the coefficient on *propresp*. Be careful to notice the units of measurement of *propresp*.

    (iv)   Now add the variable *avggift* to the equation. What happens to the estimated effect of *mailsyear*?

    (v)   In the equation from part (iv), what has happened to the coefficient on *giftlast*? What do you think is happening?

C10 Use the data in HTV to answer this question. The data set includes information on wages, education, parents' education, and several other variables for 1,230 working men in 1991.

    (i)   What is the range of the *educ* variable in the sample? What percentage of men completed twelfth grade but no higher grade? Do the men or their parents have, on average, higher levels of education?

    (ii)   Estimate the regression model

$$educ = \beta_0 + \beta_1 motheduc + \beta_2 fatheduc + u$$

by OLS and report the results in the usual form. How much sample variation in *educ* is explained by parents' education? Interpret the coefficient on *motheduc*.

    (iii)   Add the variable *abil* (a measure of cognitive ability) to the regression from part (ii), and report the results in equation form. Does "ability" help to explain variations in education, even after controlling for parents' education? Explain.

    (iv)   (Requires calculus) Now estimate an equation where *abil* appears in quadratic form:

$$educ = \beta_0 + \beta_1 motheduc + \beta_2 fatheduc + \beta_3 abil + \beta_4 abil^2 + u.$$

Using the estimates $\hat{\beta}_3$ and $\hat{\beta}_4$, use calculus to find the value of *abil*, call it $abil^*$, where *educ* is minimized. (The other coefficients and values of parents' education variables have no effect; we are holding parents' education fixed.) Notice that *abil* is measured so that negative values are permissible. You might also verify that the second derivative is positive so that you do indeed have a minimum.

    (v)   Argue that only a small fraction of men in the sample have "ability" less than the value calculated in part (iv). Why is this important?

    (vi)   If you have access to a statistical program that includes graphing capabilities, use the estimates in part (iv) to graph the relationship between the predicted education and *abil*. Set *motheduc* and *fatheduc* at their average values in the sample, 12.18 and 12.45, respectively.

C11 Use the data in MEAPSINGLE to study the effects of single-parent households on student math performance. These data are for a subset of schools in southeast Michigan for the year 2000. The socioeconomic variables are obtained at the ZIP code level (where ZIP code is assigned to schools based on their mailing addresses).

    (i)   Run the simple regression of *math4* on *pctsgle* and report the results in the usual format. Interpret the slope coefficient. Does the effect of single parenthood seem large or small?

    (ii)   Add the variables *lmedinc* and *free* to the equation. What happens to the coefficient on *pctsgle*? Explain what is happening.

    (iii)   Find the sample correlation between *lmedinc* and *free*. Does it have the sign you expect?

    (vi)   Does the substantial correlation between *lmedinc* and *free* mean that you should drop one from the regression to better estimate the causal effect of single parenthood on student performance? Explain.

    (v)   Find the variance inflation factors (VIFs) for each of the explanatory variables appearing in the regression in part (ii). Which variable has the largest VIF? Does this knowledge affect the model you would use to study the causal effect of single parenthood on math performance?

C12 The data in ECONMATH contain grade point averages and standardized test scores, along with performance in an introductory economics course, for students at a large public university. The variable to be explained is *score*, the final score in the course measured as a percentage.

(i)   How many students received a perfect score for the course? What was the average score? Find the means and standard deviations of *actmth* and *acteng*, and discuss how they compare.

(ii)   Estimate a linear equation relating *score* to *colgpa*, *actmth*, and *acteng*, where *colgpa* is measured at the beginning of the term. Report the results in the usual form.

(iii) Would you say the math or English ACT score is a better predictor of performance in the economics course? Explain.

(iv)   Discuss the size of the *R*-squared in the regression.

APPENDIX 3A

3A.1 Derivation of the First Order Conditions in Equation (3.13)

The analysis is very similar to the simple regression case. We must characterize the solutions to the problem

$$\min_{b_0, b_1, \ldots, b_k} \sum_{i=1}^{n} (y_i - b_0 - b_1 x_{i1} - \ldots - b_k x_{ik})^2.$$

Taking the partial derivatives with respect to each of the b_j (see Appendix A), evaluating them at the solutions, and setting them equal to zero gives

$$-2 \sum_{i=1}^{n} (y_i - \hat{\beta}_0 - \hat{\beta}_1 x_{i1} - \ldots - \hat{\beta}_k x_{ik}) = 0$$

$$-2 \sum_{i=1}^{n} x_{ij} (y_i - \hat{\beta}_0 - \hat{\beta}_1 x_{i1} - \ldots - \hat{\beta}_k x_{ik}) = 0, \quad \text{for all } j = 1, \ldots, k.$$

Canceling the -2 gives the first order conditions in (3.13).

3A.2 Derivation of Equation (3.22)

To derive (3.22), write x_{i1} in terms of its fitted value and its residual from the regression of x_1 on $x_2, \ldots, x_k$: $x_{i1} = \hat{x}_{i1} + \hat{r}_{i1}$, for all $i = 1, \ldots, n$. Now, plug this into the second equation in (3.13):

$$\sum_{i=1}^{n} (\hat{x}_{i1} + \hat{r}_{i1})(y_i - \hat{\beta}_0 - \hat{\beta}_1 x_{i1} - \ldots - \hat{\beta}_k x_{ik}) = 0. \qquad [3.63]$$

By the definition of the OLS residual $\hat{u}_i$, since $\hat{x}_{i1}$ is just a linear function of the explanatory variables $x_{i2}, \ldots, x_{ik}$, it follows that $\sum_{i=1}^{n} \hat{x}_{i1} \hat{u}_i = 0$. Therefore, equation (3.63) can be expressed as

$$\sum_{i=1}^{n} \hat{r}_{i1}(y_i - \hat{\beta}_0 - \hat{\beta}_1 x_{i1} - \ldots - \hat{\beta}_k x_{ik}) = 0. \qquad [3.64]$$

Since the $\hat{r}_{i1}$ are the residuals from regressing x_1 on $x_2, \ldots, x_k$, $\sum_{i=1}^{n} x_{ij} \hat{r}_{i1} = 0$, for all $j = 2, \ldots, k$. Therefore, (3.64) is equivalent to $\sum_{i=1}^{n} \hat{r}_{i1}(y_i - \hat{\beta}_1 x_{i1}) = 0$. Finally, we use the fact that $\sum_{i=1}^{n} \hat{x}_{i1} \hat{r}_{i1} = 0$, which means that $\hat{\beta}_1$ solves

$$\sum_{i=1}^{n} \hat{r}_{i1}(y_i - \hat{\beta}_1 \hat{r}_{i1}) = 0.$$

Now, straightforward algebra gives (3.22), provided, of course, that $\sum_{i=1}^{n} \hat{r}_{i1}^2 > 0$; this is ensured by Assumption MLR.3.

3A.3 Proof of Theorem 3.1

We prove Theorem 3.1 for $\hat{\beta}_1$; the proof for the other slope parameters is virtually identical. (See Appendix E for a more succinct proof using matrices.) Under Assumption MLR.3, the OLS estimators exist, and we can write $\hat{\beta}_1$ as in (3.22). Under Assumption MLR.1, we can write y_i as in (3.32); substitute this for y_i in (3.22). Then, using $\sum_{i=1}^{n} \hat{r}_{i1} = 0$, $\sum_{i=1}^{n} x_{ij}\hat{r}_{i1} = 0$, for all $j = 2, \ldots, k$, and $\sum_{i=1}^{n} x_{i1}\hat{r}_{i1} = \sum_{i=1}^{n} \hat{r}_{i1}^2$, we have

$$\hat{\beta}_1 = \beta_1 + \left(\sum_{i=1}^{n} \hat{r}_{i1} u_i\right)\bigg/\left(\sum_{i=1}^{n} \hat{r}_{i1}^2\right). \qquad [3.65]$$

Now, under Assumptions MLR.2 and MLR.4, the expected value of each u_i, given all independent variables in the sample, is zero. Since the $\hat{r}_{i1}$ are just functions of the sample independent variables, it follows that

$$\mathrm{E}(\hat{\beta}_1|\mathbf{X}) = \beta_1 + \left(\sum_{i=1}^{n} \hat{r}_{i1}\mathrm{E}(u_i|\mathbf{X})\right)\bigg/\left(\sum_{i=1}^{n} \hat{r}_{i1}^2\right)$$

$$= \beta_1 + \left(\sum_{i=1}^{n} \hat{r}_{i1} \cdot 0\right)\bigg/\left(\sum_{i=1}^{n} \hat{r}_{i1}^2\right) = \beta_1,$$

where $\mathbf{X}$ denotes the data on all independent variables and $\mathrm{E}(\hat{\beta}_1|\mathbf{X})$ is the expected value of $\hat{\beta}_1$, given $x_{i1}, \ldots, x_{ik}$, for all $i = 1, \ldots, n$. This completes the proof.

3A.4 General Omitted Variable Bias

We can derive the omitted variable bias in the general model in equation (3.31) under the first four Gauss-Markov assumptions. In particular, let the $\hat{\beta}_j$, $j = 0, 1, \ldots, k$ be the OLS estimators from the regression using the full set of explanatory variables. Let the $\tilde{\beta}_j$, $j = 0, 1, \ldots, k - 1$ be the OLS estimators from the regression that leaves out x_k. Let $\tilde{\delta}_j$, $j = 1, \ldots, k - 1$ be the slope coefficient on x_j in the auxiliary regression of x_{ik} on $x_{i1}, x_{i2}, \ldots x_{i,k-1}$, $i = 1, \ldots, n$. A useful fact is that

$$\tilde{\beta}_j = \hat{\beta}_j + \hat{\beta}_k\tilde{\delta}_j. \qquad [3.66]$$

This shows explicitly that, when we do not control for x_k in the regression, the estimated partial effect of x_j equals the partial effect when we include x_k plus the partial effect of x_k on $\hat{y}$ times the partial relationship between the omitted variable, x_k, and x_j, $j < k$. Conditional on the entire set of explanatory variables, $\mathbf{X}$, we know that the $\hat{\beta}_j$ are all unbiased for the corresponding β_j, $j = 1, \ldots, k$. Further, since $\tilde{\delta}_j$ is just a function of $\mathbf{X}$, we have

$$\mathrm{E}(\tilde{\beta}_j|\mathbf{X}) = \mathrm{E}(\hat{\beta}_j|\mathbf{X}) + \mathrm{E}(\hat{\beta}_k|\mathbf{X})\tilde{\delta}_j$$

$$= \beta_j + \beta_k\tilde{\delta}_j. \qquad [3.67]$$

Equation (3.67) shows that $\tilde{\beta}_j$ is biased for β_j unless $\beta_k = 0$—in which case x_k has no partial effect in the population—or $\tilde{\delta}_j$ equals zero, which means that x_{ik} and x_{ij} are partially uncorrelated in the sample. The key to obtaining equation (3.67) is equation (3.66). To show equation (3.66), we can use equation (3.22) a couple of times. For simplicity, we look at $j = 1$. Now, $\tilde{\beta}_1$ is the slope coefficient in the simple regression of y_i on $\tilde{r}_{i1}$, $i = 1, \ldots, n$, where the $\tilde{r}_{i1}$ are the OLS residuals from the regression of x_{i1} on $x_{i2}, x_{i3}, \ldots, x_{i,k-1}$. Consider the numerator of the expression for $\tilde{\beta}_1$: $\sum_{i=1}^{n} \tilde{r}_{i1}y_i$. But for each i, we can write $y_i = \hat{\beta}_0 + \hat{\beta}_1 x_{i1} + \ldots + \hat{\beta}_k x_{ik} + \hat{u}_i$ and plug in for y_i. Now, by properties of the OLS residuals, the $\tilde{r}_{i1}$ have zero sample average and are uncorrelated with $x_{i2}, x_{i3}, \ldots, x_{i,k-1}$ in the sample. Similarly, the $\hat{u}_i$ have zero sample average and zero sample correlation with $x_{i1}, x_{i2}, \ldots, x_{ik}$. It follows that the $\tilde{r}_{i1}$ and $\hat{u}_i$ are uncorrelated in the sample (since the $\tilde{r}_{i1}$ are just linear combinations of $x_{i1}, x_{i2}, \ldots, x_{i,k-1}$). So

$$\sum_{i=1}^{n} \tilde{r}_{i1} y_i = \hat{\beta}_1 \left(\sum_{i=1}^{n} \tilde{r}_{i1} x_{i1} \right) + \hat{\beta}_k \left(\sum_{i=1}^{n} \tilde{r}_{i1} x_{ik} \right). \qquad [3.68]$$

Now, $\sum_{i=1}^{n} \tilde{r}_{i1} x_{i1} = \sum_{i=1}^{n} \tilde{r}_{i1}^2$, which is also the denominator of $\tilde{\beta}_1$. Therefore, we have shown that

$$\tilde{\beta}_1 = \hat{\beta}_1 + \hat{\beta}_k \left(\sum_{i=1}^{n} \tilde{r}_{i1} x_{ik} \right) \Big/ \left(\sum_{i=1}^{n} \tilde{r}_{i1}^2 \right)$$

$$= \hat{\beta}_1 + \hat{\beta}_k \tilde{\delta}_1.$$

This is the relationship we wanted to show.

3A.5 Proof of Theorem 3.2

Again, we prove this for $j = 1$. Write $\hat{\beta}_1$ as in equation (3.65). Now, under MLR.5, $\mathrm{Var}(u_i|\mathbf{X}) = \sigma^2$, for all $i = 1, \ldots, n$. Under random sampling, the u_i are independent, even conditional on $\mathbf{X}$, and the $\hat{r}_{i1}$ are nonrandom conditional on $\mathbf{X}$. Therefore,

$$\mathrm{Var}(\hat{\beta}_1|\mathbf{X}) = \left(\sum_{i=1}^{n} \hat{r}_{i1}^2 \, \mathrm{Var}(u_i|\mathbf{X}) \right) \Big/ \left(\sum_{i=1}^{n} \hat{r}_{i1}^2 \right)^2$$

$$= \left(\sum_{i=1}^{n} \hat{r}_{i1}^2 \sigma^2 \right) \Big/ \left(\sum_{i=1}^{n} \hat{r}_{i1}^2 \right)^2 = \sigma^2 \Big/ \left(\sum_{i=1}^{n} \hat{r}_{i1}^2 \right).$$

Now, since $\sum_{i=1}^{n} \hat{r}_{i1}^2$ is the sum of squared residuals from regressing x_1 on $x_2, \ldots, x_k$, $\sum_{i=1}^{n} \hat{r}_{i1}^2 = \mathrm{SST}_1(1 - R_1^2)$. This completes the proof.

3A.6 Proof of Theorem 3.4

We show that, for any other linear unbiased estimator $\tilde{\beta}_1$ of β_1, $\mathrm{Var}(\tilde{\beta}_1) \geq \mathrm{Var}(\hat{\beta}_1)$, where $\hat{\beta}_1$ is the OLS estimator. The focus on $j = 1$ is without loss of generality.

For $\tilde{\beta}_1$ as in equation (3.60), we can plug in for y_i to obtain

$$\tilde{\beta}_1 = \beta_0 \sum_{i=1}^{n} w_{i1} + \beta_1 \sum_{i=1}^{n} w_{i1} x_{i1} + \beta_2 \sum_{i=1}^{n} w_{i1} x_{i2} + \ldots + \beta_k \sum_{i=1}^{n} w_{i1} x_{ik} + \sum_{i=1}^{n} w_{i1} u_i.$$

Now, since the w_{i1} are functions of the x_{ij},

$$\mathrm{E}(\tilde{\beta}_1|\mathbf{X}) = \beta_0 \sum_{i=1}^{n} w_{i1} + \beta_1 \sum_{i=1}^{n} w_{i1} x_{i1} + \beta_2 \sum_{i=1}^{n} w_{i1} x_{i2} + \ldots + \beta_k \sum_{i=1}^{n} w_{i1} x_{ik} + \sum_{i=1}^{n} w_{i1} \mathrm{E}(u_i|\mathbf{X})$$

$$= \beta_0 \sum_{i=1}^{n} w_{i1} + \beta_1 \sum_{i=1}^{n} w_{i1} x_{i1} + \beta_2 \sum_{i=1}^{n} w_{i1} x_{i2} + \ldots + \beta_k \sum_{i=1}^{n} w_{i1} x_{ik}$$

because $\mathrm{E}(u_i|\mathbf{X}) = 0$, for all $i = 1, \ldots, n$ under MLR.2 and MLR.4. Therefore, for $\mathrm{E}(\tilde{\beta}_1|\mathbf{X})$ to equal β_1 for any values of the parameters, we must have

$$\sum_{i=1}^{n} w_{i1} = 0, \ \sum_{i=1}^{n} w_{i1} x_{i1} = 1, \ \sum_{i=1}^{n} w_{i1} x_{ij} = 0, \ j = 2, \ldots, k. \qquad [3.69]$$

Now, let $\hat{r}_{i1}$ be the residuals from the regression of x_{i1} on $x_{i2}, \ldots, x_{ik}$. Then, from (3.69), it follows that

$$\sum_{i=1}^{n} w_{i1} r_{i1} = 1 \qquad [3.70]$$

because $x_{i1} = \hat{x}_{i1} + \hat{r}_{i1}$ and $\sum_{i=1}^{n} w_{i1}\hat{x}_{i1} = 0$. Now, consider the difference between $\text{Var}(\tilde{\beta}_1|\mathbf{X})$ and $\text{Var}(\hat{\beta}_1|\mathbf{X})$ under MLR.1 through MLR.5:

$$\sigma^2 \sum_{i=1}^{n} w_{i1}^2 - \sigma^2 \bigg/ \left(\sum_{i=1}^{n} \hat{r}_{i1}^2 \right). \tag{3.71}$$

Because of (3.70), we can write the difference in (3.71), without σ^2, as

$$\sum_{i=1}^{n} w_{i1}^2 - \left(\sum_{i=1}^{n} w_{i1}\hat{r}_{i1} \right)^2 \bigg/ \left(\sum_{i=1}^{n} \hat{r}_{i1}^2 \right). \tag{3.72}$$

But (3.72) is simply

$$\sum_{i=1}^{n} (w_{i1} - \hat{\gamma}_1 \hat{r}_{i1})^2, \tag{3.73}$$

where $\hat{\gamma}_1 = (\sum_{i=1}^{n} w_{i1}\hat{r}_{i1})/(\sum_{i=1}^{n} \hat{r}_{i1}^2)$, as can be seen by squaring each term in (3.73), summing, and then canceling terms. Because (3.73) is just the sum of squared residuals from the simple regression of w_{i1} on $\hat{r}_{i1}$—remember that the sample average of $\hat{r}_{i1}$ is zero—(3.73) must be nonnegative. This completes the proof.

CHAPTER 4

Multiple Regression Analysis: Inference

This chapter continues our treatment of multiple regression analysis. We now turn to the problem of testing hypotheses about the parameters in the population regression model. We begin in Section 4-1 by finding the distributions of the OLS estimators under the added assumption that the population error is normally distributed. Sections 4-2 and 4-3 cover hypothesis testing about individual parameters, while Section 4-4 discusses how to test a single hypothesis involving more than one parameter. We focus on testing multiple restrictions in Section 4-5 and pay particular attention to determining whether a group of independent variables can be omitted from a model.

4-1 Sampling Distributions of the OLS Estimators

Up to this point, we have formed a set of assumptions under which OLS is unbiased; we have also derived and discussed the bias caused by omitted variables. In Section 3-4, we obtained the variances of the OLS estimators under the Gauss-Markov assumptions. In Section 3-5, we showed that this variance is smallest among linear unbiased estimators.

Knowing the expected value and variance of the OLS estimators is useful for describing the precision of the OLS estimators. However, in order to perform statistical inference, we need to know more than just the first two moments of $\hat{\beta}_j$; we need to know the full sampling distribution of the $\hat{\beta}_j$. Even under the Gauss-Markov assumptions, the distribution of $\hat{\beta}_j$ can have virtually any shape.

When we condition on the values of the independent variables in our sample, it is clear that the sampling distributions of the OLS estimators depend on the underlying distribution of the errors. To make the sampling distributions of the $\hat{\beta}_j$ tractable, we now assume that the unobserved error is *normally distributed* in the population. We call this the **normality assumption**.

Assumption MLR.6	Normality

The population error u is *independent* of the explanatory variables $x_1, x_2,..., x_k$ and is normally distributed with zero mean and variance σ^2: $u \sim \text{Normal}(0,\sigma^2)$.

Assumption MLR.6 is much stronger than any of our previous assumptions. In fact, since u is independent of the x_j under MLR.6, $\text{E}(u|x_1,...,x_k) = \text{E}(u) = 0$ and $\text{Var}(u|x_1,...,x_k) = \text{Var}(u) = \sigma^2$. Thus, if we make Assumption MLR.6, then we are necessarily assuming MLR.4 and MLR.5. To emphasize that we are assuming more than before, we will refer to the full set of Assumptions MLR.1 through MLR.6.

For cross-sectional regression applications, Assumptions MLR.1 through MLR.6 are called the **classical linear model (CLM) assumptions**. Thus, we will refer to the model under these six assumptions as the **classical linear model**. It is best to think of the CLM assumptions as containing all of the Gauss-Markov assumptions *plus* the assumption of a normally distributed error term.

Under the CLM assumptions, the OLS estimators $\hat{\beta}_0, \hat{\beta}_1, ..., \hat{\beta}_k$ have a stronger efficiency property than they would under the Gauss-Markov assumptions. It can be shown that the OLS estimators are the **minimum variance unbiased estimators**, which means that OLS has the smallest variance among unbiased estimators; we no longer have to restrict our comparison to estimators that are linear in the y_i. This property of OLS under the CLM assumptions is discussed further in Appendix E.

A succinct way to summarize the population assumptions of the CLM is

$$y|\mathbf{x} \sim \text{Normal}(\beta_0 + \beta_1 x_1 + \beta_2 x_2 + ... + \beta_k x_k, \sigma^2),$$

where $\mathbf{x}$ is again shorthand for $(x_1, ..., x_k)$. Thus, conditional on $\mathbf{x}$, y has a normal distribution with mean linear in $x_1, ..., x_k$ and a constant variance. For a single independent variable x, this situation is shown in Figure 4.1.

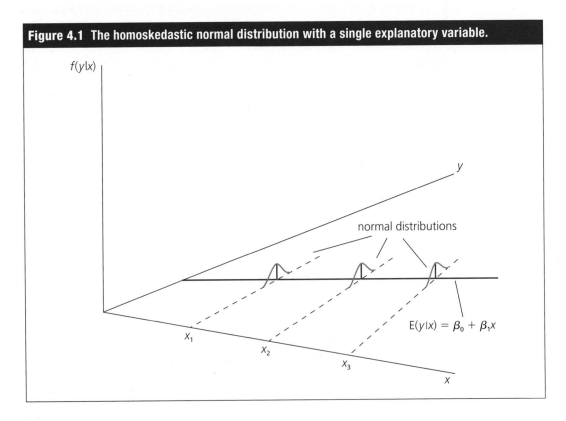

Figure 4.1 The homoskedastic normal distribution with a single explanatory variable.

The argument justifying the normal distribution for the errors usually runs something like this: Because u is the sum of many different unobserved factors affecting y, we can invoke the central limit theorem (CLT) (see Appendix C) to conclude that u has an approximate normal distribution. This argument has some merit, but it is not without weaknesses. First, the factors in u can have very different distributions in the population (for example, ability and quality of schooling in the error in a wage equation). Although the CLT can still hold in such cases, the normal approximation can be poor depending on how many factors appear in u and how different their distributions are.

A more serious problem with the CLT argument is that it assumes that all unobserved factors affect y in a separate, additive fashion. Nothing guarantees that this is so. If u is a complicated function of the unobserved factors, then the CLT argument does not really apply.

In any application, whether normality of u can be assumed is really an empirical matter. For example, there is no theorem that says *wage* conditional on *educ*, *exper*, and *tenure* is normally distributed. If anything, simple reasoning suggests that the opposite is true: since *wage* can never be less than zero, it cannot, strictly speaking, have a normal distribution. Further, because there are minimum wage laws, some fraction of the population earns exactly the minimum wage, which also violates the normality assumption. Nevertheless, as a practical matter, we can ask whether the conditional wage distribution is "close" to being normal. Past empirical evidence suggests that normality is *not* a good assumption for wages.

Often, using a transformation, especially taking the log, yields a distribution that is closer to normal. For example, something like log(*price*) tends to have a distribution that looks more normal than the distribution of *price*. Again, this is an empirical issue. We will discuss the consequences of nonnormality for statistical inference in Chapter 5.

There are some applications where MLR.6 is clearly false, as can be demonstrated with simple introspection. Whenever y takes on just a few values it cannot have anything close to a normal distribution. The dependent variable in Example 3.5 provides a good example. The variable *narr86*, the number of times a young man was arrested in 1986, takes on a small range of integer values and is zero for most men. Thus, *narr86* is far from being normally distributed. What can be done in these cases? As we will see in Chapter 5—and this is important—nonnormality of the errors is not a serious problem with large sample sizes. For now, we just make the normality assumption.

Normality of the error term translates into normal sampling distributions of the OLS estimators:

THEOREM 4.1	**NORMAL SAMPLING DISTRIBUTIONS**
	Under the CLM assumptions MLR.1 through MLR.6, conditional on the sample values of the independent variables,

$$\hat{\beta}_j \sim \text{Normal}[\beta_j, \text{Var}(\hat{\beta}_j)], \qquad \qquad [4.1]$$

where $\text{Var}(\hat{\beta}_j)$ was given in Chapter 3 [equation (3.51)]. Therefore,

$$(\hat{\beta}_j - \beta_j)/\text{sd}(\hat{\beta}_j) \sim \text{Normal}(0,1).$$

The proof of (4.1) is not that difficult, given the properties of normally distributed random variables in Appendix B. Each $\hat{\beta}_j$ can be written as $\hat{\beta}_j = \beta_j + \sum_{i=1}^{n} w_{ij}u_i$, where $w_{ij} = \hat{r}_{ij}/\text{SSR}_j$, $\hat{r}_{ij}$ is the ith residual from the regression of the x_j on all the other independent variables, and SSR_j is the sum of squared residuals from this regression [see equation (3.62)]. Since the w_{ij} depend only on the independent variables, they can be treated as nonrandom. Thus, $\hat{\beta}_j$ is just a linear combination of the errors in the sample $\{u_i: i = 1, 2, ..., n\}$. Under Assumption MLR.6 (and the random sampling Assumption MLR.2), the errors are independent, identically distributed Normal$(0,\sigma^2)$ random variables. An important fact about independent normal random variables is that a linear combination of such random variables is

---

EXPLORING FURTHER 4.1

Suppose that u is independent of the explanatory variables, and it takes on the values -2, -1, 0, 1, and 2 with equal probability of $1/5$. Does this violate the Gauss-Markov assumptions? Does this violate the CLM assumptions?

---

normally distributed (see Appendix B). This basically completes the proof. In Section 3-3, we showed that $E(\hat{\beta}_j) = \beta_j$, and we derived $\text{Var}(\hat{\beta}_j)$ in Section 3-4; there is no need to re-derive these facts.

The second part of this theorem follows immediately from the fact that when we standardize a normal random variable by subtracting off its mean and dividing by its standard deviation, we end up with a standard normal random variable.

The conclusions of Theorem 4.1 can be strengthened. In addition to (4.1), any linear combination of the $\hat{\beta}_0, \hat{\beta}_1, \ldots, \hat{\beta}_k$ is also normally distributed, and any subset of the $\hat{\beta}_j$ has a *joint* normal distribution. These facts underlie the testing results in the remainder of this chapter. In Chapter 5, we will show that the normality of the OLS estimators is still *approximately* true in large samples even without normality of the errors.

4-2 Testing Hypotheses about a Single Population Parameter: The *t* Test

This section covers the very important topic of testing hypotheses about any single parameter in the population regression function. The population model can be written as

$$y = \beta_0 + \beta_1 x_1 + \ldots + \beta_k x_k + u, \qquad [4.2]$$

and we assume that it satisfies the CLM assumptions. We know that OLS produces unbiased estimators of the β_j. In this section, we study how to test hypotheses about a particular β_j. For a full understanding of hypothesis testing, one must remember that the β_j are unknown features of the population, and we will never know them with certainty. Nevertheless, we can *hypothesize* about the value of β_j and then use statistical inference to test our hypothesis.

In order to construct hypotheses tests, we need the following result:

THEOREM 4.2

_t_ DISTRIBUTION FOR THE STANDARDIZED ESTIMATORS

Under the CLM assumptions MLR.1 through MLR.6,

$$(\hat{\beta}_j - \beta_j)/\text{se}(\hat{\beta}_j) \sim t_{n-k-1} = t_{df}, \qquad [4.3]$$

where $k + 1$ is the number of unknown parameters in the population model $y = \beta_0 + \beta_1 x_1 + \ldots + \beta_k x_k + u$ (k slope parameters and the intercept β_0) and $n - k - 1$ is the degrees of freedom (*df*).

This result differs from Theorem 4.1 in some notable respects. Theorem 4.1 showed that, under the CLM assumptions, $(\hat{\beta}_j - \beta_j)/\text{sd}(\hat{\beta}_j) \sim \text{Normal}(0,1)$. The t distribution in (4.3) comes from the fact that the constant σ in $\text{sd}(\hat{\beta}_j)$ has been replaced with the random variable $\hat{\sigma}$. The proof that this leads to a t distribution with $n - k - 1$ degrees of freedom is difficult and not especially instructive. Essentially, the proof shows that (4.3) can be written as the ratio of the standard normal random variable $(\hat{\beta}_j - \beta_j)/\text{sd}(\hat{\beta}_j)$ over the square root of $\hat{\sigma}^2/\sigma^2$. These random variables can be shown to be independent, and $(n - k - 1)\hat{\sigma}^2/\sigma^2 \sim \chi^2_{n-k-1}$. The result then follows from the definition of a t random variable (see Section B.5).

Theorem 4.2 is important in that it allows us to test hypotheses involving the β_j. In most applications, our primary interest lies in testing the **null hypothesis**

$$H_0: \beta_j = 0, \qquad [4.4]$$

where j corresponds to any of the k independent variables. It is important to understand what (4.4) means and to be able to describe this hypothesis in simple language for a particular application. Since β_j measures the partial effect of x_j on (the expected value of) y, after controlling for all other independent variables, (4.4) means that, once $x_1, x_2, \ldots, x_{j-1}, x_{j+1}, \ldots, x_k$ have been accounted for, x_j has *no effect* on the expected value of y. We cannot state the null hypothesis as "x_j does have a partial effect on y" because this is true for any value of β_j other than zero. Classical testing is suited for testing *simple hypotheses* like (4.4).

As an example, consider the wage equation

$$\log(wage) = \beta_0 + \beta_1 educ + \beta_2 exper + \beta_3 tenure + u.$$

The null hypothesis $H_0: \beta_2 = 0$ means that, once education and tenure have been accounted for, the number of years in the workforce (*exper*) has no effect on hourly wage. This is an economically interesting hypothesis. If it is true, it implies that a person's work history prior to the current employment does not affect wage. If $\beta_2 > 0$, then prior work experience contributes to productivity, and hence to wage.

You probably remember from your statistics course the rudiments of hypothesis testing for the mean from a normal population. (This is reviewed in Appendix C.) The mechanics of testing (4.4) in the multiple regression context are very similar. The hard part is obtaining the coefficient estimates, the standard errors, and the critical values, but most of this work is done automatically by econometrics software. Our job is to learn how regression output can be used to test hypotheses of interest.

The statistic we use to test (4.4) (against any alternative) is called "the" *t* **statistic** or "the" *t* **ratio** of $\hat{\beta}_j$ and is defined as

$$t_{\hat{\beta}_j} \equiv \hat{\beta}_j / se(\hat{\beta}_j). \qquad \qquad [4.5]$$

We have put "the" in quotation marks because, as we will see shortly, a more general form of the *t* statistic is needed for testing other hypotheses about β_j. For now, it is important to know that (4.5) is suitable only for testing (4.4). For particular applications, it is helpful to index *t* statistics using the name of the independent variable; for example, t_{educ} would be the *t* statistic for $\hat{\beta}_{educ}$.

The *t* statistic for $\hat{\beta}_j$ is simple to compute given $\hat{\beta}_j$ and its standard error. In fact, most regression packages do the division for you and report the *t* statistic along with each coefficient and its standard error.

Before discussing how to use (4.5) formally to test $H_0: \beta_j = 0$, it is useful to see why $t_{\hat{\beta}_j}$ has features that make it reasonable as a test statistic to detect $\beta_j \neq 0$. First, since $se(\hat{\beta}_j)$ is always positive, $t_{\hat{\beta}_j}$ has the same sign as $\hat{\beta}_j$: if $\hat{\beta}_j$ is positive, then so is $t_{\hat{\beta}_j}$ and if $\hat{\beta}_j$ is negative, so is $t_{\hat{\beta}_j}$. Second, for a given value of $se(\hat{\beta}_j)$, a larger value of $\hat{\beta}_j$ leads to larger values of $t_{\hat{\beta}_j}$. If $\hat{\beta}_j$ becomes more negative, so does $t_{\hat{\beta}_j}$.

Since we are testing $H_0: \beta_j = 0$, it is only natural to look at our unbiased estimator of β_j, $\hat{\beta}_j$, for guidance. In any interesting application, the point estimate $\hat{\beta}_j$ will *never* exactly be zero, whether or not H_0 is true. The question is: How far is $\hat{\beta}_j$ from zero? A sample value of $\hat{\beta}_j$ very far from zero provides evidence against $H_0: \beta_j = 0$. However, we must recognize that there is a sampling error in our estimate $\hat{\beta}_j$, so the size of $\hat{\beta}_j$ must be weighed against its sampling error. Since the standard error of $\hat{\beta}_j$ is an estimate of the standard deviation of $\hat{\beta}_j$, $t_{\hat{\beta}_j}$ measures how many estimated standard deviations $\hat{\beta}_j$ is away from zero. This is precisely what we do in testing whether the mean of a population is zero, using the standard t statistic from introductory statistics. Values of $t_{\hat{\beta}_j}$ sufficiently far from zero will result in a rejection of H_0. The precise rejection rule depends on the alternative hypothesis and the chosen significance level of the test.

Determining a rule for rejecting (4.4) at a given significance level—that is, the probability of rejecting H_0 when it is true—requires knowing the sampling distribution of $t_{\hat{\beta}_j}$ when H_0 is true. From Theorem 4.2, we know this to be t_{n-k-1}. This is the key theoretical result needed for testing (4.4).

Before proceeding, it is important to remember that we are testing hypotheses about the *population* parameters. We are *not* testing hypotheses about the estimates from a particular sample. Thus, it never makes sense to state a null hypothesis as "H_0: $\hat{\beta}_1 = 0$" or, even worse, as "H_0: .237 = 0" when the estimate of a parameter is .237 in the sample. We are testing whether the unknown population value, β_1, is zero.

Some treatments of regression analysis define the t statistic as the *absolute value* of (4.5), so that the t statistic is always positive. This practice has the drawback of making testing against one-sided alternatives clumsy. Throughout this text, the t statistic always has the same sign as the corresponding OLS coefficient estimate.

4-2a Testing against One-Sided Alternatives

to determine a rule for rejecting H_0, we need to decide on the relevant **alternative hypothesis**. First, consider a **one-sided alternative** of the form

$$H_1: \beta_j > 0. \tag{4.6}$$

When we state the alternative as in equation (4.6), we are really saying that the null hypothesis is H_0: $\beta_j \leq 0$. For example, if β_j is the coefficient on education in a wage regression, we only care about detecting that β_j is different from zero when β_j is actually positive. You may remember from introductory statistics that the null value that is hardest to reject in favor of (4.6) is $\beta_j = 0$. In other words, if we reject the null $\beta_j = 0$ then we automatically reject $\beta_j < 0$. Therefore, it suffices to act as if we are testing H_0: $\beta_j = 0$ against H_1: $\beta_j > 0$, effectively ignoring $\beta_j < 0$, and that is the approach we take in this book.

How should we choose a rejection rule? We must first decide on a **significance level** ("level" for short) or the probability of rejecting H_0 when it is in fact true. For concreteness, suppose we have decided on a 5% significance level, as this is the most popular choice. Thus, we are willing to mistakenly reject H_0 when it is true 5% of the time. Now, while $t_{\hat{\beta}_j}$ has a t distribution under H_0—so that it has zero mean—under the alternative $\beta_j > 0$, the expected value of $t_{\hat{\beta}_j}$ is positive. Thus, we are looking for a "sufficiently large" positive value of $t_{\hat{\beta}_j}$ in order to reject H_0: $\beta_j = 0$ in favor of H_1: $\beta_j > 0$. Negative values of $t_{\hat{\beta}_j}$ provide no evidence in favor of H_1.

The definition of "sufficiently large," with a 5% significance level, is the 95th percentile in a t distribution with $n - k - 1$ degrees of freedom; denote this by c. In other words, the **rejection rule** is that H_0 is rejected in favor of H_1 at the 5% significance level if

$$t_{\hat{\beta}_j} > c. \tag{4.7}$$

By our choice of the **critical value** c, rejection of H_0 will occur for 5% of all random samples when H_0 is true.

The rejection rule in (4.7) is an example of a **one-tailed test**. To obtain c, we only need the significance level and the degrees of freedom. For example, for a 5% level test and with $n - k - 1 = 28$ degrees of freedom, the critical value is $c = 1.701$. If $t_{\hat{\beta}_j} \leq 1.701$, then we fail to reject H_0 in favor of (4.6) at the 5% level. Note that a negative value for $t_{\hat{\beta}_j}$, no matter how large in absolute value, leads to a failure in rejecting H_0 in favor of (4.6). (See Figure 4.2.)

The same procedure can be used with other significance levels. For a 10% level test and if $df = 21$, the critical value is $c = 1.323$. For a 1% significance level and if $df = 21$, $c = 2.518$. All of these critical values are obtained directly from Table G.2. You should note a pattern in the critical values: As the significance level falls, the critical value increases, so that we require a larger and larger value of $t_{\hat{\beta}_j}$ in order to reject H_0. Thus, if H_0 is rejected at, say, the 5% level, then it is automatically rejected at the 10% level as well. It makes no sense to reject the null hypothesis at, say, the 5% level and then to redo the test to determine the outcome at the 10% level.

As the degrees of freedom in the t distribution get large, the t distribution approaches the standard normal distribution. For example, when $n - k - 1 = 120$, the 5% critical value for the one-sided alternative (4.7) is 1.658, compared with the standard normal value of 1.645. These are close enough for practical purposes; for degrees of freedom greater than 120, one can use the standard normal critical values.

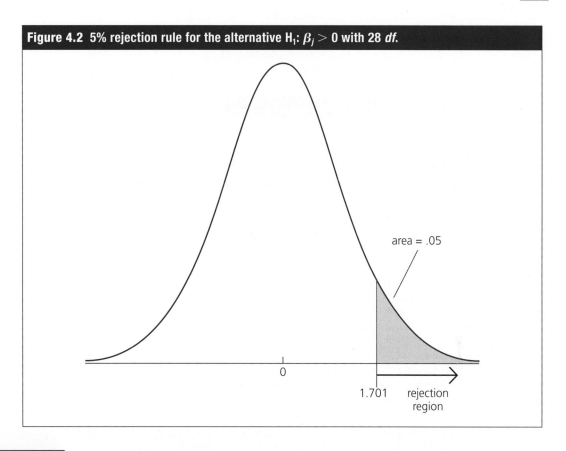

Figure 4.2 5% rejection rule for the alternative H_1: $\beta_j > 0$ with 28 *df*.

area = .05

0

1.701   rejection region

EXAMPLE 4.1   **Hourly Wage Equation**

Using the data in WAGE1 gives the estimated equation

$$\widehat{\log(wage)} = .284 + .092\ educ + .0041\ exper + .022\ tenure$$
$$(.104)\ (.007)\qquad (.0017)\qquad (.003)$$
$$n = 526,\ R^2 = .316,$$

where standard errors appear in parentheses below the estimated coefficients. We will follow this convention throughout the text. This equation can be used to test whether the return to *exper*, controlling for *educ* and *tenure*, is zero in the population, against the alternative that it is positive. Write this as H_0: $\beta_{exper} = 0$ versus H_1: $\beta_{exper} > 0$. (In applications, indexing a parameter by its associated variable name is a nice way to label parameters, since the numerical indices that we use in the general model are arbitrary and can cause confusion.) Remember that β_{exper} denotes the unknown population parameter. It is nonsense to write "H_0: .0041 = 0" or "H_0: $\hat{\beta}_{exper} = 0$."

Since we have 522 degrees of freedom, we can use the standard normal critical values. The 5% critical value is 1.645, and the 1% critical value is 2.326. The *t* statistic for $\hat{\beta}_{exper}$ is

$$t_{exper} = .0041/.0017 \approx 2.41,$$

and so $\hat{\beta}_{exper}$, or *exper*, is statistically significant even at the 1% level. We also say that "$\hat{\beta}_{exper}$ is statistically greater than zero at the 1% significance level."

The estimated return for another year of experience, holding tenure and education fixed, is not especially large. For example, adding three more years increases log(*wage*) by 3(.0041) = .0123, so wage is only about 1.2% higher. Nevertheless, we have persuasively shown that the partial effect of experience *is* positive in the population.

The one-sided alternative that the parameter is less than zero,

$$H_1: \beta_j < 0, \quad [4.8]$$

also arises in applications. The rejection rule for alternative (4.8) is just the mirror image of the previous case. Now, the critical value comes from the left tail of the t distribution. In practice, it is easiest to think of the rejection rule as

$$t_{\hat{\beta}_j} < -c, \quad [4.9]$$

where c is the critical value for the alternative $H_1: \beta_j > 0$. For simplicity, we always assume c is positive, since this is how critical values are reported in t tables, and so the critical value $-c$ is a negative number.

For example, if the significance level is 5% and the degrees of freedom is 18, then $c = 1.734$, and so $H_0: \beta_j = 0$ is rejected in favor of $H_1: \beta_j < 0$ at the 5% level if $t_{\hat{\beta}_j} < -1.734$. It is important to remember that, to reject H_0 against the negative alternative (4.8), we must get a negative t statistic. A positive t ratio, no matter how large, provides no evidence in favor of (4.8). The rejection rule is illustrated in Figure 4.3.

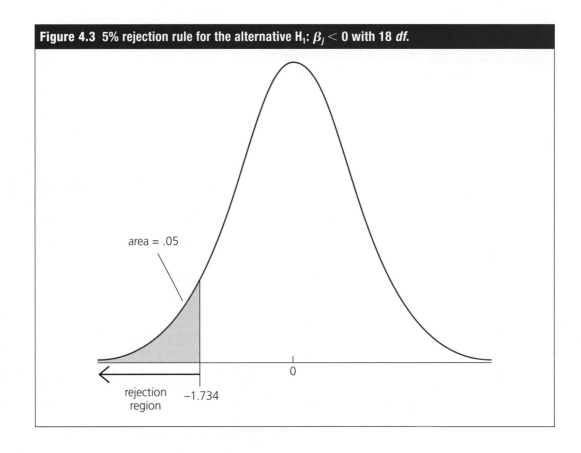

Figure 4.3 5% rejection rule for the alternative H₁: $\beta_j < 0$ with 18 *df*.

| **EXAMPLE 4.2** | **Student Performance and School Size** |

There is much interest in the effect of school size on student performance. (See, for example, *The New York Times Magazine*, 5/28/95.) One claim is that, everything else being equal, students at smaller schools fare better than those at larger schools. This hypothesis is assumed to be true even after accounting for differences in class sizes across schools.

The file MEAP93 contains data on 408 high schools in Michigan for the year 1993. We can use these data to test the null hypothesis that school size has no effect on standardized test scores against the alternative that size has a negative effect. Performance is measured by the percentage of students receiving a passing score on the Michigan Educational Assessment Program (MEAP) standardized tenth-grade math test (*math10*). School size is measured by student enrollment (*enroll*). The null hypothesis is $H_0: \beta_{enroll} = 0$, and the alternative is $H_1: \beta_{enroll} < 0$. For now, we will control for two other factors, average annual teacher compensation (*totcomp*) and the number of staff per one thousand students (*staff*). Teacher compensation is a measure of teacher quality, and staff size is a rough measure of how much attention students receive.

The estimated equation, with standard errors in parentheses, is

$$\widehat{math10} = 2.274 + .00046\,totcomp + .048\,staff - .00020\,enroll$$
$$\phantom{\widehat{math10} = }(6.113)\ (.00010)(.040)(.00022)$$
$$n = 408, R^2 = .0541.$$

The coefficient on *enroll*, $-.00020$, is in accordance with the conjecture that larger schools hamper performance: higher enrollment leads to a lower percentage of students with a passing tenth-grade math score. (The coefficients on *totcomp* and *staff* also have the signs we expect.) The fact that *enroll* has an estimated coefficient different from zero could just be due to sampling error; to be convinced of an effect, we need to conduct a t test.

Since $n - k - 1 = 408 - 4 = 404$, we use the standard normal critical value. At the 5% level, the critical value is -1.65; the t statistic on *enroll* must be *less* than -1.65 to reject H_0 at the 5% level.

The t statistic on *enroll* is $-.00020/.00022 \approx -.91$ which is larger than -1.65: we *fail* to reject H_0 in favor of H_1 at the 5% level. In fact, the 15% critical value is -1.04, and since $-.91 > -1.04$, we fail to reject H_0 even at the 15% level. We conclude that *enroll* is not statistically significant at the 15% level.

The variable *totcomp* is statistically significant even at the 1% significance level because its t statistic is 4.6. On the other hand, the t statistic for *staff* is 1.2, and so we cannot reject $H_0: \beta_{staff} = 0$ against $H_1: \beta_{staff} > 0$ even at the 10% significance level. (The critical value is $c = 1.28$ from the standard normal distribution.)

To illustrate how changing functional form can affect our conclusions, we also estimate the model with all independent variables in logarithmic form. This allows, for example, the school size effect to diminish as school size increases. The estimated equation is

$$\widehat{math10} = -207.66 + 21.16\log(totcomp) + 3.98\log(staff) - 1.29\log(enroll)$$
$$\phantom{\widehat{math10} = }(48.70)(4.06)(4.19)(0.69)$$
$$n = 408, R^2 = .0654.$$

The t statistic on $\log(enroll)$ is about -1.87; since this is below the 5% critical value -1.65, we reject $H_0: \beta_{\log(enroll)} = 0$ in favor of $H_1: \beta_{\log(enroll)} < 0$ at the 5% level.

In Chapter 2, we encountered a model where the dependent variable appeared in its original form (called *level* form), while the independent variable appeared in log form (called *level-log* model). The interpretation of the parameters is the same in the multiple regression context, except, of course, that we can give the parameters a ceteris paribus interpretation. Holding *totcomp* and *staff* fixed, we have $\widehat{\Delta math10} = -1.29[\Delta\log(enroll)]$, so that

$$\widehat{\Delta math10} \approx -(1.29/100)(\%\Delta enroll) \approx -.013(\%\Delta enroll).$$

Once again, we have used the fact that the change in log(*enroll*), when multiplied by 100, is approximately the percentage change in *enroll*. Thus, if enrollment is 10% higher at a school, $\widehat{math10}$ is predicted to be $.013(10) = 0.13$ percentage points lower (*math10* is measured as a percentage).

Which model do we prefer: the one using the level of *enroll* or the one using log(*enroll*)? In the level-level model, enrollment does not have a statistically significant effect, but in the level-log model it does. This translates into a higher *R*-squared for the level-log model, which means we explain more of the variation in *math10* by using *enroll* in logarithmic form (6.5% to 5.4%). The level-log model is preferred because it more closely captures the relationship between *math10* and *enroll*. We will say more about using *R*-squared to choose functional form in Chapter 6.

4-2b Two-Sided Alternatives

In applications, it is common to test the null hypothesis $H_0: \beta_j = 0$ against a **two-sided alternative**; that is,

$$H_1: \beta_j \neq 0. \qquad [4.10]$$

Under this alternative, x_j has a ceteris paribus effect on y without specifying whether the effect is positive or negative. This is the relevant alternative when the sign of β_j is not well determined by theory (or common sense). Even when we know whether β_j is positive or negative under the alternative, a two-sided test is often prudent. At a minimum, using a two-sided alternative prevents us from looking at the estimated equation and then basing the alternative on whether $\hat{\beta}_j$ is positive or negative. Using the regression estimates to help us formulate the null or alternative hypotheses is not allowed

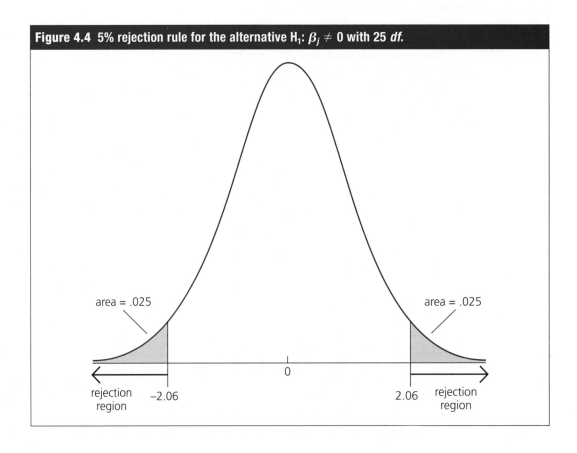

Figure 4.4 5% rejection rule for the alternative H₁: $\beta_j \neq 0$ with 25 *df*.

area = .025

area = .025

0

rejection region   −2.06

2.06   rejection region

because classical statistical inference presumes that we state the null and alternative about the population before looking at the data. For example, we should not first estimate the equation relating math performance to enrollment, note that the estimated effect is negative, and then decide the relevant alternative is $H_1: \beta_{enroll} < 0$.

When the alternative is two-sided, we are interested in the *absolute value* of the t statistic. The rejection rule for $H_0: \beta_j = 0$ against (4.10) is

$$|t_{\hat{\beta}_j}| > c, \qquad\qquad [4.11]$$

where $|\cdot|$ denotes absolute value and c is an appropriately chosen critical value. To find c, we again specify a significance level, say 5%. For a **two-tailed test**, c is chosen to make the area in each tail of the t distribution equal 2.5%. In other words, c is the 97.5th percentile in the t distribution with $n - k - 1$ degrees of freedom. When $n - k - 1 = 25$, the 5% critical value for a two-sided test is $c = 2.060$. Figure 4.4 provides an illustration of this distribution.

When a specific alternative is not stated, it is usually considered to be two-sided. In the remainder of this text, the default will be a two-sided alternative, and 5% will be the default significance level. When carrying out empirical econometric analysis, it is always a good idea to be explicit about the alternative and the significance level. If H_0 is rejected in favor of (4.10) at the 5% level, we usually say that "x_j is **statistically significant**, or statistically different from zero, at the 5% level." If H_0 is not rejected, we say that "x_j is **statistically insignificant** at the 5% level."

| **EXAMPLE 4.3** | **Determinants of College GPA** |

We use the data in GPA1 to estimate a model explaining college GPA (*colGPA*), with the average number of lectures missed per week (*skipped*) as an additional explanatory variable. The estimated model is

$$\widehat{colGPA} = 1.39 + .412\,hsGPA + .015\,ACT - .083\,skipped$$
$$\quad\;(.33)\quad(.094)\qquad\quad(.011)\qquad\;(.026)$$
$$n = 141, R^2 = .234.$$

We can easily compute t statistics to see which variables are statistically significant, using a two-sided alternative in each case. The 5% critical value is about 1.96, since the degrees of freedom $(141 - 4 = 137)$ is large enough to use the standard normal approximation. The 1% critical value is about 2.58.

The t statistic on *hsGPA* is 4.38, which is significant at very small significance levels. Thus, we say that "*hsGPA* is statistically significant at any *conventional* significance level." The t statistic on *ACT* is 1.36, which is not statistically significant at the 10% level against a two-sided alternative. The coefficient on *ACT* is also practically small: a 10-point increase in *ACT*, which is large, is predicted to increase *colGPA* by only .15 points. Thus, the variable *ACT* is practically, as well as statistically, insignificant.

The coefficient on *skipped* has a t statistic of $-.083/.026 = -3.19$, so *skipped* is statistically significant at the 1% significance level $(3.19 > 2.58)$. This coefficient means that another lecture missed per week lowers predicted *colGPA* by about .083. Thus, holding *hsGPA* and *ACT* fixed, the predicted difference in *colGPA* between a student who misses no lectures per week and a student who misses five lectures per week is about .42. Remember that this says nothing about specific students; rather, .42 is the estimated average across a subpopulation of students.

In this example, for each variable in the model, we could argue that a one-sided alternative is appropriate. The variables *hsGPA* and *skipped* are very significant using a two-tailed test and have the signs that we expect, so there is no reason to do a one-tailed test. On the other hand, against a one-sided alternative $(\beta_3 > 0)$, *ACT* is significant at the 10% level but not at the 5% level. This does not change the fact that the coefficient on *ACT* is pretty small.

4-2c Testing Other Hypotheses about β_j

Although H_0: $\beta_j = 0$ is the most common hypothesis, we sometimes want to test whether β_j is equal to some other given constant. Two common examples are $\beta_j = 1$ and $\beta_j = -1$. Generally, if the null is stated as

$$H_0: \beta_j = a_j, \quad \text{[4.12]}$$

where a_j is our hypothesized value of β_j, then the appropriate t statistic is

$$t = (\hat{\beta}_j - a_j)/\text{se}(\hat{\beta}_j).$$

As before, t measures how many estimated standard deviations $\hat{\beta}_j$ is away from the hypothesized value of β_j. The general t statistic is usefully written as

$$t = \frac{(estimate - hypothesized\ value)}{standard\ error}. \quad \text{[4.13]}$$

Under (4.12), this t statistic is distributed as t_{n-k-1} from Theorem 4.2. The usual t statistic is obtained when $a_j = 0$.

We can use the general t statistic to test against one-sided or two-sided alternatives. For example, if the null and alternative hypotheses are H_0: $\beta_j = 1$ and H_1: $\beta_j > 1$, then we find the critical value for a one-sided alternative *exactly* as before: the difference is in how we compute the t statistic, not in how we obtain the appropriate c. We reject H_0 in favor of H_1 if $t > c$. In this case, we would say that "$\hat{\beta}_j$ is statistically greater than one" at the appropriate significance level.

EXAMPLE 4.4 **Campus Crime and Enrollment**

Consider a simple model relating the annual number of crimes on college campuses (*crime*) to student enrollment (*enroll*):

$$\log(crime) = \beta_0 + \beta_1 \log(enroll) + u.$$

This is a constant elasticity model, where β_1 is the elasticity of crime with respect to enrollment. It is not much use to test H_0: $\beta_1 = 0$, as we expect the total number of crimes to increase as the size of the campus increases. A more interesting hypothesis to test would be that the elasticity of crime with respect to enrollment is one: H_0: $\beta_1 = 1$. This means that a 1% increase in enrollment leads to, on average, a 1% increase in crime. A noteworthy alternative is H_1: $\beta_1 > 1$, which implies that a 1% increase in enrollment increases campus crime by *more* than 1%. If $\beta_1 > 1$, then, in a relative sense—not just an absolute sense—crime is more of a problem on larger campuses. One way to see this is to take the exponential of the equation:

$$crime = \exp(\beta_0) enroll^{\beta_1} \exp(u).$$

(See Appendix A for properties of the natural logarithm and exponential functions.) For $\beta_0 = 0$ and $u = 0$, this equation is graphed in Figure 4.5 for $\beta_1 < 1$, $\beta_1 = 1$, and $\beta_1 > 1$.

We test $\beta_1 = 1$ against $\beta_1 > 1$ using data on 97 colleges and universities in the United States for the year 1992, contained in the data file CAMPUS. The data come from the FBI's *Uniform Crime Reports*, and the average number of campus crimes in the sample is about 394, while the average enrollment is about 16,076. The estimated equation (with estimates and standard errors rounded to two decimal places) is

$$\widehat{\log(crime)} = -6.63 + 1.27 \log(enroll)$$
$$(1.03) \quad (0.11) \quad \text{[4.14]}$$
$$n = 97, R^2 = .585.$$

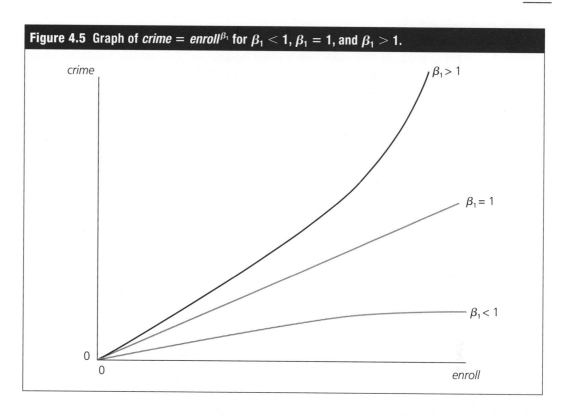

Figure 4.5 Graph of *crime* = *enroll$^{\beta_1}$* for $\beta_1 < 1$, $\beta_1 = 1$, and $\beta_1 > 1$.

The estimated elasticity of *crime* with respect to *enroll*, 1.27, is in the direction of the alternative $\beta_1 > 1$. But is there enough evidence to conclude that $\beta_1 > 1$? We need to be careful in testing this hypothesis, especially because the statistical output of standard regression packages is much more complex than the simplified output reported in equation (4.14). Our first instinct might be to construct "the" t statistic by taking the coefficient on log(*enroll*) and dividing it by its standard error, which is the t statistic reported by a regression package. But this is the *wrong* statistic for testing H_0: $\beta_1 = 1$. The correct t statistic is obtained from (4.13): we subtract the hypothesized value, unity, from the estimate and divide the result by the standard error of $\hat{\beta}_1$: $t = (1.27 - 1)/.11 = .27/.11 \approx 2.45$. The one-sided 5% critical value for a t distribution with $97 - 2 = 95$ *df* is about 1.66 (using *df* = 120), so we clearly reject $\beta_1 = 1$ in favor of $\beta_1 > 1$ at the 5% level. In fact, the 1% critical value is about 2.37, and so we reject the null in favor of the alternative at even the 1% level.

We should keep in mind that this analysis holds no other factors constant, so the elasticity of 1.27 is not necessarily a good estimate of ceteris paribus effect. It could be that larger enrollments are correlated with other factors that cause higher crime: larger schools might be located in higher crime areas. We could control for this by collecting data on crime rates in the local city.

For a two-sided alternative, for example H_0: $\beta_j = -1$, H_1: $\beta_1 \neq -1$, we still compute the t statistic as in (4.13): $t = (\hat{\beta}_j + 1)/\text{se}(\hat{\beta}_j)$ (notice how subtracting -1 means adding 1). The rejection rule is the usual one for a two-sided test: reject H_0 if $|t| > c$, where c is a two-tailed critical value. If H_0 is rejected, we say that "$\hat{\beta}_j$ is statistically different from negative one" at the appropriate significance level.

EXAMPLE 4.5	**Housing Prices and Air Pollution**

For a sample of 506 communities in the Boston area, we estimate a model relating median housing price (*price*) in the community to various community characteristics: *nox* is the amount of nitrogen oxide in the air, in parts per million; *dist* is a weighted distance of the community from five employment centers, in miles; *rooms* is the average number of rooms in houses in the community; and *stratio* is the average student-teacher ratio of schools in the community. The population model is

$$\log(price) = \beta_0 + \beta_1 \log(nox) + \beta_2 \log(dist) + \beta_3 rooms + \beta_4 stratio + u.$$

Thus, β_1 is the elasticity of *price* with respect to *nox*. We wish to test $H_0: \beta_1 = -1$ against the alternative $H_1: \beta_1 \neq -1$. The t statistic for doing this test is $t = (\hat{\beta}_1 + 1)/\text{se}(\hat{\beta}_1)$.

Using the data in HPRICE2, the estimated model is

$$\widehat{\log(price)} = 11.08 - .954 \log(nox) - .134 \log(dist) + .255 \, rooms - .052 \, stratio$$
$$(0.32) \quad (.117) \qquad\qquad (.043) \qquad\qquad (.019) \qquad\quad (.006)$$
$$n = 506, R^2 = .581.$$

The slope estimates all have the anticipated signs. Each coefficient is statistically different from zero at very small significance levels, including the coefficient on $\log(nox)$. But we do not want to test that $\beta_1 = 0$. The null hypothesis of interest is $H_0: \beta_1 = -1$, with corresponding t statistic $(-.954 + 1)/.117 = .393$. There is little need to look in the t table for a critical value when the t statistic is this small: the estimated elasticity is not statistically different from -1 even at very large significance levels. Controlling for the factors we have included, there is little evidence that the elasticity is different from -1.

4-2d Computing *p*-Values for *t* Tests

So far, we have talked about how to test hypotheses using a classical approach: after stating the alternative hypothesis, we choose a significance level, which then determines a critical value. Once the critical value has been identified, the value of the t statistic is compared with the critical value, and the null is either rejected or not rejected at the given significance level.

Even after deciding on the appropriate alternative, there is a component of arbitrariness to the classical approach, which results from having to choose a significance level ahead of time. Different researchers prefer different significance levels, depending on the particular application. There is no "correct" significance level.

Committing to a significance level ahead of time can hide useful information about the outcome of a hypothesis test. For example, suppose that we wish to test the null hypothesis that a parameter is zero against a two-sided alternative, and with 40 degrees of freedom we obtain a t statistic equal to 1.85. The null hypothesis is not rejected at the 5% level, since the t statistic is less than the two-tailed critical value of $c = 2.021$. A researcher whose agenda is not to reject the null could simply report this outcome along with the estimate: the null hypothesis is not rejected at the 5% level. Of course, if the t statistic, or the coefficient and its standard error, are reported, then we can also determine that the null hypothesis would be rejected at the 10% level, since the 10% critical value is $c = 1.684$.

Rather than testing at different significance levels, it is more informative to answer the following question: Given the observed value of the t statistic, what is the *smallest* significance level at which the null hypothesis would be rejected? This level is known as the **p-value** for the test (see Appendix C). In the previous example, we know the p-value is greater than .05, since the null is not rejected at the 5% level, and we know that the p-value is less than .10, since the null is rejected at the 10% level. We obtain the actual p-value by computing the probability that a t random variable, with 40 df, is larger than 1.85 in absolute value. That is, the p-value is the significance level of the test when we use the value of the test statistic, 1.85 in the above example, as the critical value for the test. This p-value is shown in Figure 4.6.

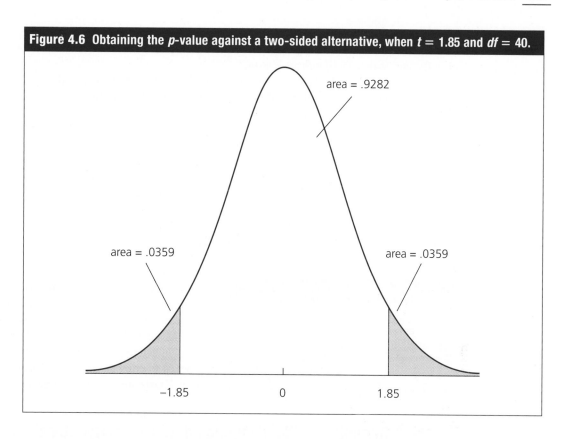

Figure 4.6 Obtaining the *p*-value against a two-sided alternative, when *t* = 1.85 and *df* = 40.

area = .9282

area = .0359

area = .0359

−1.85

0

1.85

Because a *p*-value is a probability, its value is always between zero and one. In order to compute *p*-values, we either need extremely detailed printed tables of the *t* distribution—which is not very practical—or a computer program that computes areas under the probability density function of the *t* distribution. Most modern regression packages have this capability. Some packages compute *p*-values routinely with each OLS regression, but only for certain hypotheses. If a regression package reports a *p*-value along with the standard OLS output, it is almost certainly the *p*-value for testing the null hypothesis $H_0: \beta_j = 0$ against the two-sided alternative. The *p*-value in this case is

$$P(|T| > |t|),$$ [4.15]

where, for clarity, we let *T* denote a *t* distributed random variable with $n - k - 1$ degrees of freedom and let *t* denote the numerical value of the test statistic.

The *p*-value nicely summarizes the strength or weakness of the empirical evidence against the null hypothesis. Perhaps its most useful interpretation is the following: the *p*-value is the probability of observing a *t* statistic as extreme as we did *if the null hypothesis is true*. This means that *small p*-values are evidence *against* the null; large *p*-values provide little evidence against H_0. For example, if the *p*-value = .50 (reported always as a decimal, not a percentage), then we would observe a value of the *t* statistic as extreme as we did in 50% of all random samples when the null hypothesis is true; this is pretty weak evidence against H_0.

In the example with *df* = 40 and *t* = 1.85, the *p*-value is computed as

$$p\text{-value} = P(|T| > 1.85) = 2P(T > 1.85) = 2(.0359) = .0718,$$

where $P(T > 1.85)$ is the area to the right of 1.85 in a *t* distribution with 40 *df*. (This value was computed using the econometrics package Stata; it is not available in Table G.2.) This means that, if the null hypothesis is true, we would observe an absolute value of the t statistic as large as 1.85 about 7.2 percent of the time. This provides some evidence against the null hypothesis, but we would not reject the null at the 5% significance level.

The previous example illustrates that once the p-value has been computed, a classical test can be carried out at any desired level. If α denotes the significance level of the test (in decimal form), then H_0 is rejected if p-value $< \alpha$; otherwise, H_0 is not rejected at the $100 \cdot \alpha\%$ level.

Computing p-values for one-sided alternatives is also quite simple. Suppose, for example, that we test $H_0: \beta_j = 0$ against $H_1: \beta_j > 0$. If $\hat{\beta}_j < 0$, then computing a p-value is not important: we know that the p-value is greater than .50, which will never cause us to reject H_0 in favor of H_1. If $\hat{\beta}_j > 0$, then $t > 0$ and the p-value is just the probability that a t random variable with the appropriate df exceeds the value t. Some regression packages only compute p-values for two-sided alternatives. But it is simple to obtain the one-sided p-value: just divide the two-sided p-value by 2.

If the alternative is $H_1: \beta_j < 0$, it makes sense to compute a p-value if $\hat{\beta}_j < 0$ (and hence $t < 0$): p-value $= P(T < t) = P(T > |t|)$ because the t distribution is symmetric about zero. Again, this can be obtained as one-half of the p-value for the two-tailed test.

Because you will quickly become familiar with the magnitudes of t statistics that lead to statistical significance, especially for large sample sizes, it is not always crucial to report p-values for t statistics. But it does not hurt to report them. Further, when we discuss F testing in Section 4-5, we will see that it is important to compute p-values, because critical values for F tests are not so easily memorized.

> ### EXPLORING FURTHER 4.3
>
> Suppose you estimate a regression model and obtain $\hat{\beta}_1 = .56$ and p-value $= .086$ for testing $H_0: \beta_1 = 0$ against $H_1: \beta_1 \neq 0$. What is the p-value for testing $H_0: \beta_1 = 0$ against $H_1: \beta_1 > 0$?

4-2e A Reminder on the Language of Classical Hypothesis Testing

When H_0 is not rejected, we prefer to use the language "we fail to reject H_0 at the x% level," rather than "H_0 is accepted at the x% level." We can use Example 4.5 to illustrate why the former statement is preferred. In this example, the estimated elasticity of *price* with respect to *nox* is $-.954$, and the t statistic for testing $H_0: \beta_{nox} = -1$ is $t = .393$; therefore, we cannot reject H_0. But there are many other values for β_{nox} (more than we can count) that cannot be rejected. For example, the t statistic for $H_0: \beta_{nox} = -.9$ is $(-.954 + .9)/.117 = -.462$, and so this null is not rejected either. Clearly $\beta_{nox} = -1$ and $\beta_{nox} = -.9$ cannot both be true, so it makes no sense to say that we "accept" either of these hypotheses. All we can say is that the data do not allow us to reject either of these hypotheses at the 5% significance level.

4-2f Economic, or Practical, versus Statistical Significance

Because we have emphasized *statistical significance* throughout this section, now is a good time to remember that we should pay attention to the magnitude of the *coefficient* estimates in addition to the size of the t statistics. The statistical significance of a variable x_j is determined entirely by the size of $t_{\hat{\beta}_j}$, whereas the **economic significance** or **practical significance** of a variable is related to the size (and sign) of $\hat{\beta}_j$.

Recall that the t statistic for testing $H_0: \beta_j = 0$ is defined by dividing the estimate by its standard error: $t_{\hat{\beta}_j} = \hat{\beta}_j/\text{se}(\hat{\beta}_j)$. Thus, $t_{\hat{\beta}_j}$ can indicate statistical significance either because $\hat{\beta}_j$ is "large" or because $\text{se}(\hat{\beta}_j)$ is "small." It is important in practice to distinguish between these reasons for statistically significant t statistics. Too much focus on statistical significance can lead to the false conclusion that a variable is "important" for explaining y even though its estimated effect is modest.

| EXAMPLE 4.6 | **Participation Rates in 401(k) Plans** |

In Example 3.3, we used the data on 401(k) plans to estimate a model describing participation rates in terms of the firm's match rate and the age of the plan. We now include a measure of firm size, the total number of firm employees (*totemp*). The estimated equation is

$$\widehat{prate} = 80.29 + 5.44\, mrate + .269\, age - .00013\, totemp$$
$$\qquad\quad (0.78)\ (0.52) \qquad\quad (.045) \qquad\quad (.00004)$$
$$n = 1{,}534, R^2 = .100.$$

The smallest t statistic in absolute value is that on the variable *totemp*: $t = -.00013/.00004 = -3.25$, and this is statistically significant at very small significance levels. (The two-tailed p-value for this t statistic is about .001.) Thus, all of the variables are statistically significant at rather small significance levels.

How big, in a practical sense, is the coefficient on *totemp*? Holding *mrate* and *age* fixed, if a firm grows by 10,000 employees, the participation rate falls by $10{,}000(.00013) = 1.3$ percentage points. This is a huge increase in number of employees with only a modest effect on the participation rate. Thus, although firm size does affect the participation rate, the effect is not practically very large.

The previous example shows that it is especially important to interpret the magnitude of the coefficient, in addition to looking at t statistics, when working with large samples. With large sample sizes, parameters can be estimated very precisely: standard errors are often quite small relative to the coefficient estimates, which usually results in statistical significance.

Some researchers insist on using smaller significance levels as the sample size increases, partly as a way to offset the fact that standard errors are getting smaller. For example, if we feel comfortable with a 5% level when n is a few hundred, we might use the 1% level when n is a few thousand. Using a smaller significance level means that economic and statistical significance are more likely to coincide, but there are no guarantees: In the previous example, even if we use a significance level as small as .1% (one-tenth of 1%), we would still conclude that *totemp* is statistically significant.

Many researchers are also willing to entertain larger significance levels in applications with small sample sizes, reflecting the fact that it is harder to find significance with smaller sample sizes. (Smaller sample sizes lead to less precise estimators, and the critical values are larger in magnitude, two factors that make it harder to find statistical significance.) Unfortunately, one's willingness to consider higher significance levels can depend on one's underlying agenda.

| EXAMPLE 4.7 | **Effect of Job Training on Firm Scrap Rates** |

The scrap rate for a manufacturing firm is the number of defective items—products that must be discarded—out of every 100 produced. Thus, for a given number of items produced, a decrease in the scrap rate reflects higher worker productivity.

We can use the scrap rate to measure the effect of worker training on productivity. Using the data in JTRAIN, but only for the year 1987 and for nonunionized firms, we obtain the following estimated equation:

$$\widehat{\log(scrap)} = 12.46 - .029\, hrsemp - .962\, \log(sales) + .761\, \log(employ)$$
$$\qquad\qquad\quad (5.69)\ (.023) \qquad\quad (.453) \qquad\qquad (.407)$$
$$n = 29, R^2 = .262.$$

The variable *hrsemp* is annual hours of training per employee, *sales* is annual firm sales (in dollars), and *employ* is the number of firm employees. For 1987, the average scrap rate in the sample is about 4.6 and the average of *hrsemp* is about 8.9.

The main variable of interest is *hrsemp*. One more hour of training per employee lowers log(*scrap*) by .029, which means the scrap rate is about 2.9% lower. Thus, if *hrsemp* increases by 5—each employee is trained 5 more hours per year—the scrap rate is estimated to fall by 5(2.9) = 14.5%. This seems like a reasonably large effect, but whether the additional training is worthwhile to the firm depends on the cost of training and the benefits from a lower scrap rate. We do not have the numbers needed to do a cost benefit analysis, but the estimated effect seems nontrivial.

What about the *statistical significance* of the training variable? The t statistic on *hrsemp* is $-.029/.023 = -1.26$, and now you probably recognize this as not being large enough in magnitude to conclude that *hrsemp* is statistically significant at the 5% level. In fact, with $29 - 4 = 25$ degrees of freedom for the one-sided alternative, $H_1: \beta_{hrsemp} < 0$, the 5% critical value is about -1.71. Thus, using a strict 5% level test, we must conclude that *hrsemp* is not statistically significant, even using a one-sided alternative.

Because the sample size is pretty small, we might be more liberal with the significance level. The 10% critical value is -1.32, and so *hrsemp* is almost significant against the one-sided alternative at the 10% level. The p-value is easily computed as $P(T_{25} < -1.26) = .110$. This may be a low enough p-value to conclude that the estimated effect of training is not just due to sampling error, but opinions would legitimately differ on whether a one-sided p-value of .11 is sufficiently small.

Remember that large standard errors can also be a result of multicollinearity (high correlation among some of the independent variables), even if the sample size seems fairly large. As we discussed in Section 3-4, there is not much we can do about this problem other than to collect more data or change the scope of the analysis by dropping or combining certain independent variables. As in the case of a small sample size, it can be hard to precisely estimate partial effects when some of the explanatory variables are highly correlated. (Section 4-5 contains an example.)

We end this section with some guidelines for discussing the economic and statistical significance of a variable in a multiple regression model:

1. Check for statistical significance. If the variable is statistically significant, discuss the magnitude of the coefficient to get an idea of its practical or economic importance. This latter step can require some care, depending on how the independent and dependent variables appear in the equation. (In particular, what are the units of measurement? Do the variables appear in logarithmic form?)

2. If a variable is not statistically significant at the usual levels (10%, 5%, or 1%), you might still ask if the variable has the expected effect on y and whether that effect is practically large. If it is large, you should compute a p-value for the t statistic. For small sample sizes, you can sometimes make a case for p-values as large as .20 (but there are no hard rules). With large p-values, that is, small t statistics, we are treading on thin ice because the practically large estimates may be due to sampling error: a different random sample could result in a very different estimate.

3. It is common to find variables with small t statistics that have the "wrong" sign. For practical purposes, these can be ignored: we conclude that the variables are statistically insignificant. A significant variable that has the unexpected sign and a practically large effect is much more troubling and difficult to resolve. One must usually think more about the model and the nature of the data to solve such problems. Often, a counterintuitive, significant estimate results from the omission of a key variable or from one of the important problems we will discuss in Chapters 9 and 15.

4-3 Confidence Intervals

Under the CLM assumptions, we can easily construct a **confidence interval (CI)** for the population parameter β_j. Confidence intervals are also called *interval estimates* because they provide a range of likely values for the population parameter, and not just a point estimate.

Using the fact that $(\hat{\beta}_j - \beta_j)/se(\hat{\beta}_j)$ has a t distribution with $n - k - 1$ degrees of freedom [see (4.3)], simple manipulation leads to a CI for the unknown β_j: a *95% confidence interval*, given by

$$\hat{\beta}_j \pm c \cdot se(\hat{\beta}_j), \qquad\qquad [4.16]$$

where the constant c is the 97.5[th] percentile in a t_{n-k-1} distribution. More precisely, the lower and upper bounds of the confidence interval are given by

$$\underline{\beta}_j \equiv \hat{\beta}_j - c \cdot se(\hat{\beta}_j)$$

and

$$\overline{\beta}_j \equiv \hat{\beta}_j + c \cdot se(\hat{\beta}_j),$$

respectively.

At this point, it is useful to review the meaning of a confidence interval. If random samples were obtained over and over again, with $\underline{\beta}_j$ and $\overline{\beta}_j$ computed each time, then the (unknown) population value β_j would lie in the interval $(\underline{\beta}_j, \overline{\beta}_j)$ for 95% of the samples. Unfortunately, for the single sample that we use to construct the CI, we do not know whether β_j is actually contained in the interval. We hope we have obtained a sample that is one of the 95% of all samples where the interval estimate contains β_j, but we have no guarantee.

Constructing a confidence interval is very simple when using current computing technology. Three quantities are needed: $\hat{\beta}_j$, $se(\hat{\beta}_j)$, and c. The coefficient estimate and its standard error are reported by any regression package. To obtain the value c, we must know the degrees of freedom, $n - k - 1$, and the level of confidence—95% in this case. Then, the value for c is obtained from the t_{n-k-1} distribution.

As an example, for $df = n - k - 1 = 25$, a 95% confidence interval for any β_j is given by $[\hat{\beta}_j - 2.06 \cdot se(\hat{\beta}_j), \hat{\beta}_j + 2.06 \cdot se(\hat{\beta}_j)]$.

When $n - k - 1 > 120$, the t_{n-k-1} distribution is close enough to normal to use the 97.5[th] percentile in a standard normal distribution for constructing a 95% CI: $\hat{\beta}_j \pm 1.96 \cdot se(\hat{\beta}_j)$. In fact, when $n - k - 1 > 50$, the value of c is so close to 2 that we can use a simple *rule of thumb* for a 95% confidence interval: $\hat{\beta}_j$ plus or minus two of its standard errors. For small degrees of freedom, the exact percentiles should be obtained from the t tables.

It is easy to construct confidence intervals for any other level of confidence. For example, a 90% CI is obtained by choosing c to be the 95th percentile in the t_{n-k-1} distribution. When $df = n - k - 1 = 25$, $c = 1.71$, and so the 90% CI is $\hat{\beta}_j \pm 1.71 \cdot se(\hat{\beta}_j)$, which is necessarily narrower than the 95% CI. For a 99% CI, c is the 99.5[th] percentile in the t_{25} distribution. When $df = 25$, the 99% CI is roughly $\hat{\beta}_j \pm 2.79 \cdot se(\hat{\beta}_j)$, which is inevitably wider than the 95% CI.

Many modern regression packages save us from doing any calculations by reporting a 95% CI along with each coefficient and its standard error. Once a confidence interval is constructed, it is easy to carry out two-tailed hypotheses tests. If the null hypothesis is $H_0: \beta_j = a_j$, then H_0 is rejected against $H_1: \beta_j \neq a_j$ at (say) the 5% significance level if, and only if, a_j is *not* in the 95% confidence interval.

| **EXAMPLE 4.8** | **Model of R&D Expenditures** |

Economists studying industrial organization are interested in the relationship between firm size—often measured by annual sales—and spending on research and development (R&D). Typically, a constant elasticity model is used. One might also be interested in the ceteris paribus effect of the profit margin—that is, profits as a percentage of sales—on R&D spending. Using the data in RDCHEM on 32 U.S. firms in the chemical industry, we estimate the following equation (with standard errors in parentheses below the coefficients):

$$\widehat{\log(rd)} = -4.38 + 1.084 \log(sales) + .0217 \, profmarg$$
$$\quad\quad (.47) \quad (.060) \quad\quad\quad (.0128)$$
$$n = 32, R^2 = .918.$$

The estimated elasticity of R&D spending with respect to firm sales is 1.084, so that, holding profit margin fixed, a 1% increase in sales is associated with a 1.084% increase in R&D spending. (Incidentally, R&D and sales are both measured in millions of dollars, but their units of measurement have no effect on the elasticity estimate.) We can construct a 95% confidence interval for the sales elasticity once we note that the estimated model has $n - k - 1 = 32 - 2 - 1 = 29$ degrees of freedom. From Table G.2, we find the 97.5^{th} percentile in a t_{29} distribution: $c = 2.045$. Thus, the 95% confidence interval for $\beta_{\log(sales)}$ is $1.084 \pm .060(2.045)$, or about $(.961, 1.21)$. That zero is well outside this interval is hardly surprising: we expect R&D spending to increase with firm size. More interesting is that unity is included in the 95% confidence interval for $\beta_{\log(sales)}$, which means that we cannot reject H_0: $\beta_{\log(sales)} = 1$ against H_1: $\beta_{\log(sales)} \neq 1$ at the 5% significance level. In other words, the estimated R&D-sales elasticity is not statistically different from 1 at the 5% level. (The estimate is not practically different from 1, either.)

The estimated coefficient on *profmarg* is also positive, and the 95% confidence interval for the population parameter, $\beta_{profmarg}$, is $.0217 \pm .0128(2.045)$, or about $(-.0045, .0479)$. In this case, zero is included in the 95% confidence interval, so we fail to reject H_0: $\beta_{profmarg} = 0$ against H_1: $\beta_{profmarg} \neq 0$ at the 5% level. Nevertheless, the t statistic is about 1.70, which gives a two-sided p-value of about .10, and so we would conclude that *profmarg* is statistically significant at the 10% level against the two-sided alternative, or at the 5% level against the one-sided alternative H_1: $\beta_{profmarg} > 0$. Plus, the economic size of the profit margin coefficient is not trivial: holding *sales* fixed, a one percentage point increase in *profmarg* is estimated to increase R&D spending by $100(.0217) \approx 2.2\%$. A complete analysis of this example goes beyond simply stating whether a particular value, zero in this case, is or is not in the 95% confidence interval.

You should remember that a confidence interval is only as good as the underlying assumptions used to construct it. If we have omitted important factors that are correlated with the explanatory variables, then the coefficient estimates are not reliable: OLS is biased. If heteroskedasticity is present—for instance, in the previous example, if the variance of $\log(rd)$ depends on any of the explanatory variables—then the standard error is not valid as an estimate of $\text{sd}(\hat{\beta}_j)$ (as we discussed in Section 3-4), and the confidence interval computed using these standard errors will not truly be a 95% CI. We have also used the normality assumption on the errors in obtaining these CIs, but, as we will see in Chapter 5, this is not as important for applications involving hundreds of observations.

4-4 Testing Hypotheses about a Single Linear Combination of the Parameters

The previous two sections have shown how to use classical hypothesis testing or confidence intervals to test hypotheses about a single β_j at a time. In applications, we must often test hypotheses involving more than one of the population parameters. In this section, we show how to test a single hypothesis involving more than one of the β_j. Section 4-5 shows how to test multiple hypotheses.

To illustrate the general approach, we will consider a simple model to compare the returns to education at junior colleges and four-year colleges; for simplicity, we refer to the latter as "universities." [Kane and Rouse (1995) provide a detailed analysis of the returns to two- and four-year colleges.] The population includes working people with a high school degree, and the model is

$$\log(wage) = \beta_0 + \beta_1 jc + \beta_2 univ + \beta_3 exper + u, \qquad [4.17]$$

where

$$jc = \text{number of years attending a two-year college.}$$
$$univ = \text{number of years at a four-year college.}$$
$$exper = \text{months in the workforce.}$$

Note that any combination of junior college and four-year college is allowed, including $jc = 0$ and $univ = 0$.

The hypothesis of interest is whether one year at a junior college is worth one year at a university: this is stated as

$$H_0: \beta_1 = \beta_2. \qquad [4.18]$$

Under H_0, another year at a junior college and another year at a university lead to the same ceteris paribus percentage increase in *wage*. For the most part, the alternative of interest is one-sided: a year at a junior college is worth less than a year at a university. This is stated as

$$H_1: \beta_1 < \beta_2. \qquad [4.19]$$

The hypotheses in (4.18) and (4.19) concern *two* parameters, β_1 and β_2, a situation we have not faced yet. We cannot simply use the individual t statistics for $\hat{\beta}_1$ and $\hat{\beta}_2$ to test H_0. However, conceptually, there is no difficulty in constructing a t statistic for testing (4.18). To do so, we rewrite the null and alternative as $H_0: \beta_1 - \beta_2 = 0$ and $H_1: \beta_1 - \beta_2 < 0$, respectively. The t statistic is based on whether the estimated difference $\hat{\beta}_1 - \hat{\beta}_2$ is sufficiently less than zero to warrant rejecting (4.18) in favor of (4.19). To account for the sampling error in our estimators, we standardize this difference by dividing by the standard error:

$$t = \frac{\hat{\beta}_1 - \hat{\beta}_2}{\text{se}(\hat{\beta}_1 - \hat{\beta}_2)}. \qquad [4.20]$$

Once we have the t statistic in (4.20), testing proceeds as before. We choose a significance level for the test and, based on the df, obtain a critical value. Because the alternative is of the form in (4.19), the rejection rule is of the form $t < -c$, where c is a positive value chosen from the appropriate t distribution. Or we compute the t statistic and then compute the p-value (see Section 4-2).

The only thing that makes testing the equality of two different parameters more difficult than testing about a single β_j is obtaining the standard error in the denominator of (4.20). Obtaining the numerator is trivial once we have performed the OLS regression. Using the data in TWOYEAR, which comes from Kane and Rouse (1995), we estimate equation (4.17):

$$\widehat{\log(wage)} = 1.472 + .0667\, jc + .0769\, univ + .0049\, exper$$
$$(.021)\ (.0068)\quad\ (.0023)\qquad\ (.0002) \qquad [4.21]$$
$$n = 6{,}763,\ R^2 = .222.$$

It is clear from (4.21) that jc and *univ* have both economically and statistically significant effects on wage. This is certainly of interest, but we are more concerned about testing whether the estimated *difference* in the coefficients is statistically significant. The difference is estimated as $\hat{\beta}_1 - \hat{\beta}_2 = -.0102$, so the return to a year at a junior college is about one percentage point less than a year at a university. Economically, this is not a trivial difference. The difference of $-.0102$ is the numerator of the t statistic in (4.20).

Unfortunately, the regression results in equation (4.21) do *not* contain enough information to obtain the standard error of $\hat{\beta}_1 - \hat{\beta}_2$. It might be tempting to claim that $\text{se}(\hat{\beta}_1 - \hat{\beta}_2) = \text{se}(\hat{\beta}_1) - \text{se}(\hat{\beta}_2)$, but this is not true. In fact, if we reversed the roles of $\hat{\beta}_1$ and $\hat{\beta}_2$, we would wind up with a negative standard error of the difference using the difference in standard errors. Standard errors must *always* be positive because they are estimates of standard deviations. Although the standard error of the difference $\hat{\beta}_1 - \hat{\beta}_2$ certainly depends on $\text{se}(\hat{\beta}_1)$ and $\text{se}(\hat{\beta}_2)$, it does so in a somewhat complicated way. To find $\text{se}(\hat{\beta}_1 - \hat{\beta}_2)$, we first obtain the variance of the difference. Using the results on variances in Appendix B, we have

$$\text{Var}(\hat{\beta}_1 - \hat{\beta}_2) = \text{Var}(\hat{\beta}_1) + \text{Var}(\hat{\beta}_2) - 2\,\text{Cov}(\hat{\beta}_1, \hat{\beta}_2). \qquad [4.22]$$

Observe carefully how the two variances are *added* together, and twice the covariance is then subtracted. The standard deviation of $\hat{\beta}_1 - \hat{\beta}_2$ is just the square root of (4.22), and, since $[se(\hat{\beta}_1)]^2$ is an unbiased estimator of $Var(\hat{\beta}_1)$, and similarly for $[se(\hat{\beta}_2)]^2$, we have

$$se(\hat{\beta}_1 - \hat{\beta}_2) = \{[se(\hat{\beta}_1)]^2 + [se(\hat{\beta}_2)]^2 - 2s_{12}\}^{1/2}, \qquad \text{[4.23]}$$

where s_{12} denotes an estimate of $Cov(\hat{\beta}_1, \hat{\beta}_2)$. We have not displayed a formula for $Cov(\hat{\beta}_1, \hat{\beta}_2)$. Some regression packages have features that allow one to obtain s_{12}, in which case one can compute the standard error in (4.23) and then the t statistic in (4.20). Appendix E shows how to use matrix algebra to obtain s_{12}.

Some of the more sophisticated econometrics programs include special commands that can be used for testing hypotheses about linear combinations. Here, we cover an approach that is simple to compute in virtually any statistical package. Rather than trying to compute $se(\hat{\beta}_1 - \hat{\beta}_2)$ from (4.23), it is much easier to estimate a different model that directly delivers the standard error of interest. Define a new parameter as the difference between β_1 and β_2: $\theta_1 = \beta_1 - \beta_2$. Then, we want to test

$$H_0: \theta_1 = 0 \text{ against } H_1: \theta_1 < 0. \qquad \text{[4.24]}$$

The t statistic in (4.20) in terms of $\hat{\theta}_1$ is just $t = \hat{\theta}_1/se(\hat{\theta}_1)$. The challenge is finding $se(\hat{\theta}_1)$.

We can do this by rewriting the model so that θ_1 appears directly on one of the independent variables. Because $\theta_1 = \beta_1 - \beta_2$, we can also write $\beta_1 = \theta_1 + \beta_2$. Plugging this into (4.17) and rearranging gives the equation

$$\begin{aligned} log(wage) &= \beta_0 + (\theta_1 + \beta_2)jc + \beta_2 univ + \beta_3 exper + u \\ &= \beta_0 + \theta_1 jc + \beta_2(jc + univ) + \beta_3 exper + u. \end{aligned} \qquad \text{[4.25]}$$

The key insight is that the parameter we are interested in testing hypotheses about, θ_1, now multiplies the variable *jc*. The intercept is still β_0, and *exper* still shows up as being multiplied by β_3. More importantly, there is a new variable multiplying β_2, namely $jc + univ$. Thus, if we want to directly estimate θ_1 and obtain the standard error of $\hat{\theta}_1$, then we must construct the new variable $jc + univ$ and include it in the regression model in place of *univ*. In this example, the new variable has a natural interpretation: it is *total* years of college, so define $totcoll = jc + univ$ and write (4.25) as

$$log(wage) = \beta_0 + \theta_1 jc + \beta_2 totcoll + \beta_3 exper + u. \qquad \text{[4.26]}$$

The parameter β_1 has disappeared from the model, while θ_1 appears explicitly. This model is really just a different way of writing the original model. The only reason we have defined this new model is that, when we estimate it, the coefficient on *jc* is $\hat{\theta}_1$, and, more importantly, $se(\hat{\theta}_1)$ is reported along with the estimate. The t statistic that we want is the one reported by any regression package on the variable *jc* (*not* the variable *totcoll*).

When we do this with the 6,763 observations used earlier, the result is

$$\widehat{log(wage)} = 1.472 - .0102 \, jc + .0769 \, totcoll + .0049 \, exper$$
$$\qquad\quad (.021) \quad (.0069) \qquad (.0023) \qquad\quad (.0002) \qquad \text{[4.27]}$$
$$n = 6{,}763, \, R^2 = .222.$$

The only number in this equation that we could not get from (4.21) is the standard error for the estimate $-.0102$, which is .0069. The t statistic for testing (4.18) is $-.0102/.0069 = -1.48$. Against the one-sided alternative (4.19), the p-value is about .070, so there is some, but not strong, evidence against (4.18).

The intercept and slope estimate on *exper*, along with their standard errors, are the same as in (4.21). This fact *must* be true, and it provides one way of checking whether the transformed equation has been properly estimated. The coefficient on the new variable, *totcoll*, is the same as the coefficient on *univ* in (4.21), and the standard error is also the same. We know that this must happen by comparing (4.17) and (4.25).

It is quite simple to compute a 95% confidence interval for $\theta_1 = \beta_1 - \beta_2$. Using the standard normal approximation, the CI is obtained as usual: $\hat{\theta}_1 \pm 1.96 \, se(\hat{\theta}_1)$, which in this case leads to $-.0102 \pm .0135$.

The strategy of rewriting the model so that it contains the parameter of interest works in all cases and is easy to implement. (See Computer Exercises C1 and C3 for other examples.)

4-5 Testing Multiple Linear Restrictions: The *F* Test

The t statistic associated with any OLS coefficient can be used to test whether the corresponding unknown parameter in the population is equal to any given constant (which is usually, but not always, zero). We have just shown how to test hypotheses about a single linear combination of the β_j by rearranging the equation and running a regression using transformed variables. But so far, we have only covered hypotheses involving a *single* restriction. Frequently, we wish to test *multiple* hypotheses about the underlying parameters $\beta_0, \beta_1, \ldots, \beta_k$. We begin with the leading case of testing whether a set of independent variables has no partial effect on a dependent variable.

4-5a Testing Exclusion Restrictions

We already know how to test whether a particular variable has no partial effect on the dependent variable: use the t statistic. Now, we want to test whether a *group* of variables has no effect on the dependent variable. More precisely, the null hypothesis is that a set of variables has no effect on y, once another set of variables has been controlled.

As an illustration of why testing significance of a group of variables is useful, we consider the following model that explains major league baseball players' salaries:

$$\log(salary) = \beta_0 + \beta_1 years + \beta_2 gamesyr + \beta_3 bavg + \beta_4 hrunsyr + \beta_5 rbisyr + u, \qquad [4.28]$$

where *salary* is the 1993 total salary, *years* is years in the league, *gamesyr* is average games played per year, *bavg* is career batting average (for example, *bavg* = 250), *hrunsyr* is home runs per year, and *rbisyr* is runs batted in per year. Suppose we want to test the null hypothesis that, once years in the league and games per year have been controlled for, the statistics measuring performance—*bavg*, *hrunsyr*, and *rbisyr*—have no effect on salary. Essentially, the null hypothesis states that productivity as measured by baseball statistics has no effect on salary.

In terms of the parameters of the model, the null hypothesis is stated as

$$H_0: \beta_3 = 0, \beta_4 = 0, \beta_5 = 0. \qquad [4.29]$$

The null (4.29) constitutes three **exclusion restrictions**: if (4.29) is true, then *bavg*, *hrunsyr*, and *rbisyr* have no effect on log(*salary*) after *years* and *gamesyr* have been controlled for and therefore should be excluded from the model. This is an example of a set of **multiple restrictions** because we are putting more than one restriction on the parameters in (4.28); we will see more general examples of multiple restrictions later. A test of multiple restrictions is called a **multiple hypotheses test** or a **joint hypotheses test**.

What should be the alternative to (4.29)? If what we have in mind is that "performance statistics matter, even after controlling for years in the league and games per year," then the appropriate alternative is simply

$$H_1: H_0 \text{ is not true.} \qquad [4.30]$$

The alternative (4.30) holds if at least one of β_3, β_4, or β_5 is different from zero. (Any or all could be different from zero.) The test we study here is constructed to detect any violation of H_0. It is also valid when the alternative is something like $H_1: \beta_3 > 0$, or $\beta_4 > 0$, or $\beta_5 > 0$, but it will not be the best possible test under such alternatives. We do not have the space or statistical background necessary to cover tests that have more power under multiple one-sided alternatives.

How should we proceed in testing (4.29) against (4.30)? It is tempting to test (4.29) by using the t statistics on the variables *bavg*, *hrunsyr*, and *rbisyr* to determine whether each variable is *individually* significant. This option is not appropriate. A particular t statistic tests a hypothesis that puts no restrictions on the other parameters. Besides, we would have three outcomes to contend with—one for each t statistic. What would constitute rejection of (4.29) at, say, the 5% level? Should all three or only one of the three t statistics be required to be significant at the 5% level? These are hard questions, and fortunately we do not have to answer them. Furthermore, using separate t statistics to test a multiple hypothesis like (4.29) can be very misleading. We need a way to test the exclusion restrictions *jointly*.

To illustrate these issues, we estimate equation (4.28) using the data in MLB1. This gives

$$
\begin{aligned}
\widehat{\log(salary)} &= 11.19 + .0689\ years + .0126\ gamesyr \\
&\qquad (0.29)\ (.0121) \qquad\quad (.0026) \\
&\qquad + .00098\ bavg + .0144\ hrunsyr + .0108\ rbisyr \\
&\qquad\quad (.00110) \qquad\ (.0161) \qquad\qquad (.0072) \\
&\ n = 353,\ SSR = 183.186,\ R^2 = .6278,
\end{aligned}
$$

[4.31]

where SSR is the sum of squared residuals. (We will use this later.) We have left several terms after the decimal in SSR and R-squared to facilitate future comparisons. Equation (4.31) reveals that, whereas *years* and *gamesyr* are statistically significant, none of the variables *bavg*, *hrunsyr*, and *rbisyr* has a statistically significant t statistic against a two-sided alternative, at the 5% significance level. (The t statistic on *rbisyr* is the closest to being significant; its two-sided p-value is .134.) Thus, based on the three t statistics, it appears that we cannot reject H_0.

This conclusion turns out to be wrong. To see this, we must derive a test of multiple restrictions whose distribution is known and tabulated. The sum of squared residuals now turns out to provide a very convenient basis for testing multiple hypotheses. We will also show how the R-squared can be used in the special case of testing for exclusion restrictions.

Knowing the sum of squared residuals in (4.31) tells us nothing about the truth of the hypothesis in (4.29). However, the factor that will tell us something is how much the SSR increases when we drop the variables *bavg*, *hrunsyr*, and *rbisyr* from the model. Remember that, because the OLS estimates are chosen to minimize the sum of squared residuals, the SSR *always* increases when variables are dropped from the model; this is an algebraic fact. The question is whether this increase is large enough, *relative* to the SSR in the model with all of the variables, to warrant rejecting the null hypothesis.

The model without the three variables in question is simply

$$
\log(salary) = \beta_0 + \beta_1 years + \beta_2 gamesyr + u. \tag{4.32}
$$

In the context of hypothesis testing, equation (4.32) is the **restricted model** for testing (4.29); model (4.28) is called the **unrestricted model**. The restricted model always has fewer parameters than the unrestricted model.

When we estimate the restricted model using the data in MLB1, we obtain

$$
\begin{aligned}
\widehat{\log(salary)} &= 11.22 + .0713\ years + .0202\ gamesyr \\
&\qquad (.11)\ (.0125) \qquad\quad (.0013) \\
&\ n = 353,\ SSR = 198.311,\ R^2 = .5971.
\end{aligned}
$$

[4.33]

As we surmised, the SSR from (4.33) is greater than the SSR from (4.31), and the R-squared from the restricted model is less than the R-squared from the unrestricted model. What we need to decide is whether the increase in the SSR in going from the unrestricted model to the restricted model (183.186 to 198.311) is large enough to warrant rejection of (4.29). As with all testing, the answer depends on the significance level of the test. But we cannot carry out the test at a chosen significance level until we have a statistic whose distribution is known, and can be tabulated, under H_0. Thus, we need a way to combine the information in the two SSRs to obtain a test statistic with a known distribution under H_0.

Because it is no more difficult, we might as well derive the test for the general case. Write the *unrestricted* model with k independent variables as

$$y = \beta_0 + \beta_1 x_1 + \ldots + \beta_k x_k + u; \qquad [4.34]$$

the number of parameters in the unrestricted model is $k + 1$. (Remember to add one for the intercept.) Suppose that we have q exclusion restrictions to test: that is, the null hypothesis states that q of the variables in (4.34) have zero coefficients. For notational simplicity, assume that it is the last q variables in the list of independent variables: $x_{k-q+1}, \ldots, x_k$. (The order of the variables, of course, is arbitrary and unimportant.) The null hypothesis is stated as

$$H_0: \beta_{k-q+1} = 0, \ldots, \beta_k = 0, \qquad [4.35]$$

which puts q exclusion restrictions on the model (4.34). The alternative to (4.35) is simply that it is false; this means that at least one of the parameters listed in (4.35) is different from zero. When we impose the restrictions under H_0, we are left with the restricted model:

$$y = \beta_0 + \beta_1 x_1 + \ldots + \beta_{k-q} x_{k-q} + u. \qquad [4.36]$$

In this subsection, we assume that both the unrestricted and restricted models contain an intercept, since that is the case most widely encountered in practice.

Now, for the test statistic itself. Earlier, we suggested that looking at the relative increase in the SSR when moving from the unrestricted to the restricted model should be informative for testing the hypothesis (4.35). The **F statistic** (or *F ratio*) is defined by

$$F \equiv \frac{(\text{SSR}_r - \text{SSR}_{ur})/q}{\text{SSR}_{ur}/(n - k - 1)}, \qquad [4.37]$$

EXPLORING FURTHER 4.4

Consider relating individual performance on a standardized test, *score*, to a variety of other variables. School factors include average class size, per-student expenditures, average teacher compensation, and total school enrollment. Other variables specific to the student are family income, mother's education, father's education, and number of siblings. The model is

$$\begin{aligned} score = \beta_0 &+ \beta_1 classize + \beta_2 expend \\ &+ \beta_3 tchcomp + \beta_4 enroll \\ &+ \beta_5 faminc + \beta_6 motheduc \\ &+ \beta_7 fatheduc + \beta_8 siblings + u. \end{aligned}$$

State the null hypothesis that student-specific variables have no effect on standardized test performance once school-related factors have been controlled for. What are k and q for this example? Write down the restricted version of the model.

where SSR_r is the sum of squared residuals from the restricted model and SSR_{ur} is the sum of squared residuals from the unrestricted model.

You should immediately notice that, since SSR_r can be no smaller than SSR_{ur}, the F statistic is *always* nonnegative (and almost always strictly positive). Thus, if you compute a negative F statistic, then something is wrong; the order of the SSRs in the numerator of F has usually been reversed. Also, the SSR in the denominator of F is the SSR from the *unrestricted* model. The easiest way to remember where the SSRs appear is to think of F as measuring the relative increase in SSR when moving from the unrestricted to the restricted model.

The difference in SSRs in the numerator of F is divided by q, which is the number of restrictions imposed in moving from the unrestricted to the restricted model (q independent variables are dropped). Therefore, we can write

$$q = \textbf{numerator degrees of freedom} = df_r - df_{ur}, \quad [4.38]$$

which also shows that q is the difference in degrees of freedom between the restricted and unrestricted models. (Recall that df = number of observations − number of estimated parameters.)

Since the restricted model has fewer parameters—and each model is estimated using the same n observations—df_r is always greater than df_{ur}.

The SSR in the denominator of F is divided by the degrees of freedom in the unrestricted model:

$$n - k - 1 = \textbf{denominator degrees of freedom} = df_{ur}. \qquad \text{[4.39]}$$

In fact, the denominator of F is just the unbiased estimator of $\sigma^2 = \text{Var}(u)$ in the unrestricted model.

In a particular application, computing the F statistic is easier than wading through the somewhat cumbersome notation used to describe the general case. We first obtain the degrees of freedom in the unrestricted model, df_{ur}. Then, we count how many variables are excluded in the restricted model; this is q. The SSRs are reported with every OLS regression, and so forming the F statistic is simple.

In the major league baseball salary regression, $n = 353$, and the full model (4.28) contains six parameters. Thus, $n - k - 1 = df_{ur} = 353 - 6 = 347$. The restricted model (4.32) contains three fewer independent variables than (4.28), and so $q = 3$. Thus, we have all of the ingredients to compute the F statistic; we hold off doing so until we know what to do with it.

To use the F statistic, we must know its sampling distribution under the null in order to choose critical values and rejection rules. It can be shown that, under H_0 (and assuming the CLM assumptions hold), F is distributed as an F random variable with $(q, n - k - 1)$ degrees of freedom. We write this as

$$F \sim F_{q,n-k-1}.$$

The distribution of $F_{q,n-k-1}$ is readily tabulated and available in statistical tables (see Table G.3) and, even more importantly, in statistical software.

We will not derive the F distribution because the mathematics is very involved. Basically, it can be shown that equation (4.37) is actually the ratio of two independent chi-square random variables, divided by their respective degrees of freedom. The numerator chi-square random variable has q degrees of freedom, and the chi-square in the denominator has $n - k - 1$ degrees of freedom. This is the definition of an F distributed random variable (see Appendix B).

It is pretty clear from the definition of F that we will reject H_0 in favor of H_1 when F is sufficiently "large." How large depends on our chosen significance level. Suppose that we have decided on a 5% level test. Let c be the 95th percentile in the $F_{q,n-k-1}$ distribution. This critical value depends on q (the numerator df) and $n - k - 1$ (the denominator df). It is important to keep the numerator and denominator degrees of freedom straight.

The 10%, 5%, and 1% critical values for the F distribution are given in Table G.3. The rejection rule is simple. Once c has been obtained, we reject H_0 in favor of H_1 at the chosen significance level if

$$F > c. \qquad \text{[4.40]}$$

With a 5% significance level, $q = 3$, and $n - k - 1 = 60$, the critical value is $c = 2.76$. We would reject H_0 at the 5% level if the computed value of the F statistic exceeds 2.76. The 5% critical value and rejection region are shown in Figure 4.7. For the same degrees of freedom, the 1% critical value is 4.13.

In most applications, the numerator degrees of freedom (q) will be notably smaller than the denominator degrees of freedom ($n - k - 1$). Applications where $n - k - 1$ is small are unlikely to be successful because the parameters in the unrestricted model will probably not be precisely estimated. When the denominator df reaches about 120, the F distribution is no longer sensitive to it. (This is entirely analogous to the t distribution being well approximated by the standard normal distribution as the df gets large.) Thus, there is an entry in the table for the denominator $df = \infty$, and this is what we use with large samples (because $n - k - 1$ is then large). A similar statement holds for a very large numerator df, but this rarely occurs in applications.

If H_0 is rejected, then we say that $x_{k-q+1}, \ldots, x_k$ are **jointly statistically significant** (or just *jointly significant*) at the appropriate significance level. This test alone does not allow us to say which of the variables has a partial effect on y; they may all affect y or maybe only one affects y. If

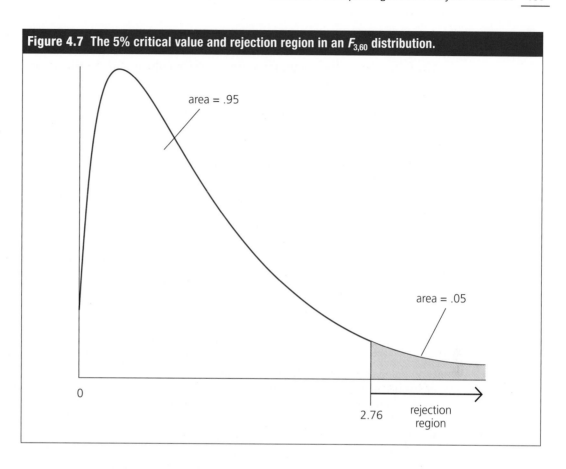

Figure 4.7 The 5% critical value and rejection region in an $F_{3,60}$ distribution.

area = .95

area = .05

0

2.76   rejection region

the null is not rejected, then the variables are **jointly insignificant**, which often justifies dropping them from the model.

For the major league baseball example with three numerator degrees of freedom and 347 denominator degrees of freedom, the 5% critical value is 2.60, and the 1% critical value is 3.78. We reject H_0 at the 1% level if F is above 3.78; we reject at the 5% level if F is above 2.60.

We are now in a position to test the hypothesis that we began this section with: after controlling for *years* and *gamesyr*, the variables *bavg*, *hrunsyr*, and *rbisyr* have no effect on players' salaries. In practice, it is easiest to first compute $(\text{SSR}_r - \text{SSR}_{ur})/\text{SSR}_{ur}$ and to multiply the result by $(n - k - 1)/q$; the reason the formula is stated as in (4.37) is that it makes it easier to keep the numerator and denominator degrees of freedom straight. Using the SSRs in (4.31) and (4.33), we have

$$F = \frac{(198.311 - 183.186)}{183.186} \cdot \frac{347}{3} \approx 9.55.$$

This number is well above the 1% critical value in the F distribution with 3 and 347 degrees of freedom, and so we soundly reject the hypothesis that *bavg*, *hrunsyr*, and *rbisyr* have no effect on salary.

The outcome of the joint test may seem surprising in light of the insignificant t statistics for the three variables. What is happening is that the two variables *hrunsyr* and *rbisyr* are highly correlated, and this multicollinearity makes it difficult to uncover the partial effect of each variable; this is reflected in the individual t statistics. The F statistic tests whether these variables (including *bavg*) are *jointly* significant, and multicollinearity between *hrunsyr* and *rbisyr* is much less relevant for testing this hypothesis. In Problem 16, you are asked to reestimate the model while dropping *rbisyr*, in which case *hrunsyr* becomes very significant. The same is true for *rbisyr* when *hrunsyr* is dropped from the model.

The *F* statistic is often useful for testing exclusion of a group of variables when the variables in the group are highly correlated. For example, suppose we want to test whether firm performance affects the salaries of chief executive officers. There are many ways to measure firm performance, and it probably would not be clear ahead of time which measures would be most important. Since measures of firm performance are likely to be highly correlated, hoping to find individually significant measures might be asking too much due to multicollinearity. But an *F* test can be used to determine whether, as a group, the firm performance variables affect salary.

4-5b Relationship between *F* and *t* Statistics

We have seen in this section how the *F* statistic can be used to test whether a group of variables should be included in a model. What happens if we apply the *F* statistic to the case of testing significance of a *single* independent variable? This case is certainly not ruled out by the previous development. For example, we can take the null to be $H_0: \beta_k = 0$ and $q = 1$ (to test the single exclusion restriction that x_k can be excluded from the model). From Section 4-2, we know that the *t* statistic on β_k can be used to test this hypothesis. The question, then, is: do we have two separate ways of testing hypotheses about a single coefficient? The answer is no. It can be shown that the *F* statistic for testing exclusion of a single variable is equal to the *square* of the corresponding *t* statistic. Since t_{n-k-1}^2 has an $F_{1,n-k-1}$ distribution, the two approaches lead to exactly the same outcome, provided that the alternative is two-sided. The *t* statistic is more flexible for testing a single hypothesis because it can be directly used to test against one-sided alternatives. Since *t* statistics are also easier to obtain than *F* statistics, there is really no reason to use an *F* statistic to test hypotheses about a single parameter.

We have already seen in the salary regressions for major league baseball players that two (or more) variables that each have insignificant *t* statistics can be jointly very significant. It is also possible that, in a group of several explanatory variables, one variable has a significant *t* statistic but the group of variables is jointly insignificant at the usual significance levels. What should we make of this kind of outcome? For concreteness, suppose that in a model with many explanatory variables we cannot reject the null hypothesis that $\beta_1, \beta_2, \beta_3, \beta_4,$ and β_5 are all equal to zero at the 5% level, yet the *t* statistic for $\hat{\beta}_1$ is significant at the 5% level. Logically, we cannot have $\beta_1 \neq 0$ but also have $\beta_1, \beta_2, \beta_3, \beta_4,$ and β_5 all equal to zero! But as a matter of testing, it is possible that we can group a bunch of insignificant variables with a significant variable and conclude that the entire set of variables is jointly insignificant. (Such possible conflicts between a *t* test and a joint *F* test give another example of why we should not "accept" null hypotheses; we should only fail to reject them.) The *F* statistic is intended to detect whether a set of coefficients is different from zero, but it is never the best test for determining whether a single coefficient is different from zero. The *t* test is best suited for testing a single hypothesis. (In statistical terms, an *F* statistic for joint restrictions including $\beta_1 = 0$ will have less power for detecting $\beta_1 \neq 0$ than the usual *t* statistic. See Section C.6 in Appendix C for a discussion of the power of a test.)

Unfortunately, the fact that we can sometimes hide a statistically significant variable along with some insignificant variables could lead to abuse if regression results are not carefully reported. For example, suppose that, in a study of the determinants of loan-acceptance rates at the city level, x_1 is the fraction of black households in the city. Suppose that the variables $x_2, x_3, x_4,$ and x_5 are the fractions of households headed by different age groups. In explaining loan rates, we would include measures of income, wealth, credit ratings, and so on. Suppose that age of household head has no effect on loan approval rates, once other variables are controlled for. Even if race has a marginally significant effect, it is possible that the race and age variables could be jointly insignificant. Someone wanting to conclude that race is not a factor could simply report something like "Race and age variables were added to the equation, but they were jointly insignificant at the 5% level."

Hopefully, peer review prevents these kinds of misleading conclusions, but you should be aware that such outcomes are possible.

Often, when a variable is very statistically significant and it is tested jointly with another set of variables, the set will be jointly significant. In such cases, there is no logical inconsistency in rejecting both null hypotheses.

4-5c The *R*-Squared Form of the *F* Statistic

For testing exclusion restrictions, it is often more convenient to have a form of the *F* statistic that can be computed using the *R*-squareds from the restricted and unrestricted models. One reason for this is that the *R*-squared is always between zero and one, whereas the SSRs can be very large depending on the unit of measurement of *y*, making the calculation based on the SSRs tedious. Using the fact that $SSR_r = SST(1 - R_r^2)$ and $SSR_{ur} = SST(1 - R_{ur}^2)$, we can substitute into (4.37) to obtain

$$F = \frac{(R_{ur}^2 - R_r^2)/q}{(1 - R_{ur}^2)/(n - k - 1)} = \frac{(R_{ur}^2 - R_r^2)/q}{(1 - R_{ur}^2)/df_{ur}} \qquad [4.41]$$

(note that the SST terms cancel everywhere). This is called the **R-squared form of the F statistic**. [At this point, you should be cautioned that although equation (4.41) is very convenient for testing exclusion restrictions, it cannot be applied for testing all linear restrictions. As we will see when we discuss testing general linear restrictions, the sum of squared residuals form of the *F* statistic is sometimes needed.]

Because the *R*-squared is reported with almost all regressions (whereas the SSR is not), it is easy to use the *R*-squareds from the unrestricted and restricted models to test for exclusion of some variables. Particular attention should be paid to the order of the *R*-squareds in the numerator: the *unrestricted* *R*-squared comes first [contrast this with the SSRs in (4.37)]. Because $R_{ur}^2 > R_r^2$, this shows again that *F* will always be positive.

In using the *R*-squared form of the test for excluding a set of variables, it is important to *not* square the *R*-squared before plugging it into formula (4.41); the squaring has already been done. All regressions report R^2, and these numbers are plugged directly into (4.41). For the baseball salary example, we can use (4.41) to obtain the *F* statistic:

$$F = \frac{(.6278 - .5971)}{(1 - .6278)} \cdot \frac{347}{3} \approx 9.54,$$

which is very close to what we obtained before. (The difference is due to rounding error.)

EXAMPLE 4.9   **Parents' Education in a Birth Weight Equation**

As another example of computing an *F* statistic, consider the following model to explain child birth weight in terms of various factors:

$$bwght = \beta_0 + \beta_1 cigs + \beta_2 parity + \beta_3 faminc$$
$$+ \beta_4 motheduc + \beta_5 fatheduc + u, \qquad [4.42]$$

where

$$bwght = \text{birth weight, in pounds.}$$
$$cigs = \text{average number of cigarettes the mother smoked per day during pregnancy.}$$
$$parity = \text{the birth order of this child.}$$
$$faminc = \text{annual family income.}$$
$$motheduc = \text{years of schooling for the mother.}$$
$$fatheduc = \text{years of schooling for the father.}$$

Let us test the null hypothesis that, after controlling for *cigs*, *parity*, and *faminc*, parents' education has no effect on birth weight. This is stated as $H_0: \beta_4 = 0, \beta_5 = 0$, and so there are $q = 2$ exclusion restrictions to be tested. There are $k + 1 = 6$ parameters in the unrestricted model (4.42); so the *df* in the unrestricted model is $n - 6$, where n is the sample size.

We will test this hypothesis using the data in BWGHT. This data set contains information on 1,388 births, but we must be careful in counting the observations used in testing the null hypothesis. It turns out that information on at least one of the variables *motheduc* and *fatheduc* is missing for 197 births in the sample; these observations cannot be included when estimating the unrestricted model. Thus, we really have $n = 1,191$ observations, and so there are $1,191 - 6 = 1,185$ *df* in the unrestricted model. We must be sure to use these *same* 1,191 observations when estimating the restricted model (not the full 1,388 observations that are available). Generally, when estimating the restricted model to compute an *F* test, we must use the same observations to estimate the unrestricted model; otherwise, the test is not valid. When there are no missing data, this will not be an issue.

The numerator *df* is 2, and the denominator *df* is 1,185; from Table G.3, the 5% critical value is $c = 3.0$. Rather than report the complete results, for brevity, we present only the *R*-squareds. The *R*-squared for the full model turns out to be $R_{ur}^2 = .0387$. When *motheduc* and *fatheduc* are dropped from the regression, the *R*-squared falls to $R_r^2 = .0364$. Thus, the *F* statistic is $F = [(.0387 - .0364)/(1 - .0387)](1,185/2) = 1.42$; since this is well below the 5% critical value, we fail to reject H_0. In other words, *motheduc* and *fatheduc* are jointly insignificant in the birth weight equation. Most statistical packages these days have built-in commands for testing multiple hypotheses after OLS estimation, and so one need not worry about making the mistake of running the two regressions on different data sets. Typically, the commands are applied after estimation of the unrestricted model, which means the smaller subset of data is used whenever there are missing values on some variables. Formulas for computing the *F* statistic using matrix algebra—see Appendix E—do not require estimation of the retricted model.

4-5d Computing *p*-Values for *F* Tests

For reporting the outcomes of *F* tests, *p*-values are especially useful. Since the *F* distribution depends on the numerator and denominator *df*, it is difficult to get a feel for how strong or weak the evidence is against the null hypothesis simply by looking at the value of the *F* statistic and one or two critical values.

In the *F* testing context, the *p*-value is defined as

$$p\text{-value} = P(\mathcal{F} > F), \qquad [4.43]$$

where, for emphasis, we let $\mathcal{F}$ denote an *F* random variable with $(q, n - k - 1)$ degrees of freedom, and *F* is the actual value of the test statistic. The *p*-value still has the same interpretation as it did for *t* statistics: it is the probability of observing a value of *F* at least as large as we did, *given* that the null hypothesis is true. A small *p*-value is evidence against H_0. For example, *p*-value = .016 means that the chance of observing a value of *F* as large as we did when the null hypothesis was true is only 1.6%; we usually reject H_0 in such cases. If the *p*-value = .314, then the chance of observing a value of the *F* statistic as large as we did under the null hypothesis is 31.4%. Most would find this to be pretty weak evidence against H_0.

> ### EXPLORING FURTHER 4.5
>
> The data in ATTEND were used to estimate the two equations
>
> $$\widehat{atndrte} = 47.13 + 13.37 \, priGPA$$
> $$\quad (2.87) \quad (1.09)$$
> $$n = 680, R^2 = .183$$
>
> and
>
> $$\widehat{atndrte} = 75.70 + 17.26 \, priGPA - 1.72 \, ACT$$
> $$\quad (3.88) \quad (1.08) \qquad\quad (?)$$
> $$n = 680, R^2 = .291,$$
>
> where, as always, standard errors are in parentheses; the standard error for *ACT* is missing in the second equation. What is the *t* statistic for the coefficient on *ACT*? (*Hint:* First compute the *F* statistic for significance of *ACT*.)

As with t testing, once the p-value has been computed, the F test can be carried out at any significance level. For example, if the p-value $= .024$, we reject H_0 at the 5% significance level but not at the 1% level.

The p-value for the F test in Example 4.9 is .238, and so the null hypothesis that $\beta_{motheduc}$ and $\beta_{fatheduc}$ are both zero is not rejected at even the 20% significance level.

Many econometrics packages have a built-in feature for testing multiple exclusion restrictions. These packages have several advantages over calculating the statistics by hand: we will less likely make a mistake, p-values are computed automatically, and the problem of missing data, as in Example 4.9, is handled without any additional work on our part.

4-5e The *F* Statistic for Overall Significance of a Regression

A special set of exclusion restrictions is routinely tested by most regression packages. These restrictions have the same interpretation, regardless of the model. In the model with k independent variables, we can write the null hypothesis as

$$H_0: x_1, x_2, \ldots, x_k \text{ do not help to explain } y.$$

This null hypothesis is, in a way, very pessimistic. It states that *none* of the explanatory variables has an effect on y. Stated in terms of the parameters, the null is that all slope parameters are zero:

$$H_0: \beta_1 = \beta_2 = \ldots = \beta_k = 0, \tag{4.44}$$

and the alternative is that at least one of the β_j is different from zero. Another useful way of stating the null is that $H_0: E(y|x_1, x_2, \ldots, x_k) = E(y)$, so that knowing the values of $x_1, x_2, \ldots, x_k$ does not affect the expected value of y.

There are k restrictions in (4.44), and when we impose them, we get the restricted model

$$y = \beta_0 + u; \tag{4.45}$$

all independent variables have been dropped from the equation. Now, the R-squared from estimating (4.45) is zero; none of the variation in y is being explained because there are no explanatory variables. Therefore, the F statistic for testing (4.44) can be written as

$$\frac{R^2/k}{(1 - R^2)/(n - k - 1)}, \tag{4.46}$$

where R^2 is just the usual R-squared from the regression of y on $x_1, x_2, \ldots, x_k$.

Most regression packages report the F statistic in (4.46) automatically, which makes it tempting to use this statistic to test general exclusion restrictions. You must avoid this temptation. The F statistic in (4.41) is used for general exclusion restrictions; it depends on the R-squareds from the restricted and unrestricted models. The special form of (4.46) is valid only for testing joint exclusion of *all* independent variables. This is sometimes called determining the **overall significance of the regression**.

If we fail to reject (4.44), then there is no evidence that any of the independent variables help to explain y. This usually means that we must look for other variables to explain y. For Example 4.9, the F statistic for testing (4.44) is about 9.55 with $k = 5$ and $n - k - 1 = 1{,}185$ *df*. The p-value is zero to four places after the decimal point, so that (4.44) is rejected very strongly. Thus, we conclude that the variables in the *bwght* equation *do* explain some variation in *bwght*. The amount explained is not large: only 3.87%. But the seemingly small R-squared results in a highly significant F statistic. That is why we must compute the F statistic to test for joint significance and not just look at the size of the R-squared.

Occasionally, the F statistic for the hypothesis that all independent variables are jointly insignificant is the focus of a study. Problem 10 asks you to use stock return data to test whether stock returns over a four-year horizon are predictable based on information known only at the beginning of the period. Under the *efficient markets hypothesis*, the returns should not be predictable; the null hypothesis is precisely (4.44).

4-5f Testing General Linear Restrictions

Testing exclusion restrictions is by far the most important application of F statistics. Sometimes, however, the restrictions implied by a theory are more complicated than just excluding some independent variables. It is still straightforward to use the F statistic for testing.

As an example, consider the following equation:

$$\log(price) = \beta_0 + \beta_1 \log(assess) + \beta_2 \log(lotsize) + \beta_3 \log(sqrft) + \beta_4 bdrms + u,$$ [4.47]

where

$price$ = house price.
$assess$ = the assessed housing value (before the house was sold).
$lotsize$ = size of the lot, in square feet.
$sqrft$ = square footage.
$bdrms$ = number of bedrooms.

Now, suppose we would like to test whether the assessed housing price is a rational valuation. If this is the case, then a 1% change in *assess* should be associated with a 1% change in *price*; that is, $\beta_1 = 1$. In addition, *lotsize*, *sqrft*, and *bdrms* should not help to explain log(*price*), once the assessed value has been controlled for. Together, these hypotheses can be stated as

$$H_0: \beta_1 = 1, \beta_2 = 0, \beta_3 = 0, \beta_4 = 0.$$ [4.48]

Four restrictions have to be tested; three are exclusion restrictions, but $\beta_1 = 1$ is not. How can we test this hypothesis using the F statistic?

As in the exclusion restriction case, we estimate the unrestricted model, (4.47) in this case, and then impose the restrictions in (4.48) to obtain the restricted model. It is the second step that can be a little tricky. But all we do is plug in the restrictions. If we write (4.47) as

$$y = \beta_0 + \beta_1 x_1 + \beta_2 x_2 + \beta_3 x_3 + \beta_4 x_4 + u,$$ [4.49]

then the restricted model is $y = \beta_0 + x_1 + u$. Now, to impose the restriction that the coefficient on x_1 is unity, we must estimate the following model:

$$y - x_1 = \beta_0 + u.$$ [4.50]

This is just a model with an intercept (β_0) but with a different dependent variable than in (4.49). The procedure for computing the F statistic is the same: estimate (4.50), obtain the SSR(SSR_r), and use this with the unrestricted SSR from (4.49) in the F statistic (4.37). We are testing $q = 4$ restrictions, and there are $n - 5$ *df* in the unrestricted model. The F statistic is simply $[(SSR_r - SSR_{ur})/SSR_{ur}][(n - 5)/4]$.

Before illustrating this test using a data set, we must emphasize one point: we cannot use the R-squared form of the F statistic for this example because the dependent variable in (4.50) is different from the one in (4.49). This means the total sum of squares from the two regressions will be different, and (4.41) is no longer equivalent to (4.37). As a general rule, the SSR form of the F statistic should be used if a different dependent variable is needed in running the restricted regression.

The estimated unrestricted model using the data in HPRICE1 is

$$\widehat{\log(price)} = .264 + 1.043 \log(assess) + .0074 \log(lotsize)$$
$$(.570) \quad (.151) \qquad\qquad (.0386)$$
$$- .1032 \log(sqrft) + .0338\ bdrms$$
$$(.1384) \qquad\qquad (.0221)$$
$$n = 88,\ SSR = 1.822,\ R^2 = .773.$$

If we use separate t statistics to test each hypothesis in (4.48), we fail to reject each one. But rationality of the assessment is a joint hypothesis, so we should test the restrictions jointly. The SSR from the restricted model turns out to be $SSR_r = 1.880$, and so the F statistic is $[(1.880 - 1.822)/1.822](83/4) = .661$. The 5% critical value in an F distribution with $(4,83)$ df is about 2.50, and so we fail to reject H_0. There is essentially no evidence against the hypothesis that the assessed values are rational.

4-6 Reporting Regression Results

We end this chapter by providing a few guidelines on how to report multiple regression results for relatively complicated empirical projects. This should help you to read published works in the applied social sciences, while also preparing you to write your own empirical papers. We will expand on this topic in the remainder of the text by reporting results from various examples, but many of the key points can be made now.

Naturally, the estimated OLS coefficients should always be reported. For the key variables in an analysis, you should *interpret* the estimated coefficients (which often requires knowing the units of measurement of the variables). For example, is an estimate an elasticity, or does it have some other interpretation that needs explanation? The economic or practical importance of the estimates of the key variables should be discussed.

The standard errors should always be included along with the estimated coefficients. Some authors prefer to report the t statistics rather than the standard errors (and sometimes just the absolute value of the t statistics). Although nothing is really wrong with this, there is some preference for reporting standard errors. First, it forces us to think carefully about the null hypothesis being tested; the null is not always that the population parameter is zero. Second, having standard errors makes it easier to compute confidence intervals.

The R-squared from the regression should always be included. We have seen that, in addition to providing a goodness-of-fit measure, it makes calculation of F statistics for exclusion restrictions simple. Reporting the sum of squared residuals and the standard error of the regression is sometimes a good idea, but it is not crucial. The number of observations used in estimating any equation should appear near the estimated equation.

If only a couple of models are being estimated, the results can be summarized in equation form, as we have done up to this point. However, in many papers, several equations are estimated with many different sets of independent variables. We may estimate the same equation for different groups of people, or even have equations explaining different dependent variables. In such cases, it is better to summarize the results in one or more tables. The dependent variable should be indicated clearly in the table, and the independent variables should be listed in the first column. Standard errors (or t statistics) can be put in parentheses below the estimates.

EXAMPLE 4.10   **Salary-Pension Tradeoff for Teachers**

Let *totcomp* denote average total annual compensation for a teacher, including salary and all fringe benefits (pension, health insurance, and so on). Extending the standard wage equation, total compensation should be a function of productivity and perhaps other characteristics. As is standard, we use logarithmic form:

$$\log(totcomp) = f(productivity\ characteristics, other\ factors),$$

where $f(\cdot)$ is some function (unspecified for now). Write

$$totcomp = salary + benefits = salary\left(1 + \frac{benefits}{salary}\right).$$

This equation shows that total compensation is the product of two terms: *salary* and $1 + b/s$, where b/s is shorthand for the "benefits to salary ratio." Taking the log of this equation gives $\log(totcomp) = \log(salary) + \log(1 + b/s)$. Now, for "small" b/s, $\log(1 + b/s) \approx b/s$; we will use this approximation. This leads to the econometric model

$$\log(salary) = \beta_0 + \beta_1(b/s) + other\,factors.$$

Testing the salary-benefits tradeoff then is the same as a test of $H_0: \beta_1 = -1$ against $H_1: \beta_1 \neq -1$.

We use the data in MEAP93 to test this hypothesis. These data are averaged at the school level, and we do not observe very many other factors that could affect total compensation. We will include controls for size of the school (*enroll*), staff per thousand students (*staff*), and measures such as the school dropout and graduation rates. The average b/s in the sample is about .205, and the largest value is .450.

The estimated equations are given in Table 4.1, where standard errors are given in parentheses below the coefficient estimates. The key variable is b/s, the benefits-salary ratio.

From the first column in Table 4.1, we see that, without controlling for any other factors, the OLS coefficient for b/s is $-.825$. The t statistic for testing the null hypothesis $H_0: \beta_1 = -1$ is $t = (-.825 + 1)/.200 = .875$, and so the simple regression fails to reject H_0. After adding controls for school size and staff size (which roughly captures the number of students taught by each teacher), the estimate of the b/s coefficient becomes $-.605$. Now, the test of $\beta_1 = -1$ gives a t statistic of about 2.39; thus, H_0 is rejected at the 5% level against a two-sided alternative. The variables $\log(enroll)$ and $\log(staff)$ are very statistically significant.

> **EXPLORING FURTHER 4.6**
>
> How does adding *droprate* and *gradrate* affect the estimate of the salary-benefits tradeoff? Are these variables jointly significant at the 5% level? What about the 10% level?

TABLE 4.1 Testing the Salary-Benefits Tradeoff

Independent Variables	Dependent Variable: log(*salary*)		
	(1)	(2)	(3)
b/s	−.825	−.605	−.589
	(.200)	(.165)	(.165)
log(*enroll*)	——	.0874	.0881
		(.0073)	(.0073)
log(*staff*)	——	−.222	−.218
		(.050)	(.050)
droprate	——	——	−.00028
			(.00161)
gradrate	——	——	.00097
			.00066)
intercept	10.523	10.884	10.738
	(0.042)	(0.252)	(0.258)
Observations	408	408	408
R-squared	.040	.353	.361

Summary

In this chapter, we have covered the very important topic of statistical inference, which allows us to infer something about the population model from a random sample. We summarize the main points:

1. Under the classical linear model assumptions MLR.1 through MLR.6, the OLS estimators are normally distributed.
2. Under the CLM assumptions, the t statistics have t distributions under the null hypothesis.
3. We use t statistics to test hypotheses about a single parameter against one- or two-sided alternatives, using one- or two-tailed tests, respectively. The most common null hypothesis is $H_0: \beta_j = 0$, but we sometimes want to test other values of β_j under H_0.
4. In classical hypothesis testing, we first choose a significance level, which, along with the df and alternative hypothesis, determines the critical value against which we compare the t statistic. It is more informative to compute the p-value for a t test—the smallest significance level for which the null hypothesis is rejected—so that the hypothesis can be tested at any significance level.
5. Under the CLM assumptions, confidence intervals can be constructed for each β_j. These CIs can be used to test any null hypothesis concerning β_j against a two-sided alternative.
6. Single hypothesis tests concerning more than one β_j can always be tested by rewriting the model to contain the parameter of interest. Then, a standard t statistic can be used.
7. The F statistic is used to test multiple exclusion restrictions, and there are two equivalent forms of the test. One is based on the SSRs from the restricted and unrestricted models. A more convenient form is based on the R-squareds from the two models.
8. When computing an F statistic, the numerator df is the number of restrictions being tested, while the denominator df is the degrees of freedom in the unrestricted model.
9. The alternative for F testing is two-sided. In the classical approach, we specify a significance level which, along with the numerator df and the denominator df, determines the critical value. The null hypothesis is rejected when the statistic, F, exceeds the critical value, c. Alternatively, we can compute a p-value to summarize the evidence against H_0.
10. General multiple linear restrictions can be tested using the sum of squared residuals form of the F statistic.
11. The F statistic for the overall significance of a regression tests the null hypothesis that *all* slope parameters are zero, with the intercept unrestricted. Under H_0, the explanatory variables have no effect on the expected value of y.
12. When data are missing on one or more explanatory variables, one must be careful when computing F statistics "by hand," that is, using either the sum of squared residuals or R-squareds from the two regressions. Whenever possible it is best to leave the calculations to statistical packages that have built-in commands, which work with or without missing data.

THE CLASSICAL LINEAR MODEL ASSUMPTIONS

Now is a good time to review the full set of classical linear model (CLM) assumptions for cross-sectional regression. Following each assumption is a comment about its role in multiple regression analysis.

Assumption MLR.1 (Linear in Parameters)

The model in the population can be written as

$$y = \beta_0 + \beta_1 x_1 + \beta_2 x_2 + \ldots + \beta_k x_k + u,$$

where $\beta_0, \beta_1, \ldots, \beta_k$ are the unknown parameters (constants) of interest and u is an unobserved random error or disturbance term.

Assumption MLR.1 describes the population relationship we hope to estimate, and explicitly sets out the β_j—the ceteris paribus population effects of the x_j on y—as the parameters of interest.

Assumption MLR.2 (Random Sampling)

We have a random sample of n observations, $\{(x_{i1}, x_{i2}, ..., x_{ik}, y_i): i = 1, ..., n\}$, following the population model in Assumption MLR.1.

This random sampling assumption means that we have data that can be used to estimate the β_j, and that the data have been chosen to be representative of the population described in Assumption MLR.1.

Assumption MLR.3 (No Perfect Collinearity)

In the sample (and therefore in the population), none of the independent variables is constant, and there are no exact *linear* relationships among the independent variables.

Once we have a sample of data, we need to know that we can use the data to compute the OLS estimates, the $\hat{\beta}_j$. This is the role of Assumption MLR.3: if we have sample variation in each independent variable and no exact linear relationships among the independent variables, we can compute the $\hat{\beta}_j$.

Assumption MLR.4 (Zero Conditional Mean)

The error u has an expected value of zero given any values of the explanatory variables. In other words, $E(u|x_1, x_2, ..., x_k) = 0$.

As we discussed in the text, assuming that the unobserved factors are, on average, unrelated to the explanatory variables is key to deriving the first statistical property of each OLS estimator: its unbiasedness for the corresponding population parameter. Of course, all of the previous assumptions are used to show unbiasedness.

Assumption MLR.5 (Homoskedasticity)

The error u has the same variance given any values of the explanatory variables. In other words,

$$\text{Var}(u|x_1, x_2, ..., x_k) = \sigma^2.$$

Compared with Assumption MLR.4, the homoskedasticity assumption is of secondary importance; in particular, Assumption MLR.5 has no bearing on the unbiasedness of the $\hat{\beta}_j$. Still, homoskedasticity has two important implications: (1) We can derive formulas for the sampling variances whose components are easy to characterize; (2) We can conclude, under the Gauss-Markov assumptions MLR.1 through MLR.5, that the OLS estimators have smallest variance among *all* linear, unbiased estimators.

Assumption MLR.6 (Normality)

The population error u is *independent* of the explanatory variables $x_1, x_2, ..., x_k$ and is normally distributed with zero mean and variance σ^2: $u \sim \text{Normal}(0, \sigma^2)$.

In this chapter, we added Assumption MLR.6 to obtain the exact sampling distributions of t statistics and F statistics, so that we can carry out exact hypotheses tests. In the next chapter, we will see that MLR.6 can be dropped if we have a reasonably large sample size. Assumption MLR.6 does imply a stronger efficiency property of OLS: the OLS estimators have smallest variance among *all* unbiased estimators; the comparison group is no longer restricted to estimators linear in the $\{y_i: i = 1, 2, ..., n\}$.

Key Terms

Alternative Hypothesis	*F* Statistic	Null Hypothesis
Classical Linear Model	Joint Hypotheses Test	Numerator Degrees of Freedom
Classical Linear Model (CLM)	Jointly Insignificant	One-Sided Alternative
Assumptions	Jointly Statistically Significant	One-Tailed Test
Confidence Interval (CI)	Minimum Variance Unbiased	Overall Significance of the Regression
Critical Value	Estimators	*p*-Value
Denominator Degrees of Freedom	Multiple Hypotheses Test	Practical Significance
Economic Significance	Multiple Restrictions	*R*-squared Form of the *F* Statistic
Exclusion Restrictions	Normality Assumption	Rejection Rule

Restricted Model	Statistically Significant	Two-Sided Alternative
Significance Level	t Ratio	Two-Tailed Test
Statistically Insignificant	t Statistic	Unrestricted Model

Problems

1 Which of the following can cause the usual OLS t statistics to be invalid (that is, not to have t distributions under H_0)?

(i)   Heteroskedasticity.

(ii)   A sample correlation coefficient of .95 between two independent variables that are in the model.

(iii)   Omitting an important explanatory variable.

2 Consider an equation to explain salaries of CEOs in terms of annual firm sales, return on equity (*roe*, in percentage form), and return on the firm's stock (*ros*, in percentage form):

$$\log(salary) = \beta_0 + \beta_1\log(sales) + \beta_2 roe + \beta_3 ros + u.$$

(i)   In terms of the model parameters, state the null hypothesis that, after controlling for *sales* and *roe*, *ros* has no effect on CEO salary. State the alternative that better stock market performance increases a CEO's salary.

(ii)   Using the data in CEOSAL1, the following equation was obtained by OLS:

$$\widehat{\log(salary)} = 4.32 + .280 \log(sales) + .0174\, roe + .00024\, ros$$
$$\phantom{\widehat{\log(salary)} = } (.32)\ \ (.035)\ \ (.0041)\ \ (.00054)$$
$$n = 209, R^2 = .283.$$

By what percentage is *salary* predicted to increase if *ros* increases by 50 points? Does *ros* have a practically large effect on *salary*?

(iii)   Test the null hypothesis that *ros* has no effect on *salary* against the alternative that *ros* has a positive effect. Carry out the test at the 10% significance level.

(iv)   Would you include *ros* in a final model explaining CEO compensation in terms of firm performance? Explain.

3 The variable *rdintens* is expenditures on research and development (R&D) as a percentage of sales. Sales are measured in millions of dollars. The variable *profmarg* is profits as a percentage of sales.

Using the data in RDCHEM for 32 firms in the chemical industry, the following equation is estimated:

$$\widehat{rdintens} = .472 + .321 \log(sales) + .050\, profmarg$$
$$\phantom{\widehat{rdintens} = } (1.369)\ \ (.216)\ \ (.046)$$
$$n = 32, R^2 = .099.$$

(i)   Interpret the coefficient on log(*sales*). In particular, if *sales* increases by 10%, what is the estimated percentage point change in *rdintens*? Is this an economically large effect?

(ii)   Test the hypothesis that R&D intensity does not change with *sales* against the alternative that it does increase with sales. Do the test at the 5% and 10% levels.

(iii)   Interpret the coefficient on *profmarg*. Is it economically large?

(iv)   Does *profmarg* have a statistically significant effect on *rdintens*?

4 Are rent rates influenced by the student population in a college town? Let *rent* be the average monthly rent paid on rental units in a college town in the United States. Let *pop* denote the total city population, *avginc* the average city income, and *pctstu* the student population as a percentage of the total population. One model to test for a relationship is

$$\log(rent) = \beta_0 + \beta_1\log(pop) + \beta_2\log(avginc) + \beta_3 pctstu + u.$$

(i) State the null hypothesis that size of the student body relative to the population has no ceteris paribus effect on monthly rents. State the alternative that there is an effect.

(ii) What signs do you expect for β_1 and β_2?

(iii) The equation estimated using 1990 data from RENTAL for 64 college towns is

$$\widehat{\log(rent)} = .043 + .066 \log(pop) + .507 \log(avginc) + .0056 \, pctstu$$
$$(.844) \quad (.039) \qquad\qquad (.081) \qquad\qquad (.0017)$$
$$n = 64, R^2 = .458.$$

What is wrong with the statement: "A 10% increase in population is associated with about a 6.6% increase in rent"?

(iv) Test the hypothesis stated in part (i) at the 1% level.

5 Consider the estimated equation from Example 4.3, which can be used to study the effects of skipping class on college GPA:

$$\widehat{colGPA} = 1.39 + .412 \, hsGPA + .015 \, ACT - .083 \, skipped$$
$$(.33) \quad (.094) \qquad (.011) \qquad (.026)$$
$$n = 141, R^2 = .234.$$

(i) Using the standard normal approximation, find the 95% confidence interval for β_{hsGPA}.

(ii) Can you reject the hypothesis $H_0: \beta_{hsGPA} = .4$ against the two-sided alternative at the 5% level?

(iii) Can you reject the hypothesis $H_0: \beta_{hsGPA} = 1$ against the two-sided alternative at the 5% level?

6 In Section 4-5, we used as an example testing the rationality of assessments of housing prices. There, we used a log-log model in *price* and *assess* [see equation (4.47)]. Here, we use a level-level formulation.

(i) In the simple regression model

$$price = \beta_0 + \beta_1 assess + u,$$

the assessment is rational if $\beta_1 = 1$ and $\beta_0 = 0$. The estimated equation is

$$\widehat{price} = -14.47 + .976 \, assess$$
$$(16.27) \quad (.049)$$
$$n = 88, SSR = 165,644.51, R^2 = .820.$$

First, test the hypothesis that $H_0: \beta_0 = 0$ against the two-sided alternative. Then, test $H_0: \beta_1 = 1$ against the two-sided alternative. What do you conclude?

(ii) To test the joint hypothesis that $\beta_0 = 0$ and $\beta_0 = 1$, we need the SSR in the restricted model. This amounts to computing $\sum_{i=1}^{n}(price_i - assess_i)^2$, where $n = 88$, since the residuals in the restricted model are just $price_i - assess_i$. (No estimation is needed for the restricted model because both parameters are specified under H_0.) This turns out to yield SSR = 209,448.99. Carry out the F test for the joint hypothesis.

(iii) Now, test $H_0: \beta_2 = 0, \beta_3 = 0$, and $\beta_4 = 0$ in the model

$$price = \beta_0 + \beta_1 assess + \beta_2 lotsize + \beta_3 sqrft + \beta_4 bdrms + u.$$

The R-squared from estimating this model using the same 88 houses is .829.

(iv) If the variance of *price* changes with *assess*, *lotsize*, *sqrft*, or *bdrms*, what can you say about the F test from part (iii)?

7 In Example 4.7, we used data on nonunionized manufacturing firms to estimate the relationship between the scrap rate and other firm characteristics. We now look at this example more closely and use all available firms.

(i) The population model estimated in Example 4.7 can be written as

$$\log(scrap) = \beta_0 + \beta_1 hrsemp + \beta_2 \log(sales) + \beta_3 \log(employ) + u.$$

Using the 43 observations available for 1987, the estimated equation is

$$\widehat{\log(scrap)} = 11.74 - .042 \ hrsemp - .951 \log(sales) + .992 \log(employ)$$
$$\quad\quad (4.57) \ (.019) \quad\quad\quad (.370) \quad\quad\quad\quad (.360)$$
$$n = 43, R^2 = .310.$$

Compare this equation to that estimated using only the 29 nonunionized firms in the sample.

(ii) Show that the population model can also be written as

$$\log(scrap) = \beta_0 + \beta_1 hrsemp + \beta_2 \log(sales/employ) + \theta_3 \log(employ) + u,$$

where $\theta_3 = \beta_2 + \beta_3$. [*Hint:* Recall that $\log(x_2/x_3) = \log(x_2) - \log(x_3)$.] Interpret the hypothesis $H_0: \theta_3 = 0$.

(iii) When the equation from part (ii) is estimated, we obtain

$$\widehat{\log(scrap)} = 11.74 - .042 \ hrsemp - .951 \ \log(sales/employ) + .041 \ \log(employ)$$
$$\quad\quad (4.57) \ (.019) \quad\quad\quad (.370) \quad\quad\quad\quad (.205)$$
$$n = 43, R^2 = .310.$$

Controlling for worker training and for the sales-to-employee ratio, do bigger firms have larger statistically significant scrap rates?

(iv) Test the hypothesis that a 1% increase in *sales/employ* is associated with a 1% drop in the scrap rate.

8 Consider the multiple regression model with three independent variables, under the classical linear model assumptions MLR.1 through MLR.6:

$$y = \beta_0 + \beta_1 x_1 + \beta_2 x_2 + \beta_3 x_3 + u.$$

You would like to test the null hypothesis $H_0: \beta_1 - 3\beta_2 = 1$.

(i) Let $\hat{\beta}_1$ and $\hat{\beta}_2$ denote the OLS estimators of β_1 and β_2. Find $\text{Var}(\hat{\beta}_1 - 3\hat{\beta}_2)$ in terms of the variances of $\hat{\beta}_1$ and $\hat{\beta}_2$ and the covariance between them. What is the standard error of $\hat{\beta}_1 - 3\hat{\beta}_2$?

(ii) Write the t statistic for testing $H_0: \beta_1 - 3\beta_2 = 1$.

(iii) Define $\theta_1 = \beta_1 - 3\beta_2$ and $\hat{\theta}_1 = \hat{\beta}_1 - 3\hat{\beta}_2$. Write a regression equation involving $\beta_0, \theta_1, \beta_2$, and β_3 that allows you to directly obtain $\hat{\theta}_1$ and its standard error.

9 In Problem 3 in Chapter 3, we estimated the equation

$$\widehat{sleep} = 3{,}638.25 - .148 \ totwrk - 11.13 \ educ + 2.20 \ age$$
$$\quad\quad (112.28) \ (.017) \quad\quad (5.88) \quad\quad (1.45)$$
$$n = 706, R^2 = .113,$$

where we now report standard errors along with the estimates.

(i) Is either *educ* or *age* individually significant at the 5% level against a two-sided alternative? Show your work.

(ii) Dropping *educ* and *age* from the equation gives

$$\widehat{sleep} = 3{,}586.38 - .151 \ totwrk$$
$$\quad\quad (38.91) \ (.017)$$
$$n = 706, R^2 = .103.$$

Are *educ* and *age* jointly significant in the original equation at the 5% level? Justify your answer.

(iii) Does including *educ* and *age* in the model greatly affect the estimated tradeoff between sleeping and working?

(iv) Suppose that the sleep equation contains heteroskedasticity. What does this mean about the tests computed in parts (i) and (ii)?

10 Regression analysis can be used to test whether the market efficiently uses information in valuing stocks. For concreteness, let *return* be the total return from holding a firm's stock over the four-year period from the end of 1990 to the end of 1994. The *efficient markets hypothesis* says that these returns should not be systematically related to information known in 1990. If firm characteristics known at the beginning of the period help to predict stock returns, then we could use this information in choosing stocks.

For 1990, let *dkr* be a firm's debt to capital ratio, let *eps* denote the earnings per share, let *netinc* denote net income, and let *salary* denote total compensation for the CEO.

(i) Using the data in RETURN, the following equation was estimated:

$$\widehat{return} = -14.37 + .321 \; dkr + .043 \; eps - .0051 \; nentinc + .0035 \; salary$$
$$(6.89) \; (.201) \qquad (.078) \qquad (.0047) \qquad (.0022)$$
$$n = 142, R^2 = .0395.$$

Test whether the explanatory variables are jointly significant at the 5% level. Is any explanatory variable individually significant?

(ii) Now, reestimate the model using the log form for *netinc* and *salary*:

$$\widehat{return} = -36.30 + .327 \; dkr + .069 \; eps - 4.74 \; \log(netinc) + 7.24 \; \log(salary)$$
$$(39.37) \; (.203) \qquad (.080) \qquad (3.39) \qquad (6.31)$$
$$n = 142, R^2 = .0330.$$

Do any of your conclusions from part (i) change?

(iii) In this sample, some firms have zero debt and others have negative earnings. Should we try to use log(*dkr*) or log(*eps*) in the model to see if these improve the fit? Explain.

(iv) Overall, is the evidence for predictability of stock returns strong or weak?

11 The following table was created using the data in CEOSAL2, where standard errors are in parentheses below the coefficients:

Independent Variables	Dependent Variable: log(*salary*)		
	(1)	(2)	(3)
log(*sales*)	.224	.158	.188
	(.027)	(.040)	(.040)
log(*mktval*)	———	.112	.100
		(.050)	(.049)
Profmarg	———	−.0023	−.0022
		(.0022)	(.0021)
Ceoten	———	———	.0171
			(.0055)
comten	———	———	−.0092
			(.0033)
intercept	4.94	4.62	4.57
	(0.20)	(0.25)	(0.25)
Observations	177	177	177
R-squared	.281	.304	.353

The variable *mktval* is market value of the firm, *profmarg* is profit as a percentage of sales, *ceoten* is years as CEO with the current company, and *comten* is total years with the company.

(i) Comment on the effect of *profmarg* on CEO salary.

(ii) Does market value have a significant effect? Explain.

(iii) Interpret the coefficients on *ceoten* and *comten*. Are these explanatory variables statistically significant?

(iv) What do you make of the fact that longer tenure with the company, holding the other factors fixed, is associated with a lower salary?

12 The following analysis was obtained using data in MEAP93, which contains school-level pass rates (as a percent) on a tenth-grade math test.

(i) The variable *expend* is expenditures per student, in dollars, and *math*10 is the pass rate on the exam. The following simple regression relates *math*10 to *lexpend* = log(*expend*):

$$\widehat{math10} = -69.34 + 11.16 \ lexpend$$
$$(25.53) \quad (3.17)$$
$$n = 408, R^2 = .0297.$$

Interpret the coefficient on *lexpend*. In particular, if *expend* increases by 10%, what is the estimated percentage point change in *math*10? What do you make of the large negative intercept estimate? (The minimum value of *lexpend* is 8.11 and its average value is 8.37.)

(ii) Does the small R-squared in part (i) imply that spending is correlated with other factors affecting *math*10? Explain. Would you expect the R-squared to be much higher if expenditures were randomly assigned to schools—that is, independent of other school and student characteristics—rather than having the school districts determine spending?

(iii) When log of enrollment and the percent of students eligible for the federal free lunch program are included, the estimated equation becomes

$$\widehat{math10} = -23.14 + 7.75 \ lexpend - 1.26 \ lenroll - .324 \ lnchprg$$
$$(24.99) \quad (3.04) \qquad (0.58) \qquad (0.36)$$
$$n = 408, R^2 = .1893.$$

Comment on what happens to the coefficient on *lexpend*. Is the spending coefficient still statistically different from zero?

(iv) What do you make of the R-squared in part (iii)? What are some other factors that could be used to explain *math*10 (at the school level)?

13 The data in MEAPSINGLE were used to estimate the following equations relating school-level performance on a fourth-grade math test to socioeconomic characteristics of students attending school. The variable *free*, measured at the school level, is the percentage of students eligible for the federal free lunch program. The variable *medinc* is median income in the ZIP code, and *pctsgle* is percent of students not living with two parents (also measured at the ZIP code level). See also Computer Exercise C11 in Chapter 3.

$$\widehat{math4} = 96.77 - .833 \ pctsgle$$
$$(1.60) \ (.071)$$
$$n = 299, R^2 = .380$$

$$\widehat{math4} = 93.00 - .275 \ pctsgle - .402 \ free$$
$$(1.63) \ (.117) \qquad (.070)$$
$$n = 299, R^2 = .459$$

$$\widehat{math4} = 24.49 - .274 \ pctsgle - .422 \ free - .752 \ lmedinc + 9.01 \ lexppp$$
$$(59.24) \ (.161) \qquad (.071) \qquad (5.358) \qquad (4.04)$$
$$n = 299, R^2 = .472$$

$$\widehat{math4} = 17.52 - .259 \ pctsgle - .420 \ free + 8.80 \ lexppp$$
$$(32.25) \ (.117) \qquad (.070) \qquad (3.76)$$
$$n = 299, R^2 = .472.$$

(i) Interpret the coefficient on the variable *pctsgle* in the first equation. Comment on what happens when *free* is added as an explanatory variable.

(ii) Does expenditure per pupil, entered in logarithmic form, have a statistically significant effect on performance? How big is the estimated effect?

(iii) If you had to choose among the four equations as your best estimate of the effect of *pctsgle* and obtain a 95% confidence interval of $\beta_{pctsgle}$, which would you choose? Why?

Computer Exercises

C1 The following model can be used to study whether campaign expenditures affect election outcomes:

$$voteA = \beta_0 + \beta_1 \log(expendA) + \beta_2 \log(expendB) + \beta_3 prtystrA + u,$$

where *voteA* is the percentage of the vote received by Candidate A, *expendA* and *expendB* are campaign expenditures by Candidates A and B, and *prtystrA* is a measure of party strength for Candidate A (the percentage of the most recent presidential vote that went to A's party).

(i) What is the interpretation of β_1?

(ii) In terms of the parameters, state the null hypothesis that a 1% increase in A's expenditures is offset by a 1% increase in B's expenditures.

(iii) Estimate the given model using the data in VOTE1 and report the results in usual form. Do A's expenditures affect the outcome? What about B's expenditures? Can you use these results to test the hypothesis in part (ii)?

(iv) Estimate a model that directly gives the *t* statistic for testing the hypothesis in part (ii). What do you conclude? (Use a two-sided alternative.)

C2 Use the data in LAWSCH85 for this exercise.

(i) Using the same model as in Problem 4 in Chapter 3, state and test the null hypothesis that the rank of law schools has no ceteris paribus effect on median starting salary.

(ii) Are features of the incoming class of students—namely, *LSAT* and *GPA*—individually or jointly significant for explaining *salary*? (Be sure to account for missing data on *LSAT* and *GPA*.)

(iii) Test whether the size of the entering class (*clsize*) or the size of the faculty (*faculty*) needs to be added to this equation; carry out a single test. (Be careful to account for missing data on *clsize* and *faculty*.)

(iv) What factors might influence the rank of the law school that are not included in the salary regression?

C3 Refer to Computer Exercise C2 in Chapter 3. Now, use the log of the housing price as the dependent variable:

$$\log(price) = \beta_0 + \beta_1 sqrft + \beta_2 bdrms + u.$$

(i) You are interested in estimating and obtaining a confidence interval for the percentage change in *price* when a 150-square-foot bedroom is added to a house. In decimal form, this is $\theta_1 = 150\beta_1 + \beta_2$. Use the data in HPRICE1 to estimate θ_1.

(ii) Write β_2 in terms of θ_1 and β_1 and plug this into the log(*price*) equation.

(iii) Use part (ii) to obtain a standard error for $\hat{\theta}_2$ and use this standard error to construct a 95% confidence interval.

C4 In Example 4.9, the restricted version of the model can be estimated using all 1,388 observations in the sample. Compute the *R*-squared from the regression of *bwght* on *cigs*, *parity*, and *faminc* using all observations. Compare this to the *R*-squared reported for the restricted model in Example 4.9.

C5 Use the data in MLB1 for this exercise.

(i) Use the model estimated in equation (4.31) and drop the variable *rbisyr*. What happens to the statistical significance of *hrunsyr*? What about the size of the coefficient on *hrunsyr*?

(ii)   Add the variables *runsyr* (runs per year), *fldperc* (fielding percentage), and *sbasesyr* (stolen bases per year) to the model from part (i). Which of these factors are individually significant?

(iii)   In the model from part (ii), test the joint significance of *bavg*, *fldperc*, and *sbasesyr*.

C6 Use the data in WAGE2 for this exercise.

(i)   Consider the standard wage equation

$$\log(wage) = \beta_0 + \beta_1 educ + \beta_2 exper + \beta_3 tenure + u.$$

State the null hypothesis that another year of general workforce experience has the same effect on log(*wage*) as another year of tenure with the current employer.

(ii)   Test the null hypothesis in part (i) against a two-sided alternative, at the 5% significance level, by constructing a 95% confidence interval. What do you conclude?

C7 Refer to the example used in Section 4-4. You will use the data set TWOYEAR.

(i)   The variable *phsrank* is the person's high school percentile. (A higher number is better. For example, 90 means you are ranked better than 90 percent of your graduating class.) Find the smallest, largest, and average *phsrank* in the sample.

(ii)   Add *phsrank* to equation (4.26) and report the OLS estimates in the usual form. Is *phsrank* statistically significant? How much is 10 percentage points of high school rank worth in terms of wage?

(iii)   Does adding *phsrank* to (4.26) substantively change the conclusions on the returns to two- and four-year colleges? Explain.

(iv)   The data set contains a variable called *id*. Explain why if you add *id* to equation (4.17) or (4.26) you expect it to be statistically insignificant. What is the two-sided *p*-value?

C8 The data set 401KSUBS contains information on net financial wealth (*nettfa*), age of the survey respondent (*age*), annual family income (*inc*), family size (*fsize*), and participation in certain pension plans for people in the United States. The wealth and income variables are both recorded in thousands of dollars. For this question, use only the data for single-person households (so *fsize* = 1).

(i)   How many single-person households are there in the data set?

(ii)   Use OLS to estimate the model

$$nettfa = \beta_0 + \beta_1 inc + \beta_2 age + u,$$

and report the results using the usual format. Be sure to use only the single-person households in the sample. Interpret the slope coefficients. Are there any surprises in the slope estimates?

(iii)   Does the intercept from the regression in part (ii) have an interesting meaning? Explain.

(iv)   Find the *p*-value for the test $H_0: \beta_2 = 1$ against $H_1: \beta_2 < 1$. Do you reject H_0 at the 1% significance level?

(v)   If you do a simple regression of *nettfa* on *inc*, is the estimated coefficient on *inc* much different from the estimate in part (ii)? Why or why not?

C9 Use the data in DISCRIM to answer this question. (See also Computer Exercise C8 in Chapter 3.)

(i)   Use OLS to estimate the model

$$\log(psoda) = \beta_0 + \beta_1 prpblck + \beta_2 \log(income) + \beta_3 prppov + u,$$

and report the results in the usual form. Is $\hat{\beta}_1$ statistically different from zero at the 5% level against a two-sided alternative? What about at the 1% level?

(ii)   What is the correlation between log(*income*) and *prppov*? Is each variable statistically significant in any case? Report the two-sided *p*-values.

(iii)   To the regression in part (i), add the variable log(*hseval*). Interpret its coefficient and report the two-sided *p*-value for $H_0: \beta_{\log(hseval)} = 0$.

(iv) In the regression in part (iii), what happens to the individual statistical significance of log(*income*) and *prppov*? Are these variables jointly significant? (Compute a *p*-value.) What do you make of your answers?

(v) Given the results of the previous regressions, which one would you report as most reliable in determining whether the racial makeup of a zip code influences local fast-food prices?

C10 Use the data in ELEM94_95 to answer this question. The findings can be compared with those in Table 4.1. The dependent variable *lavgsal* is the log of average teacher salary and *bs* is the ratio of average benefits to average salary (by school).

(i) Run the simple regression of *lavgsal* on *bs*. Is the estimated slope statistically different from zero? Is it statistically different from -1?

(ii) Add the variables *lenrol* and *lstaff* to the regression from part (i). What happens to the coefficient on *bs*? How does the situation compare with that in Table 4.1?

(iii) How come the standard error on the *bs* coefficient is smaller in part (ii) than in part (i)? (*Hint:* What happens to the error variance versus multicollinearity when *lenrol* and *lstaff* are added?)

(iv) How come the coefficient on *lstaff* is negative? Is it large in magnitude?

(v) Now add the variable *lunch* to the regression. Holding other factors fixed, are teachers being compensated for teaching students from disadvantaged backgrounds? Explain.

(vi) Overall, is the pattern of results that you find with ELEM94_95 consistent with the pattern in Table 4.1?

C11 Use the data in HTV to answer this question. See also Computer Exercise C10 in Chapter 3.

(i) Estimate the regression model

$$educ = \beta_0 + \beta_1 motheduc + \beta_2 fatheduc + \beta_3 abil + \beta_4 abil^2 + u$$

by OLS and report the results in the usual form. Test the null hypothesis that *educ* is linearly related to *abil* against the alternative that the relationship is quadratic.

(ii) Using the equation in part (i), test $H_0: \beta_1 = \beta_2$ against a two-sided alternative. What is the *p*-value of the test?

(iii) Add the two college tuition variables to the regression from part (i) and determine whether they are jointly statistically significant.

(iv) What is the correlation between *tuit17* and *tuit18*? Explain why using the average of the tuition over the two years might be preferred to adding each separately. What happens when you do use the average?

(v) Do the findings for the average tuition variable in part (iv) make sense when interpreted causally? What might be going on?

C12 Use the data in ECONMATH to answer the following questions.

(i) Estimate a model explaining *colgpa* to *hsgpa*, *actmth*, and *acteng*. Report the results in the usual form. Are all explanatory variables statistically significant?

(ii) Consider an increase in *hsgpa* of one standard deviation, about .343. By how much does $\widehat{colgpa}$ increase, holding *actmth* and *acteng* fixed. About how many standard deviations would the *actmth* have to increase to change $\widehat{colgpa}$ by the same amount as a one standard deviation in *hsgpa*? Comment.

(iii) Test the null hypothesis that *actmth* and *acteng* have the same effect (in the population) against a two-sided alternative. Report the *p*-value and describe your conclusions.

(iv) Suppose the college admissions officer wants you to use the data on the variables in part (i) to create an equation that explains at least 50 percent of the variation in *colgpa*. What would you tell the officer?

CHAPTER 5

Multiple Regression Analysis: OLS Asymptotics

In Chapters 3 and 4, we covered what are called *finite sample*, *small sample*, or *exact* properties of the OLS estimators in the population model

$$y = \beta_0 + \beta_1 x_1 + \beta_2 x_2 + \ldots + \beta_k x_k + u. \qquad [5.1]$$

For example, the unbiasedness of OLS (derived in Chapter 3) under the first four Gauss-Markov assumptions is a finite sample property because it holds for *any* sample size n (subject to the mild restriction that n must be at least as large as the total number of parameters in the regression model, $k + 1$). Similarly, the fact that OLS is the best linear unbiased estimator under the full set of Gauss-Markov assumptions (MLR.1 through MLR.5) is a finite sample property.

In Chapter 4, we added the classical linear model Assumption MLR.6, which states that the error term u is normally distributed and independent of the explanatory variables. This allowed us to derive the *exact* sampling distributions of the OLS estimators (conditional on the explanatory variables in the sample). In particular, Theorem 4.1 showed that the OLS estimators have normal sampling distributions, which led directly to the t and F distributions for t and F statistics. If the error is not normally distributed, the distribution of a t statistic is not exactly t, and an F statistic does not have an exact F distribution for any sample size.

In addition to finite sample properties, it is important to know the **asymptotic properties** or **large sample properties** of estimators and test statistics. These properties are not defined for a particular sample size; rather, they are defined as the sample size grows without bound. Fortunately, under the assumptions we have made, OLS has satisfactory large sample properties. One practically important finding is that even without the normality assumption (Assumption MLR.6), t and F statistics have *approximately t and F* distributions, at least in large sample sizes. We discuss this in more detail in Section 5-2, after we cover the consistency of OLS in Section 5-1.

Because the material in this chapter is more difficult to understand, and because one can conduct empirical work without a deep understanding of its contents, this chapter may be skipped. However, we will necessarily refer to large sample properties of OLS when we study discrete response variables in Chapter 7, relax the homoskedasticity assumption in Chapter 8, and delve into estimation with time series data in Part 2. Furthermore, virtually all advanced econometric methods derive their justification using large-sample analysis, so readers who will continue into Part 3 should be familiar with the contents of this chapter.

5-1 Consistency

Unbiasedness of estimators, although important, cannot always be obtained. For example, as we discussed in Chapter 3, the standard error of the regression, $\hat{\sigma}$, is not an unbiased estimator for σ, the standard deviation of the error u in a multiple regression model. Although the OLS estimators are unbiased under MLR.1 through MLR.4, in Chapter 11 we will find that there are time series regressions where the OLS estimators are not unbiased. Further, in Part 3 of the text, we encounter several other estimators that are biased yet useful.

Although not all useful estimators are unbiased, virtually all economists agree that **consistency** is a minimal requirement for an estimator. The Nobel Prize–winning econometrician Clive W. J. Granger once remarked, "If you can't get it right as n goes to infinity, you shouldn't be in this business." The implication is that, if your estimator of a particular population parameter is not consistent, then you are wasting your time.

There are a few different ways to describe consistency. Formal definitions and results are given in Appendix C; here, we focus on an intuitive understanding. For concreteness, let $\hat{\beta}_j$ be the OLS estimator of β_j for some j. For each n, $\hat{\beta}_j$ has a probability distribution (representing its possible values in different random samples of size n). Because $\hat{\beta}_j$ is unbiased under Assumptions MLR.1 through MLR.4, this distribution has mean value β_j. If this estimator is consistent, then the distribution of $\hat{\beta}_j$ becomes more and more tightly distributed around β_j as the sample size grows. As n tends to infinity, the distribution of $\hat{\beta}_j$ collapses to the single point β_j. In effect, this means that we can make our estimator arbitrarily close to β_j if we can collect as much data as we want. This convergence is illustrated in Figure 5.1.

Naturally, for any application, we have a fixed sample size, which is a major reason an asymptotic property such as consistency can be difficult to grasp. Consistency involves a thought experiment about what would happen as the sample size gets large (while, at the same time, we obtain numerous random samples for each sample size). If obtaining more and more data does not generally get us closer to the parameter value of interest, then we are using a poor estimation procedure.

Conveniently, the same set of assumptions implies both unbiasedness and consistency of OLS. We summarize with a theorem.

THEOREM 5.1	**CONSISTENCY OF OLS**
	Under Assumptions MLR.1 through MLR.4, the OLS estimator $\hat{\beta}_j$ is consistent for β_j, for all $j = 0, 1, \ldots, k$.

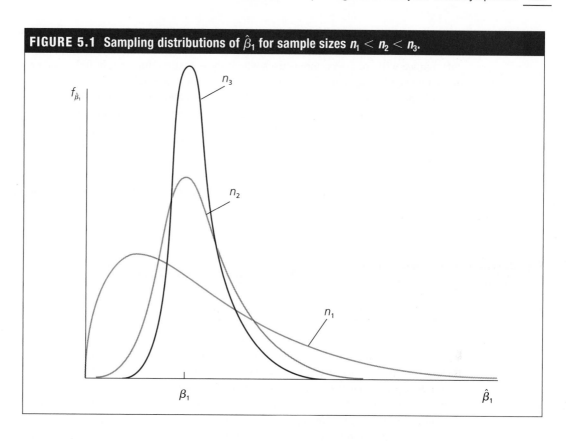

FIGURE 5.1 Sampling distributions of $\hat{\beta}_1$ for sample sizes $n_1 < n_2 < n_3$.

A general proof of this result is most easily developed using the matrix algebra methods described in Appendices D and E. But we can prove Theorem 5.1 without difficulty in the case of the simple regression model. We focus on the slope estimator, $\hat{\beta}_1$.

The proof starts out the same as the proof of unbiasedness: we write down the formula for $\hat{\beta}_1$, and then plug in $y_i = \beta_0 + \beta_1 x_{i1} + u_i$:

$$\hat{\beta}_1 = \left(\sum_{i=1}^{n}(x_{i1} - \bar{x}_1)y_i\right)\bigg/\left(\sum_{i=1}^{n}(x_{i1} - \bar{x}_1)^2\right)$$

$$= \beta_1 + \left(n^{-1}\sum_{i=1}^{n}(x_{i1} - \bar{x}_1)u_i\right)\bigg/\left(n^{-1}\sum_{i=1}^{n}(x_{i1} - \bar{x}_1)^2\right), \qquad [5.2]$$

where dividing both the numerator and denominator by n does not change the expression but allows us to directly apply the law of large numbers. When we apply the law of large numbers to the averages in the second part of equation (5.2), we conclude that the numerator and denominator converge in probability to the population quantities, $\text{Cov}(x_1, u)$ and $\text{Var}(x_1)$, respectively. Provided that $\text{Var}(x_1) \neq 0$—which is assumed in MLR.3—we can use the properties of *probability limits* (see Appendix C) to get

$$\text{plim } \hat{\beta}_1 = \beta_1 + \text{Cov}(x_1, u)/\text{Var}(x_1)$$

$$= \beta_1 \text{ because } \text{Cov}(x_1, u) = 0. \qquad [5.3]$$

We have used the fact, discussed in Chapters 2 and 3, that $\text{E}(u|x_1) = 0$ (Assumption MLR.4) implies that x_1 and u are uncorrelated (have zero covariance).

As a technical matter, to ensure that the probability limits exist, we should assume that $\text{Var}(x_1) < \infty$ and $\text{Var}(u) < \infty$ (which means that their probability distributions are not too spread out), but we will not worry about cases where these assumptions might fail. Further, we could—and, in an advanced treatment of econometrics, we would—explicitly relax Assumption MLR.3 to rule out only perfect collinearity in the population. As stated, Assumption MLR.3 also disallows perfect collinearity among the regressors in the sample we have at hand. Technically, for the thought experiment we can show consistency with no perfect collinearity in the population, allowing for the unlucky possibility that we draw a data set that does exhibit perfect collinearity. From a practical perspective the distinction is unimportant, as we cannot compute the OLS estimates for our sample if MLR.3 fails.

The previous arguments, and equation (5.3) in particular, show that OLS is consistent in the simple regression case if we assume only zero correlation. This is also true in the general case. We now state this as an assumption.

Assumption MLR.4'   Zero Mean and Zero Correlation

$E(u) = 0$ and $\text{Cov}(x_j, u) = 0$, for $j = 1, 2, ..., k$.

Assumption MLR.4' is weaker than Assumption MLR.4 in the sense that the latter implies the former. One way to characterize the zero conditional mean assumption, $E(u|x_1, ..., x_k) = 0$, is that *any* function of the explanatory variables is uncorrelated with u. Assumption MLR.4' requires only that each x_j is uncorrelated with u (and that u has a zero mean in the population). In Chapter 2, we actually motivated the OLS estimator for simple regression using Assumption MLR.4', and the first order conditions for OLS in the multiple regression case, given in equation (3.13), are simply the sample analogs of the population zero correlation assumptions (and zero mean assumption). Therefore, in some ways, Assumption MLR.4' is more natural an assumption because it leads directly to the OLS estimates. Further, when we think about violations of Assumption MLR.4, we usually think in terms of $\text{Cov}(x_j, u) \neq 0$ for some j. So how come we have used Assumption MLR.4 until now? There are two reasons, both of which we have touched on earlier. First, OLS turns out to be biased (but consistent) under Assumption MLR.4' if $E(u|x_1, ..., x_k)$ depends on any of the x_j. Because we have previously focused on finite sample, or exact, sampling properties of the OLS estimators, we have needed the stronger zero conditional mean assumption.

Second, and probably more important, is that the zero conditional mean assumption means that we have properly modeled the population regression function (PRF). That is, under Assumption MLR.4 we can write

$$E(y|x_1, ..., x_k) = \beta_0 + \beta_1 x_1 + ... + \beta_k x_k,$$

and so we can obtain partial effects of the explanatory variables on the average or expected value of y. If we instead only assume Assumption MLR.4', $\beta_0 + \beta_1 x_1 + ... + \beta_k x_k$ need not represent the PRF, and we face the possibility that some nonlinear functions of the x_j, such as x_j^2, could be correlated with the error u. A situation like this means that we have neglected nonlinearities in the model that could help us better explain y; if we knew that, we would usually include such nonlinear functions. In other words, most of the time we hope to get a good estimate of the PRF, and so the zero conditional mean assumption is natural. Nevertheless, the weaker zero correlation assumption turns out to be useful in interpreting OLS estimation of a linear model as providing the best linear approximation to the PRF. It is also used in more advanced settings, such as in Chapter 15, where we have no interest in modeling a PRF. For further discussion of this somewhat subtle point, see Wooldridge (2010, Chapter 4).

5-1a Deriving the Inconsistency in OLS

Just as failure of $E(u|x_1, \ldots, x_k) = 0$ causes bias in the OLS estimators, correlation between u and *any* of $x_1, x_2, \ldots, x_k$ generally causes *all* of the OLS estimators to be inconsistent. This simple but important observation is often summarized as: *if the error is correlated with any of the independent variables, then OLS is biased and inconsistent*. This is very unfortunate because it means that any bias persists as the sample size grows.

In the simple regression case, we can obtain the inconsistency from the first part of equation (5.3), which holds whether or not u and x_1 are uncorrelated. The **inconsistency** in $\hat{\beta}_1$ (sometimes loosely called the **asymptotic bias**) is

$$\text{plim } \hat{\beta}_1 - \beta_1 = \text{Cov}(x_1, u)/\text{Var}(x_1). \qquad [5.4]$$

Because $\text{Var}(x_1) > 0$, the inconsistency in $\hat{\beta}_1$ is positive if x_1 and u are positively correlated, and the inconsistency is negative if x_1 and u are negatively correlated. If the covariance between x_1 and u is small relative to the variance in x_1, the inconsistency can be negligible; unfortunately, we cannot even estimate how big the covariance is because u is unobserved.

We can use (5.4) to derive the asymptotic analog of the omitted variable bias (see Table 3.2 in Chapter 3). Suppose the true model,

$$y = \beta_0 + \beta_1 x_1 + \beta_2 x_2 + v,$$

satisfies the first four Gauss-Markov assumptions. Then v has a zero mean and is uncorrelated with x_1 and x_2. If $\hat{\beta}_0$, $\hat{\beta}_1$, and $\hat{\beta}_2$ denote the OLS estimators from the regression of y on x_1 and x_2, then Theorem 5.1 implies that these estimators are consistent. If we omit x_2 from the regression and do the simple regression of y on x_1, then $u = \beta_2 x_2 + v$. Let $\tilde{\beta}_1$ denote the simple regression slope estimator. Then

$$\text{plim } \tilde{\beta}_1 = \beta_1 + \beta_2 \delta_1, \qquad [5.5]$$

where

$$\delta_1 = \text{Cov}(x_1, x_2)/\text{Var}(x_1). \qquad [5.6]$$

Thus, for practical purposes, we can view the inconsistency as being the same as the bias. The difference is that the inconsistency is expressed in terms of the population variance of x_1 and the population covariance between x_1 and x_2, while the bias is based on their sample counterparts (because we condition on the values of x_1 and x_2 in the sample).

If x_1 and x_2 are uncorrelated (in the population), then $\delta_1 = 0$, and $\tilde{\beta}_1$ is a consistent estimator of β_1 (although not necessarily unbiased). If x_2 has a positive partial effect on y, so that $\beta_2 > 0$, and x_1 and x_2 are positively correlated, so that $\delta_1 > 0$, then the inconsistency in $\tilde{\beta}_1$ is positive, and so on. We can obtain the direction of the inconsistency or asymptotic bias from Table 3.2. If the covariance between x_1 and x_2 is small relative to the variance of x_1, the inconsistency can be small.

EXAMPLE 5.1   **Housing Prices and Distance from an Incinerator**

Let y denote the price of a house (*price*), let x_1 denote the distance from the house to a new trash incinerator (*distance*), and let x_2 denote the "quality" of the house (*quality*). The variable *quality* is left vague so that it can include things like size of the house and lot, number of bedrooms and bathrooms, and intangibles such as attractiveness of the neighborhood. If the incinerator depresses house prices, then β_1 should be positive: everything else being equal, a house that is farther away from the incinerator is worth more. By definition, β_2 is positive since higher quality houses sell for more, other factors being equal. If the incinerator was built farther away, on average, from better homes, then *distance* and *quality* are positively correlated, and so $\delta_1 > 0$. A simple regression of *price* on *distance* [or log(*price*) on log(*distance*)] will tend to overestimate the effect of the incinerator: $\beta_1 + \beta_2 \delta_1 > \beta_1$.

EXPLORING FURTHER 5.1

Suppose that the model

$score = \beta_0 + \beta_1 skipped + \beta_2 priGPA + u$

satisfies the first four Gauss-Markov assumptions, where *score* is score on a final exam, *skipped* is number of classes skipped, and *priGPA* is GPA prior to the current semester. If $\tilde{\beta}_1$ is from the simple regression of *score* on *skipped*, what is the direction of the asymptotic bias in $\tilde{\beta}_1$?

An important point about inconsistency in OLS estimators is that, by definition, the problem does not go away by adding more observations to the sample. If anything, the problem gets worse with more data: the OLS estimator gets closer and closer to $\beta_1 + \beta_2\delta_1$ as the sample size grows.

Deriving the sign and magnitude of the inconsistency in the general k regressor case is harder, just as deriving the bias is more difficult. We need to remember that if we have the model in equation (5.1) where, say, x_1 is correlated with u but the other independent variables are uncorrelated with u, *all* of the OLS estimators are generally inconsistent. For example, in the $k = 2$ case,

$$y = \beta_0 + \beta_1 x_1 + \beta_2 x_2 + u, \qquad [5.4]$$

suppose that x_2 and u are uncorrelated but x_1 and u are correlated. Then the OLS estimators $\hat{\beta}_1$ and $\hat{\beta}_2$ will generally both be inconsistent. (The intercept will also be inconsistent.) The inconsistency in $\hat{\beta}_2$ arises when x_1 and x_2 are correlated, as is usually the case. If x_1 and x_2 are uncorrelated, then any correlation between x_1 and u does *not* result in the inconsistency of $\hat{\beta}_2$: plim $\hat{\beta}_2 = \beta_2$. Further, the inconsistency in $\hat{\beta}_1$ is the same as in (5.4). The same statement holds in the general case: if x_1 is correlated with u, but x_1 and u are uncorrelated with the other independent variables, then only $\hat{\beta}_1$ is inconsistent, and the inconsistency is given by (5.4). The general case is very similar to the omitted variable case in Section 3A.4 of Appendix 3A.

5-2 Asymptotic Normality and Large Sample Inference

Consistency of an estimator is an important property, but it alone does not allow us to perform statistical inference. Simply knowing that the estimator is getting closer to the population value as the sample size grows does not allow us to test hypotheses about the parameters. For testing, we need the sampling distribution of the OLS estimators. Under the classical linear model assumptions MLR.1 through MLR.6, Theorem 4.1 shows that the sampling distributions are normal. This result is the basis for deriving the t and F distributions that we use so often in applied econometrics.

The exact normality of the OLS estimators hinges crucially on the normality of the distribution of the error, u, in the population. If the errors $u_1, u_2, \ldots, u_n$ are random draws from some distribution other than the normal, the $\hat{\beta}_j$ will not be normally distributed, which means that the t statistics will not have t distributions and the F statistics will not have F distributions. This is a potentially serious problem because our inference hinges on being able to obtain critical values or p-values from the t or F distributions.

Recall that Assumption MLR.6 is equivalent to saying that the distribution of y given $x_1, x_2, \ldots, x_k$ is normal. Because y is observed and u is not, in a particular application, it is much easier to think about whether the distribution of y is likely to be normal. In fact, we have already seen a few examples where y definitely cannot have a conditional normal distribution. A normally distributed random variable is symmetrically distributed about its mean, it can take on any positive or negative value, and more than 95% of the area under the distribution is within two standard deviations.

FIGURE 5.2 Histogram of *prate* using the data in 401K.

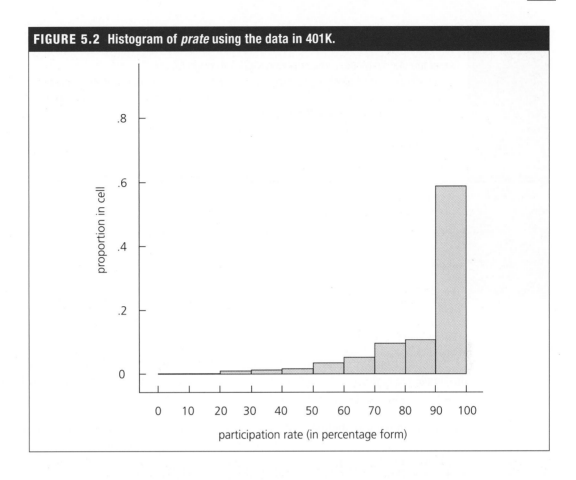

In Example 3.5, we estimated a model explaining the number of arrests of young men during a particular year (*narr86*). In the population, most men are not arrested during the year, and the vast majority are arrested one time at the most. (In the sample of 2,725 men in the data set CRIME1, fewer than 8% were arrested more than once during 1986.) Because *narr86* takes on only two values for 92% of the sample, it cannot be close to being normally distributed in the population.

In Example 4.6, we estimated a model explaining participation percentages (*prate*) in 401(k) pension plans. The frequency distribution (also called a *histogram*) in Figure 5.2 shows that the distribution of *prate* is heavily skewed to the right, rather than being normally distributed. In fact, over 40% of the observations on *prate* are at the value 100, indicating 100% participation. This violates the normality assumption even conditional on the explanatory variables.

We know that normality plays no role in the unbiasedness of OLS, nor does it affect the conclusion that OLS is the best linear unbiased estimator under the Gauss-Markov assumptions. But exact inference based on *t* and *F* statistics requires MLR.6. Does this mean that, in our prior analysis of *prate* in Example 4.6, we must abandon the *t* statistics for determining which variables are statistically significant? Fortunately, the answer to this question is *no*. Even though the y_i are not from a normal distribution, we can use the central limit theorem from Appendix C to conclude that the OLS estimators satisfy **asymptotic normality**, which means they are approximately normally distributed in large enough sample sizes.

THEOREM 5.2	**ASYMPTOTIC NORMALITY OF OLS**

Under the Gauss-Markov Assumptions MLR.1 through MLR.5,

(i) $\sqrt{n}(\hat{\beta}_j - \beta_j) \overset{a}{\sim} \text{Normal}(0, \sigma^2/a_j^2)$, where $\sigma^2/a_j^2 > 0$ is the **asymptotic variance** of $\sqrt{n}(\hat{\beta}_j - \beta_j)$; for the slope coefficients, $a_j^2 = \text{plim}(n^{-1}\sum_{i=1}^{n} \hat{r}_{ij}^2)$, where the $\hat{r}_{ij}$ are the residuals from regressing x_j on the other independent variables. We say that $\hat{\beta}_j$ is *asymptotically normally distributed* (see Appendix C);

(ii) $\hat{\sigma}^2$ is a consistent estimator of $\sigma^2 = \text{Var}(u)$;

(iii) For each j,

$$(\hat{\beta}_j - \beta_j)/\text{sd}(\hat{\beta}_j) \overset{a}{\sim} \text{Normal}(0,1)$$

and

$$(\hat{\beta}_j - \beta_j)/\text{se}(\hat{\beta}_j) \overset{a}{\sim} \text{Normal}(0,1), \qquad [5.7]$$

where $\text{se}(\hat{\beta}_j)$ is the usual OLS standard error.

The proof of asymptotic normality is somewhat complicated and is sketched in the appendix for the simple regression case. Part (ii) follows from the law of large numbers, and part (iii) follows from parts (i) and (ii) and the asymptotic properties discussed in Appendix C.

Theorem 5.2 is useful because the normality Assumption MLR.6 has been dropped; the only restriction on the distribution of the error is that it has finite variance, something we will always assume. We have also assumed zero conditional mean (MLR.4) and homoskedasticity of u (MLR.5).

In trying to understand the meaning of Theorem 5.2, it is important to keep separate the notions of the population distribution of the error term, u, and the sampling distributions of the $\hat{\beta}_j$ as the sample size grows. A common mistake is to think that something is happening to the distribution of u—namely, that it is getting "closer" to normal—as the sample size grows. But remember that the population distribution is immutable and has nothing to do with the sample size. For example, we previously discussed *narr*86, the number of times a young man is arrested during the year 1986. The nature of this variable—it takes on small, nonnegative integer values—is fixed in the population. Whether we sample 10 men or 1,000 men from this population obviously has no effect on the population distribution.

What Theorem 5.2 says is that, regardless of the population distribution of u, the OLS estimators, when properly standardized, have approximate standard normal distributions. This approximation comes about by the central limit theorem because the OLS estimators involve—in a complicated way—the use of sample averages. Effectively, the sequence of distributions of averages of the underlying errors is approaching normality for virtually any population distribution.

Notice how the standardized $\hat{\beta}_j$ has an asymptotic standard normal distribution whether we divide the difference $\hat{\beta}_j - \beta_j$ by $\text{sd}(\hat{\beta}_j)$ (which we do not observe because it depends on σ) or by $\text{se}(\hat{\beta}_j)$ (which we can compute from our data because it depends on $\hat{\sigma}$). In other words, from an asymptotic point of view it does not matter that we have to replace σ with $\hat{\sigma}$. Of course, replacing σ with $\hat{\sigma}$ affects the exact distribution of the standardized $\hat{\beta}_j$. We just saw in Chapter 4 that under the classical linear model assumptions, $(\hat{\beta}_j - \beta_j)/\text{sd}(\hat{\beta}_j)$ has an exact Normal(0,1) distribution and $(\hat{\beta}_j - \beta_j)/\text{sd}(\hat{\beta}_j)$ has an exact t_{n-k-1} distribution.

How should we use the result in equation (5.7)? It may seem one consequence is that, if we are going to appeal to large-sample analysis, we should now use the standard normal distribution for inference rather than the t distribution. But from a practical perspective it is just as legitimate to write

$$(\hat{\beta}_j - \beta_j)/\text{se}(\hat{\beta}_j) \overset{a}{\sim} t_{n-k-1} = t_{df}, \tag{5.8}$$

because t_{df} approaches the Normal(0,1), distribution as df gets large. Because we know under the CLM assumptions the t_{n-k-1} distribution holds exactly, it makes sense to treat $(\hat{\beta}_j - \beta_j)/\text{se}(\hat{\beta}_j)$ as a t_{n-k-1} random variable generally, even when MLR.6 does not hold.

Equation (5.8) tells us that t testing and the construction of confidence intervals are carried out *exactly* as under the classical linear model assumptions. This means that our analysis of dependent variables like *prate* and *narr86* does not have to change at all if the Gauss-Markov assumptions hold: in both cases, we have at least 1,500 observations, which is certainly enough to justify the approximation of the central limit theorem.

If the sample size is not very large, then the t distribution can be a poor approximation to the distribution of the t statistics when u is not normally distributed. Unfortunately, there are no general prescriptions on how big the sample size must be before the approximation is good enough. Some econometricians think that $n = 30$ is satisfactory, but this cannot be sufficient for all possible distributions of u. Depending on the distribution of u, more observations may be necessary before the central limit theorem delivers a useful approximation. Further, the quality of the approximation depends not just on n, but on the df, $n - k - 1$: With more independent variables in the model, a larger sample size is usually needed to use the t approximation. Methods for inference with small degrees of freedom and nonnormal errors are outside the scope of this text. We will simply use the t statistics as we always have without worrying about the normality assumption.

It is very important to see that Theorem 5.2 *does* require the homoskedasticity assumption (along with the zero conditional mean assumption). If $\text{Var}(y|\mathbf{x})$ is not constant, the usual t statistics and confidence intervals are invalid no matter how large the sample size is; the central limit theorem does not bail us out when it comes to heteroskedasticity. For this reason, we devote all of Chapter 8 to discussing what can be done in the presence of heteroskedasticity.

One conclusion of Theorem 5.2 is that $\hat{\sigma}^2$ is a consistent estimator of σ^2; we already know from Theorem 3.3 that $\hat{\sigma}^2$ is unbiased for σ^2 under the Gauss-Markov assumptions. The consistency implies that $\hat{\sigma}$ is a consistent estimator of σ, which is important in establishing the asymptotic normality result in equation (5.7).

Remember that $\hat{\sigma}$ appears in the standard error for each $\hat{\beta}_j$. In fact, the estimated variance of $\hat{\beta}_j$ is

$$\widehat{\text{Var}(\hat{\beta}_j)} = \frac{\hat{\sigma}^2}{\text{SST}_j(1 - R_j^2)}, \tag{5.9}$$

> **EXPLORING FURTHER 5.2**
>
> In a regression model with a large sample size, what is an approximate 95% confidence interval for $\hat{\beta}_j$ under MLR.1 through MLR.5? We call this an **asymptotic confidence interval**.

where SST_j is the total sum of squares of x_j in the sample, and R_j^2 is the R-squared from regressing x_j on all of the other independent variables. In Section 3-4, we studied each component of (5.9), which we will now expound on in the context of asymptotic analysis. As the sample size grows, $\hat{\sigma}^2$ converges in probability to the constant σ^2. Further, R_j^2 approaches a number strictly between zero and unity (so that $1 - R_j^2$ converges to some number between zero and one). The sample variance of x_j is SST_j/n, and so SST_j/n converges to $\text{Var}(x_j)$ as the sample size grows. This means that SST_j grows at approximately the same rate as the sample size: $\text{SST}_j \approx n\sigma_j^2$, where σ_j^2 is the population variance of x_j. When we combine these facts, we find that $\widehat{\text{Var}(\hat{\beta}_j)}$ shrinks to zero at the rate of $1/n$; this is why larger sample sizes are better.

When u is not normally distributed, the square root of (5.9) is sometimes called the **asymptotic standard error**, and t statistics are called **asymptotic t statistics**. Because these are the same quantities we dealt with in Chapter 4, we will just call them standard errors and t statistics, with the understanding that sometimes they have only large-sample justification. A similar comment holds for an asymptotic confidence interval constructed from the asymptotic standard error.

Using the preceding argument about the estimated variance, we can write

$$\text{se}(\hat{\beta}_j) \approx c_j / \sqrt{n}, \qquad\qquad [5.10]$$

where c_j is a positive constant that does *not* depend on the sample size. In fact, the constant c_j can be shown to be

$$c_j = \frac{\sigma}{\sigma_j \sqrt{1 - \rho_j^2}},$$

where $\sigma = \text{sd}(u)$, $\sigma_j = \text{sd}(x_j)$, and ρ_j^2 is the population R-squared from regressing x_j on the other explanatory variables. Just like studying equation (5.9) to see which variables affect $\text{Var}(\hat{\beta}_j)$ under the Gauss-Markov assumptions, we can use this expression for c_j to study the impact of larger error standard deviation (σ), more population variation in x_j (σ_j), and multicollinearity in the population (ρ_j^2).

Equation (5.10) is only an approximation, but it is a useful rule of thumb: standard errors can be expected to shrink at a rate that is the inverse of the *square root* of the sample size.

EXAMPLE 5.2   **Standard Errors in a Birth Weight Equation**

We use the data in BWGHT to estimate a relationship where log of birth weight is the dependent variable, and cigarettes smoked per day (*cigs*) and log of family income are independent variables. The total number of observations is 1,388. Using the first half of the observations (694), the standard error for $\hat{\beta}_{cigs}$ is about .0013. The standard error using all of the observations is about .00086. The ratio of the latter standard error to the former is $.00086/.0013 \approx .662$. This is pretty close to $\sqrt{694/1,388} \approx .707$, the ratio obtained from the approximation in (5.10). In other words, equation (5.10) implies that the standard error using the larger sample size should be about 70.7% of the standard error using the smaller sample. This percentage is pretty close to the 66.2% we actually compute from the ratio of the standard errors.

The asymptotic normality of the OLS estimators also implies that the F statistics have approximate F distributions in large sample sizes. Thus, for testing exclusion restrictions or other multiple hypotheses, nothing changes from what we have done before.

5-2a Other Large Sample Tests: The Lagrange Multiplier Statistic

Once we enter the realm of asymptotic analysis, other test statistics can be used for hypothesis testing. For most purposes, there is little reason to go beyond the usual t and F statistics: as we just saw, these statistics have large sample justification without the normality assumption. Nevertheless, sometimes it is useful to have other ways to test multiple exclusion restrictions, and we now cover the **Lagrange multiplier (LM) statistic**, which has achieved some popularity in modern econometrics.

The name "Lagrange multiplier statistic" comes from constrained optimization, a topic beyond the scope of this text. [See Davidson and MacKinnon (1993).] The name **score statistic**—which also comes from optimization using calculus—is used as well. Fortunately, in the linear regression framework, it is simple to motivate the LM statistic without delving into complicated mathematics.

The form of the LM statistic we derive here relies on the Gauss-Markov assumptions, the same assumptions that justify the F statistic in large samples. We do not need the normality assumption.

To derive the LM statistic, consider the usual multiple regression model with k independent variables:

$$y = \beta_0 + \beta_1 x_1 + \ldots + \beta_k x_k + u. \qquad\qquad [5.11]$$

We would like to test whether, say, the last q of these variables all have zero population parameters: the null hypothesis is

$$H_0: \beta_{k-q+1} = 0, \dots, \beta_k = 0,$$ [5.12]

which puts q exclusion restrictions on the model (5.11). As with F testing, the alternative to (5.12) is that at least one of the parameters is different from zero.

The *LM* statistic requires estimation of the *restricted* model only. Thus, assume that we have run the regression

$$y = \tilde{\beta}_0 + \tilde{\beta}_1 x_1 + \dots + \tilde{\beta}_{k-q} x_{k-q} + \tilde{u},$$ [5.13]

where "~" indicates that the estimates are from the restricted model. In particular, $\tilde{u}$ indicates the residuals from the restricted model. (As always, this is just shorthand to indicate that we obtain the restricted residual for each observation in the sample.)

If the omitted variables x_{k-q+1} through x_k truly have zero population coefficients, then, at least approximately, $\tilde{u}$ should be uncorrelated with each of these variables in the sample. This suggests running a regression of these residuals on those independent variables excluded under H_0, which is almost what the *LM* test does. However, it turns out that, to get a usable test statistic, we must include *all* of the independent variables in the regression. (We must include all regressors because, in general, the omitted regressors in the restricted model are correlated with the regressors that appear in the restricted model.) Thus, we run the regression of

$$\tilde{u} \text{ on } x_1, x_2, \dots, x_k.$$ [5.14]

This is an example of an **auxiliary regression**, a regression that is used to compute a test statistic but whose coefficients are not of direct interest.

How can we use the regression output from (5.14) to test (5.12)? If (5.12) is true, the R-squared from (5.14) should be "close" to zero, subject to sampling error, because $\tilde{u}$ will be approximately uncorrelated with all the independent variables. The question, as always with hypothesis testing, is how to determine when the statistic is large enough to reject the null hypothesis at a chosen significance level. It turns out that, under the null hypothesis, the sample size multiplied by the usual R-squared from the auxiliary regression (5.14) is distributed asymptotically as a chi-square random variable with q degrees of freedom. This leads to a simple procedure for testing the joint significance of a set of q independent variables.

The Lagrange Multiplier Statistic for q Exclusion Restrictions:

(i)   Regress y on the *restricted* set of independent variables and save the residuals, $\tilde{u}$.

(ii)   Regress $\tilde{u}$ on *all* of the independent variables and obtain the R-squared, say, R_u^2 (to distinguish it from the R-squareds obtained with y as the dependent variable).

(iii)   Compute $LM = nR_u^2$ [the sample size times the R-squared obtained from step (ii)].

(iv)   Compare LM to the appropriate critical value, c, in a χ_q^2 distribution; if $LM > c$, the null hypothesis is rejected. Even better, obtain the p-value as the probability that a χ_q^2 random variable exceeds the value of the test statistic. If the p-value is less than the desired significance level, then H_0 is rejected. If not, we fail to reject H_0. The rejection rule is essentially the same as for F testing.

Because of its form, the *LM* statistic is sometimes referred to as the **n-R-squared statistic**. Unlike with the F statistic, the degrees of freedom in the unrestricted model plays no role in carrying out the *LM* test. All that matters is the number of restrictions being tested (q), the size of the auxiliary R-squared (R_u^2), and the sample size (n). The df in the unrestricted model plays no role because of the asymptotic nature of the *LM* statistic. But we must be sure to multiply R_u^2 by the sample size to obtain *LM*; a seemingly low value of the *R*-squared can still lead to joint significance if n is large.

Before giving an example, a word of caution is in order. If in step (i), we mistakenly regress *y* on all of the independent variables and obtain the residuals from this unrestricted regression to be used in step (ii), we do not get an interesting statistic: the resulting *R*-squared will be exactly zero! This is because OLS chooses the estimates so that the residuals are uncorrelated in samples with all included independent variables [see equations in (3.13)]. Thus, we can only test (5.12) by regressing the restricted residuals on *all* of the independent variables. (Regressing the restricted residuals on the restricted set of independent variables will also produce $R^2 = 0$.)

EXAMPLE 5.3 **Economic Model of Crime**

We illustrate the *LM* test by using a slight extension of the crime model from Example 3.5:

$$narr86 = \beta_0 + \beta_1 pcnv + \beta_2 avgsen + \beta_3 tottime + \beta_4 ptime86 + \beta_5 qemp86 + u,$$

where

> *narr86* = the number of times a man was arrested.
> *pcnv* = the proportion of prior arrests leading to conviction.
> *avgsen* = average sentence served from past convictions.
> *tottime* = total time the man has spent in prison prior to 1986 since reaching the age of 18.
> *ptime86* = months spent in prison in 1986.
> *qemp86* = number of quarters in 1986 during which the man was legally employed.

We use the *LM* statistic to test the null hypothesis that *avgsen* and *tottime* have no effect on *narr86* once the other factors have been controlled for.

In step (i), we estimate the restricted model by regressing *narr86* on *pcnv*, *ptime86*, and *qemp86*; the variables *avgsen* and *tottime* are excluded from this regression. We obtain the residuals $\tilde{u}$ from this regression, 2,725 of them. Next, we run the regression of

$$\tilde{u} \text{ on } pcnv, ptime86, qemp86, avgsen, \text{ and } tottime; \qquad [5.15]$$

as always, the order in which we list the independent variables is irrelevant. This second regression produces R_u^2, which turns out to be about .0015. This may seem small, but we must multiply it by n to get the *LM* statistic: $LM = 2,725(.0015) \approx 4.09$. The 10% critical value in a chi-square distribution with two degrees of freedom is about 4.61 (rounded to two decimal places; see Table G.4). Thus, we fail to reject the null hypothesis that $\beta_{avgsen} = 0$ and $\beta_{tottime} = 0$ at the 10% level. The *p*-value is $P(\chi_2^2 > 4.09) \approx .129$, so we would reject H_0 at the 15% level.

As a comparison, the *F* test for joint significance of *avgsen* and *tottime* yields a *p*-value of about .131, which is pretty close to that obtained using the *LM* statistic. This is not surprising since, asymptotically, the two statistics have the same probability of Type I error. (That is, they reject the null hypothesis with the same frequency when the null is true.)

As the previous example suggests, with a large sample, we rarely see important discrepancies between the outcomes of *LM* and *F* tests. We will use the *F* statistic for the most part because it is computed routinely by most regression packages. But you should be aware of the *LM* statistic as it is used in applied work.

One final comment on the *LM* statistic. As with the *F* statistic, we must be sure to use the same observations in steps (i) and (ii). If data are missing for some of the independent variables that are excluded under the null hypothesis, the residuals from step (i) should be obtained from a regression on the reduced data set.

5-3 Asymptotic Efficiency of OLS

We know that, under the Gauss-Markov assumptions, the OLS estimators are best linear unbiased. OLS is also **asymptotically efficient** among a certain class of estimators under the Gauss-Markov assumptions. A general treatment requires matrix algebra and advanced asymptotic analysis. First, we describe the result in the simple regression case.

In the model

$$y = \beta_0 + \beta_1 x + u, \tag{5.16}$$

u has a zero conditional mean under MLR.4: $E(u|x) = 0$. This opens up a variety of consistent estimators for β_0 and β_1; as usual, we focus on the slope parameter, β_1. Let $g(x)$ be any function of x; for example, $g(x) = x^2$ or $g(x) = 1/(1 + |x|)$. Then u is uncorrelated with $g(x)$ (see Property CE.5 in Appendix B). Let $z_i = g(x_i)$ for all observations i. Then the estimator

$$\tilde{\beta}_1 = \left(\sum_{i=1}^{n} (z_i - \bar{z}) y_i \right) \bigg/ \left(\sum_{i=1}^{n} (z_i - \bar{z}) x_i \right) \tag{5.17}$$

is consistent for β_1, provided $g(x)$ and x are correlated. [Remember, it is possible that $g(x)$ and x are uncorrelated because correlation measures *linear* dependence.] To see this, we can plug in $y_i = \beta_0 + \beta_1 x_i + u_i$ and write $\tilde{\beta}_1$ as

$$\tilde{\beta}_1 = \beta_1 + \left(n^{-1} \sum_{i=1}^{n} (z_i - \bar{z}) u_i \right) \bigg/ \left(n^{-1} \sum_{i=1}^{n} (z_i - \bar{z}) x_i \right). \tag{5.18}$$

Now, we can apply the law of large numbers to the numerator and denominator, which converge in probability to $\text{Cov}(z,u)$ and $\text{Cov}(z,x)$, respectively. Provided that $\text{Cov}(z,x) \neq 0$—so that z and x are correlated—we have

$$\text{plim } \tilde{\beta}_1 = \beta_1 + \text{Cov}(z,u)/\text{Cov}(z,x) = \beta_1,$$

because $\text{Cov}(z,u) = 0$ under MLR.4.

It is more difficult to show that $\tilde{\beta}_1$ is asymptotically normal. Nevertheless, using arguments similar to those in the appendix, it can be shown that $\sqrt{n}(\tilde{\beta}_1 - \beta_1)$ is asymptotically normal with mean zero and asymptotic variance $\sigma^2 \text{Var}(z)/[\text{Cov}(z,x)]^2$. The asymptotic variance of the OLS estimator is obtained when $z = x$, in which case, $\text{Cov}(z,x) = \text{Cov}(x,x) = \text{Var}(x)$. Therefore, the asymptotic variance of $\sqrt{n}(\hat{\beta}_1 - \beta_1)$, where $\hat{\beta}_1$ is the OLS estimator, is $\sigma^2 \text{Var}(x)/[\text{Var}(x)]^2 = \sigma^2/\text{Var}(x)$. Now, the Cauchy-Schwartz inequality (see Appendix B.4) implies that $[\text{Cov}(z,x)]^2 \leq \text{Var}(z)\text{Var}(x)$, which implies that the asymptotic variance of $\sqrt{n}(\hat{\beta}_1 - \beta_1)$ is no larger than that of $\sqrt{n}(\tilde{\beta}_1 - \beta_1)$. We have shown in the simple regression case that, under the Gauss-Markov assumptions, the OLS estimator has a smaller asymptotic variance than any estimator of the form (5.17). [The estimator in (5.17) is an example of an *instrumental variables estimator*, which we will study extensively in Chapter 15.] If the homoskedasticity assumption fails, then there are estimators of the form (5.17) that have a smaller asymptotic variance than OLS. We will see this in Chapter 8.

The general case is similar but much more difficult mathematically. In the k regressor case, the class of consistent estimators is obtained by generalizing the OLS first order conditions:

$$\sum_{i=1}^{n} g_j(\boldsymbol{x}_i)(y_i - \tilde{\beta}_0 - \tilde{\beta}_1 x_{i1} - \dots - \tilde{\beta}_k x_{ik}) = 0, j = 0, 1, \dots, k, \tag{5.19}$$

where $g_j(\boldsymbol{x}_i)$ denotes any function of all explanatory variables for observation i. As can be seen by comparing (5.19) with the OLS first order conditions in (3.13), we obtain the OLS estimators when $g_0(\boldsymbol{x}_i) = 1$ and $g_j(\boldsymbol{x}_i) = x_{ij}$ for $j = 1, 2, \dots, k$. The class of estimators in (5.19) is infinite, because we can use any functions of the x_{ij} that we want.

> | THEOREM 5.3 | **ASYMPTOTIC EFFICIENCY OF OLS** |
> |---|---|
> | | Under the Gauss-Markov assumptions, let $\tilde{\beta}_j$ denote estimators that solve equations of the form (5.19) and let $\hat{\beta}_j$ denote the OLS estimators. Then for $j = 0, 1, 2, ..., k$, the OLS estimators have the smallest asymptotic variances: $\text{Avar}\sqrt{n}(\hat{\beta}_j - \beta_j) \le \text{Avar}\sqrt{n}(\tilde{\beta}_j - \beta_j)$. |

Proving consistency of the estimators in (5.19), let alone showing they are asymptotically normal, is mathematically difficult. See Wooldridge (2010, Chapter 5).

Summary

The claims underlying the material in this chapter are fairly technical, but their practical implications are straightforward. We have shown that the first four Gauss-Markov assumptions imply that OLS is consistent. Furthermore, all of the methods of testing and constructing confidence intervals that we learned in Chapter 4 are approximately valid without assuming that the errors are drawn from a normal distribution (equivalently, the distribution of y given the explanatory variables is not normal). This means that we can apply OLS and use previous methods for an array of applications where the dependent variable is not even approximately normally distributed. We also showed that the *LM* statistic can be used instead of the *F* statistic for testing exclusion restrictions.

Before leaving this chapter, we should note that examples such as Example 5.3 may very well have problems that *do* require special attention. For a variable such as *narr86*, which is zero or one for most men in the population, a linear model may not be able to adequately capture the functional relationship between *narr86* and the explanatory variables. Moreover, even if a linear model does describe the expected value of arrests, heteroskedasticity might be a problem. Problems such as these are not mitigated as the sample size grows, and we will return to them in later chapters.

Key Terms

Asymptotic Bias	Asymptotic *t* Statistics	Lagrange Multiplier (*LM*)
Asymptotic Confidence	Asymptotic Variance	Statistic
Interval	Asymptotically Efficient	Large Sample Properties
Asymptotic Normality	Auxiliary Regression	*n-R*-Squared Statistic
Asymptotic Properties	Consistency	Score Statistic
Asymptotic Standard Error	Inconsistency	

Problems

1 In the simple regression model under MLR.1 through MLR.4, we argued that the slope estimator, $\hat{\beta}_1$, is consistent for β_1. Using $\hat{\beta}_0 = \bar{y} - \hat{\beta}_1\bar{x}_1$, show that plim $\hat{\beta}_0 = \beta_0$. [You need to use the consistency of $\hat{\beta}_1$ and the law of large numbers, along with the fact that $\beta_0 = E(y) - \beta_1 E(x_1)$.]

2 Suppose that the model

$$pctstck = \beta_0 + \beta_1 funds + \beta_2 risktol + u$$

satisfies the first four Gauss-Markov assumptions, where *pctstck* is the percentage of a worker's pension invested in the stock market, *funds* is the number of mutual funds that the worker can choose from, and *risktol* is some measure of risk tolerance (larger *risktol* means the person has a higher tolerance for risk). If *funds* and *risktol* are positively correlated, what is the inconsistency in $\tilde{\beta}_1$, the slope coefficient in the simple regression of *pctstck* on *funds*?

3 The data set SMOKE contains information on smoking behavior and other variables for a random sample of single adults from the United States. The variable *cigs* is the (average) number of cigarettes smoked per day. Do you think *cigs* has a normal distribution in the U.S. adult population? Explain.

4 In the simple regression model (5.16), under the first four Gauss-Markov assumptions, we showed that estimators of the form (5.17) are consistent for the slope, β_1. Given such an estimator, define an estimator of β_0 by $\tilde{\beta}_0 = \bar{y} - \tilde{\beta}_1\bar{x}$. Show that plim $\tilde{\beta}_0 = \beta_0$.

5 The following histogram was created using the variable *score* in the data file ECONMATH. Thirty bins were used to create the histogram, and the height of each cell is the proportion of observations falling within the corresponding interval. The best-fitting normal distribution—that is, using the sample mean and sample standard deviation—has been superimposed on the histogram.

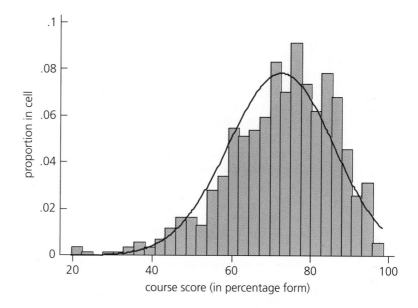

(i) If you use the normal distribution to estimate the probability that *score* exceeds 100, would the answer be zero? Why does your answer contradict the assumption of a normal distribution for *score*?

(ii) Explain what is happening in the left tail of the histogram. Does the normal distribution fit well in the left tail?

Computer Exercises

C1 Use the data in WAGE1 for this exercise.

(i) Estimate the equation

$$wage = \beta_0 + \beta_1 educ + \beta_2 exper + \beta_3 tenure + u.$$

Save the residuals and plot a histogram.

(ii) Repeat part (i), but with log(*wage*) as the dependent variable.

(iii) Would you say that Assumption MLR.6 is closer to being satisfied for the level-level model or the log-level model?

C2 Use the data in GPA2 for this exercise.

(i) Using all 4,137 observations, estimate the equation

$$colgpa = \beta_0 + \beta_1 hsperc + \beta_2 sat + u$$

and report the results in standard form.

(ii) Reestimate the equation in part (i), using the first 2,070 observations.

(iii) Find the ratio of the standard errors on *hsperc* from parts (i) and (ii). Compare this with the result from (5.10).

C3 In equation (4.42) of Chapter 4, using the data set BWGHT, compute the *LM* statistic for testing whether *motheduc* and *fatheduc* are jointly significant. In obtaining the residuals for the restricted model, be sure that the restricted model is estimated using only those observations for which all variables in the unrestricted model are available (see Example 4.9).

C4 Several statistics are commonly used to detect nonnormality in underlying population distributions. Here we will study one that measures the amount of skewness in a distribution. Recall that any normally distributed random variable is symmetric about its mean; therefore, if we standardize a symmetrically distributed random variable, say $z = (y - \mu_y)/\sigma_y$, where $\mu_y = E(y)$ and $\sigma_y = sd(y)$, then z has mean zero, variance one, and $E(z^3) = 0$. Given a sample of data $\{y_i: i = 1, \dots, n\}$, we can standardize y_i in the sample by using $z_i = (y_i - \hat{\mu}_y)/\hat{\sigma}_y$, where $\hat{\mu}_y$ is the sample mean and $\hat{\sigma}_y$ is the sample standard deviation. (We ignore the fact that these are estimates based on the sample.) A sample statistic that measures skewness is $n^{-1}\sum_{i=1}^{n} z_i^3$, or where n is replaced with $(n - 1)$ as a degrees-of-freedom adjustment. If y has a normal distribution in the population, the skewness measure in the sample for the standardized values should not differ significantly from zero.

(i) First use the data set 401KSUBS, keeping only observations with $fsize = 1$. Find the skewness measure for *inc*. Do the same for log(*inc*). Which variable has more skewness and therefore seems less likely to be normally distributed?

(ii) Next use BWGHT2. Find the skewness measures for *bwght* and log(*bwght*). What do you conclude?

(iii) Evaluate the following statement: "The logarithmic transformation always makes a positive variable look more normally distributed."

(iv) If we are interested in the normality assumption in the context of regression, should we be evaluating the unconditional distributions of y and log(y)? Explain.

C5 Consider the analysis in Computer Exercise C11 in Chapter 4 using the data in HTV, where *educ* is the dependent variable in a regression.

(i) How many different values are taken on by *educ* in the sample? Does *educ* have a continuous distribution?

(ii) Plot a histogram of *educ* with a normal distribution overlay. Does the distribution of *educ* appear anything close to normal?

(iii) Which of the CLM assumptions seems clearly violated in the model

$$educ = \beta_0 + \beta_1 motheduc + \beta_2 fatheduc + \beta_3 abil + \beta_4 abil^2 + u?$$

How does this violation change the statistical inference procedures carried out in Computer Exercise C11 in Chapter 4?

C6 Use the data in ECONMATH to answer this question.

(i) Logically, what are the smallest and largest values that can be taken on by the variable *score*? What are the smallest and largest values in the sample?

(ii) Consider the linear model

$$score = \beta_0 + \beta_1 colgpa + \beta_2 actmth + \beta_3 acteng + u.$$

Why cannot Assumption MLR.6 hold for the error term u? What consequences does this have for using the usual t statistic to test $H_0: \beta_3 = 0$?

(iii) Estimate the model from part (ii) and obtain the t statistic and associated p-value for testing $H_0: \beta_3 = 0$. How would you defend your findings to someone who makes the following statement: "You cannot trust that p-value because clearly the error term in the equation cannot have a normal distribution."

APPENDIX 5A

Asymptotic Normality of OLS

We sketch a proof of the asymptotic normality of OLS [Theorem 5.2(i)] in the simple regression case. Write the simple regression model as in equation (5.16). Then, by the usual algebra of simple regression, we can write

$$\sqrt{n}(\hat{\beta}_1 - \beta_1) = (1/s_x^2)\left[n^{-1/2}\sum_{i=1}^{n}(x_i - \bar{x})u_i\right],$$

where we use s_x^2 to denote the sample variance of $\{x_i: i = 1, 2, ..., n\}$. By the law of large numbers (see Appendix C), $s_x^2 \xrightarrow{p} \sigma_x^2 = \text{Var}(x)$. Assumption MLR.3 rules out perfect collinearity, which means that $\text{Var}(x) > 0$ (x_i varies in the sample, and therefore x is not constant in the population). Next, $n^{-1/2}\sum_{i=1}^{n}(x_i - \bar{x})u_i = n^{-1/2}\sum_{i=1}^{n}(x_i - \mu)u_i + (\mu - \bar{x})[n^{-1/2}\sum_{i=1}^{n}u_i]$, where $\mu = \text{E}(x)$ is the population mean of x. Now $\{u_i\}$ is a sequence of i.i.d. random variables with mean zero and variance σ^2, and so $n^{-1/2}\sum_{i=1}^{n}u_i$ converges to the Normal$(0,\sigma^2)$ distribution as $n \to \infty$; this is just the central limit theorem from Appendix C. By the law of large numbers, $\text{plim}(\bar{u} - \bar{x}) = 0$. A standard result in asymptotic theory is that if $\text{plim}(w_n) = 0$ and z_n has an asymptotic normal distribution, then $\text{plim}(w_n z_n) = 0$. [See Wooldridge (2010, Chapter 3) for more discussion.] This implies that $(\mu - \bar{x})[n^{-1/2}\sum_{i=1}^{n}u_i]$ has zero plim. Next, $\{(x_i - \mu)u_i: i = 1, 2, ...\}$ is an indefinite sequence of i.i.d. random variables with mean zero—because u and x are uncorrelated under Assumption MLR.4—and variance $\sigma^2\sigma_x^2$ by the homoskedasticity Assumption MLR.5. Therefore, $n^{-1/2}\sum_{i=1}^{n}(x_i - \mu)u_i$ has an asymptotic Normal$(0,\sigma^2\sigma_x^2)$ distribution. We just showed that the difference between $n^{-1/2}\sum_{i=1}^{n}(x_i - \bar{x})u_i$ and $n^{-1/2}\sum_{i=1}^{n}(x_i - \mu)u_i$ has zero plim. A result in asymptotic theory is that if z_n has an asymptotic normal distribution and $\text{plim}(v_n - z_n) = 0$, then v_n has the same asymptotic normal distribution as z_n. It follows that $n^{-1/2}\sum_{i=1}^{n}(x_i - \bar{x})u_i$ also has an asymptotic Normal$(0,\sigma^2\sigma_x^2)$ distribution. Putting all of the pieces together gives

$$\sqrt{n}(\hat{\beta}_1 - \beta_1) = (1/\sigma_x^2)\left[n^{-1/2}\sum_{i=1}^{n}(x_i - \bar{x})u_i\right]$$

$$+ [(1/s_x^2) - (1/\sigma_x^2)]\left[n^{-1/2}\sum_{i=1}^{n}(x_i - \bar{x})u_i\right],$$

and since $\text{plim}(1/s_x^2) = 1/\sigma_x^2$, the second term has zero plim. Therefore, the asymptotic distribution of $\sqrt{n}(\hat{\beta}_1 - \beta_1)$ is Normal$(0,\{\sigma^2\sigma_x^2\}/\{\sigma_x^2\}^2) = \text{Normal}(0,\sigma^2/\sigma_x^2)$. This completes the proof in the simple regression case, as $a_1^2 = \sigma_x^2$ in this case. See Wooldridge (2010, Chapter 4) for the general case.

CHAPTER 6

Multiple Regression Analysis: Further Issues

This chapter brings together several issues in multiple regression analysis that we could not conveniently cover in earlier chapters. These topics are not as fundamental as the material in Chapters 3 and 4, but they are important for applying multiple regression to a broad range of empirical problems.

6-1 Effects of Data Scaling on OLS Statistics

In Chapter 2 on bivariate regression, we briefly discussed the effects of changing the units of measurement on the OLS intercept and slope estimates. We also showed that changing the units of measurement did not affect R-squared. We now return to the issue of data scaling and examine the effects of rescaling the dependent or independent variables on standard errors, t statistics, F statistics, and confidence intervals.

We will discover that everything we expect to happen, does happen. When variables are rescaled, the coefficients, standard errors, confidence intervals, t statistics, and F statistics change in ways that preserve all measured effects and testing outcomes. Although this is no great surprise—in fact, we would be very worried if it were not the case—it is useful to see what occurs explicitly. Often, data scaling is used for cosmetic purposes, such as to reduce the number of zeros after a decimal point in an estimated coefficient. By judiciously choosing units of measurement, we can improve the appearance of an estimated equation while changing nothing that is essential.

We could treat this problem in a general way, but it is much better illustrated with examples. Likewise, there is little value here in introducing an abstract notation.

We begin with an equation relating infant birth weight to cigarette smoking and family income:

$$\widehat{bwght} = \hat{\beta}_0 + \hat{\beta}_1 cigs + \hat{\beta}_2 faminc, \tag{6.1}$$

where

$bwght$ = child birth weight, in ounces.
$cigs$ = number of cigarettes smoked by the mother while pregnant, per day.
$faminc$ = annual family income, in thousands of dollars.

The estimates of this equation, obtained using the data in BWGHT, are given in the first column of Table 6.1. Standard errors are listed in parentheses. The estimate on *cigs* says that if a woman smoked five more cigarettes per day, birth weight is predicted to be about .4634(5) = 2.317 ounces less. The *t* statistic on *cigs* is −5.06, so the variable is very statistically significant.

Now, suppose that we decide to measure birth weight in pounds, rather than in ounces. Let *bwghtlbs* = *bwght*/16 be birth weight in pounds. What happens to our OLS statistics if we use this as the dependent variable in our equation? It is easy to find the effect on the coefficient estimates by simple manipulation of equation (6.1). Divide this entire equation by 16:

$$\widehat{bwght}/16 = \hat{\beta}_0/16 + (\hat{\beta}_1/16)cigs + (\hat{\beta}_2/16)faminc.$$

Since the left-hand side is birth weight in pounds, it follows that each new coefficient will be the corresponding old coefficient divided by 16. To verify this, the regression of *bwghtlbs* on *cigs*, and *faminc* is reported in column (2) of Table 6.1. Up to the reported digits (and any digits beyond), the intercept and slopes in column (2) are just those in column (1) divided by 16. For example, the coefficient on *cigs* is now −.0289; this means that if *cigs* were higher by five, birth weight would be .0289(5) = .1445 *pounds* lower. In terms of ounces, we have .1445(16) = 2.312, which is slightly different from the 2.317 we obtained earlier due to rounding error. The point is, once the effects are transformed into the same units, we get exactly the same answer, regardless of how the dependent variable is measured.

What about statistical significance? As we expect, changing the dependent variable from ounces to pounds has no effect on how statistically important the independent variables are. The standard errors in column (2) are 16 times smaller than those in column (1). A few quick calculations show

TABLE 6.1 Effects of Data Scaling

Dependent Variable	(1) *bwght*	(2) *bwghtlbs*	(3) *bwght*
Independent Variables			
cigs	−.4634	−.0289	—
	(.0916)	(.0057)	
packs	—	—	−9.268
			(1.832)
faminc	.0927	.0058	.0927
	(.0292)	(.0018)	(.0292)
intercept	116.974	7.3109	116.974
	(1.049)	(.0656)	(1.049)
Observations	1,388	1,388	1,388
R-Squared	.0298	.0298	.0298
SSR	557,485.51	2,177.6778	557,485.51
SER	20.063	1.2539	20.063

that the t statistics in column (2) are indeed identical to the t statistics in column (1). The endpoints for the confidence intervals in column (2) are just the endpoints in column (1) divided by 16. This is because the CIs change by the same factor as the standard errors. [Remember that the 95% CI here is $\hat{\beta}_j \pm 1.96 \ \text{se}(\hat{\beta}_j)$.]

In terms of goodness-of-fit, the R-squareds from the two regressions are identical, as should be the case. Notice that the sum of squared residuals, SSR, and the standard error of the regression, SER, do differ across equations. These differences are easily explained. Let $\hat{u}_i$ denote the residual for observation i in the original equation (6.1). Then the residual when $bwghtlbs$ is the dependent variable is simply $\hat{u}_i/16$. Thus, the *squared* residual in the second equation is $(\hat{u}_i/16)^2 = \hat{u}_i^2/256$. This is why the sum of squared residuals in column (2) is equal to the SSR in column (1) divided by 256.

Since $\text{SER} = \hat{\sigma} = \sqrt{\text{SSR}/(n - k - 1)} = \sqrt{\text{SSR}/1{,}385}$, the SER in column (2) is 16 times smaller than that in column (1). Another way to think about this is that the error in the equation with $bwghtlbs$ as the dependent variable has a standard deviation 16 times smaller than the standard deviation of the original error. This does not mean that we have reduced the error by changing how birth weight is measured; the smaller SER simply reflects a difference in units of measurement.

Next, let us return the dependent variable to its original units: $bwght$ is measured in ounces. Instead, let us change the unit of measurement of one of the independent variables, $cigs$. Define $packs$ to be the number of packs of cigarettes smoked per day. Thus, $packs = cigs/20$. What happens to the coefficients and other OLS statistics now? Well, we can write

$$\widehat{bwght} = \hat{\beta}_0 + (20\hat{\beta}_1)(cigs/20) + \hat{\beta}_2 \, faminc = \hat{\beta}_0 + (20\hat{\beta}_1)packs + \hat{\beta}_2 \, faminc.$$

Thus, the intercept and slope coefficient on $faminc$ are unchanged, but the coefficient on $packs$ is 20 times that on $cigs$. This is intuitively appealing. The results from the regression of $bwght$ on $packs$ and $faminc$ are in column (3) of Table 6.1. Incidentally, remember that it would make no sense to include both $cigs$ and $packs$ in the same equation; this would induce perfect multicollinearity and would have no interesting meaning.

Other than the coefficient on $packs$, there is one other statistic in column (3) that differs from that in column (1): the standard error on $packs$ is 20 times larger than that on $cigs$ in column (1). This means that the t statistic for testing the significance of cigarette smoking is the same whether we measure smoking in terms of cigarettes or packs. This is only natural.

> ### EXPLORING FURTHER 6.1
>
> In the original birth weight equation (6.1), suppose that $faminc$ is measured in dollars rather than in thousands of dollars. Thus, define the variable $fincdol = 1{,}000 \cdot faminc$. How will the OLS statistics change when $fincdol$ is substituted for $faminc$? For the purpose of presenting the regression results, do you think it is better to measure income in dollars or in thousands of dollars?

The previous example spells out most of the possibilities that arise when the dependent and independent variables are rescaled. Rescaling is often done with dollar amounts in economics, especially when the dollar amounts are very large.

In Chapter 2, we argued that, if the dependent variable appears in logarithmic form, changing the unit of measurement does not affect the slope coefficient. The same is true here: changing the unit of measurement of the dependent variable, when it appears in logarithmic form, does not affect any of the slope estimates. This follows from the simple fact that $\log(c_1 y_i) = \log(c_1) + \log(y_i)$ for any constant $c_1 > 0$. The new intercept will be $\log(c_1) + \hat{\beta}_0$. Similarly, changing the unit of measurement of any x_j, where $\log(x_j)$ appears in the regression, only affects the intercept. This corresponds to what we know about percentage changes and, in particular, elasticities: they are invariant to the units of measurement of either y or the x_j. For example, if we had specified the dependent variable in (6.1) to be $\log(bwght)$, estimated the equation, and then reestimated it with $\log(bwghtlbs)$ as the dependent variable, the coefficients on $cigs$ and $faminc$ would be the same in both regressions; only the intercept would be different.

6-1a Beta Coefficients

Sometimes, in econometric applications, a key variable is measured on a scale that is difficult to interpret. Labor economists often include test scores in wage equations, and the scale on which these tests are scored is often arbitrary and not easy to interpret (at least for economists!). In almost all cases, we are interested in how a particular individual's score compares with the population. Thus, instead of asking about the effect on hourly wage if, say, a test score is 10 points higher, it makes more sense to ask what happens when the test score is one *standard deviation* higher.

Nothing prevents us from seeing what happens to the dependent variable when an independent variable in an estimated model increases by a certain number of standard deviations, assuming that we have obtained the sample standard deviation of the independent variable (which is easy in most regression packages). This is often a good idea. So, for example, when we look at the effect of a standardized test score, such as the SAT score, on college GPA, we can find the standard deviation of SAT and see what happens when the SAT score increases by one or two standard deviations.

Sometimes, it is useful to obtain regression results when *all* variables involved, the dependent as well as all the independent variables, have been *standardized*. A variable is standardized in the sample by subtracting off its mean and dividing by its standard deviation (see Appendix C). This means that we compute the *z-score* for every variable in the sample. Then, we run a regression using the *z*-scores.

Why is standardization useful? It is easiest to start with the original OLS equation, with the variables in their original forms:

$$y_i = \hat{\beta}_0 + \hat{\beta}_1 x_{i1} + \hat{\beta}_2 x_{i2} + \ldots + \hat{\beta}_k x_{ik} + \hat{u}_i. \qquad [6.2]$$

We have included the observation subscript i to emphasize that our standardization is applied to all sample values. Now, if we average (6.2), use the fact that the $\hat{u}_i$ have a zero sample average, and subtract the result from (6.2), we get

$$y_i - \bar{y} = \hat{\beta}_1(x_{i1} - \bar{x}_1) + \hat{\beta}_2(x_{i2} - \bar{x}_2) + \ldots + \hat{\beta}_k(x_{ik} - \bar{x}_k) + \hat{u}_i.$$

Now, let $\hat{\sigma}_y$ be the sample standard deviation for the dependent variable, let $\hat{\sigma}_1$ be the sample *sd* for x_1, let $\hat{\sigma}_2$ be the sample *sd* for x_2, and so on. Then, simple algebra gives the equation

$$(y_i - \bar{y})/\hat{\sigma}_y = (\hat{\sigma}_1/\hat{\sigma}_y)\hat{\beta}_1[(x_{i1} - \bar{x}_1)/\hat{\sigma}_1] + \ldots$$
$$+ (\hat{\sigma}_k/\hat{\sigma}_y)\hat{\beta}_k[(x_{ik} - \bar{x}_k)/\hat{\sigma}_k] + (\hat{u}_i/\hat{\sigma}_y). \qquad [6.3]$$

Each variable in (6.3) has been standardized by replacing it with its *z*-score, and this has resulted in new slope coefficients. For example, the slope coefficient on $(x_{i1} - \bar{x}_1)/\hat{\sigma}_1$ is $(\hat{\sigma}_1/\hat{\sigma}_y)\hat{\beta}_1$. This is simply the original coefficient, $\hat{\beta}_1$, multiplied by the ratio of the standard deviation of x_1 to the standard deviation of y. The intercept has dropped out altogether.

It is useful to rewrite (6.3), dropping the i subscript, as

$$z_y = \hat{b}_1 z_1 + \hat{b}_2 z_2 + \ldots + \hat{b}_k z_k + error, \qquad [6.4]$$

where z_y denotes the *z*-score of y, z_1 is the *z*-score of x_1, and so on. The new coefficients are

$$\hat{b}_j = (\hat{\sigma}_j/\hat{\sigma}_y)\hat{\beta}_j \text{ for } j = 1, \ldots, k. \qquad [6.5]$$

These $\hat{b}_j$ are traditionally called **standardized coefficients** or **beta coefficients**. (The latter name is more common, which is unfortunate because we have been using beta hat to denote the *usual* OLS estimates.)

Beta coefficients receive their interesting meaning from equation (6.4): If x_1 increases by one standard deviation, then $\hat{y}$ changes by $\hat{b}_1$ standard deviations. Thus, we are measuring effects not in terms of the original units of y or the x_j, but in standard deviation units. Because it makes the scale of the regressors irrelevant, this equation puts the explanatory variables on equal footing. In a standard OLS equation, it is not possible to simply look at the size of different coefficients and conclude that the explanatory variable with the largest coefficient is "the most important." We just saw that the magnitudes of coefficients can be changed at will by changing the units of measurement of the x_j. But, when each x_j has been standardized, comparing the magnitudes of the resulting beta coefficients is more compelling. When the regression equation has only a single explanatory variable, x_1, its standardized coefficient is simply the sample correlation coefficient between y and x_1, which means it must lie in the range -1 to 1.

Even in situations where the coefficients are easily interpretable—say, the dependent variable and independent variables of interest are in logarithmic form, so the OLS coefficients of interest are estimated elasticities—there is still room for computing beta coefficients. Although elasticities are free of units of measurement, a change in a particular explanatory variable by, say, 10% may represent a larger or smaller change over a variable's range than changing another explanatory variable by 10%. For example, in a state with wide income variation but relatively little variation in spending per student, it might not make much sense to compare performance elasticities with respect to the income and spending. Comparing beta coefficient magnitudes can be helpful.

To obtain the beta coefficients, we can always standardize $y, x_1, \ldots, x_k$ and then run the OLS regression of the z-score of y on the z-scores of $x_1, \ldots, x_k$—where it is not necessary to include an intercept, as it will be zero. This can be tedious with many independent variables. Many regression packages provide beta coefficients via a simple command. The following example illustrates the use of beta coefficients.

EXAMPLE 6.1   **Effects of Pollution on Housing Prices**

We use the data from Example 4.5 (in the file HPRICE2) to illustrate the use of beta coefficients. Recall that the key independent variable is *nox*, a measure of the nitrogen oxide in the air over each community. One way to understand the size of the pollution effect—without getting into the science underlying nitrogen oxide's effect on air quality—is to compute beta coefficients. (An alternative approach is contained in Example 4.5: we obtained a price elasticity with respect to *nox* by using *price* and *nox* in logarithmic form.)

The population equation is the level-level model

$$price = \beta_0 + \beta_1 nox + \beta_2 crime + \beta_3 rooms + \beta_4 dist + \beta_5 stratio + u,$$

where all the variables except *crime* were defined in Example 4.5; *crime* is the number of reported crimes per capita. The beta coefficients are reported in the following equation (so each variable has been converted to its z-score):

$$\widehat{zprice} = -.340\, znox - .143\, zcrime + .514\, zrooms - .235\, zdist - .270\, zstratio.$$

This equation shows that a one standard deviation increase in *nox* decreases price by .34 standard deviation; a one standard deviation increase in *crime* reduces price by .14 standard deviation. Thus, the same relative movement of pollution in the population has a larger effect on housing prices than crime does. Size of the house, as measured by number of rooms (*rooms*), has the largest standardized effect. If we want to know the effects of each independent variable on the dollar value of median house price, we should use the unstandardized variables.

Whether we use standardized or unstandardized variables does not affect statistical significance: the t statistics are the same in both cases.

6-2 More on Functional Form

In several previous examples, we have encountered the most popular device in econometrics for allowing nonlinear relationships between the explained and explanatory variables: using logarithms for the dependent or independent variables. We have also seen models containing quadratics in some explanatory variables, but we have yet to provide a systematic treatment of them. In this section, we cover some variations and extensions on functional forms that often arise in applied work.

6-2a More on Using Logarithmic Functional Forms

We begin by reviewing how to interpret the parameters in the model

$$\log(price) = \beta_0 + \beta_1 \log(nox) + \beta_2 rooms + u, \tag{6.6}$$

where these variables are taken from Example 4.5. Recall that throughout the text $\log(x)$ is the *natural log* of x. The coefficient β_1 is the elasticity of *price* with respect to *nox* (pollution). The coefficient β_2 is the change in $\log(price)$, when $\Delta rooms = 1$; as we have seen many times, when multiplied by 100, this is the approximate percentage change in *price*. Recall that $100 \cdot \beta_2$ is sometimes called the semi-elasticity of *price* with respect to *rooms*.

When estimated using the data in HPRICE2, we obtain

$$\widehat{\log(price)} = 9.23 - .718 \log(nox) + .306 \, rooms$$
$$\quad\quad\quad (0.19) \;\; (.066) \quad\quad\quad\quad (.019) \tag{6.7}$$
$$n = 506, R^2 = .514.$$

Thus, when *nox* increases by 1%, *price* falls by .718%, holding only *rooms* fixed. When *rooms* increases by one, *price* increases by approximately $100(.306) = 30.6\%$.

The estimate that one more room increases price by about 30.6% turns out to be somewhat inaccurate for this application. The approximation error occurs because, as the change in $\log(y)$ becomes larger and larger, the approximation $\%\Delta y \approx 100 \cdot \Delta \log(y)$ becomes more and more inaccurate. Fortunately, a simple calculation is available to compute the exact percentage change.

To describe the procedure, we consider the general estimated model

$$\widehat{\log(y)} = \hat{\beta}_0 + \hat{\beta}_1 \log(x_1) + \hat{\beta}_2 x_2.$$

(Adding additional independent variables does not change the procedure.) Now, fixing x_1, we have $\widehat{\Delta \log(y)} = \hat{\beta}_2 \Delta x_2$. Using simple algebraic properties of the exponential and logarithmic functions gives the *exact* percentage change in the predicted y as

$$\%\Delta\hat{y} = 100 \cdot [\exp(\hat{\beta}_2 \Delta x_2) - 1], \tag{6.8}$$

where the multiplication by 100 turns the proportionate change into a percentage change. When $\Delta x_2 = 1$,

$$\%\Delta\hat{y} = 100 \cdot [\exp(\hat{\beta}_2) - 1]. \tag{6.9}$$

Applied to the housing price example with $x_2 = $ rooms and $\hat{\beta}_2 = .306$, $\%\widehat{\Delta price} = 100[\exp(.306) - 1] = 35.8\%$, which is notably larger than the approximate percentage change, 30.6%, obtained directly from (6.7). {Incidentally, this is not an unbiased estimator because $\exp(\cdot)$ is a nonlinear function; it is, however, a consistent estimator of $100[\exp(\beta_2) - 1]$. This is because the probability limit passes through continuous functions, while the expected value operator does not. See Appendix C.}

The adjustment in equation (6.8) is not as crucial for small percentage changes. For example, when we include the student-teacher ratio in equation (6.7), its estimated coefficient is −.052, which means that if *stratio* increases by one, *price* decreases by approximately 5.2%. The exact proportionate change is $\exp(-.052)-1 \approx -.051$, or −5.1%. On the other hand, if we increase *stratio* by five, then the approximate percentage change in price is −26%, while the exact change obtained from equation (6.8) is $100[\exp(-.26)-1] \approx -22.9\%$.

The logarithmic approximation to percentage changes has an advantage that justifies its reporting even when the percentage change is large. To describe this advantage, consider again the effect on price of changing the number of rooms by one. The logarithmic approximation is just the coefficient on rooms in equation (6.7) multiplied by 100, namely, 30.6%. We also computed an estimate of the exact percentage change for *increasing* the number of rooms by one as 35.8%. But what if we want to estimate the percentage change for *decreasing* the number of rooms by one? In equation (6.8) we take $\Delta x_2 = -1$ and $\hat{\beta}_2 = .306$, and so $\%\widehat{\Delta price} = 100[\exp(-.306)-1] = -26.4$, or a drop of 26.4%. Notice that the approximation based on using the coefficient on *rooms* is between 26.4 and 35.8—an outcome that always occurs. In other words, simply using the coefficient (multiplied by 100) gives us an estimate that is always between the absolute value of the estimates for an increase and a decrease. If we are specifically interested in an increase or a decrease, we can use the calculation based on equation (6.8).

The point just made about computing percentage changes is essentially the one made in introductory economics when it comes to computing, say, price elasticities of demand based on large price changes: the result depends on whether we use the beginning or ending price and quantity in computing the percentage changes. Using the logarithmic approximation is similar in spirit to calculating an arc elasticity of demand, where the averages of prices and quantities are used in the denominators in computing the percentage changes.

We have seen that using natural logs leads to coefficients with appealing interpretations, and we can be ignorant about the units of measurement of variables appearing in logarithmic form because the slope coefficients are invariant to rescalings. There are several other reasons logs are used so much in applied work. First, when $y > 0$, models using $\log(y)$ as the dependent variable often satisfy the CLM assumptions more closely than models using the level of y. Strictly positive variables often have conditional distributions that are heteroskedastic or skewed; taking the log can mitigate, if not eliminate, both problems.

Another potential benefit of using logs is that taking the log of a variable often narrows its range. This is particularly true of variables that can be large monetary values, such as firms' annual sales or baseball players' salaries. Population variables also tend to vary widely. Narrowing the range of the dependent and independent variables can make OLS estimates less sensitive to outlying (or extreme values); we take up the issue of outlying observations in Chapter 9.

However, one must not indiscriminately use the logarithmic transformation because in some cases it can actually create extreme values. An example is when a variable y is between zero and one (such as a proportion) and takes on values close to zero. In this case, $\log(y)$ (which is necessarily negative) can be very large in magnitude whereas the original variable, y, is bounded between zero and one.

There are some standard rules of thumb for taking logs, although none is written in stone. When a variable is a positive dollar amount, the log is often taken. We have seen this for variables such as wages, salaries, firm sales, and firm market value. Variables such as population, total number of employees, and school enrollment often appear in logarithmic form; these have the common feature of being large integer values.

Variables that are measured in years—such as education, experience, tenure, age, and so on— usually appear in their original form. A variable that is a proportion or a percent—such as the unemployment rate, the participation rate in a pension plan, the percentage of students passing a standardized exam, and the arrest rate on reported crimes—can appear in either original or logarithmic form, although there is a tendency to use them in level forms. This is because any regression coefficients involving the *original* variable—whether it is the dependent or independent variable—will have a *percentage point* change interpretation. (See Appendix A for a review of the distinction between a percentage change and a percentage point change.) If we use, say, log(*unem*) in a regression, where *unem* is the percentage of unemployed individuals, we must be very careful to distinguish between a percentage point change and a percentage change. Remember, if *unem* goes from 8 to 9, this is an increase of one percentage point, but a 12.5% increase from the initial unemployment level. Using the log means that we are looking at the percentage change in the unemployment rate: log(9) − log(8) ≈ .118 or 11.8%, which is the logarithmic approximation to the actual 12.5% increase.

One limitation of the log is that it cannot be used if a variable takes on zero or negative values. In cases where a variable *y* is nonnegative but can take on the value 0, log(1+*y*) is sometimes used. The percentage change interpretations are often closely preserved, except for changes beginning at *y* = 0 (where the percentage change is not even defined). Generally, using log(1+*y*) and then interpreting the estimates as if the variable were log(*y*) is acceptable when the data on *y* contain relatively few zeros. An example might be where *y* is hours of training per employee for the population of manufacturing firms, if a large fraction of firms provides training to at least one worker. Technically, however, log(1+*y*) cannot be normally distributed (although it might be less heteroskedastic than *y*). Useful, albeit more advanced, alternatives are the Tobit and Poisson models in Chapter 17.

> ## EXPLORING FURTHER 6.2
>
> Suppose that the annual number of drunk driving arrests is determined by
>
> $$\log(arrests) = \beta_0 + \beta_1 \log(pop) + \beta_2 age16\_25 + other \ factors,$$
>
> where *age 16_25* is the proportion of the population between 16 and 25 years of age. Show that β_2 has the following (ceteris paribus) interpretation: it is the percentage change in *arrests* when the percentage of the people aged 16 to 25 increases by one *percentage point*.

One drawback to using a dependent variable in logarithmic form is that it is more difficult to predict the original variable. The original model allows us to predict log(*y*), not *y*. Nevertheless, it is fairly easy to turn a prediction for log(*y*) into a prediction for *y* (see Section 6-4). A related point is that it is *not* legitimate to compare *R*-squareds from models where *y* is the dependent variable in one case and log(*y*) is the dependent variable in the other. These measures explain variations in different variables. We discuss how to compute comparable goodness-of-fit measures in Section 6-4.

6-2b Models with Quadratics

Quadratic functions are also used quite often in applied economics to capture decreasing or increasing marginal effects. You may want to review properties of quadratic functions in Appendix A.

In the simplest case, *y* depends on a single observed factor *x*, but it does so in a quadratic fashion:

$$y = \beta_0 + \beta_1 x + \beta_2 x^2 + u.$$

For example, take *y* = *wage* and *x* = *exper*. As we discussed in Chapter 3, this model falls outside of simple regression analysis but is easily handled with multiple regression.

It is important to remember that β_1 does not measure the change in *y* with respect to *x*; it makes no sense to hold x^2 fixed while changing *x*. If we write the estimated equation as

$$\hat{y} = \hat{\beta}_0 + \hat{\beta}_1 x + \hat{\beta}_2 x^2, \tag{6.10}$$

then we have the approximation

$$\Delta \hat{y} \approx (\hat{\beta}_1 + 2\hat{\beta}_2 x)\Delta x, \ so \ \Delta \hat{y}/\Delta x \approx \hat{\beta}_1 + 2\hat{\beta}_2 x. \tag{6.11}$$

This says that the slope of the relationship between x and y depends on the value of x; the estimated slope is $\hat{\beta}_1 + 2\hat{\beta}_2 x$. If we plug in $x = 0$, we see that $\hat{\beta}_1$ can be interpreted as the approximate slope in going from $x = 0$ to $x = 1$. After that, the second term, $2\hat{\beta}_2 x$, must be accounted for.

If we are only interested in computing the predicted change in y given a starting value for x and a change in x, we could use (6.10) directly: there is no reason to use the calculus approximation at all. However, we are usually more interested in quickly summarizing the effect of x on y, and the interpretation of $\hat{\beta}_1$ and $\hat{\beta}_2$ in equation (6.11) provides that summary. Typically, we might plug in the average value of x in the sample, or some other interesting values, such as the median or the lower and upper quartile values.

In many applications, $\hat{\beta}_1$ is positive and $\hat{\beta}_2$ is negative. For example, using the wage data in WAGE1, we obtain

$$\widehat{wage} = 3.73 + .298 \; exper - .0061 \; exper^2$$
$$\quad\quad (.35) \;\; (.041) \quad\quad\;\; (.0009) \quad\quad\quad\quad\quad\quad\quad\quad \text{[6.12]}$$
$$n = 526, R^2 = .093.$$

This estimated equation implies that *exper* has a diminishing effect on *wage*. The first year of experience is worth roughly 30¢ per hour ($.298). The second year of experience is worth less [about $.298 - 2(.0061)(1) \approx .286$, or 28.6¢, according to the approximation in (6.11) with $x = 1$]. In going from 10 to 11 years of experience, *wage* is predicted to increase by about $.298 - 2(.0061)(10) = .176$, or 17.6¢. And so on.

When the coefficient on x is positive and the coefficient on x^2 is negative, the quadratic has a parabolic shape. There is always a positive value of x where the effect of x on y is zero; before this point, x has a positive effect on y; after this point, x has a negative effect on y. In practice, it can be important to know where this turning point is.

In the estimated equation (6.10) with $\hat{\beta}_1 > 0$ and $\hat{\beta}_2 < 0$, the turning point (or maximum of the function) is always achieved at the coefficient on x over *twice* the absolute value of the coefficient on x^2:

$$x^* = |\hat{\beta}_1/(2\hat{\beta}_2)|. \quad\quad\quad\quad\quad\quad\quad\quad \text{[6.13]}$$

In the wage example, $x^* = exper^*$ is $.298/[2(.0061)] \approx 24.4$. (Note how we just drop the minus sign on $-.0061$ in doing this calculation.) This quadratic relationship is illustrated in Figure 6.1.

In the wage equation (6.12), the return to experience becomes zero at about 24.4 years. What should we make of this? There are at least three possible explanations. First, it may be that few people in the sample have more than 24 years of experience, and so the part of the curve to the right of 24 can be ignored. The cost of using a quadratic to capture diminishing effects is that the quadratic must eventually turn around. If this point is beyond all but a small percentage of the people in the sample, then this is not of much concern. But in the data set WAGE1, about 28% of the people in the sample have more than 24 years of experience; this is too high a percentage to ignore.

It is possible that the return to *exper* really becomes negative at some point, but it is hard to believe that this happens at 24 years of experience. A more likely possibility is that the estimated effect of *exper* on *wage* is biased because we have controlled for no other factors, or because the functional relationship between *wage* and *exper* in equation (6.12) is not entirely correct. Computer Exercise C2 asks you to explore this possibility by controlling for education, in addition to using log(*wage*) as the dependent variable.

When a model has a dependent variable in logarithmic form and an explanatory variable entering as a quadratic, some care is needed in reporting the partial effects. The following example also shows that the quadratic can have a U-shape, rather than a parabolic shape. A U-shape arises in equation (6.10) when $\hat{\beta}_1$ is negative and $\hat{\beta}_2$ is positive; this captures an increasing effect of x on y.

FIGURE 6.1 Quadratic relationship between $\widehat{wage}$ and *exper*.

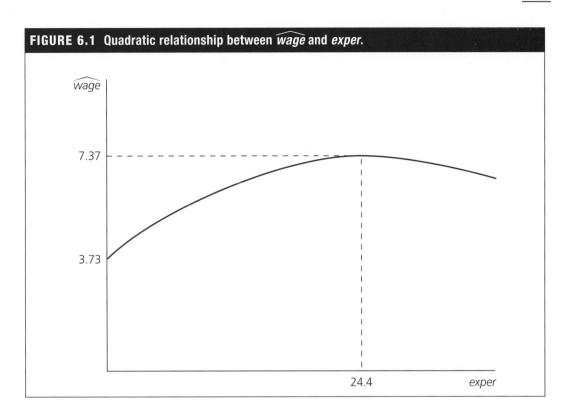

EXAMPLE 6.2   **Effects of Pollution on Housing Prices**

We modify the housing price model from Example 4.5 to include a quadratic term in *rooms*:

$$\log(price) = \beta_0 + \beta_1\log(nox) + \beta_2\log(dist) + \beta_3 rooms$$
$$+ \beta_4 rooms^2 + \beta_5 stratio + u. \qquad [6.14]$$

The model estimated using the data in HPRICE2 is

$$\widehat{\log(price)} = 13.39 - .902\log(nox) - .087\log(dist)$$
$$\quad (.57) \quad (.115) \qquad\qquad (.043)$$
$$- .545\,rooms + .062\,rooms^2 - .048\,stratio$$
$$(.165) \qquad (.013) \qquad\qquad (.006)$$
$$n = 506, R^2 = .603.$$

The quadratic term $rooms^2$ has a t statistic of about 4.77, and so it is very statistically significant. But what about interpreting the effect of *rooms* on $\log(price)$? Initially, the effect appears to be strange. Because the coefficient on *rooms* is negative and the coefficient on $rooms^2$ is positive, this equation literally implies that, at low values of *rooms*, an additional room has a *negative* effect on $\log(price)$. At some point, the effect becomes positive, and the quadratic shape means that the semi-elasticity of *price* with respect to *rooms* is increasing as *rooms* increases. This situation is shown in Figure 6.2.

   We obtain the turnaround value of *rooms* using equation (6.13) (even though $\hat{\beta}_1$ is negative and $\hat{\beta}_2$ is positive). The absolute value of the coefficient on *rooms*, .545, divided by twice the coefficient on $rooms^2$, .062, gives $rooms^* = .545/[2(.062)] \approx 4.4$; this point is labeled in Figure 6.2.

   Do we really believe that starting at three rooms and increasing to four rooms actually reduces a house's expected value? Probably not. It turns out that only five of the 506 communities in the sample

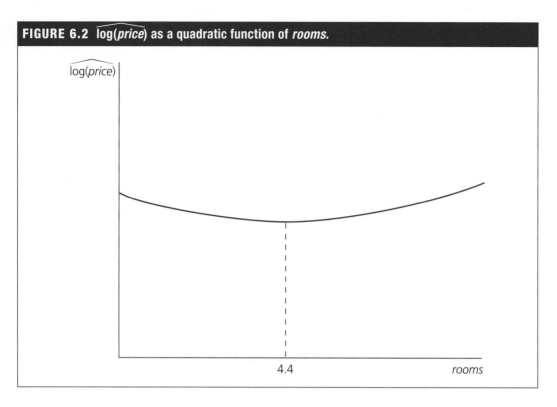

FIGURE 6.2 $\widehat{\log(price)}$ as a quadratic function of *rooms*.

have houses averaging 4.4 rooms or less, about 1% of the sample. This is so small that the quadratic to the left of 4.4 can, for practical purposes, be ignored. To the right of 4.4, we see that adding another room has an increasing effect on the percentage change in price:

$$\Delta\widehat{\log(price)} \approx \{[-.545 + 2(.062)]rooms\}\Delta rooms$$

and so

$$\%\Delta\widehat{price} \approx 100\{[-.545 + 2(.062)]rooms\}\Delta rooms$$

$$= (-54.5 + 12.4\ rooms)\Delta rooms.$$

Thus, an increase in *rooms* from, say, five to six increases price by about $-54.5 + 12.4(5) = 7.5\%$; the increase from six to seven increases price by roughly $-54.5 + 12.4(6) = 19.9\%$. This is a very strong increasing effect.

The strong increasing effect of rooms on log(*price*) in this example illustrates an important lesson: one cannot simply look at the coefficient on the quadratic term—in this case, .062—and declare that it is too small to bother with, based only on its magnitude. In many applications with quadratics the coefficient on the squared variable has one or more zeros after the decimal point: after all, this coefficient measures how the slope is changing as x (*rooms*) changes. A seemingly small coefficient can have practically important consequences, as we just saw. As a general rule, one must compute the partial effect and see how it varies with x to determine if the quadratic term is practically important. In doing so, it is useful to compare the changing slope implied by the quadratic model with the constant slope obtained from the model with only a linear term. If we drop $rooms^2$ from the equation, the coefficient on *rooms* becomes about .255, which implies that each additional room— starting from any number of rooms—increases median price by about 25.5%. This is very different from the quadratic model, where the effect becomes 25.5% at *rooms* = 6.45 but changes rapidly as *rooms* gets smaller or larger. For example, at *rooms* = 7, the return to the next room is about 32.3%.

What happens generally if the coefficients on the level and squared terms have the *same* sign (either both positive or both negative) and the explanatory variable is necessarily nonnegative (as in the case of *rooms* or *exper*)? In either case, there is no turning point for values $x > 0$. For example, if β_1 and β_2 are both positive, the smallest expected value of y is at $x = 0$, and increases in x always have a positive and increasing effect on y. (This is also true if $\beta_1 = 0$ and $\beta_2 > 0$, which means that the partial effect is zero at $x = 0$ and increasing as x increases.) Similarly, if β_1 and β_2 are both negative, the largest expected value of y is at $x = 0$, and increases in x have a negative effect on y, with the magnitude of the effect increasing as x gets larger.

The general formula for the turning point of any quadratic is $x^* = -\hat{\beta}_1/(2\hat{\beta}_2)$, which leads to a positive value if $\hat{\beta}_1$ and $\hat{\beta}_2$ have opposite signs and a negative value when $\hat{\beta}_1$ and $\hat{\beta}_2$ have the same sign. Knowing this simple formula is useful in cases where x may take on both positive and negative values; one can compute the turning point and see if it makes sense, taking into account the range of x in the sample.

There are many other possibilities for using quadratics along with logarithms. For example, an extension of (6.14) that allows a nonconstant elasticity between *price* and *nox* is

$$\log(price) = \beta_0 + \beta_1\log(nox) + \beta_2[\log(nox)]^2$$
$$+ \beta_3 crime + \beta_4 rooms + \beta_5 rooms^2 + \beta_6 stratio + u. \tag{6.15}$$

If $\beta_2 = 0$, then β_1 is the elasticity of *price* with respect to *nox*. Otherwise, this elasticity depends on the level of *nox*. To see this, we can combine the arguments for the partial effects in the quadratic and logarithmic models to show that

$$\%\Delta price \approx [\beta_1 + 2\beta_2\log(nox)]\%\Delta nox; \tag{6.16}$$

therefore, the elasticity of *price* with respect to *nox* is $\beta_1 + 2\beta_2\log(nox)$, so that it depends on $\log(nox)$.

Finally, other polynomial terms can be included in regression models. Certainly, the quadratic is seen most often, but a cubic and even a quartic term appear now and then. An often reasonable functional form for a total cost function is

$$cost = \beta_0 + \beta_1 quantity + \beta_2 quantity^2 + \beta_3 quantity^3 + u.$$

Estimating such a model causes no complications. Interpreting the parameters is more involved (though straightforward using calculus); we do not study these models further.

6-2c Models with Interaction Terms

Sometimes, it is natural for the partial effect, elasticity, or semi-elasticity of the dependent variable with respect to an explanatory variable to depend on the magnitude of yet *another* explanatory variable. For example, in the model

$$price = \beta_0 + \beta_1 sqrft + \beta_2 bdrms + \beta_3 sqrft \cdot bdrms + \beta_4 bthrms + u,$$

the partial effect of *bdrms* on *price* (holding all other variables fixed) is

$$\frac{\Delta price}{\Delta bdrms} = \beta_2 + \beta_3 sqrft. \tag{6.17}$$

If $\beta_3 > 0$, then (6.17) implies that an additional bedroom yields a higher increase in housing price for larger houses. In other words, there is an **interaction effect** between square footage and number of bedrooms. In summarizing the effect of *bdrms* on *price*, we must evaluate (6.17) at interesting values of *sqrft*, such as the mean value, or the lower and upper quartiles in the sample. Whether or not β_3 is zero is something we can easily test.

The parameters on the original variables can be tricky to interpret when we include an interaction term. For example, in the previous housing price equation, equation (6.17) shows that β_2 is the effect of *bdrms* on *price* for a home with zero square feet! This effect is clearly not of much interest. Instead, we must be careful to put interesting values of *sqrft*, such as the mean or median values in the sample, into the estimated version of equation (6.17).

Often, it is useful to reparameterize a model so that the coefficients on the original variables have an interesting meaning. Consider a model with two explanatory variables and an interaction:

$$y = \beta_0 + \beta_1 x_1 + \beta_2 x_2 + \beta_3 x_1 x_2 + u.$$

As just mentioned, β_2 is the partial effect of x_2 on y when $x_1 = 0$. Often, this is not of interest. Instead, we can reparameterize the model as

$$y = \alpha_0 + \delta_1 x_1 + \delta_2 x_2 + \beta_3 (x_1 - \mu_1)(x_2 - \mu_2) + u,$$

where μ_1 is the population mean of x_1 and μ_2 is the population mean of x_2. We can easily see that now the coefficient on x_2, δ_2, is the partial effect of x_2 on y at the mean value of x_1. (By multiplying out the interaction in the second equation and comparing the coefficients, we can easily show that $\delta_2 = \beta_2 + \beta_3 \mu_1$. The parameter δ_1 has a similar interpretation.) Therefore, if we subtract the means of the variables—in practice, these would typically be the sample means—before creating the interaction term, the coefficients on the original variables have a useful interpretation. Plus, we immediately obtain standard errors for the partial effects at the mean values. Nothing prevents us from replacing μ_1 or μ_2 with other values of the explanatory variables that may be of interest. The following example illustrates how we can use interaction terms.

EXAMPLE 6.3   **Effects of Attendance on Final Exam Performance**

A model to explain the standardized outcome on a final exam (*stndfnl*) in terms of percentage of classes attended, prior college grade point average, and ACT score is

$$stndfnl = \beta_0 + \beta_1 atndrte + \beta_2 priGPA + \beta_3 ACT + \beta_4 priGPA^2$$
$$+ \beta_5 ACT^2 + \beta_6 priGPA \cdot atndrte + u. \qquad [6.18]$$

(We use the standardized exam score for the reasons discussed in Section 6-1: it is easier to interpret a student's performance relative to the rest of the class.) In addition to quadratics in *priGPA* and *ACT*, this model includes an interaction between *priGPA* and the attendance rate. The idea is that class attendance might have a different effect for students who have performed differently in the past, as measured by *priGPA*. We are interested in the effects of attendance on final exam score: $\Delta stndfnl / \Delta atndrte = \beta_1 + \beta_6 priGPA$.

Using the 680 observations in ATTEND, for students in a course on microeconomic principles, the estimated equation is

$$\widehat{stndfnl} = 2.05 - .0067\, atndrte - 1.63\, priGPA - .128\, ACT$$
$$(1.36)\ (.0102) \qquad (.48) \qquad (.098)$$
$$+ .296\, priGPA^2 + .0045\, ACT^2 + .0056\, priGPA \cdot atndrte \qquad [6.19]$$
$$(.101) \qquad (.0022) \qquad (.0043)$$
$$n = 680,\ R^2 = .229,\ \bar{R}^2 = .222.$$

We must interpret this equation with extreme care. If we simply look at the coefficient on *atndrte*, we will incorrectly conclude that attendance has a *negative* effect on final exam score. But this coefficient supposedly measures the effect when *priGPA* = 0, which is not interesting (in this sample, the small-est prior GPA is about .86). We must also take care not to look separately at the estimates of β_1 and β_6 and conclude that, because each *t* statistic is insignificant, we cannot reject H_0: $\beta_1 = 0$, $\beta_6 = 0$. In fact, the *p*-value for the *F* test of this joint hypothesis is .014, so we certainly reject H_0 at the 5% level. This is a good example of where looking at separate *t* statistics when testing a joint hypothesis can lead one far astray.

How should we estimate the partial effect of *atndrte* on *stndfnl*? We must plug in interesting values of *priGPA* to obtain the partial effect. The mean value of *priGPA* in the sample is 2.59, so at the mean *priGPA*, the effect of *atndrte* on *stndfnl* is $-.0067 + .0056(2.59) \approx .0078$. What does this mean? Because *atndrte* is measured as a percentage, it means that a 10 percentage point increase in *atndrte* increases $\widehat{stndfnl}$ by .078 standard deviations from the mean final exam score.

How can we tell whether the estimate .0078 is statistically different from zero? We need to rerun the regression, where we replace *priGPA·atndrte* with (*priGPA* − 2.59)·*atndrte*. This gives, as the new coefficient on *atndrte*, the estimated effect at *priGPA* = 2.59, along with its standard error; nothing else in the regression changes. (We described this device in Section 4.4.) Running this new regres-sion gives the standard error of $\hat{\beta}_1 + \hat{\beta}_6(2.59) = .0078$ as .0026, which yields $t = .0078/.0026 = 3$. Therefore, at the average *priGPA*, we conclude that attendance has a statistically significant positive effect on final exam score.

Things are even more complicated for finding the effect of *priGPA* on *stndfnl* because of the quadratic term $priGPA^2$. To find the effect at the mean value of *priGPA* and the mean attend-ance rate, 82, we would replace $priGPA^2$ with $(priGPA − 2.59)^2$ and *priGPA·atndrte* with *priGPA·*(*atndrte* − 82). The coefficient on *priGPA* becomes the partial effect at the mean values, and we would have its standard error. (See Computer Exercise C7.)

> ## EXPLORING FURTHER 6.3
>
> If we add the term β_7 *ACT·atndrte* to equation (6.18), what is the partial effect of *atndrte* on *stndfnl*?

6-2d Computing Average Partial Effects

The hallmark of models with quadratics, interactions, and other nonlinear functional forms is that the partial effects depend on the values of one or more explanatory variables. For example, we just saw in Example 6.3 that the effect of *atndrte* depends on the value of *priGPA*. It is easy to see that the partial effect of *priGPA* in equation (6.18) is

$$\beta_2 + 2\beta_4 priGPA + \beta_6 atndrte$$

(something that can be verified with simple calculus or just by combining the quadratic and interac-tion formulas). The embellishments in equation (6.18) can be useful for seeing how the strength of associations between *stndfnl* and each explanatory variable changes with the values of all explanatory variables. The flexibility afforded by a model such as (6.18) does have a cost: it is tricky to describe the partial effects of the explanatory variables on *stndfnl* with a single number.

Often, one wants a single value to describe the relationship between the dependent variable *y* and each explanatory variable. One popular summary measure is the **average partial effect (APE)**, also called the *average marginal effect*. The idea behind the APE is simple for models such as (6.18). After computing the partial effect and plugging in the estimated parameters, we average the partial effects for each unit across the sample. So, the estimated partial effect of *atndrte* on *stndfnl* is

$$\hat{\beta}_1 + \hat{\beta}_6 priGPA_i.$$

We do not want to report this partial effect for each of the 680 students in our sample. Instead, we average these partial effects to obtain

$$\text{APE}_{stndfnl} = \hat{\beta}_1 + \hat{\beta}_6 \overline{priGPA},$$

where $\overline{priGPA}$ is the sample average of $priGPA$. The single number $\text{APE}_{stndfnl}$ is the (estimated) APE. The APE of $priGPA$ is only a little more complicated:

$$\text{APE}_{priGPA} = \hat{\beta}_2 + 2\hat{\beta}_4 \overline{priGPA} + \hat{\beta}_6 \overline{atndrte}.$$

Both $\text{APE}_{stndfnl}$ and APE_{priGPA} tell us the size of the partial effects on average.

The centering of explanatory variables about their sample averages before creating quadratics or interactions forces the coefficient on the levels to be the APEs. This can be cumbersome in complicated models. Fortunately, some commonly used regression packages compute APEs with a simple command after OLS estimation. Just as importantly, proper standard errors are computed using the fact that an APE is a linear combination of the OLS coefficients. For example, the APEs and their standard errors for models with both quadratics and interactions, as in Example 6.3, are easy to obtain.

APEs are also useful in models that are inherently nonlinear in parameters, which we treat in Chapter 17. At that point we will revisit the definition and calculation of APEs.

6-3 More on Goodness-of-Fit and Selection of Regressors

Until now, we have not focused much on the size of R^2 in evaluating our regression models, primarily because beginning students tend to put too much weight on R-squared. As we will see shortly, choosing a set of explanatory variables based on the size of the R-squared can lead to nonsensical models. In Chapter 10, we will discover that R-squareds obtained from time series regressions can be artificially high and can result in misleading conclusions.

Nothing about the classical linear model assumptions requires that R^2 be above any particular value; R^2 is simply an estimate of how much variation in y is explained by $x_1, x_2, \ldots, x_k$ in the population. We have seen several regressions that have had pretty small R-squareds. Although this means that we have not accounted for several factors that affect y, this does not mean that the factors in u are correlated with the independent variables. The zero conditional mean assumption MLR.4 is what determines whether we get unbiased estimators of the ceteris paribus effects of the independent variables, and the size of the R-squared has no direct bearing on this.

A small R-squared does imply that the error variance is large relative to the variance of y, which means we may have a hard time precisely estimating the β_j. But remember, we saw in Section 3.4 that a large error variance can be offset by a large sample size: if we have enough data, we may be able to precisely estimate the partial effects even though we have not controlled for many unobserved factors. Whether or not we can get precise enough estimates depends on the application. For example, suppose that some incoming students at a large university are randomly given grants to buy computer equipment. If the amount of the grant is truly randomly determined, we can estimate the ceteris paribus effect of the grant amount on subsequent college grade point average by using simple regression analysis. (Because of random assignment, all of the other factors that affect GPA would be uncorrelated with the amount of the grant.) It seems likely that the grant amount would explain little of the variation in GPA, so the R-squared from such a regression would probably be very small. But, if we have a large sample size, we still might get a reasonably precise estimate of the effect of the grant.

Another good illustration of where poor explanatory power has nothing to do with unbiased estimation of the β_j is given by analyzing the data set APPLE. Unlike the other data sets we have used, the key explanatory variables in APPLE were set experimentally—that is, without regard to other factors that might affect the dependent variable. The variable we would like to explain, *ecolbs*, is the (hypothetical) pounds of "ecologically friendly" ("ecolabeled") apples a family would demand.

Each family (actually, family head) was presented with a description of ecolabeled apples, along with prices of regular apples (*regprc*) and prices of the hypothetical ecolabeled apples (*ecoprc*). Because the price pairs were randomly assigned to each family, they are unrelated to other observed factors (such as family income) and unobserved factors (such as desire for a clean environment). Therefore, the regression of *ecolbs* on *ecoprc*, *regprc* (across all samples generated in this way) produces unbiased estimators of the price effects. Nevertheless, the *R*-squared from the regression is only .0364: the price variables explain only about 3.6% of the total variation in *ecolbs*. So, here is a case where we explain very little of the variation in *y*, yet we are in the rare situation of knowing that the data have been generated so that unbiased estimation of the β_j is possible. (Incidentally, adding observed family characteristics has a very small effect on explanatory power. See Computer Exercise C11.)

Remember, though, that the relative *change* in the *R*-squared when variables are added to an equation is very useful: the *F* statistic in (4.41) for testing the joint significance crucially depends on the difference in *R*-squareds between the unrestricted and restricted models.

As we will see in Section 6.4, an important consequence of a low *R*-squared is that prediction is difficult. Because most of the variation in *y* is explained by unobserved factors (or at least factors we do not include in our model), we will generally have a hard time using the OLS equation to predict individual future outcomes on *y* given a set of values for the explanatory variables. In fact, the low *R*-squared means that we would have a hard time predicting *y* even if we knew the β_j, the population coefficients. Fundamentally, most of the factors that explain *y* are unaccounted for in the explanatory variables, making prediction difficult.

6-3a Adjusted *R*-Squared

Most regression packages will report, along with the *R*-squared, a statistic called the **adjusted *R*-squared**. Because the adjusted *R*-squared is reported in much applied work, and because it has some useful features, we cover it in this subsection.

To see how the usual *R*-squared might be adjusted, it is usefully written as

$$R^2 = 1 - (\text{SSR}/n)/(\text{SST}/n), \qquad [6.20]$$

where SSR is the sum of squared residuals and SST is the total sum of squares; compared with equation (3.28), all we have done is divide both SSR and SST by *n*. This expression reveals what R^2 is actually estimating. Define σ_y^2 as the population variance of *y* and let σ_u^2 denote the population variance of the error term, *u*. (Until now, we have used σ^2 to denote σ_u^2, but it is helpful to be more specific here.) The **population *R*-squared** is defined as $\rho^2 = 1 - \sigma_u^2/\sigma_y^2$; this is the proportion of the variation in *y* in the population explained by the independent variables. This is what R^2 is supposed to be estimating.

R^2 estimates σ_u^2 by SSR/*n*, which we know to be biased. So why not replace SSR/*n* with SSR/(*n* − *k* − 1)? Also, we can use SST/(*n* − 1) in place of SST/*n*, as the former is the unbiased estimator of σ_y^2. Using these estimators, we arrive at the adjusted *R*-squared:

$$\bar{R}^2 = 1 - [\text{SSR}/(n - k - 1)]/[\text{SST}/(n - 1)]$$
$$= 1 - \hat{\sigma}^2/[\text{SST}/(n - 1)], \qquad [6.21]$$

because $\hat{\sigma}^2 = \text{SSR}/(n - k - 1)$. Because of the notation used to denote the adjusted *R*-squared, it is sometimes called *R-bar squared*.

The adjusted *R*-squared is sometimes called the *corrected R-squared*, but this is not a good name because it implies that $\bar{R}^2$ is somehow better than R^2 as an estimator of the population *R*-squared. Unfortunately, $\bar{R}^2$ is *not* generally known to be a better estimator. It is tempting to think that $\bar{R}^2$ corrects the bias in R^2 for estimating the population *R*-squared, ρ^2, but it does not: the ratio of two unbiased estimators is not an unbiased estimator.

The primary attractiveness of $\overline{R}^2$ is that it imposes a penalty for adding additional independent variables to a model. We know that R^2 can never fall when a new independent variable is added to a regression equation: this is because SSR never goes up (and usually falls) as more independent variables are added (assuming we use the same set of observations). But the formula for $\overline{R}^2$ shows that it depends explicitly on k, the number of independent variables. If an independent variable is added to a regression, SSR falls, but so does the *df* in the regression, $n - k - 1$. SSR/$(n - k - 1)$ can go up or down when a new independent variable is added to a regression.

An interesting algebraic fact is the following: if we add a new independent variable to a regression equation, $\overline{R}^2$ increases if, and only if, the *t* statistic on the new variable is greater than one in absolute value. (An extension of this is that $\overline{R}^2$ increases when a group of variables is added to a regression if, and only if, the *F* statistic for joint significance of the new variables is greater than unity.) Thus, we see immediately that using $\overline{R}^2$ to decide whether a certain independent variable (or set of variables) belongs in a model gives us a different answer than standard *t* or *F* testing (because a *t* or *F* statistic of unity is not statistically significant at traditional significance levels).

It is sometimes useful to have a formula for $\overline{R}^2$ in terms of R^2. Simple algebra gives

$$\overline{R}^2 = 1 - (1 - R^2)(n - 1)/(n - k - 1). \qquad [6.22]$$

For example, if $R^2 = .30$, $n = 51$, and $k = 10$, then $\overline{R}^2 = 1 - .70(50)/40 = .125$. Thus, for small n and large k, $\overline{R}^2$ can be substantially below R^2. In fact, if the usual R-squared is small, and $n - k - 1$ is small, $\overline{R}^2$ can actually be negative! For example, you can plug in $R^2 = .10$, $n = 51$, and $k = 10$ to verify that $\overline{R}^2 = -.125$. A negative $\overline{R}^2$ indicates a very poor model fit relative to the number of degrees of freedom.

The adjusted R-squared is sometimes reported along with the usual R-squared in regressions, and sometimes $\overline{R}^2$ is reported in place of R^2. It is important to remember that it is R^2, not $\overline{R}^2$, that appears in the F statistic in (4.41). The same formula with $\overline{R}^2_r$ and $\overline{R}^2_{ur}$ is *not* valid.

6-3b Using Adjusted *R*-Squared to Choose between Nonnested Models

In Section 4-5, we learned how to compute an F statistic for testing the joint significance of a group of variables; this allows us to decide, at a particular significance level, whether at least one variable in the group affects the dependent variable. This test does not allow us to decide *which* of the variables has an effect. In some cases, we want to choose a model without redundant independent variables, and the adjusted R-squared can help with this.

In the major league baseball salary example in Section 4-5, we saw that neither *hrunsyr* nor *rbisyr* was individually significant. These two variables are highly correlated, so we might want to choose between the models

$$\log(salary) = \beta_0 + \beta_1 years + \beta_2 gamesyr + \beta_3 bavg + \beta_4 hrunsyr + u$$

and

$$\log(salary) = \beta_0 + \beta_1 years + \beta_2 gamesyr + \beta_3 bavg + \beta_4 rbisyr + u.$$

These two equations are **nonnested models** because neither equation is a special case of the other. The F statistics we studied in Chapter 4 only allow us to test *nested* models: one model (the restricted model) is a special case of the other model (the unrestricted model). See equations (4.32) and (4.28) for examples of restricted and unrestricted models. One possibility is to create a composite model that contains *all* explanatory variables from the original models and then to test each model against the general model using the F test. The problem with this process is that either both models might be rejected or neither model might be rejected (as happens with the major league baseball salary example in Section 4-5). Thus, it does not always provide a way to distinguish between models with nonnested regressors.

In the baseball player salary regression using the data in MLB1, $\bar{R}^2$ for the regression containing *hrunsyr* is .6211, and $\bar{R}^2$ for the regression containing *rbisyr* is .6226. Thus, based on the adjusted R-squared, there is a very slight preference for the model with *rbisyr*. But the difference is practically very small, and we might obtain a different answer by controlling for some of the variables in Computer Exercise C5 in Chapter 4. (Because both nonnested models contain five parameters, the usual R-squared can be used to draw the same conclusion.)

Comparing $\bar{R}^2$ to choose among different nonnested sets of independent variables can be valuable when these variables represent different functional forms. Consider two models relating R&D intensity to firm sales:

$$rdintens = \beta_0 + \beta_1 \log(sales) + u. \qquad [6.23]$$

$$rdintens = \beta_0 + \beta_1 sales + \beta_2 sales^2 + u. \qquad [6.24]$$

The first model captures a diminishing return by including *sales* in logarithmic form; the second model does this by using a quadratic. Thus, the second model contains one more parameter than the first.

When equation (6.23) is estimated using the 32 observations on chemical firms in RDCHEM, R^2 is .061, and R^2 for equation (6.24) is .148. Therefore, it appears that the quadratic fits much better. But a comparison of the usual R-squareds is unfair to the first model because it contains one fewer parameter than (6.24). That is, (6.23) is a more parsimonious model than (6.24).

Everything else being equal, simpler models are better. Since the usual R-squared does not penalize more complicated models, it is better to use $\bar{R}^2$. The $\bar{R}^2$ for (6.23) is .030, while $\bar{R}^2$ for (6.24) is .090. Thus, even after adjusting for the difference in degrees of freedom, the quadratic model wins out. The quadratic model is also preferred when profit margin is added to each regression.

There is an important limitation in using $\bar{R}^2$ to choose between nonnested models: we cannot use it to choose between different functional forms for the dependent variable. This is unfortunate, because we often want to decide on whether y or $\log(y)$ (or maybe some other transformation) should be used as the dependent variable based on goodness-of-fit. But neither R^2 nor $\bar{R}^2$ can be used for this purpose. The reason is simple: these R-squareds measure the explained proportion of the total variation in whatever dependent variable we are using in the regression, and different nonlinear functions of the dependent variable will have different amounts of variation to explain. For example, the total variations in y and $\log(y)$ are not the same and are often very different. Comparing the adjusted R-squareds from regressions with these different forms of the dependent variables does not tell us anything about which model fits better; they are fitting two separate dependent variables.

> **EXPLORING FURTHER 6.4**
>
> Explain why choosing a model by maximizing $\bar{R}^2$ or minimizing $\hat{\sigma}$ (the standard error of the regression) is the same thing.

EXAMPLE 6.4   **CEO Compensation and Firm Performance**

Consider two estimated models relating CEO compensation to firm performance:

$$\widehat{salary} = 830.63 + .0163\ sales + 19.63\ roe$$
$$\phantom{\widehat{salary} = 830.63} (223.90)\ \ (.0089) \qquad (11.08) \qquad [6.25]$$
$$n = 209, R^2 = .029, \bar{R}^2 = .020$$

and

$$\widehat{lsalary} = 4.36 + .275\, lsales + .0179\, roe$$
$$\phantom{\widehat{lsalary} =} (0.29)\ (.033)\qquad (.0040) \tag{6.26}$$
$$n = 209,\, R^2 = .282,\, \overline{R}^2 = .275,$$

where *roe* is the return on equity discussed in Chapter 2. For simplicity, *lsalary* and *lsales* denote the natural logs of *salary* and *sales*. We already know how to interpret these different estimated equations. But can we say that one model fits better than the other?

The R-squared for equation (6.25) shows that *sales* and *roe* explain only about 2.9% of the variation in CEO salary in the sample. Both *sales* and *roe* have marginal statistical significance.

Equation (6.26) shows that log(*sales*) and *roe* explain about 28.2% of the variation in log(*salary*). In terms of goodness-of-fit, this much higher R-squared would seem to imply that model (6.26) is much better, but this is not necessarily the case. The total sum of squares for *salary* in the sample is 391,732,982, while the total sum of squares for log(*salary*) is only 66.72. Thus, there is much less variation in log(*salary*) that needs to be explained.

At this point, we can use features other than R^2 or $\overline{R}^2$ to decide between these models. For example, log(*sales*) and *roe* are much more statistically significant in (6.26) than are *sales* and *roe* in (6.25), and the coefficients in (6.26) are probably of more interest. To be sure, however, we will need to make a valid goodness-of-fit comparison.

In Section 6-4, we will offer a goodness-of-fit measure that does allow us to compare models where *y* appears in both level and log form.

6-3c Controlling for Too Many Factors in Regression Analysis

In many of the examples we have covered, and certainly in our discussion of omitted variables bias in Chapter 3, we have worried about omitting important factors from a model that might be correlated with the independent variables. It is also possible to control for too *many* variables in a regression analysis.

If we overemphasize goodness-of-fit, we open ourselves to controlling for factors in a regression model that should not be controlled for. To avoid this mistake, we need to remember the ceteris paribus interpretation of multiple regression models.

To illustrate this issue, suppose we are doing a study to assess the impact of state beer taxes on traffic fatalities. The idea is that a higher tax on beer will reduce alcohol consumption, and likewise drunk driving, resulting in fewer traffic fatalities. To measure the ceteris paribus effect of taxes on fatalities, we can model *fatalities* as a function of several factors, including the beer *tax*:

$$fatalities = \beta_0 + \beta_1 tax + \beta_2 miles + \beta_3 percmale + \beta_4 perc16\_21 + \ldots,$$

where

$$miles = \text{total miles driven.}$$
$$percmale = \text{percentage of the state population that is male.}$$
$$perc16\_21 = \text{percentage of the population between ages 16 and 21, and so on.}$$

Notice how we have not included a variable measuring per capita beer consumption. Are we committing an omitted variables error? The answer is no. If we control for beer consumption in this equation, then how would beer taxes affect traffic fatalities? In the equation

$$fatalities = \beta_0 + \beta_1 tax + \beta_2 beercons + \ldots,$$

β_1 measures the difference in fatalities due to a one percentage point increase in *tax*, holding *beercons* fixed. It is difficult to understand why this would be interesting. We should not be controlling for differences in *beercons* across states, unless we want to test for some sort of indirect effect of beer taxes. Other factors, such as gender and age distribution, should be controlled for.

As a second example, suppose that, for a developing country, we want to estimate the effects of pesticide usage among farmers on family health expenditures. In addition to pesticide usage amounts, should we include the number of doctor visits as an explanatory variable? No. Health expenditures include doctor visits, and we would like to pick up all effects of pesticide use on health expenditures. If we include the number of doctor visits as an explanatory variable, then we are only measuring the effects of pesticide use on health expenditures other than doctor visits. It makes more sense to use number of doctor visits as a dependent variable in a separate regression on pesticide amounts.

The previous examples are what can be called **over controlling** for factors in multiple regression. Often this results from nervousness about potential biases that might arise by leaving out an important explanatory variable. But it is important to remember the ceteris paribus nature of multiple regression. In some cases, it makes no sense to hold some factors fixed precisely because they should be allowed to change when a policy variable changes.

Unfortunately, the issue of whether or not to control for certain factors is not always clear-cut. For example, Betts (1995) studies the effect of high school quality on subsequent earnings. He points out that, if better school quality results in more education, then controlling for education in the regression along with measures of quality will underestimate the return to quality. Betts does the analysis with and without years of education in the equation to get a range of estimated effects for quality of schooling.

To see explicitly how pursuing high R-squareds can lead to trouble, consider the housing price example from Section 4-5 that illustrates the testing of multiple hypotheses. In that case, we wanted to test the rationality of housing price assessments. We regressed log(*price*) on log(*assess*), log(*lotsize*), log(*sqrft*), and *bdrms* and tested whether the latter three variables had zero population coefficients while log(*assess*) had a coefficient of unity. But what if we change the purpose of the analysis and estimate a *hedonic price model*, which allows us to obtain the marginal values of various housing attributes? Should we include log(*assess*) in the equation? The adjusted R-squared from the regression with log(*assess*) is .762, while the adjusted R-squared without it is .630. Based on goodness-of-fit only, we should include log(*assess*). But this is incorrect if our goal is to determine the effects of lot size, square footage, and number of bedrooms on housing values. Including log(*assess*) in the equation amounts to holding one measure of value fixed and then asking how much an additional bedroom would change another measure of value. This makes no sense for valuing housing attributes.

If we remember that different models serve different purposes, and we focus on the ceteris paribus interpretation of regression, then we will not include the wrong factors in a regression model.

6-3d Adding Regressors to Reduce the Error Variance

We have just seen some examples of where certain independent variables should not be included in a regression model, even though they are correlated with the dependent variable. From Chapter 3, we know that adding a new independent variable to a regression can exacerbate the multicollinearity problem. On the other hand, since we are taking something out of the error term, adding a variable generally reduces the error variance. Generally, we cannot know which effect will dominate.

However, there is one case that is clear: we should always include independent variables that affect y and are *uncorrelated* with all of the independent variables of interest. Why? Because adding such a variable does not induce multicollinearity in the population (and therefore multicollinearity in the sample should be negligible), but it will reduce the error variance. In large sample sizes, the standard errors of all OLS estimators will be reduced.

As an example, consider estimating the individual demand for beer as a function of the average county beer price. It may be reasonable to assume that individual characteristics are uncorrelated with county-level prices, and so a simple regression of beer consumption on county price would suffice for estimating the effect of price on individual demand. But it is possible to get a more precise estimate of the price elasticity of beer demand by including individual characteristics, such as age and amount of education. If these factors affect demand and are uncorrelated with price, then the standard error of the price coefficient will be smaller, at least in large samples.

As a second example, consider the grants for computer equipment given at the beginning of Section 6-3. If, in addition to the grant variable, we control for other factors that can explain college GPA, we can probably get a more precise estimate of the effect of the grant. Measures of high school grade point average and rank, SAT and ACT scores, and family background variables are good candidates. Because the grant amounts are randomly assigned, all additional control variables are uncorrelated with the grant amount; in the sample, multicollinearity between the grant amount and other independent variables should be minimal. But adding the extra controls might significantly reduce the error variance, leading to a more precise estimate of the grant effect. Remember, the issue is not unbiasedness here: we obtain an unbiased and consistent estimator whether or not we add the high school performance and family background variables. The issue is getting an estimator with a smaller sampling variance.

A related point is that when we have random assignment of a policy, we need not worry about whether some of our explanatory variables are "endogenous"—provided these variables themselves are not affected by the policy. For example, in studying the effect of hours in a job training program on labor earnings, we can include the amount of education reported prior to the job training program. We need not worry that schooling might be correlated with omitted factors, such as "ability," because we are not trying to estimate the return to schooling. We are trying to estimate the effect of the job training program, and we can include any controls that are not themselves affected by job training without biasing the job training effect. What we must avoid is including a variable such as the amount of education *after* the job training program, as some people may decide to get more education because of how many hours they were assigned to the job training program.

Unfortunately, cases where we have information on additional explanatory variables that are uncorrelated with the explanatory variables of interest are somewhat rare in the social sciences. But it is worth remembering that when these variables are available, they can be included in a model to reduce the error variance without inducing multicollinearity.

6-4 Prediction and Residual Analysis

In Chapter 3, we defined the OLS predicted or fitted values and the OLS residuals. **Predictions** are certainly useful, but they are subject to sampling variation, because they are obtained using the OLS estimators. Thus, in this section, we show how to obtain confidence intervals for a prediction from the OLS regression line.

From Chapters 3 and 4, we know that the residuals are used to obtain the sum of squared residuals and the R-squared, so they are important for goodness-of-fit and testing. Sometimes, economists study the residuals for particular observations to learn about individuals (or firms, houses, etc.) in the sample.

6.4a Confidence Intervals for Predictions

Suppose we have estimated the equation

$$\hat{y} = \hat{\beta}_0 + \hat{\beta}_1 x_1 + \hat{\beta}_2 x_2 + \dots + \hat{\beta}_k x_k. \qquad [6.27]$$

When we plug in particular values of the independent variables, we obtain a prediction for y, which is an estimate of the *expected value* of y given the particular values for the explanatory variables. For emphasis, let $c_1, c_2, \dots, c_k$ denote particular values for each of the k independent variables; these may or may not correspond to an actual data point in our sample. The parameter we would like to estimate is

$$
\begin{aligned}
\theta_0 &= \beta_0 + \beta_1 c_1 + \beta_2 c_2 + \dots + \beta_k c_k \\
&= E(y|x_1 = c_1, x_2 = c_2, \dots, x_k = c_k).
\end{aligned}
$$
[6.28]

The estimator of θ_0 is

$$
\hat{\theta}_0 = \hat{\beta}_0 + \hat{\beta}_1 c_1 + \hat{\beta}_2 c_2 + \dots + \hat{\beta}_k c_k.
$$
[6.29]

In practice, this is easy to compute. But what if we want some measure of the uncertainty in this predicted value? It is natural to construct a confidence interval for θ_0, which is centered at $\hat{\theta}_0$.

To obtain a confidence interval for θ_0, we need a standard error for $\hat{\theta}_0$. Then, with a large df, we can construct a 95% confidence interval using the rule of thumb $\hat{\theta}_0 \pm 2 \cdot se(\hat{\theta}_0)$. (As always, we can use the exact percentiles in a t distribution.)

How do we obtain the standard error of $\hat{\theta}_0$? This is the same problem we encountered in Section 4-4: we need to obtain a standard error for a linear combination of the OLS estimators. Here, the problem is even more complicated, because all of the OLS estimators generally appear in $\hat{\theta}_0$ (unless some c_j are zero). Nevertheless, the same trick that we used in Section 4-4 will work here. Write $\beta_0 = \theta_0 - \beta_1 c_1 - \dots - \beta_k c_k$ and plug this into the equation

$$
y = \beta_0 + \beta_1 x_1 + \dots + \beta_k x_k + u
$$

to obtain

$$
y = \theta_0 + \beta_1(x_1 - c_1) + \beta_2(x_2 - c_2) + \dots + \beta_k(x_k - c_k) + u.
$$
[6.30]

In other words, we subtract the value c_j from each observation on x_j, and then we run the regression of

$$
y_i \text{ on } (x_{i1} - c_1), \dots, (x_{ik} - c_k), i = 1, 2, \dots, n.
$$
[6.31]

The predicted value in (6.29) and, more importantly, its standard error, are obtained from the *intercept* (or constant) in regression (6.31).

As an example, we obtain a confidence interval for a prediction from a college GPA regression, where we use high school information.

EXAMPLE 6.5	**Confidence Interval for Predicted College GPA**

Using the data in GPA2, we obtain the following equation for predicting college GPA:

$$
\begin{aligned}
\widehat{colgpa} = \; &1.493 + .00149 \, sat - .01386 \, hsperc \\
&(0.075) \;\; (.00007) \qquad (.00056) \\
&- .06088 \, hsize + .00546 \, hsize^2 \\
&\;\;(.01650) \qquad\quad (.00227) \\
&n = 4{,}137, R^2 = .278, \overline{R}^2 = .277, \hat{\sigma} = .560,
\end{aligned}
$$
[6.32]

where we have reported estimates to several digits to reduce round-off error. What is predicted college GPA, when $sat = 1{,}200$, $hsperc = 30$, and $hsize = 5$ (which means 500)? This is easy to get by plugging these values into equation (6.32): $\widehat{colgpa} = 2.70$ (rounded to two digits). Unfortunately, we cannot use equation (6.32) directly to get a confidence interval for the expected $colgpa$ at the given values of the independent variables. One simple way to obtain a confidence interval is to define a new set of independent variables: $sat0 = sat - 1{,}200$, $hsperc0 = hsperc - 30$, $hsize0 = hsize - 5$, and $hsizesq0 = hsize^2 - 25$. When we regress $colgpa$ on these new independent variables, we get

$$\widehat{colgpa} = 2.700 + .00149\ sat0 - .01386\ hsperc0$$
$$(0.020)\ (.00007)\qquad (.00056)$$
$$-\ .06088\ hsize0 + .00546\ hsizesq0$$
$$(.01650)\qquad\quad (.00227)$$
$$n = 4{,}137, R^2 = .278, \overline{R}^2 = .277, \hat{\sigma} = .560.$$

The only difference between this regression and that in (6.32) is the intercept, which is the prediction we want, along with its standard error, .020. It is not an accident that the slope coefficients, their standard errors, R-squared, and so on are the same as before; this provides a way to check that the proper transformations were done. We can easily construct a 95% confidence interval for the expected college GPA: $2.70 \pm 1.96(.020)$ or about 2.66 to 2.74. This confidence interval is rather narrow due to the very large sample size.

Because the variance of the intercept estimator is smallest when each explanatory variable has zero sample mean (see Question 2.5 for the simple regression case), it follows from the regression in (6.31) that the variance of the prediction is smallest at the mean values of the x_j. (That is, $c_j = \overline{x}_j$ for all j.) This result is not too surprising, since we have the most faith in our regression line near the middle of the data. As the values of the c_j get farther away from the $\overline{x}_j$, $\text{Var}(\hat{y})$ gets larger and larger.

The previous method allows us to put a confidence interval around the OLS estimate of $E(y|x_1, \ldots, x_k)$ for any values of the explanatory variables. In other words, we obtain a confidence interval for the *average* value of y for the subpopulation with a given set of covariates. But a confidence interval for the average person in the subpopulation is not the same as a confidence interval for a particular unit (individual, family, firm, and so on) from the population. In forming a confidence interval for an unknown outcome on y, we must account for another very important source of variation: the variance in the unobserved error, which measures our ignorance of the unobserved factors that affect y.

Let y^0 denote the value for which we would like to construct a confidence interval, which we sometimes call a **prediction interval**. For example, y^0 could represent a person or firm not in our original sample. Let $x_1^0, \ldots, x_k^0$ be the new values of the independent variables, which we assume we observe, and let u^0 be the unobserved error. Therefore, we have

$$y^0 = \beta_0 + \beta_1 x_1^0 + \beta_2 x_2^0 + \ldots + \beta_k x_k^0 + u^0. \qquad [6.33]$$

As before, our best prediction of y^0 is the expected value of y^0 given the explanatory variables, which we estimate from the OLS regression line: $\hat{y}^0 = \hat{\beta}_0 + \hat{\beta}_1 x_1^0 + \hat{\beta}_2 x_2^0 + \ldots + \hat{\beta}_k x_k^0$. The **prediction error** in using $\hat{y}^0$ to predict y^0 is

$$\hat{e}^0 = y^0 - \hat{y}^0 = (\beta_0 + \beta_1 x_1^0 + \ldots + \beta_k x_k^0) + u^0 - \hat{y}^0. \qquad [6.34]$$

Now, $E(\hat{y}^0) = E(\hat{\beta}_0) + E(\hat{\beta}_1)x_1^0 + E(\hat{\beta}_2)x_2^0 + \ldots + E(\hat{\beta}_k)x_k^0 = \beta_0 + \beta_1 x_1^0 + \ldots + \beta_k x_k^0$, because the $\hat{\beta}_j$ are unbiased. (As before, these expectations are all conditional on the sample values of the independent variables.) Because u^0 has zero mean, $E(\hat{e}^0) = 0$. We have shown that the expected prediction error is zero.

In finding the variance of $\hat{e}^0$, note that u^0 is uncorrelated with each $\hat{\beta}_j$, because u^0 is uncorrelated with the errors in the sample used to obtain the $\hat{\beta}_j$. By basic properties of covariance (see Appendix B),

u^0 and $\hat{y}^0$ are uncorrelated. Therefore, the **variance of the prediction error** (conditional on all in-sample values of the independent variables) is the sum of the variances:

$$\text{Var}(\hat{e}^0) = \text{Var}(\hat{y}^0) + \text{Var}(u^0) = \text{Var}(\hat{y}^0) + \sigma^2, \qquad [6.35]$$

where $\sigma^2 = \text{Var}(u^0)$ is the error variance. There are two sources of variation in $\hat{e}^0$. The first is the sampling error in $\hat{y}^0$, which arises because we have estimated the β_j. Because each $\hat{\beta}_j$ has a variance proportional to $1/n$, where n is the sample size, $\text{Var}(\hat{y}^0)$ is proportional to $1/n$. This means that, for large samples, $\text{Var}(\hat{y}^0)$ can be very small. By contrast, σ^2 is the variance of the error in the population; it does not change with the sample size. In many examples, σ^2 will be the dominant term in (6.35).

Under the classical linear model assumptions, the $\hat{\beta}_j$ and u^0 are normally distributed, and so $\hat{e}^0$ is also normally distributed (conditional on all sample values of the explanatory variables). Earlier, we described how to obtain an unbiased estimator of $\text{Var}(\hat{y}^0)$, and we obtained our unbiased estimator of σ^2 in Chapter 3. By using these estimators, we can define the standard error of $\hat{e}^0$ as

$$\text{se}(\hat{e}^0) = \{[\text{se}(\hat{y}^0)]^2 + \hat{\sigma}^2\}^{1/2}. \qquad [6.36]$$

Using the same reasoning for the t statistics of the $\hat{\beta}_j$, $\hat{e}^0/\text{se}(\hat{e}^0)$ has a t distribution with $n - (k + 1)$ degrees of freedom. Therefore,

$$P[-t_{.025} \le \hat{e}^0/\text{se}(\hat{e}^0) \le t_{.025}] = .95,$$

where $t_{.025}$ is the 97.5[th] percentile in the t_{n-k-1} distribution. For large $n - k - 1$, remember that $t_{.025} \approx 1.96$. Plugging in $\hat{e}^0 = y^0 - \hat{y}^0$ and rearranging gives a 95% prediction interval for y^0:

$$\hat{y}^0 \pm t_{.025} \cdot \text{se}(\hat{e}^0); \qquad [6.37]$$

as usual, except for small df, a good rule of thumb is $\hat{y}^0 \pm 2\text{se}(\hat{e}^0)$. This is wider than the confidence interval for $\hat{y}^0$ itself because of $\hat{\sigma}^2$ in (6.36); it often is much wider to reflect the factors in u^0 that we have not accounted for.

EXAMPLE 6.6   **Confidence Interval for Future College GPA**

Suppose we want a 95% CI for the future college GPA of a high school student with *sat* = 1,200, *hsperc* = 30, and *hsize* = 5. In Example 6.5, we obtained a 95% confidence interval for the *average* college GPA among all students with the particular characteristics *sat* = 1,200, *hsperc* = 30, and *hsize* = 5. Now, we want a 95% confidence interval for any *particular* student with these characteristics. The 95% prediction interval must account for the variation in the individual, unobserved characteristics that affect college performance. We have everything we need to obtain a CI for *colgpa*. $\text{se}(\hat{y}^0) = .020$ and $\hat{\sigma} = .560$ and so, from (6.36), $\text{se}(\hat{e}^0) = [(.020)^2 + (.560)^2]^{1/2} \approx .560$. Notice how small $\text{se}(\hat{y}^0)$ is relative to $\hat{\sigma}$: virtually all of the variation in $\hat{e}^0$ comes from the variation in u^0. The 95% CI is $2.70 \pm 1.96(.560)$ or about 1.60 to 3.80. This is a wide confidence interval and shows that, based on the factors we included in the regression, we cannot accurately pin down an individual's future college grade point average. (In one sense, this is good news, as it means that high school rank and performance on the SAT do not preordain one's performance in college.) Evidently, the unobserved characteristics that affect college GPA vary widely among individuals with the same observed SAT score and high school rank.

6-4b Residual Analysis

Sometimes, it is useful to examine individual observations to see whether the actual value of the dependent variable is above or below the predicted value; that is, to examine the residuals for the individual observations. This process is called **residual analysis**. Economists have been known to examine the residuals from a regression in order to aid in the purchase of a home. The following housing price example illustrates residual analysis. Housing price is related to various observable characteristics of the house. We can list all of the characteristics that we find important, such as size, number of bedrooms, number of bathrooms, and so on. We can use a sample of houses to estimate a relationship between price and attributes, where we end up with a predicted value and an actual value for each house. Then, we can construct the residuals, $\hat{u}_i = y_i - \hat{y}_i$. The house with the most negative residual is, at least based on the factors we have controlled for, the most underpriced one relative to its *observed* characteristics. Of course, a selling price substantially below its predicted price could indicate some undesirable feature of the house that we have failed to account for, and which is therefore contained in the unobserved error. In addition to obtaining the prediction and residual, it also makes sense to compute a confidence interval for what the future selling price of the home could be, using the method described in equation (6.37).

Using the data in HPRICE1, we run a regression of *price* on *lotsize*, *sqrft*, and *bdrms*. In the sample of 88 homes, the most negative residual is −120.206, for the 81st house. Therefore, the asking price for this house is $120,206 below its predicted price.

There are many other uses of residual analysis. One way to rank law schools is to regress median starting salary on a variety of student characteristics (such as median LSAT scores of entering class, median college GPA of entering class, and so on) and to obtain a predicted value and residual for each law school. The law school with the largest residual has the highest predicted value added. (Of course, there is still much uncertainty about how an individual's starting salary would compare with the median for a law school overall.) These residuals can be used along with the costs of attending each law school to determine the best value; this would require an appropriate discounting of future earnings.

Residual analysis also plays a role in legal decisions. A *New York Times* article entitled "Judge Says Pupil's Poverty, Not Segregation, Hurts Scores" (6/28/95) describes an important legal case. The issue was whether the poor performance on standardized tests in the Hartford School District, relative to performance in surrounding suburbs, was due to poor school quality at the highly segregated schools. The judge concluded that "the disparity in test scores does not indicate that Hartford is doing an inadequate or poor job in educating its students or that its schools are failing, because the predicted scores based upon the relevant socioeconomic factors are about at the levels that one would expect." This conclusion is based on a regression analysis of average or median scores on socioeconomic characteristics of various school districts in Connecticut. The judge's conclusion suggests that, given the poverty levels of students at Hartford schools, the actual test scores were similar to those predicted from a regression analysis: the residual for Hartford was not sufficiently negative to conclude that the schools themselves were the cause of low test scores.

> **EXPLORING FURTHER 6.5**
>
> How would you use residual analysis to determine which professional athletes are overpaid or underpaid relative to their performance?

6-4c Predicting *y* When log(*y*) Is the Dependent Variable

Because the natural log transformation is used so often for the dependent variable in empirical economics, we devote this subsection to the issue of predicting *y* when log(*y*) is the dependent variable. As a byproduct, we will obtain a goodness-of-fit measure for the log model that can be compared with the *R*-squared from the level model.

To obtain a prediction, it is useful to define $logy = \log(y)$; this emphasizes that it is the log of y that is predicted in the model

$$logy = \beta_0 + \beta_1 x_1 + \beta_2 x_2 + \ldots + \beta_k x_k + u. \tag{6.38}$$

In this equation, the x_j might be transformations of other variables; for example, we could have $x_1 = \log(sales)$, $x_2 = \log(mktval)$, $x_3 = ceoten$ in the CEO salary example.

Given the OLS estimators, we know how to predict $logy$ for any value of the independent variables:

$$\widehat{logy} = \hat{\beta}_0 + \hat{\beta}_1 x_1 + \hat{\beta}_2 x_2 + \ldots + \hat{\beta}_k x_k. \tag{6.39}$$

Now, since the exponential undoes the log, our first guess for predicting y is to simply exponentiate the predicted value for $\log(y)$: $\hat{y} = \exp(\widehat{logy})$. This does not work; in fact, it will systematically *underestimate* the expected value of y. In fact, if model (6.38) follows the CLM assumptions MLR.1 through MLR.6, it can be shown that

$$\mathrm{E}(y|\boldsymbol{x}) = \exp(\sigma^2/2) \cdot \exp(\beta_0 + \beta_1 x_1 + \beta_2 x_2 + \ldots + \beta_k x_k),$$

where $\boldsymbol{x}$ denotes the independent variables and σ^2 is the variance of u. [*If $u \sim$ Normal$(0, \sigma^2)$, then the expected value of $\exp(u)$ is $\exp(\sigma^2/2)$.*] This equation shows that a simple adjustment is needed to predict y:

$$\hat{y} = \exp(\hat{\sigma}^2/2)\exp(\widehat{logy}), \tag{6.40}$$

where $\hat{\sigma}^2$ is simply the unbiased estimator of σ^2. Because $\hat{\sigma}$, the standard error of the regression, is always reported, obtaining predicted values for y is easy. Because $\hat{\sigma}^2 > 0$, $\exp(\hat{\sigma}^2/2) > 1$. For large $\hat{\sigma}^2$, this adjustment factor can be substantially larger than unity.

The prediction in (6.40) is not unbiased, but it is consistent. There are no unbiased predictions of y, and in many cases, (6.40) works well. However, it does rely on the normality of the error term, u. In Chapter 5, we showed that OLS has desirable properties, even when u is not normally distributed. Therefore, it is useful to have a prediction that does not rely on normality. If we just assume that u is independent of the explanatory variables, then we have

$$\mathrm{E}(y|\boldsymbol{x}) = \alpha_0 \exp(\beta_0 + \beta_1 x_1 + \beta_2 x_2 + \ldots + \beta_k x_k), \tag{6.41}$$

where α_0 is the expected value of $\exp(u)$, which must be greater than unity.

Given an estimate $\hat{\alpha}_0$, we can predict y as

$$\hat{y} = \hat{\alpha}_0 \exp(\widehat{logy}), \tag{6.42}$$

which again simply requires exponentiating the predicted value from the log model and multiplying the result by $\hat{\alpha}_0$.

Two approaches suggest themselves for estimating α_0 without the normality assumption. The first is based on $\alpha_0 = \mathrm{E}[\exp(u)]$. To estimate α_0 we replace the population expectation with a sample average and then we replace the unobserved errors, u_i, with the OLS residuals, $\hat{u}_i = \log(y_i) - \hat{\beta}_0 - \hat{\beta}_1 x_{i1} - \ldots - \hat{\beta}_k x_{ik}$. This leads to the method of moments estimator (see Appendix C)

$$\hat{\alpha}_0 = n^{-1} \sum_{i=1}^{n} \exp(\hat{u}_i). \tag{6.43}$$

Not surprisingly, $\hat{\alpha}_0$ is a consistent estimator of α_0, but it is not unbiased because we have replaced u_i with $\hat{u}_i$ inside a nonlinear function. This version of $\hat{\alpha}_0$ is a special case of what Duan (1983) called a **smearing estimate**. Because the OLS residuals have a zero sample average, it can be shown that, for any data set, $\hat{\alpha}_0 > 1$. (Technically, $\hat{\alpha}_0$ would equal one if all the OLS residuals were zero, but this never happens in any interesting application.) That $\hat{\alpha}_0$ is necessarily greater than one is convenient because it must be that $\alpha_0 > 1$.

A different estimate of α_0 is based on a simple regression through the origin. To see how it works, define $m_i = \exp(\beta_0 + \beta_1 x_{i1} + \ldots + \beta_k x_{ik})$, so that, from equation (6.41), $E(y_i|m_i) = \alpha_0 m_i$. If we could observe the m_i, we could obtain an unbiased estimator of α_0 from the regression y_i on m_i without an intercept. Instead, we replace the β_j with their OLS estimates and obtain $\hat{m}_i = \exp(\widehat{logy_i})$, where, of course, the $\widehat{logy_i}$ are the fitted values from the regression $logy_i$ on $x_{i1}, \ldots, x_{ik}$ (with an intercept). Then $\check{\alpha}_0$ [to distinguish it from $\hat{\alpha}_0$ in equation (6.43)] is the OLS slope estimate from the simple regression y_i on $\hat{m}_i$ (no intercept):

$$\check{\alpha}_0 = \left(\sum_{i=1}^{n} \hat{m}_i^2 \right)^{-1} \left(\sum_{i=1}^{n} \hat{m}_i y_i \right).$$ [6.44]

We will call $\check{\alpha}_0$ the regression estimate of α_0. Like $\hat{\alpha}_0$, $\check{\alpha}_0$ is consistent but not unbiased. Interestingly, $\check{\alpha}_0$ is not guaranteed to be greater than one, although it will be in most applications. If $\check{\alpha}_0$ is less than one, and especially if it is much less than one, it is likely that the assumption of independence between u and the x_j is violated. If $\check{\alpha}_0 < 1$, one possibility is to just use the estimate in (6.43), although this may simply be masking a problem with the linear model for $\log(y)$. We summarize the steps:

6-4d Predicting y When the Dependent Variable Is $\log(y)$:

1. Obtain the fitted values, $\widehat{logy_i}$, and residuals, $\hat{u}_i$, from the regression $logy$ on $x_1, \ldots, x_k$.
2. Obtain $\hat{\alpha}_0$ as in equation (6.43) or $\check{\alpha}_0$ in equation (6.44).
3. For given values of $x_1, \ldots, x_k$, obtain $\widehat{logy}$ from (6.42).
4. Obtain the prediction $\hat{y}$ from (6.42) (with $\hat{\alpha}_0$ or $\check{\alpha}_0$).

We now show how to predict CEO salaries using this procedure.

EXAMPLE 6.7   **Predicting CEO Salaries**

The model of interest is

$$\log(salary) = \beta_0 + \beta_1 \log(sales) + \beta_2 \log(mktval) + \beta_3 ceoten + u,$$

so that β_1 and β_2 are elasticities and $100 \cdot \beta_3$ is a semi-elasticity. The estimated equation using CEOSAL2 is

$$\widehat{lsalary} = 4.504 + .163\ lsales + .109\ lmktval + .0117\ ceoten$$
$$\quad\quad (.257)\ (.039) \quad\quad (.050) \quad\quad\quad (.0053)$$ [6.45]
$$n = 177, R^2 = .318,$$

where, for clarity, we let $lsalary$ denote the log of $salary$, and similarly for $lsales$ and $lmktval$. Next, we obtain $\hat{m}_i = \exp(\widehat{lsalary_i})$ for each observation in the sample.

The Duan smearing estimate from (6.43) is about $\hat{\alpha}_0 = 1.136$, and the regression estimate from (6.44) is $\check{\alpha}_0 = 1.117$. We can use either estimate to predict $salary$ for any values of $sales$, $mktval$, and $ceoten$. Let us find the prediction for $sales = 5,000$ (which means \$5 billion because $sales$ is in millions), $mktval = 10,000$ (or \$10 billion), and $ceoten = 10$. From (6.45), the prediction for $lsalary$ is $4.504 + .163 \cdot \log(5,000) + .109 \cdot \log(10.000) + .0117(10) \approx 7.013$, and $\exp(7.013) \approx 1,110.983$. Using the estimate of α_0 from (6.43), the predicted salary is about 1,262.077, or \$1,262,077. Using the estimate from (6.44) gives an estimated salary of about \$1,240,968. These differ from each other by much less than each differs from the naive prediction of \$1,110,983.

We can use the previous method of obtaining predictions to determine how well the model with $\log(y)$ as the dependent variable explains y. We already have measures for models when y is the dependent variable: the R-squared and the adjusted R-squared. The goal is to find a goodness-of-fit measure in the $\log(y)$ model that can be compared with an R-squared from a model where y is the dependent variable.

There are different ways to define a goodness-of-fit measure after retransforming a model for $\log(y)$ to predict y. Here we present two approaches that are easy to implement. The first gives the same goodness-of-fit measures whether we estimate α_0 as in (6.40), (6.43), or (6.44). To motivate the measure, recall that in the linear regression equation estimated by OLS,

$$\hat{y} = \hat{\beta}_0 + \hat{\beta}_1 x_1 + \ldots + \hat{\beta}_k x_k, \qquad [6.46]$$

the usual R-squared is simply the square of the correlation between y_i and $\hat{y}_i$ (see Section 3-2). Now, if instead we compute fitted values from (6.42)—that is, $\hat{y}_i = \hat{\alpha}_0 m_i$ for all observations i—then it makes sense to use the square of the correlation between y_i and these fitted values as an R-squared. Because correlation is unaffected if we multiply by a constant, it does not matter which estimate of α_0 we use. In fact, this R-squared measure for y [not $\log(y)$] is just the squared correlation between y_i and $\hat{m}_i$. We can compare this directly with the R-squared from equation (6.46).

The squared correlation measure does not depend on how we estimate α_0. A second approach is to compute an R-squared for y based on a sum of squared residuals. For concreteness, suppose we use equation (6.43) to estimate α_0. Then the residual for predicting y_i is

$$\hat{r}_i = y_i - \hat{\alpha}_0 \exp(\widehat{\log y_i}), \qquad [6.47]$$

and we can use these residuals to compute a sum of squared residuals. Using the formula for R-squared from linear regression, we are led to

$$1 - \frac{\sum_{i=1}^{n} \hat{r}_i^2}{\sum_{i=1}^{n}(y_i - \bar{y})} \qquad [6.48]$$

as an alternative goodness-of-fit measure that can be compared with the R-squared from the linear model for y. Notice that we can compute such a measure for the alternative estimates of α_0 in equation (6.40) and (6.44) by inserting those estimates in place of $\hat{\alpha}_0$ in (6.47). Unlike the squared correlation between y_i and $\hat{m}_i$, the R-squared in (6.48) will depend on how we estimate α_0. The estimate that minimizes $\sum_{i=1}^{n}\hat{r}_i^2$ is that in equation (6.44), but that does not mean we should prefer it (and certainly not if $\check{\alpha}_0 < 1$). We are not really trying to choose among the different estimates of α_0; rather, we are finding goodness-of-fit measures that can be compared with the linear model for y.

| EXAMPLE 6.8 | **Predicting CEO Salaries** |

After we obtain the $\hat{m}_i$, we just obtain the correlation between $salary_i$ and $\hat{m}_i$; it is .493. The square of it is about .243, and this is a measure of how well the log model explains the variation in $salary$, not $\log(salary)$. [The R^2 from (6.45), .318, tells us that the log model explains about 31.8% of the variation in $\log(salary)$.]

As a competing linear model, suppose we estimate a model with all variables in levels:

$$salary = \beta_0 + \beta_1 sales + \beta_2 mktval + \beta_3 ceoten + u. \qquad [6.49]$$

The key is that the dependent variable is $salary$. We could use logs of $sales$ or $mktval$ on the right-hand side, but it makes more sense to have all dollar values in levels if one ($salary$) appears as a level. The R-squared from estimating this equation using the same 177 observations is .201. Thus, the log model explains more of the variation in $salary$, and so we prefer it to (6.49) on goodness-of-fit grounds. The log model is also preferred because it seems more realistic and its parameters are easier to interpret.

If we maintain the full set of classical linear model assumptions in the model (6.38), we can easily obtain prediction intervals for $y^0 = \exp(\beta_0 + \beta_1 x_1^0 + \dots + \beta_k x_k^0 + u^0)$ when we have estimated a linear model for $\log(y)$. Recall that $x_1^0, x_2^0, \dots, x_k^0$ are known values and u^0 is the unobserved error that partly determines y^0. From equation (6.37), a 95% prediction interval for $logy^0 = \log(y^0)$ is simply $\widehat{logy^0} \pm t_{.025} \cdot \text{se}(\hat{e}^0)$, where $\text{se}(\hat{e}^0)$ is obtained from the regression of $\log(y)$ on $x_1, \dots, x_k$ using the original n observations. Let $c_l = \widehat{logy^0} - t_{.025} \cdot \text{se}(\hat{e}^0)$ and $c_u = \widehat{logy^0} + t_{.025} \cdot \text{se}(\hat{e}^0)$ be the lower and upper bounds of the prediction interval for $logy^0$. That is, $P(c_l \leq logy^0 \leq c_u) = .95$. Because the exponential function is strictly increasing, it is also true that $P[\exp(c_l) \leq \exp(logy^0) \leq \exp(c_u)] = .95$, that is, $P[\exp(c_l) \leq y^0 \leq \exp(c_u)] = .95$. Therefore, we can take $\exp(c_l)$ and $\exp(c_u)$ as the lower and upper bounds, respectively, for a 95% prediction interval for y^0. For large n, $t_{.025} = 1.96$, and so a 95% prediction interval for y^0 is $\exp[-1.96 \cdot \text{se}(\hat{e}^0)]\exp(\hat{\beta}_0 + \mathbf{x}^0\hat{\boldsymbol{\beta}})$ to $\exp[-1.96 \cdot \text{se}(\hat{e}^0)]\exp(\hat{\beta}_0 + \mathbf{x}^0\hat{\boldsymbol{\beta}})$, where $\mathbf{x}^0\hat{\boldsymbol{\beta}}$ is shorthand for $\hat{\beta}_1 x_1^0 + \dots + \hat{\beta}_k x_k^0$. Remember, the $\hat{\beta}_j$ and $\text{se}(\hat{e}^0)$ are obtained from the regression with $\log(y)$ as the dependent variable. Because we assume normality of u in (6.38), we probably would use (6.40) to obtain a point prediction for y^0. Unlike in equation (6.37), this point prediction will not lie halfway between the lower and upper bounds $\exp(c_l)$ and $\exp(c_u)$. One can obtain different 95% prediction intervalues by choosing different quantiles in the t_{n-k-1} distribution. If $q_{\alpha 1}$ and $q_{\alpha 2}$ are quantiles with $\alpha_2 - \alpha_1 = .95$, then we can choose $c_l = q_{\alpha 1}\text{se}(\hat{e}^0)$ and $c_u = q_{\alpha 2}\text{se}(\hat{e}^0)$.

As an example, consider the CEO salary regression, where we make the prediction at the same values of *sales*, *mktval*, and *ceoten* as in Example 6.7. The standard error of the regression for (6.43) is about .505, and the standard error of $\widehat{logy^0}$ is about .075. Therefore, using equation (6.36), $\text{se}(\hat{e}^0) \approx .511$; as in the GPA example, the error variance swamps the estimation error in the parameters, even though here the sample size is only 177. A 95% prediction interval for *salary*^{0} is $\exp[-1.96 \cdot (.511)]\exp(7.013)$ to $\exp[1.96 \cdot (.511)]\exp(7.013)$, or about 408.071 to 3,024.678, that is, \$408,071 to \$3,024,678. This very wide 95% prediction interval for CEO salary at the given sales, market value, and tenure values shows that there is much else that we have not included in the regression that determines salary. Incidentally, the point prediction for salary, using (6.40), is about \$1,262,075—higher than the predictions using the other estimates of α_0 and closer to the lower bound than the upper bound of the 95% prediction interval.

Summary

In this chapter, we have covered some important multiple regression analysis topics.

Section 6-1 showed that a change in the units of measurement of an independent variable changes the OLS coefficient in the expected manner: if x_j is multiplied by c, its coefficient is divided by c. If the dependent variable is multiplied by c, *all* OLS coefficients are multiplied by c. Neither t nor F statistics are affected by changing the units of measurement of any variables.

We discussed beta coefficients, which measure the effects of the independent variables on the dependent variable in standard deviation units. The beta coefficients are obtained from a standard OLS regression after the dependent and independent variables have been transformed into z-scores.

We provided a detailed discussion of functional form, including the logarithmic transformation, quadratics, and interaction terms. It is helpful to summarize some of our conclusions.

CONSIDERATIONS WHEN USING LOGARITHMS

1. The coefficients have percentage change interpretations. We can be ignorant of the units of measurement of any variable that appears in logarithmic form, and changing units from, say, dollars to thousands of dollars has no effect on a variable's coefficient when that variable appears in logarithmic form.

2. Logs are often used for dollar amounts that are always positive, as well as for variables such as population, especially when there is a lot of variation. They are used less often for variables measured in years, such as schooling, age, and experience. Logs are used infrequently for variables that are already percents or proportions, such as an unemployment rate or a pass rate on a test.

3. Models with log(y) as the dependent variable often more closely satisfy the classical linear model assumptions. For example, the model has a better chance of being linear, homoskedasticity is more likely to hold, and normality is often more plausible.

4. In many cases, taking the log greatly reduces the variation of a variable, making OLS estimates less prone to outlier influence. However, in cases where y is a fraction and close to zero for many observations, log(y_i) can have much more variability than y_i. For values y_i very close to zero, log(y_i) is a negative number very large in magnitude.

5. If $y \geq 0$ but $y = 0$ is possible, we cannot use log(y). Sometimes log($1 + y$) is used, but interpretation of the coefficients is difficult.

6. For large changes in an explanatory variable, we can compute a more accurate estimate of the percentage change effect.

7. It is harder (but possible) to predict y when we have estimated a model for log(y).

CONSIDERATIONS WHEN USING QUADRATICS

1. A quadratic function in an explanatory variable allows for an increasing or decreasing effect.

2. The turning point of a quadratic is easily calculated, and it should be calculated to see if it makes sense.

3. Quadratic functions where the coefficients have the opposite sign have a strictly positive turning point; if the signs of the coefficients are the same, the turning point is at a negative value of x.

4. A seemingly small coefficient on the square of a variable can be practically important in what it implies about a changing slope. One can use a t test to see if the quadratic is statistically significant, and compute the slope at various values of x to see if it is practically important.

5. For a model quadratic in a variable x, the coefficient on x measures the partial effect starting from $x = 0$, as can be seen in equation (6.11). If zero is not a possible or interesting value of x, one can center x about a more interesting value, such as the average in the sample, before computing the square. This is the same as computing the average partial effect. Computing Exercise 6.12 provides an example.

CONSIDERATIONS WHEN USING INTERACTIONS

1. Interaction terms allow the partial effect of an explanatory variable, say x_1, to depend on the level of another variable, say x_2—and vice versa.

2. Interpreting models with interactions can be tricky. The coefficient on x_1, say β_1, measures the partial effect of x_1 on y when $x_2 = 0$, which may be impossible or uninteresting. Centering x_1 and x_2 around interesting values before constructing the interaction term typically leads to an equation that is visually more appealing. When the variables are centered about their sample averages, the coefficients on the levels become estimated average partial effects.

3. A standard t test can be used to determine if an interaction term is statistically significant. Computing the partial effects at different values of the explanatory variables can be used to determine the practical importance of interactions.

We introduced the adjusted R-squared, $\overline{R}^2$, as an alternative to the usual R-squared for measuring goodness-of-fit. Whereas R^2 can never fall when another variable is added to a regression, $\overline{R}^2$ penalizes the number of regressors and can drop when an independent variable is added. This makes $\overline{R}^2$ preferable for choosing between nonnested models with different numbers of explanatory variables. Neither R^2 nor $\overline{R}^2$ can be used to compare models with different dependent variables. Nevertheless, it is fairly easy to obtain goodness-of-fit measures for choosing between y and log(y) as the dependent variable, as shown in Section 6-4.

In Section 6-3, we discussed the somewhat subtle problem of relying too much on R^2 or $\overline{R}^2$ in arriving at a final model: it is possible to control for too many factors in a regression model. For this reason, it is important to think ahead about model specification, particularly the ceteris paribus nature of the multiple regression equation. Explanatory variables that affect y and are uncorrelated with all the other explanatory variables can be used to reduce the error variance without inducing multicollinearity.

In Section 6-4, we demonstrated how to obtain a confidence interval for a prediction made from an OLS regression line. We also showed how a confidence interval can be constructed for a future, unknown value of y.

Occasionally, we want to predict y when $\log(y)$ is used as the dependent variable in a regression model. Section 6-4 explains this simple method. Finally, we are sometimes interested in knowing about the sign and magnitude of the residuals for particular observations. Residual analysis can be used to determine whether particular members of the sample have predicted values that are well above or well below the actual outcomes.

Key Terms

Adjusted R-Squared	Nonnested Models	Quadratic Functions
Average Partial Effect (APE)	Over Controlling	Resampling Method
Beta Coefficients	Population R-Squared	Residual Analysis
Bootstrap	Prediction Error	Smearing Estimate
Bootstrap Standard Error	Prediction Interval	Standardized Coefficients
Interaction Effect	Predictions	Variance of the Prediction Error

Problems

1 The following equation was estimated using the data in CEOSAL1:

$$\widehat{\log(salary)} = 4.322 + .276 \log(sales) + .0215\, roe - .00008\, roe^2$$
$$(.324)\quad (.033)\qquad\qquad (.0129)\qquad (.00026)$$
$$n = 209,\, R^2 = .282.$$

This equation allows *roe* to have a diminishing effect on $\log(salary)$. Is this generality necessary? Explain why or why not.

2 Let $\hat{\beta}_0, \hat{\beta}_1, \ldots, \hat{\beta}_k$ be the OLS estimates from the regression of y_i on $x_{i1}, \ldots, x_{ik}$, $i = 1, 2, \ldots, n$. For nonzero constants $c_1, \ldots, c_k$, argue that the OLS intercept and slopes from the regression of $c_0 y_i$ on $c_1 x_{i1}, \ldots, c_k x_{ik}$, $i = 1, 2, \ldots, n$, are given by $\tilde{\beta}_0 = c_0\hat{\beta}_0$, $\tilde{\beta}_1 = (c_0/c_1)\hat{\beta}_1, \ldots, \tilde{\beta}_k = (c_0/c_k)\hat{\beta}_k$. [*Hint*: Use the fact that the $\hat{\beta}_j$ solve the first order conditions in (3.13), and the $\tilde{\beta}_j$ must solve the first order conditions involving the rescaled dependent and independent variables.]

3 Using the data in RDCHEM, the following equation was obtained by OLS:

$$\widehat{rdintens} = 2.613 + .00030\, sales - .0000000070\, sales^2$$
$$(.429)\quad (.00014)\qquad (.0000000037)$$
$$n = 32,\, R^2 = .1484.$$

(i) At what point does the marginal effect of *sales* on *rdintens* become negative?

(ii) Would you keep the quadratic term in the model? Explain.

(iii)   Define *salesbil* as sales measured in billions of dollars: *salesbil* = *sales*/1,000. Rewrite the estimated equation with *salesbil* and *salesbil²* as the independent variables. Be sure to report standard errors and the *R*-squared. [*Hint*: Note that $salesbil^2 = sales^2/(1,000)^2$.]

(iv)   For the purpose of reporting the results, which equation do you prefer?

4 The following model allows the return to education to depend upon the total amount of both parents' education, called *pareduc*:

$$\log(wage) = \beta_0 + \beta_1 educ + \beta_2 educ \cdot pareduc + \beta_3 exper + \beta_4 tenure + u.$$

(i)   Show that, in decimal form, the return to another year of education in this model is

$$\Delta\log(wage)/\Delta educ = \beta_1 + \beta_2 pareduc.$$

What sign do you expect for β_2? Why?

(ii)   Using the data in WAGE2, the estimated equation is

$$\widehat{\log(wage)} = 5.65 + .047\ educ + .00078\ educ \cdot pareduc +$$
$$\quad\ (.13)\ \ (.010)\qquad\quad (.00021)$$
$$.019\ exper + .010\ tenure$$
$$(.004)\qquad\ (.003)$$
$$n = 722, R^2 = .169.$$

(Only 722 observations contain full information on parents' education.) Interpret the coefficient on the interaction term. It might help to choose two specific values for *pareduc*—for example, *pareduc* = 32 if both parents have a college education, or *pareduc* = 24 if both parents have a high school education—and to compare the estimated return to *educ*.

(iii)   When *pareduc* is added as a separate variable to the equation, we get:

$$\widehat{\log(wage)} = 4.94 + .097\ educ + .033\ pareduc - .0016\ educ \cdot pareduc$$
$$\quad\ (.38)\ \ (.027)\qquad (.017)\qquad\quad (.0012)$$
$$+ .020\ exper + .010\ tenure$$
$$(.004)\qquad\ (.003)$$
$$n = 722, R^2 = .174.$$

Does the estimated return to education now depend positively on parent education? Test the null hypothesis that the return to education does not depend on parent education.

5 In Example 4.2, where the percentage of students receiving a passing score on a tenth-grade math exam (*math*10) is the dependent variable, does it make sense to include *sci*11—the percentage of eleventh graders passing a science exam—as an additional explanatory variable?

6 When *atndrte²* and *ACT·atndrte* are added to the equation estimated in (6.19), the *R*-squared becomes .232. Are these additional terms jointly significant at the 10% level? Would you include them in the model?

7 The following three equations were estimated using the 1,534 observations in 401K:

$$\widehat{prate} = 80.29 + 5.44\ mrate + .269\ age - .00013\ totemp$$
$$\quad\ (.78)\ \ (.52)\qquad\ (.045)\qquad (.00004)$$
$$R^2 = .100, \overline{R}^2 = .098.$$

$$\widehat{prate} = 97.32 + 5.02 \, mrate + .314 \, age - 2.66 \log(totemp)$$
$$(1.95) \quad (0.51) \qquad\qquad (.044) \qquad (.28)$$
$$R^2 = .144, \, \overline{R}^2 = .142.$$

$$\widehat{prate} = 80.62 + 5.34 \, mrate + .290 \, age - .00043 \, totemp$$
$$(.78) \quad (.52) \qquad\qquad (.045) \qquad (.00009)$$
$$+ .0000000039 \, totemp^2$$
$$(.00000000010)$$
$$R^2 = .108, \, \overline{R}^2 = .106.$$

Which of these three models do you prefer? Why?

8 Suppose we want to estimate the effects of alcohol consumption (*alcohol*) on college grade point average (*colGPA*). In addition to collecting information on grade point averages and alcohol usage, we also obtain attendance information (say, percentage of lectures attended, called *attend*). A standardized test score (say, *SAT*) and high school GPA (*hsGPA*) are also available.
   (i) Should we include *attend* along with *alcohol* as explanatory variables in a multiple regression model? (Think about how you would interpret $\beta_{alcohol}$.)
   (ii) Should *SAT* and *hsGPA* be included as explanatory variables? Explain.

9 If we start with (6.38) under the CLM assumptions, assume large n, and ignore the estimation error in the $\hat{\beta}_j$, a 95% prediction interval for y^0 is $[\exp(-1.96\hat{\sigma})\exp(\widehat{logy^0}), \exp(1.96\hat{\sigma})\exp(\widehat{logy^0})]$. The point prediction for y^0 is $\hat{y}^0 = \exp(\hat{\sigma}_2)\exp(\widehat{logy^0})$.
   (i) For what values of $\hat{\sigma}$ will the point prediction be in the 95% prediction interval? Does this condition seem likely to hold in most applications?
   (ii) Verify that the condition from part (i) is satisfied in the CEO salary example.

10 The following two equations were estimated using the data in MEAPSINGLE. The key explanatory variable is *lexppp*, the log of expenditures per student at the school level.

$$\widehat{math4} = 24.49 + 9.01 \, lexppp - .422 \, free - .752 \, lmedinc - .274 \, pctsgle$$
$$(59.24) \quad (4.04) \qquad (.071) \qquad (5.358) \qquad (.161)$$
$$n = 229, \, R^2 = .472, \, \overline{R}^2 = .462.$$

$$\widehat{math4} = 149.38 + 1.93 \, lexppp - .060 \, free - 10.78 \, lmedinc - .397 \, pctsgle + .667 \, read4$$
$$(41.70) \quad (2.82) \qquad (.054) \qquad (3.76) \qquad (.111) \qquad (.042)$$
$$n = 229, \, R^2 = .749, \, \overline{R}^2 = .743.$$

   (i) If you are a policy maker trying to estimate the causal effect of per-student spending on math test performance, explain why the first equation is more relevant than the second. What is the estimated effect of a 10% increase in expenditures per student?
   (ii) Does adding *read4* to the regression have strange effects on coefficients and statistical significance other than β_{lexppp}?
   (iii) How would you explain to someone with only basic knowledge of regression why, in this case, you prefer the equation with the smaller adjusted R-squared?

Computer Exercises

C1 Use the data in KIELMC, only for the year 1981, to answer the following questions. The data are for houses that sold during 1981 in North Andover, Massachusetts; 1981 was the year construction began on a local garbage incinerator.

(i) To study the effects of the incinerator location on housing price, consider the simple regression model

$$\log(price) = \beta_0 + \beta_1 \log(dist) + u,$$

where *price* is housing price in dollars and *dist* is distance from the house to the incinerator measured in feet. Interpreting this equation causally, what sign do you expect for β_1 if the presence of the incinerator depresses housing prices? Estimate this equation and interpret the results.

(ii) To the simple regression model in part (i), add the variables log(*intst*), log(*area*), log(*land*), *rooms*, *baths*, and *age*, where *intst* is distance from the home to the interstate, *area* is square footage of the house, *land* is the lot size in square feet, *rooms* is total number of rooms, *baths* is number of bathrooms, and *age* is age of the house in years. Now, what do you conclude about the effects of the incinerator? Explain why (i) and (ii) give conflicting results.

(iii) Add $[\log(intst)]^2$ to the model from part (ii). Now what happens? What do you conclude about the importance of functional form?

(iv) Is the square of log(*dist*) significant when you add it to the model from part (iii)?

C2 Use the data in WAGE1 for this exercise.

(i) Use OLS to estimate the equation

$$\log(wage) = \beta_0 + \beta_1 educ + \beta_2 exper + \beta_3 exper^2 + u$$

and report the results using the usual format.

(ii) Is *exper²* statistically significant at the 1% level?

(iii) Using the approximation

$$\%\widehat{\Delta wage} \approx 100(\hat{\beta}_2 + 2\hat{\beta}_3 exper)\Delta exper,$$

find the approximate return to the fifth year of experience. What is the approximate return to the twentieth year of experience?

(iv) At what value of *exper* does additional experience actually lower predicted log(*wage*)? How many people have more experience in this sample?

C3 Consider a model where the return to education depends upon the amount of work experience (and vice versa):

$$\log(wage) = \beta_0 + \beta_1 educ + \beta_2 exper + \beta_3 educ \cdot exper + u.$$

(i) Show that the return to another year of education (in decimal form), holding *exper* fixed, is $\beta_1 + \beta_3 exper$.

(ii) State the null hypothesis that the return to education does not depend on the level of *exper*. What do you think is the appropriate alternative?

(iii) Use the data in WAGE2 to test the null hypothesis in (ii) against your stated alternative.

(iv) Let θ_1 denote the return to education (in decimal form), when *exper* = 10: $\theta_1 = \beta_1 + 10\beta_3$. Obtain $\hat{\theta}_1$ and a 95% confidence interval for θ_1. (*Hint:* Write $\beta_1 = \theta_1 - 10\beta_3$ and plug this into the equation; then rearrange. This gives the regression for obtaining the confidence interval for θ_1.)

C4 Use the data in GPA2 for this exercise.
   (i) Estimate the model

$$sat = \beta_0 + \beta_1 hsize + \beta_2 hsize^2 + u,$$

   where *hsize* is the size of the graduating class (in hundreds), and write the results in the usual form. Is the quadratic term statistically significant?
   (ii) Using the estimated equation from part (i), what is the "optimal" high school size? Justify your answer.
   (iii) Is this analysis representative of the academic performance of *all* high school seniors? Explain.
   (iv) Find the estimated optimal high school size, using log(*sat*) as the dependent variable. Is it much different from what you obtained in part (ii)?

C5 Use the housing price data in HPRICE1 for this exercise.
   (i) Estimate the model

$$\log(price) = \beta_0 + \beta_1 \log(lotsize) + \beta_2 \log(sqrft) + \beta_3 bdrms + u$$

   and report the results in the usual OLS format.
   (ii) Find the predicted value of log(*price*), when *lotsize* = 20,000, *sqrft* = 2,500, and *bdrms* = 4. Using the methods in Section 6-4, find the predicted value of *price* at the same values of the explanatory variables.
   (iii) For explaining variation in *price*, decide whether you prefer the model from part (i) or the model

$$price = \beta_0 + \beta_1 lotsize + \beta_2 sqrft + \beta_3 bdrms + u.$$

C6 Use the data in VOTE1 for this exercise.
   (i) Consider a model with an interaction between expenditures:

$$voteA = \beta_0 + \beta_1 prtystrA + \beta_2 expendA + \beta_3 expendB + \beta_4 expendA \cdot expendB + u.$$

   What is the partial effect of *expendB* on *voteA*, holding *prtystrA* and *expendA* fixed? What is the partial effect of *expendA* on *voteA*? Is the expected sign for β_4 obvious?
   (ii) Estimate the equation in part (i) and report the results in the usual form. Is the interaction term statistically significant?
   (iii) Find the average of *expendA* in the sample. Fix *expendA* at 300 (for $300,000). What is the estimated effect of another $100,000 spent by Candidate B on *voteA*? Is this a large effect?
   (iv) Now fix *expendB* at 100. What is the estimated effect of $\Delta expendA = 100$ on *voteA*? Does this make sense?
   (v) Now, estimate a model that replaces the interaction with *shareA*, Candidate A's percentage share of total campaign expenditures. Does it make sense to hold both *expendA* and *expendB* fixed, while changing *shareA*?
   (vi) (Requires calculus) In the model from part (v), find the partial effect of *expendB* on *voteA*, holding *prtystrA* and *expendA* fixed. Evaluate this at *expendA* = 300 and *expendB* = 0 and comment on the results.

C7 Use the data in ATTEND for this exercise.
   (i) In the model of Example 6.3, argue that

$$\Delta stndfnl / \Delta priGPA \approx \beta_2 + 2\beta_4 priGPA + \beta_6 atndrte.$$

   Use equation (6.19) to estimate the partial effect when *priGPA* = 2.59 and *atndrte* = 82. Interpret your estimate.

(ii)   Show that the equation can be written as

$$stndfnl = \theta_0 + \beta_1 atndrte + \theta_2 priGPA + \beta_3 ACT + \beta_4(priGPA - 2.59)^2$$
$$+ \beta_5 ACT^2 + \beta_6 priGPA(atndrte - 82) + u,$$

where $\theta_2 = \beta_2 + 2\beta_4(2.59) + \beta_6(82)$. (Note that the intercept has changed, but this is unimportant.) Use this to obtain the standard error of $\hat{\theta}_2$ from part (i).

(iii)   Suppose that, in place of $priGPA(atndrte - 82)$, you put $(priGPA - 2.59) \cdot (atndrte - 82)$. Now how do you interpret the coefficients on $atndrte$ and $priGPA$?

C8   Use the data in HPRICE1 for this exercise.

(i)   Estimate the model

$$price = \beta_0 + \beta_1 lotsize + \beta_2 sqrft + \beta_3 bdrms + u$$

and report the results in the usual form, including the standard error of the regression. Obtain predicted price, when we plug in $lotsize = 10{,}000$, $sqrft = 2{,}300$, and $bdrms = 4$; round this price to the nearest dollar.

(ii)   Run a regression that allows you to put a 95% confidence interval around the predicted value in part (i). Note that your prediction will differ somewhat due to rounding error.

(iii)   Let $price^0$ be the unknown future selling price of the house with the characteristics used in parts (i) and (ii). Find a 95% CI for $price^0$ and comment on the width of this confidence interval.

C9   The data set NBASAL contains salary information and career statistics for 269 players in the National Basketball Association (NBA).

(i)   Estimate a model relating points-per-game (*points*) to years in the league (*exper*), *age*, and years played in college (*coll*). Include a quadratic in *exper*; the other variables should appear in level form. Report the results in the usual way.

(ii)   Holding college years and age fixed, at what value of experience does the next year of experience actually reduce points-per-game? Does this make sense?

(iii)   Why do you think *coll* has a negative and statistically significant coefficient? (*Hint:* NBA players can be drafted before finishing their college careers and even directly out of high school.)

(iv)   Add a quadratic in *age* to the equation. Is it needed? What does this appear to imply about the effects of age, once experience and education are controlled for?

(v)   Now regress log(*wage*) on *points*, *exper*, *exper²*, *age*, and *coll*. Report the results in the usual format.

(vi)   Test whether *age* and *coll* are jointly significant in the regression from part (v). What does this imply about whether age and education have separate effects on wage, once productivity and seniority are accounted for?

C10   Use the data in BWGHT2 for this exercise.

(i)   Estimate the equation

$$\log(bwght) = \beta_0 + \beta_1 npvis + \beta_2 npvis^2 + u$$

by OLS, and report the results in the usual way. Is the quadratic term significant?

(ii)   Show that, based on the equation from part (i), the number of prenatal visits that maximizes log(*bwght*) is estimated to be about 22. How many women had at least 22 prenatal visits in the sample?

(iii)   Does it make sense that birth weight is actually predicted to decline after 22 prenatal visits? Explain.

(iv)   Add mother's age to the equation, using a quadratic functional form. Holding *npvis* fixed, at what mother's age is the birth weight of the child maximized? What fraction of women in the sample are older than the "optimal" age?

(v)   Would you say that mother's age and number of prenatal visits explain a lot of the variation in log(*bwght*)?

(vi)   Using quadratics for both *npvis* and *age*, decide whether using the natural log or the level of *bwght* is better for predicting *bwght*.

C11 Use APPLE to verify some of the claims made in Section 6-3.

(i)   Run the regression *ecolbs* on *ecoprc*, *regprc* and report the results in the usual form, including the *R*-squared and adjusted *R*-squared. Interpret the coefficients on the price variables and comment on their signs and magnitudes.

(ii)   Are the price variables statistically significant? Report the *p*-values for the individual *t* tests.

(iii) What is the range of fitted values for *ecolbs*? What fraction of the sample reports *ecolbs* $= 0$? Comment.

(iv)   Do you think the price variables together do a good job of explaining variation in *ecolbs*? Explain.

(v)   Add the variables *faminc*, *hhsize* (household size), *educ*, and *age* to the regression from part (i). Find the *p*-value for their joint significance. What do you conclude?

(vi)   Run separate simple regressions of *ecolbs* on *ecoprc* and then *ecolbs* on *regprc*. How do the simple regression coefficients compare with the multiple regression from part (i)? Find the correlation coefficient between *ecoprc* and *regprc* to help explain your findings.

(vii) Consider a model that adds family income and the quantity demanded for regular apples:

$$ecolbs = \beta_0 + \beta_1 ecoprc + \beta_2 regprc + \beta_3 faminc + \beta_4 reglbs + u.$$

From basic economic theory, which explanatory variable does not belong to the equation? When you drop the variables one at a time time, do the sizes of the adjusted *R*-squareds affect your answer?

C12 Use the subset of 401KSUBS with *fsize* $= 1$; this restricts the analysis to single-person households; see also Computer Exercise C8 in Chapter 4.

(i)   What is the youngest age of people in this sample? How many people are at that age?

(ii)   In the model

$$nettfa = \beta_0 + \beta_1 inc + \beta_2 age + \beta_3 age^2 + u,$$

what is the literal interpretation of β_2? By itself, is it of much interest?

(iii) Estimate the model from part (ii) and report the results in standard form. Are you concerned that the coefficient on *age* is negative? Explain.

(iv)   Because the youngest people in the sample are 25, it makes sense to think that, for a given level of income, the lowest average amount of net total financial assets is at age 25. Recall that the partial effect of *age* on *nettfa* is $\beta_2 + 2\beta_3 age$, so the partial effect at age 25 is $\beta_2 + 2\beta_3(25) = \beta_2 + 50\beta_3$; call this θ_2. Find $\hat{\theta}_2$ and obtain the two-sided *p*-value for testing $H_0: \theta_2 = 0$. You should conclude that $\hat{\theta}_2$ is small and very statistically insignificant. [*Hint:* One way to do this is to estimate the model *nettfa* $= \alpha_0 + \beta_1 inc + \theta_2 age + \beta_3(age - 25)^2 + u$, where the intercept, α_0 is different from β_0. There are other ways, too.]

(v)   Because the evidence against $H_0: \theta_2 = 0$ is very weak, set it to zero and estimate the model

$$nettfa = \alpha_0 + \beta_1 inc + \beta_3(age - 25)^2 + u.$$

In terms of goodness-of-fit, does this model fit better than that in part (ii)?

(vi)   For the estimated equation in part (v), set *inc* $= 30$ (roughly, the average value) and graph the relationship between *nettfa* and *age*, but only for *age* ≥ 25. Describe what you see.

(vii) Check to see whether including a quadratic in *inc* is necessary.

C13 Use the data in MEAP00 to answer this question.

(i) Estimate the model

$$math4 = \beta_0 + \beta_1 lexppp + \beta_2 lenroll + \beta_3 lunch + u$$

by OLS, and report the results in the usual form. Is each explanatory variable statistically significant at the 5% level?

(ii) Obtain the fitted values from the regression in part (i). What is the range of fitted values? How does it compare with the range of the actual data on *math4*?

(iii) Obtain the residuals from the regression in part (i). What is the building code of the school that has the largest (positive) residual? Provide an interpretation of this residual.

(iv) Add quadratics of all explanatory variables to the equation, and test them for joint significance. Would you leave them in the model?

(v) Returning to the model in part (i), divide the dependent variable and each explanatory variable by its sample standard deviation, and rerun the regression. (Include an intercept unless you also first subtract the mean from each variable.) In terms of standard deviation units, which explanatory variable has the largest effect on the math pass rate?

C14 Use the data in BENEFITS to answer this question. It is a school-level data set at the K–5 level on average teacher salary and benefits. See Example 4.10 for background.

(i) Regress *lavgsal* on *bs* and report the results in the usual form. Can you reject $H_0: \beta_{bs} = 0$ against a two-sided alternative? Can you reject $H_0: \beta_{bs} = -1$ against $H_1: \beta_{bs} > -1$? Report the *p*-values for both tests.

(ii) Define $lbs = \log(bs)$. Find the range of values for *lbs* and find its standard deviation. How do these compare to the range and standard deviation for *bs*?

(iii) Regress *lavgsal* on *lbs*. Does this fit better than the regression from part (i)?

(iv) Estimate the equation

$$lavgsal = \beta_0 + \beta_1 bs + \beta_2 lenroll + \beta_3 lstaff + \beta_4 lunch + u$$

and report the results in the usual form. What happens to the coefficient on *bs*? Is it now statistically different from zero?

(v) Interpret the coefficient on *lstaff*. Why do you think it is negative?

(vi) Add $lunch^2$ to the equation from part (iv). Is it statistically significant? Compute the turning point (minimum value) in the quadratic, and show that it is within the range of the observed data on *lunch*. How many values of *lunch* are higher than the calculated turning point?

(vii) Based on the findings from part (vi), describe how teacher salaries relate to school poverty rates. In terms of teacher salary, and holding other factors fixed, is it better to teach at a school with *lunch* = 0 (no poverty), *lunch* = 50, or *lunch* = 100 (all kids eligible for the free lunch program)?

APPENDIX 6A

6A. A Brief Introduction to Bootstrapping

In many cases where formulas for standard errors are hard to obtain mathematically, or where they are thought not to be very good approximations to the true sampling variation of an estimator, we can rely on a **resampling method**. The general idea is to treat the observed data as a population that we can draw samples from. The most common resampling method is the **bootstrap**. (There are actually several versions of the bootstrap, but the most general, and most easily applied, is called the *nonparametric bootstrap*, and that is what we describe here.)

Suppose we have an estimate, $\hat{\theta}$, of a population parameter, θ. We obtained this estimate, which could be a function of OLS estimates (or estimates that we cover in later chapters), from a random sample of size n. We would like to obtain a standard error for $\hat{\theta}$ that can be used for constructing t statistics or confidence intervals. Remarkably, we can obtain a valid standard error by computing the estimate from different random samples drawn from the original data.

Implementation is easy. If we list our observations from 1 through n, we draw n numbers randomly, with replacement, from this list. This produces a new data set (of size n) that consists of the original data, but with many observations appearing multiple times (except in the rather unusual case that we resample the original data). Each time we randomly sample from the original data, we can estimate θ using the same procedure that we used on the original data. Let $\hat{\theta}^{(b)}$ denote the estimate from bootstrap sample b. Now, if we repeat the resampling and estimation m times, we have m new estimates, $\{\hat{\theta}^{(b)}: b = 1, 2, ..., m\}$. The **bootstrap standard error** of $\hat{\theta}$ is just the sample standard deviation of the $\hat{\theta}^{(b)}$, namely,

$$\text{bse}(\hat{\theta}) = \left[(m-1)^{-1} \sum_{b=1}^{m} (\hat{\theta}^{(b)} - \overline{\hat{\theta}})^2 \right]^{1/2}, \qquad [6.50]$$

where $\overline{\hat{\theta}}$ is the average of the bootstrap estimates.

If obtaining an estimate of θ on a sample of size n requires little computational time, as in the case of OLS and all the other estimators we encounter in this text, we can afford to choose m—the number of bootstrap replications—to be large. A typical value is $m = 1,000$, but even $m = 500$ or a somewhat smaller value can produce a reliable standard error. Note that the size of m—the number of times we resample the original data—has nothing to do with the sample size, n. (For certain estimation problems beyond the scope of this text, a large n can force one to do fewer bootstrap replications.) Many statistics and econometrics packages have built-in bootstrap commands, and this makes the calculation of bootstrap standard errors simple, especially compared with the work often required to obtain an analytical formula for an asymptotic standard error.

One can actually do better in most cases by using the bootstrap sample to compute p-values for t statistics (and F statistics), or for obtaining confidence intervals, rather than obtaining a bootstrap standard error to be used in the construction of t statistics or confidence intervals. See Horowitz (2001) for a comprehensive treatment.

Multiple Regression Analysis with Qualitative Information: Binary (or Dummy) Variables

In previous chapters, the dependent and independent variables in our multiple regression models have had *quantitative* meaning. Just a few examples include hourly wage rate, years of education, college grade point average, amount of air pollution, level of firm sales, and number of arrests. In each case, the magnitude of the variable conveys useful information. In empirical work, we must also incorporate *qualitative* factors into regression models. The gender or race of an individual, the industry of a firm (manufacturing, retail, and so on), and the region in the United States where a city is located (South, North, West, and so on) are all considered to be qualitative factors.

Most of this chapter is dedicated to qualitative *independent* variables. After we discuss the appropriate ways to describe qualitative information in Section 7-1, we show how qualitative explanatory variables can be easily incorporated into multiple regression models in Sections 7-2, 7-3, and 7-4. These sections cover almost all of the popular ways that qualitative independent variables are used in cross-sectional regression analysis.

In Section 7-5, we discuss a binary dependent variable, which is a particular kind of qualitative dependent variable. The multiple regression model has an interesting interpretation in this case and is called the linear probability model. While much maligned by some econometricians, the simplicity of the linear probability model makes it useful in many empirical contexts. We will describe its drawbacks in Section 7-5, but they are often secondary in empirical work.

7-1 Describing Qualitative Information

Qualitative factors often come in the form of binary information: a person is female or male; a person does or does not own a personal computer; a firm offers a certain kind of employee pension plan or it does not; a state administers capital punishment or it does not. In all of these examples, the relevant

TABLE 7.1 A Partial Listing of the Data in WAGE1					
person	wage	educ	exper	female	married
1	3.10	11	2	1	0
2	3.24	12	22	1	1
3	3.00	11	2	0	0
4	6.00	8	44	0	1
5	5.30	12	7	0	1
·	·	·	·	·	·
·	·	·	·	·	·
·	·	·	·	·	·
525	11.56	16	5	0	1
526	3.50	14	5	1	0

information can be captured by defining a **binary variable** or a **zero-one variable**. In econometrics, binary variables are most commonly called **dummy variables**, although this name is not especially descriptive.

> **EXPLORING FURTHER 7.1**
>
> Suppose that, in a study comparing election outcomes between Democratic and Republican candidates, you wish to indicate the party of each candidate. Is a name such as *party* a wise choice for a binary variable in this case? What would be a better name?

In defining a dummy variable, we must decide which event is assigned the value one and which is assigned the value zero. For example, in a study of individual wage determination, we might define *female* to be a binary variable taking on the value one for females and the value zero for males. The name in this case indicates the event with the value one. The same information is captured by defining *male* to be one if the person is male and zero if the person is female. Either of these is better than using *gender* because this name does not make it clear when the dummy variable is one: does *gender* = 1 correspond to male or female? What we call our variables is unimportant for getting regression results, but it always helps to choose names that clarify equations and expositions.

Suppose in the wage example that we have chosen the name *female* to indicate gender. Further, we define a binary variable *married* to equal one if a person is married and zero if otherwise. Table 7.1 gives a partial listing of a wage data set that might result. We see that Person 1 is female and not married, Person 2 is female and married, Person 3 is male and not married, and so on.

Why do we use the values zero and one to describe qualitative information? In a sense, these values are arbitrary: any two different values would do. The real benefit of capturing qualitative information using zero-one variables is that it leads to regression models where the parameters have very natural interpretations, as we will see now.

7-2 A Single Dummy Independent Variable

How do we incorporate binary information into regression models? In the simplest case, with only a single dummy explanatory variable, we just add it as an independent variable in the equation. For example, consider the following simple model of hourly wage determination:

$$wage = \beta_0 + \delta_0 female + \beta_1 educ + u. \tag{7.1}$$

We use δ_0 as the parameter on *female* in order to highlight the interpretation of the parameters multiplying dummy variables; later, we will use whatever notation is most convenient.

In model (7.1), only two observed factors affect wage: gender and education. Because *female* = 1 when the person is female, and *female* = 0 when the person is male, the parameter δ_0 has the following interpretation: δ_0 is the difference in hourly wage between females and males, *given* the same amount of education (and the same error term *u*). Thus, the coefficient δ_0 determines whether there is discrimination against women: if $\delta_0 < 0$, then for the same level of other factors, women earn less than men on average.

In terms of expectations, if we assume the zero conditional mean assumption $E(u|female, educ) = 0$, then

$$\delta_0 = E(wage|female = 1, educ) - E(wage|female = 0, educ).$$

Because *female* = 1 corresponds to females and *female* = 0 corresponds to males, we can write this more simply as

$$\delta_0 = E(wage|female, educ) - E(wage|male, educ). \tag{7.2}$$

The key here is that the level of education is the same in both expectations; the difference, δ_0, is due to gender only.

The situation can be depicted graphically as an **intercept shift** between males and females. In Figure 7.1, the case $\delta_0 < 0$ is shown, so that men earn a fixed amount more per hour than women. The difference does not depend on the amount of education, and this explains why the wage-education profiles for women and men are parallel.

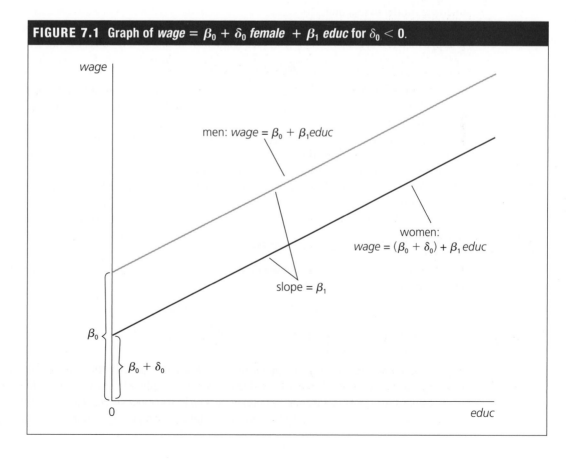

FIGURE 7.1 Graph of *wage* = β_0 + δ_0 *female* + β_1 *educ* for $\delta_0 < 0$.

At this point, you may wonder why we do not also include in (7.1) a dummy variable, say *male*, which is one for males and zero for females. This would be redundant. In (7.1), the intercept for males is β_0, and the intercept for females is $\beta_0 + \delta_0$. Because there are just two groups, we only need two different intercepts. This means that, in addition to β_0, we need to use only *one* dummy variable; we have chosen to include the dummy variable for females. Using two dummy variables would introduce perfect collinearity because *female* + *male* = 1, which means that *male* is a perfect linear function of *female*. Including dummy variables for both genders is the simplest example of the so-called **dummy variable trap**, which arises when too many dummy variables describe a given number of groups. We will discuss this problem in detail later.

In (7.1), we have chosen males to be the **base group** or **benchmark group**, that is, the group against which comparisons are made. This is why β_0 is the intercept for males, and δ_0 is the *difference* in intercepts between females and males. We could choose females as the base group by writing the model as

$$wage = \alpha_0 + \gamma_0 male + \beta_1 educ + u,$$

where the intercept for females is α_0 and the intercept for males is $\alpha_0 + \gamma_0$; this implies that $\alpha_0 = \beta_0 + \delta_0$ and $\alpha_0 + \gamma_0 = \beta_0$. In any application, it does not matter how we choose the base group, but it is important to keep track of which group is the base group.

Some researchers prefer to drop the overall intercept in the model and to include dummy variables for each group. The equation would then be $wage = \beta_0 male + \alpha_0 female + \beta_1 educ + u$, where the intercept for men is β_0 and the intercept for women is α_0. There is no dummy variable trap in this case because we do not have an overall intercept. However, this formulation has little to offer, since testing for a difference in the intercepts is more difficult, and there is no generally agreed upon way to compute R-squared in regressions without an intercept. Therefore, we will always include an overall intercept for the base group.

Nothing much changes when more explanatory variables are involved. Taking males as the base group, a model that controls for experience and tenure in addition to education is

$$wage = \beta_0 + \delta_0 female + \beta_1 educ + \beta_2 exper + \beta_3 tenure + u. \qquad \text{[7.3]}$$

If *educ*, *exper*, and *tenure* are all relevant productivity characteristics, the null hypothesis of *no* difference between men and women is $H_0: \delta_0 = 0$. The alternative that there is discrimination against women is $H_1: \delta_0 < 0$.

How can we actually test for wage discrimination? The answer is simple: just estimate the model by OLS, *exactly* as before, and use the usual t statistic. Nothing changes about the mechanics of OLS or the statistical theory when some of the independent variables are defined as dummy variables. The only difference with what we have done up until now is in the interpretation of the coefficient on the dummy variable.

| **EXAMPLE 7.1** | **Hourly Wage Equation** |

Using the data in WAGE1, we estimate model (7.3). For now, we use *wage*, rather than log(*wage*), as the dependent variable:

$$\widehat{wage} = -1.57 - 1.81\,female + .572\,educ + 0.25\,exper + .141\,tenure$$
$$\phantom{\widehat{wage} = } (.72) \quad (.26) \qquad (.049) \qquad (.012) \qquad (.021) \qquad \text{[7.4]}$$
$$n = 526, R^2 = .364.$$

The negative intercept—the intercept for men, in this case—is not very meaningful because no one has zero values for all of *educ*, *exper*, and *tenure* in the sample. The coefficient on *female* is interesting because it measures the average difference in hourly wage between a man and a woman who have the *same* levels of *educ*, *exper*, and *tenure*. If we take a woman and a man with the same levels of education, experience, and tenure, the woman earns, on average, $1.81 less per hour than the man. (Recall that these are 1976 wages.)

It is important to remember that, because we have performed multiple regression and controlled for *educ*, *exper*, and *tenure*, the $1.81 wage differential cannot be explained by different average levels of education, experience, or tenure between men and women. We can conclude that the differential of $1.81 is due to gender or factors associated with gender that we have not controlled for in the regression. [In 2013 dollars, the wage differential is about $4.09(1.81) \approx 7.40$.]

It is informative to compare the coefficient on *female* in equation (7.4) to the estimate we get when all other explanatory variables are dropped from the equation:

$$\widehat{wage} = 7.10 - 2.51 \, female$$
$$(.21) \quad (.30) \tag{7.5}$$
$$n = 526, R^2 = .116.$$

The coefficients in (7.5) have a simple interpretation. The intercept is the average wage for men in the sample (let *female* = 0), so men earn $7.10 per hour on average. The coefficient on *female* is the difference in the average wage between women and men. Thus, the average wage for women in the sample is $7.10 - 2.51 = 4.59$, or $4.59 per hour. (Incidentally, there are 274 men and 252 women in the sample.)

Equation (7.5) provides a simple way to carry out a *comparison-of-means test* between the two groups, which in this case are men and women. The estimated difference, -2.51, has a *t* statistic of -8.37, which is very statistically significant (and, of course, $2.51 is economically large as well). Generally, simple regression on a constant and a dummy variable is a straightforward way to compare the means of two groups. For the usual *t* test to be valid, we must assume that the homoskedasticity assumption holds, which means that the population variance in wages for men is the same as that for women.

The estimated wage differential between men and women is larger in (7.5) than in (7.4) because (7.5) does not control for differences in education, experience, and tenure, and these are lower, on average, for women than for men in this sample. Equation (7.4) gives a more reliable estimate of the ceteris paribus gender wage gap; it still indicates a very large differential.

In many cases, dummy independent variables reflect choices of individuals or other economic units (as opposed to something predetermined, such as gender). In such situations, the matter of causality is again a central issue. In the following example, we would like to know whether personal computer ownership *causes* a higher college grade point average.

EXAMPLE 7.2   **Effects of Computer Ownership on College GPA**

In order to determine the effects of computer ownership on college grade point average, we estimate the model

$$colGPA = \beta_0 + \delta_0 PC + \beta_1 hsGPA + \beta_2 ACT + u,$$

where the dummy variable *PC* equals one if a student owns a personal computer and zero otherwise. There are various reasons PC ownership might have an effect on *colGPA*. A student's schoolwork might be of higher quality if it is done on a computer, and time can be saved by not having to wait at a computer lab. Of course, a student might be more inclined to play computer games or surf the Internet if he or she owns a PC, so it is not obvious that δ_0 is positive. The variables *hsGPA* (high school GPA) and *ACT* (achievement test score) are used as controls: it could be that stronger students, as measured by high school *GPA* and *ACT* scores, are more likely to own computers. We control for these factors because we would like to know the average effect on *colGPA* if a student is picked at random and given a personal computer.

Using the data in GPA1, we obtain

$$\widehat{colGPA} = 1.26 + .157\,PC + .447\,hsGPA + .0087\,ACT$$
$$\phantom{\widehat{colGPA} = 1.26 + }(.33)\ (.057)\ (.094)\ (.0105) \qquad \text{[7.6]}$$
$$n = 141, R^2 = .219.$$

This equation implies that a student who owns a PC has a predicted GPA about .16 points higher than a comparable student without a PC (remember, both *colGPA* and *hsGPA* are on a four-point scale). The effect is also very statistically significant, with $t_{PC} = .157/.057 \approx 2.75$.

What happens if we drop *hsGPA* and *ACT* from the equation? Clearly, dropping the latter variable should have very little effect, as its coefficient and *t* statistic are very small. But *hsGPA* is very significant, and so dropping it could affect the estimate of β_{PC}. Regressing *colGPA* on *PC* gives an estimate on *PC* equal to about .170, with a standard error of .063; in this case, $\hat{\beta}_{PC}$ and its *t* statistic do not change by much.

In the exercises at the end of the chapter, you will be asked to control for other factors in the equation to see if the computer ownership effect disappears, or if it at least gets notably smaller.

Each of the previous examples can be viewed as having relevance for **policy analysis**. In the first example, we were interested in gender discrimination in the workforce. In the second example, we were concerned with the effect of computer ownership on college performance. A special case of policy analysis is **program evaluation**, where we would like to know the effect of economic or social programs on individuals, firms, neighborhoods, cities, and so on.

In the simplest case, there are two groups of subjects. The **control group** does not participate in the program. The **experimental group** or **treatment group** does take part in the program. These names come from literature in the experimental sciences, and they should not be taken literally. Except in rare cases, the choice of the control and treatment groups is not random. However, in some cases, multiple regression analysis can be used to control for enough other factors in order to estimate the causal effect of the program.

EXAMPLE 7.3   **Effects of Training Grants on Hours of Training**

Using the 1988 data for Michigan manufacturing firms in JTRAIN, we obtain the following estimated equation:

$$\widehat{hrsemp} = 46.67 + 26.25\,grant - .98\,\log(sales) - 6.07\,\log(employ)$$
$$\phantom{\widehat{hrsemp} = }(43.41)\ \ (5.59)\ (3.54)\ (3.88) \qquad \text{[7.7]}$$
$$n = 105, R^2 = .237.$$

The dependent variable is hours of training per employee, at the firm level. The variable *grant* is a dummy variable equal to one if the firm received a job training grant for 1988, and zero otherwise. The variables *sales* and *employ* represent annual sales and number of employees, respectively. We cannot enter *hrsemp* in logarithmic form because *hrsemp* is zero for 29 of the 105 firms used in the regression.

The variable *grant* is very statistically significant, with $t_{grant} = 4.70$. Controlling for sales and employment, firms that received a grant trained each worker, on average, 26.25 hours more. Because the average number of hours of per worker training in the sample is about 17, with a maximum value of 164, *grant* has a large effect on training, as is expected.

The coefficient on log(*sales*) is small and very insignificant. The coefficient on log(*employ*) means that, if a firm is 10% larger, it trains its workers about .61 hour less. Its *t* statistic is −1.56, which is only marginally statistically significant.

As with any other independent variable, we should ask whether the measured effect of a qualitative variable is causal. In equation (7.7), is the difference in training between firms that receive grants and those that do not due to the grant, or is grant receipt simply an indicator of something else? It might be that the firms receiving grants would have, on average, trained their workers more even in the absence of a grant. Nothing in this analysis tells us whether we have estimated a causal effect; we must know how the firms receiving grants were determined. We can only hope we have controlled for as many factors as possible that might be related to whether a firm received a grant and to its levels of training.

We will return to policy analysis with dummy variables in Section 7-6, as well as in later chapters.

7-2a Interpreting Coefficients on Dummy Explanatory Variables When the Dependent Variable Is log(y)

A common specification in applied work has the dependent variable appearing in logarithmic form, with one or more dummy variables appearing as independent variables. How do we interpret the dummy variable coefficients in this case? Not surprisingly, the coefficients have a *percentage* interpretation.

EXAMPLE 7.4 **Housing Price Regression**

Using the data in HPRICE1, we obtain the equation

$$\widehat{\log(price)} = -1.35 + .168 \log(lotsize) + .707 \log(sqrft)$$
$$(.65) \quad (.038) \qquad\qquad (.093)$$
$$+ .027\, bdrms + .054\, colonial \qquad\qquad [7.8]$$
$$(.029) \qquad\quad (.045)$$
$$n = 88, R^2 = .649.$$

All the variables are self-explanatory except colonial, which is a binary variable equal to one if the house is of the colonial style. What does the coefficient on *colonial* mean? For given levels of *lotsize*, *sqrft*, and *bdrms*, the difference in $\widehat{\log(price)}$ between a house of colonial style and that of another style is .054. This means that a colonial-style house is predicted to sell for about 5.4% more, holding other factors fixed.

This example shows that, when log(*y*) is the dependent variable in a model, the coefficient on a dummy variable, when multiplied by 100, is interpreted as the percentage difference in *y*, holding all other factors fixed. When the coefficient on a dummy variable suggests a large proportionate change in y, the exact percentage difference can be obtained exactly as with the semi-elasticity calculation in Section 6-2.

| **EXAMPLE 7.5** | **Log Hourly Wage Equation** |

Let us reestimate the wage equation from Example 7.1, using log(*wage*) as the dependent variable and adding quadratics in *exper* and *tenure*:

$$\widehat{\log(wage)} = .417 - .297 \, female + .080 \, educ + .029 \, exper$$
$$\quad (.099) \quad (.036) \qquad (.007) \qquad (.005)$$
$$\quad - .00058 \, exper^2 + .032 \, tenure - .00059 \, tenure^2 \qquad [7.9]$$
$$\quad (.00010) \qquad\quad (.007) \qquad\quad (.00023)$$
$$n = 526, R^2 = .441.$$

Using the same approximation as in Example 7.4, the coefficient on *female* implies that, for the same levels of *educ*, *exper*, and *tenure*, women earn about $100(.297) = 29.7\%$ less than men. We can do better than this by computing the exact percentage difference in predicted wages. What we want is the proportionate difference in wages between females and males, holding other factors fixed: $(\widehat{wage}_F - \widehat{wage}_M)/\widehat{wage}_M$. What we have from (7.9) is

$$\widehat{\log(wage_F)} - \widehat{\log(wage_M)} = -.297.$$

Exponentiating and subtracting one gives

$$(\widehat{wage}_F - \widehat{wage}_M)/\widehat{wage}_M = \exp(-.297) - 1 \approx -.257.$$

This more accurate estimate implies that a woman's wage is, on average, 25.7% below a comparable man's wage.

If we had made the same correction in Example 7.4, we would have obtained $\exp(.054) - 1 \approx .0555$, or about 5.6%. The correction has a smaller effect in Example 7.4 than in the wage example because the magnitude of the coefficient on the dummy variable is much smaller in (7.8) than in (7.9).

Generally, if $\hat{\beta}_1$ is the coefficient on a dummy variable, say x_1, when log(y) is the dependent variable, the exact percentage difference in the predicted y when $x_1 = 1$ versus when $x_1 = 0$ is

$$100 \cdot [\exp(\hat{\beta}_1) - 1]. \qquad [7.10]$$

The estimate $\hat{\beta}_1$ can be positive or negative, and it is important to preserve its sign in computing (7.10).

The logarithmic approximation has the advantage of providing an estimate between the magnitudes obtained by using each group as the base group. In particular, although equation (7.10) gives us a better estimate than $100 \cdot \hat{\beta}_1$ of the percentage by which y for $x_1 = 1$ is greater than y for $x_1 = 0$, (7.10) is not a good estimate if we switch the base group. In Example 7.5, we can estimate the percentage by which a man's wage exceeds a comparable woman's wage, and this estimate is $100 \cdot [\exp(-\hat{\beta}_1) - 1] = 100 \cdot [\exp(.297) - 1] \approx 34.6$. The approximation, based on $100 \cdot \hat{\beta}_1$, 29.7, is between 25.7 and 34.6 (and close to the middle). Therefore, it makes sense to report that "the difference in predicted wages between men and women is about 29.7%," without having to take a stand on which is the base group.

7-3 Using Dummy Variables for Multiple Categories

We can use several dummy independent variables in the same equation. For example, we could add the dummy variable *married* to equation (7.9). The coefficient on *married* gives the (approximate) proportional differential in wages between those who are and are not married, holding gender, *educ*, *exper*, and *tenure* fixed. When we estimate this model, the coefficient on *married* (with standard error in parentheses) is .053 (.041), and the coefficient on *female* becomes $-.290(.036)$. Thus, the "marriage premium" is estimated to be about 5.3%, but it is not statistically different from zero $(t = 1.29)$. An important limitation of this model is that the marriage premium is assumed to be the same for men and women; this is relaxed in the following example.

EXAMPLE 7.6   **Log Hourly Wage Equation**

Let us estimate a model that allows for wage differences among four groups: married men, married women, single men, and single women. To do this, we must select a base group; we choose single men. Then, we must define dummy variables for each of the remaining groups. Call these *marrmale*, *marrfem*, and *singfem*. Putting these three variables into (7.9) (and, of course, dropping *female*, since it is now redundant) gives

$$
\widehat{\log(wage)} = .321 + .213\ marrmale - .198\ marrfem
$$
$$
\quad (.100) \quad (.055) \qquad\qquad (.058)
$$
$$
\quad - .110\ singfem + .079\ educ + .027\ exper - .00054\ exper^2
$$
$$
\quad (.056) \qquad\qquad (.007) \qquad (.005) \qquad\quad (.00011) \qquad\qquad [7.11]
$$
$$
\quad + .029\ tenure - .00053\ tenure^2
$$
$$
\quad (.007) \qquad\quad (.00023)
$$
$$
\quad n = 526, R^2 = .461.
$$

All of the coefficients, with the exception of *singfem*, have t statistics well above two in absolute value. The t statistic for *singfem* is about -1.96, which is just significant at the 5% level against a two-sided alternative.

To interpret the coefficients on the dummy variables, we must remember that the base group is single males. Thus, the estimates on the three dummy variables measure the proportionate difference in wage *relative* to single males. For example, married men are estimated to earn about 21.3% more than single men, holding levels of education, experience, and tenure fixed. [The more precise estimate from (7.10) is about 23.7%.] A married woman, on the other hand, earns a predicted 19.8% less than a single man with the same levels of the other variables.

Because the base group is represented by the intercept in (7.11), we have included dummy variables for only three of the four groups. If we were to add a dummy variable for single males to (7.11), we would fall into the dummy variable trap by introducing perfect collinearity. Some regression packages will automatically correct this mistake for you, while others will just tell you there is perfect collinearity. It is best to carefully specify the dummy variables because then we are forced to properly interpret the final model.

Even though single men is the base group in (7.11), we can use this equation to obtain the estimated difference between any two groups. Because the overall intercept is common to all groups, we can ignore that in finding differences. Thus, the estimated proportionate difference between single and married women is $-.110 - (-.198) = .088$, which means that single women earn about 8.8% more than married women. Unfortunately, we cannot use equation (7.11) for testing whether the estimated difference between single and married women is statistically significant. Knowing the standard errors on *marrfem* and *singfem* is not enough to carry out the test (see Section 4-4). The easiest thing to do is to choose one of these groups to be the base group and to reestimate the equation. Nothing substantive changes, but we get the needed estimate and its standard error directly. When we use married women as the base group, we obtain

$$
\widehat{\log(wage)} = .123 + .411\ marrmale + .198\ singmale + .088\ singfem + \ldots,
$$
$$
\quad (.106) \quad (.056) \qquad\qquad (.058) \qquad\qquad (.052)
$$

where, of course, none of the unreported coefficients or standard errors have changed. The estimate on *singfem* is, as expected, .088. Now, we have a standard error to go along with this estimate. The *t* statistic for the null that there is no difference in the population between married and single women is $t_{singfem} = .088/.052 \approx 1.69$. This is marginal evidence against the null hypothesis. We also see that the estimated difference between married men and married women is very statistically significant ($t_{marrmale} = 7.34$).

The previous example illustrates a general principle for including dummy variables to indicate different groups: if the regression model is to have different intercepts for, say, *g* groups or categories, we need to include $g - 1$ dummy variables in the model along with an intercept. The intercept for the base group is the overall intercept in the model, and the dummy variable coefficient for a particular group represents the estimated difference in intercepts between that group and the base group. Including *g* dummy variables along with an intercept will result in the dummy variable trap. An alternative is to include *g* dummy variables and to exclude an overall intercept. Including *g* dummies without an overall intercept is sometimes useful, but it has two practical drawbacks. First, it makes it more cumbersome to test for differences relative to a base group. Second, regression packages usually change the way *R*-squared is computed when an overall intercept is not included. In particular, in the formula $R^2 = 1 - SSR/SST$, the total sum of squares, SST, is replaced with a total sum of squares that does not center y_i about its mean, say, $SST_0 = \sum_{i=1}^{n} y_i^2$. The resulting *R*-squared, say $R_0^2 = 1 - SSR/SST_0$, is sometimes called the **uncentered *R*-squared**. Unfortunately, R_0^2 is rarely suitable as a goodness-of-fit measure. It is always true that $SST_0 \geq SST$ with equality only if $\bar{y} = 0$. Often, SST_0 is much larger that SST, which means that R_0^2 is much larger than R^2. For example, if in the previous example we regress log(*wage*) on *marrmale*, *singmale*, *marrfem*, *singfem*, and the other explanatory variables—without an intercept—the reported *R*-squared from Stata, which is R_0^2, is .948. This high *R*-squared is an artifact of not centering the total sum of squares in the calculation. The correct *R*-squared is given in equation (7.11) as .461. Some regression packages, including Stata, have an option to force calculation of the centered *R*-squared even though an overall intercept has not been included, and using this option is generally a good idea. In the vast majority of cases, any *R*-squared based on comparing an SSR and SST should have SST computed by centering the y_i about $\bar{y}$. We can think of this SST as the sum of squared residuals obtained if we just use the sample average, $\bar{y}$, to predict each y_i. Surely we are setting the bar pretty low for any model if all we measure is its fit relative to using a constant predictor. For a model without an intercept that fits poorly, it is possible that SSR > SST, which means R^2 would be negative. The uncentered *R*-squared will always be between zero and one, which likely explains why it is usually the default when an intercept is not estimated in regression models.

> **EXPLORING FURTHER 7.2**
>
> In the baseball salary data found in MLB1, players are given one of six positions: *frstbase, scndbase, thrdbase, shrtstop, outfield,* or *catcher*. To allow for salary differentials across position, with outfielders as the base group, which dummy variables would you include as independent variables?

7-3a Incorporating Ordinal Information by Using Dummy Variables

Suppose that we would like to estimate the effect of city credit ratings on the municipal bond interest rate (*MBR*). Several financial companies, such as Moody's Investors Service and Standard and Poor's, rate the quality of debt for local governments, where the ratings depend on things like probability of default. (Local governments prefer lower interest rates in order to reduce their costs of borrowing.) For simplicity, suppose that rankings take on the integer values {0, 1, 2, 3, 4}, with zero being the worst credit rating and four being the best. This is an example of an **ordinal variable**. Call this variable *CR* for concreteness. The question we need to address is: How do we incorporate the variable *CR* into a model to explain *MBR*?

One possibility is to just include *CR* as we would include any other explanatory variable:

$$MBR = \beta_0 + \beta_1 CR + other\ factors,$$

where we do not explicitly show what other factors are in the model. Then β_1 is the percentage point change in *MBR* when *CR* increases by one unit, holding other factors fixed. Unfortunately, it is rather hard to interpret a one-unit increase in *CR*. We know the quantitative meaning of another year of education, or another dollar spent per student, but things like credit ratings typically have only ordinal meaning. We know that a *CR* of four is better than a *CR* of three, but is the difference between four and three the same as the difference between one and zero? If not, then it might not make sense to assume that a one-unit increase in *CR* has a constant effect on *MBR*.

A better approach, which we can implement because *CR* takes on relatively few values, is to define dummy variables for each value of *CR*. Thus, let $CR_1 = 1$ if $CR = 1$, and $CR_1 = 0$ otherwise; $CR_2 = 1$ if $CR = 2$, and $CR_2 = 0$ otherwise; and so on. Effectively, we take the single credit rating and turn it into five categories. Then, we can estimate the model

$$MBR = \beta_0 + \delta_1 CR_1 + \delta_2 CR_2 + \delta_3 CR_3 + \delta_4 CR_4 + other\ factors. \qquad [7.12]$$

Following our rule for including dummy variables in a model, we include four dummy variables because we have five categories. The omitted category here is a credit rating of zero, and so it is the base group. (This is why we do not need to define a dummy variable for this category.) The coefficients are easy to interpret: δ_1 is the difference in *MBR* (other factors fixed) between a municipality with a credit rating of one and a municipality with a credit rating of zero; δ_2 is the difference in *MBR* between a municipality with a credit rating of two and a municipality with a credit rating of zero; and so on. The movement between each credit rating is allowed to have a different effect, so using (7.12) is much more flexible than simply putting *CR* in as a single variable. Once the dummy variables are defined, estimating (7.12) is straightforward.

> **EXPLORING FURTHER 7.3**
>
> In model (7.12), how would you test the null hypothesis that credit rating has no effect on *MBR*?

Equation (7.12) contains the model with a constant partial effect as a special case. One way to write the three restrictions that imply a constant partial effect is $\delta_2 = 2\delta_1$, $\delta_3 = 3\delta_1$, and $\delta_4 = 4\delta_1$. When we plug these into equation (7.12) and rearrange, we get $MBR = \beta_0 + \delta_1(CR_1 + 2CR_2 + 3CR_3 + 4CR_4) + other\ factors$. Now, the term multiplying δ_1 is simply the original credit rating variable, *CR*. To obtain the *F* statistic for testing the constant partial effect restrictions, we obtain the unrestricted *R*-squared from (7.12) and the restricted *R*-squared from the regression of *MBR* on *CR* and the other factors we have controlled for. The *F* statistic is obtained as in equation (4.41) with $q = 3$.

EXAMPLE 7.7	**Effects of Physical Attractiveness on Wage**

Hamermesh and Biddle (1994) used measures of physical attractiveness in a wage equation. (The file BEAUTY contains fewer variables but more observations than used by Hamermesh and Biddle. See Computer Exercise C12.) Each person in the sample was ranked by an interviewer for physical attractiveness, using five categories (homely, quite plain, average, good looking, and strikingly beautiful or handsome). Because there are so few people at the two extremes, the authors put people into one of three groups for the regression analysis: average, below average, and above average, where the base group is *average*. Using data from the 1977 Quality of Employment Survey, after controlling for the usual productivity characteristics, Hamermesh and Biddle estimated an equation for men:

$$\widehat{\log(wage)} = \hat{\beta}_0 - .164 \, belavg + .016 \, abvavg + other \, factors$$
$$(.046) \qquad (.033)$$
$$n = 700, \overline{R}^2 = .403$$

and an equation for women:

$$\widehat{\log(wage)} = \hat{\beta}_0 - .124 \, belavg + .035 \, abvavg + other \, factors$$
$$(.066) \qquad (.049)$$
$$n = 409, \overline{R}^2 = .330.$$

The other factors controlled for in the regressions include education, experience, tenure, marital status, and race; see Table 3 in Hamermesh and Biddle's paper for a more complete list. In order to save space, the coefficients on the other variables are not reported in the paper and neither is the intercept.

For men, those with below average looks are estimated to earn about 16.4% less than an average-looking man who is the same in other respects (including education, experience, tenure, marital status, and race). The effect is statistically different from zero, with $t = -3.57$. Men with above average looks are estimated to earn only 1.6% more than men with average looks, and the effect is not statistically significant ($t < .5$).

A woman with below average looks earns about 12.4% less than an otherwise comparable average-looking woman, with $t = -1.88$. As was the case for men, the estimate on *abvavg* is much smaller in magnitude and not statistically different from zero.

In related work, Biddle and Hamermesh (1998) revisit the effects of looks on earnings using a more homogeneous group: graduates of a particular law school. The authors continue to find that physical appearance has an effect on annual earnings, something that is perhaps not too surprising among people practicing law.

In some cases, the ordinal variable takes on too many values so that a dummy variable cannot be included for each value. For example, the file LAWSCH85 contains data on median starting salaries for law school graduates. One of the key explanatory variables is the rank of the law school. Because each law school has a different rank, we clearly cannot include a dummy variable for each rank. If we do not wish to put the rank directly in the equation, we can break it down into categories. The following example shows how this is done.

EXAMPLE 7.8   **Effects of Law School Rankings on Starting Salaries**

Define the dummy variables *top10, r11_25, r26_40, r41_60, r61_100* to take on the value unity when the variable *rank* falls into the appropriate range. We let schools ranked below 100 be the base group. The estimated equation is

$$\widehat{\log(salary)} = 9.17 + .700 \, top10 + .594 \, r11\_25 + .375 \, r26\_40$$
$$(.41) \quad (.053) \qquad (.039) \qquad\quad (.034)$$
$$+ .263 \, r41\_60 + .132 \, r61\_100 + .0057 \, LSAT$$
$$(.028) \qquad\quad (.021) \qquad\qquad (.0031) \qquad\qquad\qquad [7.13]$$
$$+ .041 \, GPA + .036 \, \log(libvol) + .0008 \, \log(cost)$$
$$(.074) \qquad (.026) \qquad\qquad (.0251)$$
$$n = 136, R^2 = .911, \overline{R}^2 = .905.$$

We see immediately that all of the dummy variables defining the different ranks are very statistically significant. The estimate on *r61_100* means that, holding *LSAT*, *GPA*, *libvol*, and *cost* fixed, the median salary at a law school ranked between 61 and 100 is about 13.2% higher than that at a law school ranked below 100. The difference between a top 10 school and a below 100 school is quite large. Using the exact calculation given in equation (7.10) gives $\exp(.700) - 1 \approx 1.014$, and so the predicted median salary is more than 100% higher at a top 10 school than it is at a below 100 school.

As an indication of whether breaking the rank into different groups is an improvement, we can compare the adjusted R-squared in (7.13) with the adjusted R-squared from including *rank* as a single variable: the former is .905 and the latter is .836, so the additional flexibility of (7.13) is warranted.

Interestingly, once the rank is put into the (admittedly somewhat arbitrary) given categories, all of the other variables become insignificant. In fact, a test for joint significance of *LSAT*, *GPA*, log(*libvol*), and log(*cost*) gives a p-value of .055, which is borderline significant. When *rank* is included in its original form, the p-value for joint significance is zero to four decimal places.

One final comment about this example: In deriving the properties of ordinary least squares, we assumed that we had a random sample. The current application violates that assumption because of the way *rank* is defined: a school's rank necessarily depends on the rank of the other schools in the sample, and so the data cannot represent independent draws from the population of all law schools. This does not cause any serious problems provided the error term is uncorrelated with the explanatory variables.

7-4 Interactions Involving Dummy Variables

7-4a Interactions among Dummy Variables

Just as variables with quantitative meaning can be interacted in regression models, so can dummy variables. We have effectively seen an example of this in Example 7.6, where we defined four categories based on marital status and gender. In fact, we can recast that model by adding an **interaction term** between *female* and *married* to the model where *female* and *married* appear separately. This allows the marriage premium to depend on gender, just as it did in equation (7.11). For purposes of comparison, the estimated model with the *female-married* interaction term is

$$
\begin{aligned}
\widehat{\log(wage)} = {} & .321 - .110\,female + .231\,married \\
& (.100)\ (.056) \qquad\quad (.055) \\
& - .301\,female{\cdot}married + ..., \\
& (.072)
\end{aligned}
$$

[7.14]

where the rest of the regression is necessarily identical to (7.11). Equation (7.14) shows explicitly that there is a statistically significant interaction between gender and marital status. This model also allows us to obtain the estimated wage differential among all four groups, but here we must be careful to plug in the correct combination of zeros and ones.

Setting *female* = 0 and *married* = 0 corresponds to the group single men, which is the base group, since this eliminates *female*, *married*, and *female · married*. We can find the intercept for married men by setting *female* = 0 and *married* = 1 in (7.14); this gives an intercept of .321 + .213 = .534, and so on.

Equation (7.14) is just a different way of finding wage differentials across all gender–marital status combinations. It allows us to easily test the null hypothesis that the gender differential does not depend on marital status (equivalently, that the marriage differential does not depend on gender). Equation (7.11) is more convenient for testing for wage differentials between any group and the base group of single men.

EXAMPLE 7.9 Effects of Computer Usage on Wages

Krueger (1993) estimates the effects of computer usage on wages. He defines a dummy variable, which we call *compwork*, equal to one if an individual uses a computer at work. Another dummy variable, *comphome*, equals one if the person uses a computer at home. Using 13,379 people from the 1989 Current Population Survey, Krueger (1993, Table 4) obtains

$$\widehat{\log(wage)} = \hat{\beta}_0 + .177 \, compwork + .070 \, comphome$$
$$(.009) \qquad\qquad (.019)$$
$$+ .017 \, compwork{\cdot}comphome + other \, factors.$$
$$(.023)$$

[7.15]

(The other factors are the standard ones for wage regressions, including education, experience, gender, and marital status; see Krueger's paper for the exact list.) Krueger does not report the intercept because it is not of any importance; all we need to know is that the base group consists of people who do not use a computer at home or at work. It is worth noticing that the estimated return to using a computer at work (but not at home) is about 17.7%. (The more precise estimate is 19.4%.) Similarly, people who use computers at home but not at work have about a 7% wage premium over those who do not use a computer at all. The differential between those who use a computer at both places, relative to those who use a computer in neither place, is about 26.4% (obtained by adding all three coefficients and multiplying by 100), or the more precise estimate 30.2% obtained from equation (7.10).

The interaction term in (7.15) is not statistically significant, nor is it very big economically. But it is causing little harm by being in the equation.

7-4b Allowing for Different Slopes

We have now seen several examples of how to allow different intercepts for any number of groups in a multiple regression model. There are also occasions for interacting dummy variables with explanatory variables that are not dummy variables to allow for **a difference in slopes**. Continuing with the wage example, suppose that we wish to test whether the return to education is the same for men and women, allowing for a constant wage differential between men and women (a differential for which we have already found evidence). For simplicity, we include only education and gender in the model. What kind of model allows for different returns to education? Consider the model

$$\log(wage) = (\beta_0 + \delta_0 female) + (\beta_1 + \delta_1 female)educ + u.$$

[7.16]

If we plug *female* = 0 into (7.16), then we find that the intercept for males is β_0, and the slope on education for males is β_1. For females, we plug in *female* = 1; thus, the intercept for females is $\beta_0 + \delta_0$, and the slope is $\beta_1 + \delta_1$. Therefore, δ_0 measures the difference in intercepts between women and men, and δ_1 measures the difference in the return to education between women and men. Two of the four cases for the signs of δ_0 and δ_1 are presented in Figure 7.2.

Graph (a) shows the case where the intercept for women is below that for men, and the slope of the line is smaller for women than for men. This means that women earn less than men at all levels of education, and the gap increases as *educ* gets larger. In graph (b), the intercept for women is below that for men, but the slope on education is larger for women. This means that women earn less than men at low levels of education, but the gap narrows as education increases. At some point, a woman earns more than a man with the same level of education, and this amount of education is easily found once we have the estimated equation.

How can we estimate model (7.16)? To apply OLS, we must write the model with an interaction between *female* and *educ*:

$$\log(wage) = \beta_0 + \delta_0 female + \beta_1 educ + \delta_1 female{\cdot}educ + u.$$

[7.17]

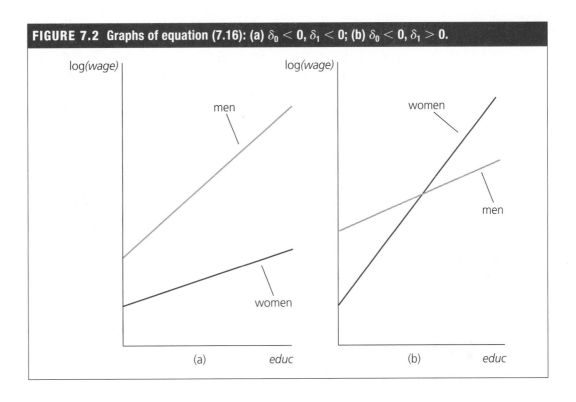

FIGURE 7.2 Graphs of equation (7.16): (a) $\delta_0 < 0$, $\delta_1 < 0$; (b) $\delta_0 < 0$, $\delta_1 > 0$.

The parameters can now be estimated from the regression of log(*wage*) on *female*, *educ*, and *female·educ*. Obtaining the interaction term is easy in any regression package. Do not be daunted by the odd nature of *female·educ*, which is zero for any man in the sample and equal to the level of education for any woman in the sample.

An important hypothesis is that the return to education is the same for women and men. In terms of model (7.17), this is stated as H_0: $\delta_1 = 0$, which means that the slope of log(*wage*) with respect to *educ* is the same for men and women. Note that this hypothesis puts no restrictions on the difference in intercepts, δ_0. A wage differential between men and women is allowed under this null, but it must be the same at all levels of education. This situation is described by Figure 7.1.

We are also interested in the hypothesis that average wages are identical for men and women who have the same levels of education. This means that δ_0 and δ_1 must *both* be zero under the null hypothesis. In equation (7.17), we must use an F test to test H_0: $\delta_0 = 0$, $\delta_1 = 0$. In the model with just an intercept difference, we reject this hypothesis because H_0: $\delta_0 = 0$ is soundly rejected against H_1: $\delta_0 < 0$.

EXAMPLE 7.10   **Log Hourly Wage Equation**

We add quadratics in experience and tenure to (7.17):

$$\widehat{\log(wage)} = .389 - .227\,female + .082\,educ$$
$$(.119)\;\;(.168)\qquad\quad(.008)$$
$$- .0056\,female·educ + .029\,exper - .00058\,exper^2$$
$$(.0131)\qquad\qquad\quad(.005)\qquad\quad(.00011)\qquad\qquad\qquad[7.18]$$
$$+ .032\,tenure - .00059\,tenure^2$$
$$(.007)\qquad\quad(.00024)$$
$$n = 526, R^2 = .441.$$

The estimated return to education for men in this equation is .082, or 8.2%. For women, it is .082 − .0056 = .0764, or about 7.6%. The difference, −.56%, or just over one-half a percentage point less for women, is not economically large nor statistically significant: the t statistic is −.0056/.0131 ≈ −.43. Thus, we conclude that there is no evidence against the hypothesis that the return to education is the same for men and women.

The coefficient on *female*, while remaining economically large, is no longer significant at conventional levels ($t = -1.35$). Its coefficient and t statistic in the equation without the interaction were −.297 and −8.25, respectively [see equation (7.9)]. Should we now conclude that there is no statistically significant evidence of lower pay for women at the same levels of *educ*, *exper*, and *tenure*? This would be a serious error. Because we have added the interaction *female·educ* to the equation, the coefficient on *female* is now estimated much less precisely than it was in equation (7.9): the standard error has increased by almost fivefold (.168/.036 ≈ 4.67). This occurs because *female* and *female·educ* are highly correlated in the sample. In this example, there is a useful way to think about the multicollinearity: in equation (7.17) and the more general equation estimated in (7.18), δ_0 measures the wage differential between women and men when *educ* = 0. Very few people in the sample have very low levels of education, so it is not surprising that we have a difficult time estimating the differential at *educ* = 0 (nor is the differential at zero years of education very informative). More interesting would be to estimate the gender differential at, say, the average education level in the sample (about 12.5). To do this, we would replace *female·educ* with *female·(educ* −12.5) and rerun the regression; this only changes the coefficient on *female* and its standard error. (See Computer Exercise C7.)

If we compute the F statistic for H_0: $\delta_0 = 0$, $\delta_1 = 0$, we obtain $F = 34.33$, which is a huge value for an F random variable with numerator $df = 2$ and denominator $df = 518$: the p-value is zero to four decimal places. In the end, we prefer model (7.9), which allows for a constant wage differential between women and men.

EXPLORING FURTHER 7.4

How would you augment the model estimated in (7.18) to allow the return to *tenure* to differ by gender?

As a more complicated example involving interactions, we now look at the effects of race and city racial composition on major league baseball player salaries.

EXAMPLE 7.11   **Effects of Race on Baseball Player Salaries**

Using MLB1, the following equation is estimated for the 330 major league baseball players for which city racial composition statistics are available. The variables *black* and *hispan* are binary indicators for the individual players. (The base group is white players.) The variable *percblck* is the percentage of the team's city that is black, and *perchisp* is the percentage of Hispanics. The other variables measure aspects of player productivity and longevity. Here, we are interested in race effects after controlling for these other factors.

In addition to including *black* and *hispan* in the equation, we add the interactions *black·percblck* and *hispan·perchisp*. The estimated equation is

$$\widehat{\log(salary)} = 10.34 + .0673 \; years + .0089 \; gamesyr$$
$$(2.18) \; (.0129) \qquad (.0034)$$
$$+ \; .00095 \; bavg + .0146 \; hrunsyr + .0045 \; rbisyr$$
$$(.00151) \qquad (.0164) \qquad \;\;\; (.0076)$$
$$+ \; .0072 \; runsyr + .0011 \; fldperc + .0075 \; allstar$$
$$(.0046) \qquad \;\; (.0021) \qquad \;\; (.0029)$$

$$- .198 \, black - .190 \, hispan + .0125 \, black \cdot percblck$$
$$\quad (.125) \qquad (.153) \qquad (.0050)$$
$$+ .0201 \, hispan \cdot perchisp$$
$$\quad (.0098)$$
$$n = 330, R^2 = .638. \qquad\qquad\qquad\qquad [7.19]$$

First, we should test whether the four race variables, *black*, *hispan*, *black·percblck*, and *hispan·perchisp*, are jointly significant. Using the same 330 players, the *R*-squared when the four race variables are dropped is .626. Since there are four restrictions and *df* = 330 − 13 in the unrestricted model, the *F* statistic is about 2.63, which yields a *p*-value of .034. Thus, these variables are jointly significant at the 5% level (though not at the 1% level).

How do we interpret the coefficients on the race variables? In the following discussion, all productivity factors are held fixed. First, consider what happens for black players, holding *perchisp* fixed. The coefficient −.198 on *black* literally means that, if a black player is in a city with no blacks (*percblck* = 0), then the black player earns about 19.8% less than a comparable white player. As *percblck* increases—which means the white population decreases, since *perchisp* is held fixed—the salary of blacks increases relative to that for whites. In a city with 10% blacks, log(*salary*) for blacks compared to that for whites is −.198 + .0125(10) = −.073, so salary is about 7.3% less for blacks than for whites in such a city. When *percblck* = 20, blacks earn about 5.2% more than whites. The largest percentage of blacks in a city is about 74% (Detroit).

Similarly, Hispanics earn less than whites in cities with a low percentage of Hispanics. But we can easily find the value of *perchisp* that makes the differential between whites and Hispanics equal zero: it must make −.190 + .0201 *perchisp* = 0, which gives *perchisp* ≈ 9.45. For cities in which the percentage of Hispanics is less than 9.45%, Hispanics are predicted to earn less than whites (for a given black population), and the opposite is true if the percentage of Hispanics is above 9.45%. Twelve of the 22 cities represented in the sample have Hispanic populations that are less than 9.45% of the total population. The largest percentage of Hispanics is about 31%.

How do we interpret these findings? We cannot simply claim discrimination exists against blacks and Hispanics, because the estimates imply that whites earn less than blacks and Hispanics in cities heavily populated by minorities. The importance of city composition on salaries might be due to player preferences: perhaps the best black players live disproportionately in cities with more blacks and the best Hispanic players tend to be in cities with more Hispanics. The estimates in (7.19) allow us to determine that some relationship is present, but we cannot distinguish between these two hypotheses.

7-4c Testing for Differences in Regression Functions across Groups

The previous examples illustrate that interacting dummy variables with other independent variables can be a powerful tool. Sometimes, we wish to test the null hypothesis that two populations or groups follow the same regression function, against the alternative that one or more of the slopes differ across the groups. We will also see examples of this in Chapter 13, when we discuss pooling different cross sections over time.

Suppose we want to test whether the same regression model describes college grade point averages for male and female college athletes. The equation is

$$cumgpa = \beta_0 + \beta_1 sat + \beta_2 hsperc + \beta_3 tothrs + u,$$

where *sat* is SAT score, *hsperc* is high school rank percentile, and *tothrs* is total hours of college courses. We know that, to allow for an intercept difference, we can include a dummy variable for either males or females. If we want any of the slopes to depend on gender, we simply interact the appropriate variable with, say, *female*, and include it in the equation.

If we are interested in testing whether there is *any* difference between men and women, then we must allow a model where the intercept and all slopes can be different across the two groups:

$$cumgpa = \beta_0 + \delta_0 female + \beta_1 sat + \delta_1 female \cdot sat + \beta_2 hsperc$$
$$+ \delta_2 female \cdot hsperc + \beta_3 tothrs + \delta_3 female \cdot tothrs + u. \qquad [7.20]$$

The parameter δ_0 is the difference in the intercept between women and men, δ_1 is the slope difference with respect to *sat* between women and men, and so on. The null hypothesis that *cumgpa* follows the same model for males and females is stated as

$$H_0: \delta_0 = 0, \delta_1 = 0, \delta_2 = 0, \delta_3 = 0. \qquad [7.21]$$

If one of the δ_j is different from zero, then the model is different for men and women.

Using the spring semester data from the file GPA3, the full model is estimated as

$$\widehat{cumgpa} = 1.48 - .353\, female + .0011\, sat + .00075\, female \cdot sat$$
$$(0.21)\ (.411) \qquad\quad (.0002) \qquad (.00039)$$
$$- .0085\, hsperc - .00055\, female \cdot hsperc + .0023\, tothrs$$
$$(.0014) \qquad\quad (.00316) \qquad\qquad\qquad (.0009) \qquad\qquad [7.22]$$
$$- .00012\, female \cdot tothrs$$
$$(.00163)$$
$$n = 366, R^2 = .406, \bar{R}^2 = .394.$$

None of the four terms involving the female dummy variable is very statistically significant; only the *female·sat* interaction has a t statistic close to two. But we know better than to rely on the individual t statistics for testing a joint hypothesis such as (7.21). To compute the F statistic, we must estimate the restricted model, which results from dropping *female* and all of the interactions; this gives an R^2 (the restricted R^2) of about .352, so the F statistic is about 8.14; the p-value is zero to five decimal places, which causes us to soundly reject (7.21). Thus, men and women athletes do follow different GPA models, even though each term in (7.22) that allows women and men to be different is individually insignificant at the 5% level.

The large standard errors on *female* and the interaction terms make it difficult to tell exactly how men and women differ. We must be very careful in interpreting equation (7.22) because, in obtaining differences between women and men, the interaction terms must be taken into account. If we look only at the *female* variable, we would wrongly conclude that *cumgpa* is about .353 less for women than for men, holding other factors fixed. This is the estimated difference only when *sat*, *hsperc*, and *tothrs* are all set to zero, which is not close to being a possible scenario. At *sat* = 1, 100, *hsperc* = 10, and *tothrs* = 50, the predicted *difference* between a woman and a man is $-.353 + .00075(1,100) - .00055(10) - .00012(50) \approx .461$. That is, the female athlete is predicted to have a GPA that is almost one-half a point higher than the comparable male athlete.

In a model with three variables, *sat*, *hsperc*, and *tothrs*, it is pretty simple to add all of the interactions to test for group differences. In some cases, many more explanatory variables are involved, and then it is convenient to have a different way to compute the statistic. It turns out that the sum of squared residuals form of the F statistic can be computed easily even when many independent variables are involved.

In the general model with k explanatory variables and an intercept, suppose we have two groups; call them $g = 1$ and $g = 2$. We would like to test whether the intercept and all slopes are the same across the two groups. Write the model as

$$y = \beta_{g,0} + \beta_{g,1}x_1 + \beta_{g,2}x_2 + \ldots + \beta_{g,k}x_k + u, \qquad [7.23]$$

for $g = 1$ and $g = 2$. The hypothesis that each beta in (7.23) is the same across the two groups involves $k + 1$ restrictions (in the GPA example, $k + 1 = 4$). The unrestricted model, which we can think of as having a group dummy variable and k interaction terms in addition to the intercept and variables themselves, has $n - 2(k + 1)$ degrees of freedom. [In the GPA example, $n - 2(k + 1) = 366 - 2(4) = 358$.] So far, there is nothing new. The key insight is that the sum of squared residuals from the unrestricted model can be obtained from two *separate* regressions, one for each group. Let SSR_1 be the sum of squared residuals obtained estimating (7.23) for the first group; this involves n_1 observations. Let SSR_2 be the sum of squared residuals obtained from estimating the model using the second group (n_2 observations). In the previous example, if group 1 is females, then $n_1 = 90$ and $n_2 = 276$. Now, the sum of squared residuals for the unrestricted model is simply $SSR_{ur} = SSR_1 + SSR_2$. The restricted sum of squared residuals is just the SSR from pooling the groups and estimating a single equation, say SSR_P. Once we have these, we compute the F statistic as usual:

$$F = \frac{[SSR_P - (SSR_1 + SSR_2)]}{SSR_1 + SSR_2} \cdot \frac{[n - 2(k + 1)]}{k + 1},$$ [7.24]

where n is the *total* number of observations. This particular F statistic is usually called the **Chow statistic** in econometrics. Because the Chow test is just an F test, it is only valid under homoskedasticity. In particular, under the null hypothesis, the error variances for the two groups must be equal. As usual, normality is not needed for asymptotic analysis.

To apply the Chow statistic to the GPA example, we need the SSR from the regression that pooled the groups together: this is $SSR_P = 85.515$. The SSR for the 90 women in the sample is $SSR_1 = 19.603$, and the SSR for the men is $SSR_2 = 58.752$. Thus, $SSR_{ur} = 19.603 + 58.752 = 78.355$. The F statistic is $[(85.515 - 78.355)/78.355](358/4) \approx 8.18]$; of course, subject to rounding error, this is what we get using the R-squared form of the test in the models with and without the interaction terms. (A word of caution: there is no simple R-squared form of the test if separate regressions have been estimated for each group; the R-squared form of the test can be used only if interactions have been included to create the unrestricted model.)

One important limitation of the traditional Chow test, regardless of the method used to implement it, is that the null hypothesis allows for no differences at all between the groups. In many cases, it is more interesting to allow for an intercept difference between the groups and then to test for slope differences; we saw one example of this in the wage equation in Example 7.10. There are two ways to allow the intercepts to differ under the null hypothesis. One is to include the group dummy and all interaction terms, as in equation (7.22), but then test joint significance of the interaction terms only. The second approach, which produces an identical statistic, is to form a sum-of-squared-residuals F statistic, as in equation (7.24), but where the restricted SSR, called "SSR_P" in equation (7.24), is obtained using a regression that contains only an intercept shift. Because we are testing k restrictions, rather than $k + 1$, the F statistic becomes

$$F = \frac{[SSR_P - (SSR_1 + SSR_2)]}{SSR_1 + SSR_2} \cdot \frac{[n - 2(k + 1)]}{k}.$$

Using this approach in the GPA example, SSR_P is obtained from the regression *cumgpa* on *female*, *sat*, *hsperc*, and *tothrs* using the data for both male and female student-athletes.

Because there are relatively few explanatory variables in the GPA example, it is easy to estimate (7.20) and test $H_0: \delta_1 = 0, \delta_2 = 0, \delta_3 = 0$ (with δ_0 unrestricted under the null). The F statistic for the three exclusion restrictions gives a p-value equal to .205, and so we do not reject the null hypothesis at even the 20% significance level.

Failure to reject the hypothesis that the parameters multiplying the interaction terms are all zero suggests that the best model allows for an intercept difference only:

$$\widehat{cumgpa} = 1.39 + .310\,female + .0012\,sat - .0084\,hsperc$$
$$(.18)\ (.059)\qquad (.0002)\qquad (.0012)$$
$$+ .0025\,tothrs \qquad\qquad\qquad\qquad\qquad\text{[7.25]}$$
$$(.0007)$$
$$n = 366, R^2 = .398, \bar{R}^2 = .392.$$

The slope coefficients in (7.25) are close to those for the base group (males) in (7.22); dropping the interactions changes very little. However, *female* in (7.25) is highly significant: its *t* statistic is over 5, and the estimate implies that, at given levels of *sat*, *hsperc*, and *tothrs*, a female athlete has a predicted GPA that is .31 point higher than that of a male athlete. This is a practically important difference.

7-5 A Binary Dependent Variable: The Linear Probability Model

By now, we have learned much about the properties and applicability of the multiple linear regression model. In the last several sections, we studied how, through the use of binary independent variables, we can incorporate qualitative information as explanatory variables in a multiple regression model. In all of the models up until now, the dependent variable *y* has had *quantitative* meaning (for example, *y* is a dollar amount, a test score, a percentage, or the logs of these). What happens if we want to use multiple regression to *explain* a qualitative event?

In the simplest case, and one that often arises in practice, the event we would like to explain is a binary outcome. In other words, our dependent variable, *y*, takes on only two values: zero and one. For example, *y* can be defined to indicate whether an adult has a high school education; *y* can indicate whether a college student used illegal drugs during a given school year; or *y* can indicate whether a firm was taken over by another firm during a given year. In each of these examples, we can let $y = 1$ denote one of the outcomes and $y = 0$ the other outcome.

What does it mean to write down a multiple regression model, such as

$$y = \beta_0 + \beta_1 x_1 + \dots + \beta_k x_k + u, \qquad\qquad\text{[7.26]}$$

when *y* is a binary variable? Because *y* can take on only two values, β_j cannot be interpreted as the change in *y* given a one-unit increase in x_j, holding all other factors fixed: *y* either changes from zero to one or from one to zero (or does not change). Nevertheless, the β_j still have useful interpretations. If we assume that the zero conditional mean assumption MLR.4 holds, that is, $E(u|x_1, \dots, x_k) = 0$, then we have, as always,

$$E(y|\mathbf{x}) = \beta_0 + \beta_1 x_1 + \dots + \beta_k x_k,$$

where **x** is shorthand for all of the explanatory variables.

The key point is that when y is a binary variable taking on the values zero and one, it is always true that $P(y = 1|\mathbf{x}) = E(y|\mathbf{x})$: the probability of "success"—that is, the probability that $y = 1$—is the same as the expected value of *y*. Thus, we have the important equation

$$P(y = 1|\mathbf{x}) = \beta_0 + \beta_1 x_1 + \dots + \beta_k x_k, \qquad\qquad\text{[7.27]}$$

which says that the probability of success, say, $p(\mathbf{x}) = P(y = 1|\mathbf{x})$, is a linear function of the x_j. Equation (7.27) is an example of a binary response model, and $P(y = 1|\mathbf{x})$ is also called the **response**

probability. (We will cover other binary response models in Chapter 17.) Because probabilities must sum to one, $P(y = 0|\mathbf{x}) = 1 - P(y = 1|\mathbf{x})$ is also a linear function of the x_j.

The multiple linear regression model with a binary dependent variable is called the **linear probability model (LPM)** because the response probability is linear in the parameters β_j, In the LPM, β_j measures the change in the probability of success when x_j changes, holding other factors fixed:

$$\Delta P(y = 1|\mathbf{x}) = \beta_j \Delta x_j. \qquad [7.28]$$

With this in mind, the multiple regression model can allow us to estimate the effect of various explanatory variables on qualitative events. The mechanics of OLS are the same as before.

If we write the estimated equation as

$$\hat{y} = \hat{\beta}_0 + \hat{\beta}_1 x_1 + \ldots + \hat{\beta}_k x_k,$$

we must now remember that $\hat{y}$ is the predicted probability of success. Therefore, $\hat{\beta}_0$ is the predicted probability of success when each x_j is set to zero, which may or may not be interesting. The slope coefficient $\hat{\beta}_1$ measures the predicted change in the probability of success when x_1 increases by one unit.

To correctly interpret a linear probability model, we must know what constitutes a "success." Thus, it is a good idea to give the dependent variable a name that describes the event $y = 1$. As an example, let *inlf* ("in the labor force") be a binary variable indicating labor force participation by a married woman during 1975: *inlf* = 1 if the woman reports working for a wage outside the home at some point during the year, and zero otherwise. We assume that labor force participation depends on other sources of income, including husband's earnings (*nwifeinc*, measured in thousands of dollars), years of education (*educ*), past years of labor market experience (*exper*), *age*, number of children less than six years old (*kidslt6*), and number of kids between 6 and 18 years of age (*kidsge6*). Using the data in MROZ from Mroz (1987), we estimate the following linear probability model, where 428 of the 753 women in the sample report being in the labor force at some point during 1975:

$$\widehat{inlf} = .586 - .0034 \, nwifeinc + .038 \, educ + .039 \, exper$$
$$\qquad (.154) \quad (.0014) \qquad\quad (.007) \qquad (.006)$$
$$\qquad - .00060 \, exper^2 - .016 \, age - .262 \, kidslt6 + .013 \, kidsge6 \qquad [7.29]$$
$$\qquad (.00018) \qquad\quad (.002) \qquad (.034) \qquad\quad (.013)$$
$$n = 753, R^2 = .264.$$

Using the usual t statistics, all variables in (7.29) except *kidsge6* are statistically significant, and all of the significant variables have the effects we would expect based on economic theory (or common sense).

To interpret the estimates, we must remember that a change in the independent variable changes the probability that *inlf* = 1. For example, the coefficient on *educ* means that, everything else in (7.29) held fixed, another year of education increases the probability of labor force participation by .038. If we take this equation literally, 10 more years of education increases the probability of being in the labor force by .038(10) = .38, which is a pretty large increase in a probability. The relationship between the probability of labor force participation and *educ* is plotted in Figure 7.3. The other independent variables are fixed at the values *nwifeinc* = 50, *exper* = 5, *age* = 30, *kidslt6* = 1, and *kidsge6* = 0 for illustration purposes. The predicted probability is negative until education equals 3.84 years. This should not cause too much concern because, in this sample, no woman has less than five years of education. The largest reported education is 17 years, and this leads to a predicted probability of .5. If we set the other independent variables at different values, the range of predicted probabilities would change. But the marginal effect of another year of education on the probability of labor force participation is always .038.

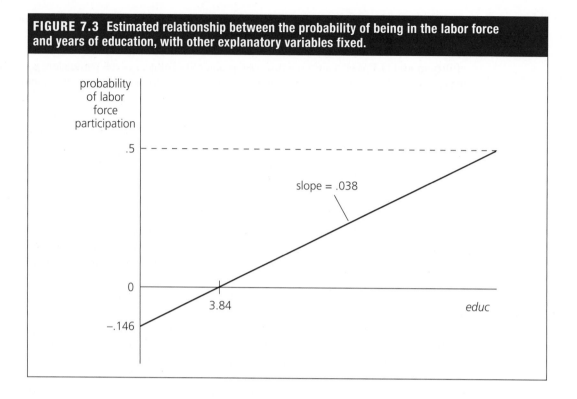

FIGURE 7.3 Estimated relationship between the probability of being in the labor force and years of education, with other explanatory variables fixed.

The coefficient on *nwifeinc* implies that, if Δ*nwifeinc* = 10 (which means an increase of $10,000), the probability that a woman is in the labor force falls by .034. This is not an especially large effect given that an increase in income of $10,000 is substantial in terms of 1975 dollars. Experience has been entered as a quadratic to allow the effect of past experience to have a diminishing effect on the labor force participation probability. Holding other factors fixed, the estimated change in the probability is approximated as .039 − 2(.0006)*exper* = .039 − .0012 *exper*. The point at which past experience has no effect on the probability of labor force participation is .039/.0012 = 32.5, which is a high level of experience: only 13 of the 753 women in the sample have more than 32 years of experience.

Unlike the number of older children, the number of young children has a huge impact on labor force participation. Having one additional child less than six years old reduces the probability of participation by −.262, at given levels of the other variables. In the sample, just under 20% of the women have at least one young child.

This example illustrates how easy linear probability models are to estimate and interpret, but it also highlights some shortcomings of the LPM. First, it is easy to see that, if we plug certain combinations of values for the independent variables into (7.29), we can get predictions either less than zero or greater than one. Since these are predicted probabilities, and probabilities must be between zero and one, this can be a little embarrassing. For example, what would it mean to predict that a woman is in the labor force with a probability of −.10? In fact, of the 753 women in the sample, 16 of the fitted values from (7.29) are less than zero, and 17 of the fitted values are greater than one.

A related problem is that a probability cannot be linearly related to the independent variables for all their possible values. For example, (7.29) predicts that the effect of going from zero children to one young child reduces the probability of working by .262. This is also the predicted drop if the woman goes from having one young child to two. It seems more realistic that the first small child would reduce the probability by a large amount, but subsequent children would have a smaller marginal effect. In fact, when taken to the extreme, (7.29) implies that going from zero to four young children reduces the probability of working by $\Delta \widehat{inlf} = .262(\Delta kidslt6) = .262(4) = 1.048$, which is impossible.

Even with these problems, the linear probability model is useful and often applied in economics. It usually works well for values of the independent variables that are near the averages in the sample. In the labor force participation example, no women in the sample have four young children; in fact, only three women have three young children. Over 96% of the women have either no young children or one small child, and so we should probably restrict attention to this case when interpreting the estimated equation.

Predicted probabilities outside the unit interval are a little troubling when we want to make predictions. Still, there are ways to use the estimated probabilities (even if some are negative or greater than one) to predict a zero-one outcome. As before, let $\hat{y}_i$ denote the fitted values—which may not be bounded between zero and one. Define a predicted value as $\tilde{y}_i = 1$ if $\hat{y}_i \geq .5$ and $\tilde{y}_i = 0$ if $\hat{y}_i < .5$. Now we have a set of predicted values, $\tilde{y}_i, i = 1, ..., n$, that, like the y_i, are either zero or one. We can use the data on y_i and $\tilde{y}_i$ to obtain the frequencies with which we correctly predict $y_i = 1$ and $y_i = 0$, as well as the proportion of overall correct predictions. The latter measure, when turned into a percentage, is a widely used goodness-of-fit measure for binary dependent variables: the **percent correctly predicted**. An example is given in Computer Exercise C9(v), and further discussion, in the context of more advanced models, can be found in Section 17-1.

Due to the binary nature of y, the linear probability model does violate one of the Gauss-Markov assumptions. When y is a binary variable, its variance, conditional on $\mathbf{x}$, is

$$\text{Var}(y|\mathbf{x}) = p(\mathbf{x})[1 - p(\mathbf{x})], \qquad [7.30]$$

where $p(\mathbf{x})$ is shorthand for the probability of success: $p(\mathbf{x}) = \beta_0 + \beta_1 x_1 + ... + \beta_k x_k$. This means that, except in the case where the probability does not depend on any of the independent variables, there *must* be heteroskedasticity in a linear probability model. We know from Chapter 3 that this does not cause bias in the OLS estimators of the β_j. But we also know from Chapters 4 and 5 that homoskedasticity is crucial for justifying the usual t and F statistics, even in large samples. Because the standard errors in (7.29) are not generally valid, we should use them with caution. We will show how to correct the standard errors for heteroskedasticity in Chapter 8. It turns out that, in many applications, the usual OLS statistics are not far off, and it is still acceptable in applied work to present a standard OLS analysis of a linear probability model.

EXAMPLE 7.12   A Linear Probability Model of Arrests

Let *arr86* be a binary variable equal to unity if a man was arrested during 1986, and zero otherwise. The population is a group of young men in California born in 1960 or 1961 who have at least one arrest prior to 1986. A linear probability model for describing *arr86* is

$$arr86 = \beta_0 + \beta_1 pcnv + \beta_2 avgsen + \beta_3 tottime + \beta_4 ptime86 + \beta_5 qemp86 + u,$$

where

    pcnv = the proportion of prior arrests that led to a conviction.

avgsen = the average sentence served from prior convictions (in months).

tottime = months spent in prison since age 18 prior to 1986.

ptime86 = months spent in prison in 1986.

qemp86 = the number of quarters (0 to 4) that the man was legally employed in 1986.

The data we use are in CRIME1, the same data set used for Example 3.5. Here, we use a binary dependent variable because only 7.2% of the men in the sample were arrested more than once. About 27.7% of the men were arrested at least once during 1986. The estimated equation is

$$\widehat{arr86} = .441 - .162\,pcnv + .0061\,avgsen - .0023\,tottime$$
$$\phantom{\widehat{arr86} = } (.017)\ (.021) \qquad (.0065) \qquad\quad (.0050)$$
$$\phantom{\widehat{arr86} = } - .022\,ptime86 - .043\,qemp86 \qquad\qquad\qquad\qquad [7.31]$$
$$\phantom{\widehat{arr86} = } (.005) \qquad\quad (.005)$$
$$n = 2{,}725,\ R^2 = .0474.$$

The intercept, .441, is the predicted probability of arrest for someone who has not been convicted (and so *pcnv* and *avgsen* are both zero), has spent no time in prison since age 18, spent no time in prison in 1986, and was unemployed during the entire year. The variables *avgsen* and *tottime* are insignificant both individually and jointly (the *F* test gives *p-value* = .347), and *avgsen* has a counterintuitive sign if longer sentences are supposed to deter crime. Grogger (1991), using a superset of these data and different econometric methods, found that *tottime* has a statistically significant *positive* effect on arrests and concluded that *tottime* is a measure of human capital built up in criminal activity.

Increasing the probability of conviction does lower the probability of arrest, but we must be careful when interpreting the magnitude of the coefficient. The variable *pcnv* is a proportion between zero and one; thus, changing *pcnv* from zero to one essentially means a change from no chance of being convicted to being convicted with certainty. Even this large change reduces the probability of arrest only by .162; increasing *pcnv* by .5 decreases the probability of arrest by .081.

The incarcerative effect is given by the coefficient on *ptime86*. If a man is in prison, he cannot be arrested. Since *ptime86* is measured in months, six more months in prison reduces the probability of arrest by .022(6) = .132. Equation (7.31) gives another example of where the linear probability model cannot be true over all ranges of the independent variables. If a man is in prison all 12 months of 1986, he cannot be arrested in 1986. Setting all other variables equal to zero, the predicted probability of arrest when *ptime86* = 12 is .441 − .022(12) = .177, which is not zero. Nevertheless, if we start from the unconditional probability of arrest, .277, 12 months in prison reduces the probability to essentially zero: .277 − .022(12) = .013.

Finally, employment reduces the probability of arrest in a significant way. All other factors fixed, a man employed in all four quarters is .172 less likely to be arrested than a man who is not employed at all.

We can also include dummy independent variables in models with dummy dependent variables. The coefficient measures the predicted difference in probability relative to the base group. For example, if we add two race dummies, *black* and *hispan*, to the arrest equation, we obtain

$$\widehat{arr86} = .380 - .152\,pcnv + .0046\,avgsen - .0026\,tottime$$
$$\phantom{\widehat{arr86} = } (.019)\ (.021) \qquad (.0064) \qquad\quad (.0049)$$
$$\phantom{\widehat{arr86} = } - .024\,ptime86 - .038\,qemp86 + .170\,black + .096\,hispan \qquad [7.32]$$
$$\phantom{\widehat{arr86} = } (.005) \qquad\quad (.005) \qquad\quad (.024) \qquad\quad (.021)$$
$$n = 2{,}725,\ R^2 = .0682.$$

EXPLORING FURTHER 7.5

What is the predicted probability of arrest for a black man with no prior convictions—so that *pcnv, avgsen, tottime,* and *ptime86* are all zero—who was employed all four quarters in 1986? Does this seem reasonable?

The coefficient on *black* means that, all other factors being equal, a black man has a .17 higher chance of being arrested than a white man (the base group). Another way to say this is that the probability of arrest is 17 percentage points higher for blacks than for whites. The difference is statistically significant as well. Similarly, Hispanic men have a .096 higher chance of being arrested than white men.

7-6 More on Policy Analysis and Program Evaluation

We have seen some examples of models containing dummy variables that can be useful for evaluating policy. Example 7.3 gave an example of program evaluation, where some firms received job training grants and others did not.

As we mentioned earlier, we must be careful when evaluating programs because in most examples in the social sciences the control and treatment groups are not randomly assigned. Consider again the Holzer et al. (1993) study, where we are now interested in the effect of the job training grants on worker productivity (as opposed to amount of job training). The equation of interest is

$$\log(scrap) = \beta_0 + \beta_1 grant + \beta_2 \log(sales) + \beta_3 \log(employ) + u,$$

where *scrap* is the firm's scrap rate, and the latter two variables are included as controls. The binary variable *grant* indicates whether the firm received a grant in 1988 for job training.

Before we look at the estimates, we might be worried that the unobserved factors affecting worker productivity—such as average levels of education, ability, experience, and tenure—might be correlated with whether the firm receives a grant. Holzer et al. point out that grants were given on a first-come, first-served basis. But this is not the same as giving out grants randomly. It might be that firms with less productive workers saw an opportunity to improve productivity and therefore were more diligent in applying for the grants.

Using the data in JTRAIN for 1988—when firms actually were eligible to receive the grants—we obtain

$$\widehat{\log(scrap)} = 4.99 - .052\, grant - .455 \log(sales)$$
$$(4.66)\quad (.431)\qquad (.373)$$
$$+ .639 \log(employ) \qquad\qquad [7.33]$$
$$(.365)$$
$$n = 50, R^2 = .072.$$

(Seventeen out of the 50 firms received a training grant, and the average scrap rate is 3.47 across all firms.) The point estimate of −.052 on *grant* means that, for given *sales* and *employ*, firms receiving a grant have scrap rates about 5.2% lower than firms without grants. This is the direction of the expected effect if the training grants are effective, but the *t* statistic is very small. Thus, from this cross-sectional analysis, we must conclude that the grants had no effect on firm productivity. We will return to this example in Chapter 9 and show how adding information from a prior year leads to a much different conclusion.

Even in cases where the policy analysis does not involve assigning units to a control group and a treatment group, we must be careful to include factors that might be systematically related to the binary independent variable of interest. A good example of this is testing for racial discrimination. Race is something that is not determined by an individual or by government administrators. In fact, race would appear to be the perfect example of an exogenous explanatory variable, given that it is determined at birth. However, for historical reasons, race is often related to other relevant factors: there are systematic differences in backgrounds across race, and these differences can be important in testing for *current* discrimination.

As an example, consider testing for discrimination in loan approvals. If we can collect data on, say, individual mortgage applications, then we can define the dummy dependent variable *approved* as equal to one if a mortgage application was approved, and zero otherwise. A systematic difference in approval rates across races is an indication of discrimination. However, since approval depends on many other factors, including income, wealth, credit ratings, and a general ability to pay back the loan, we must control for them *if* there are systematic differences in these factors across race. A linear probability model to test for discrimination might look like the following:

$$approved = \beta_0 + \beta_1 nonwhite + \beta_2 income + \beta_3 wealth + \beta_4 credrate + other\ factors.$$

Discrimination against minorities is indicated by a rejection of $H_0: \beta_1 = 0$ in favor of $H_0: \beta_1 < 0$, because β_1 is the amount by which the probability of a nonwhite getting an approval differs from the probability of a white getting an approval, given the same levels of other variables in the equation. If *income*, *wealth*, and so on are systematically different across races, then it is important to control for these factors in a multiple regression analysis.

Another problem that often arises in policy and program evaluation is that individuals (or firms or cities) choose whether or not to participate in certain behaviors or programs. For example, individuals choose to use illegal drugs or drink alcohol. If we want to examine the effects of such behaviors on unemployment status, earnings, or criminal behavior, we should be concerned that drug usage might be correlated with other factors that can affect employment and criminal outcomes. Children eligible for programs such as Head Start participate based on parental decisions. Since family background plays a role in Head Start decisions and affects student outcomes, we should control for these factors when examining the effects of Head Start [see, for example, Currie and Thomas (1995)]. Individuals selected by employers or government agencies to participate in job training programs can participate or not, and this decision is unlikely to be random [see, for example, Lynch (1992)]. Cities and states choose whether to implement certain gun control laws, and it is likely that this decision is systematically related to other factors that affect violent crime [see, for example, Kleck and Patterson (1993)].

The previous paragraph gives examples of what are generally known as **self-selection** problems in economics. Literally, the term comes from the fact that individuals self-select into certain behaviors or programs: participation is not randomly determined. The term is used generally when a binary indicator of participation might be systematically related to unobserved factors. Thus, if we write the simple model

$$y = \beta_0 + \beta_1 partic + u, \qquad [7.34]$$

where *y* is an outcome variable and *partic* is a binary variable equal to unity if the individual, firm, or city participates in a behavior or a program or has a certain kind of law, then we are worried that the average value of *u* depends on participation: $E(u|partic = 1) \neq E(u|partic = 0)$. As we know, this causes the simple regression estimator of β_1 to be biased, and so we will not uncover the true effect of participation. Thus, the self-selection problem is another way that an explanatory variable (*partic* in this case) can be endogenous.

By now, we know that multiple regression analysis can, to some degree, alleviate the self-selection problem. Factors in the error term in (7.34) that are correlated with *partic* can be included in a multiple regression equation, assuming, of course, that we can collect data on these factors. Unfortunately, in many cases, we are worried that unobserved factors are related to participation, in which case multiple regression produces biased estimators.

With standard multiple regression analysis using cross-sectional data, we must be aware of finding spurious effects of programs on outcome variables due to the self-selection problem. A good example of this is contained in Currie and Cole (1993). These authors examine the effect of AFDC (Aid to Families with Dependent Children) participation on the birth weight of a child. Even after controlling for a variety of family and background characteristics, the authors obtain OLS estimates that imply participation in AFDC *lowers* birth weight. As the authors point out, it is hard to believe that AFDC participation itself *causes* lower birth weight. [See Currie (1995) for additional examples.] Using a different econometric method that we will discuss in Chapter 15, Currie and Cole find evidence for either no effect or a *positive* effect of AFDC participation on birth weight.

When the self-selection problem causes standard multiple regression analysis to be biased due to a lack of sufficient control variables, the more advanced methods covered in Chapters 13, 14, and 15, can be used instead.

7-7 Interpreting Regression Results with Discrete Dependent Variables

A binary response is the most extreme form of a discrete random variable: it takes on only two values, zero and one. As we discussed in Section 7-5, the parameters in a linear probability model can be interpreted as measuring the change in the *probability* that $y = 1$ due to a one-unit increase in an explanatory variable. We also discussed that, because y is a zero-one outcome, $P(y = 1) = E(y)$, and this equality continues to hold when we condition on explanatory variables.

Other discrete dependent variables arise in practice, and we have already seen some examples, such as the number of times someone is arrested in a given year (Example 3.5). Studies on factors affecting fertility often use the number of living children as the dependent variable in a regression analysis. As with number of arrests, the number of living children takes on a small set of integer values, and zero is a common value. The data in FERTIL2, which contains information on a large sample of women in Botswana is one such example. Often demographers are interested in the effects of education on fertility, with special attention to trying to determine whether education has a causal effect on fertility. Such examples raise a question about how one interprets regression coefficients: after all, one cannot have a fraction of a child.

To illustrate the issues, the regression below uses the data in FERTIL2:

$$\widehat{children} = -1.997 + .175\,age - .090\,educ$$
$$\phantom{\widehat{children} = } (.094)\ (.003)\quad\ (.006) \qquad\qquad [7.35]$$
$$n = 4,361, R^2 = .560.$$

At this time, we ignore the issue of whether this regression adequately controls for all factors that affect fertility. Instead we focus on interpreting the regression coefficients.

Consider the main coefficient of interest, $\hat{\beta}_{educ} = -.090$. If we take this estimate literally, it says that each additional year of education reduces the estimated number of children by .090—something obviously impossible for any particular woman. A similar problem arises when trying to interpret $\hat{\beta}_{age} = .175$. How can we make sense of these coefficients?

To interpret regression results generally, even in cases where y is discrete and takes on a small number of values, it is useful to remember the interpretation of OLS as estimating the effects of the x_j on the *expected* (or *average*) value of y. Generally, under Assumptions MLR.1 and MLR.4,

$$E(y|x_1, x_2, \ldots, x_k) = \beta_0 + \beta_1 x_1 + \ldots + \beta_k x_k. \qquad\qquad [7.36]$$

Therefore, β_j is the effect of a ceteris paribus increase of x_j on the expected value of y. As we discussed in Section 6-4, for a given set of x_j values we interpret the predicted value, $\hat{\beta}_0 + \hat{\beta}_1 x_1 + \ldots + \hat{\beta}_k x_k$, as an estimate of $E(y|x_1, x_2, \ldots, x_k)$. Therefore, $\hat{\beta}_j$ is our estimate of how the *average* of y changes when $\Delta x_j = 1$ (keeping other factors fixed).

Seen in this light, we can now provide meaning to regression results as in equation (7.35). The coefficient $\hat{\beta}_{educ} = -.090$ means that we estimate that *average* fertility falls by .09 children given one more year of education. A nice way to summarize this interpretation is that if each woman in a group of 100 obtains another year of education, we estimate there will be nine fewer children among them.

Adding dummy variables to regressions when y is itself discrete causes no problems when we interpret the estimated effect in terms of average values. Using the data in FERTIL2 we get

$$\widehat{children} = -2.071 + .177\,age - .079\,educ - .362\,electric \qquad [7.37]$$
$$(.095)\ (.003) \qquad (.006) \qquad (.068)$$
$$n = 4{,}358,\ R^2 = .562,$$

where *electric* is a dummy variable equal to one if the woman lives in a home with electricity. Of course it cannot be true that a particular woman who has electricity has .362 less children than an otherwise comparable woman who does not. But we can say that when comparing 100 women with electricity to 100 women without—at the same age and level of education—we estimate the former group to have about 36 fewer children.

Incidentally, when y is discrete the linear model does not always provide the best estimates of partial effects on $E(y|x_1, x_2, \ldots, x_k)$. Chapter 17 contains more advanced models and estimation methods that tend to fit the data better when the range of y is limited in some substantive way. Nevertheless, a linear model estimated by OLS often provides a good approximation to the true partial effects, at least on average.

Summary

In this chapter, we have learned how to use qualitative information in regression analysis. In the simplest case, a dummy variable is defined to distinguish between two groups, and the coefficient estimate on the dummy variable estimates the ceteris paribus difference between the two groups. Allowing for more than two groups is accomplished by defining a set of dummy variables: if there are g groups, then $g - 1$ dummy variables are included in the model. All estimates on the dummy variables are interpreted relative to the base or benchmark group (the group for which no dummy variable is included in the model).

Dummy variables are also useful for incorporating ordinal information, such as a credit or a beauty rating, in regression models. We simply define a set of dummy variables representing different outcomes of the ordinal variable, allowing one of the categories to be the base group.

Dummy variables can be interacted with quantitative variables to allow slope differences across different groups. In the extreme case, we can allow each group to have its own slope on every variable, as well as its own intercept. The Chow test can be used to detect whether there are any differences across groups. In many cases, it is more interesting to test whether, after allowing for an intercept difference, the slopes for two different groups are the same. A standard F test can be used for this purpose in an unrestricted model that includes interactions between the group dummy and all variables.

The linear probability model, which is simply estimated by OLS, allows us to explain a binary response using regression analysis. The OLS estimates are now interpreted as changes in the probability of "success" $(y = 1)$, given a one-unit increase in the corresponding explanatory variable. The LPM does have some drawbacks: it can produce predicted probabilities that are less than zero or greater than one, it implies a constant marginal effect of each explanatory variable that appears in its original form, and it contains heteroskedasticity. The first two problems are often not serious when we are obtaining estimates of the partial effects of the explanatory variables for the middle ranges of the data. Heteroskedasticity does invalidate the usual OLS standard errors and test statistics, but, as we will see in the next chapter, this is easily fixed in large enough samples.

Section 7.6 provides a discussion of how binary variables are used to evaluate policies and programs. As in all regression analysis, we must remember that program participation, or some other binary regressor with policy implications, might be correlated with unobserved factors that affect the dependent variable, resulting in the usual omitted variables bias.

We ended this chapter with a general discussion of how to interpret regression equations when the dependent variable is discrete. The key is to remember that the coefficients can be interpreted as the effects on the expected value of the dependent variable.

Key Terms

Base Group	Dummy Variables	Policy Analysis
Benchmark Group	Experimental Group	Program Evaluation
Binary Variable	Interaction Term	Response Probability
Chow Statistic	Intercept Shift	Self-Selection
Control Group	Linear Probability Model (LPM)	Treatment Group
Difference in Slopes	Ordinal Variable	Uncentered R-Squared
Dummy Variable Trap	Percent Correctly Predicted	Zero-One Variable

Problems

1 Using the data in SLEEP75 (see also Problem 3 in Chapter 3), we obtain the estimated equation

$$\widehat{sleep} = 3{,}840.83 - .163\ totwrk - 11.71\ educ - 8.70\ age$$
$$(235.11)\ (.018)\qquad (5.86)\qquad (11.21)$$
$$+ .128\ age^2 + 87.75\ male$$
$$(.134)\qquad (34.33)$$
$$n = 706,\ R^2 = .123,\ \bar{R}^2 = .117.$$

The variable *sleep* is total minutes per week spent sleeping at night, *totwrk* is total weekly minutes spent working, *educ* and *age* are measured in years, and *male* is a gender dummy.
  (i)   All other factors being equal, is there evidence that men sleep more than women? How strong is the evidence?
  (ii)   Is there a statistically significant tradeoff between working and sleeping? What is the estimated tradeoff?
  (iii)   What other regression do you need to run to test the null hypothesis that, holding other factors fixed, age has no effect on sleeping?

2 The following equations were estimated using the data in BWGHT:

$$\widehat{\log(bwght)} = 4.66 - .0044\ cigs + .0093\ \log(faminc) + .016\ parity$$
$$(.22)\ (.0009)\qquad (.0059)\qquad\qquad (.006)$$
$$+ .027\ male + .055\ white$$
$$(.010)\qquad (.013)$$
$$n = 1{,}388,\ R^2 = .0472$$

and

$$\widehat{\log(bwght)} = 4.65 - .0052\,cigs + .0110\,\log(faminc) + .017\,parity$$
$$\phantom{\widehat{\log(bwght)} =} (.38)\ \ (.0010) \qquad (.0085) \qquad\qquad (.006)$$
$$\phantom{\widehat{\log(bwght)} =} + .034\,male + .045\,white - .0030\,motheduc + .0032\,fatheduc$$
$$\phantom{\widehat{\log(bwght)} =} (.011) \qquad (.015) \qquad (.0030) \qquad\qquad (.0026)$$
$$n = 1{,}191,\ R^2 = .0493.$$

The variables are defined as in Example 4.9, but we have added a dummy variable for whether the child is male and a dummy variable indicating whether the child is classified as white.

(i)   In the first equation, interpret the coefficient on the variable *cigs*. In particular, what is the effect on birth weight from smoking 10 more cigarettes per day?

(ii) How much more is a white child predicted to weigh than a nonwhite child, holding the other factors in the first equation fixed? Is the difference statistically significant?

(iii) Comment on the estimated effect and statistical significance of *motheduc*.

(iv) From the given information, why are you unable to compute the F statistic for joint significance of *motheduc* and *fatheduc*? What would you have to do to compute the F statistic?

3 Using the data in GPA2, the following equation was estimated:

$$\widehat{sat} = 1{,}028.10 + 19.30\,hsize - 2.19\,hsize^2 - 45.09\,female$$
$$\phantom{\widehat{sat} =} (6.29)\ \ (3.83) \qquad (.53) \qquad (4.29)$$
$$\phantom{\widehat{sat} =} - 169.81\,black + 62.31\,female{\cdot}black$$
$$\phantom{\widehat{sat} =} (12.71) \qquad (18.15)$$
$$n = 4{,}137,\ R^2 = .0858.$$

The variable *sat* is the combined SAT score; *hsize* is size of the student's high school graduating class, in hundreds; *female* is a gender dummy variable; and *black* is a race dummy variable equal to one for blacks, and zero otherwise.

(i)   Is there strong evidence that $hsize^2$ should be included in the model? From this equation, what is the optimal high school size?

(ii) Holding *hsize* fixed, what is the estimated difference in SAT score between nonblack females and nonblack males? How statistically significant is this estimated difference?

(iii) What is the estimated difference in SAT score between nonblack males and black males? Test the null hypothesis that there is no difference between their scores, against the alternative that there is a difference.

(iv) What is the estimated difference in SAT score between black females and nonblack females? What would you need to do to test whether the difference is statistically significant?

4 An equation explaining chief executive officer salary is

$$\widehat{\log(salary)} = 4.59 + .257\,\log(sales) + .011\,roe + .158\,finance$$
$$\phantom{\widehat{\log(salary)} =} (.30)\ \ (.032) \qquad\qquad (.004) \qquad (.089)$$
$$\phantom{\widehat{\log(salary)} =} + .181\,consprod - .283\,utility$$
$$\phantom{\widehat{\log(salary)} =} (.085) \qquad\qquad (.099)$$
$$n = 209,\ R^2 = .357.$$

The data used are in CEOSAL1, where *finance*, *consprod*, and *utility* are binary variables indicating the financial, consumer products, and utilities industries. The omitted industry is transportation.

(i) Compute the approximate percentage difference in estimated salary between the utility and transportation industries, holding *sales* and *roe* fixed. Is the difference statistically significant at the 1% level?

(ii) Use equation (7.10) to obtain the exact percentage difference in estimated salary between the utility and transportation industries and compare this with the answer obtained in part (i).

(iii) What is the approximate percentage difference in estimated salary between the consumer products and finance industries? Write an equation that would allow you to test whether the difference is statistically significant.

5 In Example 7.2, let *noPC* be a dummy variable equal to one if the student does not own a PC, and zero otherwise.

(i) If *noPC* is used in place of *PC* in equation (7.6), what happens to the intercept in the estimated equation? What will be the coefficient on *noPC*? (*Hint:* Write $PC = 1 - noPC$ and plug this into the equation $\widehat{colGPA} = \hat{\beta}_0 + \hat{\delta}_0 PC + \hat{\beta}_1 hsGPA + \hat{\beta}_2 ACT$.)

(ii) What will happen to the *R*-squared if *noPC* is used in place of *PC*?

(iii) Should *PC* and *noPC* both be included as independent variables in the model? Explain.

6 To test the effectiveness of a job training program on the subsequent wages of workers, we specify the model

$$\log(wage) = \beta_0 + \beta_1 train + \beta_2 educ + \beta_3 exper + u,$$

where *train* is a binary variable equal to unity if a worker participated in the program. Think of the error term *u* as containing unobserved worker ability. If less able workers have a greater chance of being selected for the program, and you use an OLS analysis, what can you say about the likely bias in the OLS estimator of β_1? (*Hint:* Refer back to Chapter 3.)

7 In the example in equation (7.29), suppose that we define *outlf* to be one if the woman is out of the labor force, and zero otherwise.

(i) If we regress *outlf* on all of the independent variables in equation (7.29), what will happen to the intercept and slope estimates? (*Hint: inlf* $= 1 - outlf$. Plug this into the population equation $inlf = \beta_0 + \beta_1 nwifeinc + \beta_2 educ + \dots$ and rearrange.)

(ii) What will happen to the standard errors on the intercept and slope estimates?

(iii) What will happen to the *R*-squared?

8 Suppose you collect data from a survey on wages, education, experience, and gender. In addition, you ask for information about marijuana usage. The original question is: "On how many separate occasions last month did you smoke marijuana?"

(i) Write an equation that would allow you to estimate the effects of marijuana usage on wage, while controlling for other factors. You should be able to make statements such as, "Smoking marijuana five more times per month is estimated to change wage by *x*%."

(ii) Write a model that would allow you to test whether drug usage has different effects on wages for men and women. How would you test that there are no differences in the effects of drug usage for men and women?

(iii) Suppose you think it is better to measure marijuana usage by putting people into one of four categories: nonuser, light user (1 to 5 times per month), moderate user (6 to 10 times per month), and heavy user (more than 10 times per month). Now, write a model that allows you to estimate the effects of marijuana usage on wage.

(iv) Using the model in part (iii), explain in detail how to test the null hypothesis that marijuana usage has no effect on wage. Be very specific and include a careful listing of degrees of freedom.

(v) What are some potential problems with drawing causal inference using the survey data that you collected?

9 Let d be a dummy (binary) variable and let z be a quantitative variable. Consider the model

$$y = \beta_0 + \delta_0 d + \beta_1 z + \delta_1 d \cdot z + u;$$

this is a general version of a model with an interaction between a dummy variable and a quantitative variable. [An example is in equation (7.17).]

(i)   Since it changes nothing important, set the error to zero, $u = 0$. Then, when $d = 0$ we can write the relationship between y and z as the function $f_0(z) = \beta_0 + \beta_1 z$. Write the same relationship when $d = 1$, where you should use $f_1(z)$ on the left-hand side to denote the linear function of z.

(ii)   Assuming that $\delta_1 \neq 0$ (which means the two lines are not parallel), show that the value of z^* such that $f_0(z^*) = f_1(z^*)$ is $z^* = -\delta_0/\delta_1$. This is the point at which the two lines intersect [as in Figure 7.2 (b)]. Argue that z^* is positive if and only if δ_0 and δ_1 have opposite signs.

(iii)   Using the data in TWOYEAR, the following equation can be estimated:

$$\widehat{\log(wage)} = 2.289 - .357\, female + .50\, totcoll + .030\, female \cdot totcoll$$
$$(0.011)\ (.015)\qquad\quad (.003)\qquad\quad (.005)$$
$$n = 6{,}763,\ R^2 = .202,$$

where all coefficients and standard errors have been rounded to three decimal places. Using this equation, find the value of *totcoll* such that the predicted values of log(*wage*) are the same for men and women.

(iv)   Based on the equation in part (iii), can women realistically get enough years of college so that their earnings catch up to those of men? Explain.

10 For a child i living in a particular school district, let $voucher_i$ be a dummy variable equal to one if a child is selected to participate in a school voucher program, and let $score_i$ be that child's score on a subsequent standardized exam. Suppose that the participation variable, $voucher_i$, is completely randomized in the sense that it is independent of both observed and unobserved factors that can affect the test score.

(i)   If you run a simple regression $score_i$ on $voucher_i$ using a random sample of size n, does the OLS estimator provide an unbiased estimator of the effect of the voucher program?

(ii)   Suppose you can collect additional background information, such as family income, family structure (e.g., whether the child lives with both parents), and parents' education levels. Do you need to control for these factors to obtain an unbiased estimator of the effects of the voucher program? Explain.

(iii)   Why should you include the family background variables in the regression? Is there a situation in which you would not include the background variables?

11 The following equations were estimated using the data in ECONMATH, with standard errors reported under coefficients. The average class score, measured as a percentage, is about 72.2; exactly 50% of the students are male; and the average of *colgpa* (grade point average at the start of the term) is about 2.81.

$$\widehat{score} = 32.31 + 14.32\, colgpa$$
$$(2.00)\quad (0.70)$$
$$n = 856,\ R^2 = .329,\ \bar{R}^2 = .328.$$

$$\widehat{score} = 29.66 + 3.83\, male + 14.57\, colgpa$$
$$(2.04)\quad (0.74)\qquad\quad (0.69)$$
$$n = 856,\ R^2 = .349,\ \bar{R}^2 = .348.$$

$$\widehat{score} = 30.36 + 2.47 \, male + 14.33 \, colgpa + 0.479 \, male \cdot colgpa$$
$$\quad (2.86) \ (3.96) \quad\quad (0.98) \quad\quad (1.383)$$
$$n = 856, R^2 = .349, \overline{R}^2 = .347.$$

$$\widehat{score} = 30.36 + 3.82 \, male + 14.33 \, colgpa + 0.479 \, male \cdot (colgpa - 2.81)$$
$$\quad (2.86) \ (0.74) \quad\quad (0.98) \quad\quad (1.383)$$
$$n = 856, R^2 = .349, \overline{R}^2 = .347.$$

(i) Interpret the coefficient on *male* in the second equation and construct a 95% confidence interval for β_{male}. Does the confidence interval exclude zero?

(ii) In the second equation, how come the estimate on *male* is so imprecise? Should we now conclude that there are no gender differences in *score* after controlling for *colgpa*? [*Hint:* You might want to compute an F statistic for the null hypothesis that there is no gender difference in the model with the interaction.]

(iii) Compared with the third equation, how come the coefficient on *male* in the last equation is so much closer to that in the second equation and just as precisely estimated?

Computer Exercises

C1 Use the data in GPA1 for this exercise.

(i) Add the variables *mothcoll* and *fathcoll* to the equation estimated in (7.6) and report the results in the usual form. What happens to the estimated effect of PC ownership? Is *PC* still statistically significant?

(ii) Test for joint significance of *mothcoll* and *fathcoll* in the equation from part (i) and be sure to report the *p*-value.

(iii) Add $hsGPA^2$ to the model from part (i) and decide whether this generalization is needed.

C2 Use the data in WAGE2 for this exercise.

(i) Estimate the model

$$\log(wage) = \beta_0 + \beta_1 educ + \beta_2 exper + \beta_3 tenure + \beta_4 married$$
$$+ \beta_5 black + \beta_6 south + \beta_7 urban + u$$

and report the results in the usual form. Holding other factors fixed, what is the approximate difference in monthly salary between blacks and nonblacks? Is this difference statistically significant?

(ii) Add the variables $exper^2$ and $tenure^2$ to the equation and show that they are jointly insignificant at even the 20% level.

(iii) Extend the original model to allow the return to education to depend on race and test whether the return to education does depend on race.

(iv) Again, start with the original model, but now allow wages to differ across four groups of people: married and black, married and nonblack, single and black, and single and nonblack. What is the estimated wage differential between married blacks and married nonblacks?

C3 A model that allows major league baseball player salary to differ by position is

$$\log(salary) = \beta_0 + \beta_1 years + \beta_2 gamesyr + \beta_3 bavg + \beta_4 hrunsyr$$
$$+ \beta_5 rbisyr + \beta_6 runsyr + \beta_7 fldperc + \beta_8 allstar$$
$$+ \beta_9 frstbase + \beta_{10} scndbase + \beta_{11} thrdbase + \beta_{12} shrtstop$$
$$+ \beta_{13} catcher + u,$$

where outfield is the base group.

(i)   State the null hypothesis that, controlling for other factors, catchers and outfielders earn, on average, the same amount. Test this hypothesis using the data in MLB1 and comment on the size of the estimated salary differential.

(ii) State and test the null hypothesis that there is no difference in average salary across positions, once other factors have been controlled for.

(iii) Are the results from parts (i) and (ii) consistent? If not, explain what is happening.

C4 Use the data in GPA2 for this exercise.

(i)   Consider the equation

$$colgpa = \beta_0 + \beta_1 hsize + \beta_2 hsize^2 + \beta_3 hsperc + \beta_4 sat$$
$$+ \beta_5 female + \beta_6 athlete + u,$$

where *colgpa* is cumulative college grade point average; *hsize* is size of high school graduating class, in hundreds; *hsperc* is academic percentile in graduating class; *sat* is combined SAT score; *female* is a binary gender variable; and *athlete* is a binary variable, which is one for student-athletes. What are your expectations for the coefficients in this equation? Which ones are you unsure about?

(ii) Estimate the equation in part (i) and report the results in the usual form. What is the estimated GPA differential between athletes and nonathletes? Is it statistically significant?

(iii) Drop *sat* from the model and reestimate the equation. Now, what is the estimated effect of being an athlete? Discuss why the estimate is different than that obtained in part (ii).

(iv) In the model from part (i), allow the effect of being an athlete to differ by gender and test the null hypothesis that there is no ceteris paribus difference between women athletes and women nonathletes.

(v)   Does the effect of *sat* on *colgpa* differ by gender? Justify your answer.

C5 In Problem 2 in Chapter 4, we added the return on the firm's stock, *ros*, to a model explaining CEO salary; *ros* turned out to be insignificant. Now, define a dummy variable, *rosneg*, which is equal to one if *ros* < 0 and equal to zero if *ros* ≥ 0. Use CEOSAL1 to estimate the model

$$\log(salary) = \beta_0 + \beta_1 \log(sales) + \beta_2 roe + \beta_3 rosneg + u.$$

Discuss the interpretation and statistical significance of $\hat{\beta}_3$.

C6 Use the data in SLEEP75 for this exercise. The equation of interest is

$$sleep = \beta_0 + \beta_1 totwrk + \beta_2 educ + \beta_3 age + \beta_4 age^2 + \beta_5 yngkid + u.$$

(i)   Estimate this equation separately for men and women and report the results in the usual form. Are there notable differences in the two estimated equations?

(ii) Compute the Chow test for equality of the parameters in the sleep equation for men and women. Use the form of the test that adds *male* and the interaction terms *male·totwrk*, …, *male·yngkid* and uses the full set of observations. What are the relevant *df* for the test? Should you reject the null at the 5% level?

(iii) Now, allow for a different intercept for males and females and determine whether the interaction terms involving *male* are jointly significant.

(iv) Given the results from parts (ii) and (iii), what would be your final model?

C7 Use the data in WAGE1 for this exercise.

(i)   Use equation (7.18) to estimate the gender differential when *educ* = 12.5. Compare this with the estimated differential when *educ* = 0.

(ii) Run the regression used to obtain (7.18), but with *female·*(*educ* − 12.5) replacing *female·educ*. How do you interpret the coefficient on *female* now?

(iii) Is the coefficient on *female* in part (ii) statistically significant? Compare this with (7.18) and comment.

C8 Use the data in LOANAPP for this exercise. The binary variable to be explained is *approve*, which is equal to one if a mortgage loan to an individual was approved. The key explanatory variable is *white*, a dummy variable equal to one if the applicant was white. The other applicants in the data set are black and Hispanic.

To test for discrimination in the mortgage loan market, a linear probability model can be used:

$$approve = \beta_0 + \beta_1 white + other\ factors.$$

(i) If there is discrimination against minorities, and the appropriate factors have been controlled for, what is the sign of β_1?

(ii) Regress *approve* on *white* and report the results in the usual form. Interpret the coefficient on *white*. Is it statistically significant? Is it practically large?

(iii) As controls, add the variables *hrat*, *obrat*, *loanprc*, *unem*, *male*, *married*, *dep*, *sch*, *cosign*, *chist*, *pubrec*, *mortlat1*, *mortlat2*, and *vr*. What happens to the coefficient on *white*? Is there still evidence of discrimination against nonwhites?

(iv) Now, allow the effect of race to interact with the variable measuring other obligations as a percentage of income (*obrat*). Is the interaction term significant?

(v) Using the model from part (iv), what is the effect of being white on the probability of approval when *obrat* = 32, which is roughly the mean value in the sample? Obtain a 95% confidence interval for this effect.

C9 There has been much interest in whether the presence of 401(k) pension plans, available to many U.S. workers, increases net savings. The data set 401KSUBS contains information on net financial assets (*nettfa*), family income (*inc*), a binary variable for eligibility in a 401(k) plan (*e401k*), and several other variables.

(i) What fraction of the families in the sample are eligible for participation in a 401(k) plan?

(ii) Estimate a linear probability model explaining 401(k) eligibility in terms of income, age, and gender. Include income and age in quadratic form, and report the results in the usual form.

(iii) Would you say that 401(k) eligibility is independent of income and age? What about gender? Explain.

(iv) Obtain the fitted values from the linear probability model estimated in part (ii). Are any fitted values negative or greater than one?

(v) Using the fitted values $\widehat{e401k}_i$ from part (iv), define $\widetilde{e401k}_i = 1$ if $\widehat{e401k}_i \geq .5$ and $\widetilde{e401k}_i = 0$ if $\widehat{e401k}_i < .5$. Out of 9,275 families, how many are predicted to be eligible for a 401(k) plan?

(vi) For the 5,638 families not eligible for a 401(k), what percentage of these are predicted not to have a 401(k), using the predictor $\widetilde{e401k}_i$? For the 3,637 families eligible for a 401(k) plan, what percentage are predicted to have one? (It is helpful if your econometrics package has a "tabulate" command.)

(vii) The overall percent correctly predicted is about 64.9%. Do you think this is a complete description of how well the model does, given your answers in part (vi)?

(viii) Add the variable *pira* as an explanatory variable to the linear probability model. Other things equal, if a family has someone with an individual retirement account, how much higher is the estimated probability that the family is eligible for a 401(k) plan? Is it statistically different from zero at the 10% level?

C10 Use the data in NBASAL for this exercise.

   (i)   Estimate a linear regression model relating points per game to experience in the league and position (guard, forward, or center). Include experience in quadratic form and use centers as the base group. Report the results in the usual form.

   (ii)   Why do you not include all three position dummy variables in part (i)?

   (iii) Holding experience fixed, does a guard score more than a center? How much more? Is the difference statistically significant?

   (iv)   Now, add marital status to the equation. Holding position and experience fixed, are married players more productive (based on points per game)?

   (v)   Add interactions of marital status with both experience variables. In this expanded model, is there strong evidence that marital status affects points per game?

   (vi)   Estimate the model from part (iv) but use assists per game as the dependent variable. Are there any notable differences from part (iv)? Discuss.

C11 Use the data in 401KSUBS for this exercise.

   (i)   Compute the average, standard deviation, minimum, and maximum values of *nettfa* in the sample.

   (ii)   Test the hypothesis that average *nettfa* does not differ by 401(k) eligibility status; use a two-sided alternative. What is the dollar amount of the estimated difference?

   (iii) From part (ii) of Computer Exercise C9, it is clear that *e401k* is not exogenous in a simple regression model; at a minimum, it changes by income and age. Estimate a multiple linear regression model for *nettfa* that includes income, age, and *e401k* as explanatory variables. The income and age variables should appear as quadratics. Now, what is the estimated dollar effect of 401(k) eligibility?

   (iv)   To the model estimated in part (iii), add the interactions $e401k \cdot (age - 41)$ and $e401k \cdot (age - 41)^2$. Note that the average age in the sample is about 41, so that in the new model, the coefficient on *e401k* is the estimated effect of 401(k) eligibility at the average age. Which interaction term is significant?

   (v)   Comparing the estimates from parts (iii) and (iv), do the estimated effects of 401(k) eligibility at age 41 differ much? Explain.

   (vi)   Now, drop the interaction terms from the model, but define five family size dummy variables: *fsize1, fsize2, fsize3, fsize4,* and *fsize5.* The variable *fsize5* is unity for families with five or more members. Include the family size dummies in the model estimated from part (iii); be sure to choose a base group. Are the family dummies significant at the 1% level?

   (vii) Now, do a Chow test for the model

$$nettfa = \beta_0 + \beta_1 inc + \beta_2 inc^2 + \beta_3 age + \beta_4 age^2 + \beta_5 e401k + u$$

   across the five family size categories, allowing for intercept differences. The restricted sum of squared residuals, SSR_r, is obtained from part (vi) because that regression assumes all slopes are the same. The unrestricted sum of squared residuals is $SSR_{ur} = SSR_1 + SSR_2 + \ldots + SSR_5$, where SSR_f is the sum of squared residuals for the equation estimated using only family size *f*. You should convince yourself that there are 30 parameters in the unrestricted model (5 intercepts plus 25 slopes) and 10 parameters in the restricted model (5 intercepts plus 5 slopes). Therefore, the number of restrictions being tested is $q = 20$, and the *df* for the unrestricted model is $9{,}275 - 30 = 9{,}245$.

C12 Use the data set in BEAUTY, which contains a subset of the variables (but more usable observations than in the regressions) reported by Hamermesh and Biddle (1994).

   (i)   Find the separate fractions of men and women that are classified as having above average looks. Are more people rated as having above average or below average looks?

(ii) Test the null hypothesis that the population fractions of above-average-looking women and men are the same. Report the one-sided *p*-value that the fraction is higher for women. (*Hint:* Estimating a simple linear probability model is easiest.)

(iii) Now estimate the model

$$\log(wage) = \beta_0 + \beta_1 belavg + \beta_2 abvavg + u$$

separately for men and women, and report the results in the usual form. In both cases, interpret the coefficient on *belavg*. Explain in words what the hypothesis $H_0: \beta_1 = 0$ against $H_1: \beta_1 < 0$ means, and find the *p*-values for men and women.

(iv) Is there convincing evidence that women with above average looks earn more than women with average looks? Explain.

(v) For both men and women, add the explanatory variables *educ*, *exper*, *exper*^{2}, *union*, *goodhlth*, *black*, *married*, *south*, *bigcity*, *smllcity*, and *service*. Do the effects of the "looks" variables change in important ways?

(vi) Use the SSR form of the Chow *F* statistic to test whether the slopes of the regression functions in part (v) differ across men and women. Be sure to allow for an intercept shift under the null.

C13 Use the data in APPLE to answer this question.

(i) Define a binary variable as *ecobuy* = 1 if *ecolbs* > 0 and *ecobuy* = 0 if *ecolbs* = 0. In other words, *ecobuy* indicates whether, at the prices given, a family would buy any ecologically friendly apples. What fraction of families claim they would buy ecolabeled apples?

(ii) Estimate the linear probability model

$$ecobuy = \beta_0 + \beta_1 ecoprc + \beta_2 regprc + \beta_3 faminc$$
$$+ \beta_4 hhsize + \beta_5 educ + \beta_6 age + u,$$

and report the results in the usual form. Carefully interpret the coefficients on the price variables.

(iii) Are the nonprice variables jointly significant in the LPM? (Use the usual *F* statistic, even though it is not valid when there is heteroskedasticity.) Which explanatory variable other than the price variables seems to have the most important effect on the decision to buy ecolabeled apples? Does this make sense to you?

(iv) In the model from part (ii), replace *faminc* with log(*faminc*). Which model fits the data better, using *faminc* or log(*faminc*)? Interpret the coefficient on log(*faminc*).

(v) In the estimation in part (iv), how many estimated probabilities are negative? How many are bigger than one? Should you be concerned?

(vi) For the estimation in part (iv), compute the percent correctly predicted for each outcome, *ecobuy* = 0 and *ecobuy* = 1. Which outcome is best predicted by the model?

C14 Use the data in CHARITY to answer this question. The variable *respond* is a dummy variable equal to one if a person responded with a contribution on the most recent mailing sent by a charitable organization. The variable *resplast* is a dummy variable equal to one if the person responded to the previous mailing, *avggift* is the average of past gifts (in Dutch guilders), and *propresp* is the proportion of times the person has responded to past mailings.

(i) Estimate a linear probability model relating *respond* to *resplast* and *avggift*. Report the results in the usual form, and interpret the coefficient on *resplast*.

(ii) Does the average value of past gifts seem to affect the probability of responding?

(iii) Add the variable *propresp* to the model, and interpret its coefficient. (Be careful here: an increase of one in *propresp* is the largest possible change.)

(iv) What happened to the coefficient on *resplast* when *propresp* was added to the regression? Does this make sense?

(v) Add *mailsyear*, the number of mailings per year, to the model. How big is its estimated effect? Why might this not be a good estimate of the causal effect of mailings on responding?

C15 Use the data in FERTIL2 to answer this question.

(i) Find the smallest and largest values of *children* in the sample. What is the average of *children*? Does any woman have exactly the average number of children?

(ii) What percentage of women have electricity in the home?

(iii) Compute the average of *children* for those without electricity and do the same for those with electricity. Comment on what you find. Test whether the population means are the same using a simple regression.

(iv) From part (iii), can you infer that having electricity "causes" women to have fewer children? Explain.

(v) Estimate a multiple regression model of the kind reported in equation (7.37), but add age^2, *urban*, and the three religious affiliation dummies. How does the estimated effect of having electricity compare with that in part (iii)? Is it still statistically significant?

(vi) To the equation in part (v), add an interaction between *electric* and *educ*. Is its coefficient statistically significant? What happens to the coefficient on *electric*?

(vii) The median and mode value for *educ* is 7. In the equation from part (vi), use the centered interaction term $electric \cdot (educ - 7)$ in place of $electric \cdot educ$. What happens to the coefficient on *electric* compared with part (vi)? Why? How does the coefficient on *electric* compare with that in part (v)?

C16 Use the data in CATHOLIC to answer this question.

(i) In the entire sample, what percentage of the students attend a Catholic high school? What is the average of *math*12 in the entire sample?

(ii) Run a simple regression of *math*12 on *cathhs* and report the results in the usual way. Interpret what you have found.

(iii) Now add the variables *lfaminc*, *motheduc*, and *fatheduc* to the regression from part (ii). How many observations are used in the regression? What happens to the coefficient on *cathhs*, along with its statistical significance?

(iv) Return to the simple regression of *math*12 on *cathhs*, but restrict the regression to observations used in the multiple regression from part (iii). Do any important conclusions change?

(v) To the multiple regression in part (iii), add interactions between *cathhs* and each of the other explanatory variables. Are the interaction terms individually or jointly significant?

(vi) What happens to the coefficient on *cathhs* in the regression from part (v). Explain why this coefficient is not very interesting.

(vii) Compute the average partial effect of *cathhs* in the model estimated in part (v). How does it compare with the coefficients on *cathhs* in parts (iii) and (v)?

CHAPTER 8

Heteroskedasticity

The homoskedasticity assumption, introduced in Chapter 3 for multiple regression, states that the variance of the unobserved error, u, conditional on the explanatory variables, is constant. Homoskedasticity fails whenever the variance of the unobserved factors changes across different segments of the population, where the segments are determined by the different values of the explanatory variables. For example, in a savings equation, heteroskedasticity is present if the variance of the unobserved factors affecting savings increases with income.

In Chapters 4 and 5, we saw that homoskedasticity is needed to justify the usual t tests, F tests, and confidence intervals for OLS estimation of the linear regression model, even with large sample sizes. In this chapter, we discuss the available remedies when heteroskedasticity occurs, and we also show how to test for its presence. We begin by briefly reviewing the consequences of heteroskedasticity for ordinary least squares estimation.

8-1 Consequences of Heteroskedasticity for OLS

Consider again the multiple linear regression model:

$$y = \beta_0 + \beta_1 x_1 + \beta_2 x_2 + \ldots + \beta_k x_k + u. \qquad [8.1]$$

In Chapter 3, we proved unbiasedness of the OLS estimators $\hat{\beta}_0, \hat{\beta}_1, \hat{\beta}_2, \ldots, \hat{\beta}_k$ under the first four Gauss-Markov assumptions, MLR.1 through MLR.4. In Chapter 5, we showed that the same four assumptions imply consistency of OLS. The homoskedasticity assumption MLR.5, stated in terms of the error variance as $\text{Var}(u|x_1, x_2, \ldots, x_k) = \sigma^2$, played no role in showing whether OLS was unbiased or consistent. It is important to remember that heteroskedasticity does not cause bias or inconsistency in the OLS estimators of the β_j, whereas something like omitting an important variable would have this effect.

The interpretation of our goodness-of-fit measures, R^2 and $\overline{R}^2$, is also unaffected by the presence of heteroskedasticity. Why? Recall from Section 6-3 that the usual R-squared and the adjusted R-squared are different ways of estimating the population R-squared, which is simply $1 - \sigma_u^2/\sigma_y^2$, where σ_u^2 is the population error variance and σ_y^2 is the population variance of y. The key point is that because both variances in the population R-squared are unconditional variances, the population R-squared is unaffected by the presence of heteroskedasticity in $\text{Var}(u|x_1, ..., x_k)$. Further, SSR/$n$ consistently estimates σ_u^2, and SST/n consistently estimates σ_y^2, whether or not $\text{Var}(u|x_1, ..., x_k)$ is constant. The same is true when we use the degrees of freedom adjustments. Therefore, R^2 and $\overline{R}^2$ are both consistent estimators of the population R-squared whether or not the homoskedasticity assumption holds.

If heteroskedasticity does not cause bias or inconsistency in the OLS estimators, why did we introduce it as one of the Gauss-Markov assumptions? Recall from Chapter 3 that the estimators of the *variances*, $\text{Var}(\hat{\beta}_j)$, are biased without the homoskedasticity assumption. Since the OLS standard errors are based directly on these variances, they are no longer valid for constructing confidence intervals and t statistics. The usual OLS t statistics do not have t distributions in the presence of heteroskedasticity, and the problem is not resolved by using large sample sizes. We will see this explicitly for the simple regression case in the next section, where we derive the variance of the OLS slope estimator under heteroskedasticity and propose a valid estimator in the presence of heteroskedasticity. Similarly, F statistics are no longer F distributed, and the LM statistic no longer has an asymptotic chi-square distribution. In summary, the statistics we used to test hypotheses under the Gauss-Markov assumptions are not valid in the presence of heteroskedasticity.

We also know that the Gauss-Markov Theorem, which says that OLS is best linear unbiased, relies crucially on the homoskedasticity assumption. If $\text{Var}(u|\mathbf{x})$ is not constant, OLS is no longer BLUE. In addition, OLS is no longer asymptotically efficient in the class of estimators described in Theorem 5.3. As we will see in Section 8-4, it is possible to find estimators that are more efficient than OLS in the presence of heteroskedasticity (although it requires knowing the form of the heteroskedasticity). With relatively large sample sizes, it might not be so important to obtain an efficient estimator. In the next section, we show how the usual OLS test statistics can be modified so that they are valid, at least asymptotically.

8-2 Heteroskedasticity-Robust Inference after OLS Estimation

Because testing hypotheses is such an important component of any econometric analysis and the usual OLS inference is generally faulty in the presence of heteroskedasticity, we must decide if we should entirely abandon OLS. Fortunately, OLS is still useful. In the last two decades, econometricians have learned how to adjust standard errors and t, F, and LM statistics so that they are valid in the presence of **heteroskedasticity of unknown form**. This is very convenient because it means we can report new statistics that work regardless of the kind of heteroskedasticity present in the population. The methods in this section are known as *heteroskedasticity-robust* procedures because they are valid—at least in large samples—whether or not the errors have constant variance, and we do not need to know which is the case.

We begin by sketching how the variances, $\text{Var}(\hat{\beta}_j)$, can be estimated in the presence of heteroskedasticity. A careful derivation of the theory is well beyond the scope of this text, but the application of heteroskedasticity-robust methods is very easy now because many statistics and econometrics packages compute these statistics as an option.

First, consider the model with a single independent variable, where we include an i subscript for emphasis:

$$y_i = \beta_0 + \beta_1 x_i + u_i.$$

We assume throughout that the first four Gauss-Markov assumptions hold. If the errors contain heteroskedasticity, then

$$\text{Var}(u_i|x_i) = \sigma_i^2,$$

where we put an i subscript on σ^2 to indicate that the variance of the error depends upon the particular value of x_i.

Write the OLS estimator as

$$\hat{\beta}_1 = \beta_1 + \frac{\sum_{i=1}^{n}(x_i - \bar{x})u_i}{\sum_{i=1}^{n}(x_i - \bar{x})^2}.$$

Under Assumptions MLR.1 through MLR.4 (that is, without the homoskedasticity assumption), and conditioning on the values x_i in the sample, we can use the same arguments from Chapter 2 to show that

$$\text{Var}(\hat{\beta}_1) = \frac{\sum_{i=1}^{n}(x_i - \bar{x})^2\sigma_i^2}{\text{SST}_x^2}, \tag{8.2}$$

where $\text{SST}_x = \sum_{i=1}^{n}(x_i - \bar{x})^2$ is the total sum of squares of the x_i. When $\sigma_i^2 = \sigma^2$ for all i, this formula reduces to the usual form, σ^2/SST_x. Equation (8.2) explicitly shows that, for the simple regression case, the variance formula derived under homoskedasticity is no longer valid when heteroskedasticity is present.

Since the standard error of $\hat{\beta}_1$ is based directly on estimating $\text{Var}(\hat{\beta}_1)$, we need a way to estimate equation (8.2) when heteroskedasticity is present. White (1980) showed how this can be done. Let $\hat{u}_i$ denote the OLS residuals from the initial regression of y on x. Then, a valid estimator of $\text{Var}(\hat{\beta}_1)$, for heteroskedasticity of *any* form (including homoskedasticity), is

$$\frac{\sum_{i=1}^{n}(x_i - \bar{x})^2\hat{u}_i^2}{\text{SST}_x^2}, \tag{8.3}$$

which is easily computed from the data after the OLS regression.

In what sense is (8.3) a valid estimator of $\text{Var}(\hat{\beta}_1)$? This is pretty subtle. Briefly, it can be shown that when equation (8.3) is multiplied by the sample size n, it converges in probability to $E[(x_i - \mu_x)^2 u_i^2]/(\sigma_x^2)^2$, which is the probability limit of n times (8.2). Ultimately, this is what is necessary for justifying the use of standard errors to construct confidence intervals and t statistics. The law of large numbers and the central limit theorem play key roles in establishing these convergences. You can refer to White's original paper for details, but that paper is quite technical. See also Wooldridge (2010, Chapter 4).

A similar formula works in the general multiple regression model

$$y = \beta_0 + \beta_1 x_1 + \ldots + \beta_k x_k + u.$$

It can be shown that a valid estimator of $\text{Var}(\hat{\beta}_j)$, under Assumptions MLR.1 through MLR.4, is

$$\widehat{\text{Var}}(\hat{\beta}_j) = \frac{\sum_{i=1}^{n}\hat{r}_{ij}^2\hat{u}_i^2}{\text{SSR}_j^2}, \tag{8.4}$$

where $\hat{r}_{ij}$ denotes the ith residual from regressing x_j on all other independent variables, and SSR$_j$ is the sum of squared residuals from this regression (see Section 3-2 for the partialling out representation of the OLS estimates). The square root of the quantity in (8.4) is called the **heteroskedasticity-robust standard error** for $\hat{\beta}_j$. In econometrics, these robust standard errors are usually attributed to White (1980). Earlier works in statistics, notably those by Eicker (1967) and Huber (1967), pointed to the possibility of obtaining such robust standard errors. In applied work, these are sometimes called *White, Huber,* or *Eicker standard errors* (or some hyphenated combination of these names). We will just refer to them as *heteroskedasticity-robust standard errors*, or even just *robust standard errors* when the context is clear.

Sometimes, as a degrees of freedom correction, (8.4) is multiplied by $n/(n - k - 1)$ before taking the square root. The reasoning for this adjustment is that, if the squared OLS residuals $\hat{u}_i^2$ were the same for all observations i—the strongest possible form of homoskedasticity in a sample—we would get the usual OLS standard errors. Other modifications of (8.4) are studied in MacKinnon and White (1985). Since all forms have only asymptotic justification and they are asymptotically equivalent, no form is uniformly preferred above all others. Typically, we use whatever form is computed by the regression package at hand.

Once heteroskedasticity-robust standard errors are obtained, it is simple to construct a **heteroskedasticity-robust t statistic**. Recall that the general form of the t statistic is

$$t = \frac{estimate - hypothesized\ value}{standard\ error}. \qquad [8.5]$$

Because we are still using the OLS estimates and we have chosen the hypothesized value ahead of time, the only difference between the usual OLS t statistic and the heteroskedasticity-robust t statistic is in how the standard error in the denominator is computed.

The term SSR$_j$ in equation (8.4) can be replaced with SST$_j(1 - R_j^2)$, where SST$_j$ is the total sum of squares of x_j and R_j^2 is the usual R-squared from regressing x_j on all other explanatory variables. [We implicitly used this equivalence in deriving equation (3.51).] Consequently, little sample variation in x_j, or a strong linear relationship between x_j and the other explanatory variables—that is, multicollinearity—can cause the heteroskedasticity-robust standard errors to be large. We discussed these issues with the usual OLS standard errors in Section 3-4.

EXAMPLE 8.1	**Log Wage Equation with Heteroskedasticity-Robust Standard Errors**

We estimate the model in Example 7.6, but we report the heteroskedasticity-robust standard errors along with the usual OLS standard errors. Some of the estimates are reported to more digits so that we can compare the usual standard errors with the heteroskedasticity-robust standard errors:

$$\widehat{\log(wage)} = .321 + .213\ marrmale - .198\ marrfem - .110\ singfem$$
$$\qquad\qquad (.100)\ (.055) \qquad\quad (.058) \qquad\qquad (.056)$$
$$\qquad\qquad [.109]\ [.057] \qquad\quad [.058] \qquad\qquad [.057]$$
$$\qquad + .0789\ educ + .0268\ exper - .00054\ exper^2$$
$$\qquad\qquad (.0067) \qquad\ (.0055) \qquad\ (.00011) \qquad\qquad\quad [8.6]$$
$$\qquad\qquad [.0074] \qquad\ [.0051] \qquad\ [.00011]$$
$$\qquad + .0291\ tenure - .00053\ tenure^2$$
$$\qquad\qquad (.0068) \qquad\ (.00023)$$
$$\qquad\qquad [.0069] \qquad\ [.00024]$$
$$n = 526, R^2 = .461.$$

The usual OLS standard errors are in parentheses, ( ), below the corresponding OLS estimate, and the heteroskedasticity-robust standard errors are in brackets, [ ]. The numbers in brackets are the only new things, since the equation is still estimated by OLS.

Several things are apparent from equation (8.6). First, in this particular application, any variable that was statistically significant using the usual t statistic is still statistically significant using the heteroskedasticity-robust t statistic. This occurs because the two sets of standard errors are not very different. (The associated p-values will differ slightly because the robust t statistics are not identical to the usual, nonrobust t statistics.) The largest relative change in standard errors is for the coefficient on *educ:* the usual standard error is .0067, and the robust standard error is .0074. Still, the robust standard error implies a robust t statistic above 10.

Equation (8.6) also shows that the robust standard errors can be either larger or smaller than the usual standard errors. For example, the robust standard error on *exper* is .0051, whereas the usual standard error is .0055. We do not know which will be larger ahead of time. As an empirical matter, the robust standard errors are often found to be larger than the usual standard errors.

Before leaving this example, we must emphasize that we do not know, at this point, whether heteroskedasticity is even present in the population model underlying equation (8.6). All we have done is report, along with the usual standard errors, those that are valid (asymptotically) whether or not heteroskedasticity is present. We can see that no important conclusions are overturned by using the robust standard errors in this example. This often happens in applied work, but in other cases, the differences between the usual and robust standard errors are much larger. As an example of where the differences are substantial, see Computer Exercise C2.

At this point, you may be asking the following question: if the heteroskedasticity-robust standard errors are valid more often than the usual OLS standard errors, why do we bother with the usual standard errors at all? This is a sensible question. One reason the usual standard errors are still used in cross-sectional work is that, if the homoskedasticity assumption holds and the errors are normally distributed, then the usual t statistics have *exact* t distributions, regardless of the sample size (see Chapter 4). The robust standard errors and robust t statistics are justified only as the sample size becomes large, even if the CLM assumptions are true. With small sample sizes, the robust t statistics can have distributions that are not very close to the t distribution, and that could throw off our inference.

In large sample sizes, we can make a case for always reporting only the heteroskedasticity-robust standard errors in cross-sectional applications, and this practice is being followed more and more in applied work. It is also common to report both standard errors, as in equation (8.6), so that a reader can determine whether any conclusions are sensitive to the standard error in use.

It is also possible to obtain F and LM statistics that are robust to heteroskedasticity of an unknown, arbitrary form. The **heteroskedasticity-robust F statistic** (or a simple transformation of it) is also called a *heteroskedasticity-robust Wald statistic*. A general treatment of the Wald statistic requires matrix algebra and is sketched in Appendix E; see Wooldridge (2010, Chapter 4) for a more detailed treatment. Nevertheless, using heteroskedasticity-robust statistics for multiple exclusion restrictions is straightforward because many econometrics packages now compute such statistics routinely.

EXAMPLE 8.2   **Heteroskedasticity-Robust F Statistic**

Using the data for the spring semester in GPA3, we estimate the following equation:

$$\widehat{cumgpa} = 1.47 + .00114\,sat - .00857\,hsperc + .00250\,tothrs$$
$$\qquad\quad (.23)\ \ (.00018)\quad (.00124)\qquad (.00073)$$
$$\qquad\quad [.22]\ \ [.00019]\quad [.00140]\qquad [.00073]$$
$$\qquad\quad + .303\,female - .128\,black - .059\,white \qquad\qquad\qquad [8.7]$$
$$\qquad\quad (.059)\qquad\quad (.147)\qquad (.141)$$
$$\qquad\quad [.059]\qquad\quad [.118]\qquad [.110]$$
$$n = 366,\ R^2 = .4006,\ \bar{R}^2 = .3905.$$

Again, the differences between the usual standard errors and the heteroskedasticity-robust standard errors are not very big, and use of the robust t statistics does not change the statistical significance of any independent variable. Joint significance tests are not much affected either. Suppose we wish to test the null hypothesis that, after the other factors are controlled for, there are no differences in *cumgpa* by race. This is stated as H_0: $\beta_{black} = 0$, $\beta_{white} = 0$. The usual F statistic is easily obtained, once we have the R-squared from the restricted model; this turns out to be .3983. The F statistic is then $[(.4006 - .3983)/(1 - .4006)](359/2) \approx .69$. If heteroskedasticity is present, this version of the test is invalid. The heteroskedasticity-robust version has no simple form, but it can be computed using certain statistical packages. The value of the heteroskedasticity-robust F statistic turns out to be .75, which differs only slightly from the nonrobust version. The p-value for the robust test is .474, which is not close to standard significance levels. We fail to reject the null hypothesis using either test.

Because the usual sum of squared residuals form of the F statistic is not valid under heteroskedasticity, we must be careful in computing a Chow test of common coefficients across two groups. The form of the statistic in equation (7.24) is not valid if heteroskedasticity is present, including the simple case where the error variance differs across the two groups. Instead, we can obtain a heteroskedasticity-robust Chow test by including a dummy variable distinguishing the two groups along with interactions between that dummy variable and all other explanatory variables. We can then test whether there is no difference in the two regression functions—by testing that the coefficients on the dummy variable and all interactions are zero—or just test whether the slopes are all the same, in which case we leave the coefficient on the dummy variable unrestricted. See Computer Exercise C14 for an example.

8-2a Computing Heteroskedasticity-Robust *LM* Tests

> **EXPLORING FURTHER 8.1**
>
> Evaluate the following statement: The heteroskedasticity-robust standard errors are always bigger than the usual standard errors.

Not all regression packages compute F statistics that are robust to heteroskedasticity. Therefore, it is sometimes convenient to have a way of obtaining a test of multiple exclusion restrictions that is robust to heteroskedasticity and does not require a particular kind of econometric software. It turns out that a **heteroskedasticity-robust *LM* statistic** is easily obtained using virtually any regression package.

To illustrate computation of the robust *LM* statistic, consider the model

$$y = \beta_0 + \beta_1 x_1 + \beta_2 x_2 + \beta_3 x_3 + \beta_4 x_4 + \beta_5 x_5 + u,$$

and suppose we would like to test H_0: $\beta_4 = 0$, $\beta_5 = 0$. To obtain the usual *LM* statistic, we would first estimate the restricted model (that is, the model without x_4 and x_5) to obtain the residuals, $\tilde{u}$. Then, we would regress $\tilde{u}$ on all of the independent variables and the $LM = n \cdot R_{\tilde{u}}^2$, where $R_{\tilde{u}}^2$ is the usual R-squared from this regression.

Obtaining a version that is robust to heteroskedasticity requires more work. One way to compute the statistic requires only OLS regressions. We need the residuals, say, $\tilde{r}_1$, from the regression of x_4 on x_1, x_2, x_3. Also, we need the residuals, say, $\tilde{r}_2$, from the regression of x_5 on x_1, x_2, x_3. Thus, we regress each of the independent variables excluded under the null on all of the included independent variables. We keep the residuals each time. The final step appears odd, but it is, after all, just a computational device. Run the regression of

$$1 \text{ on } \tilde{r}_1 \tilde{u}, \tilde{r}_2 \tilde{u}, \tag{8.8}$$

without an intercept. Yes, we actually define a dependent variable equal to the value one for all observations. We regress this onto the products $\tilde{r}_1 \tilde{u}$ and $\tilde{r}_2 \tilde{u}$. The robust *LM* statistic turns out to be $n - SSR_1$, where SSR_1 is just the usual sum of squared residuals from regression (8.8).

The reason this works is somewhat technical. Basically, this is doing for the *LM* test what the robust standard errors do for the *t* test. [See Wooldridge (1991b) or Davidson and MacKinnon (1993) for a more detailed discussion.]

We now summarize the computation of the heteroskedasticity-robust *LM* statistic in the general case.

A Heteroskedasticity-Robust *LM* Statistic:

1. Obtain the residuals $\tilde{u}$ from the restricted model.

2. Regress each of the independent variables excluded under the null on all of the included independent variables; if there are q excluded variables, this leads to q sets of residuals $(\tilde{r}_1, \tilde{r}_2, ..., \tilde{r}_q)$.

3. Find the products between each $\tilde{r}_j$ and $\tilde{u}$ (for all observations).

4. Run the regression of 1 on $\tilde{r}_1 \tilde{u}$, $\tilde{r}_2 \tilde{u}$, ..., $\tilde{r}_q \tilde{u}$, without an intercept. The heteroskedasticity-robust *LM* statistic is $n - \text{SSR}_1$, where SSR_1 is just the usual sum of squared residuals from this final regression. Under H_0, *LM* is distributed approximately as χ^2_q.

Once the robust *LM* statistic is obtained, the rejection rule and computation of *p*-values are the same as for the usual *LM* statistic in Section 5-2.

EXAMPLE 8.3　　**Heteroskedasticity-Robust *LM* Statistic**

We use the data in CRIME1 to test whether the average sentence length served for past convictions affects the number of arrests in the current year (1986). The estimated model is

$$\widehat{narr86} = .561 - .136\, pcnv + .0178\, avgsen - .00052\, avgsen^2$$
$$\qquad\quad (.036)\ \ (.040)\qquad (.0097)\qquad (.00030)$$
$$\qquad\quad [.040]\ \ [.034]\qquad [.0101]\qquad [.00021]$$
$$\qquad - .0394\, ptime86 - .0505\, qemp86 - .00148\, inc86$$
$$\qquad\quad (.0087)\qquad\quad (.0144)\qquad\quad (.00034)\qquad\qquad [8.9]$$
$$\qquad\quad [.0062]\qquad\quad [.0142]\qquad\quad [.00023]$$
$$\qquad + .325\, black + .193\, hispan$$
$$\qquad\quad (.045)\qquad\ (.040)$$
$$\qquad\quad [.058]\qquad\ [.040]$$
$$n = 2{,}725,\ R^2 = .0728.$$

In this example, there are more substantial differences between some of the usual standard errors and the robust standard errors. For example, the usual *t* statistic on $avgsen^2$ is about -1.73, while the robust *t* statistic is about -2.48. Thus, $avgsen^2$ is more significant using the robust standard error.

The effect of *avgsen* on *narr86* is somewhat difficult to reconcile. Because the relationship is quadratic, we can figure out where *avgsen* has a positive effect on *narr86* and where the effect becomes negative. The turning point is $.0178/[2(.00052)] \approx 17.12$; recall that this is measured in months. Literally, this means that *narr86* is positively related to *avgsen* when *avgsen* is less than 17 months; then *avgsen* has the expected deterrent effect after 17 months.

To see whether average sentence length has a statistically significant effect on *narr86*, we must test the joint hypothesis $H_0: \beta_{avgsen} = 0, \beta_{avgsen^2} = 0$. Using the usual *LM* statistic (see Section 5-2), we obtain $LM = 3.54$; in a chi-square distribution with two *df*, this yields a *p*-value $= .170$. Thus, we do not reject H_0 at even the 15% level. The heteroskedasticity-robust *LM* statistic is $LM = 4.00$ (rounded to two decimal places), with a *p*-value $= .135$. This is still not very strong evidence against H_0; *avgsen* does not appear to have a strong effect on *narr86*. [Incidentally, when *avgsen* appears alone in (8.9), that is, without the quadratic term, its usual *t* statistic is .658, and its robust *t* statistic is .592.]

8-3 Testing for Heteroskedasticity

The heteroskedasticity-robust standard errors provide a simple method for computing t statistics that are asymptotically t distributed whether or not heteroskedasticity is present. We have also seen that heteroskedasticity-robust F and LM statistics are available. Implementing these tests does not require knowing whether or not heteroskedasticity is present. Nevertheless, there are still some good reasons for having simple tests that can detect its presence. First, as we mentioned in the previous section, the usual t statistics have exact t distributions under the classical linear model assumptions. For this reason, many economists still prefer to see the usual OLS standard errors and test statistics reported, unless there is evidence of heteroskedasticity. Second, if heteroskedasticity is present, the OLS estimator is no longer the best linear unbiased estimator. As we will see in Section 8-4, it is possible to obtain a better estimator than OLS when the form of heteroskedasticity is known.

Many tests for heteroskedasticity have been suggested over the years. Some of them, while having the ability to detect heteroskedasticity, do not directly test the assumption that the variance of the error does not depend upon the independent variables. We will restrict ourselves to more modern tests, which detect the kind of heteroskedasticity that invalidates the usual OLS statistics. This also has the benefit of putting all tests in the same framework.

As usual, we start with the linear model

$$y = \beta_0 + \beta_1 x_1 + \beta_2 x_2 + \ldots + \beta_k x_k + u, \qquad [8.10]$$

where Assumptions MLR.1 through MLR.4 are maintained in this section. In particular, we assume that $E(u|x_1, x_2, \ldots, x_k) = 0$, so that OLS is unbiased and consistent.

We take the null hypothesis to be that Assumption MLR.5 is true:

$$H_0: \text{Var}(u|x_1, x_2, \ldots, x_k) = \sigma^2. \qquad [8.11]$$

That is, we assume that the ideal assumption of homoskedasticity holds, and we require the data to tell us otherwise. If we cannot reject (8.11) at a sufficiently small significance level, we usually conclude that heteroskedasticity is not a problem. However, remember that we never accept H_0; we simply fail to reject it.

Because we are assuming that u has a zero conditional expectation, $\text{Var}(u|\mathbf{x}) = E(u^2|\mathbf{x})$, and so the null hypothesis of homoskedasticity is equivalent to

$$H_0: E(u^2|x_1, x_2, \ldots, x_k) = E(u^2) = \sigma^2.$$

This shows that, in order to test for violation of the homoskedasticity assumption, we want to test whether u^2 is related (in expected value) to one or more of the explanatory variables. If H_0 is false, the expected value of u^2, given the independent variables, can be virtually any function of the x_j. A simple approach is to assume a linear function:

$$u^2 = \delta_0 + \delta_1 x_1 + \delta_2 x_2 + \ldots + \delta_k x_k + v, \qquad [8.12]$$

where v is an error term with mean zero given the x_j. Pay close attention to the dependent variable in this equation: it is the *square* of the error in the original regression equation, (8.10). The null hypothesis of homoskedasticity is

$$H_0: \delta_1 = \delta_2 = \ldots = \delta_k = 0. \qquad [8.13]$$

Under the null hypothesis, it is often reasonable to assume that the error in (8.12), v, is independent of $x_1, x_2, \ldots, x_k$. Then, we know from Section 5-2 that either the F or LM statistics for the overall significance of the independent variables in explaining u^2 can be used to test (8.13). Both statistics would have asymptotic justification, even though u^2 cannot be normally distributed. (For example, if u is normally distributed, then u^2/σ^2 is distributed as χ_1^2.) If we could observe the u^2 in the sample, then we could easily compute this statistic by running the OLS regression of u^2 on $x_1, x_2, \ldots, x_k$, using all n observations.

As we have emphasized before, we never know the actual errors in the population model, but we do have estimates of them: the OLS residual, $\hat{u}_i$, is an estimate of the error u_i for observation i. Thus, we can estimate the equation

$$\hat{u}^2 = \delta_0 + \delta_1 x_1 + \delta_2 x_2 + \ldots + \delta_k x_k + error \qquad [8.14]$$

and compute the F or LM statistics for the joint significance of $x_1, \ldots, x_k$. It turns out that using the OLS residuals in place of the errors does not affect the large sample distribution of the F or LM statistics, although showing this is pretty complicated.

The F and LM statistics both depend on the R-squared from regression (8.14); call this $R^2_{\hat{u}^2}$ to distinguish it from the R-squared in estimating equation (8.10). Then, the F statistic is

$$F = \frac{R^2_{\hat{u}^2}/k}{(1 - R^2_{\hat{u}^2})/(n - k - 1)}, \qquad [8.15]$$

where k is the number of regressors in (8.14); this is the same number of independent variables in (8.10). Computing (8.15) by hand is rarely necessary, because most regression packages automatically compute the F statistic for overall significance of a regression. This F statistic has (approximately) an $F_{k, n-k-1}$ distribution under the null hypothesis of homoskedasticity.

The LM statistic for heteroskedasticity is just the sample size times the R-squared from (8.14):

$$LM = n \cdot R^2_{\hat{u}^2}. \qquad [8.16]$$

Under the null hypothesis, LM is distributed asymptotically as χ^2_k. This is also very easy to obtain after running regression (8.14).

The LM version of the test is typically called the **Breusch-Pagan test for heteroskedasticity (BP test)**. Breusch and Pagan (1979) suggested a different form of the test that assumes the errors are normally distributed. Koenker (1981) suggested the form of the LM statistic in (8.16), and it is generally preferred due to its greater applicability.

We summarize the steps for testing for heteroskedasticity using the BP test:

The Breusch-Pagan Test for Heteroskedasticity:

1. Estimate the model (8.10) by OLS, as usual. Obtain the squared OLS residuals, $\hat{u}^2$ (one for each observation).

2. Run the regression in (8.14). Keep the R-squared from this regression, $R^2_{\hat{u}^2}$.

3. Form either the F statistic or the LM statistic and compute the p-value (using the $F_{k,n-k-1}$ distribution in the former case and the χ^2_k distribution in the latter case). If the p-value is sufficiently small, that is, below the chosen significance level, then we reject the null hypothesis of homoskedasticity.

If the BP test results in a small enough p-value, some corrective measure should be taken. One possibility is to just use the heteroskedasticity-robust standard errors and test statistics discussed in the previous section. Another possibility is discussed in Section 8-4.

EXAMPLE 8.4   **Heteroskedasticity in Housing Price Equations**

We use the data in HPRICE1 to test for heteroskedasticity in a simple housing price equation. The estimated equation using the levels of all variables is

$$\widehat{price} = -21.77 + .00207 \, lotsize + .123 \, sqrft + 13.85 \, bdrms$$
$$\phantom{\widehat{price} = } (29.48) \quad (.00064) \qquad\quad (.013) \qquad\quad (9.01) \qquad [8.17]$$
$$n = 88, R^2 = .672.$$

This equation tells us *nothing* about whether the error in the population model is heteroskedastic. We need to regress the squared OLS residuals on the independent variables. The R-squared from the regression of $\hat{u}^2$ on *lotsize*, *sqrft*, and *bdrms* is $R_{\hat{u}^2}^2 = .1601$. With $n = 88$ and $k = 3$, this produces an F statistic for significance of the independent variables of $F = [.1601/(1 - .1601)](84/3) \approx 5.34$. The associated p-value is .002, which is strong evidence against the null. The LM statistic is $88(.1601) \approx 14.09$; this gives a $p\text{-value} \approx .0028$ (using the χ_3^2 distribution), giving essentially the same conclusion as the F statistic. This means that the usual standard errors reported in (8.17) are not reliable.

In Chapter 6, we mentioned that one benefit of using the logarithmic functional form for the dependent variable is that heteroskedasticity is often reduced. In the current application, let us put *price*, *lotsize*, and *sqrft* in logarithmic form, so that the elasticities of *price*, with respect to *lotsize* and *sqrft*, are constant. The estimated equation is

$$\widehat{\log(price)} = -1.30 + .168 \log(lotsize) + .700 \log(sqrft) + 0.37\, bdrms$$
$$(.65)\quad (.038) \qquad\qquad (.093) \qquad\qquad (.028) \qquad\qquad \text{[8.18]}$$
$$n = 88, R^2 = .643.$$

Regressing the squared OLS residuals from this regression on $\log(lotsize)$, $\log(sqrft)$, and *bdrms* gives $R_{\hat{u}^2}^2 = .0480$. Thus, $F = 1.41$ (p-value = .245), and $LM = 4.22$ (p-value = .239). Therefore, we fail to reject the null hypothesis of homoskedasticity in the model with the logarithmic functional forms. The occurrence of less heteroskedasticity with the dependent variable in logarithmic form has been noticed in many empirical applications.

EXPLORING FURTHER 8.2

Consider wage equation (7.11), where you think that the conditional variance of log(*wage*) does not depend on *educ*, *exper*, or *tenure*. However, you are worried that the variance of log(*wage*) differs across the four demographic groups of married males, married females, single males, and single females. What regression would you run to test for heteroskedasticity? What are the degrees of freedom in the F test?

If we suspect that heteroskedasticity depends only upon certain independent variables, we can easily modify the Breusch-Pagan test: we simply regress $\hat{u}^2$ on whatever independent variables we choose and carry out the appropriate F or LM test. Remember that the appropriate degrees of freedom depends upon the number of independent variables in the regression with $\hat{u}^2$ as the dependent variable; the number of independent variables showing up in equation (8.10) is irrelevant.

If the squared residuals are regressed on only a single independent variable, the test for heteroskedasticity is just the usual t statistic on the variable. A significant t statistic suggests that heteroskedasticity is a problem.

8-3a The White Test for Heteroskedasticity

In Chapter 5, we showed that the usual OLS standard errors and test statistics are asymptotically valid, provided all of the Gauss-Markov assumptions hold. It turns out that the homoskedasticity assumption, $\text{Var}(u_1|x_1, \ldots, x_k) = \sigma^2$, can be replaced with the weaker assumption that the squared error, u^2, is *uncorrelated* with all the independent variables (x_j), the squares of the independent variables (x_j^2) and all the cross products $(x_j x_h \text{ for } j \neq h)$. This observation motivated White (1980) to propose a test for heteroskedasticity that adds the squares and cross products of all the independent variables to equation (8.14). The test is explicitly intended to test for forms of heteroskedasticity that invalidate the usual OLS standard errors and test statistics.

When the model contains $k = 3$ independent variables, the White test is based on an estimation of

$$\hat{u}^2 = \delta_0 + \delta_1 x_1 + \delta_2 x_2 + \delta_3 x_3 + \delta_4 x_1^2 + \delta_5 x_2^2 + \delta_6 x_3^2$$
$$+ \delta_7 x_1 x_2 + \delta_8 x_1 x_3 + \delta_9 x_2 x_3 + error.$$

[8.19]

Compared with the Breusch-Pagan test, this equation has six more regressors. The **White test for heteroskedasticity** is the *LM* statistic for testing that all of the δ_j in equation (8.19) are zero, except for the intercept. Thus, nine restrictions are being tested in this case. We can also use an *F* test of this hypothesis; both tests have asymptotic justification.

With only three independent variables in the original model, equation (8.19) has nine independent variables. With six independent variables in the original model, the White regression would generally involve 27 regressors (unless some are redundant). This abundance of regressors is a weakness in the pure form of the White test: it uses many degrees of freedom for models with just a moderate number of independent variables.

It is possible to obtain a test that is easier to implement than the White test and more conserving on degrees of freedom. To create the test, recall that the difference between the White and Breusch-Pagan tests is that the former includes the squares and cross products of the independent variables. We can preserve the spirit of the White test while conserving on degrees of freedom by using the OLS fitted values in a test for heteroskedasticity. Remember that the fitted values are defined, for each observation i, by

$$\hat{y}_i = \hat{\beta}_0 + \hat{\beta}_1 x_{i1} + \hat{\beta}_2 x_{i2} + \ldots + \hat{\beta}_k x_{ik}.$$

These are just linear functions of the independent variables. If we square the fitted values, we get a particular function of all the squares and cross products of the independent variables. This suggests testing for heteroskedasticity by estimating the equation

$$\hat{u}^2 = \delta_0 + \delta_1 \hat{y} + \delta_2 \hat{y}^2 + error,$$

[8.20]

where $\hat{y}$ stands for the fitted values. It is important not to confuse $\hat{y}$ and y in this equation. We use the fitted values because they are functions of the independent variables (and the estimated parameters); using y in (8.20) does not produce a valid test for heteroskedasticity.

We can use the *F* or *LM* statistic for the null hypothesis $H_0: \delta_1 = 0, \delta_2 = 0$ in equation (8.20). This results in two restrictions in testing the null of homoskedasticity, regardless of the number of independent variables in the original model. Conserving on degrees of freedom in this way is often a good idea, and it also makes the test easy to implement.

Since $\hat{y}$ is an estimate of the expected value of y, given the x_j, using (8.20) to test for heteroskedasticity is useful in cases where the variance is thought to change with the level of the expected value, $E(y|\mathbf{x})$. The test from (8.20) can be viewed as a special case of the White test, since equation (8.20) can be shown to impose restrictions on the parameters in equation (8.19).

A Special Case of the White Test for Heteroskedasticity:

1. Estimate the model (8.10) by OLS, as usual. Obtain the OLS residuals $\hat{u}$ and the fitted values $\hat{y}$. Compute the squared OLS residuals $\hat{u}^2$ and the squared fitted values $\hat{y}^2$.
2. Run the regression in equation (8.20). Keep the *R*-squared from this regression, $R_{\hat{u}^2}^2$.
3. Form either the *F* or *LM* statistic and compute the *p*-value (using the $F_{2,n-3}$ distribution in the former case and the χ_2^2 distribution in the latter case).

EXAMPLE 8.5	Special Form of the White Test in the Log Housing Price Equation

We apply the special case of the White test to equation (8.18), where we use the *LM* form of the statistic. The important thing to remember is that the chi-square distribution always has two *df*. The regression of $\hat{u}^2$ on $\widehat{lprice}$, $(\widehat{lprice})^2$, where $\widehat{lprice}$ denotes the fitted values from (8.18), produces $R_{\hat{u}^2}^2 = .0392$; thus, $LM = 88(.0392) \approx 3.45$, and the *p*-value = .178. This is stronger evidence of heteroskedasticity than is provided by the Breusch-Pagan test, but we still fail to reject homoskedasticity at even the 15% level.

Before leaving this section, we should discuss one important caveat. We have interpreted a rejection using one of the heteroskedasticity tests as evidence of heteroskedasticity. This is appropriate provided we maintain Assumptions MLR.1 through MLR.4. But, if MLR.4 is violated—in particular, if the functional form of $E(y|\mathbf{x})$ is misspecified—then a test for heteroskedasticity can reject H_0, even if $Var(y|\mathbf{x})$ is constant. For example, if we omit one or more quadratic terms in a regression model or use the level model when we should use the log, a test for heteroskedasticity can be significant. This has led some economists to view tests for heteroskedasticity as general misspecification tests. However, there are better, more direct tests for functional form misspecification, and we will cover some of them in Section 9-1. It is better to use explicit tests for functional form first, since functional form misspecification is more important than heteroskedasticity. Then, once we are satisfied with the functional form, we can test for heteroskedasticity.

8-4 Weighted Least Squares Estimation

If heteroskedasticity is detected using one of the tests in Section 8-3, we know from Section 8-2 that one possible response is to use heteroskedasticity-robust statistics after estimation by OLS. Before the development of heteroskedasticity-robust statistics, the response to a finding of heteroskedasticity was to specify its form and use a *weighted least squares* method, which we develop in this section. As we will argue, if we have correctly specified the form of the variance (as a function of explanatory variables), then weighted least squares (WLS) is more efficient than OLS, and WLS leads to new *t* and *F* statistics that have *t* and *F* distributions. We will also discuss the implications of using the wrong form of the variance in the WLS procedure.

8-4a The Heteroskedasticity Is Known up to a Multiplicative Constant

Let $\mathbf{x}$ denote all the explanatory variables in equation (8.10) and assume that

$$Var(u|\mathbf{x}) = \sigma^2 h(\mathbf{x}),$$ [8.21]

where $h(\mathbf{x})$ is some function of the explanatory variables that determines the heteroskedasticity. Since variances must be positive, $h(\mathbf{x}) > 0$ for all possible values of the independent variables. For now, we assume that the function $h(\mathbf{x})$ is known. The population parameter σ^2 is unknown, but we will be able to estimate it from a data sample.

For a random drawing from the population, we can write $\sigma_i^2 = Var(u_i|\mathbf{x}_i) = \sigma^2 h(\mathbf{x}_i) = \sigma^2 h_i$, where we again use the notation $\mathbf{x}_i$ to denote all independent variables for observation *i*, and h_i changes with each observation because the independent variables change across observations. For example, consider the simple savings function

$$sav_i = \beta_0 + \beta_1 inc_i + u_i$$ [8.22]

$$Var(u_i|inc_i) = \sigma^2 inc_i.$$ [8.23]

Here, $h(x) = h(inc) = inc$: the variance of the error is proportional to the level of income. This means that, as income increases, the variability in savings increases. (If $\beta_1 > 0$, the expected value of savings also increases with income.) Because inc is always positive, the variance in equation (8.23) is always guaranteed to be positive. The standard deviation of u_i, conditional on inc_i, is $\sigma\sqrt{inc_i}$.

How can we use the information in equation (8.21) to estimate the β_j? Essentially, we take the original equation,

$$y_i = \beta_0 + \beta_1 x_{i1} + \beta_2 x_{i2} + \ldots + \beta_k x_{ik} + u_i, \qquad [8.24]$$

which contains heteroskedastic errors, and transform it into an equation that has homoskedastic errors (and satisfies the other Gauss-Markov assumptions). Since h_i is just a function of $\mathbf{x}_i$, $u_i/\sqrt{h_i}$ has a zero expected value conditional on $\mathbf{x}_i$. Further, since $\text{Var}(u_i|\mathbf{x}_i) = \text{E}(u_i^2|\mathbf{x}_i) = \sigma^2 h_i$, the variance of $u_i/\sqrt{h_i}$ (conditional on $\mathbf{x}_i$) is σ^2:

$$\text{E}((u_i/\sqrt{h_i})^2) = \text{E}(u_i^2)/h_i = (\sigma^2 h_i)/h_i = \sigma^2,$$

where we have suppressed the conditioning on $\mathbf{x}_i$ for simplicity. We can divide equation (8.24) by $\sqrt{h_i}$ to get

$$\begin{aligned} y_i/\sqrt{h_i} = \beta_0/\sqrt{h_i} + \beta_1(x_{i1}/\sqrt{h_i}) + \beta_2(x_{i2}/\sqrt{h_i}) + \ldots \\ + \beta_k(x_{ik}/\sqrt{h_i}) + (u_i/\sqrt{h_i}) \end{aligned} \qquad [8.25]$$

or

$$y_i^* = \beta_0 x_{i0}^* + \beta_1 x_{i1}^* + \ldots + \beta_k x_{ik}^* + u_i^*, \qquad [8.26]$$

where $x_{i0}^* = 1/\sqrt{h_i}$ and the other starred variables denote the corresponding original variables divided by $\sqrt{h_i}$.

Equation (8.26) looks a little peculiar, but the important thing to remember is that we derived it so we could obtain estimators of the β_j that have better efficiency properties than OLS. The intercept β_0 in the original equation (8.24) is now multiplying the variable $x_{i0}^* = 1/\sqrt{h_i}$. Each slope parameter in β_j multiplies a new variable that rarely has a useful interpretation. This should not cause problems if we recall that, for interpreting the parameters and the model, we always want to return to the original equation (8.24).

In the preceding savings example, the transformed equation looks like

$$sav_i/\sqrt{inc_i} = \beta_0(1/\sqrt{inc_i}) + \beta_1\sqrt{inc_i} + u_i^*,$$

where we use the fact that $inc_i/\sqrt{inc_i} = \sqrt{inc_i}$. Nevertheless, β_1 is the marginal propensity to save out of income, an interpretation we obtain from equation (8.22).

Equation (8.26) is linear in its parameters (so it satisfies MLR.1), and the random sampling assumption has not changed. Further, u_i^* has a zero mean and a constant variance (σ^2), conditional on $\mathbf{x}_i^*$. This means that if the original equation satisfies the first four Gauss-Markov assumptions, then the transformed equation (8.26) satisfies all five Gauss-Markov assumptions. Also, if u_i has a normal distribution, then u_i^* has a normal distribution with variance σ^2. Therefore, the transformed equation satisfies the classical linear model assumptions (MLR.1 through MLR.6) if the original model does so except for the homoskedasticity assumption.

Since we know that OLS has appealing properties (is BLUE, for example) under the Gauss-Markov assumptions, the discussion in the previous paragraph suggests estimating the parameters in equation (8.26) by ordinary least squares. These estimators, $\beta_0^*, \beta_1^*, \ldots, \beta_k^*$, will be different from the OLS estimators in the original equation. The β_j^* are examples of **generalized least squares (GLS) estimators**. In this case, the GLS estimators are used to account for heteroskedasticity in the errors. We will encounter other GLS estimators in Chapter 12.

Because equation (8.26) satisfies all of the ideal assumptions, standard errors, t statistics, and F statistics can all be obtained from regressions using the transformed variables. The sum of squared residuals from (8.26) divided by the degrees of freedom is an unbiased estimator of σ^2. Further, the

GLS estimators, because they are the best linear unbiased estimators of the β_j, are necessarily more efficient than the OLS estimators $\hat{\beta}_j$ obtained from the untransformed equation. Essentially, after we have transformed the variables, we simply use standard OLS analysis. But we must remember to interpret the estimates in light of the original equation.

The GLS estimators for correcting heteroskedasticity are called **weighted least squares (WLS) estimators**. This name comes from the fact that the β_j^* minimize the *weighted* sum of squared residuals, where each squared residual is weighted by $1/h_i$. The idea is that less weight is given to observations with a higher error variance; OLS gives each observation the same weight because it is best when the error variance is identical for all partitions of the population. Mathematically, the WLS estimators are the values of the b_j that make

$$\sum_{i=1}^{n}(y_i - b_0 - b_1 x_{i1} - b_2 x_{i2} - \ldots - b_k x_{ik})^2/h_i \qquad [8.27]$$

as small as possible. Bringing the square root of $1/h_i$ inside the squared residual shows that the weighted sum of squared residuals is identical to the sum of squared residuals in the transformed variables:

$$\sum_{i=1}^{n}(y_i^* - b_0 x_{i0}^* - b_1 x_{i1}^* - b_2 x_{i2}^* - \ldots - b_k x_{ik}^*)^2.$$

Since OLS minimizes the sum of squared residuals (regardless of the definitions of the dependent variable and independent variable), it follows that the WLS estimators that minimize (8.27) are simply the OLS estimators from (8.26). Note carefully that the squared residuals in (8.27) are weighted by $1/h_i$, whereas the transformed variables in (8.26) are weighted by $1/\sqrt{h_i}$.

A weighted least squares estimator can be defined for any set of positive weights. OLS is the special case that gives equal weight to all observations. The efficient procedure, GLS, weights each squared residual by the *inverse* of the conditional variance of u_i given $\mathbf{x}_i$.

Obtaining the transformed variables in equation (8.25) in order to manually perform weighted least squares can be tedious, and the chance of making mistakes is nontrivial. Fortunately, most modern regression packages have a feature for computing weighted least squares. Typically, along with the dependent and independent variables in the original model, we just specify the weighting function, $1/h_i$, appearing in (8.27). That is, we specify weights proportional to the inverse of the variance. In addition to making mistakes less likely, this forces us to interpret weighted least squares estimates in the original model. In fact, we can write out the estimated equation in the usual way. The estimates and standard errors will be different from OLS, but the way we *interpret* those estimates, standard errors, and test statistics is the same.

Econometrics packages that have a built-in WLS option will report an R-squared (and adjusted R-squared) along with WLS estimates and standard errors. Typically, the WLS R-squared is obtained from the weighted SSR, obtained from minimizing equation (8.27), and a weighted total sum of squares (SST), obtained by using the same weights but setting all of the slope coefficients in equation (8.27), $b_1, b_2, \ldots, b_k$, to zero. As a goodness-of-fit measure, this R-squared is not especially useful, as it effectively measures explained variation in y_i^* rather than y_i. Nevertheless, the WLS R-squareds computed as just described are appropriate for computing F statistics for exclusion restrictions (provided we have properly specified the variance function). As in the case of OLS, the SST terms cancel, and so we obtain the F statistic based on the weighted SSR.

The R-squared from running the OLS regression in equation (8.26) is even less useful as a goodness-of-fit measure, as the computation of SST would make little sense: one would necessarily exclude an intercept from the regression, in which case regression packages typically compute the SST without properly centering the y_i^*. This is another reason for using a WLS option that is pre-programmed in a regression package because at least the reported R-squared properly compares the model with all of the independent variables to a model with only an intercept. Because the SST cancels out when testing exclusion restrictions, improperly computing SST does not affect the R-squared form of the F statistic. Nevertheless, computing such an R-squared tempts one to think the equation fits better than it does.

EXAMPLE 8.6 Financial Wealth Equation

We now estimate equations that explain net total financial wealth (*nettfa*, measured in $1,000s) in terms of income (*inc*, also measured in $1,000s) and some other variables, including age, gender, and an indicator for whether the person is eligible for a 401(k) pension plan. We use the data on single people (*fsize* = 1) in 401KSUBS. In Computer Exercise C12 in Chapter 6, it was found that a specific quadratic function in *age*, namely $(age - 25)^2$, fit the data just as well as an unrestricted quadratic. Plus, the restricted form gives a simplified interpretation because the minimum age in the sample is 25: *nettfa* is an increasing function of *age* after *age* = 25.

The results are reported in Table 8.1. Because we suspect heteroskedasticity, we report the heteroskedasticity-robust standard errors for OLS. The weighted least squares estimates, and their standard errors, are obtained under the assumption $\text{Var}(u|inc) = \sigma^2 inc$.

Without controlling for other factors, another dollar of income is estimated to increase *nettfa* by about 82¢ when OLS is used; the WLS estimate is smaller, about 79¢. The difference is not large; we certainly do not expect them to be identical. The WLS coefficient does have a smaller standard error than OLS, almost 40% smaller, provided we assume the model $\text{Var}(nettfa|inc) = \sigma^2 inc$ is correct.

Adding the other controls reduced the *inc* coefficient somewhat, with the OLS estimate still larger than the WLS estimate. Again, the WLS estimate of β_{inc} is more precise. Age has an increasing effect starting at *age* = 25, with the OLS estimate showing a larger effect. The WLS estimate of β_{age} is more precise in this case. Gender does not have a statistically significant effect on *nettfa*, but being eligible for a 401(k) plan does: the OLS estimate is that those eligible, holding fixed income, age, and gender, have net total financial assets about $6,890 higher. The WLS estimate is substantially below the OLS estimate and suggests a misspecification of the functional form in the mean equation. (One possibility is to interact *e401k* and *inc*; see Computer Exercise C11.)

Using WLS, the F statistic for joint significance of $(age - 25)^2$, *male*, and *e401k* is about 30.8 if we use the R-squareds reported in Table 8.1. With 3 and 2,012 degrees of freedom, the p-value is zero to more than 15 decimal places; of course, this is not surprising given the very large t statistics for the age and 401(k) variables.

EXPLORING FURTHER 8.3

Using the OLS residuals obtained from the OLS regression reported in column (1) of Table 8.1, the regression of $\hat{u}^2$ on *inc* yields a t statistic of 2.96. Does it appear we should worry about heteroskedasticity in the financial wealth equation?

TABLE 8.1 Dependent Variable: *nettfa*

Independent Variables	(1) OLS	(2) WLS	(3) OLS	(4) WLS
inc	.821 (.104)	.787 (.063)	.771 (.100)	.740 (.064)
$(age - 25)^2$	—	—	.0251 (.0043)	.0175 (.0019)
male	—	—	2.48 (2.06)	1.84 (1.56)
e401k	—	—	6.89 (2.29)	5.19 (1.70)
intercept	−10.57 (2.53)	−9.58 (1.65)	−20.98 (3.50)	−16.70 (1.96)
Observations	2,017	2,017	2,017	2,017
R-squared	.0827	.0709	.1279	.1115

Assuming that the error variance in the financial wealth equation has a variance proportional to income is essentially arbitrary. In fact, in most cases, our choice of weights in WLS has a degree of arbitrariness. However, there is one case where the weights needed for WLS arise naturally from an underlying econometric model. This happens when, instead of using individual-level data, we only have averages of data across some group or geographic region. For example, suppose we are interested in determining the relationship between the amount a worker contributes to his or her 401(k) pension plan as a function of the plan generosity. Let i denote a particular firm and let e denote an employee within the firm. A simple model is

$$contrib_{i,e} = \beta_0 + \beta_1 earns_{i,e} + \beta_2 age_{i,e} + \beta_3 mrate_i + u_{i,e}, \qquad [8.28]$$

where $contrib_{i,e}$ is the annual contribution by employee e who works for firm i, $earns_{i,e}$ is annual earnings for this person, and $age_{i,e}$ is the person's age. The variable $mrate_i$ is the amount the firm puts into an employee's account for every dollar the employee contributes.

If (8.28) satisfies the Gauss-Markov assumptions, then we could estimate it, given a sample on individuals across various employers. Suppose, however, that we only have *average* values of contributions, earnings, and age by employer. In other words, individual-level data are not available. Thus, let $\overline{contrib}_i$ denote average contribution for people at firm i, and similarly for $\overline{earns}_i$ and $\overline{age}_i$. Let m_i denote the number of employees at firm i; we assume that this is a known quantity. Then, if we average equation (8.28) across all employees at firm i, we obtain the firm-level equation

$$\overline{contrib}_i = \beta_0 + \beta_1 \overline{earns}_i + \beta_2 \overline{age}_i + \beta_3 mrate_i + \overline{u}_i, \qquad [8.29]$$

where $\overline{u}_i = m_i^{-1} \sum_{e=1}^{mi} u_{i,e}$ is the average error across all employees in firm i. If we have n firms in our sample, then (8.29) is just a standard multiple linear regression model that can be estimated by OLS. The estimators are unbiased if the original model (8.28) satisfies the Gauss-Markov assumptions and the individual errors $u_{i,e}$ are independent of the firm's size, m_i [because then the expected value of $\overline{u}_i$, given the explanatory variables in (8.29), is zero].

If the individual-level equation (8.28) satisfies the homoskedasticity assumption, and the errors within firm i are uncorrelated across employees, then we can show that the firm-level equation (8.29) has a particular kind of heteroskedasticity. Specifically, if $Var(u_{i,e}) = \sigma^2$ for all i and e, and $Cov(u_{i,e}, u_{i,g}) = 0$ for every pair of employees $e \neq g$ within firm i, then $Var(\overline{u}_i) = \sigma^2/m_i$; this is just the usual formula for the variance of an average of uncorrelated random variables with common variance. In other words, the variance of the error term $\overline{u}_i$ decreases with firm size. In this case, $h_i = 1/m_i$, and so the most efficient procedure is weighted least squares, with weights equal to the number of employees at the firm $(1/h_i = m_i)$. This ensures that larger firms receive more weight. This gives us an efficient way of estimating the parameters in the individual-level model when we only have averages at the firm level.

A similar weighting arises when we are using per capita data at the city, county, state, or country level. If the individual-level equation satisfies the Gauss-Markov assumptions, then the error in the per capita equation has a variance proportional to one over the size of the population. Therefore, weighted least squares with weights equal to the population is appropriate. For example, suppose we have city-level data on per capita beer consumption (in ounces), the percentage of people in the population over 21 years old, average adult education levels, average income levels, and the city price of beer. Then, the city-level model

$$beerpc = \beta_0 + \beta_1 perc21 + \beta_2 avgeduc + \beta_3 incpc + \beta_4 price + u$$

can be estimated by weighted least squares, with the weights being the city population.

The advantage of weighting by firm size, city population, and so on relies on the underlying individual equation being homoskedastic. If heteroskedasticity exists at the individual level, then the proper weighting depends on the form of heteroskedasticity. Further, if there is correlation across errors within a group (say, firm), then $Var(\overline{u}_i) \neq \sigma^2/m_i$; see Problem 7. Uncertainty about the form of $Var(\overline{u}_i)$ in equations such as (8.29) is why more and more researchers simply use OLS and compute robust standard errors and test statistics when estimating models using per capita data. An alternative is to weight by group size but to report the heteroskedasticity-robust statistics in the WLS estimation. This ensures that, while the estimation is efficient if the individual-level model satisfies the Gauss-Markov assumptions, heteroskedasticity at the individual level or within-group correlation are accounted for through robust inference.

8-4b The Heteroskedasticity Function Must Be Estimated: Feasible GLS

In the previous subsection, we saw some examples of where the heteroskedasticity is known up to a multiplicative form. In most cases, the exact form of heteroskedasticity is not obvious. In other words, it is difficult to find the function $h(\mathbf{x}_i)$ of the previous section. Nevertheless, in many cases we can model the function h and use the data to estimate the unknown parameters in this model. This results in an estimate of each h_i, denoted as $\hat{h}_i$. Using $\hat{h}_i$ instead of h_i in the GLS transformation yields an estimator called the **feasible GLS (FGLS) estimator**. Feasible GLS is sometimes called *estimated GLS*, or EGLS.

There are many ways to model heteroskedasticity, but we will study one particular, fairly flexible approach. Assume that

$$\text{Var}(u|\mathbf{x}) = \sigma^2\exp(\delta_0 + \delta_1 x_1 + \delta_2 x_2 + \ldots + \delta_k x_k), \qquad [8.30]$$

where $x_1, x_2, \ldots, x_k$ are the independent variables appearing in the regression model [see equation (8.1)], and the δ_j are unknown parameters. Other functions of the x_j can appear, but we will focus primarily on (8.30). In the notation of the previous subsection, $h(\mathbf{x}) = \exp(\delta_0 + \delta_1 x_1 + \delta_2 x_2 + \ldots + \delta_k x_k)$.

You may wonder why we have used the exponential function in (8.30). After all, when *testing* for heteroskedasticity using the Breusch-Pagan test, we assumed that heteroskedasticity was a linear function of the x_j. Linear alternatives such as (8.12) are fine when testing for heteroskedasticity, but they can be problematic when correcting for heteroskedasticity using weighted least squares. We have encountered the reason for this problem before: linear models do not ensure that predicted values are positive, and our estimated variances must be positive in order to perform WLS.

If the parameters δ_j were known, then we would just apply WLS, as in the previous subsection. This is not very realistic. It is better to use the data to estimate these parameters, and then to use these estimates to construct weights. How can we estimate the δ_j? Essentially, we will transform this equation into a linear form that, with slight modification, can be estimated by OLS.

Under assumption (8.30), we can write

$$u^2 = \sigma^2\exp(\delta_0 + \delta_1 x_1 + \delta_2 x_2 + \ldots + \delta_k x_k)v,$$

where v has a mean equal to unity, conditional on $\mathbf{x} = (x_1, x_2, \ldots, x_k)$. If we assume that v is actually independent of $\mathbf{x}$, we can write

$$\log(u^2) = \alpha_0 + \delta_1 x_1 + \delta_2 x_2 + \ldots + \delta_k x_k + e, \qquad [8.31]$$

where e has a zero mean and is independent of $\mathbf{x}$; the intercept in this equation is different from δ_0, but this is not important in implementing WLS. The dependent variable is the log of the squared error. Since (8.31) satisfies the Gauss-Markov assumptions, we can get unbiased estimators of the δ_j by using OLS.

As usual, we must replace the unobserved u with the OLS residuals. Therefore, we run the regression of

$$\log(\hat{u}^2) \text{ on } x_1, x_2, \ldots, x_k. \qquad [8.32]$$

Actually, what we need from this regression are the fitted values; call these $\hat{g}_i$. Then, the estimates of h_i are simply

$$\hat{h}_i = \exp(\hat{g}_i). \qquad [8.33]$$

We now use WLS with weights $1/\hat{h}_i$ in place of $1/h_i$ in equation (8.27). We summarize the steps.

A Feasible GLS Procedure to Correct for Heteroskedasticity:

1. Run the regression of y on $x_1, x_2, \ldots, x_k$ and obtain the residuals, $\hat{u}$.
2. Create $\log(\hat{u}^2)$ by first squaring the OLS residuals and then taking the natural log.
3. Run the regression in equation (8.32) and obtain the fitted values, $\hat{g}$.
4. Exponentiate the fitted values from (8.32): $\hat{h} = \exp(\hat{g})$.
5. Estimate the equation

$$y = \beta_0 + \beta_1 x_1 + \ldots + \beta_k x_k + u$$

by WLS, using weights $1/\hat{h}$. In other words, we replace h_i with $\hat{h}_i$ in equation (8.27). Remember, the *squared* residual for observation i gets weighted by $1/\hat{h}_i$. If instead we first transform all variables and run OLS, each variable gets multiplied by $1/\sqrt{\hat{h}_i}$, including the intercept.

If we could use h_i rather than $\hat{h}_i$ in the WLS procedure, we know that our estimators would be unbiased; in fact, they would be the best linear unbiased estimators, assuming that we have properly modeled the heteroskedasticity. Having to estimate h_i using the same data means that the FGLS estimator is no longer unbiased (so it cannot be BLUE, either). Nevertheless, the FGLS estimator is consistent and *asymptotically* more efficient than OLS. This is difficult to show because of estimation of the variance parameters. But if we ignore this—as it turns out we may—the proof is similar to showing that OLS is efficient in the class of estimators in Theorem 5.3. At any rate, for large sample sizes, FGLS is an attractive alternative to OLS when there is evidence of heteroskedasticity that inflates the standard errors of the OLS estimates.

We must remember that the FGLS estimators are estimators of the parameters in the usual population model

$$y = \beta_0 + \beta_1 x_1 + \ldots + \beta_k x_k + u.$$

Just as the OLS estimates measure the marginal impact of each x_j on y, so do the FGLS estimates. We use the FGLS estimates in place of the OLS estimates because the FGLS estimators are more efficient and have associated test statistics with the usual t and F distributions, at least in large samples. If we have some doubt about the variance specified in equation (8.30), we can use heteroskedasticity-robust standard errors and test statistics in the transformed equation.

Another useful alternative for estimating h_i is to replace the independent variables in regression (8.32) with the OLS fitted values and their squares. In other words, obtain the $\hat{g}_i$ as the fitted values from the regression of

$$\log(\hat{u}^2) \text{ on } \hat{y}, \hat{y}^2 \qquad\qquad [8.34]$$

and then obtain the $\hat{h}_i$ exactly as in equation (8.33). This changes only step (3) in the previous procedure.

If we use regression (8.32) to estimate the variance function, you may be wondering if we can simply test for heteroskedasticity using this same regression (an F or LM test can be used). In fact, Park (1966) suggested this. Unfortunately, when compared with the tests discussed in Section 8-3, the Park test has some problems. First, the null hypothesis must be something stronger than homoskedasticity: effectively, u and $\mathbf{x}$ must be independent. This is not required in the Breusch-Pagan or White tests. Second, using the OLS residuals $\hat{u}$ in place of u in (8.32) can cause the F statistic to deviate from the F distribution, even in large sample sizes. This is not an issue in the other tests we have covered. For these reasons, the Park test is not recommended when testing for heteroskedasticity. Regression (8.32) works well for weighted least squares because we only need consistent estimators of the δ_j, and regression (8.32) certainly delivers those.

| EXAMPLE 8.7 | **Demand for Cigarettes** |

We use the data in SMOKE to estimate a demand function for daily cigarette consumption. Since most people do not smoke, the dependent variable, *cigs*, is zero for most observations. A linear model is not ideal because it can result in negative predicted values. Nevertheless, we can still learn something about the determinants of cigarette smoking by using a linear model.

The equation estimated by ordinary least squares, with the usual OLS standard errors in parentheses, is

$$\widehat{cigs} = -3.64 + .880 \log(income) - .751 \log(cigpric)$$
$$\phantom{\widehat{cigs} = } (24.08) \quad (.728) \quad\quad\quad (5.773)$$
$$\phantom{\widehat{cigs} = } - .501\, educ + .771\, age - .0090\, age^2 - 2.83\, restaurn \quad\quad [8.35]$$
$$\phantom{\widehat{cigs} = } (.167) \quad\quad (.160) \quad\quad (.0017) \quad\quad (1.11)$$
$$\phantom{\widehat{cigs} = } n = 807, R^2 = .0526,$$

where

$$cigs = \text{number of cigarettes smoked per day.}$$
$$income = \text{annual income.}$$
$$cigpric = \text{the per-pack price of cigarettes (in cents).}$$
$$educ = \text{years of schooling.}$$
$$age = \text{age measured in years.}$$
$$restaurn = \text{a binary indicator equal to unity if the person resides in a state with restaurant}$$
$$ \text{smoking restrictions.}$$

Since we are also going to do weighted least squares, we do not report the heteroskedasticity-robust standard errors for OLS. (Incidentally, 13 out of the 807 fitted values are less than zero; this is less than 2% of the sample and is not a major cause for concern.)

Neither income nor cigarette price is statistically significant in (8.35), and their effects are not practically large. For example, if income increases by 10%, *cigs* is predicted to increase by $(.880/100)(10) = .088$, or less than one-tenth of a cigarette per day. The magnitude of the price effect is similar.

Each year of education reduces the average cigarettes smoked per day by one-half of a cigarette, and the effect is statistically significant. Cigarette smoking is also related to age, in a quadratic fashion. Smoking increases with age up until $age = .771/[2(.009)] \approx 42.83$, and then smoking decreases with age. Both terms in the quadratic are statistically significant. The presence of a restriction on smoking in restaurants decreases cigarette smoking by almost three cigarettes per day, on average.

Do the errors underlying equation (8.35) contain heteroskedasticity? The Breusch-Pagan regression of the squared OLS residuals on the independent variables in (8.35) [see equation (8.14)] produces $R_{\hat{u}^2}^2 = .040$. This small R-squared may seem to indicate no heteroskedasticity, but we must remember to compute either the F or LM statistic. If the sample size is large, a seemingly small $R_{\hat{u}^2}^2$ can result in a very strong rejection of homoskedasticity. The LM statistic is $LM = 807(.040) = 32.28$, and this is the outcome of a χ_6^2 random variable. The p-value is less than .000015, which is very strong evidence of heteroskedasticity.

Therefore, we estimate the equation using the feasible GLS procedure based on equation (8.32). The weighted least squares estimates are

$$\widehat{cigs} = 5.64 + 1.30 \log(income) - 2.94 \log(cigpric)$$
$$\phantom{\widehat{cigs} = } (17.80) \quad (.44) \quad\quad\quad (4.46)$$
$$\phantom{\widehat{cigs} = } - .463\, educ + .482\, age - .0056\, age^2 - 3.46\, restaurn \quad\quad [8.36]$$
$$\phantom{\widehat{cigs} = } (.120) \quad\quad (.097) \quad\quad (.0009) \quad\quad (.80)$$
$$\phantom{\widehat{cigs} = } n = 807, R^2 = .1134.$$

The income effect is now statistically significant and larger in magnitude. The price effect is also notably bigger, but it is still statistically insignificant. [One reason for this is that *cigpric* varies only across states in the sample, and so there is much less variation in log(*cigpric*) than in log(*income*), *educ*, and *age*.]

The estimates on the other variables have, naturally, changed somewhat, but the basic story is still the same. Cigarette smoking is negatively related to schooling, has a quadratic relationship with *age*, and is negatively affected by restaurant smoking restrictions.

We must be a little careful in computing F statistics for testing multiple hypotheses after estimation by WLS. (This is true whether the sum of squared residuals or R-squared form of the F statistic is used.) It is important that the same weights be used to estimate the unrestricted and restricted models. We should first estimate the unrestricted model by OLS. Once we have obtained the weights, we can use them to estimate the restricted model as well. The F statistic can be computed as usual. Fortunately, many regression packages have a simple command for testing joint restrictions after WLS estimation, so we need not perform the restricted regression ourselves.

Example 8.7 hints at an issue that sometimes arises in applications of weighted least squares: the OLS and WLS estimates can be substantially different. This is not such a big problem in the demand for cigarettes equation because all the coefficients maintain the same signs, and the biggest changes are on variables that were statistically insignificant when the equation was estimated by OLS. The OLS and WLS estimates will always differ due to sampling error. The issue is whether their difference is enough to change important conclusions.

If OLS and WLS produce statistically significant estimates that differ in sign—for example, the OLS price elasticity is positive and significant, while the WLS price elasticity is negative and significant— or the difference in magnitudes of the estimates is practically large, we should be suspicious. Typically, this indicates that one of the *other* Gauss-Markov assumptions is false, particularly the zero conditional mean assumption on the error (MLR.4). If $E(y|\mathbf{x}) \neq \beta_0 + \beta_1 x_1 + \dots + \beta_k x_k$, then OLS and WLS have different expected values and probability limits. For WLS to be consistent for the β_j, it is not enough for u to be uncorrelated with each x_j; we need the stronger assumption MLR.4 in the linear model MLR.1. Therefore, a significant difference between OLS and WLS can indicate a functional form misspecification in $E(y|\mathbf{x})$. The *Hausman test* [Hausman (1978)] can be used to formally compare the OLS and WLS estimates to see if they differ by more than sampling error suggests they should, but this test is beyond the scope of this text. In many cases, an informal "eyeballing" of the estimates is sufficient to detect a problem.

> ### EXPLORING FURTHER 8.4
>
> Let $\hat{u}_i$ be the WLS residuals from (8.36), which are not weighted, and let $\widehat{cigs}_i$ be the fitted values. (These are obtained using the same formulas as OLS; they differ because of different estimates of the β_j.) One way to determine whether heteroskedasticity has been eliminated is to use the $\hat{u}_i^2/\hat{h}_i = (\hat{u}_i/\sqrt{\hat{h}_i})^2$ in a test for heteroskedasticity. [If $h_i = \text{Var}(u_i|\mathbf{x}_i)$, then the transformed residuals should have little evidence of heteroskedasticity.] There are many possibilities, but one—based on White's test in the transformed equation—is to regress $\hat{u}_i^2/\hat{h}_i$ on $\widehat{cigs}_i/\sqrt{\hat{h}_i}$ and $\widehat{cigs}_i^2/\hat{h}_i$ (including an intercept). The joint F statistic when we use SMOKE is 11.15. Does it appear that our correction for heteroskedasticity has actually eliminated the heteroskedasticity?

8-4c What If the Assumed Heteroskedasticity Function Is Wrong?

We just noted that if OLS and WLS produce very different estimates, it is likely that the conditional mean $E(y|\mathbf{x})$ is misspecified. What are the properties of WLS if the variance function we use is misspecified in the sense that $\text{Var}(y|\mathbf{x}) \neq \sigma^2 h(\mathbf{x})$ for our chosen function $h(\mathbf{x})$? The most important issue is whether misspecification of $h(\mathbf{x})$ causes bias or inconsistency in the WLS estimator. Fortunately, the answer is no, at least under MLR.4. Recall that, if $\mathrm{E}(u|\mathbf{x}) = 0$, then any function of $\mathbf{x}$ is uncorrelated with u, and so the weighted error, $u/\sqrt{h(\mathbf{x})}$, is uncorrelated with the weighted regressors, $x_j/\sqrt{h(\mathbf{x})}$, for *any* function $h(\mathbf{x})$ that is always positive. This is why, as we just discussed, we can take large differences between the OLS and WLS estimators as indicative of functional form misspecification. If we estimate parameters in the function, say $h(\mathbf{x}, \hat{\boldsymbol{\delta}})$, then we can no longer claim that WLS is unbiased, but it will generally be consistent (whether or not the variance function is correctly specified).

If WLS is at least consistent under MLR.1 to MLR.4, what are the consequences of using WLS with a misspecified variance function? There are two. The first, which is very important, is that the usual WLS standard errors and test statistics, computed under the assumption that $\mathrm{Var}(y|\mathbf{x}) = \sigma^2 h(\mathbf{x})$, are no longer valid, even in large samples. For example, the WLS estimates and standard errors in column (4) of Table 8.1 assume that $\mathrm{Var}(nettfa|inc, age, male, e401k) = \mathrm{Var}(nettfa|inc) = \sigma^2 inc$; so we are assuming not only that the variance depends just on income, but also that it is a linear function of income. If this assumption is false, the standard errors (and any statistics we obtain using those standard errors) are not valid. Fortunately, there is an easy fix: just as we can obtain standard errors for the OLS estimates that are robust to arbitrary heteroskedasticity, we can obtain standard errors for WLS that allow the variance function to be arbitrarily misspecified. It is easy to see why this works. Write the transformed equation as

$$y_i/\sqrt{h_i} = \beta_0(1/\sqrt{h_i}) + \beta_1(x_{i1}/\sqrt{h_i}) + \ldots + \beta_k(x_{ik}/\sqrt{h_i}) + u_i/\sqrt{h_i}.$$

Now, if $\mathrm{Var}(u_i|\mathbf{x}_i) \neq \sigma^2 h_i$, then the weighted error $u_i/\sqrt{h_i}$ is heteroskedastic. So we can just apply the usual heteroskedasticity-robust standard errors after estimating this equation by OLS—which, remember, is identical to WLS.

To see how robust inference with WLS works in practice, column (1) of Table 8.2 reproduces the last column of Table 8.1, and column (2) contains standard errors robust to $\mathrm{Var}(u_i|\mathbf{x}_i) \neq \sigma^2 inc_i$.

The standard errors in column (2) allow the variance function to be misspecified. We see that, for the income and age variables, the robust standard errors are somewhat above the usual WLS standard errors—certainly by enough to stretch the confidence intervals. On the other hand, the robust standard errors for *male* and *e401k* are actually smaller than those that assume a correct variance function. We saw this could happen with the heteroskedasticity-robust standard errors for OLS, too.

Even if we use flexible forms of variance functions, such as that in (8.30), there is no guarantee that we have the correct model. While exponential heteroskedasticity is appealing and reasonably flexible, it is, after all, just a model. Therefore, it is always a good idea to compute fully robust standard errors and test statistics after WLS estimation.

TABLE 8.2 WLS Estimation of the *nettfa* Equation		
Independent Variables	With Nonrobust Standard Errors	With Robust Standard Errors
inc	.740 (.064)	.740 (.075)
$(age - 25)^2$	.0175 (.0019)	.0175 (.0026)
male	1.84 (1.56)	1.84 (1.31)
e401k	5.19 (1.70)	5.19 (1.57)
intercept	−16.70 (1.96)	−16.70 (2.24)
Observations	2,017	2,017
R-squared	.1115	.1115

A modern criticism of WLS is that if the variance function is misspecified, it is not guaranteed to be more efficient than OLS. In fact, that is the case: if $\text{Var}(y|\mathbf{x})$ is neither constant nor equal to $\sigma^2 h(\mathbf{x})$, where $h(\mathbf{x})$ is the proposed model of heteroskedasticity, then we cannot rank OLS and WLS in terms of variances (or asymptotic variances when the variance parameters must be estimated). However, this theoretically correct criticism misses an important practical point. Namely, in cases of strong heteroskedasticity, it is often better to use a wrong form of heteroskedasticity and apply WLS than to ignore heteroskedasticity altogether in estimation and use OLS. Models such as (8.30) can well approximate a variety of heteroskedasticity functions and may produce estimators with smaller (asymptotic) variances. Even in Example 8.6, where the form of heteroskedasticity was assumed to have the simple form $\text{Var}(nettfa|\mathbf{x}) = \sigma^2 inc$, the fully robust standard errors for WLS are well below the fully robust standard errors for OLS. (Comparing robust standard errors for the two estimators puts them on equal footing: we assume neither homoskedasticity nor that the variance has the form $\sigma^2 inc$.) For example, the robust standard error for the WLS estimator of β_{inc} is about .075, which is 25% lower than the robust standard error for OLS (about .100). For the coefficient on $(age - 25)^2$, the robust standard error of WLS is about .0026, almost 40% below the robust standard error for OLS (about .0043).

8-4d Prediction and Prediction Intervals with Heteroskedasticity

If we start with the standard linear model under MLR.1 to MLR.4, but allow for heteroskedasticity of the form $\text{Var}(y|\mathbf{x}) = \sigma^2 h(\mathbf{x})$ [see equation (8.21)], the presence of heteroskedasticity affects the point prediction of y only insofar as it affects estimation of the β_j. Of course, it is natural to use WLS on a sample of size n to obtain the $\hat{\beta}_j$. Our prediction of an unobserved outcome, y^0, given known values of the explanatory variables $\mathbf{x}^0$, has the same form as in Section 6-4: $\hat{y}^0 = \hat{\beta}_0 + \mathbf{x}^0\hat{\boldsymbol{\beta}}$. This makes sense: once we know $E(y|\mathbf{x})$, we base our prediction on it; the structure of $\text{Var}(y|\mathbf{x})$ plays no direct role.

On the other hand, prediction *intervals* do depend directly on the nature of $\text{Var}(y|\mathbf{x})$. Recall in Section 6-4 that we constructed a prediction interval under the classical linear model assumptions. Suppose now that all the CLM assumptions hold except that (8.21) replaces the homoskedasticity assumption, MLR.5. We know that the WLS estimators are BLUE and, because of normality, have (conditional) normal distributions. We can obtain $\text{se}(\hat{y}^0)$ using the same method in Section 6-4, except that now we use WLS. [A simple approach is to write $y_i = \theta_0 + \beta_1(x_{i1} - x_1^0) + \ldots + \beta_k(x_{ik} - x_k^0) + u_i$, where the x_j^0 are the values of the explanatory variables for which we want a predicted value of y. We can estimate this equation by WLS and then obtain $\hat{y}^0 = \hat{\theta}_0$ and $\text{se}(\hat{y}^0) = \text{se}(\hat{\theta}_0)$.] We also need to estimate the standard deviation of u^0, the unobserved part of y^0. But $\text{Var}(u^0|\mathbf{x} = \mathbf{x}^0) = \sigma^2 h(\mathbf{x}^0)$, and so $\text{se}(u^0) = \hat{\sigma}\sqrt{h(\mathbf{x}^0)}$, where $\hat{\sigma}$ is the standard error of the regression from the WLS estimation. Therefore, a 95% prediction interval is

$$\hat{y}^0 \pm t_{.025} \cdot \text{se}(\hat{e}^0), \qquad [8.37]$$

where $\text{se}(\hat{e}^0) = \{[\text{se}(\hat{y}^0)]^2 + \hat{\sigma}^2 h(\mathbf{x}^0)\}^{1/2}$.

This interval is exact only if we do not have to estimate the variance function. If we estimate parameters, as in model (8.30), then we cannot obtain an exact interval. In fact, accounting for the estimation error in the $\hat{\beta}_j$ and the $\hat{\delta}_j$ (the variance parameters) becomes very difficult. We saw two examples in Section 6-4 where the estimation error in the parameters was swamped by the variation in the unobservables, u^0. Therefore, we might still use equation (8.37) with $h(\mathbf{x}^0)$ simply replaced by $\hat{h}(\mathbf{x}^0)$. In fact, if we are to ignore the parameter estimation error entirely, we can drop $\text{se}(\hat{y}^0)$ from $\text{se}(\hat{e}^0)$. [Remember, $\text{se}(\hat{y}^0)$ converges to zero at the rate $1/\sqrt{n}$, while $\text{se}(\hat{u}^0)$ is roughly constant.]

We can also obtain a prediction for y in the model

$$\log(y) = \beta_0 + \beta_1 x_1 + \ldots + \beta_k x_k + u, \qquad [8.38]$$

where u is heteroskedastic. We assume that u has a conditional normal distribution with a specific form of heteroskedasticity. We assume the exponential form in equation (8.30), but add the normality assumption:

$$u|x_1, x_2, \ldots, x_k \sim \text{Normal}[0, \exp(\delta_0 + \delta_1 x_1 + \ldots + \delta_k x_k)]. \qquad [8.39]$$

As a notational shorthand, write the variance function as $\exp(\delta_0 + \mathbf{x}\boldsymbol{\delta})$. Then, because $\log(y)$ given $\mathbf{x}$ has a normal distribution with mean $\beta_0 + \mathbf{x}\boldsymbol{\beta}$ and variance $\exp(\delta_0 + \mathbf{x}\boldsymbol{\delta})$, it follows that

$$\text{E}(y|\mathbf{x}) = \exp(\beta_0 + \mathbf{x}\boldsymbol{\beta} + \exp(\delta_0 + \mathbf{x}\boldsymbol{\delta})/2). \qquad [8.40]$$

Now, we estimate the β_j and δ_j using WLS estimation of (8.38). That is, after using OLS to obtain the residuals, run the regression in (8.32) to obtain fitted values,

$$\hat{g}_i = \hat{\alpha}_0 + \hat{\delta}_1 x_{i1} + \ldots + \hat{\delta}_k x_{ik}, \qquad [8.41]$$

and then compute the $\hat{h}_i$ as in (8.33). Using these $\hat{h}_i$, obtain the WLS estimates, $\hat{\beta}_j$, and also compute $\hat{\sigma}^2$ from the weighted squared residuals. Now, compared with the original model for $\text{Var}(u|\mathbf{x})$, $\delta_0 = \alpha_0 + \log(\sigma^2)$, and so $\text{Var}(u|\mathbf{x}) = \sigma^2 \exp(\alpha_0 + \delta_1 x_1 + \ldots + \delta_k x_k)$. Therefore, the estimated variance is $\hat{\sigma}^2 \exp(\hat{g}_i) = \hat{\sigma}^2 \hat{h}_i$, and the fitted value for y_i is

$$\hat{y}_i = \exp(\widehat{\log y_i} + \hat{\sigma}^2 \hat{h}_i/2). \qquad [8.42]$$

We can use these fitted values to obtain an R-squared measure, as described in Section 6-4: use the squared correlation coefficient between y_i and $\hat{y}_i$.

For any values of the explanatory variables $\mathbf{x}^0$, we can estimate $\text{E}(y|\mathbf{x} = \mathbf{x}^0)$ as

$$\hat{\text{E}}(y|\mathbf{x} = \mathbf{x}^0) = \exp(\hat{\beta}_0 + \mathbf{x}^0\hat{\boldsymbol{\beta}} + \hat{\sigma}^2 \exp(\hat{\alpha}_0 + \mathbf{x}^0\hat{\boldsymbol{\delta}})/2), \qquad [8.43]$$

where

$\hat{\beta}_j$ = the WLS estimates.
$\hat{\alpha}_0$ = the intercept in (8.41).
$\hat{\delta}_j$ = the slopes from the same regression.
$\hat{\sigma}^2$ is obtained from the WLS estimation.

Obtaining a proper standard error for the prediction in (8.42) is very complicated analytically, but, as in Section 6-4, it would be fairly easy to obtain a standard error using a resampling method such as the bootstrap described in Appendix 6A.

Obtaining a prediction interval is more of a challenge when we estimate a model for heteroskedasticity, and a full treatment is complicated. Nevertheless, we saw in Section 6-4 two examples where the error variance swamps the estimation error, and we would make only a small mistake by ignoring the estimation error in all parameters. Using arguments similar to those in Section 6-4, an approximate 95% prediction interval (for large sample sizes) is $\exp[-1.96 \cdot \hat{\sigma}\sqrt{\hat{h}(\mathbf{x}^0)}] \exp(\hat{\beta}_0 + \mathbf{x}^0\hat{\boldsymbol{\beta}})$ to $\exp[1.96 \cdot \hat{\sigma}\sqrt{\hat{h}(\mathbf{x}^0)}] \exp(\hat{\beta}_0 + \mathbf{x}^0\hat{\boldsymbol{\beta}})$, where $\hat{h}(\mathbf{x}^0)$ is the estimated variance function evaluated at $\mathbf{x}^0$, $\hat{h}(\mathbf{x}^0) = \exp(\hat{\alpha}_0 + \hat{\delta}_1 x_1^0 + \ldots + \hat{\delta}_k x_k^0)$. As in Section 6-4, we obtain this approximate interval by simply exponentiating the endpoints.

8-5 The Linear Probability Model Revisited

As we saw in Section 7-5, when the dependent variable y is a binary variable, the model must contain heteroskedasticity, unless all of the slope parameters are zero. We are now in a position to deal with this problem.

The simplest way to deal with heteroskedasticity in the linear probability model is to continue to use OLS estimation, but to also compute robust standard errors in test statistics. This ignores the fact that we actually know the form of heteroskedasticity for the LPM. Nevertheless, OLS estimation of the LPM is simple and often produces satisfactory results.

EXAMPLE 8.8	**Labor Force Participation of Married Women**

In the labor force participation example in Section 7-5 [see equation (7.29)], we reported the usual OLS standard errors. Now, we compute the heteroskedasticity-robust standard errors as well. These are reported in brackets below the usual standard errors:

$$\widehat{inlf} = .586 - .0034 \, nwifeinc + .038 \, educ + .039 \, exper$$
$$\phantom{\widehat{inlf} =}(.154) \ (.0014) \qquad\quad (.007) \qquad\quad (.006)$$
$$\phantom{\widehat{inlf} =}[.151] \ [.0015] \qquad\quad [.007] \qquad\quad [.006]$$
$$\phantom{\widehat{inlf} =}- .00060 \, exper^2 - .016 \, age - .262 \, kidslt6 + .0130 \, kidsge6 \qquad [8.44]$$
$$\phantom{\widehat{inlf} =}(.00018) \qquad (.002) \qquad (.034) \qquad\quad (.0132)$$
$$\phantom{\widehat{inlf} =}[.00019] \qquad [.002] \qquad [.032] \qquad\quad [.0135]$$
$$n = 753, R^2 = .264.$$

Several of the robust and OLS standard errors are the same to the reported degree of precision; in all cases, the differences are practically very small. Therefore, while heteroskedasticity is a problem in theory, it is not in practice, at least not for this example. It often turns out that the usual OLS standard errors and test statistics are similar to their heteroskedasticity-robust counterparts. Furthermore, it requires a minimal effort to compute both.

Generally, the OLS estimators are inefficient in the LPM. Recall that the conditional variance of y in the LPM is

$$\text{Var}(y|\mathbf{x}) = p(\mathbf{x})[1 - p(\mathbf{x})], \qquad\qquad [8.45]$$

where

$$p(\mathbf{x}) = \beta_0 + \beta_1 x_1 + \dots + \beta_k x_k \qquad\qquad [8.46]$$

is the response probability (probability of success, $y = 1$). It seems natural to use weighted least squares, but there are a couple of hitches. The probability $p(\mathbf{x})$ clearly depends on the unknown population parameters, β_j. Nevertheless, we do have unbiased estimators of these parameters, namely the OLS estimators. When the OLS estimators are plugged into equation (8.46), we obtain the OLS fitted values. Thus, for each observation i, $\text{Var}(y_i|\mathbf{x}_i)$ is estimated by

$$\hat{h}_i = \hat{y}_i(1 - \hat{y}_i), \qquad\qquad [8.47]$$

where $\hat{y}_i$ is the OLS fitted value for observation i. Now, we apply feasible GLS, just as in Section 8-4.

Unfortunately, being able to estimate h_i for each i does not mean that we can proceed directly with WLS estimation. The problem is one that we briefly discussed in Section 7-5: the fitted values $\hat{y}_i$ need not fall in the unit interval. If either $\hat{y}_i < 0$ or $\hat{y}_i > 1$, equation (8.47) shows that $\hat{h}_i$ will be negative. Since WLS proceeds by multiplying observation i by $1/\sqrt{\hat{h}_i}$, the method will fail if $\hat{h}_i$ is negative (or zero) for any observation. In other words, all of the weights for WLS must be positive.

In some cases, $0 < \hat{y}_i < 1$ for all i, in which case WLS can be used to estimate the LPM. In cases with many observations and small probabilities of success or failure, it is very common to find some fitted values outside the unit interval. If this happens, as it does in the labor force participation example in equation (8.44), it is easiest to abandon WLS and to report the heteroskedasticity-robust statistics. An alternative is to adjust those fitted values that are less than zero or greater than unity, and then to apply WLS. One suggestion is to set $\hat{y}_i = .01$ if $\hat{y}_i < 0$ and $\hat{y}_i = .99$ if $\hat{y}_i > 1$. Unfortunately, this requires an arbitrary choice on the part of the researcher—for example, why not use .001 and .999 as the adjusted values? If many fitted values are outside the unit interval, the adjustment to the fitted values can affect the results; in this situation, it is probably best to just use OLS.

Estimating the Linear Probability Model by Weighted Least Squares:

1. Estimate the model by OLS and obtain the fitted values, $\hat{y}$.

2. Determine whether all of the fitted values are inside the unit interval. If so, proceed to step (3). If not, some adjustment is needed to bring all fitted values into the unit interval.

3. Construct the estimated variances in equation (8.47).

4. Estimate the equation

$$y = \beta_0 + \beta_1 x_1 + \dots + \beta_k x_k + u$$

by WLS, using weights $1/\hat{h}$.

EXAMPLE 8.9 **Determinants of Personal Computer Ownership**

We use the data in GPA1 to estimate the probability of owning a computer. Let PC denote a binary indicator equal to unity if the student owns a computer, and zero otherwise. The variable $hsGPA$ is high school GPA, ACT is achievement test score, and $parcoll$ is a binary indicator equal to unity if at least one parent attended college. (Separate college indicators for the mother and the father do not yield individually significant results, as these are pretty highly correlated.)

The equation estimated by OLS is

$$\widehat{PC} = -.0004 + .065\ hsGPA + .0006\ ACT + .221\ parcoll$$
$$\phantom{\widehat{PC} = }(.4905)\ \ (.137)(.0155)(.093)$$
$$\phantom{\widehat{PC} = }[.4888]\ \ [.139][.0158][.087]$$
$$n = 141,\ R^2 = .0415.$$

[8.48]

Just as with Example 8.8, there are no striking differences between the usual and robust standard errors. Nevertheless, we also estimate the model by WLS. Because all of the OLS fitted values are inside the unit interval, no adjustments are needed:

$$\widehat{PC} = .026 + .033\ hsGPA + .0043\ ACT + .215\ parcoll$$
$$\phantom{\widehat{PC} = }(.477)\ \ (.130)(.0155)(.086)$$
$$n = 142,\ R^2 = .0464.$$

[8.49]

There are no important differences in the OLS and WLS estimates. The only significant explanatory variable is *parcoll*, and in both cases we estimate that the probability of PC ownership is about .22 higher if at least one parent attended college.

Summary

We began by reviewing the properties of ordinary least squares in the presence of heteroskedasticity. Heteroskedasticity does not cause bias or inconsistency in the OLS estimators, but the usual standard errors and test statistics are no longer valid. We showed how to compute heteroskedasticity-robust standard errors and t statistics, something that is routinely done by many regression packages. Most regression packages also compute a heteroskedasticity-robust F-type statistic.

We discussed two common ways to test for heteroskedasticity: the Breusch-Pagan test and a special case of the White test. Both of these statistics involve regressing the *squared* OLS residuals on either the independent variables (BP) or the fitted and squared fitted values (White). A simple F test is asymptotically valid; there are also Lagrange multiplier versions of the tests.

OLS is no longer the best linear unbiased estimator in the presence of heteroskedasticity. When the form of heteroskedasticity is known, GLS estimation can be used. This leads to weighted least squares as a means of obtaining the BLUE estimator. The test statistics from the WLS estimation are either exactly valid when the error term is normally distributed or asymptotically valid under nonnormality. This assumes, of course, that we have the proper model of heteroskedasticity.

More commonly, we must estimate a model for the heteroskedasticity before applying WLS. The resulting *feasible* GLS estimator is no longer unbiased, but it is consistent and asymptotically efficient. The usual statistics from the WLS regression are asymptotically valid. We discussed a method to ensure that the estimated variances are strictly positive for all observations, something needed to apply WLS.

As we discussed in Chapter 7, the linear probability model for a binary dependent variable necessarily has a heteroskedastic error term. A simple way to deal with this problem is to compute heteroskedasticity-robust statistics. Alternatively, if all the fitted values (that is, the estimated probabilities) are strictly between zero and one, weighted least squares can be used to obtain asymptotically efficient estimators.

Key Terms

Breusch-Pagan Test for Heteroskedasticity (BP Test)	Heteroskedasticity of Unknown Form	Heteroskedasticity-Robust t Statistic
Feasible GLS (FGLS) Estimator	Heteroskedasticity-Robust F Statistic	Weighted Least Squares (WLS) Estimators
Generalized Least Squares (GLS) Estimators	Heteroskedasticity-Robust LM Statistic	White Test for Heteroskedasticity
	Heteroskedasticity-Robust Standard Error	

Problems

1 Which of the following are consequences of heteroskedasticity?
(i)   The OLS estimators, $\hat{\beta}_j$, are inconsistent.
(ii)   The usual F statistic no longer has an F distribution.
(iii) The OLS estimators are no longer BLUE.

2 Consider a linear model to explain monthly beer consumption:

$$beer = \beta_0 + \beta_1 inc + \beta_2 price + \beta_3 educ + \beta_4 female + u$$

$$\text{E}(u|inc, price, educ, female) = 0$$
$$\text{Var}(u|inc, price, educ, female) = \sigma^2 inc^2.$$

Write the transformed equation that has a homoskedastic error term.

3 True or False: WLS is preferred to OLS when an important variable has been omitted from the model.

4 Using the data in GPA3, the following equation was estimated for the fall and second semester students:

$$\widehat{trmgpa} = -2.12 + .900\ crsgpa + .193\ cumgpa + .0014\ tothrs$$
$$\qquad\quad (.55)\ (.175) \qquad\quad (.064) \qquad\qquad (.0012)$$
$$\qquad\quad [.55]\ [.166] \qquad\quad [.074] \qquad\qquad [.0012]$$
$$\qquad + .0018\ sat - .0039\ hsperc + .351\ female - .157\ season$$
$$\qquad\quad (.0002) \qquad (.0018) \qquad\quad (.085) \qquad\qquad (.098)$$
$$\qquad\quad [.0002] \qquad [.0019] \qquad\quad [.079] \qquad\qquad [.080]$$
$$n = 269,\ R^2 = .465.$$

Here, *trmgpa* is term GPA, *crsgpa* is a weighted average of overall GPA in courses taken, *cumgpa* is GPA prior to the current semester, *tothrs* is total credit hours prior to the semester, *sat* is SAT score, *hsperc* is graduating percentile in high school class, *female* is a gender dummy, and *season* is a dummy variable equal to unity if the student's sport is in season during the fall. The usual and heteroskedasticity-robust standard errors are reported in parentheses and brackets, respectively.

(i)   Do the variables *crsgpa*, *cumgpa*, and *tothrs* have the expected estimated effects? Which of these variables are statistically significant at the 5% level? Does it matter which standard errors are used?

(ii)   Why does the hypothesis $H_0: \beta_{crsgpa} = 1$ make sense? Test this hypothesis against the two-sided alternative at the 5% level, using both standard errors. Describe your conclusions.

(iii)   Test whether there is an in-season effect on term GPA, using both standard errors. Does the significance level at which the null can be rejected depend on the standard error used?

5   The variable *smokes* is a binary variable equal to one if a person smokes, and zero otherwise. Using the data in SMOKE, we estimate a linear probability model for *smokes*:

$$\widehat{smokes} = .656 - .069 \log(cigpric) + .012 \log(income) - .029 \; educ$$
$$\qquad (.855) \; (.204) \qquad\qquad (.026) \qquad\qquad (.006)$$
$$\qquad [.856] \; [.207] \qquad\qquad [.026] \qquad\qquad [.006]$$
$$\qquad + .020 \; age - .00026 \; age^2 - .101 \; restaurn - .026 \; white$$
$$\qquad\quad (.006) \qquad (.00006) \qquad (.039) \qquad\quad (.052)$$
$$\qquad\quad [.005] \qquad\; [.00006] \qquad [.038] \qquad\quad [.050]$$
$$n = 807, R^2 = .062.$$

The variable *white* equals one if the respondent is white, and zero otherwise; the other independent variables are defined in Example 8.7. Both the usual and heteroskedasticity-robust standard errors are reported.

(i)   Are there any important differences between the two sets of standard errors?

(ii)   Holding other factors fixed, if education increases by four years, what happens to the estimated probability of smoking?

(iii)   At what point does another year of age reduce the probability of smoking?

(iv)   Interpret the coefficient on the binary variable *restaurn* (a dummy variable equal to one if the person lives in a state with restaurant smoking restrictions).

(v)   Person number 206 in the data set has the following characteristics: *cigpric* = 67.44, *income* = 6,500, *educ* = 16, *age* = 77, *restaurn* = 0, *white* = 0, and *smokes* = 0. Compute the predicted probability of smoking for this person and comment on the result.

6   There are different ways to combine features of the Breusch-Pagan and White tests for heteroskedasticity. One possibility not covered in the text is to run the regression

$$\hat{u}_i^2 \text{ on } x_{i1}, x_{i2}, \dots, x_{ik}, \hat{y}_i^2, \; i = 1, \dots, n,$$

where the $\hat{u}_i$ are the OLS residuals and the $\hat{y}_i$ are the OLS fitted values. Then, we would test joint significance of $x_{i1}, x_{i2}, \dots, x_{ik}$ and $\hat{y}_i^2$. (Of course, we always include an intercept in this regression.)

(i)   What are the *df* associated with the proposed F test for heteroskedasticity?

(ii)   Explain why the R-squared from the regression above will always be at least as large as the R-squareds for the BP regression and the special case of the White test.

(iii)   Does part (ii) imply that the new test always delivers a smaller p-value than either the BP or special case of the White statistic? Explain.

(iv)   Suppose someone suggests also adding $\hat{y}_i$ to the newly proposed test. What do you think of this idea?

7   Consider a model at the employee level,

$$y_{i,e} = \beta_0 + \beta_1 x_{i,e,1} + \beta_2 x_{i,e,2} + \dots + \beta_k x_{i,e,k} + f_i + v_{i,e},$$

where the unobserved variable f_i is a "firm effect" to each employee at a given firm i. The error term $v_{i,e}$ is specific to employee e at firm i. The *composite error* is $u_{i,e} = f_i + v_{i,e}$, such as in equation (8.28).

(i)   Assume that $\text{Var}(f_i) = \sigma_f^2$, $\text{Var}(v_{i,e}) = \sigma_v^2$, and f_i and $v_{i,e}$ are uncorrelated. Show that $\text{Var}(u_{i,e}) = \sigma_f^2 + \sigma_v^2$; call this σ^2.

(ii) Now suppose that for $e \neq g$, $v_{i,e}$ and $v_{i,g}$ are uncorrelated. Show that $\text{Cov}(u_{i,e}, u_{i,g}) = \sigma_f^2$.

(iii) Let $\bar{u}_i = m_i^{-1}\sum_{e=1}^{mi} u_{i,e}$ be the average of the composite errors within a firm. Show that $\text{Var}(\bar{u}_i) = \sigma_f^2 + \sigma_v^2/m_i$.

(iv) Discuss the relevance of part (iii) for WLS estimation using data averaged at the firm level, where the weight used for observation i is the usual firm size.

8 The following equations were estimated using the data in ECONMATH. The first equation is for men and the second is for women. The third and fourth equations combine men and women.

$$\widehat{score} = 20.52 + 13.60\,colgpa + 0.670\,act$$
$$(3.72) \quad (0.94) \qquad\qquad (0.150)$$
$$n = 406.\ R^2 = .4025,\ \text{SSR} = 38{,}781.38.$$

$$\widehat{score} = 13.79 + 11.89\,colgpa + 1.03\,act$$
$$(4.11) \quad (1.09) \qquad\qquad (0.18)$$
$$n = 408,\ R^2 = .3666,\ \text{SSR} = 48{,}029.82.$$

$$\widehat{score} = 15.60 + 3.17\,male + 12.82\,colgpa + 0.838\,act$$
$$(2.80) \quad (0.73) \qquad\quad (0.72) \qquad\qquad (0.116)$$
$$n = 814,\ R^2 = .3946,\ \text{SSR} = 87{,}128.96.$$

$$\widehat{score} = 13.79 + 6.73\,male + 11.89\,colgpa + 1.03\,act + 1.72\,male \cdot colgpa - 0.364\,male \cdot act$$
$$(3.91) \quad (5.55) \qquad\quad (1.04) \qquad\qquad (0.17) \qquad (1.44) \qquad\qquad\qquad (0.232)$$
$$n = 814,\ R^2 = .3968,\ \text{SSR} = 86{,}811.20.$$

(i)   Compute the usual Chow statistic for testing the null hypothesis that the regression equations are the same for men and women. Find the p-value of the test.

(ii) Compute the usual Chow statistic for testing the null hypothesis that the slope coefficients are the same for men and women, and report the p-value.

(iii) Do you have enough information to compute heteroskedasticity-robust versions of the tests in (ii) and (iii)? Explain.

Computer Exercises

C1 Consider the following model to explain sleeping behavior:

$$sleep = \beta_0 + \beta_1 totwrk + \beta_2 educ + \beta_3 age + \beta_4 age^2 + \beta_5 yngkid + \beta_6 male + u.$$

(i)   Write down a model that allows the variance of u to differ between men and women. The variance should not depend on other factors.

(ii) Use the data in SLEEP75 to estimate the parameters of the model for heteroskedasticity. (You have to estimate the *sleep* equation by OLS, first, to obtain the OLS residuals.) Is the estimated variance of u higher for men or for women?

(iii) Is the variance of u statistically different for men and for women?

C2 (i)   Use the data in HPRICE1 to obtain the heteroskedasticity-robust standard errors for equation (8.17). Discuss any important differences with the usual standard errors.

(ii) Repeat part (i) for equation (8.18).

(iii) What does this example suggest about heteroskedasticity and the transformation used for the dependent variable?

C3 Apply the full White test for heteroskedasticity [see equation (8.19)] to equation (8.18). Using the chi-square form of the statistic, obtain the *p*-value. What do you conclude?

C4 Use VOTE1 for this exercise.

(i) Estimate a model with *voteA* as the dependent variable and *prtystrA*, *democA*, log(*expendA*), and log(*expendB*) as independent variables. Obtain the OLS residuals, $\hat{u}_i$, and regress these on all of the independent variables. Explain why you obtain $R^2 = 0$.

(ii) Now, compute the Breusch-Pagan test for heteroskedasticity. Use the *F* statistic version and report the *p*-value.

(iii) Compute the special case of the White test for heteroskedasticity, again using the *F* statistic form. How strong is the evidence for heteroskedasticity now?

C5 Use the data in PNTSPRD for this exercise.

(i) The variable *sprdcvr* is a binary variable equal to one if the Las Vegas point spread for a college basketball game was covered. The expected value of *sprdcvr*, say μ, is the probability that the spread is covered in a randomly selected game. Test H_0: $\mu = .5$ against H_1: $\mu \neq .5$ at the 10% significance level and discuss your findings. (*Hint:* This is easily done using a *t* test by regressing *sprdcvr* on an intercept only.)

(ii) How many games in the sample of 553 were played on a neutral court?

(iii) Estimate the linear probability model

$$sprdcvr = \beta_0 + \beta_1 favhome + \beta_2 neutral + \beta_3 fav25 + \beta_4 und25 + u$$

and report the results in the usual form. (Report the usual OLS standard errors and the heteroskedasticity-robust standard errors.) Which variable is most significant, both practically and statistically?

(iv) Explain why, under the null hypothesis H_0: $\beta_1 = \beta_2 = \beta_3 = \beta_4 = 0$, there is no heteroskedasticity in the model.

(v) Use the usual *F* statistic to test the hypothesis in part (iv). What do you conclude?

(vi) Given the previous analysis, would you say that it is possible to systematically predict whether the Las Vegas spread will be covered using information available prior to the game?

C6 In Example 7.12, we estimated a linear probability model for whether a young man was arrested during 1986:

$$arr86 = \beta_0 + \beta_1 pcnv + \beta_2 avgsen + \beta_3 tottime + \beta_4 ptime86 + \beta_5 qemp86 + u.$$

(i) Using the data in CRIME1, estimate this model by OLS and verify that all fitted values are strictly between zero and one. What are the smallest and largest fitted values?

(ii) Estimate the equation by weighted least squares, as discussed in Section 8-5.

(iii) Use the WLS estimates to determine whether *avgsen* and *tottime* are jointly significant at the 5% level.

C7 Use the data in LOANAPP for this exercise.

(i) Estimate the equation in part (iii) of Computer Exercise C8 in Chapter 7, computing the heteroskedasticity-robust standard errors. Compare the 95% confidence interval on β_{white} with the nonrobust confidence interval.

(ii) Obtain the fitted values from the regression in part (i). Are any of them less than zero? Are any of them greater than one? What does this mean about applying weighted least squares?

C8 Use the data set GPA1 for this exercise.

(i) Use OLS to estimate a model relating *colGPA* to *hsGPA*, *ACT*, *skipped*, and *PC*. Obtain the OLS residuals.

(ii) Compute the special case of the White test for heteroskedasticity. In the regression of $\hat{u}_i^2$ on $\widehat{colGPA}_i$, $\widehat{colGPA}_i^2$, obtain the fitted values, say $\hat{h}_i$.

(iii) Verify that the fitted values from part (ii) are all strictly positive. Then, obtain the weighted least squares estimates using weights $1/\hat{h}_i$. Compare the weighted least squares estimates for the effect of skipping lectures and the effect of PC ownership with the corresponding OLS estimates. What about their statistical significance?

(iv) In the WLS estimation from part (iii), obtain heteroskedasticity-robust standard errors. In other words, allow for the fact that the variance function estimated in part (ii) might be misspecified. (See Question 8.4.) Do the standard errors change much from part (iii)?

C9 In Example 8.7, we computed the OLS and a set of WLS estimates in a cigarette demand equation.

(i) Obtain the OLS estimates in equation (8.35).

(ii) Obtain the $\hat{h}_i$ used in the WLS estimation of equation (8.36) and reproduce equation (8.36). From this equation, obtain the *unweighted* residuals and fitted values; call these $\hat{u}_i$ and $\hat{y}_i$, respectively. (For example, in Stata, the unweighted residuals and fitted values are given by default.)

(iii) Let $\breve{u}_i = \hat{u}_i/\sqrt{\hat{h}_i}$ and $\breve{y}_i = \hat{y}_i/\sqrt{\hat{h}_i}$ be the weighted quantities. Carry out the special case of the White test for heteroskedasticity by regressing $\breve{u}_i^2$ on $\breve{y}_i$, $\breve{y}_i^2$, being sure to include an intercept, as always. Do you find heteroskedasticity in the weighted residuals?

(iv) What does the finding from part (iii) imply about the proposed form of heteroskedasticity used in obtaining (8.36)?

(v) Obtain valid standard errors for the WLS estimates that allow the variance function to be misspecified.

C10 Use the data set 401KSUBS for this exercise.

(i) Using OLS, estimate a linear probability model for *e401k*, using as explanatory variables *inc*, inc^2, *age*, age^2, and *male*. Obtain both the usual OLS standard errors and the heteroskedasticity-robust versions. Are there any important differences?

(ii) In the special case of the White test for heteroskedasticity, where we regress the squared OLS residuals on a quadratic in the OLS fitted values, $\hat{u}_i^2$ on $\hat{y}_i$, $\hat{y}_i^2$, $i = 1, \ldots, n$, argue that the probability limit of the coefficient on $\hat{y}_i$ should be one, the probability limit of the coefficient on $\hat{y}_i^2$ should be -1, and the probability limit of the intercept should be zero. {*Hint:* Remember that $\text{Var}(y|x_1, \ldots, x_k) = p(\mathbf{x})[1 - p(\mathbf{x})]$, where $p(\mathbf{x}) = \beta_0 + \beta_1 x_1 + \ldots + \beta_k x_k$.}

(iii) For the model estimated from part (i), obtain the White test and see if the coefficient estimates roughly correspond to the theoretical values described in part (ii).

(iv) After verifying that the fitted values from part (i) are all between zero and one, obtain the weighted least squares estimates of the linear probability model. Do they differ in important ways from the OLS estimates?

C11 Use the data in 401KSUBS for this question, restricting the sample to *fsize* = 1.

(i) To the model estimated in Table 8.1, add the interaction term, $e401k \cdot inc$. Estimate the equation by OLS and obtain the usual and robust standard errors. What do you conclude about the statistical significance of the interaction term?

(ii) Now estimate the more general model by WLS using the same weights, $1/inc_i$, as in Table 8.1. Compute the usual and robust standard error for the WLS estimator. Is the interaction term statistically significant using the robust standard error?

(iii) Discuss the WLS coefficient on *e401k* in the more general model. Is it of much interest by itself? Explain.

(iv) Reestimate the model by WLS but use the interaction term $e401k \cdot (inc - 30)$; the average income in the sample is about 29.44. Now interpret the coefficient on *e401k*.

C12 Use the data in MEAP00 to answer this question.

(i) Estimate the model

$$math4 = \beta_0 + \beta_1 lunch + \beta_2 \log(enroll) + \beta_3 \log(exppp) + u$$

by OLS and obtain the usual standard errors and the fully robust standard errors. How do they generally compare?

(ii) Apply the special case of the White test for heteroskedasticity. What is the value of the F test? What do you conclude?

(iii) Obtain $\hat{g}_i$ as the fitted values from the regression $\log(\hat{u}_i^2)$ on $\widehat{math4}_i$, $\widehat{math4}_i^2$, where $\widehat{math4}_i$ are the OLS fitted values and the $\hat{u}_i$ are the OLS residuals. Let $\hat{h}_i = \exp(\hat{g}_i)$. Use the $\hat{h}_i$ to obtain WLS estimates. Are there big differences with the OLS coefficients?

(iv) Obtain the standard errors for WLS that allow misspecification of the variance function. Do these differ much from the usual WLS standard errors?

(v) For estimating the effect of spending on *math4*, does OLS or WLS appear to be more precise?

C13 Use the data in FERTIL2 to answer this question.

(i) Estimate the model

$$children = \beta_0 + \beta_1 age + \beta_2 age^2 + \beta_3 educ + \beta_4 electric + \beta_5 urban + u$$

and report the usual and heteroskedasticity-robust standard errors. Are the robust standard errors always bigger than the nonrobust ones?

(ii) Add the three religious dummy variables and test whether they are jointly significant. What are the p-values for the nonrobust and robust tests?

(iii) From the regression in part (ii), obtain the fitted values $\hat{y}$ and the residuals, $\hat{u}$. Regress $\hat{u}^2$ on $\hat{y}$, $\hat{y}_2$ and test the joint significance of the two regressors. Conclude that heteroskedasticity is present in the equation for *children*.

(iv) Would you say the heteroskedasticity you found in part (iii) is practically important?

C14 Use the data in BEAUTY for this question.

(i) Using the data pooled for men and women, estimate the equation

$$lwage = \beta_0 + \beta_1 belavg + \beta_2 abvavg + \beta_3 female + \beta_4 educ + \beta_5 exper + \beta_5 exper^2 + u,$$

and report the results using heteroskedasticity-robust standard errors below coefficients. Are any of the coefficients surprising in either their signs or magnitudes? Is the coefficient on *female* practically large and statistically significant?

(ii) Add interactions of *female* with all other explanatory variables in the equation from part (i) (five interactions in all). Compute the usual F test of joint significance of the five interactions and a heteroskedasticity-robust version. Does using the heteroskedasticity-robust version change the outcome in any important way?

(iii) In the full model with interactions, determine whether those involving the looks variables— *female* • *belavg* and *female* • *abvavg*—are jointly significant. Are their coefficients practically small?

CHAPTER 9

More on Specification and Data Issues

In Chapter 8, we dealt with one failure of the Gauss-Markov assumptions. While heteroskedasticity in the errors can be viewed as a problem with a model, it is a relatively minor one. The presence of heteroskedasticity does not cause bias or inconsistency in the OLS estimators. Also, it is fairly easy to adjust confidence intervals and t and F statistics to obtain valid inference after OLS estimation, or even to get more efficient estimators by using weighted least squares.

In this chapter, we return to the much more serious problem of correlation between the error, u, and one or more of the explanatory variables. Remember from Chapter 3 that if u is, for whatever reason, correlated with the explanatory variable x_j, then we say that x_j is an **endogenous explanatory variable**. We also provide a more detailed discussion on three reasons why an explanatory variable can be endogenous; in some cases, we discuss possible remedies.

We have already seen in Chapters 3 and 5 that omitting a key variable can cause correlation between the error and some of the explanatory variables, which generally leads to bias and inconsistency in *all* of the OLS estimators. In the special case that the omitted variable is a function of an explanatory variable in the model, the model suffers from **functional form misspecification**.

We begin in the first section by discussing the consequences of functional form misspecification and how to test for it. In Section 9-2, we show how the use of proxy variables can solve, or at least mitigate, omitted variables bias. In Section 9-3, we derive and explain the bias in OLS that can arise under certain forms of **measurement error**. Additional data problems are discussed in Section 9-4.

All of the procedures in this chapter are based on OLS estimation. As we will see, certain problems that cause correlation between the error and some explanatory variables cannot be solved by using OLS on a single cross section. We postpone a treatment of alternative estimation methods until Part 3.

9-1 Functional Form Misspecification

A multiple regression model suffers from functional form misspecification when it does not properly account for the relationship between the dependent and the observed explanatory variables. For example, if hourly wage is determined by $\log(wage) = \beta_0 + \beta_1 educ + \beta_2 exper + \beta_3 exper^2 + u$, but we omit the squared experience term, $exper^2$, then we are committing a functional form misspecification. We already know from Chapter 3 that this generally leads to biased estimators of β_0, β_1, and β_2. (We do not estimate β_3 because $exper^2$ is excluded from the model.) Thus, misspecifying how $exper$ affects $\log(wage)$ generally results in a biased estimator of the return to education, β_1. The amount of this bias depends on the size of β_3 and the correlation among $educ$, $exper$, and $exper^2$.

Things are worse for estimating the return to experience: even if we could get an unbiased estimator of β_2, we would not be able to estimate the return to experience because it equals $\beta_2 + 2\beta_3 exper$ (in decimal form). Just using the biased estimator of β_2 can be misleading, especially at extreme values of $exper$.

As another example, suppose the $\log(wage)$ equation is

$$
\begin{aligned}
\log(wage) = \beta_0 + \beta_1 educ + \beta_2 exper + \beta_3 exper^2 \\
+ \beta_4 female + \beta_5 female \cdot educ + u,
\end{aligned}
\tag{9.1}
$$

where $female$ is a binary variable. If we omit the interaction term, $female \cdot educ$, then we are misspecifying the functional form. In general, we will not get unbiased estimators of any of the other parameters, and since the return to education depends on gender, it is not clear what return we would be estimating by omitting the interaction term.

Omitting functions of independent variables is not the only way that a model can suffer from misspecified functional form. For example, if (9.1) is the true model satisfying the first four Gauss-Markov assumptions, but we use $wage$ rather than $\log(wage)$ as the dependent variable, then we will not obtain unbiased or consistent estimators of the partial effects. The tests that follow have some ability to detect this kind of functional form problem, but there are better tests that we will mention in the subsection on testing against nonnested alternatives.

Misspecifying the functional form of a model can certainly have serious consequences. Nevertheless, in one important respect, the problem is minor: by definition, we have data on all the necessary variables for obtaining a functional relationship that fits the data well. This can be contrasted with the problem addressed in the next section, where a key variable is omitted on which we cannot collect data.

We already have a very powerful tool for detecting misspecified functional form: the F test for joint exclusion restrictions. It often makes sense to add quadratic terms of any significant variables to a model and to perform a joint test of significance. If the additional quadratics are significant, they can be added to the model (at the cost of complicating the interpretation of the model). However, significant quadratic terms can be symptomatic of other functional form problems, such as using the level of a variable when the logarithm is more appropriate, or vice versa. It can be difficult to pinpoint the precise reason that a functional form is misspecified. Fortunately, in many cases, using logarithms of certain variables and adding quadratics are sufficient for detecting many important nonlinear relationships in economics.

EXAMPLE 9.1   **Economic Model of Crime**

Table 9.1 contains OLS estimates of the economic model of crime (see Example 8.3). We first estimate the model without any quadratic terms; those results are in column (1).

In column (2), the squares of $pcnv$, $ptime86$, and $inc86$ are added; we chose to include the squares of these variables because each level term is significant in column (1). The variable $qemp86$ is a discrete variable taking on only five values, so we do not include its square in column (2).

TABLE 9.1 Dependent Variable: *narr86*		
Independent Variables	(1)	(2)
pcnv	−.133	.533
	(.040)	(.154)
pcnv^2	—	−.730
		(.156)
avgsen	−.011	−.017
	(.012)	(.012)
tottime	.012	.012
	(.009)	(.009)
ptime86	−.041	.287
	(.009)	(.004)
ptime86^2	—	−.0296
		(.0039)
qemp86	−.051	−.014
	(.014)	(.017)
inc86	−.0015	−.0034
	(.0003)	(.0008)
inc86^2	—	−.000007
		(.000003)
black	.327	.292
	(.045)	(.045)
hispan	.194	.164
	(.040)	(.039)
intercept	.596	.505
	(.036)	(.037)
Observations	2,725	2,725
R-squared	.0723	.1035

Each of the squared terms is significant, and together they are jointly very significant ($F = 31.37$, with $df = 3$ and 2,713; the p-value is essentially zero). Thus, it appears that the initial model overlooked some potentially important nonlinearities.

> **EXPLORING FURTHER 9.1**
>
> Why do we not include the squares of *black* and *hispan* in column (2) of Table 9.1?
> Would it make sense to add interactions of *black* and *hispan* with some of the other variables reported in the table?

The presence of the quadratics makes interpreting the model somewhat difficult. For example, *pcnv* no longer has a strict deterrent effect: the relationship between *narr86* and *pcnv* is positive up until *pcnv* = .365, and then the relationship is negative. We might conclude that there is little or no deterrent effect at lower values of *pcnv*; the effect only kicks in at higher prior conviction rates. We would have to use more sophisticated functional forms than the quadratic to verify this conclusion. It may be that *pcnv* is not entirely exogenous. For example, men who have not been convicted in the past (so that *pcnv* = 0) are perhaps casual criminals, and so they are less likely to be arrested in 1986. This could be biasing the estimates.

Similarly, the relationship between *narr86* and *ptime86* is positive up until *ptime86* = 4.85 (almost five months in prison), and then the relationship is negative. The vast majority of men in the sample spent no time in prison in 1986, so again we must be careful in interpreting the results.

Legal income has a negative effect on *narr86* until *inc86* = 242.85; since income is measured in hundreds of dollars, this means an annual income of $24,285. Only 46 of the men in the sample have incomes above this level. Thus, we can conclude that *narr86* and *inc86* are negatively related with a diminishing effect.

Example 9.1 is a tricky functional form problem due to the nature of the dependent variable. Other models are theoretically better suited for handling dependent variables taking on a small number of integer values. We will briefly cover these models in Chapter 17.

9-1a RESET as a General Test for Functional Form Misspecification

Some tests have been proposed to detect general functional form misspecification. Ramsey's (1969) **regression specification error test (RESET)** has proven to be useful in this regard.

The idea behind RESET is fairly simple. If the original model

$$y = \beta_0 + \beta_1 x_1 + \ldots + \beta_k x_k + u \quad\quad [9.2]$$

satisfies MLR.4, then no nonlinear functions of the independent variables should be significant when added to equation (9.2). In Example 9.1, we added quadratics in the significant explanatory variables. Although this often detects functional form problems, it has the drawback of using up many degrees of freedom if there are many explanatory variables in the original model (much as the straight form of the White test for heteroskedasticity consumes degrees of freedom). Further, certain kinds of neglected nonlinearities will not be picked up by adding quadratic terms. RESET adds polynomials in the OLS fitted values to equation (9.2) to detect general kinds of functional form misspecification.

To implement RESET, we must decide how many functions of the fitted values to include in an expanded regression. There is no right answer to this question, but the squared and cubed terms have proven to be useful in most applications.

Let $\hat{y}$ denote the OLS fitted values from estimating (9.2). Consider the expanded equation

$$y = \beta_0 + \beta_1 x_1 + \ldots + \beta_k x_k + \delta_1 \hat{y}^2 + \delta_2 \hat{y}^3 + error. \quad\quad [9.3]$$

This equation seems a little odd, because functions of the fitted values from the initial estimation now appear as explanatory variables. In fact, we will not be interested in the estimated parameters from (9.3); we only use this equation to test whether (9.2) has missed important nonlinearities. The thing to remember is that $\hat{y}^2$ and $\hat{y}^3$ are just nonlinear functions of the x_j.

The null hypothesis is that (9.2) is correctly specified. Thus, RESET is the F statistic for testing H_0: $\delta_1 = 0, \delta_2 = 0$ in the expanded model (9.3). A significant F statistic suggests some sort of functional form problem. The distribution of the F statistic is approximately $F_{2,n-k-3}$ in large samples under the null hypothesis (and the Gauss-Markov assumptions). The *df* in the expanded equation (9.3) is $n - k - 1 - 2 = n - k - 3$. An *LM* version is also available (and the chi-square distribution will have two *df*). Further, the test can be made robust to heteroskedasticity using the methods discussed in Section 8-2.

| EXAMPLE 9.2 | **Housing Price Equation** |

We estimate two models for housing prices. The first one has all variables in level form:

$$price = \beta_0 + \beta_1 lotsize + \beta_2 sqrft + \beta_3 bdrms + u. \quad\quad [9.4]$$

The second one uses the logarithms of all variables except *bdrms*:

$$lprice = \beta_0 + \beta_1 llotsize + \beta_2 lsqrft + \beta_3 bdrms + u. \quad\quad [9.5]$$

Using $n = 88$ houses in HPRICE1, the RESET statistic for equation (9.4) turns out to be 4.67; this is the value of an $F_{2,82}$ random variable ($n = 88, k = 3$), and the associated p-value is .012. This is evidence of functional form misspecification in (9.4).

The RESET statistic in (9.5) is 2.56, with p-value $= .084$. Thus, we do not reject (9.5) at the 5% significance level (although we would at the 10% level). On the basis of RESET, the log-log model in (9.5) is preferred.

In the previous example, we tried two models for explaining housing prices. One was rejected by RESET, while the other was not (at least at the 5% level). Often, things are not so simple. A drawback with RESET is that it provides no real direction on how to proceed if the model is rejected. Rejecting (9.4) by using RESET does not immediately suggest that (9.5) is the next step. Equation (9.5) was estimated because constant elasticity models are easy to interpret and can have nice statistical properties. In this example, it so happens that it passes the functional form test as well.

Some have argued that RESET is a very general test for model misspecification, including unobserved omitted variables and heteroskedasticity. Unfortunately, such use of RESET is largely misguided. It can be shown that RESET has no power for detecting omitted variables whenever they have expectations that are linear in the included independent variables in the model [see Wooldridge (2001, Section 2-1) for a precise statement]. Further, if the functional form is properly specified, RESET has no power for detecting heteroskedasticity. The bottom line is that RESET is a functional form test, and nothing more.

9-1b Tests against Nonnested Alternatives

Obtaining tests for other kinds of functional form misspecification—for example, trying to decide whether an independent variable should appear in level or logarithmic form—takes us outside the realm of classical hypothesis testing. It is possible to test the model

$$y = \beta_0 + \beta_1 x_1 + \beta_2 x_2 + u \qquad [9.6]$$

against the model

$$y = \beta_0 + \beta_1 \log(x_1) + \beta_2 \log(x_2) + u, \qquad [9.7]$$

and vice versa. However, these are **nonnested models** (see Chapter 6), and so we cannot simply use a standard F test. Two different approaches have been suggested. The first is to construct a comprehensive model that contains each model as a special case and then to test the restrictions that led to each of the models. In the current example, the comprehensive model is

$$y = \gamma_0 + \gamma_1 x_1 + \gamma_2 x_2 + \gamma_3 \log(x_1) + \gamma_4 \log(x_2) + u. \qquad [9.8]$$

We can first test $H_0: \gamma_3 = 0, \gamma_4 = 0$ as a test of (9.6). We can also test $H_0: \gamma_1 = 0, \gamma_2 = 0$ as a test of (9.7). This approach was suggested by Mizon and Richard (1986).

Another approach has been suggested by Davidson and MacKinnon (1981). They point out that if model (9.6) holds with $E(u|x_1, x_2) = 0$, the fitted values from the other model, (9.7), should be insignificant when added to equation (9.6). Therefore, to test whether (9.6) is the correct model, we first estimate model (9.7) by OLS to obtain the fitted values; call these $\check{y}$. The **Davidson-MacKinnon test** is obtained from the t statistic on $\check{y}$ in the auxiliary equation

$$y = \beta_0 + \beta_1 x_1 + \beta_2 x_2 + \theta_1 \check{y} + error.$$

Because the $\check{y}$ are just nonlinear functions of x_1 and x_2, they should be insignificant if (9.6) is the correct conditional mean model. Therefore, a significant t statistic (against a two-sided alternative) is a rejection of (9.6).

Similarly, if $\hat{y}$ denotes the fitted values from estimating (9.6), the test of (9.7) is the t statistic on $\hat{y}$ in the model

$$y = \beta_0 + \beta_1 \log(x_1) + \beta_2 \log(x_2) + \theta_1 \hat{y} + error;$$

a significant t statistic is evidence against (9.7). The same two tests can be used for testing any two nonnested models with the same dependent variable.

There are a few problems with nonnested testing. First, a clear winner need not emerge. Both models could be rejected or neither model could be rejected. In the latter case, we can use the adjusted R-squared to choose between them. If both models are rejected, more work needs to be done. However, it is important to know the practical consequences from using one form or the other: if the effects of key independent variables on y are not very different, then it does not really matter which model is used.

A second problem is that rejecting (9.6) using, say, the Davidson-MacKinnon test does not mean that (9.7) is the correct model. Model (9.6) can be rejected for a variety of functional form misspecifications.

An even more difficult problem is obtaining nonnested tests when the competing models have different dependent variables. The leading case is y versus $\log(y)$. We saw in Chapter 6 that just obtaining goodness-of-fit measures that can be compared requires some care. Tests have been proposed to solve this problem, but they are beyond the scope of this text. [See Wooldridge (1994a) for a test that has a simple interpretation and is easy to implement.]

9-2 Using Proxy Variables for Unobserved Explanatory Variables

A more difficult problem arises when a model excludes a key variable, usually because of data unavailability. Consider a wage equation that explicitly recognizes that ability (*abil*) affects $\log(wage)$:

$$\log(wage) = \beta_0 + \beta_1 educ + \beta_2 exper + \beta_3 abil + u. \qquad [9.9]$$

This model shows explicitly that we want to hold ability fixed when measuring the return to *educ* and *exper*. If, say, *educ* is correlated with *abil*, then putting *abil* in the error term causes the OLS estimator of β_1 (and β_2) to be biased, a theme that has appeared repeatedly.

Our primary interest in equation (9.9) is in the slope parameters β_1 and β_2. We do not really care whether we get an unbiased or consistent estimator of the intercept β_0; as we will see shortly, this is not usually possible. Also, we can never hope to estimate β_3 because *abil* is not observed; in fact, we would not know how to interpret β_3 anyway, since ability is at best a vague concept.

How can we solve, or at least mitigate, the omitted variables bias in an equation like (9.9)? One possibility is to obtain a **proxy variable** for the omitted variable. Loosely speaking, a proxy variable is something that is related to the unobserved variable that we would like to control for in our analysis. In the wage equation, one possibility is to use the intelligence quotient, or IQ, as a proxy for ability. This *does not* require IQ to be the same thing as ability; what we need is for IQ to be correlated with ability, something we clarify in the following discussion.

All of the key ideas can be illustrated in a model with three independent variables, two of which are observed:

$$y = \beta_0 + \beta_1 x_1 + \beta_2 x_2 + \beta_3 x_3^* + u. \qquad [9.10]$$

We assume that data are available on y, x_1, and x_2—in the wage example, these are $\log(wage)$, $educ$, and $exper$, respectively. The explanatory variable x_3^* is unobserved, but we have a proxy variable for x_3^*. Call the proxy variable x_3.

What do we require of x_3? At a minimum, it should have some relationship to x_3^*. This is captured by the simple regression equation

$$x_3^* = \delta_0 + \delta_3 x_3 + v_3, \qquad \qquad \text{[9.11]}$$

where v_3 is an error due to the fact that x_3^* and x_3 are not exactly related. The parameter δ_3 measures the relationship between x_3^* and x_3; typically, we think of x_3^* and x_3 as being positively related, so that $\delta_3 > 0$. If $\delta_3 = 0$, then x_3 is not a suitable proxy for x_3^*. The intercept δ_0 in (9.11), which can be positive or negative, simply allows x_3^* and x_3 to be measured on different scales. (For example, unobserved ability is certainly not required to have the same average value as IQ in the U.S. population.)

How can we use x_3 to get unbiased (or at least consistent) estimators of β_1 and β_2? The proposal is to pretend that x_3 and x_3^* are the same, so that we run the regression of

$$y \text{ on } x_1, x_2, x_3. \qquad \qquad \text{[9.12]}$$

We call this the **plug-in solution to the omitted variables problem** because x_3 is just plugged in for x_3^* before we run OLS. If x_3 is truly related to x_3^*, this seems like a sensible thing. However, since x_3 and x_3^* are not the same, we should determine when this procedure does in fact give consistent estimators of β_1 and β_2.

The assumptions needed for the plug-in solution to provide consistent estimators of β_1 and β_2 can be broken down into assumptions about u and v_3:

(1) The error u is uncorrelated with x_1, x_2, and x_3^*, which is just the standard assumption in model (9.10). In addition, u is uncorrelated with x_3. This latter assumption just means that x_3 is irrelevant in the population model, once x_1, x_2, and x_3^* have been included. This is essentially true by definition, since x_3 is a proxy variable for x_3^*: it is x_3^* that directly affects y, not x_3. Thus, the assumption that u is uncorrelated with x_1, x_2, x_3^*, and x_3 is not very controversial. (Another way to state this assumption is that the expected value of u, given all these variables, is zero.)

(2) The error v_3 is uncorrelated with x_1, x_2, and x_3. Assuming that v_3 is uncorrelated with x_1 and x_2 requires x_3 to be a "good" proxy for x_3^*. This is easiest to see by writing the analog of these assumptions in terms of conditional expectations:

$$\mathrm{E}(x_3^*|x_1,x_2,x_3) = \mathrm{E}(x_3^*|x_3) = \delta_0 + \delta_3 x_3. \qquad \qquad \text{[9.13]}$$

The first equality, which is the most important one, says that, once x_3 is controlled for, the expected value of x_3^* does not depend on x_1 or x_2. Alternatively, x_3^* has zero correlation with x_1 and x_2 once x_3 is partialled out.

In the wage equation (9.9), where IQ is the proxy for ability, condition (9.13) becomes

$$\mathrm{E}(abil|educ,exper,IQ) = \mathrm{E}(abil|IQ) = \delta_0 + \delta_3 IQ.$$

Thus, the average level of ability only changes with IQ, not with $educ$ and $exper$. Is this reasonable? Maybe it is not exactly true, but it may be close to being true. It is certainly worth including IQ in the wage equation to see what happens to the estimated return to education.

We can easily see why the previous assumptions are enough for the plug-in solution to work. If we plug equation (9.11) into equation (9.10) and do simple algebra, we get

$$y = (\beta_0 + \beta_3\delta_0) + \beta_1 x_1 + \beta_2 x_2 + \beta_3\delta_3 x_3 + u + \beta_3 v_3.$$

Call the composite error in this equation $e = u + \beta_3 v_3$; it depends on the error in the model of interest, (9.10), and the error in the proxy variable equation, v_3. Since u and v_3 both have zero mean and each is uncorrelated with x_1, x_2, and x_3, e also has zero mean and is uncorrelated with x_1, x_2, and x_3. Write this equation as

$$y = \alpha_0 + \beta_1 x_1 + \beta_2 x_2 + \alpha_3 x_3 + e,$$

where $\alpha_0 = (\beta_0 + \beta_3 \delta_0)$ is the new intercept and $\alpha_3 = \beta_3 \delta_3$ is the slope parameter on the proxy variable x_3. As we alluded to earlier, when we run the regression in (9.12), we will not get unbiased estimators of β_0 and β_3; instead, we will get unbiased (or at least consistent) estimators of α_0, β_1, β_2, and α_3. The important thing is that we get good estimates of the parameters β_1 and β_2.

In most cases, the estimate of α_3 is actually more interesting than an estimate of β_3 anyway. For example, in the wage equation, α_3 measures the return to wage given one more point on IQ score.

EXAMPLE 9.3 IQ as a Proxy for Ability

The file WAGE2, from Blackburn and Neumark (1992), contains information on monthly earnings, education, several demographic variables, and IQ scores for 935 men in 1980. As a method to account for omitted ability bias, we add *IQ* to a standard log wage equation. The results are shown in Table 9.2.

Our primary interest is in what happens to the estimated return to education. Column (1) contains the estimates without using *IQ* as a proxy variable. The estimated return to education is 6.5%. If we think omitted ability is positively correlated with *educ*, then we assume that this estimate is too high. (More precisely, the average estimate across all random samples would be too high.) When *IQ* is

TABLE 9.2 Dependent Variable: log(*wage*)			
Independent Variables	(1)	(2)	(3)
educ	.065	.054	.018
	(.006)	(.007)	(.041)
exper	.014	.014	.014
	(.003)	(.003)	(.003)
tenure	.012	.011	.011
	(.002)	(.002)	(.002)
married	.199	.200	.201
	(.039)	(.039)	(.039)
south	−.091	−.080	−.080
	(.026)	(.026)	(.026)
urban	.184	.182	.184
	(.027)	(.027)	(.027)
black	−.188	−.143	−.147
	(.038)	(.039)	(.040)
IQ	—	.0036	−.0009
		(.0010)	(.0052)
educ · IQ	—	—	.00034
			(.00038)
intercept	5.395	5.176	5.648
	(.113)	(.128)	(.546)
Observations	935	935	935
R-squared	.253	.263	.263

added to the equation, the return to education falls to 5.4%, which corresponds with our prior beliefs about omitted ability bias.

The effect of IQ on socioeconomic outcomes has been documented in the controversial book *The Bell Curve*, by Herrnstein and Murray (1994). Column (2) shows that IQ does have a statistically significant, positive effect on earnings, after controlling for several other factors. Everything else being equal, an increase of 10 IQ points is predicted to raise monthly earnings by 3.6%. The standard deviation of IQ in the U.S. population is 15, so a one standard deviation increase in IQ is associated with higher earnings of 5.4%. This is identical to the predicted increase in wage due to another year of education. It is clear from column (2) that education still has an important role in increasing earnings, even though the effect is not as large as originally estimated.

Some other interesting observations emerge from columns (1) and (2). Adding *IQ* to the equation only increases the *R*-squared from .253 to .263. Most of the variation in $\log(wage)$ is not explained by the factors in column (2). Also, adding *IQ* to the equation does not eliminate the estimated earnings difference between black and white men: a black man with the same IQ, education, experience, and so on, as a white man is predicted to earn about 14.3% less, and the difference is very statistically significant.

> ### EXPLORING FURTHER 9.2
>
> What do you make of the small and statistically insignificant coefficient on *educ* in column (3) of Table 9.2? (*Hint:* When *educ · IQ* is in the equation, what is the interpretation of the coefficient on *educ*?)

Column (3) in Table 9.2 includes the interaction term *educ·IQ*. This allows for the possibility that *educ* and *abil* interact in determining $\log(wage)$. We might think that the return to education is higher for people with more ability, but this turns out not to be the case: the interaction term is not significant, and its addition makes *educ* and *IQ* individually insignificant while complicating the model. Therefore, the estimates in column (2) are preferred.

There is no reason to stop at a single proxy variable for ability in this example. The data set WAGE2 also contains a score for each man on the *Knowledge of the World of Work* (KWW) test. This provides a different measure of ability, which can be used in place of IQ or along with IQ, to estimate the return to education (see Computer Exercise C2).

It is easy to see how using a proxy variable can still lead to bias if the proxy variable does not satisfy the preceding assumptions. Suppose that, instead of (9.11), the unobserved variable, x_3^*, is related to all of the observed variables by

$$x_3^* = \delta_0 + \delta_1 x_1 + \delta_2 x_2 + \delta_3 x_3 + v_3, \quad \text{[9.14]}$$

where v_3 has a zero mean and is uncorrelated with x_1, x_2, and x_3. Equation (9.11) assumes that δ_1 and δ_2 are both zero. By plugging equation (9.14) into (9.10), we get

$$y = (\beta_0 + \beta_3 \delta_0) + (\beta_1 + \beta_3 \delta_1)x_1 + (\beta_2 + \beta_3 \delta_2)x_2 \\ + \beta_3 \delta_3 x_3 + u + \beta_3 v_3, \quad \text{[9.15]}$$

from which it follows that $\text{plim}(\hat{\beta}_1) = \beta_1 + \beta_3\delta_1$ and $\text{plim}(\hat{\beta}_2) = \beta_2 + \beta_3\delta_2$. [This follows because the error in (9.15), $u + \beta_3 v_3$, has zero mean and is uncorrelated with x_1, x_2, and x_3.] In the previous example where $x_1 = educ$ and $x_3^* = abil$, $\beta_3 > 0$, so there is a positive bias (inconsistency) if *abil* has a positive partial correlation with *educ* $(\delta_1 > 0)$. Thus, we could still be getting an upward bias in the return to education by using *IQ* as a proxy for *abil* if *IQ* is not a good proxy. But we can reasonably hope that this bias is smaller than if we ignored the problem of omitted ability entirely.

A complaint that is sometimes aired about including variables such as *IQ* in a regression that includes *educ* is that it exacerbates the problem of multicollinearity, likely leading to a less precise estimate of β_{educ}. But this complaint misses two important points. First, the inclusion of *IQ* reduces the error variance because the part of ability explained by *IQ* has been removed from the error. Typically, this will be reflected in a smaller standard error of the regression (although it need not get smaller because of its degrees-of-freedom adjustment). Second, and most importantly, the added multicollinearity is a necessary evil if we want to get an estimator of β_{educ} with less bias: the reason *educ* and *IQ* are correlated is that *educ* and *abil* are thought to be correlated, and *IQ* is a proxy for *abil*. If we could observe *abil* we would include it in the regression, and of course there would be unavoidable multicollinearity caused by correlation between *educ* and *abil*.

Proxy variables can come in the form of binary information as well. In Example 7.9 [see equation (7.15)], we discussed Krueger's (1993) estimates of the return to using a computer on the job. Krueger also included a binary variable indicating whether the worker uses a computer at home (as well as an interaction term between computer usage at work and at home). His primary reason for including computer usage at home in the equation was to proxy for unobserved "technical ability" that could affect wage directly and be related to computer usage at work.

9-2a Using Lagged Dependent Variables as Proxy Variables

In some applications, like the earlier wage example, we have at least a vague idea about which unobserved factor we would like to control for. This facilitates choosing proxy variables. In other applications, we suspect that one or more of the independent variables is correlated with an omitted variable, but we have no idea how to obtain a proxy for that omitted variable. In such cases, we can include, as a control, the value of the dependent variable from an earlier time period. This is especially useful for policy analysis.

Using a **lagged dependent variable** in a cross-sectional equation increases the data requirements, but it also provides a simple way to account for historical factors that cause *current* differences in the dependent variable that are difficult to account for in other ways. For example, some cities have had high crime rates in the past. Many of the same unobserved factors contribute to both high current and past crime rates. Likewise, some universities are traditionally better in academics than other universities. Inertial effects are also captured by putting in lags of *y*.

Consider a simple equation to explain city crime rates:

$$crime = \beta_0 + \beta_1 unem + \beta_2 expend + \beta_3 crime_{-1} + u, \qquad \text{[9.16]}$$

where *crime* is a measure of per capita crime, *unem* is the city unemployment rate, *expend* is per capita spending on law enforcement, and $crime_{-1}$ indicates the crime rate measured in some earlier year (this could be the past year or several years ago). We are interested in the effects of *unem* on *crime*, as well as of law enforcement expenditures on crime.

What is the purpose of including $crime_{-1}$ in the equation? Certainly, we expect that $\beta_3 > 0$ because crime has inertia. But the main reason for putting this in the equation is that cities with high historical crime rates may spend more on crime prevention. Thus, factors unobserved to us (the econometricians) that affect *crime* are likely to be correlated with *expend* (and *unem*). If we use a pure cross-sectional analysis, we are unlikely to get an unbiased estimator of the causal effect of law enforcement expenditures on crime. But, by including $crime_{-1}$ in the equation, we can at least do the following experiment: if two cities have the same previous crime rate and current unemployment rate, then β_2 measures the effect of another dollar of law enforcement on crime.

EXAMPLE 9.4   **City Crime Rates**

We estimate a constant elasticity version of the crime model in equation (9.16) (*unem*, because it is a percentage, is left in level form). The data in CRIME2 are from 46 cities for the year 1987. The crime rate is also available for 1982, and we use that as an additional independent variable in trying to control for city unobservables that affect crime and may be correlated with current law enforcement expenditures. Table 9.3 contains the results.

TABLE 9.3 Dependent Variable: $\log(crmrte_{87})$

Independent Variables	(1)	(2)
$unem_{87}$	−.029	.009
	(.032)	(.020)
$\log(lawexpc_{87})$	.203	−.140
	(.173)	(.109)
$\log(crmrte_{82})$	—	1.194
		(.132)
intercept	3.34	.076
	(1.25)	(.821)
Observations	46	46
R-squared	.057	.680

Without the lagged crime rate in the equation, the effects of the unemployment rate and expenditures on law enforcement are counterintuitive; neither is statistically significant, although the t statistic on $\log(lawexpc_{87})$ is 1.17. One possibility is that increased law enforcement expenditures improve reporting conventions, and so more crimes are *reported*. But it is also likely that cities with high recent crime rates spend more on law enforcement.

Adding the log of the crime rate from five years earlier has a large effect on the expenditures coefficient. The elasticity of the crime rate with respect to expenditures becomes −.14, with $t = -1.28$. This is not strongly significant, but it suggests that a more sophisticated model with more cities in the sample could produce significant results.

Not surprisingly, the current crime rate is strongly related to the past crime rate. The estimate indicates that if the crime rate in 1982 was 1% higher, then the crime rate in 1987 is predicted to be about 1.19% higher. We cannot reject the hypothesis that the elasticity of current crime with respect to past crime is unity $[t = (1.194 - 1)/.132 \approx 1.47]$. Adding the past crime rate increases the explanatory power of the regression markedly, but this is no surprise. The primary reason for including the lagged crime rate is to obtain a better estimate of the ceteris paribus effect of $\log(lawexpc_{87})$ on $\log(crmrte_{87})$.

The practice of putting in a lagged y as a general way of controlling for unobserved variables is hardly perfect. But it can aid in getting a better estimate of the effects of policy variables on various outcomes. When the data are available, additional lags also can be included.

Adding lagged values of y is not the only way to use two years of data to control for omitted factors. When we discuss panel data methods in Chapters 13 and 14, we will cover other ways to use repeated data on the same cross-sectional units at different points in time.

9-2b A Different Slant on Multiple Regression

The discussion of proxy variables in this section suggests an alternative way of interpreting a multiple regression analysis when we do not necessarily observe all relevant explanatory variables. Until now, we have specified the population model of interest with an additive error, as in equation (9.9). Our discussion of that example hinged upon whether we have a suitable proxy variable (IQ score in this case, other test scores more generally) for the unobserved explanatory variable, which we called "ability."

A less structured, more general approach to multiple regression is to forego specifying models with unobservables. Rather, we begin with the premise that we have access to a set of observable explanatory variables—which includes the variable of primary interest, such as years of schooling, and controls, such as observable test scores. We then model the mean of *y* conditional on the observed explanatory variables. For example, in the wage example with *lwage* denoting log(*wage*), we can estimate E(*lwage*|*educ,exper,tenure,south,urban,black,IQ*)—exactly what is reported in Table 9.2. The difference now is that we set our goals more modestly. Namely, rather than introduce the nebulous concept of "ability" in equation (9.9), we state from the outset that we will estimate the ceteris paribus effect of education holding *IQ* (and the other observed factors) fixed. There is no need to discuss whether *IQ* is a suitable proxy for ability. Consequently, while we may not be answering the question underlying equation (9.9), we are answering a question of interest: if two people have the same *IQ* levels (and same values of experience, tenure, and so on), yet they differ in education levels by a year, what is the expected difference in their log wages?

As another example, if we include as an explanatory variable the poverty rate in a school-level regression to assess the effects of spending on standardized test scores, we should recognize that the poverty rate only crudely captures the relevant differences in children and parents across schools. But often it is all we have, and it is better to control for the poverty rate than to do nothing because we cannot find suitable proxies for student "ability," parental "involvement," and so on. Almost certainly controlling for the poverty rate gets us closer to the ceteris paribus effects of spending than if we leave the poverty rate out of the analysis.

In some applications of regression analysis, we are interested simply in predicting the outcome, *y*, given a set of explanatory variables, $(x_1, \ldots, x_k)$. In such cases, it makes little sense to think in terms of "bias" in estimated coefficients due to omitted variables. Instead, we should focus on obtaining a model that predicts as well as possible, and make sure we do not include as regressors variables that cannot be observed at the time of prediction. For example, an admissions officer for a college or university might be interested in predicting success in college, as measured by grade point average, in terms of variables that can be measured at application time. Those variables would include high school performance (maybe just grade point average, but perhaps performance in specific kinds of courses), standardized test scores, participation in various activities (such as debate or math club), and even family background variables. We would not include a variable measuring college class attendance because we do not observe attendance in college at application time. Nor would we wring our hands about potential "biases" caused by omitting an attendance variable: we have no interest in, say, measuring the effect of high school GPA holding attendance in college fixed. Likewise, we would not worry about biases in coefficients because we cannot observe factors such as motivation. Naturally, for predictive purposes it would probably help substantially if we had a measure of motivation, but in its absence we fit the best model we can with observed explanatory variables.

9-3 Models with Random Slopes

In our treatment of regression so far, we have assumed that the slope coefficients are the same across individuals in the population, or that, if the slopes differ, they differ by measurable characteristics, in which case we are led to regression models containing interaction terms. For example, as we saw in Section 7-4, we can allow the return to education to differ by men and women by interacting education with a gender dummy in a log wage equation.

Here we are interested in a related but different question: What if the partial effect of a variable depends on unobserved factors that vary by population unit? If we have only one explanatory variable, *x*, we can write a general model (for a random draw, *i*, from the population, for emphasis) as

$$y_i = a_i + b_i x_i, \qquad [9.17]$$

where a_i is the intercept for unit *i* and b_i is the slope. In the simple regression model from Chapter 2 we assumed $b_i = \beta$ and labeled a_i as the error, u_i. The model in (9.17) is sometimes called a **random coefficient model** or **random slope model** because the unobserved slope coefficient, b_i, is viewed as a random draw from the population along with the observed data, (x_i, y_i), and the unobserved intercept, a_i. As an example, if $y_i = \log(wage_i)$ and $x_i = educ_i$, then (9.17) allows the return to education, b_i, to vary by person. If, say, b_i contains unmeasured ability (just as a_i would), the partial effect of another year of schooling can depend on ability.

With a random sample of size n, we (implicitly) draw n values of b_i along with n values of a_i (and the observed data on x and y). Naturally, we cannot estimate a slope—or, for that matter, an intercept—for each i. But we can hope to estimate the average slope (and average intercept), where the average is across the population. Therefore, define $\alpha = E(a_i)$ and $\beta = E(b_i)$. Then β is the average of the partial effect of x on y, and so we call β the **average partial effect (APE)**, or the **average marginal effect (AME)**. In the context of a log wage equation, β is the average return to a year of schooling in the population.

If we write $a_i = \alpha + c_i$ and $b_i = \beta + d_i$, then d_i is the individual-specific deviation from the APE. By construction, $E(c_i) = 0$ and $E(d_i) = 0$. Substituting into (9.17) gives

$$y_i = \alpha + \beta x_i + c_i + d_i x_i \equiv \alpha + \beta x_i + u_i, \qquad \textbf{[9.18]}$$

where $u_i = c_i + d_i x_i$. (To make the notation easier to follow, we now use α, the mean value of a_i, as the intercept, and β, the mean of b_i, as the slope.) In other words, we can write the random coefficient as a constant coefficient model but where the error term contains an interaction between an unobservable, d_i, and the observed explanatory variable, x_i.

When would a simple regression of y_i on x_i provide an unbiased estimate of β (and α)? We can apply the result for unbiasedness from Chapter 2. If $E(u_i|x_i) = 0$, then OLS is generally unbiased. When $u_i = c_i + d_i x_i$, sufficient is $E(c_i|x_i) = E(c_i) = 0$ and $E(d_i|x_i) = E(d_i) = 0$. We can write these in terms of the unit-specific intercept and slope as

$$E(a_i|x_i) = E(a_i) \quad \text{and} \quad E(b_i|x_i) = E(b_i); \qquad \textbf{[9.19]}$$

that is, a_i and b_i are both mean independent of x_i. This is a useful finding: if we allow for unit-specific slopes, OLS consistently estimates the population average of those slopes when they are mean independent of the explanatory variable. (See Problem 6 for a weaker set of conditions that imply consistency of OLS.)

The error term in (9.18) almost certainly contains heteroskedasticity. In fact, if $Var(c_i|x_i) = \sigma_c^2$, $Var(d_i|x_i) = \sigma_d^2$, and $Cov(c_i, d_i|x_i) = 0$, then

$$Var(u_i|x_i) = \sigma_c^2 + \sigma_d^2 x_i^2, \qquad \textbf{[9.20]}$$

and so there must be heteroskedasticity in u_i unless $\sigma_d^2 = 0$, which means $b_i = \beta$ for all i. We know how to account for heteroskedasticity of this kind. We can use OLS and compute heteroskedasticity-robust standard errors and test statistics, or we can estimate the variance function in (9.20) and apply weighted least squares. Of course the latter strategy imposes homoskedasticity on the random intercept and slope, and so we would want to make a WLS analysis fully robust to violations of (9.20).

Because of equation (9.20), some authors like to view heteroskedasticity in regression models generally as arising from random slope coefficients. But we should remember that the form of (9.20) is special, and it does not allow for heteroskedasticity in a_i or b_i. We cannot convincingly distinguish between a random slope model, where the intercept and slope are independent of x_i, and a constant slope model with heteroskedasticity in a_i.

The treatment for multiple regression is similar. Generally, write

$$y_i = a_i + b_{i1}x_{i1} + b_{i2}x_{i2} + \ldots + b_{ik}x_{ik}. \qquad \textbf{[9.21]}$$

Then, by writing $a_i = \alpha + c_i$ and $b_{ij} = \beta_j + d_{ij}$, we have

$$y_i = \alpha + \beta_1 x_{i1} + \ldots + \beta_k x_{ik} + u_i, \qquad \textbf{[9.22]}$$

where $u_i = c_i + d_{i1}x_{i1} + \ldots + d_{ik}x_{ik}$. If we maintain the mean independence assumptions $E(a_i|\mathbf{x}_i) = E(a_i)$ and $E(b_{ij}|\mathbf{x}_i) = E(b_{ij}), j = 1, \ldots, k$, then $E(y_i|\mathbf{x}_i) = \alpha + \beta_1 x_{i1} + \ldots + \beta_k x_{ik}$, and so OLS using a random sample produces unbiased estimators of α and the β_j. As in the simple regression case, $\text{Var}(u_i|\mathbf{x}_i)$ is almost certainly heteroskedastic.

We can allow the b_{ij} to depend on observable explanatory variables as well as unobservables. For example, suppose with $k = 2$ the effect of x_{i2} depends on x_{i1}, and we write $b_{i2} = \beta_2 + \delta_1(x_{i1} - \mu_1) + d_{i2}$, where $\mu_1 = E(x_{i1})$. If we assume $E(d_{i2}|\mathbf{x}_i) = 0$ (and similarly for c_i and d_{i1}), then $E(y_i|x_{i1}, x_{i2}) = \alpha + \beta_1 x_{i1} + \beta_2 x_{i2} + \delta_1(x_{i1} - \mu_1)x_{i2}$, which means we have an interaction between x_{i1} and x_{i2}. Because we have subtracted the mean μ_1 from x_{i1}, β_2 is the APE of x_{i2}.

The bottom line of this section is that allowing for random slopes is fairly straightforward if the slopes are independent, or at least mean independent, of the explanatory variables. In addition, we can easily model the slopes as functions of the exogenous variables, which leads to models with squares and interactions. Of course, in Chapter 6 we discussed how such models can be useful without ever introducing the notion of a random slope. The random slopes specification provides a separate justification for such models. Estimation becomes considerably more difficult if the random intercept as well as some slopes are correlated with some of the regressors. We cover the problem of endogenous explanatory variables in Chapter 15.

9-4 Properties of OLS under Measurement Error

Sometimes, in economic applications, we cannot collect data on the variable that truly affects economic behavior. A good example is the marginal income tax rate facing a family that is trying to choose how much to contribute to charity in a given year. The marginal rate may be hard to obtain or summarize as a single number for all income levels. Instead, we might compute the average tax rate based on total income and tax payments.

When we use an imprecise measure of an economic variable in a regression model, then our model contains measurement error. In this section, we derive the consequences of measurement error for ordinary least squares estimation. OLS will be consistent under certain assumptions, but there are others under which it is inconsistent. In some of these cases, we can derive the size of the asymptotic bias.

As we will see, the measurement error problem has a similar statistical structure to the omitted variable–proxy variable problem discussed in the previous section, but they are conceptually different. In the proxy variable case, we are looking for a variable that is somehow associated with the unobserved variable. In the measurement error case, the variable that we do not observe has a well-defined, quantitative meaning (such as a marginal tax rate or annual income), but our recorded measures of it may contain error. For example, reported annual income is a measure of actual annual income, whereas IQ score is a proxy for ability.

Another important difference between the proxy variable and measurement error problems is that, in the latter case, often the mismeasured independent variable is the one of primary interest. In the proxy variable case, the partial effect of the omitted variable is rarely of central interest: we are usually concerned with the effects of the other independent variables.

Before we consider details, we should remember that measurement error is an issue only when the variables for which the econometrician can collect data differ from the variables that influence decisions by individuals, families, firms, and so on.

9-4a Measurement Error in the Dependent Variable

We begin with the case where only the dependent variable is measured with error. Let y^* denote the variable (in the population, as always) that we would like to explain. For example, y^* could be annual family savings. The regression model has the usual form

$$y^* = \beta_0 + \beta_1 x_1 + \ldots + \beta_k x_k + u, \tag{9.23}$$

and we assume it satisfies the Gauss-Markov assumptions. We let y represent the observable measure of y^*. In the savings case, y is reported annual savings. Unfortunately, families are not perfect in their reporting of annual family savings; it is easy to leave out categories or to overestimate the amount contributed to a fund. Generally, we can expect y and y^* to differ, at least for some subset of families in the population.

The **measurement error** (in the population) is defined as the difference between the observed value and the actual value:

$$e_0 = y - y^*. \tag{9.24}$$

For a random draw i from the population, we can write $e_{i0} = y_i - y_i^*$, but the important thing is how the measurement error in the population is related to other factors. To obtain an estimable model, we write $y^* = y - e_0$, plug this into equation (9.23), and rearrange:

$$y = \beta_0 + \beta_1 x_1 + \dots + \beta_k x_k + u + e_0. \tag{9.25}$$

The error term in equation (9.25) is $u + e_0$. Because $y, x_1, x_2, \dots, x_k$ are observed, we can estimate this model by OLS. In effect, we just ignore the fact that y is an imperfect measure of y^* and proceed as usual.

When does OLS with y in place of y^* produce consistent estimators of the β_j? Since the original model (9.23) satisfies the Gauss-Markov assumptions, u has zero mean and is uncorrelated with each x_j. It is only natural to assume that the measurement error has zero mean; if it does not, then we simply get a biased estimator of the intercept, β_0, which is rarely a cause for concern. Of much more importance is our assumption about the relationship between the measurement error, e_0, and the explanatory variables, x_j. The usual assumption is that the measurement error in y is statistically independent of each explanatory variable. If this is true, then the OLS estimators from (9.25) are unbiased and consistent. Further, the usual OLS inference procedures (t, F, and LM statistics) are valid.

If e_0 and u are uncorrelated, as is usually assumed, then $\text{Var}(u + e_0) = \sigma_u^2 + \sigma_0^2 > \sigma_u^2$. This means that measurement error in the dependent variable results in a larger error variance than when no error occurs; this, of course, results in larger variances of the OLS estimators. This is to be expected and there is nothing we can do about it (except collect better data). The bottom line is that, if the measurement error is uncorrelated with the independent variables, then OLS estimation has good properties.

EXAMPLE 9.5   **Savings Function with Measurement Error**

Consider a savings function

$$sav^* = \beta_0 + \beta_1 inc + \beta_2 size + \beta_3 educ + \beta_4 age + u,$$

but where actual savings (sav^*) may deviate from reported savings (sav). The question is whether the size of the measurement error in sav is systematically related to the other variables. It might be reasonable to assume that the measurement error is not correlated with inc, $size$, $educ$, and age. On the other hand, we might think that families with higher incomes, or more education, report their savings more accurately. We can never know whether the measurement error is correlated with inc or $educ$, unless we can collect data on sav^*; then, the measurement error can be computed for each observation as $e_{i0} = sav_i - sav_i^*$.

When the dependent variable is in logarithmic form, so that $\log(y^*)$ is the dependent variable, it is natural for the measurement error equation to be of the form

$$\log(y) = \log(y^*) + e_0. \tag{9.26}$$

This follows from a **multiplicative measurement error** for y: $y = y^* a_0$, where $a_0 > 0$ and $e_0 = \log(a_0)$.

EXAMPLE 9.6   **Measurement Error in Scrap Rates**

In Section 7-6, we discussed an example where we wanted to determine whether job training grants reduce the scrap rate in manufacturing firms. We certainly might think the scrap rate reported by firms is measured with error. (In fact, most firms in the sample do not even report a scrap rate.) In a simple regression framework, this is captured by

$$\log(scrap^*) = \beta_0 + \beta_1 grant + u,$$

where $scrap^*$ is the true scrap rate and $grant$ is the dummy variable indicating whether a firm received a grant. The measurement error equation is

$$\log(scrap) = \log(scrap^*) + e_0.$$

Is the measurement error, e_0, independent of whether the firm receives a grant? A cynical person might think that a firm receiving a grant is more likely to underreport its scrap rate in order to make the grant look effective. If this happens, then, in the estimable equation,

$$\log(scrap) = \beta_0 + \beta_1 grant + u + e_0,$$

the error $u + e_0$ is negatively correlated with $grant$. This would produce a downward bias in β_1, which would tend to make the training program look more effective than it actually was. (Remember, a more negative β_1 means the program was more effective, since increased worker productivity is associated with a lower scrap rate.)

The bottom line of this subsection is that measurement error in the dependent variable *can* cause biases in OLS if it is systematically related to one or more of the explanatory variables. If the measurement error is just a random reporting error that is independent of the explanatory variables, as is often assumed, then OLS is perfectly appropriate.

9-4b Measurement Error in an Explanatory Variable

Traditionally, measurement error in an explanatory variable has been considered a much more important problem than measurement error in the dependent variable. In this subsection, we will see why this is the case.

We begin with the simple regression model

$$y = \beta_0 + \beta_1 x_1^* + u, \tag{9.27}$$

and we assume that this satisfies at least the first four Gauss-Markov assumptions. This means that estimation of (9.27) by OLS would produce unbiased and consistent estimators of β_0 and β_1. The problem is that x_1^* is not observed. Instead, we have a measure of x_1^*; call it x_1. For example, x_1^* could be actual income and x_1 could be reported income.

The measurement error in the population is simply

$$e_1 = x_1 - x_1^*,$$ [9.28]

and this can be positive, negative, or zero. We assume that the *average* measurement error in the population is zero: $E(e_1) = 0$. This is natural, and, in any case, it does not affect the important conclusions that follow. A maintained assumption in what follows is that u is uncorrelated with x_1^* and x_1. In conditional expectation terms, we can write this as $E(y|x_1^*, x_1) = E(y|x_1^*)$, which just says that x_1 does not affect y after x_1^* has been controlled for. We used the same assumption in the proxy variable case, and it is not controversial; it holds almost by definition.

We want to know the properties of OLS if we simply replace x_1^* with x_1 and run the regression of y on x_1. They depend crucially on the assumptions we make about the measurement error. Two assumptions have been the focus in econometrics literature, and they both represent polar extremes. The first assumption is that e_1 is uncorrelated with the *observed* measure, x_1:

$$\text{Cov}(x_1, e_1) = 0.$$ [9.29]

From the relationship in (9.28), if assumption (9.29) is true, then e_1 must be correlated with the unobserved variable x_1^*. To determine the properties of OLS in this case, we write $x_1^* = x_1 - e_1$ and plug this into equation (9.27):

$$y = \beta_0 + \beta_1 x_1 + (u - \beta_1 e_1).$$ [9.30]

Because we have assumed that u and e_1 both have zero mean and are uncorrelated with x_1, $u - \beta_1 e_1$ has zero mean and is uncorrelated with x_1. It follows that OLS estimation with x_1 in place of x_1^* produces a consistent estimator of β_1 (and also β_0). Since u is uncorrelated with e_1, the variance of the error in (9.30) is $\text{Var}(u - \beta_1 e_1) = \sigma_u^2 + \beta_1^2 \sigma_{e_1}^2$. Thus, except when $\beta_1 = 0$, measurement error increases the error variance. But this does not affect any of the OLS properties (except that the variances of the $\hat{\beta}_j$ will be larger than if we observe x_1^* directly).

The assumption that e_1 is uncorrelated with x_1 is analogous to the proxy variable assumption we made in Section 9-2. Since this assumption implies that OLS has all of its nice properties, this is not usually what econometricians have in mind when they refer to measurement error in an explanatory variable. The **classical errors-in-variables (CEV)** assumption is that the measurement error is uncorrelated with the *unobserved* explanatory variable:

$$\text{Cov}(x_1^*, e_1) = 0.$$ [9.31]

This assumption comes from writing the observed measure as the sum of the true explanatory variable and the measurement error,

$$x_1 = x_1^* + e_1,$$

and then assuming the two components of x_1 are uncorrelated. (This has nothing to do with assumptions about u; we always maintain that u is uncorrelated with x_1^* and x_1, and therefore with e_1.)

If assumption (9.31) holds, then x_1 and e_1 *must* be correlated:

$$\text{Cov}(x_1, e_1) = E(x_1 e_1) = E(x_1^* e_1) + E(e_1^2) = 0 + \sigma_{e_1}^2 = \sigma_{e_1}^2.$$ [9.32]

Thus, the covariance between x_1 and e_1 is equal to the variance of the measurement error under the CEV assumption.

Referring to equation (9.30), we can see that correlation between x_1 and e_1 is going to cause problems. Because u and x_1 are uncorrelated, the covariance between x_1 and the composite error $u - \beta_1 e_1$ is

$$\text{Cov}(x_1, u - \beta_1 e_1) = -\beta_1 \text{Cov}(x_1, e_1) = -\beta_1 \sigma_{e_1}^2.$$

Thus, in the CEV case, the OLS regression of y on x_1 gives a biased and inconsistent estimator.

Using the asymptotic results in Chapter 5, we can determine the amount of inconsistency in OLS. The probability limit of $\hat{\beta}_1$ is β_1 plus the ratio of the covariance between x_1 and $u - \beta_1 e_1$ and the variance of x_1:

$$\text{plim}(\hat{\beta}_1) = \beta_1 + \frac{\text{Cov}(x_1, u - \beta_1 e_1)}{\text{Var}(x_1)}$$

$$= \beta_1 - \frac{\beta_1 \sigma_{e_1}^2}{\sigma_{x_1^*}^2 + \sigma_{e_1}^2}$$

$$= \beta_1 \left(1 - \frac{\sigma_{e_1}^2}{\sigma_{x_1^*}^2 + \sigma_{e_1}^2} \right) \qquad [9.33]$$

$$= \beta_1 \left(\frac{\sigma_{x_1^*}^2}{\sigma_{x_1^*}^2 + \sigma_{e_1}^2} \right),$$

where we have used the fact that $\text{Var}(x_1) = \text{Var}(x_1^*) + \text{Var}(e_1)$.

Equation (9.33) is very interesting. The term multiplying β_1, which is the ratio $\text{Var}(x_1^*)/\text{Var}(x_1)$, is always less than one [an implication of the CEV assumption (9.31)]. Thus, $\text{plim}(\hat{\beta}_1)$ is always closer to zero than is β_1. This is called the **attenuation bias** in OLS due to CEV: on average (or in large samples), the estimated OLS effect will be *attenuated*. In particular, if β_1 is positive, $\hat{\beta}_1$ will tend to underestimate β_1. This is an important conclusion, but it relies on the CEV setup.

If the variance of x_1^* is large relative to the variance in the measurement error, then the inconsistency in OLS will be small. This is because $\text{Var}(x_1^*)/\text{Var}(x_1)$ will be close to unity when $\sigma_{x_1^*}^2/\sigma_{e_1}^2$ is large. Therefore, depending on how much variation there is in x_1^* relative to e_1, measurement error need not cause large biases.

Things are more complicated when we add more explanatory variables. For illustration, consider the model

$$y = \beta_0 + \beta_1 x_1^* + \beta_2 x_2 + \beta_2 x_3 + u, \qquad [9.34]$$

where the first of the three explanatory variables is measured with error. We make the natural assumption that u is uncorrelated with x_1^*, x_2, x_3, and x_1. Again, the crucial assumption concerns the measurement error e_1. In almost all cases, e_1 is assumed to be uncorrelated with x_2 and x_3—the explanatory variables not measured with error. The key issue is whether e_1 is uncorrelated with x_1. If it is, then the OLS regression of y on x_1, x_2, and x_3 produces consistent estimators. This is easily seen by writing

$$y = \beta_0 + \beta_1 x_1 + \beta_2 x_2 + \beta_2 x_3 + u - \beta_1 e_1, \qquad [9.35]$$

where u and e_1 are both uncorrelated with all the explanatory variables.

Under the CEV assumption in (9.31), OLS will be biased and inconsistent, because e_1 is correlated with x_1 in equation (9.35). Remember, this means that, in general, *all* OLS estimators will be biased, not just $\hat{\beta}_1$. What about the attenuation bias derived in equation (9.33)? It turns out that there is still an attenuation bias for estimating β_1: it can be shown that

$$\text{plim}(\hat{\beta}_1) = \beta_1 \left(\frac{\sigma_{r_1^*}^2}{\sigma_{r_1^*}^2 + \sigma_{e_1}^2} \right), \qquad [9.36]$$

where r_1^* is the population error in the equation $x_1^* = \alpha_0 + \alpha_1 x_2 + \alpha_2 x_3 + r_1^*$. Formula (9.36) also works in the general k variable case when x_1 is the only mismeasured variable.

Things are less clear-cut for estimating the β_j on the variables not measured with error. In the special case that x_1^* is uncorrelated with x_2 and x_3, $\hat{\beta}_2$ and $\hat{\beta}_3$ are consistent. But this is rare in practice. Generally, measurement error in a single variable causes inconsistency in all estimators. Unfortunately, the sizes, and even the directions of the biases, are not easily derived.

| EXAMPLE 9.7 | GPA Equation with Measurement Error |

Consider the problem of estimating the effect of family income on college grade point average, after controlling for *hsGPA* (high school grade point average) and *SAT* (scholastic aptitude test). It could be that, though family income is important for performance before college, it has no direct effect on college performance. To test this, we might postulate the model

$$colGPA = \beta_0 + \beta_1 faminc^* + \beta_2 hsGPA + \beta_3 SAT + u,$$

where *faminc** is actual annual family income. (This might appear in logarithmic form, but for the sake of illustration we leave it in level form.) Precise data on *colGPA*, *hsGPA*, and *SAT* are relatively easy to obtain. But family income, especially as reported by students, could be easily mismeasured. If *faminc = faminc** + e_1 and the CEV assumptions hold, then using reported family income in place of actual family income will bias the OLS estimator of β_1 toward zero. One consequence of the downward bias is that a test of H_0: $\beta_1 = 0$ will have less chance of detecting $\beta_1 > 0$.

Of course, measurement error can be present in more than one explanatory variable, or in some explanatory variables and the dependent variable. As we discussed earlier, any measurement error in the dependent variable is usually assumed to be uncorrelated with all the explanatory variables, whether it is observed or not. Deriving the bias in the OLS estimators under extensions of the CEV assumptions is complicated and does not lead to clear results.

In some cases, it is clear that the CEV assumption in (9.31) cannot be true. Consider a variant on Example 9.7:

$$colGPA = \beta_0 + \beta_1 smoked^* + \beta_2 hsGPA + \beta_3 SAT + u,$$

where *smoked** is the actual number of times a student smoked marijuana in the last 30 days. The variable *smoked* is the answer to this question: On how many separate occasions did you smoke marijuana in the last 30 days? Suppose we postulate the standard measurement error model

$$smoked = smoked^* + e_1.$$

Even if we assume that students try to report the truth, the CEV assumption is unlikely to hold. People who do not smoke marijuana at all—so that *smoked** = 0—are likely to report *smoked* = 0, so the measurement error is probably zero for students who never smoke marijuana. When *smoked** > 0, it is much more likely that the student miscounts how many times he or she smoked marijuana in the last 30 days. This means that the measurement error e_1 and the *actual* number of times smoked, *smoked**, are correlated, which violates the CEV assumption in (9.31). Unfortunately, deriving the implications of measurement error that do not satisfy (9.29) or (9.31) is difficult and beyond the scope of this text.

| EXPLORING FURTHER 9.3 |

Let *educ** be actual amount of schooling, measured in years (which can be a noninteger), and let *educ* be reported highest grade completed. Do you think *educ* and *educ** are related by the CEV model?

Before leaving this section, we emphasize that the CEV assumption (9.31), while more believable than assumption (9.29), is still a strong assumption. The truth is probably somewhere in between, and if e_1 is correlated with both x_1^* and x_1, OLS is inconsistent. This raises an important question: must we live with inconsistent estimators under CEV, or other kinds of measurement error that are correlated with x_1? Fortunately, the answer is no. Chapter 15 shows how, under certain assumptions, the parameters can be consistently estimated in the presence of general measurement error. We postpone this discussion until later because it requires us to leave the realm of OLS estimation. (See Problem 7 for how multiple measures can be used to reduce the attenuation bias.)

9-5 Missing Data, Nonrandom Samples, and Outlying Observations

The measurement error problem discussed in the previous section can be viewed as a data problem: we cannot obtain data on the variables of interest. Further, under the CEV model, the composite error term is correlated with the mismeasured independent variable, violating the Gauss-Markov assumptions.

Another data problem we discussed frequently in earlier chapters is multicollinearity among the explanatory variables. Remember that correlation among the explanatory variables does not violate any assumptions. When two independent variables are highly correlated, it can be difficult to estimate the partial effect of each. But this is properly reflected in the usual OLS statistics.

In this section, we provide an introduction to data problems that can violate the random sampling assumption, MLR.2. We can isolate cases in which nonrandom sampling has no practical effect on OLS. In other cases, nonrandom sampling causes the OLS estimators to be biased and inconsistent. A more complete treatment that establishes several of the claims made here is given in Chapter 17.

9-5a Missing Data

The **missing data** problem can arise in a variety of forms. Often, we collect a random sample of people, schools, cities, and so on, and then discover later that information is missing on some key variables for several units in the sample. For example, in the data set BWGHT, 196 of the 1,388 observations have no information on father's education. In the data set on median starting law school salaries, LAWSCH85, six of the 156 schools have no reported information on median LSAT scores for the entering class; other variables are also missing for some of the law schools.

If data are missing for an observation on either the dependent variable or one of the independent variables, then the observation cannot be used in a standard multiple regression analysis. In fact, provided missing data have been properly indicated, all modern regression packages keep track of missing data and simply ignore observations when computing a regression. We saw this explicitly in the birth weight scenario in Example 4.9, when 197 observations were dropped due to missing information on parents' education.

In the literature on missing data, an estimator that uses only observations with a complete set of data on y and $x_1, \ldots, x_k$ is called a **complete cases estimator**; as mentioned earlier, this estimator is computed as the default for OLS (and all estimators covered later in the text). Other than reducing the sample size, are there any *statistical* consequences of using the OLS estimator and ignoring the missing data? If, in the language of the missing data literature (see, for example, Little and Rubin (2002, Chapter 1)) the data are **missing completely at random** (sometimes called **MCAR**), then missing data cause no statistical problems. The MCAR assumption implies that the reason the data are missing is independent, in a statistical sense, of both the observed and unobserved factors affecting y. In effect, we can still assume that the data have been obtained by random sampling from the population, so that Assumption MLR.2 continues to hold.

When MCAR holds, there are ways to use partial information obtained from units that are dropped from the complete case estimation. For example, that for a multiple regression model, data are always available for y and $x_1, x_2, \ldots, x_{k-1}$ but are sometimes missing for the explanatory variable x_k. A common "solution" is to create two new variables. For a unit i, the first variable, say z_{ik}, is defined to be x_{ik} when x_{ik} is observed, and zero otherwise. The second variable is a "missing data indicator," say m_{ik}, which equals one when x_{ik} is missing and equals zero when x_{ik} is observed. Having defined these two variables, all of the units are used in the regression

$$y_i \text{ on } x_{i1}, x_{i2}, \ldots, x_{i,k-1}, z_{ik}, m_{ik}, i = 1, \ldots, n.$$

This procedure can be shown to produce unbiased and consistent estimators of all parameters, provided the missing data mechanism for x_k is MCAR. Incidentally, it is a very poor idea to omit m_{ik} from the regression, as that is the same thing as assuming x_{ik} is zero whenever it is missing. Replacing missing values with zero and not including the missing data indicator can cause substantial bias in the OLS estimators. A similar trick can be used when data are missing on more than one explanatory variable (but not on *y*). Problem 9.10 provides the argument in the simple regression model.

An important point is that the estimator that uses all of the data and adds missing data indicators is actually less robust than the complete cases estimator. As will be seen in the next subsection, the complete cases estimator turns out to be consistent even when the reason the data are missing is systematically related to $(x_1, \ldots, x_k)$, is a function of $(x_1, x_2, \ldots, x_k)$, provided it does not depend on the unobserved error, *u*. There are more complicated schemes for using partial information that are based on filling in the missing data, but these are beyond the scope of this text. The reader is referred to Little and Rubin (2002).

9-5b Nonrandom Samples

The MCAR assumption ensures that units for which we observe a full set of data are not systematically different from units for which some variables are missing. Unfortunately, MCAR is often unrealistic. An example of a missing data mechanism that does not satisfy MCAR can be gotten by looking at the data set CARD, where the measure of IQ is missing for 949 men. If the probability that the IQ score is missing is, say, higher for men with lower IQ scores, the mechanism violates MCAR. For example, in the birth weight data set, what if the probability that education is missing is higher for those people with lower than average levels of education? Or, in Section 9-2, we used a wage data set that included IQ scores. This data set was constructed by omitting several people from the sample for whom IQ scores were not available. If obtaining an IQ score is easier for those with higher IQs, the sample is not representative of the population. The random sampling assumption MLR.2 is violated, and we must worry about these consequences for OLS estimation.

Fortunately, certain types of nonrandom sampling do *not* cause bias or inconsistency in OLS. Under the Gauss-Markov assumptions (but without MLR.2), it turns out that the sample can be chosen on the basis of the *independent* variables without causing any statistical problems. This is called *sample selection based on the independent variables*, and it is an example of **exogenous sample selection**.

In the statistics literature, exogenous sample selection due to missing data is often called **missing at random** (but this is not a particularly good label because the probability of missing data is allowed to depend on the explanatory variables). See Little and Rubin (2002, Chapter 1).

To illustrate exogenously missing data, suppose that we are estimating a saving function, where annual saving depends on income, age, family size, and some unobserved factors, *u*. A simple model is

$$saving = \beta_0 + \beta_1 income + \beta_2 age + \beta_3 size + u. \qquad [9.37]$$

Suppose that our data set was based on a survey of people over 35 years of age, thereby leaving us with a nonrandom sample of all adults. While this is not ideal, we can still get unbiased and consistent estimators of the parameters in the population model (9.37), using the nonrandom sample. We will not show this formally here, but the reason OLS on the nonrandom sample is unbiased is that the regression function E(*saving*|*income*,*age*,*size*) is the same for any subset of the population described by *income*, *age*, or *size*. Provided there is enough variation in the independent variables in the subpopulation, selection on the basis of the independent variables is not a serious problem, other than that it results in smaller sample sizes.

In the IQ example just mentioned, things are not so clear-cut, because no fixed rule based on IQ is used to include someone in the sample. Rather, the *probability* of being in the sample increases with IQ. If the other factors determining selection into the sample are independent of the error term in the wage equation, then we have another case of exogenous sample selection, and OLS using the selected sample will have all of its desirable properties under the other Gauss-Markov assumptions.

The situation is much different when selection is based on the dependent variable, *y*, which is called *sample selection based on the dependent variable* and is an example of **endogenous sample selection**. If the sample is based on whether the dependent variable is above or below a given value, bias always occurs in OLS in estimating the population model. For example, suppose we wish to estimate the relationship between individual wealth and several other factors in the population of all adults:

$$wealth = \beta_0 + \beta_1 educ + \beta_2 exper + \beta_3 age + u. \qquad [9.38]$$

Suppose that only people with wealth below \$250,000 are included in the sample. This is a nonrandom sample from the population of interest, and it is based on the value of the dependent variable. Using a sample on people with wealth below \$250,000 will result in biased and inconsistent estimators of the parameters in (9.32). Briefly, this occurs because the population regression $E(wealth|educ,exper,age)$ is not the same as the expected value conditional on *wealth* being less than \$250,000.

Other sampling schemes lead to **nonrandom samples** from the population, usually intentionally. A common method of data collection is **stratified sampling**, in which the population is divided into nonoverlapping, exhaustive groups, or strata. Then, some groups are sampled more frequently than is dictated by their population representation, and some groups are sampled less frequently. For example, some surveys purposely oversample minority groups or low-income groups. Whether special methods are needed again hinges on whether the stratification is exogenous (based on exogenous explanatory variables) or endogenous (based on the dependent variable). Suppose that a survey of military personnel oversampled women because the initial interest was in studying the factors that determine pay for women in the military. (Oversampling a group that is relatively small in the population is common in collecting stratified samples.) Provided men were sampled as well, we can use OLS on the stratified sample to estimate any gender differential, along with the returns to education and experience for all military personnel. (We might be willing to assume that the returns to education and experience are not gender specific.) OLS is unbiased and consistent because the stratification is with respect to an explanatory variable, namely, gender.

If, instead, the survey oversampled lower-paid military personnel, then OLS using the stratified sample does not consistently estimate the parameters of the military wage equation because the stratification is endogenous. In such cases, special econometric methods are needed [see Wooldridge (2010, Chapter 19)].

Stratified sampling is a fairly obvious form of nonrandom sampling. Other sample selection issues are more subtle. For instance, in several previous examples, we have estimated the effects of various variables, particularly education and experience, on hourly wage. The data set WAGE1 that we have used throughout is essentially a random sample of *working* individuals. Labor economists are often interested in estimating the effect of, say, education on the wage *offer*. The idea is this: every person of working age faces an hourly wage offer, and he or she can either work at that wage or not work. For someone who does work, the wage offer is just the wage earned. For people who do not work, we usually cannot observe the wage offer. Now, since the wage offer equation

$$\log(wage^o) = \beta_0 + \beta_1 educ + \beta_2 exper + u \qquad [9.39]$$

represents the population of all working-age people, we cannot estimate it using a random sample from this population; instead, we have data on the wage offer only for working people (although we can get data on *educ* and *exper* for nonworking people). If we use a random sample on working people

---

EXPLORING FURTHER 9.4

Suppose we are interested in the effects of campaign expenditures by incumbents on voter support. Some incumbents choose not to run for reelection. If we can only collect voting and spending outcomes on incumbents that actually do run, is there likely to be endogenous sample selection?

---

to estimate (9.39), will we get unbiased estimators? This case is not clear-cut. Since the sample is selected based on someone's decision to work (as opposed to the size of the wage offer), this is not like the previous case. However, since the decision to work might be related to unobserved factors that affect the wage offer, selection might be endogenous, and this can result in a sample selection bias in the OLS estimators. We will cover methods that can be used to test and correct for sample selection bias in Chapter 17.

9-5c Outliers and Influential Observations

In some applications, especially, but not only, with small data sets, the OLS estimates are sensitive to the inclusion of one or several observations. A complete treatment of **outliers** and **influential observations** is beyond the scope of this book, because a formal development requires matrix algebra. Loosely speaking, an observation is an influential observation if dropping it from the analysis changes the key OLS estimates by a practically "large" amount. The notion of an outlier is also a bit vague, because it requires comparing values of the variables for one observation with those for the remaining sample. Nevertheless, one wants to be on the lookout for "unusual" observations because they can greatly affect the OLS estimates.

OLS is susceptible to outlying observations because it minimizes the sum of squared residuals: large residuals (positive or negative) receive a lot of weight in the least squares minimization problem. If the estimates change by a practically large amount when we slightly modify our sample, we should be concerned.

When statisticians and econometricians study the problem of outliers theoretically, sometimes the data are viewed as being from a random sample from a given population—albeit with an unusual distribution that can result in extreme values—and sometimes the outliers are assumed to come from a different population. From a practical perspective, outlying observations can occur for two reasons. The easiest case to deal with is when a mistake has been made in entering the data. Adding extra zeros to a number or misplacing a decimal point can throw off the OLS estimates, especially in small sample sizes. It is always a good idea to compute summary statistics, especially minimums and maximums, in order to catch mistakes in data entry. Unfortunately, incorrect entries are not always obvious.

Outliers can also arise when sampling from a small population if one or several members of the population are very different in some relevant aspect from the rest of the population. The decision to keep or drop such observations in a regression analysis can be a difficult one, and the statistical properties of the resulting estimators are complicated. Outlying observations can provide important information by increasing the variation in the explanatory variables (which reduces standard errors). But OLS results should probably be reported with and without outlying observations in cases where one or several data points substantially change the results.

| EXAMPLE 9.8 | **R&D Intensity and Firm Size** |

Suppose that R&D expenditures as a percentage of sales (*rdintens*) are related to *sales* (in millions) and profits as a percentage of sales (*profmarg*):

$$rdintens = \beta_0 + \beta_1 sales + \beta_2 profmarg + u. \qquad [9.40]$$

The OLS equation using data on 32 chemical companies in RDCHEM is

$$\widehat{rdintens} = 2.625 + .000053\ sales + .0446\ profmarg$$
$$(0.586)\quad (.000044)\qquad\quad (.0462)$$
$$n = 32, R^2 = .0761, \bar{R}^2 = .0124.$$

Neither *sales* nor *profmarg* is statistically significant at even the 10% level in this regression.

Of the 32 firms, 31 have annual sales less than \$20 billion. One firm has annual sales of almost \$40 billion. Figure 9.1 shows how far this firm is from the rest of the sample. In terms of sales, this firm is over twice as large as every other firm, so it might be a good idea to estimate the model without it. When we do this, we obtain

$$\widehat{rdintens} = 2.297 + .000186\ sales + .0478\ profmarg$$
$$(0.592)\quad (.000084)\qquad\quad (.0445)$$
$$n = 31, R^2 = .1728, \bar{R}^2 = .1137.$$

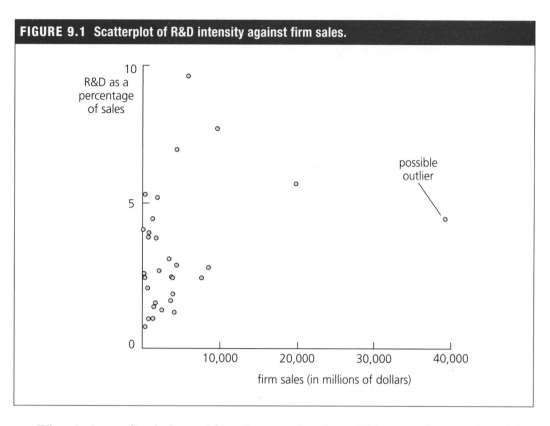

FIGURE 9.1 Scatterplot of R&D intensity against firm sales.

When the largest firm is dropped from the regression, the coefficient on *sales* more than triples, and it now has a *t* statistic over two. Using the sample of smaller firms, we would conclude that there is a statistically significant positive effect between R&D intensity and firm size. The profit margin is still not significant, and its coefficient has not changed by much.

Sometimes, outliers are defined by the size of the residual in an OLS regression, where all of the observations are used. Generally, this is *not* a good idea because the OLS estimates adjust to make the sum of squared residuals as small as possible. In the previous example, including the largest firm flattened the OLS regression line considerably, which made the residual for that estimation not especially large. In fact, the residual for the largest firm is −1.62 when all 32 observations are used. This value of the residual is not even one estimated standard deviation, $\hat{\sigma} = 1.82$, from the mean of the residuals, which is zero by construction.

Studentized residuals are obtained from the original OLS residuals by dividing them by an estimate of their standard deviation (conditional on the explanatory variables in the sample). The formula for the studentized residuals relies on matrix algebra, but it turns out there is a simple trick to compute a studentized residual for any observation. Namely, define a dummy variable equal to one for that observation—say, observation h—and then include the dummy variable in the regression (using all observations) along with the other explanatory variables. The coefficient on the dummy variable has a useful interpretation: it is the residual for observation h computed from the regression line using only the *other* observations. Therefore, the dummy's coefficient can be used to see how far off the observation is from the regression line obtained without using that observation. Even better, the *t* statistic on the dummy variable is equal to the studentized residual for observation h. Under the classical linear model assumptions, this *t* statistic has a t_{n-k-2} distribution. Therefore, a large value of the *t* statistic (in absolute value) implies a large residual relative to its estimated standard deviation.

For Example 9.8, if we define a dummy variable for the largest firm (observation 10 in the data file), and include it as an additional regressor, its coefficient is −6.57, verifying that the observation for the largest firm is very far from the regression line obtained using the other observations. However, when studentized, the residual is only −1.82. While this is a marginally significant t statistic (two-sided p-value = .08), it is not close to being the largest studentized residual in the sample. If we use the same method for the observation with the highest value of *rdintens*—the first observation, with *rdintens* ≈ 9.42—the coefficient on the dummy variable is 6.72 with a t statistic of 4.56. Therefore, by this measure, the first observation is more of an outlier than the tenth. Yet dropping the first observation changes the coefficient on *sales* by only a small amount (to about .000051 from .000053), although the coefficient on *profmarg* becomes larger and statistically significant. So, is the first observation an "outlier" too? These calculations show the conundrum one can enter when trying to determine observations that should be excluded from a regression analysis, even when the data set is small. Unfortunately, the size of the studentized residual need not correspond to how influential an observation is for the OLS slope estimates, and certainly not for all of them at once.

A general problem with using studentized residuals is that, in effect, all other observations are used to estimate the regression line to compute the residual for a particular observation. In other words, when the studentized residual is obtained for the first observation, the tenth observation has been used in estimating the intercept and slope. Given how flat the regression line is with the largest firm (tenth observation) included, it is not too surprising that the first observation, with its high value of *rdintens*, is far off the regression line.

Of course, we can add two dummy variables at the same time—one for the first observation and one for the tenth—which has the effect of using only the remaining 30 observations to estimate the regression line. If we estimate the equation without the first and tenth observations, the results are

$$\widehat{rdintens} = 1.939 + .000160\,sales + .0701\,profmarg$$
$$\qquad\quad (0.459)\ (.00065)\qquad\quad (.0343)$$
$$n = 30, R^2 = .2711, \overline{R}^2 = .2171$$

The coefficient on the dummy for the first observation is 6.47 ($t = 4.58$), and for the tenth observation it is −5.41 ($t = -1.95$). Notice that the coefficients on the *sales* and *profmarg* are both statistically significant, the latter at just about the 5% level against a two-sided alternative (p-value = .051). Even in this regression there are still two observations with studentized residuals greater than two (corresponding to the two remaining observations with R&D intensities above six).

Certain functional forms are less sensitive to outlying observations. In Section 6-2 we mentioned that, for most economic variables, the logarithmic transformation significantly narrows the range of the data and also yields functional forms—such as constant elasticity models—that can explain a broader range of data.

EXAMPLE 9.9   **R&D Intensity**

We can test whether R&D intensity increases with firm size by starting with the model

$$rd = sales^{\beta_1}\exp(\beta_0 + \beta_2 profmarg + u). \tag{9.41}$$

Then, holding other factors fixed, R&D intensity increases with *sales* if and only if $\beta_1 > 1$. Taking the log of (9.41) gives

$$\log(rd) = \beta_0 + \beta_1\log(sales) + \beta_2 profmarg + u. \tag{9.42}$$

When we use all 32 firms, the regression equation is

$$\widehat{\log(rd)} = -4.378 + 1.084 \log(sales) + .0217 \, profmarg,$$
$$\qquad\qquad (.468) \quad (.060) \qquad\qquad (.0128)$$
$$n = 32, R^2 = .9180, \bar{R}^2 = .9123,$$

while dropping the largest firm gives

$$\widehat{\log(rd)} = -4.404 + 1.088 \log(sales) + .0218 \, profmarg,$$
$$\qquad\qquad (.511) \quad (.067) \qquad\qquad (.0130)$$
$$n = 31, R^2 = .9037, \bar{R}^2 = .8968.$$

Practically, these results are the same. In neither case do we reject the null $H_0: \beta_1 = 1$ against $H_1: \beta_1 > 1$. (Why?)

In some cases, certain observations are suspected at the outset of being fundamentally different from the rest of the sample. This often happens when we use data at very aggregated levels, such as the city, county, or state level. The following is an example.

EXAMPLE 9.10   **State Infant Mortality Rates**

Data on infant mortality, per capita income, and measures of health care can be obtained at the state level from the *Statistical Abstract of the United States*. We will provide a fairly simple analysis here just to illustrate the effect of outliers. The data are for the year 1990, and we have all 50 states in the United States, plus the District of Columbia (D.C.). The variable *infmort* is number of deaths within the first year per 1,000 live births, *pcinc* is per capita income, *physic* is physicians per 100,000 members of the civilian population, and *popul* is the population (in thousands). The data are contained in INFMRT. We include all independent variables in logarithmic form:

$$\widehat{infmort} = 33.86 - 4.68 \log(pcinc) + 4.15 \log(physic)$$
$$\qquad\quad (20.43) \quad (2.60) \qquad\qquad (1.51)$$
$$\qquad\quad - .088 \log(popul) \qquad\qquad\qquad\qquad\qquad\text{[9.43]}$$
$$\qquad\quad (.287)$$
$$n = 51, R^2 = .139, \bar{R}^2 = .084.$$

Higher per capita income is estimated to lower infant mortality, an expected result. But more physicians per capita is associated with *higher* infant mortality rates, something that is counterintuitive. Infant mortality rates do not appear to be related to population size.

The District of Columbia is unusual in that it has pockets of extreme poverty and great wealth in a small area. In fact, the infant mortality rate for D.C. in 1990 was 20.7, compared with 12.4 for the highest state. It also has 615 physicians per 100,000 of the civilian population, compared with 337 for the highest state. The high number of physicians coupled with the high infant mortality rate in D.C. could certainly influence the results. If we drop D.C. from the regression, we obtain

$$\widehat{infmort} = 23.95 - .57 \log(pcinc) - 2.74 \log(physic)$$
$$\qquad\quad (12.42)(1.64) \qquad\qquad (1.19)$$
$$\qquad\quad + .629 \log(popul) \qquad\qquad\qquad\qquad\qquad\text{[9.44]}$$
$$\qquad\quad (.191)$$
$$n = 50, R^2 = .273, \bar{R}^2 = .226.$$

We now find that more physicians per capita lowers infant mortality, and the estimate is statistically different from zero at the 5% level. The effect of per capita income has fallen sharply and is no longer statistically significant. In equation (9.44), infant mortality rates are higher in more populous states, and the relationship is very statistically significant. Also, much more variation in *infmort* is explained when D.C. is dropped from the regression. Clearly, D.C. had substantial influence on the initial estimates, and we would probably leave it out of any further analysis.

As Example 9.8 demonstrates, inspecting observations in trying to determine which are outliers, and even which ones have substantial influence on the OLS estimates, is a difficult endeavor. More advanced treatments allow more formal approaches to determine which observations are likely to be influential observations. Using matrix algebra, Belsley, Kuh, and Welsh (1980) define the *leverage* of an observation, which formalizes the notion that an observation has a large or small influence on the OLS estimates. These authors also provide a more in-depth discussion of standardized and studentized residuals.

9-6 Least Absolute Deviations Estimation

Rather than trying to determine which observations, if any, have undue influence on the OLS estimates, a different approach to guarding against outliers is to use an estimation method that is less sensitive to outliers than OLS. One such method, which has become popular among applied econometricians, is called **least absolute deviations (LAD)**. The LAD estimators of the β_j in a linear model minimize the sum of the absolute values of the residuals,

$$\min_{b_0, b_1, \ldots, b_k} \sum_{i=1}^{n} |y_i - b_0 - b_1 x_{i1} - \ldots - b_k x_{ik}|. \qquad [9.45]$$

Unlike OLS, which minimizes the sum of squared residuals, the LAD estimates are not available in closed form—that is, we cannot write down formulas for them. In fact, historically, solving the problem in equation (9.45) was computationally difficult, especially with large sample sizes and many explanatory variables. But with the vast improvements in computational speed over the past two decades, LAD estimates are fairly easy to obtain even for large data sets.

Figure 9.2 shows the OLS and LAD objective functions. The LAD objective function is linear on either side of zero, so that if, say, a positive residual increases by one unit, the LAD objective function increases by one unit. By contrast, the OLS objective function gives increasing importance to large residuals, and this makes OLS more sensitive to outlying observations.

Because LAD does not give increasing weight to larger residuals, it is much less sensitive to changes in the extreme values of the data than OLS. In fact, it is known that LAD is designed to estimate the parameters of the **conditional median** of y given $x_1, x_2, \ldots, x_k$ rather than the conditional mean. Because the median is not affected by large changes in the extreme observations, it follows that the LAD parameter estimates are more resilient to outlying observations. (See Section A-1 for a brief discussion of the sample median.) In choosing the estimates, OLS squares each residual, and so the OLS estimates can be very sensitive to outlying observations, as we saw in Examples 9.8 and 9.10.

In addition to LAD being more computationally intensive than OLS, a second drawback of LAD is that all statistical inference involving the LAD estimators is justified only as the sample size grows. [The formulas are somewhat complicated and require matrix algebra, and we do not need them here. Koenker (2005) provides a comprehensive treatment.] Recall that, under the classical linear model assumptions, the OLS t statistics have exact t distributions, and F statistics have exact F distributions. While asymptotic versions of these statistics are available for LAD—and reported routinely by software packages that compute LAD estimates—these are justified only in large samples. Like the additional computational burden involved in computing LAD estimates, the lack of exact inference for LAD is only of minor concern, because most applications of LAD involve several hundred, if not

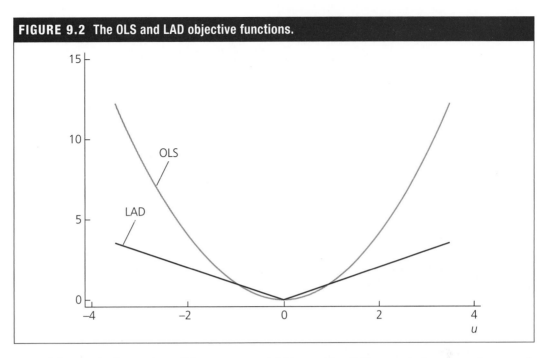

FIGURE 9.2 The OLS and LAD objective functions.

several thousand, observations. Of course, we might be pushing it if we apply large-sample approximations in an example such as Example 9.8, with $n = 32$. In a sense, this is not very different from OLS because, more often than not, we must appeal to large sample approximations to justify OLS inference whenever any of the CLM assumptions fail.

A more subtle but important drawback to LAD is that it does not always consistently estimate the parameters appearing in the conditional mean function, $E(y|x_1, ..., x_k)$. As mentioned earlier, LAD is intended to estimate the effects on the conditional median. Generally, the mean and median are the same only when the distribution of y given the covariates $x_1, ..., x_k$ is symmetric about $\beta_0 + \beta_1 x_1 + ... + \beta_k x_k$. (Equivalently, the population error term, u, is symmetric about zero.) Recall that OLS produces unbiased and consistent estimators of the parameters in the conditional mean whether or not the error distribution is symmetric; symmetry does not appear among the Gauss-Markov assumptions. When LAD and OLS are applied to cases with asymmetric distributions, the estimated partial effect of, say, x_1, obtained from LAD can be very different from the partial effect obtained from OLS. But such a difference could just reflect the difference between the median and the mean and might not have anything to do with outliers. See Computer Exercise C9 for an example.

If we assume that the population error u in model (9.2) is *independent* of $(x_1, ..., x_k)$, then the OLS and LAD slope estimates should differ only by sampling error whether or not the distribution of u is symmetric. The intercept estimates generally will be different to reflect the fact that, if the mean of u is zero, then its median is different from zero under asymmetry. Unfortunately, independence between the error and the explanatory variables is often unrealistically strong when LAD is applied. In particular, independence rules out heteroskedasticity, a problem that often arises in applications with asymmetric distributions.

An advantage that LAD has over OLS is that, because LAD estimates the median, it is easy to obtain partial effects—and predictions—using monotonic transformations. Here we consider the most common transformation, taking the natural log. Suppose that $\log(y)$ follows a linear model where the error has a zero conditional median:

$$\log(y) = \beta_0 + \mathbf{x}\boldsymbol{\beta} + u \qquad [9.46]$$

$$\text{Med}(u|\mathbf{x}) = 0, \qquad [9.47]$$

which implies that

$$\text{Med}[\log(y)|\mathbf{x}] = \beta_0 + \mathbf{x}\boldsymbol{\beta}.$$

A well-known feature of the conditional median—see, for example, Wooldridge (2010, Chapter 12)—is that it passes through increasing functions. Therefore,

$$\text{Med}(y|\mathbf{x}) = \exp(\beta_0 + \mathbf{x}\boldsymbol{\beta}). \tag{9.48}$$

It follows that β_j is the semi-elasticity of $\text{Med}(y|\mathbf{x})$ with respect to x_j. In other words, the partial effect of x_j in the linear equation (9.46) can be used to uncover the partial effect in the nonlinear model (9.48). It is important to understand that this holds for any distribution of u such that (9.47) holds, and we need not assume u and $\mathbf{x}$ are independent. By contrast, if we specify a linear model for $\text{E}[\log(y)|\mathbf{x}]$ then, in general, there is no way to uncover $\text{E}(y|\mathbf{x})$. If we make a full distributional assumption for u given $\mathbf{x}$ then, in principle, we can recover $\text{E}(y|\mathbf{x})$. We covered the special case in equation (6.40) under the assumption that $\log(y)$ follows a classical linear model. However, in general there is no way to find $\text{E}(y|\mathbf{x})$ from a model for $\text{E}[\log(y)|\mathbf{x}]$, even though we can always obtain $\text{Med}(y|\mathbf{x})$ from $\text{Med}[\log(y)|\mathbf{x}]$. Problem 9 investigates how heteroskedasticity in a linear model for $\log(y)$ confounds our ability to find $\text{E}(y|\mathbf{x})$.

LAD is a special case of what is often called *robust regression*. Unfortunately, the way "robust" is used here can be confusing. In the statistics literature, a robust regression estimator is relatively insensitive to extreme observations. Effectively, observations with large residuals are given less weight than in least squares. [Berk (1990) contains an introductory treatment of estimators that are robust to outlying observations.] Based on our earlier discussion, in econometric parlance, LAD is not a robust estimator of the conditional mean because it requires extra assumptions in order to consistently estimate the conditional mean parameters. In Equation (9.2), either the distribution of u given $(x_1, \ldots, x_k)$ has to be symmetric about zero, or u must be independent of $(x_1, \ldots, x_k)$. Neither of these is required for OLS.

LAD is also a special case of *quantile regression*, which is used to estimate the effect of the x_j on different parts of the distribution—not just the median (or mean). For example, in a study to see how having access to a particular pension plan affects wealth, it could be that access affects high-wealth people differently from low-wealth people, and these effects both differ from the median person. Wooldridge (2010, Chapter 12) contains a treatment and examples of quantile regression.

Summary

We have further investigated some important specification and data issues that often arise in empirical cross-sectional analysis. Misspecified functional form makes the estimated equation difficult to interpret. Nevertheless, incorrect functional form can be detected by adding quadratics, computing RESET, or testing against a nonnested alternative model using the Davidson-MacKinnon test. No additional data collection is needed.

Solving the omitted variables problem is more difficult. In Section 9-2, we discussed a possible solution based on using a proxy variable for the omitted variable. Under reasonable assumptions, including the proxy variable in an OLS regression eliminates, or at least reduces, bias. The hurdle in applying this method is that proxy variables can be difficult to find. A general possibility is to use data on a dependent variable from a prior year.

Applied economists are often concerned with measurement error. Under the classical errors-in-variables (CEV) assumptions, measurement error in the dependent variable has no effect on the statistical properties of OLS. In contrast, under the CEV assumptions for an independent variable, the OLS estimator for the coefficient on the mismeasured variable is biased toward zero. The bias in coefficients on the other variables can go either way and is difficult to determine.

Nonrandom samples from an underlying population can lead to biases in OLS. When sample selection is correlated with the error term u, OLS is generally biased and inconsistent. On the other hand, exogenous sample selection—which is either based on the explanatory variables or is otherwise independent of u—does not cause problems for OLS. Outliers in data sets can have large impacts on the OLS estimates, especially in small samples. It is important to at least informally identify outliers and to reestimate models with the suspected outliers excluded.

Least absolute deviations estimation is an alternative to OLS that is less sensitive to outliers and that delivers consistent estimates of conditional median parameters. In the past 20 years, with computational advances and improved understanding of the pros and cons of LAD and OLS, LAD is used more and more in empirical research–often as a supplement to OLS.

Key Terms

Attenuation Bias	Functional Form Misspecification	Nonrandom Sample
Average Marginal Effect	Influential Observations	Outliers
Average Partial Effect (APE)	Lagged Dependent Variable	Plug-In Solution to the Omitted
Classical Errors-in-Variables	Least Absolute Deviations (LAD)	Variables Problem
(CEV)	Measurement Error	Proxy Variable
Complete Cases Estimator	Missing at Random	Random Coefficient (Slope)
Conditional Median	Missing Completely at Random	Model
Davidson-MacKinnon Test	(MCAR)	Regression Specification Error
Endogenous Explanatory Variable	Missing Data	Test (RESET)
Endogenous Sample Selection	Multiplicative Measurement Error	Stratified Sampling
Exogenous Sample Selection	Nonnested Models	Studentized Residuals

Problems

1 In Problem 11 in Chapter 4, the R-squared from estimating the model

$$\log(salary) = \beta_0 + \beta_1\log(sales) + \beta_2\log(mktval) + \beta_3 profmarg$$
$$+ \beta_4 ceoten + \beta_5 comten + u,$$

using the data in CEOSAL2, was $R^2 = .353$ ($n = 177$). When $ceoten^2$ and $comten^2$ are added, $R^2 = .375$. Is there evidence of functional form misspecification in this model?

2 Let us modify Computer Exercise C4 in Chapter 8 by using voting outcomes in 1990 for incumbents who were elected in 1988. Candidate A was elected in 1988 and was seeking reelection in 1990; *voteA90* is Candidate A's share of the two-party vote in 1990. The 1988 voting share of Candidate A is used as a proxy variable for quality of the candidate. All other variables are for the 1990 election. The following equations were estimated, using the data in VOTE2:

$$\widehat{voteA90} = 75.71 + .312\, prtystrA + 4.93\, democA$$
$$(9.25)\ (.046)\qquad\quad (1.01)$$
$$-.929\log(expendA) - 1.950\log(expendB)$$
$$(.684)\qquad\qquad (.281)$$
$$n = 186, R^2 = .495, \overline{R}^2 = .483,$$

and

$$\widehat{voteA90} = 70.81 + .282\,prtystrA + 4.52\,democA$$
$$(10.01)\quad(.052)\qquad\qquad(1.06)$$
$$-.839\log(expendA) - 1.846\log(expendB) + .067\,voteA88$$
$$(.687)\qquad\qquad\qquad(.292)\qquad\qquad\qquad(.053)$$
$$n = 186,\, R^2 = .499,\, \bar{R}^2 = .485.$$

(i) Interpret the coefficient on *voteA88* and discuss its statistical significance.

(ii) Does adding *voteA88* have much effect on the other coefficients?

3 Let *math10* denote the percentage of students at a Michigan high school receiving a passing score on a standardized math test (see also Example 4.2). We are interested in estimating the effect of per-student spending on math performance. A simple model is

$$math10 = \beta_0 + \beta_1\log(expend) + \beta_2\log(enroll) + \beta_3 poverty + u,$$

where *poverty* is the percentage of students living in poverty.

(i) The variable *lnchprg* is the percentage of students eligible for the federally funded school lunch program. Why is this a sensible proxy variable for *poverty*?

(ii) The table that follows contains OLS estimates, with and without *lnchprg* as an explanatory variable.

Dependent Variable: *math10*		
Independent Variables	(1)	(2)
log(*expend*)	11.13	7.75
	(3.30)	(3.04)
log(*enroll*)	.022	−1.26
	(.615)	(.58)
lnchprg	—	−.324
		(.036)
intercept	−69.24	−23.14
	(26.72)	(24.99)
Observations	428	428
R-squared	.0297	.1893

Explain why the effect of expenditures on *math10* is lower in column (2) than in column (1). Is the effect in column (2) still statistically greater than zero?

(iii) Does it appear that pass rates are lower at larger schools, other factors being equal? Explain.

(iv) Interpret the coefficient on *lnchprg* in column (2).

(v) What do you make of the substantial increase in R^2 from column (1) to column (2)?

4 The following equation explains weekly hours of television viewing by a child in terms of the child's age, mother's education, father's education, and number of siblings:

$$tvhours^* = \beta_0 + \beta_1 age + \beta_2 age^2 + \beta_3 motheduc + \beta_4 fatheduc + \beta_5 sibs + u.$$

We are worried that *tvhours** is measured with error in our survey. Let *tvhours* denote the reported hours of television viewing per week.

(i) What do the classical errors-in-variables (CEV) assumptions require in this application?

(ii) Do you think the CEV assumptions are likely to hold? Explain.

5 In Example 4.4, we estimated a model relating number of campus crimes to student enrollment for a sample of colleges. The sample we used was not a random sample of colleges in the United States, because many schools in 1992 did not report campus crimes. Do you think that college failure to report crimes can be viewed as exogenous sample selection? Explain.

6 In the model (9.17), show that OLS consistently estimates α and β if a_i is uncorrelated with x_i and b_i is uncorrelated with x_i and x_i^2, which are weaker assumptions than (9.19). [*Hint*: Write the equation as in (9.18) and recall from Chapter 5 that sufficient for consistency of OLS for the intercept and slope is $E(u_i) = 0$ and $Cov(x_i, u_i) = 0$.]

7 Consider the simple regression model with classical measurement error, $y = \beta_0 + \beta_1 x^* + u$, where we have m measures on x^*. Write these as $z_h = x^* + e_h, h = 1, \ldots, m$. Assume that x^* is uncorrelated with $u, e_1, \ldots, e_m$, that the measurement errors are pairwise uncorrelated, and have the same variance, σ_e^2. Let $w = (z_1 + \ldots + z_m)/m$ be the average of the measures on x^*, so that, for each observation $i, w_i = (z_{i1} + \ldots + z_{im})/m$ is the average of the m measures. Let $\bar{\beta}_1$ be the OLS estimator from the simple regression y_i on 1, $w_i, i = 1, \ldots, n$, using a random sample of data.
(i)   Show that

$$\text{plim}(\bar{\beta}_1) = \beta_1 \left\{ \frac{\sigma_{x^*}^2}{[\sigma_{x^*}^2 + (\sigma_e^2/m)]} \right\}.$$

[*Hint:* The plim of $\bar{\beta}_1$ is $Cov(w,y)/Var(w)$.]
(ii)   How does the inconsistency in $\bar{\beta}_1$ compare with that when only a single measure is available (that is, $m = 1$)? What happens as m grows? Comment.

8 The point of this exercise is to show that tests for functional form cannot be relied on as a general test for omitted variables. Suppose that, conditional on the explanatory variables x_1 and x_2, a linear model relating y to x_1 and x_2 satisfies the Gauss-Markov assumptions:

$$y = \beta_0 + \beta_1 x_1 + \beta_2 x_2 + u$$
$$E(u|x_1, x_2) = 0$$
$$Var(u|x_1, x_2) = \sigma^2.$$

To make the question interesting, assume $\beta_2 \neq 0$.

Suppose further that x_2 has a simple linear relationship with x_1:

$$x_2 = \delta_0 + \delta_1 x_1 + r$$
$$E(r|x_1) = 0$$
$$Var(r|x_1) = \tau^2.$$

(i)   Show that

$$E(y|x_1) = (\beta_0 + \beta_2 \delta_0) + (\beta_1 + \beta_2 \delta_1) x_1.$$

Under random sampling, what is the probability limit of the OLS estimator from the simple regression of y on x_1? Is the simple regression estimator generally consistent for β_1?
(ii)   If you run the regression of y on x_1, x_1^2, what will be the probability limit of the OLS estimator of the coefficient on x_1^2? Explain.
(iii)   Using substitution, show that we can write

$$y = (\beta_0 + \beta_2 \delta_0) + (\beta_1 + \beta_2 \delta_1) x_1 + u + \beta_2 r.$$

It can be shown that, if we define $v = u + \beta_2 r$ then $E(v|x_1) = 0$, $Var(v|x_1) = \sigma^2 + \beta_2^2 \tau^2$. What consequences does this have for the t statistic on x_1^2 from the regression in part (ii)?
(iv)   What do you conclude about adding a nonlinear function of x_1—in particular, x_1^2—in an attempt to detect omission of x_2?

9 Suppose that $\log(y)$ follows a linear model with a linear form of heteroskedasticity. We write this as

$$\log(y) = \beta_0 + \mathbf{x}\boldsymbol{\beta} + u$$
$$u|\mathbf{x} \sim \text{Normal}(0, h(\mathbf{x})),$$

so that, conditional on $\mathbf{x}$, u has a normal distribution with mean (and median) zero but with variance $h(\mathbf{x})$ that depends on $\mathbf{x}$. Because $\text{Med}(u|\mathbf{x}) = 0$, equation (9.48) holds: $\text{Med}(y|\mathbf{x}) = \exp(\beta_0 + \mathbf{x}\boldsymbol{\beta})$. Further, using an extension of the result from Chapter 6, it can be shown that

$$E(y|\mathbf{x}) = \exp[\beta_0 + \mathbf{x}\boldsymbol{\beta} + h(\mathbf{x})/2].$$

(i) Given that $h(\mathbf{x})$ can be any positive function, is it possible to conclude $\partial E(y|\mathbf{x})/\partial x_j$ is the same sign as β_j?

(ii) Suppose $h(\mathbf{x}) = \delta_0 + \mathbf{x}\boldsymbol{\delta}$ (and ignore the problem that linear functions are not necessarily always positive). Show that a particular variable, say x_1, can have a negative effect on $\text{Med}(y|\mathbf{x})$ but a positive effect on $E(y|\mathbf{x})$.

(iii) Consider the case covered in Section 6-4, where $h(\mathbf{x}) = \sigma^2$. How would you predict y using an estimate of $E(y|\mathbf{x})$? How would you predict y using an estimate of $\text{Med}(y|\mathbf{x})$? Which prediction is always larger?

10 This exercise shows that in a simple regression model, adding a dummy variable for missing data on the explanatory variable produces a consistent estimator of the slope coefficient if the "missingness" is unrelated to both the unobservable and observable factors affecting y. Let m be a variable such that $m = 1$ if we do not observe x and $m = 0$ if we observe x. We assume that y is always observed. The population model is

$$y = \beta_0 + \beta_1 x + u$$
$$E(u|x) = 0.$$

(i) Provide an interpretation of the stronger assumption

$$E(u|x,m) = 0.$$

In particular, what kind of missing data schemes would cause this assumption to fail?

(ii) Show that we can always write

$$y = \beta_0 + \beta_1(1 - m)x + \beta_1 mx + u.$$

(iii) Let $\{(x_i, y_i, m_i): i = 1, ..., n\}$ be random draws from the population, where x_i is missing when $m_i = 1$. Explain the nature of the variable $z_i = (1 - m_i)x_i$. In particular, what does this variable equal when x_i is missing?

(iv) Let $\rho = P(m = 1)$ and assume that m and x are independent. Show that

$$\text{Cov}[(1 - m)x, mx] = -\rho(1 - \rho)\mu_x,$$

where $\mu_x = E(x)$. What does this imply about estimating β_1 from the regression y_i on $z_i, i = 1, ..., n$?

(v) If m and x are independent, it can be shown that

$$mx = \delta_0 + \delta_1 m + v,$$

where v is uncorrelated with m and $z = (1 - m)x$. Explain why this makes m a suitable proxy variable for mx. What does this mean about the coefficient on z_i in the regression

$$y_i \text{ on } z_i, m_i, i = 1, ..., n?$$

(vi) Suppose for a population of children, y is a standardized test score, obtained from school records, and x is family income, which is reported voluntarily by families (and so some families do not report their income). Is it realistic to assume m and x are independent? Explain.

Computer Exercises

C1 (i) Apply RESET from equation (9.3) to the model estimated in Computer Exercise C5 in Chapter 7. Is there evidence of functional form misspecification in the equation?

(ii) Compute a heteroskedasticity-robust form of RESET. Does your conclusion from part (i) change?

C2 Use the data set WAGE2 for this exercise.

(i) Use the variable *KWW* (the "knowledge of the world of work" test score) as a proxy for ability in place of *IQ* in Example 9.3. What is the estimated return to education in this case?

(ii) Now, use *IQ* and *KWW* together as proxy variables. What happens to the estimated return to education?

(iii) In part (ii), are *IQ* and *KWW* individually significant? Are they jointly significant?

C3 Use the data from JTRAIN for this exercise.

(i) Consider the simple regression model

$$\log(scrap) = \beta_0 + \beta_1 grant + u,$$

where *scrap* is the firm scrap rate and *grant* is a dummy variable indicating whether a firm received a job training grant. Can you think of some reasons why the unobserved factors in u might be correlated with *grant*?

(ii) Estimate the simple regression model using the data for 1988. (You should have 54 observations.) Does receiving a job training grant significantly lower a firm's scrap rate?

(iii) Now, add as an explanatory variable $\log(scrap_{87})$. How does this change the estimated effect of *grant*? Interpret the coefficient on *grant*. Is it statistically significant at the 5% level against the one-sided alternative $H_1: \beta_{grant} < 0$?

(iv) Test the null hypothesis that the parameter on $\log(scrap_{87})$ is one against the two-sided alternative. Report the p-value for the test.

(v) Repeat parts (iii) and (iv), using heteroskedasticity-robust standard errors, and briefly discuss any notable differences.

C4 Use the data for the year 1990 in INFMRT for this exercise.

(i) Reestimate equation (9.43), but now include a dummy variable for the observation on the District of Columbia (called *DC*). Interpret the coefficient on *DC* and comment on its size and significance.

(ii) Compare the estimates and standard errors from part (i) with those from equation (9.44). What do you conclude about including a dummy variable for a single observation?

C5 Use the data in RDCHEM to further examine the effects of outliers on OLS estimates and to see how LAD is less sensitive to outliers. The model is

$$rdintens = \beta_0 + \beta_1 sales + \beta_2 sales^2 + \beta_3 profmarg + u,$$

where you should first change *sales* to be in billions of dollars to make the estimates easier to interpret.

(i) Estimate the above equation by OLS, both with and without the firm having annual sales of almost $40 billion. Discuss any notable differences in the estimated coefficients.

(ii) Estimate the same equation by LAD, again with and without the largest firm. Discuss any important differences in estimated coefficients.

(iii) Based on your findings in (i) and (ii), would you say OLS or LAD is more resilient to outliers?

C6 Redo Example 4.10 by dropping schools where teacher benefits are less than 1% of salary.

(i) How many observations are lost?

(ii) Does dropping these observations have any important effects on the estimated tradeoff?

C7 Use the data in LOANAPP for this exercise.

(i) How many observations have $obrat > 40$, that is, other debt obligations more than 40% of total income?

(ii) Reestimate the model in part (iii) of Computer Exercise C8, excluding observations with $obrat > 40$. What happens to the estimate and t statistic on $white$?

(iii) Does it appear that the estimate of β_{white} is overly sensitive to the sample used?

C8 Use the data in TWOYEAR for this exercise.

(i) The variable $stotal$ is a standardized test variable, which can act as a proxy variable for unobserved ability. Find the sample mean and standard deviation of $stotal$.

(ii) Run simple regressions of jc and $univ$ on $stotal$. Are both college education variables statistically related to $stotal$? Explain.

(iii) Add $stotal$ to equation (4.17) and test the hypothesis that the returns to two- and four-year colleges are the same against the alternative that the return to four-year colleges is greater. How do your findings compare with those from Section 4-4?

(iv) Add $stotal^2$ to the equation estimated in part (iii). Does a quadratic in the test score variable seem necessary?

(v) Add the interaction terms $stotal \cdot jc$ and $stotal \cdot univ$ to the equation from part (iii). Are these terms jointly significant?

(vi) What would be your final model that controls for ability through the use of $stotal$? Justify your answer.

C9 In this exercise, you are to compare OLS and LAD estimates of the effects of 401(k) plan eligibility on net financial assets. The model is

$$nettfa = \beta_0 + \beta_1 inc + \beta_2 inc^2 + \beta_3 age + \beta_4 age^2 + \beta_5 male + \beta_6 e401k + u.$$

(i) Use the data in 401KSUBS to estimate the equation by OLS and report the results in the usual form. Interpret the coefficient on $e401k$.

(ii) Use the OLS residuals to test for heteroskedasticity using the Breusch-Pagan test. Is u independent of the explanatory variables?

(iii) Estimate the equation by LAD and report the results in the same form as for OLS. Interpret the LAD estimate of β_6.

(iv) Reconcile your findings from parts (i) and (iii).

C10 You need to use two data sets for this exercise, JTRAIN2 and JTRAIN3. The former is the outcome of a job training experiment. The file JTRAIN3 contains observational data, where individuals themselves largely determine whether they participate in job training. The data sets cover the same time period.

(i) In the data set JTRAIN2, what fraction of the men received job training? What is the fraction in JTRAIN3? Why do you think there is such a big difference?

(ii) Using JTRAIN2, run a simple regression of $re78$ on $train$. What is the estimated effect of participating in job training on real earnings?

(iii) Now add as controls to the regression in part (ii) the variables $re74$, $re75$, $educ$, age, $black$, and $hisp$. Does the estimated effect of job training on $re78$ change much? How come? (*Hint:* Remember that these are experimental data.)

(iv) Do the regressions in parts (ii) and (iii) using the data in JTRAIN3, reporting only the estimated coefficients on $train$, along with their t statistics. What is the effect now of controlling for the extra factors, and why?

(v) Define $avgre = (re74 + re75)/2$. Find the sample averages, standard deviations, and minimum and maximum values in the two data sets. Are these data sets representative of the same populations in 1978?

(vi) Almost 96% of men in the data set JTRAIN2 have $avgre$ less than $10,000. Using only these men, run the regression

$$re78 \text{ on } train, re74, re75, educ, age, black, hisp$$

and report the training estimate and its t statistic. Run the same regression for JTRAIN3, using only men with $avgre \leq 10$. For the subsample of low-income men, how do the estimated training effects compare across the experimental and nonexperimental data sets?

(vii) Now use each data set to run the simple regression $re78$ on $train$, but only for men who were unemployed in 1974 and 1975. How do the training estimates compare now?

(viii) Using your findings from the previous regressions, discuss the potential importance of having comparable populations underlying comparisons of experimental and nonexperimental estimates.

C11 Use the data in MURDER only for the year 1993 for this question, although you will need to first obtain the lagged murder rate, say $mrdrte_{-1}$.

(i) Run the regression of $mrdrte$ on $exec$, $unem$. What are the coefficient and t statistic on $exec$? Does this regression provide any evidence for a deterrent effect of capital punishment?

(ii) How many executions are reported for Texas during 1993? (Actually, this is the sum of executions for the current and past two years.) How does this compare with the other states? Add a dummy variable for Texas to the regression in part (i). Is its t statistic unusually large? From this, does it appear Texas is an "outlier"?

(iii) To the regression in part (i) add the lagged murder rate. What happens to $\hat{\beta}_{exec}$ and its statistical significance?

(iv) For the regression in part (iii), does it appear Texas is an outlier? What is the effect on $\hat{\beta}_{exec}$ from dropping Texas from the regression?

C12 Use the data in ELEM94_95 to answer this question. See also Computer Exercise C10 in Chapter 4.

(i) Using all of the data, run the regression $lavgsal$ on bs, $lenrol$, $lstaff$, and $lunch$. Report the coefficient on bs along with its usual and heteroskedasticity-robust standard errors. What do you conclude about the economic and statistical significance of $\hat{\beta}_{bs}$?

(ii) Now drop the four observations with $bs > .5$, that is, where average benefits are (supposedly) more than 50% of average salary. What is the coefficient on bs? Is it statistically significant using the heteroskedasticity-robust standard error?

(iii) Verify that the four observations with $bs > .5$ are 68, 1,127, 1,508, and 1,670. Define four dummy variables for each of these observations. (You might call them $d68$, $d1127$, $d1508$, and $d1670$.) Add these to the regression from part (i) and verify that the OLS coefficients and standard errors on the other variables are identical to those in part (ii). Which of the four dummies has a t statistic statistically different from zero at the 5% level?

(iv) Verify that, in this data set, the data point with the largest studentized residual (largest t statistic on the dummy variable) in part (iii) has a large influence on the OLS estimates. (That is, run OLS using all observations except the one with the large studentized residual.) Does dropping, in turn, each of the other observations with $bs > .5$ have important effects?

(v) What do you conclude about the sensitivity of OLS to a single observation, even with a large sample size?

(vi) Verify that the LAD estimator is not sensitive to the inclusion of the observation identified in part (iii).

C13 Use the data in CEOSAL2 to answer this question.

(i) Estimate the model

$$lsalary = \beta_0 + \beta_1 lsales + \beta_2 lmktval + \beta_3 ceoten + \beta_4 ceoten^2 + u$$

by OLS using all of the observations, where $lsalary$, $lsales$, and $lmktvale$ are all natural logarithms. Report the results in the usual form with the usual OLS standard errors. (You may verify that the heteroskedasticity-robust standard errors are similar.)

(ii) In the regression from part (i) obtain the studentized residuals; call these str_i. How many studentized residuals are above 1.96 in absolute value? If the studentized residuals were independent draws from a standard normal distribution, about how many would you expect to be above two in absolute value with 177 draws?

(iii) Reestimate the equation in part (i) by OLS using only the observations with $|str_i| \leq 1.96$. How do the coefficients compare with those in part (i)?

(iv) Estimate the equation in part (i) by LAD, using all of the data. Is the estimate of β_1 closer to the OLS estimate using the full sample or the restricted sample? What about for β_3?

(v) Evaluate the following statement: "Dropping outliers based on extreme values of studentized residuals makes the resulting OLS estimates closer to the LAD estimates on the full sample."

C14 Use the data in ECONMATH to answer this question. The population model is

$$score = \beta_0 + \beta_1 act + u.$$

(i) For how many students is the ACT score missing? What is the fraction of the sample? Define a new variable, *actmiss*, which equals one if *act* is missing, and zero otherwise.

(ii) Create a new variable, say *act0*, which is the *act* score when *act* is reported and zero when *act* is missing. Find the average of *act0* and compare it with the average for *act*.

(iii) Run the simple regression of *score* on *act* using only the complete cases. What do you obtain for the slope coefficient and its heteroskedasticity-robust standard error?

(iv) Run the simple regression of *score* on *act0* using all of the cases. Compare the slope coefficient with that in part (iii) and comment.

(v) Now use all of the cases and run the regression

$$score_i \text{ on } act0_i, actmiss_i.$$

What is the slope estimate on $act0_i$? How does it compare with the answers in parts (iii) and (iv)?

(vi) Comparing regressions (iii) and (v), does using all cases and adding the missing data estimator improve estimation of β_1?

(vii) If you add the variable *colgpa* to the regressions in parts (iii) and (v), does this change your answer to part (vi)?

PART 2

Regression Analysis with Time Series Data

Now that we have a solid understanding of how to use the multiple regression model for cross-sectional applications, we can turn to the econometric analysis of time series data. Since we will rely heavily on the method of ordinary least squares, most of the work concerning mechanics and inference has already been done. However, as we noted in Chapter 1, time series data have certain characteristics that cross-sectional data do not, and these can require special attention when applying OLS.

Chapter 10 covers basic regression analysis and gives attention to problems unique to time series data. We provide a set of Gauss-Markov and classical linear model assumptions for time series applications. The problems of functional form, dummy variables, trends, and seasonality are also discussed.

Because certain time series models necessarily violate the Gauss-Markov assumptions, Chapter 11 describes the nature of these violations and presents the large sample properties of ordinary least squares. As we can no longer assume random sampling, we must cover conditions that restrict the temporal correlation in a time series in order to ensure that the usual asymptotic analysis is valid.

Chapter 12 turns to an important new problem: serial correlation in the error terms in time series regressions. We discuss the consequences, ways of testing, and methods for dealing with serial correlation. Chapter 12 also contains an explanation of how heteroskedasticity can arise in time series models.

CHAPTER 10

Basic Regression Analysis with Time Series Data

In this chapter, we begin to study the properties of OLS for estimating linear regression models using time series data. In Section 10-1, we discuss some conceptual differences between time series and cross-sectional data. Section 10-2 provides some examples of time series regressions that are often estimated in the empirical social sciences. We then turn our attention to the finite sample properties of the OLS estimators and state the Gauss-Markov assumptions and the classical linear model assumptions for time series regression. Although these assumptions have features in common with those for the cross-sectional case, they also have some significant differences that we will need to highlight.

In addition, we return to some issues that we treated in regression with cross-sectional data, such as how to use and interpret the logarithmic functional form and dummy variables. The important topics of how to incorporate trends and account for seasonality in multiple regression are taken up in Section 10-5.

10-1 The Nature of Time Series Data

An obvious characteristic of time series data that distinguishes them from cross-sectional data is temporal ordering. For example, in Chapter 1, we briefly discussed a time series data set on employment, the minimum wage, and other economic variables for Puerto Rico. In this data set, we must know that the data for 1970 immediately precede the data for 1971. For analyzing time series data in the social sciences, we must recognize that the past can affect the future, but not vice versa (unlike in the *Star Trek* universe). To emphasize the proper ordering of time series data, Table 10.1 gives a partial listing

TABLE 10.1 Partial Listing of Data on U.S. Inflation and Unemployment Rates, 1948–2003		
Year	Inflation	Unemployment
1948	8.1	3.8
1949	−1.2	5.9
1950	1.3	5.3
1951	7.9	3.3
.	.	.
.	.	.
.	.	.
1998	1.6	4.5
1999	2.2	4.2
2000	3.4	4.0
2001	2.8	4.7
2002	1.6	5.8
2003	2.3	6.0

of the data on U.S. inflation and unemployment rates from various editions of the *Economic Report of the President*, including the 2004 *Report* (Tables B-42 and B-64).

Another difference between cross-sectional and time series data is more subtle. In Chapters 3 and 4, we studied statistical properties of the OLS estimators based on the notion that samples were randomly drawn from the appropriate population. Understanding why cross-sectional data should be viewed as random outcomes is fairly straightforward: a different sample drawn from the population will generally yield different values of the independent and dependent variables (such as education, experience, wage, and so on). Therefore, the OLS estimates computed from different random samples will generally differ, and this is why we consider the OLS estimators to be random variables.

How should we think about randomness in time series data? Certainly, economic time series satisfy the intuitive requirements for being outcomes of random variables. For example, today we do not know what the Dow Jones Industrial Average will be at the close of the next trading day. We do not know what the annual growth in output will be in Canada during the coming year. Since the outcomes of these variables are not foreknown, they should clearly be viewed as random variables.

Formally, a sequence of random variables indexed by time is called a **stochastic process** or a **time series process**. ("Stochastic" is a synonym for random.) When we collect a time series data set, we obtain one possible outcome, or *realization*, of the stochastic process. We can only see a single realization because we cannot go back in time and start the process over again. (This is analogous to cross-sectional analysis where we can collect only one random sample.) However, if certain conditions in history had been different, we would generally obtain a different realization for the stochastic process, and this is why we think of time series data as the outcome of random variables. The set of all possible realizations of a time series process plays the role of the population in cross-sectional analysis. The sample size for a time series data set is the number of time periods over which we observe the variables of interest.

10-2 Examples of Time Series Regression Models

In this section, we discuss two examples of time series models that have been useful in empirical time series analysis and that are easily estimated by ordinary least squares. We will study additional models in Chapter 11.

10-2a Static Models

Suppose that we have time series data available on two variables, say y and z, where y_t and z_t are dated contemporaneously. A **static model** relating y to z is

$$y_t = \beta_0 + \beta_1 z_t + u_t, \ t = 1, 2, \ldots, n. \tag{10.1}$$

The name "static model" comes from the fact that we are modeling a contemporaneous relationship between y and z. Usually, a static model is postulated when a change in z at time t is believed to have an immediate effect on y: $\Delta y_t = \beta_1 \Delta z_t$, when $\Delta u_t = 0$. Static regression models are also used when we are interested in knowing the tradeoff between y and z.

An example of a static model is the *static Phillips curve*, given by

$$inf_t = \beta_0 + \beta_1 unem_t + u_t, \tag{10.2}$$

where inf_t is the annual inflation rate and $unem_t$ is the annual unemployment rate. This form of the Phillips curve assumes a constant *natural rate of unemployment* and constant inflationary expectations, and it can be used to study the contemporaneous tradeoff between inflation and unemployment. [See, for example, Mankiw (1994, Section 11-2).]

Naturally, we can have several explanatory variables in a static regression model. Let $mrdrte_t$ denote the murders per 10,000 people in a particular city during year t, let $convrte_t$ denote the murder conviction rate, let $unem_t$ be the local unemployment rate, and let $yngmle_t$ be the fraction of the population consisting of males between the ages of 18 and 25. Then, a static multiple regression model explaining murder rates is

$$mrdrte_t = \beta_0 + \beta_1 convrte_t + \beta_2 unem_t + \beta_3 yngmle_t + u_t. \tag{10.3}$$

Using a model such as this, we can hope to estimate, for example, the ceteris paribus effect of an increase in the conviction rate on a particular criminal activity.

10-2b Finite Distributed Lag Models

In a **finite distributed lag (FDL) model**, we allow one or more variables to affect y with a lag. For example, for annual observations, consider the model

$$gfr_t = \alpha_0 + \delta_0 pe_t + \delta_1 pe_{t-1} + \delta_2 pe_{t-2} + u_t, \tag{10.4}$$

where gfr_t is the general fertility rate (children born per 1,000 women of childbearing age) and pe_t is the real dollar value of the personal tax exemption. The idea is to see whether, in the aggregate, the decision to have children is linked to the tax value of having a child. Equation (10.4) recognizes that, for both biological and behavioral reasons, decisions to have children would not immediately result from changes in the personal exemption.

Equation (10.4) is an example of the model

$$y_t = \alpha_0 + \delta_0 z_t + \delta_1 z_{t-1} + \delta_2 z_{t-2} + u_t, \tag{10.5}$$

which is an FDL *of order two*. To interpret the coefficients in (10.5), suppose that z is a constant, equal to c, in all time periods before time t. At time t, z increases by one unit to $c + 1$ and then reverts to its previous level at time $t + 1$. (That is, the increase in z is temporary.) More precisely,

$$\ldots, z_{t-2} = c, z_{t-1} = c, z_t = c + 1, z_{t+1} = c, z_{t+2} = c, \ldots.$$

To focus on the ceteris paribus effect of z on y, we set the error term in each time period to zero. Then,

$$y_{t-1} = \alpha_0 + \delta_0 c + \delta_1 c + \delta_2 c,$$
$$y_t = \alpha_0 + \delta_0 (c + 1) + \delta_1 c + \delta_2 c,$$
$$y_{t+1} = \alpha_0 + \delta_0 c + \delta_1 (c + 1) + \delta_2 c,$$
$$y_{t+2} = \alpha_0 + \delta_0 c + \delta_1 c + \delta_2 (c + 1),$$
$$y_{t+3} = \alpha_0 + \delta_0 c + \delta_1 c + \delta_2 c,$$

and so on. From the first two equations, $y_t - y_{t-1} = \delta_0$, which shows that δ_0 is the immediate change in y due to the one-unit increase in z at time t. δ_0 is usually called the **impact propensity** or **impact multiplier**.

Similarly, $\delta_1 = y_{t+1} - y_{t-1}$ is the change in y one period after the temporary change and $\delta_2 = y_{t+2} - y_{t-1}$ is the change in y two periods after the change. At time $t + 3$, y has reverted back to its initial level: $y_{t+3} = y_{t-1}$. This is because we have assumed that only two lags of z appear in (10.5). When we graph the δ_j as a function of j, we obtain the **lag distribution**, which summarizes the dynamic effect that a temporary increase in z has on y. A possible lag distribution for the FDL of order two is given in Figure 10.1. (Of course, we would never know the parameters δ_j; instead, we will estimate the δ_j and then plot the estimated lag distribution.)

The lag distribution in Figure 10.1 implies that the largest effect is at the first lag. The lag distribution has a useful interpretation. If we standardize the initial value of y at $y_{t-1} = 0$, the lag distribution traces out all subsequent values of y due to a one-unit, temporary increase in z.

We are also interested in the change in y due to a *permanent* increase in z. Before time t, z equals the constant c. At time t, z increases permanently to $c + 1$: $z_s = c$, $s < t$ and $z_s = c + 1$, $s \geq t$. Again, setting the errors to zero, we have

$$y_{t-1} = \alpha_0 + \delta_0 c + \delta_1 c + \delta_2 c,$$
$$y_t = \alpha_0 + \delta_0 (c + 1) + \delta_1 c + \delta_2 c,$$
$$y_{t+1} = \alpha_0 + \delta_0 (c + 1) + \delta_1 (c + 1) + \delta_2 c,$$
$$y_{t+2} = \alpha_0 + \delta_0 (c + 1) + \delta_1 (c + 1) + \delta_2 (c + 1),$$

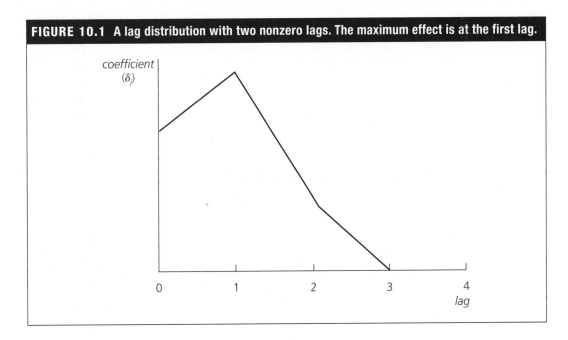

FIGURE 10.1 A lag distribution with two nonzero lags. The maximum effect is at the first lag.

and so on. With the permanent increase in z, after one period, y has increased by $\delta_0 + \delta_1$, and after two periods, y has increased by $\delta_0 + \delta_1 + \delta_2$. There are no further changes in y after two periods. This shows that the sum of the coefficients on current and lagged z, $\delta_0 + \delta_1 + \delta_2$, is the *long-run* change in y given a permanent increase in z and is called the **long-run propensity (LRP)** or **long-run multiplier**. The LRP is often of interest in distributed lag models.

As an example, in equation (10.4), δ_0 measures the immediate change in fertility due to a one-dollar increase in pe. As we mentioned earlier, there are reasons to believe that δ_0 is small, if not zero. But δ_1 or δ_2, or both, might be positive. If pe *permanently* increases by one dollar, then, after two years, gfr will have changed by $\delta_0 + \delta_1 + \delta_2$. This model assumes that there are no further changes after two years. Whether this is actually the case is an empirical matter.

An FDL of order q is written as

$$y_t = \alpha_0 + \delta_0 z_t + \delta_1 z_{t-1} + \ldots + \delta_q z_{t-q} + u_t. \qquad [10.6]$$

This contains the static model as a special case by setting $\delta_1, \delta_2, \ldots, \delta_q$ equal to zero. Sometimes, a primary purpose for estimating a distributed lag model is to test whether z has a lagged effect on y. The impact propensity is always the coefficient on the contemporaneous z, δ_0. Occasionally, we omit z_t from (10.6), in which case the impact propensity is zero. In the general case, the lag distribution can be plotted by graphing the (estimated) δ_j as a function of j. For any horizon h, we can define the **cumulative effect** as $\delta_0 + \delta_1 + \ldots + \delta_h$, which is interpreted as the change in the expected outcome h periods after a permanent, one-unit increase in x. Once the δ_j have been estimated, one may plot the estimated cumulative effects as a function of h. The LRP is the cumulative effect after all changes have taken place; it is simply the sum of all of the coefficients on the z_{t-j}:

$$\text{LRP} = \delta_0 + \delta_1 + \ldots + \delta_q. \qquad [10.7]$$

> **EXPLORING FURTHER 10.1**
>
> In an equation for annual data, suppose that
>
> $$int_t = 1.6 + .48\,inf_t - .15\,inf_{t-1} + .32\,inf_{t-2} + u_t$$
>
> where int is an interest rate and inf is the inflation rate. What are the impact and long-run propensities?

Because of the often substantial correlation in z at different lags—that is, due to multicollinearity in (10.6)—it can be difficult to obtain precise estimates of the individual δ_j. Interestingly, even when the δ_j cannot be precisely estimated, we can often get good estimates of the LRP. We will see an example later.

We can have more than one explanatory variable appearing with lags, or we can add contemporaneous variables to an FDL model. For example, the average education level for women of childbearing age could be added to (10.4), which allows us to account for changing education levels for women.

10-2c A Convention about the Time Index

When models have lagged explanatory variables (and, as we will see in the next chapter, for models with lagged y), confusion can arise concerning the treatment of initial observations. For example, if in (10.5) we assume that the equation holds starting at $t = 1$, then the explanatory variables for the first time period are z_1, z_0, and z_{-1}. Our convention will be that these are the initial values in our sample, so that we can always start the time index at $t = 1$. In practice, this is not very important because regression packages automatically keep track of the observations available for estimating models with lags. But for this and the next two chapters, we need some convention concerning the first time period being represented by the regression equation.

10-3 Finite Sample Properties of OLS under Classical Assumptions

In this section, we give a complete listing of the finite sample, or small sample, properties of OLS under standard assumptions. We pay particular attention to how the assumptions must be altered from our cross-sectional analysis to cover time series regressions.

10-3a Unbiasedness of OLS

The first assumption simply states that the time series process follows a model that is linear in its parameters.

Assumption TS.1 **Linear in Parameters**

The stochastic process $\{(x_{t1}, x_{t2}, \ldots, x_{tk}, y_t): t = 1, 2, \ldots, n\}$ follows the linear model

$$y_t = \beta_0 + \beta_1 x_{t1} + \ldots + \beta_k x_{tk} + u_t, \qquad [10.8]$$

where $\{u_t: t = 1, 2, \ldots, n\}$ is the sequence of errors or disturbances. Here, n is the number of observations (time periods).

In the notation x_{tj}, t denotes the time period, and j is, as usual, a label to indicate one of the k explanatory variables. The terminology used in cross-sectional regression applies here: y_t is the dependent variable, explained variable, or regressand; the x_{tj} are the independent variables, explanatory variables, or regressors.

We should think of Assumption TS.1 as being essentially the same as Assumption MLR.1 (the first cross-sectional assumption), but we are now specifying a linear model for time series data. The examples covered in Section 10-2 can be cast in the form of (10.8) by appropriately defining x_{tj}. For example, equation (10.5) is obtained by setting $x_{t1} = z_t$, $x_{t2} = z_{t-1}$, and $x_{t3} = z_{t-2}$.

To state and discuss several of the remaining assumptions, we let $\mathbf{x}_t = (x_{t1}, x_{t2}, \ldots, x_{tk})$ denote the set of all independent variables in the equation at time t. Further, $\mathbf{X}$ denotes the collection of all independent variables for all time periods. It is useful to think of $\mathbf{X}$ as being an array, with n rows and k columns. This reflects how time series data are stored in econometric software packages: the tth row of $\mathbf{X}$ is $\mathbf{x}_t$, consisting of all independent variables for time period t. Therefore, the first row of $\mathbf{X}$ corresponds to $t = 1$, the second row to $t = 2$, and the last row to $t = n$. An example is given in Table 10.2, using $n = 8$ and the explanatory variables in equation (10.3).

TABLE 10.2 Example of X for the Explanatory Variables in Equation (10.3)			
t	convrte	unem	yngmle
1	.46	.074	.12
2	.42	.071	.12
3	.42	.063	.11
4	.47	.062	.09
5	.48	.060	.10
6	.50	.059	.11
7	.55	.058	.12
8	.56	.059	.13

Naturally, as with cross-sectional regression, we need to rule out perfect collinearity among the regressors.

Assumption TS.2 **No Perfect Collinearity**

In the sample (and therefore in the underlying time series process), no independent variable is constant nor a perfect linear combination of the others.

We discussed this assumption at length in the context of cross-sectional data in Chapter 3. The issues are essentially the same with time series data. Remember, Assumption TS.2 does allow the explanatory variables to be correlated, but it rules out *perfect* correlation in the sample.

The final assumption for unbiasedness of OLS is the time series analog of Assumption MLR.4, and it also obviates the need for random sampling in Assumption MLR.2.

Assumption TS.3 **Zero Conditional Mean**

For each t, the expected value of the error u_t, given the explanatory variables for *all* time periods, is zero. Mathematically,

$$E(u_t|\mathbf{X}) = 0, t = 1, 2, ..., n. \qquad [10.9]$$

This is a crucial assumption, and we need to have an intuitive grasp of its meaning. As in the cross-sectional case, it is easiest to view this assumption in terms of uncorrelatedness: Assumption TS.3 implies that the error at time t, u_t, is uncorrelated with each explanatory variable in *every* time period. The fact that this is stated in terms of the conditional expectation means that we must also correctly specify the functional relationship between y_t and the explanatory variables. If u_t is independent of $\mathbf{X}$ and $E(u_t) = 0$, then Assumption TS.3 automatically holds.

Given the cross-sectional analysis from Chapter 3, it is not surprising that we require u_t to be uncorrelated with the explanatory variables also dated at time t: in conditional mean terms,

$$E(u_t|x_{t1}, ..., x_{tk}) = E(u_t|\mathbf{x}_t) = 0. \qquad [10.10]$$

When (10.10) holds, we say that the x_{tj} are **contemporaneously exogenous**. Equation (10.10) implies that u_t and the explanatory variables are contemporaneously uncorrelated: $\text{Corr}(x_{tj}, u_t) = 0$, for all j.

Assumption TS.3 requires more than contemporaneous exogeneity: u_t must be uncorrelated with x_{sj}, even when $s \neq t$. This is a strong sense in which the explanatory variables must be exogenous, and when TS.3 holds, we say that the explanatory variables are **strictly exogenous**. In Chapter 11, we will demonstrate that (10.10) is sufficient for proving consistency of the OLS estimator. But to show that OLS is unbiased, we need the strict exogeneity assumption.

In the cross-sectional case, we did not explicitly state how the error term for, say, person i, u_i, is related to the explanatory variables for *other* people in the sample. This was unnecessary because with random sampling (Assumption MLR.2), u_i is *automatically* independent of the explanatory variables for observations other than i. In a time series context, random sampling is almost never appropriate, so we must explicitly assume that the expected value of u_t is not related to the explanatory variables in any time periods.

It is important to see that Assumption TS.3 puts no restriction on correlation in the independent variables or in the u_t across time. Assumption TS.3 only says that the average value of u_t is unrelated to the independent variables in all time periods.

Anything that causes the unobservables at time t to be correlated with any of the explanatory variables in any time period causes Assumption TS.3 to fail. Two leading candidates for failure are omitted variables and measurement error in some of the regressors. But the strict exogeneity assumption can also fail for other, less obvious reasons. In the simple static regression model

$$y_t = \beta_0 + \beta_1 z_t + u_t,$$

Assumption TS.3 requires not only that u_t and z_t are uncorrelated, but that u_t is also uncorrelated with past and future values of z. This has two implications. First, z can have no lagged effect on y. If z does have a lagged effect on y, then we should estimate a distributed lag model. A more subtle point is that strict exogeneity excludes the possibility that changes in the error term today can cause future changes in z. This effectively rules out feedback from y to future values of z. For example, consider a simple static model to explain a city's murder rate in terms of police officers per capita:

$$mrdrte_t = \beta_0 + \beta_1 polpc_t + u_t.$$

It may be reasonable to assume that u_t is uncorrelated with $polpc_t$ and even with past values of $polpc_t$; for the sake of argument, assume this is the case. But suppose that the city adjusts the size of its police force based on past values of the murder rate. This means that, say, $polpc_{t+1}$ might be correlated with u_t (since a higher u_t leads to a higher $mrdrte_t$). If this is the case, Assumption TS.3 is generally violated.

There are similar considerations in distributed lag models. Usually, we do not worry that u_t might be correlated with past z because we are controlling for past z in the model. But feedback from u to future z is always an issue.

Explanatory variables that are strictly exogenous cannot react to what has happened to y in the past. A factor such as the amount of rainfall in an agricultural production function satisfies this requirement: rainfall in any future year is not influenced by the output during the current or past years. But something like the amount of labor input might not be strictly exogenous, as it is chosen by the farmer, and the farmer may adjust the amount of labor based on last year's yield. Policy variables, such as growth in the money supply, expenditures on welfare, and highway speed limits, are often influenced by what has happened to the outcome variable in the past. In the social sciences, many explanatory variables may very well violate the strict exogeneity assumption.

Even though Assumption TS.3 can be unrealistic, we begin with it in order to conclude that the OLS estimators are unbiased. Most treatments of static and FDL models assume TS.3 by making the stronger assumption that the explanatory variables are nonrandom, or fixed in repeated samples. The nonrandomness assumption is obviously false for time series observations; Assumption TS.3 has the advantage of being more realistic about the random nature of the x_{tj}, while it isolates the necessary assumption about how u_t and the explanatory variables are related in order for OLS to be unbiased.

THEOREM 10.1

UNBIASEDNESS OF OLS

Under Assumptions TS.1, TS.2, and TS.3, the OLS estimators are unbiased conditional on **X**, and therefore unconditionally as well when the expectations exist: $E(\hat{\beta}_j) = \beta_j, j = 0, 1, ..., k$.

EXPLORING FURTHER 10.2

In the FDL model $y_t = \alpha_0 + \delta_0 z_t + \delta_1 z_{t-1} + u_t$, what do we need to assume about the sequence $\{z_0, z_1, ..., z_n\}$ in order for Assumption TS.3 to hold?

The proof of this theorem is essentially the same as that for Theorem 3.1 in Chapter 3, and so we omit it. When comparing Theorem 10.1 to Theorem 3.1, we have been able to drop the random sampling assumption by assuming that, for each t, u_t has zero mean given the explanatory variables at all time periods. If this assumption does not hold, OLS cannot be shown to be unbiased.

The analysis of omitted variables bias, which we covered in Section 3-3, is essentially the same in the time series case. In particular, Table 3.2 and the discussion surrounding it can be used as before to determine the directions of bias due to omitted variables.

10-3b The Variances of the OLS Estimators and the Gauss-Markov Theorem

We need to add two assumptions to round out the Gauss-Markov assumptions for time series regressions. The first one is familiar from cross-sectional analysis.

Assumption TS.4   **Homoskedasticity**

Conditional on $\mathbf{X}$, the variance of u_t is the same for all t: $\mathrm{Var}(u_t|\mathbf{X}) = \mathrm{Var}(u_t) = \sigma^2, t = 1, 2, ..., n$.

This assumption means that $\mathrm{Var}(u_t|\mathbf{X})$ cannot depend on $\mathbf{X}$—it is sufficient that u_t and $\mathbf{X}$ are independent—*and* that $\mathrm{Var}(u_t)$ is constant over time. When TS.4 does not hold, we say that the errors are *heteroskedastic*, just as in the cross-sectional case. For example, consider an equation for determining three-month T-bill rates $(i3_t)$ based on the inflation rate (inf_t) and the federal deficit as a percentage of gross domestic product (def_t):

$$i3_t = \beta_0 + \beta_1 inf_t + \beta_2 def_t + u_t. \qquad [10.11]$$

Among other things, Assumption TS.4 requires that the unobservables affecting interest rates have a constant variance over time. Since policy regime changes are known to affect the variability of interest rates, this assumption might very well be false. Further, it could be that the variability in interest rates depends on the level of inflation or relative size of the deficit. This would also violate the homoskedasticity assumption.

When $\mathrm{Var}(u_t|\mathbf{X})$ does depend on $\mathbf{X}$, it often depends on the explanatory variables at time t, $\mathbf{x}_t$. In Chapter 12, we will see that the tests for heteroskedasticity from Chapter 8 can also be used for time series regressions, at least under certain assumptions.

The final Gauss-Markov assumption for time series analysis is new.

Assumption TS.5   **No Serial Correlation**

Conditional on $\mathbf{X}$, the errors in two different time periods are uncorrelated: $\mathrm{Corr}(u_t,u_s|\mathbf{X}) = 0$, for all $t \neq s$.

The easiest way to think of this assumption is to ignore the conditioning on $\mathbf{X}$. Then, Assumption TS.5 is simply

$$\mathrm{Corr}(u_t,u_s) = 0, \text{ for all } t \neq s. \qquad [10.12]$$

(This is how the no serial correlation assumption is stated when $\mathbf{X}$ is treated as nonrandom.) When considering whether Assumption TS.5 is likely to hold, we focus on equation (10.12) because of its simple interpretation.

When (10.12) is false, we say that the errors in (10.8) suffer from **serial correlation**, or **autocorrelation**, because they are correlated across time. Consider the case of errors from adjacent time periods. Suppose that when $u_{t-1} > 0$ then, on average, the error in the next time period, u_t, is also positive. Then, $\mathrm{Corr}(u_t,u_{t-1}) > 0$, and the errors suffer from serial correlation. In equation (10.11), this means that if interest rates are unexpectedly high for this period, then they are likely to be above average (for the given levels of inflation and deficits) for the next period. This turns out to be a reasonable characterization for the error terms in many time series applications, which we will see in Chapter 12. For now, we assume TS.5.

Importantly, Assumption TS.5 assumes nothing about temporal correlation in the *independent* variables. For example, in equation (10.11), inf_t is almost certainly correlated across time. But this has nothing to do with whether TS.5 holds.

A natural question that arises is: in Chapters 3 and 4, why did we not assume that the errors for different cross-sectional observations are uncorrelated? The answer comes from the random sampling assumption: under random sampling, u_i and u_h are independent for any two observations i and h. It can also be shown that, under random sampling, the errors for different observations are independent conditional on the explanatory variables in the sample. Thus, for our purposes, we consider serial correlation only to be a potential problem for regressions with times series data. (In Chapters 13 and 14, the serial correlation issue will come up in connection with panel data analysis.)

Assumptions TS.1 through TS.5 are the appropriate Gauss-Markov assumptions for time series applications, but they have other uses as well. Sometimes, TS.1 through TS.5 are satisfied in cross-sectional applications, even when random sampling is not a reasonable assumption, such as when the cross-sectional units are large relative to the population. Suppose that we have a cross-sectional data set at the city level. It might be that correlation exists across cities within the same state in some of the explanatory variables, such as property tax rates or per capita welfare payments. Correlation of the explanatory variables across observations does not cause problems for verifying the Gauss-Markov assumptions, provided the error terms are uncorrelated across cities. However, in this chapter, we are primarily interested in applying the Gauss-Markov assumptions to time series regression problems.

THEOREM 10.2	**OLS SAMPLING VARIANCES**

Under the time series Gauss-Markov Assumptions TS.1 through TS.5, the variance of $\hat{\beta}_j$, conditional on **X**, is

$$\text{Var}(\hat{\beta}_j|\mathbf{X}) = \sigma^2/[\text{SST}_j(1 - R_j^2)], j = 1, \dots, k, \qquad [10.13]$$

where SST_j is the total sum of squares of x_{tj} and R_j^2 is the R-squared from the regression of x_j on the other independent variables.

Equation (10.13) is the same variance we derived in Chapter 3 under the cross-sectional Gauss-Markov assumptions. Because the proof is very similar to the one for Theorem 3.2, we omit it. The discussion from Chapter 3 about the factors causing large variances, including multicollinearity among the explanatory variables, applies immediately to the time series case.

The usual estimator of the error variance is also unbiased under Assumptions TS.1 through TS.5, and the Gauss-Markov Theorem holds.

THEOREM 10.3	**UNBIASED ESTIMATION OF σ^2**

Under Assumptions TS.1 through TS.5, the estimator $\hat{\sigma}^2 = \text{SSR}/df$ is an unbiased estimator of σ^2, where $df = n - k - 1$.

THEOREM 10.4	**GAUSS-MARKOV THEOREM**

Under Assumptions TS.1 through TS.5, the OLS estimators are the best linear unbiased estimators conditional on **X**.

> **EXPLORING FURTHER 10.3**
>
> In the FDL model $y_t = \alpha_0 + \delta_0 z_t + \delta_1 z_{t-1} + u_t$, explain the nature of any multicollinearity in the explanatory variables.

The bottom line here is that OLS has the same desirable finite sample properties under TS.1 through TS.5 that it has under MLR.1 through MLR.5.

10-3c Inference under the Classical Linear Model Assumptions

In order to use the usual OLS standard errors, t statistics, and F statistics, we need to add a final assumption that is analogous to the normality assumption we used for cross-sectional analysis.

Assumption TS.6   Normality

The errors u_t are independent of **X** and are independently and identically distributed as Normal$(0,\sigma^2)$.

Assumption TS.6 implies TS.3, TS.4, and TS.5, but it is stronger because of the independence and normality assumptions.

THEOREM 10.5   NORMAL SAMPLING DISTRIBUTIONS

Under Assumptions TS.1 through TS.6, the CLM assumptions for time series, the OLS estimators are normally distributed, conditional on **X**. Further, under the null hypothesis, each t statistic has a t distribution, and each F statistic has an F distribution. The usual construction of confidence intervals is also valid.

The implications of Theorem 10.5 are of utmost importance. It implies that, when Assumptions TS.1 through TS.6 hold, everything we have learned about estimation and inference for cross-sectional regressions applies directly to time series regressions. Thus, t statistics can be used for testing statistical significance of individual explanatory variables, and F statistics can be used to test for joint significance.

Just as in the cross-sectional case, the usual inference procedures are only as good as the underlying assumptions. The classical linear model assumptions for time series data are much more restrictive than those for cross-sectional data—in particular, the strict exogeneity and no serial correlation assumptions can be unrealistic. Nevertheless, the CLM framework is a good starting point for many applications.

EXAMPLE 10.1   Static Phillips Curve

To determine whether there is a tradeoff, on average, between unemployment and inflation, we can test $H_0: \beta_1 = 0$ against $H_1: \beta_1 < 0$ in equation (10.2). If the classical linear model assumptions hold, we can use the usual OLS t statistic.

We use the file PHILLIPS to estimate equation (10.2), restricting ourselves to the data through 1996. (In later exercises, for example, Computer Exercises C12 and C10 in Chapter 11 you are asked to use all years through 2003. In Chapter 18, we use the years 1997 through 2003 in various forecasting exercises.) The simple regression estimates are

$$\widehat{inf_t} = 1.42 + .468 \, unem_t$$
$$(1.72) \quad (.289) \tag{10.14}$$
$$n = 49, R^2 = .053, \bar{R}^2 = .033.$$

This equation does not suggest a tradeoff between *unem* and *inf*: $\hat{\beta}_1 > 0$. The *t* statistic for $\hat{\beta}_1$ is about 1.62, which gives a *p*-value against a two-sided alternative of about .11. Thus, if anything, there is a positive relationship between inflation and unemployment.

There are some problems with this analysis that we cannot address in detail now. In Chapter 12, we will see that the CLM assumptions do not hold. In addition, the static Phillips curve is probably not the best model for determining whether there is a short-run tradeoff between inflation and unemployment. Macroeconomists generally prefer the expectations augmented Phillips curve, a simple example of which is given in Chapter 11.

As a second example, we estimate equation (10.11) using annual data on the U.S. economy.

EXAMPLE 10.2   **Effects of Inflation and Deficits on Interest Rates**

The data in INTDEF come from the 2004 *Economic Report of the President* (Tables B-73 and B-79) and span the years 1948 through 2003. The variable *i3* is the three-month T-bill rate, *inf* is the annual inflation rate based on the consumer price index (CPI), and *def* is the federal budget deficit as a percentage of GDP. The estimated equation is

$$\widehat{i3}_t = 1.73 + .606\ inf_t + .513\ def_t$$
$$(0.43)\quad (.082)\qquad (.118) \qquad\qquad [10.15]$$
$$n = 56,\ R^2 = .602,\ \bar{R}^2 = .587.$$

These estimates show that increases in inflation or the relative size of the deficit increase short-term interest rates, both of which are expected from basic economics. For example, a ceteris paribus one percentage point increase in the inflation rate increases *i3* by .606 points. Both *inf* and *def* are very statistically significant, assuming, of course, that the CLM assumptions hold.

10-4 Functional Form, Dummy Variables, and Index Numbers

All of the functional forms we learned about in earlier chapters can be used in time series regressions. The most important of these is the natural logarithm: time series regressions with constant percentage effects appear often in applied work.

EXAMPLE 10.3   **Puerto Rican Employment and the Minimum Wage**

Annual data on the Puerto Rican employment rate, minimum wage, and other variables are used by Castillo-Freeman and Freeman (1992) to study the effects of the U.S. minimum wage on employment in Puerto Rico. A simplified version of their model is

$$\log(prepop_t) = \beta_0 + \beta_1 \log(mincov_t) + \beta_2 \log(usgnp_t) + u_t, \qquad [10.16]$$

where *prepop_t* is the employment rate in Puerto Rico during year *t* (ratio of those working to total population), *usgnp_t* is real U.S. gross national product (in billions of dollars), and *mincov* measures the importance of the minimum wage relative to average wages. In particular, *mincov* = (*avgmin/avgwage*)·*avgcov*, where *avgmin* is the average minimum wage, *avgwage* is the average overall wage, and *avgcov* is the average coverage rate (the proportion of workers actually covered by the minimum wage law).

Using the data in PRMINWGE for the years 1950 through 1987 gives

$$\widehat{\log(prepop_t)} = -1.05 - .154 \log(mincov_t) - .012 \log(usgnp_t)$$
$$(0.77) \quad (.065) \qquad\qquad (.089) \qquad\qquad\qquad \textbf{[10.17]}$$
$$n = 38, R^2 = .661, \bar{R}^2 = .641.$$

The estimated elasticity of *prepop* with respect to *mincov* is $-.154$, and it is statistically significant with $t = -2.37$. Therefore, a higher minimum wage lowers the employment rate, something that classical economics predicts. The GNP variable is not statistically significant, but this changes when we account for a time trend in the next section.

We can use logarithmic functional forms in distributed lag models, too. For example, for quarterly data, suppose that money demand (M_t) and gross domestic product (GDP_t) are related by

$$\log(M_t) = \alpha_0 + \delta_0\log(GDP_t) + \delta_1\log(GDP_{t-1}) + \delta_2\log(GDP_{t-2})$$
$$+ \delta_3\log(GDP_{t-3}) + \delta_4\log(GDP_{t-4}) + u_t.$$

The impact propensity in this equation, δ_0, is also called the **short-run elasticity**: it measures the immediate percentage change in money demand given a 1% increase in *GDP*. The LRP, $\delta_0 + \delta_1 + ... + \delta_4$, is sometimes called the **long-run elasticity**: it measures the percentage increase in money demand after four quarters given a permanent 1% increase in *GDP*.

Binary or dummy independent variables are also quite useful in time series applications. Since the unit of observation is time, a dummy variable represents whether, in each time period, a certain event has occurred. For example, for annual data, we can indicate in each year whether a Democrat or a Republican is president of the United States by defining a variable *democ_t*, which is unity if the president is a Democrat, and zero otherwise. Or, in looking at the effects of capital punishment on murder rates in Texas, we can define a dummy variable for each year equal to one if Texas had capital punishment during that year, and zero otherwise.

Often, dummy variables are used to isolate certain periods that may be systematically different from other periods covered by a data set.

EXAMPLE 10.4   Effects of Personal Exemption on Fertility Rates

The general fertility rate (*gfr*) is the number of children born to every 1,000 women of childbearing age. For the years 1913 through 1984, the equation,

$$gfr_t = \beta_0 + \beta_1 pe_t + \beta_2 ww2_t + \beta_3 pill_t + u_t,$$

explains *gfr* in terms of the average real dollar value of the personal tax exemption (*pe*) and two binary variables. The variable *ww2* takes on the value unity during the years 1941 through 1945, when the United States was involved in World War II. The variable *pill* is unity from 1963 onward, when the birth control pill was made available for contraception.

Using the data in FERTIL3, which were taken from the article by Whittington, Alm, and Peters (1990)

$$\widehat{gfr_t} = 98.68 + .083\,pe_t - 24.24\,ww2_t - 31.59\,pill_t$$
$$(3.21) \quad (.030) \qquad (7.46) \qquad\quad (4.08) \qquad\qquad \textbf{[10.18]}$$
$$n = 72, R^2 = .473, \bar{R}^2 = .450.$$

Each variable is statistically significant at the 1% level against a two-sided alternative. We see that the fertility rate was lower during World War II: given *pe*, there were about 24 fewer births for every 1,000 women of childbearing age, which is a large reduction. (From 1913 through 1984, *gfr* ranged from about 65 to 127.) Similarly, the fertility rate has been substantially lower since the introduction of the birth control pill.

The variable of economic interest is *pe*. The average *pe* over this time period is $100.40, ranging from zero to $243.83. The coefficient on *pe* implies that a $12.00 increase in *pe* increases *gfr* by about one birth per 1,000 women of childbearing age. This effect is hardly trivial.

In Section 10-2, we noted that the fertility rate may react to changes in *pe* with a lag. Estimating a distributed lag model with two lags gives

$$\widehat{gfr}_t = 95.87 + .073\, pe_t - .0058\, pe_{t-1} + .034\, pe_{t-2} - 22.12\, ww2_t - 31.30\, pill_t$$
$$\quad (3.28)\ (.126)\quad (.1557)\quad\ (.126)\qquad (10.73)\qquad (3.98) \qquad \textbf{[10.19]}$$
$$n = 70,\, R^2 = .499,\, \bar{R}^2 = .459.$$

In this regression, we only have 70 observations because we lose two when we lag *pe* twice. The coefficients on the *pe* variables are estimated very imprecisely, and each one is individually insignificant. It turns out that there is substantial correlation between pe_t, pe_{t-1}, and pe_{t-2}, and this multicollinearity makes it difficult to estimate the effect at each lag. However, pe_t, pe_{t-1}, and pe_{t-2} are jointly significant: the F statistic has a p-value $= .012$. Thus, *pe* does have an effect on *gfr* [as we already saw in (10.18)], but we do not have good enough estimates to determine whether it is contemporaneous or with a one- or two-year lag (or some of each). Actually, pe_{t-1} and pe_{t-2} are jointly insignificant in this equation (p-value $= .95$), so at this point, we would be justified in using the static model. But for illustrative purposes, let us obtain a confidence interval for the LRP in this model.

The estimated LRP in (10.19) is $.073 - .0058 + .034 \approx .101$. However, we do not have enough information in (10.19) to obtain the standard error of this estimate. To obtain the standard error of the estimated LRP, we use the trick suggested in Section 4-4. Let $\theta_0 = \delta_0 + \delta_1 + \delta_2$ denote the LRP and write δ_0 in terms of θ_0, δ_1, and δ_2 as $\delta_0 = \theta_0 - \delta_1 - \delta_2$. Next, substitute for δ_0 in the model

$$gfr_t = \alpha_0 + \delta_0 pe_t + \delta_1 pe_{t-1} + \delta_2 pe_{t-2} + \dots$$

to get

$$gfr_t = \alpha_0 + (\theta_0 - \delta_1 - \delta_2)pe_t + \delta_1 pe_{t-1} + \delta_2 pe_{t-2} + \dots$$
$$= \alpha_0 + \theta_0 pe_t + \delta_1(pe_{t-1} - pe_t) + \delta_2(pe_{t-2} - pe_t) + \dots.$$

From this last equation, we can obtain $\hat{\theta}_0$ and its standard error by regressing gfr_t on pe_t, $(pe_{t-1} - pe_t)$, $(pe_{t-2} - pe_t)$, $ww2_t$, and $pill_t$. The coefficient and associated standard error on pe_t are what we need. Running this regression gives $\hat{\theta}_0 = .101$ as the coefficient on pe_t (as we already knew) and $se(\hat{\theta}_0) = .030$ [which we could not compute from (10.19)]. Therefore, the t statistic for $\hat{\theta}_0$ is about 3.37, so $\hat{\theta}_0$ is statistically different from zero at small significance levels. Even though none of the $\hat{\delta}_j$ is individually significant, the LRP is very significant. The 95% confidence interval for the LRP is about .041 to .160.

Whittington, Alm, and Peters (1990) allow for further lags but restrict the coefficients to help alleviate the multicollinearity problem that hinders estimation of the individual δ_j. (See Problem 6 for an example of how to do this.) For estimating the LRP, which would seem to be of primary interest here, such restrictions are unnecessary. Whittington, Alm, and Peters also control for additional variables, such as average female wage and the unemployment rate.

Binary explanatory variables are the key component in what is called an **event study**. In an event study, the goal is to see whether a particular event influences some outcome. Economists who study industrial organization have looked at the effects of certain events on firm stock prices. For example, Rose (1985) studied the effects of new trucking regulations on the stock prices of trucking companies.

A simple version of an equation used for such event studies is

$$R_t^f = \beta_0 + \beta_1 R_t^m + \beta_2 d_t + u_t,$$

where R_t^f is the stock return for firm f during period t (usually a week or a month), R_t^m is the market return (usually computed for a broad stock market index), and d_t is a dummy variable indicating when the event occurred. For example, if the firm is an airline, d_t might denote whether the airline experienced a publicized accident or near accident during week t. Including R_t^m in the equation controls for the possibility that broad market movements might coincide with airline accidents. Sometimes, multiple dummy variables are used. For example, if the event is the imposition of a new regulation that might affect a certain firm, we might include a dummy variable that is one for a few weeks before the regulation was publicly announced and a second dummy variable for a few weeks after the regulation was announced. The first dummy variable might detect the presence of inside information.

Before we give an example of an event study, we need to discuss the notion of an **index number** and the difference between nominal and real economic variables. An index number typically aggregates a vast amount of information into a single quantity. Index numbers are used regularly in time series analysis, especially in macroeconomic applications. An example of an index number is the index of industrial production (IIP), computed monthly by the Board of Governors of the Federal Reserve. The IIP is a measure of production across a broad range of industries, and, as such, its magnitude in a particular year has no quantitative meaning. In order to interpret the magnitude of the IIP, we must know the **base period** and the **base value**. In the 1997 *Economic Report of the President* (*ERP*), the base year is 1987, and the base value is 100. (Setting IIP to 100 in the base period is just a convention; it makes just as much sense to set IIP = 1 in 1987, and some indexes are defined with 1 as the base value.) Because the IIP was 107.7 in 1992, we can say that industrial production was 7.7% higher in 1992 than in 1987. We can use the IIP in any two years to compute the percentage difference in industrial output during those two years. For example, because IIP = 61.4 in 1970 and IIP = 85.7 in 1979, industrial production grew by about 39.6% during the 1970s.

It is easy to change the base period for any index number, and sometimes we must do this to give index numbers reported with different base years a common base year. For example, if we want to change the base year of the IIP from 1987 to 1982, we simply divide the IIP for each year by the 1982 value and then multiply by 100 to make the base period value 100. Generally, the formula is

$$newindex_t = 100(oldindex_t/oldindex_{newbase}), \qquad [10.20]$$

where $oldindex_{newbase}$ is the original value of the index in the new base year. For example, with base year 1987, the IIP in 1992 is 107.7; if we change the base year to 1982, the IIP in 1992 becomes $100(107.7/81.9) = 131.5$ (because the IIP in 1982 was 81.9).

Another important example of an index number is a *price index*, such as the CPI. We already used the CPI to compute annual inflation rates in Example 10.1. As with the industrial production index, the CPI is only meaningful when we compare it across different years (or months, if we are using monthly data). In the 1997 *ERP*, CPI = 38.8 in 1970 and CPI = 130.7 in 1990. Thus, the general price level grew by almost 237% over this 20-year period. (In 1997, the CPI is defined so that its average in 1982, 1983, and 1984 equals 100; thus, the base period is listed as 1982–1984.)

In addition to being used to compute inflation rates, price indexes are necessary for turning a time series measured in *nominal dollars* (or *current dollars*) into *real dollars* (or *constant dollars*). Most economic behavior is assumed to be influenced by real, not nominal, variables. For example, classical labor economics assumes that labor supply is based on the real hourly wage, not the nominal wage. Obtaining the real wage from the nominal wage is easy if we have a price index such as the CPI. We must be a little careful to first divide the CPI by 100, so that the value in the base year is 1. Then, if w denotes the average hourly wage in nominal dollars and $p = CPI/100$, the *real wage* is simply w/p. This wage is measured in dollars for the base period of the CPI. For example, in Table B-45 in the 1997 *ERP*, average hourly earnings are reported in nominal terms and in 1982 dollars (which means that the CPI used in computing the real wage had the base year 1982). This table reports that the nominal hourly wage in 1960 was $2.09, but measured in 1982 dollars, the wage was $6.79. The real hourly wage had peaked in 1973, at $8.55 in 1982 dollars, and had fallen to $7.40 by 1995. Thus, there was a nontrivial decline in real wages over those 22 years. (If we compare nominal wages from 1973 and 1995, we get a very misleading picture: $3.94 in 1973 and $11.44 in 1995. Because the real wage fell, the increase in the nominal wage was due entirely to inflation.)

Standard measures of economic output are in real terms. The most important of these is *gross domestic product*, or *GDP*. When growth in GDP is reported in the popular press, it is always *real* GDP growth. In the 2012 *ERP*, Table B-2, GDP is reported in billions of 2005 dollars. We used a similar measure of output, real gross national product, in Example 10.3.

Interesting things happen when real dollar variables are used in combination with natural logarithms. Suppose, for example, that average weekly hours worked are related to the real wage as

$$\log(hours) = \beta_0 + \beta_1 \log(w/p) + u.$$

Using the fact that $\log(w/p) = \log(w) - \log(p)$, we can write this as

$$\log(hours) = \beta_0 + \beta_1 \log(w) + \beta_2 \log(p) + u, \qquad [10.21]$$

but with the restriction that $\beta_2 = -\beta_1$. Therefore, the assumption that only the real wage influences labor supply imposes a restriction on the parameters of model (10.21). If $\beta_2 \neq -\beta_1$, then the price level has an effect on labor supply, something that can happen if workers do not fully understand the distinction between real and nominal wages.

There are many practical aspects to the actual computation of index numbers, but it would take us too far afield to cover those here. Detailed discussions of price indexes can be found in most intermediate macroeconomic texts, such as Mankiw (1994, Chapter 2). For us, it is important to be able to use index numbers in regression analysis. As mentioned earlier, since the magnitudes of index numbers are not especially informative, they often appear in logarithmic form, so that regression coefficients have percentage change interpretations.

We now give an example of an event study that also uses index numbers.

EXAMPLE 10.5   Antidumping Filings and Chemical Imports

Krupp and Pollard (1996) analyzed the effects of antidumping filings by U.S. chemical industries on imports of various chemicals. We focus here on one industrial chemical, barium chloride, a cleaning agent used in various chemical processes and in gasoline production. The data are contained in the file BARIUM. In the early 1980s, U.S. barium chloride producers believed that China was offering its U.S. imports an unfairly low price (an action known as *dumping*), and the barium chloride industry filed a complaint with the U.S. International Trade Commission (ITC) in October 1983. The ITC ruled in favor of the U.S. barium chloride industry in October 1984. There are several questions of interest in this case, but we will touch on only a few of them. First, were imports unusually high in the period immediately preceding the initial filing? Second, did imports change noticeably after an antidumping filing? Finally, what was the reduction in imports after a decision in favor of the U.S. industry?

To answer these questions, we follow Krupp and Pollard by defining three dummy variables: *befile6* is equal to 1 during the six months before filing, *affile6* indicates the six months after filing, and *afdec6* denotes the six months after the positive decision. The dependent variable is the volume of imports of barium chloride from China, *chnimp*, which we use in logarithmic form. We include as explanatory variables, all in logarithmic form, an index of chemical production, *chempi* (to control for overall demand for barium chloride), the volume of gasoline production, *gas* (another demand variable), and an exchange rate index, *rtwex*, which measures the strength of the dollar against several other currencies. The chemical production index was defined to be 100 in June 1977. The analysis here differs somewhat from Krupp and Pollard in that we use natural logarithms of all variables (except the dummy variables, of course), and we include all three dummy variables in the same regression.

Using monthly data from February 1978 through December 1988 gives the following:

$$\widehat{\log(chnimp)} = -17.80 + 3.12 \log(chempi) + .196 \log(gas)$$
$$(21.05) \quad (.48) \qquad\qquad (.907)$$
$$+ .983 \log(rtwex) + .060 \, befile6 - .032 \, affile6 - .565 \, afdec6 \qquad [10.22]$$
$$(.400) \qquad\qquad (.261) \qquad\quad (.264) \qquad\quad (.286)$$
$$n = 131, R^2 = .305, \overline{R}^2 = .271.$$

The equation shows that *befile6* is statistically insignificant, so there is no evidence that Chinese imports were unusually high during the six months before the suit was filed. Further, although the estimate on *affile6* is negative, the coefficient is small (indicating about a 3.2% fall in Chinese imports), and it is statistically very insignificant. The coefficient on *afdec6* shows a substantial fall in Chinese imports of barium chloride after the decision in favor of the U.S. industry, which is not surprising. Since the effect is so large, we compute the exact percentage change: $100[\exp(-.565) - 1] \approx -43.2\%$. The coefficient is statistically significant at the 5% level against a two-sided alternative.

The coefficient signs on the control variables are what we expect: an increase in overall chemical production increases the demand for the cleaning agent. Gasoline production does not affect Chinese imports significantly. The coefficient on $\log(rtwex)$ shows that an increase in the value of the dollar relative to other currencies increases the demand for Chinese imports, as is predicted by economic theory. (In fact, the elasticity is not statistically different from 1. Why?)

Interactions among qualitative and quantitative variables are also used in time series analysis. An example with practical importance follows.

EXAMPLE 10.6 **Election Outcomes and Economic Performance**

Fair (1996) summarizes his work on explaining presidential election outcomes in terms of economic performance. He explains the proportion of the two-party vote going to the Democratic candidate using data for the years 1916 through 1992 (every four years) for a total of 20 observations. We estimate a simplified version of Fair's model (using variable names that are more descriptive than his):

$$demvote = \beta_0 + \beta_1 partyWH + \beta_2 incum + \beta_3 partyWH \cdot gnews$$
$$+ \beta_4 partyWH \cdot inf + u,$$

where *demvote* is the proportion of the two-party vote going to the Democratic candidate. The explanatory variable *partyWH* is similar to a dummy variable, but it takes on the value 1 if a Democrat is in the White House and -1 if a Republican is in the White House. Fair uses this variable to impose the restriction that the effects of a Republican or a Democrat being in the White House have the same magnitude but the opposite sign. This is a natural restriction because the party shares must sum to one, by definition. It also saves two degrees of freedom, which is important with so few observations. Similarly, the variable *incum* is defined to be 1 if a Democratic incumbent is running, -1 if a Republican incumbent is running, and zero otherwise. The variable *gnews* is the number of quarters, during the administration's first 15 quarters, when the quarterly growth in real per capita output was above 2.9% (at an annual rate), and *inf* is the average annual inflation rate over the first 15 quarters of the administration. See Fair (1996) for precise definitions.

Economists are most interested in the interaction terms *partyWH·gnews* and *partyWH·inf*. Since *partyWH* equals 1 when a Democrat is in the White House, β_3 measures the effect of good economic news on the party in power; we expect $\beta_3 > 0$. Similarly, β_4 measures the effect that inflation has on the party in power. Because inflation during an administration is considered to be bad news, we expect $\beta_4 < 0$.

The estimated equation using the data in FAIR is

$$\widehat{demvote} = .481 - .0435\,partyWH + .0544\,incum$$
$$(.012)\quad(.0405)\qquad\qquad(.0234)$$
$$+\ .0108\,partyWH \cdot gnews - .0077\,partyWH \cdot inf \qquad\qquad \textbf{[10.23]}$$
$$(.0041)\qquad\qquad\qquad(.0033)$$
$$n = 20,\ R^2 = .663,\ \overline{R}^2 = .573.$$

All coefficients, except that on *partyWH*, are statistically significant at the 5% level. Incumbency is worth about 5.4 percentage points in the share of the vote. (Remember, *demvote* is measured as a proportion.) Further, the economic news variable has a positive effect: one more quarter of good news is worth about 1.1 percentage points. Inflation, as expected, has a negative effect: if average annual inflation is, say, two percentage points higher, the party in power loses about 1.5 percentage points of the two-party vote.

We could have used this equation to predict the outcome of the 1996 presidential election between Bill Clinton, the Democrat, and Bob Dole, the Republican. (The independent candidate, Ross Perot, is excluded because Fair's equation is for the two-party vote only.) Because Clinton ran as an incumbent, *partyWH* = 1 and *incum* = 1. To predict the election outcome, we need the variables *gnews* and *inf*. During Clinton's first 15 quarters in office, the annual growth rate of per capita real GDP exceeded 2.9% three times, so *gnews* = 3. Further, using the GDP price deflator reported in Table B-4 in the 1997 *ERP*, the average annual inflation rate (computed using Fair's formula) from the fourth quarter in 1991 to the third quarter in 1996 was 3.019. Plugging these into (10.23) gives

$$\widehat{demvote} = .481 - .0435 + .0544 + .0108(3) - .0077(3.019) \approx .5011.$$

Therefore, based on information known before the election in November, Clinton was predicted to receive a very slight majority of the two-party vote: about 50.1%. In fact, Clinton won more handily: his share of the two-party vote was 54.65%.

10-5 Trends and Seasonality

10-5a Characterizing Trending Time Series

Many economic time series have a common tendency of growing over time. We must recognize that some series contain a **time trend** in order to draw causal inference using time series data. Ignoring the fact that two sequences are trending in the same or opposite directions can lead us to falsely conclude that changes in one variable are actually caused by changes in another variable. In many cases, two time series processes appear to be correlated only because they are both trending over time for reasons related to other unobserved factors.

Figure 10.2 contains a plot of labor productivity (output per hour of work) in the United States for the years 1947 through 1987. This series displays a clear upward trend, which reflects the fact that workers have become more productive over time.

Other series, at least over certain time periods, have clear downward trends. Because positive trends are more common, we will focus on those during our discussion.

What kind of statistical models adequately capture trending behavior? One popular formulation is to write the series $\{y_t\}$ as

$$y_t = \alpha_0 + \alpha_1 t + e_t,\ t = 1, 2, \ldots, \qquad\qquad \textbf{[10.24]}$$

where, in the simplest case, $\{e_t\}$ is an independent, identically distributed (i.i.d.) sequence with $\mathrm{E}(et) = 0$ and $\mathrm{Var}(e_t) = \sigma_e^2$. Note how the parameter α_1 multiplies time, t, resulting in a **linear time trend**.

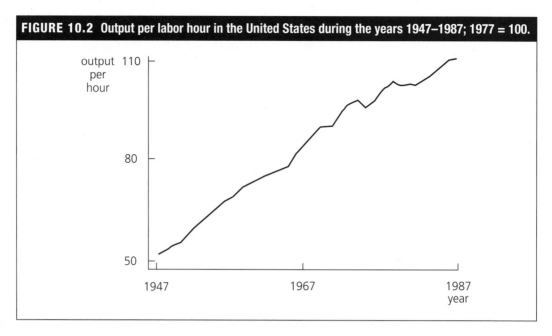

FIGURE 10.2 Output per labor hour in the United States during the years 1947–1987; 1977 = 100.

Interpreting α_1 in (10.24) is simple: holding all other factors (those in e_t) fixed, α_1 measures the change in y_t from one period to the next due to the passage of time. We can write this mathematically by defining the change in e_t from period $t-1$ to t as $\Delta e_t = e_t - e_{t-1}$. Equation (10.24) implies that if $\Delta e_t = 0$ then

$$\Delta y_t = y_t - y_{t-1} = \alpha_1.$$

Another way to think about a sequence that has a linear time trend is that its average value is a linear function of time:

$$E(y_t) = \alpha_0 + \alpha_1 t. \qquad [10.25]$$

If $\alpha_1 > 0$, then, on average, y_t is growing over time and therefore has an upward trend. If $\alpha_1 < 0$, then y_t has a downward trend. The values of y_t do not fall exactly on the line in (10.25) due to randomness, but the expected values are on the line. Unlike the mean, the variance of y_t is constant across time: $\text{Var}(y_t) = \text{Var}(e_t) = \sigma_e^2$.

> **EXPLORING FURTHER 10.4**
>
> In Example 10.4, we used the general fertility rate as the dependent variable in an FDL model. From 1950 through the mid-1980s, the *gfr* has a clear downward trend. Can a linear trend with $\alpha_1 < 0$ be realistic for all future time periods? Explain.

If $\{e_t\}$ is an i.i.d. sequence, then $\{y_t\}$ is an independent, though not identically, distributed sequence. A more realistic characterization of trending time series allows $\{e_t\}$ to be correlated over time, but this does not change the flavor of a linear time trend. In fact, what is important for regression analysis under the classical linear model assumptions is that $E\{y_t\}$ is linear in t. When we cover large sample properties of OLS in Chapter 11, we will have to discuss how much temporal correlation in $\{e_t\}$ is allowed.

Many economic time series are better approximated by an **exponential trend**, which follows when a series has the same average growth rate from period to period. Figure 10.3 plots data on annual nominal imports for the United States during the years 1948 through 1995 (*ERP* 1997, Table B-101).

In the early years, we see that the change in imports over each year is relatively small, whereas the change increases as time passes. This is consistent with a *constant average growth rate*: the percentage change is roughly the same in each period.

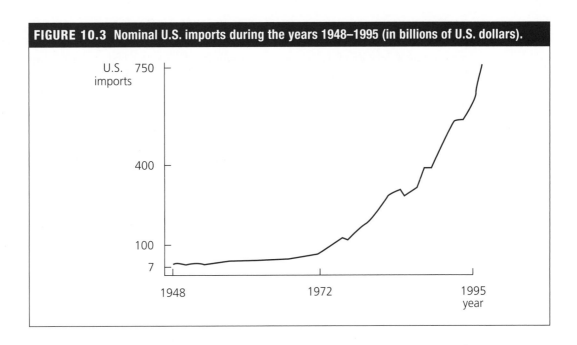

FIGURE 10.3 Nominal U.S. imports during the years 1948–1995 (in billions of U.S. dollars).

In practice, an exponential trend in a time series is captured by modeling the natural logarithm of the series as a linear trend (assuming that $y_t > 0$):

$$\log(y_t) = \beta_0 + \beta_1 t + e_t, t = 1, 2, ... \qquad [10.26]$$

Exponentiating shows that y_t itself has an exponential trend: $y_t = \exp(\beta_0 + \beta_1 t + e_t)$. Because we will want to use exponentially trending time series in linear regression models, (10.26) turns out to be the most convenient way for representing such series.

How do we interpret β_1 in (10.26)? Remember that, for small changes, $\Delta\log(y_t) = \log(y_t) - \log(y_{t-1})$ is approximately the proportionate change in y_t:

$$\Delta\log(y_t) \approx (y_t - y_{t-1})/y_{t-1}. \qquad [10.27]$$

The right-hand side of (10.27) is also called the **growth rate** in y from period $t-1$ to period t. To turn the growth rate into a percentage, we simply multiply by 100. If y_t follows (10.26), then, taking changes and setting $\Delta e_t = 0$,

$$\Delta\log(y_t) = \beta_1, \text{ for all } t. \qquad [10.28]$$

In other words, β_1 is approximately the average per period growth rate in y_t. For example, if t denotes year and $\beta_1 = .027$, then y_t grows about 2.7% per year on average.

Although linear and exponential trends are the most common, time trends can be more complicated. For example, instead of the linear trend model in (10.24), we might have a quadratic time trend:

$$y_t = \alpha_0 + \alpha_1 t + \alpha_2 t^2 + e_t. \qquad [10.29]$$

If α_1 and α_2 are positive, then the slope of the trend is increasing, as is easily seen by computing the approximate slope (holding e_t fixed):

$$\frac{\Delta y_t}{\Delta t} \approx \alpha_1 + 2\alpha_2 t. \qquad [10.30]$$

[If you are familiar with calculus, you recognize the right-hand side of (10.30) as the derivative of $\alpha_0 + \alpha_1 t + \alpha_2 t^2$ with respect to t.] If $\alpha_1 > 0$, but $\alpha_2 < 0$, the trend has a hump shape. This may not be a very good description of certain trending series because it requires an increasing trend to be followed, eventually, by a decreasing trend. Nevertheless, over a given time span, it can be a flexible way of modeling time series that have more complicated trends than either (10.24) or (10.26).

10-5b Using Trending Variables in Regression Analysis

Accounting for explained or explanatory variables that are trending is fairly straightforward in regression analysis. First, nothing about trending variables necessarily violates the classical linear model Assumptions TS.1 through TS.6. However, we must be careful to allow for the fact that unobserved, trending factors that affect y_t might also be correlated with the explanatory variables. If we ignore this possibility, we may find a spurious relationship between y_t and one or more explanatory variables. The phenomenon of finding a relationship between two or more trending variables simply because each is growing over time is an example of a **spurious regression problem**. Fortunately, adding a time trend eliminates this problem.

For concreteness, consider a model where two observed factors, x_{t1} and x_{t2}, affect y_t. In addition, there are unobserved factors that are systematically growing or shrinking over time. A model that captures this is

$$y_t = \beta_0 + \beta_1 x_{t1} + \beta_2 x_{t2} + \beta_3 t + u_t. \qquad [10.31]$$

This fits into the multiple linear regression framework with $x_{t3} = t$. Allowing for the trend in this equation explicitly recognizes that y_t may be growing $(\beta_3 > 0)$ or shrinking $(\beta_3 < 0)$ over time for reasons essentially unrelated to x_{t1} and x_{t2}. If (10.31) satisfies assumptions TS.1, TS.2, and TS.3, then omitting t from the regression and regressing y_t on x_{t1}, x_{t2} will generally yield biased estimators of β_1 and β_2: we have effectively omitted an important variable, t, from the regression. This is especially true if x_{t1} and x_{t2} are themselves trending, because they can then be highly correlated with t. The next example shows how omitting a time trend can result in spurious regression.

EXAMPLE 10.7   **Housing Investment and Prices**

The data in HSEINV are annual observations on housing investment and a housing price index in the United States for 1947 through 1988. Let *invpc* denote real per capita housing investment (in thousands of dollars) and let *price* denote a housing price index (equal to 1 in 1982). A simple regression in constant elasticity form, which can be thought of as a supply equation for housing stock, gives

$$\widehat{\log(invpc)} = -.550 + 1.241 \log(price)$$
$$(.043) \quad (.382) \qquad [10.32]$$
$$n = 42, R^2 = .208, \overline{R}^2 = .189.$$

The elasticity of per capita investment with respect to price is very large and statistically significant; it is not statistically different from one. We must be careful here. Both *invpc* and *price* have upward trends. In particular, if we regress $\log(invpc)$ on t, we obtain a coefficient on the trend equal to .0081 (standard error = .0018); the regression of $\log(price)$ on t yields a trend coefficient equal to .0044 (standard error = .0004). Although the standard errors on the trend coefficients are not necessarily reliable—these regressions tend to contain substantial serial correlation—the coefficient estimates do reveal upward trends.

To account for the trending behavior of the variables, we add a time trend:

$$\widehat{\log(invpc)} = -.913 - .381 \log(price) + .0098\, t$$
$$\qquad\qquad (1.36) \quad (.679) \qquad\qquad\qquad (.0035) \qquad\qquad \textbf{[10.33]}$$
$$n = 42,\ R^2 = .341,\ \overline{R}^2 = .307.$$

The story is much different now: the estimated price elasticity is negative and not statistically different from zero. The time trend is statistically significant, and its coefficient implies an approximate 1% increase in *invpc* per year, on average. From this analysis, we cannot conclude that real per capita housing investment is influenced at all by price. There are other factors, captured in the time trend, that affect *invpc*, but we have not modeled these. The results in (10.32) show a spurious relationship between *invpc* and *price* due to the fact that price is also trending upward over time.

In some cases, adding a time trend can make a key explanatory variable *more* significant. This can happen if the dependent and independent variables have different kinds of trends (say, one upward and one downward), but movement in the independent variable *about* its trend line causes movement in the dependent variable away from its trend line.

EXAMPLE 10.8   **Fertility Equation**

If we add a linear time trend to the fertility equation (10.18), we obtain

$$\widehat{gfr_t} = 111.77 + .279\, pe_t - 35.59\, ww2_t + .997\, pill_t - 1.15\, t$$
$$\qquad\qquad (3.36) \ (.040) \qquad (6.30) \qquad (6.626) \qquad (.19) \qquad\qquad \textbf{[10.34]}$$
$$n = 72,\ R^2 = .662,\ \overline{R}^2 = .642.$$

The coefficient on *pe* is more than triple the estimate from (10.18), and it is much more statistically significant. Interestingly, *pill* is not significant once an allowance is made for a linear trend. As can be seen by the estimate, *gfr* was falling, on average, over this period, other factors being equal.

Since the general fertility rate exhibited both upward and downward trends during the period from 1913 through 1984, we can see how robust the estimated effect of *pe* is when we use a quadratic trend:

$$\widehat{gfr_t} = 124.09 + .348\, pe_t - 35.88\, ww2_t - 10.12\, pill_t - 2.53\, t + .0196\, t^2$$
$$\qquad\qquad (4.36) \ (.040) \qquad (5.71) \qquad (6.34) \qquad (.39) \ (.0050) \qquad \textbf{[10.35]}$$
$$n = 72,\ R^2 = .727,\ \overline{R}^2 = .706.$$

The coefficient on *pe* is even larger and more statistically significant. Now, *pill* has the expected negative effect and is marginally significant, and both trend terms are statistically significant. The quadratic trend is a flexible way to account for the unusual trending behavior of *gfr*.

You might be wondering in Example 10.8: why stop at a quadratic trend? Nothing prevents us from adding, say, t^3 as an independent variable, and, in fact, this might be warranted (see Computer Exercise C6). But we have to be careful not to get carried away when including trend terms in a model. We want relatively simple trends that capture broad movements in the dependent variable that are not explained by the independent variables in the model. If we include enough polynomial terms in *t*, then we can track any series pretty well. But this offers little help in finding which explanatory variables affect y_t.

10-5c A Detrending Interpretation of Regressions with a Time Trend

Including a time trend in a regression model creates a nice interpretation in terms of **detrending** the original data series before using them in regression analysis. For concreteness, we focus on model (10.31), but our conclusions are much more general.

When we regress y_t on x_{t1}, x_{t2}, and t, we obtain the fitted equation

$$\hat{y}_t = \hat{\beta}_0 + \hat{\beta}_1 x_{t1} + \hat{\beta}_2 x_{t2} + \hat{\beta}_3 t. \qquad [10.36]$$

We can extend the Frisch-Waugh result on the partialling out interpretation of OLS that we covered in Section 3-2 to show that $\hat{\beta}_1$ and $\hat{\beta}_2$ can be obtained as follows.

(i) Regress each of y_t, x_{t1}, and x_{t2} on a constant and the time trend t and save the residuals, say, $\ddot{y}_t, \ddot{x}_{t1}, \ddot{x}_{t2}, t = 1, 2, \ldots, n$. For example,

$$\ddot{y}_t = y_t - \hat{\alpha}_0 - \hat{\alpha}_1 t.$$

Thus, we can think of $\ddot{y}_t$ as being *linearly detrended.* In detrending y_t, we have estimated the model

$$y_t = \alpha_0 + \alpha_1 t + e_t$$

by OLS; the residuals from this regression, $\hat{e}_t = \ddot{y}_t$, have the time trend removed (at least in the sample). A similar interpretation holds for $\ddot{x}_{t1}$ and $\ddot{x}_{t2}$.

(ii) Run the regression of

$$\ddot{y}_t \text{ on } \ddot{x}_{t1}, \ddot{x}_{t2}. \qquad [10.37]$$

(No intercept is necessary, but including an intercept affects nothing: the intercept will be estimated to be zero.) This regression exactly yields $\hat{\beta}_1$ and $\hat{\beta}_2$ from (10.36).

This means that the estimates of primary interest, $\hat{\beta}_1$ and $\hat{\beta}_2$, can be interpreted as coming from a regression *without* a time trend, but where we first detrend the dependent variable and all other independent variables. The same conclusion holds with any number of independent variables and if the trend is quadratic or of some other polynomial degree.

If t is omitted from (10.36), then no detrending occurs, and y_t might seem to be related to one or more of the x_{tj} simply because each contains a trend; we saw this in Example 10.7. If the trend term is statistically significant, and the results change in important ways when a time trend is added to a regression, then the initial results without a trend should be treated with suspicion.

The interpretation of $\hat{\beta}_1$ and $\hat{\beta}_2$ shows that it is a good idea to include a trend in the regression if any independent variable is trending, even if y_t is not. If y_t has no noticeable trend, but, say, x_{t1} is growing over time, then excluding a trend from the regression may make it look as if x_{t1} has no effect on y_t, even though movements of x_{t1} about its trend may affect y_t. This will be captured if t is included in the regression.

EXAMPLE 10.9   **Puerto Rican Employment**

When we add a linear trend to equation (10.17), the estimates are

$$\widehat{\log(prepop_t)} = -8.70 - .169 \log(mincov_t) + 1.06 \log(usgnp_t)$$
$$\phantom{\widehat{\log(prepop_t)} = } (1.30) \ (.044) (0.18)$$
$$\phantom{\widehat{\log(prepop_t)} = } - .032\, t \qquad [10.38]$$
$$\phantom{\widehat{\log(prepop_t)} = } (.005)$$
$$n = 38, R^2 = .847, \overline{R}^2 = .834.$$

The coefficient on log(*usgnp*) has changed dramatically: from $-.012$ and insignificant to 1.06 and very significant. The coefficient on the minimum wage has changed only slightly, although the standard error is notably smaller, making log(*mincov*) more significant than before.

The variable *prepop*$_t$ displays no clear upward or downward trend, but log(*usgnp*) has an upward, linear trend. [A regression of log(*usgnp*) on t gives an estimate of about .03, so that *usgnp* is growing by about 3% per year over the period.] We can think of the estimate 1.06 as follows: when *usgnp* increases by 1% *above* its long-run trend, *prepop* increases by about 1.06%.

10-5d Computing *R*-Squared When the Dependent Variable Is Trending

R-squareds in time series regressions are often very high, especially compared with typical *R*-squareds for cross-sectional data. Does this mean that we learn more about factors affecting *y* from time series data? Not necessarily. On one hand, time series data often come in aggregate form (such as average hourly wages in the U.S. economy), and aggregates are often easier to explain than outcomes on individuals, families, or firms, which is often the nature of cross-sectional data. But the usual and adjusted *R*-squareds for time series regressions can be artificially high when the dependent variable is trending. Remember that R^2 is a measure of how large the error variance is relative to the variance of *y*. The formula for the adjusted *R*-squared shows this directly:

$$\bar{R}^2 = 1 - (\hat{\sigma}_u^2/\hat{\sigma}_y^2),$$

where $\hat{\sigma}_u^2$ is the unbiased estimator of the error variance, $\hat{\sigma}_y^2 = \text{SST}/(n-1)$, and $\text{SST} = \sum_{t=1}^{n}(y_t - \bar{y})^2$. Now, estimating the error variance when y_t is trending is no problem, provided a time trend is included in the regression. However, when $E(y_t)$ follows, say, a linear time trend [see (10.24)], $\text{SST}/(n-1)$ is no longer an unbiased or consistent estimator of $\text{Var}(y_t)$. In fact, $\text{SST}/(n-1)$ can substantially overestimate the variance in y_t, because it does not account for the trend in y_t.

When the dependent variable satisfies linear, quadratic, or any other polynomial trends, it is easy to compute a goodness-of-fit measure that first nets out the effect of any time trend on y_t. The simplest method is to compute the usual *R*-squared in a regression where the dependent variable has already been detrended. For example, if the model is (10.31), then we first regress y_t on t and obtain the residuals $\ddot{y}_t$. Then, we regress

$$\ddot{y}_t \text{ on } x_{t1}, x_{t2}, \text{ and } t. \tag{10.39}$$

The *R*-squared from this regression is

$$1 - \frac{\text{SSR}}{\sum_{t=1}^{n} \ddot{y}_t^2}, \tag{10.40}$$

where SSR is identical to the sum of squared residuals from (10.36). Since $\sum_{t=1}^{n} \ddot{y}_t^2 \leq \sum_{t=1}^{n}(y_t - \bar{y})^2$ (and usually the inequality is strict), the *R*-squared from (10.40) is no greater than, and usually less than, the *R*-squared from (10.36). (The sum of squared residuals is identical in both regressions.) When y_t contains a strong linear time trend, (10.40) can be much less than the usual *R*-squared.

The *R*-squared in (10.40) better reflects how well x_{t1} and x_{t2} explain y_t because it nets out the effect of the time trend. After all, we can always explain a trending variable with some sort of trend, but this does not mean we have uncovered any factors that cause movements in y_t. An adjusted *R*-squared can also be computed based on (10.40): divide SSR by $(n-4)$ because this is the *df* in (10.36) and divide $\sum_{t=1}^{n} \ddot{y}_t^2$ by $(n-2)$, as there are two trend parameters estimated in detrending y_t.

In general, SSR is divided by the *df* in the usual regression (that includes any time trends), and $\sum_{t=1}^{n} \ddot{y}_t^2$ is divided by $(n - p)$, where *p* is the number of trend parameters estimated in detrending y_t. Wooldridge (1991a) provides detailed suggestions for degrees-of-freedom corrections, but a computationally simple approach is fine as an approximation: use the adjusted *R*-squared from the regression $\ddot{y}_t$ on $t, t^2, \ldots, t^p, x_{t1}, \ldots, x_{tk}$. This requires us only to remove the trend from y_t to obtain $\ddot{y}_t$, and then we can use $\ddot{y}_t$ to compute the usual kinds of goodness-of-fit measures.

EXAMPLE 10.10   **Housing Investment**

In Example 10.7, we saw that including a linear time trend along with log(*price*) in the housing investment equation had a substantial effect on the price elasticity. But the *R*-squared from regression (10.33), taken literally, says that we are "explaining" 34.1% of the variation in log(*invpc*). This is misleading. If we first detrend log(*invpc*) and regress the detrended variable on log(*price*) and *t*, the *R*-squared becomes .008, and the adjusted *R*-squared is actually negative. Thus, movements in log(*price*) about its trend have virtually no explanatory power for movements in log(*invpc*) about its trend. This is consistent with the fact that the *t* statistic on log(*price*) in equation (10.33) is very small.

Before leaving this subsection, we must make a final point. In computing the *R*-squared form of an *F* statistic for testing multiple hypotheses, we just use the usual *R*-squareds without any detrending. Remember, the *R*-squared form of the *F* statistic is just a computational device, and so the usual formula is always appropriate.

10-5e Seasonality

If a time series is observed at monthly or quarterly intervals (or even weekly or daily), it may exhibit **seasonality**. For example, monthly housing starts in the Midwest are strongly influenced by weather. Although weather patterns are somewhat random, we can be sure that the weather during January will usually be more inclement than in June, and so housing starts are generally higher in June than in January. One way to model this phenomenon is to allow the expected value of the series, y_t, to be different in each month. As another example, retail sales in the fourth quarter are typically higher than in the previous three quarters because of the Christmas holiday. Again, this can be captured by allowing the average retail sales to differ over the course of a year. This is in addition to possibly allowing for a trending mean. For example, retail sales in the most recent first quarter were higher than retail sales in the fourth quarter from 30 years ago, because retail sales have been steadily growing. Nevertheless, if we compare average sales within a typical year, the seasonal holiday factor tends to make sales larger in the fourth quarter.

Even though many monthly and quarterly data series display seasonal patterns, not all of them do. For example, there is no noticeable seasonal pattern in monthly interest or inflation rates. In addition, series that do display seasonal patterns are often **seasonally adjusted** before they are reported for public use. A seasonally adjusted series is one that, in principle, has had the seasonal factors removed from it. Seasonal adjustment can be done in a variety of ways, and a careful discussion is beyond the scope of this text. [See Harvey (1990) and Hylleberg (1992) for detailed treatments.]

Seasonal adjustment has become so common that it is not possible to get seasonally unadjusted data in many cases. Quarterly U.S. GDP is a leading example. In the annual *Economic Report of the President*, many macroeconomic data sets reported at monthly frequencies (at least for the most recent years) and those that display seasonal patterns are all seasonally adjusted. The major sources for macroeconomic time series, including *Citibase*, also seasonally adjust many of the series. Thus, the scope for using our own seasonal adjustment is often limited.

Sometimes, we do work with seasonally unadjusted data, and it is useful to know that simple methods are available for dealing with seasonality in regression models. Generally, we can include a set of **seasonal dummy variables** to account for seasonality in the dependent variable, the independent variables, or both.

The approach is simple. Suppose that we have monthly data, and we think that seasonal patterns within a year are roughly constant across time. For example, since Christmas always comes at the same time of year, we can expect retail sales to be, on average, higher in months late in the year than in earlier months. Or, since weather patterns are broadly similar across years, housing starts in the Midwest will be higher on average during the summer months than the winter months. A general model for monthly data that captures these phenomena is

$$y_t = \beta_0 + \delta_1 feb_t + \delta_2 mar_t + \delta_3 apr_t + \ldots + \delta_{11} dec_t$$
$$+ \beta_1 x_{t1} + \ldots + \beta_k x_{tk} + u_t, \quad [10.41]$$

EXPLORING FURTHER 10.5

In equation (10.41), what is the intercept for March? Explain why seasonal dummy variables satisfy the strict exogeneity assumption.

where $feb_t, mar_t, \ldots, dec_t$ are dummy variables indicating whether time period t corresponds to the appropriate month. In this formulation, January is the base month, and β_0 is the intercept for January. If there is no seasonality in y_t, once the x_{tj} have been controlled for, then δ_1 through δ_{11} are all zero. This is easily tested via an F test.

EXAMPLE 10.11   Effects of Antidumping Filings

In Example 10.5, we used monthly data (in the file BARIUM) that have not been seasonally adjusted. Therefore, we should add seasonal dummy variables to make sure none of the important conclusions change. It could be that the months just before the suit was filed are months where imports are higher or lower, on average, than in other months. When we add the 11 monthly dummy variables as in (10.41) and test their joint significance, we obtain p-value = .59, and so the seasonal dummies are jointly insignificant. In addition, nothing important changes in the estimates once statistical significance is taken into account. Krupp and Pollard (1996) actually used three dummy variables for the seasons (fall, spring, and summer, with winter as the base season), rather than a full set of monthly dummies; the outcome is essentially the same.

If the data are quarterly, then we would include dummy variables for three of the four quarters, with the omitted category being the base quarter. Sometimes, it is useful to interact seasonal dummies with some of the x_{tj} to allow the effect of x_{tj} on y_t to differ across the year.

Just as including a time trend in a regression has the interpretation of initially detrending the data, including seasonal dummies in a regression can be interpreted as **deseasonalizing** the data. For concreteness, consider equation (10.41) with $k = 2$. The OLS slope coefficients $\hat{\beta}_1$ and $\hat{\beta}_2$ on x_1 and x_2 can be obtained as follows:

(i) Regress each of y_t, x_{t1}, and x_{t2} on a constant and the monthly dummies, $feb_t, mar_t, \ldots, dec_t$, and save the residuals, say, $\ddot{y}_t$, $\ddot{x}_{t1}$, and $\ddot{x}_{t2}$, for all $t = 1, 2, \ldots, n$. For example,

$$\ddot{y}_t = y_t - \hat{\alpha}_0 - \hat{\alpha}_1 feb_t - \hat{\alpha}_2 mar_t - \ldots - \hat{\alpha}_{11} dec_t.$$

This is one method of deseasonalizing a monthly time series. A similar interpretation holds for $\ddot{x}_{t1}$ and $\ddot{x}_{t2}$.

(ii) Run the regression, without the monthly dummies, of $\ddot{y}_t$ on $\ddot{x}_{t1}$ and $\ddot{x}_{t2}$ [just as in (10.37)]. This gives $\hat{\beta}_1$ and $\hat{\beta}_2$.

In some cases, if y_t has pronounced seasonality, a better goodness-of-fit measure is an R-squared based on the deseasonalized y_t. This nets out any seasonal effects that are not explained by the x_{tj}.

Wooldridge (1991a) suggests specific degrees-of-freedom adjustments, or one may simply use the adjusted R-squared where the dependent variable has been deseasonalized.

Time series exhibiting seasonal patterns can be trending as well, in which case we should estimate a regression model with a time trend and seasonal dummy variables. The regressions can then be interpreted as regressions using both detrended and deseasonalized series. Goodness-of-fit statistics are discussed in Wooldridge (1991a): essentially, we detrend and deseasonalize y_t by regressing on both a time trend and seasonal dummies before computing R-squared or adjusted R-squared.

Summary

In this chapter, we have covered basic regression analysis with time series data. Under assumptions that parallel those for cross-sectional analysis, OLS is unbiased (under TS.1 through TS.3), OLS is BLUE (under TS.1 through TS.5), and the usual OLS standard errors, t statistics, and F statistics can be used for statistical inference (under TS.1 through TS.6). Because of the temporal correlation in most time series data, we must explicitly make assumptions about how the errors are related to the explanatory variables in all time periods and about the temporal correlation in the errors themselves. The classical linear model assumptions can be pretty restrictive for time series applications, but they are a natural starting point. We have applied them to both static regression and finite distributed lag models.

Logarithms and dummy variables are used regularly in time series applications and in event studies. We also discussed index numbers and time series measured in terms of nominal and real dollars.

Trends and seasonality can be easily handled in a multiple regression framework by including time and seasonal dummy variables in our regression equations. We presented problems with the usual R-squared as a goodness-of-fit measure and suggested some simple alternatives based on detrending or deseasonalizing.

CLASSICAL LINEAR MODEL ASSUMPTIONS FOR TIME SERIES REGRESSION

Following is a summary of the six classical linear model (CLM) assumptions for time series regression applications. Assumptions TS.1 through TS.5 are the time series versions of the Gauss-Markov assumptions (which implies that OLS is BLUE and has the usual sampling variances). We only needed TS.1, TS.2, and TS.3 to establish unbiasedness of OLS. As in the case of cross-sectional regression, the normality assumption, TS.6, was used so that we could perform exact statistical inference for any sample size.

Assumption TS.1 (Linear in Parameters)

The stochastic process $\{(x_{t1}, x_{t2}, \ldots, x_{tk}, y_t): t = 1, 2, \ldots, n\}$ follows the linear model

$$y_t = \beta_0 + \beta_1 x_{t1} + \beta_2 x_{t2} + \ldots + \beta_k x_{tk} + u_t,$$

where $\{u_t: t = 1, 2, \ldots, n\}$ is the sequence of errors or disturbances. Here, n is the number of observations (time periods).

Assumption TS.2 (No Perfect Collinearity)

In the sample (and therefore in the underlying time series process), no independent variable is constant nor a perfect linear combination of the others.

Assumption TS.3 (Zero Conditional Mean)

For each t, the expected value of the error u_t, given the explanatory variables for *all* time periods, is zero. Mathematically, $\mathrm{E}(u_t|\mathbf{X}) = 0, t = 1, 2, \ldots, n$.

Assumption TS.3 replaces MLR.4 for cross-sectional regression, and it also means we do not have to make the random sampling assumption MLR.2. Remember, Assumption TS.3 implies that the error in each time period t is uncorrelated with all explanatory variables in *all* time periods (including, of course, time period t).

Assumption TS.4 (Homoskedasticity)

Conditional on $\mathbf{X}$, the variance of u_t is the same for all t: $\text{Var}(u_t|\mathbf{X}) = \text{Var}(u_t) = \sigma^2$, $t = 1, 2, \ldots, n$.

Assumption TS.5 (No Serial Correlation)

Conditional on $\mathbf{X}$, the errors in two different time periods are uncorrelated: $\text{Corr}(u_t, u_s|\mathbf{X}) = 0$, for all $t \neq s$.

Recall that we added the no serial correlation assumption, along with the homoskedasticity assumption, to obtain the same variance formulas that we derived for cross-sectional regression under random sampling. As we will see in Chapter 12, Assumption TS.5 is often violated in ways that can make the usual statistical inference very unreliable.

Assumption TS.6 (Normality)

The errors u_t are independent of $\mathbf{X}$ and are independently and identically distributed as $\text{Normal}(0,\sigma^2)$.

Key Terms

Autocorrelation	Growth Rate	Seasonally Adjusted
Base Period	Impact Multiplier	Serial Correlation
Base Value	Impact Propensity	Short-Run Elasticity
Contemporaneously Exogenous	Index Number	Spurious Regression Problem
Cumulative Effect	Lag Distribution	Static Model
Deseasonalizing	Linear Time Trend	Stochastic Process
Detrending	Long-Run Elasticity	Strictly Exogenous
Event Study	Long-Run Multiplier	Time Series Process
Exponential Trend	Long-Run Propensity (LRP)	Time Trend
Finite Distributed Lag (FDL)	Seasonal Dummy Variables	
Model	Seasonality	

Problems

1 Decide if you agree or disagree with each of the following statements and give a brief explanation of your decision:
   (i) Like cross-sectional observations, we can assume that most time series observations are independently distributed.
   (ii) The OLS estimator in a time series regression is unbiased under the first three Gauss-Markov assumptions.
   (iii) A trending variable cannot be used as the dependent variable in multiple regression analysis.
   (iv) Seasonality is not an issue when using annual time series observations.

2 Let $gGDP_t$ denote the annual percentage change in gross domestic product and let int_t denote a short-term interest rate. Suppose that $gGDP_t$ is related to interest rates by

$$gGDP_t = \alpha_0 + \delta_0 int_t + \delta_1 int_{t-1} + u_t,$$

where u_t is uncorrelated with int_t, int_{t-1}, and all other past values of interest rates. Suppose that the Federal Reserve follows the policy rule:

$$int_t = \gamma_0 + \gamma_1(gGDP_{t-1} - 3) + v_t,$$

where $\gamma_1 > 0$. (When last year's GDP growth is above 3%, the Fed increases interest rates to prevent an "overheated" economy.) If v_t is uncorrelated with all past values of int_t and u_t, argue that int_t must be correlated with u_{t-1}. (*Hint*: Lag the first equation for one time period and substitute for $gGDP_{t-1}$ in the second equation.) Which Gauss-Markov assumption does this violate?

3 Suppose y_t follows a second order FDL model:

$$y_t = \alpha_0 + \delta_0 z_t + \delta_1 z_{t-1} + \delta_2 z_{t-2} + u_t.$$

Let z^* denote the *equilibrium value* of z_t and let y^* be the equilibrium value of y_t, such that

$$y^* = \alpha_0 + \delta_0 z^* + \delta_1 z^* + \delta_2 z^*.$$

Show that the change in y^*, due to a change in z^*, equals the long-run propensity times the change in z^*:

$$\Delta y^* = LRP \cdot \Delta z^*.$$

This gives an alternative way of interpreting the LRP.

4 When the three event indicators *befile6*, *affile6*, and *afdec6* are dropped from equation (10.22), we obtain $R^2 = .281$ and $\bar{R}^2 = .264$. Are the event indicators jointly significant at the 10% level?

5 Suppose you have quarterly data on new housing starts, interest rates, and real per capita income. Specify a model for housing starts that accounts for possible trends and seasonality in the variables.

6 In Example 10.4, we saw that our estimates of the individual lag coefficients in a distributed lag model were very imprecise. One way to alleviate the multicollinearity problem is to assume that the δ_j follow a relatively simple pattern. For concreteness, consider a model with four lags:

$$y_t = \alpha_0 + \delta_0 z_t + \delta_1 z_{t-1} + \delta_2 z_{t-2} + \delta_3 z_{t-3} + \delta_4 z_{t-4} + u_t.$$

Now, let us assume that the δ_j follow a quadratic in the lag, j:

$$\delta_j = \gamma_0 + \gamma_1 j + \gamma_2 j^2,$$

for parameters γ_0, γ_1, and γ_2. This is an example of a *polynomial distributed lag (PDL) model*.
  (i)   Plug the formula for each δ_j into the distributed lag model and write the model in terms of the parameters γ_h, for $h = 0, 1, 2$.
  (ii) Explain the regression you would run to estimate the γ_h.
  (iii) The polynomial distributed lag model is a restricted version of the general model. How many restrictions are imposed? How would you test these? (*Hint:* Think F test.)

7 In Example 10.4, we wrote the model that explicitly contains the long-run propensity, θ_0, as

$$gfr_t = \alpha_0 + \theta_0 pe_t + \delta_1(pe_{t-1} - pe_t) + \delta_2(pe_{t-2} - pe_t) + u,$$

where we omit the other explanatory variables for simplicity. As always with multiple regression analysis, θ_0 should have a ceteris paribus interpretation. Namely, if pe_t increases by one (dollar) holding $(pe_{t-1} - pe_t)$ and $(pe_{t-2} - pe_t)$ fixed, gfr_t should change by θ_0.
  (i)   If $(pe_{t-1} - pe_t)$ and $(pe_{t-2} - pe_t)$ are held fixed but pe_t is increasing, what must be true about changes in pe_{t-1} and pe_{t-2}?
  (ii) How does your answer in part (i) help you to interpret θ_0 in the above equation as the LRP?

8 In the linear model given in equation (10.8), the explanatory variables $\mathbf{x}_t = (x_{t1}, \ldots, x_{tk})$ are said to be *sequentially exogenous* (sometimes called *weakly exogenous*) if

$$E(u_t|\mathbf{x}_t, \mathbf{x}_{t-1}, \ldots, \mathbf{x}_1) = 0, t = 1, 2, \ldots,$$

so that the errors are unpredictable given current and all *past* values of the explanatory variables.
  (i)   Explain why sequential exogeneity is implied by strict exogeneity.
  (ii) Explain why contemporaneous exogeneity is implied by sequential exogeneity.

(iii) Are the OLS estimators generally unbiased under the sequential exogeneity assumption? Explain.

(iv) Consider a model to explain the annual rate of HIV infections (*HIVrate*) as a distributed lag of per capita condom usage (*pccon*) for a state, region, or province:

$$E(HIVrate_t|pccon_t, pccon_{t-1}, \dots) = \alpha_0 + \delta_0 pccon_t + \delta_1 pccon_{t-1}$$
$$+ \delta_2 pccon_{t-2} + \delta_3 pccon_{t-3}.$$

Explain why this model satisfies the sequential exogeneity assumption. Does it seem likely that strict exogeneity holds too?

Computer Exercises

C1 In October 1979, the Federal Reserve changed its policy of using finely tuned interest rate adjustments and instead began targeting the money supply. Using the data in INTDEF, define a dummy variable equal to 1 for years after 1979. Include this dummy in equation (10.15) to see if there is a shift in the interest rate equation after 1979. What do you conclude?

C2 Use the data in BARIUM for this exercise.
(i) Add a linear time trend to equation (10.22). Are any variables, other than the trend, statistically significant?
(ii) In the equation estimated in part (i), test for joint significance of all variables except the time trend. What do you conclude?
(iii) Add monthly dummy variables to this equation and test for seasonality. Does including the monthly dummies change any other estimates or their standard errors in important ways?

C3 Add the variable log(*prgnp*) to the minimum wage equation in (10.38). Is this variable significant? Interpret the coefficient. How does adding log(*prgnp*) affect the estimated minimum wage effect?

C4 Use the data in FERTIL3 to verify that the standard error for the LRP in equation (10.19) is about .030.

C5 Use the data in EZANDERS for this exercise. The data are on monthly unemployment claims in Anderson Township in Indiana, from January 1980 through November 1988. In 1984, an enterprise zone (EZ) was located in Anderson (as well as other cities in Indiana). [See Papke (1994) for details.]
(i) Regress log(*uclms*) on a linear time trend and 11 monthly dummy variables. What was the overall trend in unemployment claims over this period? (Interpret the coefficient on the time trend.) Is there evidence of seasonality in unemployment claims?
(ii) Add *ez*, a dummy variable equal to one in the months Anderson had an EZ, to the regression in part (i). Does having the enterprise zone seem to decrease unemployment claims? By how much? [You should use formula (7.10) from Chapter 7.]
(iii) What assumptions do you need to make to attribute the effect in part (ii) to the creation of an EZ?

C6 Use the data in FERTIL3 for this exercise.
(i) Regress *gfr_t* on *t* and *t²* and save the residuals. This gives a detrended *gfr_t*, say, $\ddot{gf}_t$.
(ii) Regress $\ddot{gf}_t$ on all of the variables in equation (10.35), including *t* and *t²*. Compare the *R*-squared with that from (10.35). What do you conclude?
(iii) Reestimate equation (10.35) but add *t³* to the equation. Is this additional term statistically significant?

C7 Use the data set CONSUMP for this exercise.
(i) Estimate a simple regression model relating the growth in real per capita consumption (of nondurables and services) to the growth in real per capita disposable income. Use the change in the logarithms in both cases. Report the results in the usual form. Interpret the equation and discuss statistical significance.

(ii) Add a lag of the growth in real per capita disposable income to the equation from part (i). What do you conclude about adjustment lags in consumption growth?

(iii) Add the real interest rate to the equation in part (i). Does it affect consumption growth?

C8 Use the data in FERTIL3 for this exercise.

(i) Add pe_{t-3} and pe_{t-4} to equation (10.19). Test for joint significance of these lags.

(ii) Find the estimated long-run propensity and its standard error in the model from part (i). Compare these with those obtained from equation (10.19).

(iii) Estimate the polynomial distributed lag model from Problem 6. Find the estimated LRP and compare this with what is obtained from the unrestricted model.

C9 Use the data in VOLAT for this exercise. The variable *rsp500* is the monthly return on the Standard & Poor's 500 stock market index, at an annual rate. (This includes price changes as well as dividends.) The variable *i3* is the return on three-month T-bills, and *pcip* is the percentage change in industrial production; these are also at an annual rate.

(i) Consider the equation

$$rsp500_t = \beta_0 + \beta_1 pcip_t + \beta_2 i3_t + u_t.$$

What signs do you think β_1 and β_2 should have?

(ii) Estimate the previous equation by OLS, reporting the results in standard form. Interpret the signs and magnitudes of the coefficients.

(iii) Which of the variables is statistically significant?

(iv) Does your finding from part (iii) imply that the return on the S&P 500 is predictable? Explain.

C10 Consider the model estimated in (10.15); use the data in INTDEF.

(i) Find the correlation between *inf* and *def* over this sample period and comment.

(ii) Add a single lag of *inf* and *def* to the equation and report the results in the usual form.

(iii) Compare the estimated LRP for the effect of inflation with that in equation (10.15). Are they vastly different?

(iv) Are the two lags in the model jointly significant at the 5% level?

C11 The file TRAFFIC2 contains 108 monthly observations on automobile accidents, traffic laws, and some other variables for California from January 1981 through December 1989. Use this data set to answer the following questions.

(i) During what month and year did California's seat belt law take effect? When did the highway speed limit increase to 65 miles per hour?

(ii) Regress the variable log(*totacc*) on a linear time trend and 11 monthly dummy variables, using January as the base month. Interpret the coefficient estimate on the time trend. Would you say there is seasonality in total accidents?

(iii) Add to the regression from part (ii) the variables *wkends*, *unem*, *spdlaw*, and *beltlaw*. Discuss the coefficient on the unemployment variable. Does its sign and magnitude make sense to you?

(iv) In the regression from part (iii), interpret the coefficients on *spdlaw* and *beltlaw*. Are the estimated effects what you expected? Explain.

(v) The variable *prcfat* is the percentage of accidents resulting in at least one fatality. Note that this variable is a percentage, not a proportion. What is the average of *prcfat* over this period? Does the magnitude seem about right?

(vi) Run the regression in part (iii) but use *prcfat* as the dependent variable in place of log(*totacc*). Discuss the estimated effects and significance of the speed and seat belt law variables.

C12 (i) Estimate equation (10.2) using all the data in PHILLIPS and report the results in the usual form. How many observations do you have now?

(ii) Compare the estimates from part (i) with those in equation (10.14). In particular, does adding the extra years help in obtaining an estimated tradeoff between inflation and unemployment? Explain.

(iii) Now run the regression using only the years 1997 through 2003. How do these estimates differ from those in equation (10.14)? Are the estimates using the most recent seven years precise enough to draw any firm conclusions? Explain.

(iv) Consider a simple regression setup in which we start with n time series observations and then split them into an early time period and a later time period. In the first time period we have n_1 observations and in the second period n_2 observations. Draw on the previous parts of this exercise to evaluate the following statement: "Generally, we can expect the slope estimate using all n observations to be roughly equal to a weighted average of the slope estimates on the early and later subsamples, where the weights are n_1/n and n_2/n, respectively."

C13 Use the data in MINWAGE for this exercise. In particular, use the employment and wage series for sector 232 (Men's and Boys' Furnishings). The variable *gwage232* is the monthly growth (change in logs) in the average wage in sector 232, *gemp232* is the growth in employment in sector 232, *gmwage* is the growth in the federal minimum wage, and *gcpi* is the growth in the (urban) Consumer Price Index.

(i) Run the regression *gwage232* on *gmwage*, *gcpi*. Do the sign and magnitude of $\hat{\beta}_{gmwage}$ make sense to you? Explain. Is *gmwage* statistically significant?

(ii) Add lags 1 through 12 of *gmwage* to the equation in part (i). Do you think it is necessary to include these lags to estimate the long-run effect of minimum wage growth on wage growth in sector 232? Explain.

(iii) Run the regression *gemp232* on *gmwage*, *gcpi*. Does minimum wage growth appear to have a contemporaneous effect on *gemp232*?

(iv) Add lags 1 through 12 to the employment growth equation. Does growth in the minimum wage have a statistically significant effect on employment growth, either in the short run or long run? Explain.

C14 Use the data in APPROVAL to answer the following questions. The data set consists of 78 months of data during the presidency of George W. Bush. (The data end in July 2007, before Bush left office.) In addition to economic variables and binary indicators of various events, it includes an approval rate, *approve*, collected by Gallup. (Caution: One should also attempt Computer Exercise C14 in Chapter 11 to gain a more complete understanding of the econometric issues involved in analyzing these data.)

(i) What is the range of the variable *approve*? What is its average value?

(ii) Estimate the model

$$approve_t = \beta_0 + \beta_1 lcpifood_t + \beta_2 lrgasprice_t + \beta_3 unemploy_t + u_t,$$

where the first two variables are in logarithmic form, and report the estimates in the usual way.

(iii) Interpret the coefficients in the estimates from part (ii). Comment on the signs and sizes of the effects, as well as statistical significance.

(iv) Add the binary variables *sep11* and *iraqinvade* to the equation from part (ii). Interpret the coefficients on the dummy variables. Are they statistically significant?

(v) Does adding the dummy variables in part (iv) change the other estimates much? Are any of the coefficients in part (iv) hard to rationalize?

(vi) Add *lsp500* to the regression in part (iv). Controlling for other factors, does the stock market have an important effect on the presidential approval rating?

CHAPTER 11

Further Issues in Using OLS with Time Series Data

In Chapter 10, we discussed the finite sample properties of OLS for time series data under increasingly stronger sets of assumptions. Under the full set of classical linear model assumptions for time series, TS.1 through TS.6, OLS has *exactly* the same desirable properties that we derived for cross-sectional data. Likewise, statistical inference is carried out in the same way as it was for cross-sectional analysis.

From our cross-sectional analysis in Chapter 5, we know that there are good reasons for studying the large sample properties of OLS. For example, if the error terms are not drawn from a normal distribution, then we must rely on the central limit theorem (CLT) to justify the usual OLS test statistics and confidence intervals.

Large sample analysis is even more important in time series contexts. (This is somewhat ironic given that large time series samples can be difficult to come by; but we often have no choice other than to rely on large sample approximations.) In Section 10-3, we explained how the strict exogeneity assumption (TS.3) might be violated in static and distributed lag models. As we will show in Section 11-2, models with lagged dependent variables must violate Assumption TS.3.

Unfortunately, large sample analysis for time series problems is fraught with many more difficulties than it was for cross-sectional analysis. In Chapter 5, we obtained the large sample properties of OLS in the context of random sampling. Things are more complicated when we allow the observations to be correlated across time. Nevertheless, the major limit theorems hold for certain, although not all, time series processes. The key is whether the correlation between the variables at different time periods tends to zero quickly enough. Time series that have substantial temporal correlation require special attention in regression analysis. This chapter will alert you to certain issues pertaining to such series in regression analysis.

11-1 Stationary and Weakly Dependent Time Series

In this section, we present the key concepts that are needed to apply the usual large sample approximations in regression analysis with time series data. The details are not as important as a general understanding of the issues.

11-1a Stationary and Nonstationary Time Series

Historically, the notion of a **stationary process** has played an important role in the analysis of time series. A stationary time series process is one whose probability distributions are stable over time in the following sense: If we take any collection of random variables in the sequence and then shift that sequence ahead h time periods, the joint probability distribution must remain unchanged. A formal definition of stationarity follows.

Stationary Stochastic Process. The stochastic process $\{x_t: t = 1, 2, \ldots\}$ is *stationary* if for every collection of time indices $1 \leq t_1 < t_2 < \ldots < t_m$, the joint distribution of $(x_{t_1}, x_{t_2}, \ldots, x_{t_m})$ is the same as the joint distribution of $(x_{t_1+h}, x_{t_2+h}, \ldots, x_{t_m+h})$ for all integers $h \geq 1$.

This definition is a little abstract, but its meaning is pretty straightforward. One implication (by choosing $m = 1$ and $t_1 = 1$) is that x_t has the same distribution as x_1 for all $t = 2, 3, \ldots$. In other words, the sequence $\{x_t: t = 1, 2, \ldots\}$ is *identically distributed*. Stationarity requires even more. For example, the joint distribution of (x_1, x_2) (the first two terms in the sequence) must be the same as the joint distribution of (x_t, x_{t+1}) for any $t \geq 1$. Again, this places no restrictions on how x_t and x_{t+1} are related to one another; indeed, they may be highly correlated. Stationarity does require that the nature of any correlation between adjacent terms is the same across all time periods.

A stochastic process that is not stationary is said to be a **nonstationary process**. Since stationarity is an aspect of the underlying stochastic process and not of the available single realization, it can be very difficult to determine whether the data we have collected were generated by a stationary process. However, it is easy to spot certain sequences that are not stationary. A process with a time trend of the type covered in Section 10-5 is clearly nonstationary: at a minimum, its mean changes over time.

Sometimes, a weaker form of stationarity suffices. If $\{x_t: t = 1, 2, \ldots\}$ has a finite second moment, that is, $E(x_t^2) < \infty$ for all t, then the following definition applies.

Covariance Stationary Process. A stochastic process $\{x_t: t = 1, 2, \ldots\}$ with a finite second moment $[E(x_t^2) < \infty]$ is **covariance stationary** if (i) $E(x_t)$ is constant; (ii) $Var(x_t)$ is constant; and (iii) for any $t, h \geq 1$, $Cov(x_t, x_{t+h})$ depends only on h and not on t.

> **EXPLORING FURTHER 11.1**
>
> Suppose that $\{y_t: t = 1, 2, \ldots\}$ is generated by $y_t = \delta_0 + \delta_1 t + e_t$, where $\delta_1 \neq 0$, and $\{e_t: t = 1, 2, \ldots\}$ is an i.i.d. sequence with mean zero and variance σ_e^2. (i) Is $\{y_t\}$ covariance stationary? (ii) Is $y_t - E(y_t)$ covariance stationary?

Covariance stationarity focuses only on the first two moments of a stochastic process: the mean and variance of the process are constant across time, and the covariance between x_t and x_{t+h} depends only on the distance between the two terms, h, and not on the location of the initial time period, t. It follows immediately that the correlation between x_t and x_{t+h} also depends only on h.

If a stationary process has a finite second moment, then it must be covariance stationary, but the converse is certainly not true. Sometimes, to emphasize that stationarity is a stronger requirement than covariance stationarity, the former is referred to as *strict stationarity*. Because strict stationarity simplifies the statements of some of our subsequent assumptions, "stationarity" for us will always mean the strict form.

How is stationarity used in time series econometrics? On a technical level, stationarity simplifies statements of the law of large numbers (LLN) and the CLT, although we will not worry about formal statements in this chapter. On a practical level, if we want to understand the relationship between two or more variables using regression analysis, we need to assume some sort of stability over time. If we allow the relationship between two variables (say, y_t and x_t) to change arbitrarily in each time period, then we cannot hope to learn much about how a change in one variable affects the other variable if we only have access to a single time series realization.

In stating a multiple regression model for time series data, we are assuming a certain form of stationarity in that the β_j do not change over time. Further, Assumptions TS.4 and TS.5 imply that the variance of the error process is constant over time and that the correlation between errors in two adjacent periods is equal to zero, which is clearly constant over time.

11-1b Weakly Dependent Time Series

Stationarity has to do with the joint distributions of a process as it moves through time. A very different concept is that of weak dependence, which places restrictions on how strongly related the random variables x_t and x_{t+h} can be as the time distance between them, h, gets large. The notion of weak dependence is most easily discussed for a stationary time series: loosely speaking, a stationary time series process $\{x_t: t = 1, 2, \ldots\}$ is said to be **weakly dependent** if x_t and x_{t+h} are "almost independent" as h increases without bound. A similar statement holds true if the sequence is nonstationary, but then we must assume that the concept of being almost independent does not depend on the starting point, t.

The description of weak dependence given in the previous paragraph is necessarily vague. We cannot formally define weak dependence because there is no definition that covers all cases of interest. There are many specific forms of weak dependence that are formally defined, but these are well beyond the scope of this text. [See White (1984), Hamilton (1994), and Wooldridge (1994b) for advanced treatments of these concepts.]

For our purposes, an intuitive notion of the meaning of weak dependence is sufficient. Covariance stationary sequences can be characterized in terms of correlations: a covariance stationary time series is weakly dependent if the correlation between x_t and x_{t+h} goes to zero "sufficiently quickly" as $h \to \infty$. (Because of covariance stationarity, the correlation does not depend on the starting point, t.) In other words, as the variables get farther apart in time, the correlation between them becomes smaller and smaller. Covariance stationary sequences where $\text{Corr}(x_t, x_{t+h}) \to 0$ as $h \to \infty$ are said to be **asymptotically uncorrelated**. Intuitively, this is how we will usually characterize weak dependence. Technically, we need to assume that the correlation converges to zero fast enough, but we will gloss over this.

Why is weak dependence important for regression analysis? Essentially, it replaces the assumption of random sampling in implying that the LLN and the CLT hold. The most well-known CLT for time series data requires stationarity and some form of weak dependence: thus, stationary, weakly dependent time series are ideal for use in multiple regression analysis. In Section 11-2, we will argue that OLS can be justified quite generally by appealing to the LLN and the CLT. Time series that are not weakly dependent—examples of which we will see in Section 11-3—do not generally satisfy the CLT, which is why their use in multiple regression analysis can be tricky.

The simplest example of a weakly dependent time series is an independent, identically distributed sequence: a sequence that is independent is trivially weakly dependent. A more interesting example of a weakly dependent sequence is

$$x_t = e_t + \alpha_1 e_{t-1}, t = 1, 2, \ldots, \qquad [11.1]$$

where $\{e_t: t = 0, 1, \ldots\}$ is an i.i.d. sequence with zero mean and variance σ_e^2. The process $\{x_t\}$ is called a **moving average process of order one [MA(1)]**: x_t is a weighted average of e_t and e_{t-1}; in the next period, we drop e_{t-1}, and then x_{t+1} depends on e_{t+1} and e_t. Setting the coefficient of e_t to 1 in (11.1) is done without loss of generality. [In equation (11.1), we use x_t and e_t as generic labels for time series processes. They need have nothing to do with the explanatory variables or errors in a time series regression model, although both the explanatory variables and errors could be MA(1) processes.]

Why is an MA(1) process weakly dependent? Adjacent terms in the sequence are correlated: because $x_{t+1} = e_{t+1} + \alpha_1 e_t$, $\text{Cov}(x_t, x_{t+1}) = \alpha_1 \text{Var}(e_t) = \alpha_1 \sigma_e^2$. Because $\text{Var}(x_t) = (1 + \alpha_1^2)\sigma_e^2$, $\text{Corr}(x_t, x_{t+1}) = \alpha_1/(1 + \alpha_1^2)$. For example, if $\alpha_1 = .5$, then $\text{Corr}(x_t, x_{t+1}) = .4$. [The maximum positive correlation occurs when $\alpha_1 = 1$, in which case, $\text{Corr}(x_t, x_{t+1}) = .5$.] However, once we look at variables in the sequence that are two or more time periods apart, these variables are uncorrelated because they are independent. For example, $x_{t+2} = e_{t+2} + \alpha_1 e_{t+1}$ is independent of x_t because $\{e_t\}$ is independent across t. Due to the identical distribution assumption on the e_t, $\{x_t\}$ in (11.1) is actually stationary. Thus, an MA(1) is a stationary, weakly dependent sequence, and the LLN and the CLT can be applied to $\{x_t\}$.

A more popular example is the process

$$y_t = \rho_1 y_{t-1} + e_t, \, t = 1, 2, \dots. \qquad [11.2]$$

The starting point in the sequence is y_0 (at $t = 0$), and $\{e_t: t = 1, 2, \dots\}$ is an i.i.d. sequence with zero mean and variance σ_e^2. We also assume that the e_t are independent of y_0 and that $\text{E}(y_0) = 0$. This is called an **autoregressive process of order one [AR(1)]**.

The crucial assumption for weak dependence of an AR(1) process is the *stability condition* $|\rho_1| < 1$. Then, we say that $\{y_t\}$ is a **stable AR(1) process**.

To see that a stable AR(1) process is asymptotically uncorrelated, it is useful to assume that the process is covariance stationary. (In fact, it can generally be shown that $\{y_t\}$ is strictly stationary, but the proof is somewhat technical.) Then, we know that $\text{E}(y_t) = \text{E}(y_{t-1})$, and from (11.2) with $\rho_1 \neq 1$, this can happen only if $\text{E}(y_t) = 0$. Taking the variance of (11.2) and using the fact that e_t and y_{t-1} are independent (and therefore uncorrelated), $\text{Var}(y_t) = \rho_1^2 \text{Var}(y_{t-1}) + \text{Var}(e_t)$, and so, under covariance stationarity, we must have $\sigma_y^2 = \rho_1^2 \sigma_y^2 + \sigma_e^2$. Since $\rho_1^2 < 1$ by the stability condition, we can easily solve for σ_y^2:

$$\sigma_y^2 = \sigma_e^2/(1 - \rho_1^2). \qquad [11.3]$$

Now, we can find the covariance between y_t and y_{t+h} for $h \geq 1$. Using repeated substitution,

$$\begin{aligned}
y_{t+h} &= \rho_1 y_{t+h-1} + e_{t+h} = \rho_1(\rho_1 y_{t+h-2} + e_{t+h-1}) + e_{t+h} \\
&= \rho_1^2 y_{t+h-2} + \rho_1 e_{t+h-1} + e_{t+h} = \dots \\
&= \rho_1^h y_t + \rho_1^{h-1} e_{t+1} + \dots + \rho_1 e_{t+h-1} + e_{t+h}.
\end{aligned}$$

Because $\text{E}(y_t) = 0$ for all t, we can multiply this last equation by y_t and take expectations to obtain $\text{Cov}(y_t, y_{t+h})$. Using the fact that e_{t+j} is uncorrelated with y_t for all $j \geq 1$ gives

$$\begin{aligned}
\text{Cov}(y_t, y_{t+h}) &= \text{E}(y_t y_{t+h}) = \rho_1^h \text{E}(y_t^2) + \rho_1^{h-1} \text{E}(y_t e_{t+1}) + \dots + \text{E}(y_t e_{t+h}) \\
&= \rho_1^h \text{E}(y_t^2) = \rho_1^h \sigma_y^2.
\end{aligned}$$

Because σ_y is the standard deviation of both y_t and y_{t+h}, we can easily find the correlation between y_t and y_{t+h} for any $h \geq 1$:

$$\text{Corr}(y_t, y_{t+h}) = \text{Cov}(y_t, y_{t+h})/(\sigma_y \sigma_y) = \rho_1^h. \qquad [11.4]$$

In particular, $\text{Corr}(y_t, y_{t+1}) = \rho_1$, so ρ_1 is the correlation coefficient between any two adjacent terms in the sequence.

Equation (11.4) is important because it shows that, although y_t and y_{t+h} are correlated for any $h \geq 1$, this correlation gets very small for large h: because $|\rho_1| < 1$, $\rho_1^h \to 0$ as $h \to \infty$. Even when ρ_1 is large—say, .9, which implies a very high, positive correlation between adjacent terms—the correlation between y_t and y_{t+h} tends to zero fairly rapidly. For example, $\text{Corr}(y_t, y_{t+5}) = .591$,

$\text{Corr}(y_t, y_{t+10}) = .349$, and $\text{Corr}(y_t, y_{t+20}) = .122$. If t indexes year, this means that the correlation between the outcome of two y that are 20 years apart is about .122. When ρ_1 is smaller, the correlation dies out much more quickly. (You might try $\rho_1 = .5$ to verify this.)

This analysis heuristically demonstrates that a stable AR(1) process is weakly dependent. The AR(1) model is especially important in multiple regression analysis with time series data. We will cover additional applications in Chapter 12 and the use of it for forecasting in Chapter 18.

There are many other types of weakly dependent time series, including hybrids of autoregressive and moving average processes. But the previous examples work well for our purposes.

Before ending this section, we must emphasize one point that often causes confusion in time series econometrics. A trending series, though certainly nonstationary, *can* be weakly dependent. In fact, in the simple linear time trend model in Chapter 10 [see equation (10.24)], the series $\{y_t\}$ was actually independent. A series that is stationary about its time trend, as well as weakly dependent, is often called a **trend-stationary process**. (Notice that the name is not completely descriptive because we assume weak dependence along with stationarity.) Such processes can be used in regression analysis just as in Chapter 10, *provided* appropriate time trends are included in the model.

11-2 Asymptotic Properties of OLS

In Chapter 10, we saw some cases in which the classical linear model assumptions are not satisfied for certain time series problems. In such cases, we must appeal to large sample properties of OLS, just as with cross-sectional analysis. In this section, we state the assumptions and main results that justify OLS more generally. The proofs of the theorems in this chapter are somewhat difficult and therefore omitted. See Wooldridge (1994b).

Assumption TS.1′   Linearity and Weak Dependence

We assume the model is exactly as in Assumption TS.1, but now we add the assumption that $\{(\mathbf{x}_t, y_t): t = 1, 2, ...\}$ is stationary and weakly dependent. In particular, the LLN and the CLT can be applied to sample averages.

The linear in parameters requirement again means that we can write the model as

$$y_t = \beta_0 + \beta_1 x_{t1} + ... + \beta_k x_{tk} + u_t, \qquad [11.5]$$

where the β_j are the parameters to be estimated. Unlike in Chapter 10, the x_{tj} can include lags of the dependent variable. As usual, lags of explanatory variables are also allowed.

We have included stationarity in Assumption TS.1′ for convenience in stating and interpreting assumptions. If we were carefully working through the asymptotic properties of OLS, as we do in Appendix E, stationarity would also simplify those derivations. But stationarity is not at all critical for OLS to have its standard asymptotic properties. (As mentioned in Section 11-1, by assuming the β_j are constant across time, we are already assuming some form of stability in the distributions over time.) The important extra restriction in Assumption TS.1′ as compared with Assumption TS.1 is the weak dependence assumption. In Section 11-1, we spent some effort discussing weak dependence for a time series process because it is by no means an innocuous assumption. Technically, Assumption TS.1′ requires weak dependence on multiple time series (y_t and elements of $\mathbf{x}_t$), and this entails putting restrictions on the joint distribution across time. The details are not particularly important and are anyway beyond the scope of this text; see Wooldridge (1994). It is more important to understand the kinds of persistent time series processes that violate the weak dependence requirement, and we will turn to that in the next section. There we also discuss the use of persistent processes in multiple regression models.

Naturally, we still rule out perfect collinearity.

Assumption TS.2′   **No Perfect Collinearity**

Same as Assumption TS.2.

Assumption TS.3′   **Zero Conditional Mean**

The explanatory variables $\mathbf{x}_t = (x_{t1}, x_{t2}, \ldots, x_{tk})$ are **contemporaneously exogenous** as in equation (10.10): $E(u_t | \mathbf{x}_t) = 0$.

This is the most natural assumption concerning the relationship between u_t and the explanatory variables. It is much weaker than Assumption TS.3 because it puts no restrictions on how u_t is related to the explanatory variables in other time periods. We will see examples that satisfy TS.3′ shortly. By stationarity, if contemporaneous exogeneity holds for one time period, it holds for them all. Relaxing stationarity would simply require us to assume the condition holds for all $t = 1, 2, \ldots$.

For certain purposes, it is useful to know that the following consistency result only requires u_t to have zero unconditional mean and to be uncorrelated with each x_{tj}:

$$E(u_t) = 0, \operatorname{Cov}(x_{tj}, u_t) = 0, j = 1, \ldots, k. \tag{11.6}$$

We will work mostly with the zero conditional mean assumption because it leads to the most straightforward asymptotic analysis.

THEOREM 11.1   **CONSISTENCY OF OLS**

Under TS.1′, TS.2′, and TS.3′, the OLS estimators are consistent: $\operatorname{plim} \hat{\beta}_j = \beta_j, j = 0, 1, \ldots, k$.

There are some key practical differences between Theorems 10.1 and 11.1. First, in Theorem 11.1, we conclude that the OLS estimators are consistent, but not necessarily unbiased. Second, in Theorem 11.1, we have weakened the sense in which the explanatory variables must be exogenous, but weak dependence is required in the underlying time series. Weak dependence is also crucial in obtaining approximate distributional results, which we cover later.

EXAMPLE 11.1   **Static Model**

Consider a static model with two explanatory variables:

$$y_t = \beta_0 + \beta_1 z_{t1} + \beta_2 z_{t2} + u_t. \tag{11.7}$$

Under weak dependence, the condition sufficient for consistency of OLS is

$$E(u_t | z_{t1}, z_{t2}) = 0. \tag{11.8}$$

This rules out omitted variables that are in u_t and are correlated with either z_{t1} or z_{t2}. Also, no function of z_{t1} or z_{t2} can be correlated with u_t, and so Assumption TS.3′ rules out misspecified functional form, just as in the cross-sectional case. Other problems, such as measurement error in the variables z_{t1} or z_{t2}, can cause (11.8) to fail.

Importantly, Assumption TS.3' *does not* rule out correlation between, say, u_{t-1} and z_{t1}. This type of correlation could arise if z_{t1} is related to past y_{t-1}, such as

$$z_{t1} = \delta_0 + \delta_1 y_{t-1} + v_t. \tag{11.9}$$

For example, z_{t1} might be a policy variable, such as monthly percentage change in the money supply, and this change might depend on last month's rate of inflation (y_{t-1}). Such a mechanism generally causes z_{t1} and u_{t-1} to be correlated (as can be seen by plugging in for y_{t-1}). This kind of feedback *is* allowed under Assumption TS.3'.

EXAMPLE 11.2   **Finite Distributed Lag Model**

In the finite distributed lag model,

$$y_t = \alpha_0 + \delta_0 z_t + \delta_1 z_{t-1} + \delta_2 z_{t-2} + u_t, \tag{11.10}$$

a very natural assumption is that the expected value of u_t, given current and *all past* values of z, is zero:

$$E(u_t | z_t, z_{t-1}, z_{t-2}, z_{t-3}, \ldots) = 0. \tag{11.11}$$

This means that, once z_t, z_{t-1}, and z_{t-2} are included, no further lags of z affect $E(y_t | z_t, z_{t-1}, z_{t-2}, z_{t-3}, \ldots)$; if this were not true, we would put further lags into the equation. For example, y_t could be the annual percentage change in investment and z_t a measure of interest rates during year t. When we set $\mathbf{x}_t = (z_t, z_{t-1}, z_{t-2})$, Assumption TS.3' is then satisfied: OLS will be consistent. As in the previous example, TS.3' does not rule out feedback from y to future values of z.

The previous two examples do not necessarily require asymptotic theory because the explanatory variables *could* be strictly exogenous. The next example clearly violates the strict exogeneity assumption; therefore, we can only appeal to large sample properties of OLS.

EXAMPLE 11.3   **AR(1) Model**

Consider the AR(1) model,

$$y_t = \beta_0 + \beta_1 y_{t-1} + u_t, \tag{11.12}$$

where the error u_t has a zero expected value, given all past values of y:

$$E(u_t | y_{t-1}, y_{t-2}, \ldots) = 0. \tag{11.13}$$

Combined, these two equations imply that

$$E(y_t | y_{t-1}, y_{t-2}, \ldots) = E(y_t | y_{t-1}) = \beta_0 + \beta_1 y_{t-1}. \tag{11.14}$$

This result is very important. First, it means that, once y lagged one period has been controlled for, no further lags of y affect the expected value of y_t. (This is where the name "first order" originates.) Second, the relationship is assumed to be linear.

Because $\mathbf{x}_t$ contains only y_{t-1}, equation (11.13) implies that Assumption TS.3' holds. By contrast, the strict exogeneity assumption needed for unbiasedness, Assumption TS.3, does not hold. Since the set of explanatory variables for all time periods includes all of the values on y except the last, $(y_0, y_1, \ldots, y_{n-1})$, Assumption TS.3 requires that, for all t, u_t is uncorrelated with each of $y_0, y_1, \ldots, y_{n-1}$. This cannot be true. In fact, because u_t is uncorrelated with y_{t-1} under (11.13), u_t and y_t must be correlated. In fact, it is easily seen that $\text{Cov}(y_t, u_t) = \text{Var}(u_t) > 0$. Therefore, a model with a lagged dependent variable cannot satisfy the strict exogeneity Assumption TS.3.

For the weak dependence condition to hold, we must assume that $|\beta_1| < 1$, as we discussed in Section 11-1. If this condition holds, then Theorem 11.1 implies that the OLS estimator from the regression of y_t on y_{t-1} produces consistent estimators of β_0 and β_1. Unfortunately, $\hat{\beta}_1$ is biased, and this bias can be large if the sample size is small or if β_1 is near 1. (For β_1 near 1, $\hat{\beta}_1$ can have a severe downward bias.) In moderate to large samples, $\hat{\beta}_1$ should be a good estimator of β_1.

When using the standard inference procedures, we need to impose versions of the homoskedasticity and no serial correlation assumptions. These are less restrictive than their classical linear model counterparts from Chapter 10.

Assumption TS.4′   Homoskedasticity

The errors are **contemporaneously homoskedastic**, that is, $\text{Var}(u_t|\mathbf{x}_t) = \sigma^2$.

Assumption TS.5′   No Serial Correlation

For all $t \neq s$, $\text{E}(u_t u_s|\mathbf{x}_t, \mathbf{x}_s) = 0$.

In TS.4′, note how we condition only on the explanatory variables at time t (compare to TS.4). In TS.5′, we condition only on the explanatory variables in the time periods coinciding with u_t and u_s. As stated, this assumption is a little difficult to interpret, but it is the right condition for studying the large sample properties of OLS in a variety of time series regressions. When considering TS.5′, we often ignore the conditioning on $\mathbf{x}_t$ and $\mathbf{x}_s$, and we think about whether u_t and u_s are uncorrelated, for all $t \neq s$.

Serial correlation is often a problem in static and finite distributed lag regression models: nothing guarantees that the unobservables u_t are uncorrelated over time. Importantly, Assumption TS.5′ *does* hold in the AR(1) model stated in equations (11.12) and (11.13). Since the explanatory variable at time t is y_{t-1}, we must show that $\text{E}(u_t u_s|y_{t-1}, y_{s-1}) = 0$ for all $t \neq s$. To see this, suppose that $s < t$. (The other case follows by symmetry.) Then, since $u_s = y_s - \beta_0 - \beta_1 y_{s-1}$, u_s is a function of y dated before time t. But by (11.13), $\text{E}(u_t|u_s, y_{t-1}, y_{s-1}) = 0$, and so $\text{E}(u_t u_s|u_s, y_{t-1}, y_{s-1}) = u_s\text{E}(u_t|y_{t-1}, y_{s-1}) = 0$. By the law of iterated expectations (see Appendix B), $\text{E}(u_t u_s|y_{t-1}, y_{s-1}) = 0$. This is very important: as long as only one lag belongs in (11.12), the errors must be serially uncorrelated. We will discuss this feature of dynamic models more generally in Section 11-4.

We now obtain an asymptotic result that is practically identical to the cross-sectional case.

THEOREM 11.2   ASYMPTOTIC NORMALITY OF OLS

Under TS.1′ through TS.5′, the OLS estimators are asymptotically normally distributed. Further, the usual OLS standard errors, t statistics, F statistics, and LM statistics are asymptotically valid.

This theorem provides additional justification for at least some of the examples estimated in Chapter 10: even if the classical linear model assumptions do not hold, OLS is still consistent, and the usual inference procedures are valid. Of course, this hinges on TS.1′ through TS.5′ being true. In the next section, we discuss ways in which the weak dependence assumption can fail. The problems of serial correlation and heteroskedasticity are treated in Chapter 12.

| EXAMPLE 11.4 | **Efficient Markets Hypothesis** |

We can use asymptotic analysis to test a version of the *efficient markets hypothesis* (EMH). Let y_t be the weekly percentage return (from Wednesday close to Wednesday close) on the New York Stock Exchange composite index. A strict form of the EMH states that information observable to the market prior to week t should not help to predict the return during week t. If we use only past information on y, the EMH is stated as

$$E(y_t|y_{t-1}, y_{t-2}, \ldots) = E(y_t). \qquad [11.15]$$

If (11.15) is false, then we could use information on past weekly returns to predict the current return. The EMH presumes that such investment opportunities will be noticed and will disappear almost instantaneously.

One simple way to test (11.15) is to specify the AR(1) model in (11.12) as the alternative model. Then, the null hypothesis is easily stated as $H_0: \beta_1 = 0$. Under the null hypothesis, Assumption TS.3′ is true by (11.15), and, as we discussed earlier, serial correlation is not an issue. The homoskedasticity assumption is $\text{Var}(y_t|y_{t-1}) = \text{Var}(y_t) = \sigma^2$, which we just assume is true for now. Under the null hypothesis, stock returns are serially uncorrelated, so we can safely assume that they are weakly dependent. Then, Theorem 11.2 says we can use the usual OLS t statistic for $\hat{\beta}_1$ to test $H_0: \beta_1 = 0$ against $H_1: \beta_1 \neq 0$.

The weekly returns in NYSE are computed using data from January 1976 through March 1989. In the rare case that Wednesday was a holiday, the close at the next trading day was used. The average weekly return over this period was .196 in percentage form, with the largest weekly return being 8.45% and the smallest being -15.32% (during the stock market crash of October 1987). Estimation of the AR(1) model gives

$$\widehat{return}_t = .180 + .059\ return_{t-1}$$
$$(.081)\ \ (.038) \qquad [11.16]$$
$$n = 689, R^2 = .0035, \overline{R}^2 = .0020.$$

The t statistic for the coefficient on $return_{t-1}$ is about 1.55, and so $H_0: \beta_1 = 0$ cannot be rejected against the two-sided alternative, even at the 10% significance level. The estimate does suggest a slight positive correlation in the NYSE return from one week to the next, but it is not strong enough to warrant rejection of the EMH.

In the previous example, using an AR(1) model to test the EMH might not detect correlation between weekly returns that are more than one week apart. It is easy to estimate models with more than one lag. For example, an *autoregressive model of order two*, or AR(2) model, is

$$y_t = \beta_0 + \beta_1 y_{t-1} + \beta_2 y_{t-2} + u_t$$
$$E(u_t|y_{t-1}, y_{t-2}, \ldots) = 0. \qquad [11.17]$$

There are stability conditions on β_1 and β_2 that are needed to ensure that the AR(2) process is weakly dependent, but this is not an issue here because the null hypothesis states that the EMH holds:

$$H_0: \beta_1 = \beta_2 = 0. \qquad [11.18]$$

If we add the homoskedasticity assumption $\text{Var}(u_t|y_{t-1}, y_{t-2}) = \sigma^2$, we can use a standard F statistic to test (11.18). If we estimate an AR(2) model for $return_t$, we obtain

$$\widehat{return}_t = .186 + .060\ return_{t-1} - .038\ return_{t-2}$$
$$(.081)\ \ (.038) \qquad\qquad (.038)$$
$$n = 688, R^2 = .0048, \overline{R}^2 = .0019$$

(where we lose one more observation because of the additional lag in the equation). The two lags are individually insignificant at the 10% level. They are also jointly insignificant: using $R^2 = .0048$, we find the F statistic is approximately $F = 1.65$; the p-value for this F statistic (with 2 and 685 degrees of freedom) is about .193. Thus, we do not reject (11.18) at even the 15% significance level.

EXAMPLE 11.5   **Expectations Augmented Phillips Curve**

A linear version of the *expectations augmented Phillips curve* can be written as

$$inf_t - inf_t^e = \beta_1(unem_t - \mu_0) + e_t,$$

where μ_0 is the *natural rate of unemployment* and inf_t^e is the *expected* rate of inflation formed in year $t - 1$. This model assumes that the natural rate is constant, something that macroeconomists question. The difference between actual unemployment and the natural rate is called *cyclical unemployment*, while the difference between actual and expected inflation is called *unanticipated inflation*. The error term, e_t, is called a *supply shock* by macroeconomists. If there is a tradeoff between unanticipated inflation and cyclical unemployment, then $\beta_1 < 0$. [For a detailed discussion of the expectations augmented Phillips curve, see Mankiw (1994, Section 11-2).]

To complete this model, we need to make an assumption about inflationary expectations. Under *adaptive expectations*, the expected value of current inflation depends on recently observed inflation. A particularly simple formulation is that expected inflation this year is last year's inflation: $inf_t^e = inf_{t-1}$. (See Section 18-1 for an alternative formulation of adaptive expectations.) Under this assumption, we can write

$$inf_t - inf_{t-1} = \beta_0 + \beta_1 unem_t + e_t$$

or

$$\Delta inf_t = \beta_0 + \beta_1 unem_t + e_t,$$

where $\Delta inf_t = inf_t - inf_{t-1}$ and $\beta_0 = -\beta_1\mu_0$. (β_0 is expected to be positive, since $\beta_1 < 0$ and $\mu_0 > 0$.) Therefore, under adaptive expectations, the expectations augmented Phillips curve relates the *change* in inflation to the level of unemployment and a supply shock, e_t. If e_t is uncorrelated with $unem_t$, as is typically assumed, then we can consistently estimate β_0 and β_1 by OLS. (We do not have to assume that, say, future unemployment rates are unaffected by the current supply shock.) We assume that TS.1' through TS.5' hold. Using the data through 1996 in PHILLIPS we estimate

$$\widehat{\Delta inf_t} = 3.03 - .543\, unem_t$$
$$(1.38)\ \ (.230) \tag{11.19}$$
$$n = 48, R^2 = .108, \bar{R}^2 = .088.$$

The tradeoff between cyclical unemployment and unanticipated inflation is pronounced in equation (11.19): a one-point increase in *unem* lowers unanticipated inflation by over one-half of a point. The effect is statistically significant (two-sided p-value $\approx .023$). We can contrast this with the static Phillips curve in Example 10.1, where we found a slightly positive relationship between inflation and unemployment.

Because we can write the natural rate as $\mu_0 = \beta_0/(-\beta_1)$, we can use (11.19) to obtain our own estimate of the natural rate: $\hat{\mu}_0 = \hat{\beta}_0/(-\hat{\beta}_1) = 3.03/.543 \approx 5.58$. Thus, we estimate the natural rate to be about 5.6, which is well within the range suggested by macroeconomists: historically, 5% to 6% is a common range cited for the natural rate of unemployment. A standard error of this estimate is difficult to obtain because we have a nonlinear function of the OLS estimators. Wooldridge (2010, Chapter 3) contains the theory for general nonlinear functions. In the current application, the standard error is .657, which leads to an asymptotic 95% confidence interval (based on the standard normal distribution) of about 4.29 to 6.87 for the natural rate.

> ### EXPLORING FURTHER 11.2
>
> Suppose that expectations are formed as $inf_t^e = (1/2)inf_{t-1} + (1/2)inf_{t-2}$. What regression would you run to estimate the expectations augmented Phillips curve?

Under Assumptions TS.1′ through TS.5′, we can show that the OLS estimators are asymptotically efficient in the class of estimators described in Theorem 5.3, but we replace the cross-sectional observation index i with the time series index t. Finally, models with trending explanatory variables can effectively satisfy Assumptions TS.1′ through TS.5′, provided they are trend stationary. As long as time trends are included in the equations when needed, the usual inference procedures are asymptotically valid.

11-3 Using Highly Persistent Time Series in Regression Analysis

The previous section shows that, provided the time series we use are weakly dependent, usual OLS inference procedures are valid under assumptions weaker than the classical linear model assumptions. Unfortunately, many economic time series cannot be characterized by weak dependence. Using time series with strong dependence in regression analysis poses no problem, *if* the CLM assumptions in Chapter 10 hold. But the usual inference procedures are very susceptible to violation of these assumptions when the data are not weakly dependent, because then we cannot appeal to the LLN and the CLT. In this section, we provide some examples of **highly persistent** (or **strongly dependent**) time series and show how they can be transformed for use in regression analysis.

11-3a Highly Persistent Time Series

In the simple AR(1) model (11.2), the assumption $|\rho_1| < 1$ is crucial for the series to be weakly dependent. It turns out that many economic time series are better characterized by the AR(1) model with $\rho_1 = 1$. In this case, we can write

$$y_t = y_{t-1} + e_t, \, t = 1, 2, \ldots, \tag{11.20}$$

where we again assume that $\{e_t: t = 1, 2, \ldots\}$ is independent and identically distributed with mean zero and variance σ_e^2. We assume that the initial value, y_0, is independent of e_t for all $t \geq 1$.

The process in (11.20) is called a **random walk**. The name comes from the fact that y at time t is obtained by starting at the previous value, y_{t-1}, and adding a zero mean random variable that is independent of y_{t-1}. Sometimes, a random walk is defined differently by assuming different properties of the innovations, e_t (such as lack of correlation rather than independence), but the current definition suffices for our purposes.

First, we find the expected value of y_t. This is most easily done by using repeated substitution to get

$$y_t = e_t + e_{t-1} + \ldots + e_1 + y_0.$$

Taking the expected value of both sides gives

$$E(y_t) = E(e_t) + E(e_{t-1}) + \ldots + E(e_1) + E(y_0)$$
$$= E(y_0), \text{ for all } t \geq 1.$$

Therefore, the expected value of a random walk does *not* depend on t. A popular assumption is that $y_0 = 0$—the process begins at zero at time zero—in which case, $E(y_t) = 0$ for all t.

By contrast, the variance of a random walk does change with t. To compute the variance of a random walk, for simplicity we assume that y_0 is nonrandom so that $\text{Var}(y_0) = 0$; this does not affect any important conclusions. Then, by the i.i.d. assumption for $\{e_t\}$,

$$\text{Var}(y_t) = \text{Var}(e_t) + \text{Var}(e_{t-1}) + \ldots + \text{Var}(e_1) = \sigma_e^2 t. \tag{11.21}$$

In other words, the variance of a random walk increases as a linear function of time. This shows that the process cannot be stationary.

Even more importantly, a random walk displays highly persistent behavior in the sense that the value of y today is important for determining the value of y in the very distant future. To see this, write for h periods hence,

$$y_{t+h} = e_{t+h} + e_{t+h-1} + \ldots + e_{t+1} + y_t.$$

Now, suppose at time t, we want to compute the expected value of y_{t+h} given the current value y_t. Since the expected value of e_{t+j}, given y_t, is zero for all $j \geq 1$, we have

$$E(y_{t+h}|y_t) = y_t, \text{ for all } h \geq 1. \tag{11.22}$$

This means that, no matter how far in the future we look, our best prediction of y_{t+h} is today's value, y_t. We can contrast this with the stable AR(1) case, where a similar argument can be used to show that

$$E(y_{t+h}|y_t) = \rho_1^h y_t, \text{ for all } h \geq 1.$$

Under stability, $|\rho_1| < 1$, and so $E(y_{t+h}|y_t)$ approaches zero as $h \to \infty$: the value of y_t becomes less and less important, and $E(y_{t+h}|y_t)$ gets closer and closer to the unconditional expected value, $E(y_t) = 0$.

When $h = 1$, equation (11.22) is reminiscent of the adaptive expectations assumption we used for the inflation rate in Example 11.5: if inflation follows a random walk, then the expected value of inf_t, given past values of inflation, is simply inf_{t-1}. Thus, a random walk model for inflation justifies the use of adaptive expectations.

We can also see that the correlation between y_t and y_{t+h} is close to one for large t when $\{y_t\}$ follows a random walk. If $\text{Var}(y_0) = 0$, it can be shown that

$$\text{Corr}(y_t, y_{t+h}) = \sqrt{t/(t + h)}.$$

Thus, the correlation depends on the starting point, t (so that $\{y_t\}$ is not covariance stationary). Further, although for fixed t the correlation tends to zero as $h \to \infty$, it does not do so very quickly. In fact, the larger t is, the more slowly the correlation tends to zero as h gets large. If we choose h to be something large—say, $h = 100$—we can always choose a large enough t such that the correlation between y_t and y_{t+h} is arbitrarily close to one. (If $h = 100$ and we want the correlation to be greater than .95, then $t > 1,000$ does the trick.) Therefore, a random walk does not satisfy the requirement of an asymptotically uncorrelated sequence.

Figure 11.1 plots two realizations of a random walk, generated from a computer, with initial value $y_0 = 0$ and $e_t \sim$ Normal $(0, 1)$. Generally, it is not easy to look at a time series plot and determine whether it is a random walk. Next, we will discuss an informal method for making the distinction between weakly and highly dependent sequences; we will study formal statistical tests in Chapter 18.

A series that is generally thought to be well characterized by a random walk is the three-month T-bill rate. Annual data are plotted in Figure 11.2 for the years 1948 through 1996.

A random walk is a special case of what is known as a **unit root process**. The name comes from the fact that $\rho_1 = 1$ in the AR(1) model. A more general class of unit root processes is generated as in (11.20), but $\{e_t\}$ is now allowed to be a general, weakly dependent series. [For example, $\{e_t\}$ could itself follow an MA(1) or a stable AR(1) process.] When $\{e_t\}$ is not an i.i.d. sequence, the properties of the random walk we derived earlier no longer hold. But the key feature of $\{y_t\}$ is preserved: the value of y today is highly correlated with y even in the distant future.

From a policy perspective, it is often important to know whether an economic time series is highly persistent or not. Consider the case of gross domestic product in the United States. If GDP is asymptotically uncorrelated, then the level of GDP in the coming year is at best weakly related to what GDP was, say, 30 years ago. This means a policy that affected GDP long ago has very little lasting impact. On the other hand, if GDP is strongly dependent, then next year's GDP can be highly correlated with the GDP from many years ago. Then, we should recognize that a policy that causes a discrete change in GDP can have long-lasting effects.

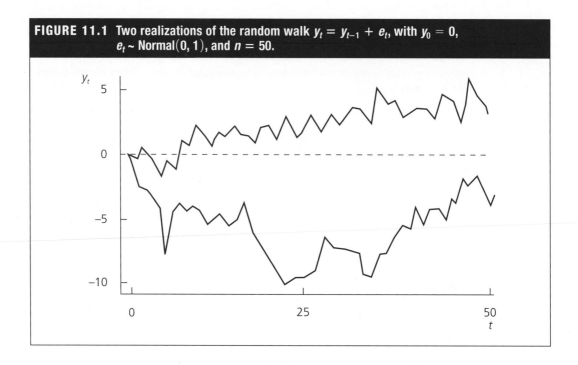

FIGURE 11.1 Two realizations of the random walk $y_t = y_{t-1} + e_t$, with $y_0 = 0$, $e_t \sim \text{Normal}(0, 1)$, and $n = 50$.

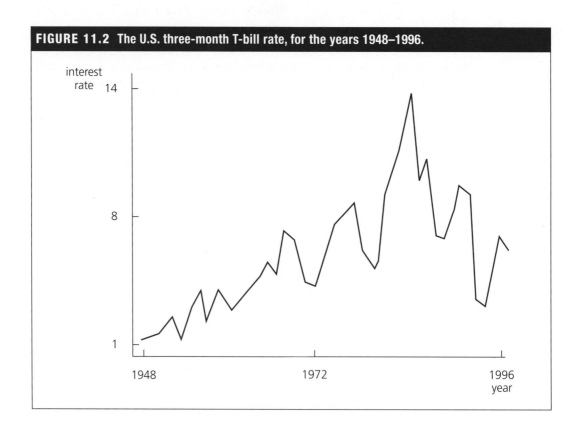

FIGURE 11.2 The U.S. three-month T-bill rate, for the years 1948–1996.

It is extremely important not to confuse trending and highly persistent behaviors. A series can be trending but not highly persistent, as we saw in Chapter 10. Further, factors such as interest rates, inflation rates, and unemployment rates are thought by many to be highly persistent, but they have no obvious upward or downward trend. However, it is often the case that a highly persistent series also contains a clear trend. One model that leads to this behavior is the **random walk with drift**:

$$y_t = \alpha_0 + y_{t-1} + e_t, \, t = 1, 2, \ldots, \qquad [11.23]$$

where $\{e_t: t = 1, 2, \ldots\}$ and y_0 satisfy the same properties as in the random walk model. What is new is the parameter α_0, which is called the *drift term*. Essentially, to generate y_t, the constant α_0 is added along with the random noise e_t to the previous value y_{t-1}. We can show that the expected value of y_t follows a linear time trend by using repeated substitution:

$$y_t = \alpha_0 t + e_t + e_{t-1} + \ldots + e_1 + y_0.$$

Therefore, if $y_0 = 0$, $\mathrm{E}(y_t) = \alpha_0 t$: the expected value of y_t is growing over time if $\alpha_0 > 0$ and shrinking over time if $\alpha_0 < 0$. By reasoning as we did in the pure random walk case, we can show that $\mathrm{E}(y_{t+h}|y_t) = \alpha_0 h + y_t$, and so the best prediction of y_{t+h} at time t is y_t plus the drift $\alpha_0 h$. The variance of y_t is the same as it was in the pure random walk case.

Figure 11.3 contains a realization of a random walk with drift, where $n = 50$, $y_0 = 0$, $\alpha_0 = 2$, and the e_t are Normal(0, 9) random variables. As can be seen from this graph, y_t tends to grow over time, but the series does not regularly return to the trend line.

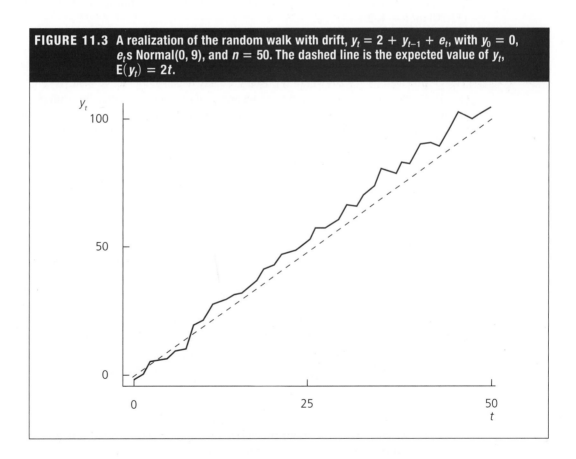

FIGURE 11.3 A realization of the random walk with drift, $y_t = 2 + y_{t-1} + e_t$, with $y_0 = 0$, e_ts Normal(0, 9), and $n = 50$. The dashed line is the expected value of y_t, $\mathrm{E}(y_t) = 2t$.

A random walk with drift is another example of a unit root process, because it is the special case $\rho_1 = 1$ in an AR(1) model with an intercept:

$$y_t = \alpha_0 + \rho_1 y_{t-1} + e_t.$$

When $\rho_1 = 1$ and $\{e_t\}$ is any weakly dependent process, we obtain a whole class of highly persistent time series processes that also have linearly trending means.

11-3b Transformations on Highly Persistent Time Series

Using time series with strong persistence of the type displayed by a unit root process in a regression equation can lead to very misleading results if the CLM assumptions are violated. We will study the spurious regression problem in more detail in Chapter 18, but for now we must be aware of potential problems. Fortunately, simple transformations are available that render a unit root process weakly dependent.

Weakly dependent processes are said to be **integrated of order zero**, or **I(0)**. Practically, this means that nothing needs to be done to such series before using them in regression analysis: averages of such sequences already satisfy the standard limit theorems. Unit root processes, such as a random walk (with or without drift), are said to be **integrated of order one**, or **I(1)**. This means that the **first difference** of the process is weakly dependent (and often stationary). A time series that is I(1) is often said to be a **difference-stationary process**, although the name is somewhat misleading with its emphasis on stationarity after differencing rather than weak dependence in the differences.

The concept of an I(1) process is easiest to see for a random walk. With $\{y_t\}$ generated as in (11.20) for $t = 1, 2, \ldots$,

$$\Delta y_t = y_t - y_{t-1} = e_t, \, t = 2, 3, \ldots; \qquad\qquad \text{[11.24]}$$

therefore, the first-differenced series $\{\Delta y_t: t = 2, 3, \ldots\}$ is actually an i.i.d. sequence. More generally, if $\{y_t\}$ is generated by (11.24) where $\{e_t\}$ is any weakly dependent process, then $\{\Delta y_t\}$ is weakly dependent. Thus, when we suspect processes are integrated of order one, we often first difference in order to use them in regression analysis; we will see some examples later. (Incidentally, the symbol "Δ" can mean "change" as well as "difference." In actual data sets, if an original variable is named y then its change or difference is often denoted cy or dy. For example, the change in *price* might be denoted *cprice*.)

Many time series y_t that are strictly positive are such that $\log(y_t)$ is integrated of order one. In this case, we can use the first difference in the logs, $\Delta \log(y_t) = \log(y_t) - \log(y_{t-1})$, in regression analysis. Alternatively, since

$$\Delta \log(y_t) \approx (y_t - y_{t-1})/y_{t-1}, \qquad\qquad \text{[11.25]}$$

we can use the proportionate or percentage change in y_t directly; this is what we did in Example 11.4 where, rather than stating the EMH in terms of the stock price, p_t, we used the weekly percentage change, $return_t = 100[(p_t - p_{t-1})/p_{t-1}]$. The quantity in equation (11.25) is often called the **growth rate**, measured as a proportionate change. When using a particular data set it is important to know how the growth rates are measured—whether as a proportionate or a percentage change. Sometimes if an original variable is y its growth rate is denoted gy, so that for each t, $gy_t = \log(y_t) - \log(y_{t-1})$ or $gy_t = (y_t - y_{t-1})/y_{t-1}$. Often these quantities are multiplied by 100 to turn a proportionate change into a percentage change.

Differencing time series before using them in regression analysis has another benefit: it removes any linear time trend. This is easily seen by writing a linearly trending variable as

$$y_t = \gamma_0 + \gamma_1 t + v_t,$$

where v_t has a zero mean. Then, $\Delta y_t = \gamma_1 + \Delta v_t$, and so $E(\Delta y_t) = \gamma_1 + E(\Delta v_t) = \gamma_1$. In other words, $E(\Delta y_t)$ is constant. The same argument works for $\Delta \log(y_t)$ when $\log(y_t)$ follows a linear time trend. Therefore, rather than including a time trend in a regression, we can instead difference those variables that show obvious trends.

11-3c Deciding Whether a Time Series Is I(1)

Determining whether a particular time series realization is the outcome of an I(1) versus an I(0) process can be quite difficult. Statistical tests can be used for this purpose, but these are more advanced; we provide an introductory treatment in Chapter 18.

There are informal methods that provide useful guidance about whether a time series process is roughly characterized by weak dependence. A very simple tool is motivated by the AR(1) model: if $|\rho_1| < 1$, then the process is I(0), but it is I(1) if $\rho_1 = 1$. Earlier, we showed that, when the AR(1) process is stable, $\rho_1 = \text{Corr}(y_t, y_{t-1})$. Therefore, we can estimate ρ_1 from the sample correlation between y_t and y_{t-1}. This sample correlation coefficient is called the **first order autocorrelation** of $\{y_t\}$; we denote this by $\hat{\rho}_1$. By applying the LLN, $\hat{\rho}_1$ can be shown to be consistent for ρ_1 *provided* $|\rho_1| < 1$. (However, $\hat{\rho}_1$ is not an unbiased estimator of ρ_1.)

We can use the value of $\hat{\rho}_1$ to help decide whether the process is I(1) or I(0). Unfortunately, because $\hat{\rho}_1$ is an estimate, we can never know for sure whether $\rho_1 < 1$. Ideally, we could compute a confidence interval for ρ_1 to see if it excludes the value $\rho_1 = 1$, but this turns out to be rather difficult: the sampling distributions of the estimator of $\hat{\rho}_1$ are extremely different when ρ_1 is close to one and when ρ_1 is much less than one. (In fact, when ρ_1 is close to one, $\hat{\rho}_1$ can have a severe downward bias.)

In Chapter 18, we will show how to test $H_0: \rho_1 = 1$ against $H_1: \rho_1 < 1$. For now, we can only use $\hat{\rho}_1$ as a rough guide for determining whether a series needs to be differenced. No hard-and-fast rule exists for making this choice. Most economists think that differencing is warranted if $\hat{\rho}_1 > .9$; some would difference when $\hat{\rho}_1 > .8$.

EXAMPLE 11.6	**Fertility Equation**

In Example 10.4, we explained the general fertility rate, *gfr*, in terms of the value of the personal exemption, *pe*. The first order autocorrelations for these series are very large: $\hat{\rho}_1 = .977$ for *gfr* and $\hat{\rho}_1 = .964$ for *pe*. These autocorrelations are highly suggestive of unit root behavior, and they raise serious questions about our use of the usual OLS t statistics for this example back in Chapter 10. Remember, the t statistics only have exact t distributions under the full set of classical linear model assumptions. To relax those assumptions in any way and apply asymptotics, we generally need the underlying series to be I(0) processes.

We now estimate the equation using first differences (and drop the dummy variable, for simplicity):

$$\widehat{\Delta gfr} = -.785 - .043\,\Delta pe$$
$$(.502)\quad(.028)$$
[11.26]
$$n = 71, R^2 = .032, \overline{R}^2 = .018.$$

Now, an increase in *pe* is estimated to lower *gfr* contemporaneously, although the estimate is not statistically different from zero at the 5% level. This gives very different results than when we estimated the model in levels, and it casts doubt on our earlier analysis.

If we add two lags of Δpe, things improve:

$$\widehat{\Delta gfr} = -.964 - .036\,\Delta pe - .014\,\Delta pe_{-1} + .110\,\Delta pe_{-2}$$
$$(.468)\quad(.027)\qquad(.028)\qquad(.027)$$
[11.27]
$$n = 69, R^2 = .233, \overline{R}^2 = .197.$$

Even though Δpe and Δpe_{-1} have negative coefficients, their coefficients are small and jointly insignificant (p-value = .28). The second lag is very significant and indicates a positive relationship between changes in *pe* and subsequent changes in *gfr* two years hence. This makes more sense than having a contemporaneous effect. See Computer Exercise C5 for further analysis of the equation in first differences.

When the series in question has an obvious upward or downward trend, it makes more sense to obtain the first order autocorrelation after detrending. If the data are not detrended, the autoregressive correlation tends to be overestimated, which biases toward finding a unit root in a trending process.

EXAMPLE 11.7 | **Wages and Productivity**

The variable *hrwage* is average hourly wage in the U.S. economy, and *outphr* is output per hour. One way to estimate the elasticity of hourly wage with respect to output per hour is to estimate the equation,

$$\log(hrwage_t) = \beta_0 + \beta_1 \log(outphr_t) + \beta_2 t + u_t,$$

where the time trend is included because $\log(hrwage_t)$ and $\log(outphr_t)$ both display clear, upward, linear trends. Using the data in EARNS for the years 1947 through 1987, we obtain

$$\widehat{\log(hrwage_t)} = -5.33 + 1.64 \log(outphr_t) - .018\, t$$
$$\quad\quad\quad (.37)\quad (.09)\quad\quad\quad\quad\quad (.002)\quad\quad\quad\quad \text{[11.28]}$$
$$n = 41, R^2 = .971, \overline{R}^2 = .970.$$

(We have reported the usual goodness-of-fit measures here; it would be better to report those based on the detrended dependent variable, as in Section 10-5.) The estimated elasticity seems too large: a 1% increase in productivity increases real wages by about 1.64%. Because the standard error is so small, the 95% confidence interval easily excludes a unit elasticity. U.S. workers would probably have trouble believing that their wages increase by more than 1.5% for every 1% increase in productivity.

The regression results in (11.28) must be viewed with caution. Even after linearly detrending $\log(hrwage)$, the first order autocorrelation is .967, and for detrended $\log(outphr)$, $\hat{\rho}_1 = .945$. These suggest that both series have unit roots, so we reestimate the equation in first differences (and we no longer need a time trend):

$$\widehat{\Delta\log(hrwage_t)} = -.0036 + .809\, \Delta\log(outphr)$$
$$\quad\quad\quad\quad (.0042)\quad (.173)\quad\quad\quad\quad\quad\quad \text{[11.29]}$$
$$n = 40, R^2 = .364, \overline{R}^2 = .348.$$

Now, a 1% increase in productivity is estimated to increase real wages by about .81%, and the estimate is not statistically different from one. The adjusted *R*-squared shows that the growth in output explains about 35% of the growth in real wages. See Computer Exercise C2 for a simple distributed lag version of the model in first differences.

In the previous two examples, both the dependent and independent variables appear to have unit roots. In other cases, we might have a mixture of processes with unit roots and those that are weakly dependent (though possibly trending). An example is given in Computer Exercise C1.

11-4 Dynamically Complete Models and the Absence of Serial Correlation

In the AR(1) model in (11.12), we showed that, under assumption (11.13), the errors $\{u_t\}$ *must* be **serially uncorrelated** in the sense that Assumption TS.5′ is satisfied: assuming that no serial correlation exists is practically the same thing as assuming that only one lag of *y* appears in $E(y_t|y_{t-1}, y_{t-2}, \ldots)$.

Can we make a similar statement for other regression models? The answer is yes, although the assumptions required for the errors to be serially uncorrelated might be implausible. Consider, for example, the simple static regression model

$$y_t = \beta_0 + \beta_1 z_t + u_t, \tag{11.30}$$

where y_t and z_t are contemporaneously dated. For consistency of OLS, we only need $E(u_t|z_t) = 0$. Generally, the $\{u_t\}$ will be serially correlated. However, if we *assume* that

$$E(u_t|z_t, y_{t-1}, z_{t-1}, \ldots) = 0, \tag{11.31}$$

then (as we will show generally later) Assumption TS.5′ holds. In particular, the $\{u_t\}$ are serially uncorrelated. Naturally, assumption (11.31) implies that z_t is contemporaneously exogenous, that is, $E(u_t|z_t) = 0$.

To gain insight into the meaning of (11.31), we can write (11.30) and (11.31) equivalently as

$$E(y_t|z_t, y_{t-1}, z_{t-1}, \ldots) = E(y_t|z_t) = \beta_0 + \beta_1 z_t, \tag{11.32}$$

where the first equality is the one of current interest. It says that, once z_t has been controlled for, no lags of either y or z help to explain current y. This is a strong requirement and is implausible when the lagged dependent variable has predictive power, which is often the case, if it is false, then we can expect the errors to be serially correlated.

Next, consider a finite distributed lag model with two lags:

$$y_t = \beta_0 + \beta_1 z_t + \beta_2 z_{t-1} + \beta_3 z_{t-2} + u_t. \tag{11.33}$$

Since we are hoping to capture the lagged effects that z has on y, we would naturally assume that (11.33) captures the *distributed lag dynamics*:

$$E(y_t|z_t, z_{t-1}, z_{t-2}, z_{t-3}, \ldots) = E(y_t|z_t, z_{t-1}, z_{t-2}); \tag{11.34}$$

that is, at most two lags of z matter. If (11.31) holds, we can make a stronger statement: once we have controlled for z and its two lags, no lags of y or additional lags of z affect current y:

$$E(y_t|z_t, y_{t-1}, z_{t-1}, \ldots) = E(y_t|z_t, z_{t-1}, z_{t-2}). \tag{11.35}$$

Equation (11.35) is more likely than (11.32), but it still rules out lagged y having extra predictive power for current y.

Next, consider a model with one lag of both y and z:

$$y_t = \beta_0 + \beta_1 z_t + \beta_2 y_{t-1} + \beta_3 z_{t-1} + u_t.$$

Since this model includes a lagged dependent variable, (11.31) is a natural assumption, as it implies that

$$E(y_t|z_t, y_{t-1}, z_{t-1}, y_{t-2}, \ldots) = E(y_t|z_t, y_{t-1}, z_{t-1});$$

in other words, once z_t, y_{t-1}, and z_{t-1} have been controlled for, no further lags of either y or z affect current y.

In the general model

$$y_t = \beta_0 + \beta_1 x_{t1} + \ldots + \beta_k x_{tk} + u_t, \tag{11.36}$$

where the explanatory variables $\mathbf{x}_t = (x_{t1}, \ldots, x_{tk})$ may or may not contain lags of y or z, (11.31) becomes

$$E(u_t|\mathbf{x}_t, y_{t-1}, \mathbf{x}_{t-1}, \ldots) = 0. \tag{11.37}$$

Written in terms of y_t,

$$E(y_t|\mathbf{x}_t, y_{t-1}, \mathbf{x}_{t-1}, \ldots) = E(y_t|\mathbf{x}_t). \tag{11.38}$$

In other words, whatever is in $\mathbf{x}_t$, enough lags have been included so that further lags of y and the explanatory variables do not matter for explaining y_t. When this condition holds, we have a **dynamically complete model**. As we saw earlier, dynamic completeness can be a very strong assumption for static and finite distributed lag models.

Once we start putting lagged y as explanatory variables, we often think that the model should be dynamically complete. We will touch on some exceptions to this claim in Chapter 18.

Since (11.37) is equivalent to

$$E(u_t|\mathbf{x}_t, u_{t-1}, \mathbf{x}_{t-1}, u_{t-2}, \ldots) = 0, \tag{11.39}$$

we can show that a dynamically complete model *must* satisfy Assumption TS.5′. (This derivation is not crucial and can be skipped without loss of continuity.) For concreteness, take $s < t$. Then, by the law of iterated expectations (see Appendix B),

$$\begin{aligned}
E(u_t u_s|\mathbf{x}_t, \mathbf{x}_s) &= E[E(u_t u_s|\mathbf{x}_t, \mathbf{x}_s, u_s)|\mathbf{x}_t, \mathbf{x}_s] \\
&= E[u_s E(u_t|\mathbf{x}_t, \mathbf{x}_s, u_s)|\mathbf{x}_t, \mathbf{x}_s],
\end{aligned}$$

where the second equality follows from $E(u_t u_s|\mathbf{x}_t, \mathbf{x}_s, u_s) = u_s E(u_t|\mathbf{x}_t, \mathbf{x}_s, u_s)$. Now, since $s < t$, $(\mathbf{x}_t, \mathbf{x}_s, u_s)$ is a subset of the conditioning set in (11.39). Therefore, (11.39) implies that $E(u_t|\mathbf{x}_t, \mathbf{x}_s, u_s) = 0$, and so

$$E(u_t u_s|\mathbf{x}_t, \mathbf{x}_s) = E(u_s \cdot 0|\mathbf{x}_t, \mathbf{x}_s) = 0,$$

which says that Assumption TS.5′ holds.

> **EXPLORING FURTHER 11.3**
>
> If (11.33) holds where $u_t = e_t + \alpha_1 e_{t-1}$ and where $\{e_t\}$ is an i.i.d. sequence with mean zero and variance σ_e^2, can equation (11.33) be dynamically complete?

Since specifying a dynamically complete model means that there is no serial correlation, does it follow that all models should be dynamically complete? As we will see in Chapter 18, for forecasting purposes, the answer is yes. Some think that all models should be dynamically complete and that serial correlation in the errors of a model is a sign of misspecification. This stance is too rigid. Sometimes, we really are interested in a static model (such as a Phillips curve) or a finite distributed lag model (such as measuring the long-run percentage change in wages given a 1% increase in productivity). In the next chapter, we will show how to detect and correct for serial correlation in such models.

EXAMPLE 11.8 Fertility Equation

In equation (11.27), we estimated a distributed lag model for Δgfr on Δpe, allowing for two lags of Δpe. For this model to be dynamically complete in the sense of (11.38), neither lags of Δgfr nor further lags of Δpe should appear in the equation. We can easily see that this is false by adding Δgf_{r-1}: the coefficient estimate is .300, and its t statistic is 2.84. Thus, the model is not dynamically complete in the sense of (11.38).

What should we make of this? We will postpone an interpretation of general models with lagged dependent variables until Chapter 18. But the fact that (11.27) is not dynamically complete suggests that there may be serial correlation in the errors. We will see how to test and correct for this in Chapter 12.

The notion of dynamic completeness should not be confused with a weaker assumption concerning including the appropriate lags in a model. In the model (11.36), the explanatory variables $\mathbf{x}_t$ are said to be **sequentially exogenous** if

$$\mathrm{E}(u_t | \mathbf{x}_t, \mathbf{x}_{t-1}, \dots) = \mathrm{E}(u_t) = 0, t = 1, 2, \dots. \qquad [11.40]$$

As discussed in Problem 8 in Chapter 10, sequential exogeneity is implied by strict exogeneity and sequential exogeneity implies contemporaneous exogeneity. Further, because $(\mathbf{x}_t, \mathbf{x}_{t-1}, \dots)$ is a subset of $(\mathbf{x}_t, y_{t-1}, \mathbf{x}_{t-1}, \dots)$, sequential exogeneity is implied by dynamic completeness. If $\mathbf{x}_t$ contains y_{t-1}, the dynamic completeness and sequential exogeneity are the same condition. The key point is that, when $\mathbf{x}_t$ does not contain y_{t-1}, sequential exogeneity allows for the possibility that the dynamics are not complete in the sense of capturing the relationship between y_t and all past values of y and other explanatory variables. But in finite distributed lag models—such as that estimated in equation (11.27)—we may not care whether past y has predictive power for current y. We are primarily interested in whether we have included enough lags of the explanatory variables to capture the distributed lag dynamics. For example, if we assume $\mathrm{E}(y_t | z_t, z_{t-1}, z_{t-2}, z_{t-3}, \dots) = \mathrm{E}(y_t | z_t, z_{t-1}, z_{t-2}) = \alpha_0 + \delta_0 z_t + \delta_1 z_{t-1} + \delta_2 z_{t-2}$, then the regressors $\mathbf{x}_t = (z_t, z_{t-1}, z_{t-2})$ are sequentially exogenous because we have assumed that two lags suffice for the distributed lag dynamics. But typically the model would not be dynamically complete in the sense that $\mathrm{E}(y_t | z_t, y_{t-1}, z_{t-1}, y_{t-2}, z_{t-2}, \dots) = \mathrm{E}(y_t | z_t, z_{t-1}, z_{t-2})$, and we may not care. In addition, the explanatory variables in an FDL model may or may not be strictly exogenous.

11-5 The Homoskedasticity Assumption for Time Series Models

The homoskedasticity assumption for time series regressions, particularly TS.4′, looks very similar to that for cross-sectional regressions. However, since $\mathbf{x}_t$ can contain lagged y as well as lagged explanatory variables, we briefly discuss the meaning of the homoskedasticity assumption for different time series regressions.

In the simple static model, say,

$$y_t = \beta_0 + \beta_1 z_t + u_t, \qquad [11.41]$$

Assumption TS.4′ requires that

$$\mathrm{Var}(u_t | z_t) = \sigma^2.$$

Therefore, even though $\mathrm{E}(y_t | z_t)$ is a linear function of z_t, $\mathrm{Var}(y_t | z_t)$ must be constant. This is pretty straightforward.

In Example 11.4, we saw that, for the AR(1) model in (11.12), the homoskedasticity assumption is

$$\mathrm{Var}(u_t | y_{t-1}) = \mathrm{Var}(y_t | y_{t-1}) = \sigma^2;$$

even though $\mathrm{E}(y_t | y_{t-1})$ depends on y_{t-1}, $\mathrm{Var}(y_t | y_{t-1})$ does not. Thus, the spread in the distribution of y_t cannot depend on y_{t-1}.

Hopefully, the pattern is clear now. If we have the model

$$y_t = \beta_0 + \beta_1 z_t + \beta_2 y_{t-1} + \beta_3 z_{t-1} + u_t,$$

the homoskedasticity assumption is

$$\text{Var}(u_t|z_t, y_{t-1}, z_{t-1}) = \text{Var}(y_t|z_t, y_{t-1}, z_{t-1}) = \sigma^2,$$

so that the variance of u_t cannot depend on z_t, y_{t-1}, or z_{t-1} (or some other function of time). Generally, whatever explanatory variables appear in the model, we must assume that the variance of y_t given these explanatory variables is constant. If the model contains lagged y or lagged explanatory variables, then we are explicitly ruling out dynamic forms of heteroskedasticity (something we study in Chapter 12). But, in a static model, we are only concerned with $\text{Var}(y_t|z_t)$. In equation (11.41), no direct restrictions are placed on, say, $\text{Var}(y_t|y_{t-1})$.

Summary

In this chapter, we have argued that OLS can be justified using asymptotic analysis, provided certain conditions are met. Ideally, the time series processes are stationary and weakly dependent, although stationarity is not crucial. Weak dependence is necessary for applying the standard large sample results, particularly the central limit theorem.

Processes with deterministic trends that are weakly dependent can be used directly in regression analysis, provided time trends are included in the model (as in Section 10-5). A similar statement holds for processes with seasonality.

When the time series are highly persistent (they have unit roots), we must exercise extreme caution in using them directly in regression models (unless we are convinced the CLM assumptions from Chapter 10 hold). An alternative to using the levels is to use the first differences of the variables. For most highly persistent economic time series, the first difference is weakly dependent. Using first differences changes the nature of the model, but this method is often as informative as a model in levels. When data are highly persistent, we usually have more faith in first-difference results. In Chapter 18, we will cover some recent, more advanced methods for using I(1) variables in multiple regression analysis.

When models have complete dynamics in the sense that no further lags of any variable are needed in the equation, we have seen that the errors will be serially uncorrelated. This is useful because certain models, such as autoregressive models, are assumed to have complete dynamics. In static and distributed lag models, the dynamically complete assumption is often false, which generally means the errors will be serially correlated. We will see how to address this problem in Chapter 12.

THE "ASYMPTOTIC" GAUSS-MARKOV ASSUMPTIONS FOR TIME SERIES REGRESSION

Following is a summary of the five assumptions that we used in this chapter to perform large-sample inference for time series regressions. Recall that we introduced this new set of assumptions because the time series versions of the classical linear model assumptions are often violated, especially the strict exogeneity, no serial correlation, and normality assumptions. A key point in this chapter is that some sort of weak dependence is required to ensure that the central limit theorem applies. We only used Assumptions TS.1' through TS.3' for consistency (not unbiasedness) of OLS. When we add TS.4' and TS.5', we can use the usual confidence intervals, t statistics, and F statistics as being approximately valid in large samples. Unlike the Gauss-Markov and classical linear model assumptions, there is no historically significant name attached to Assumptions TS.1' to TS.5'. Nevertheless, the assumptions are the analogs to the Gauss-Markov assumptions that allow us to use standard inference. As usual for large-sample analysis, we dispense with the normality assumption entirely.

Assumption TS.1′ (Linearity and Weak Dependence)

The stochastic process $\{(x_{t1}, x_{t2}, ..., x_{tk}, y_t): t = 1, 2, ..., n\}$ is stationary, weakly dependent, and follows the linear model

$$y_t = \beta_0 + \beta_1 x_{t1} + \beta_2 x_{t2} + ... + \beta_k x_{tk} + u_t,$$

where $\{u_t: t = 1, 2, ..., n\}$ is the sequence of errors or disturbances. Here, n is the number of observations (time periods).

Assumption TS.2′ (No Perfect Collinearity)

In the sample (and therefore in the underlying time series process), no independent variable is constant nor a perfect linear combination of the others.

Assumption TS.3′ (Zero Conditional Mean)

The explanatory variables are *contemporaneously exogenous*, that is, $E(u_t|x_{t1}, ..., x_{tk}) = 0$. Remember, TS.3′ is notably weaker than the strict exogeneity Assumption TS.3′.

Assumption TS.4′ (Homoskedasticity)

The errors are *contemporaneously homoskedastic*, that is, $\text{Var}(u_t|\mathbf{x}_t) = \sigma^2$, where $\mathbf{x}_t$ is shorthand for $(x_{t1}, x_{t2}, ..., x_{tk})$.

Assumption TS.5′ (No Serial Correlation)

For all $t \neq s$, $E(u_t u_s|\mathbf{x}_t, \mathbf{x}_s) = 0$.

Key Terms

Asymptotically Uncorrelated	First Order Autocorrelation	Sequentially Exogenous
Autoregressive Process of Order One [AR(1)]	Growth Rate	Serially Uncorrelated
	Highly Persistent	Stable AR(1) Process
Contemporaneously Exogenous	Integrated of Order One [I(1)]	Stationary Process
Contemporaneously Homoskedastic	Integrated of Order Zero [I(0)]	Strongly Dependent
	Moving Average Process of Order One [MA(1)]	Trend-Stationary Process
Covariance Stationary		Unit Root Process
Difference-Stationary Process	Nonstationary Process	Weakly Dependent
Dynamically Complete Model	Random Walk	
First Difference	Random Walk with Drift	

Problems

1 Let $\{x_t: t = 1, 2, ...\}$ be a covariance stationary process and define $\gamma_h = \text{Cov}(x_t, x_{t+h})$ for $h \geq 0$. [Therefore, $\gamma_0 = \text{Var}(x_t)$.] Show that $\text{Corr}(x_t, x_{t+h}) = \gamma_h/\gamma_0$.

2 Let $\{e_t: t = -1, 0, 1, ...\}$ be a sequence of independent, identically distributed random variables with mean zero and variance one. Define a stochastic process by

$$x_t = e_t - (1/2)e_{t-1} + (1/2)e_{t-2}, \quad t = 1, 2, ...$$

(i) Find $E(x_t)$ and $\text{Var}(x_t)$. Do either of these depend on t?

(ii) Show that $\text{Corr}(x_t, x_{t+1}) = -1/2$ and $\text{Corr}(x_t, x_{t+2}) = 1/3$. (*Hint:* It is easiest to use the formula in Problem 1.)

(iii) What is $\text{Corr}(x_t, x_{t+h})$ for $h > 2$?

(iv) Is $\{x_t\}$ an asymptotically uncorrelated process?

3 Suppose that a time series process $\{y_t\}$ is generated by $y_t = z + e_t$, for all $t = 1, 2, \ldots$, where $\{e_t\}$ is an i.i.d. sequence with mean zero and variance σ_e^2. The random variable z does not change over time; it has mean zero and variance σ_z^2. Assume that each e_t is uncorrelated with z.

(i) Find the expected value and variance of y_t. Do your answers depend on t?

(ii) Find $\text{Cov}(y_t, y_{t+h})$ for any t and h. Is $\{y_t\}$ covariance stationary?

(iii) Use parts (i) and (ii) to show that $\text{Corr}(y_t, y_{t+h}) = \sigma_z^2/(\sigma_z^2 + \sigma_e^2)$ for all t and h.

(iv) Does y_t satisfy the intuitive requirement for being asymptotically uncorrelated? Explain.

4 Let $\{y_t: t = 1, 2, \ldots\}$ follow a random walk, as in (11.20), with $y_0 = 0$. Show that $\text{Corr}(y_t, y_{t+h}) = \sqrt{t/(t + h)}$ for $t \geq 1, h > 0$.

5 For the U.S. economy, let *gprice* denote the monthly growth in the overall price level and let *gwage* be the monthly growth in hourly wages. [These are both obtained as differences of logarithms: *gprice* $= \Delta\log(price)$ and *gwage* $= \Delta\log(wage)$.] Using the monthly data in WAGEPRC we estimate the following distributed lag model:

$$gprice = -.00093 + .119\, gwage + .097\, gwage_{-1} + .040\, gwage_{-2}$$
$$(.00057)\ (.052)\qquad (.039)\qquad\quad (.039)$$
$$+ .038\, gwage_{-3} + .081\, gwage_{-4} + .107\, gwage_{-5} + .095\, gwage_{-6}$$
$$(.039)\qquad\quad (.039)\qquad\quad (.039)\qquad\quad (.039)$$
$$+ .104\, gwage_{-7} + .103\, gwage_{-8} + .159\, gwage_{-9} + .110\, gwage_{-10}$$
$$(.039)\qquad\quad (.039)\qquad\quad (.039)\qquad\quad (.039)$$
$$+ .103\, gwage_{-11} + .016\, gwage_{-12}$$
$$(.039)\qquad\quad\ (.052)$$
$$n = 273, R^2 = .317, \overline{R}^2 = .283.$$

(i) Sketch the estimated lag distribution. At what lag is the effect of *gwage* on *gprice* largest? Which lag has the smallest coefficient?

(ii) For which lags are the t statistics less than two?

(iii) What is the estimated long-run propensity? Is it much different than one? Explain what the LRP tells us in this example.

(iv) What regression would you run to obtain the standard error of the LRP directly?

(v) How would you test the joint significance of six more lags of *gwage*? What would be the *df*s in the F distribution? (Be careful here; you lose six more observations.)

6 Let $hy6_t$ denote the three-month holding yield (in percent) from buying a six-month T-bill at time $(t - 1)$ and selling it at time t (three months hence) as a three-month T-bill. Let $hy3_{t-1}$ be the three-month holding yield from buying a three-month T-bill at time $(t - 1)$. At time $(t - 1)$, $hy3_{t-1}$ is known, whereas $hy6_t$ is unknown because $p3_t$ (the price of three-month T-bills) is unknown at time $(t - 1)$. The *expectations hypothesis* (EH) says that these two different three-month investments should be the same, on average. Mathematically, we can write this as a conditional expectation:

$$E(hy6_t|I_{t-1}) = hy3_{t-1},$$

where I_{t-1} denotes all observable information up through time $t - 1$. This suggests estimating the model

$$hy6_t = \beta_0 + \beta_1 hy3_{t-1} + u_t,$$

and testing $H_0: \beta_1 = 1$. (We can also test $H_0: \beta_0 = 0$, but we often allow for a *term premium* for buying assets with different maturities, so that $\beta_0 \neq 0$.)

(i) Estimating the previous equation by OLS using the data in INTQRT (spaced every three months) gives

$$\widehat{hy6_t} = -.058 + 1.104\ hy3_{t-1}$$
$$\qquad\qquad (.070)\quad (.039)$$
$$n = 123,\ R^2 = .866.$$

Do you reject $H_0: \beta_1 = 1$ against $H_0: \beta_1 \neq 1$ at the 1% significance level? Does the estimate seem practically different from one?

(ii) Another implication of the EH is that no other variables dated as $t - 1$ or earlier should help explain $hy6_t$, once $hy3_{t-1}$ has been controlled for. Including one lag of the *spread* between six-month and three-month T-bill rates gives

$$\widehat{hy6_t} = -.123 + 1.053\ hy3_{t-1} + .480\ (r6_{t-1} - r3_{t-1})$$
$$\qquad\qquad (.067)\quad (.039)\qquad\qquad (.109)$$
$$n = 123,\ R^2 = .885.$$

Now, is the coefficient on $hy3_{t-1}$ statistically different from one? Is the lagged spread term significant? According to this equation, if, at time $t - 1$, $r6$ is above $r3$, should you invest in six-month or three-month T-bills?

(iii) The sample correlation between $hy3_t$ and $hy3_{t-1}$ is .914. Why might this raise some concerns with the previous analysis?

(iv) How would you test for seasonality in the equation estimated in part (ii)?

7 A *partial adjustment model* is

$$y_t^* = \gamma_0 + \gamma_1 x_t + e_t$$
$$y_t - y_{t-1} = \lambda(y_t^* - y_{t-1}) + a_t,$$

where y_t^* is the desired or optimal level of y and y_t is the actual (observed) level. For example, y_t^* is the desired growth in firm inventories, and x_t is growth in firm sales. The parameter γ_1 measures the effect of x_t on y_t^*. The second equation describes how the actual y adjusts depending on the relationship between the desired y in time t and the actual y in time $t - 1$. The parameter λ measures the speed of adjustment and satisfies $0 < \lambda < 1$.

(i) Plug the first equation for y_t^* into the second equation and show that we can write

$$y_t = \beta_0 + \beta_1 y_{t-1} + \beta_2 x_t + u_t.$$

In particular, find the β_j in terms of the γ_j and λ and find u_t in terms of e_t and a_t. Therefore, the partial adjustment model leads to a model with a lagged dependent variable and a contemporaneous x.

(ii) If $E(e_t | x_t, y_{t-1}, x_{t-1}, \ldots) = E(a_t | x_t, y_{t-1}, x_{t-1}, \ldots) = 0$ and all series are weakly dependent, how would you estimate the β_j?

(iii) If $\hat{\beta}_1 = .7$ and $\hat{\beta}_2 = .2$, what are the estimates of γ_1 and λ?

8 Suppose that the equation

$$y_t = \alpha + \delta t + \beta_1 x_{t1} + \ldots + \beta_k x_{tk} + u_t$$

satisfies the sequential exogeneity assumption in equation (11.40).

(i) Suppose you difference the equation to obtain

$$\Delta y_t = \delta + \beta_1 \Delta x_{t1} + \ldots + \beta_k \Delta x_{tk} + \Delta u_t.$$

How come applying OLS on the differenced equation does not generally result in consistent estimators of the β_j?

(ii)   What assumption on the explanatory variables in the original equation would ensure that OLS on the differences consistently estimates the β_j?

(iii)   Let $z_{t1}, \ldots, z_{tk}$ be a set of explanatory variables dated contemporaneously with y_t. If we specify the static regression model $y_t = \beta_0 + \beta_1 z_{t1} + \ldots + \beta_k z_{tk} + u_t$, describe what we need to assume for $\mathbf{x}_t = \mathbf{z}_t$ to be sequentially exogenous. Do you think the assumptions are likely to hold in economic applications?

Computer Exercises

C1 Use the data in HSEINV for this exercise.

(i)   Find the first order autocorrelation in log($invpc$). Now, find the autocorrelation *after* linearly detrending log($invpc$). Do the same for log($price$). Which of the two series may have a unit root?

(ii)   Based on your findings in part (i), estimate the equation

$$\log(invpc_t) = \beta_0 + \beta_1 \Delta\log(price_t) + \beta_2 t + u_t$$

and report the results in standard form. Interpret the coefficient $\hat{\beta}_1$ and determine whether it is statistically significant.

(iii) Linearly detrend log($invpc_t$) and use the detrended version as the dependent variable in the regression from part (ii) (see Section 10-5). What happens to R^2?

(iv)   Now use $\Delta\log(invpc_t)$ as the dependent variable. How do your results change from part (ii)? Is the time trend still significant? Why or why not?

C2 In Example 11.7, define the growth in hourly wage and output per hour as the change in the natural log: $ghrwage = \Delta\log(hrwage)$ and $goutphr = \Delta\log(outphr)$. Consider a simple extension of the model estimated in (11.29):

$$ghrwage_t = \beta_0 + \beta_1 goutphr_t + \beta_2 goutphr_{t-1} + u_t.$$

This allows an increase in productivity growth to have both a current and lagged effect on wage growth.

(i)   Estimate the equation using the data in EARNS and report the results in standard form. Is the lagged value of $goutphr$ statistically significant?

(ii)   If $\beta_1 + \beta_2 = 1$, a permanent increase in productivity growth is fully passed on in higher wage growth after one year. Test H_0: $\beta_1 + \beta_2 = 1$ against the two-sided alternative. Remember, one way to do this is to write the equation so that $\theta = \beta_1 + \beta_2$ appears directly in the model, as in Example 10.4 from Chapter 10.

(iii) Does $goutphr_{t-2}$ need to be in the model? Explain.

C3 (i)   In Example 11.4, it may be that the expected value of the return at time t, given past returns, is a quadratic function of $return_{t-1}$. To check this possibility, use the data in NYSE to estimate

$$return_t = \beta_0 + \beta_1 return_{t-1} + \beta_2 return_{t-1}^2 + u_t;$$

report the results in standard form.

(ii)   State and test the null hypothesis that $E(return_t | return_{t-1})$ does not depend on $return_{t-1}$. (*Hint:* There are two restrictions to test here.) What do you conclude?

(iii) Drop $return_{t-1}^2$ from the model, but add the interaction term $return_{t-1} \cdot return_{t-2}$. Now test the efficient markets hypothesis.

(iv)   What do you conclude about predicting weekly stock returns based on past stock returns?

C4 Use the data in PHILLIPS for this exercise, but only through 1996.

(i)   In Example 11.5, we assumed that the natural rate of unemployment is constant. An alternative form of the expectations augmented Phillips curve allows the natural rate of unemployment to depend on past levels of unemployment. In the simplest case, the natural rate at time t equals

$unem_{t-1}$. If we assume adaptive expectations, we obtain a Phillips curve where inflation and unemployment are in first differences:

$$\Delta inf = \beta_0 + \beta_1 \Delta unem + u.$$

Estimate this model, report the results in the usual form, and discuss the sign, size, and statistical significance of $\hat{\beta}_1$.

(ii) Which model fits the data better, (11.19) or the model from part (i)? Explain.

C5 (i) Add a linear time trend to equation (11.27). Is a time trend necessary in the first-difference equation?

(ii) Drop the time trend and add the variables $ww2$ and $pill$ to (11.27) (do not difference these dummy variables). Are these variables jointly significant at the 5% level?

(iii) Add the linear time trend, $ww2$, and $pill$ all to equation (11.27). What happens to the magnitude and statistical significance of the time trend as compared with that in part (i)? What about the coefficient on $pill$ as compared with that in part (ii)?

(iv) Using the model from part (iii), estimate the LRP and obtain its standard error. Compare this to (10.19), where gfr and pe appeared in levels rather than in first differences. Would you say that the link between fertility and the value of the personal exemption is a particularly robust finding?

C6 Let $inven_t$ be the real value inventories in the United States during year t, let GDP_t denote real gross domestic product, and let $r3_t$ denote the (ex post) real interest rate on three-month T-bills. The ex post real interest rate is (approximately) $r3_t = i3_t - inf_t$, where $i3_t$ is the rate on three-month T-bills and inf_t is the annual inflation rate [see Mankiw (1994, Section 6-4)]. The change in inventories, $cinven_t$, is the *inventory investment* for the year. The *accelerator model* of inventory investment relates $cinven$ to the $cGDP$, the change in GDP:

$$cinven_t = \beta_0 + \beta_1 cGDP_t + u_t,$$

where $\beta_1 > 0$. [See, for example, Mankiw (1994), Chapter 17.]

(i) Use the data in INVEN to estimate the accelerator model. Report the results in the usual form and interpret the equation. Is $\hat{\beta}_1$ statistically greater than zero?

(ii) If the real interest rate rises, then the opportunity cost of holding inventories rises, and so an increase in the real interest rate should decrease inventories. Add the real interest rate to the accelerator model and discuss the results.

(iii) Does the level of the real interest rate work better than the first difference, $cr3_t$?

C7 Use CONSUMP for this exercise. One version of the *permanent income hypothesis* (PIH) of consumption is that the *growth* in consumption is unpredictable. [Another version is that the change in consumption itself is unpredictable; see Mankiw (1994, Chapter 15) for discussion of the PIH.] Let $gc_t = \log(c_t) - \log(c_{t-1})$ be the growth in real per capita consumption (of nondurables and services). Then the PIH implies that $E(gc_t|I_{t-1}) = E(gc_t)$, where I_{t-1} denotes information known at time $(t-1)$; in this case, t denotes a year.

(i) Test the PIH by estimating $gc_t = \beta_0 + \beta_1 gc_{t-1} + u_t$. Clearly state the null and alternative hypotheses. What do you conclude?

(ii) To the regression in part (i) add the variables gy_{t-1}, $i3_{t-1}$, and inf_{t-1}. Are these new variables individually or jointly significant at the 5% level? (Be sure to report the appropriate p-values.)

(iii) In the regression from part (ii), what happens to the p-value for the t statistic on gc_{t-1}? Does this mean the PIH hypothesis is now supported by the data?

(iv) In the regression from part (ii), what is the F statistic and its associated p-value for joint significance of the four explanatory variables? Does your conclusion about the PIH now agree with what you found in part (i)?

C8 Use the data in PHILLIPS for this exercise.
  (i) Estimate an AR(1) model for the unemployment rate. Use this equation to predict the unemployment rate for 2004. Compare this with the actual unemployment rate for 2004. (You can find this information in a recent *Economic Report of the President*.)
  (ii) Add a lag of inflation to the AR(1) model from part (i). Is inf_{t-1} statistically significant?
  (iii) Use the equation from part (ii) to predict the unemployment rate for 2004. Is the result better or worse than in the model from part (i)?
  (iv) Use the method from Section 6-4 to construct a 95% prediction interval for the 2004 unemployment rate. Is the 2004 unemployment rate in the interval?

C9 Use the data in TRAFFIC2 for this exercise. Computer Exercise C11 in Chapter 10 previously asked for an analysis of these data.
  (i) Compute the first order autocorrelation coefficient for the variable *prcfat*. Are you concerned that *prcfat* contains a unit root? Do the same for the unemployment rate.
  (ii) Estimate a multiple regression model relating the first difference of *prcfat*, $\Delta prcfat$, to the same variables in part (vi) of Computer Exercise C11 in Chapter 10, except you should first difference the unemployment rate, too. Then, include a linear time trend, monthly dummy variables, the weekend variable, and the two policy variables; do not difference these. Do you find any interesting results?
  (iii) Comment on the following statement: "We should always first difference any time series we suspect of having a unit root before doing multiple regression because it is the safe strategy and should give results similar to using the levels." [In answering this, you may want to do the regression from part (vi) of Computer Exercise C11 in Chapter 10, if you have not already.]

C10 Use all the data in PHILLIPS to answer this question. You should now use 56 years of data.
  (i) Reestimate equation (11.19) and report the results in the usual form. Do the intercept and slope estimates change notably when you add the recent years of data?
  (ii) Obtain a new estimate of the natural rate of unemployment. Compare this new estimate with that reported in Example 11.5.
  (iii) Compute the first order autocorrelation for *unem*. In your opinion, is the root close to one?
  (iv) Use *cunem* as the explanatory variable instead of *unem*. Which explanatory variable gives a higher R-squared?

C11 Okun's Law—see, for example, Mankiw (1994, Chapter 2)—implies the following relationship between the annual percentage change in real GDP, *pcrgdp*, and the change in the annual unemployment rate, *cunem*:

$$pcrgdp = 3 - 2 \cdot cunem.$$

If the unemployment rate is stable, real GDP grows at 3% annually. For each percentage point increase in the unemployment rate, real GDP grows by two percentage points less. (This should not be interpreted in any causal sense; it is more like a statistical description.)
  To see if the data on the U.S. economy support Okun's Law, we specify a model that allows deviations via an error term, $pcrgdp_t = \beta_0 + \beta_1 cunem_t + u_t$.
  (i) Use the data in OKUN to estimate the equation. Do you get exactly 3 for the intercept and –2 for the slope? Did you expect to?
  (ii) Find the t statistic for testing $H_0: \beta_1 = -2$. Do you reject H_0 against the two-sided alternative at any reasonable significance level?
  (iii) Find the t statistic for testing $H_0: \beta_0 = 3$. Do you reject H_0 at the 5% level against the two-sided alternative? Is it a "strong" rejection?
  (iv) Find the F statistic and p-value for testing $H_0: \beta_0 = 3, \beta_1 = -2$ against the alternative that H_0 is false. Does the test reject at the 10% level? Overall, would you say the data reject or tend to support Okun's Law?

C12 Use the data in MINWAGE for this exercise, focusing on the wage and employment series for sector 232 (Men's and Boys' Furnishings). The variable $gwage232$ is the monthly growth (change in logs) in the average wage in sector 232; $gemp232$ is the growth in employment in sector 232; $gmwage$ is the growth in the federal minimum wage; and $gcpi$ is the growth in the (urban) Consumer Price Index.

(i) Find the first order autocorrelation in $gwage232$. Does this series appear to be weakly dependent?

(ii) Estimate the dynamic model

$$gwage232_t = \beta_0 + \beta_1 gwage232_{t-1} + \beta_2 gmwage_t + \beta_3 gcpi_t + u_t$$

by OLS. Holding fixed last month's growth in wage and the growth in the CPI, does an increase in the federal minimum result in a contemporaneous increase in $gwage232_t$? Explain.

(iii) Now add the lagged growth in employment, $gemp232_{t-1}$, to the equation in part (ii). Is it statistically significant?

(iv) Compared with the model without $gwage232_{t-1}$ and $gemp232_{t-1}$, does adding the two lagged variables have much of an effect on the $gmwage$ coefficient?

(v) Run the regression of $gmwage_t$ on $gwage232_{t-1}$ and $gemp232_{t-1}$, and report the R-squared. Comment on how the value of R-squared helps explain your answer to part (iv).

C13 Use the data in BEVERIDGE to answer this question. The data set includes monthly observations on vacancy rates and unemployment rates for the United States from December 2000 through February 2012.

(i) Find the correlation between $urate$ and $urate\_1$. Would you say the correlation points more toward a unit root process or a weakly dependent process?

(ii) Repeat part (i) but with the vacancy rate, $vrate$.

(iii) The Beveridge Curve relates the unemployment rate to the vacancy rate, with the simplest relationship being linear:

$$urate_t = \beta_0 + \beta_1 vrate_t + u_t,$$

where $\beta_1 < 0$ is expected. Estimate β_0 and β_1 by OLS and report the results in the usual form. Do you find a negative relationship?

(iv) Explain why you cannot trust the confidence interval for β_1 reported by the OLS output in part (iii). [The tools needed to study regressions of this type are presented in Chapter 18.]

(v) If you difference $urate$ and $vrate$ before running the regression, how does the estimated slope coefficient compare with part (iii)? Is it statistically different from zero? [This example shows that differencing before running an OLS regression is not always a sensible strategy. But we cannot say more until Chapter 18.]

C14 Use the data in APPROVAL to answer the following questions. See also Computer Exercise C14 in Chapter 10.

(i) Compute the first order autocorrelations for the variables $approve$ and $lrgasprice$. Do they seem close enough to unity to worry about unit roots?

(ii) Consider the model

$$approve_t = \beta_0 + \beta_1 lcpifood_t + \beta_2 lrgasprice_t + \beta_3 unemploy_t$$
$$+ \beta_4 sep11_t + \beta_5 iraqinvade_t + u_t,$$

where the first two variables are in logarithmic form. Given what you found in part (i), why might you hesitate to estimate this model by OLS?

(iii) Estimate the equation in part (ii) by differencing all variables (including the dummy variables). How do you interpret your estimate of β_2? Is it statistically significant? (Report the p-value.)

(iv) Interpret your estimate of β_4 and discuss its statistical significance.

(v) Add $lsp500$ to the model in part (ii) and estimate the equation by first differencing. Discuss what you find for the stock market variable.

CHAPTER 12

Serial Correlation and Heteroskedasticity in Time Series Regressions

In this chapter, we discuss the critical problem of serial correlation in the error terms of a multiple regression model. We saw in Chapter 11 that when, in an appropriate sense, the dynamics of a model have been completely specified, the errors will not be serially correlated. Thus, testing for serial correlation can be used to detect dynamic misspecification. Furthermore, static and finite distributed lag models often have serially correlated errors even if there is no underlying misspecification of the model. Therefore, it is important to know the consequences and remedies for serial correlation for these useful classes of models.

In Section 12-1, we present the properties of OLS when the errors contain serial correlation. In Section 12-2, we demonstrate how to test for serial correlation. We cover tests that apply to models with strictly exogenous regressors and tests that are asymptotically valid with general regressors, including lagged dependent variables. Section 12-3 explains how to correct for serial correlation under the assumption of strictly exogenous explanatory variables, while Section 12-4 shows how using differenced data often eliminates serial correlation in the errors. Section 12-5 covers more recent advances on how to adjust the usual OLS standard errors and test statistics in the presence of very general serial correlation.

In Chapter 8, we discussed testing and correcting for heteroskedasticity in cross-sectional applications. In Section 12-6, we show how the methods used in the cross-sectional case can be extended to the time series case. The mechanics are essentially the same, but there are a few subtleties associated with the temporal correlation in time series observations that must be addressed. In addition, we briefly touch on the consequences of dynamic forms of heteroskedasticity.

12-1 Properties of OLS with Serially Correlated Errors

12-1a Unbiasedness and Consistency

In Chapter 10, we proved unbiasedness of the OLS estimator under the first three Gauss-Markov assumptions for time series regressions (TS.1 through TS.3). In particular, Theorem 10.1 assumed nothing about serial correlation in the errors. It follows that, as long as the explanatory variables are strictly exogenous, the $\hat{\beta}_j$ are unbiased, regardless of the degree of serial correlation in the errors. This is analogous to the observation that heteroskedasticity in the errors does not cause bias in the $\hat{\beta}_j$.

In Chapter 11, we relaxed the strict exogeneity assumption to $E(u_t|\mathbf{x}_t) = 0$ and showed that, when the data are weakly dependent, the $\hat{\beta}_j$ are still consistent (although not necessarily unbiased). This result did not hinge on any assumption about serial correlation in the errors.

12-1b Efficiency and Inference

Because the Gauss-Markov Theorem (Theorem 10.4) requires both homoskedasticity and serially uncorrelated errors, OLS is no longer BLUE in the presence of serial correlation. Even more importantly, the usual OLS standard errors and test statistics are not valid, even asymptotically. We can see this by computing the variance of the OLS estimator under the first four Gauss-Markov assumptions and the **AR(1) serial correlation** model for the error terms. More precisely, we assume that

$$u_t = \rho u_{t-1} + e_t, \; t = 1, 2, \ldots, n \tag{12.1}$$

$$|\rho| < 1, \tag{12.2}$$

where the e_t are uncorrelated random variables with mean zero and variance σ_e^2; recall from Chapter 11 that assumption (12.2) is the stability condition.

We consider the variance of the OLS slope estimator in the simple regression model

$$y_t = \beta_0 + \beta_1 x_t + u_t,$$

and, just to simplify the formula, we assume that the sample average of the x_t is zero ($\bar{x} = 0$). Then, the OLS estimator $\hat{\beta}_1$ of β_1 can be written as

$$\hat{\beta}_1 = \beta_1 + \text{SST}_x^{-1} \sum_{t=1}^{n} x_t u_t, \tag{12.3}$$

where $\text{SST}_x = \sum_{t=1}^{n} x_t^2$. Now, in computing the variance of $\hat{\beta}_1$ (conditional on $\mathbf{X}$), we must account for the serial correlation in the u_t:

$$\begin{aligned}
\text{Var}(\hat{\beta}_1) &= \text{SST}_x^{-2} \text{Var}\left(\sum_{t=1}^{n} x_t u_t \right) \\
&= \text{SST}_x^{-2} \left(\sum_{t=1}^{n} x_t^2 \text{Var}(u_t) + 2 \sum_{t=1}^{n-1} \sum_{j=1}^{n-t} x_t x_{t+j} E(u_t u_{t+j}) \right) \\
&= \sigma^2/\text{SST}_x + 2(\sigma^2/\text{SST}_x^2) \sum_{t=1}^{n-1} \sum_{j=1}^{n-t} \rho^j x_t x_{t+j},
\end{aligned} \tag{12.4}$$

where $\sigma^2 = \text{Var}(u_t)$ and we have used the fact that $E(u_t u_{t+j}) = \text{Cov}(u_t, u_{t+j}) = \rho^j \sigma^2$ [see equation (11.4)]. The first term in equation (12.4), σ^2/SST_x, is the variance of $\hat{\beta}_1$ when $\rho = 0$, which is the familiar OLS variance under the Gauss-Markov assumptions. If we ignore the serial correlation and estimate the variance in the usual way, the variance estimator will usually be biased when $\rho \neq 0$

because it ignores the second term in (12.4). As we will see through later examples, $\rho > 0$ is most common, in which case, $\rho^j > 0$ for all j. Further, the independent variables in regression models are often positively correlated over time, so that $x_t x_{t+j}$ is positive for most pairs t and $t+j$. Therefore, in most economic applications, the term $\sum_{t=1}^{n-1}\sum_{j=1}^{n-t}\rho^j x_t x_{t+j}$ is positive, and so the usual OLS variance formula σ^2/SST_x *understates* the true variance of the OLS estimator. If ρ is large or x_t has a high degree of positive serial correlation—a common case—the bias in the usual OLS variance estimator can be substantial. We will tend to think the OLS slope estimator is more precise than it actually is.

> ### ■ EXPLORING FURTHER 12.1
>
> Suppose that, rather than the AR(1) model, u_t follows the MA(1) model $u_t = e_t + \alpha e_{t-1}$. Find $\text{Var}(\hat{\beta}_1)$ and show that it is different from the usual formula if $\alpha \neq 0$.

When $\rho < 0$, ρ^j is negative when j is odd and positive when j is even, and so it is difficult to determine the sign of $\sum_{t=1}^{n-1}\sum_{j=1}^{n-t}\rho^j x_t x_{t+j}$. In fact, it is possible that the usual OLS variance formula actually *overstates* the true variance of $\hat{\beta}_1$. In either case, the usual variance estimator will be biased for $\text{Var}(\hat{\beta}_1)$ in the presence of serial correlation.

Because the standard error of $\hat{\beta}_1$ is an estimate of the standard deviation of $\hat{\beta}_1$, using the usual OLS standard error in the presence of serial correlation is invalid. Therefore, t statistics are no longer valid for testing single hypotheses. Since a smaller standard error means a larger t statistic, the usual t statistics will often be too large when $\rho > 0$. The usual F and LM statistics for testing multiple hypotheses are also invalid.

12-1c Goodness of Fit

Sometimes one sees the claim that serial correlation in the errors of a time series regression model invalidates our usual goodness-of-fit measures, R-squared and adjusted R-squared. Fortunately, this is not the case, provided the data are stationary and weakly dependent. To see why these measures are still valid, recall that we defined the population R-squared in a cross-sectional context to be $1 - \sigma_u^2/\sigma_y^2$ (see Section 6-3). This definition is still appropriate in the context of time series regressions with stationary, weakly dependent data: the variances of both the error and the dependent variable do not change over time. By the law of large numbers, R^2 and $\bar{R}^2$ both consistently estimate the population R-squared. The argument is essentially the same as in the cross-sectional case in the presence of heteroskedasticity (see Section 8-1). Because there is never an unbiased estimator of the population R-squared, it makes no sense to talk about bias in R^2 caused by serial correlation. All we can really say is that our goodness-of-fit measures are still consistent estimators of the population parameter. This argument does not go through if $\{y_t\}$ is an I(1) process because $\text{Var}(y_t)$ grows with t; goodness of fit does not make much sense in this case. As we discussed in Section 10-5, trends in the mean of y_t, or seasonality, can and should be accounted for in computing an R-squared. Other departures from stationarity do not cause difficulty in interpreting R^2 and $\bar{R}^2$ in the usual ways.

12-1d Serial Correlation in the Presence of Lagged Dependent Variables

Beginners in econometrics are often warned of the dangers of serially correlated errors in the presence of lagged dependent variables. Almost every textbook on econometrics contains some form of the statement "OLS is inconsistent in the presence of lagged dependent variables and serially correlated errors." Unfortunately, as a general assertion, this statement is false. There is a version of the statement that is correct, but it is important to be very precise.

To illustrate, suppose that the expected value of y_t given y_{t-1} is linear:

$$E(y_t|y_{t-1}) = \beta_0 + \beta_1 y_{t-1},$$ [12.5]

where we assume stability, $|\beta_1| < 1$. We know we can always write this with an error term as

$$y_t = \beta_0 + \beta_1 y_{t-1} + u_t, \tag{12.6}$$

$$E(u_t|y_{t-1}) = 0. \tag{12.7}$$

By construction, this model satisfies the key zero conditional mean Assumption TS.3′ for consistency of OLS; therefore, the OLS estimators $\hat{\beta}_0$ and $\hat{\beta}_1$ are consistent. It is important to see that, without further assumptions, the errors $\{u_t\}$ *can* be serially correlated. Condition (12.7) ensures that u_t is uncorrelated with y_{t-1}, but u_t and y_{t-2} could be correlated. Then, because $u_{t-1} = y_{t-1} - \beta_0 - \beta_1 y_{t-2}$, the covariance between u_t and u_{t-1} is $-\beta_1 \text{Cov}(u_t, y_{t-2})$, which is not necessarily zero. Thus, the errors exhibit serial correlation and the model contains a lagged dependent variable, but OLS consistently estimates β_0 and β_1 because these are the parameters in the conditional expectation (12.5). The serial correlation in the errors will cause the usual OLS statistics to be invalid for testing purposes, but it will not affect consistency.

So when is OLS inconsistent if the errors are serially correlated and the regressors contain a lagged dependent variable? This happens when we write the model in error form, exactly as in (12.6), but then we *assume* that $\{u_t\}$ follows a stable AR(1) model as in (12.1) and (12.2), where

$$E(e_t|u_{t-1}, u_{t-2}, \ldots) = E(e_t|y_{t-1}, y_{t-2}, \ldots) = 0. \tag{12.8}$$

Because e_t is uncorrelated with y_{t-1} by assumption, $\text{Cov}(y_{t-1}, u_t) = \rho \text{Cov}(y_{t-1}, u_{t-1})$ which is not zero unless $\rho = 0$. This causes the OLS estimators of β_0 and β_1 from the regression of y_t on y_{t-1} to be inconsistent.

We now see that OLS estimation of (12.6) when the errors u_t also follow an AR(1) model leads to inconsistent estimators. However, the correctness of this statement makes it no less wrongheaded. We have to ask: What would be the point in estimating the parameters in (12.6) when the errors follow an AR(1) model? It is difficult to think of cases where this would be interesting. At least in (12.5) the parameters tell us the expected value of y_t given y_{t-1}. When we combine (12.6) and (12.1), we see that y_t really follows a second order autoregressive model, or AR(2) model. To see this, write $u_{t-1} = y_{t-1} - \beta_0 - \beta_1 y_{t-2}$ and plug this into $u_t = \rho u_{t-1} + e_t$. Then, (12.6) can be rewritten as

$$
\begin{aligned}
y_t &= \beta_0 + \beta_1 y_{t-1} + \rho(y_{t-1} - \beta_0 - \beta_1 y_{t-2}) + e_t \\
&= \beta_0(1 - \rho) + (\beta_1 + \rho)y_{t-1} - \rho\beta_1 y_{t-2} + e_t \\
&= \alpha_0 + \alpha_1 y_{t-1} + \alpha_2 y_{t-2} + e_t,
\end{aligned}
$$

where $\alpha_0 = \beta_0(1 - \rho)$, $\alpha_1 = \beta_1 + \rho$, and $\alpha_2 = -\rho\beta_1$. Given (12.8), it follows that

$$E(y_t|y_{t-1}, y_{t-2}, \ldots) = E(y_t|y_{t-1}, y_{t-2}) = \alpha_0 + \alpha_1 y_{t-1} + \alpha_2 y_{t-2}. \tag{12.9}$$

This means that the expected value of y_t, given all past y, depends on *two* lags of y. It is equation (12.9) that we would be interested in using for any practical purpose, including forecasting, as we will see in Chapter 18. We are especially interested in the parameters α_j. Under the appropriate stability conditions for an AR(2) model—which we will cover in Section 12-3—OLS estimation of (12.9) produces consistent and asymptotically normal estimators of the α_j.

The bottom line is that you need a good reason for having both a lagged dependent variable in a model and a particular model of serial correlation in the errors. Often, serial correlation in the errors of a dynamic model simply indicates that the dynamic regression function has not been completely specified: in the previous example, we should add y_{t-2} to the equation.

In Chapter 18, we will see examples of models with lagged dependent variables where the errors are serially correlated and are also correlated with y_{t-1}. But even in these cases the errors do not follow an autoregressive process.

12-2 Testing for Serial Correlation

In this section, we discuss several methods of testing for serial correlation in the error terms in the multiple linear regression model

$$y_t = \beta_0 + \beta_1 x_{t1} + \dots + \beta_k x_{tk} + u_t.$$

We first consider the case when the regressors are strictly exogenous. Recall that this requires the error, u_t, to be uncorrelated with the regressors in all time periods (see Section 10-3), so, among other things, it rules out models with lagged dependent variables.

12-2a A *t* Test for AR(1) Serial Correlation with Strictly Exogenous Regressors

Although there are numerous ways in which the error terms in a multiple regression model can be serially correlated, the most popular model—and the simplest to work with—is the AR(1) model in equations (12.1) and (12.2). In the previous section, we explained the implications of performing OLS when the errors are serially correlated in general, and we derived the variance of the OLS slope estimator in a simple regression model with AR(1) errors. We now show how to test for the presence of AR(1) serial correlation. The null hypothesis is that there is *no* serial correlation. Therefore, just as with tests for heteroskedasticity, we assume the best and require the data to provide reasonably strong evidence that the ideal assumption of no serial correlation is violated.

We first derive a large-sample test under the assumption that the explanatory variables are strictly exogenous: the expected value of u_t, given the entire history of independent variables, is zero. In addition, in (12.1), we must assume that

$$\mathrm{E}(e_t | u_{t-1}, u_{t-2}, \dots) = 0 \qquad [12.10]$$

and

$$\mathrm{Var}(e_t | u_{t-1}) = \mathrm{Var}(e_t) = \sigma_e^2. \qquad [12.11]$$

These are standard assumptions in the AR(1) model (which follow when $\{e_t\}$ is an i.i.d. sequence), and they allow us to apply the large-sample results from Chapter 11 for dynamic regression.

As with testing for heteroskedasticity, the null hypothesis is that the appropriate Gauss-Markov assumption is true. In the AR(1) model, the null hypothesis that the errors are serially uncorrelated is

$$\mathrm{H}_0: \rho = 0. \qquad [12.12]$$

How can we test this hypothesis? If the u_t were observed, then, under (12.10) and (12.11), we could immediately apply the asymptotic normality results from Theorem 11.2 to the dynamic regression model

$$u_t = \rho u_{t-1} + e_t, t = 2, \dots, n. \qquad [12.13]$$

(Under the null hypothesis $\rho = 0$, $\{u_t\}$ is clearly weakly dependent.) In other words, we could estimate ρ from the regression of u_t on u_{t-1}, for all $t = 2, \dots, n$, without an intercept, and use the usual t statistic for $\hat{\rho}$. This does not work because the errors u_t are not observed. Nevertheless, just as with testing for heteroskedasticity, we can replace u_t with the corresponding OLS residual, $\hat{u}_t$. Since $\hat{u}_t$ depends on the OLS estimators $\hat{\beta}_0, \hat{\beta}_1, \dots, \hat{\beta}_k$, it is not obvious that using $\hat{u}_t$ for u_t in the regression has no effect on the distribution of the t statistic. Fortunately, it turns out that, because of the strict exogeneity assumption, the large-sample distribution of the t statistic is not affected by using the OLS residuals in place of the errors. A proof is well beyond the scope of this text, but it follows from the work of Wooldridge (1991b).

We can summarize the asymptotic test for AR(1) serial correlation very simply.

Testing for AR(1) Serial Correlation with Strictly Exogenous Regressors:

(i) Run the OLS regression of y_t on $x_{t1}, \ldots, x_{tk}$ and obtain the OLS residuals, $\hat{u}_t$, for all $t = 1, 2, \ldots, n$.

(ii) Run the regression of

$$\hat{u}_t \text{ on } \hat{u}_{t-1}, \text{ for all } t = 2, \ldots, n, \qquad [12.14]$$

obtaining the coefficient $\hat{\rho}$ on $\hat{u}_{t-1}$ and its t statistic, $t_{\hat{\rho}}$. (This regression may or may not contain an intercept; the t statistic for $\hat{\rho}$ will be slightly affected, but it is asymptotically valid either way.)

(iii) Use $t_{\hat{\rho}}$ to test H_0: $\rho = 0$ against H_1: $\rho \neq 0$ in the usual way. (Actually, since $\rho > 0$ is often expected a priori, the alternative can be H_1: $\rho > 0$.) Typically, we conclude that serial correlation is a problem to be dealt with only if H_0 is rejected at the 5% level. As always, it is best to report the p-value for the test.

In deciding whether serial correlation needs to be addressed, we should remember the difference between practical and statistical significance. With a large sample size, it is possible to find serial correlation even though $\hat{\rho}$ is practically small; when $\hat{\rho}$ is close to zero, the usual OLS inference procedures will not be far off [see equation (12.4)]. Such outcomes are somewhat rare in time series applications because time series data sets are usually small.

| **EXAMPLE 12.1** | **Testing for AR(1) Serial Correlation in the Phillips Curve** |

In Chapter 10, we estimated a static Phillips curve that explained the inflation-unemployment tradeoff in the United States (see Example 10.1). In Chapter 11, we studied a particular expectations augmented Phillips curve, where we assumed adaptive expectations (see Example 11.5). We now test the error term in each equation for serial correlation. Since the expectations augmented curve uses $\Delta inf_t = inf_t - inf_{t-1}$ as the dependent variable, we have one fewer observation.

For the static Phillips curve, the regression in (12.14) yields $\hat{\rho} = .573$, $t = 4.93$, and p-value $= .000$ (with 48 observations through 1996). This is very strong evidence of positive, first order serial correlation. One consequence of this is that the standard errors and t statistics from Chapter 10 are not valid. By contrast, the test for AR(1) serial correlation in the expectations augmented curve gives $\hat{\rho} = -.036$, $t = -.287$, and p-value $= .775$ (with 47 observations): there is no evidence of AR(1) serial correlation in the expectations augmented Phillips curve.

Although the test from (12.14) is derived from the AR(1) model, the test can detect other kinds of serial correlation. Remember, $\hat{\rho}$ is a consistent estimator of the correlation between u_t and u_{t-1}. Any serial correlation that causes adjacent errors to be correlated can be picked up by this test. On the other hand, it does not detect serial correlation where adjacent errors are uncorrelated, $\text{Corr}(u_t, u_{t-1}) = 0$. (For example, u_t and u_{t-2} could be correlated.)

In using the usual t statistic from (12.14), we must assume that the errors in (12.13) satisfy the appropriate homoskedasticity assumption, (12.11). In fact, it is easy to make the test robust to heteroskedasticity in e_t: we simply use the usual, heteroskedasticity-robust t statistic from Chapter 8. For the static Phillips curve in Example 12.1, the heteroskedasticity-robust t statistic is 4.03, which is

> **EXPLORING FURTHER 12.2**
>
> How would you use regression (12.14) to construct an approximate 95% confidence interval for ρ?

smaller than the nonrobust t statistic but still very significant. In Section 12-7, we further discuss heteroskedasticity in time series regressions, including its dynamic forms.

12-2b The Durbin-Watson Test under Classical Assumptions

Another test for AR(1) serial correlation is the Durbin-Watson test. The **Durbin-Watson (DW) statistic** is also based on the OLS residuals:

$$DW = \frac{\sum_{t=2}^{n}(\hat{u}_t - \hat{u}_{t-1})^2}{\sum_{t=1}^{n}\hat{u}_t^2}. \qquad [12.15]$$

Simple algebra shows that DW and $\hat{\rho}$ from (12.14) are closely linked:

$$DW \approx 2(1 - \hat{\rho}). \qquad [12.16]$$

One reason this relationship is not exact is that $\hat{\rho}$ has $\sum_{t=2}^{n}\hat{u}_{t-1}^2$ in its denominator, while the DW statistic has the sum of squares of all OLS residuals in its denominator. Even with moderate sample sizes, the approximation in (12.16) is often pretty close. Therefore, tests based on DW and the t test based on $\hat{\rho}$ are conceptually the same.

Durbin and Watson (1950) derive the distribution of DW (conditional on $\mathbf{X}$), something that requires the full set of classical linear model assumptions, including normality of the error terms. Unfortunately, this distribution depends on the values of the independent variables. (It also depends on the sample size, the number of regressors, and whether the regression contains an intercept.) Although some econometrics packages tabulate critical values and p-values for DW, many do not. In any case, they depend on the full set of CLM assumptions.

Several econometrics texts report upper and lower bounds for the critical values that depend on the desired significance level, the alternative hypothesis, the number of observations, and the number of regressors. (We assume that an intercept is included in the model.) Usually, the DW test is computed for the alternative

$$H_1: \rho > 0. \qquad [12.17]$$

From the approximation in (12.16), $\hat{\rho} \approx 0$ implies that $DW \approx 2$, and $\hat{\rho} = 0$ implies that $DW < 2$. Thus, to reject the null hypothesis (12.12) in favor of (12.17), we are looking for a value of DW that is significantly less than two. Unfortunately, because of the problems in obtaining the null distribution of DW, we must compare DW with two sets of critical values. These are usually labeled as d_U (for *upper*) and d_L (for *lower*). If $DW < d_L$, then we reject H_0 in favor of (12.17); if $DW > d_U$, we fail to reject H_0. If $d_L \leq DW \leq d_U$, the test is inconclusive.

As an example, if we choose a 5% significance level with $n = 45$ and $k = 4$, $d_U = 1.720$ and $d_L = 1.336$ [see Savin and White (1977)]. If $DW < 1.336$, we reject the null of no serial correlation at the 5% level; if $DW > 1.72$, we fail to reject H_0; if $1.336 \leq DW \leq 1.72$, the test is inconclusive.

In Example 12.1, for the static Phillips curve, DW is computed to be $DW = .80$. We can obtain the lower 1% critical value from Savin and White (1977) for $k = 1$ and $n = 50$: $d_L = 1.32$. Therefore, we reject the null of no serial correlation against the alternative of positive serial correlation at the 1% level. (Using the previous t test, we can conclude that the p-value equals zero to three decimal places.) For the expectations augmented Phillips curve, $DW = 1.77$, which is well within the fail-to-reject region at even the 5% level ($d_U = 1.59$).

The fact that an exact sampling distribution for DW can be tabulated is the only advantage that DW has over the t test from (12.14). Given that the tabulated critical values are exactly valid only under the full set of CLM assumptions and that they can lead to a wide inconclusive region, the practical disadvantages of the *DW* statistic are substantial. The *t* statistic from (12.14) is simple to compute and asymptotically valid without normally distributed errors. The *t* statistic is also valid in the presence of heteroskedasticity that depends on the x_{tj}. Plus, it is easy to make it robust to any form of heteroskedasticity.

12-2c Testing for AR(1) Serial Correlation without Strictly Exogenous Regressors

When the explanatory variables are not strictly exogenous, so that one or more x_{tj} are correlated with u_{t-1}, neither the *t* test from regression (12.14) nor the Durbin-Watson statistic are valid, even in large samples. The leading case of nonstrictly exogenous regressors occurs when the model contains a lagged dependent variable: y_{t-1} and u_{t-1} are obviously correlated. Durbin (1970) suggested two alternatives to the *DW* statistic when the model contains a lagged dependent variable and the other regressors are nonrandom (or, more generally, strictly exogenous). The first is called *Durbin's* h *statistic*. This statistic has a practical drawback in that it cannot always be computed, so we do not cover it here.

Durbin's alternative statistic is simple to compute and is valid when there are any number of nonstrictly exogenous explanatory variables. The test also works if the explanatory variables happen to be strictly exogenous.

Testing for Serial Correlation with General Regressors:

(i) Run the OLS regression of y_t on $x_{t1}, \ldots, x_{tk}$ and obtain the OLS residuals, $\hat{u}_t$, for all $t = 1, 2, \ldots, n$.

(ii) Run the regression of

$$\hat{u}_t \text{ on } x_{t1}, x_{t2}, \ldots, x_{tk}, \hat{u}_{t-1}, \text{ for all } t = 2, \ldots, n \qquad \text{[12.18]}$$

to obtain the coefficient $\hat{\rho}$ on $\hat{u}_{t-1}$ and its *t* statistic, $t_{\hat{\rho}}$.

(iii) Use $t_{\hat{\rho}}$ to test H_0: $\rho = 0$ against H_1: $\rho \neq 0$ in the usual way (or use a one-sided alternative).

In equation (12.18), we regress the OLS residuals on *all* independent variables, including an intercept, and the lagged residual. The *t* statistic on the lagged residual is a valid test of (12.12) in the AR(1) model (12.13) [when we add $\text{Var}(u_t|\mathbf{x}_t, u_{t-1}) = \sigma^2$ under H_0]. Any number of lagged dependent variables may appear among the x_{tj}, and other nonstrictly exogenous explanatory variables are allowed as well.

The inclusion of $x_{t1}, \ldots, x_{tk}$ explicitly allows for each x_{tj} to be correlated with u_{t-1}, and this ensures that $t_{\hat{\rho}}$ has an approximate *t* distribution in large samples. The *t* statistic from (12.14) ignores possible correlation between x_{tj} and u_{t-1}, so it is not valid without strictly exogenous regressors. Incidentally, because $\hat{u}_t = y_t - \hat{\beta}_0 - \hat{\beta}_1 x_{t1} - \ldots - \hat{\beta}_k x_{tk}$, it can be shown that the *t* statistic on $\hat{u}_{t-1}$ is the same if y_t is used in place of $\hat{u}_t$ as the dependent variable in (12.18).

The *t* statistic from (12.18) is easily made robust to heteroskedasticity of unknown form [in particular, when $\text{Var}(u_t|\mathbf{x}_t, u_{t-1})$ is not constant]: just use the heteroskedasticity-robust *t* statistic on $\hat{u}_{t-1}$.

| **EXAMPLE 12.2** | **Testing for AR(1) Serial Correlation in the Minimum Wage Equation** |

In Chapter 10 (see Example 10.9), we estimated the effect of the minimum wage on the Puerto Rican employment rate. We now check whether the errors appear to contain serial correlation, using the test that does not assume strict exogeneity of the minimum wage or GNP variables. [We add the log of Puerto Rican real GNP to equation (10.38), as in Computer Exercise C3 in Chapter 10.] We are assuming that the underlying stochastic processes are weakly dependent, but we allow them to contain a linear time trend by including *t* in the regression.

Letting $\hat{u}_t$ denote the OLS residuals, we run the regression of

$$\hat{u}_t \text{ on } \log(mincov_t), \log(prgnp_t), \log(usgnp_t), t, \text{ and } \hat{u}_{t-1},$$

using the 37 available observations. The estimated coefficient on $\hat{u}_{t-1}$ is $\hat{\rho} = .481$ with $t = 2.89$ (two-sided p-value $= .007$). Therefore, there is strong evidence of AR(1) serial correlation in the errors, which means the t statistics for the $\hat{\beta}_j$ that we obtained before are not valid for inference. Remember, though, the $\hat{\beta}_j$ are still consistent if u_t is contemporaneously uncorrelated with each explanatory variable. Incidentally, if we use regression (12.14) instead, we obtain $\hat{\rho} = .417$ and $t = 2.63$, so the outcome of the test is similar in this case.

12-2d Testing for Higher Order Serial Correlation

The test from (12.18) is easily extended to higher orders of serial correlation. For example, suppose that we wish to test

$$H_0: \rho_1 = 0, \rho_2 = 0 \qquad [12.19]$$

in the AR(2) model,

$$u_t = \rho_1 u_{t-1} + \rho_2 u_{t-2} + e_t.$$

This alternative model of serial correlation allows us to test for *second order serial correlation*. As always, we estimate the model by OLS and obtain the OLS residuals, $\hat{u}_t$. Then, we can run the regression of

$$\hat{u}_t \text{ on } x_{t1}, x_{t2}, \ldots, x_{tk}, \hat{u}_{t-1}, \text{ and } \hat{u}_{t-2}, \text{ for all } t = 3, \ldots, n,$$

to obtain the F test for joint significance of $\hat{u}_{t-1}$ and $\hat{u}_{t-2}$. If these two lags are jointly significant at a small enough level, say, 5%, then we reject (12.19) and conclude that the errors are serially correlated.

More generally, we can test for serial correlation in the autoregressive model of order q:

$$u_t = \rho_1 u_{t-1} + \rho_2 u_{t-2} + \ldots + \rho_q u_{t-q} + e_t. \qquad [12.20]$$

The null hypothesis is

$$H_0: \rho_1 = 0, \rho_2 = 0, \ldots, \rho_q = 0. \qquad [12.21]$$

Testing for AR(q) Serial Correlation:

(i) Run the OLS regression of y_t on $x_{t1}, \ldots, x_{tk}$ and obtain the OLS residuals, $\hat{u}_t$, for all $t = 1, 2, \ldots, n$.

(ii) Run the regression of

$$\hat{u}_t \text{ on } x_{t1}, x_{t2}, \ldots, x_{tk}, \hat{u}_{t-1}, \hat{u}_{t-2}, \ldots, \hat{u}_{t-q}, \text{ for all } t = (q+1), \ldots, n. \qquad [12.22]$$

(iii) Compute the F test for joint significance of $\hat{u}_{t-1}, \hat{u}_{t-2}, \ldots, \hat{u}_{t-q}$ in (12.22). [The F statistic with y_t as the dependent variable in (12.22) can also be used, as it gives an identical answer.]

If the x_{tj} are assumed to be strictly exogenous, so that each x_{tj} is uncorrelated with $u_{t-1}, u_{t-2}, \ldots, u_{t-q}$, then the x_{tj} can be omitted from (12.22). Including the x_{tj} in the regression makes the test valid with or without the strict exogeneity assumption. The test requires the homoskedasticity assumption

$$\text{Var}(u_t | \mathbf{x}_t, u_{t-1}, \ldots, u_{t-q}) = \sigma^2. \qquad [12.23]$$

A heteroskedasticity-robust version can be computed as described in Chapter 8.

An alternative to computing the F test is to use the Lagrange multiplier (LM) form of the statistic. (We covered the LM statistic for testing exclusion restrictions in Chapter 5 for cross-sectional analysis.) The LM statistic for testing (12.21) is simply

$$LM = (n - q)R_{\hat{u}}^2,$$ [12.24]

where $R_{\hat{u}}^2$ is just the usual R-squared from regression (12.22). Under the null hypothesis, $LM \overset{a}{\sim} \chi_q^2$. This is usually called the **Breusch-Godfrey test** for AR(q) serial correlation. The LM statistic also requires (12.23), but it can be made robust to heteroskedasticity. [For details, see Wooldridge (1991b).]

EXAMPLE 12.3   **Testing for AR(3) Serial Correlation**

In the event study of the barium chloride industry (see Example 10.5), we used monthly data, so we may wish to test for higher orders of serial correlation. For illustration purposes, we test for AR(3) serial correlation in the errors underlying equation (10.22). Using regression (12.22), we find the F statistic for joint significance of $\hat{u}_{t-1}$, $\hat{u}_{t-2}$, and $\hat{u}_{t-3}$ is $F = 5.12$. Originally, we had $n = 131$, and we lose three observations in the auxiliary regression (12.22). Because we estimate 10 parameters in (12.22) for this example, the df in the F statistic are 3 and 118. The p-value of the F statistic is .0023, so there is strong evidence of AR(3) serial correlation.

With quarterly or monthly data that have not been seasonally adjusted, we sometimes wish to test for seasonal forms of serial correlation. For example, with quarterly data, we might postulate the autoregressive model

$$u_t = \rho_4 u_{t-4} + e_t.$$ [12.25]

From the AR(1) serial correlation tests, it is pretty clear how to proceed. When the regressors are strictly exogenous, we can use a t test on $\hat{u}_{t-4}$ in the regression of

$$\hat{u}_t \text{ on } \hat{u}_{t-4}, \text{ for all } t = 5, \ldots, n.$$

A modification of the Durbin-Watson statistic is also available [see Wallis (1972)]. When the x_{tj} are not strictly exogenous, we can use the regression in (12.18), with $\hat{u}_{t-4}$ replacing $\hat{u}_{t-1}$.

> **EXPLORING FURTHER 12.3**
>
> Suppose you have quarterly data and you want to test for the presence of first order or fourth order serial correlation. With strictly exogenous regressors, how would you proceed?

In Example 12.3, the data are monthly and are not seasonally adjusted. Therefore, it makes sense to test for correlation between u_t and u_{t-12}. A regression of $\hat{u}_t$ on $\hat{u}_{t-12}$ yields $\hat{\rho}_{12} = -.187$ and p-value = .028, so there is evidence of *negative* seasonal autocorrelation. (Including the regressors changes things only modestly: $\hat{\rho}_{12} = -.170$ and p-value = .052.) This is somewhat unusual and does not have an obvious explanation.

12-3 Correcting for Serial Correlation with Strictly Exogenous Regressors

If we detect serial correlation after applying one of the tests in Section 12-2, we have to do something about it. If our goal is to estimate a model with complete dynamics, we need to respecify the model. In applications where our goal is not to estimate a fully dynamic model, we need to find a way to carry out statistical inference: as we saw in Section 12-1, the usual OLS test statistics are no longer valid. In this section, we begin with the important case of AR(1) serial correlation. The traditional approach to this problem assumes fixed regressors. What are actually needed are strictly exogenous regressors. Therefore, at a minimum, we should not use these corrections when the explanatory variables include lagged dependent variables.

12-3a Obtaining the Best Linear Unbiased Estimator in the AR(1) Model

We assume the Gauss-Markov assumptions TS.1 through TS.4, but we relax Assumption TS.5. In particular, we assume that the errors follow the AR(1) model

$$u_t = \rho u_{t-1} + e_t, \text{ for all } t = 1, 2, \dots. \qquad [12.26]$$

Remember that Assumption TS.3 implies that u_t has a zero mean conditional on **X**. In the following analysis, we let the conditioning on **X** be implied in order to simplify the notation. Thus, we write the variance of u_t as

$$\text{Var}(u_t) = \sigma_e^2/(1 - \rho^2). \qquad [12.27]$$

For simplicity, consider the case with a single explanatory variable:

$$y_t = \beta_0 + \beta_1 x_t + u_t, \text{ for all } t = 1, 2, \dots, n.$$

Because the problem in this equation is serial correlation in the u_t, it makes sense to transform the equation to eliminate the serial correlation. For $t \geq 2$, we write

$$y_{t-1} = \beta_0 + \beta_1 x_{t-1} + u_{t-1}$$
$$y_t = \beta_0 + \beta_1 x_t + u_t.$$

Now, if we multiply this first equation by ρ and subtract it from the second equation, we get

$$y_t - \rho y_{t-1} = (1 - \rho)\beta_0 + \beta_1(x_t - \rho x_{t-1}) + e_t, t \geq 2,$$

where we have used the fact that $e_t = u_t - \rho u_{t-1}$. We can write this as

$$\tilde{y}_1 = (1 - \rho)\beta_0 + \beta_1 \tilde{x}_t + e_t, t \geq 2, \qquad [12.28]$$

where

$$\tilde{y}_1 = y_t - \rho y_{t-1}, \tilde{x}_t = x_t - \rho x_{t-1} \qquad [12.29]$$

are called the **quasi-differenced data**. (If $\rho = 1$, these are differenced data, but remember we are assuming $|\rho| < 1$.) The error terms in (12.28) are serially uncorrelated; in fact, this equation satisfies all of the Gauss-Markov assumptions. This means that, if we knew ρ, we could estimate β_0 and β_1 by regressing $\tilde{y}_t$ on $\tilde{x}_t$, provided we divide the estimated intercept by $(1 - \rho)$.

The OLS estimators from (12.28) are not quite BLUE because they do not use the first time period. This is easily fixed by writing the equation for $t = 1$ as

$$y_1 = \beta_0 + \beta_1 x_1 + u_1. \qquad [12.30]$$

Since each e_t is uncorrelated with u_1, we can add (12.30) to (12.28) and still have serially uncorrelated errors. However, using (12.27), $\text{Var}(u_1) = \sigma_e^2/(1 - \rho^2) > \sigma_e^2 = \text{Var}(e_t)$. [Equation (12.27) clearly does not hold when $|\rho| \geq 1$, which is why we assume the stability condition.] Thus, we must multiply (12.30) by $(1 - \rho^2)^{1/2}$ to get errors with the same variance:

$$(1 - \rho^2)^{1/2}y_1 = (1 - \rho^2)^{1/2}\beta_0 + \beta_1(1 - \rho^2)^{1/2}x_1 + (1 - \rho^2)^{1/2}u_1$$

or

$$\tilde{y}_1 = (1 - \rho^2)^{1/2}\beta_0 + \beta_1\tilde{x}_1 + \tilde{u}_1, \qquad [12.31]$$

where $\tilde{u}_1 = (1 - \rho^2)^{1/2}u_1$, $\tilde{y}_1 = (1 - \rho^2)^{1/2}y_1$, and so on. The error in (12.31) has variance $\text{Var}(\tilde{u}_1) = (1 - \rho^2)\text{Var}(u_1) = \sigma_e^2$, so we can use (12.31) along with (12.28) in an OLS regression. This gives the BLUE estimators of β_0 and β_1 under Assumptions TS.1 through TS.4 and the AR(1) model for u_t. This is another example of a *generalized least squares* (or GLS) estimator. We saw other GLS estimators in the context of heteroskedasticity in Chapter 8.

Adding more regressors changes very little. For $t \geq 2$, we use the equation

$$\tilde{y}_t = (1 - \rho)\beta_0 + \beta_1\tilde{x}_{t1} + \ldots + \beta_k\tilde{x}_{tk} + e_t, \qquad [12.32]$$

where $\tilde{x}_{tj} = x_{tj} - \rho x_{t-1,j}$. For $t = 1$, we have $\tilde{y}_1 = (1 - \rho^2)^{1/2}y_1$, $\tilde{x}_{1j} = (1 - \rho^2)^{1/2}x_{1j}$, and the intercept is $(1 - \rho^2)^{1/2}\beta_0$. For given ρ, it is fairly easy to transform the data and to carry out OLS. Unless $\rho = 0$, the GLS estimator, that is, OLS on the transformed data, will generally be different from the original OLS estimator. The GLS estimator turns out to be BLUE, and, since the errors in the transformed equation are serially uncorrelated and homoskedastic, t and F statistics from the transformed equation are valid (at least asymptotically, and exactly if the errors e_t are normally distributed).

12-3b Feasible GLS Estimation with AR(1) Errors

The problem with the GLS estimator is that ρ is rarely known in practice. However, we already know how to get a consistent estimator of ρ: we simply regress the OLS residuals on their lagged counterparts, exactly as in equation (12.14). Next, we use this estimate, $\hat{\rho}$, in place of ρ to obtain the quasi-differenced variables. We then use OLS on the equation

$$\tilde{y}_t = \beta_0\tilde{x}_{t0} + \beta_1\tilde{x}_{t1} + \ldots + \beta_k\tilde{x}_{tk} + error_t, \qquad [12.33]$$

where $\tilde{x}_{t0} = (1 - \hat{\rho})$ for $t \geq 2$, and $\tilde{x}_{10} = (1 - \hat{\rho}^2)^{1/2}$. This results in the **feasible GLS(FGLS)** estimator of the β_j. The error term in (12.33) contains e_t and also the terms involving the estimation error in $\hat{\rho}$. Fortunately, the estimation error in $\hat{\rho}$ does not affect the asymptotic distribution of the FGLS estimators.

Feasible GLS Estimation of the AR(1) Model:

    (i) Run the OLS regression of y_t on $x_{t1}, \ldots, x_{tk}$ and obtain the OLS residuals, $\hat{u}_t$, $t = 1, 2, \ldots, n$.

    (ii) Run the regression in equation (12.14) and obtain $\hat{\rho}$.

    (iii) Apply OLS to equation (12.33) to estimate $\beta_0, \beta_1, \ldots, \beta_k$. The usual standard errors, t statistics, and F statistics are asymptotically valid.

The cost of using $\hat{\rho}$ in place of ρ is that the FGLS estimator has no tractable finite sample properties. In particular, it is not unbiased, although it is consistent when the data are weakly dependent. Further, even if e_t in (12.32) is normally distributed, the t and F statistics are only approximately t and F distributed because of the estimation error in $\hat{\rho}$. This is fine for most purposes, although we must be careful with small sample sizes.

Since the FGLS estimator is not unbiased, we certainly cannot say it is BLUE. Nevertheless, it is asymptotically more efficient than the OLS estimator when the AR(1) model for serial correlation holds (and the explanatory variables are strictly exogenous). Again, this statement assumes that the time series are weakly dependent.

There are several names for FGLS estimation of the AR(1) model that come from different methods of estimating ρ and different treatment of the first observation. **Cochrane-Orcutt (CO) estimation** omits the first observation and uses $\hat{\rho}$ from (12.14), whereas **Prais-Winsten (PW) estimation** uses the first observation in the previously suggested way. Asymptotically, it makes no difference whether or not the first observation is used, but many time series samples are small, so the differences can be notable in applications.

In practice, both the Cochrane-Orcutt and Prais-Winsten methods are used in an iterative scheme. That is, once the FGLS estimator is found using $\hat{\rho}$ from (12.14), we can compute a new set of residuals, obtain a new estimator of ρ from (12.14), transform the data using the new estimate of ρ, and estimate (12.33) by OLS. We can repeat the whole process many times, until the estimate of ρ changes by very little from the previous iteration. Many regression packages implement an iterative procedure automatically, so there is no additional work for us. It is difficult to say whether more than one iteration helps. It seems to be helpful in some cases, but, theoretically, the large-sample properties of the iterated estimator are the same as the estimator that uses only the first iteration. For details on these and other methods, see Davidson and MacKinnon (1993, Chapter 10).

EXAMPLE 12.4   **Prais-Winsten Estimation in the Event Study**

Again using the data in BARIUM, we estimate the equation in Example 10.5 using iterated Prais-Winsten estimation. For comparison, we also present the OLS results in Table 12.1.

The coefficients that are statistically significant in the Prais-Winsten estimation do not differ by much from the OLS estimates [in particular, the coefficients on log(*chempi*), log(*rtwex*), and *afdec6*]. It is not surprising for statistically insignificant coefficients to change, perhaps markedly, across different estimation methods.

Notice how the standard errors in the second column are uniformly higher than the standard errors in column (1). This is common. The Prais-Winsten standard errors account for serial correlation; the OLS standard errors do not. As we saw in Section 12-1, the OLS standard errors usually understate the actual sampling variation in the OLS estimates and should not be relied upon when significant serial correlation is present. Therefore, the effect on Chinese imports after the International Trade Commission's decision is now less statistically significant than we thought ($t_{afdec6} = -1.69$).

Finally, an R-squared is reported for the PW estimation that is well below the R-squared for the OLS estimation in this case. However, these R-squareds should not be compared. For OLS, the R-squared, as usual, is based on the regression with the untransformed dependent and independent variables. For PW, the R-squared comes from the final regression of the *transformed* dependent variable on the transformed independent variables. It is not clear what this R^2 is actually measuring; nevertheless, it is traditionally reported.

TABLE 12.1 Dependent Variable: log(*chnimp*)		
Coefficient	OLS	Prais-Winsten
log(*chempi*)	3.12	2.94
	(0.48)	(0.63)
log(*gas*)	.196	1.05
	(.907)	(0.98)
log(*rtwex*)	.983	1.13
	(.400)	(0.51)
befile6	.060	−.016
	(.261)	(.322)
affile6	−.032	−.033
	(.264)	(.322)
afdec6	−.565	−.577
	(.286)	(.342)
intercept	−17.80	−37.08
	(21.05)	(22.78)
$\hat{\rho}$	—	.293
Observations	131	131
R-squared	.305	.202

12-3c Comparing OLS and FGLS

In some applications of the Cochrane-Orcutt or Prais-Winsten methods, the FGLS estimates differ in practically important ways from the OLS estimates. (This was not the case in Example 12.4.) Typically, this has been interpreted as a verification of FGLS's superiority over OLS. Unfortunately, things are not so simple. To see why, consider the regression model

$$y_t = \beta_0 + \beta_1 x_t + u_t,$$

where the time series processes are stationary. Now, assuming that the law of large numbers holds, consistency of OLS for β_1 holds if

$$\text{Cov}(x_t, u_t) = 0. \qquad \qquad \textbf{[12.34]}$$

Earlier, we asserted that FGLS was consistent under the strict exogeneity assumption, which is more restrictive than (12.34). In fact, it can be shown that the weakest assumption that must hold for FGLS to be consistent, *in addition to* (12.34), is that the sum of x_{t-1} and x_{t+1} is uncorrelated with u_t:

$$\text{Cov}[(x_{t-1} + x_{t+1}), u_t] = 0. \qquad \qquad \textbf{[12.35]}$$

Practically speaking, consistency of FGLS requires u_t to be uncorrelated with x_{t-1}, x_t, and x_{t+1}.

How can we show that condition (12.35) is needed along with (12.34)? The argument is simple if we assume ρ is known and drop the first time period, as in Cochrane-Orcutt. The argument when we use $\hat{\rho}$ is technically harder and yields no additional insights. Since one observation cannot affect the asymptotic properties of an estimator, dropping it does not affect the argument. Now, with known ρ, the GLS estimator uses $x_t - \rho x_{t-1}$ as the regressor in an equation where $u_t - \rho u_{t-1}$ is the error. From Theorem 11.1, we know the key condition for consistency of OLS is that the error and the regressor are uncorrelated. In this case, we need $E[(x_t - \rho x_{t-1})(u_t - \rho u_{t-1})] = 0$. If we expand the expectation, we get

$$E[(x_t - \rho x_{t-1})(u_t - \rho u_{t-1})] = E(x_t u_t) - \rho E(x_{t-1} u_t) - \rho E(x_t u_{t-1}) + \rho^2 E(x_{t-1} u_{t-1})$$
$$= -\rho[E(x_{t-1} u_t) + E(x_t u_{t-1})]$$

because $E(x_t u_t) = E(x_{t-1} u_{t-1}) = 0$ by assumption (12.34). Now, under stationarity, $E(x_t u_{t-1}) = E(x_{t+1} u_t)$ because we are just shifting the time index one period forward. Therefore,

$$E(x_{t-1} u_t) + E(x_t u_{t-1}) = E[(x_{t-1} + x_{t+1}) u_t],$$

and the last expectation is the covariance in equation (12.35) because $E(u_t) = 0$. We have shown that (12.35) is necessary along with (12.34) for GLS to be consistent for β_1. [Of course, if $\rho = 0$, we do not need (12.35) because we are back to doing OLS.]

Our derivation shows that OLS and FGLS might give significantly different estimates because (12.35) fails. In this case, OLS—which is still consistent under (12.34)—is preferred to FGLS (which is inconsistent). If x has a lagged effect on y, or x_{t+1} reacts to changes in u_t, FGLS can produce misleading results.

Because OLS and FGLS are different estimation procedures, we never expect them to give the same estimates. If they provide similar estimates of the β_j, then FGLS is preferred if there is evidence of serial correlation because the estimator is more efficient and the FGLS test statistics are at least asymptotically valid. A more difficult problem arises when there are practical differences in the OLS and FGLS estimates: it is hard to determine whether such differences are statistically significant. The general method proposed by Hausman (1978) can be used, but it is beyond the scope of this text.

The next example gives a case where OLS and FGLS are different in practically important ways.

EXAMPLE 12.5	**Static Phillips Curve**

Table 12.2 presents OLS and iterated Prais-Winsten estimates of the static Phillips curve from Example 10.1, using the observations through 1996.

TABLE 12.2 Dependent Variable: *inf*		
Coefficient	OLS	Prais-Winsten
unem	.468	−.716
	(.289)	(.313)
intercept	1.424	8.296
	(1.719)	(2.231)
$\hat{\rho}$	———	.781
Observations	49	49
R-squared	.053	.136

The coefficient of interest is on *unem*, and it differs markedly between PW and OLS. Because the PW estimate is consistent with the inflation-unemployment tradeoff, our tendency is to focus on the PW estimates. In fact, these estimates are fairly close to what is obtained by first differencing both *inf* and *unem* (see Computer Exercise C4 in Chapter 11), which makes sense because the quasi-differencing used in PW with $\hat{\rho} = .781$ is similar to first differencing. It may just be that *inf* and *unem* are not related in levels, but they have a negative relationship in first differences.

Examples like the static Phillips curve can pose difficult problems for empirical researchers. On the one hand, if we are truly interested in a static relationship, and if unemployment and inflation are I(0) processes, then OLS produces consistent estimators without additional assumptions. But it could be that unemployment, inflation, or both have unit roots, in which case OLS need not have its usual desirable properties; we discuss this further in Chapter 18. In Example 12.5, FGLS gives more economically sensible estimates; because it is similar to first differencing, FGLS has the advantage of (approximately) eliminating unit roots.

12-3d Correcting for Higher Order Serial Correlation

It is also possible to correct for higher orders of serial correlation. A general treatment is given in Harvey (1990). Here, we illustrate the approach for AR(2) serial correlation:

$$u_t = \rho_1 u_{t-1} + \rho_2 u_{t-2} + e_t,$$

where $\{e_t\}$ satisfies the assumptions stated for the AR(1) model. The stability conditions are more complicated now. They can be shown to be [see Harvey (1990)]

$$\rho_2 > -1, \rho_2 - \rho_1 < 1, \text{ and } \rho_1 + \rho_2 < 1.$$

For example, the model is stable if $\rho_1 = .8$ and $\rho_2 = -.3$; the model is unstable if $\rho_1 = .7$ and $\rho_2 = .4$. Assuming the stability conditions hold, we can obtain the transformation that eliminates the serial correlation. In the simple regression model, this is easy when $t > 2$:

$$y_t - \rho_1 y_{t-1} - \rho_2 y_{t-2} = \beta_0(1 - \rho_1 - \rho_2) + \beta_1(x_t - \rho_1 x_{t-1} - \rho_2 x_{t-2}) + e_t$$

or

$$\tilde{y}_t = \beta_0(1 - \rho_1 - \rho_2) + \beta_1 \tilde{x}_t + e_t, t = 3, 4, \ldots, n. \qquad [12.36]$$

If we know ρ_1 and ρ_2, we can easily estimate this equation by OLS after obtaining the transformed variables. Since we rarely know ρ_1 and ρ_2, we have to estimate them. As usual, we can use the OLS residuals, $\hat{u}_t$: obtain $\hat{\rho}_1$ and $\hat{\rho}_2$ from the regression of

$$\hat{u}_t \text{ on } \hat{u}_{t-1}, \hat{u}_{t-2}, t = 3, \ldots, n.$$

[This is the same regression used to test for AR(2) serial correlation with strictly exogenous regressors.] Then, we use $\hat{\rho}_1$ and $\hat{\rho}_2$ in place of ρ_1 and ρ_2 to obtain the transformed variables. This gives one version of the FGLS estimator. If we have multiple explanatory variables, then each one is transformed by $\tilde{x}_{tj} = x_{tj} - \hat{\rho}_1 x_{t-1,j} - \hat{\rho}_2 x_{t-2,j}$, when $t > 2$.

The treatment of the first two observations is a little tricky. It can be shown that the dependent variable and each independent variable (including the intercept) should be transformed by

$$\tilde{z}_1 = \{(1 + \rho_2)[(1 - \rho_2)^2 - \rho_1^2]/(1 - \rho_2)\}^{1/2} z_1$$
$$\tilde{z}_2 = (1 - \rho_2^2)^{1/2} z_2 - [\rho_1(1 - \rho_1^2)^{1/2}/(1 - \rho_2)] z_1,$$

where z_1 and z_2 denote either the dependent or an independent variable at $t = 1$ and $t = 2$, respectively. We will not derive these transformations. Briefly, they eliminate the serial correlation between the first two observations and make their error variances equal to σ_e^2.

Fortunately, econometrics packages geared toward time series analysis easily estimate models with general AR(q) errors; we rarely need to directly compute the transformed variables ourselves.

12-4 Differencing and Serial Correlation

In Chapter 11, we presented differencing as a transformation for making an integrated process weakly dependent. There is another way to see the merits of differencing when dealing with highly persistent data. Suppose that we start with the simple regression model:

$$y_t = \beta_0 + \beta_1 x_t + u_t, t = 1, 2, \ldots, \qquad [12.37]$$

where u_t follows the AR(1) process in (12.26). As we mentioned in Section 11-3, and as we will discuss more fully in Chapter 18, the usual OLS inference procedures can be very misleading when the variables y_t and x_t are integrated of order one, or I(1). In the extreme case where the errors $\{u_t\}$ in (12.37) follow a random walk, the equation makes no sense because, among other things, the variance of u_t grows with t. It is more logical to difference the equation:

$$\Delta y_t = \beta_1 \Delta x_t + \Delta u_t, t = 2, \ldots, n. \qquad [12.38]$$

If u_t follows a random walk, then $e_t \equiv \Delta u_t$ has zero mean and a constant variance and is serially uncorrelated. Thus, assuming that e_t and Δx_t are uncorrelated, we can estimate (12.38) by OLS, where we lose the first observation.

Even if u_t does not follow a random walk, but ρ is positive and large, first differencing is often a good idea: it will eliminate most of the serial correlation. Of course, equation (12.38) is different from (12.37), but at least we can have more faith in the OLS standard errors and t statistics in (12.38). Allowing for multiple explanatory variables does not change anything.

EXAMPLE 12.6 | **Differencing the Interest Rate Equation**

In Example 10.2, we estimated an equation relating the three-month T-bill rate to inflation and the federal deficit [see equation (10.15)]. If we obtain the residuals obtained from estimating (10.15) and regress them on a single lag, we obtain $\hat{\rho} = .623(.110)$, which is large and very statistically significant. Therefore, at a minimum, serial correlation is a problem in this equation.

If we difference the data and run the regression, we obtain

$$\Delta i3_t = .042 + .149 \ \Delta inf_t - .181 \ \Delta def_t + \hat{e}_t$$
$$(.171) \ (.092) \qquad (.148) \qquad \qquad \textbf{[12.39]}$$
$$n = 55, R^2 = .176, \bar{R}^2 = .145.$$

The coefficients from this regression are very different from the equation in levels, suggesting either that the explanatory variables are not strictly exogenous or that one or more of the variables has a unit root. In fact, the correlation between $i3_t$ and $i3_{t-1}$ is about .885, which may indicate a problem with interpreting (10.15) as a meaningful regression. Plus, the regression in differences has essentially no serial correlation: a regression of $\hat{e}_t$ on $\hat{e}_{t-1}$ gives $\hat{\rho} = .072$ (.134). Because first differencing eliminates possible unit roots as well as serial correlation, we probably have more faith in the estimates and standard errors from (12.39) than (10.15). The equation in differences shows that annual changes in interest rates are only weakly, positively related to annual changes in inflation, and the coefficient on Δdef_t is actually negative (though not statistically significant at even the 20% significance level against a two-sided alternative).

> **EXPLORING FURTHER 12.4**
>
> Suppose after estimating a model by OLS that you estimate ρ from regression (12.14) and you obtain $\hat{\rho} = .92$. What would you do about this?

As we explained in Chapter 11, the decision of whether or not to difference is a tough one. But this discussion points out another benefit of differencing, which is that it removes serial correlation. We will come back to this issue in Chapter 18.

12-5 Serial Correlation–Robust Inference after OLS

In recent years, it has become more popular to estimate models by OLS but to correct the standard errors for fairly arbitrary forms of serial correlation (and heteroskedasticity). Even though we know OLS will be inefficient, there are some good reasons for taking this approach. First, the explanatory variables may not be strictly exogenous. In this case, FGLS is not even consistent, let alone efficient. Second, in most applications of FGLS, the errors are assumed to follow an AR(1) model. It may be better to compute standard errors for the OLS estimates that are robust to more general forms of serial correlation.

To get the idea, consider equation (12.4), which is the variance of the OLS slope estimator in a simple regression model with AR(1) errors. We can estimate this variance very simply by plugging in our standard estimators of ρ and σ^2. The only problems with this are that it assumes the AR(1) model holds and also assumes homoskedasticity. It is possible to relax both of these assumptions.

A general treatment of standard errors that are both heteroskedasticity- and serial correlation–robust is given in Davidson and MacKinnon (1993). Here, we provide a simple method to compute the robust standard error of any OLS coefficient.

Our treatment here follows Wooldridge (1989). Consider the standard multiple linear regression model

$$y_t = \beta_0 + \beta_1 x_{t1} + \ldots + \beta_k x_{tk} + u_t, t = 1, 2, \ldots, n, \qquad \textbf{[12.40]}$$

which we have estimated by OLS. For concreteness, we are interested in obtaining a serial correlation–robust standard error for $\hat{\beta}_1$. This turns out to be fairly easy. Write x_{t1} as a linear function of the remaining independent variables and an error term,

$$x_{t1} = \delta_0 + \delta_2 x_{t2} + \ldots + \delta_k x_{tk} + r_t,$$

where the error r_t has zero mean and is uncorrelated with $x_{t2}, x_{t3}, \ldots, x_{tk}$.

Then, it can be shown that the asymptotic variance of the OLS estimator $\hat{\beta}_1$ is

$$\text{AVar}(\hat{\beta}_1) = \left(\sum_{t=1}^{n} \text{E}(r_t^2)\right)^{-2} \text{Var}\left(\sum_{t=1}^{n} r_t u_t\right).$$

Under the no serial correlation Assumption TS.5′, $\{a_t \equiv r_t u_t\}$ is serially uncorrelated, so either the usual OLS standard errors (under homoskedasticity) or the heteroskedasticity-robust standard errors will be valid. But if TS.5′ fails, our expression for $\text{AVar}(\hat{\beta}_1)$ must account for the correlation between a_t and a_s, when $t \neq s$. In practice, it is common to assume that, once the terms are farther apart than a few periods, the correlation is essentially zero. Remember that under weak dependence, the correlation must be approaching zero, so this is a reasonable approach.

Following the general framework of Newey and West (1987), Wooldridge (1989) shows that $\text{AVar}(\hat{\beta}_1)$ can be estimated as follows. Let "$\text{se}(\hat{\beta}_1)$" denote the usual (but incorrect) OLS standard error and let $\hat{\sigma}$ be the usual standard error of the regression (or root mean squared error) from estimating (12.40) by OLS. Let $\hat{r}_t$ denote the residuals from the auxiliary regression of

$$x_{t1} \text{ on } x_{t2}, x_{t3}, \ldots, x_{tk} \tag{12.41}$$

(including a constant, as usual). For a chosen integer $g > 0$, define

$$\hat{\nu} = \sum_{t=1}^{n} \hat{a}_t^2 + 2\sum_{h=1}^{g}\left[1 - h/(g+1)\right]\left(\sum_{t=h+1}^{n} \hat{a}_t \hat{a}_{t-h}\right), \tag{12.42}$$

where

$$\hat{a}_t = \hat{r}_t \hat{u}_t, \ t = 1, 2, \ldots, n.$$

This looks somewhat complicated, but in practice it is easy to obtain. The integer g in (12.42) controls how much serial correlation we are allowing in computing the standard error. Once we have $\hat{\nu}$ the **serial correlation–robust standard error** of $\hat{\beta}_1$ is simply

$$\text{se}(\hat{\beta}_1) = [\text{"se}(\hat{\beta}_1)\text{"}/\hat{\sigma}]^2 \sqrt{\hat{\nu}}. \tag{12.43}$$

In other words, we take the usual OLS standard error of $\hat{\beta}_1$, divide it by $\hat{\sigma}$, square the result, and then multiply by the square root of $\hat{\nu}$. This can be used to construct confidence intervals and t statistics for $\hat{\beta}_1$.

It is useful to see what $\hat{\nu}$ looks like in some simple cases. When $g = 1$,

$$\hat{\nu} = \sum_{t=1}^{n} \hat{a}_t^2 + \sum_{t=2}^{n} \hat{a}_t \hat{a}_{t-1}, \tag{12.44}$$

and when $g = 2$,

$$\hat{\nu} = \sum_{t=1}^{n} \hat{a}_t^2 + (4/3)\left(\sum_{t=2}^{n} \hat{a}_t \hat{a}_{t-1}\right) + (2/3)\left(\sum_{t=3}^{n} \hat{a}_t \hat{a}_{t-2}\right). \tag{12.45}$$

The larger that g is, the more terms are included to correct for serial correlation. The purpose of the factor $[1 - h/(g+1)]$ in (12.42) is to ensure that $\hat{\nu}$ is in fact nonnegative [Newey and West (1987) verify this]. We clearly need $\hat{\nu} \geq 0$, since $\hat{\nu}$ is estimating a variance and the square root of $\hat{\nu}$ appears in (12.43).

The standard error in (12.43) is also robust to arbitrary heteroskedasticity. (In the time series literature, the serial correlation–robust standard errors are sometimes called *heteroskedasticity and autocorrelation consistent*, or *HAC*, standard errors.) In fact, if we drop the second term in (12.42), then (12.43) becomes the usual heteroskedasticity-robust standard error that we discussed in Chapter 8 (without the degrees of freedom adjustment).

The theory underlying the standard error in (12.43) is technical and somewhat subtle. Remember, we started off by claiming we do not know the form of serial correlation. If this is the case, how can we select the integer g? Theory states that (12.43) works for fairly arbitrary forms of serial correlation, provided g grows with sample size n. The idea is that, with larger sample sizes, we can be more flexible about the amount of correlation in (12.42). There has been much recent work on the relationship between g and n, but we will not go into that here. For annual data, choosing a small g, such as $g = 1$ or $g = 2$, is likely to account for most of the serial correlation. For quarterly or monthly data, g should probably be larger (such as $g = 4$ or 8 for quarterly and $g = 12$ or 24 for monthly), assuming that we have enough data. Newey and West (1987) recommend taking g to be the integer part of $4(n/100)^{2/9}$; others have suggested the integer part of $n^{1/4}$. The Newey-West suggestion is implemented by the econometrics program Eviews®. For, say, $n = 50$ (which is reasonable for annual, postwar data from World War II), $g = 3$. (The integer part of $n^{1/4}$ gives $g = 2$.)

We summarize how to obtain a serial correlation–robust standard error for $\hat{\beta}_1$. Of course, since we can list any independent variable first, the following procedure works for computing a standard error for any slope coefficient.

Serial Correlation–Robust Standard Error for $\hat{\beta}_1$:

(i) Estimate (12.40) by OLS, which yields "se$(\hat{\beta}_1)$", $\hat{\sigma}$, and the OLS residuals $\{\hat{u}_t: t = 1, ..., n\}$.

(ii) Compute the residuals $\{\hat{r}_t: t = 1, ..., n\}$ from the auxiliary regression (12.41). Then, form $\hat{a}_t = \hat{r}_t \hat{u}_t$ (for each t).

(iii) For your choice of g, compute $\hat{v}$ as in (12.42).

(iv) Compute se$(\hat{\beta}_1)$ from (12.43).

Empirically, the serial correlation–robust standard errors are typically larger than the usual OLS standard errors when there is serial correlation. This is true because, in most cases, the errors are positively serially correlated. However, it is possible to have substantial serial correlation in $\{u_t\}$ but to also have similarities in the usual and serial correlation–robust (SC-robust) standard errors of some coefficients: it is the sample autocorrelations of $\hat{a}_t = \hat{r}_t \hat{u}_t$ that determine the robust standard error for $\hat{\beta}_1$.

The use of SC-robust standard errors has somewhat lagged behind the use of standard errors robust only to heteroskedasticity for several reasons. First, large cross sections, where the heteroskedasticity-robust standard errors will have good properties, are more common than large time series. The SC-robust standard errors can be poorly behaved when there is substantial serial correlation and the sample size is small (where small can even be as large as, say, 100). Second, since we must choose the integer g in equation (12.42), computation of the SC-robust standard errors is not automatic. As mentioned earlier, some econometrics packages have automated the selection, but you still have to abide by the choice.

Another important reason that SC-robust standard errors are not yet routinely reported is that, in the presence of severe serial correlation, OLS can be very inefficient, especially in small sample sizes. After performing OLS and correcting the standard errors for serial correlation, we find the coefficients are often insignificant, or at least less significant than they were with the usual OLS standard errors.

If we are confident that the explanatory variables are strictly exogenous, yet are skeptical about the errors following an AR(1) process, we can still get estimators more efficient than OLS by using a standard FGLS estimator, such as Prais-Winsten or Cochrane-Orcutt. With substantial serial correlation, the quasi-differencing transformation used by PW and CO is likely to be better than doing nothing and just using OLS. But, if the errors do not follow an AR(1) model, then the standard errors reported from PW or CO estimation will be incorrect. Nevertheless, we can manually quasi-difference the data after estimating ρ, use pooled OLS on the transformed data, and then use SC-robust standard errors in the transformed equation. Computing an SC-robust standard error after quasi-differencing would ensure that any extra serial correlation is accounted for in statistical inference. In fact, the SC-robust standard errors probably work better after much serial correlation has been eliminated using quasi-differencing [or some other transformation, such as that used for AR(2) serial correlation]. Such an approach is analogous to using weighted least squares in the presence of heteroskedasticity but then computing standard errors that are robust to having the variance function incorrectly specified; see Section 8-4.

The SC-robust standard errors after OLS estimation are most useful when we have doubts about some of the explanatory variables being strictly exogenous, so that methods such as Prais-Winsten and Cochrane-Orcutt are not even consistent. It is also valid to use the SC-robust standard errors in models with lagged dependent variables, assuming, of course, that there is good reason for allowing serial correlation in such models.

EXAMPLE 12.7 **The Puerto Rican Minimum Wage**

We obtain an SC-robust standard error for the minimum wage effect in the Puerto Rican employment equation. In Example 12.2, we found pretty strong evidence of AR(1) serial correlation. As in that example, we use as additional controls log(*usgnp*), log(*prgnp*), and a linear time trend.

The OLS estimate of the elasticity of the employment rate with respect to the minimum wage is $\hat{\beta}_1 = -.2123$, and the usual OLS standard error is "se$(\hat{\beta}_1)$" = .0402. The standard error of the regression is $\hat{\sigma} = .0328$. Further, using the previous procedure with $g = 2$ [see (12.45)], we obtain $\hat{v} = .000805$. This gives the SC-robust standard error as se$(\hat{\beta}_1) = [(.0402/.0328)^2]\sqrt{.000805} \approx .0426$. Interestingly, the robust standard error is only slightly greater than the usual OLS standard error. The robust t statistic is about -4.98, and so the estimated elasticity is still very statistically significant.

For comparison, the iterated PW estimate of β_1 is $-.1477$, with a standard error of .0458. Thus, the FGLS estimate is closer to zero than the OLS estimate, and we might suspect violation of the strict exogeneity assumption. Or, the difference in the OLS and FGLS estimates might be explainable by sampling error. It is very difficult to tell.

Kiefer and Vogelsang (2005) provide a different way to obtain valid inference in the presence of arbitrary serial correlation. Rather than worry about the rate at which g is allowed to grow (as a function of n) in order for the t statistics to have asymptotic standard normal distributions, Kiefer and Vogelsang derive the large-sample distribution of the t statistic when $b = (g + 1)/n$ is allowed to settle down to a nonzero fraction. [In the Newey-West setup, $(g + 1)/n$ always converges to zero.] For example, when $b = 1$, $g = n - 1$, which means that we include *every* covariance term in equation (12.42). The resulting t statistic does not have a large-sample standard normal distribution, but Kiefer and Vogelsang show that it does have an asymptotic distribution, and they tabulate the appropriate critical values. For a two-sided, 5% level test, the critical value is 4.771, and for a two-sided 10% level test, the critical value is 3.764. Compared with the critical values from the standard normal distribution, we need a t statistic substantially larger. But we do not have to worry about choosing the number of covariances in (12.42).

Before leaving this section, we note that it is possible to construct SC-robust F-type statistics for testing multiple hypotheses, but these are too advanced to cover here. [See Wooldridge (1991b, 1995) and Davidson and MacKinnon (1993) for treatments.]

12-6 Heteroskedasticity in Time Series Regressions

We discussed testing and correcting for heteroskedasticity for cross-sectional applications in Chapter 8. Heteroskedasticity can also occur in time series regression models, and the presence of heteroskedasticity, while not causing bias or inconsistency in the $\hat{\beta}_j$, does invalidate the usual standard errors, t statistics, and F statistics. This is just as in the cross-sectional case.

In time series regression applications, heteroskedasticity often receives little, if any, attention: the problem of serially correlated errors is usually more pressing. Nevertheless, it is useful to briefly cover some of the issues that arise in applying tests and corrections for heteroskedasticity in time series regressions.

Because the usual OLS statistics are asymptotically valid under Assumptions TS.1′ through TS.5′, we are interested in what happens when the homoskedasticity assumption TS.4′, does not hold. Assumption TS.3′ rules out misspecifications such as omitted variables and certain kinds of measurement error, while TS.5′ rules out serial correlation in the errors. It is important to remember that serially correlated errors cause problems that adjustments for heteroskedasticity are not able to address.

12-6a Heteroskedasticity-Robust Statistics

In studying heteroskedasticity for cross-sectional regressions, we noted how it has no bearing on the unbiasedness or consistency of the OLS estimators. Exactly the same conclusions hold in the time series case, as we can see by reviewing the assumptions needed for unbiasedness (Theorem 10.1) and consistency (Theorem 11.1).

In Section 8-2, we discussed how the usual OLS standard errors, t statistics, and F statistics can be adjusted to allow for the presence of heteroskedasticity of unknown form. These same adjustments work for time series regressions under Assumptions TS.1′, TS.2′, TS.3′, and TS.5′. Thus, provided the only assumption violated is the homoskedasticity assumption, valid inference is easily obtained in most econometric packages.

12-6b Testing for Heteroskedasticity

Sometimes, we wish to test for heteroskedasticity in time series regressions, especially if we are concerned about the performance of heteroskedasticity-robust statistics in relatively small sample sizes. The tests we covered in Chapter 8 can be applied directly, but with a few caveats. First, the errors u_t should *not* be serially correlated; any serial correlation will generally invalidate a test for heteroskedasticity. Thus, it makes sense to test for serial correlation first, using a heteroskedasticity-robust test if heteroskedasticity is suspected. Then, after something has been done to correct for serial correlation, we can test for heteroskedasticity.

Second, consider the equation used to motivate the Breusch-Pagan test for heteroskedasticity:

$$u_t^2 = \delta_0 + \delta_1 x_{t1} + \ldots + \delta_k x_{tk} + v_t, \qquad [12.46]$$

where the null hypothesis is $H_0: \delta_1 = \delta_2 = \ldots = \delta_k = 0$. For the F statistic—with $\hat{u}_t^2$ replacing u_t^2 as the dependent variable—to be valid, we must assume that the errors $\{v_t\}$ are themselves homoskedastic (as in the cross-sectional case) *and* serially uncorrelated. These are implicitly assumed in computing all standard tests for heteroskedasticity, including the version of the White test we covered in Section 8-3. Assuming that the $\{v_t\}$ are serially uncorrelated rules out certain forms of dynamic heteroskedasticity, something we will treat in the next subsection.

> **EXPLORING FURTHER 12.5**
>
> How would you compute the White test for heteroskedasticity in equation (12.47)?

If heteroskedasticity is found in the u_t (and the u_t are not serially correlated), then the heteroskedasticity-robust test statistics can be used. An alternative is to use **weighted least squares**, as in Section 8-4. The mechanics of weighted least squares for the time series case are identical to those for the cross-sectional case.

EXAMPLE 12.8 **Heteroskedasticity and the Efficient Markets Hypothesis**

In Example 11.4, we estimated the simple model

$$return_t = \beta_0 + \beta_1 return_{t-1} + u_t.$$ [12.47]

The EMH states that $\beta_1 = 0$. When we tested this hypothesis using the data in NYSE, we obtained $t_{\beta_1} = 1.55$ with $n = 689$. With such a large sample, this is not much evidence against the EMH. Although the EMH states that the expected return given past observable information should be constant, it says nothing about the conditional variance. In fact, the Breusch-Pagan test for heteroskedasticity entails regressing the squared OLS residuals $\hat{u}_t^2$ on $return_{t-1}$:

$$\hat{u}_t^2 = 4.66 - 1.104\,return_{t-1} + residual_t$$
$$\quad\;\;(0.43)\;\;(0.201) \qquad\qquad\qquad\qquad [12.48]$$
$$n = 689, R^2 = .042.$$

The t statistic on $return_{t-1}$ is about -5.5, indicating strong evidence of heteroskedasticity. Because the coefficient on $return_{t-1}$ is negative, we have the interesting finding that volatility in stock returns is lower when the previous return was high, and vice versa. Therefore, we have found what is common in many financial studies: the expected value of stock returns does not depend on past returns, but the variance of returns does.

12-6c Autoregressive Conditional Heteroskedasticity

In recent years, economists have become interested in dynamic forms of heteroskedasticity. Of course, if $\mathbf{x}_t$ contains a lagged dependent variable, then heteroskedasticity as in (12.46) is dynamic. But dynamic forms of heteroskedasticity can appear even in models with no dynamics in the regression equation.

To see this, consider a simple static regression model:

$$y_t = \beta_0 + \beta_1 z_t + u_t,$$

and assume that the Gauss-Markov assumptions hold. This means that the OLS estimators are BLUE. The homoskedasticity assumption says that $Var(u_t|\mathbf{Z})$ is constant, where $\mathbf{Z}$ denotes all n outcomes of z_t. Even if the variance of u_t given $\mathbf{Z}$ is constant, there are other ways that heteroskedasticity can arise. Engle (1982) suggested looking at the conditional variance of u_t given past errors (where the conditioning on $\mathbf{Z}$ is left implicit). Engle suggested what is known as the **autoregressive conditional heteroskedasticity (ARCH)** model. The first order ARCH model is

$$E(u_t^2|u_{t-1}, u_{t-2}, \ldots) = E(u_t^2|u_{t-1}) = \alpha_0 + \alpha_1 u_{t-1}^2,$$ [12.49]

where we leave the conditioning on $\mathbf{Z}$ implicit. This equation represents the conditional variance of u_t given past u_t only if $E(u_t|u_{t-1}, u_{t-2}, \ldots) = 0$, which means that the errors are serially uncorrelated. Since conditional variances must be positive, this model only makes sense if $\alpha_0 > 0$ and $\alpha_1 \geq 0$; if $\alpha_1 = 0$, there are no dynamics in the variance equation.

It is instructive to write (12.49) as

$$u_t^2 = \alpha_0 + \alpha_1 u_{t-1}^2 + v_t,$$ [12.50]

where the expected value of v_t (given $u_{t-1}, u_{t-2}, \ldots$) is zero by definition. (However, the v_t are not independent of past u_t because of the constraint $v_t \geq -\alpha_0 - \alpha_1 u_{t-1}^2$.) Equation (12.50) looks like an autoregressive model in u_t^2 (hence the name ARCH). The stability condition for this equation is $\alpha_1 < 1$, just as in the usual AR(1) model. When $\alpha_1 > 0$, the squared errors contain (positive) serial correlation even though the u_t themselves do not.

What implications does (12.50) have for OLS? Because we began by assuming the Gauss-Markov assumptions hold, OLS is BLUE. Further, even if u_t is not normally distributed, we know that the usual OLS test statistics are asymptotically valid under Assumptions TS.1' through TS.5', which are satisfied by static and distributed lag models with ARCH errors.

If OLS still has desirable properties under ARCH, why should we care about ARCH forms of heteroskedasticity in static and distributed lag models? We should be concerned for two reasons. First, it is possible to get consistent (but not unbiased) estimators of the β_j that are *asymptotically* more efficient than the OLS estimators. A weighted least squares procedure, based on estimating (12.50), will do the trick. A maximum likelihood procedure also works under the assumption that the errors u_t have a conditional normal distribution. Second, economists in various fields have become interested in dynamics in the conditional variance. Engle's original application was to the variance of United Kingdom inflation, where he found that a larger magnitude of the error in the previous time period (larger u_{t-1}^2) was associated with a larger error variance in the current period. Since variance is often used to measure volatility, and volatility is a key element in asset pricing theories, ARCH models have become important in empirical finance.

ARCH models also apply when there are dynamics in the conditional mean. Suppose we have the dependent variable, y_t, a contemporaneous exogenous variable, z_t, and

$$E(y_t|z_t, y_{t-1}, z_{t-1}, y_{t-2}, \ldots) = \beta_0 + \beta_1 z_t + \beta_2 y_{t-1} + \beta_3 z_{t-1},$$

so that at most one lag of y and z appears in the dynamic regression. The typical approach is to assume that $\text{Var}(y_t|z_t, y_{t-1}, z_{t-1}, y_{t-2}, \ldots)$ is constant, as we discussed in Chapter 11. But this variance could follow an ARCH model:

$$\text{Var}(y_t|z_t, y_{t-1}, z_{t-1}, y_{t-2}, \ldots) = \text{Var}(u_t|z_t, y_{t-1}, z_{t-1}, y_{t-2}, \ldots)$$
$$= \alpha_0 + \alpha_1 u_{t-1}^2,$$

where $u_t = y_t - E(y_t|z_t, y_{t-1}, z_{t-1}, y_{t-2}, \ldots)$. As we know from Chapter 11, the presence of ARCH does not affect consistency of OLS, and the usual heteroskedasticity-robust standard errors and test statistics are valid. (Remember, these are valid for any form of heteroskedasticity, and ARCH is just one particular form of heteroskedasticity.)

If you are interested in the ARCH model and its extensions, see Bollerslev, Chou, and Kroner (1992) and Bollerslev, Engle, and Nelson (1994) for recent surveys.

EXAMPLE 12.9	**ARCH in Stock Returns**

In Example 12.8, we saw that there was heteroskedasticity in weekly stock returns. This heteroskedasticity is actually better characterized by the ARCH model in (12.50). If we compute the OLS residuals from (12.47), square these, and regress them on the lagged squared residual, we obtain

$$\hat{u}_t^2 = 2.95 + .337\ \hat{u}_{t-1}^2 + residual_t$$

$$(.44)\ (.036) \qquad\qquad \text{[12.51]}$$

$$n = 688, R^2 = .114.$$

The t statistic on $\hat{u}_{t-1}^2$ is over nine, indicating strong ARCH. As we discussed earlier, a larger error at time $t-1$ implies a larger variance in stock returns today.

It is important to see that, though the *squared* OLS residuals are autocorrelated, the OLS residuals themselves are not (as is consistent with the EMH). Regressing $\hat{u}_t$ on $\hat{u}_{t-1}$ gives $\hat{\rho} = .0014$ with $t_{\hat{\rho}} = .038$.

12-6d Heteroskedasticity and Serial Correlation in Regression Models

Nothing rules out the possibility of both heteroskedasticity and serial correlation being present in a regression model. If we are unsure, we can always use OLS and compute fully robust standard errors, as described in Section 12-5.

Much of the time serial correlation is viewed as the most important problem, because it usually has a larger impact on standard errors and the efficiency of estimators than does heteroskedasticity. As we concluded in Section 12-2, obtaining tests for serial correlation that are robust to arbitrary heteroskedasticity is fairly straightforward. If we detect serial correlation using such a test, we can employ the Cochrane-Orcutt (or Prais-Winsten) transformation [see equation (12.32)] and, in the transformed equation, use heteroskedasticity-robust standard errors and test statistics. Or, we can even test for heteroskedasticity in (12.32) using the Breusch-Pagan or White tests.

Alternatively, we can model heteroskedasticity and serial correlation and correct for both through a combined weighted least squares AR(1) procedure. Specifically, consider the model

$$
\begin{aligned}
y_t &= \beta_0 + \beta_1 x_{t1} + \ldots + \beta_k x_{tk} + u_t \\
u_t &= \sqrt{h_t} v_t \\
v_t &= \rho v_{t-1} + e_t, |\rho| < 1,
\end{aligned}
\qquad \text{[12.52]}
$$

where the explanatory variables **X** are independent of e_t for all t, and h_t is a function of the x_{tj}. The process $\{e_t\}$ has zero mean and constant variance σ_e^2 and is serially uncorrelated. Therefore, $\{v_t\}$ satisfies a stable AR(1) process. The error u_t is heteroskedastic, in addition to containing serial correlation:

$$
\text{Var}(u_t|\mathbf{x}_t) = \sigma_v^2 h_t,
$$

where $\sigma_v^2 = \sigma_e^2/(1 - \rho^2)$. But $v_t = u_t/\sqrt{h_t}$ is homoskedastic and follows a stable AR(1) model. Therefore, the transformed equation

$$
y_t/\sqrt{h_t} = \beta_0(1/\sqrt{h_t}) + \beta_1(x_{t1}/\sqrt{h_t}) + \ldots + \beta_k(x_{tk}/\sqrt{h_t}) + v_t \qquad \text{[12.53]}
$$

has AR(1) errors. Now, if we have a particular kind of heteroskedasticity in mind—that is, we know h_t—we can estimate (12.53) using standard CO or PW methods.

In most cases, we have to estimate h_t first. The following method combines the weighted least squares method from Section 8-4 with the AR(1) serial correlation correction from Section 12-3.

Feasible GLS with Heteroskedasticity and AR(1) Serial Correlation:

(i) Estimate (12.52) by OLS and save the residuals, $\hat{u}_t$.
(ii) Regress $\log(\hat{u}_t^2)$ on $x_{t1}, \ldots, x_{tk}$ (or on $\hat{y}_t, \hat{y}_t^2$) and obtain the fitted values, say, $\hat{g}_t$.
(iii) Obtain the estimates of h_t: $\hat{h}_t = \exp(\hat{g}_t)$.
(iv) Estimate the transformed equation

$$
\hat{h}_t^{-1/2} y_t = \hat{h}_t^{-1/2}\beta_0 + \beta_1\hat{h}_t^{-1/2}x_{t1} + \ldots + \beta_k\hat{h}_t^{-1/2}x_{tk} + error_t \qquad \text{[12.54]}
$$

by standard Cochrane-Orcutt or Prais-Winsten methods.

The FGLS estimators obtained from the procedure are asymptotically efficient provided the assumptions in model (12.52) hold. More importantly, all standard errors and test statistics from the CO or PW estimation are asymptotically valid. If we allow the variance function to be misspecified, or allow the possibility that any serial correlation does not follow an AR(1) model, then we can apply quasi-differencing to (12.54), estimating the resulting equation by OLS, and then obtain the Newey-West standard errors. By doing so, we would be using a procedure that could be asymptotically efficient while ensuring that our inference is valid (asymptotically) if we have misspecified our model of either heteroskedasticity or serial correlation.

Summary

We have covered the important problem of serial correlation in the errors of multiple regression models. Positive correlation between adjacent errors is common, especially in static and finite distributed lag models. This causes the usual OLS standard errors and statistics to be misleading (although the $\hat{\beta}_j$ can still be unbiased, or at least consistent). Typically, the OLS standard errors underestimate the true uncertainty in the parameter estimates.

The most popular model of serial correlation is the AR(1) model. Using this as the starting point, it is easy to test for the presence of AR(1) serial correlation using the OLS residuals. An asymptotically valid t statistic is obtained by regressing the OLS residuals on the lagged residuals, assuming the regressors are strictly exogenous and a homoskedasticity assumption holds. Making the test robust to heteroskedasticity is simple. The Durbin-Watson statistic is available under the classical linear model assumptions, but it can lead to an inconclusive outcome, and it has little to offer over the t test.

For models with a lagged dependent variable or other nonstrictly exogenous regressors, the standard t test on $\hat{u}_{t-1}$ is still valid, provided all independent variables are included as regressors along with $\hat{u}_{t-1}$. We can use an F or an LM statistic to test for higher order serial correlation.

In models with strictly exogenous regressors, we can use a feasible GLS procedure—Cochrane-Orcutt or Prais-Winsten—to correct for AR(1) serial correlation. This gives estimates that are different from the OLS estimates: the FGLS estimates are obtained from OLS on *quasi-differenced* variables. All of the usual test statistics from the transformed equation are asymptotically valid. Almost all regression packages have built-in features for estimating models with AR(1) errors.

Another way to deal with serial correlation, especially when the strict exogeneity assumption might fail, is to use OLS but to compute serial correlation–robust standard errors (that are also robust to heteroskedasticity). Many regression packages follow a method suggested by Newey and West (1987); it is also possible to use standard regression packages to obtain one standard error at a time.

Finally, we discussed some special features of heteroskedasticity in time series models. As in the cross-sectional case, the most important kind of heteroskedasticity is that which depends on the explanatory variables; this is what determines whether the usual OLS statistics are valid. The Breusch-Pagan and White tests covered in Chapter 8 can be applied directly, with the caveat that the errors should not be serially correlated. In recent years, economists—especially those who study the financial markets—have become interested in dynamic forms of heteroskedasticity. The ARCH model is the leading example.

Key Terms

AR(1) Serial Correlation	Cochrane-Orcutt (CO) Estimation	Quasi-Differenced Data
Autoregressive Conditional Heteroskedasticity (ARCH)	Durbin-Watson (*DW*) Statistic	Serial Correlation–Robust Standard Error
Breusch-Godfrey Test	Feasible GLS (FGLS)	Weighted Least Squares
	Prais-Winsten (PW) Estimation	

Problems

1 When the errors in a regression model have AR(1) serial correlation, why do the OLS standard errors tend to underestimate the sampling variation in the $\hat{\beta}_j$? Is it always true that the OLS standard errors are too small?

2 Explain what is wrong with the following statement: "The Cochrane-Orcutt and Prais-Winsten methods are both used to obtain valid standard errors for the OLS estimates when there is a serial correlation."

3 In Example 10.6, we used the data in FAIR to estimate a variant on Fair's model for predicting presidential election outcomes in the United States.

(i) What argument can be made for the error term in this equation being serially uncorrelated? (*Hint:* How often do presidential elections take place?)

(ii) When the OLS residuals from (10.23) are regressed on the lagged residuals, we obtain $\hat{\rho} = -.068$ and $se(\hat{\rho}) = .240$. What do you conclude about serial correlation in the u_t?

(iii) Does the small sample size in this application worry you in testing for serial correlation?

4 True or false: "If the errors in a regression model contain ARCH, they must be serially correlated."

5 (i) In the enterprise zone event study in Computer Exercise C5 in Chapter 10, a regression of the OLS residuals on the lagged residuals produces $\hat{\rho} = .841$ and $se(\hat{\rho}) = .053$. What implications does this have for OLS?

(ii) If you want to use OLS but also want to obtain a valid standard error for the EZ coefficient, what would you do?

6 In Example 12.8, we found evidence of heteroskedasticity in u_t in equation (12.47). Thus, we compute the heteroskedasticity-robust standard errors (in $[\cdot]$) along with the usual standard errors:

$$\widehat{return_t} = .180 + .059\ return_{t-1}$$
$$(.081)\ (.038)$$
$$[.085]\ [.069]$$
$$n = 689, R^2 = .0035, \bar{R}^2 = .0020.$$

What does using the heteroskedasticity-robust t statistic do to the significance of $return_{t-1}$?

7 Consider a standard multiple linear regression model with time series data:

$$y_t = \beta_0 + \beta_1 x_{t1} + \ldots + \beta_k x_{tk} + u_t.$$

Assume that Assumptions TS.1, TS.2, TS.3, and TS.4 all hold.

(i) Suppose we think that the errors $\{u_t\}$ follow an AR(1) model with parameter ρ and so we apply the Prais-Winsten method. If the errors do not follow an AR(1) model–for example, suppose they follow an AR(2) model, or an MA(1) model–why will the usual Prais-Winsten standard errors be incorrect?

(ii) Can you think of a way to use the Newey-West procedure, in conjunction with Prais-Winsten estimation, to obtain valid standard errors? Be very specific about the steps you would follow. [*Hint*: It may help to study equation (12.32) and note that, if $\{u_t\}$ does not follow an AR(1) process, e_t generally should be replaced by $u_t - \rho u_{t-1}$, where ρ is the probability limit of the estimator $\hat{\rho}$. Now, is the error $\{u_t - \rho u_{t-1}\}$ serially uncorrelated in general? What can you do if it is not?]

(iii) Explain why your answer to part (ii) should not change if we drop Assumption TS.4.

Computer Exercises

C1 In Example 11.6, we estimated a finite DL model in first differences (changes):

$$cgfr_t = \gamma_0 + \delta_0 cpe_t + \delta_1 cpe_{t-1} + \delta_2 cpe_{t-2} + u_t.$$

Use the data in FERTIL3 to test whether there is AR(1) serial correlation in the errors.

C2 (i) Using the data in WAGEPRC, estimate the distributed lag model from Problem 5 in Chapter 11. Use regression (12.14) to test for AR(1) serial correlation.

(ii) Reestimate the model using iterated Cochrane-Orcutt estimation. What is your new estimate of the long-run propensity?

    (iii)   Using iterated CO, find the standard error for the LRP. (This requires you to estimate a modified equation.) Determine whether the estimated LRP is statistically different from one at the 5% level.

C3 (i)   In part (i) of Computer Exercise C6 in Chapter 11, you were asked to estimate the accelerator model for inventory investment. Test this equation for AR(1) serial correlation.

    (ii)   If you find evidence of serial correlation, reestimate the equation by Cochrane-Orcutt and compare the results.

C4 (i)   Use NYSE to estimate equation (12.48). Let $\hat{h}_t$ be the fitted values from this equation (the estimates of the conditional variance). How many $\hat{h}_t$ are negative?

    (ii)   Add $return_{t-1}^2$ to (12.48) and again compute the fitted values, $\hat{h}_t$. Are any $\hat{h}_t$ negative?

    (iii)   Use the $\hat{h}_t$ from part (ii) to estimate (12.47) by weighted least squares (as in Section 8-4). Compare your estimate of β_1 with that in equation (11.16). Test $H_0: \beta_1 = 0$ and compare the outcome when OLS is used.

    (iv)   Now, estimate (12.47) by WLS, using the estimated ARCH model in (12.51) to obtain the $\hat{h}_t$. Does this change your findings from part (iii)?

C5 Consider the version of Fair's model in Example 10.6. Now, rather than predicting the proportion of the two-party vote received by the Democrat, estimate a linear probability model for whether or not the Democrat wins.

    (i)   Use the binary variable *demwins* in place of *demvote* in (10.23) and report the results in standard form. Which factors affect the probability of winning? Use the data only through 1992.

    (ii)   How many fitted values are less than zero? How many are greater than one?

    (iii)   Use the following prediction rule: if $\widehat{demwins} > .5$, you predict the Democrat wins; otherwise, the Republican wins. Using this rule, determine how many of the 20 elections are correctly predicted by the model.

    (iv)   Plug in the values of the explanatory variables for 1996. What is the predicted probability that Clinton would win the election? Clinton did win; did you get the correct prediction?

    (v)   Use a heteroskedasticity-robust t test for AR(1) serial correlation in the errors. What do you find?

    (vi)   Obtain the heteroskedasticity-robust standard errors for the estimates in part (i). Are there notable changes in any t statistics?

C6 (i)   In Computer Exercise C7 in Chapter 10, you estimated a simple relationship between consumption growth and growth in disposable income. Test the equation for AR(1) serial correlation (using CONSUMP).

    (ii)   In Computer Exercise C7 in Chapter 11, you tested the permanent income hypothesis by regressing the growth in consumption on one lag. After running this regression, test for heteroskedasticity by regressing the squared residuals on gc_{t-1} and gc_{t-1}^2. What do you conclude?

C7 (i)   For Example 12.4, using the data in BARIUM, obtain the iterative Cochrane-Orcutt estimates.

    (ii)   Are the Prais-Winsten and Cochrane-Orcutt estimates similar? Did you expect them to be?

C8 Use the data in TRAFFIC2 for this exercise.

    (i)   Run an OLS regression of *prcfat* on a linear time trend, monthly dummy variables, and the variables *wkends*, *unem*, *spdlaw*, and *beltlaw*. Test the errors for AR(1) serial correlation using the regression in equation (12.14). Does it make sense to use the test that assumes strict exogeneity of the regressors?

    (ii)   Obtain serial correlation- and heteroskedasticity-robust standard errors for the coefficients on *spdlaw* and *beltlaw*, using four lags in the Newey-West estimator. How does this affect the statistical significance of the two policy variables?

    (iii)   Now, estimate the model using iterative Prais-Winsten and compare the estimates with the OLS estimates. Are there important changes in the policy variable coefficients or their statistical significance?

C9 The file FISH contains 97 daily price and quantity observations on fish prices at the Fulton Fish Market in New York City. Use the variable log(*avgprc*) as the dependent variable.

(i) Regress log(*avgprc*) on four daily dummy variables, with Friday as the base. Include a linear time trend. Is there evidence that price varies systematically within a week?

(ii) Now, add the variables *wave2* and *wave3*, which are measures of wave heights over the past several days. Are these variables individually significant? Describe a mechanism by which stormy seas would increase the price of fish.

(iii) What happened to the time trend when *wave2* and *wave3* were added to the regression? What must be going on?

(iv) Explain why all explanatory variables in the regression are safely assumed to be strictly exogenous.

(v) Test the errors for AR(1) serial correlation.

(vi) Obtain the Newey-West standard errors using four lags. What happens to the *t* statistics on *wave2* and *wave3*? Did you expect a bigger or smaller change compared with the usual OLS *t* statistics?

(vii) Now, obtain the Prais-Winsten estimates for the model estimated in part (ii). Are *wave2* and *wave3* jointly statistically significant?

C10 Use the data in PHILLIPS to answer these questions.

(i) Using the entire data set, estimate the static Phillips curve equation $inf_t = \beta_0 + \beta_1 unem_t + u_t$ by OLS and report the results in the usual form.

(ii) Obtain the OLS residuals from part (i), $\hat{u}_t$, and obtain ρ from the regression $\hat{u}_t$ on $\hat{u}_{t-1}$. (It is fine to include an intercept in this regression.) Is there strong evidence of serial correlation?

(iii) Now estimate the static Phillips curve model by iterative Prais-Winsten. Compare the estimate of β_1 with that obtained in Table 12.2. Is there much difference in the estimate when the later years are added?

(iv) Rather than using Prais-Winsten, use iterative Cochrane-Orcutt. How similar are the final estimates of ρ? How similar are the PW and CO estimates of β_1?

C11 Use the data in NYSE to answer these questions.

(i) Estimate the model in equation (12.47) and obtain the squared OLS residuals. Find the average, minimum, and maximum values of $\hat{u}_t^2$ over the sample.

(ii) Use the squared OLS residuals to estimate the following model of heteroskedasticity:

$$\text{Var}(u_t | return_{t-1}, return_{t-2}, \ldots) = \text{Var}(u_t | return_{t-1}) = \delta_0 + \delta_1 return_{t-1} + \delta_2 return_{t-1}^2.$$

Report the estimated coefficients, the reported standard errors, the *R*-squared, and the adjusted *R*-squared.

(iii) Sketch the conditional variance as a function of the lagged $return_{-1}$. For what value of $return_{-1}$ is the variance the smallest, and what is the variance?

(iv) For predicting the dynamic variance, does the model in part (ii) produce any negative variance estimates?

(v) Does the model in part (ii) seem to fit better or worse than the ARCH(1) model in Example 12.9? Explain.

(vi) To the ARCH(1) regression in equation (12.51), add the second lag, $\hat{u}_{t-2}^2$. Does this lag seem important? Does the ARCH(2) model fit better than the model in part (ii)?

C12 Use the data in INVEN for this exercise; see also Computer Exercise C6 in Chapter 11.

(i) Obtain the OLS residuals from the accelerator model $\Delta inven_t = \beta_0 + \beta_1 \Delta GDP_t + u_t$ and use the regression $\hat{u}_t$ on $\hat{u}_{t-1}$ to test for serial correlation. What is the estimate of ρ? How big a problem does serial correlation seem to be?

(ii) Estimate the accelerator model by PW, and compare the estimate of β_1 to the OLS estimate. Why do you expect them to be similar?

C13 Use the data in OKUN to answer this question; see also Computer Exercise C11 in Chapter 11.

(i) Estimate the equation $pcrgdp_t = \beta_0 + \beta_1 cunem_t + u_t$ and test the errors for AR(1) serial correlation, without assuming $\{cunem_t: t = 1, 2, ...\}$ is strictly exogenous. What do you conclude?

(ii) Regress the squared residuals, $\hat{u}_t^2$, on $cunem_t$ (this is the Breusch-Pagan test for heteroskedasticity in the simple regression case). What do you conclude?

(iii) Obtain the heteroskedasticity-robust standard error for the OLS estimate $\hat{\beta}_1$. Is it substantially different from the usual OLS standard error?

C14 Use the data in MINWAGE for this exercise, focusing on sector 232.

(i) Estimate the equation

$$gwage232_t = \beta_0 + \beta_1 gmwage_t + \beta_2 gcpi_t + u_t,$$

and test the errors for AR(1) serial correlation. Does it matter whether you assume $gmwage_t$ and $gcpi_t$ are strictly exogenous? What do you conclude overall?

(ii) Obtain the Newey-West standard error for the OLS estimates in part (i), using a lag of 12. How do the Newey-West standard errors compare to the usual OLS standard errors?

(iii) Now obtain the heteroskedasticity-robust standard errors for OLS, and compare them with the usual standard errors and the Newey-West standard errors. Does it appear that serial correlation or heteroskedasticity is more of a problem in this application?

(iv) Use the Breusch-Pagan test in the original equation to verify that the errors exhibit strong heteroskedasticity.

(v) Add lags 1 through 12 of $gmwage$ to the equation in part (i). Obtain the p-value for the joint F test for lags 1 through 12, and compare it with the p-value for the heteroskedasticity-robust test. How does adjusting for heteroskedasticity affect the significance of the lags?

(vi) Obtain the p-value for the joint significance test in part (v) using the Newey-West approach. What do you conclude now?

(vii) If you leave out the lags of $gmwage$, is the estimate of the long-run propensity much different?

C15 Use the data in BARIUM to answer this question.

(i) In Table 12.1 the reported standard errors for OLS are uniformly below those of the corresponding standard errors for GLS (Prais-Winsten). Explain why comparing the OLS and GLS standard errors is flawed.

(ii) Reestimate the equation represented by the column labeled "OLS" in Table 12.1 by OLS, but now find the Newey-West standard errors using a window $g = 4$ (four months). How does the Newey-West standard error on $lchempi$ compare to the usual OLS standard error? How does it compare to the P-W standard error? Make the same comparisons for the $afdec6$ variable.

(iii) Redo part (ii) now using a window $g = 12$. What happens to the standard errors on $lchempi$ and $afdec6$ when the window increases from 4 to 12?

C16 Use the data in APPROVAL to answer the following questions. See also Computer Exercise C14 in Chapter 11.

(i) Estimate the equation

$$approve_t = \beta_0 + \beta_1 lcpifood_t + \beta_2 lrgasprice_t + \beta_3 unemploy_t + \beta_4 sep11_t + \beta_5 iraqinvade_t + u_t$$

using first differencing and test the errors in the first-differenced (FD) equation for AR(1) serial correlation. In particular, let $\hat{e}_t$ be the OLS residuals in the FD estimation and regress $\hat{e}_t$ on $\hat{e}_{t-1}$; report the p-value of the test. What is the estimate of ρ?

(ii) Estimate the FD equation using Prais-Winsten. How does the estimate of β_2 compare with the OLS estimate on the FD equation? What about its statistical significance?

(iii) Return to estimating the FD equation by OLS. Now obtain the Newey-West standard errors using lags of one, four, and eight. Discuss the statistical significance of the estimate of β_2 using each of the three standard errors.

PART 3

Advanced Topics

W e now turn to some more specialized topics that are not usually covered in a one-term, introductory course. Some of these topics require few more mathematical skills than the multiple regression analysis did in Parts 1 and 2. In Chapter 13, we show how to apply multiple regression to independently pooled cross sections. The issues raised are very similar to standard cross-sectional analysis, except that we can study how relationships change over time by including time dummy variables. We also illustrate how panel data sets can be analyzed in a regression framework. Chapter 14 covers more advanced panel data methods that are nevertheless used routinely in applied work.

Chapters 15 and 16 investigate the problem of endogenous explanatory variables. In Chapter 15, we introduce the method of instrumental variables as a way of solving the omitted variable problem as well as the measurement error problem. The method of two-stage least squares is used quite often in empirical economics and is indispensable for estimating simultaneous equation models, a topic we turn to in Chapter 16.

Chapter 17 covers some fairly advanced topics that are typically used in cross-sectional analysis, including models for limited dependent variables and methods for correcting sample selection bias. Chapter 18 heads in a different direction by covering some recent advances in time series econometrics that have proven to be useful in estimating dynamic relationships.

Chapter 19 should be helpful to students who must write either a term paper or some other paper in the applied social sciences. The chapter offers suggestions for how to select a topic, collect and analyze the data, and write the paper.

CHAPTER 13

Pooling Cross Sections across Time: Simple Panel Data Methods

ntil now, we have covered multiple regression analysis using pure cross-sectional or pure time series data. Although these two cases arise often in applications, data sets that have both cross-sectional and time series dimensions are being used more and more often in empirical research. Multiple regression methods can still be used on such data sets. In fact, data with cross-sectional and time series aspects can often shed light on important policy questions. We will see several examples in this chapter.

We will analyze two kinds of data sets in this chapter. An **independently pooled cross section** is obtained by sampling randomly from a large population at different points in time (usually, but not necessarily, different years). For instance, in each year, we can draw a random sample on hourly wages, education, experience, and so on, from the population of working people in the United States. Or, in every other year, we draw a random sample on the selling price, square footage, number of bathrooms, and so on, of houses sold in a particular metropolitan area. From a statistical standpoint, these data sets have an important feature: they consist of *independently* sampled observations. This was also a key aspect in our analysis of cross-sectional data: among other things, it rules out correlation in the error terms across different observations.

An independently pooled cross section differs from a single random sample in that sampling from the population at different points in time likely leads to observations that are not identically distributed. For example, distributions of wages and education have changed over time in most countries. As we will see, this is easy to deal with in practice by allowing the intercept in a multiple regression model, and in some cases the slopes, to change over time. We cover such models in Section 13-1. In Section 13-1, we discuss how pooling cross sections over time can be used to evaluate policy changes.

A **panel data** set, while having both a cross-sectional and a time series dimension, differs in some important respects from an independently pooled cross section. To collect panel data—sometimes called **longitudinal data**—we follow (or attempt to follow) the *same* individuals, families, firms, cities, states, or whatever, across time. For example, a panel data set on individual wages, hours, education, and other factors is collected by randomly selecting people from a population at a given point in time. Then, these *same* people are reinterviewed at several subsequent points in time. This gives us data on wages, hours, education, and so on, for the same group of people in different years.

Panel data sets are fairly easy to collect for school districts, cities, counties, states, and countries, and policy analysis is greatly enhanced by using panel data sets; we will see some examples in the following discussion. For the econometric analysis of panel data, we cannot assume that the observations are independently distributed across time. For example, unobserved factors (such as ability) that affect someone's wage in 1990 will also affect that person's wage in 1991; unobserved factors that affect a city's crime rate in 1985 will also affect that city's crime rate in 1990. For this reason, special models and methods have been developed to analyze panel data. In Sections 13-3, 13-4, and 13-5, we describe the straightforward method of differencing to remove time-constant, unobserved attributes of the units being studied. Because panel data methods are somewhat more advanced, we will rely mostly on intuition in describing the statistical properties of the estimation procedures, leaving detailed assumptions to the chapter appendix. We follow the same strategy in Chapter 14, which covers more complicated panel data methods.

13-1 Pooling Independent Cross Sections across Time

Many surveys of individuals, families, and firms are repeated at regular intervals, often each year. An example is the *Current Population Survey* (or CPS), which randomly samples households each year. (See, for example, CPS78_85, which contains data from the 1978 and 1985 CPS.) If a random sample is drawn at each time period, pooling the resulting random samples gives us an independently pooled cross section.

One reason for using independently pooled cross sections is to increase the sample size. By pooling random samples drawn from the same population, but at different points in time, we can get more precise estimators and test statistics with more power. Pooling is helpful in this regard only insofar as the relationship between the dependent variable and at least some of the independent variables remain constant over time.

As mentioned in the introduction, using pooled cross sections raises only minor statistical complications. Typically, to reflect the fact that the population may have different distributions in different time periods, we allow the intercept to differ across periods, usually years. This is easily accomplished by including dummy variables for all but one year, where the earliest year in the sample is usually chosen as the base year. It is also possible that the error variance changes over time, something we discuss later.

Sometimes, the pattern of coefficients on the year dummy variables is itself of interest. For example, a demographer may be interested in the following question: *After* controlling for education, has the pattern of fertility among women over age 35 changed between 1972 and 1984? The following example illustrates how this question is simply answered by using multiple regression analysis with **year dummy variables**.

EXAMPLE 13.1	**Women's Fertility over Time**

The data set in FERTIL1, which is similar to that used by Sander (1992), comes from the National Opinion Research Center's *General Social Survey* for the even years from 1972 to 1984, inclusively. We use these data to estimate a model explaining the total number of kids born to a woman (*kids*).

One question of interest is: After controlling for other observable factors, what has happened to fertility rates over time? The factors we control for are years of education, age, race, region of the country where living at age 16, and living environment at age 16. The estimates are given in Table 13.1.

The base year is 1972. The coefficients on the year dummy variables show a sharp drop in fertility in the early 1980s. For example, the coefficient on *y82* implies that, holding education, age, and other factors fixed, a woman had on average .52 less children, or about one-half a child, in 1982 than in 1972. This is a very large drop: holding *educ*, *age*, and the other factors fixed, 100 women in 1982 are predicted to have about 52 fewer children than 100 comparable women in 1972. Since we are controlling for education, this drop is separate from the decline in fertility that is due to the increase in average education levels. (The average years of education are 12.2 for 1972 and 13.3 for 1984.) The coefficients on *y82* and *y84* represent drops in fertility for reasons that are not captured in the explanatory variables.

Given that the 1982 and 1984 year dummies are individually quite significant, it is not surprising that as a group the year dummies are jointly very significant: the R-squared for the regression without the year dummies is .1019, and this leads to $F_{6,1111} = 5.87$ and p-value ≈ 0.

TABLE 13.1 Determinants of Women's Fertility

Dependent Variable: *kids*

Independent Variables	Coefficients	Standard Errors
educ	−.128	.018
age	.532	.138
age^2	−.0058	.0016
black	1.076	.174
east	.217	.133
northcen	.363	.121
west	.198	.167
farm	−.053	.147
othrural	−.163	.175
town	.084	.124
smcity	.212	.160
y74	.268	.173
y76	−.097	.179
y78	−.069	.182
y80	−.071	.183
y82	−.522	.172
y84	−.545	.175
constant	−7.742	3.052

$n = 1,129$
$R^2 = .1295$
$\bar{R}^2 = .1162$

Women with more education have fewer children, and the estimate is very statistically significant. Other things being equal, 100 women with a college education will have about 51 fewer children on average than 100 women with only a high school education: $.128(4) = .512$. Age has a diminishing effect on fertility. (The turning point in the quadratic is at about $age = 46$, by which time most women have finished having children.)

The model estimated in Table 13.1 assumes that the effect of each explanatory variable, particularly education, has remained constant. This may or may not be true; you will be asked to explore this issue in Computer Exercise C1.

Finally, there may be heteroskedasticity in the error term underlying the estimated equation. This can be dealt with using the methods in Chapter 8. There is one interesting difference here: now, the error variance may change over time even if it does not change with the values of *educ*, *age*, *black*, and so on. The heteroskedasticity-robust standard errors and test statistics are nevertheless valid. The Breusch-Pagan test would be obtained by regressing the squared OLS residuals on *all* of the independent variables in Table 13.1, including the year dummies. (For the special case of the White statistic, the fitted values $\widehat{kids}$ and the squared fitted values are used as the independent variables, as always.) A weighted least squares procedure should account for variances that possibly change over time. In the procedure discussed in Section 8-4, year dummies would be included in equation (8.32).

EXPLORING FURTHER 13.1

In reading Table 13.1, someone claims that, if everything else is equal in the table, a black woman is expected to have one more child than a nonblack woman. Do you agree with this claim?

We can also interact a year dummy variable with key explanatory variables to see if the effect of that variable has changed over a certain time period. The next example examines how the return to education and the gender gap have changed from 1978 to 1985.

EXAMPLE 13.2 **Changes in the Return to Education and the Gender Wage Gap**

A log(*wage*) equation (where *wage* is hourly wage) pooled across the years 1978 (the base year) and 1985 is

$$\log(wage) = \beta_0 + \delta_0 y85 + \beta_1 educ + \delta_1 y85 \cdot educ + \beta_2 exper$$
$$+ \beta_3 exper^2 + \beta_4 union + \beta_5 female + \delta_5 y85 \cdot female + u, \qquad [13.1]$$

where most explanatory variables should by now be familiar. The variable *union* is a dummy variable equal to one if the person belongs to a union, and zero otherwise. The variable *y85* is a dummy variable equal to one if the observation comes from 1985 and zero if it comes from 1978. There are 550 people in the sample in 1978 and a different set of 534 people in 1985.

The intercept for 1978 is β_0, and the intercept for 1985 is $\beta_0 + \delta_0$. The return to education in 1978 is β_1, and the return to education in 1985 is $\beta_1 + \delta_1$. Therefore, δ_1 measures how the return to another year of education has changed over the seven-year period. Finally, in 1978, the log(*wage*) differential between women and men is β_5; the differential in 1985 is $\beta_5 + \delta_5$. Thus, we can test the null hypothesis that nothing has happened to the gender differential over this seven-year period by testing $H_0: \delta_5 = 0$. The alternative that the gender differential has been *reduced* is $H_1: \delta_5 > 0$. For simplicity, we have assumed that experience and union membership have the same effect on wages in both time periods.

Before we present the estimates, there is one other issue we need to address—namely, hourly wage here is in nominal (or current) dollars. Since nominal wages grow simply due to inflation, we are really interested in the effect of each explanatory variable on real wages. Suppose that we settle on measuring wages in 1978 dollars. This requires deflating 1985 wages to 1978 dollars. (Using the Consumer Price Index for the 1997 *Economic Report of the President*, the deflation factor is $107.6/65.2 \approx 1.65$.) Although we can easily divide each 1985 wage by 1.65, it turns out that this is not necessary, *provided* a 1985 year dummy is included in the regression *and* log(*wage*) (as opposed to *wage*) is used as the dependent variable. Using real or nominal wage in a logarithmic functional form only affects the coefficient on the year dummy, *y85*. To see this, let *P85* denote the deflation factor for 1985 wages (1.65, if we use the CPI). Then, the log of the real wage for each person *i* in the 1985 sample is

$$\log(wage_i/P85) = \log(wage_i) - \log(P85).$$

Now, while *wage_i* differs across people, *P85* does not. Therefore, $\log(P85)$ will be absorbed into the intercept for 1985. (This conclusion would change if, for example, we used a different price index for people living in different parts of the country.) The bottom line is that, for studying how the return to education or the gender gap has changed, we do not need to turn nominal wages into real wages in equation (13.1). Computer Exercise C2 asks you to verify this for the current example.

If we forget to allow different intercepts in 1978 and 1985, the use of nominal wages can produce seriously misleading results. If we use *wage* rather than log(*wage*) as the dependent variable, it is important to use the real wage and to include a year dummy.

The previous discussion generally holds when using dollar values for either the dependent or independent variables. Provided the dollar amounts appear in logarithmic form and dummy variables are used for all time periods (except, of course, the base period), the use of aggregate price deflators will only affect the intercepts; none of the slope estimates will change.

Now, we use the data in CPS78_85 to estimate the equation:

$$
\begin{aligned}
\log(wage) = \;.459 &+ .118\,y85 + .0747\,educ + .0185\,y85 \cdot educ \\
(.093)\;\; &(.124) \quad\;\; (.0067) \qquad\;\; (.0094) \\
&+ .0296\,exper - .00040\,exper^2 + .202\,union \\
&(.0036) \qquad\;\; (.00008) \qquad\;\;\; (.030) \\
&- .317\,female + .085\,y85 \cdot female \\
&(.037) \qquad\quad\; (.051) \\
n = 1{,}084, &\; R^2 = .426, \; \bar{R}^2 = .422.
\end{aligned}
$$

[13.2]

The return to education in 1978 is estimated to be about 7.5%; the return to education in 1985 is about 1.85 percentage points *higher*, or about 9.35%. Because the *t* statistic on the interaction term is $.0185/.0094 \approx 1.97$, the difference in the return to education is statistically significant at the 5% level against a two-sided alternative.

What about the gender gap? In 1978, other things being equal, a woman earned about 31.7% less than a man (27.2% is the more accurate estimate). In 1985, the gap in log(*wage*) is $-.317 + .085 = -.232$. Therefore, the gender gap appears to have fallen from 1978 to 1985 by about 8.5 percentage points. The *t* statistic on the interaction term is about 1.67, which means it is significant at the 5% level against the positive one-sided alternative.

What happens if we interact *all* independent variables with *y85* in equation (13.2)? This is identical to estimating two separate equations, one for 1978 and one for 1985. Sometimes, this is desirable. For example, in Chapter 7, we discussed a study by Krueger (1993), in which he estimated the return to using a computer on the job. Krueger estimates two separate equations, one using the 1984 CPS and the other using the 1989 CPS. By comparing how the return to education changes across time and whether or not computer usage is controlled for, he estimates that one-third to one-half of the observed increase in the return to education over the five-year period can be attributed to increased computer usage. [See Tables VIII and IX in Krueger (1993).]

13-1a The Chow Test for Structural Change across Time

In Chapter 7, we discussed how the Chow test—which is simply an F test—can be used to determine whether a multiple regression function differs across two groups. We can apply that test to two different time periods as well. One form of the test obtains the sum of squared residuals from the pooled estimation as the restricted SSR. The unrestricted SSR is the sum of the SSRs for the two separately estimated time periods. The mechanics of computing the statistic are exactly as they were in Section 7-4. A heteroskedasticity-robust version is also available (see Section 8-2).

Example 13.2 suggests another way to compute the Chow test for two time periods by interacting each variable with a year dummy for one of the two years and testing for joint significance of the year dummy and all of the interaction terms. Since the intercept in a regression model often changes over time (due to, say, inflation in the housing price example), this full-blown Chow test can detect such changes. It is usually more interesting to allow for an intercept difference and then to test whether certain slope coefficients change over time (as we did in Example 13.2).

A Chow test can also be computed for more than two time periods. Just as in the two-period case, it is usually more interesting to allow the intercepts to change over time and then test whether the slope coefficients have changed over time. We can test the constancy of slope coefficients generally by interacting all of the time-period dummies (except that defining the base group) with one, several, or all of the explanatory variables and test the joint significance of the interaction terms. Computer Exercises C1 and C2 are examples. For many time periods and explanatory variables, constructing a full set of interactions can be tedious. Alternatively, we can adapt the approach described in part (vi) of Computer Exercise C11 in Chapter 7. First, estimate the restricted model by doing a pooled regression allowing for different time intercepts; this gives SSR_r. Then, run a regression for each of the, say, T time periods and obtain the sum of squared residuals for each time period. The unrestricted sum of squared residuals is obtained as $SSR_{ur} = SSR_1 + SSR_2 + \ldots + SSR_T$. If there are k explanatory variables (not including the intercept or the time dummies) with T time periods, then we are testing $(T - 1)k$ restrictions, and there are $T + Tk$ parameters estimated in the unrestricted model. So, if $n = n_1 + n_2 + \ldots + n_T$ is the total number of observations, then the df of the F test are $(T - 1)k$ and $n - T - Tk$. We compute the F statistic as usual: $[(SSR_r - SSR_{ur})/SSR_{ur}][(n - T - Tk)/(T - 1)k]$. Unfortunately, as with any F test based on sums of squared residuals or R-squareds, this test is not robust to heteroskedasticity (including changing variances across time). To obtain a heteroskedasticity-robust test, we must construct the interaction terms and do a pooled regression.

13-2 Policy Analysis with Pooled Cross Sections

Pooled cross sections can be very useful for evaluating the impact of a certain event or policy. The following example of an event study shows how two cross-sectional data sets, collected before and after the occurrence of an event, can be used to determine the effect on economic outcomes.

| EXAMPLE 13.3 | **Effect of a Garbage Incinerator's Location on Housing Prices** |

Kiel and McClain (1995) studied the effect that a new garbage incinerator had on housing values in North Andover, Massachusetts. They used many years of data and a fairly complicated econometric analysis. We will use two years of data and some simplified models, but our analysis is similar.

The rumor that a new incinerator would be built in North Andover began after 1978, and construction began in 1981. The incinerator was expected to be in operation soon after the start of construction; the incinerator actually began operating in 1985. We will use data on prices of houses that sold in 1978 and another sample on those that sold in 1981. The hypothesis is that the price of houses located near the incinerator would fall relative to the price of more distant houses.

For illustration, we define a house to be near the incinerator if it is within three miles. [In Computer Exercise C3, you are instead asked to use the actual distance from the house to the incinerator, as in Kiel and McClain (1995).] We will start by looking at the dollar effect on housing prices. This requires us to measure price in constant dollars. We measure all housing prices in 1978 dollars, using the Boston housing price index. Let *rprice* denote the house price in real terms.

A naive analyst would use only the 1981 data and estimate a very simple model:

$$rprice = \gamma_0 + \gamma_1 nearinc + u,$$ [13.3]

where *nearinc* is a binary variable equal to one if the house is near the incinerator, and zero otherwise. Estimating this equation using the data in KIELMC gives

$$\widehat{rprice} = 101{,}307.5 - 30{,}688.27\ nearinc$$
$$(3{,}093.0)\quad (5{,}827.71)$$ [13.4]
$$n = 142,\ R^2 = .165.$$

Since this is a simple regression on a single dummy variable, the intercept is the average selling price for homes not near the incinerator, and the coefficient on *nearinc* is the difference in the average selling price between homes near the incinerator and those that are not. The estimate shows that the average selling price for the former group was $30,688.27 less than for the latter group. The *t* statistic is greater than five in absolute value, so we can strongly reject the hypothesis that the average value for homes near and far from the incinerator are the same.

Unfortunately, equation (13.4) does *not* imply that the siting of the incinerator is causing the lower housing values. In fact, if we run the same regression for 1978 (before the incinerator was even rumored), we obtain

$$\widehat{rprice} = 82{,}517.23 - 18{,}824.37\ nearinc$$
$$(2{,}653.79)\quad (4{,}744.59)$$ [13.5]
$$n = 179,\ R^2 = .082.$$

Therefore, even *before* there was any talk of an incinerator, the average value of a home near the site was $18,824.37 less than the average value of a home not near the site ($82,517.23); the difference is statistically significant, as well. This is consistent with the view that the incinerator was built in an area with lower housing values.

How, then, can we tell whether building a new incinerator depresses housing values? The key is to look at how the coefficient on *nearinc* changed between 1978 and 1981. The difference in average housing value was much larger in 1981 than in 1978 ($30,688.27 versus $18,824.37), even as a percentage of the average value of homes not near the incinerator site. The difference in the two coefficients on *nearinc* is

$$\hat{\delta}_1 = -30{,}688.27 - (-18{,}824.37) = -11{,}863.9.$$

This is our estimate of the effect of the incinerator on values of homes near the incinerator site. In empirical economics, $\hat{\delta}_1$ has become known as the **difference-in-differences estimator** because it can be expressed as

$$\hat{\delta}_1 = (\overline{rprice}_{81,\,nr} - \overline{rprice}_{81,\,fr}) - (\overline{rprice}_{78,\,nr} - \overline{rprice}_{78,\,fr}),$$ [13.6]

where *nr* stands for "near the incinerator site" and *fr* stands for "farther away from the site." In other words, $\hat{\delta}_1$ is the difference over time in the average difference of housing prices in the two locations.

To test whether $\hat{\delta}_1$ is statistically different from zero, we need to find its standard error by using a regression analysis. In fact, $\hat{\delta}_1$ can be obtained by estimating

$$rprice = \beta_0 + \delta_0 y81 + \beta_1 nearinc + \delta_1 y81 \cdot nearinc + u,$$ [13.7]

using the data pooled over both years. The intercept, β_0, is the average price of a home not near the incinerator in 1978. The parameter δ_0 captures changes in *all* housing values in North Andover from 1978 to 1981. [A comparison of equations (13.4) and (13.5) shows that housing values in North Andover, relative to the Boston housing price index, increased sharply over this period.] The coefficient on *nearinc*, β_1, measures the location effect that is *not* due to the presence of the incinerator: as we saw in equation (13.5), even in 1978, homes near the incinerator site sold for less than homes farther away from the site.

The parameter of interest is on the interaction term *y81·nearinc*: δ_1 measures the decline in housing values due to the new incinerator, provided we assume that houses both near and far from the site did not appreciate at different rates for other reasons.

The estimates of equation (13.7) are given in column (1) of Table 13.2. The only number we could not obtain from equations (13.4) and (13.5) is the standard error of $\hat{\delta}_1$. The t statistic on $\hat{\delta}_1$ is about -1.59, which is marginally significant against a one-sided alternative (p-value $\approx .057$).

Kiel and McClain (1995) included various housing characteristics in their analysis of the incinerator siting. There are two good reasons for doing this. First, the kinds of homes selling near the incinerator in 1981 might have been systematically different than those selling near the incinerator in 1978; if so, it can be important to control for such characteristics. Second, even if the relevant house characteristics did not change, including them can greatly reduce the error variance, which can then shrink the standard error of $\hat{\delta}_1$. (See Section 6-3 for discussion.) In column (2), we control for the age of the houses, using a quadratic. This substantially increases the R-squared (by reducing the residual variance). The coefficient on *y81·nearinc* is now much larger in magnitude, and its standard error is lower.

In addition to the age variables in column (2), column (3) controls for distance to the interstate in feet (*intst*), land area in feet (*land*), house area in feet (*area*), number of rooms (*rooms*), and number of baths (*baths*). This produces an estimate on *y81·nearinc* closer to that without any controls, but it yields a much smaller standard error: the t statistic for $\hat{\delta}_1$ is about -2.84. Therefore, we find a much more significant effect in column (3) than in column (1). The column (3) estimates are preferred because they control for the most factors and have the smallest standard errors (except in the constant, which is not important here). The fact that *nearinc* has a much smaller coefficient and is insignificant in column (3) indicates that the characteristics included in column (3) largely capture the housing characteristics that are most important for determining housing prices.

TABLE 13.2 Effects of Incinerator Location on Housing Prices

Dependent Variable: *rprice*

Independent Variable	(1)	(2)	(3)
constant	82,517.23 (2,726.91)	89,116.54 (2,406.05)	13,807.67 (11,166.59)
y81	18,790.29 (4,050.07)	21,321.04 (3,443.63)	13,928.48 (2,798.75)
nearinc	−18,824.37 (4,875.32)	9,397.94 (4,812.22)	3,780.34 (4,453.42)
y81·nearinc	−11,863.90 (7,456.65)	−21,920.27 (6,359.75)	−14,177.93 (4,987.27)
Other controls	No	age, age²	Full Set
Observations	321	321	321
R-squared	.174	.414	.660

For the purpose of introducing the method, we used the level of real housing prices in Table 13.2. It makes more sense to use log($price$) [or log($rprice$)] in the analysis in order to get an approximate percentage effect. The basic model becomes

$$\log(price) = \beta_0 + \delta_0 y81 + \beta_1 nearinc + \delta_1 y81 \cdot nearinc + u. \qquad [13.8]$$

Now, $100 \cdot \delta_1$ is the approximate percentage reduction in housing value due to the incinerator. [Just as in Example 13.2, using log($price$) versus log($rprice$) only affects the coefficient on $y81$.] Using the same 321 pooled observations gives

$$\widehat{\log(price)} = 11.29 + .457 \, y81 - .340 \, nearinc - .063 \, y81 \cdot nearinc$$
$$\qquad\qquad (.31) \quad (.045) \qquad (.055) \qquad\qquad (.083) \qquad\qquad\qquad [13.9]$$
$$n = 321, R^2 = .409.$$

The coefficient on the interaction term implies that, because of the new incinerator, houses near the incinerator lost about 6.3% in value. However, this estimate is not statistically different from zero. But when we use a full set of controls, as in column (3) of Table 13.2 (but with *intst*, *land*, and *area* appearing in logarithmic form), the coefficient on $y81 \cdot nearinc$ becomes $-.132$ with a t statistic of about -2.53. Again, controlling for other factors turns out to be important. Using the logarithmic form, we estimate that houses near the incinerator were devalued by about 13.2%.

The methodology used in the previous example has numerous applications, especially when the data arise from a **natural experiment** (or a **quasi-experiment**). A natural experiment occurs when some exogenous event—often a change in government policy—changes the environment in which individuals, families, firms, or cities operate. A natural experiment always has a control group, which is not affected by the policy change, and a treatment group, which is thought to be affected by the policy change. Unlike a true experiment, in which treatment and control groups are randomly and explicitly chosen, the control and treatment groups in natural experiments arise from the particular policy change. To control for systematic differences between the control and treatment groups, we need two years of data, one before the policy change and one after the change. Thus, our sample is usefully broken down into four groups: the control group before the change, the control group after the change, the treatment group before the change, and the treatment group after the change.

Call C the control group and T the treatment group, letting dT equal unity for those in the treatment group T, and zero otherwise. Then, letting $d2$ denote a dummy variable for the second (post-policy change) time period, the equation of interest is

$$y = \beta_0 + \delta_0 d2 + \beta_1 dT + \delta_1 d2 \cdot dT + other \, factors, \qquad [13.10]$$

where y is the outcome variable of interest. As in Example 13.3, δ_1 measures the effect of the policy. Without other factors in the regression, $\hat{\delta}_1$ will be the difference-in-differences estimator:

$$\hat{\delta}_1 = (\bar{y}_{2,T} - \bar{y}_{2,C}) - (\bar{y}_{1,T} - \bar{y}_{1,C}), \qquad [13.11]$$

where the bar denotes average, the first subscript denotes the year, and the second subscript denotes the group.

The general difference-in-differences setup is shown in Table 13.3. Table 13.3 suggests that the parameter δ_1, sometimes called the **average treatment effect** (because it measures the effect of the "treatment" or policy on the average outcome of y), can be estimated in two ways: (1) Compute the differences in averages between the treatment and control groups in each time period, and then difference the results over time; this is just as in equation (13.11); (2) Compute the change in averages over time for each of the treatment and control groups, and then difference these changes, which means we simply write $\hat{\delta}_1 = (\bar{y}_{2,T} - \bar{y}_{1,T}) - (\bar{y}_{2,C} - \bar{y}_{1,C})$. Naturally, the estimate $\hat{\delta}_1$ does not depend on how we do the differencing, as is seen by simple rearrangement.

TABLE 13.3 Illustration of the Difference-in-Differences Estimator

	Before	After	After − Before
Control	β_0	$\beta_0 + \delta_0$	δ_0
Treatment	$\beta_0 + \beta_1$	$\beta_0 + \delta_0 + \beta_1 + \delta_1$	$\delta_0 + \delta_1$
Treatment—Control	β_1	$\beta_1 + \delta_1$	δ_1

When explanatory variables are added to equation (13.10) (to control for the fact that the populations sampled may differ systematically over the two periods), the OLS estimate of δ_1 no longer has the simple form of (13.11), but its interpretation is similar.

EXAMPLE 13.4   **Effect of Worker Compensation Laws on Weeks out of Work**

Meyer, Viscusi, and Durbin (1995) (hereafter, MVD) studied the length of time (in weeks) that an injured worker receives workers' compensation. On July 15, 1980, Kentucky raised the cap on weekly earnings that were covered by workers' compensation. An increase in the cap has no effect on the benefit for low-income workers, but it makes it less costly for a high-income worker to stay on workers' compensation. Therefore, the control group is low-income workers, and the treatment group is high-income workers; high-income workers are defined as those who were subject to the pre-policy change cap. Using random samples both before and after the policy change, MVD were able to test whether more generous workers' compensation causes people to stay out of work longer (everything else fixed). They started with a difference-in-differences analysis, using log(*durat*) as the dependent variable. Let *afchnge* be the dummy variable for observations after the policy change and *highearn* the dummy variable for high earners. Using the data in INJURY, the estimated equation, with standard errors in parentheses, is

$$\widehat{\log(durat)} = 1.126 + .0077 \, afchnge + .256 \, highearn$$
$$(0.031) \quad (.0447) \qquad\qquad (.047)$$
$$+ .191 \, afchnge \cdot highearn \qquad\qquad\qquad [13.12]$$
$$(.069)$$
$$n = 5{,}626, R^2 = .021.$$

Therefore, $\hat{\delta}_1 = .191 (t = 2.77)$, which implies that the average length of time on workers' compensation for high earners increased by about 19% due to the increased earnings cap. The coefficient on *afchnge* is small and statistically insignificant: as is expected, the increase in the earnings cap has no effect on duration for low-income workers.

This is a good example of how we can get a fairly precise estimate of the effect of a policy change even though we cannot explain much of the variation in the dependent variable. The dummy variables in (13.12) explain only 2.1% of the variation in log(*durat*). This makes sense: there are clearly many factors, including severity of the injury, that affect how long someone receives workers' compensation. Fortunately, we have a very large sample size, and this allows us to get a significant t statistic.

MVD also added a variety of controls for gender, marital status, age, industry, and type of injury. This allows for the fact that the kinds of people and types of injuries may differ systematically by earnings group across the two years. Controlling for these factors turns out to have little effect on the estimate of δ_1. (See Computer Exercise C4.)

Sometimes, the two groups consist of people living in two neighboring states in the United States. For example, to assess the impact of changing cigarette taxes on cigarette consumption, we can obtain random samples from two states for two years. In State A, the control group, there was no change in

EXPLORING FURTHER 13.2

What do you make of the coefficient and t statistic on *highearn* in equation (13.12)?

the cigarette tax. In State B, the treatment group, the tax increased (or decreased) between the two years. The outcome variable would be a measure of cigarette consumption, and equation (13.10) can be estimated to determine the effect of the tax on cigarette consumption.

For an interesting survey on natural experiment methodology and several additional examples, see Meyer (1995).

13-3 Two-Period Panel Data Analysis

We now turn to the analysis of the simplest kind of panel data: for a cross section of individuals, schools, firms, cities, or whatever, we have two years of data; call these $t = 1$ and $t = 2$. These years need not be adjacent, but $t = 1$ corresponds to the earlier year. For example, the file CRIME2 contains data on (among other things) crime and unemployment rates for 46 cities for 1982 and 1987. Therefore, $t = 1$ corresponds to 1982, and $t = 2$ corresponds to 1987.

What happens if we use the 1987 cross section and run a simple regression of *crmrte* on *unem*? We obtain

$$\widehat{crmrte} = 128.38 - 4.16 \, unem$$
$$(20.76) \quad (3.42)$$
$$n = 46, R^2 = .033.$$

If we interpret the estimated equation causally, it implies that an increase in the unemployment rate *lowers* the crime rate. This is certainly not what we expect. The coefficient on *unem* is not statistically significant at standard significance levels: at best, we have found no link between crime and unemployment rates.

As we have emphasized throughout this text, this simple regression equation likely suffers from omitted variable problems. One possible solution is to try to control for more factors, such as age distribution, gender distribution, education levels, law enforcement efforts, and so on, in a multiple regression analysis. But many factors might be hard to control for. In Chapter 9, we showed how including the *crmrte* from a previous year—in this case, 1982—can help to control for the fact that different cities have historically different crime rates. This is one way to use two years of data for estimating a causal effect.

An alternative way to use panel data is to view the unobserved factors affecting the dependent variable as consisting of two types: those that are constant and those that vary over time. Letting i denote the cross-sectional unit and t the time period, we can write a model with a single observed explanatory variable as

$$y_{it} = \beta_0 + \delta_0 d2_t + \beta_1 x_{it} + a_i + u_{it}, t = 1, 2. \qquad [13.13]$$

In the notation y_{it}, i denotes the person, firm, city, and so on, and t denotes the time period. The variable $d2_t$ is a dummy variable that equals zero when $t = 1$ and one when $t = 2$; it does not change across i, which is why it has no i subscript. Therefore, the intercept for $t = 1$ is β_0, and the intercept for $t = 2$ is $\beta_0 + \delta_0$. Just as in using independently pooled cross sections, allowing the intercept to change over time is important in most applications. In the crime example, secular trends in the United States will cause crime rates in all U.S. cities to change, perhaps markedly, over a five-year period.

The variable a_i captures all unobserved, time-constant factors that affect y_{it}. (The fact that a_i has no t subscript tells us that it does not change over time.) Generically, a_i is called an **unobserved effect**. It is also common in applied work to find a_i referred to as a **fixed effect**, which helps us to remember that a_i is fixed over time. The model in (13.13) is called an **unobserved effects model** or a **fixed effects model**. In applications, you might see a_i referred to as **unobserved heterogeneity** as well (or *individual heterogeneity*, *firm heterogeneity*, *city heterogeneity*, and so on).

The error u_{it} is often called the **idiosyncratic error** or time-varying error, because it represents unobserved factors that change over time and affect y_{it}. These are very much like the errors in a straight time series regression equation.

A simple unobserved effects model for city crime rates for 1982 and 1987 is

$$crmrte_{it} = \beta_0 + \delta_0 d87_t + \beta_1 unem_{it} + a_i + u_{it}, \qquad [13.14]$$

where $d87$ is a dummy variable for 1987. Since i denotes different cities, we call a_i an *unobserved city effect* or a *city fixed effect*: it represents all factors affecting city crime rates that do not change over time. Geographical features, such as the city's location in the United States, are included in a_i. Many other factors may not be exactly constant, but they might be roughly constant over a five-year period. These might include certain demographic features of the population (age, race, and education). Different cities may have their own methods for reporting crimes, and the people living in the cities might have different attitudes toward crime; these are typically slow to change. For historical reasons, cities can have very different crime rates, and historical factors are effectively captured by the unobserved effect a_i.

How should we estimate the parameter of interest, β_1, given two years of panel data? One possibility is just to pool the two years and use OLS, essentially as in Section 13-1. This method has two drawbacks. The most important of these is that, in order for pooled OLS to produce a consistent estimator of β_1, we would have to assume that the unobserved effect, a_i, is uncorrelated with x_{it}. We can easily see this by writing (13.13) as

$$y_{it} = \beta_0 + \delta_0 d2_t + \beta_1 x_{it} + v_{it}, \quad t = 1, 2, \qquad [13.15]$$

> **EXPLORING FURTHER 13.3**
>
> Suppose that a_i, u_{i1}, and u_{i2} have zero means and are pairwise uncorrelated. Show that $Cov(v_{i1}, v_{i2}) = Var(a_i)$, so that the composite errors are positively serially correlated across time, unless $a_i = 0$. What does this imply about the usual OLS standard errors from pooled OLS estimation?

where $v_{it} = a_i + u_{it}$ is often called the **composite error**. From what we know about OLS, we must assume that v_{it} is uncorrelated with x_{it}, where $t = 1$ or 2, for OLS to estimate β_1 (and the other parameters consistently). This is true whether we use a single cross section or pool the two cross sections. Therefore, even if we assume that the idiosyncratic error u_{it} is uncorrelated with x_{it}, pooled OLS is biased and inconsistent if a_i and x_{it} are correlated. The resulting bias in pooled OLS is sometimes called **heterogeneity bias**, but it is really just bias caused from omitting a time-constant variable.

To illustrate what happens, we use the data in CRIME2 to estimate (13.14) by pooled OLS. Since there are 46 cities and two years for each city, there are 92 total observations:

$$\widehat{crmrte} = 93.42 + 7.94\,d87 + .427\,unem$$
$$\phantom{\widehat{crmrte} =} (12.74)\ (7.98)\quad\ (1.188) \qquad [13.16]$$
$$n = 92, R^2 = .012.$$

(When reporting the estimated equation, we usually drop the i and t subscripts.) The coefficient on *unem*, though positive in (13.16), has a very small t statistic. Thus, using pooled OLS on the two years has not substantially changed anything from using a single cross section. This is not surprising since using pooled OLS does not solve the omitted variables problem. (The standard errors in this equation are incorrect because of the serial correlation described in Question 13.3, but we ignore this since pooled OLS is not the focus here.)

In most applications, the main reason for collecting panel data is to allow for the unobserved effect, a_i, to be correlated with the explanatory variables. For example, in the crime equation, we want to allow the unmeasured city factors in a_i that affect the crime rate also to be correlated with the unemployment rate. It turns out that this is simple to allow: because a_i is constant over time, we can difference the data across the two years. More precisely, for a cross-sectional observation i, write the two years as

$$y_{i2} = (\beta_0 + \delta_0) + \beta_1 x_{i2} + a_i + u_{i2} \quad (t = 2)$$
$$y_{i1} = \beta_0 + \beta_1 x_{i1} + a_i + u_{i1} \quad (t = 1).$$

If we subtract the *second* equation from the *first*, we obtain

$$(y_{i2} - y_{i1}) = \delta_0 + \beta_1(x_{i2} - x_{i1}) + (u_{i2} - u_{i1}),$$

or

$$\Delta y_i = \delta_0 + \beta_1 \Delta x_i + \Delta u_i, \qquad\qquad\qquad \text{[13.17]}$$

where Δ denotes the change from $t = 1$ to $t = 2$. The unobserved effect, a_i, does not appear in (13.17): it has been "differenced away." Also, the intercept in (13.17) is actually the *change* in the intercept from $t = 1$ to $t = 2$.

Equation (13.17), which we call the **first-differenced equation**, is very simple. It is just a single cross-sectional equation, but each variable is differenced over time. We can analyze (13.17) using the methods we developed in Part 1, provided the key assumptions are satisfied. The most important of these is that Δu_i is uncorrelated with Δx_i. This assumption holds if the idiosyncratic error at each time t, u_{it}, is uncorrelated with the explanatory variable in *both* time periods. This is another version of the **strict exogeneity** assumption that we encountered in Chapter 10 for time series models. In particular, this assumption rules out the case where x_{it} is the lagged dependent variable, $y_{i, t-1}$. Unlike in Chapter 10, we allow x_{it} to be correlated with unobservables that are constant over time. When we obtain the OLS estimator of β_1 from (13.17), we call the resulting estimator the **first-differenced estimator**.

In the crime example, assuming that Δu_i and $\Delta unem_i$ are uncorrelated may be reasonable, but it can also fail. For example, suppose that law enforcement effort (which is in the idiosyncratic error) increases more in cities where the unemployment rate decreases. This can cause negative correlation between Δu_i and $\Delta unem_i$, which would then lead to bias in the OLS estimator. Naturally, this problem can be overcome to some extent by including more factors in the equation, something we will cover later. As usual, it is always possible that we have not accounted for enough time-varying factors.

Another crucial condition is that Δx_i must have some variation across i. This qualification fails if the explanatory variable does not change over time for any cross-sectional observation, or if it changes by the same amount for every observation. This is not an issue in the crime rate example because the unemployment rate changes across time for almost all cities. But, if i denotes an individual and x_{it} is a dummy variable for gender, $\Delta x_i = 0$ for all i; we clearly cannot estimate (13.17) by OLS in this case. This actually makes perfectly good sense: since we allow a_i to be correlated with x_{it}, we cannot hope to separate the effect of a_i on y_{it} from the effect of any variable that does not change over time.

The only other assumption we need to apply to the usual OLS statistics is that (13.17) satisfies the homoskedasticity assumption. This is reasonable in many cases, and, if it does not hold, we know how to test and correct for heteroskedasticity using the methods in Chapter 8. It is sometimes fair to assume that (13.17) fulfills all of the classical linear model assumptions. The OLS estimators are unbiased and all statistical inference is exact in such cases.

When we estimate (13.17) for the crime rate example, we get

$$\widehat{\Delta crmrte} = 15.40 + 2.22\,\Delta unem$$
$$\phantom{\widehat{\Delta crmrte} = } (4.70) \quad (.88) \qquad\qquad\qquad \text{[13.18]}$$
$$n = 46, R^2 = .127,$$

which now gives a positive, statistically significant relationship between the crime and unemployment rates. Thus, differencing to eliminate time-constant effects makes a big difference in this example. The intercept in (13.18) also reveals something interesting. Even if $\Delta unem = 0$, we predict an increase in the crime rate (crimes per 1,000 people) of 15.40. This reflects a secular increase in crime rates throughout the United States from 1982 to 1987.

Even if we do not begin with the unobserved effects model (13.13), using differences across time makes intuitive sense. Rather than estimating a standard cross-sectional relationship—which may suffer from omitted variables, thereby making ceteris paribus conclusions difficult—equation (13.17) explicitly considers how changes in the explanatory variable over time affect the change in y over the same time period. Nevertheless, it is still very useful to have (13.13) in mind: it explicitly shows that we can estimate the effect of x_{it} on y_{it}, holding a_i fixed.

Although differencing two years of panel data is a powerful way to control for unobserved effects, it is not without cost. First, panel data sets are harder to collect than a single cross section, especially for individuals. We must use a survey and keep track of the individual for a follow-up survey. It is often difficult to locate some people for a second survey. For units such as firms, some will go bankrupt or merge with other firms. Panel data are much easier to obtain for schools, cities, counties, states, and countries.

Even if we have collected a panel data set, the differencing used to eliminate a_i can greatly reduce the variation in the explanatory variables. While x_{it} frequently has substantial variation in the cross section for each t, Δx_i may not have much variation. We know from Chapter 3 that a little variation in Δx_i can lead to a large standard error for $\hat{\beta}_1$ when estimating (13.17) by OLS. We can combat this by using a large cross section, but this is not always possible. Also, using longer differences over time is sometimes better than using year-to-year changes.

As an example, consider the problem of estimating the return to education, now using panel data on individuals for two years. The model for person i is

$$\log(wage_{it}) = \beta_0 + \delta_0 d2_t + \beta_1 educ_{it} + a_i + u_{it}, \quad t = 1, 2,$$

where a_i contains unobserved ability—which is probably correlated with $educ_{it}$. Again, we allow different intercepts across time to account for aggregate productivity gains (and inflation, if $wage_{it}$ is in nominal terms). Since, by definition, innate ability does not change over time, panel data methods seem ideally suited to estimate the return to education. The equation in first differences is

$$\Delta \log(wage_i) = \delta_0 + \beta_1 \Delta educ_i + \Delta u_i, \qquad \text{[13.19]}$$

and we can estimate this by OLS. The problem is that we are interested in working adults, and for most employed individuals, education does not change over time. If only a small fraction of our sample has $\Delta educ_i$ different from zero, it will be difficult to get a precise estimator of β_1 from (13.19), unless we have a rather large sample size. In theory, using a first-differenced equation to estimate the return to education is a good idea, but it does not work very well with most currently available panel data sets.

Adding several explanatory variables causes no difficulties. We begin with the unobserved effects model

$$y_{it} = \beta_0 + \delta_0 d2_t + \beta_1 x_{it1} + \beta_2 x_{it2} + \ldots + \beta_k x_{itk} + a_i + u_{it}, \qquad \text{[13.20]}$$

for $t = 1$ and 2. This equation looks more complicated than it is because each explanatory variable has three subscripts. The first denotes the cross-sectional observation number, the second denotes the time period, and the third is just a variable label.

EXAMPLE 13.5   Sleeping versus Working

We use the two years of panel data in SLP75_81, from Biddle and Hamermesh (1990), to estimate the tradeoff between sleeping and working. In Problem 3 in Chapter 3, we used just the 1975 cross section. The panel data set for 1975 and 1981 has 239 people, which is much smaller than the 1975 cross section that includes over 700 people. An unobserved effects model for total minutes of sleeping per week is

$$slpnap_{it} = \beta_0 + \delta_0 d81_t + \beta_1 totwrk_{it} + \beta_2 educ_{it} + \beta_3 marr_{it}$$
$$+ \beta_4 yngkid_{it} + \beta_5 gdhlth_{it} + a_i + u_{it}, \quad t = 1, 2.$$

The unobserved effect, a_i, would be called an *unobserved individual effect* or an *individual fixed effect*. It is potentially important to allow a_i to be correlated with $totwrk_{it}$: the same factors (some biological) that cause people to sleep more or less (captured in a_i) are likely correlated with the amount of time spent working. Some people just have more energy, and this causes them to sleep less and work more. The variable *educ* is years of education, *marr* is a marriage dummy variable, *yngkid* is a dummy variable indicating the presence of a small child, and *gdhlth* is a "good health" dummy variable. Notice that we do not include gender or race (as we did in the cross-sectional analysis), since these do not change over time; they are part of a_i. Our primary interest is in β_1.

Differencing across the two years gives the estimable equation

$$\Delta slpnap_i = \delta_0 + \beta_1 \Delta totwrk_i + \beta_2 \Delta educ_i + \beta_3 \Delta marr_i$$
$$+ \beta_4 \Delta yngkid_i + \beta_5 \Delta gdhlth_i + \Delta u_i.$$

Assuming that the change in the idiosyncratic error, Δu_i, is uncorrelated with the changes in all explanatory variables, we can get consistent estimators using OLS. This gives

$$\widehat{\Delta slpnap} = -92.63 - .227\,\Delta totwrk - .024\,\Delta educ$$
$$(45.87)\ (.036) \qquad (48.759)$$
$$+ 104.21\,\Delta marr + 94.67\,\Delta yngkid + 87.58\,\Delta gdhlth \qquad [13.21]$$
$$(92.86) \qquad (87.65) \qquad (76.60)$$
$$n = 239, R^2 = .150.$$

The coefficient on $\Delta totwrk$ indicates a tradeoff between sleeping and working: holding other factors fixed, one more hour of work is associated with $.227(60) = 13.62$ fewer minutes of sleeping. The t statistic (-6.31) is very significant. No other estimates, except the intercept, are statistically different from zero. The F test for joint significance of all variables except $\Delta totwrk$ gives p-value $= .49$, which means they are jointly insignificant at any reasonable significance level and could be dropped from the equation.

The standard error on $\Delta educ$ is especially large relative to the estimate. This is the phenomenon described earlier for the wage equation. In the sample of 239 people, 183 (76.6%) have no change in education over the six-year period; 90% of the people have a change in education of at most one year. As reflected by the extremely large standard error of $\hat{\beta}_2$, there is not nearly enough variation in education to estimate β_2 with any precision. Anyway, $\hat{\beta}_2$ is practically very small.

Panel data can also be used to estimate finite distributed lag models. Even if we specify the equation for only two years, we need to collect more years of data to obtain the lagged explanatory variables. The following is a simple example.

EXAMPLE 13.6	**Distributed Lag of Crime Rate on Clear-Up Rate**

Eide (1994) uses panel data from police districts in Norway to estimate a distributed lag model for crime rates. The single explanatory variable is the "clear-up percentage" (*clrprc*)—the percentage of crimes that led to a conviction. The crime rate data are from the years 1972 and 1978. Following

Eide, we lag *clrprc* for one and two years: it is likely that past clear-up rates have a deterrent effect on current crime. This leads to the following unobserved effects model for the two years:

$$\log(crime_{it}) = \beta_0 + \delta_0 d78_t + \beta_1 clrprc_{i, t-1} + \beta_2 clrprc_{i, t-2} + a_i + u_{it}.$$

When we difference the equation and estimate it using the data in CRIME3, we get

$$\widehat{\Delta\log(crime)} = .086 - .0040\,\Delta clrprc_{-1} - .0132\,\Delta clrprc_{-2}$$
$$(.064)\ (.0047)\qquad\qquad (.0052) \qquad\qquad\qquad \text{[13.22]}$$
$$n = 53,\ R^2 = .193,\ \bar{R}^2 = .161.$$

The second lag is negative and statistically significant, which implies that a higher clear-up percentage two years ago would deter crime this year. In particular, a 10 percentage point increase in *clrprc* two years ago would lead to an estimated 13.2% drop in the crime rate this year. This suggests that using more resources for solving crimes and obtaining convictions can reduce crime in the future.

13-3a Organizing Panel Data

In using panel data in an econometric study, it is important to know how the data should be stored. We must be careful to arrange the data so that the different time periods for the same cross-sectional unit (person, firm, city, and so on) are easily linked. For concreteness, suppose that the data set is on cities for two different years. For most purposes, the best way to enter the data is to have *two* records for each city, one for each year: the first record for each city corresponds to the early year, and the second record is for the later year. These two records should be adjacent. Therefore, a data set for 100 cities and two years will contain 200 records. The first two records are for the first city in the sample, the next two records are for the second city, and so on. (See Table 1.5 in Chapter 1 for an example.) This makes it easy to construct the differences to store these in the second record for each city and to do a pooled cross-sectional analysis, which can be compared with the differencing estimation.

Most of the two-period panel data sets accompanying this text are stored in this way (for example, CRIME2, CRIME3, GPA3, LOWBRTH, and RENTAL). We use a direct extension of this scheme for panel data sets with more than two time periods.

A second way of organizing two periods of panel data is to have only one record per cross-sectional unit. This requires two entries for each variable, one for each time period. The panel data in SLP75_81 are organized in this way. Each individual has data on the variables *slpnap75*, *slpnap81*, *totwrk75*, *totwrk81*, and so on. Creating the differences from 1975 to 1981 is easy. Other panel data sets with this structure are TRAFFIC1 and VOTE2. Putting the data in one record, however, does not allow a pooled OLS analysis using the two time periods on the original data. Also, this organizational method does not work for panel data sets with more than two time periods, a case we will consider in Section 13-5.

13-4 Policy Analysis with Two-Period Panel Data

Panel data sets are very useful for policy analysis and, in particular, program evaluation. In the simplest program evaluation setup, a sample of individuals, firms, cities, and so on, is obtained in the first time period. Some of these units, those in the treatment group, then take part in a particular program in a later time period; the ones that do not are the control group. This is similar to the natural experiment literature discussed earlier, with one important difference: the *same* cross-sectional units appear in each time period.

As an example, suppose we wish to evaluate the effect of a Michigan job training program on worker productivity of manufacturing firms (see also Computer Exercise C3) in Chapter 9. Let *scrap*$_{it}$ denote the scrap rate of firm *i* during year *t* (the number of items, per 100, that must be scrapped due to defects). Let $grant_{it}$ be a binary indicator equal to one if firm i in year t received a job training grant. For the years 1987 and 1988, the model is

$$scrap_{it} = \beta_0 + \delta_0 y88_t + \beta_1 grant_{it} + a_i + u_{it}, \quad t = 1, 2, \quad [13.23]$$

where $y88_t$ is a dummy variable for 1988 and a_i is the *unobserved firm effect* or the *firm fixed effect*. The unobserved effect contains such factors as average employee ability, capital, and managerial skill; these are roughly constant over a two-year period. We are concerned about a_i being systematically related to whether a firm receives a grant. For example, administrators of the program might give priority to firms whose workers have lower skills. Or, the opposite problem could occur: to make the job training program appear effective, administrators may give the grants to employers with more productive workers. Actually, in this particular program, grants were awarded on a first-come, first-served basis. But whether a firm applied early for a grant could be correlated with worker productivity. In that case, an analysis using a single cross section or just a pooling of the cross sections will produce biased and inconsistent estimators.

Differencing to remove a_i gives

$$\Delta scrap_i = \delta_0 + \beta_1 \Delta grant_i + \Delta u_i. \quad [13.24]$$

Therefore, we simply regress the change in the scrap rate on the change in the grant indicator. Because no firms received grants in 1987, $grant_{i1} = 0$ for all i, and so $\Delta grant_i = grant_{i2} - grant_{i1} = grant_{i2}$, which simply indicates whether the firm received a grant in 1988. However, it is generally important to difference all variables (dummy variables included) because this is necessary for removing a_i in the unobserved effects model (13.23).

Estimating the first-differenced equation using the data in JTRAIN gives

$$\widehat{\Delta scrap} = -.564 - .739\,\Delta grant$$
$$(.405) \quad (.683)$$
$$n = 54, R^2 = .022.$$

Therefore, we estimate that having a job training grant lowered the scrap rate on average by $-.739$. But the estimate is not statistically different from zero.

We get stronger results by using $\log(scrap)$ and estimating the percentage effect:

$$\widehat{\Delta\log(scrap)} = -.057 - .317\Delta grant$$
$$(.097) \quad (.164)$$
$$n = 54, R^2 = .067.$$

Having a job training grant is estimated to lower the scrap rate by about 27.2%. [We obtain this estimate from equation (7.10): $\exp(-.317) - 1 \approx -.272$.] The t statistic is about -1.93, which is marginally significant. By contrast, using pooled OLS of $\log(scrap)$ on $y88$ and $grant$ gives $\hat{\beta}_1 = .057$ (standard error $= .431$). Thus, we find no significant relationship between the scrap rate and the job training grant. Since this differs so much from the first-difference estimates, it suggests that firms that have lower-ability workers are more likely to receive a grant.

It is useful to study the program evaluation model more generally. Let y_{it} denote an outcome variable and let $prog_{it}$ be a program participation dummy variable. The simplest unobserved effects model is

$$y_{it} = \beta_0 + \delta_0 d2_t + \beta_1 prog_{it} + a_i + u_{it}. \quad [13.25]$$

If program participation only occurred in the second period, then the OLS estimator of β_1 in the differenced equation has a very simple representation:

$$\hat{\beta}_1 = \overline{\Delta y}_{treat} - \overline{\Delta y}_{control}. \quad [13.26]$$

That is, we compute the average change in y over the two time periods for the treatment and control groups. Then, $\hat{\beta}_1$ is the difference of these. This is the panel data version of the difference-in-differences estimator in equation (13.11) for two pooled cross sections. With panel data, we have a potentially important advantage: we can difference y across time for the *same* cross-sectional units. This allows us to control for person-, firm-, or city-specific effects, as the model in (13.25) makes clear.

If program participation takes place in both periods, $\hat{\beta}_1$ cannot be written as in (13.26), but we interpret it in the same way: it is the change in the average value of y due to program participation.

Controlling for time-varying factors does not change anything of significance. We simply difference those variables and include them along with $\Delta prog$. This allows us to control for time-varying variables that might be correlated with program designation.

The same differencing method works for analyzing the effects of any policy that varies across city or state. The following is a simple example.

EXAMPLE 13.7 **Effect of Drunk Driving Laws on Traffic Fatalities**

Many states in the United States have adopted different policies in an attempt to curb drunk driving. Two types of laws that we will study here are *open container laws*—which make it illegal for passengers to have open containers of alcoholic beverages—and *administrative per se laws*—which allow courts to suspend licenses after a driver is arrested for drunk driving but before the driver is convicted. One possible analysis is to use a single cross section of states to regress driving fatalities (or those related to drunk driving) on dummy variable indicators for whether each law is present. This is unlikely to work well because states decide, through legislative processes, whether they need such laws. Therefore, the presence of laws is likely to be related to the average drunk driving fatalities in recent years. A more convincing analysis uses panel data over a time period where some states adopted new laws (and some states may have repealed existing laws). The file TRAFFIC1 contains data for 1985 and 1990 for all 50 states and the District of Columbia. The dependent variable is the number of traffic deaths per 100 million miles driven (*dthrte*). In 1985, 19 states had open container laws, while 22 states had such laws in 1990. In 1985, 21 states had per se laws; the number had grown to 29 by 1990.

Using OLS after first differencing gives

$$\widehat{\Delta dthrte} = -.497 - .420\ \Delta open - .151\Delta admn$$
$$\qquad\qquad (.052)\ (.206)\qquad\quad (.117) \qquad\qquad\qquad [13.27]$$
$$n = 51,\ R^2 = .119.$$

EXPLORING FURTHER 13.4

In Example 13.7, $\Delta admn = -1$ for the state of Washington. Explain what this means.

The estimates suggest that adopting an open container law lowered the traffic fatality rate by .42, a nontrivial effect given that the average death rate in 1985 was 2.7 with a standard deviation of about .6. The estimate is statistically significant at the 5% level against a two-sided alternative. The administrative per se law has a smaller effect, and its t statistic is only -1.29; but the estimate is the sign we expect. The intercept in this equation shows that traffic fatalities fell substantially for all states over the five-year period, whether or not there were any law changes. The states that adopted an open container law over this period saw a further drop, on average, in fatality rates.

Other laws might also affect traffic fatalities, such as seat belt laws, motorcycle helmet laws, and maximum speed limits. In addition, we might want to control for age and gender distributions, as well as measures of how influential an organization such as Mothers Against Drunk Driving is in each state.

13-5 Differencing with More Than Two Time Periods

We can also use differencing with more than two time periods. For illustration, suppose we have N individuals and $T = 3$ time periods for each individual. A general fixed effects model is

$$y_{it} = \delta_1 + \delta_2 d2_t + \delta_3 d3_t + \beta_1 x_{it1} + \dots + \beta_k x_{itk} + a_i + u_{it}, \qquad [13.28]$$

for $t = 1$, 2, and 3. (The total number of observations is therefore $3N$.) Notice that we now include two time-period dummies in addition to the intercept. It is a good idea to allow a separate intercept for each time period, especially when we have a small number of them. The base period, as always, is $t = 1$. The intercept for the second time period is $\delta_1 + \delta_2$, and so on. We are primarily interested in $\beta_1, \beta_2, \dots, \beta_k$. If the unobserved effect a_i is correlated with any of the explanatory variables, then using pooled OLS on the three years of data results in biased and inconsistent estimates.

The key assumption is that the idiosyncratic errors are uncorrelated with the explanatory variable in each time period:

$$\text{Cov}(x_{itj}, u_{is}) = 0, \quad \text{for all, } t, s, \text{ and } j. \qquad [13.29]$$

That is, the explanatory variables are *strictly exogenous* after we take out the unobserved effect, a_i. (The strict exogeneity assumption stated in terms of a zero conditional expectation is given in the chapter appendix.) Assumption (13.29) rules out cases where future explanatory variables react to current changes in the idiosyncratic errors, as must be the case if x_{itj} is a lagged dependent variable. If we have omitted an important time-varying variable, then (13.29) is generally violated. Measurement error in one or more explanatory variables can cause (13.29) to be false, just as in Chapter 9. In Chapters 15 and 16, we will discuss what can be done in such cases.

If a_i is correlated with x_{itj}, then x_{itj} will be correlated with the *composite* error, $v_{it} = a_i + u_{it}$, under (13.29). We can eliminate a_i by differencing adjacent periods. In the $T = 3$ case, we subtract time period one from time period two and time period two from time period three. This gives

$$\Delta y_{it} = \delta_2 \Delta d2_t + \delta_3 \Delta d3_t + \beta_1 \Delta x_{it1} + \dots + \beta_k \Delta x_{itk} + \Delta u_{it}, \qquad [13.30]$$

for $t = 2$ and 3. We do not have a differenced equation for $t = 1$ because there is nothing to subtract from the $t = 1$ equation. Now, (13.30) represents *two* time periods for each individual in the sample. If this equation satisfies the classical linear model assumptions, then pooled OLS gives unbiased estimators, and the usual t and F statistics are valid for hypothesis. We can also appeal to asymptotic results. The important requirement for OLS to be consistent is that Δu_{it} is uncorrelated with Δx_{itj} for all j and $t = 2$ and 3. This is the natural extension from the two time period case.

Notice how (13.30) contains the differences in the year dummies, $d2_t$ and $d3_t$. For $t = 2$, $\Delta d2_t = 1$ and $\Delta d3_t = 0$; for $t = 3$, $\Delta d2_t = -1$ and $\Delta d3_t = 1$. Therefore, (13.30) does not contain an intercept. This is inconvenient for certain purposes, including the computation of R-squared. Unless the time intercepts in the original model (13.28) are of direct interest—they rarely are—it is better to estimate the first-differenced equation with an intercept and a single time-period dummy, usually for the third period. In other words, the equation becomes

$$\Delta y_{it} = \alpha_0 + \alpha_3 d3_t + \beta_1 \Delta x_{it1} + \dots + \beta_k \Delta x_{itk} + \Delta u_{it}, \quad \text{for } t = 2 \text{ and } 3.$$

The estimates of the β_j are identical in either formulation.

With more than three time periods, things are similar. If we have the same T time periods for each of N cross-sectional units, we say that the data set is a **balanced panel**: we have the same time periods for all individuals, firms, cities, and so on. When T is small relative to N, we should include a dummy variable for each time period to account for secular changes that are not being modeled. Therefore, after first differencing, the equation looks like

$$\Delta y_{it} = \alpha_0 + \alpha_3 d3_t + \alpha_4 d4_t + \dots + \alpha_T dT_t + \beta_1 \Delta x_{it1} + \dots$$
$$+ \beta_k \Delta x_{itk} + \Delta u_{it}, \quad t = 2, 3, \dots, T, \qquad [13.31]$$

where we have $T - 1$ time periods on each unit i for the first-differenced equation. The total number of observations is $N(T - 1)$.

It is simple to estimate (13.31) by pooled OLS, provided the observations have been properly organized and the differencing carefully done. To facilitate first differencing, the data file should consist of NT records. The first T records are for the first cross-sectional observation, arranged chronologically; the second T records are for the second cross-sectional observations, arranged chronologically; and so on. Then, we compute the differences, with the change from $t - 1$ to t stored in the time t record. Therefore, the differences for $t = 1$ should be missing values for all N cross-sectional observations. Without doing this, you run the risk of using bogus observations in the regression analysis. An invalid observation is created when the last observation for, say, person $i - 1$ is subtracted from the first observation for person i. If you do the regression on the differenced data, and NT or $NT - 1$ observations are reported, then you forgot to set the $t = 1$ observations as missing.

When using more than two time periods, we must assume that Δu_{it} is uncorrelated over time for the usual standard errors and test statistics to be valid. This assumption is sometimes reasonable, but it does not follow if we assume that the original idiosyncratic errors, u_{it}, are uncorrelated over time (an assumption we will use in Chapter 14). In fact, if we assume the u_{it} are serially uncorrelated with constant variance, then the correlation between Δu_{it} and $\Delta u_{i, t+1}$ can be shown to be $-.5$. If u_{it} follows a stable AR(1) model, then Δu_{it} will be serially correlated. Only when u_{it} follows a random walk will Δu_{it} be serially uncorrelated.

It is easy to test for serial correlation in the first-differenced equation. Let $r_{it} = \Delta u_{it}$ denote the first difference of the original error. If r_{it} follows the AR(1) model $r_{it} = \rho r_{i, t-1} + e_{it}$, then we can easily test $H_0: \rho = 0$. First, we estimate (13.31) by pooled OLS and obtain the residuals, $\hat{r}_{it}$.

Then, we run a simple pooled OLS regression of $\hat{r}_{it}$ on $\hat{r}_{i, t-1}$, $t = 3, ..., T$, $i = 1, ..., N$, and compute a standard t test for the coefficient on $\hat{r}_{i, t-1}$. (Or we can make the t statistic robust to heteroskedasticity.) The coefficient $\hat{\rho}$ on $\hat{r}_{i, t-1}$ is a consistent estimator of ρ. Because we are using the lagged residual, we lose another time period. For example, if we started with $T = 3$, the differenced equation has two time periods, and the test for serial correlation is just a cross-sectional regression of the residuals from the third time period on the residuals from the second time period. We will give an example later.

We can correct for the presence of AR(1) serial correlation in r_{it} by using feasible GLS. Essentially, within each cross-sectional observation, we would use the Prais-Winsten transformation based on $\hat{\rho}$ described in the previous paragraph. (We clearly prefer Prais-Winsten to Cochrane-Orcutt here, as dropping the first time period would now mean losing N cross-sectional observations.) Unfortunately, standard packages that perform AR(1) corrections for time series regressions will not work. Standard Prais-Winsten methods will treat the observations as if they followed an AR(1) process across i and t; this makes no sense, as we are assuming the observations are independent across i. Corrections to the OLS standard errors that allow arbitrary forms of serial correlation (and heteroskedasticity) can be computed when N is large (and N should be notably larger than T). A detailed treatment of standard errors and test statistics that are robust to any forms of serial correlation and heteroskedasticity is beyond the scope of this text; see, for example, Wooldridge (2010, Chapter 10). Nevertheless, such statistics are easy to compute in many econometrics software packages, and the appendix contains an intuitive discussion.

> **EXPLORING FURTHER 13.5**
>
> Does serial correlation in Δu_{it} cause the first-differenced estimator to be biased and inconsistent? Why is serial correlation a concern?

If there is no serial correlation in the errors, the usual methods for dealing with heteroskedasticity are valid. We can use the Breusch-Pagan and White tests for heteroskedasticity from Chapter 8, and we can also compute robust standard errors.

Differencing more than two years of panel data is very useful for policy analysis, as shown by the following example.

| EXAMPLE 13.8 | **Effect of Enterprise Zones on Unemployment Claims** |

Papke (1994) studied the effect of the Indiana enterprise zone (EZ) program on unemployment claims. She analyzed 22 cities in Indiana over the period from 1980 to 1988. Six enterprise zones were designated in 1984, and four more were assigned in 1985. Twelve of the cities in the sample did not receive an enterprise zone over this period; they served as the control group.

A simple policy evaluation model is

$$\log(uclms_{it}) = \theta_t + \beta_1 ez_{it} + a_i + u_{it},$$

where $uclms_{it}$ is the number of unemployment claims filed during year t in city i. The parameter θ_t just denotes a different intercept for each time period. Generally, unemployment claims were falling statewide over this period, and this should be reflected in the different year intercepts. The binary variable ez_{it} is equal to one if city i at time t was an enterprise zone; we are interested in β_1. The unobserved effect a_i represents fixed factors that affect the economic climate in city i. Because enterprise zone designation was not determined randomly—enterprise zones are usually economically depressed areas—it is likely that ez_{it} and a_i are positively correlated (high a_i means higher unemployment claims, which lead to a higher chance of being given an EZ). Thus, we should difference the equation to eliminate a_i:

$$\Delta\log(uclms_{it}) = \alpha_0 + \alpha_1 d82_t + \ldots + \alpha_7 d88_t + \beta_1 \Delta ez_{it} + \Delta u_{it}. \qquad [13.32]$$

The dependent variable in this equation, the change in $\log(uclms_{it})$, is the approximate annual growth rate in unemployment claims from year $t - 1$ to t. We can estimate this equation for the years 1981 to 1988 using the data in EZUNEM; the total sample size is $22 \cdot 8 = 176$. The estimate of β_1 is $\hat{\beta}_1 = -.182$ (standard error $= .078$). Therefore, it appears that the presence of an EZ causes about a 16.6% $[\exp(-.182) - 1 \approx -.166]$ fall in unemployment claims. This is an economically large and statistically significant effect.

There is no evidence of heteroskedasticity in the equation: the Breusch-Pagan F test yields $F = .85$, p-value $= .557$. However, when we add the lagged OLS residuals to the differenced equation (and lose the year 1981), we get $\hat{\rho} = -.197$ ($t = -2.44$), so there is evidence of minimal negative serial correlation in the first-differenced errors. Unlike with positive serial correlation, the usual OLS standard errors may not greatly understate the correct standard errors when the errors are negatively correlated (see Section 12-1). Thus, the significance of the enterprise zone dummy variable will probably not be affected.

| EXAMPLE 13.9 | **County Crime Rates in North Carolina** |

Cornwell and Trumbull (1994) used data on 90 counties in North Carolina, for the years 1981 through 1987, to estimate an unobserved effects model of crime; the data are contained in CRIME4. Here, we estimate a simpler version of their model, and we difference the equation over time to eliminate a_i, the unobserved effect. (Cornwell and Trumbull use a different transformation, which we will cover in Chapter 14.) Various factors including geographical location, attitudes toward crime, historical records, and reporting conventions might be contained in a_i. The crime rate is number of crimes per person, *prbarr* is the estimated probability of arrest, *prbconv* is the estimated probability of conviction (given an arrest), *prbpris* is the probability of serving time in prison (given a conviction), *avgsen* is the average sentence length served, and *polpc* is the number of police officers per capita. As is standard in criminometric studies, we use the logs of all variables to estimate elasticities. We also include a full set of year dummies to control for state trends in crime rates. We can use the years 1982 through 1987 to estimate the differenced equation. The quantities in parentheses are the usual OLS standard errors; the quantities in brackets are standard errors robust to both serial correlation and heteroskedasticity:

$$\widehat{\Delta\log(crmrte)} = .008 - .100\ d83 - .048\ d84 - .005\ d85$$
$$(.017)\ (.024)\qquad (.024)\qquad (.023)$$
$$[.014]\ [.022]\qquad [.020]\qquad [.025]$$
$$+ .028\ d86 + .041\ d87 - .327\ \Delta\log(prbarr)$$
$$(.024)\qquad (.024)\qquad (.030)$$
$$[.021]\qquad [.024]\qquad [.056]$$
$$- .238\ \Delta\log(prbconv) - .165\ \Delta\log(prbpris)\qquad\qquad [13.33]$$
$$(.018)\qquad\qquad (.026)$$
$$[.040]\qquad\qquad [.046]$$
$$- .022\ \Delta\log(avgsen) + .398\ \Delta\log(polpc)$$
$$(.022)\qquad\qquad (.027)$$
$$[.026]\qquad\qquad [.103]$$
$$n = 540, R^2 = .433, \overline{R}^2 = .422.$$

The three probability variables—of arrest, conviction, and serving prison time—all have the expected sign, and all are statistically significant. For example, a 1% increase in the probability of arrest is predicted to lower the crime rate by about .33%. The average sentence variable shows a modest deterrent effect, but it is not statistically significant.

The coefficient on the police per capita variable is somewhat surprising and is a feature of most studies that seek to explain crime rates. Interpreted causally, it says that a 1% increase in police per capita *increases* crime rates by about .4%. (The usual t statistic is very large, almost 15.) It is hard to believe that having more police officers causes more crime. What is going on here? There are at least two possibilities. First, the crime rate variable is calculated from *reported* crimes. It might be that, when there are additional police, more crimes are reported. Second, the police variable might be endogenous in the equation for other reasons: counties may enlarge the police force when they expect crime rates to increase. In this case, (13.33) cannot be interpreted in a causal fashion. In Chapters 15 and 16, we will cover models and estimation methods that can account for this additional form of endogeneity.

The special case of the White test for heteroskedasticity in Section 8-3 gives $F = 75.48$ and p-value $= .0000$, so there is strong evidence of heteroskedasticity. (Technically, this test is not valid if there is also serial correlation, but it is strongly suggestive.) Testing for AR(1) serial correlation yields $\hat{\rho} = -.233, t = -4.77$, so negative serial correlation exists. The standard errors in brackets adjust for serial correlation and heteroskedasticity. [We will not give the details of this; the calculations are similar to those described in Section 12-5 and are carried out by many econometric packages. See Wooldridge (2010, Chapter 10) for more discussion.] No variables lose statistical significance, but the t statistics on the significant deterrent variables get notably smaller. For example, the t statistic on the probability of conviction variable goes from -13.22 using the usual OLS standard error to -6.10 using the fully robust standard error. Equivalently, the confidence intervals constructed using the robust standard errors will, appropriately, be much wider than those based on the usual OLS standard errors.

Naturally, we can apply the Chow test to panel data models estimated by first differencing. As in the case of pooled cross sections, we rarely want to test whether the intercepts are constant over time; for many reasons, we expect the intercepts to be different. Much more interesting is to test whether slope coefficients have changed over time, and we can easily carry out such tests by interacting the explanatory variables of interest with time-period dummy variables. Interestingly, while we cannot estimate the slopes on variables that do not change over time, we can test whether the partial effects of time-constant variables have changed over time. As an illustration, suppose we observe three years of data on a random sample of people working in 2000, 2002, and 2004, and specify the model (for the log of wage, *lwage*),

$$lwage_{it} = \beta_0 + \delta_1 d02_t + \delta_2 d04_t + \beta_1 female_i + \gamma_1 d02_t female_i$$
$$+ \gamma_2 d04_t female_i + \mathbf{z}_{it}\boldsymbol{\lambda} + a_i + u_{it},$$

where $\mathbf{z}_{it}\boldsymbol{\lambda}$ is shorthand for other explanatory variables included in the model and their coefficients. When we first difference, we eliminate the intercept for 2000, β_0, and also the gender wage gap for 2000, β_1. However, the change in $d01_t female_i$ is $(\Delta d01_t)female_i$, which does not drop out. Consequently, we can estimate how the wage gap has changed in 2002 and 2004 relative to 2000, and we can test whether $\gamma_1 = 0$, or $\gamma_2 = 0$, or both. We might also ask whether the union wage premium has changed over time, in which case we include in the model $union_{it}$, $d02_t union_{it}$, and $d04_t union_{it}$. The coefficients on all of these explanatory variables can be estimated because $union_{it}$ would presumably have some time variation.

If one tries to estimate a model containing interactions by differencing by hand, it can be a bit tricky. For example, in the previous equation with union status, we must simply difference the interaction terms, $d02_t union_{it}$ and $d04_t union_{it}$. We *cannot* compute the proper differences as, say, $d02_t \Delta union_{it}$ and $d04_t \Delta union_{it}$, or even replacing $d02_t$ and $d04_t$ with their first differences.

As a general comment, it is important to return to the original model and remember that the differencing is used to eliminate a_i. It is easiest to use a built-in command that allows first differencing as an option in panel data analysis. (We will see some of the other options in Chapter 14.)

13-5a Potential Pitfalls in First Differencing Panel Data

In this and previous sections, we have argued that differencing panel data over time, in order to eliminate a time-constant unobserved effect, is a valuable method for obtaining causal effects. Nevertheless, differencing is not free of difficulties. We have already discussed potential problems with the method when the key explanatory variables do not vary much over time (and the method is useless for explanatory variables that never vary over time). Unfortunately, even when we do have sufficient time variation in the x_{itj}, first-differenced (FD) estimation can be subject to serious biases. We have already mentioned that strict exogeneity of the regressors is a critical assumption. Unfortunately, as discussed in Wooldridge (2010, Section 11-1), having more time periods generally does not reduce the inconsistency in the FD estimator when the regressors are not strictly exogenous (say, if $y_{i, t-1}$ is included among the x_{itj}).

Another important drawback to the FD estimator is that it can be worse than pooled OLS if one or more of the explanatory variables is subject to measurement error, especially the classical errors-in-variables model discussed in Section 9.3. Differencing a poorly measured regressor reduces its variation relative to its correlation with the differenced error caused by classical measurement error, resulting in a potentially sizable bias. Solving such problems can be very difficult. See Section 15-8 and Wooldridge (2010, Chapter 11).

Summary

We have studied methods for analyzing independently pooled cross-sectional and panel data sets. Independent cross sections arise when different random samples are obtained in different time periods (usually years). OLS using pooled data is the leading method of estimation, and the usual inference procedures are available, including corrections for heteroskedasticity. (Serial correlation is not an issue because the samples are independent across time.) Because of the time series dimension, we often allow different time intercepts. We might also interact time dummies with certain key variables to see how they have changed over time. This is especially important in the policy evaluation literature for natural experiments.

Panel data sets are being used more and more in applied work, especially for policy analysis. These are data sets where the same cross-sectional units are followed over time. Panel data sets are most useful when controlling for time-constant unobserved features—of people, firms, cities, and so on—which we think might be correlated with the explanatory variables in our model. One way to remove the unobserved effect is to difference the data in adjacent time periods. Then, a standard OLS analysis on the differences can be used. Using two periods of data results in a cross-sectional regression of the differenced data. The usual inference procedures are asymptotically valid under homoskedasticity; exact inference is available under normality.

For more than two time periods, we can use pooled OLS on the differenced data; we lose the first time period because of the differencing. In addition to homoskedasticity, we must assume that the *differenced* errors are serially uncorrelated in order to apply the usual t and F statistics. (The chapter appendix contains a careful listing of the assumptions.) Naturally, any variable that is constant over time drops out of the analysis.

Key Terms

Average Treatment Effect	Fixed Effect	Panel Data
Balanced Panel	Fixed Effects Model	Quasi-Experiment
Clustering	Heterogeneity Bias	Strict Exogeneity
Composite Error	Idiosyncratic Error	Unobserved Effect
Difference-in-Differences	Independently Pooled Cross	Unobserved Effects Model
Estimator	Section	Unobserved Heterogeneity
First-Differenced Equation	Longitudinal Data	Year Dummy Variables
First-Differenced Estimator	Natural Experiment	

Problems

1 In Example 13.1, assume that the averages of all factors other than *educ* have remained constant over time and that the average level of education is 12.2 for the 1972 sample and 13.3 in the 1984 sample. Using the estimates in Table 13.1, find the estimated change in average fertility between 1972 and 1984. (Be sure to account for the intercept change and the change in average education.)

2 Using the data in KIELMC, the following equations were estimated using the years 1978 and 1981:

$$\widehat{\log(price)} = 11.49 - .547\ nearinc + .394\ y81{\cdot}nearinc$$
$$(.26)\ (.058)\qquad\quad (.080)$$
$$n = 321, R^2 = .220$$

and

$$\widehat{\log(price)} = 11.18 + .563\ y81 - .403\ y81{\cdot}nearinc$$
$$(.27)\ (.044)\qquad (.067)$$
$$n = 321, R^2 = .337.$$

Compare the estimates on the interaction term *y81·nearinc* with those from equation (13.9). Why are the estimates so different?

3 Why can we not use first differences when we have independent cross sections in two years (as opposed to panel data)?

4 If we think that β_1 is positive in (13.14) and that Δu_i and $\Delta unem_i$ are negatively correlated, what is the bias in the OLS estimator of β_1 in the first-differenced equation? [*Hint:* Review equation (5.4).]

5 Suppose that we want to estimate the effect of several variables on annual saving and that we have a panel data set on individuals collected on January 31, 1990, and January 31, 1992. If we include a year dummy for 1992 and use first differencing, can we also include age in the original model? Explain.

6 In 1985, neither Florida nor Georgia had laws banning open alcohol containers in vehicle passenger compartments. By 1990, Florida had passed such a law, but Georgia had not.

 (i) Suppose you can collect random samples of the driving-age population in both states, for 1985 and 1990. Let *arrest* be a binary variable equal to unity if a person was arrested for drunk driving during the year. Without controlling for any other factors, write down a linear probability model that allows you to test whether the open container law reduced the probability of being arrested for drunk driving. Which coefficient in your model measures the effect of the law?

 (ii) Why might you want to control for other factors in the model? What might some of these factors be?

 (iii) Now, suppose that you can only collect data for 1985 and 1990 at the county level for the two states. The dependent variable would be the fraction of licensed drivers arrested for drunk driving during the year. How does this data structure differ from the individual-level data described in part (i)? What econometric method would you use?

7 (i) Using the data in INJURY for Kentucky, we find the estimated equation when *afchnge* is dropped from (13.12) is

$$\widehat{\log(durat)} = 1.129 + .253 \, highearn + .198 \, afchnge{\cdot}highearn$$
$$\phantom{\widehat{\log(durat)} = } (0.022) \; (.042) (.052)$$
$$n = 5{,}626,\, R^2 = .021.$$

Is it surprising that the estimate on the interaction is fairly close to that in (13.12)? Explain.

 (ii) When *afchnge* is included but *highearn* is dropped, the result is

$$\widehat{\log(durat)} = 1.233 - .100 \, afchnge + .447 \, afchnge{\cdot}highearn$$
$$\phantom{\widehat{\log(durat)} = } (0.023) \; (.040) (.050)$$
$$n = 5{,}626,\, R^2 = .016.$$

Why is the coefficient on the interaction term now so much larger than in (13.12)? [*Hint:* In equation (13.10), what is the assumption being made about the treatment and control groups if $\beta_1 = 0$?]

Computer Exercises

C1 Use the data in FERTIL1 for this exercise.

 (i) In the equation estimated in Example 13.1, test whether living environment at age 16 has an effect on fertility. (The base group is large city.) Report the value of the F statistic and the p-value.

 (ii) Test whether region of the country at age 16 (South is the base group) has an effect on fertility.

 (iii) Let u be the error term in the population equation. Suppose you think that the variance of u changes over time (but not with *educ*, *age*, and so on). A model that captures this is

$$u^2 = \gamma_0 + \gamma_1 y74 + \gamma_2 y76 + \ldots + \gamma_6 y84 + v.$$

Using this model, test for heteroskedasticity in u. (*Hint:* Your F test should have 6 and 1,122 degrees of freedom.)

 (iv) Add the interaction terms $y74{\cdot}educ$, $y76{\cdot}educ$, ..., $y84{\cdot}educ$ to the model estimated in Table 13.1. Explain what these terms represent. Are they jointly significant?

C2 Use the data in CPS78_85 for this exercise.

(i) How do you interpret the coefficient on $y85$ in equation (13.2)? Does it have an interesting interpretation? (Be careful here; you must account for the interaction terms $y85 \cdot educ$ and $y85 \cdot female$.)

(ii) Holding other factors fixed, what is the estimated percent increase in nominal wage for a male with 12 years of education? Propose a regression to obtain a confidence interval for this estimate. [*Hint:* To get the confidence interval, replace $y85 \cdot educ$ with $y85 \cdot (educ - 12)$; refer to Example 6.3.]

(iii) Reestimate equation (13.2) but let all wages be measured in 1978 dollars. In particular, define the real wage as $rwage = wage$ for 1978 and as $rwage = wage/1.65$ for 1985. Now, use $\log(rwage)$ in place of $\log(wage)$ in estimating (13.2). Which coefficients differ from those in equation (13.2)?

(iv) Explain why the R-squared from your regression in part (iii) is not the same as in equation (13.2). (*Hint:* The residuals, and therefore the sum of squared residuals, from the two regressions *are* identical.)

(v) Describe how union participation changed from 1978 to 1985.

(vi) Starting with equation (13.2), test whether the union wage differential changed over time. (This should be a simple t test.)

(vii) Do your findings in parts (v) and (vi) conflict? Explain.

C3 Use the data in KIELMC for this exercise.

(i) The variable *dist* is the distance from each home to the incinerator site, in feet. Consider the model

$$\log(price) = \beta_0 + \delta_0 y81 + \beta_1 \log(dist) + \delta_1 y81 \cdot \log(dist) + u.$$

If building the incinerator reduces the value of homes closer to the site, what is the sign of δ_1? What does it mean if $\beta_1 > 0$?

(ii) Estimate the model from part (i) and report the results in the usual form. Interpret the coefficient on $y81 \cdot \log(dist)$. What do you conclude?

(iii) Add *age*, age^2, *rooms*, *baths*, $\log(intst)$, $\log(land)$, and $\log(area)$ to the equation. Now, what do you conclude about the effect of the incinerator on housing values?

(iv) Why is the coefficient on $\log(dist)$ positive and statistically significant in part (ii) but not in part (iii)? What does this say about the controls used in part (iii)?

C4 Use the data in INJURY for this exercise.

(i) Using the data for Kentucky, reestimate equation (13.12), adding as explanatory variables *male*, *married*, and a full set of industry and injury type dummy variables. How does the estimate on *afchnge·highearn* change when these other factors are controlled for? Is the estimate still statistically significant?

(ii) What do you make of the small R-squared from part (i)? Does this mean the equation is useless?

(iii) Estimate equation (13.12) using the data for Michigan. Compare the estimates on the interaction term for Michigan and Kentucky. Is the Michigan estimate statistically significant? What do you make of this?

C5 Use the data in RENTAL for this exercise. The data for the years 1980 and 1990 include rental prices and other variables for college towns. The idea is to see whether a stronger presence of students affects rental rates. The unobserved effects model is

$$\log(rent_{it}) = \beta_0 + \delta_0 y90_t + \beta_1 \log(pop_{it}) + \beta_2 \log(avginc_{it}) + \beta_3 pctstu_{it} + a_i + u_{it},$$

where *pop* is city population, *avginc* is average income, and *pctstu* is student population as a percentage of city population (during the school year).

(i) Estimate the equation by pooled OLS and report the results in standard form. What do you make of the estimate on the 1990 dummy variable? What do you get for $\hat{\beta}_{pctstu}$?

(ii) Are the standard errors you report in part (i) valid? Explain.

(iii) Now, difference the equation and estimate by OLS. Compare your estimate of β_{pctstu} with that from part (ii). Does the relative size of the student population appear to affect rental prices?

(iv) Obtain the heteroskedasticity-robust standard errors for the first-differenced equation in part (iii). Does this change your conclusions?

C6 Use CRIME3 for this exercise.

(i) In the model of Example 13.6, test the hypothesis $H_0: \beta_1 = \beta_2$. (*Hint:* Define $\theta_1 = \beta_1 - \beta_2$ and write β_1 in terms of θ_1 and β_2. Substitute this into the equation and then rearrange. Do a t test on θ_1.)

(ii) If $\beta_1 = \beta_2$, show that the differenced equation can be written as

$$\Delta\log(crime_i) = \delta_0 + \delta_1\Delta avgclr_i + \Delta u_i,$$

where $\delta_1 = 2\beta_1$ and $avgclri = (clrprc_{i,-1} + clrprc_{i,-2})/2$ is the average clear-up percentage over the previous two years.

(iii) Estimate the equation from part (ii). Compare the adjusted R-squared with that in (13.22). Which model would you finally use?

C7 Use GPA3 for this exercise. The data set is for 366 student-athletes from a large university for fall and spring semesters. [A similar analysis is in Maloney and McCormick (1993), but here we use a true panel data set.] Because you have two terms of data for each student, an unobserved effects model is appropriate. The primary question of interest is this: Do athletes perform more poorly in school during the semester their sport is in season?

(i) Use pooled OLS to estimate a model with term GPA (*trmgpa*) as the dependent variable. The explanatory variables are *spring, sat, hsperc, female, black, white, frstsem, tothrs, crsgpa,* and *season*. Interpret the coefficient on *season*. Is it statistically significant?

(ii) Most of the athletes who play their sport only in the fall are football players. Suppose the ability levels of football players differ systematically from those of other athletes. If ability is not adequately captured by SAT score and high school percentile, explain why the pooled OLS estimators will be biased.

(iii) Now, use the data differenced across the two terms. Which variables drop out? Now, test for an in-season effect.

(iv) Can you think of one or more potentially important, time-varying variables that have been omitted from the analysis?

C8 VOTE2 includes panel data on House of Representatives elections in 1988 and 1990. Only winners from 1988 who are also running in 1990 appear in the sample; these are the incumbents. An unobserved effects model explaining the share of the incumbent's vote in terms of expenditures by both candidates is

$$vote_{it} = \beta_0 + \delta_0 d90_t + \beta_1\log(inexp_{it}) + \beta_2\log(chexp_{it}) + \beta_3 incshr_{it} + a_i + u_{it},$$

where $incshr_{it}$ is the incumbent's share of total campaign spending (in percentage form). The unobserved effect a_i contains characteristics of the incumbent—such as "quality"—as well as things about the district that are constant. The incumbent's gender and party are constant over time, so these are subsumed in a_i. We are interested in the effect of campaign expenditures on election outcomes.

(i) Difference the given equation across the two years and estimate the differenced equation by OLS. Which variables are individually significant at the 5% level against a two-sided alternative?

(ii) In the equation from part (i), test for joint significance of $\Delta\log(inexp)$ and $\Delta\log(chexp)$. Report the p-value.

(iii) Reestimate the equation from part (i) using $\Delta incshr$ as the only independent variable. Interpret the coefficient on $\Delta incshr$. For example, if the incumbent's share of spending increases by 10 percentage points, how is this predicted to affect the incumbent's share of the vote?

(iv)   Redo part (iii), but now use only the pairs that have repeat challengers. [This allows us to control for characteristics of the challengers as well, which would be in a_i. Levitt (1994) conducts a much more extensive analysis.]

C9   Use CRIME4 for this exercise.

(i)   Add the logs of each wage variable in the data set and estimate the model by first differencing. How does including these variables affect the coefficients on the criminal justice variables in Example 13.9?

(ii)   Do the wage variables in (i) all have the expected sign? Are they jointly significant? Explain.

C10   For this exercise, we use JTRAIN to determine the effect of the job training grant on hours of job training per employee. The basic model for the three years is

$$hrsemp_{it} = \beta_0 + \delta_1 d88_t + \delta_2 d89_t + \beta_1 grant_{it}$$
$$+ \beta_2 grant_{i, t-1} + \beta_3 \log(employ_{it}) + a_i + u_{it}.$$

(i)   Estimate the equation using first differencing. How many firms are used in the estimation? How many total observations would be used if each firm had data on all variables (in particular, *hrsemp*) for all three time periods?

(ii)   Interpret the coefficient on *grant* and comment on its significance.

(iii)   Is it surprising that $grant_{-1}$ is insignificant? Explain.

(iv)   Do larger firms train their employees more or less, on average? How big are the differences in training?

C11   The file MATHPNL contains panel data on school districts in Michigan for the years 1992 through 1998. It is the district-level analogue of the school-level data used by Papke (2005). The response variable of interest in this question is *math4*, the percentage of fourth graders in a district receiving a passing score on a standardized math test. The key explanatory variable is *rexpp*, which is real expenditures per pupil in the district. The amounts are in 1997 dollars. The spending variable will appear in logarithmic form.

(i)   Consider the static unobserved effects model

$$math4_{it} = \delta_1 y93_t + \ldots + \delta_6 y98_t + \beta_1 \log(rexpp_{it})$$
$$+ \beta_2 \log(enrol_{it}) + \beta_3 lunch_{it} + a_i + u_{it},$$

where $enrol_{it}$ is total district enrollment and $lunch_{it}$ is the percentage of students in the district eligible for the school lunch program. (So $lunch_{it}$ is a pretty good measure of the district-wide poverty rate.) Argue that $\beta_1/10$ is the percentage point change in $math4_{it}$ when real per-student spending increases by roughly 10%.

(ii)   Use first differencing to estimate the model in part (i). The simplest approach is to allow an intercept in the first-differenced equation and to include dummy variables for the years 1994 through 1998. Interpret the coefficient on the spending variable.

(iii)   Now, add one lag of the spending variable to the model and reestimate using first differencing. Note that you lose another year of data, so you are only using changes starting in 1994. Discuss the coefficients and significance on the current and lagged spending variables.

(iv)   Obtain heteroskedasticity-robust standard errors for the first-differenced regression in part (iii). How do these standard errors compare with those from part (iii) for the spending variables?

(v)   Now, obtain standard errors robust to both heteroskedasticity and serial correlation. What does this do to the significance of the lagged spending variable?

(vi)   Verify that the differenced errors $r_{it} = \Delta u_{it}$ have negative serial correlation by carrying out a test of AR(1) serial correlation.

(vii)   Based on a fully robust joint test, does it appear necessary to include the enrollment and lunch variables in the model?

C12 Use the data in MURDER for this exercise.

(i) Using the years 1990 and 1993, estimate the equation

$$mrdrte_{it} = \delta_0 + \delta_1 d93_t + \beta_1 exec_{it} + \beta_2 unem_{it} + a_i + u_{it}, t = 1, 2$$

by pooled OLS and report the results in the usual form. Do not worry that the usual OLS standard errors are inappropriate because of the presence of a_i. Do you estimate a deterrent effect of capital punishment?

(ii) Compute the FD estimates (use only the differences from 1990 to 1993; you should have 51 observations in the FD regression). Now what do you conclude about a deterrent effect?

(iii) In the FD regression from part (ii), obtain the residuals, say, $\hat{e}_i$. Run the Breusch-Pagan regression $\hat{e}_i^2$ on $\Delta exec_i$, $\Delta unem_i$ and compute the F test for heteroskedasticity. Do the same for the special case of the White test [that is, regress $\hat{e}_i^2$ on $\hat{y}_i$, $\hat{y}_i^2$, where the fitted values are from part (ii)]. What do you conclude about heteroskedasticity in the FD equation?

(iv) Run the same regression from part (ii), but obtain the heteroskedasticity-robust t statistics. What happens?

(v) Which t statistic on $\Delta exec_i$ do you feel more comfortable relying on, the usual one or the heteroskedasticity-robust one? Why?

C13 Use the data in WAGEPAN for this exercise.

(i) Consider the unobserved effects model

$$lwage_{it} = \beta_0 + \delta_1 d81_t + \ldots + \delta_7 d87_t + \beta_1 educ_i$$
$$+ \gamma_1 d81_t educ_i + \ldots + \delta_7 d87_t educ_i + \beta_2 union_{it} + a_i + u_{it},$$

where a_i is allowed to be correlated with $educ_i$ and $union_{it}$. Which parameters can you estimate using first differencing?

(ii) Estimate the equation from part (i) by FD, and test the null hypothesis that the return to education has not changed over time.

(iii) Test the hypothesis from part (ii) using a fully robust test, that is, one that allows arbitrary heteroskedasticity and serial correlation in the FD errors, Δu_{it}. Does your conclusion change?

(iv) Now allow the union differential to change over time (along with education) and estimate the equation by FD. What is the estimated union differential in 1980? What about 1987? Is the difference statistically significant?

(v) Test the null hypothesis that the union differential has not changed over time, and discuss your results in light of your answer to part (iv).

C14 Use the data in JTRAIN3 for this question.

(i) Estimate the simple regression model $re78 = \beta_0 + \beta_1 train + u$, and report the results in the usual form. Based on this regression, does it appear that job training, which took place in 1976 and 1977, had a positive effect on real labor earnings in 1978?

(ii) Now use the change in real labor earnings, $cre = re78 - re75$, as the dependent variable. (We need not difference $train$ because we assume there was no job training prior to 1975. That is, if we define $ctrain = train78 - train75$ then $ctrain = train78$ because $train75 = 0$.) Now what is the estimated effect of training? Discuss how it compares with the estimate in part (i).

(iii) Find the 95% confidence interval for the training effect using the usual OLS standard error and the heteroskedasticity-robust standard error, and describe your findings.

C15 The data set HAPPINESS contains independently pooled cross sections for the even years from 1994 through 2006, obtained from the General Social Survey. The dependent variable for this problem is a measure of "happiness," $vhappy$, which is a binary variable equal to one if the person reports being "very happy" (as opposed to just "pretty happy" or "not too happy").

(i) Which year has the largest number of observations? Which has the smallest? What is the percentage of people in the sample reporting they are "very happy"?

(ii) Regress *vhappy* on all of the year dummies, leaving out *y94* so that 1994 is the base year. Compute a heteroskedasticity-robust statistic of the null hypothesis that the proportion of very happy people has not changed over time. What is the *p*-value of the test?

(iii) To the regression in part (ii), add the dummy variables *occattend* and *regattend*. Interpret their coefficients. (Remember, the coefficients are interpreted relative to a base group.) How would you summarize the effects of church attendance on happiness?

(iv) Define a variable, say *highinc*, equal to one if family income is above $25,000. (Unfortunately, the same threshold is used in each year, and so inflation is not accounted for. Also, $25,000 is hardly what one would consider "high income.") Include *highinc*, *unem10*, *educ*, and *teens* in the regression in part (iii). Is the coefficient on *regattend* affected much? What about its statistical significance?

(v) Discuss the signs, magnitudes, and statistical significance of the four new variables in part (iv). Do the estimates make sense?

(vi) Controlling for the factors in part (iv), do there appear to be differences in happiness by gender or race? Justify your answer.

C16 Use the data in COUNTYMURDERS to answer this question. The data set covers murders and executions (capital punishment) for 2,197 counties in the United States.

(i) Find the average value of *murdrate* across all counties and years. What is the standard deviation? For what percentage of the sample is *murdrate* equal to zero?

(ii) How many observations have *execs* equal to zero? What is the maximum value of *execs*? Why is the average of *execs* so small?

(iii) Consider the model

$$murdrate_{it} = \theta_t + \beta_1 execs_{it} + \beta_2 execs_{i,t-1} + \beta_3 percblack_{it} + \beta_4 percmale_i$$
$$+ \beta_5 perc1019 + \beta_6 perc2029 + a_i + u_{it},$$

where θ_t represents a different intercept for each time period, a_i is the county fixed effect, and u_{it} is the idiosyncratic error. What do we need to assume about a_i and the execution variables in order for pooled OLS to consistently estimate the parameters, in particular, β_1 and β_2?

(iv) Apply OLS to the equation from part (ii) and report the estimates of β_1 and β_2, along with the usual pooled OLS standard errors. Do you estimate that executions have a deterrent effect on murders? What do you think is happening?

(v) Even if the pooled OLS estimators are consistent, do you trust the standard errors obtained from part (iv)? Explain.

(vi) Now estimate the equation in part (iii) using first differencing to remove a_i. What are the new estimates of β_1 and β_2? Are they very different from the estimates from part (iv)?

(vii) Using the estimates from part (vi), can you say there is evidence of a statistically significant deterrent effect of capital punishment on the murder rate? If possible, in addition to the usual OLS standard errors, use those that are robust to any kind of serial correlation or heteroskedasticity in the FD errors.

APPENDIX 13A

13A.1 Assumptions for Pooled OLS Using First Differences

In this appendix, we provide careful statements of the assumptions for the first-differencing estimator. Verification of these claims is somewhat involved, but it can be found in Wooldridge (2010, Chapter 10).

Assumption FD.1

For each i, the model is

$$y_{it} = \beta_1 x_{it1} + \ldots + \beta_k x_{itk} + a_i + u_{it}, \ t = 1, \ldots, T,$$

where the β_j are the parameters to estimate and a_i is the unobserved effect.

Assumption FD.2

We have a random sample from the cross section.

Assumption FD.3

Each explanatory variable changes over time (for at least some i), and no perfect linear relationships exist among the explanatory variables.

For the next assumption, it is useful to let $\mathbf{X}_i$ denote the explanatory variables for all time periods for cross-sectional observation i; thus, $\mathbf{X}_i$ contains x_{itj}, $t = 1, \ldots, T$, $j = 1, \ldots, k$.

Assumption FD.4

For each t, the expected value of the idiosyncratic error given the explanatory variables in *all* time periods and the unobserved effect is zero: $\mathrm{E}(u_{it}|\mathbf{X}_i, a_i) = 0$.

When Assumption FD.4 holds, we sometimes say that the x_{itj} are *strictly exogenous conditional on the unobserved effect*. The idea is that, once we control for a_i, there is no correlation between the x_{isj} and the remaining idiosyncratic error, u_{it}, for all s and t.

As stated, Assumption FD.4 is stronger than necessary. We use this form of the assumption because it emphasizes that we are interested in the equation

$$\mathrm{E}(y_{it}|\mathbf{X}_i, a_i) = \mathrm{E}(y_{it}|\mathbf{x}_{it}, a_i) = \beta_1 x_{it1} + \ldots + \beta_k x_{itk} + a_i,$$

so that the β_j measure partial effects of the observed explanatory variables holding fixed, or "controlling for," the unobserved effect, a_i. Nevertheless, an important implication of FD.4, and one that is sufficient for the unbiasedness of the FD estimator, is $\mathrm{E}(\Delta u_{it}|\mathbf{X}_i) = 0, t = 2, \ldots, T$. In fact, for consistency we can simply assume that Δx_{itj} is uncorrelated with Δu_{it} for all $t = 2, \ldots, T$ and $j = 1, \ldots, k$. See Wooldridge (2010, Chapter 10) for further discussion.

Under these first four assumptions, the first-difference estimators are unbiased. The key assumption is FD.4, which is strict exogeneity of the explanatory variables. Under these same assumptions, we can also show that the FD estimator is consistent with a fixed T and as $N \to \infty$ (and perhaps more generally).

The next two assumptions ensure that the standard errors and test statistics resulting from pooled OLS on the first differences are (asymptotically) valid.

Assumption FD.5

The variance of the differenced errors, conditional on all explanatory variables, is constant: $\text{Var}(\Delta u_{it}|\mathbf{X}_i) = \sigma^2$, $t = 2, \ldots, T$.

Assumption FD.6

For all $t \neq s$, the *differences* in the idiosyncratic errors are uncorrelated (conditional on all explanatory variables): $\text{Cov}(\Delta u_{it}, \Delta u_{is}|\mathbf{X}_i) = 0$, $t \neq s$.

Assumption FD.5 ensures that the differenced errors, Δu_{it}, are homoskedastic. Assumption FD.6 states that the differenced errors are serially uncorrelated, which means that the u_{it} follow a random walk across time (see Chapter 11). Under Assumptions FD.1 through FD.6, the FD estimator of the β_j is the best linear unbiased estimator (conditional on the explanatory variables).

Assumption FD.7

Conditional on $\mathbf{X}_i$, the Δu_{it} are independent and identically distributed normal random variables.

When we add Assumption FD.7, the FD estimators are normally distributed, and the t and F statistics from pooled OLS on the differences have exact t and F distributions. Without FD.7, we can rely on the usual asymptotic approximations.

13A.2 Computing Standard Errors Robust to Serial Correlation and Heteroskedasticity of Unknown Form

Because the FD estimator is consistent as $N \to \infty$ under Assumptions FD.1 through FD.4, it would be very handy to have a simple method of obtaining proper standard errors and test statistics that allow for any kind of serial correlation or heteroskedasticity in the FD errors, $e_{it} = \Delta u_{it}$. Fortunately, provided N is moderately large, and T is not "too large," fully robust standard errors and test statistics are readily available. As mentioned in the text, a detailed treatment is above the level of this text. The technical arguments combine the insights described in Chapters 8 and 12, where statistics robust to heteroskedasticity and serial correlation are discussed. Actually, there is one important advantage with panel data: because we have a (large) cross section, we can allow unrestricted serial correlation in the errors $\{e_{it}\}$, provided T is not too large. We can contrast this situation with the Newey-West approach in Section 12-5, where the estimated covariances must be downweighted as the observations get farther apart in time.

The general approach to obtaining fully robust standard errors and test statistics in the context of panel data is known as **clustering**, and ideas have been borrowed from the cluster sampling literature. The idea is that each cross-sectional unit is defined as a cluster of observations over time, and arbitrary correlation—serial correlation—and changing variances are allowed within each cluster. Because of the relationship to cluster sampling, many econometric software packages have options for clustering standard errors and test statistics. Most commands look something like

$$\text{regress cy cx1 cx2} \ldots \text{cxk, cluster(id)},$$

where "id" is a variable containing unique identifiers for the cross-sectional units (and the "c" before each variable denotes "change"). The option "cluster(id)" at the end of the "regress" command tells the software to report all standard errors and test statistics—including t statistics and F-type statistics—so that they are valid, in large cross sections, with any kind of serial correlation or heteroskedasticity. Reporting such statistics is very common in modern empirical work with panel data. Often the corrected standard errors will be substantially larger than either the usual standard errors or those that only correct for heteroskedasticity. The larger standard errors better reflect the sampling error in the pooled OLS coefficients.

CHAPTER 14

Advanced Panel Data Methods

I n this chapter, we focus on two methods for estimating unobserved effects panel data models that are at least as common as first differencing. Although these methods are somewhat harder to describe and implement, several econometrics packages support them.

In Section 14-1, we discuss the fixed effects estimator, which, like first differencing, uses a transformation to remove the unobserved effect a_i prior to estimation. Any time-constant explanatory variables are removed along with a_i.

The random effects estimator in Section 14-2 is attractive when we think the unobserved effect is uncorrelated with all the explanatory variables. If we have good controls in our equation, we might believe that any leftover neglected heterogeneity only induces serial correlation in the composite error term, but it does not cause correlation between the composite errors and the explanatory variables. Estimation of random effects models by generalized least squares is fairly easy and is routinely done by many econometrics packages.

Section 14-3 introduces the relatively new correlated random effects approach, which provides a synthesis of fixed effects and random effects methods, and has been shown to be practically very useful.

In Section 14-4, we show how panel data methods can be applied to other data structures, including matched pairs and cluster samples.

14-1 Fixed Effects Estimation

First differencing is just one of the many ways to eliminate the fixed effect, a_i. An alternative method, which works better under certain assumptions, is called the **fixed effects transformation**. To see what this method involves, consider a model with a single explanatory variable: for each i,

$$y_{it} = \beta_1 x_{it} + a_i + u_{it}, \quad t = 1, 2, \ldots, T. \tag{14.1}$$

Now, for each i, average this equation over time. We get

$$\bar{y}_i = \beta_1 \bar{x}_i + a_i + \bar{u}_i, \tag{14.2}$$

where $\bar{y}_i = T^{-1} \sum_{t=1}^{T} y_{it}$, and so on. Because a_i is fixed over time, it appears in both (14.1) and (14.2). If we subtract (14.2) from (14.1) for each t, we wind up with

$$y_{it} - \bar{y}_i = \beta_1(x_{it} - \bar{x}_i) + u_{it} - \bar{u}_i, \quad t = 1, 2, \ldots, T,$$

or

$$\ddot{y}_{it} = \beta_1 \ddot{x}_{it} + \ddot{u}_{it}, \quad t = 1, 2, \ldots, T, \tag{14.3}$$

where $\ddot{y}_{it} = y_{it} - \bar{y}_i$ is the **time-demeaned data** on y, and similarly for $\ddot{x}_{it}$ and $\ddot{u}_{it}$. The fixed effects transformation is also called the **within transformation**. The important thing about equation (14.3) is that the unobserved effect, a_i, has disappeared. This suggests that we should estimate (14.3) by pooled OLS. A pooled OLS estimator that is based on the time-demeaned variables is called the **fixed effects estimator** or the **within estimator**. The latter name comes from the fact that OLS on (14.3) uses the time variation in y and x *within* each cross-sectional observation.

The *between estimator* is obtained as the OLS estimator on the cross-sectional equation (14.2) (where we include an intercept, β_0): we use the time averages for both y and x and then run a cross-sectional regression. We will not study the between estimator in detail because it is biased when a_i is correlated with $\bar{x}_i$ (see Problem 2). If we think a_i is uncorrelated with x_{it}, it is better to use the random effects estimator, which we cover in Section 14-2. The between estimator ignores important information on how the variables change over time.

Adding more explanatory variables to the equation causes few changes. The original **unobserved effects model** is

$$y_{it} = \beta_1 x_{it1} + \beta_2 x_{it2} + \ldots + \beta_k x_{itk} + a_i + u_{it}, \quad t = 1, 2, \ldots, T. \tag{14.4}$$

We simply use the time-demeaning on each explanatory variable—including things like time-period dummies—and then do a pooled OLS regression using all time-demeaned variables. The general time-demeaned equation for each i is

$$\ddot{y}_{it} = \beta_1 \ddot{x}_{it1} + \beta_2 \ddot{x}_{it2} + \ldots + \beta_k \ddot{x}_{itk} + \ddot{u}_{it}, \quad t = 1, 2, \ldots, T, \tag{14.5}$$

which we estimate by pooled OLS.

> **EXPLORING FURTHER 14.1**
>
> Suppose that in a family savings equation, for the years 1990, 1991, and 1992, we let $kids_{it}$ denote the number of children in family i for year t. If the number of kids is constant over this three-year period for most families in the sample, what problems might this cause for estimating the effect that the number of kids has on savings?

Under a strict exogeneity assumption on the explanatory variables, the fixed effects estimator is unbiased: roughly, the idiosyncratic error u_{it} should be uncorrelated with each explanatory variable across *all* time periods. (See the chapter appendix for precise statements of the assumptions.) The fixed effects estimator allows for arbitrary correlation between a_i and the explanatory variables in any time period, just as with first differencing. Because of this, any explanatory variable that is constant over time for all i gets swept away by the fixed effects transformation: $\ddot{x}_{it} = 0$ for all i and t, if x_{it} is constant across t. Therefore, we cannot include variables such as gender or a city's distance from a river.

The other assumptions needed for a straight OLS analysis to be valid are that the errors u_{it} are homoskedastic and serially uncorrelated (across t); see the appendix to this chapter.

There is one subtle point in determining the degrees of freedom for the fixed effects estimator. When we estimate the time-demeaned equation (14.5) by pooled OLS, we have NT total observations and k independent variables. [Notice that there is no intercept in (14.5); it is eliminated by the fixed effects transformation.] Therefore, we should apparently have $NT - k$ degrees of freedom. This calculation is incorrect. For each cross-sectional observation i, we lose one df because of the time-demeaning. In other words, for each i, the demeaned errors $\ddot{u}_{it}$ add up to zero when summed across t, so we lose one degree of freedom. (There is no such constraint on the original idiosyncratic errors u_{it}.) Therefore, the appropriate degrees of freedom is $df = NT - N - k = N(T - 1) - k$. Fortunately, modern regression packages that have a fixed effects estimation feature properly compute the df. But if we have to do the time-demeaning and the estimation by pooled OLS ourselves, we need to correct the standard errors and test statistics.

EXAMPLE 14.1 **Effect of Job Training on Firm Scrap Rates**

We use the data for three years, 1987, 1988, and 1989, on the 54 firms that reported scrap rates in each year. No firms received grants prior to 1988; in 1988, 19 firms received grants; in 1989, 10 different firms received grants. Therefore, we must also allow for the possibility that the additional job training in 1988 made workers more productive in 1989. This is easily done by including a lagged value of the grant indicator. We also include year dummies for 1988 and 1989. The results are given in Table 14.1.

We have reported the results in a way that emphasizes the need to interpret the estimates in light of the unobserved effects model, (14.4). We are explicitly controlling for the unobserved, time-constant effects in a_i. The time-demeaning allows us to estimate the β_j, but (14.5) is not the best equation for interpreting the estimates.

Interestingly, the estimated lagged effect of the training grant is substantially larger than the contemporaneous effect: job training has an effect at least one year later. Because the dependent variable is in logarithmic form, obtaining a grant in 1988 is predicted to lower the firm scrap rate in 1989 by about 34.4% $[\exp(-.422) - 1 \approx -.344]$; the coefficient on $grant_{-1}$ is significant at the 5% level against a two-sided alternative. The coefficient on $grant$ is significant at the 10% level, and the size

TABLE 14.1 Fixed Effects Estimation of the Scrap Rate Equation

Dependent Variable: log(scrap)

Independent Variables	Coefficient (Standard Error)
d88	−.080 (.109)
d89	−.247 (.133)
grant	−.252 (.151)
grant_{-1}	−.422 (.210)
Observations	162
Degrees of freedom	104
R-squared	.201

<table>
<tr><td>

EXPLORING FURTHER 14.2

Under the Michigan program, if a firm received a grant in one year, it was not eligible for a grant the following year. What does this imply about the correlation between *grant* and *grant*$_{-1}$?

</td></tr>
</table>

of the coefficient is hardly trivial. Notice the *df* is obtained as $N(T-1) - k = 54(3-1) - 4 = 104$.

The coefficient on *d89* indicates that the scrap rate was substantially lower in 1989 than in the base year, 1987, even in the absence of job training grants. Thus, it is important to allow for these aggregate effects. If we omitted the year dummies, the secular increase in worker productivity would be attributed to the job training grants. Table 14.1 shows that, even after controlling for aggregate trends in productivity, the job training grants had a large estimated effect.

Finally, it is crucial to allow for the lagged effect in the model. If we omit *grant*$_{-1}$, then we are assuming that the effect of job training does not last into the next year. The estimate on *grant* when we drop *grant*$_{-1}$ is $-.082$ $(t = -.65)$; this is much smaller and statistically insignificant.

When estimating an unobserved effects model by fixed effects, it is not clear how we should compute a goodness-of-fit measure. The *R*-squared given in Table 14.1 is based on the within transformation: it is the *R*-squared obtained from estimating (14.5). Thus, it is interpreted as the amount of time variation in the y_{it} that is explained by the time variation in the explanatory variables. Other ways of computing *R*-squared are possible, one of which we discuss later.

Although time-constant variables cannot be included by themselves in a fixed effects model, they *can* be interacted with variables that change over time and, in particular, with year dummy variables. For example, in a wage equation where education is constant over time for each individual in our sample, we can interact education with each year dummy to see how the return to education has changed over time. But we cannot use fixed effects to estimate the return to education in the base period, which means we cannot estimate the return to education in any period; we can only see how the return to education in each year differs from that in the base period. Section 14-3 describes an approach that allows coefficients on time-constant variables to be estimated while preserving the fixed effects nature of the analysis.

When we include a full set of year dummies—that is, year dummies for all years but the first— we cannot estimate the effect of any variable whose *change* across time is constant. An example is years of experience in a panel data set where each person works in every year, so that experience always increases by one in each year, for every person in the sample. The presence of a_i accounts for differences across people in their years of experience in the initial time period. But then the effect of a one-year increase in experience cannot be distinguished from the aggregate time effects (because experience increases by the same amount for everyone). This would also be true if, in place of separate year dummies, we used a linear time trend: for each person, experience cannot be distinguished from a linear trend.

EXAMPLE 14.2   **Has the Return to Education Changed over Time?**

The data in WAGEPAN are from Vella and Verbeek (1998). Each of the 545 men in the sample worked in every year from 1980 through 1987. Some variables in the data set change over time: experience, marital status, and union status are the three important ones. Other variables do not change: race and education are the key examples. If we use fixed effects (or first differencing), we cannot include race, education, or experience in the equation. However, we can include interactions of *educ* with year dummies for 1981 through 1987 to test whether the return to education was constant over this time period. We use log(*wage*) as the dependent variable, dummy variables for marital and union status, a full set of year dummies, and the interaction terms *d81·educ*, *d82·educ*, ..., *d87·educ*.

The estimates on these interaction terms are all positive, and they generally get larger for more recent years. The largest coefficient of .030 is on *d87·educ*, with $t = 2.48$. In other words, the return to education is estimated to be about 3 percentage points larger in 1987 than in the base year, 1980. (We do not have an estimate of the return to education in the base year for the reasons given earlier.) The other significant interaction term is $d86 \cdot educ$ (coefficient = .027, $t = 2.23$). The estimates on the earlier years are smaller and insignificant at the 5% level against a two-sided alternative. If we do a joint F test for significance of all seven interaction terms, we get p-value = .28: this gives an example where a set of variables is jointly insignificant even though some variables are individually significant. [The df for the F test are 7 and 3,799; the second of these comes from $N(T - 1) - k = 545(8 - 1) - 16 = 3,799$.] Generally, the results are consistent with an increase in the return to education over this period.

14-1a The Dummy Variable Regression

A traditional view of the fixed effects approach is to assume that the unobserved effect, a_i, is a parameter to be estimated for each i. Thus, in equation (14.4), a_i is the intercept for person i (or firm i, city i, and so on) that is to be estimated along with the β_j. (Clearly, we cannot do this with a single cross section: there would be $N + k$ parameters to estimate with only N observations. We need at least two time periods.) The way we estimate an intercept for each i is to put in a dummy variable for each cross-sectional observation, along with the explanatory variables (and probably dummy variables for each time period). This method is usually called the **dummy variable regression**. Even when N is not very large (say, $N = 54$ as in Example 14.1), this results in many explanatory variables—in most cases, too many to explicitly carry out the regression. Thus, the dummy variable method is not very practical for panel data sets with many cross-sectional observations.

Nevertheless, the dummy variable regression has some interesting features. Most importantly, it gives us *exactly* the same estimates of the β_j that we would obtain from the regression on time-demeaned data, and the standard errors and other major statistics are identical. Therefore, the fixed effects estimator can be obtained by the dummy variable regression. One benefit of the dummy variable regression is that it properly computes the degrees of freedom directly. This is a minor advantage now that many econometrics packages have programmed fixed effects options.

The R-squared from the dummy variable regression is usually rather high. This occurs because we are including a dummy variable for each cross-sectional unit, which explains much of the variation in the data. For example, if we estimate the unobserved effects model in Example 13.8 by fixed effects using the dummy variable regression (which is possible with $N = 22$), then $R^2 = .933$. We should not get too excited about this large R-squared: it is not surprising that we can explain much of the variation in unemployment claims using both year and city dummies. Just as in Example 13.8, the estimate on the EZ dummy variable is more important than R^2.

The R-squared from the dummy variable regression can be used to compute F tests in the usual way, assuming, of course, that the classical linear model assumptions hold (see the chapter appendix). In particular, we can test the joint significance of all of the cross-sectional dummies ($N - 1$, since one unit is chosen as the base group). The unrestricted R-squared is obtained from the regression with all of the cross-sectional dummies; the restricted R-squared omits these. In the vast majority of applications, the dummy variables will be jointly significant.

Occasionally, the estimated intercepts, say $\hat{a}_i$, are of interest. This is the case if we want to study the distribution of the $\hat{a}_i$ across i, or if we want to pick a particular firm or city to see whether its $\hat{a}_i$ is above or below the average value in the sample. These estimates are directly available from the dummy variable regression, but they are rarely reported by packages that have fixed effects routines (for the practical reason that there are so many $\hat{a}_i$). After fixed effects estimation with N of any size, the $\hat{a}_i$ are pretty easy to compute:

$$\hat{a}_i = \bar{y}_i - \hat{\beta}_1 \bar{x}_{i1} - \ldots - \hat{\beta}_k \bar{x}_{ik}, \, i = 1, \ldots, N, \tag{14.6}$$

where the overbar refers to the time averages and the $\hat{\beta}_j$ are the fixed effects estimates. For example, if we have estimated a model of crime while controlling for various time-varying factors, we can obtain $\hat{a}_i$ for a city to see whether the unobserved fixed effects that contribute to crime are above or below average.

Some econometrics packages that support fixed effects estimation report an "intercept," which can cause confusion in light of our earlier claim that the time-demeaning eliminates all time-constant variables, including an overall intercept. [See equation (14.5).] Reporting an overall intercept in fixed effects (FE) estimation arises from viewing the a_i as parameters to estimate. Typically, the intercept reported is the average across i of the $\hat{a}_i$. In other words, the overall intercept is actually the average of the individual-specific intercepts, which is an unbiased, consistent estimator of $\alpha = \mathrm{E}(a_i)$.

In most studies, the $\hat{\beta}_j$ are of interest, and so the time-demeaned equations are used to obtain these estimates. Further, it is usually best to view the a_i as omitted variables that we control for through the within transformation. The sense in which the a_i can be estimated is generally weak. In fact, even though $\hat{a}_i$ is unbiased (under Assumptions FE.1 through FE.4 in the chapter appendix), it is not consistent with a fixed T as $N \to \infty$. The reason is that, as we add each additional cross-sectional observation, we add a new a_i. No information accumulates on each a_i when T is fixed. With larger T, we can get better estimates of the a_i, but most panel data sets are of the large N and small T variety.

14-1b Fixed Effects or First Differencing?

So far, setting aside pooled OLS, we have seen two competing methods for estimating unobserved effects models. One involves differencing the data, and the other involves time-demeaning. How do we know which one to use?

We can eliminate one case immediately: when $T = 2$, the FE and FD estimates, as well as all test statistics, are *identical*, and so it does not matter which we use. Of course, the equivalence between the FE and FD estimates requires that we estimate the same model in each case. In particular, as we discussed in Chapter 13, it is natural to include an intercept in the FD equation; this intercept is actually the intercept for the second time period in the original model written for the two time periods. Therefore, FE estimation must include a dummy variable for the second time period in order to be identical to the FD estimates that include an intercept.

With $T = 2$, FD has the advantage of being straightforward to implement in any econometrics or statistical package that supports basic data manipulation, and it is easy to compute heteroskedasticity-robust statistics after FD estimation (because when $T = 2$, FD estimation is just a cross-sectional regression).

When $T \geq 3$, the FE and FD estimators are not the same. Since both are unbiased under Assumptions FE.1 through FE.4, we cannot use unbiasedness as a criterion. Further, both are consistent (with T fixed as $N \to \infty$) under FE.1 through FE.4. For large N and small T, the choice between FE and FD hinges on the relative efficiency of the estimators, and this is determined by the serial correlation in the idiosyncratic errors, u_{it}. (We will assume homoskedasticity of the u_{it}, since efficiency comparisons require homoskedastic errors.)

When the u_{it} are serially uncorrelated, fixed effects is more efficient than first differencing (and the standard errors reported from fixed effects are valid). Since the unobserved effects model is typically stated (sometimes only implicitly) with serially uncorrelated idiosyncratic errors, the FE estimator is used more than the FD estimator. But we should remember that this assumption can be false. In many applications, we can expect the unobserved factors that change over time to be serially correlated. If u_{it} follows a random walk—which means that there is very substantial, positive serial correlation—then the difference Δu_{it} is serially uncorrelated, and first differencing is better. In many cases, the u_{it} exhibit some positive serial correlation, but perhaps not as much as a random walk. Then, we cannot easily compare the efficiency of the FE and FD estimators.

It is difficult to test whether the u_{it} are serially uncorrelated after FE estimation: we can estimate the time-demeaned errors, $\ddot{u}_{it}$, but not the u_{it}. However, in Section 13-3, we showed how to test whether the differenced errors, Δu_{it}, are serially uncorrelated. If this seems to be the case, FD can be used. If there is substantial negative serial correlation in the Δu_{it}, FE is probably better. It is often a good idea to try both: if the results are not sensitive, so much the better.

When T is large, and especially when N is not very large (for example, $N = 20$ and $T = 30$), we must exercise caution in using the fixed effects estimator. Although exact distributional results hold for any N and T under the classical fixed effects assumptions, inference can be very sensitive to violations of the assumptions when N is small and T is large. In particular, if we are using unit root processes—see Chapter 11—the spurious regression problem can arise. First differencing has the advantage of turning an integrated time series process into a weakly dependent process. Therefore, if we apply first differencing, we can appeal to the central limit theorem even in cases where T is larger than N. Normality in the idiosyncratic errors is not needed, and heteroskedasticity and serial correlation can be dealt with as we touched on in Chapter 13. Inference with the fixed effects estimator is potentially more sensitive to nonnormality, heteroskedasticity, and serial correlation in the idiosyncratic errors.

Like the first difference estimator, the fixed effects estimator can be very sensitive to classical measurement error in one or more explanatory variables. However, if each x_{itj} is uncorrelated with u_{it}, but the strict exogeneity assumption is otherwise violated—for example, a lagged dependent variable is included among the regressors or there is feedback between u_{it} and future outcomes of the explanatory variable—then the FE estimator likely has substantially less bias than the FD estimator (unless $T = 2$). The important theoretical fact is that the bias in the FD estimator does not depend on T, while that for the FE estimator tends to zero at the rate $1/T$. See Wooldridge (2010, Section 10-7) for details.

Generally, it is difficult to choose between FE and FD when they give substantively different results. It makes sense to report both sets of results and to try to determine why they differ.

14-1c Fixed Effects with Unbalanced Panels

Some panel data sets, especially on individuals or firms, have missing years for at least some cross-sectional units in the sample. In this case, we call the data set an **unbalanced panel**. The mechanics of fixed effects estimation with an unbalanced panel are not much more difficult than with a balanced panel. If T_i is the number of time periods for cross-sectional unit i, we simply use these T_i observations in doing the time-demeaning. The total number of observations is then $T_1 + T_2 + \ldots + T_N$. As in the balanced case, one degree of freedom is lost for every cross-sectional observation due to the time-demeaning. Any regression package that does fixed effects makes the appropriate adjustment for this loss. The dummy variable regression also goes through in exactly the same way as with a balanced panel, and the df is appropriately obtained.

It is easy to see that units for which we have only a single time period play no role in a fixed effects analysis. The time-demeaning for such observations yields all zeros, which are not used in the estimation. (If T_i is at most two for all i, we can use first differencing: if $T_i = 1$ for any i, we do not have two periods to difference.)

The more difficult issue with an unbalanced panel is determining why the panel is unbalanced. With cities and states, for example, data on key variables are sometimes missing for certain years. Provided the reason we have missing data for some i is not correlated with the idiosyncratic errors, u_{it}, the unbalanced panel causes no problems. When we have data on individuals, families, or firms, things are trickier. Imagine, for example, that we obtain a random sample of manufacturing firms in 1990, and we are interested in testing how unionization affects firm profitability. Ideally, we can use a panel data analysis to control for unobserved worker and management characteristics that affect profitability and might also be correlated with the fraction of the firm's workforce that is unionized. If we collect data again in subsequent years, some firms may be lost because they have gone out of business or have merged with other companies. If so, we probably have a nonrandom sample in subsequent time periods. The question is: If we apply fixed effects to the unbalanced panel, when will the estimators be unbiased (or at least consistent)?

If the reason a firm leaves the sample (called *attrition*) is correlated with the idiosyncratic error—those unobserved factors that change over time and affect profits—then the resulting sample section problem (see Chapter 9) can cause biased estimators. This is a serious consideration in this example. Nevertheless, one useful thing about a fixed effects analysis is that it *does* allow attrition to be correlated with a_i, the unobserved effect. The idea is that, with the initial sampling, some units are more likely to drop out of the survey, and this is captured by a_i.

EXAMPLE 14.3   **Effect of Job Training on Firm Scrap Rates**

We add two variables to the analysis in Table 14.1: $\log(sales_{it})$ and $\log(employ_{it})$, where *sales* is annual firm sales and *employ* is number of employees. Three of the 54 firms drop out of the analysis entirely because they do not have sales or employment data. Five additional observations are lost due to missing data on one or both of these variables for some years, leaving us with $n = 148$. Using fixed effects on the unbalanced panel does not change the basic story, although the estimated grant effect gets larger: $\hat{\beta}_{grant} = -.297$, $t_{grant} = -1.89$; $\hat{\beta}_{grant-1} = -.536$, $t_{grant-1} = -2.389$.

Solving general attrition problems in panel data is complicated and beyond the scope of this text. [See, for example, Wooldridge (2010, Chapter 19).]

14-2 Random Effects Models

We begin with the same unobserved effects model as before,

$$y_{it} = \beta_0 + \beta_1 x_{it1} + \dots + \beta_k x_{itk} + a_i + u_{it}, \qquad [14.7]$$

where we explicitly include an intercept so that we can make the assumption that the unobserved effect, a_i, has zero mean (without loss of generality). We would usually allow for time dummies among the explanatory variables as well. In using fixed effects or first differencing, the goal is to eliminate a_i because it is thought to be correlated with one or more of the x_{itj}. But suppose we think a_i is *uncorrelated* with each explanatory variable in all time periods. Then, using a transformation to eliminate a_i results in inefficient estimators.

Equation (14.7) becomes a **random effects model** when we assume that the unobserved effect a_i is uncorrelated with each explanatory variable:

$$\text{Cov}(x_{itj}, a_i) = 0, \quad t = 1, 2, \dots, T; j = 1, 2, \dots, k. \qquad [14.8]$$

In fact, the ideal random effects assumptions include all of the fixed effects assumptions plus the additional requirement that a_i is independent of all explanatory variables in all time periods. (See the chapter appendix for the actual assumptions used.) If we think the unobserved effect a_i is correlated with any explanatory variables, we should use first differencing or fixed effects.

Under (14.8) and along with the random effects assumptions, how should we estimate the β_j? It is important to see that, if we believe that a_i is uncorrelated with the explanatory variables, the β_j can be consistently estimated by using a single cross section: there is no need for panel data at all. But using a single cross section disregards much useful information in the other time periods. We can also use the data in a pooled OLS procedure: just run OLS of y_{it} on the explanatory variables and probably the time dummies. This, too, produces consistent estimators of the β_j under the random effects assumption. But it ignores a key feature of the model. If we define the **composite error term** as $v_{it} = a_i + u_{it}$, then (14.7) can be written as

$$y_{it} = \beta_0 + \beta_1 x_{it1} + \dots + \beta_k x_{itk} + v_{it}. \qquad [14.9]$$

Because a_i is in the composite error in each time period, the v_{it} are serially correlated across time. In fact, under the random effects assumptions,

$$\text{Corr}(v_{it}, v_{is}) = \sigma_a^2/(\sigma_a^2 + \sigma_u^2), \quad t \neq s,$$

where $\sigma_a^2 = \text{Var}(a_i)$ and $\sigma_u^2 = \text{Var}(u_{it})$. This (necessarily) positive serial correlation in the error term can be substantial, and, because the usual pooled OLS standard errors ignore this correlation, they will be incorrect, as will the usual test statistics. In Chapter 12, we showed how generalized least squares can be used to estimate models with autoregressive serial correlation. We can also use GLS to solve the serial correlation problem here. For the procedure to have good properties, we should have large N and relatively small T. We assume that we have a balanced panel, although the method can be extended to unbalanced panels.

Deriving the GLS transformation that eliminates serial correlation in the errors requires sophisticated matrix algebra [see, for example, Wooldridge (2010, Chapter 10)]. But the transformation itself is simple. Define

$$\theta = 1 - [\sigma_u^2/(\sigma_u^2 + T\sigma_a^2)]^{1/2}, \qquad [14.10]$$

which is between zero and one. Then, the transformed equation turns out to be

$$y_{it} - \theta\bar{y}_i = \beta_0(1 - \theta) + \beta_1(x_{it1} - \theta\bar{x}_{i1}) + \dots$$
$$+ \beta_k(x_{itk} - \theta\bar{x}_{ik}) + (v_{it} - \theta\bar{v}_i), \qquad [14.11]$$

where the overbar again denotes the time averages. This is a very interesting equation, as it involves **quasi-demeaned data** on each variable. The fixed effects estimator subtracts the time averages from the corresponding variable. The random effects transformation subtracts a fraction of that time average, where the fraction depends on σ_u^2, σ_a^2, and the number of time periods, T. The GLS estimator is simply the pooled OLS estimator of equation (14.11). It is hardly obvious that the errors in (14.11) are serially uncorrelated, but they are. (See Problem 3.)

The transformation in (14.11) allows for explanatory variables that are constant over time, and this is one advantage of random effects (RE) over either fixed effects or first differencing. This is possible because RE assumes that the unobserved effect is uncorrelated with all explanatory variables, whether the explanatory variables are fixed over time or not. Thus, in a wage equation, we can include a variable such as education even if it does not change over time. But we are assuming that education is uncorrelated with a_i, which contains ability and family background. In many applications, the whole reason for using panel data is to allow the unobserved effect to be correlated with the explanatory variables.

The parameter θ is never known in practice, but it can always be estimated. There are different ways to do this, which may be based on pooled OLS or fixed effects, for example. Generally, $\hat{\theta}$ takes the form $\hat{\theta} = 1 - \{1/[1 + T(\hat{\sigma}_a^2/\hat{\sigma}_u^2)]\}^{1/2}$, where $\hat{\sigma}_a^2$ is a consistent estimator of σ_a^2 and $\hat{\sigma}_u^2$ is a consistent estimator of σ_u^2. These estimators can be based on the pooled OLS or fixed effects residuals. One possibility is that $\hat{\sigma}_a^2 = [NT(T-1)/2 - (k+1)]^{-1}\sum_{i=1}^{N}\sum_{t=1}^{T-1}\sum_{s=t+1}^{T}\hat{v}_{it}\hat{v}_{is}$, where the $\hat{v}_{it}$ are the residuals from estimating (14.9) by pooled OLS. Given this, we can estimate σ_u^2 by using $\hat{\sigma}_u^2 = \hat{\sigma}_v^2 - \hat{\sigma}_a^2$, where $\hat{\sigma}_v^2$ is the square of the usual standard error of the regression from pooled OLS. [See Wooldridge (2010, Chapter 10) for additional discussion of these estimators.]

Many econometrics packages support estimation of random effects models and automatically compute some version of $\hat{\theta}$. The feasible GLS estimator that uses $\hat{\theta}$ in place of θ is called the **random effects estimator**. Under the random effects assumptions in the chapter appendix, the estimator is consistent (not unbiased) and asymptotically normally distributed as N gets large with fixed T. The properties of the random effects (RE) estimator with small N and large T are largely unknown, although it has certainly been used in such situations.

Equation (14.11) allows us to relate the RE estimator to both pooled OLS and fixed effects. Pooled OLS is obtained when $\theta = 0$, and FE is obtained when $\theta = 1$. In practice, the estimate $\hat{\theta}$ is never zero or one. But if $\hat{\theta}$ is close to zero, the RE estimates will be close to the pooled OLS estimates. This is the case when the unobserved effect, a_i, is relatively unimportant (because it has small variance relative to σ_u^2). It is more common for σ_a^2 to be large relative to σ_u^2, in which case $\hat{\theta}$ will be closer to unity. As T gets large, $\hat{\theta}$ tends to one, and this makes the RE and FE estimates very similar.

We can gain more insight on the relative merits of random effects versus fixed effects by writing the quasi-demeaned error in equation (14.11) as $v_{it} - \theta\bar{v}_i = (1 - \theta)a_i + u_{it} - \theta\bar{u}_i$. This simple expression makes it clear that in the transformed equation the unobserved effect is weighted by $(1 - \theta)$. Although correlation between a_i and one or more x_{itj} causes inconsistency in the random effects estimation, we see that the correlation is attenuated by the factor $(1 - \theta)$. As $\theta \to 1$, the bias term goes to zero, as it must because the RE estimator tends to the FE estimator. If θ is close to zero, we are leaving a larger fraction of the unobserved effect in the error term, and, as a consequence, the asymptotic bias of the RE estimator will be larger.

In applications of FE and RE, it is usually informative also to compute the pooled OLS estimates. Comparing the three sets of estimates can help us determine the nature of the biases caused by leaving the unobserved effect, a_i, entirely in the error term (as does pooled OLS) or partially in the error term (as does the RE transformation). But we must remember that, even if a_i is uncorrelated with all explanatory variables in all time periods, the pooled OLS standard errors and test statistics are generally invalid: they ignore the often substantial serial correlation in the composite errors, $v_{it} = a_i + u_{it}$. As we mentioned in Chapter 13 (see Example 13.9), it is possible to compute standard errors and test statistics that are robust to arbitrary serial correlation (and heteroskedasticity) in v_{it}, and popular statistics packages often allow this option. [See, for example, Wooldridge (2010, Chapter 10).]

EXAMPLE 14.4 **A Wage Equation Using Panel Data**

We again use the data in WAGEPAN to estimate a wage equation for men. We use three methods: pooled OLS, random effects, and fixed effects. In the first two methods, we can include *educ* and race dummies (*black* and *hispan*), but these drop out of the fixed effects analysis. The time-varying variables are *exper*, *exper²*, *union*, and *married*. As we discussed in Section 14-1, *exper* is dropped in the FE analysis (although *exper²* remains). Each regression also contains a full set of year dummies. The estimation results are in Table 14.2.

TABLE 14.2 Three Different Estimators of a Wage Equation

Dependent Variable: log(*wage*)

Independent Variables	Pooled OLS	Random Effects	Fixed Effects
educ	.091 (.005)	.092 (.011)	———
black	−.139 (.024)	−.139 (.048)	———
hispan	.016 (.021)	.022 (.043)	———
exper	.067 (.014)	.106 (.015)	———
exper²	−.0024 (.0008)	−.0047 (.0007)	−.0052 (.0007)
married	.108 (.016)	.064 (.017)	.047 (.018)
union	.182 (.017)	.106 (.018)	.080 (.019)

> ### EXPLORING FURTHER 14.3
>
> The union premium estimated by fixed effects is about 10 percentage points lower than the OLS estimate. What does this strongly suggest about the correlation between *union* and the unobserved effect?

The coefficients on *educ*, *black*, and *hispan* are similar for the pooled OLS and random effects estimations. The pooled OLS standard errors are the usual OLS standard errors, and these underestimate the true standard errors because they ignore the positive serial correlation; we report them here for comparison only. The experience profile is somewhat different, and both the marriage and union premiums fall notably in the random effects estimation. When we eliminate the unobserved effect entirely by using fixed effects, the marriage premium falls to about 4.7%, although it is still statistically significant. The drop in the marriage premium is consistent with the idea that men who are more able—as captured by a higher unobserved effect, a_i—are more likely to be married. Therefore, in the pooled OLS estimation, a large part of the marriage premium reflects the fact that men who are married would earn more even if they were not married. The remaining 4.7% has at least two possible explanations: (1) marriage really makes men more productive or (2) employers pay married men a premium because marriage is a signal of stability. We cannot distinguish between these two hypotheses.

The estimate of θ for the random effects estimation is $\hat{\theta} = .643$, which helps explain why, on the time-varying variables, the RE estimates lie closer to the FE estimates than to the pooled OLS estimates.

14-2a Random Effects or Fixed Effects?

Because fixed effects allows arbitrary correlation between a_i and the x_{itj}, while random effects does not, FE is widely thought to be a more convincing tool for estimating ceteris paribus effects. Still, random effects is applied in certain situations. Most obviously, if the key explanatory variable is constant over time, we cannot use FE to estimate its effect on y. For example, in Table 14.2, we must rely on the RE (or pooled OLS) estimate of the return to education. Of course, we can only use random effects because we are willing to assume the unobserved effect is uncorrelated with all explanatory variables. Typically, if one uses random effects, as many time-constant controls as possible are included among the explanatory variables. (With an FE analysis, it is not necessary to include such controls.) RE is preferred to pooled OLS because RE is generally more efficient.

If our interest is in a time-varying explanatory variable, is there ever a case to use RE rather than FE? Yes, but situations in which $\text{Cov}(x_{itj}, a_i) = 0$ should be considered the exception rather than the rule. If the key policy variable is set experimentally—say, each year, children are randomly assigned to classes of different sizes—then random effects would be appropriate for estimating the effect of class size on performance. Unfortunately, in most cases the regressors are themselves outcomes of choice processes and likely to be correlated with individual preferences and abilities as captured by a_i.

It is still fairly common to see researchers apply both random effects and fixed effects, and then formally test for statistically significant differences in the coefficients on the time-varying explanatory variables. (So, in Table 14.2, these would be the coefficients on $exper^2$, *married*, and *union*.) Hausman (1978) first proposed such a test, and some econometrics packages routinely compute the Hausman test under the full set of random effects assumptions listed in the appendix to this chapter. The idea is that one uses the random effects estimates unless the Hausman test rejects (14.8). In practice, a failure to reject means either that the RE and FE estimates are sufficiently close so that it does not matter which is used, or the sampling variation is so large in the FE estimates that one cannot conclude practically significant differences are statistically significant. In the latter case, one is left to wonder whether there is enough information in the data to provide precise estimates of the coefficients. A rejection using the Hausman test is taken to mean that the key RE assumption, (14.8), is false, and then the FE estimates are used. (Naturally, as in all applications of statistical inference, one should distinguish between a practically significant difference and a statistically significant difference.) Wooldridge (2010, Chapter 10) contains further discussion. In the next section we discuss an alternative, computationally simpler approach to choosing between the RE and FE approaches.

A final word of caution. In reading empirical work, you may find that some authors decide on FE versus RE estimation based on whether the a_i are properly viewed as parameters to estimate or as random variables. Such considerations are usually wrongheaded. In this chapter, we have treated the a_i as random variables in the unobserved effects model (14.7), regardless of how we decide to estimate the β_j. As we have emphasized, the key issue that determines whether we use FE or RE is whether we can plausibly assume a_i is uncorrelated with all x_{itj}. Nevertheless, in some applications of panel data methods, we cannot treat our sample as a random sample from a large population, especially when the unit of observation is a large geographical unit (say, states or provinces). Then, it often makes sense to think of each a_i as a separate intercept to estimate for each cross-sectional unit. In this case, we use fixed effects: remember, using FE is mechanically the same as allowing a different intercept for each cross-sectional unit. Fortunately, whether or not we engage in the philosophical debate about the nature of a_i, FE is almost always much more convincing than RE for policy analysis using aggregated data.

14-3 The Correlated Random Effects Approach

In applications where it makes sense to view the a_i (unobserved effects) as being random variables, along with the observed variables we draw, there is an alternative to fixed effects that still allows a_i to be correlated with the observed explanatory variables. To describe the approach, consider again the simple model in equation (14.1), with a single, time-varying explanatory variable x_{it}. Rather than assume a_i is uncorrelated with $\{x_{it}: t = 1, 2, ..., T\}$—which is the random effects approach—or take away time averages to remove a_i—the fixed effects approach—we might instead model correlation between a_i and $\{x_{it}: t = 1, 2, ..., T\}$. Because a_i is, by definition, constant over time, allowing it to be correlated with the average level of the x_{it} has a certain appeal. More specifically, let $\bar{x}_i = T^{-1}\sum_{t=1}^{T}x_{it}$ be the time average, as before. Suppose we assume the simple linear relationship

$$a_i = \alpha + \gamma\bar{x}_i + r_i,$$ [14.12]

where we assume r_i is uncorrelated with each x_{it}. Because $\bar{x}_i$ is a linear function of the x_{it},

$$Cov(\bar{x}_i, r_i) = 0.$$ [14.13]

Equations (14.12) and (14.13) imply that a_i and $\bar{x}_i$ are correlated whenever $\gamma \neq 0$.

The **correlated random effects** (CRE) approach uses (14.12) in conjunction with (14.1): substituting the former in the latter gives

$$y_{it} = \beta x_{it} + \alpha + \gamma\bar{x}_i + r_i + u_{it} = \alpha + \beta x_{it} + \gamma\bar{x}_i + r_i + u_{it}.$$ [14.14]

Equation (14.14) is interesting because it still has a composite error term, $r_i + u_{it}$, consisting of a time-constant unobservable r_i and the idiosyncratic shocks, u_{it}. Importantly, assumption (14.8) holds when we replace a_i with r_i. Also, because u_{it} is assumed to be uncorrelated with x_{is}, all s and t, u_{it} is also uncorrelated with $\bar{x}_i$. All of these assumptions add up to random effects estimation of the equation

$$y_{it} = \alpha + \beta x_{it} + \gamma\bar{x}_i + r_i + u_{it},$$ [14.15]

which is like the usual equation underlying RE estimation with the important addition of the time-average variable, $\bar{x}_i$. It is the addition of $\bar{x}_i$ that controls for the correlation between a_i and the sequence $\{x_{it}: t = 1, 2, ..., T\}$. What is left over, r_i, is uncorrelated with the x_{it}.

In most econometrics packages it is easy to compute the unit-specific time averages, $\bar{x}_i$. Assuming we have done that for each cross-sectional unit i, what can we expect to happen if we apply RE to equation (14.15)? Notice that estimation of (14.15) gives $\hat{\alpha}_{CRE}, \hat{\beta}_{CRE}$, and $\hat{\gamma}_{CRE}$—the CRE estimators.

As far as $\hat{\beta}_{CRE}$ goes, the answer is a bit anticlimactic. It can be shown—see, for example, Wooldridge (2010, Chapter 10)—that

$$\hat{\beta}_{CRE} = \hat{\beta}_{FE}, \qquad \text{[14.16]}$$

where $\hat{\beta}_{FE}$ denotes the FE estimator from equation (14.3). In other words, adding the time average $\bar{x}_i$ and using random effects is the same as subtracting the time averages and using pooled OLS.

Even though (14.15) is not needed to obtain $\hat{\beta}_{FE}$, the equivalence of the CRE and FE estimates of β provides a nice interpretation of FE: it controls for the average level, $\bar{x}_i$, when measuring the partial effect of x_{it} on y_{it}. As an example, suppose that x_{it} is a tax rate on firm profits in county i in year t, and y_{it} is some measure of county-level economic output. By including $\bar{x}_i$, the average tax rate in the county over the T years, we are allowing for systematic differences between historically high-tax and low-tax counties—differences that may also affect economic output.

We can also use equation (14.15) to see why the FE estimators are often much less precise than the RE estimators. If we set $\gamma = 0$ in equation (14.15) then we obtain the usual RE estimator of β, $\hat{\beta}_{RE}$. This means that correlation between x_{it} and $\bar{x}_i$ has no bearing on the variance of the RE estimator. By contrast, we know from multiple regression analysis in Chapter 3 that correlation between x_{it} and $\bar{x}_i$—that is, multicollinearity—can result in a higher variance for $\hat{\beta}_{FE}$. Sometimes the variance is much higher, particularly when there is little variation in x_{it} across t, in which case x_{it} and $\bar{x}_i$ tend to be highly (positively) correlated. In the limiting case where there is no variation across time for any i, the correlation is perfect—and FE fails to provide an estimate of β.

Apart from providing a synthesis of the FE and RE approaches, are there other reasons to consider the CRE approach even if it simply delivers the usual FE estimate of β? Yes, at least two. First, the CRE approach provides a simple, formal way of choosing between the FE and RE approaches. As we just discussed, the RE approach sets $\gamma = 0$ while FE estimates γ. Because we have $\hat{\gamma}_{CRE}$ and its standard error [obtained from RE estimation of (14.15)], we can construct a t test of $H_0: \gamma = 0$ against $H_1: \gamma \neq 0$. [The appendix discusses how to make this test robust to heteroskedasticity and serial correlation in $\{u_{it}\}$.] If we reject H_0 at a sufficiently small significance level, we reject RE in favor of FE. As usual, especially with a large cross section, it is important to distinguish between a statistical rejection and economically important differences.

A second reason to study the CRE approach is that it provides a way to include time-constant explanatory variables in what is effectively a fixed effects analysis. For example, let z_i be a variable that does not change over time—it could be gender, say, or an IQ test score determined in childhood. We can easily augment (14.15) to include z_i:

$$y_{it} = \alpha + \beta x_{it} + \gamma \bar{x}_i + \delta z_i + r_i + u_{it}, \qquad \text{[14.17]}$$

where we do not change the notation for the error term (which no longer includes z_i). If we estimate this expanded equation by RE, it can still be shown that the estimate of β is the FE estimate from (14.1). In fact, once we include $\bar{x}_i$, we can include any other time-constant variables in the equation, estimate it by RE, and obtain $\hat{\beta}_{FE}$ as the coefficient on x_{it}. In addition, we obtain an estimate of δ, although the estimate should be interpreted with caution because it does not necessarily estimate a causal effect of z_i on y_{it}.

The same CRE strategy can be applied to models with many time-varying explanatory variables (and many time-constant variables). When the equation augmented with the time averages is estimated by RE, the coefficients on the time-varying variables are identical to the FE estimates. As a practical note, when the panel is balanced there is no need to include the time averages of variables that change over time—the leading case being time period dummies. (With T time periods, the time average of a time period is just $1/T$, a constant for all i and t; clearly it makes no sense to add a bunch of constants to an equation that already has an intercept.) If the panel data set is unbalanced, then the average of variables such as time dummies can change across i—it will depend on how many periods we have for cross-sectional unit i. In such cases, the time averages of any variable that changes over time must be included.

Computer Exercise 14 in this chapter illustrates how the CRE approach can be applied to the balanced panel data set in AIRFARE and how one can test RE versus FE in the CRE framework.

14-3a Unbalanced Panels

The correlated random effects approach also can be applied to unbalanced panels, but some care is required. In order to obtain an estimator that reproduces the fixed effects estimates on the time-varying explanatory variables, one must be careful in constructing the time averages. In particular, for y or any x_j, a time period contributes to the time average, $\bar{y}_i$ or $\bar{x}_{ij}$, only if data on *all* of $(y_{it}, x_{it1}, \ldots, x_{itk})$ are observed. One way to depict the situation is to define a dummy variable, s_{it}, which equals one when a complete set of data on $(y_{it}, x_{it1}, \ldots, x_{itk})$ is observed. If any element is missing (including, of course, if the entire time period is missing), then $s_{it} = 0$. (The notion of a *selection indicator* is discussed in more detail in Chapter 17.) With this definition, the appropriate time average of $\{y_{it}\}$ can be written as

$$\bar{y}_i = T_i^{-1} \sum_{t=1}^{T} s_{it} y_{it},$$

where T_i is the total number of complete time periods for cross-sectional observation i. In other words, we only average over the time periods that have a complete set of data.

Another subtle point is that when time period dummies are included in the model, or any other variables that change only by t and not i, we must now include their time averages (unlike in the balanced case, where the time averages are just constants). For example, if $\{w_t: t = 1, \ldots, T\}$ is an aggregate time variable, such as a time dummy or a linear time trend, then

$$\bar{w}_i = T_i^{-1} \sum_{t=1}^{T} s_{it} w_t.$$

Because of the unbalanced nature of the panel, $\bar{w}_i$ almost always varies somewhat across i (unless the exact same time periods are missing for all cross-sectional units). As with variables that actually change across i and t, the time averages of aggregate time effects are easy to obtain in many software packages.

The mechanics of the random effects estimator also change somewhat when we have an unbalanced panel, and this is true whether we use the traditional random effects estimator or the CRE version. Namely, the parameter θ in equation (14.10), used in equation (14.11) to obtain the quasi-demeaned data, depends on i through the number of time periods observed for unit i. Specifically, simply replace T in equation (14.10) with T_i. Econometrics packages that support random effects estimation recognize this difference when using balanced panels, and so nothing special needs to be done from a user's perspective.

The bottom line is that, once the time averages have been properly obtained, using an equation such as (14.17) is the same as in the balanced case. We can still use a test of statistical significance on the set of time averages to choose between fixed effects and pure random effects, and the CRE approach still allows us to include time-constant variables.

As with fixed effects estimation, a key issue is understanding why the panel data set is unbalanced. In the pure random effects case, the selection indicator, s_{it}, cannot be correlated with the composite error in equation (14.7), $a_i + u_{it}$, in any time period. Otherwise, as discussed in Wooldridge (2010, Chapter 19), the RE estimator is inconsistent. As discussed in Section 14-1, the FE estimator allows for arbitrary correlation between the selection indicator, s_{it}, and the fixed effect, a_i. Therefore, FE estimator is more robust in the context of unbalanced panels. And, as we already know, FE allows arbitrary correlation between time-varying explanatory variables and a_i.

14-4 Applying Panel Data Methods to Other Data Structures

The various panel data methods can be applied to certain data structures that do not involve time. For example, it is common in demography to use siblings (sometimes twins) to account for unobserved family and background characteristics. Usually we want to allow the unobserved "family effect," which is common to all siblings within a family, to be correlated with observed explanatory variables. If those explanatory variables vary across siblings within a family, differencing across sibling pairs— or, more generally, using the within transformation within a family—is preferred as an estimation method. By removing the unobserved effect, we eliminate potential bias caused by confounding family background characteristics. Implementing fixed effects on such data structures is rather straightforward in regression packages that support FE estimation.

As an example, Geronimus and Korenman (1992) used pairs of sisters to study the effects of teen childbearing on future economic outcomes. When the outcome is income relative to needs— something that depends on the number of children—the model is

$$\log(incneeds_{fs}) = \beta_0 + \delta_0 sister2_s + \beta_1 teenbrth_{fs}$$
$$+ \beta_2 age_{fs} + other\ factors + a_f + u_{fs}, \qquad [14.18]$$

where f indexes family and s indexes a sister within the family. The intercept for the first sister is β_0, and the intercept for the second sister is $\beta_0 + \delta_0$. The variable of interest is $teenbrth_{fs}$, which is a binary variable equal to one if sister s in family f had a child while a teenager. The variable age_{fs} is the current age of sister s in family f; Geronimus and Korenman also used some other controls. The unobserved variable a_f, which changes only across family, is an *unobserved family effect* or a *family fixed effect*. The main concern in the analysis is that *teenbrth* is correlated with the family effect. If so, an OLS analysis that pools across families and sisters gives a biased estimator of the effect of teenage motherhood on economic outcomes. Solving this problem is simple: within each family, difference (14.18) across sisters to get

$$\Delta\log(incneeds) = \delta_0 + \beta_1 \Delta teenbrth + \beta_2 \Delta age + \ldots + \Delta u; \qquad [14.19]$$

> **EXPLORING FURTHER 14.4**
>
> When using the differencing method, does it make sense to include dummy variables for the mother and father's race in (14.18)? Explain.

this removes the family effect, a_f, and the resulting equation can be estimated by OLS. Notice that there is no time element here: the differencing is across sisters within a family. Also, we have allowed for differences in intercepts across sisters in (14.18), which leads to a nonzero intercept in the differenced equation, (14.19). If in entering the data the order of the sisters within each family is essentially random, the estimated intercept should be close to zero. But even in such cases it does not hurt to include an intercept in (14.19), and having the intercept allows for the fact that, say, the first sister listed might always be the neediest.

Using 129 sister pairs from the 1982 National Longitudinal Survey of Young Women, Geronimus and Korenman first estimated β_1 by pooled OLS to obtain $-.33$ or $-.26$, where the second estimate comes from controlling for family background variables (such as parents' education); both estimates are very statistically significant [see Table 3 in Geronimus and Korenman (1992)]. Therefore, teenage motherhood has a rather large impact on future family income. However, when the differenced equation is estimated, the coefficient on *teenbrth* is $-.08$, which is small and statistically insignificant. This suggests that it is largely a woman's family background that affects her future income, rather than teenage childbearing.

Geronimus and Korenman looked at several other outcomes and two other data sets; in some cases, the within family estimates were economically large and statistically significant. They also showed how the effects disappear entirely when the sisters' education levels are controlled for.

Ashenfelter and Krueger (1994) used the differencing methodology to estimate the return to education. They obtained a sample of 149 identical twins and collected information on earnings, education, and other variables. Identical twins were used because they should have the same underlying ability. This can be differenced away by using twin differences, rather than OLS on the pooled data. Because identical twins are the same in age, gender, and race, these factors all drop out of the differenced equation. Therefore, Ashenfelter and Krueger regressed the difference in log($earnings$) on the difference in education and estimated the return to education to be about 9.2% ($t = 3.83$). Interestingly, this is actually $larger$ than the pooled OLS estimate of 8.4% (which controls for gender, age, and race). Ashenfelter and Krueger also estimated the equation by random effects and obtained 8.7% as the return to education. (See Table 5 in their paper.) The random effects analysis is mechanically the same as the panel data case with two time periods.

The samples used by Geronimus and Korenman (1992) and Ashenfelter and Krueger (1994) are examples of **matched pairs samples**. More generally, fixed and random effects methods can be applied to a **cluster sample**. A cluster sample has the same appearance as a cross-sectional data set, but there is an important difference: clusters of units are sampled from a population of clusters rather than sampling individuals from the population of individuals. In the previous examples, each family is sampled from the population of families, and then we obtain data on at least two family members. Therefore, each family is a cluster.

As another example, suppose we are interested in modeling individual pension plan participation decisions. One might obtain a random sample of working individuals—say, from the United States—but it is also common to sample firms from a population of firms. Once the firms are sampled, one might collect information on all workers or a subset of workers within each firm. In either case, the resulting data set is a cluster sample because sampling was first at the firm level. Unobserved firm-level characteristics (along with observed firm characteristics) are likely to be present in participation decisions, and this within-firm correlation must be accounted for. Fixed effects estimation is preferred when we think the unobserved **cluster effect**—an example of which is a_i in (14.12)—is correlated with one or more of the explanatory variables. Then, we can only include explanatory variables that vary, at least somewhat, within clusters. The cluster sizes are rarely the same, so we are effectively using fixed effects methods for unbalanced panels.

Educational data on student outcomes can also come in the form of a cluster sample, where a sample of schools is obtained from the population of schools, and then information on students within each school is obtained. Each school acts as a cluster, and allowing a school effect to be correlated with key explanatory variables—say, whether a student participates in a state-sponsored tutoring program—is likely to be important. Because the rate at which students are tutored likely varies by school, it is probably a good idea to use fixed effects estimation. One often sees authors use, as a shorthand, "I included school fixed effects in the analysis."

The correlated random effects approach can be applied immediately to cluster samples because, for the purposes of estimation, a cluster sample acts like an unbalanced panel. Now, the averages that are added to the equation are within-cluster averages—for example, averages within schools. The only difference with panel data is that the notion of serial correlation in idiosyncratic errors is not relevant. Nevertheless, as discussed in Wooldridge (2010, Chapter 20), there are still good reasons for using cluster-robust standard errors, whether one uses fixed effects or correlated random effects.

In some cases, the key explanatory variables—often policy variables—change only at the level of the cluster, not within the cluster. In such cases the fixed effects approach is not applicable. For example, we may be interested in the effects of measured teacher quality on student performance, where each cluster is an elementary school classroom. Because all students within a cluster have the same teacher, eliminating a "class effect" also eliminates any observed measures of teacher quality. If we have good controls in the equation, we may be justified in applying random effects on the unbalanced cluster. As with panel data, the key requirement for RE to produce convincing estimates is that the explanatory variables are uncorrelated with the unobserved cluster effect. Most econometrics packages allow random effects estimation on unbalanced clusters without much effort.

Pooled OLS is also commonly applied to cluster samples when eliminating a cluster effect via fixed effects is infeasible or undesirable. However, as with panel data, the usual OLS standard errors are incorrect unless there is no cluster effect, and so robust standard errors that allow "cluster correlation" (and heteroskedasticity) should be used. Some regression packages have simple commands to correct standard errors and the usual test statistics for general within cluster correlation (as well as heteroskedasticity). These are the same corrections that work for pooled OLS on panel data sets, which we reported in Example 13.9. As an example, Papke (1999) estimates linear probability models for the continuation of defined benefit pension plans based on whether firms adopted defined contribution plans. Because there is likely to be a firm effect that induces correlation across different plans within the same firm, Papke corrects the usual OLS standard errors for cluster sampling, as well as for heteroskedasticity in the linear probability model.

Before ending this section some final comments are in order. Given the readily available tools of fixed effects, random effects, and cluster-robust standard inference, it is tempting to find reasons to use clustering methods where none may exist. For example, if a set of data is obtained from a random sample from the population, then there is usually no reason to account for cluster effects in computing standard errors after OLS estimation. The fact that the units can be put into groups ex post—that is, after the random sample has been obtained—is not a reason to make inference robust to cluster correlation.

To illustrate this point, suppose that, out of the population of fourth-grade students in the United States, a random sample of 50,000 is obtained, these data are properly studied using standard methods for cross-sectional regression. It may be tempting to group the students by, say, the 50 states plus the District of Columbia—assuming a state identifier is included—and then treat the data as a cluster sample. But this would be wrong, and clustering the standard errors at the state level can produce standard errors that are systematically too large. Or, they might be too small because the asymptotic theory underlying cluster sampling assumes that we have many clusters with each cluster size being relatively small. In any case, a simple thought experiment shows that clustering cannot be correct. For example, if we know the county of residence for each student, why not cluster at the county level? Or, at a coarser level, we can divide the United States into four census regions and treat those as the clusters—and this would give a different set of standard errors (that do not have any theoretical justification). Taking this argument to its extreme, one could argue that we have one cluster: the entire United States, in which case the clustered standard errors would not be defined and inference would be impossible. The confusion comes about because the clusters are defined ex post—that is, after the random sample is obtained. In a true cluster sample, the clusters are first drawn from a population of clusters, and then individuals are drawn from the clusters.

One might use clustering methods if, say, a district-level variable is created after the random sample is collected and then used in the student-level equation. This can create unobserved cluster correlation within each district. Recall that the fixed effects estimator (in this case, at the district level) is the same as putting in district-level averages. Thus, one might want to account for cluster correlation at the district level in addition to using fixed effects. As shown by Stock and Watson (2008) (in the context of panel data), with large cluster sizes the resulting cluster correlation is generally unimportant, but with small cluster sizes one should use the cluster-robust standard errors.

Summary

In this chapter we have continued our discussion of panel data methods, studying the fixed effects and random effects estimators, and also described the correlated random effects approach as a unifying framework. Compared with first differencing, the fixed effects estimator is efficient when the idiosyncratic errors are serially uncorrelated (as well as homoskedastic), and we make no assumptions about correlation between the unobserved effect a_i and the explanatory variables. As with first differencing, any time-constant explanatory variables drop out of the analysis. Fixed effects methods apply immediately to unbalanced panels, but we must assume that the reasons some time periods are missing are not systematically related to the idiosyncratic errors.

The random effects estimator is appropriate when the unobserved effect is thought to be uncorrelated with all the explanatory variables. Then, a_i can be left in the error term, and the resulting serial correlation over time can be handled by generalized least squares estimation. Conveniently, feasible GLS can be obtained by a pooled regression on quasi-demeaned data. The value of the estimated transformation parameter, $\hat{\theta}$, indicates whether the estimates are likely to be closer to the pooled OLS or the fixed effects estimates. If the full set of random effects assumptions holds, the random effects estimator is asymptotically—as N gets large with T fixed—more efficient than pooled OLS, first differencing, or fixed effects (which are all unbiased, consistent, and asymptotically normal).

The correlated random effects approach to panel data models has become more popular in recent years, primarily because it allows a simple test for choosing between FE and RE, and it allows one to incorporate time-constant variables in an equation that delivers the FE estimates of the time-varying variables. Finally, the panel data methods studied in Chapters 13 and 14 can be used when working with matched pairs or cluster samples. Differencing or the within transformation eliminates the cluster effect. If the cluster effect is uncorrelated with the explanatory variables, pooled OLS can be used, but the standard errors and test statistics should be adjusted for cluster correlation. Random effects estimation is also a possibility.

Key Terms

Cluster Effect	Fixed Effects Estimator	Time-Demeaned Data
Cluster Sample	Fixed Effects Transformation	Unbalanced Panel
Clustering	Matched Pairs Samples	Unobserved Effects Model
Composite Error Term	Quasi-Demeaned Data	Within Estimator
Correlated Random Effects	Random Effects Estimator	Within Transformation
Dummy Variable Regression	Random Effects Model	

Problems

1 Suppose that the idiosyncratic errors in (14.4), $\{u_{it}: t = 1, 2, ..., T\}$, are serially uncorrelated with constant variance, σ_u^2. Show that the correlation between adjacent differences, Δu_{it} and $\Delta u_{i,t+1}$, is $-.5$. Therefore, under the ideal FE assumptions, first differencing induces negative serial correlation of a known value.

2 With a single explanatory variable, the equation used to obtain the between estimator is

$$\bar{y}_i = \beta_0 + \beta_1 \bar{x}_i + a_i + \bar{u}_i,$$

where the overbar represents the average over time. We can assume that $E(a_i) = 0$ because we have included an intercept in the equation. Suppose that $\bar{u}_i$ is uncorrelated with $\bar{x}_i$, but $Cov(x_{it}, a_i) = \sigma_{xa}$ for all t (and i because of random sampling in the cross section).

(i) Letting $\tilde{\beta}_1$ be the between estimator, that is, the OLS estimator using the time averages, show that

$$\text{plim } \tilde{\beta}_1 = \beta_1 + \sigma_{xa}/\text{Var}(\bar{x}_i),$$

where the probability limit is defined as $N \to \infty$. [*Hint:* See equations (5.5) and (5.6).]

(ii) Assume further that the x_{it}, for all $t = 1, 2, ..., T$, are uncorrelated with constant variance σ_x^2. Show that $\text{plim } \tilde{\beta}_1 = \beta_1 + T(\sigma_{xa}/\sigma_x^2)$.

(iii) If the explanatory variables are not very highly correlated across time, what does part (ii) suggest about whether the inconsistency in the between estimator is smaller when there are more time periods?

3 In a random effects model, define the composite error $v_{it} = a_i + u_{it}$, where a_i is uncorrelated with u_{it} and the u_{it} have constant variance σ_u^2 and are serially uncorrelated. Define $e_{it} = v_{it} - \theta\bar{v}_i$, where θ is given in (14.10).

   (i)   Show that $E(e_{it}) = 0$.

   (ii)   Show that $\text{Var}(e_{it}) = \sigma_u^2, t = 1, \ldots, T$.

   (iii)   Show that for $t \neq s$, $\text{Cov}(e_{it}, e_{is}) = 0$.

4 In order to determine the effects of collegiate athletic performance on applicants, you collect data on applications for a sample of Division I colleges for 1985, 1990, and 1995.

   (i)   What measures of athletic success would you include in an equation? What are some of the timing issues?

   (ii)   What other factors might you control for in the equation?

   (iii)   Write an equation that allows you to estimate the effects of athletic success on the percentage change in applications. How would you estimate this equation? Why would you choose this method?

5 Suppose that, for one semester, you can collect the following data on a random sample of college juniors and seniors for each class taken: a standardized final exam score, percentage of lectures attended, a dummy variable indicating whether the class is within the student's major, cumulative grade point average prior to the start of the semester, and SAT score.

   (i)   Why would you classify this data set as a cluster sample? Roughly, how many observations would you expect for the typical student?

   (ii)   Write a model, similar to equation (14.18), that explains final exam performance in terms of attendance and the other characteristics. Use s to subscript student and c to subscript class. Which variables do not change within a student?

   (iii)   If you pool all of the data and use OLS, what are you assuming about unobserved student characteristics that affect performance and attendance rate? What roles do SAT score and prior GPA play in this regard?

   (iv)   If you think SAT score and prior GPA do not adequately capture student ability, how would you estimate the effect of attendance on final exam performance?

6 Using the "cluster" option in the econometrics package Stata® 11, the fully robust standard errors for the pooled OLS estimates in Table 14.2—that is, robust to serial correlation and heteroskedasticity in the composite errors, $\{v_{it}: t = 1, \ldots, T\}$—are obtained as $\text{se}(\hat{\beta}_{educ}) = .011$, $\text{se}(\hat{\beta}_{black}) = .051$, $\text{se}(\hat{\beta}_{hispan}) = .039$, $\text{se}(\hat{\beta}_{exper}) = .020$, $\text{se}(\hat{\beta}_{exper2}) = .0010$, $\text{se}(\hat{\beta}_{married}) = .026$, and $\text{se}(\hat{\beta}_{union}) = .027$.

   (i)   How do these standard errors generally compare with the nonrobust ones, and why?

   (ii)   How do the robust standard errors for pooled OLS compare with the standard errors for RE? Does it seem to matter whether the explanatory variable is time-constant or time-varying?

   (iii)   When the fully robust standard errors for the RE estimates are computed, Stata® 11 reports the following (where we look at only the coefficients on the time-varying variables): $\text{se}(\hat{\beta}_{exper}) = 0.16$, $\text{se}(\hat{\beta}_{expersq}) = .0008$, $\text{se}(\hat{\beta}_{married}) = 0.19$, and $\text{se}(\hat{\beta}_{union}) = 0.21$. [These are robust to any kind of serial correlation or heteroskedasticity in the idiosyncratic errors $\{u_{it}: t = 1, \ldots, T\}$ as well as heteroskedasticity in a_i.] How do the robust standard errors generally compare with the usual RE standard errors reported in Table 14.2? What conclusion might you draw?

   (iv)   Comparing the four standard errors in part (iii) with their pooled OLS counterparts, what do you make of the fact that the robust RE standard errors are all below the robust pooled OLS standard errors?

7 The data in CENSUS2000 is a random sample of individuals from the United States. Here we are interested in estimating a simple regression model relating the log of weekly income, *lweekinc*, to schooling, *educ*. There are 29,501 observations. Associated with each individual is a state identifier (*state*) for the 50 states plus the District of Columbia. A less coarse geographic identifier is *puma*, which takes on 610 different values indicating geographic regions smaller than a state.

Running the simple regression of *lweekinc* on *educ* gives a slope coefficient equal to .1083 (to four decimal places). The heteroskedasticity-robust standard error is about .0024. The standard error clustered at the *puma* level is about .0027, and the standard error clustered at the *state* level is about .0033. For computing a confidence interval, which of these standard errors is the most reliable? Explain.

Computer Exercises

C1 Use the data in RENTAL for this exercise. The data on rental prices and other variables for college towns are for the years 1980 and 1990. The idea is to see whether a stronger presence of students affects rental rates. The unobserved effects model is

$$\log(rent_{it}) = \beta_0 + \delta_0 y90_t + \beta_1 \log(pop_{it}) + \beta_2 \log(avginc_{it})$$
$$+ \beta_3 pctstu_{it} + a_i + u_{it},$$

where *pop* is city population, *avginc* is average income, and *pctstu* is student population as a percentage of city population (during the school year).
(i) Estimate the equation by pooled OLS and report the results in standard form. What do you make of the estimate on the 1990 dummy variable? What do you get for $\hat{\beta}_{pctstu}$?
(ii) Are the standard errors you report in part (i) valid? Explain.
(iii) Now, difference the equation and estimate by OLS. Compare your estimate of β_{pctstu} with that from part (i). Does the relative size of the student population appear to affect rental prices?
(iv) Estimate the model by fixed effects to verify that you get identical estimates and standard errors to those in part (iii).

C2 Use CRIME4 for this exercise.
(i) Reestimate the unobserved effects model for crime in Example 13.9 but use fixed effects rather than differencing. Are there any notable sign or magnitude changes in the coefficients? What about statistical significance?
(ii) Add the logs of each wage variable in the data set and estimate the model by fixed effects. How does including these variables affect the coefficients on the criminal justice variables in part (i)?
(iii) Do the wage variables in part (ii) all have the expected sign? Explain. Are they jointly significant?

C3 For this exercise, we use JTRAIN to determine the effect of the job training grant on hours of job training per employee. The basic model for the three years is

$$hrsemp_{it} = \beta_0 + \delta_1 d88_t + \delta_2 d89_t + \beta_1 grant_{it} + \beta_2 grant_{i,t-1}$$
$$+ \beta_3 \log(employ_{it}) + a_i + u_{it}.$$

(i) Estimate the equation using fixed effects. How many firms are used in the FE estimation? How many total observations would be used if each firm had data on all variables (in particular, *hrsemp*) for all three years?
(ii) Interpret the coefficient on *grant* and comment on its significance.
(iii) Is it surprising that $grant_{-1}$ is insignificant? Explain.
(iv) Do larger firms provide their employees with more or less training, on average? How big are the differences? (For example, if a firm has 10% more employees, what is the change in average hours of training?)

C4 In Example 13.8, we used the unemployment claims data from Papke (1994) to estimate the effect of enterprise zones on unemployment claims. Papke also uses a model that allows each city to have its own time trend:

$$\log(uclms_{it}) = a_i + c_i t + \beta_1 ez_{it} + u_{it},$$

where a_i and c_i are both unobserved effects. This allows for more heterogeneity across cities.

(i) Show that, when the previous equation is first differenced, we obtain

$$\Delta\log(uclms_{it}) = c_i + \beta_1\Delta ez_{it} + \Delta u_{it}, t = 2,\ldots, T.$$

Notice that the differenced equation contains a fixed effect, c_i.

(ii) Estimate the differenced equation by fixed effects. What is the estimate of β_1? Is it very different from the estimate obtained in Example 13.8? Is the effect of enterprise zones still statistically significant?

(iii) Add a full set of year dummies to the estimation in part (ii). What happens to the estimate of β_1?

C5 (i) In the wage equation in Example 14.4, explain why dummy variables for occupation might be important omitted variables for estimating the union wage premium.

(ii) If every man in the sample stayed in the same occupation from 1981 through 1987, would you need to include the occupation dummies in a fixed effects estimation? Explain.

(iii) Using the data in WAGEPAN include eight of the occupation dummy variables in the equation and estimate the equation using fixed effects. Does the coefficient on *union* change by much? What about its statistical significance?

C6 Add the interaction term $union_{it} \cdot t$ to the equation estimated in Table 14.2 to see if wage *growth* depends on union status. Estimate the equation by random and fixed effects and compare the results.

C7 Use the state-level data on murder rates and executions in MURDER for the following exercise.

(i) Consider the unobserved effects model

$$mrdrte_{it} = \eta_t + \beta_1 exec_{it} + \beta_2 unem_{it} + a_i + u_{it},$$

where η_t simply denotes different year intercepts and a_i is the unobserved state effect. If past executions of convicted murderers have a deterrent effect, what should be the sign of β_1? What sign do you think β_2 should have? Explain.

(ii) Using just the years 1990 and 1993, estimate the equation from part (i) by pooled OLS. Ignore the serial correlation problem in the composite errors. Do you find any evidence for a deterrent effect?

(iii) Now, using 1990 and 1993, estimate the equation by fixed effects. You may use first differencing since you are only using two years of data. Is there evidence of a deterrent effect? How strong?

(iv) Compute the heteroskedasticity-robust standard error for the estimation in part (ii).

(v) Find the state that has the largest number for the execution variable in 1993. (The variable *exec* is total executions in 1991, 1992, and 1993.) How much bigger is this value than the next highest value?

(vi) Estimate the equation using first differencing, dropping Texas from the analysis. Compute the usual and heteroskedasticity-robust standard errors. Now, what do you find? What is going on?

(vii) Use all three years of data and estimate the model by fixed effects. Include Texas in the analysis. Discuss the size and statistical significance of the deterrent effect compared with only using 1990 and 1993.

C8 Use the data in MATHPNL for this exercise. You will do a fixed effects version of the first differencing done in Computer Exercise 11 in Chapter 13. The model of interest is

$$math4_{it} = \delta_1 y94_t + \ldots + \delta_5 y98_t + \gamma_1\log(rexpp_{it}) + \gamma_2\log(rexpp_{i,t-1})$$
$$+ \psi_1\log(enrol_{it}) + \psi_2 lunch_{it} + a_i + u_{it},$$

where the first available year (the base year) is 1993 because of the lagged spending variable.

(i) Estimate the model by pooled OLS and report the usual standard errors. You should include an intercept along with the year dummies to allow a_i to have a nonzero expected value. What are the estimated effects of the spending variables? Obtain the OLS residuals, $\hat{v}_{it}$.

(ii) Is the sign of the $lunch_{it}$ coefficient what you expected? Interpret the magnitude of the coefficient. Would you say that the district poverty rate has a big effect on test pass rates?

(iii) Compute a test for AR(1) serial correlation using the regression $\hat{v}_{it}$ on $\hat{v}_{i,t-1}$. You should use the years 1994 through 1998 in the regression. Verify that there is strong positive serial correlation and discuss why.

(iv) Now, estimate the equation by fixed effects. Is the lagged spending variable still significant?

(v) Why do you think, in the fixed effects estimation, the enrollment and lunch program variables are jointly insignificant?

(vi) Define the total, or long-run, effect of spending as $\theta_1 = \gamma_1 + \gamma_2$. Use the substitution $\gamma_1 = \theta_1 - \gamma_2$ to obtain a standard error for $\hat{\theta}_1$. [*Hint:* Standard fixed effects estimation using $\log(rexpp_{it})$ and $z_{it} = \log(rexpp_{i,t-1}) - \log(rexpp_{it})$ as explanatory variables should do it.]

C9 The file PENSION contains information on participant-directed pension plans for U.S. workers. Some of the observations are for couples within the same family, so this data set constitutes a small cluster sample (with cluster sizes of two).

(i) Ignoring the clustering by family, use OLS to estimate the model

$$pctstck = \beta_0 + \beta_1 choice + \beta_2 prftshr + \beta_3 female + \beta_4 age$$
$$+ \beta_5 educ + \beta_6 finc25 + \beta_7 finc35 + \beta_8 finc50 + \beta_9 finc75$$
$$+ \beta_{10} finc100 + \beta_{11} finc101 + \beta_{12} wealth89 + \beta_{13} stckin89$$
$$+ \beta_{14} irain89 + u,$$

where the variables are defined in the data set. The variable of most interest is *choice*, which is a dummy variable equal to one if the worker has a choice in how to allocate pension funds among different investments. What is the estimated effect of *choice*? Is it statistically significant?

(ii) Are the income, wealth, stock holding, and IRA holding control variables important? Explain.

(iii) Determine how many different families there are in the data set.

(iv) Now, obtain the standard errors for OLS that are robust to cluster correlation within a family. Do they differ much from the usual OLS standard errors? Are you surprised?

(v) Estimate the equation by differencing across only the spouses within a family. Why do the explanatory variables asked about in part (ii) drop out in the first-differenced estimation?

(vi) Are any of the remaining explanatory variables in part (v) significant? Are you surprised?

C10 Use the data in AIRFARE for this exercise. We are interested in estimating the model

$$\log(fare_{it}) = \eta_t + \beta_1 concen_{it} + \beta_2 \log(dist_i) + \beta_3 [\log(dist_i)]^2$$
$$+ a_i + u_{it}, t = 1, \ldots, 4,$$

where η_t means that we allow for different year intercepts.

(i) Estimate the above equation by pooled OLS, being sure to include year dummies. If $\Delta concen = .10$, what is the estimated percentage increase in *fare*?

(ii) What is the usual OLS 95% confidence interval for β_1? Why is it probably not reliable? If you have access to a statistical package that computes fully robust standard errors, find the fully robust 95% CI for β_1. Compare it to the usual CI and comment.

(iii) Describe what is happening with the quadratic in log(*dist*). In particular, for what value of *dist* does the relationship between log(*fare*) and *dist* become positive? [*Hint:* First figure out the turning point value for log(*dist*), and then exponentiate.] Is the turning point outside the range of the data?

(iv) Now estimate the equation using random effects. How does the estimate of β_1 change?

(v) Now estimate the equation using fixed effects. What is the FE estimate of β_1? Why is it fairly similar to the RE estimate? (*Hint:* What is $\hat{\theta}$ for RE estimation?)

(vi) Name two characteristics of a route (other than distance between stops) that are captured by a_i. Might these be correlated with $concen_{it}$?

(vii) Are you convinced that higher concentration on a route increases airfares? What is your best estimate?

C11 This question assumes that you have access to a statistical package that computes standard errors robust to arbitrary serial correlation and heteroskedasticity for panel data methods.

(i) For the pooled OLS estimates in Table 14.1, obtain the standard errors that allow for arbitrary serial correlation (in the composite errors, $v_{it} = a_i + u_{it}$) and heteroskedasticity. How do the robust standard errors for *educ*, *married*, and *union* compare with the nonrobust ones?

(ii) Now obtain the robust standard errors for the fixed effects estimates that allow arbitrary serial correlation and heteroskedasticity in the idiosyncratic errors, u_{it}. How do these compare with the nonrobust FE standard errors?

(iii) For which method, pooled OLS or FE, is adjusting the standard errors for serial correlation more important? Why?

C12 Use the data in ELEM94_95 to answer this question. The data are on elementary schools in Michigan. In this exercise, we view the data as a cluster sample, where each school is part of a district cluster.

(i) What are the smallest and largest number of schools in a district? What is the average number of schools per district?

(ii) Using pooled OLS (that is, pooling across all 1,848 schools), estimate a model relating *lavgsal* to *bs*, *lenrol*, *lstaff*, and *lunch*; see also Computer Exercise 11 from Chapter 9. What are the coefficient and standard error on *bs*?

(iii) Obtain the standard errors that are robust to cluster correlation within district (and also heteroskedasticity). What happens to the t statistic for *bs*?

(iv) Still using pooled OLS, drop the four observations with $bs > .5$ and obtain $\hat{\beta}_{bs}$ and its cluster-robust standard error. Now is there much evidence for a salary-benefits tradeoff?

(v) Estimate the equation by fixed effects, allowing for a common district effect for schools within a district. Again drop the observations with $bs > .5$. Now what do you conclude about the salary-benefits tradeoff?

(vi) In light of your estimates from parts (iv) and (v), discuss the importance of allowing teacher compensation to vary systematically across districts via a district fixed effect.

C13 The data set DRIVING includes state-level panel data (for the 48 continental U.S. states) from 1980 through 2004, for a total of 25 years. Various driving laws are indicated in the data set, including the alcohol level at which drivers are considered legally intoxicated. There are also indicators for "per se" laws—where licenses can be revoked without a trial—and seat belt laws. Some economics and demographic variables are also included.

(i) How is the variable *totfatrte* defined? What is the average of this variable in the years 1980, 1992, and 2004? Run a regression of *totfatrte* on dummy variables for the years 1981 through 2004, and describe what you find. Did driving become safer over this period? Explain.

(ii) Add the variables *bac08*, *bac10*, *perse*, *sbprim*, *sbsecon*, *sl70plus*, *gdl*, *perc14_24*, *unem*, and *vehicmilespc* to the regression from part (i). Interpret the coefficients on *bac8* and *bac10*. Do per se laws have a negative effect on the fatality rate? What about having a primary seat belt law? (Note that if a law was enacted sometime within a year the fraction of the year is recorded in place of the zero-one indicator.)

(iii) Reestimate the model from part (ii) using fixed effects (at the state level). How do the coefficients on *bac08*, *bac10*, *perse*, and *sbprim* compare with the pooled OLS estimates? Which set of estimates do you think is more reliable?

(iv) Suppose that *vehicmilespc*, the number of miles driven per capita, increases by 1,000. Using the FE estimates, what is the estimated effect on *totfatrte*? Be sure to interpret the estimate as if explaining to a layperson.

(v) If there is serial correlation or heteroskedasticity in the idiosyncratic errors of the model then the standard errors in part (iii) are invalid. If possible, use "cluster" robust standard errors for the fixed effects estimates. What happens to the statistical significance of the policy variables in part (iii)?

C14 Use the data set in AIRFARE to answer this question. The estimates can be compared with those in Computer Exercise 10, in this Chapter.

(i) Compute the time averages of the variable *concen*; call these *concenbar*. How many different time averages can there be? Report the smallest and the largest.

(ii) Estimate the equation

$$lfare_{it} = \beta_0 + \delta_1 y98_t + \delta_2 y99_t + \delta_3 y00_t + \beta_1 concen_{it} + \beta_2 ldist_i + \beta_3 ldistsq_i +$$
$$\gamma_1 concenbar_i + a_i + u_{it}$$

by random effects. Verify that $\hat{\beta}_1$ is identical to the FE estimate computed in C10.

(iii) If you drop *ldist* and *ldistsq* from the estimation in part (i) but still include *concenbar*$_i$, what happens to the estimate of $\hat{\beta}_1$? What happens to the estimate of γ_1?

(iv) Using the equation in part (ii) and the usual RE standard error, test $H_0: \gamma_1 = 0$ against the two-sided alternative. Report the p-value. What do you conclude about RE versus FE for estimating β_1 in this application?

(v) If possible, for the test in part (iv) obtain a t-statistic (and, therefore, p-value) that is robust to arbitrary serial correlation and heteroskedasticity. Does this change the conclusion reached in part (iv)?

C15 Use the data in COUNTYMURDERS to answer this question. The data set covers murders and executions (capital punishment) for 2,197 counties in the United States. See also Computer Exercise C16 in Chapter 13.

(i) Consider the model

$$murdrate_{it} = \theta_t + \delta_0 execs_{it} + \delta_1 execs_{i,t-1} + \delta_2 execs_{i,t-2} + \delta_3 execs_{i,t-3} +$$
$$\beta_5 percblack_{it} + \beta_6 percmale_{it} + \beta_7 perc1019_{it} + \beta_8 perc2029_{it} + a_i + u_{it},$$

where θ_t represents a different intercept for each time period, a_i is the county fixed effect, and u_{it} is the idiosyncratic error. Why does it make sense to include lags of the key variable, *execs*, in the equation?

(ii) Apply OLS to the equation from part (i) and report the estimates of δ_0, δ_1, δ_2, and δ_3, along with the usual pooled OLS standard errors. Do you estimate that executions have a deterrent effect on murders? Provide an explanation that involves a_i.

(iii) Now estimate the equation in part (i) using fixed effects to remove a_i. What are the new estimates of the δ_j? Are they very different from the estimates from part (ii)?

(iv) Obtain the long-run propensity from estimates in part (iii). Using the usual FE standard errors, is the LRP statistically different from zero?

(v) If possible, obtain the standard errors for the FE estimates that are robust to arbitrary heteroskedasticity and serial correlation in the $\{u_{it}\}$. What happens to the statistical significance of the $\hat{\delta}_j$? What about the estimated LRP?

APPENDIX 14A

14A.1 Assumptions for Fixed and Random Effects

In this appendix, we provide statements of the assumptions for fixed and random effects estimation. We also provide a discussion of the properties of the estimators under different sets of assumptions. Verification of these claims is somewhat involved, but can be found in Wooldridge (2010, Chapter 10).

Assumption FE.1

For each i, the model is

$$y_{it} = \beta_1 x_{it1} + \ldots + \beta_k x_{itk} + a_i + u_{it}, \quad t = 1, \ldots, T,$$

where the β_j are the parameters to estimate and a_i is the unobserved effect.

Assumption FE.2

We have a random sample from the cross section.

Assumption FE.3

Each explanatory variable changes over time (for at least some i), and no perfect linear relationships exist among the explanatory variables.

Assumption FE.4

For each t, the expected value of the idiosyncratic error given the explanatory variables in *all* time periods and the unobserved effect is zero: $E(u_{it}|\mathbf{X}_i, a_i) = 0$.

Under these first four assumptions—which are identical to the assumptions for the first-differencing estimator—the fixed effects estimator is unbiased. Again, the key is the strict exogeneity assumption, FE.4. Under these same assumptions, the FE estimator is consistent with a fixed T as $N \to \infty$.

Assumption FE.5

$\text{Var}(u_{it}|\mathbf{X}_i, a_i) = \text{Var}(u_{it}) = \sigma_u^2$, for all $t = 1, \ldots, T$.

Assumption FE.6

For all $t \neq s$, the idiosyncratic errors are uncorrelated (conditional on all explanatory variables and a_i): $\text{Cov}(u_{it}, u_{is}|\mathbf{X}_i, a_i) = 0$.

Under Assumptions FE.1 through FE.6, the fixed effects estimator of the β_j is the best linear unbiased estimator. Since the FD estimator is linear and unbiased, it is necessarily worse than the FE estimator. The assumption that makes FE better than FD is FE.6, which implies that the idiosyncratic errors are serially uncorrelated.

Assumption FE.7

Conditional on $\mathbf{X}_i$ and a_i, the u_{it} are independent and identically distributed as $\text{Normal}(0, \sigma_u^2)$.

Assumption FE.7 implies FE.4, FE.5, and FE.6, but it is stronger because it assumes a normal distribution for the idiosyncratic errors. If we add FE.7, the FE estimator is normally distributed, and t and F statistics have exact t and F distributions. Without FE.7, we can rely on asymptotic approximations. But, without making special assumptions, these approximations require large N and small T.

The ideal random effects assumptions include FE.1, FE.2, FE.4, FE.5, and FE.6. (FE.7 could be added but it gains us little in practice because we have to estimate θ.) Because we are only subtracting a fraction of the time averages, we can now allow time-constant explanatory variables. So, FE.3 is replaced with the following assumption:

Assumption RE.1

There are no perfect linear relationships among the explanatory variables.
The cost of allowing time-constant regressors is that we must add assumptions about how the unobserved effect, a_i, is related to the explanatory variables.

Assumption RE.2

In addition to FE.4, the expected value of a_i given all explanatory variables is constant: $E(a_i|\mathbf{X}_i) = \beta_0$.

This is the assumption that rules out correlation between the unobserved effect and the explanatory variables, and it is the key distinction between fixed effects and random effects. Because we are assuming a_i is uncorrelated with all elements of $\mathbf{x}_{it}$, we can include time-constant explanatory variables. (Technically, the quasi-time-demeaning only removes a fraction of the time average, and not the whole time average.) We allow for a nonzero expectation for a_i in stating Assumption RE.4 so that the model under the random effects assumptions contains an intercept, β_0, as in equation (14.7). Remember, we would typically include a set of time-period intercepts, too, with the first year acting as the base year.

We also need to impose homoskedasticity on a_i as follows:

Assumption RE.3

In addition to FE.5, the variance of a_i given all explanatory variables is constant: $\mathrm{Var}(a_i|\mathbf{X}_i) = \sigma_a^2$.

Under the six random effects assumptions (FE.1, FE.2, RE.3, RE.4, RE.5, and FE.6), the RE estimator is consistent and asymptotically normally distributed as N gets large for fixed T. Actually, consistency and asymptotic normality follow under the first four assumptions, but without the last two assumptions the usual RE standard errors and test statistics would not be valid. In addition, under the six RE assumptions, the RE estimators are asymptotically efficient. This means that, in large samples, the RE estimators will have smaller standard errors than the corresponding pooled OLS estimators (when the proper, robust standard errors are used for pooled OLS). For coefficients on time-varying explanatory variables (the only ones estimable by FE), the RE estimator is more efficient than the FE estimator—often much more efficient. But FE is not meant to be efficient under the RE assumptions; FE is intended to be robust to correlation between a_i and the x_{itj}. As often happens in econometrics, there is a tradeoff between robustness and efficiency. See Wooldridge (2010, Chapter 10) for verification of the claims made here.

14A.2 Inference Robust to Serial Correlation and Heteroskedasticity for Fixed Effects and Random Effects

One of the key assumptions for performing inference using the FE, RE, and even the CRE approach to panel data models is the assumption of no serial correlation in the idiosyncratic errors, $\{u_{it}: t = 1, ..., T\}$—see Assumption FE.6. Of course, heteroskedasticity can also be an issue, but this is also ruled out for standard inference (see Assumption FE.5). As discussed in the appendix to Chapter 13, the same issues can arise with first differencing estimation when we have $T \geq 3$ time periods.

Fortunately, as with FD estimation, there are now simple solutions for fully robust inference—inference that is robust to arbitrary violations of Assumptions FE.5 and FE.6 and, when applying the RE or CRE approaches, to Assumption RE.5. As with FD estimation, the general approach to obtaining fully robust standard errors and test statistics is known as **clustering**. Now, however, the clustering is applied to a different equation. For example, for FE estimation, the clustering is applied to the time-demeaned equation (14.5). For RE estimation, the clustering gets applied to the quasi-time-demeaned equation (14.11) [and a similar comment holds for CRE, but there the time averages are included as separate explanatory variables]. The details, which can be found in Wooldridge (2010, Chapter 10) are too advanced for this text. But understanding the purpose of clustering is not: if possible, we should compute standard errors, confidence intervals, and test statistics that are valid in large cross sections under the weakest set of assumptions. The FE estimator requires only Assumptions FE.1 to FE.4 for unbiasedness and consistency (as $N \to \infty$ with T fixed). Thus, a careful researcher at least checks whether inference made robust to serial correlation and heteroskedasticity in the errors affects inference. Experience shows that it often does.

Applying cluster-robust inference to account for serial correlation within a panel data context is easily justified when N is substantially larger than T. Under certain restrictions on the time series dependence, of the sort discussed in Chapter 11, cluster-robust inference for the fixed effects estimator can be justified when T is of a similar magnitude as N, provided both are not small. This follows from the work by Hansen (2007). Generally, clustering is not theoretically justified when N is small and T is large.

Computing the cluster-robust statistics after FE or RE estimation is simple in many econometrics packages, often only requiring an option of the form "cluster(id)" appended to the end of FE and RE estimation commands. As in the FD case, "id" refers to a cross-section identifier. Similar comments hold when applying FE or RE to cluster samples, as the cluster identifier.

CHAPTER 15

Instrumental Variables Estimation and Two Stage Least Squares

I n this chapter, we further study the problem of **endogenous explanatory variables** in multiple regression models. In Chapter 3, we derived the bias in the OLS estimators when an important variable is omitted; in Chapter 5, we showed that OLS is generally inconsistent under **omitted variables**. Chapter 9 demonstrated that omitted variables bias can be eliminated (or at least mitigated) when a suitable proxy variable is given for an unobserved explanatory variable. Unfortunately, suitable proxy variables are not always available.

In the previous two chapters, we explained how fixed effects estimation or first differencing can be used with panel data to estimate the effects of time-varying independent variables in the presence of *time-constant* omitted variables. Although such methods are very useful, we do not always have access to panel data. Even if we can obtain panel data, it does us little good if we are interested in the effect of a variable that does not change over time: first differencing or fixed effects estimation eliminates time-constant explanatory variables. In addition, the panel data methods that we have studied so far do not solve the problem of time-varying omitted variables that are correlated with the explanatory variables.

In this chapter, we take a different approach to the endogeneity problem. You will see how the method of instrumental variables (IV) can be used to solve the problem of endogeneity of one or more explanatory variables. The method of two stage least squares (2SLS or TSLS) is second in popularity only to ordinary least squares for estimating linear equations in applied econometrics.

We begin by showing how IV methods can be used to obtain consistent estimators in the presence of omitted variables. IV can also be used to solve the **errors-in-variables** problem, at least under certain assumptions. The next chapter will demonstrate how to estimate simultaneous equations models using IV methods.

Our treatment of instrumental variables estimation closely follows our development of ordinary least squares in Part 1, where we assumed that we had a random sample from an underlying population. This is a desirable starting point because, in addition to simplifying the notation, it emphasizes that the important assumptions for IV estimation are stated in terms of the underlying population (just as with OLS). As we showed in Part 2, OLS can be applied to time series data, and the same is true of instrumental variables methods. Section 15-7 discusses some special issues that arise when IV methods are applied to time series data. In Section 15-8, we cover applications to pooled cross sections and panel data.

15-1 Motivation: Omitted Variables in a Simple Regression Model

When faced with the prospect of omitted variables bias (or unobserved heterogeneity), we have so far discussed three options: (1) we can ignore the problem and suffer the consequences of biased and inconsistent estimators; (2) we can try to find and use a suitable proxy variable for the unobserved variable; or (3) we can assume that the omitted variable does not change over time and use the fixed effects or first-differencing methods from Chapters 13 and 14. The first response can be satisfactory if the estimates are coupled with the direction of the biases for the key parameters. For example, if we can say that the estimator of a positive parameter, say, the effect of job training on subsequent wages, is biased toward zero and we have found a statistically significant positive estimate, we have still learned something: job training has a positive effect on wages, and it is likely that we have underestimated the effect. Unfortunately, the opposite case, where our estimates may be too large in magnitude, often occurs, which makes it very difficult for us to draw any useful conclusions.

The proxy variable solution discussed in Section 9-2 can also produce satisfying results, but it is not always possible to find a good proxy. This approach attempts to solve the omitted variable problem by replacing the unobservable with one or more proxy variables.

Another approach leaves the unobserved variable in the error term, but rather than estimating the model by OLS, it uses an estimation method that recognizes the presence of the omitted variable. This is what the method of instrumental variables does.

For illustration, consider the problem of unobserved ability in a wage equation for working adults. A simple model is

$$\log(wage) = \beta_0 + \beta_1 educ + \beta_2 abil + e,$$

where e is the error term. In Chapter 9, we showed how, under certain assumptions, a proxy variable such as IQ can be substituted for ability, and then a consistent estimator of β_1 is available from the regression of

$$\log(wage) \text{ on } educ, IQ.$$

Suppose, however, that a proxy variable is not available (or does not have the properties needed to produce a consistent estimator of β_1). Then, we put $abil$ into the error term, and we are left with the simple regression model

$$\log(wage) = \beta_0 + \beta_1 educ + u, \tag{15.1}$$

where u contains $abil$. Of course, if equation (15.1) is estimated by OLS, a biased and inconsistent estimator of β_1 results if $educ$ and $abil$ are correlated.

It turns out that we can still use equation (15.1) as the basis for estimation, provided we can find an instrumental variable for *educ*. To describe this approach, the simple regression model is written as

$$y = \beta_0 + \beta_1 x + u, \tag{15.2}$$

where we think that *x* and *u* are correlated (have nonzero covariance):

$$\text{Cov}(x,u) \neq 0. \tag{15.3}$$

The method of instrumental variables works whether or not *x* and *u* are correlated, but, for reasons we will see later, OLS should be used if *x* is uncorrelated with *u*.

In order to obtain consistent estimators of β_0 and β_1 when *x* and *u* are correlated, we need some additional information. The information comes by way of a new variable that satisfies certain properties. Suppose that we have an observable variable *z* that satisfies these two assumptions: (1) *z* is uncorrelated with *u*, that is,

$$\text{Cov}(z,u) = 0; \tag{15.4}$$

(2) *z* is correlated with *x*, that is,

$$\text{Cov}(z,x) \neq 0. \tag{15.5}$$

Then, we call *z* an **instrumental variable** for *x*, or sometimes simply an **instrument** for *x*.

The requirement that the instrument *z* satisfies (15.4) is summarized by saying "*z* is exogenous in equation (15.2)," and so we often refer to (15.4) as **instrument exogeneity**. In the context of omitted variables, instrument exogeneity means that *z* should have no partial effect on *y* (after *x* and omitted variables have been controlled for), and *z* should be uncorrelated with the omitted variables. Equation (15.5) means that *z* must be related, either positively or negatively, to the endogenous explanatory variable *x*. This condition is sometimes referred to as **instrument relevance** (as in "*z* is relevant for explaining variation in *x*").

There is a very important difference between the two requirements for an instrumental variable. Because (15.4) involves the covariance between *z* and the unobserved error *u*, we cannot generally hope to test this assumption: in the vast majority of cases, we must maintain $\text{Cov}(z,u) = 0$ by appealing to economic behavior or introspection. (In unusual cases, we might have an observable proxy variable for some factor contained in *u*, in which case we can check to see if *z* and the proxy variable are roughly uncorrelated. Of course, if we have a good proxy for an important element of *u*, we might just add the proxy as an explanatory variable and estimate the expanded equation by ordinary least squares. See Section 9-2.)

By contrast, the condition that *z* is correlated with *x* (in the population) can be tested, given a random sample from the population. The easiest way to do this is to estimate a simple regression between *x* and *z*. In the population, we have

$$x = \pi_0 + \pi_1 z + v. \tag{15.6}$$

Then, because $\pi_1 = \text{Cov}(z,x)/\text{Var}(z)$, assumption (15.5) holds if, and only if, $\pi_1 \neq 0$. Thus, we should be able to *reject* the null hypothesis

$$H_0: \pi_1 = 0 \tag{15.7}$$

against the two-sided alternative $H_0: \pi_1 \neq 0$, at a sufficiently small significance level (say, 5% or 1%). If this is the case, then we can be fairly confident that (15.5) holds.

For the log(*wage*) equation in (15.1), an instrumental variable *z* for *educ* must be (1) uncorrelated with ability (and any other unobserved factors affecting wage) and (2) correlated with education. Something such as the last digit of an individual's Social Security Number almost certainly satisfies the first requirement: it is uncorrelated with ability because it is determined randomly. However, it is precisely because of the randomness of the last digit of the SSN that it is not correlated with education, either; therefore it makes a poor instrumental variable for *educ* because it violates the instrument relevance requirement in equation (15.5).

What we have called a *proxy variable* for the omitted variable makes a poor IV for the opposite reason. For example, in the log(*wage*) example with omitted ability, a proxy variable for *abil* should be as highly correlated as possible with *abil*. An instrumental variable must be *uncorrelated* with *abil*. Therefore, while *IQ* is a good candidate as a proxy variable for *abil*, it is not a good instrumental variable for *educ* because it violates the instrument exogeneity requirement in equation (15.4).

Whether other possible instrumental variable candidates satisfy the exogeneity requirement in (15.4) is less clear-cut. In wage equations, labor economists have used family background variables as IVs for education. For example, mother's education (*motheduc*) is positively correlated with child's education, as can be seen by collecting a sample of data on working people and running a simple regression of *educ* on *motheduc*. Therefore, *motheduc* satisfies equation (15.5). The problem is that mother's education might also be correlated with child's ability (through mother's ability and perhaps quality of nurturing at an early age), in which case (15.4) fails.

Another IV choice for *educ* in (15.1) is number of siblings while growing up (*sibs*). Typically, having more siblings is associated with lower average levels of education. Thus, if number of siblings is uncorrelated with ability, it can act as an instrumental variable for *educ*.

As a second example, consider the problem of estimating the causal effect of skipping classes on final exam score. In a simple regression framework, we have

$$score = \beta_0 + \beta_1 skipped + u,$$
[15.8]

where *score* is the final exam score and *skipped* is the total number of lectures missed during the semester. We certainly might be worried that *skipped* is correlated with other factors in *u*: more able, highly motivated students might miss fewer classes. Thus, a simple regression of *score* on *skipped* may not give us a good estimate of the causal effect of missing classes.

What might be a good IV for *skipped*? We need something that has no direct effect on *score* and is not correlated with student ability and motivation. At the same time, the IV must be correlated with *skipped*. One option is to use distance between living quarters and campus. Some students at a large university will commute to campus, which may increase the likelihood of missing lectures (due to bad weather, oversleeping, and so on). Thus, *skipped* may be positively correlated with *distance*; this can be checked by regressing *skipped* on *distance* and doing a *t* test, as described earlier.

Is *distance* uncorrelated with *u*? In the simple regression model (15.8), some factors in *u* may be correlated with *distance*. For example, students from low-income families may live off campus; if income affects student performance, this could cause *distance* to be correlated with *u*. Section 15-2 shows how to use IV in the context of multiple regression, so that other factors affecting *score* can be included directly in the model. Then, *distance* might be a good IV for *skipped*. An IV approach may not be necessary at all if a good proxy exists for student ability, such as cumulative GPA prior to the semester.

There is a final point worth emphasizing before we turn to the mechanics of IV estimation: namely, in using the simple regression in equation (15.6) to test (15.7), it is important to take note of the sign (and even magnitude) of $\hat{\pi}_1$ and not just its statistical significance. Arguments for why a variable *z* makes a good IV candidate for an endogenous explanatory variable *x* should include a discussion about the nature of the relationship between *x* and *z*. For example, due to genetics and background influences it makes sense that child's education (*x*) and mother's education (*z*) are positively correlated. If in your sample of data you find that they are actually negatively correlated—that is, $\hat{\pi}_1 < 0$—then your use of mother's education as an IV for child's education is likely to be unconvincing. [And this has nothing to do with whether condition (15.4) is likely to hold.] In the example of measuring whether skipping classes has an effect on test performance, one should find a positive, statistically significant relationship between *skipped* and *distance* in order to justify using *distance* as an IV for skipped: a negative relationship would be difficult to justify [and would suggest that there are important omitted variables driving a negative correlation—variables that might themselves have to be included in the model (15.8)].

We now demonstrate that the availability of an instrumental variable can be used to estimate consistently the parameters in equation (15.2). In particular, we show that assumptions (15.4) and (15.5) serve to *identify* the parameter β_1. **Identification** of a parameter in this context means that we can write β_1 in terms of population moments that can be estimated using a sample of data. To write β_1 in terms of population covariances, we use equation (15.2): the covariance between z and y is

$$\text{Cov}(z,y) = \beta_1\text{Cov}(z,x) + \text{Cov}(z,u).$$

Now, under assumption (15.4), $\text{Cov}(z,u) = 0$, and under assumption (15.5), $\text{Cov}(z,x) \neq 0$. Thus, we can solve for β_1 as

$$\beta_1 = \frac{\text{Cov}(z,y)}{\text{Cov}(z,x)}. \tag{15.9}$$

[Notice how this simple algebra fails if z and x are uncorrelated, that is, if $\text{Cov}(z,x) = 0$.] Equation (15.9) shows that β_1 is the population covariance between z and y divided by the population covariance between z and x, which shows that β_1 is identified. Given a random sample, we estimate the population quantities by the sample analogs. After canceling the sample sizes in the numerator and denominator, we get the **instrumental variables (IV) estimator** of β_1:

$$\hat{\beta}_1 = \frac{\sum_{i=1}^{n}(z_i - \bar{z})(y_i - \bar{y})}{\sum_{i=1}^{n}(z_i - \bar{z})(x_i - \bar{x})}. \tag{15.10}$$

Given a sample of data on x, y, and z, it is simple to obtain the IV estimator in (15.10). The IV estimator of β_0 is simply $\hat{\beta}_0 = \bar{y} - \hat{\beta}_1\bar{x}$, which looks just like the OLS intercept estimator except that the slope estimator, $\hat{\beta}_1$, is now the IV estimator.

It is no accident that when $z = x$ we obtain the OLS estimator of β_1. In other words, when x is exogenous, it can be used as its own IV, and the IV estimator is then identical to the OLS estimator.

A simple application of the law of large numbers shows that the IV estimator is consistent for β_1: $\text{plim}(\hat{\beta}_1) = \beta_1$, provided assumptions (15.4) and (15.5) are satisfied. If either assumption fails, the IV estimators are not consistent (more on this later). One feature of the IV estimator is that, when x and u are in fact correlated—so that instrumental variables estimation is actually needed—it is essentially never unbiased. This means that, in small samples, the IV estimator can have a substantial bias, which is one reason why large samples are preferred.

When discussing the application of instrumental variables it is important to be careful with language. Like OLS, IV is an *estimation* method. It makes little sense to refer to "an instrumental variables model"—just as the phrase "OLS model" makes little sense. As we know, a model is an equation such as (15.8), which is a special case of the generic model in equation (15.2). When we have a model such as (15.2), we can choose to estimate the parameters of that model in many different ways. Prior to this chapter we focused primarily on OLS, but, for example, we also know from Chapter 8 that one can use weighted least squares as an alternative estimation method (and there are unlimited possibilities for the weights). If we have an instrumental variable candidate z for x, then we can instead apply instrumental variables estimation. It is certainly true that the estimation method we apply is motivated by the model and assumptions we make about that model. But the estimators are well defined and exist apart from any underlying model or assumptions: remember, an estimator is simply a rule for combining data. The bottom line is that while we probably know what a researcher means when using a phrase such as "I estimated an IV model," such language betrays a lack of understanding about the difference between a model and an estimation method.

15-1a Statistical Inference with the IV Estimator

Given the similar structure of the IV and OLS estimators, it is not surprising that the IV estimator has an approximate normal distribution in large sample sizes. To perform inference on β_1, we need a standard error that can be used to compute t statistics and confidence intervals. The usual approach is to impose a homoskedasticity assumption, just as in the case of OLS. Now, the homoskedasticity assumption is stated conditional on the instrumental variable, z, not the endogenous explanatory variable, x. Along with the previous assumptions on u, x, and z, we add

$$E(u^2|z) = \sigma^2 = \text{Var}(u). \qquad [15.11]$$

It can be shown that, under (15.4), (15.5), and (15.11), the asymptotic variance of $\hat{\beta}_1$ is

$$\frac{\sigma^2}{n\sigma_x^2\rho_{x,z}^2}, \qquad [15.12]$$

where σ_x^2 is the population variance of x, σ^2 is the population variance of u, and $\rho_{x,z}^2$ is the square of the population correlation between x and z. This tells us how highly correlated x and z are in the population. As with the OLS estimator, the asymptotic variance of the IV estimator decreases to zero at the rate of $1/n$, where n is the sample size.

Equation (15.12) is interesting for two reasons. First, it provides a way to obtain a standard error for the IV estimator. All quantities in (15.12) can be consistently estimated given a random sample. To estimate σ_x^2, we simply compute the sample variance of x_i; to estimate $\rho_{x,z}^2$, we can run the regression of x_i on z_i to obtain the R-squared, say, $R_{x,z}^2$. Finally, to estimate σ^2, we can use the IV residuals,

$$\hat{u}_i = y_i - \hat{\beta}_0 - \hat{\beta}_1 x_i, \quad i = 1, 2, \dots, n,$$

where $\hat{\beta}_0$ and $\hat{\beta}_1$ are the IV estimates. A consistent estimator of σ^2 looks just like the estimator of σ^2 from a simple OLS regression:

$$\hat{\sigma}^2 = \frac{1}{n-2}\sum_{i=1}^{n}\hat{u}_i^2,$$

where it is standard to use the degrees of freedom correction (even though this has little effect as the sample size grows).

The (asymptotic) standard error of $\hat{\beta}_1$ is the square root of the estimated asymptotic variance, the latter of which is given by

$$\frac{\hat{\sigma}^2}{\text{SST}_x \cdot R_{x,z}^2}, \qquad [15.13]$$

where SST_x is the total sum of squares of the x_i. [Recall that the sample variance of x_i is SST_x/n, and so the sample sizes cancel to give us (15.13).] The resulting standard error can be used to construct either t statistics for hypotheses involving β_1 or confidence intervals for β_1. $\hat{\beta}_0$ also has a standard error that we do not present here. Any modern econometrics package computes the standard error after any IV estimation; there is rarely any reason to perform the calculations by hand.

A second reason (15.12) is interesting is that it allows us to compare the asymptotic variances of the IV and the OLS estimators (when x and u are uncorrelated). Under the Gauss-Markov assumptions, the variance of the OLS estimator is σ^2/SST_x, while the comparable formula for the IV estimator is $\sigma^2/(\text{SST}_x \cdot R_{x,z}^2)$; they differ only in that $R_{x,z}^2$ appears in the denominator of the IV variance. Because an R-squared is always less than one, the IV variance is always larger than the OLS variance (when OLS is valid). If $R_{x,z}^2$ is small, then the IV variance can be much larger than the OLS variance. Remember, $R_{x,z}^2$ measures the strength of the linear relationship between x and z in the sample.

If x and z are only slightly correlated, $R_{x,z}^2$ can be small, and this can translate into a very large sampling variance for the IV estimator. The more highly correlated z is with x, the closer $R_{x,z}^2$ is to one, and the smaller is the variance of the IV estimator. In the case that $z = x$, $R_{x,z}^2 = 1$, and we get the OLS variance, as expected.

The previous discussion highlights an important cost of performing IV estimation when x and u are uncorrelated: the asymptotic variance of the IV estimator is always larger, and sometimes much larger, than the asymptotic variance of the OLS estimator.

EXAMPLE 15.1   **Estimating the Return to Education for Married Women**

We use the data on married working women in MROZ to estimate the return to education in the simple regression model

$$\log(wage) = \beta_0 + \beta_1 educ + u. \tag{15.14}$$

For comparison, we first obtain the OLS estimates:

$$\widehat{\log(wage)} = -.185 + .109\, educ$$
$$(.185)\ (.014) \tag{15.15}$$
$$n = 428, R^2 = .118.$$

The estimate for β_1 implies an almost 11% return for another year of education.

Next, we use father's education (*fatheduc*) as an instrumental variable for *educ*. We have to maintain that *fatheduc* is uncorrelated with u. The second requirement is that *educ* and *fatheduc* are correlated. We can check this very easily using a simple regression of *educ* on *fatheduc* (using only the working women in the sample):

$$\widehat{educ} = 10.24 + .269\, fatheduc$$
$$(.28)\ (.029) \tag{15.16}$$
$$n = 428, R^2 = .173.$$

The t statistic on *fatheduc* is 9.28, which indicates that *educ* and *fatheduc* have a statistically significant positive correlation. (In fact, *fatheduc* explains about 17% of the variation in *educ* in the sample.) Using *fatheduc* as an IV for *educ* gives

$$\widehat{\log(wage)} = .441 + .059\, educ$$
$$(.446)\ (.035) \tag{15.17}$$
$$n = 428, R^2 = .093.$$

The IV estimate of the return to education is 5.9%, which is barely more than one-half of the OLS estimate. This *suggests* that the OLS estimate is too high and is consistent with omitted ability bias. But we should remember that these are estimates from just one sample: we can never know whether .109 is above the true return to education, or whether .059 is closer to the true return to education. Further, the standard error of the IV estimate is two and one-half times as large as the OLS standard error (this is expected, for the reasons we gave earlier). The 95% confidence interval for β_1 using OLS is much tighter than that using the IV; in fact, the IV confidence interval actually contains the OLS estimate. Therefore, although the differences between (15.15) and (15.17) are practically large, we cannot say whether the difference is *statistically* significant. We will show how to test this in Section 15-5.

In the previous example, the estimated return to education using IV was less than that using OLS, which corresponds to our expectations. But this need not have been the case, as the following example demonstrates.

EXAMPLE 15.2	**Estimating the Return to Education for Men**

We now use WAGE2 to estimate the return to education for men. We use the variable *sibs* (number of siblings) as an instrument for *educ*. These are negatively correlated, as we can verify from a simple regression:

$$\widehat{educ} = 14.14 - .228 \, sibs$$
$$(.11) \quad (.030)$$
$$n = 935, R^2 = .057.$$

This equation implies that every sibling is associated with, on average, about .23 less of a year of education. If we assume that *sibs* is uncorrelated with the error term in (15.14), then the IV estimator is consistent. Estimating equation (15.14) using *sibs* as an IV for *educ* gives

$$\widehat{\log(wage)} = 5.13 + .122 \, educ$$
$$(.36) \quad (.026)$$
$$n = 935.$$

(The *R*-squared is computed to be negative, so we do not report it. A discussion of *R*-squared in the context of IV estimation follows.) For comparison, the OLS estimate of β_1 is .059 with a standard error of .006. Unlike in the previous example, the IV estimate is now much higher than the OLS estimate. While we do not know whether the difference is statistically significant, this does not mesh with the omitted ability bias from OLS. It could be that *sibs* is also correlated with ability: more siblings means, on average, less parental attention, which could result in lower ability. Another interpretation is that the OLS estimator is biased toward zero because of measurement error in *educ*. This is not entirely convincing because, as we discussed in Section 9-3, *educ* is unlikely to satisfy the classical errors-in-variables model.

In the previous examples, the endogenous explanatory variable (*educ*) and the instrumental variables (*fatheduc*, *sibs*) have quantitative meaning. But nothing prevents the explanatory variable or IV from being binary variables. Angrist and Krueger (1991), in their simplest analysis, came up with a clever binary instrumental variable for *educ*, using census data on men in the United States. Let *frstqrt* be equal to one if the man was born in the first quarter of the year, and zero otherwise. It seems that the error term in (15.14)—and, in particular, ability—should be unrelated to quarter of birth. But *frstqrt* also needs to be correlated with *educ*. It turns out that years of education *do* differ systematically in the population based on quarter of birth. Angrist and Krueger argued persuasively that this is due to compulsory school attendance laws in effect in all states. Briefly, students born early in the year typically begin school at an older age. Therefore, they reach the compulsory schooling age (16 in most states) with somewhat less education than students who begin school at a younger age. For students who finish high school, Angrist and Krueger verified that there is no relationship between years of education and quarter of birth.

Because years of education varies only slightly across quarter of birth—which means $R^2_{x,z}$ in (15.13) is very small—Angrist and Krueger needed a very large sample size to get a reasonably precise IV estimate. Using 247,199 men born between 1920 and 1929, the OLS estimate of the return to education was .0801 (standard error .0004), and the IV estimate was .0715 (.0219); these are reported in Table III of Angrist and Krueger's paper. Note how large the *t* statistic is for the OLS estimate (about 200), whereas the *t* statistic for the IV estimate is only 3.26. Thus, the IV estimate is statistically different from zero, but its confidence interval is much wider than that based on the OLS estimate.

An interesting finding by Angrist and Krueger is that the IV estimate does not differ much from the OLS estimate. In fact, using men born in the next decade, the IV estimate is somewhat higher than the OLS estimate. One could interpret this as showing that there is no omitted ability bias when wage equations are estimated by OLS. However, the Angrist and Krueger paper has been criticized on econometric grounds. As discussed by Bound, Jaeger, and Baker (1995), it is not obvious that season of birth is unrelated to unobserved factors that affect wage. As we will explain in the next subsection, even a small amount of correlation between z and u can cause serious problems for the IV estimator.

For policy analysis, the endogenous explanatory variable is often a binary variable. For example, Angrist (1990) studied the effect that being a veteran of the Vietnam War had on lifetime earnings. A simple model is

$$\log(earns) = \beta_0 + \beta_1 veteran + u, \qquad [15.18]$$

where *veteran* is a binary variable. The problem with estimating this equation by OLS is that there may be a *self-selection* problem, as we mentioned in Chapter 7: perhaps people who get the most out of the military choose to join, or the decision to join is correlated with other characteristics that affect earnings. These will cause *veteran* and u to be correlated.

EXPLORING FURTHER 15.1

If some men who were assigned low draft lottery numbers obtained additional schooling to reduce the probability of being drafted, is lottery number a good instrument for *veteran* in (15.18)?

Angrist pointed out that the Vietnam draft lottery provided a **natural experiment** (see also Chapter 13) that created an instrumental variable for *veteran*. Young men were given lottery numbers that determined whether they would be called to serve in Vietnam. Because the numbers given were (eventually) randomly assigned, it seems plausible that draft lottery number is uncorrelated with the error term u.

But those with a low enough number had to serve in Vietnam, so that the probability of being a veteran is correlated with lottery number. If both of these assertions are true, draft lottery number is a good IV candidate for *veteran*.

It is also possible to have a binary endogenous explanatory variable and a binary instrumental variable. See Problem 1 for an example.

15-1b Properties of IV with a Poor Instrumental Variable

We have already seen that, though IV is consistent when z and u are uncorrelated and z and x have any positive or negative correlation, IV estimates can have large standard errors, especially if z and x are only weakly correlated. Weak correlation between z and x can have even more serious consequences: the IV estimator can have a large asymptotic bias even if z and u are only moderately correlated.

We can see this by studying the probability limit of the IV estimator when z and u are possibly correlated. Letting $\hat{\beta}_{1,\,IV}$ denote the IV estimator, we can write

$$\text{plim } \hat{\beta}_{1,\,IV} = \beta_1 + \frac{\text{Corr}(z,u)}{\text{Corr}(z,x)} \cdot \frac{\sigma_u}{\sigma_x}, \qquad [15.19]$$

where σ_u and σ_x are the standard deviations of u and x in the population, respectively. The interesting part of this equation involves the correlation terms. It shows that, even if $\text{Corr}(z,u)$ is small, the inconsistency in the IV estimator can be very large if $\text{Corr}(z,x)$ is also small. Thus, even if we focus only on consistency, it is not necessarily better to use IV than OLS if the correlation between z and u is smaller than that between x and u. Using the fact that $\text{Corr}(x,u) = \text{Cov}(x,u)/(\sigma_x\sigma_u)$ along with equation (5.3), we can write the plim of the OLS estimator—call it $\hat{\beta}_{1,\,OLS}$—as

$$\text{plim } \hat{\beta}_{1,\,OLS} = \beta_1 + \text{Corr}(x,u) \cdot \frac{\sigma_u}{\sigma_x}. \qquad [15.20]$$

Comparing these formulas shows that it is possible for the directions of the asymptotic biases to be different for IV and OLS. For example, suppose $\text{Corr}(x,u) > 0$, $\text{Corr}(z,x) > 0$, and $\text{Corr}(z,u) < 0$.

Then the IV estimator has a downward bias, whereas the OLS estimator has an upward bias (asymptotically). In practice, this situation is probably rare. More problematic is when the direction of the bias is the same and the correlation between z and x is small. For concreteness, suppose x and z are both positively correlated with u and $\text{Corr}(z,x) > 0$. Then the asymptotic bias in the IV estimator is less than that for OLS only if $\text{Corr}(z,u)/\text{Corr}(z,x) < \text{Corr}(x,u)$. If $\text{Corr}(z,x)$ is small, then a seemingly small correlation between z and u can be magnified and make IV worse than OLS, even if we restrict attention to bias. For example, if $\text{Corr}(z,x) = .2$, $\text{Corr}(z,u)$ must be less than one-fifth of $\text{Corr}(z,u)$ before IV has less asymptotic bias than OLS. In many applications, the correlation between the instrument and x is less than .2. Unfortunately, because we rarely have an idea about the relative magnitudes of $\text{Corr}(z,u)$ and $\text{Corr}(x,u)$, we can never know for sure which estimator has the largest asymptotic bias [unless, of course, we assume $\text{Corr}(z,u) = 0$].

In the Angrist and Krueger (1991) example mentioned earlier, where x is years of schooling and z is a binary variable indicating quarter of birth, the correlation between z and x is very small. Bound, Jaeger, and Baker (1995) discussed reasons why quarter of birth and u might be somewhat correlated. From equation (15.19), we see that this can lead to a substantial bias in the IV estimator.

When z and x are not correlated at all, things are especially bad, whether or not z is uncorrelated with u. The following example illustrates why we should always check to see if the endogenous explanatory variable is correlated with the IV candidate.

EXAMPLE 15.3   **Estimating the Effect of Smoking on Birth Weight**

In Chapter 6, we estimated the effect of cigarette smoking on child birth weight. Without other explanatory variables, the model is

$$\log(bwght) = \beta_0 + \beta_1 packs + u, \qquad [15.21]$$

where *packs* is the number of packs smoked by the mother per day. We might worry that *packs* is correlated with other health factors or the availability of good prenatal care, so that *packs* and u might be correlated. A possible instrumental variable for *packs* is the average price of cigarettes in the state of residence, *cigprice*. We will assume that *cigprice* and u are uncorrelated (even though state support for health care could be correlated with cigarette taxes).

If cigarettes are a typical consumption good, basic economic theory suggests that *packs* and *cigprice* are negatively correlated, so that *cigprice* can be used as an IV for *packs*. To check this, we regress *packs* on *cigprice*, using the data in BWGHT:

$$\widehat{packs} = .067 + .0003\, cigprice$$
$$\qquad\;\; (.103)\;\; (.0008)$$
$$n = 1{,}388,\; R^2 = .0000,\; \overline{R}^2 = -.0006.$$

This indicates no relationship between smoking during pregnancy and cigarette prices, which is perhaps not too surprising given the addictive nature of cigarette smoking.

Because *packs* and *cigprice* are not correlated, we should not use *cigprice* as an IV for *packs* in (15.21). But what happens if we do? The IV results would be

$$\widehat{\log(bwght)} = 4.45 + 2.99\, packs$$
$$\qquad\qquad (.91)\;\; (8.70)$$
$$n = 1{,}388$$

(the reported R-squared is negative). The coefficient on *packs* is huge and of an unexpected sign. The standard error is also very large, so *packs* is not significant. But the estimates are meaningless because *cigprice* fails the one requirement of an IV that we can always test: assumption (15.5).

The previous example shows that IV estimation can produce strange results when the instrument relevance condition, $\text{Corr}(z,x) \neq 0$, fails. Of practically greater interest is the so-called problem of **weak instruments**, which is loosely defined as the problem of "low" (but not zero) correlation between z and x. In a particular application, it is difficult to define how low is too low, but recent theoretical research, supplemented by simulation studies, has shed considerable light on the issue. Staiger and Stock (1997) formalized the problem of weak instruments by modeling the correlation between z and x as a function of the sample size; in particular, the correlation is assumed to shrink to zero at the rate $1/\sqrt{n}$. Not surprisingly, the asymptotic distribution of the instrumental variables estimator is different compared with the usual asymptotics, where the correlation is assumed to be fixed and nonzero. One of the implications of the Stock–Staiger work is that the usual statistical inference, based on t statistics and the standard normal distribution, can be seriously misleading. We discuss this further in Section 15-3.

15-1c Computing *R*-Squared after IV Estimation

Most regression packages compute an R-squared after IV estimation, using the standard formula: $R^2 = 1 - \text{SSR/SST}$, where SSR is the sum of squared *IV residuals* and SST is the total sum of squares of y. Unlike in the case of OLS, the R-squared from IV estimation can be negative because SSR for IV can actually be larger than SST. Although it does not really hurt to report the R-squared for IV estimation, it is not very useful, either. When x and u are correlated, we cannot decompose the variance of y into $\beta_1^2 \text{Var}(x) + \text{Var}(u)$, and so the R-squared has no natural interpretation. In addition, as we will discuss in Section 15-3, these R-squareds *cannot* be used in the usual way to compute F tests of joint restrictions.

If our goal was to produce the largest R-squared, we would always use OLS. IV methods are intended to provide better estimates of the ceteris paribus effect of x on y when x and u are correlated; goodness-of-fit is not a factor. A high R-squared resulting from OLS is of little comfort if we cannot consistently estimate β_1.

15-2 IV Estimation of the Multiple Regression Model

The IV estimator for the simple regression model is easily extended to the multiple regression case. We begin with the case where only one of the explanatory variables is correlated with the error. In fact, consider a standard linear model with two explanatory variables:

$$y_1 = \beta_0 + \beta_1 y_2 + \beta_2 z_1 + u_1. \qquad [15.22]$$

We call this a **structural equation** to emphasize that we are interested in the β_j, which simply means that the equation is supposed to measure a causal relationship. We use a new notation here to distinguish endogenous from **exogenous variables**. The dependent variable y_1 is clearly endogenous, as it is correlated with u_1. The variables y_2 and z_1 are the explanatory variables, and u_1 is the error. As usual, we assume that the expected value of u_1 is zero: $\text{E}(u_1) = 0$. We use z_1 to indicate that this variable is exogenous in (15.22) (z_1 is uncorrelated with u_1). We use y_2 to indicate that this variable is suspected of being correlated with u_1. We do not specify why y_2 and u_1 are correlated, but for now it is best to think of u_1 as containing an omitted variable correlated with y_2. The notation in equation (15.22) originates in simultaneous equations models (which we cover in Chapter 16), but we use it more generally to easily distinguish exogenous from endogenous explanatory variables in a multiple regression model.

An example of (15.22) is

$$\log(wage) = \beta_0 + \beta_1 educ + \beta_2 exper + u_1, \qquad [15.23]$$

where $y_1 = \log(wage)$, $y_2 = educ$, and $z_1 = exper$. In other words, we assume that *exper* is exogenous in (15.23), but we allow that *educ*—for the usual reasons—is correlated with u_1.

We know that if (15.22) is estimated by OLS, *all* of the estimators will be biased and inconsistent. Thus, we follow the strategy suggested in the previous section and seek an instrumental variable for y_2. Since z_1 is assumed to be uncorrelated with u_1, can we use z_1 as an instrument for y_2, assuming y_2 and z_1 are correlated? The answer is no. Since z_1 itself appears as an explanatory variable in (15.22), it cannot serve as an instrumental variable for y_2. We need another exogenous variable—call it z_2—that does *not* appear in (15.22). Therefore, key assumptions are that z_1 and z_2 are uncorrelated with u_1; we also assume that u_1 has zero expected value, which is without loss of generality when the equation contains an intercept:

$$E(u_1) = 0, \ \text{Cov}(z_1, u_1) = 0, \ \text{and} \ \text{Cov}(z_2, u_1) = 0. \tag{15.24}$$

Given the zero mean assumption, the latter two assumptions are equivalent to $E(z_1 u_1) = E(z_2 u_1) = 0$, and so the method of moments approach suggests obtaining estimators $\hat{\beta}_0$, $\hat{\beta}_1$, and $\hat{\beta}_2$ by solving the sample counterparts of (15.24):

$$\sum_{i=1}^{n} (y_{i1} - \hat{\beta}_0 - \hat{\beta}_1 y_{i2} - \hat{\beta}_2 z_{i1}) = 0$$

$$\sum_{i=1}^{n} z_{i1}(y_{i1} - \hat{\beta}_0 - \hat{\beta}_1 y_{i2} - \hat{\beta}_2 z_{i1}) = 0 \tag{15.25}$$

$$\sum_{i=1}^{n} z_{i2}(y_{i1} - \hat{\beta}_0 - \hat{\beta}_1 y_{i2} - \hat{\beta}_2 z_{i1}) = 0.$$

This is a set of three linear equations in the three unknowns $\hat{\beta}_0$, $\hat{\beta}_1$, and $\hat{\beta}_2$, and it is easily solved given the data on y_1, y_2, z_1, and z_2. The estimators are called *instrumental variables estimators*. If we think y_2 is exogenous and we choose $z_2 = y_2$, equations (15.25) are exactly the first order conditions for the OLS estimators; see equations (3.13).

We still need the instrumental variable z_2 to be correlated with y_2, but the sense in which these two variables must be correlated is complicated by the presence of z_1 in equation (15.22). We now need to state the assumption in terms of *partial* correlation. The easiest way to state the condition is to write the endogenous explanatory variable as a linear function of the exogenous variables and an error term:

$$y_2 = \pi_0 + \pi_1 z_1 + \pi_2 z_2 + v_2, \tag{15.26}$$

where, by construction, $E(v_2) = 0$, $\text{Cov}(z_1, v_2) = 0$, and $\text{Cov}(z_2, v_2) = 0$, and the π_j are unknown parameters. The key identification condition [along with (15.24)] is that

$$\pi_2 \neq 0. \tag{15.27}$$

In other words, after partialling out z_1, y_2 and z_2 are still correlated. This correlation can be positive or negative, but it cannot be zero. Testing (15.27) is easy: we estimate (15.26) by OLS and use a t test (possibly making it robust to heteroskedasticity). We should always test this assumption. Unfortunately, we cannot test that z_1 and z_2 are uncorrelated with u_1; hopefully, we can make the case based on economic reasoning or introspection.

> ### EXPLORING FURTHER 15.2
>
> Suppose we wish to estimate the effect of marijuana usage on college grade point average. For the population of college seniors at a university, let *daysused* denote the number of days in the past month on which a student smoked marijuana and consider the structural equation
>
> $colGPA = \beta_0 + \beta_1 daysused + \beta_2 SAT + u.$
>
> (i) Let *percHS* denote the percentage of a student's high school graduating class that reported regular use of marijuana. If this is an IV candidate for *daysused*, write the reduced form for *daysused*. Do you think (15.27) is likely to be true?
>
> (ii) Do you think *percHS* is truly exogenous in the structural equation? What problems might there be?

Equation (15.26) is an example of a **reduced form equation**, which means that we have written an endogenous variable in terms of exogenous variables. This name comes from simultaneous equations models—which we study in the next chapter—but it is a useful concept whenever we have an endogenous explanatory variable. The name helps distinguish it from the structural equation (15.22).

Adding more **exogenous explanatory variables** to the model is straightforward. Write the structural model as

$$y_1 = \beta_0 + \beta_1 y_2 + \beta_2 z_1 + \dots + \beta_k z_{k-1} + u_1, \qquad [15.28]$$

where y_2 is thought to be correlated with u_1. Let z_k be a variable not in (15.28) that is also exogenous. Therefore, we assume that

$$E(u_1) = 0, \ \text{Cov}(z_j, u_1) = 0, \quad j = 1, \dots, k. \qquad [15.29]$$

Under (15.29), $z_1, \dots, z_{k-1}$ are the exogenous variables appearing in (15.28). In effect, these act as their own instrumental variables in estimating the β_j in (15.28). The special case of $k = 2$ is given in the equations in (15.25); along with z_2, z_1 appears in the set of moment conditions used to obtain the IV estimates. More generally, $z_1, \dots, z_{k-1}$ are used in the moment conditions along with the instrumental variable for y_2, z_k.

The reduced form for y_2 is

$$y_2 = \pi_0 + \pi_1 z_1 + \dots + \pi_{k-1} z_{k-1} + \pi_k z_k + v_2, \qquad [15.30]$$

and we need some partial correlation between z_k and y_2:

$$\pi_k \neq 0. \qquad [15.31]$$

Under (15.29) and (15.31), z_k is a valid IV for y_2. [We do not care about the remaining π_j in (15.30); some or all of them could be zero.] A minor additional assumption is that there are no perfect linear relationships among the exogenous variables; this is analogous to the assumption of no perfect collinearity in the context of OLS.

For standard statistical inference, we need to assume homoskedasticity of u_1. We give a careful statement of these assumptions in a more general setting in Section 15-3.

EXAMPLE 15.4   **Using College Proximity as an IV for Education**

Card (1995) used wage and education data for a sample of men in 1976 to estimate the return to education. He used a dummy variable for whether someone grew up near a four-year college (*nearc4*) as an instrumental variable for education. In a log(*wage*) equation, he included other standard controls: experience, a black dummy variable, dummy variables for living in an SMSA and living in the South, and a full set of regional dummy variables and an SMSA dummy for where the man was living in 1966. In order for *nearc4* to be a valid instrument, it must be uncorrelated with the error term in the wage equation—we assume this—and it must be partially correlated with *educ*. To check the latter requirement, we regress *educ* on *nearc4* and all of the exogenous variables appearing in the equation. (That is, we estimate the reduced form for *educ*.) Using the data in CARD, we obtain, in condensed form,

$$educ = 16.64 + .320 \, nearc4 - .413 \, exper + \dots$$
$$(.24) \ (.088) \qquad (.034)$$
$$n = 3{,}010, R^2 = .477.$$

We are interested in the coefficient and t statistic on *nearc4*. The coefficient implies that in 1976, other things being fixed (experience, race, region, and so on), people who lived near a college in 1966 had, on average, about one-third of a year more education than those who did not grow up near a college. The t statistic on *nearc4* is 3.64, which gives a p-value that is zero in the first three decimals.

Therefore, if *nearc4* is uncorrelated with unobserved factors in the error term, we can use *nearc4* as an IV for *educ*.

The OLS and IV estimates are given in Table 15.1. Like the OLS standard errors, the reported IV standard errors employ a degrees-of-freedom adjustment in estimating the error variance. In some statistical packages the degrees-of-freedom adjustment is the default; in others it is not.

Interestingly, the IV estimate of the return to education is almost twice as large as the OLS estimate, but the standard error of the IV estimate is over 18 times larger than the OLS standard error. The 95% confidence interval for the IV estimate is between .024 and .239, which is a very wide range. The presence of larger confidence intervals is a price we must pay to get a consistent estimator of the return to education when we think *educ* is endogenous.

TABLE 15.1 Dependent Variable: log(*wage*)

Explanatory Variables	OLS	IV
educ	.075	.132
	(.003)	(.055)
exper	.085	.108
	(.007)	(.024)
exper^2	−.0023	−.0023
	(.0003)	(.0003)
black	−.199	−.147
	(.018)	(.054)
smsa	.136	.112
	(.020)	(.032)
south	−.148	−.145
	(.026)	(.027)
Observations	3,010	3,010
R-squared	.300	.238
Other controls: *smsa66, reg662, …, reg669*		

As discussed earlier, we should not make anything of the smaller *R*-squared in the IV estimation: by definition, the OLS *R*-squared will always be larger because OLS minimizes the sum of squared residuals.

It is worth noting, especially for studying the effects of policy interventions, that a reduced form equation exists for y_1, too. In the context of equation (15.28) with z_k an IV for y_2, the reduced form for y_1 always has the form

$$y_1 = \gamma_0 + \gamma_1 z_1 + \ldots + \gamma_k z_k + e_1, \qquad [15.32]$$

where $\gamma_j = \beta_j + \beta_1 \pi_j$ for $j < k$, $\gamma_k = \beta_1 \pi_k$, and $e_1 = u_1 + \beta_1 v_2$—as can be verified by plugging (15.30) into (15.28) and rearranging. Because the z_j are exogenous in (15.32), the γ_j can be consistently estimated by OLS. In other words, we regress y_1 on all of the exogenous variables, including z_k, the IV for y_2. Only if we want to estimate β_1 in (15.28) do we need to apply IV.

When y_2 is a zero-one variable denoting participation and z_k is a zero-one variable representing *eligibility* for program participation—which is, hopefully, either randomized across individuals or, at most, a function of the other exogenous variables $z_1, \ldots, z_{k-1}$ (such as income)—the coefficient γ_k has an interesting interpretation. Rather than an estimate of the effect of the program itself, it is an estimate of the effect of *offering* the program. Unlike β_1 in (15.28)—which measures the effect of the program itself—γ_k accounts for the possibility that some units made eligible will choose not to participate. In the program evaluation literature, γ_k is an example of an *intention-to-treat* parameter: it measures the effect of being made *eligible* and not the effect of actual participation. The intention-to-treat coefficient, $\gamma_k = \beta_1 \pi_k$, depends on the effect of participating, β_1, and the change (typically, increase) in the probability of participating due to being eligible, π_k. [When y_2 is binary, equation (15.30) is a linear probability model, and therefore π_k measures the ceteris paribus change in probability that $y_2 = 1$ as z_k switches from zero to one.]

15-3 Two Stage Least Squares

In the previous section, we assumed that we had a single endogenous explanatory variable (y_2), along with one instrumental variable for y_2. It often happens that we have more than one exogenous variable that is excluded from the structural model and might be correlated with y_2, which means they are valid IVs for y_2. In this section, we discuss how to use multiple instrumental variables.

15-3a A Single Endogenous Explanatory Variable

Consider again the structural model (15.22), which has one endogenous and one exogenous explanatory variable. Suppose now that we have *two* exogenous variables excluded from (15.22): z_2 and z_3. Our assumptions that z_2 and z_3 do not appear in (15.22) and are uncorrelated with the error u_1 are known as **exclusion restrictions**.

If z_2 and z_3 are both correlated with y_2, we could just use each as an IV, as in the previous section. But then we would have two IV estimators, and neither of these would, in general, be efficient. Since each of z_1, z_2, and z_3 is uncorrelated with u_1, any linear combination is also uncorrelated with u_1, and therefore any linear combination of the exogenous variables is a valid IV. To find the best IV, we choose the linear combination that is most highly correlated with y_2. This turns out to be given by the reduced form equation for y_2. Write

$$y_2 = \pi_0 + \pi_1 z_1 + \pi_2 z_2 + \pi_3 z_3 + v_2, \qquad [15.33]$$

where

$$E(v_2) = 0, \ \operatorname{Cov}(z_1, v_2) = 0, \ \operatorname{Cov}(z_2, v_2) = 0, \ \text{and} \operatorname{Cov}(z_3, v_2) = 0.$$

Then, the best IV for y_2 (under the assumptions given in the chapter appendix) is the linear combination of the z_j in (15.33), which we call y_2^*:

$$y_2^* = \pi_0 + \pi_1 z_1 + \pi_2 z_2 + \pi_3 z_3. \qquad [15.34]$$

For this IV not to be perfectly correlated with z_1 we need at least one of π_2 or π_3 to be different from zero:

$$\pi_2 \neq 0 \text{ or } \pi_3 \neq 0. \qquad [15.35]$$

This is the key identification assumption, once we assume the z_j are all exogenous. (The value of π_1 is irrelevant.) The structural equation (15.22) is not identified if $\pi_2 = 0$ and $\pi_3 = 0$. We can test H_0: $\pi_2 = 0$ and $\pi_3 = 0$ against (15.35) using an F statistic.

A useful way to think of (15.33) is that it breaks y_2 into two pieces. The first is y_2^*; this is the part of y_2 that is uncorrelated with the error term, u_1. The second piece is v_2, and this part is possibly correlated with u_1—which is why y_2 is possibly endogenous.

Given data on the z_j, we can compute y_2^* for each observation, provided we know the population parameters π_j. This is never true in practice. Nevertheless, as we saw in the previous section, we can always estimate the reduced form by OLS. Thus, using the sample, we regress y_2 on z_1, z_2, and z_3 and obtain the fitted values:

$$\hat{y}_2 = \hat{\pi}_0 + \hat{\pi}_1 z_1 + \hat{\pi}_2 z_2 + \hat{\pi}_3 z_3 \qquad [15.36]$$

(that is, we have $\hat{y}_{i2}$ for each i). At this point, we should verify that z_2 and z_3 are jointly significant in (15.33) at a reasonably small significance level (no larger than 5%). If z_2 and z_3 are not jointly significant in (15.33), then we are wasting our time with IV estimation.

Once we have $\hat{y}_2$, we can use it as the IV for y_2. The three equations for estimating β_0, β_1, and β_2 are the first two equations of (15.25), with the third replaced by

$$\sum_{i=1}^{n} \hat{y}_{i2}(y_{i1} - \hat{\beta}_0 - \hat{\beta}_1 y_{i2} - \hat{\beta}_2 z_{i1}) = 0. \qquad [15.37]$$

Solving the three equations in three unknowns gives us the IV estimators.

With multiple instruments, the IV estimator using $\hat{y}_{i2}$ as the instrument is also called the **two stage least squares (2SLS) estimator**. The reason is simple. Using the algebra of OLS, it can be shown that when we use $\hat{y}_2$ as the IV for y_2, the IV estimates $\hat{\beta}_0$, $\hat{\beta}_1$, and $\hat{\beta}_2$ are *identical* to the OLS estimates from the regression of

$$y_1 \text{ on } \hat{y}_2 \text{ and } z_1. \qquad [15.38]$$

In other words, we can obtain the 2SLS estimator in two stages. The first stage is to run the regression in (15.36), where we obtain the fitted values $\hat{y}_2$. The second stage is the OLS regression (15.38). Because we use $\hat{y}_2$ in place of y_2, the 2SLS estimates can differ substantially from the OLS estimates.

Some economists like to interpret the regression in (15.38) as follows. The fitted value, $\hat{y}_2$, is the estimated version of y_2^*, and y_2^* is uncorrelated with u_1. Therefore, 2SLS first "purges" y_2 of its correlation with u_1 before doing the OLS regression in (15.38). We can show this by plugging $y_2 = y_2^* + v_2$ into (15.22):

$$y_1 = \beta_0 + \beta_1 y_2^* + \beta_2 z_1 + u_1 + \beta_1 v_2. \qquad [15.39]$$

Now, the composite error $u_1 + \beta_1 v_2$ has zero mean and is uncorrelated with y_2^* and z_1, which is why the OLS regression in (15.38) works.

Most econometrics packages have special commands for 2SLS, so there is no need to perform the two stages explicitly. In fact, in most cases you should avoid doing the second stage manually, as the standard errors and test statistics obtained in this way are *not* valid. [The reason is that the error term in (15.39) includes v_2, but the standard errors involve the variance of u_1 only.] Any regression software that supports 2SLS asks for the dependent variable, the list of explanatory variables (both exogenous and endogenous), and the entire list of instrumental variables (that is, all exogenous variables). The output is typically quite similar to that for OLS.

In model (15.28) with a single IV for y_2, the IV estimator from Section 15-2 is identical to the 2SLS estimator. Therefore, when we have one IV for each endogenous explanatory variable, we can call the estimation method IV or 2SLS.

Adding more exogenous variables changes very little. For example, suppose the wage equation is

$$\log(wage) = \beta_0 + \beta_1 educ + \beta_2 exper + \beta_3 exper^2 + u_1, \qquad [15.40]$$

where u_1 is uncorrelated with both *exper* and *exper²*. Suppose that we also think mother's and father's educations are uncorrelated with u_1. Then, we can use both of these as IVs for *educ*. The reduced form equation for *educ* is

$$educ = \pi_0 + \pi_1 exper + \pi_2 exper^2 + \pi_3 motheduc + \pi_4 fatheduc + v_2, \qquad [15.41]$$

and identification requires that $\pi_3 \neq 0$ or $\pi_4 \neq 0$ (or both, of course).

EXAMPLE 15.5   **Return to Education for Working Women**

We estimate equation (15.40) using the data in MROZ. First, we test $H_0: \pi_3 = 0$, $\pi_4 = 0$ in (15.41) using an F test. The result is $F = 124.76$, and p-value $= .0000$. As expected, *educ* is (partially) correlated with parents' education.

When we estimate (15.40) by 2SLS, we obtain, in equation form,

$$\widehat{\log(wage)} = .048 + .061 \, educ + .044 \, exper - .0009 \, exper^2$$
$$(.400) \quad (.031) \qquad\quad (.013) \qquad\quad (.0004)$$
$$n = 428, R^2 = .136.$$

The estimated return to education is about 6.1%, compared with an OLS estimate of about 10.8%. Because of its relatively large standard error, the 2SLS estimate is barely statistically significant at the 5% level against a two-sided alternative.

The assumptions needed for 2SLS to have the desired large sample properties are given in the chapter appendix, but it is useful to briefly summarize them here. If we write the structural equation as in (15.28),

$$y_1 = \beta_0 + \beta_1 y_2 + \beta_2 z_1 + \ldots + \beta_k z_{k-1} + u_1,$$ [15.42]

then we assume each z_j to be uncorrelated with u_1. In addition, we need at least one exogenous variable *not* in (15.42) that is partially correlated with y_2. This ensures consistency. For the usual 2SLS standard errors and t statistics to be asymptotically valid, we also need a homoskedasticity assumption: the variance of the structural error, u_1, cannot depend on any of the exogenous variables. For time series applications, we need more assumptions, as we will see in Section 15-7.

15-3b Multicollinearity and 2SLS

In Chapter 3, we introduced the problem of multicollinearity and showed how correlation among regressors can lead to large standard errors for the OLS estimates. Multicollinearity can be even more serious with 2SLS. To see why, the (asymptotic) variance of the 2SLS estimator of β_1 can be approximated as

$$\sigma^2/[\widehat{SST_2}(1 - \hat{R}_2^2)],$$ [15.43]

where $\sigma^2 = \text{Var}(u_1)$, $\widehat{SST_2}$ is the total variation in $\hat{y}_2$, and $\hat{R}_2^2$ is the R-squared from a regression of $\hat{y}_2$ on all other exogenous variables appearing in the structural equation. There are two reasons why the variance of the 2SLS estimator is larger than that for OLS. First, $\hat{y}_2$, by construction, has less variation than y_2. (Remember: Total sum of squares = explained sum of squares + residual sum of squares; the variation in y_2 is the total sum of squares, while the variation in $\hat{y}_2$ is the explained sum of squares from the first regression.) Second, the correlation between $\hat{y}_2$ and the exogenous variables in (15.42) is often much higher than the correlation between y_2 and these variables. This essentially defines the multicollinearity problem in 2SLS.

As an illustration, consider Example 15.4. When *educ* is regressed on the exogenous variables in Table 15.1 (not including *nearc4*), R-squared $= .475$; this is a moderate degree of multicollinearity, but the important thing is that the OLS standard error on $\hat{\beta}_{educ}$ is quite small. When we obtain the first stage fitted values, $\widehat{educ}$, and regress these on the exogenous variables in Table 15.1, R-squared $= .995$, which indicates a very high degree of multicollinearity between $\widehat{educ}$ and the remaining exogenous variables in the table. (This high R-squared is not too surprising because $\widehat{educ}$ is a function of all the exogenous variables in Table 15.1, plus *nearc4*.) Equation (15.43) shows that an $\hat{R}_2^2$ close to one can result in a very large standard error for the 2SLS estimator. But as with OLS, a large sample size can help offset a large $\hat{R}_2^2$.

15-3c Detecting Weak Instruments

In Section 15-1 we briefly discussed the problem of weak instruments. We focused on equation (15.19), which demonstrates how a small correlation between the instrument and error can lead to very large inconsistency (and therefore bias) if the instrument, z, also has little correlation with the explanatory variable, x. The same problem can arise in the context of the multiple equation model in equation (15.42), whether we have one instrument for y_2 or more instruments than we need.

We also mentioned the findings of Staiger and Stock (1997), and we now discuss the practical implications of this research in a bit more depth. Importantly, Staiger and Stock study the case of where all instrumental variables are exogenous. With the exogeneity requirement satisfied by the instruments, they focus on the case where the instruments are weakly correlated with y_2, and they study the validity of standard errors, confidence intervals, and t statistics involving the coefficient β_1 on y_2. The mechanism they used to model weak correlation led to an important finding: even with very large sample sizes the 2SLS estimator can be biased and a distribution that is very different from standard normal.

Building on Staiger and Stock (1997), Stock and Yogo (2005) (SY for short) proposed methods for detecting situations where weak instruments will lead to substantial bias and distorted statistical inference. Conveniently, Stock and Yogo obtained rules concerning the size of the t statistic (with one instrument) or the F statistic (with more than one instrument) from the first-stage regression. The theory is much too involved to pursue here. Instead, we describe some simple rules of thumb proposed by Stock and Yogo that are easy to implement.

The key implication of the SY work is that one needs more than just a statistical rejection of the null hypothesis in the first stage regression at the usual significance levels. For example, in equation (15.6), it is not enough to reject the null hypothesis stated in (15.7) at the 5% significance level. Using bias calculations for the instrumental variables estimator, SY recommend that one can proceed with the usual IV inference if the first-stage t statistic has absolute value larger than $\sqrt{10} \approx 3.2$. Readers will recognize this value as being well above the 95th percentile of the standard normal distribution, 1.96, which is what we would use for a standard 5% significance level. This same rule of thumb applies in the multiple regression model with a single endogenous explanatory variable, y_2, and a single instrumental variable, z_k. In particular, the t statistic in testing hypothesis (15.31) should be at least 3.2 in absolute value.

SY cover the case of 2SLS, too. In this case, we must focus on the first-stage F statistic for exclusion of the instrumental variables for y_2, and the SY rule is $F > 10$. (Notice this is the same rule based on the t statistic when there is only one instrument, as $t^2 = F$.) For example, consider equation (15.34), where we have two instruments for y_2, z_2 and z_3. Then the F statistic for the null hypothesis

$$H_0: \pi_2 = 0, \pi_3 = 0$$

should have $F > 10$. Remember, this is not the overall F statistic for all of the exogenous variables in (15.34). We test only the coefficients on the proposed IVs for y_2, that is, the exogenous variables that do not appear in (15.22). In Example 15.5 the relevant F statistic is 124.76, which is well above 10, implying that we do not have to worry about weak instruments. (Of course, the exogeneity of the parents' education variables is in doubt.)

The rule of thumb of requiring the F statistic to be larger than 10 works well in most models and is easy to remember. However, like all rules of thumb involving statistical inference, it makes no sense to use 10 as a knife-edge cutoff. For example, one can probably proceed if $F = 9.94$, as it is pretty close to 10. The rule of thumb should be used as a guideline. SY have more detailed suggestions for cases where there are many instruments for y_2, say five or more. The interested reader is referred to the SY paper. Most empirical researchers adopt 10 as the target value.

15-3d Multiple Endogenous Explanatory Variables

Two stage least squares can also be used in models with more than one endogenous explanatory variable. For example, consider the model

$$y_1 = \beta_0 + \beta_1 y_2 + \beta_2 y_3 + \beta_3 z_1 + \beta_4 z_2 + \beta_5 z_3 + u_1, \qquad [15.44]$$

where $E(u_1) = 0$ and u_1 is uncorrelated with z_1, z_2, and z_3. The variables y_2 and y_3 are endogenous explanatory variables: each may be correlated with u_1.

To estimate (15.44) by 2SLS, we need *at least two* exogenous variables that do not appear in (15.44) but that are correlated with y_2 and y_3. Suppose we have two excluded exogenous variables, say z_4 and z_5. Then, from our analysis of a single endogenous explanatory variable, we need either z_4 or z_5 to appear in each reduced form for y_2 and y_3. (As before, we can use F statistics to test this.) Although this is necessary for identification, unfortunately, it is not sufficient. Suppose that z_4 appears in each reduced form, but z_5 appears in neither. Then, we do not really have two exogenous variables partially correlated with y_2 and y_3. Two stage least squares will not produce consistent estimators of the β_j.

Generally, when we have more than one endogenous explanatory variable in a regression model, identification can fail in several complicated ways. But we can easily state a necessary condition for identification, which is called the **order condition**.

> ## EXPLORING FURTHER 15.3
>
> The following model explains violent crime rates, at the city level, in terms of a binary variable for whether gun control laws exist and other controls:
>
> $violent = \beta_0 + \beta_1 guncontrol + \beta_2 unem$
> $\quad + \beta_3 popul + \beta_4 percblck$
> $\quad + \beta_5 age18\_21 + \ldots$
>
> Some researchers have estimated similar equations using variables such as the number of National Rifle Association members in the city and the number of subscribers to gun magazines as instrumental variables for *guncontrol* [see, for example, Kleck and Patterson (1993)]. Are these convincing instruments?

Order Condition for Identification of an Equation. We need at least as many excluded exogenous variables as there are included endogenous explanatory variables in the structural equation. The order condition is simple to check, as it only involves counting endogenous and exogenous variables. The sufficient condition for identification is called the **rank condition**. We have seen special cases of the rank condition before—for example, in the discussion surrounding equation (15.35). A general statement of the rank condition requires matrix algebra and is beyond the scope of this text. [See Wooldridge (2010, Chapter 5).] It is even more difficult to obtain diagnostics for weak instruments.

15-3e Testing Multiple Hypotheses after 2SLS Estimation

We must be careful when testing multiple hypotheses in a model estimated by 2SLS. It is tempting to use either the sum of squared residuals or the R-squared form of the F statistic, as we learned with OLS in Chapter 4. The fact that the R-squared in 2SLS can be negative suggests that the usual way of computing F statistics might not be appropriate; this is the case. In fact, if we use the 2SLS residuals to compute the SSRs for both the restricted and unrestricted models, there is no guarantee that $SSR_r \geq SSR_{ur}$; if the reverse is true, the F statistic would be negative.

It is possible to combine the sum of squared residuals from the second stage regression [such as (15.38)] with SSR_{ur} to obtain a statistic with an approximate F distribution in large samples. Because many econometrics packages have simple-to-use test commands that can be used to test multiple hypotheses after 2SLS estimation, we omit the details. Davidson and MacKinnon (1993) and Wooldridge (2010, Chapter 5) contain discussions of how to compute F-type statistics for 2SLS.

15-4 IV Solutions to Errors-in-Variables Problems

In the previous sections, we presented the use of instrumental variables as a way to solve the omitted variables problem, but they can also be used to deal with the measurement error problem. As an illustration, consider the model

$$y = \beta_0 + \beta_1 x_1^* + \beta_2 x_2 + u, \qquad [15.45]$$

where y and x_2 are observed but x_1^* is not. Let x_1 be an observed measurement of x_1^*: $x_1 = x_1^* + e_1$, where e_1 is the measurement error. In Chapter 9, we showed that correlation between x_1 and e_1 causes OLS, where x_1 is used in place of x_1^*, to be biased and inconsistent. We can see this by writing

$$y = \beta_0 + \beta_1 x_1 + \beta_2 x_2 + (u - \beta_1 e_1). \qquad [15.46]$$

If the classical errors-in-variables (CEV) assumptions hold, the bias in the OLS estimator of β_1 is toward zero. Without further assumptions, we can do nothing about this.

In some cases, we can use an IV procedure to solve the measurement error problem. In (15.45), we assume that u is uncorrelated with x_1^*, x_1, and x_2; in the CEV case, we assume that e_1 is uncorrelated with x_1^* and x_2. These imply that x_2 is exogenous in (15.46), but that x_1 is correlated with e_1. What we need is an IV for x_1. Such an IV must be correlated with x_1, uncorrelated with u—so that it can be excluded from (15.45)—and uncorrelated with the measurement error, e_1.

One possibility is to obtain a second measurement on x_1^*, say, z_1. Because it is x_1^* that affects y, it is only natural to assume that z_1 is uncorrelated with u. If we write $z_1 = x_1^* + a_1$, where a_1 is the measurement error in z_1, then we must assume that a_1 and e_1 are uncorrelated. In other words, x_1 and z_1 both mismeasure x_1^*, but their measurement errors are uncorrelated. Certainly, x_1 and z_1 are correlated through their dependence on x_1^*, so we can use z_1 as an IV for x_1.

Where might we get two measurements on a variable? Sometimes, when a group of workers is asked for their annual salary, their employers can provide a second measure. For married couples, each spouse can independently report the level of savings or family income. In the Ashenfelter and Krueger (1994) study cited in Section 14-3, each twin was asked about his or her sibling's years of education; this gives a second measure that can be used as an IV for self-reported education in a wage equation. (Ashenfelter and Krueger combined differencing and IV to account for the omitted ability problem as well; more on this in Section 15-8.) Generally, though, having two measures of an explanatory variable is rare.

An alternative is to use other exogenous variables as IVs for a potentially mismeasured variable. For example, our use of *motheduc* and *fatheduc* as IVs for *educ* in Example 15.5 can serve this purpose. If we think that $educ = educ^* + e_1$, then the IV estimates in Example 15.5 do not suffer from measurement error if *motheduc* and *fatheduc* are uncorrelated with the measurement error, e_1. This is probably more reasonable than assuming *motheduc* and *fatheduc* are uncorrelated with ability, which is contained in u in (15.45).

IV methods can also be adopted when using things like test scores to control for unobserved characteristics. In Section 9-2, we showed that, under certain assumptions, proxy variables can be used to solve the omitted variables problem. In Example 9.3, we used IQ as a proxy variable for unobserved ability. This simply entails adding IQ to the model and performing an OLS regression. But there is an alternative that works when IQ does not fully satisfy the proxy variable assumptions. To illustrate, write a wage equation as

$$\log(wage) = \beta_0 + \beta_1 educ + \beta_2 exper + \beta_3 exper^2 + abil + u, \qquad [15.47]$$

where we again have the omitted ability problem. But we have two test scores that are *indicators* of ability. We assume that the scores can be written as

$$test_1 = \gamma_1 abil + e_1$$

and

$$test_2 = \delta_1 abil + e_2,$$

where $\gamma_1 > 0$, $\delta_1 > 0$. Since it is ability that affects wage, we can assume that $test_1$ and $test_2$ are uncorrelated with u. If we write $abil$ in terms of the first test score and plug the result into (15.47), we get

$$\log(wage) = \beta_0 + \beta_1 educ + \beta_2 exper + \beta_3 exper^2 + \alpha_1 test_1 + (u - \alpha_1 e_1), \qquad [15.48]$$

where $\alpha_1 = 1/\gamma_1$. Now, if we assume that e_1 is uncorrelated with all the explanatory variables in (15.47), including *abil*, then e_1 and *test*$_1$ *must* be correlated. [Notice that *educ* is *not* endogenous in (15.48); however, *test*$_1$ is.] This means that estimating (15.48) by OLS will produce inconsistent estimators of the β_j (and α_1). Under the assumptions we have made, *test*$_1$ does not satisfy the proxy variable assumptions.

If we assume that e_2 is also uncorrelated with all the explanatory variables in (15.47) *and* that e_1 and e_2 are uncorrelated, then e_1 is uncorrelated with the second test score, *test*$_2$. Therefore, *test*$_2$ can be used as an IV for *test*$_1$.

EXAMPLE 15.6   **Using Two Test Scores as Indicators of Ability**

We use the data in WAGE2 to implement the preceding procedure, where *IQ* plays the role of the first test score and *KWW* (knowledge of the world of work) is the second test score. The explanatory variables are the same as in Example 9.3: *educ, exper, tenure, married, south, urban,* and *black*. Rather than adding *IQ* and doing OLS, as in column (2) of Table 9.2, we add *IQ* and use *KWW* as its instrument. The coefficient on *educ* is .025 (se = .017). This is a low estimate, and it is not statistically different from zero. This is a puzzling finding, and it suggests that one of our assumptions fails; perhaps e_1 and e_2 are correlated.

15-5 Testing for Endogeneity and Testing Overidentifying Restrictions

In this section, we describe two important tests in the context of instrumental variables estimation.

15-5a Testing for Endogeneity

The 2SLS estimator is less efficient than OLS when the explanatory variables are exogenous; as we have seen, the 2SLS estimates can have very large standard errors. Therefore, it is useful to have a test for endogeneity of an explanatory variable that shows whether 2SLS is even necessary. Obtaining such a test is rather simple.

To illustrate, suppose we have a single suspected endogenous variable,

$$y_1 = \beta_0 + \beta_1 y_2 + \beta_2 z_1 + \beta_3 z_2 + u_1,$$ [15.49]

where z_1 and z_2 are exogenous. We have two additional exogenous variables, z_3 and z_4, which do not appear in (15.49). If y_2 is uncorrelated with u_1, we should estimate (15.49) by OLS. How can we test this? Hausman (1978) suggested directly comparing the OLS and 2SLS estimates and determining whether the differences are statistically significant. After all, both OLS and 2SLS are consistent if all variables are exogenous. If 2SLS and OLS differ significantly, we conclude that y_2 must be endogenous (maintaining that the z_j are exogenous).

It is a good idea to compute OLS and 2SLS to see if the estimates are practically different. To determine whether the differences are statistically significant, it is easier to use a regression test. This is based on estimating the reduced form for y_2, which in this case is

$$y_2 = \pi_0 + \pi_1 z_1 + \pi_2 z_2 + \pi_3 z_3 + \pi_4 z_4 + v_2.$$ [15.50]

Now, since each z_j is uncorrelated with u_1, y_2 is uncorrelated with u_1 if, and only if, v_2 is uncorrelated with u_1; this is what we wish to test. Write $u_1 = \delta_1 v_2 + e_1$, where e_1 is uncorrelated with v_2 and has zero mean. Then, u_1 and v_2 are uncorrelated if, and only if, $\delta_1 = 0$. The easiest way to test this is to include v_2 as an additional regressor in (15.49) and to do a t test. There is only one problem with implementing this: v_2 is not observed, because it is the error term in (15.50). Because we can estimate the reduced form for y_2 by OLS, we can obtain the reduced form residuals, $\hat{v}_2$. Therefore, we estimate

$$y_1 = \beta_0 + \beta_1 y_2 + \beta_2 z_1 + \beta_3 z_2 + \delta_1 \hat{v}_2 + error \qquad [15.51]$$

by OLS and test $H_0: \delta_1 = 0$ using a t statistic. If we reject H_0 at a small significance level, we conclude that y_2 is endogenous because v_2 and u_1 are correlated.

Testing for Endogeneity of a Single Explanatory Variable:

(i) Estimate the reduced form for y_2 by regressing it on *all* exogenous variables (including those in the structural equation and the additional IVs). Obtain the residuals, $\hat{v}_2$.

(ii) Add $\hat{v}_2$ to the structural equation (which includes y_2) and test for significance of $\hat{v}_2$ using an OLS regression. If the coefficient on $\hat{v}_2$ is statistically different from zero, we conclude that y_2 is indeed endogenous. We might want to use a heteroskedasticity-robust t test.

EXAMPLE 15.7   **Return to Education for Working Women**

We can test for endogeneity of *educ* in (15.40) by obtaining the residuals $\hat{v}_2$ from estimating the reduced form (15.41)—using only working women—and including these in (15.40). When we do this, the coefficient on $\hat{v}_2$ is $\hat{\delta}_1 = .058$, and $t = 1.67$. This is moderate evidence of positive correlation between u_1 and v_2. It is probably a good idea to report both estimates because the 2SLS estimate of the return to education (6.1%) is well below the OLS estimate (10.8%).

An interesting feature of the regression from step (ii) of the test for endogeneity is that the coefficient estimates on all explanatory variables (except, of course, $\hat{v}_2$) are identical to the 2SLS estimates. For example, estimating (15.51) by OLS produces the same $\hat{\beta}_j$ as estimating (15.49) by 2SLS. One benefit of this equivalence is that it provides an easy check on whether you have done the proper regression in testing for endogeneity. But it also gives a different, useful interpretation of 2SLS: adding $\hat{v}_2$ to the original equation as an explanatory variable, and applying OLS, clears up the endogeneity of y_2. So, when we start by estimating (15.49) by OLS, we can quantify the importance of allowing y_2 to be endogenous by seeing how much $\hat{\beta}_1$ changes when $\hat{v}_2$ is added to the equation. Irrespective of the outcome of the statistical tests, we can see whether the change in $\hat{\beta}_1$ is expected and is practically significant.

We can also test for endogeneity of multiple explanatory variables. For each suspected endogenous variable, we obtain the reduced form residuals, as in part (i). Then, we test for joint significance of these residuals in the structural equation, using an F test. Joint significance indicates that at least one suspected explanatory variable is endogenous. The number of exclusion restrictions tested is the number of suspected endogenous explanatory variables.

15-5b Testing Overidentification Restrictions

When we introduced the simple instrumental variables estimator in Section 15-1, we emphasized that the instrument must satisfy two requirements: it must be uncorrelated with the error (exogeneity) and correlated with the endogenous explanatory variable (relevance). We have now seen that, even in models with additional explanatory variables, the second requirement can be tested using a t test (with just one instrument) or an F test (when there are multiple instruments). In the context of the simple IV estimator, we noted that the exogeneity requirement cannot be tested. However, if we have more instruments than we need, we can effectively test whether some of them are uncorrelated with the structural error.

As a specific example, again consider equation (15.49) with two instrumental variables for y_2, z_3, and z_4. Remember, z_1 and z_2 essentially act as their own instruments. Because we have two instruments for y_2, we can estimate (15.49) using, say, only z_3 as an IV for y_2; let $\check{\beta}_1$ be the resulting IV estimator of β_1. Then, we can estimate (15.49) using only z_4 as an IV for y_2; call this IV estimator $\tilde{\beta}_1$. If all z_j are exogenous, and if z_3 and z_4 are each partially correlated with y_2, then $\check{\beta}_1$ and $\tilde{\beta}_1$ are both consistent for β_1. Therefore, if our logic for choosing the instruments is sound, $\check{\beta}_1$ and $\tilde{\beta}_1$ should differ only by sampling error. Hausman (1978) proposed basing a test of whether z_3 and z_4 are both exogenous on the difference, $\check{\beta}_1 - \tilde{\beta}_1$. Shortly, we will provide a simpler way to obtain a valid test, but, before doing so, we should understand how to interpret the outcome of the test.

If we conclude that $\check{\beta}_1$ and $\tilde{\beta}_1$ are statistically different from one another, then we have no choice but to conclude that either z_3, z_4, or both fail the exogeneity requirement. Unfortunately, we cannot know which is the case (unless we simply assert from the beginning that, say, z_3 is exogenous). For example, if y_2 denotes years of schooling in a log wage equation, z_3 is mother's education, and z_4 is father's education, a statistically significant difference in the two IV estimators implies that one or both of the parents' education variables are correlated with u_1 in (15.54).

Certainly, rejecting that one's instruments are exogenous is serious and requires a new approach. But the more serious, and subtle, problem in comparing IV estimates is that they may be similar even though both instruments fail the exogeneity requirement. In the previous example, it seems likely that if mother's education is positively correlated with u_1, then so is father's education. Therefore, the two IV estimates may be similar even though each is inconsistent. In effect, because the IVs in this example are chosen using similar reasoning, their separate use in IV procedures may very well lead to similar estimates that are nevertheless both inconsistent. The point is that we should not feel especially comfortable if our IV procedures pass the Hausman test.

Another problem with comparing two IV estimates is that often they may seem practically different yet, statistically, we cannot reject the null hypothesis that they are consistent for the same population parameter. For example, in estimating (15.40) by IV using *motheduc* as the only instrument, the coefficient on *educ* is .049 (.037). If we use only *fatheduc* as the IV for *educ*, the coefficient on *educ* is .070 (.034). [Perhaps not surprisingly, the estimate using both parents' education as IVs is in between these two, .061 (.031).] For policy purposes, the difference between 5% and 7% for the estimated return to a year of schooling is substantial. Yet, as shown in Example 15.8, the difference is not statistically significant.

The procedure of comparing different IV estimates of the same parameter is an example of testing **overidentifying restrictions**. The general idea is that we have more instruments than we need to estimate the parameters consistently. In the previous example, we had one more instrument than we need, and this results in one overidentifying restriction that can be tested. In the general case, suppose that we have q more instruments than we need. For example, with one endogenous explanatory variable, y_2, and three proposed instruments for y_2, we have $q = 3 - 1 = 2$ overidentifying restrictions. When q is two or more, comparing several IV estimates is cumbersome. Instead, we can easily compute a test statistic based on the 2SLS residuals. The idea is that, if all instruments are exogenous, the 2SLS residuals should be uncorrelated with the instruments, up to sampling error. But if there are $k + 1$ parameters and $k + 1 + q$ instruments, the 2SLS residuals have a zero mean and are identically uncorrelated with k linear combinations of the instruments. (This algebraic fact contains, as a special case, the fact that the OLS residuals have a zero mean and are uncorrelated with the k explanatory variables.) Therefore, the test checks whether the 2SLS residuals are correlated with q linear functions of the instruments, and we need not decide on the functions; the test does that for us automatically.

The following regression-based test is valid when the homoskedasticity assumption, listed as Assumption 2SLS.5 in the chapter appendix, holds.

Testing Overidentifying Restrictions:
    (i) Estimate the structural equation by 2SLS and obtain the 2SLS residuals, $\hat{u}_1$.

    (ii) Regress $\hat{u}_1$ on *all exogenous* variables. Obtain the R-squared, say, R_1^2.

    (iii) Under the null hypothesis that all IVs are uncorrelated with u_1, $nR_1^2 \overset{a}{\sim} \chi_q^2$, where q is the number of instrumental variables from outside the model minus the total number of endogenous explanatory variables. If nR_1^2 exceeds (say) the 5% critical value in the χ_q^2 distribution, we reject H_0 and conclude that at least some of the IVs are not exogenous.

EXAMPLE 15.8   Return to Education for Working Women

When we use *motheduc* and *fatheduc* as IVs for *educ* in (15.40), we have a single overidentifying restriction. Regressing the 2SLS residuals $\hat{u}_1$ on *exper*, *exper*^{2}, *motheduc*, and *fatheduc* produces $R_1^2 = .0009$. Therefore, $nR_1^2 = 428(.0009) = .3852$, which is a very small value in a χ_1^2 distribution (*p*-value $= .535$). Therefore, the parents' education variables pass the overidentification test. When we add husband's education to the IV list, we get two overidentifying restrictions, and $nR_1^2 = 1.11$ (*p*-value $= .574$). Subject to the preceding cautions, it seems reasonable to add *huseduc* to the IV list, as this reduces the standard error of the 2SLS estimate: the 2SLS estimate on *educ* using all three instruments is .080 (*se* $= .022$), so this makes *educ* much more significant than when *huseduc* is not used as an IV ($\hat{\beta}_{educ} = .061$, se $= .031$).

When $q = 1$, a natural question is: How does the test obtained from the regression-based procedure compare with a test based on directly comparing the estimates? In fact, the two procedures are asymptotically the same. As a practical matter, it makes sense to compute the two IV estimates to see how they differ. More generally, when $q \geq 2$, one can compare the 2SLS estimates using all IVs to the IV estimates using single instruments. By doing so, one can see if the various IV estimates are practically different, whether or not the overidentification test rejects or fails to reject.

In the previous example, we alluded to a general fact about 2SLS: under the standard 2SLS assumptions, adding instruments to the list improves the asymptotic efficiency of the 2SLS. But this requires that any new instruments are in fact exogenous—otherwise, 2SLS will not even be consistent— and it is only an asymptotic result. With the typical sample sizes available, adding too many instruments—that is, increasing the number of overidentifying restrictions—can cause severe biases in 2SLS. A detailed discussion would take us too far afield. A nice illustration is given by Bound, Jaeger, and Baker (1995), who argue that the 2SLS estimates of the return to education obtained by Angrist and Krueger (1991), using many instrumental variables, are likely to be seriously biased (even with hundreds of thousands of observations!).

The overidentification test can be used whenever we have more instruments than we need. If we have just enough instruments, the model is said to be *just identified*, and the R-squared in part (ii) will be identically zero. As we mentioned earlier, we cannot test exogeneity of the instruments in the just identified case.

The test can be made robust to heteroskedasticity of arbitrary form; for details, see Wooldridge (2010, Chapter 5).

15-6 2SLS with Heteroskedasticity

Heteroskedasticity in the context of 2SLS raises essentially the same issues as with OLS. Most importantly, it is possible to obtain standard errors and test statistics that are (asymptotically) robust to heteroskedasticity of arbitrary and unknown form. In fact, expression (8.4) continues to be valid if the $\hat{r}_{ij}$ are obtained as the residuals from regressing $\hat{x}_{ij}$ on the other $\hat{x}_{ih}$, where the "^" denotes fitted values from the first stage regressions (for endogenous explanatory variables). Wooldridge (2010, Chapter 5) contains more details. Some software packages do this routinely.

We can also test for heteroskedasticity, using an analog of the Breusch-Pagan test that we covered in Chapter 8. Let $\hat{u}$ denote the 2SLS residuals and let $z_1, z_2, \ldots, z_m$ denote all the exogenous variables (including those used as IVs for the endogenous explanatory variables). Then, under reasonable assumptions [spelled out, for example, in Wooldridge (2010, Chapter 5)], an asymptotically valid statistic is the usual F statistic for joint significance in a regression of $\hat{u}^2$ on $z_1, z_2, \ldots, z_m$. The null hypothesis of homoskedasticity is rejected if the z_j are jointly significant.

If we apply this test to Example 15.8, using *motheduc*, *fatheduc*, and *huseduc* as instruments for *educ*, we obtain $F_{5,422} = 2.53$ and p-value $= .029$. This is evidence of heteroskedasticity at the 5% level. We might want to compute heteroskedasticity-robust standard errors to account for this.

If we know how the error variance depends on the exogenous variables, we can use a weighted 2SLS procedure, essentially the same as in Section 8-4. After estimating a model for $\text{Var}(u|z_1, z_2, \ldots, z_m)$, we divide the dependent variable, the explanatory variables, and all the instrumental variables for observation i by $\sqrt{\hat{h}_i}$, where $\hat{h}_i$ denotes the estimated variance. (The constant, which is both an explanatory variable and an IV, is divided by $\sqrt{\hat{h}_i}$; see Section 8-4.) Then, we apply 2SLS on the transformed equation using the transformed instruments.

15-7 Applying 2SLS to Time Series Equations

When we apply 2SLS to time series data, many of the considerations that arose for OLS in Chapters 10, 11, and 12 are relevant. Write the structural equation for each time period as

$$y_t = \beta_0 + \beta_1 x_{t1} + \ldots + \beta_k x_{tk} + u_t, \qquad [15.52]$$

where one or more of the explanatory variables x_{tj} might be correlated with u_t. Denote the set of exogenous variables by $z_{t1}, \ldots, z_{tm}$:

$$\text{E}(u_t) = 0, \text{Cov}(z_{tj}, u_t) = 0, \quad j = 1, \ldots, m.$$

> **EXPLORING FURTHER 15.4**
>
> A model to test the effect of growth in government spending on growth in output is
>
> $$gGDP_t = \beta_0 + \beta_1 gGOV_t + \beta_2 INVRAT_t$$
> $$+ \beta_3 gLAB_t + u_t,$$
>
> where g indicates growth, *GDP* is real gross domestic product, *GOV* is real government spending, *INVRAT* is the ratio of gross domestic investment to GDP, and *LAB* is the size of the labor force. [See equation (6) in Ram (1986).] Under what assumptions would a dummy variable indicating whether the president in year $t - 1$ is a Republican be a suitable IV for $gGOV_t$?

Any exogenous explanatory variable is also a z_{tj}. For identification, it is necessary that $m \geq k$ (we have as many exogenous variables as explanatory variables).

The mechanics of 2SLS are identical for time series or cross-sectional data, but for time series data the statistical properties of 2SLS depend on the trending and correlation properties of the underlying sequences. In particular, we must be careful to include trends if we have trending dependent or explanatory variables. Since a time trend is exogenous, it can always serve as its own instrumental variable. The same is true of seasonal dummy variables, if monthly or quarterly data are used.

Series that have strong persistence (have unit roots) must be used with care, just as with OLS. Often, differencing the equation is warranted before estimation, and this applies to the instruments as well.

Under analogs of the assumptions in Chapter 11 for the asymptotic properties of OLS, 2SLS using time series data is consistent and asymptotically normally distributed. In fact, if we replace the explanatory variables with the instrumental variables in stating the assumptions, we only need to add the identification assumptions for 2SLS. For example, the homoskedasticity assumption is stated as

$$\text{E}(u_t^2|z_{t1}, \ldots, z_{tm}) = \sigma^2, \qquad [15.53]$$

and the no serial correlation assumption is stated as

$$\text{E}(u_t u_s|\mathbf{z}_t, \mathbf{z}_s) = 0 \quad \text{for all } t \neq s, \qquad [15.54]$$

where $\mathbf{z}_t$ denotes all exogenous variables at time t. A full statement of the assumptions is given in the chapter appendix. We will provide examples of 2SLS for time series problems in Chapter 16; see also Computer Exercise C4.

As in the case of OLS, the no serial correlation assumption can often be violated with time series data. Fortunately, it is very easy to test for AR(1) serial correlation. If we write $u_t = \rho u_{t-1} + e_t$ and plug this into equation (15.52), we get

$$y_t = \beta_0 + \beta_1 x_{t1} + \dots + \beta_k x_{tk} + \rho u_{t-1} + e_t, \quad t \geq 2. \qquad [15.55]$$

To test $H_0: \rho_1 = 0$, we must replace u_{t-1} with the 2SLS residuals, $\hat{u}_{t-1}$. Further, if x_{tj} is endogenous in (15.52), then it is endogenous in (15.55), so we still need to use an IV. Because e_t is uncorrelated with all past values of u_t, $\hat{u}_{t-1}$ can be used as its own instrument.

Testing for AR(1) Serial Correlation after 2SLS:

(i) Estimate (15.52) by 2SLS and obtain the 2SLS residuals, $\hat{u}_t$.

(ii) Estimate

$$y_t = \beta_0 + \beta_1 x_{t1} + \dots + \beta_k x_{tk} + \rho \hat{u}_{t-1} + error_t, \quad t = 2, \dots, n$$

by 2SLS, using the same instruments from part (i), in addition to $\hat{u}_{t-1}$. Use the t statistic on $\hat{\rho}$ to test $H_0: \rho = 0$.

As with the OLS version of this test from Chapter 12, the t statistic only has asymptotic justification, but it tends to work well in practice. A heteroskedasticity-robust version can be used to guard against heteroskedasticity. Further, lagged residuals can be added to the equation to test for higher forms of serial correlation using a joint F test.

What happens if we detect serial correlation? Some econometrics packages will compute standard errors that are robust to fairly general forms of serial correlation and heteroskedasticity. This is a nice, simple way to go if your econometrics package does this. The computations are very similar to those in Section 12-5 for OLS. [See Wooldridge (1995) for formulas and other computational methods.]

An alternative is to use the AR(1) model and correct for serial correlation. The procedure is similar to that for OLS and places additional restrictions on the instrumental variables. The quasi-differenced equation is the same as in equation (12.32):

$$\tilde{y}_t = \beta_0(1 - \rho) + \beta_1 \tilde{x}_{t1} + \dots + \beta_k \tilde{x}_{tk} + e_t, \quad t \geq 2, \qquad [15.56]$$

where $\tilde{x}_{tj} = x_{tj} - \rho x_{t-1,j}$. (We can use the $t = 1$ observation just as in Section 12-3, but we omit that for simplicity here.) The question is: What can we use as instrumental variables? It seems natural to use the quasi-differenced instruments, $\tilde{z}_{tj} = z_{tj} - \rho z_{t-1,j}$. This only works, however, if in (15.52) the original error u_t is uncorrelated with the instruments at times t, $t - 1$, and $t + 1$. That is, the instrumental variables must be strictly exogenous in (15.52). This rules out lagged dependent variables as IVs, for example. It also eliminates cases where future movements in the IVs react to current and past changes in the error, u_t.

2SLS with AR(1) Errors:

(i) Estimate (15.52) by 2SLS and obtain the 2SLS residuals, $\hat{u}_t, t = 1, 2, \dots, n$.

(ii) Obtain $\hat{\rho}$ from the regression of $\hat{u}_t$ on $\hat{u}_{t-1}$ $t = 2, \dots, n$ and construct the quasi-differenced variables $\tilde{y}_t = y_t - \hat{\rho} y_{t-1}$, $\tilde{x}_{tj} = x_{tj} - \hat{\rho} x_{t-1,j}$, and $\tilde{z}_{tj} = z_{tj} - \hat{\rho} z_{t-1,j}$ for $t \geq 2$. (Remember, in most cases, some of the IVs will also be explanatory variables.)

(iii) Estimate (15.56) (where ρ is replaced with $\hat{\rho}$) by 2SLS, using the $\tilde{z}_{tj}$ as the instruments. Assuming that (15.56) satisfies the 2SLS assumptions in the chapter appendix, the usual 2SLS test statistics are asymptotically valid.

We can also use the first time period as in Prais-Winsten estimation of the model with exogenous explanatory variables. The transformed variables in the first time period—the dependent variable, explanatory variables, and instrumental variables—are obtained simply by multiplying all first-period values by $(1 - \hat{\rho})^{1/2}$. (See also Section 12-3.)

15-8 Applying 2SLS to Pooled Cross Sections and Panel Data

Applying instrumental variables methods to independently pooled cross sections raises no new difficulties. As with models estimated by OLS, we should often include time period dummy variables to allow for aggregate time effects. These dummy variables are exogenous—because the passage of time is exogenous—and so they act as their own instruments.

EXAMPLE 15.9   **Effect of Education on Fertility**

In Example 13.1, we used the pooled cross section in FERTIL1 to estimate the effect of education on women's fertility, controlling for various other factors. As in Sander (1992), we allow for the possibility that *educ* is endogenous in the equation. As instrumental variables for *educ*, we use mother's and father's education levels (*meduc, feduc*). The 2SLS estimate of β_{educ} is $-.153$ (se $= .039$), compared with the OLS estimate $-.128$ (se $= .018$). The 2SLS estimate shows a somewhat larger effect of education on fertility, but the 2SLS standard error is over twice as large as the OLS standard error. (In fact, the 95% confidence interval based on 2SLS easily contains the OLS estimate.) The OLS and 2SLS estimates of β_{educ} are *not statistically* different, as can be seen by testing for endogeneity of *educ* as in Section 15-5: when the reduced form residual, $\hat{v}_2$, is included with the other regressors in Table 13.1 (including *educ*), its t statistic is .702, which is not significant at any reasonable level. Therefore, in this case, we conclude that the difference between 2SLS and OLS could be entirely due to sampling error.

Instrumental variables estimation can be combined with panel data methods, particularly first differencing, to estimate parameters consistently in the presence of unobserved effects and endogeneity in one or more time-varying explanatory variables. The following simple example illustrates this combination of methods.

EXAMPLE 15.10   **Job Training and Worker Productivity**

Suppose we want to estimate the effect of another hour of job training on worker productivity. For the two years 1987 and 1988, consider the simple panel data model

$$\log(scrap_{it}) = \beta_0 + \delta_0 d88_t + \beta_1 hrsemp_{it} + a_i + u_{it}, t = 1, 2,$$

where $scrap_{it}$ is firm i's scrap rate in year t and $hrsemp_{it}$ is hours of job training per employee. As usual, we allow different year intercepts and a constant, unobserved firm effect, a_i.

For the reasons discussed in Section 13-2, we might be concerned that $hrsemp_{it}$ is correlated with a_i, the latter of which contains unmeasured worker ability. As before, we difference to remove a_i:

$$\Delta\log(scrap_i) = \delta_0 + \beta_1\Delta hrsemp_i + \Delta u_i. \tag{15.57}$$

Normally, we would estimate this equation by OLS. But what if Δu_i is correlated with $\Delta hrsemp_i$? For example, a firm might hire more skilled workers, while at the same time reducing the level of job training. In this case, we need an instrumental variable for $\Delta hrsemp_i$. Generally, such an IV would be hard to find, but we can exploit the fact that some firms received job training grants in 1988. If we assume that grant designation is uncorrelated with Δu_i—something that is reasonable, because the grants were given at the beginning of 1988—then $\Delta grant_i$ is valid as an IV, provided $\Delta hrsemp$ and $\Delta grant$ are correlated. Using the data in JTRAIN differenced between 1987 and 1988, the first stage regression is

$$\widehat{\Delta hrsemp} = .51 + 27.88 \, \Delta grant$$
$$(1.56) \quad (3.13)$$
$$n = 45, R^2 = .392.$$

This confirms that the change in hours of job training per employee is strongly positively related to receiving a job training grant in 1988. In fact, receiving a job training grant increased per-employee training by almost 28 hours, and grant designation accounted for almost 40% of the variation in $\Delta hrsemp$. Two stage least squares estimation of (15.57) gives

$$\Delta \log(scrap) = -.033 - .014 \, \Delta hrsemp$$
$$(.127) \quad (.008)$$
$$n = 45, R^2 = .016.$$

This means that 10 more hours of job training per worker are estimated to reduce the scrap rate by about 14%. For the firms in the sample, the average amount of job training in 1988 was about 17 hours per worker, with a minimum of zero and a maximum of 88.

For comparison, OLS estimation of (15.57) gives $\hat{\beta}_1 = -.0076$ (se = .0045), so the 2SLS estimate of β_1 is almost twice as large in magnitude and is slightly more statistically significant.

When $T \geq 3$, the differenced equation may contain serial correlation. The same test and correction for AR(1) serial correlation from Section 15-7 can be used, where all regressions are pooled across i as well as t. Because we do not want to lose an entire time period, the Prais-Winsten transformation should be used for the initial time period.

Unobserved effects models containing lagged dependent variables also require IV methods for consistent estimation. The reason is that, after differencing, $\Delta y_{i,t-1}$ is correlated with Δu_{it} because $y_{i,t-1}$ and $u_{i,t-1}$ are correlated. We can use two or more lags of y as IVs for $\Delta y_{i,t-1}$. [See Wooldridge (2010, Chapter 11) for details.]

Instrumental variables after differencing can be used on matched pairs samples as well. Ashenfelter and Krueger (1994) differenced the wage equation across twins to eliminate unobserved ability:

$$\log(wage_2) - \log(wage_1) = \delta_0 + \beta_1(educ_{2,2} - educ_{1,1}) + (u_2 - u_1),$$

where $educ_{1,1}$ is years of schooling for the first twin as reported by the first twin and $educ_{2,2}$ is years of schooling for the second twin as reported by the second twin. To account for possible measurement error in the self-reported schooling measures, Ashenfelter and Krueger used $(educ_{2,1} - educ_{1,2})$ as an IV for $(educ_{2,2} - educ_{1,1})$, where $educ_{2,1}$ is years of schooling for the second twin as reported by the first twin and $educ_{1,2}$ is years of schooling for the first twin as reported by the second twin. The IV estimate of β_1 is $.167 (t = 3.88)$, compared with the OLS estimate on the first differences of $.092 (t = 3.83)$ [see Ashenfelter and Krueger (1994, Table 3)].

Summary

In Chapter 15, we have introduced the method of instrumental variables as a way to estimate the parameters in a linear model consistently when one or more explanatory variables are endogenous. An instrumental variable must have two properties: (1) it must be exogenous, that is, uncorrelated with the error term of the structural equation; (2) it must be partially correlated with the endogenous explanatory variable. Finding a variable with these two properties is usually challenging.

The method of two stage least squares, which allows for more instrumental variables than we have explanatory variables, is used routinely in the empirical social sciences. When used properly, it can allow us to estimate ceteris paribus effects in the presence of endogenous explanatory variables. This is true in cross-sectional, time series, and panel data applications. But when instruments are poor—which means they are correlated with the error term, only weakly correlated with the endogenous explanatory variable, or both—then 2SLS can be worse than OLS.

When we have valid instrumental variables, we can test whether an explanatory variable is endogenous, using the test in Section 15-5. In addition, though we can never test whether all IVs are exogenous, we can test that at least some of them are—assuming that we have more instruments than we need for consistent estimation (that is, the model is overidentified). Heteroskedasticity and serial correlation can be tested for and dealt with using methods similar to the case of models with exogenous explanatory variables.

In this chapter, we used omitted variables and measurement error to illustrate the method of instrumental variables. IV methods are also indispensable for simultaneous equations models, which we will cover in Chapter 16.

Key Terms

Endogenous Explanatory Variables	Instrumental Variable	Overidentifying Restrictions
Errors-in-Variables	Instrumental Variables (IV) Estimator	Rank Condition
Exclusion Restrictions	Instrument Exogeneity	Reduced Form Equation
Exogenous Explanatory Variables	Instrument Relevance	Structural Equation
Exogenous Variables	Natural Experiment	Two Stage Least Squares (2SLS) Estimator
Identification	Omitted Variables	Weak Instruments
Instrument	Order Condition	

Problems

1 Consider a simple model to estimate the effect of personal computer (PC) ownership on college grade point average for graduating seniors at a large public university:

$$GPA = \beta_0 + \beta_1 PC + u,$$

where PC is a binary variable indicating PC ownership.
(i) Why might PC ownership be correlated with u?
(ii) Explain why PC is likely to be related to parents' annual income. Does this mean parental income is a good IV for PC? Why or why not?
(iii) Suppose that, four years ago, the university gave grants to buy computers to roughly one-half of the incoming students, and the students who received grants were randomly chosen. Carefully explain how you would use this information to construct an instrumental variable for PC.

2 Suppose that you wish to estimate the effect of class attendance on student performance, as in Example 6.3. A basic model is

$$stndfnl = \beta_0 + \beta_1 atndrte + \beta_2 priGPA + \beta_3 ACT + u,$$

where the variables are defined as in Chapter 6.
(i) Let $dist$ be the distance from the students' living quarters to the lecture hall. Do you think $dist$ is uncorrelated with u?
(ii) Assuming that $dist$ and u are uncorrelated, what other assumption must $dist$ satisfy to be a valid IV for $atndrte$?
(iii) Suppose, as in equation (6.18), we add the interaction term $priGPA \cdot atndrte$:

$$stndfnl = \beta_0 + \beta_1 atndrte + \beta_2 priGPA + \beta_3 ACT + \beta_4 priGPA \cdot atndrte + u.$$

If $atndrte$ is correlated with u, then, in general, so is $priGPA \cdot atndrte$. What might be a good IV for $priGPA \cdot atndrte$? [*Hint*: If $E(u|priGPA, ACT, dist) = 0$, as happens when $priGPA$, ACT, and $dist$ are all exogenous, then any function of $priGPA$ and $dist$ is uncorrelated with u.]

3 Consider the simple regression model

$$y = \beta_0 + \beta_1 x + u$$

and let z be a *binary* instrumental variable for x. Use (15.10) to show that the IV estimator $\hat{\beta}_1$ can be written as

$$\hat{\beta}_1 = (\bar{y}_1 - \bar{y}_0)/(\bar{x}_1 - \bar{x}_0),$$

where $\bar{y}_0$ and $\bar{x}_0$ are the sample averages of y_i and x_i over the part of the sample with $z_i = 0$, and where $\bar{y}_1$ and $\bar{x}_1$ are the sample averages of y_i and x_i over the part of the sample with $z_i = 1$. This estimator, known as a *grouping estimator*, was first suggested by Wald (1940).

4 Suppose that, for a given state in the United States, you wish to use annual time series data to estimate the effect of the state-level minimum wage on the employment of those 18 to 25 years old (*EMP*). A simple model is

$$gEMP_t = \beta_0 + \beta_1 gMIN_t + \beta_2 gPOP_t + \beta_3 gGSP_t + \beta_4 gGDP_t + u_t,$$

where MIN_t is the minimum wage, in real dollars; POP_t is the population from 18 to 25 years old; GSP_t is gross state product; and GDP_t is U.S. gross domestic product. The g prefix indicates the growth rate from year $t - 1$ to year t, which would typically be approximated by the difference in the logs.

(i) If we are worried that the state chooses its minimum wage partly based on unobserved (to us) factors that affect youth employment, what is the problem with OLS estimation?

(ii) Let $USMIN_t$ be the U.S. minimum wage, which is also measured in real terms. Do you think $gUSMIN_t$ is uncorrelated with u_t?

(iii) By law, any state's minimum wage must be at least as large as the U.S. minimum. Explain why this makes $gUSMIN_t$ a potential IV candidate for $gMIN_t$.

5 Refer to equations (15.19) and (15.20). Assume that $\sigma_u = \sigma_x$, so that the population variation in the error term is the same as it is in x. Suppose that the instrumental variable, z, is slightly correlated with u: $\text{Corr}(z, u) = .1$. Suppose also that z and x have a somewhat stronger correlation: $\text{Corr}(z, x) = .2$.

(i) What is the asymptotic bias in the IV estimator?

(ii) How much correlation would have to exist between x and u before OLS has more asymptotic bias than 2SLS?

6 (i) In the model with one endogenous explanatory variable, one exogenous explanatory variable, and one extra exogenous variable, take the reduced form for y_2 (15.26), and plug it into the structural equation (15.22). This gives the reduced form for y_1:

$$y_1 = \alpha_0 + \alpha_1 z_1 + \alpha_2 z_2 + v_1.$$

Find the α_j in terms of the β_j and the π_j.

(ii) Find the reduced form error, v_1, in terms of u_1, v_2, and the parameters.

(iii) How would you consistently estimate the a_j?

7 The following is a simple model to measure the effect of a school choice program on standardized test performance [see Rouse (1998) for motivation and Computer Exercise C11 for an analysis of a subset of Rouse's data]:

$$score = \beta_0 + \beta_1 choice + \beta_2 faminc + u_1,$$

where *score* is the score on a statewide test, *choice* is a binary variable indicating whether a student attended a choice school in the last year, and *faminc* is family income. The IV for *choice* is *grant*, the dollar amount granted to students to use for tuition at choice schools. The grant amount differed by family income level, which is why we control for *faminc* in the equation.

(i) Even with *faminc* in the equation, why might *choice* be correlated with u_1?

(ii) If within each income class, the grant amounts were assigned randomly, is *grant* uncorrelated with u_1?

(iii) Write the reduced form equation for *choice*. What is needed for *grant* to be partially correlated with *choice*?

(iv) Write the reduced form equation for *score*. Explain why this is useful. (*Hint*: How do you interpret the coefficient on *grant*?)

8 Suppose you want to test whether girls who attend a girls' high school do better in math than girls who attend coed schools. You have a random sample of senior high school girls from a state in the United States, and *score* is the score on a standardized math test. Let *girlhs* be a dummy variable indicating whether a student attends a girls' high school.

(i) What other factors would you control for in the equation? (You should be able to reasonably collect data on these factors.)

(ii) Write an equation relating *score* to *girlhs* and the other factors you listed in part (i).

(iii) Suppose that parental support and motivation are unmeasured factors in the error term in part (ii). Are these likely to be correlated with *girlhs*? Explain.

(iv) Discuss the assumptions needed for the number of girls' high schools within a 20-mile radius of a girl's home to be a valid IV for *girlhs*.

(v) Suppose that, when you estimate the reduced form for *girlshs*, you find that the coefficient on *numghs* (the number of girls' high schools within a 20-mile radius) is negative and statistically significant. Would you feel comfortable proceeding with IV estimation where *numghs* is used as an IV for *girlshs*? Explain.

9 Suppose that, in equation (15.8), you do not have a good instrumental variable candidate for *skipped*. But you have two other pieces of information on students: combined SAT score and cumulative GPA prior to the semester. What would you do instead of IV estimation?

10 In a recent article, Evans and Schwab (1995) studied the effects of attending a Catholic high school on the probability of attending college. For concreteness, let *college* be a binary variable equal to unity if a student attends college, and zero otherwise. Let *CathHS* be a binary variable equal to one if the student attends a Catholic high school. A linear probability model is

$$college = \beta_0 + \beta_1 CathHS + other\ factors + u,$$

where the other factors include gender, race, family income, and parental education.

(i) Why might *CathHS* be correlated with u?

(ii) Evans and Schwab have data on a standardized test score taken when each student was a sophomore. What can be done with this variable to improve the ceteris paribus estimate of attending a Catholic high school?

(iii) Let *CathRel* be a binary variable equal to one if the student is Catholic. Discuss the two requirements needed for this to be a valid IV for *CathHS* in the preceding equation. Which of these can be tested?

(iv) Not surprisingly, being Catholic has a significant positive effect on attending a Catholic high school. Do you think *CathRel* is a convincing instrument for *CathHS*?

11 Consider a simple time series model where the explanatory variable has classical measurement error:

$$y_t = \beta_0 + \beta_1 x_t^* + u_t \qquad [15.58]$$
$$x_t = x_t^* + e_t,$$

where u_t has zero mean and is uncorrelated with x_t^* and e_t. We observe y_t and x_t only. Assume that e_t has zero mean and is uncorrelated with x_t^* and that x_t^* also has a zero mean (this last assumption is only to simplify the algebra).

(i) Write $x_t^* = x_t - e_t$ and plug this into (15.58). Show that the error term in the new equation, say, v_t, is negatively correlated with x_t if $\beta_1 > 0$. What does this imply about the OLS estimator of β_1 from the regression of y_t on x_t?

(ii) In addition to the previous assumptions, assume that u_t and e_t are uncorrelated with all past values of x_t^* and e_t; in particular, with $x_t^* - 1$ and e_{t-1}. Show that $E(x_{t-1}v_t) = 0$ where v_t is the error term in the model from part (i).

(iii) Are x_t and x_{t-1} likely to be correlated? Explain.

(iv) What do parts (ii) and (iii) suggest as a useful strategy for consistently estimating β_0 and β_1?

Computer Exercises

C1 Use the data in WAGE2 for this exercise.

(i) In Example 15.2, if *sibs* is used as an instrument for *educ*, the IV estimate of the return to education is .122. To convince yourself that using *sibs* as an IV for *educ* is *not* the same as just plugging *sibs* in for *educ* and running an OLS regression, run the regression of log(*wage*) on *sibs* and explain your findings.

(ii) The variable *brthord* is birth order (*brthord* is one for a first-born child, two for a second-born child, and so on). Explain why *educ* and *brthord* might be negatively correlated. Regress *educ* on *brthord* to determine whether there is a statistically significant negative correlation.

(iii) Use *brthord* as an IV for *educ* in equation (15.1). Report and interpret the results.

(iv) Now, suppose that we include number of siblings as an explanatory variable in the wage equation; this controls for family background, to some extent:

$$\log(wage) = \beta_0 + \beta_1 educ + \beta_2 sibs + u.$$

Suppose that we want to use *brthord* as an IV for *educ*, assuming that *sibs* is exogenous. The reduced form for *educ* is

$$educ = \pi_0 + \pi_1 sibs + \pi_2 brthord + v.$$

State and test the identification assumption.

(v) Estimate the equation from part (iv) using *brthord* as an IV for *educ* (and *sibs* as its own IV). Comment on the standard errors for $\hat{\beta}_{educ}$ and $\hat{\beta}_{sibs}$.

(vi) Using the fitted values from part (iv), $\widehat{educ}$, compute the correlation between $\widehat{educ}$ and *sibs*. Use this result to explain your findings from part (v).

C2 The data in FERTIL2 include, for women in Botswana during 1988, information on number of children, years of education, age, and religious and economic status variables.

(i) Estimate the model

$$children = \beta_0 + \beta_1 educ + \beta_2 age + \beta_3 age^2 + u$$

by OLS and interpret the estimates. In particular, holding *age* fixed, what is the estimated effect of another year of education on fertility? If 100 women receive another year of education, how many fewer children are they expected to have?

(ii) The variable *frsthalf* is a dummy variable equal to one if the woman was born during the first six months of the year. Assuming that *frsthalf* is uncorrelated with the error term from part (i), show that *frsthalf* is a reasonable IV candidate for *educ*. (*Hint*: You need to do a regression.)

(iii) Estimate the model from part (i) by using *frsthalf* as an IV for *educ*. Compare the estimated effect of education with the OLS estimate from part (i).

(iv) Add the binary variables *electric*, *tv*, and *bicycle* to the model and assume these are exogenous. Estimate the equation by OLS and 2SLS and compare the estimated coefficients on *educ*. Interpret the coefficient on *tv* and explain why television ownership has a negative effect on fertility.

C3 Use the data in CARD for this exercise.

(i) The equation we estimated in Example 15.4 can be written as

$$\log(wage) = \beta_0 + \beta_1 educ + \beta_2 exper + \ldots + u,$$

where the other explanatory variables are listed in Table 15.1. In order for IV to be consistent, the IV for *educ*, *nearc4*, must be uncorrelated with *u*. Could *nearc4* be correlated with things in the error term, such as unobserved ability? Explain.

(ii) For a subsample of the men in the data set, an IQ score is available. Regress *IQ* on *nearc4* to check whether average IQ scores vary by whether the man grew up near a four-year college. What do you conclude?

(iii) Now, regress *IQ* on *nearc4*, *smsa66*, and the 1966 regional dummy variables *reg662*, ..., *reg669*. Are *IQ* and *nearc4* related after the geographic dummy variables have been partialled out? Reconcile this with your findings from part (ii).

(iv) From parts (ii) and (iii), what do you conclude about the importance of controlling for *smsa66* and the 1966 regional dummies in the log(*wage*) equation?

C4 Use the data in INTDEF for this exercise. A simple equation relating the three-month T-bill rate to the inflation rate (constructed from the Consumer Price Index) is

$$i3_t = \beta_0 + \beta_1 inf_t + u_t.$$

(i) Estimate this equation by OLS, omitting the first time period for later comparisons. Report the results in the usual form.

(ii) Some economists feel that the Consumer Price Index mismeasures the true rate of inflation, so that the OLS from part (i) suffers from measurement error bias. Reestimate the equation from part (i), using inf_{t-1} as an IV for inf_t. How does the IV estimate of β_1 compare with the OLS estimate?

(iii) Now, first difference the equation:

$$\Delta i3_t = \beta_0 + \beta_1 \Delta inf_t + \Delta u_t.$$

Estimate this by OLS and compare the estimate of β_1 with the previous estimates.

(iv) Can you use Δinf_{t-1} as an IV for Δinf_t in the differenced equation in part (iii)? Explain. (*Hint*: Are Δinf_t and Δinf_{t-1} sufficiently correlated?)

C5 Use the data in CARD for this exercise.

(i) In Table 15.1, the difference between the IV and OLS estimates of the return to education is economically important. Obtain the reduced form residuals, $\hat{v}_2$, from the reduced form regression *educ* on *nearc4*, *exper*, *exper²*, *black*, *smsa*, *south*, *smsa66*, *reg662*, ..., *reg669*—see Table 15.1. Use these to test whether *educ* is exogenous; that is, determine if the difference between OLS and IV is *statistically* significant.

(ii) Estimate the equation by 2SLS, adding *nearc2* as an instrument. Does the coefficient on *educ* change much?

(iii) Test the single overidentifying restriction from part (ii).

C6 Use the data in MURDER for this exercise. The variable *mrdrte* is the murder rate, that is, the number of murders per 100,000 people. The variable *exec* is the total number of prisoners executed for the current and prior two years; *unem* is the state unemployment rate.

(i) How many states executed at least one prisoner in 1991, 1992, or 1993? Which state had the most executions?

(ii) Using the two years 1990 and 1993, do a pooled regression of *mrdrte* on *d93*, *exec*, and *unem*. What do you make of the coefficient on *exec*?

(iii) Using the changes from 1990 to 1993 only (for a total of 51 observations), estimate the equation

$$\Delta mrdrte = \delta_0 + \beta_1 \Delta exec + \beta_2 \Delta unem + \Delta u$$

by OLS and report the results in the usual form. Now, does capital punishment appear to have a deterrent effect?

(iv) The change in executions may be at least partly related to changes in the expected murder rate, so that $\Delta exec$ is correlated with Δu in part (iii). It might be reasonable to assume that $\Delta exec_{-1}$

is uncorrelated with Δu. (After all, $\Delta exec_{-1}$ depends on executions that occurred three or more years ago.) Regress $\Delta exec$ on $\Delta exec_{-1}$ to see if they are sufficiently correlated; interpret the coefficient on $\Delta exec_{-1}$.

(v) Reestimate the equation from part (iii), using $\Delta exec_{-1}$ as an IV for $\Delta exec$. Assume that $\Delta unem$ is exogenous. How do your conclusions change from part (iii)?

C7 Use the data in PHILLIPS for this exercise.

(i) In Example 11.5, we estimated an expectations augmented Phillips curve of the form

$$\Delta inf_t = \beta_0 + \beta_1 unem_t + e_t,$$

where $\Delta inf_t = inf_t - inf_{t-1}$. In estimating this equation by OLS, we assumed that the supply shock, e_t, was uncorrelated with $unem_t$. If this is false, what can be said about the OLS estimator of β_1?

(ii) Suppose that e_t is unpredictable given all past information: $E(e_t | inf_{t-1}, unem_{t-1}, \ldots) = 0$. Explain why this makes $unem_{t-1}$ a good IV candidate for $unem_t$.

(iii) Regress $unem_t$ on $unem_{t-1}$. Are $unem_t$ and $unem_{t-1}$ significantly correlated?

(iv) Estimate the expectations augmented Phillips curve by IV. Report the results in the usual form and compare them with the OLS estimates from Example 11.5.

C8 Use the data in 401KSUBS for this exercise. The equation of interest is a linear probability model:

$$pira = \beta_0 + \beta_1 p401k + \beta_2 inc + \beta_3 inc^2 + \beta_4 age + \beta_5 age^2 + u.$$

The goal is to test whether there is a tradeoff between participating in a 401(k) plan and having an individual retirement account (IRA). Therefore, we want to estimate β_1.

(i) Estimate the equation by OLS and discuss the estimated effect of $p401k$.

(ii) For the purposes of estimating the ceteris paribus tradeoff between participation in two different types of retirement savings plans, what might be a problem with ordinary least squares?

(iii) The variable $e401k$ is a binary variable equal to one if a worker is *eligible* to participate in a 401(k) plan. Explain what is required for $e401k$ to be a valid IV for $p401k$. Do these assumptions seem reasonable?

(iv) Estimate the reduced form for $p401k$ and verify that $e401k$ has significant partial correlation with $p401k$. Since the reduced form is also a linear probability model, use a heteroskedasticity-robust standard error.

(v) Now, estimate the structural equation by IV and compare the estimate of β_1 with the OLS estimate. Again, you should obtain heteroskedasticity-robust standard errors.

(vi) Test the null hypothesis that $p401k$ is in fact exogenous, using a heteroskedasticity-robust test.

C9 The purpose of this exercise is to compare the estimates and standard errors obtained by correctly using 2SLS with those obtained using inappropriate procedures. Use the data file WAGE2.

(i) Use a 2SLS routine to estimate the equation

$$\log(wage) = \beta_0 + \beta_1 educ + \beta_2 exper + \beta_3 tenure + \beta_4 black + u,$$

where $sibs$ is the IV for $educ$. Report the results in the usual form.

(ii) Now, manually carry out 2SLS. That is, first regress $educ_i$ on $sibs_i$, $exper_i$, $tenure_i$, and $black_i$ and obtain the fitted values, $\widehat{educ}_i$, $i = 1, \ldots, n$. Then, run the second stage regression $\log(wage_i)$ on $\widehat{educ}_i$, $exper_i$, $tenure_i$, and $black_i$, $i = 1, \ldots, n$. Verify that the $\hat{\beta}_j$ are identical to those obtained from part (i), but that the standard errors are somewhat different. The standard errors obtained from the second stage regression when manually carrying out 2SLS are generally inappropriate.

(iii) Now, use the following two-step procedure, which generally yields inconsistent parameter estimates of the β_j, and not just inconsistent standard errors. In step one, regress $educ_i$ on $sibs_i$ only and obtain the fitted values, say $\widetilde{educ}_i$. (Note that this is an incorrect first stage regression.) Then, in the second step, run the regression of $\log(wage_i)$ on $\widetilde{educ}_i$, $exper_i$, $tenure_i$, and $black_i$, $i = 1, \ldots, n$. How does the estimate from this incorrect, two-step procedure compare with the correct 2SLS estimate of the return to education?

C10 Use the data in HTV for this exercise.

    (i)   Run a simple OLS regression of log(*wage*) on *educ*. Without controlling for other factors, what is the 95% confidence interval for the return to another year of education?

    (ii)   The variable *ctuit,* in thousands of dollars, is the change in college tuition facing students from age 17 to age 18. Show that *educ* and *ctuit* are essentially uncorrelated. What does this say about *ctuit* as a possible IV for *educ* in a simple regression analysis?

    (iii)   Now, add to the simple regression model in part (i) a quadratic in experience and a full set of regional dummy variables for current residence and residence at age 18. Also include the urban indicators for current and age 18 residences. What is the estimated return to a year of education?

    (iv)   Again using *ctuit* as a potential IV for *educ*, estimate the reduced form for *educ*. [Naturally, the reduced form for *educ* now includes the explanatory variables in part (iii).] Show that *ctuit* is now statistically significant in the reduced form for *educ*.

    (v)   Estimate the model from part (iii) by IV, using *ctuit* as an IV for *educ*. How does the confidence interval for the return to education compare with the OLS CI from part (iii)?

    (vi)   Do you think the IV procedure from part (v) is convincing?

C11 The data set in VOUCHER, which is a subset of the data used in Rouse (1998), can be used to estimate the effect of school choice on academic achievement. Attendance at a choice school was paid for by a voucher, which was determined by a lottery among those who applied. The data subset was chosen so that any student in the sample has a valid 1994 math test score (the last year available in Rouse's sample). Unfortunately, as pointed out by Rouse, many students have missing test scores, possibly due to attrition (that is, leaving the Milwaukee public school district). These data include students who applied to the voucher program and were accepted, students who applied and were not accepted, and students who did not apply. Therefore, even though the vouchers were chosen by lottery among those who applied, we do not necessarily have a random sample from a population where being selected for a voucher has been randomly determined. (An important consideration is that students who never applied to the program may be systematically different from those who did—and in ways that we cannot know based on the data.)

    Rouse (1998) uses panel data methods of the kind we discussed in Chapter 14 to allow student fixed effects; she also uses instrumental variables methods. This problem asks you to do a cross-sectional analysis where winning the lottery for a voucher acts as an instrumental variable for attending a choice school. Actually, because we have multiple years of data on each student, we construct two variables. The first, *choiceyrs*, is the number of years from 1991 to 1994 that a student attended a choice school; this variable ranges from zero to four. The variable *selectyrs* indicates the number of years a student was selected for a voucher. If the student applied for the program in 1990 and received a voucher then *selectyrs* = 4; if he or she applied in 1991 and received a voucher then *selectyrs* = 3; and so on. The outcome of interest is *mnce*, the student's percentile score on a math test administered in 1994.

    (i)   Of the 990 students in the sample, how many were never awarded a voucher? How many had a voucher available for four years? How many students actually attended a choice school for four years?

    (ii)   Run a simple regression of *choiceyrs* on *selectyrs*. Are these variables related in the direction you expected? How strong is the relationship? Is *selectyrs* a sensible IV candidate for *choiceyrs*?

    (iii)   Run a simple regression of *mnce* on *choiceyrs*. What do you find? Is this what you expected? What happens if you add the variables *black*, *hispanic*, and *female*?

    (iv)   Why might *choiceyrs* be endogenous in an equation such as

$$mnce = \beta_0 + \beta_1 choiceyrs + \beta_2 black + \beta_3 hispanic + \beta_4 female + u_1?$$

    (v)   Estimate the equation in part (iv) by instrumental variables, using *selectyrs* as the IV for *choiceyrs*. Does using IV produce a positive effect of attending a choice school? What do you make of the coefficients on the other explanatory variables?

    (vi)   To control for the possibility that prior achievement affects participating in the lottery (as well as predicting attrition), add *mnce90*—the math score in 1990—to the equation in part (iv).

Estimate the equation by OLS and IV, and compare the results for β_1. For the IV estimate, how much is each year in a choice school worth on the math percentile score? Is this a practically large effect?

(vii) Why is the analysis from part (vi) not entirely convincing? [*Hint*: Compared with part (v), what happens to the number of observations, and why?]

(viii) The variables *choiceyrs*1, *choiceyrs*2, and so on are dummy variables indicating the different number of years a student could have been in a choice school (from 1991 to 1994). The dummy variables *selectyrs*1, *selectyrs*2, and so on have a similar definition, but for being selected from the lottery. Estimate the equation

$$mnce = \beta_0 + \beta_1 choiceyrs1 + \beta_2 choiceyrs2 + \beta_3 choiceyrs3 + \beta_4 choiceyrs4$$
$$+ \beta_5 black + \beta_6 hispanic + \beta_7 female + \beta_8 mnce90 + u_1$$

by IV, using as instruments the four *selectyrs* dummy variables. (As before, the variables *black*, *hispanic*, and *female* act as their own IVs.) Describe your findings. Do they make sense?

C12 Use the data in CATHOLIC to answer this question. The model of interest is

$$math12 = \beta_0 + \beta_1 cathhs + \beta_2 lfaminc + \beta_3 motheduc + \beta_4 fatheduc + u,$$

where *cathhs* is a binary indicator for whether a student attends a Catholic high school.

(i) How many students are in the sample? What percentage of these students attend a Catholic high school?

(ii) Estimate the above equation by OLS. What is the estimate of β_1? What is its 95% confidence interval?

(iii) Using *parcath* as an instrument for *cathhs*, estimate the reduced form *for cathhs*. What is the t statistic for *parcath*? Is there evidence of a weak instrument problem?

(iv) Estimate the above equation by IV, using *parcath* as an IV for *cathhs*. How does the estimate and 95% CI compare with the OLS quantities?

(v) Test the null hypothesis that *cathhs* is exogenous. What is the p-value of the test?

(vi) Suppose you add the interaction between *cathhs* $\cdot$ *motheduc* to the above model. Why is it generally endogenous? Why is *pareduc* $\cdot$ *motheduc* a good IV candidate for *cathhs* $\cdot$ *motheduc*?

(vii) Before you create the interactions in part (vi), first find the sample average of *motheduc* and create *cathhs* $\cdot$ ($motheduc - \overline{motheduc}$) and *parcath* $\cdot$ ($motheduc - \overline{motheduc}$). Add the first interaction to the model and use the second as an IV. Of course, *cathhs* is also instrumented. Is the interaction term statistically significant?

(viii) Compare the coefficient on *cathhs* in (vii) to that in part (iv). Is including the interaction important for estimating the average partial effect?

APPENDIX 15A

15A.1 Assumptions for Two Stage Least Squares

This appendix covers the assumptions under which 2SLS has desirable large sample properties. We first state the assumptions for cross-sectional applications under random sampling. Then, we discuss what needs to be added for them to apply to time series and panel data.

15A.2 Assumption 2SLS.1 (Linear in Parameters)

The model in the population can be written as

$$y = \beta_0 + \beta_1 x_1 + \beta_2 x_2 + \ldots + \beta_k x_k + u,$$

where $\beta_0, \beta_1, \ldots, \beta_k$ are the unknown parameters (constants) of interest and u is an unobserved random error or random disturbance term. The instrumental variables are denoted as z_j.

It is worth emphasizing that Assumption 2SLS.1 is virtually identical to MLR.1 (with the minor exception that 2SLS.1 mentions the notation for the instrumental variables, z_j). In other words, the model we are interested in is the same as that for OLS estimation of the β_j. Sometimes it is easy to lose sight of the fact that we can apply different estimation methods to the same model. Unfortunately, it is not uncommon to hear researchers say "I estimated an OLS model" or "I used a 2SLS model." Such statements are meaningless. OLS and 2SLS are different *estimation* methods that are applied to the *same* model. It is true that they have desirable statistical properties under different sets of assumptions on the model, but the relationship they are estimating is given by the equation in 2SLS.1 (or MLR.1). The point is similar to that made for the unobserved effects panel data model covered in Chapters 13 and 14: pooled OLS, first differencing, fixed effects, and random effects are different estimation methods for the same model.

15A.3 Assumption 2SLS.2 (Random Sampling)

We have a random sample on y, the x_j, and the z_j.

15A.4 Assumption 2SLS.3 (Rank Condition)

(i) There are no perfect linear relationships among the instrumental variables. (ii) The rank condition for identification holds.

With a single endogenous explanatory variable, as in equation (15.42), the rank condition is easily described. Let $z_1, \ldots, z_m$ denote the exogenous variables, where $z_k, \ldots, z_m$ do not appear in the structural model (15.42). The reduced form of y_2 is

$$y_2 = \pi_0 + \pi_1 z_1 + \pi_2 z_2 + \ldots + \pi_{k-1} z_{k-1} + \pi_k z_k + \ldots + \pi_m z_m + v_2.$$

Then, we need at least one of $\pi_k, \ldots, \pi_m$ to be nonzero. This requires at least one exogenous variable that does not appear in (15.42) (the order condition). Stating the rank condition with two or more endogenous explanatory variables requires matrix algebra. [See Wooldridge (2010, Chapter 5).]

15A.5 Assumption 2SLS.4 (Exogenous Instrumental Variables)

The error term u has zero mean, and each IV is uncorrelated with u.
Remember that any x_j that is uncorrelated with u also acts as an IV.

15A.6 Theorem 15A.1

Under Assumptions 2SLS.1 through 2SLS.4, the 2SLS estimator is consistent.

15A.7 Assumption 2SLS.5 (Homoskedasticity)

Let $\mathbf{z}$ denote the collection of all instrumental variables. Then, $E(u^2|\mathbf{z}) = \sigma^2$.

15A.8 Theorem 15A.2

Under Assumptions 2SLS.1 through 2SLS.5, the 2SLS estimators are asymptotically normally distributed. Consistent estimators of the asymptotic variance are given as in equation (15.43), where σ^2 is replaced with $\hat{\sigma}^2 = (n - k - 1)^{-1}\sum_{i=1}^{n}\hat{u}_i^2$, and the $\hat{u}_i$ are the 2SLS residuals.

The 2SLS estimator is also the best IV estimator under the five assumptions given. We state the result here. A proof can be found in Wooldridge (2010, Chapter 5).

15A.9 Theorem 15A.3

Under Assumptions 2SLS.1 through 2SLS.5, the 2SLS estimator is asymptotically efficient in the class of IV estimators that uses linear combinations of the exogenous variables as instruments.

If the homoskedasticity assumption does not hold, the 2SLS estimators are still asymptotically normal, but the standard errors (and t and F statistics) need to be adjusted; many econometrics packages do this routinely. Moreover, the 2SLS estimator is no longer the asymptotically efficient IV estimator, in general. We will not study more efficient estimators here [see Wooldridge (2010, Chapter 8)].

For time series applications, we must add some assumptions. First, as with OLS, we must assume that all series (including the IVs) are weakly dependent: this ensures that the law of large numbers and the central limit theorem hold. For the usual standard errors and test statistics to be valid, as well as for asymptotic efficiency, we must add a no serial correlation assumption.

15A.10 Assumption 2SLS.6 (No Serial Correlation)

Equation (15.54) holds.

A similar no serial correlation assumption is needed in panel data applications. Tests and corrections for serial correlation were discussed in Section 15-7.

CHAPTER 16

Simultaneous Equations Models

I n the previous chapter, we showed how the method of instrumental variables can solve two kinds of endogeneity problems: omitted variables and measurement error. Conceptually, these problems are straightforward. In the omitted variables case, there is a variable (or more than one) that we would like to hold fixed when estimating the ceteris paribus effect of one or more of the observed explanatory variables. In the measurement error case, we would like to estimate the effect of certain explanatory variables on y, but we have mismeasured one or more variables. In both cases, we could estimate the parameters of interest by OLS if we could collect better data.

Another important form of endogeneity of explanatory variables is **simultaneity**. This arises when one or more of the explanatory variables is *jointly determined* with the dependent variable, typically through an equilibrium mechanism (as we will see later). In this chapter, we study methods for estimating simple simultaneous equations models (SEMs). Although a complete treatment of SEMs is beyond the scope of this text, we are able to cover models that are widely used.

The leading method for estimating simultaneous equations models is the method of instrumental variables. Therefore, the solution to the simultaneity problem is essentially the same as the IV solutions to the omitted variables and measurement error problems. However, crafting and interpreting SEMs is challenging. Therefore, we begin by discussing the nature and scope of simultaneous equations models in Section 16-1. In Section 16-2, we confirm that OLS applied to an equation in a simultaneous system is generally biased and inconsistent.

Section 16-3 provides a general description of identification and estimation in a two-equation system, while Section 16-4 briefly covers models with more than two equations. Simultaneous equations models are used to model aggregate time series, and in Section 16-5 we include a discussion of some special issues that arise in such models. Section 16-6 touches on simultaneous equations models with panel data.

16-1 The Nature of Simultaneous Equations Models

The most important point to remember in using simultaneous equations models is that each equation in the system should have a ceteris paribus, causal interpretation. Because we only observe the outcomes in equilibrium, we are required to use counterfactual reasoning in constructing the equations of a simultaneous equations model. We must think in terms of potential as well as actual outcomes.

The classic example of an SEM is a supply and demand equation for some commodity or input to production (such as labor). For concreteness, let h_s denote the annual labor hours supplied by workers in agriculture, measured at the county level, and let w denote the average hourly wage offered to such workers. A simple labor supply function is

$$h_s = \alpha_1 w + \beta_1 z_1 + u_1,$$ [16.1]

where z_1 is some observed variable affecting labor supply—say, the average manufacturing wage in the county. The error term, u_1, contains other factors that affect labor supply. [Many of these factors are observed and could be included in equation (16.1); to illustrate the basic concepts, we include only one such factor, z_1.] Equation (16.1) is an example of a **structural equation**. This name comes from the fact that the labor supply function is derivable from economic theory and has a causal interpretation. The coefficient α_1 measures how labor supply changes when the wage changes; if h_s and w are in logarithmic form, α_1 is the labor supply elasticity. Typically, we expect α_1 to be positive (although economic theory does not rule out $\alpha_1 \leq 0$). Labor supply elasticities are important for determining how workers will change the number of hours they desire to work when tax rates on wage income change. If z_1 is the manufacturing wage, we expect $\beta_1 \leq 0$: other factors equal, if the manufacturing wage increases, more workers will go into manufacturing than into agriculture.

When we graph labor supply, we sketch hours as a function of wage, with z_1 and u_1 held fixed. A change in z_1 shifts the labor supply function, as does a change in u_1. The difference is that z_1 is observed while u_1 is not. Sometimes, z_1 is called an *observed supply shifter*, and u_1 is called an *unobserved supply shifter*.

How does equation (16.1) differ from those we have studied previously? The difference is subtle. Although equation (16.1) is supposed to hold for all possible values of wage, we cannot generally view wage as varying exogenously for a cross section of counties. If we could run an experiment where we vary the level of agricultural and manufacturing wages across a sample of counties and survey workers to obtain the labor supply h_s for each county, then we could estimate (16.1) by OLS. Unfortunately, this is not a manageable experiment. Instead, we must collect data on average wages in these two sectors along with how many person hours were spent in agricultural production. In deciding how to analyze these data, we must understand that they are best described by the interaction of labor supply *and* demand. Under the assumption that labor markets clear, we actually observe *equilibrium* values of wages and hours worked.

To describe how equilibrium wages and hours are determined, we need to bring in the demand for labor, which we suppose is given by

$$h_d = \alpha_2 w + \beta_2 z_2 + u_2,$$ [16.2]

where h_d is hours demanded. As with the supply function, we graph hours demanded as a function of wage, w, keeping z_2 and u_2 fixed. The variable z_2—say, agricultural land area—is an *observable demand shifter*, while u_2 is an *unobservable demand shifter*.

Just as with the labor supply equation, the labor demand equation is a structural equation: it can be obtained from the profit maximization considerations of farmers. If h_d and w are in logarithmic form, α_2 is the labor demand elasticity. Economic theory tells us that $\alpha_2 < 0$. Because labor and land are complements in production, we expect $\beta_2 > 0$.

Notice how equations (16.1) and (16.2) describe entirely different relationships. Labor supply is a behavioral equation for workers, and labor demand is a behavioral relationship for farmers. Each equation has a ceteris paribus interpretation and stands on its own. They become linked in an econometric analysis only because *observed* wage and hours are determined by the intersection of supply and demand. In other words, for each county i, observed hours h_i and observed wage w_i are determined by the equilibrium condition

$$h_{is} = h_{id}. \tag{16.3}$$

Because we observe only equilibrium hours for each county i, we denote observed hours by h_i.

When we combine the equilibrium condition in (16.3) with the labor supply and demand equations, we get

$$h_i = \alpha_1 w_i + \beta_1 z_{i1} + u_{i1} \tag{16.4}$$

and

$$h_i = \alpha_2 w_i + \beta_2 z_{i2} + u_{i2}, \tag{16.5}$$

where we explicitly include the i subscript to emphasize that h_i and w_i are the equilibrium observed values for county i. These two equations constitute a **simultaneous equations model (SEM)**, which has several important features. First, given z_{i1}, z_{i2}, u_{i1}, and u_{i2}, these two equations determine h_i and w_i. (Actually, we must assume that $\alpha_1 \neq \alpha_2$, which means that the slopes of the supply and demand functions differ; see Problem 1.) For this reason, h_i and w_i are the **endogenous variables** in this SEM. What about z_{i1} and z_{i2}? Because they are determined outside of the model, we view them as **exogenous variables**. From a statistical standpoint, the key assumption concerning z_{i1} and z_{i2} is that they are both uncorrelated with the supply and demand errors, u_{i1} and u_{i2}, respectively. These are examples of **structural errors** because they appear in the structural equations.

A second important point is that, without including z_1 and z_2 in the model, there is no way to tell which equation is the supply function and which is the demand function. When z_1 represents manufacturing wage, economic reasoning tells us that it is a factor in agricultural labor supply because it is a measure of the opportunity cost of working in agriculture; when z_2 stands for agricultural land area, production theory implies that it appears in the labor demand function. Therefore, we know that (16.4) represents labor supply and (16.5) represents labor demand. If z_1 and z_2 are the same—for example, average education level of adults in the county, which can affect both supply and demand—then the equations look identical, and there is no hope of estimating either one. In a nutshell, this illustrates the identification problem in simultaneous equations models, which we will discuss more generally in Section 16-3.

The most convincing examples of SEMs have the same flavor as supply and demand examples. Each equation should have a behavioral, ceteris paribus interpretation on its own. Because we only observe equilibrium outcomes, specifying an SEM requires us to ask such counterfactual questions as: How much labor *would* workers provide if the wage were different from its equilibrium value? Example 16.1 provides another illustration of an SEM where each equation has a ceteris paribus interpretation.

EXAMPLE 16.1   **Murder Rates and Size of the Police Force**

Cities often want to determine how much additional law enforcement will decrease their murder rates. A simple cross-sectional model to address this question is

$$murdpc = \alpha_1 polpc + \beta_{10} + \beta_{11} incpc + u_1, \tag{16.6}$$

where *murdpc* is murders per capita, *polpc* is number of police officers per capita, and *incpc* is income per capita. (Henceforth, we do not include an i subscript.) We take income per capita as exogenous in this equation. In practice, we would include other factors, such as age and gender distributions, education levels, perhaps geographic variables, and variables that measure severity of punishment. To fix ideas, we consider equation (16.6).

The question we hope to answer is: If a city exogenously increases its police force, will that increase, on average, lower the murder rate? If we could exogenously choose police force sizes for a random sample of cities, we could estimate (16.6) by OLS. Certainly, we cannot run such an experiment. But can we think of police force size as being exogenously determined, anyway? Probably not. A city's spending on law enforcement is at least partly determined by its expected murder rate. To reflect this, we postulate a second relationship:

$$polpc = \alpha_2 murdpc + \beta_{20} + other\, factors. \qquad [16.7]$$

We expect that $\alpha_2 > 0$: other factors being equal, cities with higher (expected) murder rates will have more police officers per capita. Once we specify the other factors in (16.7), we have a two-equation simultaneous equations model. We are really only interested in equation (16.6), but, as we will see in Section 16-3, we need to know precisely how the second equation is specified in order to estimate the first.

An important point is that (16.7) describes behavior by city officials, while (16.6) describes the actions of potential murderers. This gives each equation a clear ceteris paribus interpretation, which makes equations (16.6) and (16.7) an appropriate simultaneous equations model.

We next give an example of an inappropriate use of SEMs.

EXAMPLE 16.2 **Housing Expenditures and Saving**

Suppose that, for a random household in the population, we assume that annual housing expenditures and saving are jointly determined by

$$housing = \alpha_1 saving + \beta_{10} + \beta_{11} inc + \beta_{12} educ + \beta_{13} age + u_1 \qquad [16.8]$$

and

$$saving = \alpha_2 housing + \beta_{20} + \beta_{21} inc + \beta_{22} educ + \beta_{23} age + u_2, \qquad [16.9]$$

where *inc* is annual income and *educ* and *age* are measured in years. Initially, it may seem that these equations are a sensible way to view how housing and saving expenditures are determined. But we have to ask: What value would one of these equations be without the other? Neither has a ceteris paribus interpretation because *housing* and *saving* are chosen by the same household. For example, it makes no sense to ask this question: If annual income increases by $10,000, how would housing expenditures change, *holding saving fixed*? If family income increases, a household will generally change the optimal mix of housing expenditures and saving. But equation (16.8) makes it seem as if we want to know the effect of changing *inc*, *educ*, or *age* while keeping *saving* fixed. Such a thought experiment is not interesting. Any model based on economic principles, particularly utility maximization, would have households optimally choosing *housing* and *saving* as functions of *inc* and the relative prices of housing and saving. The variables *educ* and *age* would affect preferences for consumption, saving, and risk. Therefore, *housing* and *saving* would each be functions of income, education, age, and other variables that affect the utility maximization problem (such as different rates of return on housing and other saving).

Even if we decided that the SEM in (16.8) and (16.9) made sense, there is no way to estimate the parameters. (We discuss this problem more generally in Section 16-3.) The two equations are indistinguishable, unless we assume that income, education, or age appears in one equation but not the other, which would make no sense.

Though this makes a poor SEM example, we might be interested in testing whether, other factors being fixed, there is a tradeoff between housing expenditures and saving. But then we would just estimate, say, (16.8) by OLS, unless there is an omitted variable or measurement error problem.

Example 16.2 has the characteristics of all too many SEM applications. The problem is that the two endogenous variables are chosen by the same economic agent. Therefore, neither equation can stand on its own. Another example of an inappropriate use of an SEM would be to model weekly hours spent studying and weekly hours working. Each student will choose these variables simultaneously—presumably as a function of the wage that can be earned working, ability as a student, enthusiasm for college, and so on. Just as in Example 16.2, it makes no sense to specify two equations where each is a function of the other. The important lesson is this: just because two variables are determined simul-

taneously does *not* mean that a simultaneous equations model is suitable. For an SEM to make sense, each equation in the SEM should have a ceteris paribus interpretation in isolation from the other equation. As we discussed earlier, supply and demand examples, and Example 16.1, have this feature. Usually, basic economic reasoning, supported in some cases by simple economic models, can help us use SEMs intelligently (including knowing when not to use an SEM).

> **EXPLORING FURTHER 16.1**
>
> Pindyck and Rubinfeld (1992, Section 11-6) describe a model of advertising where monopolistic firms choose profit maximizing levels of price and advertising expenditures. Does this mean we should use an SEM to model these variables at the firm level?

16-2 Simultaneity Bias in OLS

It is useful to see, in a simple model, that an explanatory variable that is determined simultaneously with the dependent variable is generally correlated with the error term, which leads to bias and inconsistency in OLS. We consider the two-equation structural model

$$y_1 = \alpha_1 y_2 + \beta_1 z_1 + u_1 \tag{16.10}$$

$$y_2 = \alpha_2 y_1 + \beta_2 z_2 + u_2 \tag{16.11}$$

and focus on estimating the first equation. The variables z_1 and z_2 are exogenous, so that each is uncorrelated with u_1 and u_2. For simplicity, we suppress the intercept in each equation.

To show that y_2 is generally correlated with u_1, we solve the two equations for y_2 in terms of the exogenous variables and the error term. If we plug the right-hand side of (16.10) in for y_1 in (16.11), we get

$$y_2 = \alpha_2(\alpha_1 y_2 + \beta_1 z_1 + u_1) + \beta_2 z_2 + u_2$$

or

$$(1 - \alpha_2\alpha_1)y_2 = \alpha_2\beta_1 z_1 + \beta_2 z_2 + \alpha_2 u_1 + u_2. \tag{16.12}$$

Now, we must make an assumption about the parameters in order to solve for y_2:

$$\alpha_2\alpha_1 \neq 1. \tag{16.13}$$

Whether this assumption is restrictive depends on the application. In Example 16.1, we think that $\alpha_1 \leq 0$ and $\alpha_2 \geq 0$, which implies $\alpha_1\alpha_2 \leq 0$; therefore, (16.13) is very reasonable for Example 16.1.

Provided condition (16.13) holds, we can divide (16.12) by $(1 - \alpha_2\alpha_1)$ and write y_2 as

$$y_2 = \pi_{21} z_1 + \pi_{22} z_2 + v_2, \tag{16.14}$$

where $\pi_{21} = \alpha_2\beta_1/(1 - \alpha_2\alpha_1)$, $\pi_{22} = \beta_2/(1 - \alpha_2\alpha_1)$, and $v_2 = (\alpha_2 u_1 + u_2)/(1 - \alpha_2\alpha_1)$. Equation (16.14), which expresses y_2 in terms of the exogenous variables and the error terms, is the **reduced form equation** for y_2, a concept we introduced in Chapter 15 in the context of instrumental variables estimation. The parameters π_{21} and π_{22} are called **reduced form parameters**; notice how they are nonlinear functions of the **structural parameters**, which appear in the structural equations, (16.10) and (16.11).

The **reduced form error**, v_2, is a linear function of the structural error terms, u_1 and u_2. Because u_1 and u_2 are each uncorrelated with z_1 and z_2, v_2 is also uncorrelated with z_1 and z_2. Therefore, we can consistently estimate π_{21} and π_{22} by OLS, something that is used for two stage least squares estimation (which we return to in the next section). In addition, the reduced form parameters are sometimes of direct interest, although we are focusing here on estimating equation (16.10).

A reduced form also exists for y_1 under assumption (16.13); the algebra is similar to that used to obtain (16.14). It has the same properties as the reduced form equation for y_2.

We can use equation (16.14) to show that, except under special assumptions, OLS estimation of equation (16.10) will produce biased and inconsistent estimators of α_1 and β_1 in equation (16.10). Because z_1 and u_1 are uncorrelated by assumption, the issue is whether y_2 and u_1 are uncorrelated. From the reduced form in (16.14), we see that y_2 and u_1 are correlated if and only if v_2 and u_1 are correlated (because z_1 and z_2 are assumed exogenous). But v_2 is a linear function of u_1 and u_2, so it is generally correlated with u_1. In fact, if we assume that u_1 and u_2 are uncorrelated, then v_2 and u_1 *must* be correlated whenever $\alpha_2 \neq 0$. Even if α_2 equals zero—which means that y_1 does not appear in equation (16.11)— v_2 and u_1 will be correlated if u_1 and u_2 are correlated.

When $\alpha_2 = 0$ and u_1 and u_2 are uncorrelated, y_2 and u_1 are also uncorrelated. These are fairly strong requirements: if $\alpha_2 = 0$, y_2 is not simultaneously determined with y_1. If we add zero correlation between u_1 and u_2, this rules out omitted variables or measurement errors in u_1 that are correlated with y_2. We should not be surprised that OLS estimation of equation (16.10) works in this case.

When y_2 is correlated with u_1 because of simultaneity, we say that OLS suffers from **simultaneity bias**. Obtaining the direction of the bias in the coefficients is generally complicated, as we saw with omitted variables bias in Chapters 3 and 5. But in simple models, we can determine the direction of the bias. For example, suppose that we simplify equation (16.10) by dropping z_1 from the equation, and we assume that u_1 and u_2 are uncorrelated. Then, the covariance between y_2 and u_1 is

$$\text{Cov}(y_2, u_1) = \text{Cov}(v_2, u_1) = [\alpha_2/(1 - \alpha_2\alpha_1)]\text{E}(u_1^2)$$
$$= [\alpha_2/(1 - \alpha_2\alpha_1)]\sigma_1^2,$$

where $\sigma_1^2 = \text{Var}(u_1) > 0$. Therefore, the asymptotic bias (or inconsistency) in the OLS estimator of α_1 has the same sign as $\alpha_2/(1 - \alpha_2\alpha_1)$. If $\alpha_2 > 0$ and $\alpha_2\alpha_1 < 1$, the asymptotic bias is positive. (Unfortunately, just as in our calculation of omitted variables bias from Section 3-3, the conclusions do not carry over to more general models. But they do serve as a useful guide.) For example, in Example 16.1, we think $\alpha_2 > 0$ and $\alpha_2\alpha_1 \leq 0$, which means that the OLS estimator of α_1 would have a positive bias. If $\alpha_1 = 0$, OLS would, on average, estimate a *positive* impact of more police on the murder rate; generally, the estimator of α_1 is biased upward. Because we expect an increase in the size of the police force to reduce murder rates (ceteris paribus), the upward bias means that OLS will underestimate the effectiveness of a larger police force.

16-3 Identifying and Estimating a Structural Equation

As we saw in the previous section, OLS is biased and inconsistent when applied to a structural equation in a simultaneous equations system. In Chapter 15, we learned that the method of two stage least squares can be used to solve the problem of endogenous explanatory variables. We now show how 2SLS can be applied to SEMs.

The mechanics of 2SLS are similar to those in Chapter 15. The difference is that, because we specify a structural equation for each endogenous variable, we can immediately see whether sufficient IVs are available to estimate either equation. We begin by discussing the identification problem.

16-3a Identification in a Two-Equation System

We mentioned the notion of identification in Chapter 15. When we estimate a model by OLS, the key identification condition is that each explanatory variable is uncorrelated with the error term. As we demonstrated in Section 16-2, this fundamental condition no longer holds, in general, for SEMs. However, if we have some instrumental variables, we can still identify (or consistently estimate) the parameters in an SEM equation, just as with omitted variables or measurement error.

Before we consider a general two-equation SEM, it is useful to gain intuition by considering a simple supply and demand example. Write the system in equilibrium form (that is, with $q_s = q_d = q$ imposed) as

$$q = \alpha_1 p + \beta_1 z_1 + u_1 \qquad\qquad [16.15]$$

and

$$q = \alpha_2 p + u_2. \qquad\qquad [16.16]$$

For concreteness, let q be per capita milk consumption at the county level, let p be the average price per gallon of milk in the county, and let z_1 be the price of cattle feed, which we assume is exogenous to the supply and demand equations for milk. This means that (16.15) must be the supply function, as the price of cattle feed would shift supply $(\beta_1 < 0)$ but not demand. The demand function contains no observed demand shifters.

Given a random sample on (q, p, z_1), which of these equations can be estimated? That is, which is an **identified equation**? It turns out that the *demand* equation, (16.16), is identified, but the supply equation is not. This is easy to see by using our rules for IV estimation from Chapter 15: we can use z_1 as an IV for price in equation (16.16). However, because z_1 appears in equation (16.15), we have no IV for price in the supply equation.

Intuitively, the fact that the demand equation is identified follows because we have an observed variable, z_1, that shifts the supply equation while not affecting the demand equation. Given variation in z_1 and no errors, we can trace out the demand curve, as shown in Figure 16.1. The presence of the

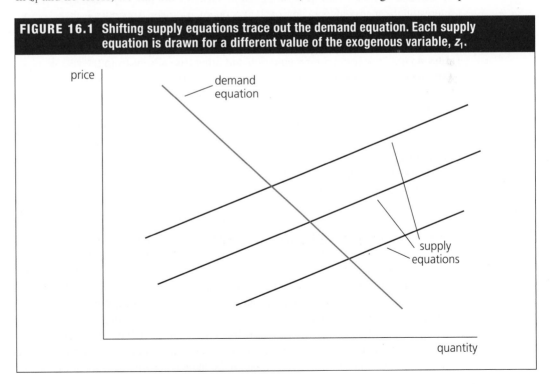

FIGURE 16.1 Shifting supply equations trace out the demand equation. Each supply equation is drawn for a different value of the exogenous variable, z_1.

unobserved demand shifter u_2 causes us to estimate the demand equation with error, but the estimators will be consistent, provided z_1 is uncorrelated with u_2.

The supply equation cannot be traced out because there are no exogenous observed factors shifting the demand curve. It does not help that there are unobserved factors shifting the demand function; we need something observed. If, as in the labor demand function (16.2), we have an observed exogenous demand shifter—such as income in the milk demand function—then the supply function would also be identified.

To summarize: *In the system of (16.15) and (16.16), it is the presence of an exogenous variable in the supply equation that allows us to estimate the demand equation.*

Extending the identification discussion to a general two-equation model is not difficult. Write the two equations as

$$y_1 = \beta_{10} + \alpha_1 y_2 + \mathbf{z}_1 \boldsymbol{\beta}_1 + u_1 \qquad [16.17]$$

and

$$y_2 = \beta_{20} + \alpha_2 y_1 + \mathbf{z}_2 \boldsymbol{\beta}_2 + u_2, \qquad [16.18]$$

where y_1 and y_2 are the endogenous variables and u_1 and u_2 are the structural error terms. The intercept in the first equation is β_{10}, and the intercept in the second equation is β_{20}. The variable $\mathbf{z}_1$ denotes a set of k_1 exogenous variables appearing in the first equation: $\mathbf{z}_1 = (z_{11}, z_{12}, ..., z_{1k_1})$. Similarly, $\mathbf{z}_2$ is the set of k_2 exogenous variables in the second equation: $\mathbf{z}_2 = (z_{21}, z_{22}, ..., z_{2k_2})$. In many cases, $\mathbf{z}_1$ and $\mathbf{z}_2$ will overlap. As a shorthand form, we use the notation

$$\mathbf{z}_1 \boldsymbol{\beta}_1 = \beta_{11} z_{11} + \beta_{12} z_{12} + ... + \beta_{1k_1} z_{1k_1}$$

and

$$\mathbf{z}_2 \boldsymbol{\beta}_2 = \beta_{21} z_{21} + \beta_{22} z_{22} + ... + \beta_{2k_2} z_{2k_2};$$

that is, $\mathbf{z}_1 \boldsymbol{\beta}_1$ stands for all exogenous variables in the first equation, with each multiplied by a coefficient, and similarly for $\mathbf{z}_2 \boldsymbol{\beta}_2$. (Some authors use the notation $\mathbf{z}_1' \boldsymbol{\beta}_1$ and $\mathbf{z}_2' \boldsymbol{\beta}_2$ instead. If you have an interest in the matrix algebra approach to econometrics, see Appendix E.)

The fact that $\mathbf{z}_1$ and $\mathbf{z}_2$ generally contain different exogenous variables means that we have imposed **exclusion restrictions** on the model. In other words, we *assume* that certain exogenous variables do not appear in the first equation and others are absent from the second equation. As we saw with the previous supply and demand examples, this allows us to distinguish between the two structural equations.

When can we solve equations (16.17) and (16.18) for y_1 and y_2 (as linear functions of all exogenous variables and the structural errors, u_1 and u_2)? The condition is the same as that in (16.13), namely, $\alpha_2 \alpha_1 \neq 1$. The proof is virtually identical to the simple model in Section 16-2. Under this assumption, reduced forms exist for y_1 and y_2.

The key question is: Under what assumptions can we estimate the parameters in, say, (16.17)? This is the identification issue. The **rank condition** for identification of equation (16.17) is easy to state.

Rank Condition for Identification of a Structural Equation.

The first equation in a two-equation simultaneous equations model is identified if, and only if, the *second* equation contains at least one exogenous variable (with a nonzero coefficient) that is excluded from the first equation.

This is the necessary and sufficient condition for equation (16.17) to be identified. The **order condition**, which we discussed in Chapter 15, is necessary for the rank condition. The order condition for identifying the first equation states that at least one exogenous variable is excluded from this equation. The order condition is trivial to check once both equations have been specified. The rank condition requires more: at least one of the exogenous variables excluded from the first equation must have a nonzero population coefficient in the second equation. This ensures that at least one of the exogenous variables omitted from the first equation actually appears in the reduced form of y_2, so that we can use these variables as instruments for y_2. We can test this using a t or an F test, as in Chapter 15; some examples follow.

Identification of the second equation is, naturally, just the mirror image of the statement for the first equation. Also, if we write the equations as in the labor supply and demand example in Section 16-1—so that y_1 appears on the left-hand side in *both* equations, with y_2 on the right-hand side—the identification condition is identical.

EXAMPLE 16.3 **Labor Supply of Married, Working Women**

To illustrate the identification issue, consider labor supply for married women already in the workforce. In place of the demand function, we write the wage offer as a function of hours and the usual productivity variables. With the equilibrium condition imposed, the two structural equations are

$$hours = \alpha_1 \log(wage) + \beta_{10} + \beta_{11}educ + \beta_{12}age + \beta_{13}kidslt6$$
$$+ \beta_{14}nwifeinc + u_1 \qquad [16.19]$$

and

$$\log(wage) = \alpha_2 hours + \beta_{20} + \beta_{21}educ + \beta_{22}exper$$
$$+ \beta_{23}exper^2 + u_2. \qquad [16.20]$$

The variable *age* is the woman's age, in years, *kidslt6* is the number of children less than six years old, *nwifeinc* is the woman's nonwage income (which includes husband's earnings), and *educ* and *exper* are years of education and prior experience, respectively. All variables except *hours* and $\log(wage)$ are assumed to be exogenous. (This is a tenuous assumption, as *educ* might be correlated with omitted ability in either equation. But for illustration purposes, we ignore the omitted ability problem.) The functional form in this system—where *hours* appears in level form but *wage* is in logarithmic form—is popular in labor economics. We can write this system as in equations (16.17) and (16.18) by defining $y_1 = hours$ and $y_2 = \log(wage)$.

The first equation is the supply function. It satisfies the order condition because two exogenous variables, *exper* and $exper^2$, are omitted from the labor supply equation. These exclusion restrictions are crucial assumptions: we are assuming that, once wage, education, age, number of small children, and other income are controlled for, past experience has no effect on current labor supply. One could certainly question this assumption, but we use it for illustration.

Given equations (16.19) and (16.20), the rank condition for identifying the first equation is that at least one of *exper* and $exper^2$ has a nonzero coefficient in equation (16.20). If $\beta_{22} = 0$ and $\beta_{23} = 0$, there are no exogenous variables appearing in the second equation that do not also appear in the first (*educ* appears in both). We can state the rank condition for identification of (16.19) equivalently in terms of the reduced form for $\log(wage)$, which is

$$\log(wage) = \pi_{20} + \pi_{21}educ + \pi_{22}age + \pi_{23}kidslt6$$
$$+ \pi_{24}nwifeinc + \pi_{25}exper + \pi_{26}exper^2 + v_2. \qquad [16.21]$$

For identification, we need $\pi_{25} \neq 0$ or $\pi_{26} \neq 0$, something we can test using a standard F statistic, as we discussed in Chapter 15.

The wage offer equation, (16.20), is identified if at least one of *age*, *kidslt6*, or *nwifeinc* has a nonzero coefficient in (16.19). This is identical to assuming that the reduced form for *hours*—which has the same form as the right-hand side of (16.21)—depends on at least one of *age*, *kidslt6*, or *nwifeinc*. In specifying the wage offer equation, we are *assuming* that *age*, *kidslt6*, and *nwifeinc* have no effect on the offered wage, once hours, education, and experience are accounted for. These would be poor assumptions if these variables somehow have direct effects on productivity, or if women are discriminated against based on their age or number of small children.

In Example 16.3, we take the population of interest to be married women who are in the workforce (so that equilibrium hours are positive). This excludes the group of married women who choose not to work outside the home. Including such women in the model raises some difficult problems. For instance, if a woman does not work, we cannot observe her wage offer. We touch on these issues in Chapter 17; but for now, we must think of equations (16.19) and (16.20) as holding only for women who have *hours* > 0.

EXAMPLE 16.4   **Inflation and Openness**

Romer (1993) proposes theoretical models of inflation that imply that more "open" countries should have lower inflation rates. His empirical analysis explains average annual inflation rates (since 1973) in terms of the average share of imports in gross domestic (or national) product since 1973—which is his measure of openness. In addition to estimating the key equation by OLS, he uses instrumental variables. While Romer does not specify both equations in a simultaneous system, he has in mind a two-equation system:

$$inf = \beta_{10} + \alpha_1 open + \beta_{11}\log(pcinc) + u_1 \qquad [16.22]$$

$$open = \beta_{20} + \alpha_2 inf + \beta_{21}\log(pcinc) + \beta_{22}\log(land) + u_2, \qquad [16.23]$$

where *pcinc* is 1980 per capita income, in U.S. dollars (assumed to be exogenous), and *land* is the land area of the country, in square miles (also assumed to be exogenous). Equation (16.22) is the one of interest, with the hypothesis that $\alpha_1 < 0$. (More open economies have lower inflation rates.) The second equation reflects the fact that the degree of openness might depend on the average inflation rate, as well as other factors. The variable $\log(pcinc)$ appears in both equations, but $\log(land)$ is *assumed* to appear only in the second equation. The idea is that, ceteris paribus, a smaller country is likely to be more open (so $\beta_{22} < 0$).

> **EXPLORING FURTHER 16.2**
>
> If we have money supply growth since 1973 for each country, which we assume is exogenous, does this help identify equation (16.23)?

Using the identification rule that was stated earlier, equation (16.22) is identified, provided $\beta_{22} \neq 0$. Equation (16.23) is *not* identified because it contains both exogenous variables. But we are interested in (16.22).

16-3b Estimation by 2SLS

Once we have determined that an equation is identified, we can estimate it by two stage least squares. The instrumental variables consist of the exogenous variables appearing in either equation.

EXAMPLE 16.5   **Labor Supply of Married, Working Women**

We use the data on working, married women in MROZ to estimate the labor supply equation (16.19) by 2SLS. The full set of instruments includes *educ*, *age*, *kidslt6*, *nwifeinc*, *exper*, and $exper^2$. The estimated labor supply curve is

$$\widehat{hours} = 2{,}225.66 + 1{,}639.56\log(wage) - 183.75\,educ$$
$$\qquad\quad (574.56) \quad\ (470.58) \qquad\qquad (59.10)$$
$$\qquad - 7.81\,age - 198.15\,kidslt6 - 10.17\,nwifeinc \qquad [16.24]$$
$$\qquad (9.38) \qquad (182.93) \qquad\quad (6.61)$$
$$n = 428,$$

where the reported standard errors are computed using a degrees-of-freedom adjustment. This equation shows that the labor supply curve slopes upward. The estimated coefficient on log(*wage*) has the following interpretation: holding other factors fixed, $\widehat{\Delta hours} \approx 16.4(\%\Delta wage)$. We can calculate labor supply elasticities by multiplying both sides of this last equation by 100/*hours*:

$$100 \cdot (\widehat{\Delta hours}/hours) \approx (1{,}640/hours)(\%\Delta wage)$$

or

$$\%\widehat{\Delta hours} \approx (1{,}640/hours)(\%\Delta wage),$$

which implies that the labor supply elasticity (with respect to wage) is simply 1,640/*hours*. [The elasticity is not constant in this model because *hours*, not log(*hours*), is the dependent variable in (16.24).] At the average hours worked, 1,303, the estimated elasticity is 1,640/ 1,303 $\approx$ 1.26, which implies a greater than 1% increase in hours worked given a 1% increase in wage. This is a large estimated elasticity. At higher hours, the elasticity will be smaller; at lower hours, such as *hours* = 800, the elasticity is over two.

For comparison, when (16.19) is estimated by OLS, the coefficient on log(*wage*) is -2.05 (se = 54.88), which implies no wage effect on hours worked. To confirm that log(*wage*) is in fact endogenous in (16.19), we can carry out the test from Section 15-5. When we add the reduced form residuals $\hat{v}_2$ to the equation and estimate by OLS, the t statistic on $\hat{v}_2$ is -6.61, which is very significant, and so log(*wage*) appears to be endogenous.

The wage offer equation (16.20) can also be estimated by 2SLS. The result is

$$\widehat{\log(wage)} = -.656 + .00013\ hours + .110\ educ$$

$$(.338)\ (.00025)\qquad (.016)$$

$$+ .035\ exper - .00071\ exper^2 \qquad\qquad \text{[16.25]}$$

$$(.019)\qquad\quad (.00045)$$

$$n = 428.$$

This differs from previous wage equations in that *hours* is included as an explanatory variable and 2SLS is used to account for endogeneity of *hours* (and we assume that *educ* and *exper* are exogenous). The coefficient on *hours* is statistically insignificant, which means that there is no evidence that the wage offer increases with hours worked. The other coefficients are similar to what we get by dropping *hours* and estimating the equation by OLS.

Estimating the effect of openness on inflation by instrumental variables is also straightforward.

EXAMPLE 16.6   **Inflation and Openness**

Before we estimate (16.22) using the data in OPENNESS, we check to see whether *open* has sufficient partial correlation with the proposed IV, log(*land*). The reduced form regression is

$$\widehat{open} = 117.08 + .546\log(pcinc) - 7.57\log(land)$$

$$(15.85)(1.493)\qquad\qquad (.81)$$

$$n = 114, R^2 = .449.$$

The t statistic on log(*land*) is over nine in absolute value, which verifies Romer's assertion that smaller countries are more open. The fact that log(*pcinc*) is so insignificant in this regression is irrelevant.

Estimating (16.22) using log(*land*) as an IV for *open* gives

$$\widehat{inf} = 26.90 - .337\,open + .376\log(pcinc)$$
$$\quad\quad\;\; (15.40)\;\; (.144)\quad\quad (2.015)$$

[16.26]

$$n = 114.$$

EXPLORING FURTHER 16.3

How would you test whether the difference between the OLS and IV estimates on *open* are statistically different?

The coefficient on *open* is statistically significant at about the 1% level against a one-sided alternative $(\alpha_1 < 0)$. The effect is economically important as well: for every percentage point increase in the import share of GDP, annual inflation is about one-third of a percentage point lower. For comparison, the OLS estimate is $-.215$ (se $= .095$).

16-4 Systems with More Than Two Equations

Simultaneous equations models can consist of more than two equations. Studying general identification of these models is difficult and requires matrix algebra. Once an equation in a general system has been shown to be identified, it can be estimated by 2SLS.

16-4a Identification in Systems with Three or More Equations

We will use a three-equation system to illustrate the issues that arise in the identification of complicated SEMs. With intercepts suppressed, write the model as

$$y_1 = \alpha_{12}y_2 + \alpha_{13}y_3 + \beta_{11}z_1 + u_1$$ [16.27]

$$y_2 = \alpha_{21}y_1 + \beta_{21}z_1 + \beta_{22}z_2 + \beta_{23}z_3 + u_2$$ [16.28]

$$y_3 = \alpha_{32}y_2 + \beta_{31}z_1 + \beta_{32}z_2 + \beta_{33}z_3 + \beta_{34}z_4 + u_3,$$ [16.29]

where the y_g are the endogenous variables and the z_j are exogenous. The first subscript on the parameters indicates the equation number, and the second indicates the variable number; we use α for parameters on endogenous variables and β for parameters on exogenous variables.

Which of these equations can be estimated? It is generally difficult to show that an equation in an SEM with more than two equations is identified, but it is easy to see when certain equations are *not* identified. In system (16.27) through (16.29), we can easily see that (16.29) falls into this category. Because every exogenous variable appears in this equation, we have no IVs for y_2. Therefore, we cannot consistently estimate the parameters of this equation. For the reasons we discussed in Section 16-2, OLS estimation will not usually be consistent.

What about equation (16.27)? Things look promising because z_2, z_3, and z_4 are all excluded from the equation—this is another example of *exclusion restrictions*. Although there are two endogenous variables in this equation, we have three potential IVs for y_2 and y_3. Therefore, equation (16.27) passes the order condition. For completeness, we state the order condition for general SEMs.

Order Condition for Identification. An equation in any SEM satisfies the order condition for identification if the number of *excluded* exogenous variables from the equation is at least as large as the number of right-hand side endogenous variables.

The second equation, (16.28), also passes the order condition because there is one excluded exogenous variable, z_4, and one right-hand side endogenous variable, y_1.

As we discussed in Chapter 15 and in the previous section, the order condition is only necessary, not sufficient, for identification. For example, if $\beta_{34} = 0$, z_4 appears nowhere in the system, which means it is not correlated with y_1, y_2, or y_3. If $\beta_{34} = 0$, then the second equation is not identified, because z_4 is useless as an IV for y_1. This again illustrates that identification of an equation depends on the values of the parameters (which we can never know for sure) in the other equations.

There are many subtle ways that identification can fail in complicated SEMs. To obtain sufficient conditions, we need to extend the rank condition for identification in two-equation systems. This is possible, but it requires matrix algebra [see, for example, Wooldridge (2010, Chapter 9)]. In many applications, one assumes that, unless there is obviously failure of identification, an equation that satisfies the order condition is identified.

The nomenclature on overidentified and just identified equations from Chapter 15 originated with SEMs. In terms of the order condition, (16.27) is an **overidentified equation** because we need only two IVs (for y_2 and y_3) but we have three available (z_2, z_3, and z_4); there is one overidentifying restriction in this equation. In general, the number of overidentifying restrictions equals the total number of exogenous variables in the system minus the total number of explanatory variables in the equation. These can be tested using the overidentification test from Section 15-5. Equation (16.28) is a **just identified equation**, and the third equation is an **unidentified equation**.

16-4b Estimation

Regardless of the number of equations in an SEM, each identified equation can be estimated by 2SLS. The instruments for a particular equation consist of the exogenous variables appearing anywhere in the system. Tests for endogeneity, heteroskedasticity, serial correlation, and overidentifying restrictions can be obtained, just as in Chapter 15.

It turns out that, when any system with two or more equations is correctly specified and certain additional assumptions hold, *system estimation methods* are generally more efficient than estimating each equation by 2SLS. The most common system estimation method in the context of SEMs is *three stage least squares*. These methods, with or without endogenous explanatory variables, are beyond the scope of this text. [See, for example, Wooldridge (2010, Chapters 7 and 8).]

16-5 Simultaneous Equations Models with Time Series

Among the earliest applications of SEMs was estimation of large systems of simultaneous equations that were used to describe a country's economy. A simple Keynesian model of aggregate demand (that ignores exports and imports) is

$$C_t = \beta_0 + \beta_1(Y_t - T_t) + \beta_2 r_t + u_{t1} \qquad [16.30]$$

$$I_t = \gamma_0 + \gamma_1 r_t + u_{t2} \qquad [16.31]$$

$$Y_t \equiv C_t + I_t + G_t, \qquad [16.32]$$

where

$$C_t = \text{consumption,}$$
$$Y_t = \text{income,}$$
$$T_t = \text{tax receipts,}$$
$$r_t = \text{the interest rate,}$$
$$I_t = \text{investment, and}$$
$$G_t = \text{government spending.}$$

[See, for example, Mankiw (1994, Chapter 9).] For concreteness, assume t represents year.

The first equation is an aggregate consumption function, where consumption depends on disposable income, the interest rate, and the unobserved structural error u_{t1}. The second equation is a very simple investment function. Equation (16.32) is an *identity* that is a result of national income accounting: it holds by definition, without error. Thus, there is no sense in which we estimate (16.32), but we need this equation to round out the model.

Because there are three equations in the system, there must also be three endogenous variables. Given the first two equations, it is clear that we intend for C_t and I_t to be endogenous. In addition, because of the accounting identity, Y_t is endogenous. We would assume, at least in this model, that T_t, r_t, and G_t are exogenous, so that they are uncorrelated with u_{t1} and u_{t2}. (We will discuss problems with this kind of assumption later.)

If r_t is exogenous, then OLS estimation of equation (16.31) is natural. The consumption function, however, depends on disposable income, which is endogenous because Y_t is. We have two instruments available under the maintained exogeneity assumptions: T_t and G_t. Therefore, if we follow our prescription for estimating cross-sectional equations, we would estimate (16.30) by 2SLS using instruments (T_t, G_t, r_t).

Models such as (16.30) through (16.32) are seldom estimated now, for several good reasons. First, it is very difficult to justify, at an aggregate level, the assumption that taxes, interest rates, and government spending are exogenous. Taxes clearly depend directly on income; for example, with a single marginal income tax rate τ_t in year t, $T_t = \tau_t Y_t$. We can easily allow this by replacing $(Y_t - T_t)$ with $(1 - \tau_t)Y_t$ in (16.30), and we can still estimate the equation by 2SLS if we assume that government spending is exogenous. We could also add the tax rate to the instrument list, if it is exogenous. But are government spending and tax rates really exogenous? They certainly could be in principle, if the government sets spending and tax rates independently of what is happening in the economy. But it is a difficult case to make in reality: government spending generally depends on the level of income, and at high levels of income, the same tax receipts are collected for lower marginal tax rates. In addition, assuming that interest rates are exogenous is extremely questionable. We could specify a more realistic model that includes money demand and supply, and then interest rates could be jointly determined with C_t, I_t, and Y_t. But then finding enough exogenous variables to identify the equations becomes quite difficult (and the following problems with these models still pertain).

Some have argued that certain components of government spending, such as defense spending—see, for example, Hall (1988) and Ramey (1991)—are exogenous in a variety of simultaneous equations applications. But this is not universally agreed upon, and, in any case, defense spending is not always appropriately correlated with the endogenous explanatory variables [see Shea (1993) for discussion and Computer Exercises C6 for an example].

A second problem with a model such as (16.30) through (16.32) is that it is completely static. Especially with monthly or quarterly data, but even with annual data, we often expect adjustment lags. (One argument in favor of static Keynesian-type models is that they are intended to describe the long run without worrying about short-run dynamics.) Allowing dynamics is not very difficult. For example, we could add lagged income to equation (16.31):

$$I_t = \gamma_0 + \gamma_1 r_t + \gamma_2 Y_{t-1} + u_{t2}. \qquad [16.33]$$

In other words, we add a **lagged endogenous variable** (but not I_{t-1}) to the investment equation. Can we treat Y_{t-1} as exogenous in this equation? Under certain assumptions on u_{t2}, the answer is yes. But we typically call a lagged endogenous variable in an SEM a **predetermined variable**. Lags of exogenous variables are also predetermined. If we assume that u_{t2} is uncorrelated with current exogenous variables (which is standard) and all *past* endogenous and exogenous variables, then Y_{t-1} is uncorrelated with u_{t2}. Given exogeneity of r_t, we can estimate (16.33) by OLS.

If we add lagged consumption to (16.30), we can treat C_{t-1} as exogenous in this equation under the same assumptions on u_{t1} that we made for u_{t2} in the previous paragraph. Current disposable income is still endogenous in

$$C_t = \beta_0 + \beta_1(Y_t - T_t) + \beta_2 r_t + \beta_3 C_{t-1} + u_{t1}, \qquad [16.34]$$

so we could estimate this equation by 2SLS using instruments (T_t, G_t, r_t, C_{t-1}); if investment is determined by (16.33), Y_{t-1} should be added to the instrument list. [To see why, use (16.32), (16.33), and (16.34) to find the reduced form for Y_t in terms of the exogenous and predetermined variables: T_t, r_t, G_t, C_{t-1}, and Y_{t-1}. Because Y_{t-1} shows up in this reduced form, it should be used as an IV.]

The presence of dynamics in aggregate SEMs is, at least for the purposes of forecasting, a clear improvement over static SEMs. But there are still some important problems with estimating SEMs using aggregate time series data, some of which we discussed in Chapters 11 and 15. Recall that the validity of the usual OLS or 2SLS inference procedures in time series applications hinges on the notion of *weak dependence*. Unfortunately, series such as aggregate consumption, income, investment, and even interest rates seem to violate the weak dependence requirements. (In the terminology of Chapter 11, they have *unit roots*.) These series also tend to have exponential trends, although this can be partly overcome by using the logarithmic transformation and assuming different functional forms. Generally, even the large sample, let alone the small sample, properties of OLS and 2SLS are complicated and dependent on various assumptions when they are applied to equations with I(1) variables. We will briefly touch on these issues in Chapter 18. An advanced, general treatment is given by Hamilton (1994).

Does the previous discussion mean that SEMs are not usefully applied to time series data? Not at all. The problems with trends and high persistence can be avoided by specifying systems in first differences or growth rates. But one should recognize that this is a different SEM than one specified in levels. [For example, if we specify consumption growth as a function of disposable income growth and interest rate changes, this is different from (16.30).] Also, as we discussed earlier, incorporating dynamics is not especially difficult. Finally, the problem of finding truly exogenous variables to include in SEMs is often easier with disaggregated data. For example, for manufacturing industries, Shea (1993) describes how output (or, more precisely, growth in output) in other industries can be used as an instrument in estimating supply functions. Ramey (1991) also has a convincing analysis of estimating industry cost functions by instrumental variables using time series data.

The next example shows how aggregate data can be used to test an important economic theory, the permanent income theory of consumption, usually called the *permanent income hypothesis* (PIH). The approach used in this example is not, strictly speaking, based on a simultaneous equations model, but we can think of consumption and income growth (as well as interest rates) as being jointly determined.

EXAMPLE 16.7 **Testing the Permanent Income Hypothesis**

Campbell and Mankiw (1990) used instrumental variables methods to test various versions of the PIH. We will use the annual data from 1959 through 1995 in CONSUMP to mimic one of their analyses. Campbell and Mankiw used quarterly data running through 1985.

One equation estimated by Campbell and Mankiw (using our notation) is

$$gc_t = \beta_0 + \beta_1 gy_t + \beta_2 r3_t + u_t, \qquad [16.35]$$

where

$gc_t = \Delta \log(c_t) =$ annual growth in real per capita consumption (excluding durables),

$gy_t =$ growth in real disposable income, and

$r3_t =$ the (ex post) real interest rate as measured by the return on three-month T-bill rates: $r3_t = i3_t - inf_t$, where the inflation rate is based on the Consumer Price Index.

The growth rates of consumption and disposable income are not trending, and they are weakly dependent; we will assume this is the case for $r3_t$ as well, so that we can apply standard asymptotic theory.

The key feature of equation (16.35) is that the PIH implies that the error term u_t has a zero mean conditional on all information observed at time $t-1$ or earlier: $E(u_t|I_{t-1}) = 0$. However, u_t is *not* necessarily uncorrelated with gy_t or $r3_t$; a traditional way to think about this is that these variables are jointly determined, but we are not writing down a full three-equation system.

Because u_t is uncorrelated with all variables dated $t - 1$ or earlier, valid instruments for estimating (16.35) are lagged values of gc, gy, and $r3$ (and lags of other observable variables, but we will not use those here). What are the hypotheses of interest? The pure form of the PIH has $\beta_1 = \beta_2 = 0$. Campbell and Mankiw argue that β_1 is positive if some fraction of the population consumes current income, rather than permanent income. The PIH with a nonconstant real interest rate implies that $\beta_2 > 0$.

When we estimate (16.35) by 2SLS, using instruments gc_{-1}, gy_{-1}, and $r3_{-1}$ for the endogenous variables gy_t and $r3_t$, we obtain

$$\widehat{gc_t} = .0081 + .586\, gy_t - .00027 r3_t$$
$$\qquad\quad (.0032) \quad (.135) \qquad (.00076) \qquad\qquad\qquad \textbf{[16.36]}$$
$$n = 35, R^2 = .678.$$

Therefore, the pure form of the PIH is strongly rejected because the coefficient on gy is economically large (a 1% increase in disposable income increases consumption by over .5%) and statistically significant ($t = 4.34$). By contrast, the real interest rate coefficient is very small and statistically insignificant. These findings are qualitatively the same as Campbell and Mankiw's.

The PIH also implies that the errors $\{u_t\}$ are serially uncorrelated. After 2SLS estimation, we obtain the residuals, $\hat{u}_t$, and include $\hat{u}_{t-1}$ as an additional explanatory variable in (16.36); we still use instruments gc_{t-1}, gy_{t-1}, $r3_{t-1}$, and $\hat{u}_{t-1}$ acts as its own instrument (see Section 15-7). The coefficient on $\hat{u}_{t-1}$ is $\hat{\rho} = .187$ (se = .133), so there is some evidence of positive serial correlation, although not at the 5% significance level. Campbell and Mankiw discuss why, with the available quarterly data, positive serial correlation might be found in the errors even if the PIH holds; some of those concerns carry over to annual data.

> **EXPLORING FURTHER 16.4**
>
> Suppose that for a particular city you have monthly data on per capita consumption of fish, per capita income, the price of fish, and the prices of chicken and beef; income and chicken and beef prices are exogenous. Assume that there is no seasonality in the demand function for fish, but there is in the supply of fish. How can you use this information to estimate a constant elasticity demand-for-fish equation? Specify an equation and discuss identification. (*Hint*: You should have 11 instrumental variables for the price of fish.)

Using growth rates of trending or I(1) variables in SEMs is fairly common in time series applications. For example, Shea (1993) estimates industry supply curves specified in terms of growth rates.

If a structural model contains a time trend—which may capture exogenous, trending factors that are not directly modeled—then the trend acts as its own IV.

16-6 Simultaneous Equations Models with Panel Data

Simultaneous equations models also arise in panel data contexts. For example, we can imagine estimating labor supply and wage offer equations, as in Example 16.3, for a group of people working over a given period of time. In addition to allowing for simultaneous determination of variables within each time period, we can allow for unobserved effects in each equation. In a labor supply function, it would be useful to allow an unobserved taste for leisure that does not change over time.

The basic approach to estimating SEMs with panel data involves two steps: (1) eliminate the unobserved effects from the equations of interest using the fixed effects transformation or first differencing and (2) find instrumental variables for the endogenous variables in the transformed equation. This can be very challenging because, for a convincing analysis, we need to find instruments that change over time. To see why, write an SEM for panel data as

$$y_{it1} = \alpha_1 y_{it2} + \mathbf{z}_{it1}\boldsymbol{\beta}_1 + a_{i1} + u_{it1} \qquad [16.37]$$

$$y_{it2} = \alpha_2 y_{it1} + \mathbf{z}_{it2}\boldsymbol{\beta}_2 + a_{i2} + u_{it2}, \qquad [16.38]$$

where i denotes cross section, t denotes time period, and $\mathbf{z}_{it1}\boldsymbol{\beta}_1$ or $\mathbf{z}_{it2}\boldsymbol{\beta}_2$ denotes linear functions of a set of exogenous explanatory variables in each equation. The most general analysis allows the unobserved effects, a_{i1} and a_{i2}, to be correlated with *all* explanatory variables, even the elements in z. However, we assume that the idiosyncratic structural errors, u_{it1} and u_{it2}, are uncorrelated with the **z** in both equations and across all time periods; this is the sense in which the **z** are exogenous. Except under special circumstances, y_{it2} is correlated with u_{it1} and y_{it1} is correlated with u_{it2}.

Suppose we are interested in equation (16.37). We cannot estimate it by OLS, as the composite error $a_{i1} + u_{it1}$ is potentially correlated with all explanatory variables. Suppose we difference over time to remove the unobserved effect, a_{i1}:

$$\Delta y_{it1} = \alpha_1 \Delta y_{it2} + \Delta \mathbf{z}_{it1}\boldsymbol{\beta}_1 + \Delta u_{it1}. \qquad [16.39]$$

(As usual with differencing or time-demeaning, we can only estimate the effects of variables that change over time for at least some cross-sectional units.) Now, the error term in this equation is uncorrelated with $\Delta \mathbf{z}_{it1}$ by assumption. But Δy_{it2} and Δu_{it1} are possibly correlated. Therefore, we need an IV for Δy_{it2}.

As with the case of pure cross-sectional or pure time series data, possible IVs come from the *other* equation: elements in $\mathbf{z}_{it2}$ that are not also in $\mathbf{z}_{it1}$. In practice, we need *time-varying* elements in $\mathbf{z}_{it2}$ that are not also in $\mathbf{z}_{it1}$. This is because we need an instrument for Δy_{it2}, and a change in a variable from one period to the next is unlikely to be highly correlated with the *level* of exogenous variables. In fact, if we difference (16.38), we see that the natural IVs for Δy_{it2} are those elements in $\Delta \mathbf{z}_{it2}$ that are not also in $\Delta \mathbf{z}_{it1}$.

As an example of the problems that can arise, consider a panel data version of the labor supply function in Example 16.3. After differencing, suppose we have the equation

$$\Delta hours_{it} = \beta_0 + \alpha_1 \Delta \log(wage_{it}) + \Delta(other\ factors_{it}),$$

and we wish to use $\Delta exper_{it}$ as an instrument for $\Delta \log(wage_{it})$. The problem is that, because we are looking at people who work in every time period, $\Delta exper_{it} = 1$ for all i and t. (Each person gets another year of experience after a year passes.) We cannot use an IV that is the same value for all i and t, and so we must look elsewhere.

Often, participation in an experimental program can be used to obtain IVs in panel data contexts. In Example 15.10, we used receipt of job training grants as an IV for the change in hours of training in determining the effects of job training on worker productivity. In fact, we could view that in an SEM context: job training and worker productivity are jointly determined, but receiving a job training grant is exogenous in equation (15.57).

We can sometimes come up with clever, convincing instrumental variables in panel data applications, as the following example illustrates.

EXAMPLE 16.8 | **Effect of Prison Population on Violent Crime Rates**

In order to estimate the causal effect of prison population increases on crime rates at the state level, Levitt (1996) used instances of prison overcrowding litigation as instruments for the growth in prison population. The equation Levitt estimated is in first differences; we can write an underlying fixed effects model as

$$\log(crime_{it}) = \theta_t + \alpha_1 \log(prison_{it}) + \mathbf{z}_{it1}\boldsymbol{\beta}_1 + a_{i1} + u_{it1}, \qquad [16.40]$$

where θ_t denotes different time intercepts, and *crime* and *prison* are measured per 100,000 people. (The prison population variable is measured on the last day of the previous year.) The vector $\mathbf{z}_{it1}$ contains log of police per capita, log of income per capita, the unemployment rate, proportions of black and those living in metropolitan areas, and age distribution proportions.

Differencing (16.40) gives the equation estimated by Levitt:

$$\Delta\log(crime_{it}) = \xi_t + \alpha_1\Delta\log(prison_{it}) + \Delta\mathbf{z}_{it1}\boldsymbol{\beta}_1 + \Delta u_{it1}. \tag{16.41}$$

Simultaneity between crime rates and prison population, or more precisely in the growth rates, makes OLS estimation of (16.41) generally inconsistent. Using the violent crime rate and a subset of the data from Levitt (in PRISON, for the years 1980 through 1993, for $51 \cdot 14 = 714$ total observations), we obtain the pooled OLS estimate of α_1, which is $-.181$ (se $= .048$). We also estimate (16.41) by pooled 2SLS, where the instruments for $\Delta \log(prison)$ are two binary variables, one each for whether a final decision was reached on overcrowding litigation in the current year or in the previous two years. The pooled 2SLS estimate of α_1 is -1.032 (se $= .370$). Therefore, the 2SLS estimated effect is much larger; not surprisingly, it is much less precise, too. Levitt found similar results when using a longer time period (but with early observations missing for some states) and more instruments.

Testing for AR(1) serial correlation in $r_{it1} = \Delta u_{it1}$ is easy. After the pooled 2SLS estimation, obtain the residuals, $\hat{r}_{it1}$. Then, include one lag of these residuals in the original equation, and estimate the equation by 2SLS, where $\hat{r}_{it1}$ acts as its own instrument. The first year is lost because of the lagging. Then, the usual 2SLS t statistic on the lagged residual is a valid test for serial correlation. In Example 16.8, the coefficient on $\hat{r}_{it1}$ is only about .076 with $t = 1.67$. With such a small coefficient and modest t statistic, we can safely assume serial independence.

An alternative approach to estimating SEMs with panel data is to use the fixed effects transformation and then to apply an IV technique such as pooled 2SLS. A simple procedure is to estimate the time-demeaned equation by pooled 2SLS, which would look like

$$\ddot{y}_{it1} = \alpha_1\ddot{y}_{t2} + \ddot{\mathbf{z}}_{it1}\boldsymbol{\beta}_1 + \ddot{u}_{it1}, \quad t = 1, 2, \ldots, T, \tag{16.42}$$

where $\ddot{\mathbf{z}}_{it1}$ and $\ddot{\mathbf{z}}_{it2}$ are IVs. This is equivalent to using 2SLS in the dummy variable formulation, where the unit-specific dummy variables act as their own instruments. Ayres and Levitt (1998) applied 2SLS to a time-demeaned equation to estimate the effect of LoJack electronic theft prevention devices on car theft rates in cities. If (16.42) is estimated directly, then the *df* needs to be corrected to $N(T - 1) - k_1$, where k_1 is the total number of elements in α_1 and $\boldsymbol{\beta}_1$. Including unit-specific dummy variables and applying pooled 2SLS to the original data produces the correct *df*. A detailed treatment of 2SLS with panel data is given in Wooldridge (2010, Chapter 11).

Summary

Simultaneous equations models are appropriate when each equation in the system has a ceteris paribus interpretation. Good examples are when separate equations describe different sides of a market or the behavioral relationships of different economic agents. Supply and demand examples are leading cases, but there are many other applications of SEMs in economics and the social sciences.

An important feature of SEMs is that, by fully specifying the system, it is clear which variables are assumed to be exogenous and which ones appear in each equation. Given a full system, we are able to determine which equations can be identified (that is, can be estimated). In the important case of a two-equation system, identification of (say) the first equation is easy to state: at least one exogenous variable must be excluded from the first equation that appears with a nonzero coefficient in the second equation.

As we know from previous chapters, OLS estimation of an equation that contains an endogenous explanatory variable generally produces biased and inconsistent estimators. Instead, 2SLS can be used to estimate any identified equation in a system. More advanced system methods are available, but they are beyond the scope of our treatment.

The distinction between omitted variables and simultaneity in applications is not always sharp. Both problems, not to mention measurement error, can appear in the same equation. A good example is the labor supply of married women. Years of education (*educ*) appears in both the labor supply and the wage offer functions [see equations (16.19) and (16.20)]. If omitted ability is in the error term of the labor supply function, then wage and education are both endogenous. The important thing is that an equation estimated by 2SLS can stand on its own.

SEMs can be applied to time series data as well. As with OLS estimation, we must be aware of trending, integrated processes in applying 2SLS. Problems such as serial correlation can be handled as in Section 15-7. We also gave an example of how to estimate an SEM using panel data, where the equation is first differenced to remove the unobserved effect. Then, we can estimate the differenced equation by pooled 2SLS, just as in Chapter 15. Alternatively, in some cases, we can use time-demeaning of all variables, including the IVs, and then apply pooled 2SLS; this is identical to putting in dummies for each cross-sectional observation and using 2SLS, where the dummies act as their own instruments. SEM applications with panel data are very powerful, as they allow us to control for unobserved heterogeneity while dealing with simultaneity. They are becoming more and more common and are not especially difficult to estimate.

Key Terms

Endogenous Variables	Overidentified Equation	Simultaneity Bias
Exclusion Restrictions	Predetermined Variable	Simultaneous Equations
Exogenous Variables	Rank Condition	Model (SEM)
Identified Equation	Reduced Form Equation	Structural Equation
Just Identified Equation	Reduced Form Error	Structural Errors
Lagged Endogenous Variable	Reduced Form Parameters	Structural Parameters
Order Condition	Simultaneity	Unidentified Equation

Problems

1 Write a two-equation system in "supply and demand form," that is, with the same variable y_t (typically, "quantity") appearing on the left-hand side:

$$y_1 = \alpha_1 y_2 + \beta_1 z_1 + u_1$$
$$y_1 = \alpha_2 y_2 + \beta_2 z_2 + u_2.$$

(i) If $\alpha_1 = 0$ or $\alpha_2 = 0$, explain why a reduced form exists for y_1. (Remember, a reduced form expresses y_1 as a linear function of the exogenous variables and the structural errors.) If $\alpha_1 \neq 0$ and $\alpha_2 = 0$, find the reduced form for y_2.

(ii) If $\alpha_1 \neq 0$, $\alpha_2 \neq 0$, and $\alpha_1 \neq \alpha_2$, find the reduced form for y_1. Does y_2 have a reduced form in this case?

(iii) Is the condition $\alpha_1 \neq \alpha_2$ likely to be met in supply and demand examples? Explain.

2 Let *corn* denote per capita consumption of corn in bushels at the county level, let *price* be the price per bushel of corn, let *income* denote per capita county income, and let *rainfall* be inches of rainfall during the last corn-growing season. The following simultaneous equations model imposes the equilibrium condition that supply equals demand:

$$corn = \alpha_1 price + \beta_1 income + u_1$$
$$corn = \alpha_2 price + \beta_2 rainfall + \gamma_2 rainfall^2 + u_2.$$

Which is the supply equation, and which is the demand equation? Explain.

3 In Problem 3 of Chapter 3, we estimated an equation to test for a tradeoff between minutes per week spent sleeping (*sleep*) and minutes per week spent working (*totwrk*) for a random sample of individuals. We also included education and age in the equation. Because *sleep* and *totwrk* are jointly chosen by each individual, is the estimated tradeoff between sleeping and working subject to a "simultaneity bias" criticism? Explain.

4 Suppose that annual earnings and alcohol consumption are determined by the SEM

$$\log(earnings) = \beta_0 + \beta_1 alcohol + \beta_2 educ + u_1$$
$$alcohol = \gamma_0 + \gamma_1 \log(earnings) + \gamma_2 educ + \gamma_3 \log(price) + u_2,$$

where *price* is a local price index for alcohol, which includes state and local taxes. Assume that *educ* and *price* are exogenous. If β_1, β_2, γ_1, γ_2, and γ_3 are all different from zero, which equation is identified? How would you estimate that equation?

5 A simple model to determine the effectiveness of condom usage on reducing sexually transmitted diseases among sexually active high school students is

$$infrate = \beta_0 + \beta_1 conuse + \beta_2 percmale + \beta_3 avginc + \beta_4 city + u_1,$$

where

  $infrate$ = the percentage of sexually active students who have contracted venereal disease.

  $conuse$ = the percentage of boys who claim to use condoms regularly.

  $avginc$ = average family income.

  $city$ = a dummy variable indicating whether a school is in a city.

The model is at the school level.
  (i)   Interpreting the preceding equation in a causal, ceteris paribus fashion, what should be the sign of β_1?
  (ii) Why might *infrate* and *conuse* be jointly determined?
  (iii) If condom usage increases with the rate of venereal disease, so that $\gamma_1 > 0$ in the equation

$$conuse = \gamma_0 + \gamma_1 infrate + other\ factors,$$

    what is the likely bias in estimating β_1 by OLS?
  (iv) Let *condis* be a binary variable equal to unity if a school has a program to distribute condoms. Explain how this can be used to estimate β_1 (and the other betas) by IV. What do we have to assume about *condis* in each equation?

6 Consider a linear probability model for whether employers offer a pension plan based on the percentage of workers belonging to a union, as well as other factors:

$$pension = \beta_0 + \beta_1 percunion + \beta_2 avgage + \beta_3 avgeduc$$
$$+ \beta_4 percmale + \beta_5 percmarr + u_1.$$

  (i)   Why might *percunion* be jointly determined with *pension*?
  (ii) Suppose that you can survey workers at firms and collect information on workers' families. Can you think of information that can be used to construct an IV for *percunion*?
  (iii) How would you test whether your variable is at least a reasonable IV candidate for *percunion*?

7 For a large university, you are asked to estimate the demand for tickets to women's basketball games. You can collect time series data over 10 seasons, for a total of about 150 observations. One possible model is

$$lATTEND_t = \beta_0 + \beta_1 lPRICE_t + \beta_2 WINPERC_t + \beta_3 RIVAL_t$$
$$+ \beta_4 WEEKEND_t + \beta_5 t + u_t,$$

where

$$PRICE_t = \text{the price of admission, probably measured in real terms—say,}$$
$$\text{deflating by a regional consumer price index.}$$

$$WINPERC_t = \text{the team's current winning percentage.}$$

$$RIVAL_t = \text{a dummy variable indicating a game against a rival.}$$

$$WEEKEND_t = \text{a dummy variable indicating whether the game is on a weekend.}$$

The l denotes natural logarithm, so that the demand function has a constant price elasticity.
(i)   Why is it a good idea to have a time trend in the equation?
(ii) The supply of tickets is fixed by the stadium capacity; assume this has not changed over the 10 years. This means that quantity supplied does not vary with price. Does this mean that price is necessarily exogenous in the demand equation? (*Hint*: The answer is no.)
(iii) Suppose that the nominal price of admission changes slowly—say, at the beginning of each season. The athletic office chooses price based partly on last season's average attendance, as well as last season's team success. Under what assumptions is last season's winning percentage $(SEASPERC_{t-1})$ a valid instrumental variable for $lPRICE_t$?
(iv) Does it seem reasonable to include the (log of the) real price of men's basketball games in the equation? Explain. What sign does economic theory predict for its coefficient? Can you think of another variable related to men's basketball that might belong in the women's attendance equation?
(v)   If you are worried that some of the series, particularly $lATTEND$ and $lPRICE$, have unit roots, how might you change the estimated equation?
(vi) If some games are sold out, what problems does this cause for estimating the demand function? (*Hint*: If a game is sold out, do you necessarily observe the true demand?)

8 How big is the effect of per-student school expenditures on local housing values? Let $HPRICE$ be the median housing price in a school district and let $EXPEND$ be per-student expenditures. Using panel data for the years 1992, 1994, and 1996, we postulate the model

$$lHPRICE_{it} = \theta_t + \beta_1 lEXPEND_{it} + \beta_2 lPOLICE_{it} + \beta_3 lMEDINC_{it}$$
$$+ \beta_4 PROPTAX_{it} + a_{i1} + u_{it1},$$

where $POLICE_{it}$ is per capita police expenditures, $MEDINC_{it}$ is median income, and $PROPTAX_{it}$ is the property tax rate; l denotes natural logarithm. Expenditures and housing price are simultaneously determined because the value of homes directly affects the revenues available for funding schools.

Suppose that, in 1994, the way schools were funded was drastically changed: rather than being raised by local property taxes, school funding was largely determined at the state level. Let $lSTATEALL_{it}$ denote the log of the state allocation for district i in year t, which is exogenous in the preceding equation, once we control for expenditures and a district fixed effect. How would you estimate the β_j?

Computer Exercises

C1 Use SMOKE for this exercise.
(i)   A model to estimate the effects of smoking on annual income (perhaps through lost work days due to illness, or productivity effects) is

$$\log(income) = \beta_0 + \beta_1 cigs + \beta_2 educ + \beta_3 age + \beta_4 age^2 + u_1,$$

where *cigs* is number of cigarettes smoked per day, on average. How do you interpret β_1?

(ii) To reflect the fact that cigarette consumption might be jointly determined with income, a demand for cigarettes equation is

$$cigs = \gamma_0 + \gamma_1 \log(income) + \gamma_2 educ + \gamma_3 age + \gamma_4 age^2$$
$$+ \gamma_5 \log(cigpric) + \gamma_6 restaurn + u_2,$$

where *cigpric* is the price of a pack of cigarettes (in cents) and *restaurn* is a binary variable equal to unity if the person lives in a state with restaurant smoking restrictions. Assuming these are exogenous to the individual, what signs would you expect for γ_5 and γ_6?

(iii) Under what assumption is the income equation from part (i) identified?

(iv) Estimate the income equation by OLS and discuss the estimate of β_1.

(v) Estimate the reduced form for *cigs*. (Recall that this entails regressing *cigs* on all exogenous variables.) Are $\log(cigpric)$ and *restaurn* significant in the reduced form?

(vi) Now, estimate the income equation by 2SLS. Discuss how the estimate of β_1 compares with the OLS estimate.

(vii) Do you think that cigarette prices and restaurant smoking restrictions are exogenous in the income equation?

C2 Use MROZ for this exercise.

(i) Reestimate the labor supply function in Example 16.5, using $\log(hours)$ as the dependent variable. Compare the estimated elasticity (which is now constant) to the estimate obtained from equation (16.24) at the average hours worked.

(ii) In the labor supply equation from part (i), allow *educ* to be endogenous because of omitted ability. Use *motheduc* and *fatheduc* as IVs for *educ*. Remember, you now have two endogenous variables in the equation.

(iii) Test the overidentifying restrictions in the 2SLS estimation from part (ii). Do the IVs pass the test?

C3 Use the data in OPENNESS for this exercise.

(i) Because $\log(pcinc)$ is insignificant in both (16.22) and the reduced form for *open*, drop it from the analysis. Estimate (16.22) by OLS and IV without $\log(pcinc)$. Do any important conclusions change?

(ii) Still leaving $\log(pcinc)$ out of the analysis, is *land* or $\log(land)$ a better instrument for *open*? (*Hint*: Regress *open* on each of these separately and jointly.)

(iii) Now, return to (16.22). Add the dummy variable *oil* to the equation and treat it as exogenous. Estimate the equation by IV. Does being an oil producer have a ceteris paribus effect on inflation?

C4 Use the data in CONSUMP for this exercise.

(i) In Example 16.7, use the method from Section 15-5 to test the single overidentifying restriction in estimating (16.35). What do you conclude?

(ii) Campbell and Mankiw (1990) use *second* lags of all variables as IVs because of potential data measurement problems and informational lags. Reestimate (16.35), using only gc_{t-2}, gy_{t-2}, and $r3_{t-2}$ as IVs. How do the estimates compare with those in (16.36)?

(iii) Regress gy_t on the IVs from part (ii) and test whether gy_t is sufficiently correlated with them. Why is this important?

C5 Use the *Economic Report of the President* (2005 or later) to update the data in CONSUMP, at least through 2003. Reestimate equation (16.35). Do any important conclusions change?

C6 Use the data in CEMENT for this exercise.

(i) A static (inverse) supply function for the monthly growth in cement price (*gprc*) as a function of growth in quantity (*gcem*) is

$$gprc_t = \alpha_1 gcem_t + \beta_0 + \beta_1 gprcpet + \beta_2 feb_t + \ldots + \beta_{12} dec_t + u_t^s,$$

where *gprcpet* (growth in the price of petroleum) is assumed to be exogenous and *feb*, ..., *dec* are monthly dummy variables. What signs do you expect for α_1 and β_1? Estimate the equation by OLS. Does the supply function slope upward?

(ii) The variable *gdefs* is the monthly growth in real defense spending in the United States. What do you need to assume about *gdefs* for it to be a good IV for *gcem*? Test whether *gcem* is partially correlated with *gdefs*. (Do not worry about possible serial correlation in the reduced form.) Can you use *gdefs* as an IV in estimating the supply function?

(iii) Shea (1993) argues that the growth in output of residential (*gres*) and nonresidential (*gnon*) construction are valid instruments for *gcem*. The idea is that these are demand shifters that should be roughly uncorrelated with the supply error u_t^s. Test whether *gcem* is partially correlated with *gres* and *gnon*; again, do not worry about serial correlation in the reduced form.

(iv) Estimate the supply function, using *gres* and *gnon* as IVs for *gcem*. What do you conclude about the static supply function for cement? [The dynamic supply function is, apparently, upward sloping; see Shea (1993).]

C7 Refer to Example 13.9 and the data in CRIME4,

(i) Suppose that, after differencing to remove the unobserved effect, you think $\Delta\log(polpc)$ is simultaneously determined with $\Delta\log(crmrte)$; in particular, increases in crime are associated with increases in police officers. How does this help to explain the positive coefficient on $\Delta\log(polpc)$ in equation (13.33)?

(ii) The variable *taxpc* is the taxes collected per person in the county. Does it seem reasonable to exclude this from the crime equation?

(iii) Estimate the reduced form for $\Delta\log(polpc)$ using pooled OLS, including the potential IV, $\Delta\log(taxpc)$. Does it look like $\Delta\log(taxpc)$ is a good IV candidate? Explain.

(iv) Suppose that, in several of the years, the state of North Carolina awarded grants to some counties to increase the size of their county police force. How could you use this information to estimate the effect of additional police officers on the crime rate?

C8 Use the data set in FISH, which comes from Graddy (1995), to do this exercise. The data set is also used in Computer Exercise C9 in Chapter 12. Now, we will use it to estimate a demand function for fish.

(i) Assume that the demand equation can be written, in equilibrium for each time period, as

$$\log(totqty_t) = \alpha_1\log(avgprc_t) + \beta_{10} + \beta_{11}mon_t + \beta_{12}tues_t$$
$$+ \beta_{13}wed_t + \beta_{14}thurs_t + u_{t1},$$

so that demand is allowed to differ across days of the week. Treating the price variable as endogenous, what additional information do we need to estimate the demand-equation parameters consistently?

(ii) The variables $wave2_t$ and $wave3_t$ are measures of ocean wave heights over the past several days. What two assumptions do we need to make in order to use $wave2_t$ and $wave3_t$ as IVs for $\log(avgprc_t)$ in estimating the demand equation?

(iii) Regress $\log(avgprc_t)$ on the day-of-the-week dummies and the two wave measures. Are $wave2_t$ and $wave3_t$ jointly significant? What is the p-value of the test?

(iv) Now, estimate the demand equation by 2SLS. What is the 95% confidence interval for the price elasticity of demand? Is the estimated elasticity reasonable?

(v) Obtain the 2SLS residuals, $\hat{u}_{t1}$. Add a single lag, $\hat{u}_{t-1,1}$ in estimating the demand equation by 2SLS. Remember, use $\hat{u}_{t-1,1}$ as its own instrument. Is there evidence of AR(1) serial correlation in the demand equation errors?

(vi) Given that the supply equation evidently depends on the wave variables, what two assumptions would we need to make in order to estimate the price elasticity of supply?

(vii) In the reduced form equation for $\log(avgprc_t)$, are the day-of-the-week dummies jointly significant? What do you conclude about being able to estimate the supply elasticity?

C9 For this exercise, use the data in AIRFARE, but only for the year 1997.

(i) A simple demand function for airline seats on routes in the United States is

$$\log(passen) = \beta_{10} + \alpha_1 \log(fare) + \beta_{11} \log(dist) + \beta_{12}[\log(dist)]^2 + u_1,$$

where

$$passen = \text{average passengers per day,}$$
$$fare = \text{average airfare, and}$$
$$dist = \text{the route distance (in miles).}$$

If this is truly a demand function, what should be the sign of α_1?

(ii) Estimate the equation from part (i) by OLS. What is the estimated price elasticity?

(iii) Consider the variable *concen*, which is a measure of market concentration. (Specifically, it is the share of business accounted for by the largest carrier.) Explain in words what we must assume to treat *concen* as exogenous in the demand equation.

(iv) Now assume *concen* is exogenous to the demand equation. Estimate the reduced form for log(*fare*) and confirm that *concen* has a positive (partial) effect on log(*fare*).

(v) Estimate the demand function using IV. Now what is the estimated price elasticity of demand? How does it compare with the OLS estimate?

(vi) Using the IV estimates, describe how demand for seats depends on route distance.

C10 Use the entire panel data set in AIRFARE for this exercise. The demand equation in a simultaneous equations unobserved effects model is

$$\log(passen_{it}) = \theta_{t1} + \alpha_1 \log(fare_{it}) + a_{i1} + u_{it1},$$

where we absorb the distance variables into a_{i1}.

(i) Estimate the demand function using fixed effects, being sure to include year dummies to account for the different intercepts. What is the estimated elasticity?

(ii) Use fixed effects to estimate the reduced form

$$\log(fare_{it}) = \theta_{t2} + \pi_{21} concen_{it} + a_{i2} + v_{it2}.$$

Perform the appropriate test to ensure that $concen_{it}$ can be used as an IV for $\log(fare_{it})$.

(iii) Now estimate the demand function using the fixed effects transformation along with IV, as in equation (16.42). What is the estimated elasticity? Is it statistically significant?

C11 A common method for estimating *Engel curves* is to model expenditure shares as a function of total expenditure, and possibly demographic variables. A common specification has the form

$$sgood = \beta_0 + \beta_1 ltotexpend + demographics + u,$$

where *sgood* is the fraction of spending on a particular good out of total expenditure and *ltotexpend* is the log of total expenditure. The sign and magnitude of β_1 are of interest across various expenditure categories.

To account for the potential endogeneity of *ltotexpend*—which can be viewed as an omitted variables or simultaneous equations problem, or both—the log of family income is often used as an instrumental variable. Let *lincome* denote the log of family income. For the remainder of this question, use the data in EXPENDSHARES, which comes from Blundell, Duncan, and Pendakur (1998).

(i) Use *sfood*, the share of spending on food, as the dependent variable. What is the range of values of *sfood*? Are you surprised there are no zeros?

(ii) Estimate the equation

$$sfood = \beta_0 + \beta_1 ltotexpend + \beta_2 age + \beta_3 kids + u \qquad [16.43]$$

by OLS and report the coefficient on *ltotexpend*, $\hat{\beta}_{OLS,1}$, along with its heteroskedasticity-robust standard error. Interpret the result.

(iii)   Using *lincome* as an IV for *ltotexpend*, estimate the reduced form equation for *ltotexpend*; be sure to include *age* and *kids*. Assuming *lincome* is exogenous in (16.43), is *lincome* a valid IV for *ltotexpend*?

(iv)   Now estimate (16.43) by instrumental variables. How does $\hat{\beta}_{IV,1}$ compare with $\hat{\beta}_{OLS,1}$? What about the robust 95% confidence intervals?

(v)   Use the test in Section 15-5 to test the null hypothesis that *ltotexpend* is exogenous in (16.43). Be sure to report and interpret the *p*-value. Are there any overidentifying restrictions to test?

(vi)   Substitute *salcohol* for *sfood* in (16.43) and estimate the equation by OLS and 2SLS. Now what do you find for the coefficients on *ltotexpend*?

CHAPTER 17

Limited Dependent Variable Models and Sample Selection Corrections

In Chapter 7, we studied the linear probability model, which is simply an application of the multiple regression model to a binary dependent variable. A binary dependent variable is an example of a **limited dependent variable (LDV)**. An LDV is broadly defined as a dependent variable whose range of values is substantively restricted. A binary variable takes on only two values, zero and one. In Section 7-7, we discussed the interpretation of multiple regression estimates for generally discrete response variables, focusing on the case where y takes on a small number of integer values—for example, the number of times a young man is arrested during a year or the number of children born to a woman. Elsewhere, we have encountered several other limited dependent variables, including the percentage of people participating in a pension plan (which must be between zero and 100) and college grade point average (which is between zero and 4.0 at most colleges).

Most economic variables we would like to explain are limited in some way, often because they must be positive. For example, hourly wage, housing price, and nominal interest rates must be greater than zero. But not all such variables need special treatment. If a strictly positive variable takes on many different values, a special econometric model is rarely necessary. When y is discrete and takes on a small number of values, it makes no sense to treat it as an approximately continuous variable. Discreteness of y does not in itself mean that linear models are inappropriate. However, as we saw in Chapter 7 for binary response, the linear probability model has certain drawbacks. In Section 17-1, we discuss logit and probit models, which overcome the shortcomings of the LPM; the disadvantage is that they are more difficult to interpret.

Other kinds of limited dependent variables arise in econometric analysis, especially when the behavior of individuals, families, or firms is being modeled. Optimizing behavior often leads to a **corner solution response** for some nontrivial fraction of the population. That is, it is optimal to choose a zero quantity or dollar value, for example. During any given year, a significant number of families will make zero charitable contributions. Therefore, annual family charitable contributions has a population distribution that is spread out over a large range of positive values, but with a pileup at the value zero. Although a linear model could be appropriate for capturing the expected value of charitable contributions, a linear model will likely lead to negative predictions for some families. Taking the natural log is not possible because many observations are zero. The Tobit model, which we cover in Section 17-2, is explicitly designed to model corner solution dependent variables.

Another important kind of LDV is a count variable, which takes on nonnegative integer values. Section 17-3 illustrates how Poisson regression models are well suited for modeling count variables.

In some cases, we encounter limited dependent variables due to data censoring, a topic we introduce in Section 17-4. The general problem of sample selection, where we observe a nonrandom sample from the underlying population, is treated in Section 17-5.

Limited dependent variable models can be used for time series and panel data, but they are most often applied to cross-sectional data. Sample selection problems are usually confined to cross-sectional or panel data. We focus on cross-sectional applications in this chapter. Wooldridge (2010) analyzes these problems in the context of panel data models and provides many more details for cross-sectional and panel data applications.

17-1 Logit and Probit Models for Binary Response

The linear probability model is simple to estimate and use, but it has some drawbacks that we discussed in Section 7-5. The two most important disadvantages are that the fitted probabilities can be less than zero or greater than one and the partial effect of any explanatory variable (appearing in level form) is constant. These limitations of the LPM can be overcome by using more sophisticated **binary response models**.

In a binary response model, interest lies primarily in the **response probability**

$$P(y = 1|\mathbf{x}) = P(y = 1|x_1, x_2, ..., x_k),$$
[17.1]

where we use $\mathbf{x}$ to denote the full set of explanatory variables. For example, when y is an employment indicator, $\mathbf{x}$ might contain various individual characteristics such as education, age, marital status, and other factors that affect employment status, including a binary indicator variable for participation in a recent job training program.

17-1a Specifying Logit and Probit Models

In the LPM, we assume that the response probability is linear in a set of parameters, β_j; see equation (7.27). To avoid the LPM limitations, consider a class of binary response models of the form

$$P(y = 1|\mathbf{x}) = G(\beta_0 + \beta_1 x_1 + ... + \beta_k x_k) = G(\beta_0 + \mathbf{x}\boldsymbol{\beta}),$$
[17.2]

where G is a function taking on values strictly between zero and one: $0 < G(z) < 1$, for all real numbers z. This ensures that the estimated response probabilities are strictly between zero and one. As in earlier chapters, we write $\mathbf{x}\boldsymbol{\beta} = \beta_1 x_1 + ... + \beta_k x_k$.

Various nonlinear functions have been suggested for the function G to make sure that the probabilities are between zero and one. The two we will cover here are used in the vast majority of applications (along with the LPM). In the **logit model**, G is the logistic function:

$$G(z) = \exp(z)/[1 + \exp(z)] = \Lambda(z), \qquad\qquad [17.3]$$

which is between zero and one for all real numbers z. This is the cumulative distribution function (cdf) for a standard logistic random variable. In the **probit model**, G is the standard normal cdf, which is expressed as an integral:

$$G(z) = \Phi(z) \equiv \int_{-\infty}^{z} \phi(v)dv, \qquad\qquad [17.4]$$

where $\phi(z)$ is the standard normal density

$$\phi(z) = (2\pi)^{-1/2}\exp(-z^2/2). \qquad\qquad [17.5]$$

This choice of G again ensures that (17.2) is strictly between zero and one for all values of the parameters and the x_j.

The G functions in (17.3) and (17.4) are both increasing functions. Each increases most quickly at $z = 0$, $G(z) \to 0$ as $z \to -\infty$, and $G(z) \to 1$ as $z \to \infty$. The logistic function is plotted in Figure 17.1. The standard normal cdf has a shape very similar to that of the logistic cdf.

Logit and probit models can be derived from an underlying **latent variable model**. Let y^* be an unobserved, or *latent*, variable, and suppose that

$$y^* = \beta_0 + \mathbf{x}\boldsymbol{\beta} + e, \; y = 1[y^* > 0], \qquad\qquad [17.6]$$

where we introduce the notation $1[\cdot]$ to define a binary outcome. The function $1[\cdot]$ is called the *indicator function*, which takes on the value one if the event in brackets is true, and zero otherwise. Therefore, y is one if $y^* > 0$, and y is zero if $y^* \leq 0$. We assume that e is independent of $\mathbf{x}$ and that e either has the standard logistic distribution or the standard normal distribution. In either case, e is

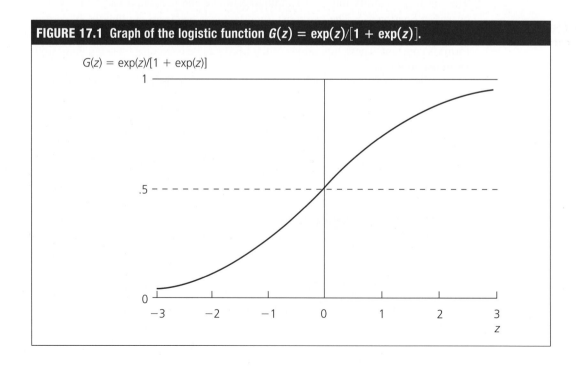

FIGURE 17.1 Graph of the logistic function $G(z) = \exp(z)/[1 + \exp(z)]$.

symmetrically distributed about zero, which means that $1 - G(-z) = G(z)$ for all real numbers z. Economists tend to favor the normality assumption for e, which is why the probit model is more popular than logit in econometrics. In addition, several specification problems, which we touch on later, are most easily analyzed using probit because of properties of the normal distribution.

From (17.6) and the assumptions given, we can derive the response probability for y:

$$P(y = 1|\mathbf{x}) = P(y^* > 0|\mathbf{x}) = P[e > -(\beta_0 + \mathbf{x}\boldsymbol{\beta})|\mathbf{x}]$$
$$= 1 - G[-(\beta_0 + \mathbf{x}\boldsymbol{\beta})] = G(\beta_0 + \mathbf{x}\boldsymbol{\beta}),$$

which is exactly the same as (17.2).

In most applications of binary response models, the primary goal is to explain the effects of the x_j on the response probability $P(y = 1|\mathbf{x})$. The latent variable formulation tends to give the impression that we are primarily interested in the effects of each x_j on y^*. As we will see, for logit and probit, the *direction* of the effect of x_j on $E(y^*|\mathbf{x}) = \beta_0 + \mathbf{x}\boldsymbol{\beta}$ and on $E(y|\mathbf{x}) = P(y = 1|\mathbf{x}) = G(\beta_0 + \mathbf{x}\boldsymbol{\beta})$ is always the same. But the latent variable y^* rarely has a well-defined unit of measurement. (For example, y^* might be the difference in utility levels from two different actions.) Thus, the magnitudes of each β_j are not, by themselves, especially useful (in contrast to the linear probability model). For most purposes, we want to estimate the effect of x_j on the probability of success $P(y = 1|\mathbf{x})$, but this is complicated by the nonlinear nature of $G(\cdot)$.

To find the partial effect of roughly continuous variables on the response probability, we must rely on calculus. If x_j is a roughly continuous variable, its partial effect on $p(\mathbf{x}) = P(y = 1|\mathbf{x})$ is obtained from the partial derivative:

$$\frac{\partial p(\mathbf{x})}{\partial x_j} = g(\beta_0 + \mathbf{x}\boldsymbol{\beta})\beta_j, \quad \text{where } g(z) \equiv \frac{dG}{dz}(z). \quad \text{[17.7]}$$

Because G is the cdf of a continuous random variable, g is a probability density function (pdf). In the logit and probit cases, $G(\cdot)$ is a strictly increasing cdf, and so $g(z) > 0$ for all z. Therefore, the partial effect of x_j on $p(\mathbf{x})$ depends on $\mathbf{x}$ through the positive quantity $g(\beta_0 + \mathbf{x}\boldsymbol{\beta})$, which means that the partial effect always has the same sign as β_j.

Equation (17.7) shows that the *relative* effects of any two continuous explanatory variables do not depend on $\mathbf{x}$: the ratio of the partial effects for x_j and x_h is β_j/β_h. In the typical case that g is a symmetric density about zero, with a unique mode at zero, the largest effect occurs when $\beta_0 + \mathbf{x}\boldsymbol{\beta} = 0$. For example, in the probit case with $g(z) = \phi(z)$, $g(0) = \phi(0) = 1/\sqrt{2\pi} \approx .40$. In the logit case, $g(z) = \exp(z)/[1 + \exp(z)]^2$, and so $g(0) = .25$.

If, say, x_1 is a binary explanatory variable, then the partial effect from changing x_1 from zero to one, holding all other variables fixed, is simply

$$G(\beta_0 + \beta_1 + \beta_2 x_2 + \dots + \beta_k x_k) - G(\beta_0 + \beta_2 x_2 + \dots + \beta_k x_k). \quad \text{[17.8]}$$

Again, this depends on all the values of the other x_j. For example, if y is an employment indicator and x_1 is a dummy variable indicating participation in a job training program, then (17.8) is the change in the probability of employment due to the job training program; this depends on other characteristics that affect employability, such as education and experience. Note that knowing the sign of β_1 is sufficient for determining whether the program had a positive or negative effect. But to find the *magnitude* of the effect, we have to estimate the quantity in (17.8).

We can also use the difference in (17.8) for other kinds of discrete variables (such as number of children). If x_k denotes this variable, then the effect on the probability of x_k going from c_k to $c_k + 1$ is simply

$$G[\beta_0 + \beta_1 x_1 + \beta_2 x_2 + \dots + \beta_k(c_k + 1)]$$
$$- G(\beta_0 + \beta_1 x_1 + \beta_2 x_2 + \dots + \beta_k c_k). \quad \text{[17.9]}$$

It is straightforward to include standard functional forms among the explanatory variables. For example, in the model

$$P(y = 1|\mathbf{z}) = G(\beta_0 + \beta_1 z_1 + \beta_2 z_1^2 + \beta_3 \log(z_2) + \beta_4 z_3),$$

the partial effect of z_1 on $P(y = 1|\mathbf{z})$ is $\partial P(y = 1|\mathbf{z})/\partial z_1 = g(\beta_0 + \mathbf{x}\boldsymbol{\beta})(\beta_1 + 2\beta_2 z_1)$, and the partial effect of z_2 on the response probability is $\partial P(y = 1|\mathbf{z})/\partial z_2 = g(\beta_0 + \mathbf{x}\boldsymbol{\beta})(\beta_3/z_2)$, where $\mathbf{x}\boldsymbol{\beta} = \beta_1 z_1 + \beta_2 z_1^2 + \beta_3 \log(z_2) + \beta_4 z_3$. Therefore, $g(\beta_0 + \mathbf{x}\boldsymbol{\beta})(\beta_3/100)$ is the approximate change in the response probability when z_2 increases by 1%.

Sometimes we want to compute the elasticity of the response probability with respect to an explanatory variable, although we must be careful in interpreting percentage changes in probabilities. For example, a change in a probability from .04 to .06 represents a 2-percentage-*point* increase in the probability, but a 50% increase relative to the initial value. Using calculus, in the preceding model the elasticity of $P(y = 1|\mathbf{z})$ with respect to z_2 can be shown to be $\beta_3[g(\beta_0 + \mathbf{x}\boldsymbol{\beta})/G(\beta_0 + \mathbf{x}\boldsymbol{\beta})]$. The elasticity with respect to z_3 is $(\beta_4 z_3)[g(\beta_0 + \mathbf{x}\boldsymbol{\beta})/G(\beta_0 + \mathbf{x}\boldsymbol{\beta})]$. In the first case, the elasticity is always the same sign as β_2, but it generally depends on all parameters and all values of the explanatory variables. If $z_3 > 0$, the second elasticity always has the same sign as the parameter β_4.

Models with interactions among the explanatory variables can be a bit tricky, but one should compute the partial derivatives and then evaluate the resulting partial effects at interesting values. When measuring the effects of discrete variables—no matter how complicated the model—we should use (17.9). We discuss this further in the subsection on interpreting the estimates on page 530.

17-1b Maximum Likelihood Estimation of Logit and Probit Models

How should we estimate nonlinear binary response models? To estimate the LPM, we can use ordinary least squares (see Section 7-5) or, in some cases, weighted least squares (see Section 8-5). Because of the nonlinear nature of $E(y|\mathbf{x})$, OLS and WLS are not applicable. We could use nonlinear versions of these methods, but it is no more difficult to use **maximum likelihood estimation (MLE)** (see Appendix 17A for a brief discussion). Up until now, we have had little need for MLE, although we did note that, under the classical linear model assumptions, the OLS estimator is the maximum likelihood estimator (conditional on the explanatory variables). For estimating limited dependent variable models, maximum likelihood methods are indispensable. Because MLE is based on the distribution of y given $\mathbf{x}$, the heteroskedasticity in $Var(y|\mathbf{x})$ is automatically accounted for.

Assume that we have a random sample of size n. To obtain the maximum likelihood estimator, conditional on the explanatory variables, we need the density of y_i given $\mathbf{x}_i$. We can write this as

$$f(y|\mathbf{x}_i;\boldsymbol{\beta}) = [G(\mathbf{x}_i\boldsymbol{\beta})]^y [1 - G(\mathbf{x}_i\boldsymbol{\beta})]^{1-y}, y = 0, 1, \qquad [17.10]$$

where, for simplicity, we absorb the intercept into the vector $\mathbf{x}_i$. We can easily see that when $y = 1$, we get $G(\mathbf{x}_i\boldsymbol{\beta})$ and when $y = 0$, we get $1 - G(\mathbf{x}_i\boldsymbol{\beta})$. The **log-likelihood function** for observation i is a function of the parameters and the data $(\mathbf{x}_i, y_i)$ and is obtained by taking the log of (17.10):

$$\ell_i(\boldsymbol{\beta}) = y_i \log[G(\mathbf{x}_i\boldsymbol{\beta})] + (1 - y_i)\log[1 - G(\mathbf{x}_i\boldsymbol{\beta})]. \qquad [17.11]$$

Because $G(\cdot)$ is strictly between zero and one for logit and probit, $\ell_i(\boldsymbol{\beta})$ is well defined for all values of $\boldsymbol{\beta}$.

The log-likelihood for a sample size of n is obtained by summing (17.11) across all observations: $\mathcal{L}(\boldsymbol{\beta}) = \sum_{i=1}^{n}\ell_i(\boldsymbol{\beta})$. The MLE of $\boldsymbol{\beta}$, denoted by $\hat{\boldsymbol{\beta}}$, maximizes this log-likelihood. If $G(\cdot)$ is the standard logit cdf, then $\hat{\boldsymbol{\beta}}$ is the *logit estimator*; if $G(\cdot)$ is the standard normal cdf, then $\hat{\boldsymbol{\beta}}$ is the *probit estimator*.

Because of the nonlinear nature of the maximization problem, we cannot write formulas for the logit or probit maximum likelihood estimates. In addition to raising computational issues, this makes the statistical theory for logit and probit much more difficult than OLS or even 2SLS. Nevertheless, the general theory of MLE for random samples implies that, under very general conditions, the MLE is consistent, asymptotically normal, and asymptotically efficient. [See Wooldridge (2010, Chapter 13) for a general discussion.] We will just use the results here; applying logit and probit models is fairly easy, provided we understand what the statistics mean.

Each $\hat{\beta}_j$ comes with an (asymptotic) standard error, the formula for which is complicated and presented in the chapter appendix. Once we have the standard errors—and these are reported along with the coefficient estimates by any package that supports logit and probit—we can construct (asymptotic) t tests and confidence intervals, just as with OLS, 2SLS, and the other estimators we have encountered. In particular, to test H_0: $\beta_j = 0$, we form the t statistic $\hat{\beta}_j / se(\hat{\beta}_j)$ and carry out the test in the usual way, once we have decided on a one- or two-sided alternative.

17-1c Testing Multiple Hypotheses

We can also test multiple restrictions in logit and probit models. In most cases, these are tests of multiple exclusion restrictions, as in Section 4-5. We will focus on exclusion restrictions here.

There are three ways to test exclusion restrictions for logit and probit models. The Lagrange multiplier or score test only requires estimating the model under the null hypothesis, just as in the linear case in Section 5-2; we will not cover the score test here, since it is rarely needed to test exclusion restrictions. [See Wooldridge (2010, Chapter 15) for other uses of the score test in binary response models.]

The Wald test requires estimation of only the unrestricted model. In the linear model case, the **Wald statistic**, after a simple transformation, is essentially the F statistic, so there is no need to cover the Wald statistic separately. The formula for the Wald statistic is given in Wooldridge (2010, Chapter 15). This statistic is computed by econometrics packages that allow exclusion restrictions to be tested after the unrestricted model has been estimated. It has an asymptotic chi-square distribution, with df equal to the number of restrictions being tested.

> **EXPLORING FURTHER 17.1**
>
> A probit model to explain whether a firm is taken over by another firm during a given year is
>
> $$P(takeover = 1|\mathbf{x}) = \Phi(\beta_0 + \beta_1 avgprof$$
> $$+ \beta_2 mktval$$
> $$+ \beta_3 debtearn$$
> $$+ \beta_4 ceoten$$
> $$+ \beta_5 ceosal$$
> $$+ \beta_5 ceoage),$$
>
> where *takeover* is a binary response variable, *avgprof* is the firm's average profit margin over several prior years, *mktval* is market value of the firm, *debtearn* is the debt-to-earnings ratio, and *ceoten*, *ceosal*, and *ceoage* are the tenure, annual salary, and age of the chief executive officer, respectively. State the null hypothesis that, other factors being equal, variables related to the CEO have no effect on the probability of takeover. How many *df* are in the chi-square distribution for the *LR* or Wald test?

If both the restricted and unrestricted models are easy to estimate—as is usually the case with exclusion restrictions—then the *likelihood ratio* (*LR*) *test* becomes very attractive. The *LR* test is based on the same concept as the F test in a linear model. The F test measures the increase in the sum of squared residuals when variables are dropped from the model. The *LR* test is based on the difference in the log-likelihood functions for the unrestricted and restricted models. The idea is this: Because the MLE maximizes the log-likelihood function, dropping variables generally leads to a *smaller*—or at least no larger—log-likelihood. (This is similar to the fact that the R-squared never increases when variables are dropped from a regression.) The question is whether the fall in the log-likelihood is large enough to conclude that the dropped variables are important. We can make this decision once we have a test statistic and a set of critical values.

The **likelihood ratio statistic** is *twice* the difference in the log-likelihoods:

$$LR = 2(\mathcal{L}_{ur} - \mathcal{L}_r), \qquad [17.12]$$

where $\mathcal{L}_{ur}$ is the log-likelihood value for the unrestricted model and $\mathcal{L}_r$ is the log-likelihood value for the restricted model. Because $\mathcal{L}_{ur} \geq \mathcal{L}_r$, *LR* is nonnegative and usually strictly positive. In computing the *LR* statistic for binary response models, it is important to know that the log-likelihood function is always a negative number. This fact follows from equation (17.11), because y_i is either zero or one and both variables inside the log function are strictly between zero and one, which means their natural logs are negative. That the log-likelihood functions are both negative does not change the way we compute the *LR* statistic; we simply preserve the negative signs in equation (17.12).

The multiplication by two in (17.12) is needed so that *LR* has an approximate chi-square distribution under H_0. If we are testing q exclusion restrictions, $LR \overset{a}{\sim} \chi_q^2$. This means that, to test H_0 at the 5% level, we use as our critical value the 95th percentile in the χ_q^2 distribution. Computing *p*-values is easy with most software packages.

17-1d Interpreting the Logit and Probit Estimates

Given modern computers, from a practical perspective the most difficult aspect of logit or probit models is presenting and interpreting the results. The coefficient estimates, their standard errors, and the value of the log-likelihood function are reported by all software packages that do logit and probit, and these should be reported in any application. The coefficients give the signs of the partial effects of each x_j on the response probability, and the statistical significance of x_j is determined by whether we can reject H_0: $\beta_j = 0$ at a sufficiently small significance level.

As we briefly discussed in Section 7-5 for the linear probability model, we can compute a goodness-of-fit measure called the **percent correctly predicted**. As before, we define a binary predictor of y_i to be one if the predicted probability is at least .5, and zero otherwise. Mathematically, $\tilde{y}_i = 1$ if $G(\hat{\beta}_0 + \mathbf{x}_i\hat{\boldsymbol{\beta}}) \geq .5$ and $\tilde{y}_i = 0$ if $G(\hat{\beta}_0 + \mathbf{x}_i\hat{\boldsymbol{\beta}}) < .5$. Given $\{\tilde{y}_i: i = 1, 2, ..., n\}$, we can see how well $\tilde{y}_i$ predicts y_i across all observations. There are four possible outcomes on each pair, $(y_i, \tilde{y}_i)$; when both are zero or both are one, we make the correct prediction. In the two cases where one of the pair is zero and the other is one, we make the incorrect prediction. The percentage correctly predicted is the percentage of times that $\tilde{y}_i = y_i$.

Although the percentage correctly predicted is useful as a goodness-of-fit measure, it can be misleading. In particular, it is possible to get rather high percentages correctly predicted even when the least likely outcome is very poorly predicted. For example, suppose that $n = 200$, 160 observations have $y_i = 0$, and, out of these 160 observations, 140 of the $\tilde{y}_i$ are also zero (so we correctly predict 87.5% of the zero outcomes). Even if *none* of the predictions is correct when $y_i = 1$, we still correctly predict 70% of all outcomes $(140/200 = .70)$. Often, we hope to have some ability to predict the least likely outcome (such as whether someone is arrested for committing a crime), and so we should be up front about how well we do in predicting each outcome. Therefore, it makes sense to also compute the percentage correctly predicted for each of the outcomes. Problem 1 asks you to show that the overall percentage correctly predicted is a weighted average of $\hat{q}_0$ (the percentage correctly predicted for $y_i = 0$) and $\hat{q}_1$ (the percentage correctly predicted for $y_i = 1$), where the weights are the fractions of zeros and ones in the sample, respectively.

Some have criticized the prediction rule just described for using a threshold value of .5, especially when one of the outcomes is unlikely. For example, if $\bar{y} = .08$ (only 8% "successes" in the sample), it could be that we *never* predict $y_i = 1$ because the estimated probability of success is never greater than .5. One alternative is to use the fraction of successes in the sample as the threshold—.08 in the previous example. In other words, define $\tilde{y}_i = 1$ when $G(\hat{\beta}_0 + \mathbf{x}_i\hat{\boldsymbol{\beta}}) \geq .08$, and zero otherwise. Using this rule will certainly increase the number of predicted successes, but not without cost: we will necessarily make more mistakes—perhaps many more—in predicting zeros ("failures"). In terms of the overall percentage correctly predicted, we may do worse than using the .5 threshold.

A third possibility is to choose the threshold such that the fraction of $\tilde{y}_i = 1$ in the sample is the same as (or very close to) $\bar{y}$. In other words, search over threshold values τ, $0 < \tau < 1$, such that if we define $\tilde{y}_i = 1$ when $G(\hat{\beta}_0 + \mathbf{x}_i\hat{\boldsymbol{\beta}}) \geq \tau$, then $\sum_{i=1}^{n}\tilde{y}_i \approx \sum_{i=1}^{n}y_i$. (The trial and error required to find the desired value of τ can be tedious, but it is feasible. In some cases, it will not be possible to make the number of predicted successes exactly the same as the number of successes in the sample.) Now, given this set of $\hat{y}_i$, we can compute the percentage correctly predicted for each of the two outcomes as well as the overall percentage correctly predicted.

There are also various **pseudo R-squared** measures for binary response. McFadden (1974) suggests the measure $1 - \mathcal{L}_{ur}/\mathcal{L}_o$, where $\mathcal{L}_{ur}$ is the log-likelihood function for the estimated model and $\mathcal{L}_0$ is the log-likelihood function in the model with only an intercept. Why does this measure make sense? Recall that the log-likelihoods are negative, and so $\mathcal{L}_{ur}/\mathcal{L}_o = |\mathcal{L}_{ur}|/|\mathcal{L}_o|$. Further, $|\mathcal{L}_{ur}| \leq |\mathcal{L}_o|$. If the covariates have no explanatory power, then $\mathcal{L}_{ur}/\mathcal{L}_o = 1$, and the pseudo R-squared is zero, just as the usual R-squared is zero in a linear regression when the covariates have no explanatory power. Usually, $|\mathcal{L}_{ur}| < |\mathcal{L}_o|$, in which $1 - \mathcal{L}_{ur}/\mathcal{L}_o > 0$. If $\mathcal{L}_{ur}$ were zero, the pseudo R-squared would equal unity. In fact, $\mathcal{L}_{ur}$ cannot reach zero in a probit or logit model, as that would require the estimated probabilities when $y_i = 1$ all to be unity and the estimated probabilities when $y_i = 0$ all to be zero.

Alternative pseudo R-squareds for probit and logit are more directly related to the usual R-squared from OLS estimation of a linear probability model. For either probit or logit, let $\hat{y}_i = G(\hat{\beta}_0 + \mathbf{x}_i\hat{\boldsymbol{\beta}})$ be the fitted probabilities. Since these probabilities are also estimates of $E(y_i|\mathbf{x}_i)$, we can base an R-squared on how close the $\hat{y}_i$ are to the y_i. One possibility that suggests itself from standard regression analysis is to compute the squared correlation between y_i and $\hat{y}_i$. Remember, in a linear regression framework, this is an algebraically equivalent way to obtain the usual R-squared; see equation (3.29). Therefore, we can compute a pseudo R-squared for probit and logit that is directly comparable to the usual R-squared from estimation of a linear probability model. In any case, goodness-of-fit is usually less important than trying to obtain convincing estimates of the ceteris paribus effects of the explanatory variables.

Often, we want to estimate the effects of the x_j on the response probabilities, $P(y = 1|\mathbf{x})$. If x_j is (roughly) continuous, then

$$\Delta\hat{P}(y = 1|\mathbf{x}) \approx [g(\hat{\beta}_0 + \mathbf{x}\hat{\boldsymbol{\beta}})\hat{\beta}_j]\Delta x_j, \qquad [17.13]$$

for "small" changes in x_j. So, for $\Delta x_j = 1$, the change in the estimated success probability is roughly $g(\hat{\beta}_0 + \mathbf{x}\hat{\boldsymbol{\beta}})\hat{\beta}_j$. Compared with the linear probability model, the cost of using probit and logit models is that the partial effects in equation (17.13) are harder to summarize because the scale factor, $g(\hat{\beta}_0 + \mathbf{x}\hat{\boldsymbol{\beta}})$, depends on $\mathbf{x}$ (that is, on all of the explanatory variables). One possibility is to plug in interesting values for the x_j—such as means, medians, minimums, maximums, and lower and upper quartiles—and then see how $g(\hat{\beta}_0 + \mathbf{x}\hat{\boldsymbol{\beta}})$ changes. Although attractive, this can be tedious and result in too much information even if the number of explanatory variables is moderate.

As a quick summary for getting at the magnitudes of the partial effects, it is handy to have a single scale factor that can be used to multiply each $\hat{\beta}_j$ (or at least those coefficients on roughly continuous variables). One method, commonly used in econometrics packages that routinely estimate probit and logit models, is to replace each explanatory variable with its sample average. In other words, the adjustment factor is

$$g(\hat{\beta}_0 + \bar{\mathbf{x}}\hat{\boldsymbol{\beta}}) = g(\hat{\beta}_0 + \hat{\beta}_1\bar{x}_1 + \hat{\beta}_2\bar{x}_2 + \ldots + \hat{\beta}_k\bar{x}_k), \qquad [17.14]$$

where $g(\cdot)$ is the standard normal density in the probit case and $g(z) = \exp(z)/[1 + \exp(z)]^2$ in the logit case. The idea behind (17.14) is that, when it is multiplied by $\hat{\beta}_j$, we obtain the partial effect of x_j for the "average" person in the sample. Thus, if we multiply a coefficient by (17.14), we generally obtain the **partial effect at the average (PEA)**.

There are at least two potential problems with using PEAs to summarize the partial effects of the explanatory variables. First, if some of the explanatory variables are discrete, the averages of them represent no one in the sample (or population, for that matter). For example, if $x_1 = $ *female* and 47.5% of the sample is female, what sense does it make to plug in $\bar{x}_1 = .475$ to represent the "average" person? Second, if a continuous explanatory variable appears as a nonlinear function—say, as a natural log or in a quadratic—it is not clear whether we want to average the nonlinear function or plug the average into the nonlinear function. For example, should we use $\overline{\log(sales)}$ or $\log\overline{(sales)}$ to represent average firm size? Econometrics packages that compute the scale factor in (17.14) default to the former: the software is written to compute the averages of the regressors included in the probit or logit estimation.

A different approach to computing a scale factor circumvents the issue of which values to plug in for the explanatory variables. Instead, the second scale factor results from averaging the individual partial effects across the sample, leading to what is called the **average partial effect (APE)** or, sometimes, the **average marginal effect (AME)**. For a continuous explanatory variable x_j, the average partial effect is $n^{-1}\sum_{i=1}^{n}[g(\hat{\beta}_0 + \mathbf{x}_i\hat{\boldsymbol{\beta}})\hat{\beta}_j] = [n^{-1}\sum_{i=1}^{n}g(\hat{\beta}_0 + \mathbf{x}_i\hat{\boldsymbol{\beta}})]\hat{\beta}_j$. The term multiplying $\hat{\beta}_j$ acts as a scale factor:

$$n^{-1}\sum_{i=1}^{n}g(\hat{\beta}_0 + \mathbf{x}_i\hat{\boldsymbol{\beta}}). \qquad [17.15]$$

Equation (17.15) is easily computed after probit or logit estimation, where $g(\hat{\beta}_0 + \mathbf{x}_i\hat{\boldsymbol{\beta}}) = \phi(\hat{\beta}_0 + \mathbf{x}_i\hat{\boldsymbol{\beta}})$ in the probit case and $g(\hat{\beta}_0 + \mathbf{x}_i\hat{\boldsymbol{\beta}}) = \exp(\hat{\beta}_0 + \mathbf{x}_i\hat{\boldsymbol{\beta}})/[1 + \exp(\hat{\beta}_0 + \mathbf{x}_i\hat{\boldsymbol{\beta}})]^2$ in the logit case. The two scale factors differ—and are possibly quite different—because in (17.15) we are using the average of the nonlinear function rather than the nonlinear function of the average [as in (17.14)].

Because both of the scale factors just described depend on the calculus approximation in (17.13), neither makes much sense for discrete explanatory variables. Instead, it is better to use equation (17.9) to directly estimate the change in the probability. For a change in x_k from c_k to $c_k + 1$, the discrete analog of the partial effect based on (17.14) is

$$\begin{aligned} &G[\hat{\beta}_0 + \hat{\beta}_1\bar{x}_1 + \ldots + \hat{\beta}_{k-1}\bar{x}_{k-1} + \hat{\beta}_k(c_k + 1)] \\ &- G(\hat{\beta}_0 + \hat{\beta}_1\bar{x}_1 + \ldots + \hat{\beta}_{k-1}\bar{x}_{k-1} + \hat{\beta}_k c_k), \end{aligned} \qquad [17.16]$$

where G is the standard normal cdf in the probit case and $G(z) = \exp(z)/[1 + \exp(z)]$ in the logit case. The average partial effect, which usually is more comparable to LPM estimates, is

$$\begin{aligned} n^{-1}\sum_{i=1}^{n}\{&G[\hat{\beta}_0 + \hat{\beta}_1 x_{i1} + \ldots + \hat{\beta}_{k-1}x_{ik-1} + \hat{\beta}_k(c_k + 1)] \\ &- G(\hat{\beta}_0 + \hat{\beta}_1 x_{i1} + \ldots + \hat{\beta}_{k-1}x_{ik-1} + \hat{\beta}_k c_k)\}. \end{aligned} \qquad [17.17]$$

The quantity in equation (17.17) is a "partial" effect because all explanatory variables other than x_k are being held fixed at their observed values. It is not necessarily a "marginal" effect because the change in x_k from c_k to $c_k + 1$ may not be a "marginal" (or "small") increase; whether it is depends on the definition of x_k. Obtaining expression (17.17) for either probit or logit is actually rather simple. First, for each observation, we estimate the probability of success for the two chosen values of x_k, plugging in the actual outcomes for the other explanatory variables. (So, we would have n estimated differences.) Then, we average the differences in estimated probabilities across all observations. For binary x_k, both (17.16) and (17.17) are easily computed using certain econometrics packages, such as Stata®.

The expression in (17.17) has a particularly useful interpretation when x_k is a binary variable. For each unit i, we estimate the predicted difference in the probability that $y_i = 1$ when $x_k = 1$ and $x_k = 0$, namely,

$$G(\hat{\beta}_0 + \hat{\beta}_1 x_{i1} + \ldots + \hat{\beta}_{k-1}x_{i,k-1} + \hat{\beta}_k) - G(\hat{\beta}_0 + \hat{\beta}_1 x_{i1} + \ldots + \hat{\beta}_{k-1}x_{i,k-1}).$$

For each i, this difference is the estimated effect of switching x_k from zero to one, whether unit i had $x_{ik} = 1$ or $x_{ik} = 0$. For example, if y is an employment indicator (equal to one if the person is employed) after participation in a job training program, indicated by x_k, then we can estimate the difference in employment probabilities for each person in both states of the world. This *counterfactual reasoning* is similar to that in Chapter 16, which we used to motivate simultaneous equations models. The estimated effect of the job training program on the employment probability is the average of the estimated differences in probabilities. As another example, suppose that *y* indicates whether a family was approved for a mortgage, and x_k is a binary race indicator (say, equal to one for nonwhites). Then for each family we can estimate the predicted difference in having the mortgage approved as a function of income, wealth, credit rating, and so on—which would be elements of $(x_{i1}, x_{i2}, ..., x_{i,k-1})$—under the two scenarios that the household head is nonwhite versus white. Hopefully, we have controlled for enough factors so that averaging the differences in probabilities results in a convincing estimate of the race effect.

In applications where one applies probit, logit, and the LPM, it makes sense to compute the scale factors described above for probit and logit in making comparisons of partial effects. Still, sometimes one wants a quicker way to compare magnitudes of the different estimates. As mentioned earlier, for probit $g(0) \approx .4$ and for logit, $g(0) = .25$. Thus, to make the magnitudes of probit and logit roughly comparable, we can multiply the probit coefficients by $.4/.25 = 1.6$, or we can multiply the logit estimates by .625. In the LPM, $g(0)$ is effectively one, so the logit slope estimates can be divided by four to make them comparable to the LPM estimates; the probit slope estimates can be divided by 2.5 to make them comparable to the LPM estimates. Still, in most cases, we want the more accurate comparisons obtained by using the scale factors in (17.15) for logit and probit.

EXAMPLE 17.1 **Married Women's Labor Force Participation**

We now use the data on 753 married women in MROZ to estimate the labor force participation model from Example 8.8—see also Section 7-5—by logit and probit. We also report the linear probability model estimates from Example 8.8, using the heteroskedasticity-robust standard errors. The results, with standard errors in parentheses, are given in Table 17.1.

TABLE 17.1 LPM, Logit, and Probit Estimates of Labor Force Participation

Independent Variables	Dependent Variable: *inlf*		
	LPM (OLS)	Logit (MLE)	Probit (MLE)
nwifeinc	−.0034 (.0015)	−.021 (.008)	−.012 (.005)
educ	.038 (.007)	.221 (.043)	.131 (.025)
exper	.039 (.006)	.206 (.032)	.123 (.019)
exper^2	−.00060 (.00019)	−.0032 (.0010)	−.0019 (.0006)
age	−.016 (.002)	−.088 (.015)	−.053 (.008)
kidslt6	−.262 (.032)	−1.443 (.204)	−.868 (.119)
kidsge6	.013 (.014)	.060 (.075)	.036 (.043)
constant	.586 (.152)	.425 (.860)	.270 (.509)
Percentage correctly predicted	73.4	73.6	73.4
Log-likelihood value	—	−401.77	−401.30
Pseudo *R*-squared	.264	.220	.221

EXPLORING FURTHER 17.2

Using the probit estimates and the calculus approximation, what is the approximate change in the response probability when *exper* increases from 10 to 11?

The estimates from the three models tell a consistent story. The signs of the coefficients are the same across models, and the same variables are statistically significant in each model. The pseudo R-squared for the LPM is just the usual R-squared reported for OLS; for logit and probit, the pseudo R-squared is the measure based on the log-likelihoods described earlier.

As we have already emphasized, the *magnitudes* of the coefficient estimates across models are not directly comparable. Instead, we compute the scale factors in equations (17.14) and (17.15). If we evaluate the standard normal pdf $\phi(\hat{\beta}_0 + \hat{\beta}_1 x_1 + \hat{\beta}_2 x_2 + \ldots + \hat{\beta}_k x_k)$ at the sample averages of the explanatory variables (including the average of $exper^2$, *kidslt6*, and *kidsge6*), the result is approximately .391. When we compute (17.14) for the logit case, we obtain about .243. The ratio of these, $.391/.243 \approx 1.61$, is very close to the simple rule of thumb for scaling up the probit estimates to make them comparable to the logit estimates: multiply the probit estimates by 1.6. Nevertheless, for comparing probit and logit to the LPM estimates, it is better to use (17.15). These scale factors are about .301 (probit) and .179 (logit). For example, the scaled logit coefficient on *educ* is about $.179(.221) \approx .040$, and the scaled probit coefficient on *educ* is about $.301(.131) \approx .039$; both are remarkably close to the LPM estimate of .038. Even on the discrete variable *kidslt6*, the scaled logit and probit coefficients are similar to the LPM coefficient of $-.262$. These are $.179(-1.443) \approx -.258$ (logit) and $.301(-.868) \approx -.261$ (probit).

Table 17.2 reports the average partial effects for all explanatory variables and for each of the three estimated models. We obtained the estimates and standard errors from the statistical package Stata® 13. These APEs treat all explanatory variables as continuous, even the variables for the number of children. Obtaining the APE for *exper* requires some care, as it must account for the quadratic functional form in *exper*. Even for the linear model we must compute the derivative and then find the average. In the LPM column, the APE of *exper* is the average of the derivative with respect to *exper*, so $.039 - .0012$ $exper_i$ averaged across all i. (The remaining APE entries for the LPM column are simply the OLS coefficients in Table 17.1.) The APEs for *exper* for the logit and probit models also account for the quadratic in *exper*. As is clear from the table, the APEs, and their statistical significance, are very similar for all explanatory variables across all three models.

The biggest difference between the LPM model and the logit and probit models is that the LPM assumes *constant* marginal effects for *educ*, *kidslt6*, and so on, while the logit and probit models

TABLE 17.2 Average Partial Effects for the Labor Force Participation Models

Independent Variables	LPM	Logit	Probit
nwifeinc	−.0034	−.0038	−.0036
	(.0015)	(.0015)	(.0014)
educ	.038	.039	.039
	(.007)	(.007)	(.007)
exper	.027	.025	.026
	(.002)	(.002)	(.002)
age	−.016	−.016	−.016
	(.002)	(.002)	(.002)
kidslt6	−.262	−.258	−.261
	(.032)	(.032)	(.032)
kidsge6	.013	.011	.011
	(.014)	(.013)	(.013)

imply diminishing magnitudes of the partial effects. In the LPM, one more small child is estimated to reduce the probability of labor force participation by about .262, regardless of how many young children the woman already has (and regardless of the levels of the other explanatory variables). We can contrast this with the estimated marginal effect from probit. For concreteness, take a woman with *nwifeinc* = 20.13, *educ* = 12.3, *exper* = 10.6, and *age* = 42.5—which are roughly the sample averages—and *kidsge6* = 1. What is the estimated decrease in the probability of working in going from zero to one small child? We evaluate the standard normal cdf, $\Phi(\hat{\beta}_0 + \hat{\beta}_1 x_1 + \ldots + \hat{\beta}_k x_k)$, with *kidslt6* = 1 and *kidslt6* = 0, and the other independent variables set at the preceding values. We get roughly $.373 - .707 = -.334$, which means that the labor force participation probability is about .334 lower when a woman has one young child. If the woman goes from one to two young children, the probability falls even more, but the marginal effect is not as large: $.117 - .373 = -.256$. Interestingly, the estimate from the linear probability model, which is supposed to estimate the effect near the average, is in fact between these two estimates. (Note that the calculations provided here, which use coefficients mostly rounded to the third decimal place, will differ somewhat from calculations obtained within a statistical package—which would be subject to less rounding error.)

Figure 17.2 illustrates how the estimated response probabilities from nonlinear binary response models can differ from the linear probability model. The estimated probability of labor force participation is graphed against years of education for the linear probability model and the probit model. (The graph for the logit model is very similar to that for the probit model.) In both cases, the explanatory variables, other than *educ*, are set at their sample averages. In particular, the two equations graphed are $\widehat{inlf} = .102 + .038 \, educ$ for the linear model and $\widehat{inlf} = \Phi(-1.403 + .131 \, educ)$. At lower levels of education, the linear probability model estimates higher labor force participation probabilities than the probit model. For example, at eight years of education, the linear probability model estimates a .406 labor force participation probability while the probit model estimates about .361.

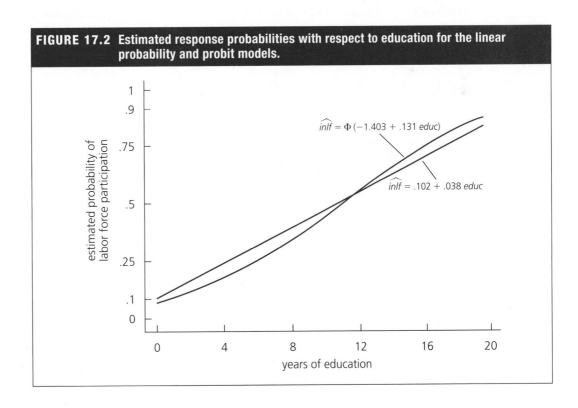

FIGURE 17.2 Estimated response probabilities with respect to education for the linear probability and probit models.

$\widehat{inlf} = \Phi(-1.403 + .131 \, educ)$

$\widehat{inlf} = .102 + .038 \, educ$

estimated probability of labor force participation

years of education

The estimates are the same at around 11⅓ years of education. At higher levels of education, the probit model gives higher labor force participation probabilities. In this sample, the smallest years of education is 5 and the largest is 17, so we really should not make comparisons outside this range.

The same issues concerning endogenous explanatory variables in linear models also arise in logit and probit models. We do not have the space to cover them, but it is possible to test and correct for endogenous explanatory variables using methods related to two stage least squares. Evans and Schwab (1995) estimated a probit model for whether a student attends college, where the key explanatory variable is a dummy variable for whether the student attends a Catholic school. Evans and Schwab estimated a model by maximum likelihood that allows attending a Catholic school to be considered endogenous. [See Wooldridge (2010, Chapter 15) for an explanation of these methods.]

Two other issues have received attention in the context of probit models. The first is nonnormality of e in the latent variable model (17.6). Naturally, if e does not have a standard normal distribution, the response probability will not have the probit form. Some authors tend to emphasize the inconsistency in estimating the β_j, but this is the wrong focus unless we are only interested in the direction of the effects. Because the response probability is unknown, we could not estimate the magnitude of partial effects even if we had consistent estimates of the β_j.

A second specification problem, also defined in terms of the latent variable model, is heteroskedasticity in e. If $\text{Var}(e|\mathbf{x})$ depends on $\mathbf{x}$, the response probability no longer has the form $G(\beta_0 + \mathbf{x}\boldsymbol{\beta})$; instead, it depends on the form of the variance and requires more general estimation. Such models are not often used in practice, since logit and probit with flexible functional forms in the independent variables tend to work well.

Binary response models apply with little modification to independently pooled cross sections or to other data sets where the observations are independent but not necessarily identically distributed. Often, year or other time period dummy variables are included to account for aggregate time effects. Just as with linear models, logit and probit can be used to evaluate the impact of certain policies in the context of a natural experiment.

The linear probability model can be applied with panel data; typically, it would be estimated by fixed effects (see Chapter 14). Logit and probit models with unobserved effects have recently become popular. These models are complicated by the nonlinear nature of the response probabilities, and they are difficult to estimate and interpret. [See Wooldridge (2010, Chapter 15).]

17-2 The Tobit Model for Corner Solution Responses

As mentioned in the chapter introduction, another important kind of limited dependent variable is a corner solution response. Such a variable is zero for a nontrivial fraction of the population but is roughly continuously distributed over positive values. An example is the amount an individual spends on alcohol in a given month. In the population of people over age 21 in the United States, this variable takes on a wide range of values. For some significant fraction, the amount spent on alcohol is zero. The following treatment omits verification of some details concerning the Tobit model. [These are given in Wooldridge (2010, Chapter 17).]

Let y be a variable that is essentially continuous over strictly positive values but that takes on a value of zero with positive probability. Nothing prevents us from using a linear model for y. In fact, a linear model might be a good approximation to $\text{E}(y|x_1, x_2, \ldots, x_k)$, especially for x_j near the mean values. But we would possibly obtain negative fitted values, which leads to negative predictions for y; this is analogous to the problems with the LPM for binary outcomes. Also, the assumption that an explanatory variable appearing in level form has a constant partial effect on $\text{E}(y|\mathbf{x})$ can be misleading. Probably, $\text{Var}(y|\mathbf{x})$ would be heteroskedastic, although we can easily deal with general heteroskedasticity by computing robust standard errors and test statistics. Because the distribution of y piles up at zero, y clearly cannot have a conditional normal distribution. So all inference would have only asymptotic justification, as with the linear probability model.

In some cases, it is important to have a model that implies nonnegative predicted values for y, and which has sensible partial effects over a wide range of the explanatory variables. Plus, we sometimes want to estimate features of the distribution of y given $x_1, \ldots, x_k$ other than the conditional expectation. The **Tobit model** is quite convenient for these purposes. Typically, the Tobit model expresses the observed response, y, in terms of an underlying latent variable:

$$y^* = \beta_0 + \mathbf{x}\boldsymbol{\beta} + u, \ u|\mathbf{x} \sim \text{Normal}(0, \sigma^2) \qquad [17.18]$$

$$y = \max(0, y^*). \qquad [17.19]$$

The latent variable y^* satisfies the classical linear model assumptions; in particular, it has a normal, homoskedastic distribution with a linear conditional mean. Equation (17.19) implies that the observed variable, y, equals y^* when $y^* \geq 0$, but $y = 0$ when $y^* < 0$. Because y^* is normally distributed, y has a continuous distribution over strictly positive values. In particular, the density of y given $\mathbf{x}$ is the same as the density of y^* given $\mathbf{x}$ for positive values. Further,

$$P(y = 0|\mathbf{x}) = P(y^* < 0|\mathbf{x}) = P(u < -\mathbf{x}\boldsymbol{\beta}|\mathbf{x})$$
$$= P(u/\sigma < -\mathbf{x}\boldsymbol{\beta}/\sigma|\mathbf{x}) = \Phi(-\mathbf{x}\boldsymbol{\beta}/\sigma) = 1 - \Phi(\mathbf{x}\boldsymbol{\beta}/\sigma),$$

because u/σ has a standard normal distribution and is independent of $\mathbf{x}$; we have absorbed the intercept into $\mathbf{x}$ for notational simplicity. Therefore, if $(\mathbf{x}_i, y_i)$ is a random draw from the population, the density of y_i given $\mathbf{x}_i$ is

$$(2\pi\sigma^2)^{-1/2}\exp[-(y - \mathbf{x}_i\boldsymbol{\beta})^2/(2\sigma^2)] = (1/\sigma)\phi[(y - \mathbf{x}_i\boldsymbol{\beta})/\sigma], y > 0 \qquad [17.20]$$

$$P(y_i = 0|\mathbf{x}_i) = 1 - \Phi(\mathbf{x}_i\boldsymbol{\beta}/\sigma), \qquad [17.21]$$

where ϕ is the standard normal density function.

From (17.20) and (17.21), we can obtain the log-likelihood function for each observation i:

$$\ell_i(\boldsymbol{\beta},\sigma) = 1(y_i = 0)\log[1 - \Phi(\mathbf{x}_i\boldsymbol{\beta}/\sigma)]$$
$$+ 1(y_i > 0)\log\{(1/\sigma)\phi[(y_i - \mathbf{x}_i\boldsymbol{\beta})/\sigma]\}; \qquad [17.22]$$

notice how this depends on σ, the standard deviation of u, as well as on the β_j. The log-likelihood for a random sample of size n is obtained by summing (17.22) across all i. The maximum likelihood estimates of $\boldsymbol{\beta}$ and σ are obtained by maximizing the log-likelihood; this requires numerical methods, although in most cases this is easily done using a packaged routine.

> **EXPLORING FURTHER 17.3**
>
> Let y be the number of extramarital affairs for a married woman from the U.S. population; we would like to explain this variable in terms of other characteristics of the woman—in particular, whether she works outside of the home, her husband, and her family. Is this a good candidate for a Tobit model?

As in the case of logit and probit, each Tobit estimate comes with a standard error, and these can be used to construct t statistics for each $\hat{\beta}_j$; the matrix formula used to find the standard errors is complicated and will not be presented here. [See, for example, Wooldridge (2010, Chapter 17).]

Testing multiple exclusion restrictions is easily done using the Wald test or the likelihood ratio test. The Wald test has a form similar to that of the logit or probit case; the *LR* test is always given by (17.12), where, of course, we use the Tobit log-likelihood functions for the restricted and unrestricted models.

17-2a Interpreting the Tobit Estimates

Using modern computers, it is usually not much more difficult to obtain the maximum likelihood estimates for Tobit models than the OLS estimates of a linear model. Further, the outputs from Tobit and OLS are often similar. This makes it tempting to interpret the $\hat{\beta}_j$ from Tobit as if these were estimates from a linear regression. Unfortunately, things are not so easy.

From equation (17.18), we see that the β_j measure the partial effects of the x_j on $E(y^*|\mathbf{x})$, where y^* is the latent variable. Sometimes, y^* has an interesting economic meaning, but more often it does not. The variable we want to explain is y, as this is the observed outcome (such as hours worked or amount of charitable contributions). For example, as a policy matter, we are interested in the sensitivity of hours worked to changes in marginal tax rates.

We can estimate $P(y = 0|\mathbf{x})$ from (17.21), which, of course, allows us to estimate $P(y > 0|\mathbf{x})$. What happens if we want to estimate the expected value of y as a function of $\mathbf{x}$? In Tobit models, two expectations are of particular interest: $E(y|y > 0, \mathbf{x})$, which is sometimes called the "conditional expectation" because it is conditional on $y > 0$, and $E(y|\mathbf{x})$, which is, unfortunately, called the "unconditional expectation." (Both expectations are conditional on the explanatory variables.) The expectation $E(y|y > 0, \mathbf{x})$ tells us, for given values of $\mathbf{x}$, the expected value of y for the subpopulation where y is positive. Given $E(y|y > 0, \mathbf{x})$, we can easily find $E(y|\mathbf{x})$:

$$E(y|\mathbf{x}) = P(y > 0|\mathbf{x}) \cdot E(y|y > 0, \mathbf{x}) = \Phi(\mathbf{x}\boldsymbol{\beta}/\sigma) \cdot E(y|y > 0, \mathbf{x}). \qquad \textbf{[17.23]}$$

To obtain $E(y|y > 0, \mathbf{x})$, we use a result for normally distributed random variables: if $z \sim \text{Normal}(0,1)$, then $E(z|z > c) = \phi(c)/[1 - \Phi(c)]$ for any constant c. But $E(y|y > 0, \mathbf{x}) = \mathbf{x}\boldsymbol{\beta} + E(u|u > -\mathbf{x}\boldsymbol{\beta}) = \mathbf{x}\boldsymbol{\beta} + \sigma E[(u/\sigma)|(u/\sigma) > -\mathbf{x}\boldsymbol{\beta}/\sigma] = \mathbf{x}\boldsymbol{\beta} + \sigma\phi(\mathbf{x}\boldsymbol{\beta}/\sigma)/\Phi(\mathbf{x}\boldsymbol{\beta}/\sigma)$, because $\phi(-c) = \phi(c)$, $1 - \Phi(-c) = \Phi(c)$, and u/σ has a standard normal distribution independent of $\mathbf{x}$.

We can summarize this as

$$E(y|y > 0, \mathbf{x}) = \mathbf{x}\boldsymbol{\beta} + \sigma\lambda(\mathbf{x}\boldsymbol{\beta}/\sigma), \qquad \textbf{[17.24]}$$

where $\lambda(c) = \phi(c)/\Phi(c)$ is called the **inverse Mills ratio**; it is the ratio between the standard normal pdf and standard normal cdf, each evaluated at c.

Equation (17.24) is important. It shows that the expected value of y conditional on $y > 0$ is equal to $\mathbf{x}\boldsymbol{\beta}$ plus a strictly positive term, which is σ times the inverse Mills ratio evaluated at $\mathbf{x}\boldsymbol{\beta}/\sigma$. This equation also shows why using OLS only for observations where $y_i > 0$ will not always consistently estimate $\boldsymbol{\beta}$; essentially, the inverse Mills ratio is an omitted variable, and it is generally correlated with the elements of $\mathbf{x}$.

Combining (17.23) and (17.24) gives

$$E(y|\mathbf{x}) = \Phi(\mathbf{x}\boldsymbol{\beta}/\sigma)[\mathbf{x}\boldsymbol{\beta} + \sigma\lambda(\mathbf{x}\boldsymbol{\beta}/\sigma)] = \Phi(\mathbf{x}\boldsymbol{\beta}/\sigma)\mathbf{x}\boldsymbol{\beta} + \sigma\phi(\mathbf{x}\boldsymbol{\beta}/\sigma), \qquad \textbf{[17.25]}$$

where the second equality follows because $\Phi(\mathbf{x}\boldsymbol{\beta}/\sigma)\lambda(\mathbf{x}\boldsymbol{\beta}/\sigma) = \phi(\mathbf{x}\boldsymbol{\beta}/\sigma)$. This equation shows that when y follows a Tobit model, $E(y|\mathbf{x})$ is a nonlinear function of $\mathbf{x}$ *and* $\boldsymbol{\beta}$. Although it is not obvious, the right-hand side of equation (17.25) can be shown to be positive for any values of $\mathbf{x}$ and $\boldsymbol{\beta}$. Therefore, once we have estimates of $\boldsymbol{\beta}$, we can be sure that predicted values for y—that is, estimates of $E(y|\mathbf{x})$—are positive. The cost of ensuring positive predictions for y is that equation (17.25) is more complicated than a linear model for $E(y|\mathbf{x})$. Even more importantly, the partial effects from (17.25) are more complicated than for a linear model. As we will see, the partial effects of x_j on $E(y|y > 0, \mathbf{x})$ and $E(y|\mathbf{x})$ have the same sign as the coefficient, β_j, but the magnitude of the effects depends on the values of *all* explanatory variables and parameters. Because σ appears in (17.25), it is not surprising that the partial effects depend on σ, too.

If x_j is a continuous variable, we can find the partial effects using calculus. First,

$$\partial E(y|y > 0, \mathbf{x})/\partial x_j = \beta_j + \beta_j \cdot \frac{d\lambda}{dc}(\mathbf{x}\boldsymbol{\beta}/\sigma),$$

assuming that x_j is not functionally related to other regressors. By differentiating $\lambda(c) = \phi(c)/\Phi(c)$ and using $d\Phi/dc = \phi(c)$ and $d\phi/dc = -c\phi(c)$, it can be shown that $d\lambda/dc = -\lambda(c)[c + \lambda(c)]$. Therefore,

$$\partial E(y|y > 0, \mathbf{x})/\partial x_j = \beta_j\{1 - \lambda(\mathbf{x}\boldsymbol{\beta}/\sigma)[\mathbf{x}\boldsymbol{\beta}/\sigma + \lambda(\mathbf{x}\boldsymbol{\beta}/\sigma)]\}. \qquad \textbf{[17.26]}$$

This shows that the partial effect of x_j on $E(y|y > 0, \mathbf{x})$ is not determined just by β_j. The adjustment factor is given by the term in brackets, $\{\cdot\}$, and depends on a linear function of $\mathbf{x}$, $\mathbf{x}\boldsymbol{\beta}/\sigma = (\beta_0 + \beta_1 x_1 + \ldots + \beta_k x_k)/\sigma$. It can be shown that the adjustment factor is strictly between zero and one. In practice, we can estimate (17.26) by plugging in the MLEs of the β_j and σ. As with logit and probit models, we must plug in values for the x_j, usually the mean values or other interesting values.

Equation (17.26) reveals a subtle point that is sometimes lost in applying the Tobit model to corner solution responses: the parameter σ appears directly in the partial effects, so having an estimate of σ is crucial for estimating the partial effects. Sometimes, σ is called an "ancillary" parameter (which means it is auxiliary, or unimportant). Although it is true that the value of σ does not affect the sign of the partial effects, it does affect the magnitudes, and we are often interested in the economic importance of the explanatory variables. Therefore, characterizing σ as ancillary is misleading and comes from a confusion between the Tobit model for corner solution applications and applications to true data censoring. (For the latter, see Section 17-4.)

All of the usual economic quantities, such as elasticities, can be computed. For example, the elasticity of y with respect to x_1, conditional on $y > 0$, is

$$\frac{\partial E(y|y > 0, \mathbf{x})}{\partial x_1} \cdot \frac{x_1}{E(y|y > 0, \mathbf{x})}. \qquad [17.27]$$

This can be computed when x_1 appears in various functional forms, including level, logarithmic, and quadratic forms.

If x_1 is a binary variable, the effect of interest is obtained as the difference between $E(y|y > 0, \mathbf{x})$, with $x_1 = 1$ and $x_1 = 0$. Partial effects involving other discrete variables (such as number of children) can be handled similarly.

We can use (17.25) to find the partial derivative of $E(y|\mathbf{x})$ with respect to continuous x_j. This derivative accounts for the fact that people starting at $y = 0$ might choose $y > 0$ when x_j changes:

$$\frac{\partial E(y|\mathbf{x})}{\partial x_j} = \frac{\partial P(y > 0|\mathbf{x})}{\partial x_j} \cdot E(y|y > 0, \mathbf{x}) + P(y > 0|\mathbf{x}) \cdot \frac{\partial E(y|y > 0, \mathbf{x})}{\partial x_j}. \qquad [17.28]$$

Because $P(y > 0|\mathbf{x}) = \Phi(\mathbf{x}\boldsymbol{\beta}/\sigma)$,

$$\frac{\partial P(y > 0|\mathbf{x})}{\partial x_j} = (\beta_j/\sigma)\phi(\mathbf{x}\boldsymbol{\beta}/\sigma), \qquad [17.29]$$

so we can estimate each term in (17.28), once we plug in the MLEs of the β_j and σ and particular values of the x_j.

Remarkably, when we plug (17.26) and (17.29) into (17.28) and use the fact that $\Phi(c)\lambda(c) = \phi(c)$ for any c, we obtain

$$\frac{\partial E(y|\mathbf{x})}{\partial x_j} = \beta_j\Phi(\mathbf{x}\boldsymbol{\beta}/\sigma). \qquad [17.30]$$

Equation (17.30) allows us to roughly compare OLS and Tobit estimates. [Equation (17.30) also can be derived directly from equation (17.25) using the fact that $d\phi(z)/dz = -z\phi(z)$.] The OLS slope coefficients, say, $\hat{\gamma}_j$, from the regression of y_i on $x_{i1}, x_{i2}, \ldots, x_{ik}$, $i = 1, \ldots, n$—that is, using all of the data—are direct estimates of $\partial E(y|\mathbf{x})/\partial x_j$. To make the Tobit coefficient, $\hat{\beta}_j$, comparable to $\hat{\gamma}_j$, we must multiply $\hat{\beta}_j$ by an adjustment factor.

As in the probit and logit cases, there are two common approaches for computing an adjustment factor for obtaining partial effects—at least for continuous explanatory variables. Both are based on equation (17.30). First, the PEA is obtained by evaluating $\Phi(\mathbf{x}\hat{\boldsymbol{\beta}}/\hat{\sigma})$, which we denote $\Phi(\overline{\mathbf{x}}\hat{\boldsymbol{\beta}}/\hat{\sigma})$. We can then use this single factor to multiply the coefficients on the continuous explanatory variables. The PEA has the same drawbacks here as in the probit and logit cases: we may not be interested in the partial effect for the "average" because the average is either uninteresting or meaningless. Plus, we must decide whether to use averages of nonlinear functions or plug the averages into the nonlinear functions.

The average partial effect, APE, is preferred in most cases. Here, we compute the scale factor as $n^{-1}\sum_{i=1}^{n}\Phi(\mathbf{x}_i\hat{\boldsymbol{\beta}}/\hat{\sigma})$. Unlike the PEA, the APE does not require us to plug in a fictitious or non-existent unit from the population, and there are no decisions to make about plugging averages into nonlinear functions. Like the PEA, the APE scale factor is always between zero and one because $0 < \Phi(\mathbf{x}\hat{\boldsymbol{\beta}}/\hat{\sigma}) < 1$ for any values of the explanatory variables. In fact, $\hat{P}(y_i > 0|\mathbf{x}_i) = \Phi(\mathbf{x}_i\hat{\boldsymbol{\beta}}/\hat{\sigma})$, and so the APE scale factor and the PEA scale factor tend to be closer to one when there are few observations with $y_i = 0$. In the case that $y_i > 0$ for all i, the Tobit and OLS estimates of the parameters are identical. [Of course, if $y_i > 0$ for all i, we cannot justify the use of a Tobit model anyway. Using log (y_i) in a linear regression model makes much more sense.]

Unfortunately, for discrete explanatory variables, comparing OLS and Tobit estimates is not so easy (although using the scale factor for continuous explanatory variables often is a useful approximation). For Tobit, the partial effect of a discrete explanatory variable, for example, a binary variable, should really be obtained by estimating $E(y|\mathbf{x})$ from equation (17.25). For example, if x_1 is a binary, we should first plug in $x_1 = 1$ and then $x_1 = 0$. If we set the other explanatory variables at their sample averages, we obtain a measure analogous to (17.16) for the logit and probit cases. If we compute the difference in expected values for each individual, and then average the difference, we get an APE analogous to (17.17). Fortunately, many modern statistical packages routinely compute the APES for fairly complicated models, including the Tobit model, and allow both continuous and discrete explanatory variables.

| **EXAMPLE 17.2** | **Married Women's Annual Labor Supply** |

The file MROZ includes data on hours worked for 753 married women, 428 of whom worked for a wage outside the home during the year; 325 of the women worked zero hours. For the women who worked positive hours, the range is fairly broad, extending from 12 to 4,950. Thus, annual hours worked is a good candidate for a Tobit model. We also estimate a linear model (using all 753 observations) by OLS, and compute the heteroskedasticity-robust standard errors. The results are given in Table 17.3.

This table has several noteworthy features. First, the Tobit coefficient estimates have the same sign as the corresponding OLS estimates, and the statistical significance of the estimates is similar. (Possible exceptions are the coefficients on *nwifeinc* and *kidsge6*, but the t statistics have similar magnitudes.) Second, though it is tempting to compare the magnitudes of the OLS and Tobit estimates, this is not very informative. We must be careful not to think that, because the Tobit coefficient on *kidslt6* is roughly twice that of the OLS coefficient, the Tobit model implies a much greater response of hours worked to young children.

We can multiply the Tobit estimates by appropriate adjustment factors to make them roughly comparable to the OLS estimates. The APE scale factor $n^{-1}\sum_{i=1}^{n}\Phi(\mathbf{x}_i\hat{\boldsymbol{\beta}}/\hat{\sigma})$ turns out to be about .589, which we can use to obtain the average partial effects for the Tobit estimation. If, for example, we multiply the *educ* coefficient by .589 we get .589(80.65) ≈ 47.50 (that is, 47.5 hours more), which is quite a bit larger than the OLS partial effect, about 28.8 hours. Table 17.4 contains the APEs for all variables, where the APEs for the linear model are simply the OLS coefficients except for the variable *exper*, which appears as a quadratic. The APEs and their standard errors, obtained from Stata® 13, are rounded to two decimal places and because of rounding can differ slightly from what is obtained by multiplying .589 by the reported Tobit coefficient. The Tobit APEs for *nwifeinc*, *educ*, and *kidslt6* are all substantially larger in magnitude than the corresponding OLS coefficients.

TABLE 17.3 OLS and Tobit Estimation of Annual Hours Worked

	Dependent Variable: *hours*	
Independent Variables	Linear (OLS)	Tobit (MLE)
nwifeinc	−3.45	−8.81
	(2.24)	(4.46)
educ	28.76	80.65
	(13.04)	(21.58)
exper	65.67	131.56
	(10.79)	(17.28)
exper^2	−.700	−1.86
	(.372)	(0.54)
age	−30.51	−54.41
	(4.24)	(7.42)
kidslt6	−442.09	−894.02
	(57.46)	(111.88)
kidsge6	−32.78	−16.22
	(22.80)	(38.64)
constant	1,330.48	965.31
	(274.88)	(446.44)
Log-likelihood value	—	−3,819.09
R-squared	.266	.274
$\hat{\sigma}$	750.18	1,122.02

The APEs for *exper* and *age* are similar, and for *kidsge*6, which is nowhere close to being statistically significant, the Tobit APE is smaller in magnitude.

If, instead, we want the estimated effect of another year of education starting at the average values of all explanatory variables, then we compute the PEA scale factor $\Phi(\bar{\mathbf{x}}\hat{\boldsymbol{\beta}}/\hat{\sigma})$. This turns out to be about .645 [when we use the squared average of experience, $\overline{(exper)}^2$, rather than the average of *exper*^{2}]. This partial effect, which is about 52 hours, is almost twice as large as the OLS estimate.

We have reported an *R*-squared for both the linear regression and the Tobit models. The *R*-squared for OLS is the usual one. For Tobit, the *R*-squared is the square of the correlation coefficient between

TABLE 17.4 Average Partial Effects for the Hours Worked Models

Independent Variables	Linear	Tobit
nwifeinc	−3.45	−5.19
	(2.24)	(2.62)
educ	28.76	47.47
	(13.04)	(12.62)
exper	50.78	48.79
	(4.45)	(3.59)
age	−30.51	−32.03
	(4.24)	(4.29)
kidslt6	−442.09	−526.28
	(57.46)	(64.71)
kidsge6	−32.78	−9.55
	(22.80)	(22.75)

y_i and $\hat{y}_i$, where $\hat{y}_i = \Phi(\mathbf{x}_i\hat{\boldsymbol{\beta}}/\hat{\sigma})\mathbf{x}_i\hat{\boldsymbol{\beta}} + \hat{\sigma}\phi(\mathbf{x}_i\hat{\boldsymbol{\beta}}/\hat{\sigma})$ is the estimate of $E(y|\mathbf{x} = \mathbf{x}_i)$. This is motivated by the fact that the usual R-squared for OLS is equal to the squared correlation between the y_i and the fitted values [see equation (3.29)]. In nonlinear models such as the Tobit model, the squared correlation coefficient is not identical to an R-squared based on a sum of squared residuals as in (3.28). This is because the fitted values, as defined earlier, and the residuals, $y_i - \hat{y}_i$, are not uncorrelated in the sample. An R-squared defined as the squared correlation coefficient between y_i and $\hat{y}_i$ has the advantage of always being between zero and one; an R-squared based on a sum of squared residuals need not have this feature.

We can see that, based on the R-squared measures, the Tobit conditional mean function fits the hours data somewhat, but not substantially, better. However, we should remember that the Tobit estimates are not chosen to maximize an R-squared—they maximize the log-likelihood function—whereas the OLS estimates are the values that do produce the highest R-squared given the linear functional form.

By construction, all of the Tobit fitted values for *hours* are positive. By contrast, 39 of the OLS fitted values are negative. Although negative predictions are of some concern, 39 out of 753 is just over 5% of the observations. It is not entirely clear how negative fitted values for OLS translate into differences in estimated partial effects. Figure 17.3 plots estimates of $E(hours|\mathbf{x})$ as a function of education; for the Tobit model, the other explanatory variables are set at their average values. For the linear model, the equation graphed is $\widehat{hours} = 387.19 + 28.76\,educ$. For the Tobit model, the equation graphed is $\widehat{hours} = \Phi[(-694.12 + 80.65\,educ)/1{,}122.02] \cdot (-694.12 + 80.65\,educ) + 1{,}122.02 \cdot \phi[(-694.12 + 80.65\,educ)/1{,}122.02]$. As can be seen from the figure, the linear model gives notably higher estimates of the expected hours worked at even fairly high levels of education. For example, at eight years of education, the OLS predicted value of hours is about 617.5, while the Tobit estimate is about 423.9. At 12 years of education, the predicted *hours* are about 732.7 and 598.3, respectively. The two prediction lines cross after 17 years of education, but no woman in the sample has more than 17 years of education. The increasing slope of the Tobit line clearly indicates the increasing marginal effect of education on expected hours worked.

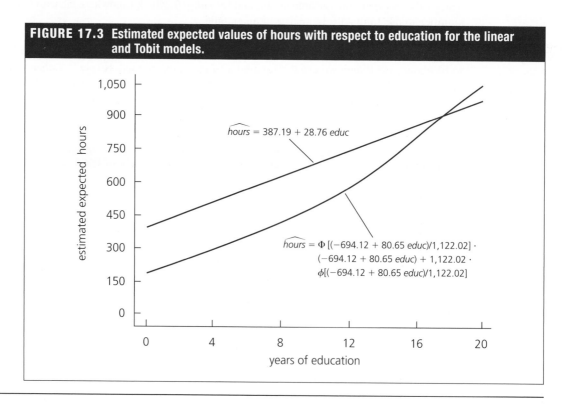

FIGURE 17.3 Estimated expected values of hours with respect to education for the linear and Tobit models.

17-2b Specification Issues in Tobit Models

The Tobit model, and in particular the formulas for the expectations in (17.24) and (17.25), rely crucially on normality and homoskedasticity in the underlying latent variable model. When $E(y|\mathbf{x}) = \beta_0 + \beta_1 x_1 + \ldots + \beta_k x_k$, we know from Chapter 5 that conditional normality of y does not play a role in unbiasedness, consistency, or large sample inference. Heteroskedasticity does not affect unbiasedness or consistency of OLS, although we must compute robust standard errors and test statistics to perform approximate inference. In a Tobit model, if any of the assumptions in (17.18) fail, then it is hard to know what the Tobit MLE is estimating. Nevertheless, for moderate departures from the assumptions, the Tobit model is likely to provide good estimates of the partial effects on the conditional means. It is possible to allow for more general assumptions in (17.18), but such models are much more complicated to estimate and interpret.

One potentially important limitation of the Tobit model, at least in certain applications, is that the expected value conditional on $y > 0$ is closely linked to the probability that $y > 0$. This is clear from equations (17.26) and (17.29). In particular, the effect of x_j on $P(y > 0|\mathbf{x})$ is proportional to β_j, as is the effect on $E(y|y > 0, \mathbf{x})$, where both functions multiplying β_j are positive and depend on $\mathbf{x}$ only through $\mathbf{x}\boldsymbol{\beta}/\sigma$. This rules out some interesting possibilities. For example, consider the relationship between amount of life insurance coverage and a person's age. Young people may be less likely to have life insurance at all, so the probability that $y > 0$ increases with age (at least up to a point). Conditional on having life insurance, the value of policies might decrease with age, since life insurance becomes less important as people near the end of their lives. This possibility is not allowed for in the Tobit model.

One way to informally evaluate whether the Tobit model is appropriate is to estimate a probit model where the binary outcome, say, w, equals one if $y > 0$, and $w = 0$ if $y = 0$. Then, from (17.21), w follows a probit model, where the coefficient on x_j is $\gamma_j = \beta_j/\sigma$. This means we can estimate the ratio of β_j to σ by probit, for each j. If the Tobit model holds, the probit estimate, $\hat{\gamma}_j$, should be "close" to $\hat{\beta}_j/\hat{\sigma}$, where $\hat{\beta}_j$ and $\hat{\sigma}$ are the Tobit estimates. These will never be identical because of sampling error. But we can look for certain problematic signs. For example, if $\hat{\gamma}_j$ is significant and negative, but $\hat{\beta}_j$ is positive, the Tobit model might not be appropriate. Or, if $\hat{\gamma}_j$ and $\hat{\beta}_j$ are the same sign, but $|\hat{\beta}_j/\hat{\sigma}|$ is much larger or smaller than $|\hat{\gamma}_j|$, this could also indicate problems. We should not worry too much about sign changes or magnitude differences on explanatory variables that are insignificant in both models.

In the annual hours worked example, $\hat{\sigma} = 1{,}122.02$. When we divide the Tobit coefficient on *nwifeinc* by $\hat{\sigma}$, we obtain $-8.81/1{,}122.02 \approx -.0079$; the probit coefficient on *nwifeinc* is about $-.012$, which is different, but not dramatically so. On *kidslt6*, the coefficient estimate over $\hat{\sigma}$ is about $-.797$, compared with the probit estimate of $-.868$. Again, this is not a huge difference, but it indicates that having small children has a larger effect on the initial labor force participation decision than on how many hours a woman chooses to work once she is in the labor force. (Tobit effectively averages these two effects together.) We do not know whether the effects are statistically different, but they are of the same order of magnitude.

What happens if we conclude that the Tobit model is inappropriate? There are models, usually called *hurdle* or *two-part* models, that can be used when Tobit seems unsuitable. These all have the property that $P(y > 0|\mathbf{x})$ and $E(y|y > 0, \mathbf{x})$ depend on different parameters, so x_j can have dissimilar effects on these two functions. [See Wooldridge (2010, Chapter 17) for a description of these models.]

17-3 The Poisson Regression Model

Another kind of nonnegative dependent variable is a **count variable**, which can take on nonnegative integer values: $\{0, 1, 2, \ldots\}$. We are especially interested in cases where y takes on relatively few values, including zero. Examples include the number of children ever born to a woman, the number of times someone is arrested in a year, or the number of patents applied for by a firm in a year. For the same reasons discussed for binary and Tobit responses, a linear model for $E(y|x_1, ..., x_k)$ might not provide the best fit over all values of the explanatory variables. (Nevertheless, it is always informative to start with a linear model, as we did in Example 3.5.)

As with a Tobit outcome, we cannot take the logarithm of a count variable because it takes on the value zero. A profitable approach is to model the expected value as an exponential function:

$$E(y|x_1, x_2, ..., x_k) = \exp(\beta_0 + \beta_1 x_1 + ... + \beta_k x_k). \qquad [17.31]$$

Because $\exp(\cdot)$ is always positive, (17.31) ensures that predicted values for y will also be positive. The exponential function is graphed in Figure A.5 of Appendix A.

Although (17.31) is more complicated than a linear model, we basically already know how to interpret the coefficients. Taking the log of equation (17.31) shows that

$$\log[E(y|x_1, x_2, ..., x_k)] = \beta_0 + \beta_1 x_1 + ... + \beta_k x_k, \qquad [17.32]$$

so that the log of the expected value is linear. Therefore, using the approximation properties of the log function that we have used often in previous chapters,

$$\%\Delta E(y|\mathbf{x}) \approx (100\beta_j)\Delta x_j.$$

In other words, $100\beta_j$ is roughly the percentage change in $E(y|\mathbf{x})$, given a one-unit increase in x_j. Sometimes, a more accurate estimate is needed, and we can easily find one by looking at discrete changes in the expected value. Keep all explanatory variables except x_k fixed and let x_k^0 be the initial value and x_k^1 the subsequent value. Then, the proportionate change in the expected value is

$$[\exp(\beta_0 + \mathbf{x}_{k-1}\boldsymbol{\beta}_{k-1} + \beta_k x_k^1)/\exp(\beta_0 + \mathbf{x}_{k-1}\boldsymbol{\beta}_{k-1} + \beta_k x_k^0)] - 1 = \exp(\beta_k \Delta x_k) - 1,$$

where $\mathbf{x}_{k-1}\boldsymbol{\beta}_{k-1}$ is shorthand for $\beta_1 x_1 + ... + \beta_{k-1} x_{k-1}$ and $\Delta x_k = x_k^1 - x_k^0$. When $\Delta x_k = 1$—for example, if x_k is a dummy variable that we change from zero to one—then the change is $\exp(\beta_k) - 1$. Given $\hat{\beta}_k$, we obtain $\exp(\hat{\beta}_k) - 1$ and multiply this by 100 to turn the proportionate change into a percentage change.

If, say, $x_j = \log(z_j)$ for some variable $z_j > 0$, then its coefficient, β_j, is interpreted as an elasticity with respect to z_j. Technically, it is an elasticity of the *expected value* of y with respect to z_j because we cannot compute the percentage change in cases where $y = 0$. For our purposes, the distinction is unimportant. The bottom line is that, for practical purposes, we can interpret the coefficients in equation (17.31) as if we have a linear model, with $\log(y)$ as the dependent variable. There are some subtle differences that we need not study here.

Because (17.31) is nonlinear in its parameters—remember, $\exp(\cdot)$ is a nonlinear function—we cannot use linear regression methods. We could use *nonlinear least squares*, which, just as with OLS, minimizes the sum of squared residuals. It turns out, however, that all standard count data distributions exhibit heteroskedasticity, and nonlinear least squares does not exploit this [see Wooldridge (2010, Chapter 12)]. Instead, we will rely on maximum likelihood and the important related method of *quasi-maximum likelihood estimation.*

In Chapter 4, we introduced normality as the standard distributional assumption for linear regression. The normality assumption is reasonable for (roughly) continuous dependent variables that can take on a large range of values. A count variable cannot have a normal distribution (because the normal distribution is for continuous variables that can take on all values, and if it takes on very few values, the distribution can be very different from normal. Instead, the nominal distribution for count data is the **Poisson distribution**.

Because we are interested in the effect of explanatory variables on y, we must look at the Poisson distribution conditional on $\mathbf{x}$. The Poisson distribution is entirely determined by its mean, so we only need to specify $E(y|\mathbf{x})$. We assume this has the same form as (17.31), which we write in shorthand as $\exp(\mathbf{x}\boldsymbol{\beta})$. Then, the probability that y equals the value h, conditional on $\mathbf{x}$, is

$$P(y = h|\mathbf{x}) = \exp[-\exp(\mathbf{x}\boldsymbol{\beta})][\exp(\mathbf{x}\boldsymbol{\beta})]^h/h!, \ h = 0, 1, ...,$$

where $h!$ denotes factorial (see Appendix B). This distribution, which is the basis for the **Poisson regression model**, allows us to find conditional probabilities for any values of the explanatory variables. For example, $P(y = 0|\mathbf{x}) = \exp[-\exp(\mathbf{x}\boldsymbol{\beta})]$. Once we have estimates of the β_j, we can plug them into the probabilities for various values of $\mathbf{x}$.

Given a random sample $\{(\mathbf{x}_i, y_i): i = 1, 2, ..., n\}$, we can construct the log-likelihood function:

$$\mathscr{L}(\boldsymbol{\beta}) = \sum_{i=1}^{n} \ell_i(\boldsymbol{\beta}) = \sum_{i=1}^{n} \{y_i \mathbf{x}_i \boldsymbol{\beta} - \exp(\mathbf{x}_i \boldsymbol{\beta})\}, \qquad [17.33]$$

where we drop the term $- \log(y_i!)$ because it does not depend on $\boldsymbol{\beta}$. This log-likelihood function is simple to maximize, although the Poisson MLEs are not obtained in closed form.

The standard errors of the Poisson estimates $\hat{\beta}_j$ are easy to obtain after the log-likelihood function has been maximized; the formula is in Appendix 17B. These are reported along with the $\hat{\beta}_j$ by any software package.

As with the probit, logit, and Tobit models, we cannot directly compare the magnitudes of the Poisson estimates of an exponential function with the OLS estimates of a linear function. Nevertheless, a rough comparison is possible, at least for continuous explanatory variables. If (17.31) holds, then the partial effect of x_j with respect to $E(y|x_1, x_2, ..., x_k)$ is $\partial E(y|x_1, x_2, ..., x_k)/x_j = \exp(\beta_0 + \beta_1 x_1 + ... + \beta_k x_k) \cdot \beta_j$. This expression follows from the chain rule in calculus because the derivative of the exponential function is just the exponential function. If we let $\hat{\gamma}_j$ denote an OLS slope coefficient from the regression y on $x_1, x_2, ..., x_k$, then we can roughly compare the magnitude of the $\hat{\gamma}_j$ and the average partial effect for an exponential regression function. Interestingly, the APE scale factor in this case, $n^{-1} \sum_{i=1}^{n} \exp(\hat{\beta}_0 + \hat{\beta}_1 x_{i1} + ... + \hat{\beta}_k x_{ik}) = n^{-1} \sum_{i=1}^{n} \hat{y}_i$, is simply the sample average $\bar{y}$ of y_i. where we define the fitted values as $\hat{y}_i = \exp(\hat{\beta}_0 + \mathbf{x}_i \hat{\boldsymbol{\beta}})$. In other words, for Poisson regression with an exponential mean function, the average of the fitted values is the same as the average of the original outcomes on y_i—just as in the linear regression case. This makes it simple to scale the Poisson estimates, $\hat{\beta}_j$, to make them comparable to the corresponding OLS estimates, $\hat{\gamma}_j$: for a continuous explanatory variable, we can compare $\hat{\gamma}_j$ to $\bar{y} \cdot \hat{\beta}_j$.

Although Poisson MLE analysis is a natural first step for count data, it is often much too restrictive. All of the probabilities and higher moments of the Poisson distribution are determined entirely by the mean. In particular, the variance is equal to the mean:

$$\text{Var}(y|\mathbf{x}) = E(y|\mathbf{x}). \qquad [17.34]$$

This is restrictive and has been shown to be violated in many applications. Fortunately, the Poisson distribution has a very nice robustness property: whether or not the Poisson distribution holds, we still get consistent, asymptotically normal estimators of the β_j. [See Wooldridge (2010, Chapter 18) for details.] This is analogous to the OLS estimator, which is consistent and asymptotically normal whether or not the normality assumption holds; yet OLS is the MLE under normality.

When we use Poisson MLE, but we do not assume that the Poisson distribution is entirely correct, we call the analysis **quasi-maximum likelihood estimation (QMLE)**. The Poisson QMLE is very handy because it is programmed in many econometrics packages. However, unless the Poisson variance assumption (17.34) holds, the standard errors need to be adjusted.

A simple adjustment to the standard errors is available when we assume that the variance is proportional to the mean:

$$\text{Var}(y|\mathbf{x}) = \sigma^2 E(y|\mathbf{x}), \qquad [17.35]$$

where $\sigma^2 > 0$ is an unknown parameter. When $\sigma^2 = 1$, we obtain the Poisson variance assumption. When $\sigma^2 > 1$, the variance is greater than the mean for all $\mathbf{x}$; this is called **overdispersion** because the variance is larger than in the Poisson case, and it is observed in many applications of count regressions. The case $\sigma^2 < 1$, called *underdispersion*, is less common but is allowed in (17.35).

Under (17.35), it is easy to adjust the usual Poisson MLE standard errors. Let $\hat{\beta}_j$ denote the Poisson QMLE and define the residuals as $\hat{u}_i = y_i - \hat{y}_i$, where $\hat{y}_i = \exp(\hat{\beta}_0 + \hat{\beta}_1 x_{i1} + \ldots + \hat{\beta}_k x_{ik})$ is the fitted value. As usual, the residual for observation i is the difference between y_i and its fitted value. A consistent estimator of σ^2 is $(n - k - 1)^{-1} \sum_{i=1}^{n} \hat{u}_i^2 / \hat{y}_i$, where the division by $\hat{y}_i$ is the proper heteroskedasticity adjustment and $n - k - 1$ is the *df* given n observations and $k + 1$ estimates $\hat{\beta}_0, \hat{\beta}_1, \ldots, \hat{\beta}_k$. Letting $\hat{\sigma}$ be the positive square root of $\hat{\sigma}^2$, we multiply the usual Poisson standard errors by $\hat{\sigma}$. If $\hat{\sigma}$ is notably greater than one, the corrected standard errors can be much bigger than the nominal, generally incorrect, Poisson MLE standard errors.

Even (17.35) is not entirely general. Just as in the linear model, we can obtain standard errors for the Poisson QMLE that do not restrict the variance at all. [See Wooldridge (2010, Chapter 18) for further explanation.]

EXPLORING FURTHER 17.4

Suppose that we obtain $\hat{\sigma}^2 = 2$. How will the adjusted standard errors compare with the usual Poisson MLE standard errors? How will the quasi-*LR* statistic compare with the usual *LR* statistic?

Under the Poisson distributional assumption, we can use the likelihood ratio statistic to test exclusion restrictions, which, as always, has the form in (17.12). If we have q exclusion restrictions, the statistic is distributed approximately as χ_q^2 under the null. Under the less restrictive assumption (17.35), a simple adjustment is available (and then we call the statistic the **quasi-likelihood ratio statistic**): we divide (17.12) by $\hat{\sigma}^2$, where $\hat{\sigma}^2$ is obtained from the unrestricted model.

EXAMPLE 17.3   Poisson Regression for Number of Arrests

We now apply the Poisson regression model to the arrest data in CRIME1, used, among other places, in Example 9.1. The dependent variable, *narr86*, is the number of times a man is arrested during 1986. This variable is zero for 1,970 of the 2,725 men in the sample, and only eight values of *narr86* are greater than five. Thus, a Poisson regression model is more appropriate than a linear regression model. Table 17.5 also presents the results of OLS estimation of a linear regression model.

The standard errors for OLS are the usual ones; we could certainly have made these robust to heteroskedasticity. The standard errors for Poisson regression are the usual maximum likelihood standard errors. Because $\hat{\sigma} = 1.232$, the standard errors for Poisson regression should be inflated by this factor (so each corrected standard error is about 23% higher). For example, a more reliable standard error for *tottime* is $1.23(.015) \approx .0185$, which gives a t statistic of about 1.3. The adjustment to the standard errors reduces the significance of all variables, but several of them are still very statistically significant.

The OLS and Poisson coefficients are not directly comparable, and they have very different meanings. For example, the coefficient on *pcnv* implies that, if $\Delta pcnv = .10$, the expected number of arrests falls by .013 (*pcnv* is the proportion of prior arrests that led to conviction). The Poisson coefficient implies that $\Delta pcnv = .10$ reduces expected arrests by about 4% [$.402(.10) = .0402$, and we multiply this by 100 to get the percentage effect]. As a policy matter, this suggests we can reduce overall arrests by about 4% if we can increase the probability of conviction by .1.

The Poisson coefficient on *black* implies that, other factors being equal, the expected number of arrests for a black man is estimated to be about $100 \cdot [\exp(.661) - 1] \approx 93.7\%$ higher than for a white man with the same values for the other explanatory variables.

As with the Tobit application in Table 17.3, we report an R-squared for Poisson regression: the squared correlation coefficient between y_i and $\hat{y}_i = \exp(\hat{\beta}_0 + \hat{\beta}_1 x_{i1} + \ldots + \hat{\beta}_k x_{ik})$. The motivation for this goodness-of-fit measure is the same as for the Tobit model. We see that the exponential regression model, estimated by Poisson QMLE, fits slightly better. Remember that the OLS estimates are chosen to maximize the R-squared, but the Poisson estimates are not. (They are selected to maximize the log-likelihood function.)

TABLE 17.5 Determinants of Number of Arrests for Young Men		
Dependent Variable: *narr86*		
Independent Variables	Linear (OLS)	Exponential (Poisson QMLE)
pcnv	−.132	−.402
	(.040)	(.085)
avgsen	−.011	−.024
	(.012)	(.020)
tottime	.012	.024
	(.009)	(.015)
ptime86	−.041	−.099
	(.009)	(.021)
qemp86	−.051	−.038
	(.014)	(.029)
inc86	−.0015	−.0081
	(.0003)	(.0010)
black	.327	.661
	(.045)	(.074)
hispan	.194	.500
	(.040)	(.074)
born60	−.022	−.051
	(.033)	(.064)
constant	.577	−.600
	(.038)	(.067)
Log-likelihood value	—	−2,248.76
R-squared	.073	.077
$\hat{\sigma}$	.829	1.232

Other count data regression models have been proposed and used in applications, which generalize the Poisson distribution in a variety of ways. If we are interested in the effects of the x_j on the mean response, there is little reason to go beyond Poisson regression: it is simple, often gives good results, and has the robustness property discussed earlier. In fact, we could apply Poisson regression to a y that is a Tobit-like outcome, provided (17.31) holds. This might give good estimates of the mean effects. Extensions of Poisson regression are more useful when we are interested in estimating probabilities, such as $P(y > 1|\mathbf{x})$. [See, for example, Cameron and Trivedi (1998).]

17-4 Censored and Truncated Regression Models

The models in Sections 17-1, 17-2, and 17-3 apply to various kinds of limited dependent variables that arise frequently in applied econometric work. In using these methods, it is important to remember that we use a probit or logit model for a binary response, a Tobit model for a corner solution outcome, or a Poisson regression model for a count response because we want models that account for important features of the distribution of y. There is no issue of data observability. For example, in the Tobit application to women's labor supply in Example 17.2, there is no problem with observing hours worked: it is simply the case that a nontrivial fraction of married women in the population choose not to work for a wage. In the Poisson regression application to annual arrests, we observe the dependent variable for every young man in a random sample from the population, but the dependent variable can be zero as well as other small integer values.

Unfortunately, the distinction between lumpiness in an outcome variable (such as taking on the value zero for a nontrivial fraction of the population) and problems of data censoring can be confusing. This is particularly true when applying the Tobit model. In this book, the standard Tobit model described in Section 17-2 is only for corner solution outcomes. But the literature on Tobit models usually treats another situation within the same framework: the response variable has been censored above or below some threshold. Typically, the censoring is due to survey design and, in some cases, institutional constraints. Rather than treat data censoring problems along with corner solution outcomes, we solve data censoring by applying a **censored regression model**. Essentially, the problem solved by a censored regression model is one of missing data on the response variable, y. Although we are able to randomly draw units from the population and obtain information on the explanatory variables for all units, the outcome on y_i is missing for some i. Still, we know whether the missing values are above or below a given threshold, and this knowledge provides useful information for estimating the parameters.

A **truncated regression model** arises when we exclude, on the basis of y, a subset of the population in our sampling scheme. In other words, we do not have a random sample from the underlying population, but we know the rule that was used to include units in the sample. This rule is determined by whether y is above or below a certain threshold. We explain more fully the difference between censored and truncated regression models later.

17-4a Censored Regression Models

While censored regression models can be defined without distributional assumptions, in this subsection we study the **censored normal regression model**. The variable we would like to explain, y, follows the classical linear model. For emphasis, we put an i subscript on a random draw from the population:

$$y_i = \beta_0 + \mathbf{x}_i\boldsymbol{\beta} + u_i, \ u_i|\mathbf{x}_i, c_i \sim \text{Normal}(0, \sigma^2) \qquad [17.36]$$

$$w_i = \min(y_i, c_i). \qquad [17.37]$$

Rather than observing y_i, we observe it only if it is less than a censoring value, c_i. Notice that (17.36) includes the assumption that u_i is independent of c_i. (For concreteness, we explicitly consider censoring from above, or *right censoring*; the problem of censoring from below, or *left censoring*, is handled similarly.)

One example of right data censoring is **top coding**. When a variable is top coded, we know its value only up to a certain threshold. For responses greater than the threshold, we only know that the variable is at least as large as the threshold. For example, in some surveys family wealth is top coded. Suppose that respondents are asked their wealth, but people are allowed to respond with "more than $500,000." Then, we observe actual wealth for those respondents whose wealth is less than $500,000 but not for those whose wealth is greater than $500,000. In this case, the censoring threshold, c_i, is the same for all i. In many situations, the censoring threshold changes with individual or family characteristics.

If we observed a random sample for $(\mathbf{x}, y)$, we would simply estimate $\boldsymbol{\beta}$ by OLS, and statistical inference would be standard. (We again absorb the intercept into $\mathbf{x}$ for simplicity.) The censoring causes problems. Using arguments similar to the Tobit model, an OLS regression using only the uncensored

---

EXPLORING FURTHER 17.5

Let mvp_i be the marginal value product for worker i; this is the price of a firm's good multiplied by the marginal product of the worker. Assume mvp_i is a linear function of exogenous variables, such as education, experience, and so on, and an unobservable error. Under perfect competition and without institutional constraints, each worker is paid his or her marginal value product. Let $minwage_i$ denote the minimum wage for worker i, which varies by state. We observe $wage_i$, which is the larger of mvp_i and $minwage_i$. Write the appropriate model for the observed wage.

observations—that is, those with $y_i < c_i$—produces inconsistent estimators of the β_j. An OLS regression of w_i on $\mathbf{x}_i$, using all observations, does not consistently estimate the β_j, unless there is no censoring. This is similar to the Tobit case, but the problem is much different. In the Tobit model, we are modeling economic behavior, which often yields zero outcomes; the Tobit model is supposed to reflect this. With censored regression, we have a data collection problem because, for some reason, the data are censored.

Under the assumptions in (17.36) and (17.37), we can estimate $\boldsymbol{\beta}$ (and σ^2) by maximum likelihood, given a random sample on $(\mathbf{x}_i, w_i)$. For this, we need the density of w_i, given $(\mathbf{x}_i, c_i)$. For uncensored observations, $w_i = y_i$, and the density of w_i is the same as that for y_i: Normal$(\mathbf{x}_i\boldsymbol{\beta}, \sigma^2)$. For censored observations, we need the probability that w_i equals the censoring value, c_i, given $\mathbf{x}_i$:

$$P(w_j = c_i|\mathbf{x}_i) = P(y_i \geq c_i|\mathbf{x}_i) = P(u_i \geq c_i - \mathbf{x}_i\boldsymbol{\beta}) = 1 - \Phi[(c_i - \mathbf{x}_i\boldsymbol{\beta})/\sigma].$$

We can combine these two parts to obtain the density of w_i, given $\mathbf{x}_i$ and c_i:

$$f(w|\mathbf{x}_i,c_i) = 1 - \Phi[(c_i - \mathbf{x}_i\boldsymbol{\beta})/\sigma], \quad w = c_i, \tag{17.38}$$

$$= (1/\sigma)\phi\,[(w - \mathbf{x}_i\boldsymbol{\beta})/\sigma], \quad w < c_i. \tag{17.39}$$

The log-likelihood for observation i is obtained by taking the natural log of the density for each i. We can maximize the sum of these across i, with respect to the β_j and σ, to obtain the MLEs.

It is important to know that we can interpret the β_j just as in a linear regression model under random sampling. This is much different than Tobit applications to corner solution responses, where the expectations of interest are nonlinear functions of the β_j.

An important application of censored regression models is **duration analysis.** A *duration* is a variable that measures the time before a certain event occurs. For example, we might wish to explain the number of days before a felon released from prison is arrested. For some felons, this may never happen, or it may happen after such a long time that we must censor the duration in order to analyze the data.

In duration applications of censored normal regression, as well as in top coding, we often use the natural log as the dependent variable, which means we also take the log of the censoring threshold in (17.37). As we have seen throughout this text, using the log transformation for the dependent variable causes the parameters to be interpreted as percentage changes. Further, as with many positive variables, the log of a duration typically has a distribution closer to (conditional) normal than the duration itself.

EXAMPLE 17.4	**Duration of Recidivism**

The file RECID contains data on the time in months until an inmate in a North Carolina prison is arrested after being released from prison; call this *durat*. Some inmates participated in a work program while in prison. We also control for a variety of demographic variables, as well as for measures of prison and criminal history.

Of 1,445 inmates, 893 had not been arrested during the period they were followed; therefore, these observations are censored. The censoring times differed among inmates, ranging from 70 to 81 months.

Table 17.6 gives the results of censored normal regression for log(*durat*). Each of the coefficients, when multiplied by 100, gives the estimated percentage change in expected duration, given a ceteris paribus increase of one unit in the corresponding explanatory variable.

Several of the coefficients in Table 17.6 are interesting. The variables *priors* (number of prior convictions) and *tserved* (total months spent in prison) have negative effects on the time until the next arrest occurs. This suggests that these variables measure proclivity for criminal activity rather than representing a deterrent effect. For example, an inmate with one more prior conviction has a duration until next arrest that is almost 14% less. A year of time served reduces duration by about $100 \cdot 12(.019) = 22.8\%$. A somewhat surprising finding is that a man serving time for a felony has an

TABLE 17.6 Censored Regression Estimation of Criminal Recidivism

Independent Variables	Coefficient (Standard Error)
workprg	−.063 (.120)
priors	−.137 (.021)
tserved	−.019 (.003)
felon	.444 (.145)
alcohol	−.635 (.144)
drugs	−.298 (.133)
black	−.543 (.117)
married	.341 (.140)
educ	.023 (.025)
age	.0039 (.0006)
constant	4.099 (.348)
Log-likelihood value $\hat{\sigma}$	−1,597.06 1.810

estimated expected duration that is almost 56% $[\exp(.444) - 1 \approx .56]$ *longer* than a man serving time for a nonfelony.

Those with a history of drug or alcohol abuse have substantially shorter expected durations until the next arrest. (The variables *alcohol* and *drugs* are binary variables.) Older men, and men who were married at the time of incarceration, are expected to have significantly longer durations until their next arrest. Black men have substantially shorter durations, on the order of 42% $[\exp(-.543) - 1 \approx -.42]$.

The key policy variable, *workprg*, does not have the desired effect. The point estimate is that, other things being equal, men who participated in the work program have estimated recidivism durations that are about 6.3% shorter than men who did not participate. The coefficient has a small t statistic, so we would probably conclude that the work program has no effect. This could be due to a self-selection problem, or it could be a product of the way men were assigned to the program. Of course, it may simply be that the program was ineffective.

In this example, it is crucial to account for the censoring, especially because almost 62% of the durations are censored. If we apply straight OLS to the entire sample and treat the censored durations as if they were uncensored, the coefficient estimates are markedly different. In fact, they are all shrunk toward zero. For example, the coefficient on *priors* becomes −.059 (se = .009), and that on *alcohol* becomes −.262 (se = .060). Although the directions of the effects are the same, the importance of these variables is greatly diminished. The censored regression estimates are much more reliable.

There are other ways of measuring the effects of each of the explanatory variables in Table 17.6 on the duration, rather than focusing only on the expected duration. A treatment of modern duration analysis is beyond the scope of this text. [For an introduction, see Wooldridge (2010, Chapter 22).]

If any of the assumptions of the censored normal regression model are violated—in particular, if there is heteroskedasticity or nonnormality in u_i—the MLEs are generally inconsistent. This shows that the censoring is potentially very costly, as OLS using an uncensored sample requires neither normality nor homoskedasticity for consistency. There are methods that do not require us to assume a distribution, but they are more advanced. [See Wooldridge (2010, Chapter 19).]

17-4b Truncated Regression Models

The truncated regression model differs in an important respect from the censored regression model. In the case of data censoring, we *do* randomly sample units from the population. The censoring problem is that, while we always observe the explanatory variables for each randomly drawn unit, we observe the outcome on y only when it is not censored above or below a given threshold. With data truncation, we restrict attention to a subset of the population prior to sampling; so there is a part of the population for which we observe no information. In particular, we have no information on explanatory variables. The truncated sampling scenario typically arises when a survey targets a particular subset of the population and, perhaps due to cost considerations, entirely ignores the other part of the population. Subsequently, researchers might want to use the truncated sample to answer questions about the entire population, but one must recognize that the sampling scheme did not generate a random sample from the whole population.

As an example, Hausman and Wise (1977) used data from a negative income tax experiment to study various determinants of earnings. To be included in the study, a family had to have income less than 1.5 times the 1967 poverty line, where the poverty line depended on family size. Hausman and Wise wanted to use the data to estimate an earnings equation for the entire population.

The **truncated normal regression model** begins with an underlying population model that satisfies the classical linear model assumptions:

$$y = \beta_0 + \mathbf{x}\boldsymbol{\beta} + u, \ u|\mathbf{x} \sim \text{Normal}(0,\sigma^2). \quad\quad\quad [17.40]$$

Recall that this is a strong set of assumptions, because u must not only be independent of $\mathbf{x}$, but also normally distributed. We focus on this model because relaxing the assumptions is difficult.

Under (17.40) we know that, given a random sample from the population, OLS is the most efficient estimation procedure. The problem arises because we do not observe a random sample from the population: Assumption MLR.2 is violated. In particular, a random draw $(\mathbf{x}_i, y_i)$ is observed only if $y_i \leq c_i$, where c_i is the truncation threshold that can depend on exogenous variables—in particular, the $\mathbf{x}_i$. (In the Hausman and Wise example, c_i depends on family size.) This means that, if $\{(\mathbf{x}_i, y_i): i = 1, ..., n\}$ is our *observed* sample, then y_i is necessarily less than or equal to c_i. This differs from the censored regression model: in a censored regression model, we observe $\mathbf{x}_i$ for any randomly drawn observation from the population; in the truncated model, we only observe $\mathbf{x}_i$ if $y_i \leq c_i$.

To estimate the β_j (along with σ), we need the distribution of y_i, given that $y_i \leq c_i$ and $\mathbf{x}_i$. This is written as

$$g(y|\mathbf{x}_i,c_i) = \frac{f(y|\mathbf{x}_i\boldsymbol{\beta},\sigma^2)}{F(c_i|\mathbf{x}_i\boldsymbol{\beta},\sigma^2)}, \quad y \leq c_i, \quad\quad\quad [17.41]$$

where $f(y|\mathbf{x}_i\boldsymbol{\beta},\sigma^2)$ denotes the normal density with mean $\beta_0 + \mathbf{x}_i\boldsymbol{\beta}$ and variance σ^2, and $F(c_i|\mathbf{x}_i\boldsymbol{\beta},\sigma^2)$ is the normal cdf with the same mean and variance, evaluated at c_i. This expression for the density, conditional on $y_i \leq c_i$, makes intuitive sense: it is the population density for y, given $\mathbf{x}$, divided by the probability that y_i is less than or equal to c_i (given $\mathbf{x}_i$), $P(y_i \leq c_i|\mathbf{x}_i)$. In effect, we renormalize the density by dividing by the area under $f(\cdot|\mathbf{x}_i\boldsymbol{\beta},\sigma^2)$ that is to the left of c_i.

If we take the log of (17.41), sum across all i, and maximize the result with respect to the β_j and σ^2, we obtain the maximum likelihood estimators. This leads to consistent, approximately normal estimators. The inference, including standard errors and log-likelihood statistics, is standard and treated in Wooldridge (2010, Chapter 19).

We could analyze the data from Example 17.4 as a truncated sample if we drop all data on an observation whenever it is censored. This would give us 552 observations from a truncated normal distribution, where the truncation point differs across i. However, we would never analyze duration data (or top-coded data) in this way, as it eliminates useful information. The fact that we know a lower bound for 893 durations, along with the explanatory variables, is useful information; censored regression uses this information, while truncated regression does not.

A better example of truncated regression is given in Hausman and Wise (1977), where they emphasize that OLS applied to a sample truncated from above generally produces estimators biased toward zero. Intuitively, this makes sense. Suppose that the relationship of interest is between income and education levels. If we only observe people whose income is below a certain threshold, we are lopping off the upper end. This tends to flatten the estimated line relative to the true regression line in the whole population. Figure 17.4 illustrates the problem when income is truncated from above at $50,000. Although we observe the data points represented by the open circles, we do not observe the data points represented by the darkened circles. A regression analysis using the truncated sample does not lead to consistent estimators. Incidentally, if the sample in Figure 17.4 were censored rather than truncated—that is, we had top-coded data—we would observe education levels for all points in Figure 17.4, but for individuals with incomes above $50,000 we would not know the exact income amount. We would only know that income was at least $50,000. In effect, all observations represented by the darkened circles would be brought down to the horizontal line at *income* = 50.

As with censored regression, if the underlying homoskedastic normal assumption in (17.40) is violated, the truncated normal MLE is biased and inconsistent. Methods that do not require these assumptions are available; see Wooldridge (2010, Chapter 19) for discussion and references.

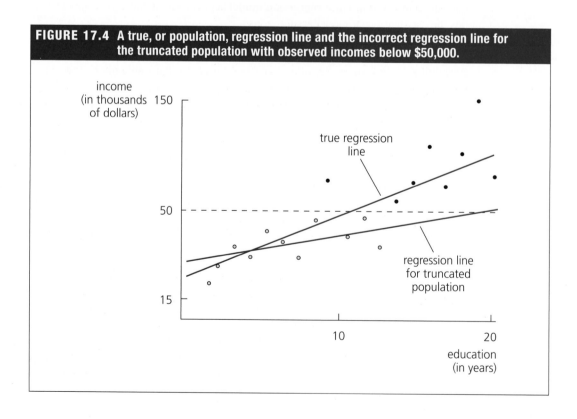

FIGURE 17.4 A true, or population, regression line and the incorrect regression line for the truncated population with observed incomes below $50,000.

17-5 Sample Selection Corrections

Truncated regression is a special case of a general problem known as **nonrandom sample selection**. But survey design is not the only cause of nonrandom sample selection. Often, respondents fail to provide answers to certain questions, which leads to missing data for the dependent or independent variables. Because we cannot use these observations in our estimation, we should wonder whether dropping them leads to bias in our estimators.

Another general example is usually called **incidental truncation**. Here, we do not observe y because of the outcome of another variable. The leading example is estimating the so-called *wage offer function* from labor economics. Interest lies in how various factors, such as education, affect the wage an individual could earn in the labor force. For people who are in the workforce, we observe the wage offer as the current wage. But for those currently out of the workforce, we do not observe the wage offer. Because working may be systematically correlated with unobservables that affect the wage offer, using only working people—as we have in all wage examples so far—might produce biased estimators of the parameters in the wage offer equation.

Nonrandom sample selection can also arise when we have panel data. In the simplest case, we have two years of data, but, due to attrition, some people leave the sample. This is particularly a problem in policy analysis, where attrition may be related to the effectiveness of a program.

17-5a When Is OLS on the Selected Sample Consistent?

In Section 9-4, we provided a brief discussion of the kinds of sample selection that can be ignored. The key distinction is between *exogenous* and *endogenous* sample selection. In the truncated Tobit case, we clearly have endogenous sample selection, and OLS is biased and inconsistent. On the other hand, if our sample is determined solely by an exogenous explanatory variable, we have exogenous sample selection. Cases between these extremes are less clear, and we now provide careful definitions and assumptions for them. The population model is

$$y = \beta_0 + \beta_1 x_1 + \ldots + \beta_k x_k + u, \, \mathrm{E}(u|x_1, x_2, \ldots, x_k) = 0. \quad\quad [17.42]$$

It is useful to write the population model for a *random* draw as

$$y_i = \mathbf{x}_i \boldsymbol{\beta} + u_i, \quad\quad [17.43]$$

where we use $\mathbf{x}_i \boldsymbol{\beta}$ as shorthand for $\beta_0 + \beta_1 x_{i1} + \beta_2 x_{i2} + \ldots + \beta_k x_{ik}$. Now, let n be the size of a *random sample* from the population. If we could observe y_i and each x_{ij} for all i, we would simply use OLS. Assume that, for some reason, either y_i or some of the independent variables are not observed for certain i. For at least some observations, we observe the full set of variables. Define a *selection indicator* s_i for each i by $s_i = 1$ if we observe all of $(y_i, \mathbf{x}_i)$, and $s_i = 0$ otherwise. Thus, $s_i = 1$ indicates that we will use the observation in our analysis; $s_i = 0$ means the observation will not be used. We are interested in the statistical properties of the OLS estimators using the **selected sample**, that is, using observations for which $s_i = 1$. Therefore, we use fewer than n observations, say, n_1.

It turns out to be easy to obtain conditions under which OLS is consistent (and even unbiased). Effectively, rather than estimating (17.43), we can only estimate the equation

$$s_i y_i = s_i \mathbf{x}_i \boldsymbol{\beta} + s_i u_i. \quad\quad [17.44]$$

When $s_i = 1$, we simply have (17.43); when $s_i = 0$, we simply have $0 = 0 + 0$, which clearly tells us nothing about $\boldsymbol{\beta}$. Regressing $s_i y_i$ on $s_i \mathbf{x}_i$ for $i = 1, 2, \ldots, n$ is the same as regressing y_i on $\mathbf{x}_i$ using the observations for which $s_i = 1$. Thus, we can learn about the consistency of the $\hat{\beta}_j$ by studying (17.44) on a random sample.

From our analysis in Chapter 5, the OLS estimators from (17.44) are consistent if the error term has zero mean and is uncorrelated with each explanatory variable. In the population, the zero mean assumption is $\mathrm{E}(su) = 0$, and the zero correlation assumptions can be stated as

$$\mathrm{E}[(sx_j)(su)] = \mathrm{E}(sx_j u) = 0, \qu\quad [17.45]$$

where s, x_j, and u are random variables representing the population; we have used the fact that $s^2 = s$ because s is a binary variable. Condition (17.45) is different from what we need if we observe all variables for a random sample: $E(x_j u) = 0$. Therefore, in the population, we need u to be uncorrelated with sx_j.

The key condition for unbiasedness is $E(su|sx_1, \ldots, sx_k) = 0$. As usual, this is a stronger assumption than that needed for consistency.

If s is a function only of the explanatory variables, then sx_j is just a function of $x_1, x_2, \ldots, x_k$; by the conditional mean assumption in (17.42), sx_j is also uncorrelated with u. In fact, $E(su|sx_1, \ldots, sx_k) = sE(u|sx_1, \ldots, sx_k) = 0$, because $E(u|x_1, \ldots, x_k) = 0$. This is the case of **exogenous sample selection**, where $s_i = 1$ is determined entirely by $x_{i1}, \ldots, x_{ik}$. As an example, if we are estimating a wage equation where the explanatory variables are education, experience, tenure, gender, marital status, and so on—which are assumed to be exogenous—we can select the sample on the basis of any or all of the explanatory variables.

If sample selection is entirely random in the sense that s_i is *independent* of $(\mathbf{x}_i, u_i)$, then $E(sx_j u) = E(s)E(x_j u) = 0$, because $E(x_j u) = 0$ under (17.42). Therefore, if we begin with a random sample and randomly drop observations, OLS is still consistent. In fact, OLS is again unbiased in this case, provided there is no perfect multicollinearity in the selected sample.

If s depends on the explanatory variables and additional random terms that are independent of $\mathbf{x}$ and u, OLS is also consistent and unbiased. For example, suppose that IQ score is an explanatory variable in a wage equation, but IQ is missing for some people. Suppose we think that selection can be described by $s = 1$ if $IQ \geq v$, and $s = 0$ if $IQ < v$, where v is an unobserved random variable that is independent of IQ, u, and the other explanatory variables. This means that we are more likely to observe an IQ that is high, but there is always some chance of not observing any IQ. Conditional on the explanatory variables, s is independent of u, which means that $E(u|x_1, \ldots, x_k, s) = E(u|x_1, \ldots, x_k)$, and the last expectation is zero by assumption on the population model. If we add the homoskedasticity assumption $E(u^2|\mathbf{x},s) = E(u^2) = \sigma^2$, then the usual OLS standard errors and test statistics are valid.

So far, we have shown several situations where OLS on the selected sample is unbiased, or at least consistent. When is OLS on the selected sample inconsistent? We already saw one example: regression using a truncated sample. When the truncation is from above, $s_i = 1$ if $y_i \leq c_i$, where c_i is the truncation threshold. Equivalently, $s_i = 1$ if $u_i \leq c_i - \mathbf{x}_i\boldsymbol{\beta}$. Because s_i depends directly on u_i, s_i and u_i will not be uncorrelated, even conditional on $\mathbf{x}_i$. This is why OLS on the selected sample does not consistently estimate the β_j. There are less obvious ways that s and u can be correlated; we consider this in the next subsection.

The results on consistency of OLS extend to instrumental variables estimation. If the IVs are denoted z_h in the population, the key condition for consistency of 2SLS is $E(sz_h u) = 0$, which holds if $E(u|\mathbf{z},s) = 0$. Therefore, if selection is determined entirely by the exogenous variables $\mathbf{z}$, or if s depends on other factors that are independent of u and $\mathbf{z}$, then 2SLS on the selected sample is generally consistent. We do need to assume that the explanatory and instrumental variables are appropriately correlated in the selected part of the population. Wooldridge (2010, Chapter 19) contains precise statements of these assumptions.

It can also be shown that, when selection is entirely a function of the exogenous variables, MLE of a nonlinear model—such as a logit or probit model—produces consistent, asymptotically normal estimators, and the usual standard errors and test statistics are valid. [Again, see Wooldridge (2010, Chapter 19).]

17-5b Incidental Truncation

As we mentioned earlier, a common form of sample selection is called incidental truncation. We again start with the population model in (17.42). However, we assume that we will always observe the explanatory variables x_j. The problem is, we only observe y for a subset of the population. The rule determining whether we observe y does *not* depend directly on the outcome of y. A leading example is when $y = \log(wage^o)$, where $wage^o$ is the *wage offer*, or the hourly wage that an individual could receive in the labor market. If the person is actually working at the time of the survey, then we observe the wage offer because we assume it is the observed wage. But for people out of the workforce, we cannot observe $wage^o$. Therefore, the truncation of wage offer is *incidental* because it depends on another variable, namely, labor force participation. Importantly, we would generally observe all other information about an individual, such as education, prior experience, gender, marital status, and so on.

The usual approach to incidental truncation is to add an explicit selection equation to the population model of interest:

$$y = \mathbf{x}\boldsymbol{\beta} + u, \quad \mathrm{E}(u|\mathbf{x}) = 0 \qquad\qquad [17.46]$$

$$s = 1[\mathbf{z}\boldsymbol{\gamma} + v \geq 0], \qquad\qquad [17.47]$$

where $s = 1$ if we observe y, and zero otherwise. We assume that elements of $\mathbf{x}$ and $\mathbf{z}$ are always observed, and we write $\mathbf{x}\boldsymbol{\beta} = \beta_0 + \beta_1 x_1 + \dots + \beta_k x_k$ and $\mathbf{z}\boldsymbol{\gamma} = \gamma_0 + \gamma_1 z_1 + \dots + \gamma_m z_m$.

The equation of primary interest is (17.46), and we could estimate $\boldsymbol{\beta}$ by OLS given a random sample. The selection equation, (17.47), depends on observed variables, z_h, and an unobserved error, v. A standard assumption, which we will make, is that $\mathbf{z}$ is exogenous in (17.46):

$$\mathrm{E}(u|\mathbf{x},\mathbf{z}) = 0.$$

In fact, for the following proposed methods to work well, we will require that $\mathbf{x}$ be a strict subset of $\mathbf{z}$: any x_j is also an element of $\mathbf{z}$, and we have some elements of $\mathbf{z}$ that are not also in $\mathbf{x}$. We will see later why this is crucial.

The error term v in the sample selection equation is assumed to be independent of $\mathbf{z}$ (and therefore $\mathbf{x}$). We also assume that v has a standard normal distribution. We can easily see that correlation between u and v generally causes a sample selection problem. To see why, assume that (u, v) is independent of $\mathbf{z}$. Then, taking the expectation of (17.46), conditional on $\mathbf{z}$ and v, and using the fact that $\mathbf{x}$ is a subset of $\mathbf{z}$ gives

$$\mathrm{E}(y|\mathbf{z},v) = \mathbf{x}\boldsymbol{\beta} + \mathrm{E}(u|\mathbf{z},v) = \mathbf{x}\boldsymbol{\beta} + \mathrm{E}(u|v),$$

where $\mathrm{E}(u|\mathbf{z},v) = \mathrm{E}(u|v)$ because (u, v) is independent of $\mathbf{z}$. Now, if u and v are jointly normal (with zero mean), then $\mathrm{E}(u|v) = \rho v$ for some parameter ρ. Therefore,

$$\mathrm{E}(y|\mathbf{z},v) = \mathbf{x}\boldsymbol{\beta} + \rho v.$$

We do not observe v, but we can use this equation to compute $\mathrm{E}(y|\mathbf{z},s)$ and then specialize this to $s = 1$. We now have:

$$\mathrm{E}(y|\mathbf{z},s) = \mathbf{x}\boldsymbol{\beta} + \rho\mathrm{E}(v|\mathbf{z},s).$$

Because s and v are related by (17.47), and v has a standard normal distribution, we can show that $\mathrm{E}(v|\mathbf{z},s)$ is simply the inverse Mills ratio, $\lambda(\mathbf{z}\boldsymbol{\gamma})$, when $s = 1$. This leads to the important equation

$$\mathrm{E}(y|\mathbf{z},s = 1) = \mathbf{x}\boldsymbol{\beta} + \rho\lambda(\mathbf{z}\boldsymbol{\gamma}). \qquad\qquad [17.48]$$

Equation (17.48) shows that the expected value of y, given $\mathbf{z}$ *and* observability of y, is equal to $\mathbf{x}\boldsymbol{\beta}$, plus an additional term that depends on the inverse Mills ratio evaluated at $\mathbf{x}\boldsymbol{\gamma}$. Remember, we hope to estimate $\boldsymbol{\beta}$. This equation shows that we can do so using only the selected sample, provided we include the term $\lambda(\mathbf{z}\boldsymbol{\gamma})$ as an additional regressor.

If $\rho = 0$, $\lambda(\mathbf{z}\boldsymbol{\gamma})$ does not appear, and OLS of y on $\mathbf{x}$ using the selected sample consistently estimates $\boldsymbol{\beta}$. Otherwise, we have effectively omitted a variable, $\lambda(\mathbf{z}\boldsymbol{\gamma})$, which is generally correlated with $\mathbf{x}$. When does $\rho = 0$? The answer is when u and v are uncorrelated.

Because $\boldsymbol{\gamma}$ is unknown, we cannot evaluate $\lambda(\mathbf{z}_i\boldsymbol{\gamma})$ for each i. However, from the assumptions we have made, s given z follows a probit model:

$$\mathrm{P}(s = 1|\mathbf{z}) = \Phi(\mathbf{z}\boldsymbol{\gamma}). \qquad\qquad [17.49]$$

Therefore, we can estimate γ by probit of s_i on $\mathbf{z}_i$, using the *entire* sample. In a second step, we can estimate β. We summarize the procedure, which has recently been dubbed the **Heckit method** in econometrics literature after the work of Heckman (1976).

Sample Selection Correction:

(i) Using all n observations, estimate a probit model of s_i on $\mathbf{z}_i$ and obtain the estimates $\hat{\gamma}_h$. Compute the inverse Mills ratio, $\hat{\lambda}_i = \lambda(\mathbf{z}_i\hat{\gamma})$ for each i. (Actually, we need these only for the i with $s_i = 1$.)

(ii) Using the selected sample, that is, the observations for which $s_i = 1$ (say, n_1 of them), run the regression of

$$y_i \text{ on } \mathbf{x}_i, \hat{\lambda}_i. \qquad [17.50]$$

The $\hat{\beta}_j$ are consistent and approximately normally distributed.

A simple test of selection bias is available from regression (17.50). Namely, we can use the usual t statistic on $\hat{\lambda}_i$ as a test of H_0: $\rho = 0$. Under H_0, there is no sample selection problem.

When $\rho \neq 0$, the usual OLS standard errors reported from (17.50) are not correct. This is because they do not account for estimation of γ, which uses the same observations in regression (17.50), and more. Some econometrics packages compute corrected standard errors. [Unfortunately, it is not as simple as a heteroskedasticity adjustment. See Wooldridge (2010, Chapter 6) for further discussion.] In many cases, the adjustments do not lead to important differences, but it is hard to know that beforehand (unless $\hat{\rho}$ is small and insignificant).

We recently mentioned that $\mathbf{x}$ should be a strict subset of $\mathbf{z}$. This has two implications. First, any element that appears as an explanatory variable in (17.46) should also be an explanatory variable in the selection equation. Although in rare cases it makes sense to exclude elements from the selection equation, including all elements of $\mathbf{x}$ in $\mathbf{z}$ is not very costly; excluding them can lead to inconsistency if they are incorrectly excluded.

A second major implication is that we have at least one element of $\mathbf{z}$ that is not also in $\mathbf{x}$. This means that we need a variable that affects selection but does *not* have a partial effect on y. This is not absolutely necessary to apply the procedure—in fact, we can mechanically carry out the two steps when $\mathbf{z} = \mathbf{x}$—but the results are usually less than convincing unless we have an *exclusion restriction* in (17.46). The reason for this is that while the inverse Mills ratio is a nonlinear function of $\mathbf{z}$, it is often well approximated by a linear function. If $\mathbf{z} = \mathbf{x}$, $\hat{\lambda}_i$ can be highly correlated with the elements of $\mathbf{x}_i$. As we know, such multicollinearity can lead to very high standard errors for the $\hat{\beta}_j$. Intuitively, if we do not have a variable that affects selection but not y, it is extremely difficult, if not impossible, to distinguish sample selection from a misspecified functional form in (17.46).

EXAMPLE 17.5   Wage Offer Equation for Married Women

We apply the sample selection correction to the data on married women in MROZ. Recall that of the 753 women in the sample, 428 worked for a wage during the year. The wage offer equation is standard, with log(*wage*) as the dependent variable and *educ*, *exper*, and *exper*^{2} as the explanatory variables. In order to test and correct for sample selection bias—due to unobservability of the wage offer for nonworking women—we need to estimate a probit model for labor force participation. In addition to the education and experience variables, we include the factors in Table 17.1: other income, age, number of young children, and number of older children. The fact that these four variables are excluded from the wage offer equation is an *assumption*: we assume that, given the productivity factors, *nwifeinc*, *age*, *kidslt6*, and *kidsge6* have no effect on the wage offer. It is clear from the probit results in Table 17.1 that at least *age* and *kidslt6* have a strong effect on labor force participation.

Table 17.7 contains the results from OLS and Heckit. [The standard errors reported for the Heckit results are just the usual OLS standard errors from regression (17.50).] There is no evidence of a sample selection problem in estimating the wage offer equation. The coefficient on $\hat{\lambda}$ has a very small *t* statistic (.239), so we fail to reject H_0: $\rho = 0$. Just as importantly, there are no practically large differences in the estimated slope coefficients in Table 17.7. The estimated returns to education differ by only one-tenth of a percentage point.

TABLE 17.7 Wage Offer Equation for Married Women		
Dependent Variable: log(*wage*)		
Independent Variables	OLS	Heckit
educ	.108	.109
	(.014)	(.016)
exper	.042	.044
	(.012)	(.016)
exper^2	−.00081	−.00086
	(.00039)	(.00044)
constant	−.522	−.578
	(.199)	(.307)
$\hat{\lambda}$	—	.032
		(.134)
Sample size *R*-squared	428	428
	.157	.157

An alternative to the preceding two-step estimation method is full MLE. This is more complicated as it requires obtaining the joint distribution of *y* and *s*. It often makes sense to test for sample selection using the previous procedure; if there is no evidence of sample selection, there is no reason to continue. If we detect sample selection bias, we can either use the two-step estimates or estimate the regression and selection equations jointly by MLE. [See Wooldridge (2010, Chapter 19).]

In Example 17.5, we know more than just whether a woman worked during the year: we know how many hours each woman worked. It turns out that we can use this information in an alternative sample selection procedure. In place of the inverse Mills ratio $\hat{\lambda}_i$, we use the Tobit residuals, say, $\hat{v}_i$, which are computed as $\hat{v}_i = y_i - \mathbf{x}_i\hat{\boldsymbol{\beta}}$ whenever $y_i > 0$. It can be shown that the regression in (17.50) with $\hat{v}_i$ in place of $\hat{\lambda}_i$ also produces consistent estimates of the β_j, and the standard *t* statistic on $\hat{v}_i$ is a valid test for sample selection bias. This approach has the advantage of using more information, but it is less widely applicable. [See Wooldridge (2010, Chapter 19).]

There are many more topics concerning sample selection. One worth mentioning is models with endogenous explanatory variables *in addition to* possible sample selection bias. Write a model with a single endogenous explanatory variable as

$$y_1 = \alpha_1 y_2 + \mathbf{z}_1\boldsymbol{\beta}_1 + u_1, \qquad [17.51]$$

where y_1 is only observed when $s = 1$ and y_2 may only be observed along with y_1. An example is when y_1 is the percentage of votes received by an incumbent, and y_2 is the percentage of total expenditures accounted for by the incumbent. For incumbents who do not run, we cannot observe y_1 or y_2. If we have exogenous factors that affect the decision to run and that are correlated with campaign expenditures, we can consistently estimate α_1 and the elements of $\boldsymbol{\beta}_1$ by instrumental variables. To be convincing, we need *two* exogenous variables that do not appear in (17.51). Effectively, one should affect the selection decision, and one should be correlated with y_2 [the usual requirement for estimating (17.51) by 2SLS]. Briefly, the method is to estimate the selection equation by probit, where *all* exogenous variables appear in the probit equation. Then, we add the inverse Mills ratio to (17.51) and estimate the equation by 2SLS. The inverse Mills ratio acts as its own instrument, as it depends only on exogenous variables. We use all exogenous variables as the other instruments. As before, we can use the t statistic on $\hat{\lambda}_i$ as a test for selection bias. [See Wooldridge (2010, Chapter 19) for further information.]

Summary

In this chapter, we have covered several advanced methods that are often used in applications, especially in microeconomics. Logit and probit models are used for binary response variables. These models have some advantages over the linear probability model: fitted probabilities are between zero and one, and the partial effects diminish. The primary cost to logit and probit is that they are harder to interpret.

The Tobit model is applicable to nonnegative outcomes that pile up at zero but also take on a broad range of positive values. Many individual choice variables, such as labor supply, amount of life insurance, and amount of pension fund invested in stocks, have this feature. As with logit and probit, the expected values of y given $\mathbf{x}$—either conditional on $y > 0$ or unconditionally—depend on $\mathbf{x}$ and $\boldsymbol{\beta}$ in nonlinear ways. We gave the expressions for these expectations as well as formulas for the partial effects of each x_j on the expectations. These can be estimated after the Tobit model has been estimated by maximum likelihood.

When the dependent variable is a count variable—that is, it takes on nonnegative, integer values—a Poisson regression model is appropriate. The expected value of y given the x_j has an exponential form. This gives the parameter interpretations as semi-elasticities or elasticities, depending on whether x_j is in level or logarithmic form. In short, we can interpret the parameters *as if* they are in a linear model with $\log(y)$ as the dependent variable. The parameters can be estimated by MLE. However, because the Poisson distribution imposes equality of the variance and mean, it is often necessary to compute standard errors and test statistics that allow for over- or underdispersion. These are simple adjustments to the usual MLE standard errors and statistics.

Censored and truncated regression models handle specific kinds of missing data problems. In censored regression, the dependent variable is censored above or below a threshold. We can use information on the censored outcomes because we always observe the explanatory variables, as in duration applications or top coding of observations. A truncated regression model arises when a part of the population is excluded entirely: we observe no information on units that are not covered by the sampling scheme. This is a special case of a sample selection problem.

Section 17-5 gave a systematic treatment of nonrandom sample selection. We showed that exogenous sample selection does not affect consistency of OLS when it is applied to the subsample, but endogenous sample selection does. We showed how to test and correct for sample selection bias for the general problem of incidental truncation, where observations are missing on y due to the outcome of another variable (such as labor force participation). Heckman's method is relatively easy to implement in these situations.

Key Terms

Average Marginal Effect (AME)	Exogenous Sample Selection	Maximum Likelihood Estimation
Average Partial Effect (APE)	Heckit Method	(MLE)
Binary Response Models	Incidental Truncation	Nonrandom Sample Selection
Censored Normal Regression	Inverse Mills Ratio	Overdispersion
Model	Latent Variable Model	Partial Effect at the Average
Censored Regression Model	Likelihood Ratio Statistic	(PEA)
Corner Solution Response	Limited Dependent Variable (LDV)	Percent Correctly Predicted
Count Variable	Logit Model	Poisson Distribution
Duration Analysis	Log-Likelihood Function	Poisson Regression Model

Probit Model   Response Probability   Truncated Normal Regression
Pseudo R-Squared   Selected Sample   Model
Quasi-Likelihood Ratio Statistic   Tobit Model   Truncated Regression Model
Quasi-Maximum Likelihood   Top Coding   Wald Statistic
   Estimation (QMLE)

Problems

1 (i) For a binary response y, let $\bar{y}$ be the proportion of ones in the sample (which is equal to the sample average of the y_j). Let $\hat{q}_0$ be the percent correctly predicted for the outcome $y = 0$ and let $\hat{q}_1$ be the percent correctly predicted for the outcome $y = 1$. If $\hat{p}$ is the overall percent correctly predicted, show that $\hat{p}$ is a weighted average of $\hat{q}_0$ and $\hat{q}_1$:

$$\hat{p} = (1 - \bar{y})\hat{q}_0 + \bar{y}\hat{q}_1.$$

(ii) In a sample of 300, suppose that $\bar{y} = .70$, so that there are 210 outcomes with $y_i = 1$ and 90 with $y_i = 0$. Suppose that the percent correctly predicted when $y = 0$ is 80, and the percent correctly predicted when $y = 1$ is 40. Find the overall percent correctly predicted.

2 Let *grad* be a dummy variable for whether a student-athlete at a large university graduates in five years. Let *hsGPA* and *SAT* be high school grade point average and SAT score, respectively. Let *study* be the number of hours spent per week in an organized study hall. Suppose that, using data on 420 student-athletes, the following logit model is obtained:

$$\hat{P}(grad = 1|hsGPA,SAT,study) = \Lambda(-1.17 + .24\,hsGPA + .00058\,SAT + .073\,study),$$

where $\Lambda(z) = \exp(z)/[1 + \exp(z)]$ is the logit function. Holding *hsGPA* fixed at 3.0 and *SAT* fixed at 1,200, compute the estimated difference in the graduation probability for someone who spent 10 hours per week in study hall and someone who spent 5 hours per week.

3 (Requires calculus)
(i) Suppose in the Tobit model that $x_1 = \log(z_1)$, and this is the only place z_1 appears in $\mathbf{x}$. Show that

$$\frac{\partial E(y|y > 0,\mathbf{x})}{\partial z_1} = (\beta_1/z_1)\{1 - \lambda(\mathbf{x}\boldsymbol{\beta}/\sigma)[\mathbf{x}\boldsymbol{\beta}/\sigma + \lambda(\mathbf{x}\boldsymbol{\beta}/\sigma)]\}, \qquad\qquad \textbf{[17.52]}$$

where β_1 is the coefficient on $\log(z_1)$.

(ii) If $x_1 = z_1$, and $x_2 = z_1^2$, show that

$$\frac{\partial E(y|y > 0,\mathbf{x})}{\partial z_1} = (\beta_1 + 2\beta_2 z_1)\{1 - \lambda(\mathbf{x}\boldsymbol{\beta}/\sigma)[\mathbf{x}\boldsymbol{\beta}/\sigma + \lambda(\mathbf{x}\boldsymbol{\beta}/\sigma)]\},$$

where β_1 is the coefficient on z_1 and β_2 is the coefficient on z_1^2.

4 Let mvp_i be the marginal value product for worker i, which is the price of a firm's good multiplied by the marginal product of the worker. Assume that

$$\log(mvp_i) = \beta_0 + \beta_1 x_{i1} + \dots + \beta_k x_{ik} + u_i$$
$$wage_i = \max(mvp_i,minwage_i),$$

where the explanatory variables include education, experience, and so on, and $minwage_i$ is the minimum wage relevant for person i. Write $\log(wage_i)$ in terms of $\log(mvp_i)$ and $\log(minwage_i)$.

5 (Requires calculus) Let *patents* be the number of patents applied for by a firm during a given year. Assume that the conditional expectation of *patents* given *sales* and *RD* is

$$E(patents|sales,RD) = \exp[\beta_0 + \beta_1\log(sales) + \beta_2 RD + \beta_3 RD^2],$$

where *sales* is annual firm sales and *RD* is total spending on research and development over the past 10 years.

(i) How would you estimate the β_j? Justify your answer by discussing the nature of *patents*.

(ii) How do you interpret β_1?

(iii) Find the partial effect of *RD* on $E(patents|sales,RD)$.

6 Consider a family saving function for the population of all families in the United States:

$$sav = \beta_0 + \beta_1 inc + \beta_2 hhsize + \beta_3 educ + \beta_4 age + u,$$

where *hhsize* is household size, *educ* is years of education of the household head, and *age* is age of the household head. Assume that $E(u|inc,hhsize,educ,age) = 0$.

(i) Suppose that the sample includes only families whose head is over 25 years old. If we use OLS on such a sample, do we get unbiased estimators of the β_j? Explain.

(ii) Now, suppose our sample includes only married couples without children. Can we estimate all of the parameters in the saving equation? Which ones can we estimate?

(iii) Suppose we exclude from our sample families that save more than $25,000 per year. Does OLS produce consistent estimators of the β_j?

7 Suppose you are hired by a university to study the factors that determine whether students admitted to the university actually come to the university. You are given a large random sample of students who were admitted the previous year. You have information on whether each student chose to attend, high school performance, family income, financial aid offered, race, and geographic variables. Someone says to you, "Any analysis of that data will lead to biased results because it is not a random sample of all college applicants, but only those who apply to this university." What do you think of this criticism?

Computer Exercises

C1 Use the data in PNTSPRD for this exercise.

(i) The variable *favwin* is a binary variable if the team favored by the Las Vegas point spread wins. A linear probability model to estimate the probability that the favored team wins is

$$P(favwin = 1|spread) = \beta_0 + \beta_1 spread.$$

Explain why, if the spread incorporates all relevant information, we expect $\beta_0 = .5$.

(ii) Estimate the model from part (i) by OLS. Test $H_0: \beta_0 = .5$ against a two-sided alternative. Use both the usual and heteroskedasticity-robust standard errors.

(iii) Is *spread* statistically significant? What is the estimated probability that the favored team wins when *spread* = 10?

(iv) Now, estimate a probit model for $P(favwin = 1|spread)$. Interpret and test the null hypothesis that the intercept is zero. [*Hint*: Remember that $\Phi(0) = .5$.]

(v) Use the probit model to estimate the probability that the favored team wins when *spread* = 10. Compare this with the LPM estimate from part (iii).

(vi) Add the variables *favhome*, *fav25*, and *und25* to the probit model and test joint significance of these variables using the likelihood ratio test. (How many *df* are in the chi-square distribution?) Interpret this result, focusing on the question of whether the spread incorporates all observable information prior to a game.

C2 Use the data in LOANAPP for this exercise; see also Computer Exercise C8 in Chapter 7.

(i) Estimate a probit model of *approve* on *white*. Find the estimated probability of loan approval for both whites and nonwhites. How do these compare with the linear probability estimates?

(ii) Now, add the variables *hrat, obrat, loanprc, unem, male, married, dep, sch, cosign, chist, pubrec, mortlat1, mortlat2,* and *vr* to the probit model. Is there statistically significant evidence of discrimination against nonwhites?

(iii) Estimate the model from part (ii) by logit. Compare the coefficient on *white* to the probit estimate.

(iv) Use equation (17.17) to estimate the sizes of the discrimination effects for probit and logit.

C3 Use the data in FRINGE for this exercise.

(i) For what percentage of the workers in the sample is *pension* equal to zero? What is the range of *pension* for workers with nonzero pension benefits? Why is a Tobit model appropriate for modeling *pension*?

(ii) Estimate a Tobit model explaining *pension* in terms of *exper, age, tenure, educ, depends, married, white,* and *male*. Do whites and males have statistically significant higher expected pension benefits?

(iii) Use the results from part (ii) to estimate the difference in expected pension benefits for a white male and a nonwhite female, both of whom are 35 years old, are single with no dependents, have 16 years of education, and have 10 years of experience.

(iv) Add *union* to the Tobit model and comment on its significance.

(v) Apply the Tobit model from part (iv) but with *peratio*, the pension-earnings ratio, as the dependent variable. (Notice that this is a fraction between zero and one, but, though it often takes on the value zero, it never gets close to being unity. Thus, a Tobit model is fine as an approximation.) Does gender or race have an effect on the pension-earnings ratio?

C4 In Example 9.1, we added the quadratic terms $pcnv^2$, $ptime86^2$, and $inc86^2$ to a linear model for *narr86*.

(i) Use the data in CRIME1 to add these same terms to the Poisson regression in Example 17.3.

(ii) Compute the estimate of σ^2 given by $\hat{\sigma}^2 = (n - k - 1)^{-1}\sum_{i=1}^{n} \hat{u}_i^2/\hat{y}_i$. Is there evidence of overdispersion? How should the Poisson MLE standard errors be adjusted?

(iii) Use the results from parts (i) and (ii) and Table 17.5 to compute the quasi-likelihood ratio statistic for joint significance of the three quadratic terms. What do you conclude?

C5 Refer to Table 13.1 in Chapter 13. There, we used the data in FERTIL1 to estimate a linear model for *kids*, the number of children ever born to a woman.

(i) Estimate a Poisson regression model for *kids*, using the same variables in Table 13.1. Interpret the coefficient on *y82*.

(ii) What is the estimated percentage difference in fertility between a black woman and a nonblack woman, holding other factors fixed?

(iii) Obtain $\hat{\sigma}$. Is there evidence of over- or underdispersion?

(iv) Compute the fitted values from the Poisson regression and obtain the *R*-squared as the squared correlation between $kids_i$ and $\widehat{kids}_i$. Compare this with the *R*-squared for the linear regression model.

C6 Use the data in RECID to estimate the model from Example 17.4 by OLS, using *only* the 552 uncensored durations. Comment generally on how these estimates compare with those in Table 17.6.

C7 Use the MROZ data for this exercise.

(i) Using the 428 women who were in the workforce, estimate the return to education by OLS including *exper, exper², nwifeinc, age, kidslt6,* and *kidsge6* as explanatory variables. Report your estimate on *educ* and its standard error.

(ii) Now, estimate the return to education by Heckit, where all exogenous variables show up in the second-stage regression. In other words, the regression is log(*wage*) on *educ, exper, exper²*, *nwifeinc*, *age*, *kidslt6*, *kidsge6*, and $\hat{\lambda}$. Compare the estimated return to education *and* its standard error to that from part (i).

(iii) Using only the 428 observations for working women, regress $\hat{\lambda}$ on *educ*, *exper*, *exper*², *nwifeinc*, *age*, *kidslt6*, and *kidsge6*. How big is the *R*-squared? How does this help explain your findings from part (ii)? (*Hint*: Think multicollinearity.)

C8 The file JTRAIN2 contains data on a job training experiment for a group of men. Men could enter the program starting in January 1976 through about mid-1977. The program ended in December 1977. The idea is to test whether participation in the job training program had an effect on unemployment probabilities and earnings in 1978.

(i) The variable *train* is the job training indicator. How many men in the sample participated in the job training program? What was the highest number of months a man actually participated in the program?

(ii) Run a linear regression of *train* on several demographic and pretraining variables: *unem74*, *unem75*, *age*, *educ*, *black*, *hisp*, and *married*. Are these variables jointly significant at the 5% level?

(iii) Estimate a probit version of the linear model in part (ii). Compute the likelihood ratio test for joint significance of all variables. What do you conclude?

(iv) Based on your answers to parts (ii) and (iii), does it appear that participation in job training can be treated as exogenous for explaining 1978 unemployment status? Explain.

(v) Run a simple regression of *unem78* on *train* and report the results in equation form. What is the estimated effect of participating in the job training program on the probability of being unemployed in 1978? Is it statistically significant?

(vi) Run a probit of *unem78* on *train*. Does it make sense to compare the probit coefficient on *train* with the coefficient obtained from the linear model in part (v)?

(vii) Find the fitted probabilities from parts (v) and (vi). Explain why they are identical. Which approach would you use to measure the effect and statistical significance of the job training program?

(viii) Add all of the variables from part (ii) as additional controls to the models from parts (v) and (vi). Are the fitted probabilities now identical? What is the correlation between them?

(ix) Using the model from part (viii), estimate the average partial effect of *train* on the 1978 unemployment probability. Use (17.17) with $c_k = 0$. How does the estimate compare with the OLS estimate from part (viii)?

C9 Use the data in APPLE for this exercise. These are telephone survey data attempting to elicit the demand for a (fictional) "ecologically friendly" apple. Each family was (randomly) presented with a set of prices for regular apples and the ecolabeled apples. They were asked how many pounds of each kind of apple they would buy.

(i) Of the 660 families in the sample, how many report wanting none of the ecolabeled apples at the set price?

(ii) Does the variable *ecolbs* seem to have a continuous distribution over strictly positive values? What implications does your answer have for the suitability of a Tobit model for *ecolbs*?

(iii) Estimate a Tobit model for *ecolbs* with *ecoprc*, *regprc*, *faminc*, and *hhsize* as explanatory variables. Which variables are significant at the 1% level?

(iv) Are *faminc* and *hhsize* jointly significant?

(v) Are the signs of the coefficients on the price variables from part (iii) what you expect? Explain.

(vi) Let β_1 be the coefficient on *ecoprc* and let β_2 be the coefficient on *regprc*. Test the hypothesis $H_0: -\beta_1 = \beta_2$ against the two-sided alternative. Report the *p*-value of the test. (You might want to refer to Section 4-4 if your regression package does not easily compute such tests.)

(vii) Obtain the estimates of $E(ecolbs|\mathbf{x})$ for all observations in the sample. [See equation (17.25).] Call these $\widehat{ecolbs}_i$. What are the smallest and largest fitted values?

(viii) Compute the squared correlation between $ecolbs_i$ and $\widehat{ecolbs_i}$.

(ix) Now, estimate a linear model for $ecolbs$ using the same explanatory variables from part (iii). Why are the OLS estimates so much smaller than the Tobit estimates? In terms of goodness-of-fit, is the Tobit model better than the linear model?

(x) Evaluate the following statement: "Because the R-squared from the Tobit model is so small, the estimated price effects are probably inconsistent."

C10 Use the data in SMOKE for this exercise.

(i) The variable $cigs$ is the number of cigarettes smoked per day. How many people in the sample do not smoke at all? What fraction of people claim to smoke 20 cigarettes a day? Why do you think there is a pileup of people at 20 cigarettes?

(ii) Given your answers to part (i), does $cigs$ seem a good candidate for having a conditional Poisson distribution?

(iii) Estimate a Poisson regression model for $cigs$, including $\log(cigpric)$, $\log(income)$, $white$, $educ$, age, and age^2 as explanatory variables. What are the estimated price and income elasticities?

(iv) Using the maximum likelihood standard errors, are the price and income variables statistically significant at the 5% level?

(v) Obtain the estimate of σ^2 described after equation (17.35). What is $\hat{\sigma}$? How should you adjust the standard errors from part (iv)?

(vi) Using the adjusted standard errors from part (v), are the price and income elasticities now statistically different from zero? Explain.

(vii) Are the education and age variables significant using the more robust standard errors? How do you interpret the coefficient on $educ$?

(viii) Obtain the fitted values, $\hat{y}_i$, from the Poisson regression model. Find the minimum and maximum values and discuss how well the exponential model predicts heavy cigarette smoking.

(ix) Using the fitted values from part (viii), obtain the squared correlation coefficient between $\hat{y}_i$ and y_i.

(x) Estimate a linear model for $cigs$ by OLS, using the explanatory variables (and same functional forms) as in part (iii). Does the linear model or exponential model provide a better fit? Is either R-squared very large?

C11 Use the data in CPS91 for this exercise. These data are for married women, where we also have information on each husband's income and demographics.

(i) What fraction of the women report being in the labor force?

(ii) Using only the data for working women—you have no choice—estimate the wage equation

$$\log(wage) = \beta_0 + \beta_1 educ + \beta_2 exper + \beta_3 exper^2 + \beta_4 black + \beta_5 hispanic + u$$

by ordinary least squares. Report the results in the usual form. Do there appear to be significant wage differences by race and ethnicity?

(iii) Estimate a probit model for $inlf$ that includes the explanatory variables in the wage equation from part (ii) as well as $nwifeinc$ and $kidlt6$. Do these last two variables have coefficients of the expected sign? Are they statistically significant?

(iv) Explain why, for the purposes of testing and, possibly, correcting the wage equation for selection into the workforce, it is important for $nwifeinc$ and $kidlt6$ to help explain $inlf$. What must you assume about $nwifeinc$ and $kidlt6$ in the wage equation?

(v) Compute the inverse Mills ratio (for each observation) and add it as an additional regressor to the wage equation from part (ii). What is its two-sided p-value? Do you think this is particularly small with 3,286 observations?

(vi) Does adding the inverse Mills ratio change the coefficients in the wage regression in important ways? Explain.

C12 Use the data in CHARITY to answer these questions.
  (i)   The variable *respond* is a binary variable equal to one if an individual responded with a donation to the most recent request. The database consists only of people who have responded at least once in the past. What fraction of people responded most recently?
  (ii) Estimate a probit model for *respond*, using *resplast*, *weekslast*, *propresp*, *mailsyear*, and *avggift* as explanatory variables. Which of the explanatory variables is statistically significant?
  (iii) Find the average partial effect for *mailsyear* and compare it with the coefficient from a linear probability model.
  (iv) Using the same explanatory variables, estimate a Tobit model for *gift*, the amount of the most recent gift (in Dutch guilders). Now which explanatory variable is statistically significant?
  (v)   Compare the Tobit APE for *mailsyear* with that from a linear regression. Are they similar?
  (vi) Are the estimates from parts (ii) and (iv) entirely compatible with at Tobit model? Explain.

C13 Use the data in HTV to answer this question.
  (i)   Using OLS on the full sample, estimate a model for log(*wage*) using explanatory variables *educ*, *abil*, *exper*, *nc*, *west*, *south*, and *urban*. Report the estimated return to education and its standard error.
  (ii) Now estimate the equation from part (i) using only people with *educ* < 16. What percentage of the sample is lost? Now what is the estimated return to a year of schooling? How does it compare with part (i)?
  (iii) Now drop all observations with *wage* ≥ 20, so that everyone remaining in the sample earns less than $20 an hour. Run the regression from part (i) and comment on the coefficient on *educ*. (Because the normal truncated regression model assumes that *y* is continuous, it does not matter in theory whether we drop observations with *wage* ≥ 20 or *wage* > 20. In practice, including in this application, it can matter slightly because there are some people who earn exactly $20 per hour.)
  (iv) Using the sample in part (iii), apply truncated regression [with the upper truncation point being log(20)]. Does truncated regression appear to recover the return to education in the full population, assuming the estimate from (i) is consistent? Explain.

C14 Use the data in HAPPINESS for this question. See also Computer Exercise C15 in Chapter 13.
  (i)   Estimate a probit probability model relating *vhappy* to *occattend* and *regattend*, and include a full set of year dummies. Find the average partial effects for *occattend* and *regattend*. How do these compare with those from estimating a linear probability model?
  (ii) Define a variable, *highinc*, equal to one if family income is above $25,000. Include *highinc*, *unem10*, *educ*, and *teens* to the probit estimation in part (ii). Is the APE of *regattend* affected much? What about its statistical significance?
  (iii) Discuss the APEs and statistical significance of the four new variables in part (ii). Do the estimates make sense?
  (iv) Controlling for the factors in part (ii), do there appear to be differences in happiness by gender or race? Justify your answer.

C15 Use the data set in ALCOHOL, obtained from Terza (2002), to answer this question. The data, on 9,822 men, includes labor market information, whether the man abuses alcohol, and demographic and background variables. In this question you will study the effects of alcohol abuse on *employ*, which is a binary variable equal to one if the man has a job. If *employ* = 0, the man is either unemployed or not in the workforce.
  (i)   What fraction of the sample is employed at the time of the interview? What fraction of the sample has abused alcohol?
  (ii) Run the simple regression of *employ* on *abuse* and report the results in the usual form, obtaining the heteroskedasticity-robust standard errors. Interpret the estimated equation. Is the relationship as you expected? Is it statistically significant?

(iii)   Run a probit of *employ* on *abuse*. Do you get the same sign and statistical significance as in part (ii)? How does the average partial effect for the probit compare with that for the linear probability model?

(iv)   Obtain the fitted values for the LPM estimated in part (ii) and report what they are when *abuse* = 0 and when *abuse* = 1. How do these compare to the probit fitted values, and why?

(v)   To the LPM in part (ii) add the variables *age*, *agesq*, *educ*, *educsq*, *married*, *famsize*, *white*, *northeast*, *midwest*, *south*, *centcity*, *outercity*, *qrt1*, *qrt2*, and *qrt3*. What happens to the coefficient on *abuse* and its statistical significance?

(vi)   Estimate a probit model using the variables in part (v). Find the APE of *abuse* and its *t* statistic. Is the estimated effect now identical to that for the linear model? Is it "close"?

(vii)   Variables indicating the overall health of each man are also included in the data set. Is it obvious that such variables should be included as controls? Explain.

(viii)   Why might *abuse* be properly thought of as endogenous in the *employ* equation? Do you think the variables *mothalc* and *fathalc*, indicating whether a man's mother or father were alcoholics, are sensible instrumental variables for *abuse*?

(ix)   Estimate the LPM underlying part (v) by 2SLS, where *mothalc* and *fathalc* act as IVs for *abuse*. Is the difference between the 2SLS and OLS coefficients practically large?

(x)   Use the test described in Section 15-5 to test whether *abuse* is endogenous in the LPM.

C16   Use the data in CRIME1 to answer this question.

(i)   For the OLS estimates reported in Table 17.5, find the heteroskedasticity-robust standard errors. In terms of statistical significance of the coefficients, are there any notable changes?

(ii)   Obtain the fully robust standard errors—that is, those that do not even require assumption (17.35)—for the Poisson regression estimates in the second column. (This requires that you have a statistical package that computes the fully robust standard errors.) Compare the fully robust 95% confidence interval for β_{pcnv} with that obtained using the standard error in Table 17.5.

(iii)   Compute the average partial effects for each variable in the Poisson regression model. Use the formula for binary explanatory variables for *black*, *hispan*, and *born60*. Compare the APEs for *qemp86* and *inc86* with the corresponding OLS coefficients.

(iv)   If your statistical package reports the robust standard errors for the APEs in part (iii), compare the robust *t* statistic for the OLS estimate of β_{pcnv} with the robust *t* statistic for the APE of *pcnv* in the Poisson regression.

APPENDIX 17A

17A.1 Maximum Likelihood Estimation with Explanatory Variables

Appendix C provides a review of maximum likelihood estimation (MLE) in the simplest case of estimating the parameters in an unconditional distribution. But most models in econometrics have explanatory variables, whether we estimate those models by OLS or MLE. The latter is indispensable for nonlinear models, and here we provide a very brief description of the general approach.

All of the models covered in this chapter can be put in the following form. Let $f(y|\mathbf{x},\boldsymbol{\beta})$ denote the density function for a random draw y_i from the population, conditional on $\mathbf{x}_i = \mathbf{x}$. The maximum likelihood estimator (MLE) of $\boldsymbol{\beta}$ maximizes the log-likelihood function,

$$\max_{\mathbf{b}} \sum_{i=1}^{n} \log f(y_i|\mathbf{x}_i, \mathbf{b}), \qquad [17.53]$$

where the vector $\mathbf{b}$ is the dummy argument in the maximization problem. In most cases, the MLE, which we write as $\hat{\boldsymbol{\beta}}$, is consistent and has an approximate normal distribution in large samples. This is true even though we cannot write down a formula for $\hat{\boldsymbol{\beta}}$ except in very special circumstances.

For the binary response case (logit and probit), the conditional density is determined by two values, $f(1|\mathbf{x},\boldsymbol{\beta}) = P(y_i = 1|\mathbf{x}_i) = G(\mathbf{x}_i\boldsymbol{\beta})$ and $f(0|\mathbf{x},\boldsymbol{\beta}) = P(y_i = 0|\mathbf{x}_i) = 1 - G(\mathbf{x}_i\boldsymbol{\beta})$. In fact, a succinct way to write the density is $f(y|\mathbf{x},\boldsymbol{\beta}) = [1 - G(\mathbf{x}\boldsymbol{\beta})]^{(1-y)}[G(\mathbf{x}\boldsymbol{\beta})]^y$ for $y = 0, 1$. Thus, we can write (17.53) as

$$\max_{\mathbf{b}} \sum_{i=1}^{n} \{(1 - y_i)\log[1 - G(\mathbf{x}_i\mathbf{b})] + y_i\log[G(\mathbf{x}_i\mathbf{b})]\}. \qquad [17.54]$$

Generally, the solutions to (17.54) are quickly found by modern computers using iterative methods to maximize a function. The total computation time even for fairly large data sets is typically quite low.

The log-likelihood function for the Tobit model and for censored and truncated regression are only slightly more complicated, depending on an additional variance parameter in addition to $\boldsymbol{\beta}$. They are easily derived from the densities obtained in the text. See Wooldridge (2010) for details.

APPENDIX 17B

17B.1 Asymptotic Standard Errors in Limited Dependent Variable Models

Derivations of the asymptotic standard errors for the models and methods introduced in this chapter are well beyond the scope of this text. Not only do the derivations require matrix algebra, but they also require advanced asymptotic theory of nonlinear estimation. The background needed for a careful analysis of these methods and several derivations are given in Wooldridge (2010).

It is instructive to see the formulas for obtaining the asymptotic standard errors for at least some of the methods. Given the binary response model $P(y = 1|\mathbf{x}) = G(\mathbf{x}\boldsymbol{\beta})$, where $G(\cdot)$ is the logit or probit function, and $\boldsymbol{\beta}$ is the $k \times 1$ vector of parameters, the asymptotic variance matrix of $\hat{\boldsymbol{\beta}}$ is estimated as

$$\widehat{\text{Avar}}(\hat{\boldsymbol{\beta}}) \equiv \left(\sum_{i=1}^{n} \frac{[g(\mathbf{x}_i\hat{\boldsymbol{\beta}})]^2 \mathbf{x}_i'\mathbf{x}_i}{G(\mathbf{x}_i\hat{\boldsymbol{\beta}})[1 - G(\mathbf{x}_i\hat{\boldsymbol{\beta}})]} \right)^{-1}, \qquad [17.55]$$

which is a $k \times k$ matrix. (See Appendix D for a summary of matrix algebra.) Without the terms involving $g(\cdot)$ and $G(\cdot)$, this formula looks a lot like the estimated variance matrix for the OLS estimator, minus the term $\hat{\sigma}^2$. The expression in (17.55) accounts for the nonlinear nature of the response probability—that is, the nonlinear nature of $G(\cdot)$—as well as the particular form of heteroskedasticity in a binary response model: $\text{Var}(y|\mathbf{x}) = G(\mathbf{x}\boldsymbol{\beta})[1 - G(\mathbf{x}\boldsymbol{\beta})]$.

The square roots of the diagonal elements of (17.55) are the asymptotic standard errors of the $\hat{\beta}_j$, and they are routinely reported by econometrics software that supports logit and probit analysis. Once we have these, (asymptotic) t statistics and confidence intervals are obtained in the usual ways.

The matrix in (17.55) is also the basis for Wald tests of multiple restrictions on $\boldsymbol{\beta}$ [see Wooldridge (2010, Chapter 15)].

The asymptotic variance matrix for Tobit is more complicated but has a similar structure. Note that we can obtain a standard error for $\hat{\sigma}$ as well. The asymptotic variance for Poisson regression, allowing for $\sigma^2 \neq 1$ in (17.35), has a form much like (17.55):

$$\widehat{\text{Avar}}(\hat{\boldsymbol{\beta}}) = \hat{\sigma}^2 \left(\sum_{i=1}^{n} \exp(\mathbf{x}_i\hat{\boldsymbol{\beta}})\mathbf{x}_i'\mathbf{x}_i \right)^{-1}. \qquad [17.56]$$

The square roots of the diagonal elements of this matrix are the asymptotic standard errors. If the Poisson assumption holds, we can drop $\hat{\sigma}^2$ from the formula (because $\sigma^2 = 1$).

The formula for the fully robust variance matrix estimator is obtained in Wooldridge (2010, Chapter 18):

$$\widehat{\text{Avar}}(\hat{\boldsymbol{\beta}}) = \left[\sum_{i=1}^{n}\exp(\mathbf{x}_i\hat{\boldsymbol{\beta}})\mathbf{x}_i'\mathbf{x}_i\right]^{-1}\left(\sum_{i=1}^{n}\hat{u}_i^2\mathbf{x}_i'\mathbf{x}_i\right)\left[\sum_{i=1}^{n}\exp(\mathbf{x}_i\hat{\boldsymbol{\beta}})\mathbf{x}_i'\mathbf{x}_i\right]^{-1},$$

where $\hat{u}_i = y_i - \exp(\mathbf{x}_i\hat{\boldsymbol{\beta}})$ are the residuals from the Poisson regression. This expression has a structure similar to the heteroskedasticity-robust standard variance matrix estimator for OLS, and it is computed routinely by many software packages to obtain the fully robust standard errors.

Asymptotic standard errors for censored regression, truncated regression, and the Heckit sample selection correction are more complicated, although they share features with the previous formulas. [See Wooldridge (2010) for details.]

CHAPTER 18

Advanced Time Series Topics

I n this chapter, we cover some more advanced topics in time series econometrics. In Chapters 10, 11, and 12, we emphasized in several places that using time series data in regression analysis requires some care due to the trending, persistent nature of many economic time series. In addition to studying topics such as infinite distributed lag models and forecasting, we also discuss some recent advances in analyzing time series processes with unit roots.

In Section 18-1, we describe infinite distributed lag models, which allow a change in an explanatory variable to affect all future values of the dependent variable. Conceptually, these models are straightforward extensions of the finite distributed lag models in Chapter 10, but estimating these models poses some interesting challenges.

In Section 18-2, we show how to formally test for unit roots in a time series process. Recall from Chapter 11 that we excluded unit root processes to apply the usual asymptotic theory. Because the presence of a unit root implies that a shock today has a long-lasting impact, determining whether a process has a unit root is of interest in its own right.

We cover the notion of spurious regression between two time series processes, each of which has a unit root, in Section 18-3. The main result is that even if two unit root series are *independent*, it is quite likely that the regression of one on the other will yield a statistically significant t statistic. This emphasizes the potentially serious consequences of using standard inference when the dependent and independent variables are integrated processes.

The notion of cointegration applies when two series are I(1), but a linear combination of them is I(0); in this case, the regression of one on the other is not spurious, but instead tells us something about the long-run relationship between them. Cointegration between two series also implies a particular kind of model, called an error correction model, for the short-term dynamics. We cover these models in Section 18-4.

In Section 18-5, we provide an overview of forecasting and bring together all of the tools in this and previous chapters to show how regression methods can be used to forecast future outcomes of a time series. The forecasting literature is vast, so we focus only on the most common regression-based methods. We also touch on the related topic of Granger causality.

18-1 Infinite Distributed Lag Models

Let $\{(y_t, z_t): t = \ldots, -2, -1, 0, 1, 2, \ldots\}$ be a bivariate time series process (which is only partially observed). An **infinite distributed lag (IDL) model** relating y_t to current and all past values of z is

$$y_t = \alpha + \delta_0 z_t + \delta_1 z_{t-1} + \delta_2 z_{t-2} + \ldots + u_t, \qquad [18.1]$$

where the sum on lagged z extends back to the indefinite past. This model is only an approximation to reality, as no economic process started infinitely far into the past. Compared with a finite distributed lag model, an IDL model does not require that we truncate the lag at a particular value.

In order for model (18.1) to make sense, the lag coefficients, δ_j, must tend to zero as $j \to \infty$. This is not to say that δ_2 is smaller in magnitude than δ_1; it only means that the impact of z_{t-j} on y_t must eventually become small as j gets large. In most applications, this makes economic sense as well: the distant past of z should be less important for explaining y than the recent past of z.

Even if we decide that (18.1) is a useful model, we clearly cannot estimate it without some restrictions. For one, we only observe a finite history of data. Equation (18.1) involves an infinite number of parameters, $\delta_0, \delta_1, \delta_2, \ldots$, which cannot be estimated without restrictions. Later, we place restrictions on the δ_j that allow us to estimate (18.1).

As with finite distributed lag (FDL) models, the impact propensity in (18.1) is simply δ_0 (see Chapter 10). Generally, the δ_h have the same interpretation as in an FDL. Suppose that $z_s = 0$ for all $s < 0$ and that $z_0 = 1$ and $z_s = 0$ for all $s > 1$; in other words, at time $t = 0$, z increases temporarily by one unit and then reverts to its initial level of zero. For any $h \geq 0$, we have $y_h = \alpha + \delta_h + u_h$ for all $h \geq 0$, and so

$$\mathrm{E}(y_h) = \alpha + \delta_h, \qquad [18.2]$$

where we use the standard assumption that u_h has zero mean. It follows that δ_h is the change in $\mathrm{E}(y_h)$ given a one-unit, temporary change in z at time zero. We just said that δ_h must be tending to zero as h gets large for the IDL to make sense. This means that a temporary change in z has *no long-run effect* on expected y: $\mathrm{E}(y_h) = \alpha + \delta_h \to \alpha$ as $h \to \infty$.

We assumed that the process z starts at $z_s = 0$ and that the one-unit increase occurred at $t = 0$. These were only for the purpose of illustration. More generally, if z temporarily increases by one unit (from any initial level) at time t, then δ_h measures the change in the expected value of y after h periods. The lag distribution, which is δ_h plotted as a function of h, shows the expected path that future outcomes on y follow given the one-unit, temporary increase in z.

The long-run propensity in model (18.1) is the sum of all of the lag coefficients:

$$LRP = \delta_0 + \delta_1 + \delta_2 + \delta_3 + \ldots, \qquad [18.3]$$

where we assume that the infinite sum is well defined. Because the δ_j must converge to zero, the LRP can often be well approximated by a finite sum of the form $\delta_0 + \delta_1 + \ldots + \delta_p$ for sufficiently large p. To interpret the LRP, suppose that the process z_t is steady at $z_s = 0$ for $s < 0$. At $t = 0$, the process permanently increases by one unit. For example, if z_t is the percentage change in the money supply and y_t is the inflation rate, then we are interested in the effects of a permanent increase of one percentage point in money supply growth. Then, by substituting $z_s = 0$ for $s < 0$ and $z_t = 1$ for $t \geq 0$, we have

$$y_h = \alpha + \delta_0 + \delta_1 + \ldots + \delta_h + u_h,$$

where $h \geq 0$ is any horizon. Because u_t has a zero mean for all t, we have

$$E(y_h) = \alpha + \delta_0 + \delta_1 + \ldots + \delta_h. \qquad [18.4]$$

[It is useful to compare (18.4) and (18.2).] As the horizon increases, that is, as $h \to \infty$, the right-hand side of (18.4) is, by definition, the long-run propensity, plus α. Thus, the LRP measures the long-run change in the expected value of y given a one-unit, *permanent* increase in z.

> **EXPLORING FURTHER 18.1**
>
> Suppose that $z_s = 0$ for $s < 0$ and that $z_0 = 1$, $z_1 = 1$, and $z_s = 0$ for $s > 1$. Find $E(y_{-1})$, $E(y_0)$, and $E(y_h)$ for $h \geq 1$. What happens as $h \to \infty$?

The previous derivation of the LRP and the interpretation of δ_j used the fact that the errors have a zero mean; as usual, this is not much of an assumption, provided an intercept is included in the model. A closer examination of our reasoning shows that we assumed that the change in z during any time period had no effect on the expected value of u_t. This is the infinite distributed lag version of the *strict exogeneity* assumption that we introduced in Chapter 10 (in particular, Assumption TS.3). Formally,

$$E(u_t | \ldots, z_{t-2}, z_{t-1}, z_t, z_{t+1}, \ldots) = 0, \qquad [18.5]$$

so that the expected value of u_t does not depend on the z in *any* time period. Although (18.5) is natural for some applications, it rules out other important possibilities. In effect, (18.5) does not allow feedback from y_t to future z because z_{t+h} must be uncorrelated with u_t for $h > 0$. In the inflation/money supply growth example, where y_t is inflation and z_t is money supply growth, (18.5) rules out future changes in money supply growth that are tied to changes in today's inflation rate. Given that money supply policy often attempts to keep interest rates and inflation at certain levels, this might be unrealistic.

One approach to estimating the δ_j, which we cover in the next subsection, requires a strict exogeneity assumption in order to produce consistent estimators of the δ_j. A weaker assumption is

$$E(u_t | z_t, z_{t-1}, \ldots) = 0. \qquad [18.6]$$

Under (18.6), the error is uncorrelated with current and *past* z, but it may be correlated with future z; this allows z_t to be a variable that follows policy rules that depend on past y. Sometimes, (18.6) is sufficient to estimate the δ_j; we explain this in the next subsection.

One thing to remember is that neither (18.5) nor (18.6) says anything about the serial correlation properties of $\{u_t\}$. (This is just as in finite distributed lag models.) If anything, we might expect the $\{u_t\}$ to be serially correlated because (18.1) is not generally dynamically complete in the sense discussed in Section 11-4. We will study the serial correlation problem later.

How do we interpret the lag coefficients and the LRP if (18.6) holds but (18.5) does not? The answer is: the same way as before. We can still do the previous thought (or counterfactual) experiment even though the data we observe are generated by some feedback between y_t and future z. For example, we can certainly ask about the long-run effect of a permanent increase in money supply growth on inflation even though the data on money supply growth cannot be characterized as strictly exogenous.

18-1a The Geometric (or Koyck) Distributed Lag

Because there are generally an infinite number of δ_j, we cannot consistently estimate them without some restrictions. The simplest version of (18.1), which still makes the model depend on an infinite number of lags, is the **geometric (or Koyck) distributed lag**. In this model, the δ_j depend on only two parameters:

$$\delta_j = \gamma\rho^j, \ |\rho| < 1, \ j = 0, 1, \ 2, \dots \quad \text{[18.7]}$$

The parameters γ and ρ may be positive or negative, but ρ must be less than one in absolute value. This ensures that $\delta_j \to 0$ as $j \to \infty$. In fact, this convergence happens at a very fast rate. (For example, with $\rho = .5$ and $j = 10$, $\rho^j = 1/1{,}024 < .001$.)

The impact propensity (IP) in the GDL is simply $\delta_0 = \gamma$, so the sign of the IP is determined by the sign of γ. If $\gamma > 0$, say, and $\rho > 0$, then all lag coefficients are positive. If $\rho < 0$, the lag coefficients alternate in sign (ρ^j is negative for odd j). The long-run propensity is more difficult to obtain, but we can use a standard result on the sum of a geometric series: for $|\rho| < 1, 1 + \rho + \rho^2 + \dots + \rho^j + \dots = 1/(1 - \rho)$, and so

$$LRP = \gamma/(1 - \rho).$$

The LRP has the same sign as γ.

If we plug (18.7) into (18.1), we still have a model that depends on the z back to the indefinite past. Nevertheless, a simple subtraction yields an estimable model. Write the IDL at times t and $t - 1$ as:

$$y_t = \alpha + \gamma z_t + \gamma\rho z_{t-1} + \gamma\rho^2 z_{t-2} + \dots + u_t \quad \text{[18.8]}$$

and

$$y_{t-1} = \alpha + \gamma z_{t-1} + \gamma\rho z_{t-2} + \gamma\rho^2 z_{t-3} + \dots + u_{t-1}. \quad \text{[18.9]}$$

If we multiply the second equation by ρ and subtract it from the first, all but a few of the terms cancel:

$$y_t - \rho y_{t-1} = (1 - \rho)\alpha + \gamma z_t + u_t - \rho u_{t-1},$$

which we can write as

$$y_t = \alpha_0 + \gamma z_t + \rho y_{t-1} + u_t - \rho u_{t-1}, \quad \text{[18.10]}$$

where $\alpha_0 = (1 - \rho)\alpha$. This equation looks like a standard model with a lagged dependent variable, where z_t appears contemporaneously. Because γ is the coefficient on z_t and ρ is the coefficient on y_{t-1}, it appears that we can estimate these parameters. [If, for some reason, we are interested in α, we can always obtain $\hat{\alpha} = \hat{\alpha}_0/(1 - \hat{\rho})$ after estimating ρ and α_0.]

The simplicity of (18.10) is somewhat misleading. The error term in this equation, $u_t - \rho u_{t-1}$, is generally correlated with y_{t-1}. From (18.9), it is pretty clear that u_{t-1} and y_{t-1} are correlated. Therefore, if we write (18.10) as

$$y_t = \alpha_0 + \gamma z_t + \rho y_{t-1} + v_t, \quad \text{[18.11]}$$

where $v_t \equiv u_t - \rho u_{t-1}$, then we generally have correlation between v_t and y_{t-1}. Without further assumptions, OLS estimation of (18.11) produces inconsistent estimates of γ and ρ.

One case where v_t *must* be correlated with y_{t-1} occurs when u_t is independent of z_t and *all* past values of z and y. Then, (18.8) is dynamically complete, so u_t is uncorrelated with y_{t-1}. From (18.9), the covariance between v_t and y_{t-1} is $-\rho\text{Var}(u_{t-1}) = -\rho\sigma_u^2$, which is zero only if $\rho = 0$. We can easily see that v_t is serially correlated: because $\{u_t\}$ is serially uncorrelated, $\text{E}(v_t v_{t-1}) = \text{E}(u_t u_{t-1}) - \rho\text{E}(u_{t-1}^2) - \rho\text{E}(u_t u_{t-2}) + \rho^2\text{E}(u_{t-1}u_{t-2}) = -\rho\sigma_u^2$. For $j > 1, \text{E}(v_t v_{t-j}) = 0$. Thus, $\{v_t\}$ is a moving average process of order one (see Section 11-1). This, and equation (18.11), gives an example of a model—which is derived from the original model of interest—that has a lagged dependent variable *and* a particular kind of serial correlation.

If we make the strict exogeneity assumption (18.5), then z_t is uncorrelated with u_t and u_{t-1}, and therefore with v_t. Thus, if we can find a suitable instrumental variable for y_{t-1}, then we can estimate (18.11) by IV. What is a good IV candidate for y_{t-1}? By assumption, u_t and u_{t-1} are both uncorrelated with z_{t-1}, so v_t is uncorrelated with z_{t-1}. If $\gamma \neq 0$, z_{t-1} and y_{t-1} are correlated, even after partialling out z_t. Therefore, we can use instruments (z_t, z_{t-1}) to estimate (18.11). Generally, the standard errors need to be adjusted for serial correlation in the $\{v_t\}$, as we discussed in Section 15-7.

An alternative to IV estimation exploits the fact that $\{u_t\}$ may contain a specific kind of serial correlation. In particular, in addition to (18.6), suppose that $\{u_t\}$ follows the AR(1) model

$$u_t = \rho u_{t-1} + e_t \qquad \text{[18.12]}$$

$$E(e_t | z_t, y_{t-1}, z_{t-1}, \ldots) = 0. \qquad \text{[18.13]}$$

It is important to notice that the ρ appearing in (18.12) is the same parameter multiplying y_{t-1} in (18.11). If (18.12) and (18.13) hold, we can write equation (18.10) as

$$y_t = \alpha_0 + \gamma z_t + \rho y_{t-1} + e_t, \qquad \text{[18.14]}$$

which is a dynamically complete model under (18.13). From Chapter 11, we can obtain consistent, asymptotically normal estimators of the parameters by OLS. This is very convenient, as there is no need to deal with serial correlation in the errors. If e_t satisfies the homoskedasticity assumption $\text{Var}(e_t | z_t, y_{t-1}) = \sigma_e^2$, the usual inference applies. Once we have estimated γ and ρ, we can easily estimate the LRP: $\widehat{LRP} = \hat{\gamma}/(1 - \hat{\rho})$. Many econometrics packages have simple commands that allow one to obtain a standard error for the estimated LRP.

The simplicity of this procedure relies on the potentially strong assumption that $\{u_t\}$ follows an AR(1) process with the *same* ρ appearing in (18.7). This is usually no worse than assuming the $\{u_t\}$ are serially uncorrelated. Nevertheless, because consistency of the estimators relies heavily on this assumption, it is a good idea to test it. A simple test begins by specifying $\{u_t\}$ as an AR(1) process with a *different* parameter, say, $u_t = \lambda u_{t-1} + e_t$. McClain and Wooldridge (1995) devised a simple Lagrange multiplier test of $H_0: \lambda = \rho$ that can be computed after OLS estimation of (18.14).

The geometric distributed lag model extends to multiple explanatory variables—so that we have an infinite DL in each explanatory variable—but then we must be able to write the coefficient on $z_{t-j, h}$ as $\gamma_h \rho^j$. In other words, though γ_h is different for each explanatory variable, ρ is the same. Thus, we can write

$$y_t = \alpha_0 + \gamma_1 z_{t1} + \ldots + \gamma_k z_{tk} + \rho y_{t-1} + v_t. \qquad \text{[18.15]}$$

The same issues that arose in the case with one z arise in the case with many z. Under the natural extension of (18.12) and (18.13)—just replace z_t with $z_t = (z_{t1}, \ldots, z_{tk})$—OLS is consistent and asymptotically normal. Or, an IV method can be used.

18-1b Rational Distributed Lag Models

The geometric DL implies a fairly restrictive lag distribution. When $\gamma > 0$ and $\rho > 0$, the δ_j are positive and monotonically declining to zero. It is possible to have more general infinite distributed lag models. The GDL is a special case of what is generally called a **rational distributed lag (RDL) model**. A general treatment is beyond our scope—Harvey (1990) is a good reference—but we can cover one simple, useful extension.

Such an RDL model is most easily described by adding a lag of z to equation (18.11):

$$y_t = \alpha_0 + \gamma_0 z_t + \rho y_{t-1} + \gamma_1 z_{t-1} + v_t, \qquad \text{[18.16]}$$

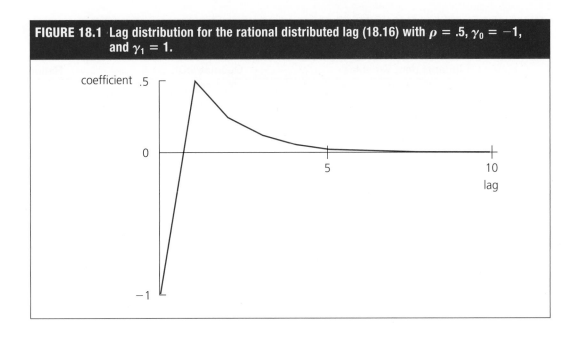

FIGURE 18.1 Lag distribution for the rational distributed lag (18.16) with $\rho = .5$, $\gamma_0 = -1$, and $\gamma_1 = 1$.

where $v_t = u_t - \rho u_{t-1}$, as before. By repeated substitution, it can be shown that (18.16) is equivalent to the infinite distributed lag model

$$
\begin{aligned}
y_t &= \alpha + \gamma_0(z_t + \rho z_{t-1} + \rho^2 z_{t-2} + \dots) \\
&\quad + \gamma_1(z_{t-1} + \rho z_{t-2} + \rho^2 z_{t-3} + \dots) + u_t \\
&= \alpha + \gamma_0 z_t + (\rho\gamma_0 + \gamma_1)z_{t-1} + \rho(\rho\gamma_0 + \gamma_1)z_{t-2} \\
&\quad + \rho^2(\rho\gamma_0 + \gamma_1)z_{t-3} + \dots + u_t,
\end{aligned}
$$

where we again need the assumption $|\rho| < 1$. From this last equation, we can read off the lag distribution. In particular, the impact propensity is γ_0, while the coefficient on z_{t-h} is $\rho^{h-1}(\rho\gamma_0 + \gamma_1)$ for $h \geq 1$. Therefore, this model allows the impact propensity to differ in sign from the other lag coefficients, even if $\rho > 0$. However, if $\rho > 0$, the δ_h have the same sign as $(\rho\gamma_0 + \gamma_1)$ for all $h \geq 1$. The lag distribution is plotted in Figure 18.1 for $\rho = .5$, $\gamma_0 = -1$, and $\gamma_1 = 1$.

The easiest way to compute the long-run propensity is to set y and z at their long-run values for all t, say, y^* and z^*, and then find the change in y^* with respect to z^* (see also Problem 3 in Chapter 10). We have $y^* = \alpha_0 + \gamma_0 z^* + \rho y^* + \gamma_1 z^*$ and solving gives $y^* = \alpha_0/(1 - \rho) + (\gamma_0 + \gamma_1)/(1 - \rho)z^*$. Now, we use the fact that $LRP = \Delta y^*/\Delta z^*$:

$$
LRP = (\gamma_0 + \gamma_1)/(1 - \rho).
$$

Because $|\rho| < 1$, the LRP has the same sign as $\gamma_0 + \gamma_1$, and the LRP is zero if, and only if, $\gamma_0 + \gamma_1 = 0$, as in Figure 18.1.

EXAMPLE 18.1 **Housing Investment and Residential Price Inflation**

We estimate both the basic geometric and the rational distributed lag models by applying OLS to (18.14) and (18.16), respectively. The dependent variable is log(*invpc*) *after* a linear time trend has been removed [that is, we linearly detrend log(*invpc*)]. For z_t, we use the growth in the price index. This allows us to estimate how residential price inflation affects movements in housing investment around its trend. The results of the estimation, using the data in HSEINV, are given in Table 18.1.

TABLE 18.1 Distributed Lag Models for Housing Investment

Dependent Variable: log(*invpc*), detrended

Independent Variables	GeometricDL	RationalDL
gprice	3.095	3.256
	(.933)	(.970)
y_{-1}	.340	.547
	(.132)	(.152)
$gprice_{-1}$	—	−2.936
		(.973)
constant	−.010	.006
	(.018)	(.017)
Long-run propensity	4.689	.706
Sample size	41	40
Adjusted *R*-squared	.375	.504

The geometric distributed lag model is clearly rejected by the data, as $gprice_{-1}$ is very significant. The adjusted R-squareds also show that the RDL model fits much better.

The two models give very different estimates of the long-run propensity. If we incorrectly use the GDL, the estimated LRP is almost five: a permanent one percentage point increase in residential price inflation increases long-term housing investment by 4.7% (above its trend value). Economically, this seems implausible. The LRP estimated from the rational distributed lag model is below one. In fact, we cannot reject the null hypothesis H_0: $\gamma_0 + \gamma_1 = 0$ at any reasonable significance level (p-value = .83), so there is no evidence that the LRP is different from zero. This is a good example of how misspecifying the dynamics of a model by omitting relevant lags can lead to erroneous conclusions.

18-2 Testing for Unit Roots

We now turn to the important problem of testing whether a time series follows a **Unit Roots**. In Chapter 11, we gave some vague, necessarily informal guidelines to decide whether a series is I(1) or not. In many cases, it is useful to have a formal test for a unit root. As we will see, such tests must be applied with caution.

The simplest approach to testing for a unit root begins with an AR(1) model:

$$y_t = \alpha + \rho y_{t-1} + e_t, t = 1, 2, \ldots, \qquad [18.17]$$

where y_0 is the observed initial value. Throughout this section, we let $\{e_t\}$ denote a process that has zero mean, given past observed y:

$$E(e_t|y_{t-1}, y_{t-2}, \ldots, y_0) = 0. \qquad [18.18]$$

[Under (18.18), $\{e_t\}$ is said to be a **martingale difference sequence** with respect to $\{y_{t-1}, y_{t-2}, \ldots\}$. If $\{e_t\}$ is assumed to be i.i.d. with zero mean and is independent of y_0, then it also satisfies (18.18).]

If $\{y_t\}$ follows (18.17), it has a unit root if, and only if, $\rho = 1$. If $\alpha = 0$ and $\rho = 1$, $\{y_t\}$ follows a random walk without drift [with the innovations e_t satisfying (18.18)]. If $\alpha \neq 0$ and $\rho = 1$, $\{y_t\}$ is a random walk with drift, which means that $E(y_t)$ is a linear function of t. A unit root process with drift behaves very differently from one without drift. Nevertheless, it is common to leave α unspecified under the null hypothesis, and this is the approach we take. Therefore, the null hypothesis is that $\{y_t\}$ has a unit root:

$$H_0: \rho = 1. \qquad \qquad [18.19]$$

In almost all cases, we are interested in the one-sided alternative

$$H_1: \rho < 1. \qquad \qquad [18.20]$$

(In practice, this means $0 < \rho < 1$, as $\rho < 0$ for a series that we suspect has a unit root would be very rare.) The alternative $H_1: \rho > 1$ is not usually considered, since it implies that y_t is explosive. In fact, if $\alpha > 0$, y_t has an exponential trend in its mean when $\rho > 1$.

When $|\rho| < 1$, $\{y_t\}$ is a stable AR(1) process, which means it is weakly dependent or asymptotically uncorrelated. Recall from Chapter 11 that $\text{Corr}(y_t, y_{t+h}) = \rho^h \to 0$ when $|\rho| < 1$. Therefore, testing (18.19) in model (18.17), with the alternative given by (18.20), is really a test of whether $\{y_t\}$ is I(1) against the alternative that $\{y_t\}$ is I(0). [We do not take the null to be I(0) in this setup because $\{y_t\}$ is I(0) for any value of ρ strictly between -1 and 1, something that classical hypothesis testing does not handle easily. There are tests where the null hypothesis is I(0) against the alternative of I(1), but these take a different approach. See, for example, Kwiatkowski, Phillips, Schmidt, and Shin (1992).]

A convenient equation for carrying out the unit root test is to subtract y_{t-1} from both sides of (18.17) and to define $\theta = \rho - 1$:

$$\Delta y_t = \alpha + \theta y_{t-1} + e_t. \qquad \qquad [18.21]$$

Under (18.18), this is a dynamically complete model, and so it seems straightforward to test $H_0: \theta = 0$ against $H_1: \theta < 0$. The problem is that, under H_0, y_{t-1} is I(1), and so the usual central limit theorem that underlies the asymptotic standard normal distribution for the t statistic does not apply: the t statistic does not have an approximate standard normal distribution even in large sample sizes. The asymptotic distribution of the t statistic under H_0 has come to be known as the **Dickey-Fuller distribution** after Dickey and Fuller (1979).

Although we cannot use the usual critical values, we *can* use the usual t statistic for $\hat{\theta}$ in (18.21), at least once the appropriate critical values have been tabulated. The resulting test is known as the **Dickey-Fuller (DF) test** for a unit root. The theory used to obtain the asymptotic critical values is rather complicated and is covered in advanced texts on time series econometrics. [See, for example, Banerjee, Dolado, Galbraith, and Hendry (1993), or BDGH for short.] By contrast, using these results is very easy. The critical values for the t statistic have been tabulated by several authors, beginning with the original work by Dickey and Fuller (1979). Table 18.2 contains the large sample critical values for various significance levels, taken from BDGH (1993, Table 4.2). (Critical values adjusted for small sample sizes are available in BDGH.)

We reject the null hypothesis $H_0: \theta = 0$ against $H_1: \theta < 0$ if $t_{\hat{\theta}} < c$, where c is one of the negative values in Table 18.2. For example, to carry out the test at the 5% significance level, we reject if $t_{\hat{\theta}} < -2.86$. This requires a t statistic with a much larger magnitude than if we used the standard normal critical value, which would be -1.65. If we use the standard normal critical value to test for a unit root, we would reject H_0 much more often than 5% of the time when H_0 is true.

TABLE 18.2 Asymptotic Critical Values for Unit Root t Test: No Time Trend				
Significance level	1%	2.5%	5%	10%
Critical value	-3.43	-3.12	-2.86	-2.57

EXAMPLE 18.2 **Unit Root Test for Three-Month T-Bill Rates**

We use the quarterly data in INTQRT to test for a unit root in three-month T-bill rates. When we estimate (18.20), we obtain

$$\widehat{\Delta r3}_t = .625 - .091 \; r3_{t-1}$$
$$(.261) \quad (.037)$$
$$n = 123, R^2 = .048,$$

[18.22]

where we keep with our convention of reporting standard errors in parentheses below the estimates. We must remember that these standard errors cannot be used to construct usual confidence intervals or to carry out traditional t tests because these do not behave in the usual ways when there is a unit root. The coefficient on $r3_{t-1}$ shows that the estimate of ρ is $\hat{\rho} = 1 + \hat{\theta} = .909$. While this is less than unity, we do not know whether it is *statistically* less than one. The t statistic on $r3_{t-1}$ is $-.091/.037 = -2.46$. From Table 18.2, the 10% critical value is -2.57; therefore, we fail to reject $H_0: \rho = 1$ against $H_1: \rho < 1$ at the 10% significance level.

As with other hypothesis tests, when we fail to reject H_0, we do *not* say that we accept H_0. Why? Suppose we test $H_0: \rho = .9$ in the previous example using a standard t test—which is asymptotically valid, because y_t is I(0) under H_0. Then, we obtain $t = .001/.037$, which is very small and provides no evidence against $\rho = .9$. Yet, it makes no sense to accept $\rho = 1$ and $\rho = .9$.

When we fail to reject a unit root, as in the previous example, we should only conclude that the data do not provide strong evidence against H_0. In this example, the test does provide *some* evidence against H_0 because the t statistic is close to the 10% critical value. (Ideally, we would compute a p-value, but this requires special software because of the nonnormal distribution.) In addition, though $\hat{\rho} \approx .91$ implies a fair amount of persistence in $\{r3_t\}$, the correlation between observations that are 10 periods apart for an AR(1) model with $\rho = .9$ is about .35, rather than almost one if $\rho = 1$.

What happens if we now want to use $r3_t$ as an explanatory variable in a regression analysis? The outcome of the unit root test implies that we should be extremely cautious: if $r3_t$ does have a unit root, the usual asymptotic approximations need not hold (as we discussed in Chapter 11). One solution is to use the first difference of $r3_t$ in any analysis. As we will see in Section 18-4, that is not the only possibility.

We also need to test for unit roots in models with more complicated dynamics. If $\{y_t\}$ follows (18.17) with $\rho = 1$, then Δy_t is serially uncorrelated. We can easily allow $\{\Delta y_t\}$ to follow an AR model by augmenting equation (18.21) with additional lags. For example,

$$\Delta y_t = \alpha + \theta y_{t-1} + \gamma_1 \Delta y_{t-1} + e_t,$$

[18.23]

where $|\gamma_1| < 1$. This ensures that, under $H_0: \theta = 0$, $\{\Delta y_t\}$ follows a stable AR(1) model. Under the alternative $H_1: \theta < 0$, it can be shown that $\{y_t\}$ follows a stable AR(2) model.

More generally, we can add p lags of Δy_t to the equation to account for the dynamics in the process. The way we test the null hypothesis of a unit root is very similar: we run the regression of

$$\Delta y_t \text{ on } y_{t-1}, \Delta y_{t-1}, \ldots, \Delta y_{t-p}$$

[18.24]

and carry out the t test on $\hat{\theta}$, the coefficient on y_{t-1}, just as before. This extended version of the Dickey-Fuller test is usually called the **augmented Dickey-Fuller test** because the regression has been augmented with the lagged changes, Δy_{t-h}. The critical values and rejection rule are the same as before. The inclusion of the lagged changes in (18.24) is intended to clean up any serial correlation in Δy_t. The more lags we include in (18.24), the more initial observations we lose. If we include too many lags, the small sample power of the test generally suffers. But if we include too few lags, the size of the test will be incorrect, even asymptotically, because the validity of the critical values in

Table 18.2 relies on the dynamics being completely modeled. Often, the lag length is dictated by the frequency of the data (as well as the sample size). For annual data, one or two lags usually suffice. For monthly data, we might include 12 lags. But there are no hard rules to follow in any case.

Interestingly, the t statistics on the lagged changes have approximate t distributions. The F statistics for joint significance of any group of terms Δy_{t-h} are also asymptotically valid. (These maintain the homoskedasticity assumption discussed in Section 11-5.) Therefore, we can use standard tests to determine whether we have enough lagged changes in (18.24).

EXAMPLE 18.3   **Unit Root Test for Annual U.S. Inflation**

We use annual data on U.S. inflation, based on the CPI, to test for a unit root in inflation (see PHILLIPS), restricting ourselves to the years from 1948 through 1996. Allowing for one lag of Δinf_t in the augmented Dickey-Fuller regression gives

$$\widehat{\Delta inf_t} = 1.36 - .310\, inf_{t-1} + .138\, \Delta inf_{t-1}$$
$$(.517)(.103) \qquad (.126)$$
$$n = 47, R^2 = .172.$$

The t statistic for the unit root test is $-.310/.103 = -3.01$. Because the 5% critical value is -2.86, we reject the unit root hypothesis at the 5% level. The estimate of ρ is about .690. Together, this is reasonably strong evidence against a unit root in inflation. The lag Δinf_{t-1} has a t statistic of about 1.10, so we do not need to include it, but we could not know this ahead of time. If we drop Δinf_{t-1}, the evidence against a unit root is slightly stronger: $\hat{\theta} = -.335$ ($\hat{\rho} = .665$) and $t_{\hat{\theta}} = -3.13$.

For series that have clear time trends, we need to modify the test for unit roots. A trend-stationary process—which has a linear trend in its mean but is I(0) about its trend—can be mistaken for a unit root process if we do not control for a time trend in the Dickey-Fuller regression. In other words, if we carry out the usual DF or augmented DF test on a trending but I(0) series, we will probably have little power for rejecting a unit root.

To allow for series with time trends, we change the basic equation to

$$\Delta y_t = \alpha + \delta t + \theta y_{t-1} + e_t, \qquad\qquad [18.25]$$

where again the null hypothesis is $H_0: \theta = 0$, and the alternative is $H_1: \theta < 0$. Under the alternative, $\{y_t\}$ is a trend-stationary process. If y_t has a unit root, then $\Delta y_t = \alpha + \delta t + e_t$, and so the *change* in y_t has a mean linear in t unless $\delta = 0$. [It can be shown that $E(y_t)$ is actually a *quadratic* in t.] It is unusual for the first difference of an economic series to have a linear trend, so a more appropriate null hypothesis is probably $H_0: \theta = 0, \delta = 0$. Although it is possible to test this joint hypothesis using an F test—but with modified critical values—it is common to test $H_0: \theta = 0$ using only a t test. We follow that approach here. [See BDGH (1993, Section 4-4) for more details on the joint test.]

When we include a time trend in the regression, the critical values of the test change. Intuitively, this occurs because detrending a unit root process tends to make it look more like an I(0) process. Therefore, we require a larger magnitude for the t statistic in order to reject H_0. The Dickey-Fuller critical values for the t test that includes a time trend are given in Table 18.3; they are taken from BDGH (1993, Table 4.2).

TABLE 18.3 Asymptotic Critical Values for Unit Root *t* Test: Linear Time Trend				
Significance level	1%	2.5%	5%	10%
Critical value	-3.96	-3.66	-3.41	-3.12

For example, to reject a unit root at the 5% level, we need the t statistic on $\hat{\theta}$, to be less than -3.41, as compared with -2.86 without a time trend.

We can augment equation (18.25) with lags of Δy_t to account for serial correlation, just as in the case without a trend.

EXAMPLE 18.4 **Unit Root in the Log of U.S. Real Gross Domestic Product**

We can apply the unit root test with a time trend to the U.S. GDP data in INVEN. These annual data cover the years from 1959 through 1995. We test whether $\log(GDP_t)$ has a unit root. This series has a pronounced trend that looks roughly linear. We include a single lag of $\Delta\log(GDP_t)$, which is simply the growth in GDP (in decimal form), to account for dynamics:

$$\widehat{gGDP_t} = 1.65 + .0059\, t - .210\, \log(GDP_{t-1}) + .264\, gGDP_{t-1}$$
$$(.67)(.0027)(.087)(.165) \text{[18.26]}$$
$$n = 35, R^2 = .268.$$

From this equation, we get $\hat{\rho} = 1 - .21 = .79$, which is clearly less than one. But we *cannot* reject a unit root in the log of GDP: the t statistic on $\log(GDP_{t-1})$ is $-.210/.087 = -2.41$, which is well above the 10% critical value of -3.12. The t statistic on $gGDP_{t-1}$ is 1.60, which is almost significant at the 10% level against a two-sided alternative.

What should we conclude about a unit root? Again, we cannot reject a unit root, but the point estimate of ρ is not especially close to one. When we have a small sample size—and $n = 35$ is considered to be pretty small—it is very difficult to reject the null hypothesis of a unit root if the process has something close to a unit root. Using more data over longer time periods, many researchers have concluded that there is little evidence against the unit root hypothesis for $\log(GDP)$. This has led most of them to assume that the *growth* in GDP is I(0), which means that $\log(GDP)$ is I(1). Unfortunately, given currently available sample sizes, we cannot have much confidence in this conclusion.

If we omit the time trend, there is much less evidence against H_0, as $\hat{\theta} = -.023$ and $t_{\hat{\theta}} = -1.92$. Here, the estimate of ρ is much closer to one, but this is misleading due to the omitted time trend.

It is tempting to compare the t statistic on the time trend in (18.26) with the critical value from a standard normal or t distribution, to see whether the time trend is significant. Unfortunately, the t statistic on the trend does not have an asymptotic standard normal distribution (unless $|\rho| < 1$). The asymptotic distribution of this t statistic is known, but it is rarely used. Typically, we rely on intuition (or plots of the time series) to decide whether to include a trend in the DF test.

There are many other variants on unit root tests. In one version that is applicable only to series that are clearly not trending, the intercept is omitted from the regression; that is, α is set to zero in (18.21). This variant of the Dickey-Fuller test is rarely used because of biases induced if $\alpha \neq 0$. Also, we can allow for more complicated time trends, such as quadratic. Again, this is seldom used.

Another class of tests attempts to account for serial correlation in Δy_t in a different manner than by including lags in (18.21) or (18.25). The approach is related to the serial correlation–robust standard errors for the OLS estimators that we discussed in Section 12-5. The idea is to be as agnostic as possible about serial correlation in Δy_t. In practice, the (augmented) Dickey-Fuller test has held up pretty well. [See BDGH (1993, Section 4-3) for a discussion on other tests.]

18-3 Spurious Regression

In a cross-sectional environment, we use the phrase "spurious correlation" to describe a situation where two variables are related through their correlation with a third variable. In particular, if we regress y on x, we find a significant relationship. But when we control for another variable, say, z, the partial effect of x on y becomes zero. Naturally, this can also happen in time series contexts with I(0) variables.

As we discussed in Section 10-5, it is possible to find a spurious relationship between time series that have increasing or decreasing trends. Provided the series are weakly dependent about their time trends, the problem is effectively solved by including a time trend in the regression model.

When we are dealing with integrated processes of order one, there is an additional complication. Even if the two series have means that are not trending, a simple regression involving two *independent* I(1) series will often result in a significant t statistic.

To be more precise, let $\{x_t\}$ and $\{y_t\}$ be random walks generated by

$$x_t = x_{t-1} + a_t, \quad t = 1, 2, \ldots, \tag{18.27}$$

and

$$y_t = y_{t-1} + e_t, \quad t = 1, 2, \ldots, \tag{18.28}$$

where $\{a_t\}$ and $\{e_t\}$ are independent, identically distributed innovations, with mean zero and variances σ_a^2 and σ_e^2, respectively. For concreteness, take the initial values to be $x_0 = y_0 = 0$. Assume further that $\{a_t\}$ and $\{e_t\}$ are independent processes. This implies that $\{x_t\}$ and $\{y_t\}$ are also independent. But what if we run the simple regression

$$\hat{y}_t = \hat{\beta}_0 + \hat{\beta}_1 x_t \tag{18.29}$$

and obtain the usual t statistic for $\hat{\beta}_1$ and the usual R-squared? Because y_t and x_t are independent, we would hope that plim $\hat{\beta}_1 = 0$. Even more importantly, if we test $H_0: \beta_1 = 0$ against $H_1: \beta_1 \neq 0$ at the 5% level, we hope that the t statistic for $\hat{\beta}_1$ is insignificant 95% of the time. Through a simulation, Granger and Newbold (1974) showed that this is *not* the case: even though y_t and x_t are *independent*, the regression of y_t on x_t yields a statistically significant t statistic a large percentage of the time, much larger than the nominal significance level. Granger and Newbold called this the **spurious regression problem**: there is no sense in which y and x are related, but an OLS regression using the usual t statistics will often indicate a relationship.

Recent simulation results are given by Davidson and MacKinnon (1993, Table 19.1), where a_t and e_t are generated as independent, identically distributed normal random variables, and 10,000 different samples are generated. For a sample size of $n = 50$ at the 5% significance level, the standard t statistic for $H_0: \beta_1 = 0$ against the two-sided alternative rejects H_0 about 66.2% of the time under H_0, rather than 5% of the time. As the sample size increases, things get *worse*: with $n = 250$, the null is rejected 84.7% of the time!

> **EXPLORING FURTHER 18.2**
>
> Under the preceding setup, where $\{x_t\}$ and $\{y_t\}$ are generated by (18.27) and (18.28) and $\{e_t\}$ and $\{a_t\}$ are i.i.d. sequences, what is the plim of the slope coefficient, say, $\hat{\gamma}_1$, from the regression of Δy_t on Δx_t? Describe the behavior of the t statistic of $\hat{\gamma}_1$.

Here is one way to see what is happening when we regress the level of y on the level of x. Write the model underlying (18.29) as

$$y_t = \beta_0 + \beta_1 x_t + u_t. \tag{18.30}$$

For the t statistic of $\hat{\beta}_1$ to have an approximate standard normal distribution in large samples, at a minimum, $\{u_t\}$ should be a mean zero, serially uncorrelated process. But under $H_0: \beta_1 = 0$, $y_t = \beta_0 + u_t$, and, because $\{y_t\}$ is a random walk starting at $y_0 = 0$, equation (18.30) holds under H_0 only if $\beta_0 = 0$ and, more importantly, if $u_t = y_t = \sum_{j=1}^{t} e_j$. In other words, $\{u_t\}$ is a random walk under H_0. This clearly violates even the asymptotic version of the Gauss-Markov assumptions from Chapter 11.

Including a time trend does not really change the conclusion. If y_t or x_t is a random walk with drift and a time trend is not included, the spurious regression problem is even worse. The same qualitative conclusions hold if $\{a_t\}$ and $\{e_t\}$ are general I(0) processes, rather than i.i.d. sequences.

In addition to the usual t statistic not having a limiting standard normal distribution—in fact, it increases to infinity as $n \to \infty$—the behavior of R-squared is nonstandard. In cross-sectional contexts or in regressions with I(0) time series variables, the R-squared converges in probability to the population R-squared: $1 - \sigma_u^2/\sigma_y^2$. This is not the case in spurious regressions with I(1) processes. Rather than the R-squared having a well-defined plim, it actually converges to a random variable. Formalizing this notion is well beyond the scope of this text. [A discussion of the asymptotic properties of the t statistic and the R-squared can be found in BDGH (Section 3-1).] The implication is that the R-squared is large with high probability, even though $\{y_t\}$ and $\{x_t\}$ are independent time series processes.

The same considerations arise with multiple independent variables, each of which may be I(1) or some of which may be I(0). If $\{y_t\}$ is I(1) and at least some of the explanatory variables are I(1), the regression results may be spurious.

The possibility of spurious regression with I(1) variables is quite important and has led economists to reexamine many aggregate time series regressions whose t statistics were very significant and whose R-squareds were extremely high. In the next section, we show that regressing an I(1) dependent variable on an I(1) independent variable *can* be informative, but only if these variables are related in a precise sense.

18-4 Cointegration and Error Correction Models

The discussion of spurious regression in the previous section certainly makes one wary of using the levels of I(1) variables in regression analysis. In earlier chapters, we suggested that I(1) variables should be differenced before they are used in linear regression models, whether they are estimated by OLS or instrumental variables. This is certainly a safe course to follow, and it is the approach used in many time series regressions after Granger and Newbold's original paper on the spurious regression problem. Unfortunately, always differencing I(1) variables limits the scope of the questions that we can answer.

18-4a Cointegration

The notion of **cointegration**, which was given a formal treatment in Engle and Granger (1987), makes regressions involving I(1) variables potentially meaningful. A full treatment of cointegration is mathematically involved, but we can describe the basic issues and methods that are used in many applications.

If $\{y_t: t = 0, 1, \ldots\}$ and $\{x_t: t = 0, 1, \ldots\}$ are two I(1) processes, then, in general, $y_t - \beta x_t$ is an I(1) process for any number β. Nevertheless, it is *possible* that for some $\beta \neq 0$, $y_t - \beta x_t$ is an I(0) process, which means it has constant mean, constant variance, and autocorrelations that depend only on the time distance between any two variables in the series, and it is asymptotically uncorrelated.

If such a β exists, we say that y and x are *cointegrated*, and we call β the cointegration parameter. [Alternatively, we could look at $x_t - \gamma y_t$ for $\gamma \neq 0$: if $y_t - \beta x_t$ is I(0), then $x_t - (1/\beta)y_t$ is I(0). Therefore, the linear combination of y_t and x_t is not unique, but if we fix the coefficient on y_t at unity, then β is unique. See Problem 3. For concreteness, we consider linear combinations of the form $y_t - \beta x_t$.]

> **EXPLORING FURTHER 18.3**
>
> Let $\{(y_t, x_t): t = 1, 2, \ldots\}$ be a bivariate time series where each series is I(1) without drift. Explain why, if y_t and x_t are cointegrated, y_t and x_{t-1} are also cointegrated.

For the sake of illustration, take $\beta = 1$, suppose that $y_0 = x_0 = 0$, and write $y_t = y_{t-1} + r_t$, $x_t = x_{t-1} + v_t$, where $\{r_t\}$ and $\{v_t\}$ are two I(0) processes with zero means. Then, y_t and x_t have a tendency to wander around and not return to the initial value of zero with any regularity. By contrast, if $y_t - x_t$ is I(0), it has zero mean and does return to zero with some regularity.

As a specific example, let $r6_t$ be the annualized interest rate for six-month T-bills (at the end of quarter t) and let $r3_t$ be the annualized interest rate for three-month T-bills. (These are typically called bond equivalent yields, and they are reported in the financial pages.) In Example 18.2, using the data in INTQRT, we found little evidence against the hypothesis that $r3_t$ has a unit root; the same is true of $r6_t$. Define the spread between six- and three-month T-bill rates as $spr_t = r6_t - r3_t$. Then, using equation (18.21), the Dickey-Fuller t statistic for spr_t is -7.71 (with $\hat{\theta} = -.67$ or $\hat{\rho} = .33$). Therefore, we strongly reject a unit root for spr_t in favor of I(0). The upshot of this is that though $r6_t$ and $r3_t$ each appear to be unit root processes, the difference between them is an I(0) process. In other words, $r6$ and $r3$ are cointegrated.

Cointegration in this example, as in many examples, has an economic interpretation. If $r6$ and $r3$ were not cointegrated, the difference between interest rates could become very large, with no tendency for them to come back together. Based on a simple arbitrage argument, this seems unlikely. Suppose that the spread spr_t continues to grow for several time periods, making six-month T-bills a much more desirable investment. Then, investors would shift away from three-month and toward six-month T-bills, driving up the price of six-month T-bills, while lowering the price of three-month T-bills. Because interest rates are inversely related to price, this would lower $r6$ and increase $r3$, until the spread is reduced. Therefore, large deviations between $r6$ and $r3$ are not expected to continue: the spread has a tendency to return to its mean value. (The spread actually has a slightly positive mean because long-term investors are more rewarded relative to short-term investors.)

There is another way to characterize the fact that spr_t will not deviate for long periods from its average value: $r6$ and $r3$ have a *long-run* relationship. To describe what we mean by this, let $\mu = E(spr_t)$ denote the expected value of the spread. Then, we can write

$$r6_t = r3_t + \mu + e_t,$$

where $\{e_t\}$ is a zero mean, I(0) process. The equilibrium or long-run relationship occurs when $e_t = 0$, or $r6^* = r3^* + \mu$. At any time period, there can be deviations from equilibrium, but they will be temporary: there are economic forces that drive $r6$ and $r3$ back toward the equilibrium relationship.

In the interest rate example, we used economic reasoning to tell us the value of β if y_t and x_t are cointegrated. If we have a hypothesized value of β, then *testing* whether two series are cointegrated is easy: we simply define a new variable, $s_t = y_t - \beta x_t$, and apply either the usual DF or augmented DF test to $\{s_t\}$. If we *reject* a unit root in $\{s_t\}$ in favor of the I(0) alternative, then we find that y_t and x_t *are cointegrated*. In other words, the null hypothesis is that y_t and x_t are *not* cointegrated.

Testing for cointegration is more difficult when the (potential) cointegration parameter β is unknown. Rather than test for a unit root in $\{s_t\}$, we must first estimate β. If y_t and x_t are cointegrated, it turns out that the OLS estimator $\hat{\beta}$ from the regression

$$y_t = \hat{\alpha} + \hat{\beta} x_t \tag{18.31}$$

is consistent for β. The problem is that the null hypothesis states that the two series are *not* cointegrated, which means that, under H_0, we are running a spurious regression. Fortunately, it is possible to tabulate critical values even when β is estimated, where we apply the Dickey-Fuller or augmented Dickey-Fuller test to the residuals, say, $\hat{u}_t = y_t - \hat{\alpha} - \hat{\beta} x_t$, from (18.31). The only difference is that the critical values account for estimation of β. The resulting test is called the **Engle-Granger test**, and the asymptotic critical values are given in Table 18.4. These are taken from Davidson and MacKinnon (1993, Table 20.2).

TABLE 18.4 Asymptotic Critical Values for Cointegration Test: No Time Trend				
Significance level	1%	2.5%	5%	10%
Critical value	-3.90	-3.59	-3.34	-3.04

TABLE 18.5 Asymptotic Critical Values for Cointegration Test: Linear Time Trend				
Significance level	1%	2.5%	5%	10%
Critical value	−4.32	−4.03	−3.78	−3.50

In the basic test, we run the regression of $\Delta\hat{u}_t$ on $\hat{u}_{t-1}$ and compare the t statistic on $\hat{u}_{t-1}$ to the desired critical value in Table 18.4. If the t statistic is below the critical value, we have evidence that $y_t - \beta x_t$ is I(0) for some β; that is, y_t and x_t are cointegrated. We can add lags of $\Delta\hat{u}_t$ to account for serial correlation. If we compare the critical values in Table 18.4 with those in Table 18.2, we must get a t statistic much larger in magnitude to find cointegration than if we used the usual DF critical values. This happens because OLS, which minimizes the sum of squared residuals, tends to produce residuals that look like an I(0) sequence even if y_t and x_t are *not* cointegrated.

As with the usual Dickey-Fuller test, we can augment the Engle-Granger test by including lags of $\Delta\hat{u}_t$ as additional regressors.

If y_t and x_t are not cointegrated, a regression of y_t on x_t is spurious and tells us nothing meaningful: there is no long-run relationship between y and x. We can still run a regression involving the first differences, Δy_t and Δx_t, including lags. But we should interpret these regressions for what they are: they explain the difference in y in terms of the difference in x and have nothing necessarily to do with a relationship in levels.

If y_t and x_t *are* cointegrated, we can use this to specify more general dynamic models, as we will see in the next subsection.

The previous discussion assumes that neither y_t nor x_t has a drift. This is reasonable for interest rates but not for other time series. If y_t and x_t contain drift terms, $E(y_t)$ and $E(x_t)$ are linear (usually increasing) functions of time. The strict definition of cointegration requires $y_t - \beta x_t$ to be I(0) *without* a trend. To see what this entails, write $y_t = \delta t + g_t$ and $x_t = \lambda t + h_t$, where $\{g_t\}$ and $\{h_t\}$ are I(1) processes, δ is the drift in $y_t[\delta = E(\Delta y_t)]$, and λ is the drift in $x_t[\lambda = E(\Delta x_t)]$. Now, if y_t and x_t are cointegrated, there must exist β such that $g_t - \beta h_t$ is I(0). But then

$$y_t - \beta x_t = (\delta - \beta\lambda)t + (g_t - \beta h_t),$$

which is generally a *trend-stationary* process. The strict form of cointegration requires that there not be a trend, which means $\delta = \beta\lambda$. For I(1) processes with drift, it is possible that the stochastic parts—that is, g_t and h_t—are cointegrated, but that the parameter β that causes $g_t - \beta h_t$ to be I(0) does not eliminate the linear time trend.

We can test for cointegration between g_t and h_t, without taking a stand on the trend part, by running the regression

$$\hat{y}_t = \hat{\alpha} + \hat{\eta}t + \hat{\beta}x_t \qquad [18.32]$$

and applying the usual DF or augmented DF test to the residuals $\hat{u}_t$. The asymptotic critical values are given in Table 18.5 [from Davidson and MacKinnon (1993, Table 20.2)].

A finding of cointegration in this case leaves open the possibility that $y_t - \beta x_t$ has a linear trend. But at least it is not I(1).

EXAMPLE 18.5   **Cointegration between Fertility and Personal Exemption**

In Chapters 10 and 11, we studied various models to estimate the relationship between the general fertility rate (*gfr*) and the real value of the personal tax exemption (*pe*) in the United States. The static regression results in levels and first differences are notably different. The regression in levels, with a time trend included, gives an OLS coefficient on *pe* equal to .187 (se = .035) and $R^2 = .500$. In first differences (without a trend), the coefficient on Δpe is −.043 (se = .028) and $R^2 = .032$. Although there are other reasons for these differences—such as misspecified distributed lag dynamics—the discrepancy between the levels and changes regressions suggests that we should test for cointegration. Of course, this presumes that *gfr* and *pe* are I(1) processes. This appears to be the case: the augmented DF tests, with a single lagged change and a linear time trend, each yield *t* statistics of about −1.47, and the estimated AR(1) coefficients are close to one.

When we obtain the residuals from the regression of *gfr* on *t* and *pe* and apply the augmented DF test with one lag, we obtain a *t* statistic on $\hat{u}_{t-1}$ of −2.43, which is nowhere near the 10% critical value, −3.50. Therefore, we must conclude that there is little evidence of cointegration between *gfr* and *pe*, even allowing for separate trends. It is very likely that the earlier regression results we obtained in levels suffer from the spurious regression problem.

The good news is that, when we used first differences and allowed for two lags—see equation (11.27)—we found an overall positive and significant long-run effect of Δpe on Δgfr.

If we think two series are cointegrated, we often want to test hypotheses about the cointegrating parameter. For example, a theory may state that the cointegrating parameter is one. Ideally, we could use a *t* statistic to test this hypothesis.

We explicitly cover the case without time trends, although the extension to the linear trend case is immediate. When y_t and x_t are I(1) and cointegrated, we can write

$$y_t = \alpha + \beta x_t + u_t, \tag{18.33}$$

where u_t is a zero mean, I(0) process. Generally, $\{u_t\}$ contains serial correlation, but we know from Chapter 11 that this does not affect consistency of OLS. As mentioned earlier, OLS applied to (18.33) consistently estimates β (and α). Unfortunately, because x_t is I(1), the usual inference procedures do not necessarily apply: OLS is not asymptotically normally distributed, and the *t* statistic for $\hat{\beta}$ does not necessarily have an approximate *t* distribution. We do know from Chapter 10 that, if $\{x_t\}$ is strictly exogenous—see Assumption TS.3—and the errors are homoskedastic, serially uncorrelated, and normally distributed, the OLS estimator is also normally distributed (conditional on the explanatory variables) *and* the *t* statistic has an exact *t* distribution. Unfortunately, these assumptions are too strong to apply to most situations. The notion of cointegration implies nothing about the relationship between $\{x_t\}$ and $\{u_t\}$—indeed, they can be arbitrarily correlated. Further, except for requiring that $\{u_t\}$ is I(0), cointegration between y_t and x_t does not restrict the serial dependence in $\{u_t\}$.

Fortunately, the feature of (18.33) that makes inference the most difficult—the lack of strict exogeneity of $\{x_t\}$—can be fixed. Because x_t is I(1), the proper notion of strict exogeneity is that u_t is uncorrelated with Δx_s, for all t and s. We can always arrange this for a *new* set of errors, at least approximately, by writing u_t as a function of the Δx_s for all s close to t. For example,

$$u_t = \eta + \phi_0 \Delta x_t + \phi_1 \Delta x_{t-1} + \phi_2 \Delta x_{t-2} \\ + \gamma_1 \Delta x_{t+1} + \gamma_2 \Delta x_{t+2} + e_t, \tag{18.34}$$

where, by construction, e_t is uncorrelated with each Δx_s appearing in the equation. The hope is that e_t is uncorrelated with further lags and leads of Δx_s. We know that, as $|s - t|$ gets large, the correlation between e_t and Δx_s approaches zero, because these are I(0) processes. Now, if we plug (18.34) into (18.33), we obtain

$$y_t = \alpha_0 + \beta x_t + \phi_0 \Delta x_t + \phi_1 \Delta x_{t-1} + \phi_2 \Delta x_{t-2} \\ + \gamma_1 \Delta x_{t+1} + \gamma_2 \Delta x_{t+2} + e_t. \tag{18.35}$$

This equation looks a bit strange because future Δx_s appear with both current and lagged Δx_t. The key is that the coefficient on x_t is still β, and, by construction, x_t is now strictly exogenous in this equation. The strict exogeneity assumption is the important condition needed to obtain an approximately normal *t* statistic for $\hat{\beta}$. If u_t is uncorrelated with all Δx_s, $s \neq t$, then we can drop the leads and lags of the changes and simply include the contemporaneous change, Δx_t. Then, the equation we estimate looks more standard but still includes the first difference of x_t along with its level: $y_t = \alpha_0 + \beta x_t + \phi_0 \Delta x_t + e_t$. In effect, adding Δx_t solves any contemporaneous endogeneity between x_t and u_t. (Remember, any endogeneity does not cause inconsistency. But we are trying to obtain an asymptotically normal t statistic.) Whether we need to include leads and lags of the changes, and how many, is really an empirical issue. Each time we add an additional lead or lag, we lose one observation, and this can be costly unless we have a large data set.

The OLS estimator of β from (18.35) is called the **leads and lags estimator** of β because of the way it employs Δx. [See, for example, Stock and Watson (1993).] The only issue we must worry about in (18.35) is the possibility of serial correlation in $\{e_t\}$. This can be dealt with by computing a serial correlation–robust standard error for $\hat{\beta}$ (as described in Section 12-5) or by using a standard AR(1) correction (such as Cochrane-Orcutt).

EXAMPLE 18.6   **Cointegrating Parameter for Interest Rates**

Earlier, we tested for cointegration between $r6$ and $r3$—six- and three-month T-bill rates—by assuming that the cointegrating parameter was equal to one. This led us to find cointegration and, naturally, to conclude that the cointegrating parameter is equal to unity. Nevertheless, let us estimate the cointegrating parameter directly and test $H_0: \beta = 1$. We apply the leads and lags estimator with two leads and two lags of $\Delta r3$, as well as the contemporaneous change. The estimate of β is $\hat{\beta} = 1.038$, and the usual OLS standard error is .0081. Therefore, the t statistic for $H_0: \beta = 1$ is $(1.038 - 1)/.0081 \approx 4.69$, which is a strong statistical rejection of H_0. (Of course, whether 1.038 is economically different from 1 is a relevant consideration.) There is little evidence of serial correlation in the residuals, so we can use this t statistic as having an approximate normal distribution. [For comparison, the OLS estimate of β without the leads, lags, or contemporaneous $\Delta r3$ terms—and using five more observations—is 1.026 (se = .0077). But the t statistic from (18.33) is not necessarily valid.]

There are many other estimators of cointegrating parameters, and this continues to be a very active area of research. The notion of cointegration applies to more than two processes, but the interpretation, testing, and estimation are much more complicated. One issue is that, even after we normalize a coefficient to be one, there can be many cointegrating relationships. BDGH provide some discussion and several references.

18-4b Error Correction Models

In addition to learning about a potential long-run relationship between two series, the concept of cointegration enriches the kinds of dynamic models at our disposal. If y_t and x_t are I(1) processes and are *not* cointegrated, we might estimate a dynamic model in first differences. As an example, consider the equation

$$\Delta y_t = \alpha_0 + \alpha_1 \Delta y_{t-1} + \gamma_0 \Delta x_t + \gamma_1 \Delta x_{t-1} + u_t, \tag{18.36}$$

where u_t has zero mean given Δx_t, Δy_{t-1}, Δx_{t-1}, and further lags. This is essentially equation (18.16), but in first differences rather than in levels. If we view this as a rational distributed lag model, we can find the impact propensity, long-run propensity, and lag distribution for Δy as a distributed lag in Δx.

If y_t and x_t are cointegrated with parameter β, then we have additional I(0) variables that we can include in (18.36). Let $s_t = y_t - \beta x_t$, so that s_t is I(0), and assume for the sake of simplicity that s_t has zero mean. Now, we can include lags of s_t in the equation. In the simplest case, we include one lag of s_t:

$$\begin{aligned} \Delta y_t &= \alpha_0 + \alpha_1 \Delta y_{t-1} + \gamma_0 \Delta x_t + \gamma_1 \Delta x_{t-1} + \delta s_{t-1} + u_t \\ &= \alpha_0 + \alpha_1 \Delta y_{t-1} + \gamma_0 \Delta x_t + \gamma_1 \Delta x_{t-1} + \delta(y_{t-1} - \beta x_{t-1}) + u_t, \end{aligned} \tag{18.37}$$

where $E(u_t|I_{t-1}) = 0$, and I_{t-1} contains information on Δx_t and all past values of x and y. The term $\delta(y_{t-1} - \beta x_{t-1})$ is called the *error correction term*, and (18.37) is an example of an **error correction model**. (In some error correction models, the contemporaneous change in x, Δx_t, is omitted. Whether it is included or not depends partly on the purpose of the equation. In forecasting, Δx_t is rarely included, for reasons we will see in Section 18-5.)

An error correction model allows us to study the short-run dynamics in the relationship between y and x. For simplicity, consider the model without lags of Δy_t and Δx_t:

$$\Delta y_t = \alpha_0 + \gamma_0 \Delta x_t + \delta(y_{t-1} - \beta x_{t-1}) + u_t, \qquad [18.38]$$

where $\delta < 0$. If $y_{t-1} > \beta x_{t-1}$, then y in the previous period has overshot the equilibrium; because $\delta < 0$, the error correction term works to push y back toward the equilibrium. Similarly, if $y_{t-1} < \beta x_{t-1}$, the error correction term induces a positive change in y back toward the equilibrium.

How do we estimate the parameters of an error correction model? If we know β, this is easy. For example, in (18.38), we simply regress Δy_t on Δx_t and s_{t-1}, where $s_{t-1} = (y_{t-1} - \beta x_{t-1})$.

EXAMPLE 18.7   **Error Correction Model for Holding Yields**

In Problem 6 in Chapter 11, we regressed $hy6_t$, the three-month holding yield (in percent) from buying a six-month T-bill at time $t - 1$ and selling it at time t as a three-month T-bill, on $hy3_{t-1}$, the three-month holding yield from buying a three-month T-bill at time $t - 1$. The expectations hypoth-

> **EXPLORING FURTHER 18.4**
>
> How would you test H_0: $\gamma_0 = 1$, $\delta = -1$ in the holding yield error correction model?

esis implies that the slope coefficient should not be statistically different from one. It turns out that there is evidence of a unit root in $\{hy3_t\}$, which calls into question the standard regression analysis. We will assume that both holding yields are I(1) processes. The expectations hypothesis implies, at a minimum, that $hy6_t$ and $hy3_{t-1}$ are cointegrated with β equal to one, which appears to be the case (see Computer Exercise C5). Under this assumption, an error correction model is

$$\Delta hy6_t = \alpha_0 + \gamma_0 \Delta hy3_{t-1} + \delta(hy6_{t-1} - hy3_{t-2}) + u_t,$$

where u_t has zero mean, given all $hy3$ and $hy6$ dated at time $t - 1$ and earlier. The lags on the variables in the error correction model are dictated by the expectations hypothesis.

Using the data in INTQRT gives

$$\widehat{\Delta hy6_t} = .090 + 1.218\ \Delta hy3_{t-1} - .840(hy6_{t-1} - hy3_{t-2})$$
$$\qquad\quad (.043)\quad (.264)\qquad\qquad (.244) \qquad\qquad\qquad [18.39]$$
$$n = 122,\ R^2 = .790.$$

The error correction coefficient is negative and very significant. For example, if the holding yield on six-month T-bills is above that for three-month T-bills by one point, $hy6$ falls by .84 points on average in the next quarter. Interestingly, $\hat{\delta} = -.84$ is not statistically different from -1, as is easily seen by computing the 95% confidence interval.

In many other examples, the cointegrating parameter must be estimated. Then, we replace s_{t-1} with $\hat{s}_{t-1} = y_{t-1} - \hat{\beta} x_{t-1}$, where $\hat{\beta}$ can be various estimators of β. We have covered the standard OLS estimator as well as the leads and lags estimator. This raises the issue about how sampling variation in $\hat{\beta}$ affects inference on the other parameters in the error correction model. Fortunately, as shown by Engle and Granger (1987), we can ignore the preliminary estimation of β (asymptotically). This property is very convenient and implies that the asymptotic efficiency of the estimators of the parameters in the error correction model is unaffected by whether we use the OLS estimator or the leads and lags estimator for $\hat{\beta}$. Of course, the choice of $\hat{\beta}$ will generally have an effect on the estimated error correction parameters in any particular sample, but we have no systematic way of deciding which preliminary estimator of β to use. The procedure of replacing β with $\hat{\beta}$ is called the **Engle-Granger two-step procedure**.

18-5 Forecasting

Forecasting economic time series is very important in some branches of economics, and it is an area that continues to be actively studied. In this section, we focus on regression-based forecasting methods. Diebold (2001) provides a comprehensive introduction to forecasting, including recent developments.

We assume in this section that the primary focus is on forecasting future values of a time series process and not necessarily on estimating causal or structural economic models.

It is useful to first cover some fundamentals of forecasting that do not depend on a specific model. Suppose that at time t we want to forecast the outcome of y at time $t + 1$, or y_{t+1}. The time period could correspond to a year, a quarter, a month, a week, or even a day. Let I_t denote information that we can observe at time t. This **information set** includes y_t, earlier values of y, and often other variables dated at time t or earlier. We can combine this information in innumerable ways to forecast y_{t+1}. Is there one best way?

The answer is yes, provided we specify the *loss* associated with forecast error. Let f_t denote the forecast of y_{t+1} made at time t. We call f_t a **one-step-ahead forecast**. The **forecast error** is $e_{t+1} = y_{t+1} - f_t$, which we observe once the outcome on y_{t+1} is observed. The most common measure of loss is the same one that leads to ordinary least squares estimation of a multiple linear regression model: the squared error, e_{t+1}^2. The squared forecast error treats positive and negative prediction errors symmetrically, and larger forecast errors receive relatively more weight. For example, errors of $+2$ and -2 yield the same loss, and the loss is four times as great as forecast errors of $+1$ or -1. The squared forecast error is an example of a **loss function**. Another popular loss function is the absolute value of the prediction error, $|e_{t+1}|$. For reasons to be seen shortly, we focus now on squared error loss.

Given the squared error loss function, we can determine how to best use the information at time t to forecast y_{t+1}. But we must recognize that at time t, we do not know e_{t+1}: it is a random variable, because y_{t+1} is a random variable. Therefore, any useful criterion for choosing f_t must be based on what we know at time t. It is natural to choose the forecast to minimize the *expected* squared forecast error, given I_t:

$$E(e_{t+1}^2|I_t) = E[(y_{t+1} - f_t)^2|I_t]. \qquad [18.40]$$

A basic fact from probability (see Property CE.6 in Appendix B) is that the conditional expectation, $E(y_{t+1}|I_t)$, minimizes (18.40). In other words, if we wish to minimize the expected squared forecast error given information at time t, our forecast should be the expected value of y_{t+1} given variables we know at time t.

For many popular time series processes, the conditional expectation is easy to obtain. Suppose that $\{y_t: t = 0, 1, \ldots\}$ is a martingale difference sequence (MDS) and take I_t to be $\{y_t, y_{t-1}, \ldots, y_0\}$, the observed past of y. By definition, $E(y_{t+1}|I_t) = 0$ for all t; the best prediction of y_{t+1} at time t is always zero! Recall from Section 18-2 that an i.i.d. sequence with zero mean is a martingale difference sequence.

A martingale difference sequence is one in which the past is not useful for predicting the future. Stock returns are widely thought to be well approximated as an MDS or, perhaps, with a positive mean. The key is that $E(y_{t+1}|y_t, y_{t-1}, \ldots) = E(y_{t+1})$: the conditional mean is equal to the unconditional mean, in which case past outcomes on y do not help to predict future y.

A process $\{y_t\}$ is a **martingale** if $E(y_{t+1}|y_t, y_{t-1}, \ldots, y_0) = y_t$ for all $t \geq 0$. [If $\{y_t\}$ is a martingale, then $\{\Delta y_t\}$ is a martingale difference sequence, which is where the latter name comes from.] The predicted value of y for the next period is always the value of y for this period.

A more complicated example is

$$E(y_{t+1}|I_t) = \alpha y_t + \alpha(1 - \alpha)y_{t-1} + \ldots + \alpha(1 - \alpha)^t y_0, \qquad [18.41]$$

where $0 < \alpha < 1$ is a parameter that we must choose. This method of forecasting is called **exponential smoothing** because the weights on the lagged y decline to zero exponentially.

The reason for writing the expectation as in (18.41) is that it leads to a very simple recurrence relation. Set $f_0 = y_0$. Then, for $t \geq 1$, the forecasts can be obtained as

$$f_t = \alpha y_t + (1 - \alpha)f_{t-1}.$$

In other words, the forecast of y_{t+1} is a weighted average of y_t and the forecast of y_t made at time $t - 1$. Exponential smoothing is suitable only for very specific time series and requires choosing α. Regression methods, which we turn to next, are more flexible.

The previous discussion has focused on forecasting y only one period ahead. The general issues that arise in forecasting y_{t+h} at time t, where h is any positive integer, are similar. In particular, if we use expected squared forecast error as our measure of loss, the best predictor is $E(y_{t+h}|I_t)$. When dealing with a **multiple-step-ahead forecast**, we use the notation $f_{t,h}$ to indicate the forecast of y_{t+h} made at time t.

18-5a Types of Regression Models Used for Forecasting

There are many different regression models that we can use to forecast future values of a time series. The first regression model for time series data from Chapter 10 was the static model. To see how we can forecast with this model, assume that we have a single explanatory variable:

$$y_t = \beta_0 + \beta_1 z_t + u_t. \qquad [18.42]$$

Suppose, for the moment, that the parameters β_0 and β_1 are known. Write this equation at time $t + 1$ as $y_{t+1} = \beta_0 + \beta_1 z_{t+1} + u_{t+1}$. Now, *if* z_{t+1} is known at time t, so that it is an element of I_t and $E(u_{t+1}|I_t) = 0$, then

$$E(y_{t+1}|I_t) = \beta_0 + \beta_1 z_{t+1},$$

where I_t contains $z_{t+1}, y_t, z_t, \ldots, y_1, z_1$. The right-hand side of this equation is the forecast of y_{t+1} at time t. This kind of forecast is usually called a **conditional forecast** because it is conditional on knowing the value of z at time $t + 1$.

Unfortunately, at any time, we rarely know the value of the explanatory variables in future time periods. Exceptions include time trends and seasonal dummy variables, which we cover explicitly below, but otherwise knowledge of z_{t+1} at time t is rare. Sometimes, we wish to generate conditional forecasts for several values of z_{t+1}.

Another problem with (18.42) as a model for forecasting is that $E(u_{t+1}|I_t) = 0$ means that $\{u_t\}$ cannot contain serial correlation, something we have seen to be false in most static regression models. [Problem 8 asks you to derive the forecast in a simple distributed lag model with AR(1) errors.]

If z_{t+1} is not known at time t, we cannot include it in I_t. Then, we have

$$E(y_{t+1}|I_t) = \beta_0 + \beta_1 E(z_{t+1}|I_t).$$

This means that in order to forecast y_{t+1}, we must first forecast z_{t+1}, based on the same information set. This is usually called an **unconditional forecast** because we do not assume knowledge of z_{t+1} at time t. Unfortunately, this is somewhat of a misnomer, as our forecast is still conditional on the information in I_t. But the name is entrenched in the forecasting literature.

For forecasting, unless we are wedded to the static model in (18.42) for other reasons, it makes more sense to specify a model that depends only on lagged values of y and z. This saves us the extra step of having to forecast a right-hand side variable before forecasting y. The kind of model we have in mind is

$$y_t = \delta_0 + \alpha_1 y_{t-1} + \gamma_1 z_{t-1} + u_t$$
$$\mathrm{E}(u_t|I_{t-1}) = 0, \qquad\qquad\qquad\qquad \text{[18.43]}$$

where I_{t-1} contains y and z dated at time $t-1$ and earlier. Now, the forecast of y_{t+1} at time t is $\delta_0 + \alpha_1 y_t + \gamma_1 z_t$; if we know the parameters, we can just plug in the values of y_t and z_t.

If we only want to use past y to predict future y, then we can drop z_{t-1} from (18.43). Naturally, we can add more lags of y or z and lags of other variables. Especially for forecasting one step ahead, such models can be very useful.

18-5b One-Step-Ahead Forecasting

Obtaining a forecast one period after the sample ends is relatively straightforward using models such as (18.43). As usual, let n be the sample size. The forecast of y_{n+1} is

$$\hat{f}_n = \hat{\delta}_0 + \hat{\alpha}_1 y_n + \hat{\gamma}_1 z_n, \qquad\qquad\qquad\qquad \text{[18.44]}$$

where we assume that the parameters have been estimated by OLS. We use a hat on f_n to emphasize that we have estimated the parameters in the regression model. (If we knew the parameters, there would be no estimation error in the forecast.) The forecast error—which we will not know until time $n+1$—is

$$\hat{e}_{n+1} = y_{n+1} - \hat{f}_n. \qquad\qquad\qquad\qquad \text{[18.45]}$$

If we add more lags of y or z to the forecasting equation, we simply lose more observations at the beginning of the sample.

The forecast $\hat{f}_n$ of y_{n+1} is usually called a **point forecast**. We can also obtain a **forecast interval**. A forecast interval is essentially the same as a prediction interval, which we studied in Section 6-4. There we showed how, under the classical linear model assumptions, to obtain an exact 95% prediction interval. A forecast interval is obtained in *exactly* the same way. If the model does not satisfy the classical linear model assumptions—for example, if it contains lagged dependent variables, as in (18.44)—the forecast interval is still approximately valid, provided u_t given I_{t-1} is normally distributed with zero mean and constant variance. (This ensures that the OLS estimators are approximately normally distributed with the usual OLS variances and that u_{n+1} is independent of the OLS estimators with mean zero and variance σ^2.) Let $\mathrm{se}(\hat{f}_n)$ be the standard error of the forecast and let $\hat{\sigma}$ be the standard error of the regression. [From Section 6-4, we can obtain $\hat{f}_n$ and $\mathrm{se}(\hat{f}_n)$ as the intercept and its standard error from the regression of y_t on $(y_{t-1} - y_n)$ and $(z_{t-1} - z_n)$, $t = 1, 2, \ldots, n$; that is, we subtract the time n value of y from each lagged y, and similarly for z, before doing the regression.] Then,

$$\mathrm{se}(\hat{e}_{n+1}) = \{[\mathrm{se}(\hat{f}_n)]^2 + \hat{\sigma}^2\}^{1/2}, \qquad\qquad\qquad\qquad \text{[18.46]}$$

and the (approximate) 95% forecast interval is

$$\hat{f}_n \pm 1.96 \cdot \mathrm{se}(\hat{e}_{n+1}). \qquad\qquad\qquad\qquad \text{[18.47]}$$

Because $\mathrm{se}(\hat{f}_n)$ is roughly proportional to $1/\sqrt{n}$, $\mathrm{se}(\hat{f}_n)$ is usually small relative to the uncertainty in the error u_{n+1}, as measured by $\hat{\sigma}$. [Some econometrics packages compute forecast intervals routinely, but others require some simple manipulations to obtain (18.47).]

EXAMPLE 18.8   **Forecasting the U.S. Unemployment Rate**

We use the data in PHILLIPS, but only for the years 1948 through 1996, to forecast the U.S. civilian unemployment rate for 1997. We use two models. The first is a simple AR(1) model for *unem*:

$$\widehat{unem}_t = 1.572 + .732\, unem_{t-1}$$
$$(.577)\quad (.097) \qquad\qquad\qquad \text{[18.48]}$$
$$n = 48,\ \overline{R}^2 = .544,\ \hat{\sigma} = 1.049.$$

In a second model, we add inflation with a lag of one year:

$$\widehat{unem}_t = 1.304 + .647\, unem_{t-1} + .184\, inf_{t-1}$$
$$(.490)\quad (.084)\qquad\qquad (.041) \qquad\qquad \text{[18.49]}$$
$$n = 48,\ \overline{R}^2 = .677,\ \hat{\sigma} = .883.$$

The lagged inflation rate is very significant in (18.49) ($t \approx 4.5$), and the adjusted *R*-squared from the second equation is much higher than that from the first. Nevertheless, this does *not* necessarily mean that the second equation will produce a better forecast for 1997. All we can say so far is that, using the data up through 1996, a lag of inflation helps to explain variation in the unemployment rate.

To obtain the forecasts for 1997, we need to know *unem* and *inf* in 1996. These are 5.4 and 3.0, respectively. Therefore, the forecast of $unem_{1997}$ from equation (18.48) is 1.572 + .732(5.4), or about 5.52. The forecast from equation (18.49) is 1.304 + .647(5.4) + .184(3.0), or about 5.35. The actual civilian unemployment rate for 1997 was 4.9, so both equations overpredict the actual rate. The second equation does provide a somewhat better forecast.

We can easily obtain a 95% forecast interval. When we regress $unem_t$ on $(unem_{t-1} - 5.4)$ and $(inf_{t-1} - 3.0)$, we obtain 5.35 as the intercept—which we already computed as the forecast—and $se(\hat{f}_n) = .137$. Therefore, because $\hat{\sigma} = .883$, we have $se(\hat{e}_{n+1}) = [(.137)^2 + (.883)^2]^{1/2} \approx .894$. The 95% forecast interval from (18.47) is $5.35 \pm 1.96(.894)$, or about [3.6, 7.1]. This is a wide interval, and the realized 1997 value, 4.9, is well within the interval. As expected, the standard error of u_{n+1}, which is .883, is a very large fraction of $se(\hat{e}_{n+1})$.

A professional forecaster must usually produce a forecast for every time period. For example, at time *n*, she or he produces a forecast of y_{n+1}. Then, when y_{n+1} and z_{n+1} become available, he or she must forecast y_{n+2}. Even if the forecaster has settled on model (18.43), there are two choices for forecasting y_{n+2}. The first is to use $\hat{\delta}_0 + \hat{\alpha}_1 y_{n+1} + \hat{\gamma}_1 z_{n+1}$, where the parameters are estimated using the first *n* observations. The second possibility is to *reestimate* the parameters using all $n + 1$ observations and then to use the same formula to forecast y_{n+2}. To forecast in subsequent time periods, we can generally use the parameter estimates obtained from the initial *n* observations, or we can update the regression parameters each time we obtain a new data point. Although the latter approach requires more computation, the extra burden is relatively minor, and it can (although it need not) work better because the regression coefficients adjust at least somewhat to the new data points.

As a specific example, suppose we wish to forecast the unemployment rate for 1998, using the model with a single lag of *unem* and *inf*. The first possibility is to just plug the 1997 values of unemployment and inflation into the right-hand side of (18.49). With *unem* = 4.9 and *inf* = 2.3 in 1997, we have a forecast for $unem_{1998}$ of about 4.9. (It is just a coincidence that this is the same as the 1997 unemployment rate.) The second possibility is to reestimate the equation by adding the 1997 observation and then using this new equation (see Computer Exercise C6).

The model in equation (18.43) is one equation in what is known as a **vector autoregressive (VAR) model**. We know what an autoregressive model is from Chapter 11: we model a single series, $\{y_t\}$, in terms of its own past. In vector autoregressive models, we model several series—which, if you are familiar with linear algebra, is where the word "vector" comes from—in terms of their own past. If we have two series, y_t and z_t, a vector autoregression consists of equations that look like

$$y_t = \delta_0 + \alpha_1 y_{t-1} + \gamma_1 z_{t-1} + \alpha_2 y_{t-2} + \gamma_2 z_{t-2} + \ldots \qquad [18.50]$$

and

$$z_t = \eta_0 + \beta_1 y_{t-1} + \rho_1 z_{t-1} + \beta_2 y_{t-2} + \rho_2 z_{t-2} + \ldots,$$

where each equation contains an error that has zero expected value given past information on y and z. In equation (18.43)—and in the example estimated in (18.49)—we assumed that one lag of each variable captured all of the dynamics. (An F test for joint significance of $unem_{t-2}$ and inf_{t-2} confirms that only one lag of each is needed.)

As Example 18.8 illustrates, VAR models can be useful for forecasting. In many cases, we are interested in forecasting only one variable, y, in which case we only need to estimate and analyze the equation for y. Nothing prevents us from adding other lagged variables, say, $w_{t-1}, w_{t-2}, \ldots$, to equation (18.50). Such equations are efficiently estimated by OLS, provided we have included enough lags of all variables and the equation satisfies the homoskedasticity assumption for time series regressions.

Equations such as (18.50) allow us to test whether, *after controlling for past values of y*, past values of z help to forecast y_t. Generally, we say that z *Granger causes* y if

$$\mathrm{E}(y_t | I_{t-1}) \neq \mathrm{E}(y_t | J_{t-1}), \qquad [18.51]$$

where I_{t-1} contains past information on y *and* z, and J_{t-1} contains only information on past y. When (18.51) holds, past z is useful, *in addition to past y*, for predicting y_t. The term "causes" in "Granger causes" should be interpreted with caution. The only sense in which z "causes" y is given in (18.51). In particular, it has nothing to say about *contemporaneous* causality between y and z, so it does not allow us to determine whether z_t is an exogenous or endogenous variable in an equation relating y_t to z_t. (This is also why the notion of **Granger causality** does not apply in pure cross-sectional contexts.)

Once we assume a linear model and decide how many lags of y should be included in $\mathrm{E}(y_t | y_{t-1}, y_{t-2}, \ldots)$, we can easily test the null hypothesis that z does *not* Granger cause y. To be more specific, suppose that $\mathrm{E}(y_t | y_{t-1}, y_{t-2}, \ldots)$ depends on only three lags:

$$y_t = \delta_0 + \alpha_1 y_{t-1} + \alpha_2 y_{t-2} + \alpha_3 y_{t-3} + u_t$$
$$\mathrm{E}(u_t | y_{t-1}, y_{t-2}, \ldots) = 0.$$

Now, under the null hypothesis that z does not Granger cause y, *any* lags of z that we add to the equation should have zero population coefficients. If we add z_{t-1}, then we can simply do a t test on z_{t-1}. If we add two lags of z, then we can do an F test for joint significance of z_{t-1} and z_{t-2} in the equation

$$y_t = \delta_0 + \alpha_1 y_{t-1} + \alpha_2 y_{t-2} + \alpha_3 y_{t-3} + \gamma_1 z_{t-1} + \gamma_2 z_{t-2} + u_t.$$

(If there is heteroskedasticity, we can use a robust form of the test. There cannot be serial correlation under H_0 because the model is dynamically complete.)

As a practical matter, how do we decide on which lags of y and z to include? First, we start by estimating an autoregressive model for y and performing t and F tests to determine how many lags of y should appear. With annual data, the number of lags is typically small, say, one or two. With quarterly or monthly data, there are usually many more lags. Once an autoregressive model for y has been chosen, we can test for lags of z. The choice of lags of z is less important because, when z does not Granger cause y, no set of lagged z's should be significant. With annual data, 1 or 2 lags are typically used; with quarterly data, usually 4 or 8; and with monthly data, perhaps 6, 12, or maybe even 24, given enough data.

We have already done one example of testing for Granger causality in equation (18.49). The autoregressive model that best fits unemployment is an AR(1). In equation (18.49), we added a single lag of inflation, and it was very significant. Therefore, inflation Granger causes unemployment.

There is an extended definition of Granger causality that is often useful. Let $\{w_t\}$ be a third series (or, it could represent several additional series). Then, z *Granger causes* y *conditional on* w if (18.51) holds, but now I_{t-1} contains past information on y, z, and w, while J_{t-1} contains past information on y and w. It is certainly possible that z Granger causes y, but z does not Granger cause y conditional on w. A test of the null that z does *not* Granger cause y conditional on w is obtained by testing for significance of lagged z in a model for y that also depends on lagged y and lagged w. For example, to test whether growth in the money supply Granger causes growth in real GDP, conditional on the change in interest rates, we would regress $gGDP_t$ on lags of $gGDP$, Δint, and gM and do significance tests on the lags of gM. [See, for example, Stock and Watson (1989).]

18-5c Comparing One-Step-Ahead Forecasts

In almost any forecasting problem, there are several competing methods for forecasting. Even when we restrict attention to regression models, there are many possibilities. Which variables should be included, and with how many lags? Should we use logs, levels of variables, or first differences?

In order to decide on a forecasting method, we need a way to choose which one is most suitable. Broadly, we can distinguish between **in-sample criteria** and **out-of-sample criteria**. In a regression context, in-sample criteria include R-squared and especially adjusted R-squared. There are many other *model selection statistics*, but we will not cover those here [see, for example, Ramanathan (1995, Chapter 4)].

For forecasting, it is better to use out-of-sample criteria, as forecasting is essentially an out-of-sample problem. A model might provide a good fit to y in the sample used to estimate the parameters. But this need not translate to good forecasting performance. An out-of-sample comparison involves using the first part of a sample to estimate the parameters of the model and saving the latter part of the sample to gauge its forecasting capabilities. This mimics what we would have to do in practice if we did not yet know the future values of the variables.

Suppose that we have $n + m$ observations, where we use the first n observations to estimate the parameters in our model and save the last m observations for forecasting. Let $\hat{f}_{n+h}$ be the one-step-ahead forecast of y_{n+h+1} for $h = 0, 1, \ldots, m - 1$. The m forecast errors are $\hat{e}_{n+h+1} = y_{n+h+1} - \hat{f}_{n+h}$. How should we measure how well our model forecasts y when it is out of sample? Two measures are most common. The first is the **root mean squared error (RMSE)**:

$$RMSE = \left(m^{-1} \sum_{h=0}^{m-1} \hat{e}_{n+h+1}^2 \right)^{1/2}. \qquad [18.52]$$

This is essentially the sample standard deviation of the forecast errors (without any degrees of freedom adjustment). If we compute RMSE for two or more forecasting methods, then we prefer the method with the smallest out-of-sample RMSE.

A second common measure is the **mean absolute error (MAE)**, which is the average of the absolute forecast errors:

$$MAE = m^{-1} \sum_{h=0}^{m-1} |\hat{e}_{n+h+1}|. \qquad [18.53]$$

Again, we prefer a smaller MAE. Other possible criteria include minimizing the largest of the absolute values of the forecast errors.

EXAMPLE 18.9   **Out-of-Sample Comparisons of Unemployment Forecasts**

In Example 18.8, we found that equation (18.49) fit notably better over the years 1948 through 1996 than did equation (18.48), and, at least for forecasting unemployment in 1997, the model that included lagged inflation worked better. Now, we use the two models, still estimated using the data only through 1996, to compare one-step-ahead forecasts for 1997 through 2003. This leaves seven out-of-sample observations ($n = 48$ and $m = 7$) to use in equations (18.52) and (18.53). For the AR(1) model, RMSE = .962 and MAE = .778. For the model that adds lagged inflation (a VAR model of order one), RMSE = .673 and MAE = .628. Thus, by either measure, the model that includes inf_{t-1} produces better out-of-sample forecasts for 1997 through 2003. In this case, the in-sample and out-of-sample criteria choose the same model.

Rather than using only the first n observations to estimate the parameters of the model, we can reestimate the models each time we add a new observation and use the new model to forecast the next time period.

18-5d Multiple-Step-Ahead Forecasts

Forecasting more than one period ahead is generally more difficult than forecasting one period ahead. We can formalize this as follows. Suppose we consider forecasting y_{t+1} at time t and at an earlier time period s (so that $s < t$). Then $\text{Var}[y_{t+1} - \text{E}(y_{t+1}|I_t)] \leq \text{Var}[y_{t+1} - \text{E}(y_{t+1}|I_s)]$, where the inequality is usually strict. We will not prove this result generally, but, intuitively, it makes sense: the forecast error variance in predicting y_{t+1} is larger when we make that forecast based on less information.

If $\{y_t\}$ follows an AR(1) model (which includes a random walk, possibly with drift), we can easily show that the error variance increases with the forecast horizon. The model is

$$y_t = \alpha + \rho y_{t-1} + u_t$$
$$\text{E}(u_t|I_{t-1}) = 0, I_{t-1} = \{y_{t-1}, y_{t-2}, \dots\},$$

and $\{u_t\}$ has constant variance σ^2 conditional on I_{t-1}. At time $t + h - 1$, our forecast of y_{t+h} is $\alpha + \rho y_{t+h-1}$, and the forecast error is simply u_{t+h}. Therefore, the one-step-ahead forecast variance is simply σ^2. To find multiple-step-ahead forecasts, we have, by repeated substitution,

$$y_{t+h} = (1 + \rho + \dots + \rho^{h-1})\alpha + \rho^h y_t$$
$$+ \rho^{h-1} u_{t+1} + \rho^{h-2} u_{t+2} + \dots + u_{t+h}.$$

At time t, the expected value of u_{t+j}, for all $j \geq 1$, is zero. So

$$\text{E}(y_{t+h}|I_t) = (1 + \rho + \dots + \rho^{h-1})\alpha + \rho^h y_t, \qquad [18.54]$$

and the forecast error is $e_{t,h} = \rho^{h-1} u_{t+1} + \rho^{h-2} u_{t+2} + \dots + u_{t+h}$. This is a sum of uncorrelated random variables, and so the variance of the sum is the sum of the variances: $\text{Var}(e_{t,h}) = \sigma^2[\rho^{2(h-1)} + \rho^{2(h-2)} + \dots + \rho^2 + 1]$. Because $\rho^2 > 0$, each term multiplying σ^2 is positive, so the forecast error variance increases with h. When $\rho^2 < 1$, as h gets large the forecast variance converges to $\sigma^2/(1 - \rho^2)$, which is just the unconditional variance of y_t. In the case of a random walk $(\rho = 1), f_{t,h} = \alpha h + y_t$, and $\text{Var}(e_{t,h}) = \sigma^2 h$: the forecast variance grows without bound as the horizon h increases. This demonstrates that it is very difficult to forecast a random walk, with or without drift, far out into the future. For example, forecasts of interest rates farther into the future become dramatically less precise.

Equation (18.54) shows that using the AR(1) model for multistep forecasting is easy, once we have estimated ρ by OLS. The forecast of y_{n+h} at time n is

$$\hat{f}_{n,h} = (1 + \hat{\rho} + \dots + \hat{\rho}^{h-1})\hat{\alpha} + \hat{\rho}^h y_n. \qquad [18.55]$$

Obtaining forecast intervals is harder, unless $h = 1$, because obtaining the standard error of $\hat{f}_{n,h}$ is difficult. Nevertheless, the standard error of $\hat{f}_{n,h}$ is usually small compared with the standard deviation of the error term, and the latter can be estimated as $\hat{\sigma}[\hat{\rho}^{2(h-1)} + \hat{\rho}^{2(h-2)} + \ldots + \hat{\rho}^2 + 1]^{1/2}$, where $\hat{\sigma}$ is the standard error of the regression from the AR(1) estimation. We can use this to obtain an approximate confidence interval. For example, when $h = 2$, an approximate 95% confidence interval (for large n) is

$$\hat{f}_{n,2} \pm 1.96\hat{\sigma}(1 + \hat{\rho}^2)^{1/2}. \qquad [18.56]$$

Because we are underestimating the standard deviation of y_{n+h}, this interval is too narrow, but perhaps not by much, especially if n is large.

A less traditional, but useful, approach is to estimate a different model for each forecast horizon. For example, suppose we wish to forecast y two periods ahead. If I_t depends only on y through time t, we might assume that $E(y_{t+2}|I_t) = \alpha_0 + \gamma_1 y_t$ [which, as we saw earlier, holds if $\{y_t\}$ follows an AR(1) model]. We can estimate α_0 and γ_1 by regressing y_t on an intercept and on y_{t-2}. Even though the errors in this equation contain serial correlation—errors in adjacent periods are correlated—we can obtain consistent and approximately normal estimators of α_0 and γ_1. The forecast of y_{n+2} at time n is simply $\hat{f}_{n,2} = \hat{\alpha}_0 + \hat{\gamma}_1 y_n$. Further, and very importantly, the standard error of the regression is just what we need for computing a confidence interval for the forecast. Unfortunately, to get the standard error of $\hat{f}_{n,2}$, using the trick for a one-step-ahead forecast requires us to obtain a serial correlation–robust standard error of the kind described in Section 12-5. This standard error goes to zero as n gets large while the variance of the error is constant. Therefore, we can get an approximate interval by using (18.56) and by putting the SER from the regression of y_t on y_{t-2} in place of $\hat{\sigma}(1 + \hat{\rho}^2)^{1/2}$. But we should remember that this ignores the estimation error in $\hat{\alpha}_0$ and $\hat{\gamma}_1$.

We can also compute multiple-step-ahead forecasts with more complicated autoregressive models. For example, suppose $\{y_t\}$ follows an AR(2) model and that at time n, we wish to forecast y_{n+2}. Now, $y_{n+2} = \alpha + \rho_1 y_{n+1} + \rho_2 y_n + u_{n+2}$, so

$$E(y_{n+2}|I_n) = \alpha + \rho_1 E(y_{n+1}|I_n) + \rho_2 y_n.$$

We can write this as

$$f_{n,2} = \alpha + \rho_1 f_{n,1} + \rho_2 y_n,$$

so that the two-step-ahead forecast at time n can be obtained once we get the one-step-ahead forecast. If the parameters of the AR(2) model have been estimated by OLS, then we operationalize this as

$$\hat{f}_{n,2} = \hat{\alpha} + \hat{\rho}_1 \hat{f}_{n,1} + \hat{\rho}_2 y_n. \qquad [18.57]$$

Now, $\hat{f}_{n,1} = \hat{\alpha} + \hat{\rho}_1 y_n + \hat{\rho}_2 y_{n-1}$, which we can compute at time n. Then, we plug this into (18.57), along with y_n, to obtain $\hat{f}_{n,2}$. For any $h > 2$, obtaining any h-step-ahead forecast for an AR(2) model is easy to find in a recursive manner: $\hat{f}_{n,h} = \hat{\alpha} + \hat{\rho}_1 \hat{f}_{n,h-1} + \hat{\rho}_2 \hat{f}_{n,h-2}$.

Similar reasoning can be used to obtain multiple-step-ahead forecasts for VAR models. To illustrate, suppose we have

$$y_t = \delta_0 + \alpha_1 y_{t-1} + \gamma_1 z_{t-1} + u_t \qquad [18.58]$$

and

$$z_t = \eta_0 + \beta_1 y_{t-1} + \rho_1 z_{t-1} + v_t.$$

Now, if we wish to forecast y_{n+1} at time n, we simply use $\hat{f}_{n,1} = \hat{\delta}_0 + \hat{\alpha}_1 y_n + \hat{\gamma}_1 z_n$. Likewise, the forecast of z_{n+1} at time n is (say) $\hat{g}_{n,1} = \hat{\eta}_0 + \hat{\beta}_1 y_n + \hat{\rho}_1 z_n$. Now, suppose we wish to obtain a two-step-ahead forecast of y at time n. From (18.58), we have

$$E(y_{n+2}|I_n) = \delta_0 + \alpha_1 E(y_{n+1}|I_n) + \gamma_1 E(z_{n+1}|I_n)$$

[because $E(u_{n+2}|I_n) = 0$], so we can write the forecast as

$$\hat{f}_{n,2} = \hat{\delta}_0 + \hat{\alpha}_1 \hat{f}_{n,1} + \hat{\gamma}_1 \hat{g}_{n,1}. \qquad [18.59]$$

This equation shows that the two-step-ahead forecast for y depends on the one-step-ahead forecasts for y *and* z. Generally, we can build up multiple-step-ahead forecasts of y by using the recursive formula

$$\hat{f}_{n,h} = \hat{\delta}_0 + \hat{\alpha}_1\hat{f}_{n,h-1} + \hat{\gamma}_1\hat{g}_{n,h-1}, \quad h \geq 2.$$

EXAMPLE 18.10   Two-Year-Ahead Forecast for the Unemployment Rate

To use equation (18.49) to forecast unemployment two years out—say, the 1998 rate using the data through 1996—we need a model for inflation. The best model for *inf* in terms of lagged *unem* and *inf* appears to be a simple AR(1) model (*unem*$_{-1}$ is not significant when added to the regression):

$$\widehat{inf_t} = 1.277 + .665\ inf_{t-1}$$
$$(.558)\quad(.107)$$
$$n = 48, R^2 = .457, \bar{R}^2 = .445.$$

If we plug the 1996 value of *inf* into this equation, we get the forecast of *inf* for 1997: $\widehat{inf}_{1997} = 3.27$. Now, we can plug this, along with $\widehat{unem}_{1997} = 5.35$ (which we obtained earlier), into (18.59) to forecast *unem*$_{1998}$:

$$\widehat{unem}_{1998} = 1.304 + .647(5.35) + .184(3.27) \approx 5.37.$$

Remember, this forecast uses information only through 1996. The one-step-ahead forecast of *unem*$_{1998}$, obtained by plugging the 1997 values of *unem* and *inf* into (18.48), was about 4.90. The actual unemployment rate in 1998 was 4.5%, which means that, in this case, the one-step-ahead forecast does quite a bit better than the two-step-ahead forecast.

Just as with one-step-ahead forecasting, an out-of-sample root mean squared error or a mean absolute error can be used to choose among multiple-step-ahead forecasting methods.

18-5e Forecasting Trending, Seasonal, and Integrated Processes

We now turn to forecasting series that either exhibit trends, have seasonality, or have unit roots. Recall from Chapters 10 and 11 that one approach to handling trending dependent or independent variables in regression models is to include time trends, the most popular being a linear trend. Trends can be included in forecasting equations as well, although they must be used with caution.

In the simplest case, suppose that $\{y_t\}$ has a linear trend but is unpredictable around that trend. Then, we can write

$$y_t = \alpha + \beta t + u_t, \mathrm{E}(u_t|I_{t-1}) = 0, t = 1, 2, \ldots, \qquad [18.60]$$

where, as usual, I_{t-1} contains information observed through time $t-1$ (which includes at least past y). How do we forecast y_{n+h} at time n for any $h \geq 1$? This is simple because $\mathrm{E}(y_{n+h}|I_n) = \alpha + \beta(n+h)$. The forecast error variance is simply $\sigma^2 = \mathrm{Var}(u_t)$ (assuming a constant variance over time). If we estimate α and β by OLS using the first n observations, then our forecast for y_{n+h} at time n is $\hat{f}_{n,h} = \hat{\alpha} + \hat{\beta}(n+h)$. In other words, we simply plug the time period corresponding to y into the estimated trend function. For example, if we use the $n = 131$ observations in BARIUM to forecast monthly imports of Chinese barium chloride to the United States from China, we obtain $\hat{\alpha} = 249.56$ and $\hat{\beta} = 5.15$. The sample period ends in December 1988, so the forecast of imports of Chinese barium chloride six months later is $249.56 + 5.15(137) = 955.11$, measured as short tons. For comparison, the December 1988 value is 1,087.81, so it is greater than the forecasted value six months later. The series and its estimated trend line are shown in Figure 18.2.

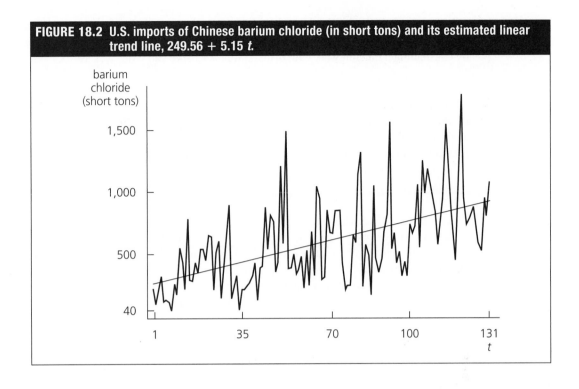

FIGURE 18.2 U.S. imports of Chinese barium chloride (in short tons) and its estimated linear trend line, 249.56 + 5.15 *t*.

As we discussed in Chapter 10, most economic time series are better characterized as having, at least approximately, a constant growth rate, which suggests that $\log(y_t)$ follows a linear time trend. Suppose we use n observations to obtain the equation

$$\log(y_t) = \hat{\alpha} + \hat{\beta}t, \ t = 1, 2, \ldots, n. \tag{18.61}$$

EXPLORING FURTHER 18.5

Suppose you model $\{y_t: t = 1, 2, \ldots, 46\}$ as a linear time trend, where data are annual starting in 1950 and ending in 1995. Define the variable $year_t$ as ranging from 50 when $t = 1$ to 95 when $t = 46$. If you estimate the equation $\hat{y}_t = \hat{\gamma} + \hat{\delta}year_t$ how do $\hat{\gamma}$ and $\hat{\delta}$ compare with $\hat{\alpha}$ and $\hat{\beta}$ in $\hat{y}_t = \hat{\alpha} + \hat{\beta}t$? How will forecasts from the two equations compare?

Then, to forecast $\log(y)$ at any future time period $n + h$, we just plug $n + h$ into the trend equation, as before. But this does not allow us to forecast y, which is usually what we want. It is tempting to simply exponentiate $\hat{\alpha} + \hat{\beta}(n + h)$ to obtain the forecast for y_{n+h}, but this is not quite right, for the same reasons we gave in Section 6-4. We must properly account for the error implicit in (18.61). The simplest way to do this is to use the n observations to regress y_t on $\exp(\widehat{logy_t})$ *without* an intercept. Let $\hat{\gamma}$ be the slope coefficient on $\exp(\widehat{logy_t})$. Then, the forecast of y in period $n + h$ is simply

$$\hat{f}_{n,h} = \hat{\gamma}\exp[\hat{\alpha} + \hat{\beta}(n + h)]. \tag{18.62}$$

As an example, if we use the first 687 weeks of data on the New York Stock Exchange index in NYSE, we obtain $\hat{\alpha} = 3.782$ and $\hat{\beta} = .0019$ [by regressing $\log(price_t)$ on a linear time trend]; this shows that the index grows about .2% per week, on average. When we regress *price* on the exponentiated fitted values, we obtain $\hat{\gamma} = 1.018$. Now, we forecast *price* four weeks out, which is the last week in the sample, using (18.62): $1.018 \cdot \exp[3.782 + .0019(691)] \approx 166.12$. The actual value turned out to be 164.25, so we have somewhat overpredicted. But this result is much better than if we estimate a linear time trend for the first 687 weeks: the forecasted value for week 691 is 152.23, which is a substantial underprediction.

Although trend models can be useful for prediction, they must be used with caution, especially for forecasting far into the future integrated series that have drift. The potential problem can be seen by considering a random walk with drift. At time $t + h$, we can write y_{t+h} as

$$y_{t+h} = \beta h + y_t + u_{t+1} + \ldots + u_{t+h},$$

where β is the drift term (usually $\beta > 0$), and each u_{t+j} has zero mean given I_t and constant variance σ^2. As we saw earlier, the forecast of y_{t+h} at time t is $E(y_{t+h}|I_t) = \beta h + y_t$, and the forecast error variance is $\sigma^2 h$. What happens if we use a linear trend model? Let y_0 be the initial value of the process at time zero, which we take as nonrandom. Then, we can also write

$$y_{t+h} = y_0 + \beta(t + h) + u_1 + u_2 + \ldots + u_{t+h}$$
$$= y_0 + \beta(t + h) + v_{t+h}.$$

This looks like a linear trend model with the intercept $\alpha = y_0$. But the error, v_{t+h}, while having mean zero, has variance $\sigma^2(t + h)$. Therefore, if we use the linear trend $y_0 + \beta(t + h)$ to forecast y_{t+h} at time t, the forecast error variance is $\sigma^2(t + h)$, compared with $\sigma^2 h$ when we use $\beta h + y_t$. The ratio of the forecast variances is $(t + h)/h$, which can be big for large t. The bottom line is that we should not use a linear trend to forecast a random walk with drift. (Computer Exercise C8 asks you to compare forecasts from a cubic trend line and those from the simple random walk model for the general fertility rate in the United States.)

Deterministic trends can also produce poor forecasts if the trend parameters are estimated using old data and the process has a subsequent shift in the trend line. Sometimes, exogenous shocks—such as the oil crises of the 1970s—can change the trajectory of trending variables. If an old trend line is used to forecast far into the future, the forecasts can be way off. This problem can be mitigated by using the most recent data available to obtain the trend line parameters.

Nothing prevents us from combining trends with other models for forecasting. For example, we can add a linear trend to an AR(1) model, which can work well for forecasting series with linear trends but which are also stable AR processes around the trend.

It is also straightforward to forecast processes with deterministic seasonality (monthly or quarterly series). For example, the file BARIUM contains the monthly production of gasoline in the United States from 1978 through 1988. This series has no obvious trend, but it does have a strong seasonal pattern. (Gasoline production is higher in the summer months and in December.) In the simplest model, we would regress *gas* (measured in gallons) on 11 month dummies, say, for February through December. Then, the forecast for any future month is simply the intercept plus the coefficient on the appropriate month dummy. (For January, the forecast is just the intercept in the regression.) We can also add lags of variables and time trends to allow for general series with seasonality.

Forecasting processes with unit roots also deserves special attention. Earlier, we obtained the expected value of a random walk conditional on information through time n. To forecast a random walk, with possible drift α, h periods into the future at time n, we use $\hat{f}_{n,h} = \hat{\alpha}_h + y_n$, where $\hat{\alpha}$ is the sample average of the Δy_t up through $t = n$. (If there is no drift, we set $\hat{\alpha} = 0$.) This approach imposes the unit root. An alternative would be to estimate an AR(1) model for $\{y_t\}$ and to use the forecast formula (18.55). This approach does not impose a unit root, but if one is present, $\hat{\rho}$ converges in probability to one as n gets large. Nevertheless, $\hat{\rho}$ can be substantially different than one, especially if the sample size is not very large. The matter of which approach produces better out-of-sample forecasts is an empirical issue. If in the AR(1) model, ρ is less than one, even slightly, the AR(1) model will tend to produce better long-run forecasts.

Generally, there are two approaches to producing forecasts for I(1) processes. The first is to impose a unit root. For a one-step-ahead forecast, we obtain a model to forecast the change in y, Δy_{t+1}, given information through time t. Then, because $y_{t+1} = \Delta y_{t+1} + y_t$, $E(y_{t+1}|I_t) = E(y_{t+1}|I_t) + y_t$. Therefore, our forecast of y_{n+1} at time n is just

$$\hat{f}_n = \hat{g}_n + y_n,$$

where $\hat{g}_n$ is the forecast of Δy_{n+1} at time n. Typically, an AR model (which is necessarily stable) is used for Δy_t, or a vector autoregression.

This can be extended to multiple-step-ahead forecasts by writing y_{n+h} as

$$y_{n+h} = (y_{n+h} - y_{n+h-1}) + (y_{n+h-1} - y_{n+h-2}) + \ldots + (y_{n+1} - y_n) + y_n,$$

or

$$y_{n+h} = \Delta y_{n+h} + \Delta y_{n+h-1} + \ldots + \Delta y_{n+1} + y_n.$$

Therefore, the forecast of y_{n+h} at time n is

$$\hat{f}_{n,h} = \hat{g}_{n,h} + \hat{g}_{n,h-1} + \ldots + \hat{g}_{n,1} + y_n, \qquad [18.63]$$

where $\hat{g}_{n,j}$ is the forecast of Δy_{n+j} at time n. For example, we might model Δy_t as a stable AR(1), obtain the multiple-step-ahead forecasts from (18.55) (but with $\hat{\alpha}$ and $\hat{\rho}$ obtained from Δy_t on Δy_{t-1}, and y_n replaced with Δy_n), and then plug these into (18.63).

The second approach to forecasting I(1) variables is to use a general AR or VAR model for $\{y_t\}$. This does not impose the unit root. For example, if we use an AR(2) model,

$$y_t = \alpha + \rho_1 y_{t-1} + \rho_2 y_{t-2} + u_t, \qquad [18.64]$$

then $\rho_1 + \rho_2 = 1$. If we plug in $\rho_1 = 1 - \rho_2$ and rearrange, we obtain $\Delta y_t = \alpha - \rho_2 \Delta y_{t-1} + u_t$, which is a stable AR(1) model in the difference that takes us back to the first approach described earlier. Nothing prevents us from estimating (18.64) directly by OLS. One nice thing about this regression is that we *can* use the usual t statistic on $\hat{\rho}_2$ to determine if y_{t-2} is significant. (This assumes that the homoskedasticity assumption holds; if not, we can use the heteroskedasticity-robust form.) We will not show this formally, but, intuitively, it follows by rewriting the equation as $y_t = \alpha + \gamma y_{t-1} - \rho_2 \Delta y_{t-1} + u_t$, where $\gamma = \rho_1 + \rho_2$. Even if $\gamma = 1$, ρ_2 is minus the coefficient on a stationary, weakly dependent process $\{\Delta y_{t-1}\}$. Because the regression results will be identical to (18.64), we can use (18.64) directly.

As an example, let us estimate an AR(2) model for the general fertility rate in FERTIL3, using the observations through 1979. (In Computer Exercise C8, you are asked to use this model for forecasting, which is why we save some observations at the end of the sample.)

$$\widehat{gfr}_t = 3.22 + 1.272\, gfr_{t-1} - .311\, gfr_{t-2}$$
$$(2.92)\quad (.120)\qquad\quad (.121) \qquad\qquad [18.65]$$
$$n = 65, R^2 = .949, \overline{R}^2 = .947.$$

The t statistic on the second lag is about -2.57, which is statistically different from zero at about the 1% level. (The first lag also has a very significant t statistic, which has an approximate t distribution by the same reasoning used for $\hat{\rho}_2$.) The R-squared, adjusted or not, is not especially informative as a goodness-of-fit measure because gfr apparently contains a unit root, and it makes little sense to ask how much of the variance in gfr we are explaining.

The coefficients on the two lags in (18.65) add up to .961, which is close to and not statistically different from one (as can be verified by applying the augmented Dickey-Fuller test to the equation $\Delta gfr_t = \alpha + \theta gfr_{t-1} + \delta_1 \Delta gfr_{t-1} + u_t$). Even though we have not imposed the unit root restriction, we can still use (18.65) for forecasting, as we discussed earlier.

Before ending this section, we point out one potential improvement in forecasting in the context of vector autoregressive models with I(1) variables. Suppose $\{y_t\}$ and $\{z_t\}$ are each I(1) processes. One approach for obtaining forecasts of y is to estimate a bivariate autoregression in the variables Δy_t and Δz_t and then to use (18.63) to generate one- or multiple-step-ahead forecasts; this is essentially the first approach we described earlier. However, if y_t and z_t are *cointegrated*, we have more stationary, stable variables in the information set that can be used in forecasting Δy: namely, lags of $y_t - \beta z_t$, where β is the cointegrating parameter. A simple error correction model is

$$\Delta y_t = \alpha_0 + \alpha_1 \Delta y_{t-1} + \gamma_1 \Delta z_{t-1} + \delta_1(y_{t-1} - \beta z_{t-1}) + e_t,$$
$$E(e_t|I_{t-1}) = 0. \tag{18.66}$$

To forecast y_{n+1}, we use observations up through n to estimate the cointegrating parameter, β, and then estimate the parameters of the error correction model by OLS, as described in Section 18-4. Forecasting Δy_{n+1} is easy: we just plug Δy_n, Δz_n, and $y_n - \hat{\beta} z_n$ into the estimated equation. Having obtained the forecast of Δy_{n+1}, we add it to y_n.

By rearranging the error correction model, we can write

$$y_t = \alpha_0 + \rho_1 y_{t-1} + \rho_2 y_{t-2} + \delta_1 z_{t-1} + \delta_2 z_{t-2} + u_t, \tag{18.67}$$

where $\rho_1 = 1 + \alpha_1 + \delta$, $\rho_2 = -\alpha_1$, and so on, which is the first equation in a VAR model for y_t and z_t. Notice that this depends on five parameters, just as many as in the error correction model. The point is that, for the purposes of forecasting, the VAR model in the levels and the error correction model are essentially the same. This is not the case in more general error correction models. For example, suppose that $\alpha_1 = \gamma_1 = 0$ in (18.66), but we have a second error correction term, $\delta_2(y_{t-2} - \beta z_{t-2})$. Then, the error correction model involves only four parameters, whereas (18.67)—which has the same order of lags for y and z—contains five parameters. Thus, error correction models can economize on parameters; that is, they are generally more *parsimonious* than VARs in levels.

If y_t and z_t are I(1) but not cointegrated, the appropriate model is (18.66) without the error correction term. This can be used to forecast Δy_{n+1}, and we can add this to y_n to forecast y_{n+1}.

Summary

The time series topics covered in this chapter are used routinely in empirical macroeconomics, empirical finance, and a variety of other applied fields. We began by showing how infinite distributed lag models can be interpreted and estimated. These can provide flexible lag distributions with fewer parameters than a similar finite distributed lag model. The geometric distributed lag and, more generally, rational distributed lag models are the most popular. They can be estimated using standard econometric procedures on simple dynamic equations.

Testing for a unit root has become very common in time series econometrics. If a series has a unit root, then, in many cases, the usual large sample normal approximations are no longer valid. In addition, a unit root process has the property that an innovation has a long-lasting effect, which is of interest in its own right. While there are many tests for unit roots, the Dickey-Fuller t test—and its extension, the augmented Dickey-Fuller test—is probably the most popular and easiest to implement. We can allow for a linear trend when testing for unit roots by adding a trend to the Dickey-Fuller regression.

When an I(1) series, y_t, is regressed on another I(1) series, x_t, there is serious concern about spurious regression, even if the series do not contain obvious trends. This has been studied thoroughly in the case of a random walk: even if the two random walks are independent, the usual t test for significance of the slope coefficient, based on the usual critical values, will reject much more than the nominal size of the test. In addition, the R^2 tends to a random variable, rather than to zero (as would be the case if we regress the difference in y_t on the difference in x_t).

In one important case, a regression involving I(1) variables is not spurious, and that is when the series are cointegrated. This means that a linear function of the two I(1) variables is I(0). If y_t and x_t are I(1) but $y_t - x_t$ is I(0), y_t and x_t cannot drift arbitrarily far apart. There are simple tests of the null of no cointegration against the alternative of cointegration, one of which is based on applying a Dickey-Fuller unit root test to the residuals from a static regression. There are also simple estimators of the cointegrating parameter that yield t statistics with approximate standard normal distributions (and asymptotically valid confidence intervals). We covered the leads and lags estimator in Section 18-4.

Cointegration between y_t and x_t implies that error correction terms may appear in a model relating Δy_t to Δx_t: the error correction terms are lags in $y_t - \beta x_t$, where β is the cointegrating parameter. A simple two-step estimation procedure is available for estimating error correction models. First, β is estimated using a static regression (or the leads and lags regression). Then, OLS is used to estimate a simple dynamic model in first differences that includes the error correction terms.

Section 18-5 contained an introduction to forecasting, with emphasis on regression-based forecasting methods. Static models or, more generally, models that contain explanatory variables dated contemporaneously with the dependent variable, are limited because then the explanatory variables need to be forecasted. If we plug in hypothesized values of unknown future explanatory variables, we obtain a conditional forecast. Unconditional forecasts are similar to simply modeling y_t as a function of *past* information we have observed at the time the forecast is needed. Dynamic regression models, including autoregressions and vector autoregressions, are used routinely. In addition to obtaining one-step-ahead point forecasts, we also discussed the construction of forecast intervals, which are very similar to prediction intervals.

Various criteria are used for choosing among forecasting methods. The most common performance measures are the root mean squared error and the mean absolute error. Both estimate the size of the average forecast error. It is most informative to compute these measures using out-of-sample forecasts.

Multiple-step-ahead forecasts present new challenges and are subject to large forecast error variances. Nevertheless, for models such as autoregressions and vector autoregressions, multiple-step-ahead forecasts can be computed, and approximate forecast intervals can be obtained.

Forecasting trending and I(1) series requires special care. Processes with deterministic trends can be forecasted by including time trends in regression models, possibly with lags of variables. A potential drawback is that deterministic trends can provide poor forecasts for long-horizon forecasts: once it is estimated, a linear trend continues to increase or decrease. The typical approach to forecasting an I(1) process is to forecast the difference in the process and to add the level of the variable to that forecasted difference. Alternatively, vector autoregressive models can be used in the levels of the series. If the series are cointegrated, error correction models can be used instead.

Key Terms

Augmented Dickey-Fuller Test	Granger Causality	Rational Distributed Lag (RDL)
Cointegration	Infinite Distributed Lag (IDL)	Model
Conditional Forecast	Model	Root Mean Squared Error
Dickey-Fuller Distribution	Information Set	(RMSE)
Dickey-Fuller (DF) Test	In-Sample Criteria	Spurious Regression Problem
Engle-Granger Test	Leads and Lags Estimator	Unconditional Forecast
Engle-Granger Two-Step	Loss Function	Unit Roots
Procedure	Martingale	Vector Autoregressive (VAR)
Error Correction Model	Martingale Difference Sequence	Model
Exponential Smoothing	Mean Absolute Error (MAE)	
Forecast Error	Multiple-Step-Ahead Forecast	
Forecast Interval	One-Step-Ahead Forecast	
Geometric (or Koyck)	Out-of-Sample Criteria	
Distributed Lag	Point Forecast	

Problems

1 Consider equation (18.15) with $k = 2$. Using the IV approach to estimating the γ_h and ρ, what would you use as instruments for y_{t-1}?

2 An interesting economic model that leads to an econometric model with a lagged dependent variable relates y_t to the *expected value* of x_t, say, x_t^*, where the expectation is based on all observed information at time $t - 1$:

$$y_t = \alpha_0 + \alpha_1 x_t^* + u_t. \qquad [18.68]$$

A natural assumption on $\{u_t\}$ is that $E(u_t|I_{t-1}) = 0$, where I_{t-1} denotes all information on y and x observed at time $t - 1$; this means that $E(y_t|I_{t-1}) = \alpha_0 + \alpha_1 x_t^*$. To complete this model, we need an assumption about how the expectation x_t^* is formed. We saw a simple example of adaptive expectations in Section 11-2, where $x_t^* = x_{t-1}$. A more complicated adaptive expectations scheme is

$$x_t^* - x_{t-1}^* = \lambda(x_{t-1} - x_{t-1}^*), \qquad [18.69]$$

where $0 < \lambda < 1$. This equation implies that the change in expectations reacts to whether last period's realized value was above or below its expectation. The assumption $0 < \lambda < 1$ implies that the change in expectations is a fraction of last period's error.

(i)　Show that the two equations imply that

$$y_t = \lambda\alpha_0 + (1 - \lambda)y_{t-1} + \lambda\alpha_1 x_{t-1} + u_t - (1 - \lambda)u_{t-1}.$$

　　[*Hint*: Lag equation (18.68) one period, multiply it by $(1 - \lambda)$, and subtract this from (18.68). Then, use (18.69).]

(ii)　Under $E(u_t|I_{t-1}) = 0$, $\{u_t\}$ is serially uncorrelated. What does this imply about the new errors, $v_t = u_t - (1 - \lambda)u_{t-1}$?

(iii)　If we write the equation from part (i) as

$$y_t = \beta_0 + \beta_1 y_{t-1} + \beta_2 x_{t-1} + v_t,$$

　　how would you consistently estimate the β_j?

(iv)　Given consistent estimators of the β_j, how would you consistently estimate λ and α_1?

3 Suppose that $\{y_t\}$ and $\{z_t\}$ are I(1) series, but $y_t - \beta z_t$ is I(0) for some $\beta \neq 0$. Show that for any $\delta \neq \beta$, $y_t - \delta z_t$ must be I(1).

4 Consider the error correction model in equation (18.37). Show that if you add another lag of the error correction term, $y_{t-2} - \beta x_{t-2}$, the equation suffers from perfect collinearity. (*Hint*: Show that $y_{t-2} - \beta x_{t-2}$ is a perfect linear function of $y_{t-1} - \beta x_{t-1}$, Δx_{t-1}, and Δy_{t-1}.)

5 Suppose the process $\{(x_t, y_t): t = 0, 1, 2, \ldots\}$ satisfies the equations

$$y_t = \beta x_t + u_t$$

and

$$\Delta x_t = \gamma\Delta x_{t-1} + v_t,$$

where $E(u_t|I_{t-1}) = E(v_t|I_{t-1}) = 0$, I_{t-1} contains information on x and y dated at time $t - 1$ and earlier, $\beta \neq 0$, and $|\gamma| < 1$ [so that x_t, and therefore y_t, is I(1)]. Show that these two equations imply an error correction model of the form

$$\Delta y_t = \gamma_1\Delta x_{t-1} + \delta(y_{t-1} - \beta x_{t-1}) + e_t,$$

where $\gamma_1 = \beta\gamma$, $\delta = -1$, and $e_t = u_t + \beta v_t$. (*Hint*: First subtract y_{t-1} from both sides of the first equation. Then, add and subtract βx_{t-1} from the right-hand side and rearrange. Finally, use the second equation to get the error correction model that contains Δx_{t-1}.)

6 Using the monthly data in VOLAT, the following model was estimated:

$$\widehat{pcip} = 1.54 + .344\, pcip_{-1} + .074\, pcip_{-2} + .073\, pcip_{-3} + .031\, pcsp_{-1}$$
$$\phantom{\widehat{pcip} =} (.56)\ \ (.042) (.045) (.042) (.013)$$
$$n = 554, R^2 = .174, \bar{R}^2 = .168,$$

where *pcip* is the percentage change in monthly industrial production, at an annualized rate, and *pcsp* is the percentage change in the Standard & Poor's 500 Index, also at an annualized rate.

   (i)   If the past three months of *pcip* are zero and $pcsp_{-1} = 0$, what is the predicted growth in industrial production for this month? Is it statistically different from zero?

   (ii) If the past three months of *pcip* are zero but $pcsp_{-1} = 10$, what is the predicted growth in industrial production?

   (iii) What do you conclude about the effects of the stock market on real economic activity?

7 Let gM_t be the annual growth in the money supply and let $unem_t$ be the unemployment rate. Assuming that $unem_t$ follows a stable AR(1) process, explain in detail how you would test whether gM Granger causes *unem*.

8 Suppose that y_t follows the model

$$y_t = \alpha + \delta_1 z_{t-1} + u_t$$
$$u_t = \rho u_{t-1} + e_t$$
$$E(e_t | I_{t-1}) = 0,$$

where I_{t-1} contains *y* and *z* dated at $t - 1$ and earlier.

   (i)   Show that $E(y_{t+1} | I_t) = (1 - \rho)\alpha + \rho y_t + \delta_1 z_t - \rho \delta_1 z_{t-1}$. (*Hint*: Write $u_{t-1} = y_{t-1} - \alpha - \delta_1 z_{t-2}$ and plug this into the second equation; then, plug the result into the first equation and take the conditional expectation.)

   (ii) Suppose that you use *n* observations to estimate α, δ_1, and ρ. Write the equation for forecasting y_{n+1}.

   (iii) Explain why the model with one lag of *z* and AR(1) serial correlation is a special case of the model

$$y_t = \alpha_0 + \rho y_{t-1} + \gamma_1 z_{t-1} + \gamma_2 z_{t-2} + e_t.$$

   (iv) What does part (iii) suggest about using models with AR(1) serial correlation for forecasting?

9 Let $\{y_t\}$ be an I(1) sequence. Suppose that $\hat{g}_n$ is the one-step-ahead forecast of Δy_{n+1} and let $\hat{f}_n = \hat{g}_n + y_n$ be the one-step-ahead forecast of y_{n+1}. Explain why the forecast errors for forecasting Δy_{n+1} and y_{n+1} are identical.

Computer Exercises

C1 Use the data in WAGEPRC for this exercise. Problem 5 in Chapter 11 gave estimates of a finite distributed lag model of *gprice* on *gwage*, where 12 lags of *gwage* are used.

   (i)   Estimate a simple geometric DL model of *gprice* on *gwage*. In particular, estimate equation (18.11) by OLS. What are the estimated impact propensity and LRP? Sketch the estimated lag distribution.

   (ii) Compare the estimated IP and LRP to those obtained in Problem 5 in Chapter 11. How do the estimated lag distributions compare?

   (iii) Now, estimate the rational distributed lag model from (18.16). Sketch the lag distribution and compare the estimated IP and LRP to those obtained in part (ii).

C2 Use the data in HSEINV for this exercise.

   (i)   Test for a unit root in $\log(invpc)$, including a linear time trend and two lags of $\Delta\log(invpc_t)$. Use a 5% significance level.

   (ii)   Use the approach from part (i) to test for a unit root in $\log(price)$.

   (iii) Given the outcomes in parts (i) and (ii), does it make sense to test for cointegration between $\log(invpc)$ and $\log(price)$?

C3 Use the data in VOLAT for this exercise.

   (i)   Estimate an AR(3) model for $pcip$. Now, add a fourth lag and verify that it is very insignificant.

   (ii)   To the AR(3) model from part (i), add three lags of $pcsp$ to test whether $pcsp$ Granger causes $pcip$. Carefully, state your conclusion.

   (iii) To the model in part (ii), add three lags of the change in $i3$, the three-month T-bill rate. Does $pcsp$ Granger cause $pcip$ conditional on past $\Delta i3$?

C4 In testing for cointegration between gfr and pe in Example 18.5, add t^2 to equation (18.32) to obtain the OLS residuals. Include one lag in the augmented DF test. The 5% critical value for the test is -4.15.

C5 Use INTQRT for this exercise.

   (i)   In Example 18.7, we estimated an error correction model for the holding yield on six-month T-bills, where one lag of the holding yield on three-month T-bills is the explanatory variable. We assumed that the cointegration parameter was one in the equation $hy6_t = \alpha + \beta hy3_{t-1} + u_t$. Now, add the lead change, $\Delta hy3_t$, the contemporaneous change, $\Delta hy3_{t-1}$, and the lagged change, $\Delta hy3_{t-2}$, of $hy3_{t-1}$. That is, estimate the equation

$$hy6_t = \alpha + \beta hy3_{t-1} + \phi_0 \Delta hy3_t + \phi_1 \Delta hy3_{t-1} + \rho_1 \Delta hy3_{t-2} + e_t$$

and report the results in equation form. Test $H_0\!: \beta = 1$ against a two-sided alternative. Assume that the lead and lag are sufficient so that $\{hy3_{t-1}\}$ is strictly exogenous in this equation and do not worry about serial correlation.

   (ii)   To the error correction model in (18.39), add $\Delta hy3_{t-2}$ and $(hy6_{t-2} - hy3_{t-3})$. Are these terms jointly significant? What do you conclude about the appropriate error correction model?

C6 Use the data in PHILLIPS to answer these questions.

   (i)   Estimate the models in (18.48) and (18.49) using the data through 1997. Do the parameter estimates change much compared with (18.48) and (18.49)?

   (ii)   Use the new equations to forecast $unem_{1998}$; round to two places after the decimal. Which equation produces a better forecast?

   (iii) As we discussed in the text, the forecast for $unem_{1998}$ using (18.49) is 4.90. Compare this with the forecast obtained using the data through 1997. Does using the extra year of data to obtain the parameter estimates produce a better forecast?

   (iv) Use the model estimated in (18.48) to obtain a two-step-ahead forecast of $unem$. That is, forecast $unem_{1998}$ using equation (18.55) with $\hat\alpha = 1.572$, $\hat\rho = .732$, and $h = 2$. Is this better or worse than the one-step-ahead forecast obtained by plugging $unem_{1997} = 4.9$ into (18.48)?

C7 Use the data in BARIUM for this exercise.

   (i)   Estimate the linear trend model $chnimp_t = \alpha + \beta t + u_t$, using the first 119 observations (this excludes the last 12 months of observations for 1988). What is the standard error of the regression?

   (ii)   Now, estimate an AR(1) model for $chnimp$, again using all data but the last 12 months. Compare the standard error of the regression with that from part (i). Which model provides a better in-sample fit?

   (iii) Use the models from parts (i) and (ii) to compute the one-step-ahead forecast errors for the 12 months in 1988. (You should obtain 12 forecast errors for each method.) Compute and compare the RMSEs and the MAEs for the two methods. Which forecasting method works better out-of-sample for one-step-ahead forecasts?

(iv)   Add monthly dummy variables to the regression from part (i). Are these jointly significant? (Do not worry about the slight serial correlation in the errors from this regression when doing the joint test.)

C8   Use the data in FERTIL3 for this exercise.

(i)   Graph *gfr* against time. Does it contain a clear upward or downward trend over the entire sample period?

(ii)   Using the data through 1979, estimate a cubic time trend model for *gfr* (that is, regress *gfr* on t, t^2, and t^3, along with an intercept). Comment on the *R*-squared of the regression.

(iii) Using the model in part (ii), compute the mean absolute error of the one-step-ahead forecast errors for the years 1980 through 1984.

(iv)   Using the data through 1979, regress Δgfr_t on a constant only. Is the constant statistically different from zero? Does it make sense to assume that any drift term is zero, if we assume that gfr_t follows a random walk?

(v)   Now, forecast *gfr* for 1980 through 1984, using a random walk model: the forecast of gfr_{n+1} is simply gfr_n. Find the MAE. How does it compare with the MAE from part (iii)? Which method of forecasting do you prefer?

(vi)   Now, estimate an AR(2) model for *gfr*, again using the data only through 1979. Is the second lag significant?

(vii) Obtain the MAE for 1980 through 1984, using the AR(2) model. Does this more general model work better out-of-sample than the random walk model?

C9   Use CONSUMP for this exercise.

(i)   Let y_t be real per capita disposable income. Use the data through 1989 to estimate the model

$$y_t = \alpha + \beta t + \rho y_{t-1} + u_t$$

and report the results in the usual form.

(ii)   Use the estimated equation from part (i) to forecast *y* in 1990. What is the forecast error?

(iii) Compute the mean absolute error of the one-step-ahead forecasts for the 1990s, using the parameters estimated in part (i).

(iv)   Now, compute the MAE over the same period, but drop y_{t-1} from the equation. Is it better to include y_{t-1} in the model or not?

C10 Use the data in INTQRT for this exercise.

(i)   Using the data from all but the last four years (16 quarters), estimate an AR(1) model for $\Delta r6_t$. (We use the difference because it appears that $r6_t$ has a unit root.) Find the RMSE of the one-step-ahead forecasts for $\Delta r6$, using the last 16 quarters.

(ii)   Now, add the error correction term $spr_{t-1} = r6_{t-1} - r3_{t-1}$ to the equation from part (i). (This assumes that the cointegrating parameter is one.) Compute the RMSE for the last 16 quarters. Does the error correction term help with out-of-sample forecasting in this case?

(iii) Now, estimate the cointegrating parameter, rather than setting it to one. Use the last 16 quarters again to produce the out-of-sample RMSE. How does this compare with the forecasts from parts (i) and (ii)?

(iv)   Would your conclusions change if you wanted to predict *r6* rather than $\Delta r6$? Explain.

C11 Use the data in VOLAT for this exercise.

(i)   Confirm that $lsp500 = \log(sp500)$ and $lip = \log(ip)$ appear to contain unit roots. Use Dickey-Fuller tests with four lagged changes and do the tests with and without a linear time trend.

(ii)   Run a simple regression of *lsp500* on *lip*. Comment on the sizes of the *t* statistic and *R*-squared.

(iii) Use the residuals from part (ii) to test whether *lsp500* and *lip* are cointegrated. Use the standard Dickey-Fuller test and the ADF test with two lags. What do you conclude?

(iv)   Add a linear time trend to the regression from part (ii) and now test for cointegration using the same tests from part (iii).

(v)   Does it appear that stock prices and real economic activity have a long-run equilibrium relationship?

C12 This exercise also uses the data from VOLAT. Computer Exercise C11 studies the long-run relationship between stock prices and industrial production. Here, you will study the question of Granger causality using the percentage changes.

(i) Estimate an AR(3) model for $pcip_t$, the percentage change in industrial production (reported at an annualized rate). Show that the second and third lags are jointly significant at the 2.5% level.

(ii) Add one lag of $pcsp_t$ to the equation estimated in part (i). Is the lag statistically significant? What does this tell you about Granger causality between the growth in industrial production and the growth in stock prices?

(iii) Redo part (ii) but obtain a heteroskedasticity-robust t statistic. Does the robust test change your conclusions from part (ii)?

C13 Use the data in TRAFFIC2 for this exercise. These monthly data, on traffic accidents in California over the years 1981 to 1989, were used in Computer Exercise C11 in Chapter 10.

(i) Using the standard Dickey-Fuller regression, test whether $ltotacc_t$ has a unit root. Can you reject a unit root at the 2.5% level?

(ii) Now, add two lagged changes to the test from part (i) and compute the augmented Dickey-Fuller test. What do you conclude?

(iii) Add a linear time trend to the ADF regression from part (ii). Now what happens?

(iv) Given the findings from parts (i) through (iii), what would you say is the best characterization of $ltotacc_t$: an I(1) process or an I(0) process about a linear time trend?

(v) Test the percentage of fatalities, $prcfat_t$, for a unit root, using two lags in an ADF regression. In this case, does it matter whether you include a linear time trend?

C14 Use the data in MINWAGE.DTA for sector 232 to answer the following questions.

(i) Confirm that $lwage232_t$ and $lemp232_t$ are best characterized as I(1) processes. Use the augmented DF test with one lag of $gwage232$ and $gemp232$, respectively, and a linear time trend. Is there any doubt that these series should be assumed to have unit roots?

(ii) Regress $lemp232_t$ on $lwage232_t$ and test for cointegration, both with and without a time trend, allowing for two lags in the augmented Engle-Granger test. What do you conclude?

(iii) Now regress $lemp232_t$ on log of the real wage rate, $lrwage232_t = lwage232_t - lcpi_t$, and a time trend. Do you find cointegration? Are they "closer" to being cointegrated when you use real wages rather than nominal wages?

(iv) What are some factors that might be missing from the cointegrating regression in part (iii)?

C15 This question asks you to study the so-called Beveridge Curve from the perspective of cointegration analysis. The U.S. monthly data from December 2000 through February 2012 are in BEVERIDGE.

(i) Test for a unit root in $urate$ using the usual Dickey-Fuller test (with a constant) and the augmented DF with two lags of $curate$. What do you conclude? Are the lags of $curate$ in the augmented DF test statistically significant? Does it matter to the outcome of the unit root test?

(ii) Repeat part (i) but with the vacancy rate, $vrate$.

(iii) Assuming that $urate$ and $vrate$ are both I(1), the Beveridge Curve,

$$urate_t = \alpha + \beta vrate + u_t,$$

only makes sense if $urate$ and $vrate$ are cointegrated (with cointegrating parameter $\beta < 0$). Test for cointegration using the Engle-Granger test with no lags. Are $urate$ and $vrate$ cointegrated at the 10% significance level? What about at the 5% level?

(iv) Obtain the leads and lags estimator with $cvrate_t$, $cvrate_{t-1}$, and $cvrate_{t+1}$ as the I(0) explanatory variables added to the equation in part (iii). Obtain the Newey-West standard error for $\hat{\beta}$ using four lags (so $g = 4$ in the notation of Section 12-5). What is the resulting 95% confidence interval for β? How does it compare with the confidence interval that is not robust to serial correlation (or heteroskedasticity)?

(v) Redo the Engle-Granger test but with two lags in the augmented DF regression. What happens? What do you conclude about the robustness of the claim that $urate$ and $vrate$ are cointegrated?$lemp232_t$

CHAPTER 19

Carrying Out an Empirical Project

I n this chapter, we discuss the ingredients of a successful empirical analysis, with emphasis on completing a term project. In addition to reminding you of the important issues that have arisen throughout the text, we emphasize recurring themes that are important for applied research. We also provide suggestions for topics as a way of stimulating your imagination. Several sources of economic research and data are given as references.

19-1 Posing a Question

The importance of posing a very specific question that, in principle, can be answered with data cannot be overstated. Without being explicit about the goal of your analysis, you cannot know where to begin. The widespread availability of rich data sets makes it tempting to launch into data collection based on half-baked ideas, but this is often counterproductive. It is likely that, without carefully formulating your hypotheses and the kind of model you will need to estimate, you will forget to collect information on important variables, obtain a sample from the wrong population, or collect data for the wrong time period.

This does not mean that you should pose your question in a vacuum. Especially for a one-term project you cannot be too ambitious. Therefore, when choosing a topic, you should be reasonably sure that data sources exist that will allow you to answer your question in the allotted time.

You need to decide what areas of economics or other social sciences interest you when selecting a topic. For example, if you have taken a course in labor economics you have probably seen theories that can be tested empirically or relationships that have some policy relevance. Labor economists are constantly coming up with new variables that can explain wage differentials. Examples include quality of high school [Card and Krueger (1992) and Betts (1995)], amount of math and science taken in high school [Levine and Zimmerman (1995)], and physical appearance [Hamermesh and Biddle (1994), Averett and Korenman (1996), Biddle and Hamermesh (1998), and Hamermesh and Parker (2005)]. Researchers in state and local public finance study how local economic activity depends on economic policy variables, such as property taxes, sales taxes, level and quality of services (such as schools, fire, and police), and so on. [See, for example, White (1986), Papke (1987), Bartik (1991), Netzer (1992), and Mark, McGuire, and Papke (2000).]

Economists that study education issues are interested in determining how spending affects performance [Hanushek (1986)], whether attending certain kinds of schools improves performance [for example, Evans and Schwab (1995)], and what factors affect where private schools choose to locate [Downes and Greenstein (1996)].

Macroeconomists are interested in relationships between various aggregate time series, such as the link between growth in gross domestic product and growth in fixed investment or machinery [see De Long and Summers (1991)] or the effect of taxes on interest rates [for example, Peek (1982)].

There are certainly reasons for estimating models that are mostly descriptive. For example, property tax assessors use models (called *hedonic price models*) to estimate housing values for homes that have not been sold recently. This involves a regression model relating the price of a house to its characteristics (size, number of bedrooms, number of bathrooms, and so on). As a topic for a term paper, this is not very exciting: we are unlikely to learn much that is surprising, and such an analysis has no obvious policy implications. Adding the crime rate in the neighborhood as an explanatory variable would allow us to determine how important a factor crime is on housing prices, something that would be useful in estimating the costs of crime.

Several relationships have been estimated using macroeconomic data that are mostly descriptive. For example, an aggregate saving function can be used to estimate the aggregate marginal propensity to save, as well as the response of saving to asset returns (such as interest rates). Such an analysis could be made more interesting by using time series data on a country that has a history of political upheavals and determining whether savings rates decline during times of political uncertainty.

Once you decide on an area of research, there are a variety of ways to locate specific papers on the topic. The *Journal of Economic Literature* (JEL) has a detailed classification system in which each paper is given a set of identifying codes that places it within certain subfields of economics. The JEL also contains a list of articles published in a wide variety of journals, organized by topic, and it even contains short abstracts of some articles.

Especially convenient for finding published papers on various topics are **Internet** services, such as *EconLit*, which many universities subscribe to. *EconLit* allows users to do a comprehensive search of almost all economics journals by author, subject, words in the title, and so on. The *Social Sciences Citation Index* is useful for finding papers on a broad range of topics in the social sciences, including popular papers that have been cited often in other published works.

Google Scholar is an Internet search engine that can be very helpful for tracking down research on various topics or research by a particular author. This is especially true of work that has not been published in an academic journal or that has not yet been published.

In thinking about a topic, you should keep some things in mind. First, for a question to be interesting, it does not need to have broad-based policy implications; rather, it can be of local interest. For example, you might be interested in knowing whether living in a fraternity at your university causes students to have lower or higher grade point averages. This may or may not be of interest to people outside your university, but it is probably of concern to at least some people within the university. On the other hand, you might study a problem that starts by being of local interest but turns out to have widespread interest, such as determining which factors affect, and which university policies can stem, alcohol abuse on college campuses.

Second, it is very difficult, especially for a quarter or semester project, to do truly original research using the standard macroeconomic aggregates on the U.S. economy. For example, the question of whether money growth, government spending growth, and so on affect economic growth has been and continues to be studied by professional macroeconomists. The question of whether stock or other asset returns can be systematically predicted using known information has, for obvious reasons, been studied pretty carefully. This does not mean that you should avoid estimating macroeconomic or empirical finance models, as even just using more recent data can add constructively to a debate. In addition, you can sometimes find a new variable that has an important effect on economic aggregates or financial returns; such a discovery can be exciting.

The point is that exercises such as using a few additional years to estimate a standard Phillips curve or an aggregate consumption function for the U.S. economy, or some other large economy, are unlikely to yield additional insights, although they can be instructive for the student. Instead, you might use data on a smaller country to estimate a static or dynamic Phillips curve or a Beveridge curve (possibly allowing the slopes of the curves to depend on information known prior to the current time period), or to test the efficient markets hypothesis, and so on.

At the nonmacroeconomic level, there are also plenty of questions that have been studied extensively. For example, labor economists have published many papers on estimating the return to education. This question is still studied because it is very important, and new data sets, as well as new econometric approaches, continue to be developed. For example, as we saw in Chapter 9, certain data sets have better proxy variables for unobserved ability than other data sets. (Compare WAGE1 and WAGE2.) In other cases, we can obtain panel data or data from a natural experiment—see Chapter 13—that allow us to approach an old question from a different perspective.

As another example, criminologists are interested in studying the effects of various laws on crime. The question of whether capital punishment has a deterrent effect has long been debated. Similarly, economists have been interested in whether taxes on cigarettes and alcohol reduce consumption (as always, in a ceteris paribus sense). As more years of data at the state level become available, a richer panel data set can be created, and this can help us better answer major policy questions. Plus, the effectiveness of fairly recent crime-fighting innovations—such as community policing—can be evaluated empirically.

While you are formulating your question, it is helpful to discuss your ideas with your classmates, instructor, and friends. You should be able to convince people that the answer to your question is of some interest. (Of course, whether you can persuasively answer your question is another issue, but you need to begin with an interesting question.) If someone asks you about your paper and you respond with "I'm doing my paper on crime" or "I'm doing my paper on interest rates," chances are you have only decided on a general area without formulating a true question. You should be able to say something like "I'm studying the effects of community policing on city crime rates in the United States" or "I'm looking at how inflation volatility affects short-term interest rates in Brazil."

19-2 Literature Review

All papers, even if they are relatively short, should contain a review of relevant literature. It is rare that one attempts an empirical project for which no published precedent exists. If you search through journals or use **online search services** such as *EconLit* to come up with a topic, you are already well on your way to a literature review. If you select a topic on your own—such as studying the effects of drug usage on college performance at your university—then you will probably have to work a little harder. But online search services make that work a lot easier, as you can search by keywords, by words in the title, by author, and so on. You can then read abstracts of papers to see how relevant they are to your own work.

When doing your literature search, you should think of related topics that might not show up in a search using a handful of keywords. For example, if you are studying the effects of drug usage on wages or grade point average, you should probably look at the literature on how alcohol usage affects such factors. Knowing how to do a thorough literature search is an acquired skill, but you can get a long way by thinking before searching.

Researchers differ on how a literature review should be incorporated into a paper. Some like to have a separate section called "literature review," while others like to include the literature review as part of the introduction. This is largely a matter of taste, although an extensive literature review probably deserves its own section. If the term paper is the focus of the course—say, in a senior seminar or an advanced econometrics course—your literature review probably will be lengthy. Term papers at the end of a first course are typically shorter, and the literature reviews are briefer.

19-3 Data Collection

19-3a Deciding on the Appropriate Data Set

Collecting data for a term paper can be educational, exciting, and sometimes even frustrating. You must first decide on the kind of data needed to answer your posed question. As we discussed in the introduction and have covered throughout this text, data sets come in a variety of forms. The most common kinds are cross-sectional, time series, pooled cross sections, and panel data sets.

Many questions can be addressed using any of the data structures we have described. For example, to study whether more law enforcement lowers crime, we could use a cross section of cities, a time series for a given city, or a panel data set of cities—which consists of data on the same cities over two or more years.

Deciding on which kind of data to collect often depends on the nature of the analysis. To answer questions at the individual or family level, we often only have access to a single cross section; typically, these are obtained via surveys. Then, we must ask whether we can obtain a rich enough data set to do a convincing ceteris paribus analysis. For example, suppose we want to know whether families who save through individual retirement accounts (IRAs)—which have certain tax advantages—have less non-IRA savings. In other words, does IRA saving simply crowd out other forms of saving? There are data sets, such as the Survey of Consumer Finances, that contain information on various kinds of saving for a different sample of families each year. Several issues arise in using such a data set. Perhaps the most important is whether there are enough controls—including income, demographics, and proxies for saving tastes—to do a reasonable ceteris paribus analysis. If these are the only kinds of data available, we must do what we can with them.

The same issues arise with cross-sectional data on firms, cities, states, and so on. In most cases, it is not obvious that we will be able to do a ceteris paribus analysis with a single cross section. For example, any study of the effects of law enforcement on crime must recognize the endogeneity of law enforcement expenditures. When using standard regression methods, it may be very hard to complete a convincing ceteris paribus analysis, no matter how many controls we have. (See Section 19-4 for more discussion.)

If you have read the advanced chapters on panel data methods, you know that having the same cross-sectional units at two or more different points in time can allow us to control for time-constant unobserved effects that would normally confound regression on a single cross section. Panel data sets are relatively hard to obtain for individuals or families—although some important ones exist, such as the Panel Study of Income Dynamics—but they can be used in very convincing ways. Panel data sets on firms also exist. For example, Compustat and the Center for Research in Security Prices (CRSP) manage very large panel data sets of financial information on firms. Easier to obtain are panel data sets on larger units, such as schools, cities, counties, and states, as these tend not to disappear over time, and government agencies are responsible for collecting information on the same variables each year. For example, the Federal Bureau of Investigation collects and reports detailed information on crime rates at the city level. Sources of data are listed at the end of this chapter.

Data come in a variety of forms. Some data sets, especially historical ones, are available only in printed form. For small data sets, entering the data yourself from the printed source is manageable and convenient. Sometimes, articles are published with small data sets—especially time series applications. These can be used in an empirical study, perhaps by supplementing the data with more recent years.

Many data sets are available in electronic form. Various government agencies provide data on their websites. Private companies sometimes compile data sets to make them user friendly, and then they provide them for a fee. Authors of papers are often willing to provide their data sets in electronic form. More and more data sets are available on the Internet. The web is a vast resource of **online databases**. Numerous websites containing economic and related data sets have been created. Several other websites contain links to data sets that are of interest to economists; some of these are listed at the end of this chapter. Generally, searching the Internet for data sources is easy and will become even more convenient in the future.

19-3b Entering and Storing Your Data

Once you have decided on a data type and have located a data source, you must put the data into a usable format. If the data came in electronic form, they are already in some format, hopefully one in widespread use. The most flexible way to obtain data in electronic form is as a standard **text (ASCII) file**. All statistics and econometrics software packages allow raw data to be stored this way. Typically, it is straightforward to read a text file directly into an econometrics package, provided the file is properly structured. The data files we have used throughout the text provide several examples of how cross-sectional, time series, pooled cross sections, and panel data sets are usually stored. As a rule, the data should have a tabular form, with each observation representing a different row; the columns in the data set represent different variables. Occasionally, you might encounter a data set stored with each column representing an observation and each row a different variable. This is not ideal, but most software packages allow data to be read in this form and then reshaped. Naturally, it is crucial to know how the data are organized before reading them into your econometrics package.

For time series data sets, there is only one sensible way to enter and store the data: namely, chronologically, with the earliest time period listed as the first observation and the most recent time period as the last observation. It is often useful to include variables indicating year and, if relevant, quarter or month. This facilitates estimation of a variety of models later on, including allowing for seasonality and breaks at different time periods. For cross sections pooled over time, it is usually best to have the cross section for the earliest year fill the first block of observations, followed by the cross section for the second year, and so on. (See FERTIL1 as an example.) This arrangement is not crucial, but it is very important to have a variable stating the year attached to each observation.

For panel data, as we discussed in Section 13-5, it is best if all the years for each cross-sectional observation are adjacent and in chronological order. With this ordering, we can use all of the panel data methods from Chapters 13 and 14. With panel data, it is important to include a unique identifier for each cross-sectional unit, along with a year variable.

If you obtain your data in printed form, you have several options for entering them into a computer. First, you can create a text file using a standard **text editor**. (This is how several of the raw data sets included with the text were initially created.) Typically, it is required that each row starts a new observation, that each row contains the same ordering of the variables—in particular, each row should have the same number of entries—and that the values are separated by at least one space. Sometimes, a different separator, such as a comma, is better, but this depends on the software you are using. If you have missing observations on some variables, you must decide how to denote that; simply leaving a blank does not generally work. Many regression packages accept a period as the missing value symbol. Some people prefer to use a number—presumably an impossible value for the variable of interest—to denote missing values. If you are not careful, this can be dangerous; we discuss this further later.

If you have nonnumerical data—for example, you want to include the names in a sample of colleges or the names of cities—then you should check the econometrics package you will use to see the best way to enter such variables (often called *strings*). Typically, strings are put between double or single quotation marks. Or the text file can follow a rigid formatting, which usually requires a small program to read in the text file. But you need to check your econometrics package for details.

Another generally available option is to use a **spreadsheet** to enter your data, such as Excel. This has a couple of advantages over a text file. First, because each observation on each variable is a cell, it is less likely that numbers will be run together (as would happen if you forget to enter a space in a text file). Second, spreadsheets allow manipulation of data, such as sorting or computing averages. This benefit is less important if you use a software package that allows sophisticated data management; many software packages, including EViews and Stata, fall into this category. If you use a spreadsheet for initial data entry, then you must often export the data in a form that can be read by your econometrics package. This is usually straightforward, as spreadsheets export to text files using a variety of formats.

A third alternative is to enter the data directly into your econometrics package. Although this obviates the need for a text editor or a spreadsheet, it can be more awkward if you cannot freely move across different observations to make corrections or additions.

Data downloaded from the Internet may come in a variety of forms. Often data come as text files, but different conventions are used for separating variables; for panel data sets, the conventions on how to order the data may differ. Some Internet data sets come as spreadsheet files, in which case you must use an appropriate spreadsheet to read them.

19-3c Inspecting, Cleaning, and Summarizing Your Data

It is extremely important to become familiar with any data set you will use in an empirical analysis. If you enter the data yourself, you will be forced to know everything about it. But if you obtain data from an outside source, you should still spend some time understanding its structure and conventions. Even data sets that are widely used and heavily documented can contain glitches. If you are using a data set obtained from the author of a paper, you must be aware that rules used for data set construction can be forgotten.

Earlier, we reviewed the standard ways that various data sets are stored. You also need to know how missing values are coded. Preferably, missing values are indicated with a nonnumeric character, such as a period. If a number is used as a missing value code, such as "999" or "−1," you must be very careful when using these observations in computing any statistics. Your econometrics package will probably not know that a certain number really represents a missing value: it is likely that such observations will be used as if they are valid, and this can produce rather misleading results. The best approach is to set any numerical codes for missing values to some other character (such as a period) that cannot be mistaken for real data.

You must also know the nature of the variables in the data set. Which are binary variables? Which are ordinal variables (such as a credit rating)? What are the units of measurement of the variables? For example, are monetary values expressed in dollars, thousands of dollars, millions of dollars, or some other units? Are variables representing a rate—such as school dropout rates, inflation rates, unionization rates, or interest rates—measured as a percentage or a proportion?

Especially for time series data, it is crucial to know if monetary values are in nominal (current) or real (constant) dollars. If the values are in real terms, what is the base year or period?

If you receive a data set from an author, some variables may already be transformed in certain ways. For example, sometimes only the log of a variable (such as wage or salary) is reported in the data set.

Detecting mistakes in a data set is necessary for preserving the integrity of any data analysis. It is always useful to find minimums, maximums, means, and standard deviations of all, or at least the most important, variables in the analysis. For example, if you find that the minimum value of education in your sample is –99, you know that at least one entry on education needs to be set to a missing value. If, upon further inspection, you find that several observations have −99 as the level of education, you can be confident that you have stumbled onto the missing value code for education. As another example, if you find that an average murder conviction rate across a sample of cities is .632, you know that conviction rate is measured as a proportion, not a percentage. Then, if the maximum value is above one, this is likely a typographical error. (It is not uncommon to find data sets where most of the entries on a rate variable were entered as a percentage, but where some were entered as a proportion, and vice versa. Such data coding errors can be difficult to detect, but it is important to try.)

We must also be careful in using time series data. If we are using monthly or quarterly data, we must know which variables, if any, have been seasonally adjusted. Transforming data also requires great care. Suppose we have a monthly data set and we want to create the change in a variable from one month to the next. To do this, we must be sure that the data are ordered chronologically, from earliest period to latest. If for some reason this is not the case, the differencing will result in garbage. To be sure the data are properly ordered, it is useful to have a time period indicator. With annual data, it is sufficient to know the year, but then we should know whether the year is entered as four digits or two digits (for example, 1998 versus 98). With monthly or quarterly data, it is also useful to have a variable or variables indicating month or quarter. With monthly data, we may have a set of dummy variables (11 or 12) or one variable indicating the month (1 through 12 or a string variable, such as *jan*, *feb*, and so on).

With or without yearly, monthly, or quarterly indicators, we can easily construct time trends in all econometrics software packages. Creating seasonal dummy variables is easy if the month or quarter is indicated; at a minimum, we need to know the month or quarter of the first observation.

Manipulating panel data can be even more challenging. In Chapter 13, we discussed pooled OLS on the differenced data as one general approach to controlling for unobserved effects. In constructing the differenced data, we must be careful not to create phantom observations. Suppose we have a balanced panel on cities from 1992 through 1997. Even if the data are ordered chronologically within each cross-sectional unit—something that should be done before proceeding—a mindless differencing will create an observation for 1992 for all cities except the first in the sample. This observation will be the 1992 value for city i, minus the 1997 value for city $i - 1$; this is clearly nonsense. Thus, we must make sure that 1992 is missing for all differenced variables.

19-4 Econometric Analysis

This text has focused on econometric analysis, and we are not about to provide a review of econometric methods in this section. Nevertheless, we can give some general guidelines about the sorts of issues that need to be considered in an empirical analysis.

As we discussed earlier, after deciding on a topic, we must collect an appropriate data set. Assuming that this has also been done, we must next decide on the appropriate econometric methods.

If your course has focused on ordinary least squares estimation of a multiple linear regression model, using either cross-sectional or time series data, the econometric approach has pretty much been decided for you. This is not necessarily a weakness, as OLS is still the most widely used econometric method. Of course, you still have to decide whether any of the variants of OLS—such as weighted least squares or correcting for serial correlation in a time series regression—are warranted.

In order to justify OLS, you must also make a convincing case that the key OLS assumptions are satisfied for your model. As we have discussed at some length, the first issue is whether the error term is uncorrelated with the explanatory variables. Ideally, you have been able to control for enough other factors to assume that those that are left in the error are unrelated to the regressors. Especially when dealing with individual-, family-, or firm-level cross-sectional data, the self-selection problem—which we discussed in Chapters 7 and 15—is often relevant. For instance, in the IRA example from Section 19-3, it may be that families with an unobserved taste for saving are also the ones that open IRAs. You should also be able to argue that the other potential sources of endogeneity—namely, measurement error and simultaneity—are not a serious problem.

When specifying your model you must also make functional form decisions. Should some variables appear in logarithmic form? (In econometric applications, the answer is often yes.) Should some variables be included in levels and squares, to possibly capture a diminishing effect? How should qualitative factors appear? Is it enough to just include binary variables for different attributes or groups? Or do these need to be interacted with quantitative variables? (See Chapter 7 for details.)

A common mistake, especially among beginners, is to incorrectly include explanatory variables in a regression model that are listed as numerical values but have no quantitative meaning. For example, in an individual-level data set that contains information on wages, education, experience, and other variables, an "occupation" variable might be included. Typically, these are just arbitrary codes that have been assigned to different occupations; the fact that an elementary school teacher is given, say, the value 453 while a computer technician is, say, 751 is relevant only in that it allows us to distinguish between the two occupations. It makes no sense to include the raw occupational variable in a regression model. (What sense would it make to measure the effect of increasing *occupation* by one unit when the one-unit increase has no quantitative meaning?) Instead, different dummy variables should be defined for different occupations (or groups of occupations, if there are many occupations). Then, the dummy variables can be included in the regression model. A less egregious problem occurs when an ordered qualitative variable is included as an explanatory variable. Suppose that in a wage data set a variable is included measuring "job satisfaction," defined on a scale from 1 to 7, with 7 being the most satisfied. Provided we have enough data, we would want to define a set of six dummy variables for, say, job satisfaction levels of 2 through 7, leaving job satisfaction level 1 as the base group. By including the six job satisfaction dummies in the regression, we allow a completely flexible relationship between the response variable and job satisfaction. Putting in the job satisfaction variable in raw form implicitly assumes that a one-unit increase in the ordinal variable has quantitative meaning. While the direction of the effect will often be estimated appropriately, interpreting the coefficient on an ordinal variable is difficult. If an ordinal variable takes on many values, then we can define a set of dummy variables for ranges of values. See Section 17-3 for an example.

Sometimes, we want to explain a variable that is an ordinal response. For example, one could think of using a job satisfaction variable of the type described above as the dependent variable in a regression model, with both worker and employer characteristics among the independent variables. Unfortunately, with the job satisfaction variable in its original form, the coefficients in the model are hard to interpret: each measures the change in job satisfaction given a unit increase in the independent variable. Certain models—*ordered probit* and *ordered logit* are the most common—are well suited for ordered responses. These models essentially extend the binary probit and logit models we discussed in Chapter 17. [See Wooldridge (2010, Chapter 16) for a treatment of ordered response models.] A simple solution is to turn any ordered response into a binary response. For example, we could define a variable equal to one if job satisfaction is at least four, and zero otherwise. Unfortunately, creating a binary variable throws away information and requires us to use a somewhat arbitrary cutoff.

For cross-sectional analysis, a secondary, but nevertheless important, issue is whether there is heteroskedasticity. In Chapter 8, we explained how this can be dealt with. The simplest way is to compute heteroskedasticity-robust statistics.

As we emphasized in Chapters 10, 11, and 12, time series applications require additional care. Should the equation be estimated in levels? If levels are used, are time trends needed? Is differencing the data more appropriate? If the data are monthly or quarterly, does seasonality have to be accounted for? If you are allowing for dynamics—for example, distributed lag dynamics—how many lags should be included? You must start with some lags based on intuition or common sense, but eventually it is an empirical matter.

If your model has some potential misspecification, such as omitted variables, and you use OLS, you should attempt some sort of **misspecification analysis** of the kinds we discussed in Chapters 3 and 5. Can you determine, based on reasonable assumptions, the direction of any bias in the estimators?

If you have studied the method of instrumental variables, you know that it can be used to solve various forms of endogeneity, including omitted variables (Chapter 15), errors-in-variables (Chapter 15), and simultaneity (Chapter 16). Naturally, you need to think hard about whether the instrumental variables you are considering are likely to be valid.

Good papers in the empirical social sciences contain **sensitivity analysis**. Broadly, this means you estimate your original model and modify it in ways that seem reasonable. Hopefully, the important conclusions do not change. For example, if you use as an explanatory variable a measure of alcohol consumption (say, in a grade point average equation), do you get qualitatively similar results if you replace the quantitative measure with a dummy variable indicating alcohol usage? If the binary usage variable is significant but the alcohol quantity variable is not, it could be that usage reflects some unobserved attribute that affects GPA and is also correlated with alcohol usage. But this needs to be considered on a case-by-case basis.

If some observations are much different from the bulk of the sample—say, you have a few firms in a sample that are much larger than the other firms—do your results change much when those observations are excluded from the estimation? If so, you may have to alter functional forms to allow for these observations or argue that they follow a completely different model. The issue of outliers was discussed in Chapter 9.

Using panel data raises some additional econometric issues. Suppose you have collected two periods. There are at least four ways to use two periods of panel data without resorting to instrumental variables. You can pool the two years in a standard OLS analysis, as discussed in Chapter 13. Although this might increase the sample size relative to a single cross section, it does not control for time-constant unobservables. In addition, the errors in such an equation are almost always serially correlated because of an unobserved effect. Random effects estimation corrects the serial correlation problem and produces asymptotically efficient estimators, provided the unobserved effect has zero mean given values of the explanatory variables in all time periods.

Another possibility is to include a lagged dependent variable in the equation for the second year. In Chapter 9, we presented this as a way to at least mitigate the omitted variables problem, as we are in any event holding fixed the initial outcome of the dependent variable. This often leads to similar results as differencing the data, as we covered in Chapter 13.

With more years of panel data, we have the same options, plus an additional choice. We can use the fixed effects transformation to eliminate the unobserved effect. (With two years of data, this is the same as differencing.) In Chapter 15, we showed how instrumental variables techniques can be combined with panel data transformations to relax exogeneity assumptions even more. As a rule, it is a good idea to apply several reasonable econometric methods and compare the results. This often allows us to determine which of our assumptions are likely to be false.

Even if you are very careful in devising your topic, postulating your model, collecting your data, and carrying out the econometrics, it is quite possible that you will obtain puzzling results—at least some of the time. When that happens, the natural inclination is to try different models, different estimation techniques, or perhaps different subsets of data until the results correspond more closely to what was expected. Virtually all applied researchers search over various models before finding the "best" model. Unfortunately, this practice of **data mining** violates the assumptions we have made in our econometric analysis. The results on unbiasedness of OLS and other estimators, as well as the t and F distributions we derived for hypothesis testing, assume that we observe a sample following the population model and we estimate that model once. Estimating models that are variants of our original model violates that assumption because we are using the same set of data in a *specification search*. In effect, we use the outcome of tests by using the data to respecify our model. The estimates and tests from different model specifications are not independent of one another.

Some specification searches have been programmed into standard software packages. A popular one is known as *stepwise regression*, where different combinations of explanatory variables are used in multiple regression analysis in an attempt to come up with the best model. There are various ways that stepwise regression can be used, and we have no intention of reviewing them here. The general idea is either to start with a large model and keep variables whose p-values are below a certain significance level or to start with a simple model and add variables that have significant p-values. Sometimes, groups of variables are tested with an F test. Unfortunately, the final model often depends on the order in which variables were dropped or added. [For more on stepwise regression, see Draper and Smith (1981).] In addition, this is a severe form of data mining, and it is difficult to interpret t and F statistics in the final model. One might argue that stepwise regression simply automates what researchers do anyway in searching over various models. However, in most applications, one or two explanatory variables are of primary interest, and then the goal is to see how robust the coefficients on those variables are to either adding or dropping other variables, or to changing functional form.

In principle, it is possible to incorporate the effects of data mining into our statistical inference; in practice, this is very difficult and is rarely done, especially in sophisticated empirical work. [See Leamer (1983) for an engaging discussion of this problem.] But we can try to minimize data mining by not searching over numerous models or estimation methods until a significant result is found and then reporting only that result. If a variable is statistically significant in only a small fraction of the models estimated, it is quite likely that the variable has no effect in the population.

19-5 Writing an Empirical Paper

Writing a paper that uses econometric analysis is very challenging, but it can also be rewarding. A successful paper combines a careful, convincing data analysis with good explanations and exposition. Therefore, you must have a good grasp of your topic, good understanding of econometric methods, and solid writing skills. Do not be discouraged if you find writing an empirical paper difficult; most professional researchers have spent many years learning how to craft an empirical analysis and to write the results in a convincing form.

While writing styles vary, many papers follow the same general outline. The following paragraphs include ideas for section headings and explanations about what each section should contain. These are only suggestions and hardly need to be strictly followed. In the final paper, each section would be given a number, usually starting with one for the introduction.

19-5a Introduction

The introduction states the basic objectives of the study and explains why it is important. It generally entails a review of the literature, indicating what has been done and how previous work can be improved upon. (As discussed in Section 19-2, an extensive literature review can be put in a separate section.) Presenting simple statistics or graphs that reveal a seemingly paradoxical relationship is a useful way to introduce the paper's topic. For example, suppose that you are writing a paper about factors affecting fertility in a developing country, with the focus on education levels of women. An appealing way to introduce the topic would be to produce a table or a graph showing that fertility has been falling (say) over time and a brief explanation of how you hope to examine the factors contributing to the decline. At this point, you may already know that, ceteris paribus, more highly educated women have fewer children and that average education levels have risen over time.

Most researchers like to summarize the findings of their paper in the introduction. This can be a useful device for grabbing the reader's attention. For example, you might state that your best estimate of the effect of missing 10 hours of lecture during a 30-hour term is about one-half a grade point. But the summary should not be too involved because neither the methods nor the data used to obtain the estimates have yet been introduced.

19-5b Conceptual (or Theoretical) Framework

In this section, you describe the general approach to answering the question you have posed. It can be formal economic theory, but in many cases, it is an intuitive discussion about what conceptual problems arise in answering your question.

Suppose you are studying the effects of economic opportunities and severity of punishment on criminal behavior. One approach to explaining participation in crime is to specify a utility maximization problem where the individual chooses the amount of time spent in legal and illegal activities, given wage rates in both kinds of activities, as well as variables measuring probability and severity of punishment for criminal activity. The usefulness of such an exercise is that it suggests which variables should be included in the empirical analysis; it gives guidance (but rarely specifics) as to how the variables should appear in the econometric model.

Often, there is no need to write down an economic theory. For econometric policy analysis, common sense usually suffices for specifying a model. For example, suppose you are interested in estimating the effects of participation in Aid to Families with Dependent Children (AFDC) on the effects of child performance in school. AFDC provides supplemental income, but participation also makes it easier to receive Medicaid and other benefits. The hard part of such an analysis is deciding on the set of variables that should be controlled for. In this example, we could control for family income (including AFDC and any other welfare income), mother's education, whether the family lives in an urban area, and other variables. Then, the inclusion of an AFDC participation indicator (hopefully) measures the nonincome benefits of AFDC participation. A discussion of which factors should be controlled for and the mechanisms through which AFDC participation might improve school performance substitute for formal economic theory.

19-5c Econometric Models and Estimation Methods

It is very useful to have a section that contains a few equations of the sort you estimate and present in the results section of the paper. This allows you to fix ideas about what the key explanatory variable is and what other factors you will control for. Writing equations containing error terms allows you to discuss whether OLS is a suitable estimation method.

The distinction between a *model* and an estimation method should be made in this section. A model represents a *population* relationship (broadly defined to allow for time series equations). For example, we should write

$$colGPA = \beta_0 + \beta_1 alcohol + \beta_2 hsGPA + \beta_3 SAT + \beta_4 female + u \qquad [19.1]$$

to describe the relationship between college GPA and alcohol consumption, with some other controls in the equation. Presumably, this equation represents a population, such as all undergraduates at a particular university. There are no "hats" (^) on the β_j or on *colGPA* because this is a model, not an estimated equation. We do not put in numbers for the β_j because we do not know (and never will know) these numbers. Later, we will *estimate* them. In this section, do not anticipate the presentation of your empirical results. In other words, do not start with a general model and then say that you omitted certain variables because they turned out to be insignificant. Such discussions should be left for the results section.

A time series model to relate city-level car thefts to the unemployment rate and conviction rates could look like

$$thefts_t = \beta_0 + \beta_1 unem_t + \beta_2 unem_{t-1} + \beta_3 cars_t$$
$$+ \beta_4 convrate_t + \beta_5 convrate_{t-1} + u_t, \qquad [19.2]$$

where the t subscript is useful for emphasizing any dynamics in the equation (in this case, allowing for unemployment and the automobile theft conviction rate to have lagged effects).

After specifying a model or models, it is appropriate to discuss estimation methods. In most cases, this will be OLS, but, for example, in a time series equation, you might use feasible GLS to do a serial correlation correction (as in Chapter 12). However, the method for estimating a model is quite distinct from the model itself. It is not meaningful, for instance, to talk about "an OLS model." Ordinary least squares is a method of estimation, and so are weighted least squares, Cochrane-Orcutt, and so on. There are usually several ways to estimate any model. You should explain why the method you are choosing is warranted.

Any assumptions that are used in obtaining an estimable econometric model from an underlying economic model should be clearly discussed. For example, in the quality of high school example mentioned in Section 19-1, the issue of how to measure school quality is central to the analysis. Should it be based on average SAT scores, percentage of graduates attending college, student-teacher ratios, average education level of teachers, some combination of these, or possibly other measures?

We always have to make assumptions about functional form whether or not a theoretical model has been presented. As you know, constant elasticity and constant semi-elasticity models are attractive because the coefficients are easy to interpret (as percentage effects). There are no hard rules on how to choose functional form, but the guidelines discussed in Section 6-2 seem to work well in practice. You do not need an extensive discussion of functional form, but it is useful to mention whether you will be estimating elasticities or a semi-elasticity. For example, if you are estimating the effect of some variable on wage or salary, the dependent variable will almost surely be in logarithmic form, and you might as well include this in any equations from the beginning. You do not have to present every one, or even most, of the functional form variations that you will report later in the results section.

Often, the data used in empirical economics are at the city or county level. For example, suppose that for the population of small to midsize cities, you wish to test the hypothesis that having a minor league baseball team causes a city to have a lower divorce rate. In this case, you must account for the fact that larger cities will have more divorces. One way to account for the size of the city is to scale divorces by the city or adult population. Thus, a reasonable model is

$$\log(div/pop) = \beta_0 + \beta_1 mlb + \beta_2 perCath + \beta_3 \log(inc/pop) + other\ factors, \qquad [19.3]$$

where mlb is a dummy variable equal to one if the city has a minor league baseball team and $perCath$ is the percentage of the population that is Catholic (so a number such as 34.6 means 34.6%). Note that div/pop is a divorce rate, which is generally easier to interpret than the absolute number of divorces.

Another way to control for population is to estimate the model

$$\log(div) = \gamma_0 + \gamma_1 mlb + \gamma_2 perCath + \gamma_3 \log(inc) + \gamma_4 \log(pop) + other\ factors. \qquad [19.4]$$

The parameter of interest, γ_1, when multiplied by 100, gives the percentage difference between divorce rates, holding population, percent Catholic, income, and whatever else is in "other factors" constant. In equation (19.3), β_1 measures the percentage effect of minor league baseball on div/pop, which can change either because the number of divorces or the population changes. Using the fact that $\log(div/pop) = \log(div) - \log(pop)$ and $\log(inc/pop) = \log(inc) - \log(pop)$, we can rewrite (19.3) as

$$\log(div) = \beta_0 + \beta_1 mlb + \beta_2 perCath + \beta_3 \log(inc) + (1 - \beta_3) \log(pop) + others\ factors,$$

which shows that (19.3) is a special case of (19.4) with $\gamma_4 = (1 - \beta_3)$ and $\gamma_j = \beta_j$, $j = 0, 1, 2, 3$. Alternatively, (19.4) is equivalent to adding $\log(pop)$ as an additional explanatory variable to (19.3). This makes it easy to test for a separate population effect on the divorce rate.

If you are using a more advanced estimation method, such as two stage least squares, you need to provide some reasons for doing so. If you use 2SLS, you must provide a careful discussion on why your IV choices for the endogenous explanatory variable (or variables) are valid. As we mentioned in Chapter 15, there are two requirements for a variable to be considered a good IV. First, it must be omitted from and exogenous to the equation of interest (structural equation). This is something we must assume. Second, it must have some partial correlation with the endogenous explanatory variable. This we can test. For example, in equation (19.1), you might use a binary variable for whether a student lives in a dormitory (*dorm*) as an IV for alcohol consumption. This requires that living situation has no direct impact on *colGPA*—so that it is omitted from (19.1)—and that it is uncorrelated with unobserved factors in u that have an effect on *colGPA*. We would also have to verify that *dorm* is partially correlated with *alcohol* by regressing *alcohol* on *dorm*, *hsGPA*, *SAT*, and *female*. (See Chapter 15 for details.)

You might account for the omitted variable problem (or omitted heterogeneity) by using panel data. Again, this is easily described by writing an equation or two. In fact, it is useful to show how to difference the equations over time to remove time-constant unobservables; this gives an equation that can be estimated by OLS. Or, if you are using fixed effects estimation instead, you simply state so.

As a simple example, suppose you are testing whether higher county tax rates reduce economic activity, as measured by per capita manufacturing output. Suppose that for the years 1982, 1987, and 1992, the model is

$$\log(manuf_{it}) = \beta_0 + \delta_1 d87_t + \delta_2 d92_t + \beta_1 tax_{it} + \ldots + a_i + u_{it},$$

where $d87_t$ and $d92_t$ are year dummy variables and tax_{it} is the tax rate for county i at time t (in percent form). We would have other variables that change over time in the equation, including measures for costs of doing business (such as average wages), measures of worker productivity (as measured by average education), and so on. The term a_i is the fixed effect, containing all factors that do not vary over time, and u_{it} is the idiosyncratic error term. To remove a_i, we can either difference across the years or use time-demeaning (the fixed effects transformation).

19-5d The Data

You should always have a section that carefully describes the data used in the empirical analysis. This is particularly important if your data are nonstandard or have not been widely used by other researchers. Enough information should be presented so that a reader could, in principle, obtain the data and redo your analysis. In particular, all applicable public data sources should be included in the references, and short data sets can be listed in an appendix. If you used your own survey to collect the data, a copy of the questionnaire should be presented in an appendix.

Along with a discussion of the data sources, be sure to discuss the units of each of the variables (for example, is income measured in hundreds or thousands of dollars?). Including a table of variable definitions is very useful to the reader. The names in the table should correspond to the names used in describing the econometric results in the following section.

It is also very informative to present a table of summary statistics, such as minimum and maximum values, means, and standard deviations for each variable. Having such a table makes it easier to interpret the coefficient estimates in the next section, and it emphasizes the units of measurement of the variables. For binary variables, the only necessary summary statistic is the fraction of ones in the sample (which is the same as the sample mean). For trending variables, things like means are less interesting. It is often useful to compute the average growth rate in a variable over the years in your sample.

You should always clearly state how many observations you have. For time series data sets, identify the years that you are using in the analysis, including a description of any special periods in history (such as World War II). If you use a pooled cross section or a panel data set, be sure to report how many cross-sectional units (people, cities, and so on) you have for each year.

19-5e Results

The results section should include your estimates of any models formulated in the models section. You might start with a very simple analysis. For example, suppose that percentage of students attending college from the graduating class (*percoll*) is used as a measure of the quality of the high school a person attended. Then, an equation to estimate is

$$\log(wage) = \beta_0 + \beta_1 percoll + u.$$

Of course, this does not control for several other factors that may determine wages and that may be correlated with *percoll*. But a simple analysis can draw the reader into the more sophisticated analysis and reveal the importance of controlling for other factors.

If only a few equations are estimated, you can present the results in equation form with standard errors in parentheses below estimated coefficients. If your model has several explanatory variables and you are presenting several variations on the general model, it is better to report the results in tabular rather than equation form. Most of your papers should have at least one table, which should always include at least the R-squared and the number of observations for each equation. Other statistics, such as the adjusted R-squared, can also be listed.

The most important thing is to discuss the interpretation and strength of your empirical results. Do the coefficients have the expected signs? Are they statistically significant? If a coefficient is statistically significant but has a counterintuitive sign, why might this be true? It might be revealing a problem with the data or the econometric method (for example, OLS may be inappropriate due to omitted variables problems).

Be sure to describe the *magnitudes* of the coefficients on the major explanatory variables. Often, one or two policy variables are central to the study. Their signs, magnitudes, and statistical significance should be treated in detail. Remember to distinguish between economic and statistical significance. If a t statistic is small, is it because the coefficient is practically small or because its standard error is large?

In addition to discussing estimates from the most general model, you can provide interesting special cases, especially those needed to test certain multiple hypotheses. For example, in a study to determine wage differentials across industries, you might present the equation without the industry dummies; this allows the reader to easily test whether the industry differentials are statistically significant (using the R-squared form of the F test). Do not worry too much about dropping various variables to find the "best" combination of explanatory variables. As we mentioned earlier, this is a difficult and not even very well-defined task. Only if eliminating a set of variables substantially alters the magnitudes and/or significance of the coefficients of interest is this important. Dropping a group of variables to simplify the model—such as quadratics or interactions—can be justified via an F test.

If you have used at least two different methods—such as OLS and 2SLS, or levels and differencing for a time series, or pooled OLS versus differencing with a panel data set—then you should comment on any critical differences. If OLS gives counterintuitive results, did using 2SLS or panel data methods improve the estimates? Or, did the opposite happen?

19.5f Conclusions

This can be a short section that summarizes what you have learned. For example, you might want to present the magnitude of a coefficient that was of particular interest. The conclusion should also discuss caveats to the conclusions drawn, and it might even suggest directions for further research. It is useful to imagine readers turning first to the conclusion to decide whether to read the rest of the paper.

19-5g Style Hints

You should give your paper a title that reflects its topic, but make sure the title is not so long as to be cumbersome. The title should be on a separate title page that also includes your name, affiliation, and—if relevant—the course number. The title page can also include a short abstract, or an abstract can be included on a separate page.

Papers should be typed and double-spaced. All equations should begin on a new line, and they should be centered and numbered consecutively, that is, (1), (2), (3), and so on. Large graphs and tables may be included after the main body. In the text, refer to papers by author and date, for example, White (1980). The reference section at the end of the paper should be done in standard format. Several examples are given in the references at the back of the text.

When you introduce an equation in the econometric models section, you should describe the important variables: the dependent variable and the key independent variable or variables. To focus on a single independent variable, you can write an equation, such as

$$GPA = \beta_0 + \beta_1 alcohol + \mathbf{x}\boldsymbol{\delta} + u$$

or

$$\log(wage) = \beta_0 + \beta_1 educ + \mathbf{x}\boldsymbol{\delta} + u,$$

where the notation $\mathbf{x}\boldsymbol{\delta}$ is shorthand for several other explanatory variables. At this point, you need only describe them generally; they can be described specifically in the data section in a table. For example, in a study of the factors affecting chief executive officer salaries, you might include a table like Table 19.1.

A table of summary statistics, obtained from Table I in Papke and Wooldridge (1996) and similar to the data in 401K, might be set up as shown in Table 19.2.

In the results section, you can write the estimates either in equation form, as we often have done, or in a table. Especially when several models have been estimated with different sets of explanatory variables, tables are very useful. If you write out the estimates as an equation, for example,

$$\widehat{\log(salary)} = 2.45 + .236 \log(sales) + .008\ roe + .061\ ceoten$$
$$(0.93)\quad (.115)\qquad\qquad (.003)\qquad (.028)$$
$$n = 204, R^2 = .351,$$

be sure to state near the first equation that standard errors are in parentheses. It is acceptable to report the t statistics for testing $H_0: \beta_j = 0$, or their absolute values, but it is most important to state what you are doing.

TABLE 19.1 Variable Descriptions	
salary	annual salary (including bonuses) in 1990 (in thousands)
sales	firm sales in 1990 (in millions)
roe	average return on equity, 1988–1990 (in percent)
pcsal	percentage change in salary, 1988–1990
pcroe	percentage change in roe, 1988–1990
indust	= 1 if an industrial company, 0 otherwise
finance	= 1 if a financial company, 0 otherwise
consprod	= 1 if a consumer products company, 0 otherwise
util	= 1 if a utility company, 0 otherwise
ceoten	number of years as CEO of the company

TABLE 19.2 Summary Statistics

Variable	Mean	Standard Deviation	Minimum	Maximum
prate	.869	.167	.023	1
mrate	.746	.844	.011	5
employ	4,621.01	16,299.64	53	443,040
age	13.14	9.63	4	76
sole	.415	.493	0	1
Number of observations = 3,784				

If you report your results in tabular form, make sure the dependent and independent variables are clearly indicated. Again, state whether standard errors or t statistics are below the coefficients (with the former preferred). Some authors like to use asterisks to indicate statistical significance at different significance levels (for example, one star means significant at 5%, two stars mean significant at 10% but not 5%, and so on). This is not necessary if you carefully discuss the significance of the explanatory variables in the text.

A sample table of results, derived from Table II in Papke and Wooldridge (1996), is shown in Table 19.3.

Your results will be easier to read and interpret if you choose the units of both your dependent and independent variables so that coefficients are not too large or too small. You should never report numbers such as $1.051\mathrm{e}-007$ or $3.524\mathrm{e}+006$ for your coefficients or standard errors, and you should not use scientific notation. If coefficients are either extremely small or large, rescale the dependent or independent variables, as we discussed in Chapter 6. You should limit the number of digits reported after the decimal point so as not to convey a false sense of precision. For example, if your regression

TABLE 19.3 OLS Results. Dependent Variable: Participation Rate

Independent Variables	(1)	(2)	(3)
mrate	.156	.239	.218
	(.012)	(.042)	(.342)
$mrate^2$	—	−.087	−.096
		(.043)	(.073)
log(emp)	−.112	−.112	−.098
	(.014)	(.014)	(.111)
$log(emp)^2$	.0057	.0057	.0052
	(.0009)	(.0009)	(.0007)
age	.0060	.0059	.0050
	(.0010)	(.0010)	(.0021)
age^2	−.00007	−.00007	−.00006
	(.00002)	(.00002)	(.00002)
sole	−.0001	.0008	.0006
	(.0058)	(.0058)	(.0061)
constant	1.213	.198	.085
	(.051)	(.052)	(.041)
industry dummies?	no	no	yes
Observations	3,784	3,784	3,784
R-squared	.143	.152	.162

Note: The quantities in parentheses below the estimates are the standard errors.

package estimates a coefficient to be .54821059, you should report this as .548, or even .55, in the paper.

As a rule, the commands that your particular econometrics package uses to produce results should not appear in the paper; only the results are important. If some special command was used to carry out a certain estimation method, this can be given in an appendix. An appendix is also a good place to include extra results that support your analysis but are not central to it.

Summary

In this chapter, we have discussed the ingredients of a successful empirical study and have provided hints that can improve the quality of an analysis. Ultimately, the success of any study depends crucially on the care and effort put into it.

Key Terms

Data Mining	Online Databases	Spreadsheet
Internet	Online Search Services	Text Editor
Misspecification Analysis	Sensitivity Analysis	Text (ASCII) File

Sample Empirical Projects

Throughout the text, we have seen examples of econometric analysis that either came from or were motivated by published works. We hope these have given you a good idea about the scope of empirical analysis. We include the following list as additional examples of questions that others have found or are likely to find interesting. These are intended to stimulate your imagination; no attempt is made to fill in all the details of specific models, data requirements, or alternative estimation methods. It should be possible to complete these projects in one term.

1   Do your own campus survey to answer a question of interest at your university. For example: What is the effect of working on college GPA? You can ask students about high school GPA, college GPA, ACT or SAT scores, hours worked per week, participation in athletics, major, gender, race, and so on. Then, use these variables to create a model that explains GPA. How much of an effect, if any, does another hour worked per week have on GPA? One issue of concern is that hours worked might be endogenous: it might be correlated with unobserved factors that affect college GPA, or lower GPAs might cause students to work more.

A better approach would be to collect cumulative GPA prior to the semester and then to obtain GPA for the most recent semester, along with amount worked during that semester, and the other variables. Now, cumulative GPA could be used as a control (explanatory variable) in the equation.

2   There are many variants on the preceding topic. You can study the effects of drug or alcohol usage, or of living in a fraternity, on grade point average. You would want to control for many family background variables, as well as previous performance variables.

3   Do gun control laws at the city level reduce violent crimes? Such questions can be difficult to answer with a single cross section because city and state laws are often endogenous. [See Kleck and Patterson (1993) for an example. They used cross-sectional data and instrumental variables methods, but their IVs are questionable.] Panel data can be very useful for inferring causality in these contexts. At a minimum, you could control for a previous year's violent crime rate.

4   Low and McPheters (1983) used city cross-sectional data on wage rates and estimates of risk of death for police officers, along with other controls. The idea is to determine whether police officers are compensated for working in cities with a higher risk of on-the-job injury or death.

5 Do parental consent laws increase the teenage birthrate? You can use state level data for this: either a time series for a given state or, even better, a panel data set of states. Do the same laws reduce abortion rates among teenagers? The *Statistical Abstract of the United States* contains all kinds of state-level data. Levine, Trainor, and Zimmerman (1996) studied the effects of abortion funding restrictions on similar outcomes. Other factors, such as access to abortions, may affect teen birth and abortion rates.

There is also recent interest in the effects of "abstinence-only" sex education curricula. One can again use state-level panel data, or maybe even panel data at the school district level, to determine the effects of abstinence-only approaches to sex education on various outcomes, including rates of sexually transmitted diseases and teen birthrates.

6 Do changes in traffic laws affect traffic fatalities? McCarthy (1994) contains an analysis of monthly time series data for the state of California. A set of dummy variables can be used to indicate the months in which certain laws were in effect. The file TRAFFIC2 contains the data used by McCarthy. An alternative is to obtain a panel data set on states in the United States, where you can exploit variation in laws across states, as well as across time. Freeman (2007) is a good example of a state-level analysis, using 25 years of data that straddle changes in various state drunk driving, seat belt, and speed limit laws. The data can be found in the file DRIVING.

Mullahy and Sindelar (1994) used individual-level data matched with state laws and taxes on alcohol to estimate the effects of laws and taxes on the probability of driving drunk.

7 Are blacks discriminated against in the lending market? Hunter and Walker (1996) looked at this question; in fact, we used their data in Computer Exercises C.8 in Chapter 7 and C.2 in Chapter 17.

8 Is there a marriage premium for professional athletes? Korenman and Neumark (1991) found a significant wage premium for married men after using a variety of econometric methods, but their analysis is limited because they cannot directly observe productivity. (Plus, Korenman and Neumark used men in a variety of occupations.) Professional athletes provide an interesting group in which to study the marriage premium because we can easily collect data on various productivity measures, in addition to salary. The data set NBASAL, on players in the National Basketball Association (NBA), is one example. For each player, we have information on points scored, rebounds, assists, playing time, and demographics. As in Computer Exercise C.9 in Chapter 6, we can use multiple regression analysis to test whether the productivity measures differ by marital status. We can also use this kind of data to test whether married men are paid more after we account for productivity differences. (For example, NBA owners may think that married men bring stability to the team, or are better for the team image.) For individual sports—such as golf and tennis—annual earnings directly reflect productivity. Such data, along with age and experience, are relatively easy to collect.

9 Answer this question: Are cigarette smokers less productive? A variant on this is: Do workers who smoke take more sick days (everything else being equal)? Mullahy and Portney (1990) use individual-level data to evaluate this question. You could use data at, say, the metropolitan level. Something like average productivity in manufacturing can be related to percentage of manufacturing workers who smoke. Other variables, such as average worker education, capital per worker, and size of the city (you can think of more), should be controlled for.

10 Do minimum wages alleviate poverty? You can use state or county data to answer this question. The idea is that the minimum wage varies across states because some states have higher minimums than the federal minimum. Further, there are changes over time in the nominal minimum within a state, some due to changes at the federal level and some because of changes at the state level. Neumark and Wascher (1995) used a panel data set on states to estimate the effects of the minimum wage on the employment rates of young workers, as well as on school enrollment rates.

11 What factors affect student performance at public schools? It is fairly easy to get school-level or at least district-level data in most states. Does spending per student matter? Do student-teacher ratios have any effects? It is difficult to estimate ceteris paribus effects because spending is related to other factors, such as family incomes or poverty rates. The data set MEAP93, for Michigan high schools, contains a measure of the poverty rates. Another possibility is to use panel data, or at least to control for a previous year's performance measure (such as average test score or percentage of students passing an exam).

You can look at less obvious factors that affect student performance. For example, after controlling for income, does family structure matter? Perhaps families with two parents, but only one working for a wage, have a positive effect on performance. (There could be at least two channels: parents spend more time with the children, and they might also volunteer at school.) What about the effect of single-parent households, controlling for income and other factors? You can merge census data for one or two years with school district data.

Do public schools with more charter or private schools nearby better educate their students because of competition? There is a tricky simultaneity issue here because private schools are probably located in areas where the public schools are already poor. Hoxby (1994) used an instrumental variables approach, where population proportions of various religions were IVs for the number of private schools.

Rouse (1998) studied a different question: Did students who were able to attend a private school due to the Milwaukee voucher program perform better than those who did not? She used panel data and was able to control for an unobserved student effect. A subset of Rouse's data is contained in the file VOUCHER.

12 Can excess returns on a stock, or a stock index, be predicted by the lagged price/dividend ratio? Or by lagged interest rates or weekly monetary policy? It would be interesting to pick a foreign stock index, or one of the less well-known U.S. indexes. Cochrane (1997) provides a nice survey of recent theories and empirical results for explaining excess stock returns.

13 Is there racial discrimination in the market for baseball cards? This involves relating the prices of baseball cards to factors that should affect their prices, such as career statistics, whether the player is in the Hall of Fame, and so on. Holding other factors fixed, do cards of black or Hispanic players sell at a discount?

14 You can test whether the market for gambling on sports is efficient. For example, does the spread on football or basketball games contain all usable information for picking against the spread? The data set PNTSPRD contains information on men's college basketball games. The outcome variable is binary. Was the spread covered or not? Then, you can try to find information that was known prior to each game's being played in order to predict whether the spread is covered. (Good luck!) A useful website that contains historical spreads and outcomes for college football and men's basketball games is www.goldsheet.com.

15 What effect, if any, does success in college athletics have on other aspects of the university (applications, quality of students, quality of nonathletic departments)? McCormick and Tinsley (1987) looked at the effects of athletic success at major colleges on changes in SAT scores of entering freshmen. Timing is important here: presumably, it is recent past success that affects current applications and student quality. One must control for many other factors—such as tuition and measures of school quality—to make the analysis convincing because, without controlling for other factors, there is a negative correlation between academics and athletic performance. A more recent examination of the link between academic and athletic performance is provided by Tucker (2004), who also looks at how alumni contributions are affected by athletic success.

A variant is to match natural rivals in football or men's basketball and to look at differences across schools as a function of which school won the football game or one or more basketball games. ATHLET1 and ATHLET2 are small data sets that could be expanded and updated.

16 Collect murder rates for a sample of counties (say, from the FBI Uniform Crime Reports) for two years. Make the latter year such that economic and demographic variables are easy to obtain from the *County and City Data Book*. You can obtain the total number of people on death row plus executions for intervening years at the county level. If the years are 1990 and 1985, you might estimate

$$mrdrte_{90} = \beta_0 + \beta_1 mrdrte_{85} + \beta_2 executions + other\ factors,$$

where interest is in the coefficient on *executions*. The lagged murder rate and other factors serve as controls. If more than two years of data are obtained, then the panel data methods in Chapters 13 and 14 can be applied.

Other factors may also act as a deterrent to crime. For example, Cloninger (1991) presented a cross-sectional analysis of the effects of lethal police response on crime rates.

As a different twist, what factors affect crime rates on college campuses? Does the fraction of students living in fraternities or sororities have an effect? Does the size of the police force matter, or the kind of policing used? (Be careful about inferring causality here.) Does having an escort program help reduce crime? What about crime rates in nearby communities? Recently, colleges and universities have been required to report crime statistics; in previous years, reporting was voluntary.

17 What factors affect manufacturing productivity at the state level? In addition to levels of capital and worker education, you could look at degree of unionization. A panel data analysis would be most convincing here, using multiple years of census data, say, 1980, 1990, 2000, and 2010. Clark (1984) provides an analysis of how unionization affects firm performance and productivity. What other variables might explain productivity?

Firm-level data can be obtained from *Compustat*. For example, other factors being fixed, do changes in unionization affect stock price of a firm?

18 Use state- or county-level data or, if possible, school district–level data to look at the factors that affect education spending per pupil. An interesting question is: Other things being equal (such as income and education levels of residents), do districts with a larger percentage of elderly people spend less on schools? Census data can be matched with school district spending data to obtain a very large cross section. The U.S. Department of Education compiles such data.

19 What are the effects of state regulations, such as motorcycle helmet laws, on motorcycle fatalities? Or do differences in boating laws—such as minimum operating age—help to explain boating accident rates? The U.S. Department of Transportation compiles such information. This can be merged with data from the *Statistical Abstract of the United States*. A panel data analysis seems to be warranted here.

20 What factors affect output growth? Two factors of interest are inflation and investment [for example, Blomström, Lipsey, and Zejan (1996)]. You might use time series data on a country you find interesting. Or you could use a cross section of countries, as in De Long and Summers (1991). Friedman and Kuttner (1992) found evidence that, at least in the 1980s, the spread between the commercial paper rate and the Treasury bill rate affects real output.

21 What is the behavior of mergers in the U.S. economy (or some other economy)? Shughart and Tollison (1984) characterize (the log of) annual mergers in the U.S. economy as a random walk by showing that the difference in logs—roughly, the growth rate—is unpredictable given past growth rates. Does this still hold? Does it hold across various industries? What past measures of economic activity can be used to forecast mergers?

22 What factors might explain racial and gender differences in employment and wages? For example, Holzer (1991) reviewed the evidence on the "spatial mismatch hypothesis" to explain differences in employment rates between blacks and whites. Korenman and Neumark (1992) examined the effects of childbearing on women's wages, while Hersch and Stratton (1997) looked at the effects of household responsibilities on men's and women's wages.

23 Obtain monthly or quarterly data on teenage employment rates, the minimum wage, and factors that affect teen employment to estimate the effects of the minimum wage on teen employment. Solon (1985) used quarterly U.S. data, while Castillo-Freeman and Freeman (1992) used annual data on Puerto Rico. It might be informative to analyze time series data on a low-wage state in the United States—where changes in the minimum wage are likely to have the largest effect.

24 At the city level, estimate a time series model for crime. An example is Cloninger and Sartorius (1979). As a twist, you might estimate the effects of community policing or midnight basketball programs,

relatively new innovations in fighting crime. Inferring causality is tricky. Including a lagged dependent variable might be helpful. Because you are using time series data, you should be aware of the spurious regression problem.

Grogger (1990) used data on daily homicide counts to estimate the deterrent effects of capital punishment. Might there be other factors—such as news on lethal response by police—that have an effect on daily crime counts?

25 Are there aggregate productivity effects of computer usage? You would need to obtain time series data, perhaps at the national level, on productivity, percentage of employees using computers, and other factors. What about spending (probably as a fraction of total sales) on research and development? What sociological factors (for example, alcohol usage or divorce rates) might affect productivity?

26 What factors affect chief executive officer salaries? The files CEOSAL1 and CEOSAL2 are data sets that have various firm performance measures as well as information such as tenure and education. You can certainly update these data files and look for other interesting factors. Rose and Shepard (1997) considered firm diversification as one important determinant of CEO compensation.

27 Do differences in tax codes across states affect the amount of foreign direct investment? Hines (1996) studied the effects of state corporate taxes, along with the ability to apply foreign tax credits, on investment from outside the United States.

28 What factors affect election outcomes? Does spending matter? Do votes on specific issues matter? Does the state of the local economy matter? See, for example, Levitt (1994) and the data sets VOTE1 and VOTE2. Fair (1996) performed a time series analysis of U.S. presidential elections.

29 Test whether stores or restaurants practice price discrimination based on race or ethnicity. Graddy (1997) used data on fast-food restaurants in New Jersey and Pennsylvania, along with ZIP code-level characteristics, to see whether prices vary by characteristics of the local population. She found that prices of standard items, such as sodas, increase when the fraction of black residents increases. (Her data are contained in the file DISCRIM.) You can collect similar data in your local area by surveying stores or restaurants for prices of common items and matching those with recent census data. See Graddy's paper for details of her analysis.

30 Do your own "audit" study to test for race or gender discrimination in hiring. (One such study is described in Example C.3 of Appendix C.) Have pairs of equally qualified friends, say, one male and one female, apply for job openings in local bars or restaurants. You can provide them with phony résumés that give each the same experience and background, where the only difference is gender (or race). Then, you can keep track of who gets the interviews and job offers. Neumark (1996) described one such study conducted in Philadelphia. A variant would be to test whether general physical attractiveness or a specific characteristic, such as being obese or having visible tattoos or body piercings, plays a role in hiring decisions. You would want to use the same gender in the matched pairs, and it may not be easy to get volunteers for such a study.

31 Following Hamermesh and Parker (2005), try to establish a link between the physical appearance of college instructors and student evaluations. This can be done on campus via a survey. Somewhat crude data can be obtained from websites that allow students to rank their professors and provide some information about appearance. Ideally, though, any evaluations of attractiveness are not done by current or former students, as those evaluations can be influenced by the grade received.

32 Use panel data to study the effects of various economic policies on regional economic growth. Studying the effects of taxes and spending is natural, but other policies may be of interest. For example, Craig, Jackson, and Thomson (2007) study the effects of Small Business Association Loan Guarantee programs on per capita income growth.

33 Blinder and Watson (2014) have recently studied explanations for systematic differences in economic variables, particularly growth in real GDP, in the United States based on the political party of the sitting president. One might update the data to the most recent quarters and also study variables other than GDP, such as unemployment.

List of Journals

The following is a partial list of popular journals containing empirical research in business, economics, and other social sciences. A complete list of journals can be found on the Internet at http://www.econlit.org.

American Economic Journal: Applied Economics
American Economic Journal: Economic Policy
American Economic Review
American Journal of Agricultural Economics
American Political Science Review
Applied Economics
Brookings Papers on Economic Activity
Canadian Journal of Economics
Demography
Economic Development and Cultural Change
Economic Inquiry
Economica
Economics of Education Review
Education Finance and Policy
Economics Letters
Empirical Economics
Federal Reserve Bulletin
International Economic Review
International Tax and Public Finance
Journal of Applied Econometrics
Journal of Business and Economic Statistics
Journal of Development Economics
Journal of Economic Education
Journal of Empirical Finance
Journal of Environmental Economics and Management
Journal of Finance
Journal of Health Economics
Journal of Human Resources
Journal of Industrial Economics
Journal of International Economics
Journal of Labor Economics
Journal of Monetary Economics
Journal of Money, Credit and Banking
Journal of Political Economy
Journal of Public Economics
Journal of Quantitative Criminology
Journal of Urban Economics
National Bureau of Economic Research Working Papers Series
National Tax Journal
Public Finance Quarterly
Quarterly Journal of Economics
Regional Science & Urban Economics
Review of Economic Studies
Review of Economics and Statistics

Data Sources

Numerous data sources are available throughout the world. Governments of most countries compile a wealth of data; some general and easily accessible data sources for the United States, such as the *Economic Report of the President*, the *Statistical Abstract of the United States*, and the *County and City Data Book*, have already been mentioned. International financial data on many countries are published annually in *International Financial Statistics*. Various magazines, like *BusinessWeek* and *U.S. News and World Report*, often publish statistics—such as CEO salaries and firm performance, or ranking of academic programs—that are novel and can be used in an econometric analysis.

Rather than attempting to provide a list here, we instead give some Internet addresses that are comprehensive sources for economists. A very useful site for economists, called Resources for Economists on the Internet, is maintained by Bill Goffe at Pennsylvania State University. The address is

http://www.rfe.org.

This site provides links to journals, data sources, and lists of professional and academic economists. It is quite simple to use.

Another very useful site is

http://econometriclinks.com,

which contains links to lots of data sources as well as to other sites of interest to empirical economists.

In addition, the *Journal of Applied Econometrics* and the *Journal of Business and Economic Statistics* have data archives that contain data sets used in most papers published in the journals over the past several years. If you find a data set that interests you, this is a good way to go, as much of the cleaning and formatting of the data have already been done. The downside is that some of these data sets are used in econometric analyses that are more advanced than we have learned about in this text. On the other hand, it is often useful to estimate simpler models using standard econometric methods for comparison.

Many universities, such as the University of California–Berkeley, the University of Michigan, and the University of Maryland, maintain very extensive data sets as well as links to a variety of data sets. Your own library possibly contains an extensive set of links to databases in business, economics, and the other social sciences. The regional Federal Reserve banks, such as the one in St. Louis, manage a variety of data. The National Bureau of Economic Research posts data sets used by some of its researchers. State and federal governments now publish a wealth of data that can be accessed via the Internet. Census data are publicly available from the U.S. Census Bureau. (Two useful publications are the *Economic Census*, published in years ending with two and seven, and the *Census of Population and Housing*, published at the beginning of each decade.) Other agencies, such as the U.S. Department of Justice, also make data available to the public.

Appendix A

Basic Mathematical Tools

T his appendix covers some basic mathematics that are used in econometric analysis. We summarize various properties of the summation operator, study properties of linear and certain nonlinear equations, and review proportions and percentages. We also present some special functions that often arise in applied econometrics, including quadratic functions and the natural logarithm. The first four sections require only basic algebra skills. Section A-5 contains a brief review of differential calculus; although a knowledge of calculus is not necessary to understand most of the text, it is used in some end-of-chapter appendices and in several of the more advanced chapters in Part 3.

A-1 The Summation Operator and Descriptive Statistics

The **summation operator** is a useful shorthand for manipulating expressions involving the sums of many numbers, and it plays a key role in statistics and econometric analysis. If $\{x_i: i = 1, \ldots, n\}$ denotes a sequence of n numbers, then we write the sum of these numbers as

$$\sum_{i=1}^{n} x_i \equiv x_1 + x_2 + \ldots + x_n. \tag{A.1}$$

With this definition, the summation operator is easily shown to have the following properties:

Property Sum.1: For any constant c,

$$\sum_{i=1}^{n} c = nc. \tag{A.2}$$

Property Sum.2: For any constant c,

$$\sum_{i=1}^{n} c x_i = c \sum_{i=1}^{n} x_i. \tag{A.3}$$

Sum.3: If $\{(x_i, y_i): i = 1, 2, \ldots, n\}$ is a set of n pairs of numbers, and a and b are
en

$$\sum_{i=1}^{n} (ax_i + by_i) = a\sum_{i=1}^{n} x_i + b\sum_{i=1}^{n} y_i. \qquad \text{[A.4]}$$

important to be aware of some things that *cannot* be done with the summation operator.
$= 1, 2, \ldots, n\}$ again be a set of n pairs of numbers with $y_i \neq 0$ for each i. Then,

$$\sum_{i=1}^{n} (x_i/y_i) \neq \left(\sum_{i=1}^{n} x_i\right) \Big/ \left(\sum_{i=1}^{n} y_i\right).$$

, the sum of the ratios is not the ratio of the sums. In the $n = 2$ case, the application of
ntary algebra also reveals this lack of equality: $x_1/y_1 + x_2/y_2 \neq (x_1 + x_2)/(y_1 + y_2)$.
e sum of the squares is not the square of the sum: $\sum_{i=1}^{n} x_i^2 \neq (\sum_{i=1}^{n} x_i)^2$, ex-
l cases. That these two quantities are not generally equal is easiest to see when
$\neq (x_1 + x_2)^2 = x_1^2 + 2x_1x_2 + x_2^2$.
mbers $\{x_i: i = 1, \ldots, n\}$, we compute their **average** or *mean* by adding them up and

$$\bar{x} = (1/n)\sum_{i=1}^{n} x_i. \qquad \text{[A.5]}$$

a sample of data on a particular variable (such as years of education), we often call
verage (or *sample mean*) to emphasize that it is computed from a particular set of
data. The sample average is an example of a **descriptive statistic**; in this case, the statistic describes
the central tendency of the set of points x_i.

There are some basic properties about averages that are important to understand. First, suppose
we take each observation on x and subtract off the average: $d_i \equiv x_i - \bar{x}$ (the "*d*" here stands for *deviation* from the average). Then, the sum of these deviations is always zero:

$$\sum_{i=1}^{n} d_i = \sum_{i=1}^{n} (x_i - \bar{x}) = \sum_{i=1}^{n} x_i - \sum_{i=1}^{n} \bar{x} = \sum_{i=1}^{n} x_i - n\bar{x} = n\bar{x} - n\bar{x} = 0.$$

We summarize this as

$$\sum_{i=1}^{n} (x_i - \bar{x}) = 0. \qquad \text{[A.6]}$$

A simple numerical example shows how this works. Suppose $n = 5$ and $x_1 = 6$, $x_2 = 1$,
$x_3 = -2$, $x_4 = 0$, and $x_5 = 5$. Then, $\bar{x} = 2$, and the demeaned sample is $\{4, -1, -4, -2, 3\}$. Adding
these gives zero, which is just what equation (A.6) says.

In our treatment of regression analysis in Chapter 2, we need to know some additional algebraic
facts involving deviations from sample averages. An important one is that the sum of squared deviations is the sum of the squared x_i minus n times the square of $\bar{x}$:

$$\sum_{i=1}^{n} (x_i - \bar{x})^2 = \sum_{i=1}^{n} x_i^2 - n(\bar{x})^2. \qquad \text{[A.7]}$$

This can be shown using basic properties of the summation operator:

$$\sum_{i=1}^{n} (x_i - \bar{x})^2 = \sum_{i=1}^{n} (x_i^2 - 2x_i\bar{x} + \bar{x}^2)$$

$$= \sum_{i=1}^{n} x_i^2 - 2\bar{x}\sum_{i=1}^{n} x_i + n(\bar{x})^2$$

$$= \sum_{i=1}^{n} x_i^2 - 2n(\bar{x})^2 + n(\bar{x})^2 = \sum_{i=1}^{n} x_i^2 - n(\bar{x})^2.$$

Given a data set on two variables, $\{(x_i, y_i): i = 1, 2, \ldots, n\}$, it can also be shown that

$$\sum_{i=1}^{n} (x_i - \bar{x})(y_i - \bar{y}) = \sum_{i=1}^{n} x_i(y_i - \bar{y}) \qquad \text{[A.8]}$$

$$= \sum_{i=1}^{n} (x_i - \bar{x})y_i = \sum_{i=1}^{n} x_i y_i - n(\bar{x}\cdot\bar{y});$$

this is a generalization of equation (A.7). (There, $y_i = x_i$ for all i.)

The average is the measure of central tendency that we will focus on in most of this text. However, it is sometimes informative to use the **median** (or *sample median*) to describe the central value. To obtain the median of the n numbers $\{x_1, \ldots, x_n\}$, we first order the values of the x_i from smallest to largest. Then, if n is odd, the sample median is the middle number of the ordered observations. For example, given the numbers $\{-4, 8, 2, 0, 21, -10, 18\}$, the median value is 2 (because the ordered sequence is $\{-10, -4, 0, 2, 8, 18, 21\}$). If we change the largest number in this list, 21, to twice its value, 42, the median is still 2. By contrast, the sample average would increase from 5 to 8, a sizable change. Generally, the median is less sensitive than the average to changes in the extreme values (large or small) in a list of numbers. This is why "median incomes" or "median housing values" are often reported, rather than averages, when summarizing income or housing values in a city or county.

If n is even, there is no unique way to define the median because there are two numbers at the center. Usually, the median is defined to be the average of the two middle values (again, after ordering the numbers from smallest to largest). Using this rule, the median for the set of numbers $\{4, 12, 2, 6\}$ would be $(4 + 6)/2 = 5$.

A-2 Properties of Linear Functions

Linear functions play an important role in econometrics because they are simple to interpret and manipulate. If x and y are two variables related by

$$y = \beta_0 + \beta_1 x, \qquad \text{[A.9]}$$

then we say that y is a **linear function** of x, and β_0 and β_1 are two parameters (numbers) describing this relationship. The **intercept** is β_0, and the **slope** is β_1.

The defining feature of a linear function is that the change in y is always β_1 times the change in x:

$$\Delta y = \beta_1 \Delta x, \qquad \text{[A.10]}$$

where Δ denotes "change." In other words, the **marginal effect** of x on y is constant and equal to β_1.

EXAMPLE A.1   Linear Housing Expenditure Function

Suppose that the relationship between monthly housing expenditure and monthly income is

$$housing = 164 + .27\, income. \qquad\qquad \text{[A.11]}$$

Then, for each additional dollar of income, 27 cents is spent on housing. If family income increases by \$200, then housing expenditure increases by $(.27)200 = \$54$. This function is graphed in Figure A.1.

According to equation (A.11), a family with no income spends \$164 on housing, which of course cannot be literally true. For low levels of income, this linear function would not describe the relationship between *housing* and *income* very well, which is why we will eventually have to use other types of functions to describe such relationships.

In (A.11), the *marginal propensity to consume* (MPC) housing out of income is .27. This is different from the *average propensity to consume* (APC), which is

$$\frac{housing}{income} = 164/income + .27.$$

The APC is not constant; it is always larger than the MPC, and it gets closer to the MPC as income increases.

Linear functions are easily defined for more than two variables. Suppose that y is related to two variables, x_1 and x_2, in the general form

$$y = \beta_0 + \beta_1 x_1 + \beta_2 x_2. \qquad\qquad \text{[A.12]}$$

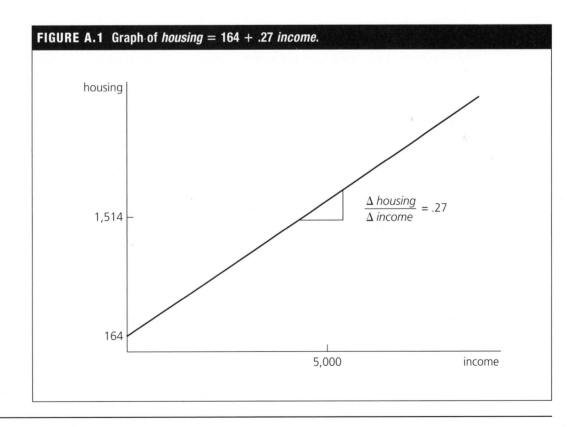

FIGURE A.1 Graph of *housing* = 164 + .27 *income.*

It is rather difficult to envision this function because its graph is three-dimensional. Nevertheless, β_0 is still the intercept (the value of y when $x_1 = 0$ and $x_2 = 0$), and β_1 and β_2 measure particular slopes. From (A.12), the change in y, for given changes in x_1 and x_2, is

$$\Delta y = \beta_1 \Delta x_1 + \beta_2 \Delta x_2. \qquad \text{[A.13]}$$

If x_2 does not change, that is, $\Delta x_2 = 0$, then we have

$$\Delta y = \beta_1 \Delta x_1 \text{ if } \Delta x_2 = 0,$$

so that β_1 is the slope of the relationship in the direction of x_1:

$$\beta_1 = \frac{\Delta y}{\Delta x_1} \text{ if } \Delta x_2 = 0.$$

Because it measures how y changes with x_1, holding x_2 fixed, β_1 is often called the **partial effect** of x_1 on y. Because the partial effect involves holding other factors fixed, it is closely linked to the notion of **ceteris paribus**. The parameter β_2 has a similar interpretation: $\beta_2 = \Delta y/\Delta x_2$ if $\Delta x_1 = 0$, so that β_2 is the partial effect of x_2 on y.

EXAMPLE A.2	**Demand for Compact Discs**

For college students, suppose that the monthly quantity demanded of compact discs is related to the price of compact discs and monthly discretionary income by

$$quantity = 120 - 9.8\, price + .03\, income,$$

where *price* is dollars per disc and *income* is measured in dollars. The *demand curve* is the relationship between *quantity* and *price*, holding *income* (and other factors) fixed. This is graphed in two dimensions in Figure A.2 at an income level of $900. The slope of the demand curve, -9.8, is the *partial effect* of price on quantity: holding income fixed, if the price of compact discs increases by one dollar, then the quantity demanded falls by 9.8. (We abstract from the fact that CDs can only be purchased in discrete units.) An increase in income simply shifts the demand curve up (changes the intercept), but the slope remains the same.

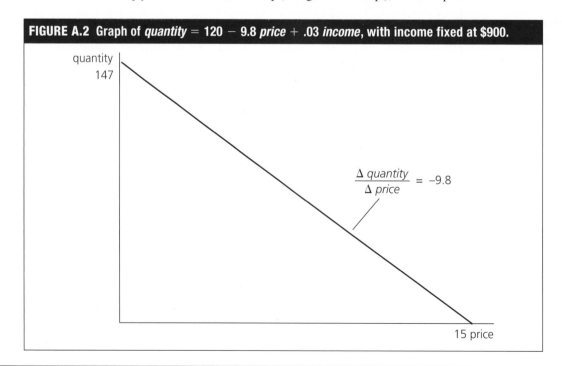

FIGURE A.2 Graph of *quantity* = 120 − 9.8 *price* + .03 *income*, with income fixed at $900.

A-3 Proportions and Percentages

Proportions and percentages play such an important role in applied economics that it is necessary to become very comfortable in working with them. Many quantities reported in the popular press are in the form of percentages; a few examples are interest rates, unemployment rates, and high school graduation rates.

An important skill is being able to convert proportions to percentages and vice versa. A percentage is easily obtained by multiplying a proportion by 100. For example, if the proportion of adults in a county with a high school degree is .82, then we say that 82% (82 percent) of adults have a high school degree. Another way to think of percentages and proportions is that a proportion is the decimal form of a percentage. For example, if the marginal tax rate for a family earning $30,000 per year is reported as 28%, then the proportion of the next dollar of income that is paid in income taxes is .28 (or 28¢).

When using percentages, we often need to convert them to decimal form. For example, if a state sales tax is 6% and $200 is spent on a taxable item, then the sales tax paid is $200(.06) = 12. If the annual return on a certificate of deposit (CD) is 7.6% and we invest $3,000 in such a CD at the beginning of the year, then our interest income is $3,000(.076) = 228. As much as we would like it, the interest income is not obtained by multiplying 3,000 by 7.6.

We must be wary of proportions that are sometimes incorrectly reported as percentages in the popular media. If we read, "The percentage of high school students who drink alcohol is .57," we know that this really means 57% (not just over one-half of a percent, as the statement literally implies). College volleyball fans are probably familiar with press clips containing statements such as "Her hitting percentage was .372." This really means that her hitting percentage was 37.2%.

In econometrics, we are often interested in measuring the *changes* in various quantities. Let x denote some variable, such as an individual's income, the number of crimes committed in a community, or the profits of a firm. Let x_0 and x_1 denote two values for x: x_0 is the initial value, and x_1 is the subsequent value. For example, x_0 could be the annual income of an individual in 1994 and x_1 the income of the same individual in 1995. The **proportionate change** in x in moving from x_0 to x_1, sometimes called the **relative change,** is simply

$$(x_1 - x_0)/x_0 = \Delta x/x_0, \qquad \text{[A.14]}$$

assuming, of course, that $x_0 \neq 0$. In other words, to get the proportionate change, we simply divide the change in x by its initial value. This is a way of standardizing the change so that it is free of units. For example, if an individual's income goes from $30,000 per year to $36,000 per year, then the proportionate change is $6,000/30,000 = .20$.

It is more common to state changes in terms of percentages. The **percentage change** in x in going from x_0 to x_1 is simply 100 times the proportionate change:

$$\%\Delta x = 100(\Delta x/x_0); \qquad \text{[A.15]}$$

the notation "$\%\Delta x$" is read as "the percentage change in x." For example, when income goes from $30,000 to $33,750, income has increased by 12.5%; to get this, we simply multiply the proportionate change, .125, by 100.

Again, we must be on guard for proportionate changes that are reported as percentage changes. In the previous example, for instance, reporting the percentage change in income as .125 is incorrect and could lead to confusion.

When we look at changes in things like dollar amounts or population, there is no ambiguity about what is meant by a percentage change. By contrast, interpreting percentage change calculations can be tricky when the variable of interest is itself a percentage, something that happens often in economics and other social sciences. To illustrate, let x denote the percentage of adults in a particular city having a college education. Suppose the initial value is $x_0 = 24$ (24% have a college education), and the new value is $x_1 = 30$. We can compute two quantities to describe how the percentage of college-educated people has changed. The first is the change in x, Δx. In this case, $\Delta x = x_1 - x_0 = 6$: the percentage of people with a college education has increased by six *percentage points*. On the other hand, we can compute the percentage change in x using equation (A.15): $\%\Delta x = 100[(30 - 24)/24] = 25$.

In this example, the percentage point change and the percentage change are very different. The **percentage point change** is just the change in the percentages. The percentage change is the change relative to the initial value. Generally, we must pay close attention to which number is being computed. The careful researcher makes this distinction perfectly clear; unfortunately, in the popular press as well as in academic research, the type of reported change is often unclear.

EXAMPLE A.3	**Michigan Sales Tax Increase**

In March 1994, Michigan voters approved a sales tax increase from 4% to 6%. In political advertisements, supporters of the measure referred to this as a two percentage point increase, or an increase of two cents on the dollar. Opponents of the tax increase called it a 50% increase in the sales tax rate. Both claims are correct; they are simply different ways of measuring the increase in the sales tax. Naturally, each group reported the measure that made its position most favorable.

For a variable such as salary, it makes no sense to talk of a "percentage point change in salary" because salary is not measured as a percentage. We can describe a change in salary either in dollar or percentage terms.

A-4 Some Special Functions and Their Properties

In Section A-2, we reviewed the basic properties of linear functions. We already indicated one important feature of functions like $y = \beta_0 + \beta_1 x$: a one-unit change in x results in the *same* change in y, regardless of the initial value of x. As we noted earlier, this is the same as saying the marginal effect of x on y is constant, something that is not realistic for many economic relationships. For example, the important economic notion of *diminishing marginal returns* is not consistent with a linear relationship.

In order to model a variety of economic phenomena, we need to study several nonlinear functions. A **nonlinear function** is characterized by the fact that the change in y for a given change in x depends on the starting value of x. Certain nonlinear functions appear frequently in empirical economics, so it is important to know how to interpret them. A complete understanding of nonlinear functions takes us into the realm of calculus. Here, we simply summarize the most significant aspects of the functions, leaving the details of some derivations for Section A-5.

A-4a Quadratic Functions

One simple way to capture diminishing returns is to add a quadratic term to a linear relationship. Consider the equation

$$y = \beta_0 + \beta_1 x + \beta_2 x^2,$$ [A.16]

where β_0, β_1, and β_2 are parameters. When $\beta_1 > 0$ and $\beta_2 < 0$, the relationship between y and x has the parabolic shape given in Figure A.3, where $\beta_0 = 6$, $\beta_1 = 8$, and $\beta_2 = -2$.

When $\beta_1 > 0$ and $\beta_2 < 0$, it can be shown (using calculus in the next section) that the *maximum* of the function occurs at the point

$$x^* = \beta_1/(-2\beta_2).$$ [A.17]

For example, if $y = 6 + 8x - 2x^2$ (so $\beta_1 = 8$ and $\beta_2 = -2$), then the largest value of y occurs at $x^* = 8/4 = 2$, and this value is $6 + 8(2) - 2(2)^2 = 14$ (see Figure A.3).

The fact that equation (A.16) implies a **diminishing marginal effect** of x on y is easily seen from its graph. Suppose we start at a low value of x and then increase x by some amount, say, c. This has a larger effect on y than if we start at a higher value of x and increase x by the same amount c. In fact, once $x > x^*$, an increase in x actually decreases y.

The statement that x has a diminishing marginal effect on y is the same as saying that the slope of the function in Figure A.3 decreases as x increases. Although this is clear from looking at the graph, we usually want to quantify how quickly the slope is changing. An application of calculus gives the approximate slope of the quadratic function as

$$slope = \frac{\Delta y}{\Delta x} \approx \beta_1 + 2\beta_2 x, \qquad \text{[A.18]}$$

for "small" changes in x. [The right-hand side of equation (A.18) is the **derivative** of the function in equation (A.16) with respect to x.] Another way to write this is

$$\Delta y \approx (\beta_1 + 2\beta_2 x)\Delta x \text{ for "small" } \Delta x. \qquad \text{[A.19]}$$

To see how well this approximation works, consider again the function $y = 6 + 8x - 2x^2$. Then, according to equation (A.19), $\Delta y \approx (8 - 4x)\Delta x$. Now, suppose we start at $x = 1$ and change x by $\Delta x = .1$. Using (A.19), $\Delta y \approx (8 - 4)(.1) = .4$. Of course, we can compute the change exactly by finding the values of y when $x = 1$ and $x = 1.1$: $y_0 = 6 + 8(1) - 2(1)^2 = 12$ and $y_1 = 6 + 8(1.1) - 2(1.1)^2 = 12.38$, so the exact change in y is .38. The approximation is pretty close in this case.

Now, suppose we start at $x = 1$ but change x by a larger amount: $\Delta x = .5$. Then, the approximation gives $\Delta y \approx 4(.5) = 2$. The exact change is determined by finding the difference in y when $x = 1$

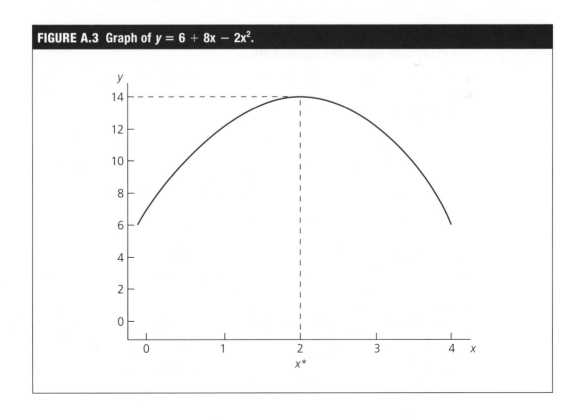

FIGURE A.3 Graph of $y = 6 + 8x - 2x^2$.

and $x = 1.5$. The former value of y was 12, and the latter value is $6 + 8(1.5) - 2(1.5)^2 = 13.5$, so the actual change is 1.5 (not 2). The approximation is worse in this case because the change in x is larger.

For many applications, equation (A.19) can be used to compute the approximate marginal effect of x on y for any initial value of x and small changes. And, we can always compute the exact change if necessary.

EXAMPLE A.4   **A Quadratic Wage Function**

Suppose the relationship between hourly wages and years in the workforce (*exper*) is given by

$$wage = 5.25 + .48\ exper - .008\ exper^2. \qquad \text{[A.20]}$$

This function has the same general shape as the one in Figure A.3. Using equation (A.17), *exper* has a positive effect on wage up to the turning point, $exper^* = .48/[2(.008)] = 30$. The first year of experience is worth approximately .48, or 48 cents [see (A.19) with $x = 0$, $\Delta x = 1$]. Each additional year of experience increases wage by less than the previous year—reflecting a diminishing marginal return to experience. At 30 years, an additional year of experience would actually lower the wage. This is not very realistic, but it is one of the consequences of using a quadratic function to capture a diminishing marginal effect: at some point, the function must reach a maximum and curve downward. For practical purposes, the point at which this happens is often large enough to be inconsequential, but not always.

The graph of the quadratic function in (A.16) has a U-shape if $\beta_1 < 0$ and $\beta_2 > 0$, in which case there is an increasing marginal return. The minimum of the function is at the point $-\beta_1/(2\beta_2)$.

A-4b The Natural Logarithm

The nonlinear function that plays the most important role in econometric analysis is the **natural logarithm**. In this text, we denote the natural logarithm, which we often refer to simply as the **log function**, as

$$y = \log(x). \qquad \text{[A.21]}$$

You might remember learning different symbols for the natural log; $\ln(x)$ or $\log_e(x)$ are the most common. These different notations are useful when logarithms with several different bases are being used. For our purposes, only the natural logarithm is important, and so $\log(x)$ denotes the natural logarithm throughout this text. This corresponds to the notational usage in many statistical packages, although some use $\ln(x)$ [and most calculators use $\ln(x)$]. Economists use both $\log(x)$ and $\ln(x)$, which is useful to know when you are reading papers in applied economics.

The function $y = \log(x)$ is defined only for $x > 0$, and it is plotted in Figure A.4. It is not very important to know how the values of $\log(x)$ are obtained. For our purposes, the function can be thought of as a black box: we can plug in any $x > 0$ and obtain $\log(x)$ from a calculator or a computer.

Several things are apparent from Figure A.4. First, when $y = \log(x)$, the relationship between y and x displays diminishing marginal returns. One important difference between the log and the quadratic function in Figure A.3 is that when $y = \log(x)$, the effect of x on y never becomes negative: the slope of the function gets closer and closer to zero as x gets large, but the slope never quite reaches zero and certainly never becomes negative.

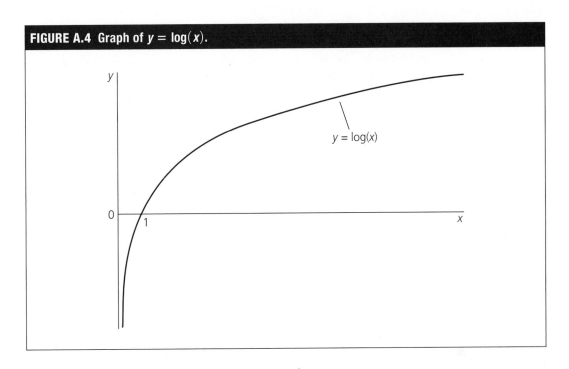

FIGURE A.4 Graph of $y = \log(x)$.

The following are also apparent from Figure A.4:

$$\log(x) < 0 \text{ for } 0 < x < 1$$
$$\log(1) = 0$$
$$\log(x) > 0 \text{ for } x > 1.$$

In particular, $\log(x)$ can be positive or negative. Some useful algebraic facts about the log function are

$$\log(x_1 \cdot x_2) = \log(x_1) + \log(x_2), x_1, x_2 > 0$$
$$\log(x_1/x_2) = \log(x_1) - \log(x_2), x_1, x_2 > 0$$
$$\log(x^c) \quad = c \log(x), x > 0, c \text{ any number.}$$

Occasionally, we will need to rely on these properties.

The logarithm can be used for various approximations that arise in econometric applications. First, $\log(1 + x) \approx x$ for $x \approx 0$. You can try this with $x = .02, .1,$ and $.5$ to see how the quality of the approximation deteriorates as x gets larger. Even more useful is the fact that the difference in logs can be used to approximate proportionate changes. Let x_0 and x_1 be positive values. Then, it can be shown (using calculus) that

$$\log(x_1) - \log(x_0) \approx (x_1 - x_0)/x_0 = \Delta x/x_0 \qquad \text{[A.22]}$$

for small changes in x. If we multiply equation (A.22) by 100 and write $\Delta \log(x) = \log(x_1) - \log(x_0)$, then

$$100 \cdot \Delta \log(x) \approx \%\Delta x \qquad \text{[A.23]}$$

for small changes in x. The meaning of "small" depends on the context, and we will encounter several examples throughout this text.

Why should we approximate the percentage change using (A.23) when the exact percentage change is so easy to compute? Momentarily, we will see why the approximation in (A.23) is useful in econometrics. First, let us see how good the approximation is in two examples.

First, suppose $x_0 = 40$ and $x_1 = 41$. Then, the percentage change in x in moving from x_0 to x_1 is 2.5%, using $100(x_1 - x_0)/x_0$. Now, $\log(41) - \log(40) = .0247$ (to four decimal places), which when multiplied by 100 is very close to 2.5. The approximation works pretty well. Now, consider a much bigger change: $x_0 = 40$ and $x_1 = 60$. The exact percentage change is 50%. However, $\log(60) - \log(40) \approx .4055$, so the approximation gives 40.55%, which is much farther off.

Why is the approximation in (A.23) useful if it is only satisfactory for small changes? To build up to the answer, we first define the **elasticity** of y with respect to x as

$$\frac{\Delta y}{\Delta x} \cdot \frac{x}{y} = \frac{\%\Delta y}{\%\Delta x}. \tag{A.24}$$

In other words, the elasticity of y with respect to x is the percentage change in y when x increases by 1%. This notion should be familiar from introductory economics.

If y is a linear function of x, $y = \beta_0 + \beta_1 x$, then the elasticity is

$$\frac{\Delta y}{\Delta x} \cdot \frac{x}{y} = \beta_1 \cdot \frac{x}{y} = \beta_1 \cdot \frac{x}{\beta_0 + \beta_1 x}, \tag{A.25}$$

which clearly depends on the value of x. (This is a generalization of the well-known result from basic demand theory: the elasticity is not constant along a straight-line demand curve.)

Elasticities are of critical importance in many areas of applied economics, not just in demand theory. It is convenient in many situations to have *constant* elasticity models, and the log function allows us to specify such models. If we use the approximation in (A.23) for both x and y, then the elasticity is approximately equal to $\Delta\log(y)/\Delta\log(x)$. Thus, a constant elasticity model is approximated by the equation

$$\log(y) = \beta_0 + \beta_1\log(x), \tag{A.26}$$

and β_1 is the elasticity of y with respect to x (assuming that $x, y > 0$).

EXAMPLE A.5	**Constant Elasticity Demand Function**

If q is quantity demanded and p is price and these variables are related by

$$\log(q) = 4.7 - 1.25 \log(p),$$

then the price elasticity of demand is -1.25. Roughly, a 1% increase in price leads to a 1.25% fall in the quantity demanded.

For our purposes, the fact that β_1 in (A.26) is only close to the elasticity is not important. In fact, when the elasticity is defined using calculus—as in Section A-5—the definition is exact. For the purposes of econometric analysis, (A.26) defines a **constant elasticity model**. Such models play a large role in empirical economics.

Other possibilities for using the log function often arise in empirical work. Suppose that $y > 0$ and

$$\log(y) = \beta_0 + \beta_1 x. \tag{A.27}$$

Then, $\Delta\log(y) = \beta_1\Delta x$, so $100 \cdot \Delta\log(y) = (100 \cdot \beta_1)\Delta x$. It follows that, when y and x are related by equation (A.27),

$$\%\Delta y \approx (100 \cdot \beta_1)\Delta x. \tag{A.28}$$

| EXAMPLE A.6 | **Logarithmic Wage Equation** |

Suppose that hourly wage and years of education are related by

$$\log(wage) = 2.78 + .094 \ educ.$$

Then, using equation (A.28),

$$\%\Delta wage \approx 100(.094)\Delta educ = 9.4 \ \Delta educ.$$

It follows that one more year of education increases hourly wage by about 9.4%.

Generally, the quantity $\%\Delta y/\Delta x$ is called the **semi-elasticity** of y with respect to x. The semi-elasticity is the percentage change in y when x increases by one *unit*. What we have just shown is that, in model (A.27), the semi-elasticity is constant and equal to $100 \cdot \beta_1$. In Example A.6, we can conveniently summarize the relationship between wages and education by saying that one more year of education—starting from any amount of education—increases the wage by about 9.4%. This is why such models play an important role in economics.

Another relationship of some interest in applied economics is

$$y = \beta_0 + \beta_1\log(x), \qquad\qquad [A.29]$$

where $x > 0$. How can we interpret this equation? If we take the change in y, we get $\Delta y = \beta_1\Delta\log(x)$, which can be rewritten as $\Delta y = (\beta_1/100)[100 \cdot \Delta\log(x)]$. Thus, using the approximation in (A.23), we have

$$\Delta y \approx (\beta_1/100)(\%\Delta x). \qquad\qquad [A.30]$$

In other words, $\beta_1/100$ is the unit change in y when x increases by 1%.

| EXAMPLE A.7 | **Labor Supply Function** |

Assume that the labor supply of a worker can be described by

$$hours = 33 + 45.1 \log(wage),$$

where *wage* is hourly wage and *hours* is hours worked per week. Then, from (A.30),

$$\Delta hours \approx (45.1/100)(\%\Delta wage) = .451 \ \%\Delta wage.$$

In other words, a 1% increase in *wage* increases the weekly hours worked by about .45, or slightly less than one-half hour. If the wage increases by 10%, then $\Delta hours = .451(10) = 4.51$, or about four and one-half hours. We would not want to use this approximation for much larger percentage changes in wages.

A-4c The Exponential Function

Before leaving this section, we need to discuss a special function that is related to the log. As motivation, consider equation (A.27). There, $\log(y)$ is a linear function of x. But how do we find y itself as a function of x? The answer is given by the **exponential function**.

We will write the exponential function as $y = \exp(x)$, which is graphed in Figure A.5. From Figure A.5, we see that $\exp(x)$ is defined for any value of x and is always greater than zero. Sometimes, the exponential function is written as $y = e^x$, but we will not use this notation. Two important values of the exponential function are $\exp(0) = 1$ and $\exp(1) = 2.7183$ (to four decimal places).

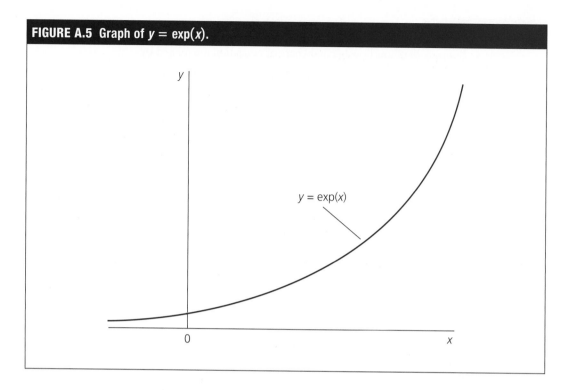

FIGURE A.5 Graph of $y = \exp(x)$.

The exponential function is the inverse of the log function in the following sense: $\log[\exp(x)] = x$ for all x, and $\exp[\log(x)] = x$ for $x > 0$. In other words, the log "undoes" the exponential, and vice versa. (This is why the exponential function is sometimes called the *anti-log* function.) In particular, note that $\log(y) = \beta_0 + \beta_1 x$ is equivalent to

$$y = \exp(\beta_0 + \beta_1 x).$$

If $\beta_1 > 0$, the relationship between x and y has the same shape as in Figure A.5. Thus, if $\log(y) = \beta_0 + \beta_1 x$ with $\beta_1 > 0$, then x has an *increasing* marginal effect on y. In Example A.6, this means that another year of education leads to a larger change in wage than the previous year of education.

Two useful facts about the exponential function are $\exp(x_1 + x_2) = \exp(x_1)\exp(x_2)$ and $\exp[c \cdot \log(x)] = x^c$.

A-5 Differential Calculus

In the previous section, we asserted several approximations that have foundations in calculus. Let $y = f(x)$ for some function f. Then, for small changes in x,

$$\Delta y \approx \frac{df}{dx} \cdot \Delta x, \qquad \text{[A.31]}$$

where df/dx is the derivative of the function f, evaluated at the initial point x_0. We also write the derivative as dy/dx.

For example, if $y = \log(x)$, then $dy/dx = 1/x$. Using (A.31), with dy/dx evaluated at x_0, we have $\Delta y \approx (1/x_0)\Delta x$, or $\Delta\log(x) \approx \Delta x/x_0$, which is the approximation given in (A.22).

In applying econometrics, it helps to recall the derivatives of a handful of functions because we use the derivative to define the slope of a function at a given point. We can then use (A.31) to find the approximate change in y for small changes in x. In the linear case, the derivative is simply the slope of the line, as we would hope: if $y = \beta_0 + \beta_1 x$, then $dy/dx = \beta_1$.

If $y = x^c$, then $dy/dx = cx^{c-1}$. The derivative of a sum of two functions is the sum of the derivatives: $d[f(x) + g(x)]/dx = df(x)/dx + dg(x)/dx$. The derivative of a constant times any function is that same constant times the derivative of the function: $d[cf(x)]/dx = c[df(x)/dx]$. These simple rules allow us to find derivatives of more complicated functions. Other rules, such as the product, quotient, and chain rules, will be familiar to those who have taken calculus, but we will not review those here.

Some functions that are often used in economics, along with their derivatives, are

$$y = \beta_0 + \beta_1 x + \beta_2 x^2; \ dy/dx = \beta_1 + 2\beta_2 x$$
$$y = \beta_0 + \beta_1/x; \ dy/dx = -\beta_1/(x^2)$$
$$y = \beta_0 + \beta_1\sqrt{x}; \ dy/dx = (\beta_1/2)x^{-1/2}$$
$$y = \beta_0 + \beta_1\log(x); \ dy/dx = \beta_1/x$$
$$y = \exp(\beta_0 + \beta_1 x); \ dy/dx = \beta_1\exp(\beta_0 + \beta_1 x).$$

If $\beta_0 = 0$ and $\beta_1 = 1$ in this last expression, we get $dy/dx = \exp(x)$, when $y = \exp(x)$.

In Section A-4, we noted that equation (A.26) defines a constant elasticity model when calculus is used. The calculus definition of elasticity is $(dy/dx) \cdot (x/y)$. It can be shown using properties of logs and exponentials that, when (A.26) holds, $(dy/dx) \cdot (x/y) = \beta_1$.

When y is a function of multiple variables, the notion of a **partial derivative** becomes important. Suppose that

$$y = f(x_1, x_2).$$ [A.32]

Then, there are two partial derivatives, one with respect to x_1 and one with respect to x_2. The partial derivative of y with respect to x_1, denoted here by $\partial y/\partial x_1$, is just the usual derivative of (A.32) with respect to x_1, where x_2 is treated as a *constant*. Similarly, $\partial y/\partial x_2$ is just the derivative of (A.32) with respect to x_2, holding x_1 fixed.

Partial derivatives are useful for much the same reason as ordinary derivatives. We can approximate the change in y as

$$\Delta y \approx \frac{\partial y}{\partial x_1} \cdot \Delta x_1, \text{ holding } x_2 \text{ fixed.}$$ [A.33]

Thus, calculus allows us to define partial effects in nonlinear models just as we could in linear models. In fact, if

$$y = \beta_0 + \beta_1 x_1 + \beta_2 x_2,$$

then

$$\frac{\partial y}{\partial x_1} = \beta_1, \frac{\partial y}{\partial x_2} = \beta_2.$$

These can be recognized as the partial effects defined in Section A-2.

A more complicated example is

$$y = 5 + 4x_1 + x_1^2 - 3x_2 + 7x_1 \cdot x_2.$$ [A.34]

Now, the derivative of (A.34), with respect to x_1 (treating x_2 as a constant), is simply

$$\frac{\partial y}{\partial x_1} = 4 + 2x_1 + 7x_2;$$

note how this depends on x_1 and x_2. The derivative of (A.34), with respect to x_2, is $\partial y/\partial x_2 = -3 + 7x_1$, so this depends only on x_1.

| EXAMPLE A.8 | **Wage Function with Interaction** |

A function relating wages to years of education and experience is

$$wage = 3.10 + .41\,educ + .19\,exper - .004\,exper^2$$
$$+ .007\,educ \cdot exper. \tag{A.35}$$

The partial effect of *exper* on *wage* is the partial derivative of (A.35):

$$\frac{\partial wage}{\partial exper} = .19 - .008\,exper + .007\,educ.$$

This is the approximate change in wage due to increasing experience by one year. Notice that this partial effect depends on the initial level of *exper* and *educ*. For example, for a worker who is starting with $educ = 12$ and $exper = 5$, the next year of experience increases wage by about $.19 - .008(5) + .007(12) = .234$, or 23.4 cents per hour. The exact change can be calculated by computing (A.35) at $exper = 5$, $educ = 12$ and at $exper = 6$, $educ = 12$, and then taking the difference. This turns out to be .23, which is very close to the approximation.

Differential calculus plays an important role in minimizing and maximizing functions of one or more variables. If $f(x_1, x_2, \ldots, x_k)$ is a differentiable function of k variables, then a necessary condition for $x_1^*, x_2^*, \ldots, x_k^*$ to either minimize or maximize f over all possible values of x_j is

$$\frac{\partial f}{\partial x_i}(x_1^*, x_2^*, \ldots, x_k^*) = 0, j = 1, 2, \ldots, k. \tag{A.36}$$

In other words, all of the partial derivatives of f must be zero when they are evaluated at the x_h*. These are called the *first order conditions* for minimizing or maximizing a function. Practically, we hope to solve equation (A.36) for the x_h*. Then, we can use other criteria to determine whether we have minimized or maximized the function. We will not need those here. [See Sydsaeter and Hammond (1995) for a discussion of multivariable calculus and its use in optimizing functions.]

Summary

The math tools reviewed here are crucial for understanding regression analysis and the probability and statistics that are covered in Appendices B and C. The material on nonlinear functions—especially quadratic, logarithmic, and exponential functions—is critical for understanding modern applied economic research. The level of comprehension required of these functions does not include a deep knowledge of calculus, although calculus is needed for certain derivations.

Key Terms

Average	Intercept	Partial Effect
Ceteris Paribus	Linear Function	Percentage Change
Constant Elasticity Model	Log Function	Percentage Point Change
Derivative	Marginal Effect	Proportionate Change
Descriptive Statistic	Median	Relative Change
Diminishing Marginal Effect	Natural Logarithm	Semi-Elasticity
Elasticity	Nonlinear Function	Slope
Exponential Function	Partial Derivative	Summation Operator

Problems

1 The following table contains monthly housing expenditures for 10 families.

Family	Monthly Housing Expenditures (Dollars)
1	300
2	440
3	350
4	1,100
5	640
6	480
7	450
8	700
9	670
10	530

(i) Find the average monthly housing expenditure.
(ii) Find the median monthly housing expenditure.
(iii) If monthly housing expenditures were measured in hundreds of dollars, rather than in dollars, what would be the average and median expenditures?
(iv) Suppose that family number 8 increases its monthly housing expenditure to $900, but the expenditures of all other families remain the same. Compute the average and median housing expenditures.

2 Suppose the following equation describes the relationship between the average number of classes missed during a semester (*missed*) and the distance from school (*distance*, measured in miles):

$$missed = 3 + 0.2 \, distance.$$

(i) Sketch this line, being sure to label the axes. How do you interpret the intercept in this equation?
(ii) What is the average number of classes missed for someone who lives five miles away?
(iii) What is the difference in the average number of classes missed for someone who lives 10 miles away and someone who lives 20 miles away?

3 In Example A.2, quantity of compact discs was related to price and income by *quantity* = $120 - 9.8 \, price + .03 \, income$. What is the demand for CDs if *price* = 15 and *income* = 200? What does this suggest about using linear functions to describe demand curves?

4 Suppose the unemployment rate in the United States goes from 6.4% in one year to 5.6% in the next.
(i) What is the percentage point decrease in the unemployment rate?
(ii) By what percentage has the unemployment rate fallen?

5 Suppose that the return from holding a particular firm's stock goes from 15% in one year to 18% in the following year. The majority shareholder claims that "the stock return only increased by 3%," while the chief executive officer claims that "the return on the firm's stock increased by 20%." Reconcile their disagreement.

6 Suppose that Person A earns $35,000 per year and Person B earns $42,000.
(i) Find the exact percentage by which Person B's salary exceeds Person A's.
(ii) Now, use the difference in natural logs to find the approximate percentage difference.

7 Suppose the following model describes the relationship between annual salary (*salary*) and the number of previous years of labor market experience (*exper*):

$$\log(salary) = 10.6 + .027\ exper.$$

(i) What is *salary* when *exper* = 0? When *exper* = 5? (*Hint*: You will need to exponentiate.)
(ii) Use equation (A.28) to approximate the percentage increase in *salary* when *exper* increases by five years.
(iii) Use the results of part (i) to compute the exact percentage difference in salary when *exper* = 5 and *exper* = 0. Comment on how this compares with the approximation in part (ii).

8 Let *grthemp* denote the proportionate growth in employment, at the county level, from 1990 to 1995, and let *salestax* denote the county sales tax rate, stated as a proportion. Interpret the intercept and slope in the equation

$$grthemp = .043 - .78\ sales\ tax.$$

9 Suppose the yield of a certain crop (in bushels per acre) is related to fertilizer amount (in pounds per acre) as

$$yield = 120 + .19\sqrt{fertilizer}.$$

(i) Graph this relationship by plugging in several values for *fertilizer*.
(ii) Describe how the shape of this relationship compares with a linear relationship between *yield* and *fertilizer*.

10 Suppose that in a particular state a standardized test is given to all graduating seniors. Let *score* denote a student's score on the test. Someone discovers that performance on the test is related to the size of the student's graduating high school class. The relationship is quadratic:

$$score = 45.6 + .082\ class - .000147\ class^2,$$

where *class* is the number of students in the graduating class.

(i) How do you literally interpret the value 45.6 in the equation? By itself, is it of much interest? Explain.
(ii) From the equation, what is the optimal size of the graduating class (the size that maximizes the test score)? (Round your answer to the nearest integer.) What is the highest achievable test score?
(iii) Sketch a graph that illustrates your solution in part (ii).
(iv) Does it seem likely that *score* and *class* would have a deterministic relationship? That is, is it realistic to think that once you know the size of a student's graduating class you know, with certainty, his or her test score? Explain.

11 Consider the line

$$y = \beta_0 + \beta_1 x.$$

(i) Let (x_1, y_1) and (x_2, y_2) be two points on the line. Show that $(\bar{x}, \bar{y})$ is also on the line, where $\bar{x} = (x_1 + x_2)/2$ is the average of the two values and $\bar{y} = (y_1 + y_2)/2$.
(ii) Extend the result of part (i) to n points on the line, $\{(x_i, y_i): i = 1, \ldots, n\}$.

Appendix B

Fundamentals of Probability

This appendix covers key concepts from basic probability. Appendices B and C are primarily for review; they are not intended to replace a course in probability and statistics. However, all of the probability and statistics concepts that we use in the text are covered in these appendices.

Probability is of interest in its own right for students in business, economics, and other social sciences. For example, consider the problem of an airline trying to decide how many reservations to accept for a flight that has 100 available seats. If fewer than 100 people want reservations, then these should all be accepted. But what if more than 100 people request reservations? A safe solution is to accept at most 100 reservations. However, because some people book reservations and then do not show up for the flight, there is some chance that the plane will not be full even if 100 reservations are booked. This results in lost revenue to the airline. A different strategy is to book more than 100 reservations and to hope that some people do not show up, so the final number of passengers is as close to 100 as possible. This policy runs the risk of the airline having to compensate people who are necessarily bumped from an overbooked flight.

A natural question in this context is: Can we decide on the optimal (or best) number of reservations the airline should make? This is a nontrivial problem. Nevertheless, given certain information (on airline costs and how frequently people show up for reservations), we can use basic probability to arrive at a solution.

B-1 Random Variables and Their Probability Distributions

Suppose that we flip a coin 10 times and count the number of times the coin turns up heads. This is an example of an **experiment**. Generally, an experiment is any procedure that can, at least in theory, be infinitely repeated and has a well-defined set of outcomes. We could, in principle, carry out the coin-flipping procedure again and again. Before we flip the coin, we know that the number of heads appearing is an integer from 0 to 10, so the outcomes of the experiment are well defined.

A **random variable** is one that takes on numerical values and has an outcome that is determined by an experiment. In the coin-flipping example, the number of heads appearing in 10 flips of a coin is an example of a random variable. Before we flip the coin 10 times, we do not know how many times the coin will come up heads. Once we flip the coin 10 times and count the number of heads, we obtain the outcome of the random variable for this particular trial of the experiment. Another trial can produce a different outcome.

In the airline reservation example mentioned earlier, the number of people showing up for their flight is a random variable: before any particular flight, we do not know how many people will show up.

To analyze data collected in business and the social sciences, it is important to have a basic understanding of random variables and their properties. Following the usual conventions in probability and statistics throughout Appendices B and C, we denote random variables by uppercase letters, usually W, X, Y, and Z; particular outcomes of random variables are denoted by the corresponding lowercase letters, w, x, y, and z. For example, in the coin-flipping experiment, let X denote the number of heads appearing in 10 flips of a coin. Then, X is not associated with any particular value, but we know X will take on a value in the set $\{0, 1, 2, \ldots, 10\}$. A particular outcome is, say, $x = 6$.

We indicate large collections of random variables by using subscripts. For example, if we record last year's income of 20 randomly chosen households in the United States, we might denote these random variables by X_1, X_2, $\ldots$, X_{20}; the particular outcomes would be denoted x_1, x_2, $\ldots$, x_{20}.

As stated in the definition, random variables are always defined to take on numerical values, even when they describe qualitative events. For example, consider tossing a single coin, where the two outcomes are heads and tails. We can define a random variable as follows: $X = 1$ if the coin turns up heads, and $X = 0$ if the coin turns up tails.

A random variable that can only take on the values zero and one is called a **Bernoulli** (or **binary**) **random variable**. In basic probability, it is traditional to call the event $X = 1$ a "success" and the event $X = 0$ a "failure." For a particular application, the success-failure nomenclature might not correspond to our notion of a success or failure, but it is a useful terminology that we will adopt.

B-1a Discrete Random Variables

A **discrete random variable** is one that takes on only a finite or countably infinite number of values. The notion of "countably infinite" means that even though an infinite number of values can be taken on by a random variable, those values can be put in a one-to-one correspondence with the positive integers. Because the distinction between "countably infinite" and "uncountably infinite" is somewhat subtle, we will concentrate on discrete random variables that take on only a finite number of values. Larsen and Marx (1986, Chapter 3) provide a detailed treatment.

A Bernoulli random variable is the simplest example of a discrete random variable. The only thing we need to completely describe the behavior of a Bernoulli random variable is the probability that it takes on the value one. In the coin-flipping example, if the coin is "fair," then $P(X = 1) = 1/2$ (read as "the probability that X equals one is one-half"). Because probabilities must sum to one, $P(X = 0) = 1/2$, also.

Social scientists are interested in more than flipping coins, so we must allow for more general situations. Again, consider the example where the airline must decide how many people to book for a flight with 100 available seats. This problem can be analyzed in the context of several Bernoulli random variables as follows: for a randomly selected customer, define a Bernoulli random variable as $X = 1$ if the person shows up for the reservation, and $X = 0$ if not.

There is no reason to think that the probability of any particular customer showing up is 1/2; in principle, the probability can be any number between 0 and 1. Call this number θ, so that

$$P(X = 1) = \theta \tag{B.1}$$
$$P(X = 0) = 1 - \theta. \tag{B.2}$$

For example, if $\theta = .75$, then there is a 75% chance that a customer shows up after making a reservation and a 25% chance that the customer does not show up. Intuitively, the value of θ is crucial in determining the airline's strategy for booking reservations. Methods for *estimating* θ, given historical data on airline reservations, are a subject of mathematical statistics, something we turn to in Appendix C.

More generally, any discrete random variable is completely described by listing its possible values and the associated probability that it takes on each value. If X takes on the k possible values $\{x_1, \ldots, x_k\}$, then the probabilities $p_1, p_2, \ldots, p_k$ are defined by

$$p_j = P(X = x_j), j = 1, 2, \ldots, k, \qquad \text{[B.3]}$$

where each p_j is between 0 and 1 and

$$p_1 + p_2 + \ldots + p_k = 1. \qquad \text{[B.4]}$$

Equation (B.3) is read as: "The probability that X takes on the value x_j is equal to p_j."

Equations (B.1) and (B.2) show that the probabilities of success and failure for a Bernoulli random variable are determined entirely by the value of θ. Because Bernoulli random variables are so prevalent, we have a special notation for them: $X \sim \text{Bernoulli}(\theta)$ is read as "X has a Bernoulli distribution with probability of success equal to θ."

The **probability density function (pdf)** of X summarizes the information concerning the possible outcomes of X and the corresponding probabilities:

$$f(x_j) = p_j, j = 1, 2, \ldots, k, \qquad \text{[B.5]}$$

with $f(x) = 0$ for any x not equal to x_j for some j. In other words, for any real number x, $f(x)$ is the probability that the random variable X takes on the particular value x. When dealing with more than one random variable, it is sometimes useful to subscript the pdf in question: f_X is the pdf of X, f_Y is the pdf of Y, and so on.

Given the pdf of any discrete random variable, it is simple to compute the probability of any event involving that random variable. For example, suppose that X is the number of free throws made by a basketball player out of two attempts, so that X can take on the three values $\{0, 1, 2\}$. Assume that the pdf of X is given by

$$f(0) = .20, f(1) = .44, \text{ and } f(2) = .36.$$

The three probabilities sum to one, as they must. Using this pdf, we can calculate the probability that the player makes *at least* one free throw: $P(X \geq 1) = P(X = 1) + P(X = 2) = .44 + .36 = .80$. The pdf of X is shown in Figure B.1.

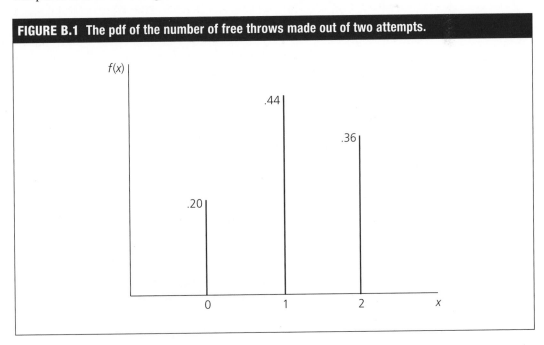

FIGURE B.1   The pdf of the number of free throws made out of two attempts.

B-1b Continuous Random Variables

A variable X is a **continuous random variable** if it takes on any real value with *zero* probability. This definition is somewhat counterintuitive because in any application we eventually observe some outcome for a random variable. The idea is that a continuous random variable X can take on so many possible values that we cannot count them or match them up with the positive integers, so logical consistency dictates that X can take on each value with probability zero. While measurements are always discrete in practice, random variables that take on numerous values are best treated as continuous. For example, the most refined measure of the price of a good is in terms of cents. We can imagine listing all possible values of price in order (even though the list may continue indefinitely), which technically makes price a discrete random variable. However, there are so many possible values of price that using the mechanics of discrete random variables is not feasible.

We can define a probability density function for continuous random variables, and, as with discrete random variables, the pdf provides information on the likely outcomes of the random variable. However, because it makes no sense to discuss the probability that a continuous random variable takes on a particular value, we use the pdf of a continuous random variable only to compute events involving a range of values. For example, if a and b are constants where $a < b$, the probability that X lies between the numbers a and b, $P(a \leq X \leq b)$, is the *area* under the pdf between points a and b, as shown in Figure B.2. If you are familiar with calculus, you recognize this as the *integral* of the function f between the points a and b. The entire area under the pdf must always equal one.

When computing probabilities for continuous random variables, it is easiest to work with the **cumulative distribution function (cdf)**. If X is any random variable, then its cdf is defined for any real number x by

$$F(x) \equiv P(X \leq x).$$

[B.6]

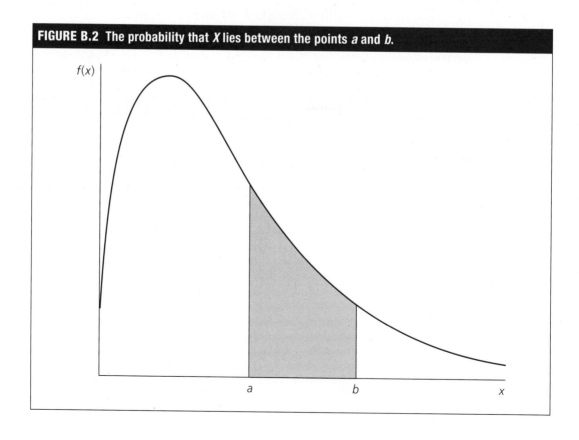

FIGURE B.2 The probability that X lies between the points a and b.

For discrete random variables, (B.6) is obtained by summing the pdf over all values x_j such that $x_j \leq x$. For a continuous random variable, $F(x)$ is the area under the pdf, f, to the left of the point x. Because $F(x)$ is simply a probability, it is always between 0 and 1. Further, if $x_1 < x_2$, then $P(X \leq x_1) \leq P(X \leq x_2)$, that is, $F(x_1) \leq F(x_2)$. This means that a cdf is an increasing (or at least a nondecreasing) function of x.

Two important properties of cdfs that are useful for computing probabilities are the following:

$$\text{For any number } c, \text{ P}(X > c) = 1 - F(c). \tag{B.7}$$

$$\text{For any numbers } a < b, \text{ P}(a < X \leq b) = F(b) - F(a). \tag{B.8}$$

In our study of econometrics, we will use cdfs to compute probabilities only for continuous random variables, in which case it does not matter whether inequalities in probability statements are strict or not. That is, for a continuous random variable X,

$$P(X \geq c) = P(X > c), \tag{B.9}$$

and

$$P(a < X < b) = P(a \leq X \leq b) = P(a \leq X < b) = P(a < X \leq b). \tag{B.10}$$

Combined with (B.7) and (B.8), equations (B.9) and (B.10) greatly expand the probability calculations that can be done using continuous cdfs.

Cumulative distribution functions have been tabulated for all of the important continuous distributions in probability and statistics. The most well known of these is the normal distribution, which we cover along with some related distributions in Section B-5.

B-2 Joint Distributions, Conditional Distributions, and Independence

In economics, we are usually interested in the occurrence of events involving more than one random variable. For example, in the airline reservation example referred to earlier, the airline might be interested in the probability that a person who makes a reservation shows up *and* is a business traveler; this is an example of a *joint probability*. Or, the airline might be interested in the following *conditional probability*: conditional on the person being a business traveler, what is the probability of his or her showing up? In the next two subsections, we formalize the notions of joint and conditional distributions and the important notion of *independence* of random variables.

B-2a Joint Distributions and Independence

Let X and Y be discrete random variables. Then, (X, Y) have a **joint distribution**, which is fully described by the *joint probability density function* of (X, Y):

$$f_{X,Y}(x, y) = P(X = x, Y = y), \tag{B.11}$$

where the right-hand side is the probability that $X = x$ and $Y = y$. When X and Y are continuous, a joint pdf can also be defined, but we will not cover such details because joint pdfs for continuous random variables are not used explicitly in this text.

In one case, it is easy to obtain the joint pdf if we are given the pdfs of X and Y. In particular, random variables X and Y are said to be independent if, and only if,

$$f_{X,Y}(x, y) = f_X(x)f_Y(y) \tag{B.12}$$

for all x and y, where f_X is the pdf of X and f_Y is the pdf of Y. In the context of more than one random variable, the pdfs f_X and f_Y are often called *marginal probability density functions* to distinguish them from the joint pdf $f_{X,Y}$. This definition of independence is valid for discrete and continuous random variables.

To understand the meaning of (B.12), it is easiest to deal with the discrete case. If X and Y are discrete, then (B.12) is the same as

$$P(X = x, Y = y) = P(X = x)P(Y = y);$$ [B.13]

in other words, the probability that $X = x$ and $Y = y$ is the product of the two probabilities $P(X = x)$ and $P(Y = y)$. One implication of (B.13) is that joint probabilities are fairly easy to compute, since they only require knowledge of $P(X = x)$ and $P(Y = y)$.

If random variables are not independent, then they are said to be *dependent*.

EXAMPLE B.1 **Free Throw Shooting**

Consider a basketball player shooting two free throws. Let X be the Bernoulli random variable equal to one if she or he makes the first free throw, and zero otherwise. Let Y be a Bernoulli random variable equal to one if he or she makes the second free throw. Suppose that she or he is an 80% free throw shooter, so that $P(X = 1) = P(Y = 1) = .8$. What is the probability of the player making both free throws?

If X and Y are independent, we can easily answer this question: $P(X = 1, Y = 1) = P(X = 1)P(Y = 1) = (.8)(.8) = .64$. Thus, there is a 64% chance of making both free throws. If the chance of making the second free throw depends on whether the first was made—that is, X and Y are not independent—then this simple calculation is not valid.

Independence of random variables is a very important concept. In the next subsection, we will show that if X and Y are independent, then knowing the outcome of X does not change the probabilities of the possible outcomes of Y, and vice versa. One useful fact about independence is that if X and Y are independent and we define new random variables $g(X)$ and $h(Y)$ for any functions g and h, then these new random variables are also independent.

There is no need to stop at two random variables. If $X_1, X_2, \ldots, X_n$ are discrete random variables, then their joint pdf is $f(x_1, x_2, \ldots, x_n) = P(X_1 = x_1, X_2 = x_2, \ldots, X_n = x_n)$. The random variables $X_1, X_2, \ldots, X_n$ are **independent random variables** if, and only if, their joint pdf is the product of the individual pdfs for any $(x_1, x_2, \ldots, x_n)$. This definition of independence also holds for continuous random variables.

The notion of independence plays an important role in obtaining some of the classic distributions in probability and statistics. Earlier, we defined a Bernoulli random variable as a zero-one random variable indicating whether or not some event occurs. Often, we are interested in the number of successes in a sequence of *independent* Bernoulli trials. A standard example of independent Bernoulli trials is flipping a coin again and again. Because the outcome on any particular flip has nothing to do with the outcomes on other flips, independence is an appropriate assumption.

Independence is often a reasonable approximation in more complicated situations. In the airline reservation example, suppose that the airline accepts n reservations for a particular flight. For each $i = 1, 2, \ldots, n$, let Y_i denote the Bernoulli random variable indicating whether customer i shows up: $Y_i = 1$ if customer i appears, and $Y_i = 0$ otherwise. Letting θ again denote the probability of success (using reservation), each Y_i has a Bernoulli(θ) distribution. As an approximation, we might assume that the Y_i are independent of one another, although this is not exactly true in reality: some people travel in groups, which means that whether or not a person shows up is not truly independent of whether all others show up. Modeling this kind of dependence is complex, however, so we might be willing to use independence as an approximation.

The variable of primary interest is the total number of customers showing up out of the n reservations; call this variable X. Since each Y_i is unity when a person shows up, we can write

$X = Y_1 + Y_2 + \ldots + Y_n$. Now, assuming that each Y_i has probability of success θ and that the Y_i are independent, X can be shown to have a **binomial distribution**. That is, the probability density function of X is

$$f(x) = \binom{n}{x}\theta^x(1 - \theta)^{n-x}, x = 0, 1, 2, \ldots, n,$$ [B.14]

where $\binom{n}{x} = \dfrac{n!}{x!(n - x)!}$, and for any integer n, $n!$ (read "n factorial") is defined as $n! = n \cdot (n - 1) \cdot (n - 2) \cdots 1$. By convention, $0! = 1$. When a random variable X has the pdf given in (B.14), we write $X \sim \text{Binomial}(n, \theta)$. Equation (B.14) can be used to compute $P(X = x)$ for any value of x from 0 to n.

If the flight has 100 available seats, the airline is interested in $P(X > 100)$. Suppose, initially, that $n = 120$, so that the airline accepts 120 reservations, and the probability that each person shows up is $\theta = .85$. Then, $P(X > 100) = P(X = 101) + P(X = 102) + \ldots + P(X = 120)$, and each of the probabilities in the sum can be found from equation (B.14) with $n = 120$, $\theta = .85$, and the appropriate value of x (101 to 120). This is a difficult hand calculation, but many statistical packages have commands for computing this kind of probability. In this case, the probability that more than 100 people will show up is about .659, which is probably more risk of overbooking than the airline wants to tolerate. If, instead, the number of reservations is 110, the probability of more than 100 passengers showing up is only about .024.

B-2b Conditional Distributions

In econometrics, we are usually interested in how one random variable, call it Y, is related to one or more other variables. For now, suppose that there is only one variable whose effects we are interested in, call it X. The most we can know about how X affects Y is contained in the **conditional distribution** of Y given X. This information is summarized by the *conditional probability density function*, defined by

$$f_{Y|X}(y|x) = f_{X,Y}(x, y)/f_X(x)$$ [B.15]

for all values of x such that $f_X(x) > 0$. The interpretation of (B.15) is most easily seen when X and Y are discrete. Then,

$$f_{Y|X}(y|x) = P(Y = y|X = x),$$ [B.16]

where the right-hand side is read as "the probability that $Y = y$ given that $X = x$." When Y is continuous, $f_{Y|X}(y|x)$ is not interpretable directly as a probability, for the reasons discussed earlier, but conditional probabilities are found by computing areas under the conditional pdf.

An important feature of conditional distributions is that, if X and Y are independent random variables, knowledge of the value taken on by X tells us nothing about the probability that Y takes on various values (and vice versa). That is, $f_{Y|X}(y|x) = f_Y(y)$, and $f_{X|Y}(x|y) = f_X(x)$.

EXAMPLE B.2	**Free Throw Shooting**

Consider again the basketball-shooting example, where two free throws are to be attempted. Assume that the conditional density is

$$f_{Y|X}(1|1) = .85, f_{Y|X}(0|1) = .15$$
$$f_{Y|X}(1|0) = .70, f_{Y|X}(0|0) = .30.$$

This means that the probability of the player making the second free throw depends on whether the first free throw was made: if the first free throw is made, the chance of making the second is .85; if the first free throw is missed, the chance of making the second is .70. This implies that X and Y are *not* independent; they are dependent.

We can still compute $P(X = 1, Y = 1)$ provided we know $P(X = 1)$. Assume that the probability of making the first free throw is .8, that is, $P(X = 1) = .8$. Then, from (B.15), we have

$$P(X = 1, Y = 1) = P(Y = 1|X = 1) \cdot P(X = 1) = (.85)(.8) = .68.$$

B-3 Features of Probability Distributions

For many purposes, we will be interested in only a few aspects of the distributions of random variables. The features of interest can be put into three categories: measures of central tendency, measures of variability or spread, and measures of association between two random variables. We cover the last of these in Section B-4.

B-3a A Measure of Central Tendency: The Expected Value

The expected value is one of the most important probabilistic concepts that we will encounter in our study of econometrics. If X is a random variable, the **expected value** (or expectation) of X, denoted $E(X)$ and sometimes μX or simply μ, is a weighted average of all possible values of X. The weights are determined by the probability density function. Sometimes, the expected value is called the *population mean*, especially when we want to emphasize that X represents some variable in a population.

The precise definition of expected value is simplest in the case that X is a discrete random variable taking on a finite number of values, say, $\{x_1, \ldots, x_k\}$. Let $f(x)$ denote the probability density function of X. The expected value of X is the weighted average

$$E(X) = x_1 f(x_1) + x_2 f(x_2) + \ldots + x_k f(x_k) \equiv \sum_{j=1}^{k} x_j f(x_j). \qquad \text{[B.17]}$$

This is easily computed given the values of the pdf at each possible outcome of X.

EXAMPLE B.3   **Computing an Expected Value**

Suppose that X takes on the values -1, 0, and 2 with probabilities $1/8$, $1/2$, and $3/8$, respectively. Then,

$$E(X) = (-1) \cdot (1/8) + 0 \cdot (1/2) + 2 \cdot (3/8) = 5/8.$$

This example illustrates something curious about expected values: the expected value of X can be a number that is not even a possible outcome of X. We know that X takes on the values -1, 0, or 2, yet its expected value is $5/8$. This makes the expected value deficient for summarizing the central tendency of certain discrete random variables, but calculations such as those just mentioned can be useful, as we will see later.

If X is a continuous random variable, then $E(X)$ is defined as an integral:

$$E(X) = \int_{-\infty}^{\infty} x f(x) dx, \qquad \text{[B.18]}$$

which we assume is well defined. This can still be interpreted as a weighted average. For the most common continuous distributions, $E(X)$ is a number that is a possible outcome of X. In this text, we will not need to compute expected values using integration, although we will draw on some well-known results from probability for expected values of special random variables.

Given a random variable X and a function $g(\cdot)$, we can create a new random variable $g(X)$. For example, if X is a random variable, then so is X^2 and $\log(X)$ (if $X > 0$). The expected value of $g(X)$ is, again, simply a weighted average:

$$E[g(X)] = \sum_{j=1}^{k} g(x_j) f_X(x_j)$$ [B.19]

or, for a continuous random variable,

$$E[g(X)] = \int_{-\infty}^{\infty} g(x) f_X(x) dx.$$ [B.20]

EXAMPLE B.4 **Expected Value of X^2**

For the random variable in Example B.3, let $g(X) = X^2$. Then,

$$E(X^2) = (-1)^2(1/8) + (0)^2(1/2) + (2)^2(3/8) = 13/8.$$

In Example B.3, we computed $E(X) = 5/8$, so that $[E(X)]^2 = 25/64$. This shows that $E(X^2)$ is *not* the same as $[E(X)]^2$. In fact, for a nonlinear function $g(X)$, $E[g(X)] \neq g[E(X)]$ (except in very special cases).

If X and Y are random variables, then $g(X, Y)$ is a random variable for any function g, and so we can define its expectation. When X and Y are both discrete, taking on values $\{x_1, x_2, \ldots, x_k\}$ and $\{y_1, y_2, \ldots, y_m\}$, respectively, the expected value is

$$E[g(X, Y)] = \sum_{h=1}^{k} \sum_{j=1}^{m} g(x_h, y_j) f_{X,Y}(x_h, y_j),$$

where $f_{X,Y}$ is the joint pdf of (X, Y). The definition is more complicated for continuous random variables since it involves integration; we do not need it here. The extension to more than two random variables is straightforward.

B-3b Properties of Expected Values

In econometrics, we are not so concerned with computing expected values from various distributions; the major calculations have been done many times, and we will largely take these on faith. We will need to manipulate some expected values using a few simple rules. These are so important that we give them labels:

Property E.1: For any constant c, $E(c) = c$.

Property E.2: For any constants a and b, $E(aX + b) = aE(X) + b$.

One useful implication of E.2 is that, if $\mu = E(X)$, and we define a new random variable as $Y = X - \mu$, then $E(Y) = 0$; in E.2, take $a = 1$ and $b = -\mu$.

As an example of Property E.2, let X be the temperature measured in Celsius at noon on a particular day at a given location; suppose the expected temperature is $E(X) = 25$. If Y is the temperature measured in Fahrenheit, then $Y = 32 + (9/5)X$. From Property E.2, the expected temperature in Fahrenheit is $E(Y) = 32 + (9/5){\cdot}E(X) = 32 + (9/5){\cdot}25 = 77$.

Generally, it is easy to compute the expected value of a linear function of many random variables.

Property E.3: If $\{a_1, a_2, \ldots, a_n\}$ are constants and $\{X_1, X_2, \ldots, X_n\}$ are random variables, then

$$E(a_1X_1 + a_2X_2 + \ldots + a_nX_n) = a_1E(X_1) + a_2E(X_2) + \ldots + a_nE(X_n).$$

Or, using summation notation,

$$E\left(\sum_{i=1}^{n} a_iX_i\right) = \sum_{i=1}^{n} a_iE(X_i). \qquad [B.21]$$

As a special case of this, we have (with each $a_i = 1$)

$$E\left(\sum_{i=1}^{n} X_i\right) = \sum_{i=1}^{n} E(X_i), \qquad [B.22]$$

so that the expected value of the sum is the sum of expected values. This property is used often for derivations in mathematical statistics.

EXAMPLE B.5   **Finding Expected Revenue**

Let $X_1, X_2,$ and X_3 be the numbers of small, medium, and large pizzas, respectively, sold during the day at a pizza parlor. These are random variables with expected values $E(X_1) = 25$, $E(X_2) = 57$, and $E(X_3) = 40$. The prices of small, medium, and large pizzas are $5.50, $7.60, and $9.15. Therefore, the expected revenue from pizza sales on a given day is

$$E(5.50\,X_1 + 7.60\,X_2 + 9.15\,X_3) = 5.50\,E(X_1) + 7.60\,E(X_2) + 9.15\,E(X_3)$$
$$= 5.50(25) + 7.60(57) + 9.15(40) = 936.70,$$

that is, $936.70. The actual revenue on any particular day will generally differ from this value, but this is the *expected* revenue.

We can also use Property E.3 to show that if $X \sim \text{Binomial}(n, \theta)$, then $E(X) = n\theta$. That is, the expected number of successes in n Bernoulli trials is simply the number of trials times the probability of success on any particular trial. This is easily seen by writing X as $X = Y_1 + Y_2 + \ldots + Y_n$, where each $Y_i \sim \text{Bernoulli}(\theta)$. Then,

$$E(X) = \sum_{i=1}^{n} E(Y_i) = \sum_{i=1}^{n} \theta = n\theta.$$

We can apply this to the airline reservation example, where the airline makes $n = 120$ reservations, and the probability of showing up is $\theta = .85$. The *expected* number of people showing up is $120(.85) = 102$. Therefore, if there are 100 seats available, the expected number of people showing up is too large; this has some bearing on whether it is a good idea for the airline to make 120 reservations.

Actually, what the airline should do is define a profit function that accounts for the net revenue earned per seat sold and the cost per passenger bumped from the flight. This profit function is random because the actual number of people showing up is random. Let r be the net revenue from each passenger. (You can think of this as the price of the ticket for simplicity.) Let c be the compensation owed to any passenger bumped from the flight. Neither r nor c is random; these are assumed to be known to the airline. Let Y denote profits for the flight. Then, with 100 seats available,

$$Y = rX \text{ if } X \le 100$$
$$= 100r - c(X - 100) \text{ if } X > 100.$$

The first equation gives profit if no more than 100 people show up for the flight; the second equation is profit if more than 100 people show up. (In the latter case, the net revenue from ticket sales is $100r$, since all 100 seats are sold, and then $c(X - 100)$ is the cost of making more than 100 reservations.) Using the fact that X has a Binomial(n,.85) distribution, where n is the number of reservations made, expected profits, E(Y), can be found as a function of n (and r and c). Computing E(Y) directly would be quite difficult, but it can be found quickly using a computer. Once values for r and c are given, the value of n that maximizes expected profits can be found by searching over different values of n.

B-3c Another Measure of Central Tendency: The Median

The expected value is only one possibility for defining the central tendency of a random variable. Another measure of central tendency is the **median**. A general definition of *median* is too complicated for our purposes. If X is continuous, then the median of X, say, m, is the value such that one-half of the area under the pdf is to the left of m, and one-half of the area is to the right of m.

When X is discrete and takes on a finite number of odd values, the median is obtained by ordering the possible values of X and then selecting the value in the middle. For example, if X can take on the values $\{-4, 0, 2, 8, 10, 13, 17\}$, then the median value of X is 8. If X takes on an even number of values, there are really two median values; sometimes, these are averaged to get a unique median value. Thus, if X takes on the values $\{-5, 3, 9, 17\}$, then the median values are 3 and 9; if we average these, we get a median equal to 6.

In general, the median, sometimes denoted Med(X), and the expected value, E(X), are different. Neither is "better" than the other as a measure of central tendency; they are both valid ways to measure the center of the distribution of X. In one special case, the median and expected value (or mean) are the same. If X has a **symmetric distribution** about the value μ, then μ is both the expected value and the median. Mathematically, the condition is $f(\mu + x) = f(\mu - x)$ for all x. This case is illustrated in Figure B.3.

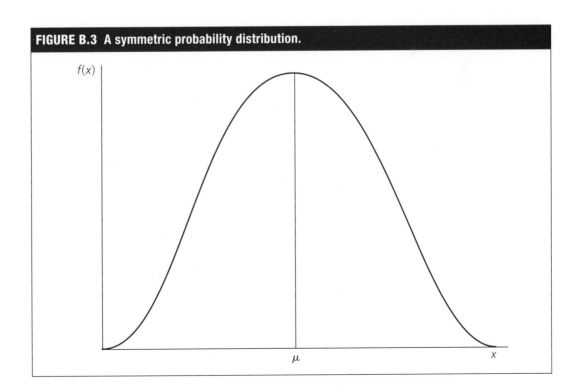

FIGURE B.3 A symmetric probability distribution.

B-3d Measures of Variability: Variance and Standard Deviation

Although the central tendency of a random variable is valuable, it does not tell us everything we want to know about the distribution of a random variable. Figure B.4 shows the pdfs of two random variables with the same mean. Clearly, the distribution of X is more tightly centered about its mean than is the distribution of Y. We would like to have a simple way of summarizing differences in the spreads of distributions.

B-3e Variance

For a random variable X, let $\mu = E(X)$. There are various ways to measure how far X is from its expected value, but the simplest one to work with algebraically is the squared difference, $(X - \mu)^2$. (The squaring eliminates the sign from the distance measure; the resulting positive value corresponds to our intuitive notion of distance and treats values above and below μ symmetrically.) This distance is itself a random variable since it can change with every outcome of X. Just as we needed a number to summarize the central tendency of X, we need a number that tells us how far X is from μ, *on average*. One such number is the **variance**, which tells us the expected distance from X to its mean:

$$\text{Var}(X) \equiv E[(X - \mu)^2].$$

[B.23]

Variance is sometimes denoted σ_X^2, or simply σ^2, when the context is clear. From (B.23), it follows that the variance is always nonnegative.

As a computational device, it is useful to observe that

$$\sigma^2 = E(X^2 - 2X\mu + \mu^2) = E(X^2) - 2\mu^2 + \mu^2 = E(X^2) - \mu^2.$$

[B.24]

In using either (B.23) or (B.24), we need not distinguish between discrete and continuous random variables: the definition of variance is the same in either case. Most often, we first compute $E(X)$, then $E(X^2)$, and then we use the formula in (B.24). For example, if $X \sim \text{Bernoulli}(\theta)$, then $E(X) = \theta$, and, since $X^2 = X$, $E(X^2) = \theta$. It follows from equation (B.24) that $\text{Var}(X) = E(X^2) - \mu^2 = \theta - \theta^2 = \theta(1 - \theta)$.

FIGURE B.4 Random variables with the same mean but different distributions.

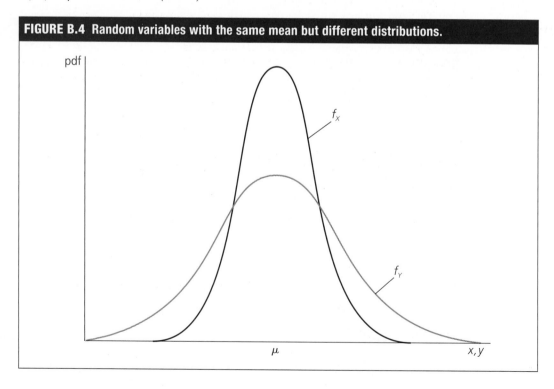

Two important properties of the variance follow.

Property VAR.1: $\text{Var}(X) = 0$ if, and only if, there is a constant c such that $P(X = c) = 1$, in which case $E(X) = c$.

This first property says that the variance of any constant is zero and if a random variable has zero variance, then it is essentially constant.

Property VAR.2: For any constants a and b, $\text{Var}(aX + b) = a^2\text{Var}(X)$.

This means that adding a constant to a random variable does not change the variance, but multiplying a random variable by a constant increases the variance by a factor equal to the *square* of that constant. For example, if X denotes temperature in Celsius and $Y = 32 + (9/5)X$ is temperature in Fahrenheit, then $\text{Var}(Y) = (9/5)^2\text{Var}(X) = (81/25)\text{Var}(X)$.

B-3f Standard Deviation

The **standard deviation** of a random variable, denoted $\text{sd}(X)$, is simply the positive square root of the variance: $\text{sd}(X) \equiv +\sqrt{\text{Var}(X)}$. The standard deviation is sometimes denoted σ_X, or simply σ, when the random variable is understood. Two standard deviation properties immediately follow from Properties VAR.1 and VAR.2.

Property SD.1: For any constant c, $\text{sd}(c) = 0$.

Property SD.2: For any constants a and b,

$$\text{sd}(aX + b) = |a|\text{sd}(X).$$

In particular, if $a > 0$, then $\text{sd}(aX) = a \cdot \text{sd}(X)$.

This last property makes the standard deviation more natural to work with than the variance. For example, suppose that X is a random variable measured in thousands of dollars, say, income. If we define $Y = 1,000X$, then Y is income measured in dollars. Suppose that $E(X) = 20$, and $\text{sd}(X) = 6$. Then, $E(Y) = 1,000E(X) = 20,000$, and $\text{sd}(Y) = 1,000 \cdot \text{sd}(X) = 6,000$, so that the expected value and standard deviation both increase by the same factor, 1,000. If we worked with variance, we would have $\text{Var}(Y) = (1,000)^2\text{Var}(X)$, so that the variance of Y is one million times larger than the variance of X.

B-3g Standardizing a Random Variable

As an application of the properties of variance and standard deviation—and a topic of practical interest in its own right—suppose that given a random variable X, we define a new random variable by subtracting off its mean m and dividing by its standard deviation σ:

$$Z \equiv \frac{X - \mu}{\sigma}, \qquad\qquad [\text{B.25}]$$

which we can write as $Z = aX + b$, where $a \equiv (1/\sigma)$ and $b \equiv -(\mu/\sigma)$. Then, from Property E.2,

$$E(Z) = aE(X) + b = (\mu/\sigma) - (\mu/\sigma) = 0.$$

From Property VAR.2,

$$\text{Var}(Z) = a^2\text{Var}(X) = (\sigma^2/\sigma^2) = 1.$$

Thus, the random variable Z has a mean of zero and a variance (and therefore a standard deviation) equal to one. This procedure is sometimes known as *standardizing* the random variable X, and Z is called a **standardized random variable**. (In introductory statistics courses, it is sometimes called the *z-transform* of X.) It is important to remember that the standard deviation, not the variance, appears in the denominator of (B.25). As we will see, this transformation is frequently used in statistical inference.

As a specific example, suppose that $E(X) = 2$, and $Var(X) = 9$. Then, $Z = (X - 2)/3$ has expected value zero and variance one.

B-3h Skewness and Kurtosis

We can use the standardized version of a random variable to define other features of the distribution of a random variable. These features are described by using what are called *higher order moments*. For example, the third moment of the random variable Z in (B.25) is used to determine whether a distribution is symmetric about its mean. We can write

$$E(Z^3) = E[(X - \mu)^3]/\sigma^3.$$

If X has a symmetric distribution about μ, then Z has a symmetric distribution about zero. (The division by σ^3 does not change whether the distribution is symmetric.) That means the density of Z at any two points z and $-z$ is the same, which means that, in computing $E(Z^3)$, positive values z^3 when $z > 0$ are exactly offset with the negative value $(-z)^3 = -z^3$. It follows that, if X is symmetric about zero, then $E(Z) = 0$. Generally, $E[(X - \mu)^3]/\sigma^3$ is viewed as a measure of **skewness** in the distribution of X. In a statistical setting, we might use data to estimate $E(Z^3)$ to determine whether an underlying population distribution appears to be symmetric. (Computer Exercise C5.4 in Chapter 5 provides an illustration.)

It also can be informative to compute the fourth moment of Z,

$$E(Z^4) = E[(X - \mu)^4]/\sigma^4.$$

Because $Z^4 \geq 0$, $E(Z^4) \geq 0$ (and, in any interesting case, strictly greater than zero). Without having a reference value, it is difficult to interpret values of $E(Z^4)$, but larger values mean that the tails in the distribution of X are thicker. The fourth moment $E(Z^4)$ is called a measure of **kurtosis** in the distribution of X. In Section B-5, we will obtain $E(Z^4)$ for the normal distribution.

B-4 Features of Joint and Conditional Distributions

B-4a Measures of Association: Covariance and Correlation

While the joint pdf of two random variables completely describes the relationship between them, it is useful to have summary measures of how, on average, two random variables vary with one another. As with the expected value and variance, this is similar to using a single number to summarize something about an entire distribution, which in this case is a joint distribution of two random variables.

B-4b Covariance

Let $\mu_X = E(X)$ and $\mu_Y = E(Y)$ and consider the random variable $(X - \mu_X)(Y - \mu_Y)$. Now, if X is above its mean and Y is above its mean, then $(X - \mu_X)(Y - \mu_Y) > 0$. This is also true if $X < \mu_X$ and $Y < \mu_Y$. On the other hand, if $X > \mu_X$ and $Y < \mu_Y$, or vice versa, then $(X - \mu_X)(Y - \mu_Y) < 0$. How, then, can this product tell us anything about the relationship between X and Y?

The **covariance** between two random variables X and Y, sometimes called the *population covariance* to emphasize that it concerns the relationship between two variables describing a population, is defined as the expected value of the product $(X - \mu_X)(Y - \mu_Y)$:

$$\text{Cov}(X, Y) \equiv \text{E}[(X - \mu_X)(Y - \mu_Y)], \qquad [\text{B.26}]$$

which is sometimes denoted σ_{XY}. If $\sigma_{XY} > 0$, then, on average, when X is above its mean, Y is also above its mean. If $\sigma_{XY} < 0$, then, on average, when X is above its mean, Y is below its mean.

Several expressions useful for computing $\text{Cov}(X, Y)$ are as follows:

$$\text{Cov}(X, Y) = \text{E}[(X - \mu_X)(Y - \mu_Y)] = \text{E}[(X - \mu_X)Y]$$
$$= \text{E}[X(Y - \mu_Y)] = \text{E}(XY) - \mu_X\mu_Y. \qquad [\text{B.27}]$$

It follows from (B.27), that if $\text{E}(X) = 0$ or $\text{E}(Y) = 0$, then $\text{Cov}(X, Y) = \text{E}(XY)$.

Covariance measures the amount of *linear* dependence between two random variables. A positive covariance indicates that two random variables move in the same direction, while a negative covariance indicates they move in opposite directions. Interpreting the *magnitude* of a covariance can be a little tricky, as we will see shortly.

Because covariance is a measure of how two random variables are related, it is natural to ask how covariance is related to the notion of independence. This is given by the following property.

Property COV.1: If X and Y are independent, then $\text{Cov}(X, Y) = 0$.

This property follows from equation (B.27) and the fact that $\text{E}(XY) = \text{E}(X)\text{E}(Y)$ when X and Y are independent. It is important to remember that the converse of COV.1 is *not* true: zero covariance between X and Y does not imply that X and Y are independent. In fact, there are random variables X such that, if $Y = X^2$, $\text{Cov}(X, Y) = 0$. [Any random variable with $\text{E}(X) = 0$ and $\text{E}(X^3) = 0$ has this property.] If $Y = X^2$, then X and Y are clearly not independent: once we know X, we know Y. It seems rather strange that X and X^2 could have zero covariance, and this reveals a weakness of covariance as a general measure of association between random variables. The covariance is useful in contexts when relationships are at least approximately linear.

The second major property of covariance involves covariances between linear functions.

Property COV.2: For any constants a_1, b_1, a_2, and b_2,

$$\text{Cov}(a_1X + b_1, a_2Y + b_2) = a_1a_2\text{Cov}(X, Y). \qquad [\text{B.28}]$$

An important implication of COV.2 is that the covariance between two random variables can be altered simply by multiplying one or both of the random variables by a constant. This is important in economics because monetary variables, inflation rates, and so on can be defined with different units of measurement without changing their meaning.

Finally, it is useful to know that the absolute value of the covariance between any two random variables is bounded by the product of their standard deviations; this is known as the *Cauchy-Schwartz inequality*.

Property COV.3: $|\text{Cov}(X, Y)| \leq \text{sd}(X)\text{sd}(Y)$.

B-4c Correlation Coefficient

Suppose we want to know the relationship between amount of education and annual earnings in the working population. We could let X denote education and Y denote earnings and then compute their covariance. But the answer we get will depend on how we choose to measure education and earnings.

Property COV.2 implies that the covariance between education and earnings depends on whether earnings are measured in dollars or thousands of dollars, or whether education is measured in months or years. It is pretty clear that how we measure these variables has no bearing on how strongly they are related. But the covariance between them does depend on the units of measurement.

The fact that the covariance depends on units of measurement is a deficiency that is overcome by the **correlation coefficient** between X and Y:

$$\text{Corr}(X, Y) \equiv \frac{\text{Cov}(X, Y)}{\text{sd}(X) \cdot \text{sd}(Y)} = \frac{\sigma_{XY}}{\sigma_X \sigma_Y}; \qquad \text{[B.29]}$$

the correlation coefficient between X and Y is sometimes denoted ρ_{XY} (and is sometimes called the *population correlation*).

Because σ_X and σ_Y are positive, $\text{Cov}(X, Y)$ and $\text{Corr}(X, Y)$ always have the same sign, and $\text{Corr}(X, Y) = 0$ if, and only if, $\text{Cov}(X, Y) = 0$. Some of the properties of covariance carry over to correlation. If X and Y are independent, then $\text{Corr}(X, Y) = 0$, but zero correlation does not imply independence. (Like the covariance, the correlation coefficient is also a measure of linear dependence.) However, the magnitude of the correlation coefficient is easier to interpret than the size of the covariance due to the following property.

Property CORR.1: $-1 \leq \text{Corr}(X, Y) \leq 1$.

If $\text{Corr}(X, Y) = 0$, or equivalently $\text{Cov}(X, Y) = 0$, then there is no linear relationship between X and Y, and X and Y are said to be **uncorrelated random variables**; otherwise, X and Y are *correlated*. $\text{Corr}(X, Y) = 1$ implies a perfect positive linear relationship, which means that we can write $Y = a + bX$ for some constant a and some constant $b > 0$. $\text{Corr}(X, Y) = -1$ implies a perfect negative linear relationship, so that $Y = a + bX$ for some $b < 0$. The extreme cases of positive or negative 1 rarely occur. Values of ρ_{XY} closer to 1 or -1 indicate stronger linear relationships.

As mentioned earlier, the correlation between X and Y is invariant to the units of measurement of either X or Y. This is stated more generally as follows.

Property CORR.2: For constants a_1, b_1, a_2, and b_2, with $a_1 a_2 > 0$,

$$\text{Corr}(a_1 X + b_1, a_2 Y + b_2) = \text{Corr}(X, Y).$$

If $a_1 a_2 < 0$, then

$$\text{Corr}(a_1 X + b_1, a_2 Y + b_2) = -\text{Corr}(X, Y).$$

As an example, suppose that the correlation between earnings and education in the working population is .15. This measure does not depend on whether earnings are measured in dollars, thousands of dollars, or any other unit; it also does not depend on whether education is measured in years, quarters, months, and so on.

B-4d Variance of Sums of Random Variables

Now that we have defined covariance and correlation, we can complete our list of major properties of the variance.

Property VAR.3: For constants a and b,

$$\text{Var}(aX + bY) = a^2 \text{Var}(X) + b^2 \text{Var}(Y) + 2ab\text{Cov}(X, Y).$$

It follows immediately that, if X and Y are uncorrelated—so that $\text{Cov}(X, Y) = 0$—then

$$\text{Var}(X + Y) = \text{Var}(X) + \text{Var}(Y) \tag{B.30}$$

and

$$\text{Var}(X - Y) = \text{Var}(X) + \text{Var}(Y). \tag{B.31}$$

In the latter case, note how the variance of the difference is the *sum of the variances*, not the difference in the variances.

As an example of (B.30), let X denote profits earned by a restaurant during a Friday night and let Y be profits earned on the following Saturday night. Then, $Z = X + Y$ is profits for the two nights. Suppose X and Y each have an expected value of $300 and a standard deviation of $15 (so that the variance is 225). Expected profits for the two nights is $E(Z) = E(X) + E(Y) = 2 \cdot (300) = 600$ dollars. If X and Y are independent, and therefore uncorrelated, then the variance of total profits is the sum of the variances: $\text{Var}(Z) = \text{Var}(X) + \text{Var}(Y) = 2 \cdot (225) = 450$. It follows that the standard deviation of total profits is $\sqrt{450}$ or about $21.21.

Expressions (B.30) and (B.31) extend to more than two random variables. To state this extension, we need a definition. The random variables $\{X_1, \ldots, X_n\}$ are **pairwise uncorrelated random variables** if each variable in the set is uncorrelated with every other variable in the set. That is, $\text{Cov}(X_i, X_j) = 0$, for all $i \neq j$.

Property VAR.4: If $\{X_1, \ldots, X_n\}$ are pairwise uncorrelated random variables and $a_i: i = 1, \ldots, n$ are constants, then

$$\text{Var}(a_1 X_1 + \ldots + a_n X_n) = a_1^2 \text{Var}(X_1) + \ldots + a_n^2 \text{Var}(X_n).$$

In summation notation, we can write

$$\text{Var}\left(\sum_{i=1}^{n} a_i X_i \right) = \sum_{i=1}^{n} a_i^2 \text{Var}(X_i). \tag{B.32}$$

A special case of Property VAR.4 occurs when we take $a_i = 1$ for all i. Then, for pairwise uncorrelated random variables, the variance of the sum is the sum of the variances:

$$\text{Var}\left(\sum_{i=1}^{n} X_i \right) = \sum_{i=1}^{n} \text{Var}(X_i). \tag{B.33}$$

Because independent random variables are uncorrelated (see Property COV.1), the variance of a sum of independent random variables is the sum of the variances.

If the X_i are not pairwise uncorrelated, then the expression for $\text{Var}(\sum_{i=1}^{n} a_i X_i)$ is much more complicated; we must add to the right-hand side of (B.32) the terms $2 a_i a_j \text{Cov}(x_i, x_j)$ for all $i > j$.

We can use (B.33) to derive the variance for a binomial random variable. Let $X \sim \text{Binomial}(n, \theta)$ and write $X = Y_1 + \ldots + Y_n$, where the Y_i are independent Bernoulli (θ) random variables. Then, by (B.33), $\text{Var}(X) = \text{Var}(Y_1) + \ldots + \text{Var}(Y_n) = n\theta(1 - \theta)$.

In the airline reservation example with $n = 120$ and $\theta = .85$, the variance of the number of passengers arriving for their reservations is $120(.85)(.15) = 15.3$, so the standard deviation is about 3.9.

B-4e Conditional Expectation

Covariance and correlation measure the linear relationship between two random variables and treat them symmetrically. More often in the social sciences, we would like to explain one variable, called Y, in terms of another variable, say, X. Further, if Y is related to X in a nonlinear fashion, we would like to know this. Call Y the explained variable and X the explanatory variable. For example, Y might be hourly wage, and X might be years of formal education.

We have already introduced the notion of the conditional probability density function of Y given X. Thus, we might want to see how the distribution of wages changes with education level. However, we usually want to have a simple way of summarizing this distribution. A single number will no longer suffice, since the distribution of Y given $X = x$ generally depends on the value of x. Nevertheless, we can summarize the relationship between Y and X by looking at the **conditional expectation** of Y given X, sometimes called the *conditional mean*. The idea is this. Suppose we know that X has taken on a particular value, say, x. Then, we can compute the expected value of Y, given that we know this outcome of X. We denote this expected value by $E(Y|X = x)$, or sometimes $E(Y|x)$ for shorthand. Generally, as x changes, so does $E(Y|x)$.

When Y is a discrete random variable taking on values $\{y_1, \ldots, y_m\}$, then

$$E(Y|x) = \sum_{j=1}^{m} y_j f_{Y|X}(y_j|x).$$

When Y is continuous, $E(Y|x)$ is defined by integrating $y f_{Y|X}(y|x)$ over all possible values of y. As with unconditional expectations, the conditional expectation is a weighted average of possible values of Y, but now the weights reflect the fact that X has taken on a specific value. Thus, $E(Y|x)$ is just some function of x, which tells us how the expected value of Y varies with x.

As an example, let (X, Y) represent the population of all working individuals, where X is years of education and Y is hourly wage. Then, $E(Y|X = 12)$ is the average hourly wage for all people in the population with 12 years of education (roughly a high school education). $E(Y|X = 16)$ is the average hourly wage for all people with 16 years of education. Tracing out the expected value for various levels of education provides important information on how wages and education are related. See Figure B.5 for an illustration.

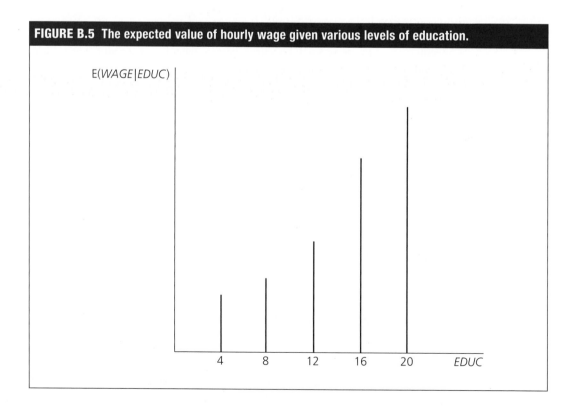

FIGURE B.5 The expected value of hourly wage given various levels of education.

In principle, the expected value of hourly wage can be found at each level of education, and these expectations can be summarized in a table. Because education can vary widely—and can even be measured in fractions of a year—this is a cumbersome way to show the relationship between average wage and amount of education. In econometrics, we typically specify simple functions that capture this relationship. As an example, suppose that the expected value of *WAGE* given *EDUC* is the linear function

$$E(WAGE|EDUC) = 1.05 + .45\ EDUC.$$

If this relationship holds in the population of working people, the average wage for people with eight years of education is $1.05 + .45(8) = 4.65$, or \$4.65. The average wage for people with 16 years of education is 8.25, or \$8.25. The coefficient on *EDUC* implies that each year of education increases the expected hourly wage by .45, or 45¢.

Conditional expectations can also be nonlinear functions. For example, suppose that $E(Y|x) = 10/x$, where *X* is a random variable that is always greater than zero. This function is graphed in Figure B.6. This could represent a demand function, where *Y* is quantity demanded and *X* is price. If *Y* and *X* are related in this way, an analysis of linear association, such as correlation analysis, would be incomplete.

B-4f Properties of Conditional Expectation

Several basic properties of conditional expectations are useful for derivations in econometric analysis.

Property CE.1: $E[c(X)|X] = c(X)$, for any function $c(X)$.

This first property means that functions of *X* behave as constants when we compute expectations conditional on *X*. For example, $E(X^2|X) = X^2$. Intuitively, this simply means that if we know *X*, then we also know X^2.

Property CE.2: For functions $a(X)$ and $b(X)$,

$$E[a(X)Y + b(X)|X] = a(X)E(Y|X) + b(X).$$

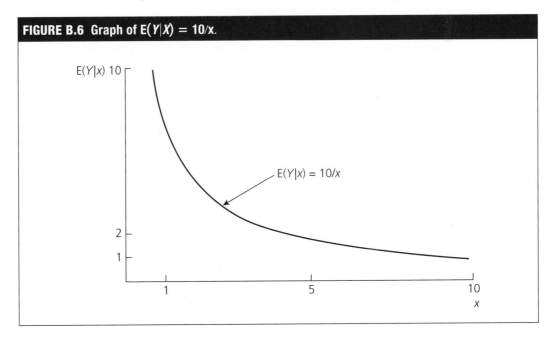

FIGURE B.6 Graph of E($Y|X$) = 10/x.

For example, we can easily compute the conditional expectation of a function such as $XY + 2X^2$: $E(XY + 2X^2|X) = XE(Y|X) + 2X^2$.

The next property ties together the notions of independence and conditional expectations.

Property CE.3: If X and Y are independent, then $E(Y|X) = E(Y)$.

This property means that, if X and Y are independent, then the expected value of Y given X does not depend on X, in which case, $E(Y|X)$ always equals the (unconditional) expected-value of Y. In the wage and education example, if wages were independent of education, then the average wages of high school and college graduates would be the same. Since this is almost certainly false, we cannot assume that wage and education are independent.

A special case of Property CE.3 is the following: if U and X are independent and $E(U) = 0$, then $E(U|X) = 0$.

There are also properties of the conditional expectation that have to do with the fact that $E(Y|X)$ is a function of X, say, $E(Y|X) = \mu(X)$. Because X is a random variable, $\mu(X)$ is also a random variable. Furthermore, $\mu(X)$ has a probability distribution and therefore an expected value. Generally, the expected value of $\mu(X)$ could be very difficult to compute directly. The **law of iterated expectations** says that the expected value of $\mu(X)$ is simply equal to the expected value of Y. We write this as follows.

Property CE.4: $E[E(Y|X)] = E(Y)$.

This property is a little hard to grasp at first. It means that, if we first obtain $E(Y|X)$ as a function of X and take the expected value of this (with respect to the distribution of X, of course), then we end up with $E(Y)$. This is hardly obvious, but it can be derived using the definition of expected values.

As an example of how to use Property CE.4, let $Y = WAGE$ and $X = EDUC$, where $WAGE$ is measured in hours and $EDUC$ is measured in years. Suppose the expected value of $WAGE$ given $EDUC$ is $E(WAGE|EDUC) = 4 + .60\ EDUC$. Further, $E(EDUC) = 11.5$. Then, the law of iterated expectations implies that $E(WAGE) = E(4 + .60\ EDUC) = 4 + .60\ E(EDUC) = 4 + .60(11.5) = 10.90$, or $10.90 an hour.

The next property states a more general version of the law of iterated expectations.

Property CE.4': $E(Y|X) = E[E(Y|X, Z)|X]$.

In other words, we can find $E(Y|X)$ in two steps. First, find $E(Y|X, Z)$ for any other random variable Z. Then, find the expected value of $E(Y|X, Z)$, conditional on X.

Property CE.5: If $E(Y|X) = E(Y)$, then $Cov(X, Y) = 0$ [and so $Corr(X, Y) = 0$]. In fact, *every* function of X is uncorrelated with Y.

This property means that, if knowledge of X does not change the expected value of Y, then X and Y *must* be uncorrelated, which implies that if X and Y are correlated, then $E(Y|X)$ must depend on X. The converse of Property CE.5 is not true: if X and Y are uncorrelated, $E(Y|X)$ *could* still depend on X. For example, suppose $Y = X^2$. Then, $E(Y|X) = X^2$, which is clearly a function of X. However, as we mentioned in our discussion of covariance and correlation, it is possible that X and X^2 are uncorrelated. The conditional expectation captures the nonlinear relationship between X and Y that correlation analysis would miss entirely.

Properties CE.4 and CE.5 have two important implications: if U and X are random variables such that $E(U|X) = 0$, then $E(U) = 0$, and U and X are uncorrelated.

Property CE.6: If $E(Y^2) < \infty$ and $E[g(X)^2] < \infty$ for some function g, then $E\{[Y - \mu(X)]^2|X\} \leq E\{[Y - g(X)]^2|X\}$ and $E\{[Y - \mu(X)]^2\} \leq E\{[Y - g(X)]^2\}$.

Property CE.6 is very useful in predicting or forecasting contexts. The first inequality says that, if we measure prediction inaccuracy as the *expected* squared prediction error, conditional on X, then the conditional mean is better than any other function of X for predicting Y. The conditional mean also minimizes the unconditional expected squared prediction error.

B-4g Conditional Variance

Given random variables X and Y, the variance of Y, conditional on $X = x$, is simply the variance associated with the conditional distribution of Y, given $X = x$: $\mathrm{E}\{[Y - \mathrm{E}(Y|x)]^2|x\}$. The formula

$$\mathrm{Var}(Y|X = x) = \mathrm{E}(Y^2|x) - [\mathrm{E}(Y|x)]^2$$

is often useful for calculations. Only occasionally will we have to compute a conditional variance. But we will have to make assumptions about and manipulate conditional variances for certain topics in regression analysis.

As an example, let $Y = SAVING$ and $X = INCOME$ (both of these measured annually for the population of all families). Suppose that $\mathrm{Var}(SAVING|INCOME) = 400 + .25\ INCOME$. This says that, as income increases, the variance in saving levels also increases. It is important to see that the relationship between the variance of $SAVING$ and $INCOME$ is totally separate from that between the *expected value* of $SAVING$ and $INCOME$.

We state one useful property about the conditional variance.

Property CV.1: If X and Y are independent, then $\mathrm{Var}(Y|X) = \mathrm{Var}(Y)$.

This property is pretty clear, since the distribution of Y given X does not depend on X, and $\mathrm{Var}(Y|X)$ is just one feature of this distribution.

B-5 The Normal and Related Distributions

B-5a The Normal Distribution

The normal distribution and those derived from it are the most widely used distributions in statistics and econometrics. Assuming that random variables defined over populations are normally distributed simplifies probability calculations. In addition, we will rely heavily on the normal and related distributions to conduct inference in statistics and econometrics—even when the underlying population is not necessarily normal. We must postpone the details, but be assured that these distributions will arise many times throughout this text.

A normal random variable is a continuous random variable that can take on any value. Its probability density function has the familiar bell shape graphed in Figure B.7.

Mathematically, the pdf of X can be written as

$$f(x) = \frac{1}{\sigma\sqrt{2\pi}}\exp[-(x - \mu)^2/2\sigma^2], \quad -\infty < x < \infty, \tag{B.34}$$

where $\mu = \mathrm{E}(X)$ and $\sigma^2 = \mathrm{Var}(X)$. We say that X has a **normal distribution** with expected value μ and variance σ^2, written as $X \sim \mathrm{Normal}(\mu, \sigma^2)$. Because the normal distribution is symmetric about μ, μ is also the median of X. The normal distribution is sometimes called the *Gaussian distribution* after the famous mathematician C. F. Gauss.

Certain random variables appear to roughly follow a normal distribution. Human heights and weights, test scores, and county unemployment rates have pdfs roughly the shape in Figure B.7. Other distributions, such as income distributions, do not appear to follow the normal probability function. In most countries, income is not symmetrically distributed about any value; the distribution is skewed toward the upper tail. In some cases, a variable can be transformed to achieve normality. A popular transformation is

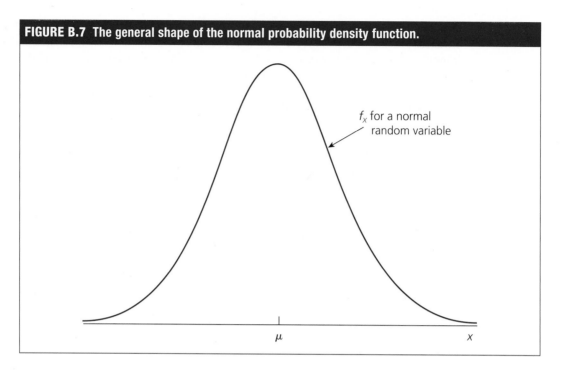

FIGURE B.7 The general shape of the normal probability density function.

f_X for a normal random variable

μ

X

the natural log, which makes sense for positive random variables. If X is a positive random variable, such as income, and $Y = \log(X)$ has a normal distribution, then we say that X has a *lognormal distribution*. It turns out that the lognormal distribution fits income distribution pretty well in many countries. Other variables, such as prices of goods, appear to be well described as lognormally distributed.

B-5b The Standard Normal Distribution

One special case of the normal distribution occurs when the mean is zero and the variance (and, therefore, the standard deviation) is unity. If a random variable Z has a Normal(0,1) distribution, then we say it has a **standard normal distribution**. The pdf of a standard normal random variable is denoted $\phi(z)$; from (B.34), with $\mu = 0$ and $\sigma^2 = 1$, it is given by

$$\phi(z) = \frac{1}{\sqrt{2\pi}} \exp(-z^2/2), \quad -\infty < z < \infty. \tag{B.35}$$

The standard normal cumulative distribution function is denoted $\Phi(z)$ and is obtained as the area under ϕ, to the left of z; see Figure B.8. Recall that $\Phi(z) = P(Z \leq z)$; because Z is continuous, $\Phi(z) = P(Z < z)$ as well.

No simple formula can be used to obtain the values of $\Phi(z)$ [because $\Phi(z)$ is the integral of the function in (B.35), and this integral has no closed form]. Nevertheless, the values for $\Phi(z)$ are easily tabulated; they are given for z between -3.1 and 3.1 in Table G.1 in Appendix G. For $z \leq -3.1$, $\Phi(z)$ is less than .001, and for $z \geq 3.1$, $\Phi(z)$ is greater than .999. Most statistics and econometrics software packages include simple commands for computing values of the standard normal cdf, so we can often avoid printed tables entirely and obtain the probabilities for any value of z.

Using basic facts from probability—and, in particular, properties (B.7) and (B.8) concerning cdfs—we can use the standard normal cdf for computing the probability of any event involving a standard normal random variable. The most important formulas are

$$P(Z > z) = 1 - \Phi(z), \tag{B.36}$$

$$P(Z < -z) = P(Z > z), \tag{B.37}$$

FIGURE B.8 The standard normal cumulative distribution function.

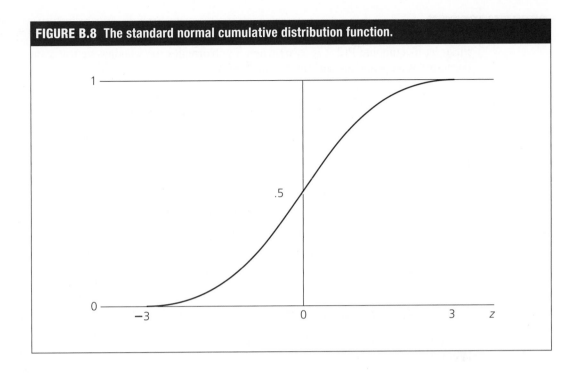

and

$$P(a \leq Z \leq b) = \Phi(b) - \Phi(a). \tag{B.38}$$

Because Z is a continuous random variable, all three formulas hold whether or not the inequalities are strict. Some examples include $P(Z > .44) = 1 - .67 = .33$, $P(Z < -.92) = P(Z > .92) = 1 - .821 = .179$, and $P(-1 < Z \leq .5) = .692 - .159 = .533$.

Another useful expression is that, for any $c > 0$,

$$P(|Z| > c) = P(Z > c) + P(Z < -c) \tag{B.39}$$
$$= 2 \cdot P(Z > c) = 2[1 - \Phi(c)].$$

Thus, the probability that the absolute value of Z is bigger than some positive constant c is simply twice the probability $P(Z > c)$; this reflects the symmetry of the standard normal distribution.

In most applications, we start with a normally distributed random variable, $X \sim \text{Normal}(\mu, \sigma^2)$, where μ is different from zero and $\sigma^2 \neq 1$. Any normal random variable can be turned into a standard normal using the following property.

Property Normal.1: If $X \sim \text{Normal}(\mu, \sigma^2)$, then $(X - \mu)/\sigma \sim \text{Normal}(0, 1)$.

Property Normal.1 shows how to turn any normal random variable into a standard normal. Thus, suppose $X \sim \text{Normal}(3, 4)$, and we would like to compute $P(X \leq 1)$. The steps always involve the normalization of X to a standard normal:

$$P(X \leq 1) = P(X - 3 \leq 1 - 3) = P\left(\frac{X - 3}{2} \leq -1\right)$$
$$= P(Z \leq -1) = \Phi(-1) = .159.$$

EXAMPLE B.6	**Probabilities for a Normal Random Variable**

First, let us compute $P(2 < X \le 6)$ when $X \sim \text{Normal}(4,9)$ (whether we use $<$ or $\le$ is irrelevant because X is a continuous random variable). Now,

$$P(2 < X \le 6) = P\left(\frac{2-4}{3} < \frac{X-4}{3} \le \frac{6-4}{3}\right) = P(-2/3 < Z \le 2/3)$$
$$= \Phi(.67) - \Phi(-.67) = .749 - .251 = .498.$$

Now, let us compute $P(|X| > 2)$:

$$P(|X| > 2) = P(X > 2) + P(X < -2)$$
$$= P[(X-4)/3 > (2-4)/3] + P[(X-4)/3 < (-2-4)/3]$$
$$= 1 - \Phi(-2/3) + \Phi(-2)$$
$$= 1 - .251 + .023 = .772.$$

B-5c Additional Properties of the Normal Distribution

We end this subsection by collecting several other facts about normal distributions that we will later use.

Property Normal.2: If $X \sim \text{Normal}(\mu, \sigma^2)$, then $aX + b \sim \text{Normal}(a\mu + b, a^2\sigma^2)$.

Thus, if $X \sim \text{Normal}(1,9)$, then $Y = 2X + 3$ is distributed as normal with mean $2E(X) + 3 = 5$ and variance $2^2 \cdot 9 = 36$; $\text{sd}(Y) = 2\text{sd}(X) = 2 \cdot 3 = 6$.

Earlier, we discussed how, in general, zero correlation and independence are not the same. In the case of normally distributed random variables, it turns out that zero correlation suffices for independence.

Property Normal.3: If X and Y are jointly normally distributed, then they are independent if, and only if, $\text{Cov}(X, Y) = 0$.

Property Normal.4: Any linear combination of independent, identically distributed normal random variables has a normal distribution.

For example, let X_i, for $i = 1, 2,$ and 3, be independent random variables distributed as $\text{Normal}(\mu, \sigma^2)$. Define $W = X_1 + 2X_2 - 3X_3$. Then, W is normally distributed; we must simply find its mean and variance. Now,

$$E(W) = E(X_1) + 2E(X_2) - 3E(X_3) = \mu + 2\mu - 3\mu = 0.$$

Also,

$$\text{Var}(W) = \text{Var}(X_1) + 4\text{Var}(X_2) + 9\text{Var}(X_3) = 14\sigma^2.$$

Property Normal.4 also implies that the average of independent, normally distributed random variables has a normal distribution. If $Y_1, Y_2, \ldots, Y_n$ are independent random variables and each is distributed as $\text{Normal}(\mu, \sigma^2)$, then

$$\bar{Y} \sim \text{Normal}(\mu, \sigma^2/n). \qquad \text{[B.40]}$$

This result is critical for statistical inference about the mean in a normal population.

Other features of the normal distribution are worth knowing, although they do not play a central role in the text. Because a normal random variable is symmetric about its mean, it has zero skewness, that is, $E[(X - \mu)^3] = 0$. Further, it can be shown that

$$E[(X - \mu)^4]/\sigma^4 = 3,$$

or $E(Z^4) = 3$, where Z has a standard normal distribution. Because the normal distribution is so prevalent in probability and statistics, the measure of kurtosis for any given random variable X (whose fourth moment exists) is often defined to be $E[(X - \mu)^4]/\sigma^4 - 3$, that is, relative to the value for the standard normal distribution. If $E[(X - \mu)^4]/\sigma^4 > 3$, then the distribution of X has fatter tails than the normal distribution (a somewhat common occurrence, such as with the t distribution to be introduced shortly); if $E[(X - \mu)^4]/\sigma^4 < 3$, then the distribution has thinner tails than the normal (a rarer situation).

B-5d The Chi-Square Distribution

The chi-square distribution is obtained directly from independent, standard normal random variables. Let Z_i, $i = 1, 2, \ldots, n$, be independent random variables, each distributed as standard normal. Define a new random variable as the sum of the squares of the Z_i:

$$X = \sum_{i=1}^{n} Z_i^2. \qquad \text{[B.41]}$$

Then, X has what is known as a **chi-square distribution** with n **degrees of freedom** (or df for short). We write this as $X \sim \chi_n^2$. The df in a chi-square distribution corresponds to the number of terms in the sum in (B.41). The concept of degrees of freedom will play an important role in our statistical and econometric analyses.

The pdf for chi-square distributions with varying degrees of freedom is given in Figure B.9; we will not need the formula for this pdf, and so we do not reproduce it here. From equation (B.41), it is clear that a chi-square random variable is always nonnegative, and that, unlike the normal distribution, the chi-square distribution is not symmetric about any point. It can be shown that if $X \sim \chi_n^2$, then the expected value of X is n [the number of terms in (B.41)], and the variance of X is $2n$.

B-5e The t Distribution

The t distribution is the workhorse in classical statistics and multiple regression analysis. We obtain a t distribution from a standard normal and a chi-square random variable.

Let Z have a standard normal distribution and let X have a chi-square distribution with n degrees of freedom. Further, assume that Z and X are independent. Then, the random variable

$$T = \frac{Z}{\sqrt{X/n}} \qquad \text{[B.42]}$$

has a t **distribution** with n degrees of freedom. We will denote this by $T \sim t_n$. The t distribution gets its degrees of freedom from the chi-square random variable in the denominator of (B.42).

The pdf of the t distribution has a shape similar to that of the standard normal distribution, except that it is more spread out and therefore has more area in the tails. The expected value of a t distributed random variable is zero (strictly speaking, the expected value exists only for $n > 1$),

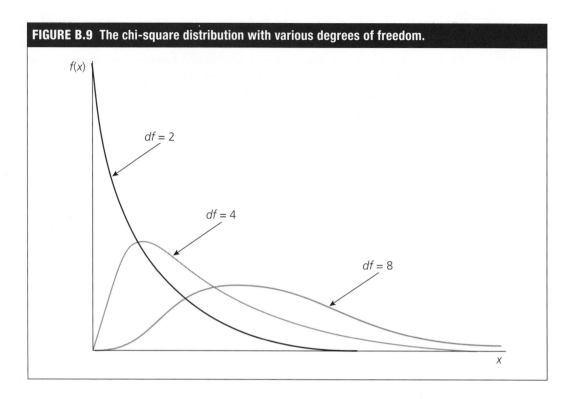

FIGURE B.9 The chi-square distribution with various degrees of freedom.

and the variance is $n/(n - 2)$ for $n > 2$. (The variance does not exist for $n \leq 2$ because the distribution is so spread out.) The pdf of the t distribution is plotted in Figure B.10 for various degrees of freedom. As the degrees of freedom gets large, the t distribution approaches the standard normal distribution.

B-5f The *F* Distribution

Another important distribution for statistics and econometrics is the F distribution. In particular, the F distribution will be used for testing hypotheses in the context of multiple regression analysis.

To define an F random variable, let $X_1 \sim \chi^2_{k_1}$ and $X_2 \sim \chi^2_{k_2}$ and assume that X_1 and X_2 are independent. Then, the random variable

$$F = \frac{(X_1/k_1)}{(X_2/k_2)}$$ [B.43]

has an **F distribution** with (k_1, k_2) degrees of freedom. We denote this as $F \sim F_{k_1, k_2}$. The pdf of the F distribution with different degrees of freedom is given in Figure B.11.

The order of the degrees of freedom in F_{k_1, k_2} is critical. The integer k_1 is called the *numerator degrees of freedom* because it is associated with the chi-square variable in the numerator. Likewise, the integer k_2 is called the *denominator degrees of freedom* because it is associated with the chi-square variable in the denominator. This can be a little tricky because (B.43) can also be written as $(X_1 k_2)/(X_2 k_1)$, so that k_1 appears in the denominator. Just remember that the numerator *df* is the integer associated with the chi-square variable in the numerator of (B.43), and similarly for the denominator *df*.

FIGURE B.10 The t distribution with various degrees of freedom.

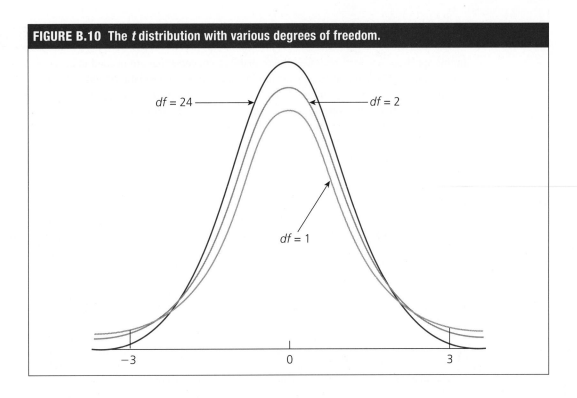

FIGURE B.11 The F_{k_1, k_2} distribution for various degrees of freedom, k_1 and k_2.

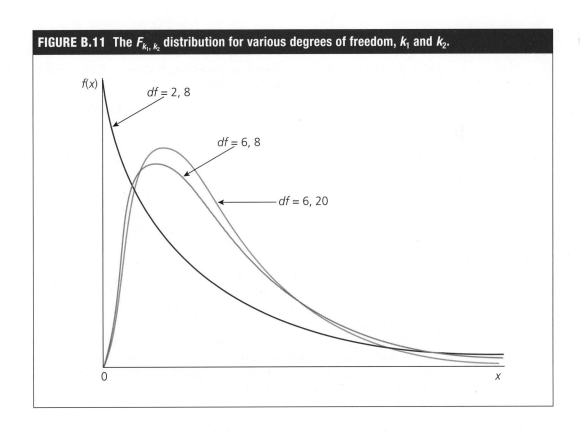

Summary

In this appendix, we have reviewed the probability concepts that are needed in econometrics. Most of the concepts should be familiar from your introductory course in probability and statistics. Some of the more advanced topics, such as features of conditional expectations, do not need to be mastered now—there is time for that when these concepts arise in the context of regression analysis in Part 1.

In an introductory statistics course, the focus is on calculating means, variances, covariances, and so on for particular distributions. In Part 1, we will not need such calculations: we mostly rely on the *properties* of expectations, variances, and so on that have been stated in this appendix.

Key Terms

Bernoulli (or Binary) Random Variable	Discrete Random Variable	Probability Density Function (pdf)
Binomial Distribution	Expected Value	Random Variable
Chi-Square Distribution	Experiment	Skewness
Conditional Distribution	*F* Distribution	Standard Deviation
Conditional Expectation	Independent Random Variables	Standard Normal Distribution
Continuous Random Variable	Joint Distribution	Standardized Random Variable
Correlation Coefficient	Kurtosis	Symmetric Distribution
Covariance	Law of Iterated Expectations	*t* Distribution
Cumulative Distribution Function (cdf)	Median	Uncorrelated Random Variables
Degrees of Freedom	Normal Distribution	Variance
	Pairwise Uncorrelated Random Variables	

Problems

1 Suppose that a high school student is preparing to take the SAT exam. Explain why his or her eventual SAT score is properly viewed as a random variable.

2 Let X be a random variable distributed as Normal(5,4). Find the probabilities of the following events:
  (i) $P(X \le 6)$.
  (ii) $P(X > 4)$.
  (iii) $P(|X - 5| > 1)$.

3 Much is made of the fact that certain mutual funds outperform the market year after year (that is, the return from holding shares in the mutual fund is higher than the return from holding a portfolio such as the S&P 500). For concreteness, consider a 10-year period and let the population be the 4,170 mutual funds reported in *The Wall Street Journal* on January 1, 1995. By saying that performance relative to the market is random, we mean that each fund has a 50–50 chance of outperforming the market in any year and that performance is independent from year to year.
  (i)   If performance relative to the market is truly random, what is the probability that any particular fund outperforms the market in all 10 years?
  (ii) Of the 4,170 mutual funds, what is the expected number of funds that will outperform the market in all 10 years?
  (iii) Find the probability that *at least* one fund out of 4,170 funds outperforms the market in all 10 years. What do you make of your answer?
  (iv) If you have a statistical package that computes binomial probabilities, find the probability that at least five funds outperform the market in all 10 years.

4 For a randomly selected county in the United States, let X represent the proportion of adults over age 65 who are employed, or the elderly employment rate. Then, X is restricted to a value between zero and one. Suppose that the cumulative distribution function for X is given by $F(x) = 3x^2 - 2x^3$ for $0 \le x \le 1$. Find the probability that the elderly employment rate is at least .6 (60%).

5 Just prior to jury selection for O. J. Simpson's murder trial in 1995, a poll found that about 20% of the adult population believed Simpson was innocent (after much of the physical evidence in the case had been revealed to the public). Ignore the fact that this 20% is an estimate based on a subsample from the population; for illustration, take it as the true percentage of people who thought Simpson was innocent prior to jury selection. Assume that the 12 jurors were selected randomly and independently from the population (although this turned out not to be true).

(i) Find the probability that the jury had at least one member who believed in Simpson's innocence prior to jury selection. [*Hint*: Define the Binomial(12,.20) random variable X to be the number of jurors believing in Simpson's innocence.]

(ii) Find the probability that the jury had at least two members who believed in Simpson's innocence. [*Hint*: $P(X \ge 2) = 1 - P(X \le 1)$ and $P(X \le 1) = P(X = 0) + P(X = 1)$.]

6 (Requires calculus) Let X denote the prison sentence, in years, for people convicted of auto theft in a particular state in the United States. Suppose that the pdf of X is given by

$$f(x) = (1/9)x^2, 0 < x < 3.$$

Use integration to find the expected prison sentence.

7 If a basketball player is a 74% free throw shooter, then, on average, how many free throws will he or she make in a game with eight free throw attempts?

8 Suppose that a college student is taking three courses: a two-credit course, a three-credit course, and a four-credit course. The expected grade in the two-credit course is 3.5, while the expected grade in the three- and four-credit courses is 3.0. What is the expected overall grade point average for the semester? (Remember that each course grade is weighted by its share of the total number of units.)

9 Let X denote the annual salary of university professors in the United States, measured in thousands of dollars. Suppose that the average salary is 52.3, with a standard deviation of 14.6. Find the mean and standard deviation when salary is measured in dollars.

10 Suppose that at a large university, college grade point average, *GPA*, and SAT score, *SAT*, are related by the conditional expectation $E(GPA|SAT) = .70 + .002\ SAT$.

(i) Find the expected *GPA* when $SAT = 800$. Find $E(GPA|SAT = 1{,}400)$. Comment on the difference.

(ii) If the average *SAT* in the university is 1,100, what is the average *GPA*? (*Hint*: Use Property CE.4.)

(iii) If a student's SAT score is 1,100, does this mean he or she will have the GPA found in part (ii)? Explain.

11 (i) Let X be a random variable taking on the values -1 and 1, each with probability 1/2. Find $E(X)$ and $E(X^2)$.

(ii) Now let X be a random variable taking on the values 1 and 2, each with probability 1/2. Find $E(X)$ and $E(1/X)$.

(iii) Conclude from parts (i) and (ii) that, in general,

$$E[g(X)] \ne g[E(X)]$$

for a nonlinear function $g(\cdot)$.

(iv) Given the definition of the F random variable in equation (B.43), show that

$$E(F) = E\left[\frac{1}{(X_2/k_2)}\right].$$

Can you conclude that $E(F) = 1$?

Appendix C

Fundamentals of Mathematical Statistics

C-1 Populations, Parameters, and Random Sampling

Statistical inference involves learning something about a population given the availability of a sample from that population. By **population**, we mean any well-defined group of subjects, which could be individuals, firms, cities, or many other possibilities. By "learning," we can mean several things, which are broadly divided into the categories of *estimation* and *hypothesis testing*.

A couple of examples may help you understand these terms. In the population of all working adults in the United States, labor economists are interested in learning about the return to education, as measured by the average percentage increase in earnings given another year of education. It would be impractical and costly to obtain information on earnings and education for the entire working population in the United States, but we can obtain data on a subset of the population. Using the data collected, a labor economist may report that his or her best estimate of the return to another year of education is 7.5%. This is an example of a *point estimate*. Or, she or he may report a range, such as "the return to education is between 5.6% and 9.4%." This is an example of an *interval estimate*.

An urban economist might want to know whether neighborhood crime watch programs are associated with lower crime rates. After comparing crime rates of neighborhoods with and without such programs in a sample from the population, he or she can draw one of two conclusions: neighborhood watch programs do affect crime, or they do not. This example falls under the rubric of hypothesis testing.

The first step in statistical inference is to identify the population of interest. This may seem obvious, but it is important to be very specific. Once we have identified the population, we can specify a model for the population relationship of interest. Such models involve probability distributions or features of probability distributions, and these depend on unknown parameters. Parameters are simply constants that determine the directions and strengths of relationships among variables. In the labor economics example just presented, the parameter of interest is the return to education in the population.

C-1a Sampling

For reviewing statistical inference, we focus on the simplest possible setting. Let Y be a random variable representing a population with a probability density function $f(y; \theta)$, which depends on the single parameter θ. The probability density function (pdf) of Y is assumed to be known except for the value of θ; different values of θ imply different population distributions, and therefore we are interested in the value of θ. If we can obtain certain kinds of samples from the population, then we can learn something about θ. The easiest sampling scheme to deal with is random sampling.

Random Sampling. If $Y_1, Y_2, \ldots, Y_n$ are independent random variables with a common probability density function $f(y; \theta)$, then $\{Y_1, \ldots, Y_n\}$ is said to be a **random sample** from $f(y; \theta)$ [or a random sample from the population represented by $f(y; \theta)$].

When $\{Y_1, \ldots, Y_n\}$ is a random sample from the density $f(y; \theta)$, we also say that the Y_i are *independent, identically distributed* (or *i.i.d.*) random variables from $f(y; \theta)$. In some cases, we will not need to entirely specify what the common distribution is.

The random nature of $Y_1, Y_2, \ldots, Y_n$ in the definition of random sampling reflects the fact that many different outcomes are possible before the sampling is actually carried out. For example, if family income is obtained for a sample of $n = 100$ families in the United States, the incomes we observe will usually differ for each different sample of 100 families. Once a sample is obtained, we have a set of numbers, say, $\{y_1, y_2, \ldots, y_n\}$, which constitute the data that we work with. Whether or not it is appropriate to assume the sample came from a random sampling scheme requires knowledge about the actual sampling process.

Random samples from a Bernoulli distribution are often used to illustrate statistical concepts, and they also arise in empirical applications. If $Y_1, Y_2, \ldots, Y_n$ are independent random variables and each is distributed as Bernoulli(θ), so that $P(Y_i = 1) = \theta$ and $P(Y_i = 0) = 1 - \theta$, then $\{Y_1, Y_2, \ldots, Y_n\}$ constitutes a random sample from the Bernoulli(θ) distribution. As an illustration, consider the airline reservation example carried along in Appendix B. Each Y_i denotes whether customer i shows up for his or her reservation; $Y_i = 1$ if passenger i shows up, and $Y_i = 0$ otherwise. Here, θ is the probability that a randomly drawn person from the population of all people who make airline reservations shows up for his or her reservation.

For many other applications, random samples can be assumed to be drawn from a normal distribution. If $\{Y_1, \ldots, Y_n\}$ is a random sample from the Normal(μ, σ^2) population, then the population is characterized by two parameters, the mean μ and the variance σ^2. Primary interest usually lies in μ, but σ^2 is of interest in its own right because making inferences about μ often requires learning about σ^2.

C-2 Finite Sample Properties of Estimators

In this section, we study what are called finite sample properties of estimators. The term "finite sample" comes from the fact that the properties hold for a sample of any size, no matter how large or small. Sometimes, these are called small sample properties. In Section C-3, we cover "asymptotic properties," which have to do with the behavior of estimators as the sample size grows without bound.

C-2a Estimators and Estimates

To study properties of estimators, we must define what we mean by an estimator. Given a random sample $\{Y_1, Y_2, \ldots, Y_n\}$ drawn from a population distribution that depends on an unknown parameter θ, an **estimator** of θ is a rule that assigns each possible outcome of the sample a value of θ. The rule is specified before any sampling is carried out; in particular, the rule is the same regardless of the data actually obtained.

As an example of an estimator, let $\{Y_1, \ldots, Y_n\}$ be a random sample from a population with mean μ. A natural estimator of μ is the average of the random sample:

$$\bar{Y} = n^{-1} \sum_{i=1}^{n} Y_i. \qquad [\text{C.1}]$$

$\bar{Y}$ is called the **sample average** but, unlike in Appendix A where we defined the sample average of a set of numbers as a descriptive statistic, $\bar{Y}$ is now viewed as an estimator. Given any outcome of the random variables $Y_1, \ldots, Y_n$, we use the same rule to estimate μ: we simply average them. For actual data outcomes $\{y_1, \ldots, y_n\}$, the **estimate** is just the average in the sample: $\bar{y} = (y_1 + y_2 + \ldots + y_n)/n$.

EXAMPLE C.1	**City Unemployment Rates**

Suppose we obtain the following sample of unemployment rates for 10 cities in the United States:

City	Unemployment Rate
1	5.1
2	6.4
3	9.2
4	4.1
5	7.5
6	8.3
7	2.6
8	3.5
9	5.8
10	7.5

Our estimate of the average city unemployment rate in the United States is $\bar{y} = 6.0$. Each sample generally results in a different estimate. But the *rule* for obtaining the estimate is the same, regardless of which cities appear in the sample, or how many.

More generally, an estimator W of a parameter θ can be expressed as an abstract mathematical formula:

$$W = h(Y_1, Y_2, \dots Y_n), \qquad [\text{C.2}]$$

for some known function h of the random variables $Y_1, Y_2, \dots, Y_n$. As with the special case of the sample average, W is a random variable because it depends on the random sample: as we obtain different random samples from the population, the value of W can change. When a particular set of numbers, say, $\{y_1, y_2, \dots, y_n\}$, is plugged into the function h, we obtain an *estimate* of θ, denoted $w = h(y_1, \dots, y_n)$. Sometimes, W is called a point estimator and w a point estimate to distinguish these from *interval* estimators and estimates, which we will come to in Section C-5.

For evaluating estimation procedures, we study various properties of the probability distribution of the random variable W. The distribution of an estimator is often called its **sampling distribution**, because this distribution describes the likelihood of various outcomes of W across different random samples. Because there are unlimited rules for combining data to estimate parameters, we need some sensible criteria for choosing among estimators, or at least for eliminating some estimators from consideration. Therefore, we must leave the realm of descriptive statistics, where we compute things such as the sample average to simply summarize a body of data. In mathematical statistics, we study the sampling distributions of estimators.

C-2b Unbiasedness

In principle, the entire sampling distribution of W can be obtained given the probability distribution of Y_i and the function h. It is usually easier to focus on a few features of the distribution of W in evaluating it as an estimator of θ. The first important property of an estimator involves its expected value.

Unbiased Estimator. An estimator, W of θ, is an **unbiased estimator** if

$$E(W) = \theta, \qquad [\text{C.3}]$$

for all possible values of θ.

If an estimator is unbiased, then its probability distribution has an expected value equal to the parameter it is supposed to be estimating. Unbiasedness does *not* mean that the estimate we get with any particular sample is equal to θ, or even very close to θ. Rather, if we could *indefinitely* draw random samples on Y from the population, compute an estimate each time, and then average these estimates over all random samples, we would obtain θ. This thought experiment is abstract because, in most applications, we just have one random sample to work with.

For an estimator that is not unbiased, we define its **bias** as follows.

Bias of an Estimator. If W is a **biased estimator** of θ, its bias is defined

$$\text{Bias}(W) \equiv \text{E}(W) - \theta. \tag{C.4}$$

Figure C.1 shows two estimators; the first one is unbiased, and the second one has a positive bias.

The unbiasedness of an estimator and the size of any possible bias depend on the distribution of Y and on the function h. The distribution of Y is usually beyond our control (although we often choose a *model* for this distribution): it may be determined by nature or social forces. But the choice of the rule h is ours, and if we want an unbiased estimator, then we must choose h accordingly.

Some estimators can be shown to be unbiased quite generally. We now show that the sample average $\overline{Y}$ is an unbiased estimator of the population mean μ, regardless of the underlying population distribution. We use the properties of expected values (E.1 and E.2) that we covered in Section B-3:

$$\text{E}(\overline{Y}) = \text{E}\left((1/n) \sum_{i=1}^{n} Y_i \right) = (1/n)\text{E}\left(\sum_{i=1}^{n} Y_i \right) = (1/n)\left(\sum_{i=1}^{n} \text{E}(Y_i) \right)$$

$$= (1/n)\left(\sum_{i=1}^{n} \mu \right) = (1/n)(n\mu) = \mu.$$

FIGURE C.1 An unbiased estimator, W_1, and an estimator with positive bias, W_2.

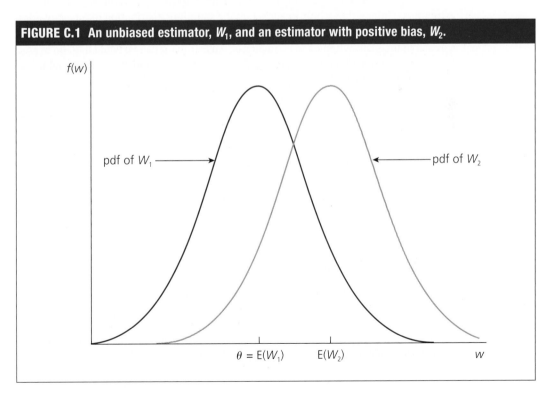

For hypothesis testing, we will need to estimate the variance σ^2 from a population with mean μ. Letting $\{Y_1, \ldots, Y_n\}$ denote the random sample from the population with $E(Y) = \mu$ and $Var(Y) = \sigma^2$, define the estimator as

$$S^2 = \frac{1}{n-1} \sum_{i=1}^{n} (Y_i - \overline{Y})^2, \qquad \text{[C.5]}$$

which is usually called the **sample variance**. It can be shown that S^2 is unbiased for σ^2: $E(S^2) = \sigma^2$. The division by $n - 1$, rather than n, accounts for the fact that the mean μ is estimated rather than known. If μ were known, an unbiased estimator of σ^2 would be $n^{-1} \sum_{i=1}^{n} (Y_i - \mu)^2$, but μ is rarely known in practice.

Although unbiasedness has a certain appeal as a property for an estimator—indeed, its antonym, "biased," has decidedly negative connotations—it is not without its problems. One weakness of unbiasedness is that some reasonable, and even some very good, estimators are not unbiased. We will see an example shortly.

Another important weakness of unbiasedness is that unbiased estimators exist that are actually quite poor estimators. Consider estimating the mean μ from a population. Rather than using the sample average $\overline{Y}$ to estimate μ, suppose that, after collecting a sample of size n, we discard all of the observations except the first. That is, our estimator of μ is simply $W \equiv Y_1$. This estimator is unbiased because $E(Y_1) = \mu$. Hopefully, you sense that ignoring all but the first observation is not a prudent approach to estimation: it throws out most of the information in the sample. For example, with $n = 100$, we obtain 100 outcomes of the random variable Y, but then we use only the first of these to estimate $E(Y)$.

C-2d The Sampling Variance of Estimators

The example at the end of the previous subsection shows that we need additional criteria to evaluate estimators. Unbiasedness only ensures that the sampling distribution of an estimator has a mean value equal to the parameter it is supposed to be estimating. This is fine, but we also need to know how spread out the distribution of an estimator is. An estimator can be equal to θ, on average, but it can also be very far away with large probability. In Figure C.2, W_1 and W_2 are both unbiased estimators of θ. But the distribution of W_1 is more tightly centered about θ: the probability that W_1 is greater than any given distance from θ is less than the probability that W_2 is greater than that same distance from θ. Using W_1 as our estimator means that it is less likely that we will obtain a random sample that yields an estimate very far from θ.

To summarize the situation shown in Figure C.2, we rely on the variance (or standard deviation) of an estimator. Recall that this gives a single measure of the dispersion in the distribution. The variance of an estimator is often called its **sampling variance** because it is the variance associated with a sampling distribution. Remember, the sampling variance is not a random variable; it is a constant, but it might be unknown.

We now obtain the variance of the sample average for estimating the mean μ from a population:

$$Var(\overline{Y}) = Var\left((1/n) \sum_{i=1}^{n} Y_i \right) = (1/n^2) Var\left(\sum_{i=1}^{n} Y_i \right) = (1/n^2) \left(\sum_{i=1}^{n} Var(Y_i) \right)$$

$$= (1/n^2) \left(\sum_{i=1}^{n} \sigma^2 \right) = (1/n^2)(n\sigma^2) = \sigma^2/n. \qquad \text{[C.6]}$$

Notice how we used the properties of variance from Sections B-3 and B-4 (VAR.2 and VAR.4), as well as the independence of the Y_i. To summarize: If $\{Y_i : i = 1, 2, \ldots, n\}$ is a random sample from a population with mean μ and variance σ^2, then $\overline{Y}$ has the same mean as the population, but its sampling variance equals the population variance, σ^2, divided by the sample size.

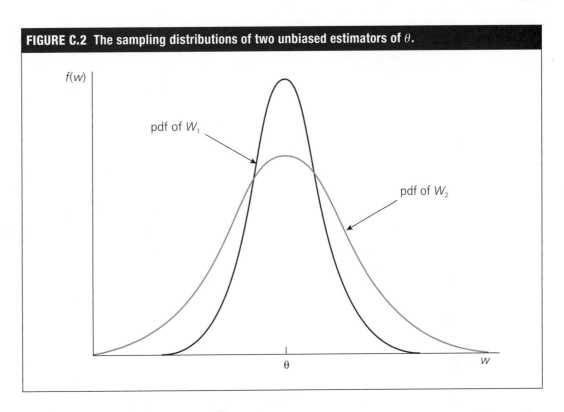

FIGURE C.2 The sampling distributions of two unbiased estimators of θ.

An important implication of $\text{Var}(\overline{Y}) = \sigma^2/n$ is that it can be made very close to zero by increasing the sample size n. This is a key feature of a reasonable estimator, and we return to it in Section C-3.

As suggested by Figure C.2, among unbiased estimators, we prefer the estimator with the smallest variance. This allows us to eliminate certain estimators from consideration. For a random sample from a population with mean μ and variance σ^2, we know that $\overline{Y}$ is unbiased and $\text{Var}(\overline{Y}) = \sigma^2/n$. What about the estimator Y_1, which is just the first observation drawn? Because Y_1 is a random draw from the population, $\text{Var}(Y_1) = \sigma^2$. Thus, the difference between $\text{Var}(Y_1)$ and $\text{Var}(\overline{Y})$ can be large even for small sample sizes. If $n = 10$, then $\text{Var}(Y_1)$ is 10 times as large as $\text{Var}(\overline{Y}) = \sigma^2/10$. This gives us a formal way of excluding Y_1 as an estimator of μ.

To emphasize this point, Table C.1 contains the outcome of a small simulation study. Using the statistical package Stata®, 20 random samples of size 10 were generated from a normal distribution, with $\mu = 2$ and $\sigma^2 = 1$; we are interested in estimating μ here. For each of the 20 random samples, we compute two estimates, y_1 and $\bar{y}$; these values are listed in Table C.1. As can be seen from the table, the values for y_1 are much more spread out than those for $\bar{y}$: y_1 ranges from -0.64 to 4.27, while $\bar{y}$ ranges only from 1.16 to 2.58. Further, in 16 out of 20 cases, $\bar{y}$ is closer than y_1 to $\mu = 2$. The average of y_1 across the simulations is about 1.89, while that for $\bar{y}$ is 1.96. The fact that these averages are close to 2 illustrates the unbiasedness of both estimators (and we could get these averages closer to 2 by doing more than 20 replications). But comparing just the average outcomes across random draws masks the fact that the sample average $\overline{Y}$ is far superior to Y_1 as an estimator of μ.

C-2e Efficiency

Comparing the variances of $\overline{Y}$ and Y_1 in the previous subsection is an example of a general approach to comparing different unbiased estimators.

Relative Efficiency. If W_1 and W_2 are two unbiased estimators of θ, W_1 is efficient relative to W_2 when $\text{Var}(W_1) \le \text{Var}(W_2)$ for all θ, with strict inequality for at least one value of θ.

TABLE C.1 Simulation of Estimators for a Normal(μ, 1) Distribution with $\mu = 2$		
Replication	y_1	$\bar{y}$
1	−0.64	1.98
2	1.06	1.43
3	4.27	1.65
4	1.03	1.88
5	3.16	2.34
6	2.77	2.58
7	1.68	1.58
8	2.98	2.23
9	2.25	1.96
10	2.04	2.11
11	0.95	2.15
12	1.36	1.93
13	2.62	2.02
14	2.97	2.10
15	1.93	2.18
16	1.14	2.10
17	2.08	1.94
18	1.52	2.21
19	1.33	1.16
20	1.21	1.75

Earlier, we showed that, for estimating the population mean μ, $\text{Var}(\bar{Y}) < \text{Var}(Y_1)$ for any value of σ^2 whenever $n > 1$. Thus, $\bar{Y}$ is efficient relative to Y_1 for estimating μ. We cannot always choose between unbiased estimators based on the smallest variance criterion: given two unbiased estimators of θ, one can have smaller variance from some values of θ, while the other can have smaller variance for other values of θ.

If we restrict our attention to a certain class of estimators, we can show that the sample average has the smallest variance. Problem C.2 asks you to show that $\bar{Y}$ has the smallest variance among all unbiased estimators that are also linear functions of $Y_1, Y_2, \ldots, Y_n$. The assumptions are that the Y_i have common mean and variance, and that they are pairwise uncorrelated.

If we do not restrict our attention to unbiased estimators, then comparing variances is meaningless. For example, when estimating the population mean μ, we can use a trivial estimator that is equal to zero, regardless of the sample that we draw. Naturally, the variance of this estimator is zero (since it is the same value for every random sample). But the bias of this estimator is $-\mu$, so it is a very poor estimator when $|\mu|$ is large.

One way to compare estimators that are not necessarily unbiased is to compute the **mean squared error (MSE)** of the estimators. If W is an estimator of θ, then the MSE of W is defined as $\text{MSE}(W) = \text{E}[(W - \theta)^2]$. The MSE measures how far, on average, the estimator is away from θ. It can be shown that $\text{MSE}(W) = \text{Var}(W) + [\text{Bias}(W)]^2$, so that $\text{MSE}(W)$ depends on the variance and bias (if any is present). This allows us to compare two estimators when one or both are biased.

C-3 Asymptotic or Large Sample Properties of Estimators

In Section C-2, we encountered the estimator Y_1 for the population mean μ, and we saw that, even though it is unbiased, it is a poor estimator because its variance can be much larger than that of the sample mean. One notable feature of Y_1 is that it has the same variance for any sample size. It seems reasonable to require any estimation procedure to improve as the sample size increases. For estimating a population mean μ, $\overline{Y}$ improves in the sense that its variance gets smaller as n gets larger; Y_1 does not improve in this sense.

We can rule out certain silly estimators by studying the *asymptotic* or *large sample* properties of estimators. In addition, we can say something positive about estimators that are not unbiased and whose variances are not easily found.

Asymptotic analysis involves approximating the features of the sampling distribution of an estimator. These approximations depend on the size of the sample. Unfortunately, we are necessarily limited in what we can say about how "large" a sample size is needed for asymptotic analysis to be appropriate; this depends on the underlying population distribution. But large sample approximations have been known to work well for sample sizes as small as $n = 20$.

C-3a Consistency

The first asymptotic property of estimators concerns how far the estimator is likely to be from the parameter it is supposed to be estimating as we let the sample size increase indefinitely.

Consistency. Let W_n be an estimator of θ based on a sample $Y_1, Y_2, \ldots, Y_n$ of size n. Then, W_n is a **consistent estimator** of θ if for every $\varepsilon > 0$,

$$P(|W_n - \theta| > \varepsilon) \to 0 \text{ as } n \to \infty. \tag{C.7}$$

If W_n is not consistent for θ, then we say it is **inconsistent**.

When W_n is consistent, we also say that θ is the **probability limit** of W_n, written as $\text{plim}(W_n) = \theta$.

Unlike unbiasedness—which is a feature of an estimator for a given sample size—consistency involves the behavior of the sampling distribution of the estimator as the sample size n gets large. To emphasize this, we have indexed the estimator by the sample size in stating this definition, and we will continue with this convention throughout this section.

Equation (C.7) looks technical, and it can be rather difficult to establish based on fundamental probability principles. By contrast, interpreting (C.7) is straightforward. It means that the distribution of W_n becomes more and more concentrated about θ, which roughly means that for larger sample sizes, W_n is less and less likely to be very far from θ. This tendency is illustrated in Figure C.3.

If an estimator is not consistent, then it does not help us to learn about θ, even with an unlimited amount of data. For this reason, consistency is a minimal requirement of an estimator used in statistics or econometrics. We will encounter estimators that are consistent under certain assumptions and inconsistent when those assumptions fail. When estimators are inconsistent, we can usually find their probability limits, and it will be important to know how far these probability limits are from θ.

As we noted earlier, unbiased estimators are not necessarily consistent, but those whose variances shrink to zero as the sample size grows *are* consistent. This can be stated formally: If W_n is an unbiased estimator of θ and $\text{Var}(W_n) \to 0$ as $n \to \infty$, then $\text{plim}(W_n) = \theta$. Unbiased estimators that use the entire data sample will usually have a variance that shrinks to zero as the sample size grows, thereby being consistent.

A good example of a consistent estimator is the average of a random sample drawn from a population with mean μ and variance σ^2. We have already shown that the sample average is unbiased for μ.

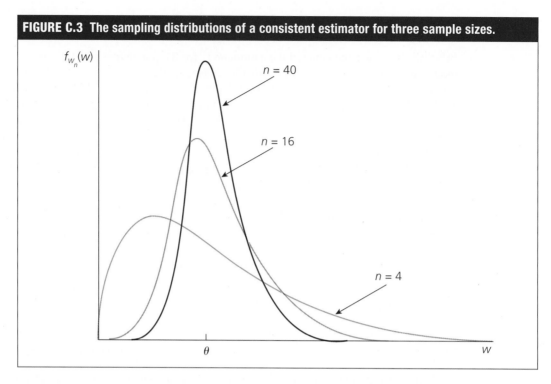

FIGURE C.3 The sampling distributions of a consistent estimator for three sample sizes.

In Equation (C.6), we derived $\text{Var}(\overline{Y}_n) = \sigma^2/n$ for any sample size n. Therefore, $\text{Var}(\overline{Y}_n) \to 0$ as $n \to \infty$, so $\overline{Y}_n$ is a consistent estimator of μ (in addition to being unbiased).

The conclusion that $\overline{Y}_n$ is consistent for μ holds even if $\text{Var}(\overline{Y}_n)$ does not exist. This classic result is known as the **law of large numbers (LLN)**.

Law of Large Numbers. Let $Y_1, Y_2, \ldots, Y_n$ be independent, identically distributed random variables with mean μ. Then,

$$\text{plim}(\overline{Y}_n) = \mu. \tag{C.8}$$

The law of large numbers means that, if we are interested in estimating the population average μ, we can get arbitrarily close to μ by choosing a sufficiently large sample. This fundamental result can be combined with basic properties of plims to show that fairly complicated estimators are consistent.

Property PLIM.1: Let θ be a parameter and define a new parameter, $\gamma = g(\theta)$, for some *continuous function* $g(\theta)$. Suppose that $\text{plim}(W_n) = \theta$. Define an estimator of γ by $G_n = g(W_n)$. Then,

$$\text{plim}(G_n) = \gamma. \tag{C.9}$$

This is often stated as

$$\text{plim } g(W_n) = g(\text{plim } W_n) \tag{C.10}$$

for a continuous function $g(\theta)$.

The assumption that $g(\theta)$ is continuous is a technical requirement that has often been described nontechnically as "a function that can be graphed without lifting your pencil from the paper." Because all the functions we encounter in this text are continuous, we do not provide a formal definition of a continuous function. Examples of continuous functions are $g(\theta) = a + b\theta$ for constants a and b, $g(\theta) = \theta^2$, $g(\theta) = 1/\theta$, $g(\theta) = \sqrt{\theta}$, $g(\theta) = \exp(\theta)$, and many variants on these. We will not need to mention the continuity assumption again.

As an important example of a consistent but biased estimator, consider estimating the standard deviation, σ, from a population with mean μ and variance σ^2. We already claimed that the sample variance $S_n^2 = (n-1)^{-1}\sum_{i=1}^{n}(Y_i - \overline{Y}_n)^2$ is unbiased for σ^2. Using the law of large numbers and some algebra, S_n^2 can also be shown to be consistent for σ^2. The natural estimator of $\sigma = \sqrt{\sigma^2}$ is $S_n = \sqrt{S_n^2}$ (where the square root is always the positive square root). S_n, which is called the **sample standard deviation**, is *not* an unbiased estimator because the expected value of the square root is *not* the square root of the expected value (see Section B-3). Nevertheless, by PLIM.1, plim $S_n = \sqrt{\text{plim } S_n^2} = \sqrt{\sigma^2} = \sigma$, so S_n is a consistent estimator of σ.

Here are some other useful properties of the probability limit:

Property PLIM.2: If $\text{plim}(T_n) = \alpha$ and $\text{plim}(U_n) = \beta$, then

   (i) $\text{plim}(T_n + U_n) = \alpha + \beta$;
   (ii) $\text{plim}(T_n U_n) = \alpha\beta$;
   (iii) $\text{plim}(T_n/U_n) = \alpha/\beta$, provided $\beta \neq 0$.

These three facts about probability limits allow us to combine consistent estimators in a variety of ways to get other consistent estimators. For example, let $\{Y_1, \ldots, Y_n\}$ be a random sample of size n on annual earnings from the population of workers with a high school education and denote the population mean by μ_Y. Let $\{Z_1, \ldots, Z_n\}$ be a random sample on annual earnings from the population of workers with a college education and denote the population mean by μ_Z. We wish to estimate the percentage difference in annual earnings between the two groups, which is $\gamma = 100 \cdot (\mu_Z - \mu_Y)/\mu_Y$. (This is the percentage by which average earnings for college graduates differs from average earnings for high school graduates.) Because $\overline{Y}_n$ is consistent for μ_Y and $\overline{Z}_n$ is consistent for μ_Z, it follows from PLIM.1 and part (iii) of PLIM.2 that

$$G_n \equiv 100 \cdot (\overline{Z}_n - \overline{Y}_n)/\overline{Y}_n$$

is a consistent estimator of γ. G_n is just the percentage difference between $\overline{Z}_n$ and $\overline{Y}_n$ in the sample, so it is a natural estimator. G_n is not an unbiased estimator of γ, but it is still a good estimator except possibly when n is small.

C-3b Asymptotic Normality

Consistency is a property of point estimators. Although it does tell us that the distribution of the estimator is collapsing around the parameter as the sample size gets large, it tells us essentially nothing about the *shape* of that distribution for a given sample size. For constructing interval estimators and testing hypotheses, we need a way to approximate the distribution of our estimators. Most econometric estimators have distributions that are well approximated by a normal distribution for large samples, which motivates the following definition.

Asymptotic Normality. Let $\{Z_n: n = 1, 2, \ldots\}$ be a sequence of random variables, such that for all numbers z,

$$P(Z_n \leq z) \to \Phi(z) \text{ as } n \to \infty, \tag{C.11}$$

where $\Phi(z)$ is the standard normal cumulative distribution function. Then, Z_n is said to have an *asymptotic standard normal distribution*. In this case, we often write $Z_n \overset{a}{\sim} \text{Normal}(0, 1)$. (The "*a*" above the tilde stands for "asymptotically" or "approximately.")

Property (C.11) means that the cumulative distribution function for Z_n gets closer and closer to the cdf of the standard normal distribution as the sample size n gets large. When **asymptotic normality** holds, for large n we have the approximation $P(Z_n \leq z) \approx \Phi(z)$. Thus, probabilities concerning Z_n can be approximated by standard normal probabilities.

The **central limit theorem (CLT)** is one of the most powerful results in probability and statistics. It states that the average from a random sample for *any* population (with finite variance), when standardized, has an asymptotic standard normal distribution.

Central Limit Theorem. Let $\{Y_1, Y_2, \ldots, Y_n\}$ be a random sample with mean μ and variance σ^2. Then,

$$Z_n = \frac{\overline{Y}_n - \mu}{\sigma/\sqrt{n}} \qquad [\text{C.12}]$$

has an asymptotic standard normal distribution.

The variable Z_n in (C.12) is the standardized version of $\overline{Y}_n$: we have subtracted off $E(\overline{Y}_n) = \mu$ and divided by $sd(\overline{Y}_n) = \sigma/\sqrt{n}$. Thus, regardless of the population distribution of Y, Z_n has mean zero and variance one, which coincides with the mean and variance of the standard normal distribution. Remarkably, the entire distribution of Z_n gets arbitrarily close to the standard normal distribution as n gets large.

We can write the standardized variable in equation (C.12) as $\sqrt{n}(\overline{Y}_n - \mu)/\sigma$, which shows that we must multiply the difference between the sample mean and the population mean by the square root of the sample size in order to obtain a useful limiting distribution. Without the multiplication by $\sqrt{n}$, we would just have $(\overline{Y}_n - \mu)/\sigma$, which converges in probability to zero. In other words, the distribution of $(\overline{Y}_n - \mu)/\sigma$ simply collapses to a single point as $n \to \infty$, which we know cannot be a good approximation to the distribution of $(\overline{Y}_n - \mu)/\sigma$ for reasonable sample sizes. Multiplying by $\sqrt{n}$ ensures that the variance of Z_n remains constant. Practically, we often treat $\overline{Y}_n$ as being approximately normally distributed with mean μ and variance σ^2/n, and this gives us the correct statistical procedures because it leads to the standardized variable in equation (C.12).

Most estimators encountered in statistics and econometrics can be written as functions of sample averages, in which case we can apply the law of large numbers and the central limit theorem. When two consistent estimators have asymptotic normal distributions, we choose the estimator with the smallest asymptotic variance.

In addition to the standardized sample average in (C.12), many other statistics that depend on sample averages turn out to be asymptotically normal. An important one is obtained by replacing σ with its consistent estimator S_n in equation (C.12):

$$\frac{\overline{Y}_n - \mu}{S_n/\sqrt{n}} \qquad [\text{C.13}]$$

also has an approximate standard normal distribution for large n. The exact (finite sample) distributions of (C.12) and (C.13) are definitely not the same, but the difference is often small enough to be ignored for large n.

Throughout this section, each estimator has been subscripted by n to emphasize the nature of asymptotic or large sample analysis. Continuing this convention clutters the notation without providing additional insight, once the fundamentals of asymptotic analysis are understood. Henceforth, we drop the n subscript and rely on you to remember that estimators depend on the sample size, and properties such as consistency and asymptotic normality refer to the growth of the sample size without bound.

C-4 General Approaches to Parameter Estimation

Until this point, we have used the sample average to illustrate the finite and large sample properties of estimators. It is natural to ask: Are there general approaches to estimation that produce estimators with good properties, such as unbiasedness, consistency, and efficiency?

The answer is yes. A detailed treatment of various approaches to estimation is beyond the scope of this text; here, we provide only an informal discussion. A thorough discussion is given in Larsen and Marx (1986, Chapter 5).

C-4a Method of Moments

Given a parameter θ appearing in a population distribution, there are usually many ways to obtain unbiased and consistent estimators of θ. Trying all different possibilities and comparing them on the basis of the criteria in Sections C-2 and C-3 is not practical. Fortunately, some methods have been shown to have good general properties, and, for the most part, the logic behind them is intuitively appealing.

In the previous sections, we have studied the sample average as an unbiased estimator of the population average and the sample variance as an unbiased estimator of the population variance. These estimators are examples of **method of moments** estimators. Generally, method of moments estimation proceeds as follows. The parameter θ is shown to be related to some expected value in the distribution of Y, usually $E(Y)$ or $E(Y^2)$ (although more exotic choices are sometimes used). Suppose, for example, that the parameter of interest, θ, is related to the population mean as $\theta = g(\mu)$ for some function g. Because the sample average $\bar{Y}$ is an unbiased and consistent estimator of μ, it is natural to replace μ with $\bar{Y}$, which gives us the estimator $g(\bar{Y})$ of θ. The estimator $g(\bar{Y})$ is consistent for θ, and if $g(\mu)$ is a linear function of μ, then $g(\bar{Y})$ is unbiased as well. What we have done is replace the population moment, μ, with its sample counterpart, $\bar{Y}$. This is where the name "method of moments" comes from.

We cover two additional method of moments estimators that will be useful for our discussion of regression analysis. Recall that the covariance between two random variables X and Y is defined as $\sigma_{XY} = E[(X - \mu_X)(Y - \mu_Y)]$. The method of moments suggests estimating σ_{XY} by $n^{-1}\sum_{i=1}^{n}(X_i - \bar{X})(Y_i - \bar{Y})$. This is a consistent estimator of σ_{XY}, but it turns out to be biased for essentially the same reason that the sample variance is biased if n, rather than $n - 1$, is used as the divisor. The **sample covariance** is defined as

$$S_{XY} = \frac{1}{n-1}\sum_{i=1}^{n}(X_i - \bar{X})(Y_i - \bar{Y}). \qquad \text{[C.14]}$$

It can be shown that this is an unbiased estimator of σ_{XY}. (Replacing n with $n - 1$ makes no difference as the sample size grows indefinitely, so this estimator is still consistent.)

As we discussed in Section B-4, the covariance between two variables is often difficult to interpret. Usually, we are more interested in correlation. Because the population correlation is $\rho_{XY} = \sigma_{XY}/(\sigma_X\sigma_Y)$, the method of moments suggests estimating ρ_{XY} as

$$R_{XY} = \frac{S_{XY}}{S_X S_Y} = \frac{\sum_{i=1}^{n}(X_i - \bar{X})(Y_i - \bar{Y})}{\left(\sum_{i=1}^{n}(X_i - \bar{X})^2\right)^{1/2}\left(\sum_{i=1}^{n}(Y_i - \bar{Y})^2\right)^{1/2}}, \qquad \text{[C.15]}$$

which is called the **sample correlation coefficient** (or *sample correlation* for short). Notice that we have canceled the division by $n - 1$ in the sample covariance and the sample standard deviations. In fact, we could divide each of these by n, and we would arrive at the same final formula.

It can be shown that the sample correlation coefficient is always in the interval $[-1, 1]$, as it should be. Because S_{XY}, S_X, and S_Y are consistent for the corresponding population parameter, R_{XY} is a consistent estimator of the population correlation, ρ_{XY}. However, R_{XY} is a biased estimator for two reasons. First, S_X and S_Y are biased estimators of σ_X and σ_Y, respectively. Second, R_{XY} is a ratio of estimators, so it would not be unbiased, even if S_X and S_Y were. For our purposes, this is not important, although the fact that no unbiased estimator of ρ_{XY} exists is a classical result in mathematical statistics.

C-4b Maximum Likelihood

Another general approach to estimation is the method of *maximum likelihood*, a topic covered in many introductory statistics courses. A brief summary in the simplest case will suffice here. Let $\{Y_1, Y_2, \ldots, Y_n\}$ be a random sample from the population distribution $f(y; \theta)$. Because of the random sampling assumption, the joint distribution of $\{Y_1, Y_2, \ldots, Y_n\}$ is simply the product of the densities: $f(y_1; \theta)f(y_2; \theta) \cdots f(y_n; \theta)$. In the discrete case, this is $P(Y_1 = y_1, Y_2 = y_2, \ldots, Y_n = y_n)$. Now, define the *likelihood function* as

$$L(\theta; Y_1, \ldots, Y_n) = f(Y_1; \theta)f(Y_2; \theta) \cdots f(Y_n; \theta),$$

which is a random variable because it depends on the outcome of the random sample $\{Y_1, Y_2, \ldots, Y_n\}$. The **maximum likelihood estimator** of θ, call it W, is the value of θ that maximizes the likelihood function. (This is why we write L as a function of θ, followed by the random sample.) Clearly, this value depends on the random sample. The maximum likelihood principle says that, out of all the possible values for θ, the value that makes the likelihood of the observed data largest should be chosen. Intuitively, this is a reasonable approach to estimating θ.

Usually, it is more convenient to work with the *log-likelihood function*, which is obtained by taking the natural log of the likelihood function:

$$\log[L(\theta; Y_1, \ldots, Y_n)] = \sum_{i=1}^{n} \log[f(Y_i; \theta)], \qquad \text{[C.16]}$$

where we use the fact that the log of the product is the sum of the logs. Because (C.16) is the sum of independent, identically distributed random variables, analyzing estimators that come from (C.16) is relatively easy.

Maximum likelihood estimation (MLE) is usually consistent and sometimes unbiased. But so are many other estimators. The widespread appeal of MLE is that it is generally the most asymptotically efficient estimator when the population model $f(y; \theta)$ is correctly specified. In addition, the MLE is sometimes the **minimum variance unbiased estimator**; that is, it has the smallest variance among all unbiased estimators of θ. [See Larsen and Marx (1986, Chapter 5) for verification of these claims.]

In Chapter 17, we will need maximum likelihood to estimate the parameters of more advanced econometric models. In econometrics, we are almost always interested in the distribution of Y conditional on a set of explanatory variables, say, $X_1, X_2, \ldots, X_k$. Then, we replace the density in (C.16) with $f(Y_i | X_{i1}, \ldots, X_{ik}; \theta_1, \ldots, \theta_p)$, where this density is allowed to depend on p parameters, $\theta_1, \ldots, \theta_p$. Fortunately, for successful application of maximum likelihood methods, we do not need to delve much into the computational issues or the large-sample statistical theory. Wooldridge (2010, Chapter 13) covers the theory of MLE.

C-4c Least Squares

A third kind of estimator, and one that plays a major role throughout the text, is called a **least squares estimator**. We have already seen an example of least squares: the sample mean, $\overline{Y}$, is a least squares estimator of the population mean, μ. We already know $\overline{Y}$ is a method of moments estimator. What makes it a least squares estimator? It can be shown that the value of m that makes the sum of squared deviations

$$\sum_{i=1}^{n} (Y_i - m)^2$$

as small as possible is $m = \overline{Y}$. Showing this is not difficult, but we omit the algebra.

For some important distributions, including the normal and the Bernoulli, the sample average $\overline{Y}$ is also the maximum likelihood estimator of the population mean μ. Thus, the principles of least squares, method of moments, and maximum likelihood often result in the *same* estimator. In other cases, the estimators are similar but not identical.

C-5 Interval Estimation and Confidence Intervals

C-5a The Nature of Interval Estimation

A point estimate obtained from a particular sample does not, by itself, provide enough information for testing economic theories or for informing policy discussions. A point estimate may be the researcher's best guess at the population value, but, by its nature, it provides no information about how close the estimate is "likely" to be to the population parameter. As an example, suppose a researcher reports, on the basis of a random sample of workers, that job training grants increase hourly wage by 6.4%. How are we to know whether or not this is close to the effect in the population of workers who could have been trained? Because we do not know the population value, we cannot know how close an estimate is for a particular sample. However, we can make statements involving probabilities, and this is where interval estimation comes in.

We already know one way of assessing the uncertainty in an estimator: find its sampling standard deviation. Reporting the standard deviation of the estimator, along with the point estimate, provides some information on the accuracy of our estimate. However, even if the problem of the standard deviation's dependence on unknown population parameters is ignored, reporting the standard deviation along with the point estimate makes no direct statement about where the population value is likely to lie in relation to the estimate. This limitation is overcome by constructing a **confidence interval**.

We illustrate the concept of a confidence interval with an example. Suppose the population has a Normal$(\mu, 1)$ distribution and let $\{Y_1, \ldots, Y_n\}$ be a random sample from this population. (We assume that the variance of the population is known and equal to unity for the sake of illustration; we then show what to do in the more realistic case that the variance is unknown.) The sample average, $\overline{Y}$, has a normal distribution with mean μ and variance $1/n$: $\overline{Y} \sim$ Normal$(\mu, 1/n)$. From this, we can standardize $\overline{Y}$, and, because the standardized version of $\overline{Y}$ has a standard normal distribution, we have

$$P\left(-1.96 < \frac{\overline{Y} - \mu}{1/\sqrt{n}} < 1.96\right) = .95.$$

The event in parentheses is identical to the event $\overline{Y} - 1.96/\sqrt{n} < \mu < \overline{Y} + 1.96/\sqrt{n}$, so

$$P(\overline{Y} - 1.96/\sqrt{n} < \mu < \overline{Y} + 1.96\sqrt{n}) = .95. \qquad \text{[C.17]}$$

Equation (C.17) is interesting because it tells us that the probability that the random interval $[\overline{Y} - 1.96/\sqrt{n}, \overline{Y} + 1.96/\sqrt{n}]$ contains the population mean μ is .95, or 95%. This information allows us to construct an *interval estimate* of μ, which is obtained by plugging in the sample outcome of the average, $\overline{y}$. Thus,

$$[\overline{y} - 1.96/\sqrt{n}, \overline{y} + 1.96/\sqrt{n}] \qquad \text{[C.18]}$$

is an example of an interval estimate of μ. It is also called a 95% confidence interval. A shorthand notation for this interval is $\overline{y} \pm 1.96/\sqrt{n}$.

The confidence interval in equation (C.18) is easy to compute, once the sample data $\{y_1, y_2, \ldots, y_n\}$ are observed; $\overline{y}$ is the only factor that depends on the data. For example, suppose that $n = 16$ and the average of the 16 data points is 7.3. Then, the 95% confidence interval for μ is $7.3 \pm 1.96/\sqrt{16} = 7.3 \pm .49$, which we can write in interval form as $[6.81, 7.79]$. By construction, $\overline{y} = 7.3$ is in the center of this interval.

Unlike its computation, the meaning of a confidence interval is more difficult to understand. When we say that equation (C.18) is a 95% confidence interval for μ, we mean that the *random* interval

$$[\overline{Y} - 1.96/\sqrt{n}, \overline{Y} + 1.96/\sqrt{n}] \qquad \text{[C.19]}$$

contains μ with probability .95. In other words, *before* the random sample is drawn, there is a 95% chance that (C.19) contains μ. Equation (C.19) is an example of an **interval estimator**. It is a random interval, since the endpoints change with different samples.

A confidence interval is often interpreted as follows: "The probability that μ is in the interval (C.18) is .95." This is incorrect. Once the sample has been observed and $\bar{y}$ has been computed, the limits of the confidence interval are simply numbers (6.81 and 7.79 in the example just given). The population parameter, μ, though unknown, is also just some number. Therefore, μ either is or is not in the interval (C.18) (and we will never know with certainty which is the case). Probability plays no role once the confidence interval is computed for the particular data at hand. The probabilistic interpretation comes from the fact that for 95% of all random samples, the constructed confidence interval will contain μ.

To emphasize the meaning of a confidence interval, Table C.2 contains calculations for 20 random samples (or replications) from the Normal(2,1) distribution with sample size $n = 10$. For each of the 20 samples, $\bar{y}$ is obtained, and (C.18) is computed as $\bar{y} \pm 1.96/\sqrt{10} = \bar{y} \pm .62$ (each rounded to two decimals). As you can see, the interval changes with each random sample. Nineteen of the twenty intervals contain the population value of μ. Only for replication number 19 is μ not in the confidence interval. In other words, 95% of the samples result in a confidence interval that contains μ. This did not have to be the case with only 20 replications, but it worked out that way for this particular simulation.

TABLE C.2 Simulated Confidence Intervals from a Normal(μ, 1) Distribution with $\mu = 2$

Replication	$\bar{y}$	95% Interval	Contains μ?
1	1.98	(1.36,2.60)	Yes
2	1.43	(0.81,2.05)	Yes
3	1.65	(1.03,2.27)	Yes
4	1.88	(1.26,2.50)	Yes
5	2.34	(1.72,2.96)	Yes
6	2.58	(1.96,3.20)	Yes
7	1.58	(.96,2.20)	Yes
8	2.23	(1.61,2.85)	Yes
9	1.96	(1.34,2.58)	Yes
10	2.11	(1.49,2.73)	Yes
11	2.15	(1.53,2.77)	Yes
12	1.93	(1.31,2.55)	Yes
13	2.02	(1.40,2.64)	Yes
14	2.10	(1.48,2.72)	Yes
15	2.18	(1.56,2.80)	Yes
16	2.10	(1.48,2.72)	Yes
17	1.94	(1.32,2.56)	Yes
18	2.21	(1.59,2.83)	Yes
19	1.16	(.54,1.78)	No
20	1.75	(1.13,2.37)	Yes

C-5b Confidence Intervals for the Mean from a Normally Distributed Population

The confidence interval derived in equation (C.18) helps illustrate how to construct and interpret confidence intervals. In practice, equation (C.18) is not very useful for the mean of a normal population because it assumes that the variance is known to be unity. It is easy to extend (C.18) to the case where the standard deviation σ is known to be any value: the 95% confidence interval is

$$[\bar{y} - 1.96\sigma/\sqrt{n}, \bar{y} + 1.96\sigma/\sqrt{n}].$$ [C.20]

Therefore, provided σ is known, a confidence interval for μ is readily constructed. To allow for unknown σ, we must use an estimate. Let

$$s = \left(\frac{1}{n-1}\sum_{i=1}^{n}(y_i - \bar{y})^2\right)^{1/2}$$ [C.21]

denote the sample standard deviation. Then, we obtain a confidence interval that depends entirely on the observed data by replacing σ in equation (C.20) with its estimate, s. Unfortunately, this does not preserve the 95% level of confidence because s depends on the particular sample. In other words, the random interval $[\bar{Y} \pm 1.96(S/\sqrt{n})]$ no longer contains μ with probability .95 because the constant σ has been replaced with the random variable S.

How should we proceed? Rather than using the standard normal distribution, we must rely on the t distribution. The t distribution arises from the fact that

$$\frac{\bar{Y} - \mu}{S/\sqrt{n}} \sim t_{n-1},$$ [C.22]

where $\bar{Y}$ is the sample average and S is the sample standard deviation of the random sample $\{Y_1, \ldots, Y_n\}$. We will not prove (C.22); a careful proof can be found in a variety of places [for example, Larsen and Marx (1986, Chapter 7)].

To construct a 95% confidence interval, let c denote the 97.5th percentile in the t_{n-1} distribution. In other words, c is the value such that 95% of the area in the t_{n-1} is between $-c$ and c: $P(-c < t_{n-1} < c) = .95$. (The value of c depends on the degrees of freedom $n - 1$, but we do not

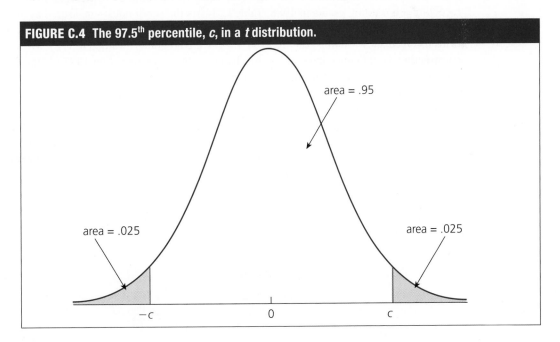

FIGURE C.4 The 97.5th percentile, **c**, in a **t** distribution.

area = .95

area = .025

area = .025

$-c$

0

c

make this explicit.) The choice of c is illustrated in Figure C.4. Once c has been properly chosen, the random interval $[\bar{Y} - c \cdot S/\sqrt{n}, \bar{Y} + c \cdot S/\sqrt{n}]$ contains μ with probability .95. For a particular sample, the 95% confidence interval is calculated as

$$[\bar{y} - c \cdot s/\sqrt{n}, \bar{y} + c \cdot s/\sqrt{n}]. \qquad \text{[C.23]}$$

The values of c for various degrees of freedom can be obtained from Table G.2 in Appendix G. For example, if $n = 20$, so that the df is $n - 1 = 19$, then $c = 2.093$. Thus, the 95% confidence interval is $[\bar{y} \pm 2.093(s/\sqrt{20})]$, where $\bar{y}$ and s are the values obtained from the sample. Even if $s = \sigma$ (which is very unlikely), the confidence interval in (C.23) is wider than that in (C.20) because $c > 1.96$. For small degrees of freedom, (C.23) is much wider.

More generally, let c_α denote the $100(1 - \alpha)$ percentile in the t_{n-1} distribution. Then, a $100(1 - \alpha)\%$ confidence interval is obtained as

$$[\bar{y} - c_{\alpha/2} S/\sqrt{n}, \bar{y} + c_{\alpha/2} S/\sqrt{n}]. \qquad \text{[C.24]}$$

Obtaining $c_{\alpha/2}$ requires choosing α and knowing the degrees of freedom $n - 1$; then, Table G.2 can be used. For the most part, we will concentrate on 95% confidence intervals.

There is a simple way to remember how to construct a confidence interval for the mean of a normal distribution. Recall that $\text{sd}(\bar{Y}) = \sigma/\sqrt{n}$. Thus, $s/\sqrt{n}$ is the point estimate of $\text{sd}(\bar{Y})$. The associated random variable, $S/\sqrt{n}$, is sometimes called the **standard error** of $\bar{Y}$. Because what shows up in formulas is the point estimate $s/\sqrt{n}$, we define the standard error of $\bar{y}$ as $\text{se}(\bar{y}) = s/\sqrt{n}$. Then, (C.24) can be written in shorthand as

$$[\bar{y} \pm c_{\alpha/2} \cdot \text{se}(\bar{y})]. \qquad \text{[C.25]}$$

This equation shows why the notion of the standard error of an estimate plays an important role in econometrics.

EXAMPLE C.2   Effect of Job Training Grants on Worker Productivity

Holzer, Block, Cheatham, and Knott (1993) studied the effects of job training grants on worker productivity by collecting information on "scrap rates" for a sample of Michigan manufacturing firms receiving job training grants in 1988. Table C.3 lists the scrap rates—measured as number of items per 100 produced that are not usable and therefore need to be scrapped—for 20 firms. Each of these firms received a job training grant in 1988; there were no grants awarded in 1987. We are interested in constructing a confidence interval for the change in the scrap rate from 1987 to 1988 for the population of all manufacturing firms that could have received grants.

We assume that the change in scrap rates has a normal distribution. Since $n = 20$, a 95% confidence interval for the mean change in scrap rates μ is $[\bar{y} \pm 2.093 \cdot \text{se}(\bar{y})]$, where $\text{se}(\bar{y}) = s/\sqrt{n}$. The value 2.093 is the 97.5^{th} percentile in a t_{19} distribution. For the particular sample values, $\bar{y} = -1.15$ and $\text{se}(\bar{y}) = .54$ (each rounded to two decimals), so the 95% confidence interval is $[-2.28, -.02]$. The value zero is excluded from this interval, so we conclude that, with 95% confidence, the average change in scrap rates in the population is not zero.

TABLE C.3 Scrap Rates for 20 Michigan Manufacturing Firms			
Firm	1987	1988	Change
1	10	3	−7
2	1	1	0
3	6	5	−1
4	.45	.5	.05
5	1.25	1.54	.29
6	1.3	1.5	.2
7	1.06	.8	−.26
8	3	2	−1
9	8.18	.67	−7.51
10	1.67	1.17	−.5
11	.98	.51	−.47
12	1	.5	−.5
13	.45	.61	.16
14	5.03	6.7	1.67
15	8	4	−4
16	9	7	−2
17	18	19	1
18	.28	.2	−.08
19	7	5	−2
20	3.97	3.83	−.14
Average	4.38	3.23	−1.15

At this point, Example C.2 is mostly illustrative because it has some potentially serious flaws as an econometric analysis. Most importantly, it assumes that any systematic reduction in scrap rates is due to the job training grants. But many things can happen over the course of the year to change worker productivity. From this analysis, we have no way of knowing whether the fall in average scrap rates is attributable to the job training grants or if, at least partly, some external force is responsible.

C.5c A Simple Rule of Thumb for a 95% Confidence Interval

The confidence interval in (C.25) can be computed for any sample size and any confidence level. As we saw in Section B-5, the t distribution approaches the standard normal distribution as the degrees of freedom gets large. In particular, for $\alpha = .05$, $c_{\alpha/2} \to 1.96$ as $n \to \infty$, although $c_{\alpha/2}$ is always greater than 1.96 for each n. A *rule of thumb* for an approximate 95% confidence interval is

$$[\bar{y} \pm 2 \cdot se(\bar{y})]. \qquad \text{[C.26]}$$

In other words, we obtain $\bar{y}$ and its standard error and then compute $\bar{y}$ plus or minus twice its standard error to obtain the confidence interval. This is slightly too wide for very large n, and it is too narrow for small n. As we can see from Example C.2, even for n as small as 20, (C.26) is in the ballpark for a 95% confidence interval for the mean from a normal distribution. This means we can get pretty close to a 95% confidence interval without having to refer to t tables.

C.5d Asymptotic Confidence Intervals for Nonnormal Populations

In some applications, the population is clearly nonnormal. A leading case is the Bernoulli distribution, where the random variable takes on only the values zero and one. In other cases, the nonnormal population has no standard distribution. This does not matter, provided the sample size is sufficiently large for the central limit theorem to give a good approximation for the distribution of the sample average $\bar{Y}$. For large n, an *approximate* 95% confidence interval is

$$[\bar{y} \pm 1.96 \cdot \text{se}(\bar{y})], \qquad\qquad \text{[C.27]}$$

where the value 1.96 is the 97.5th percentile in the standard normal distribution. Mechanically, computing an approximate confidence interval does not differ from the normal case. A slight difference is that the number multiplying the standard error comes from the standard normal distribution, rather than the t distribution, because we are using asymptotics. Because the t distribution approaches the standard normal as the *df* increases, equation (C.25) is also perfectly legitimate as an approximate 95% interval; some prefer this to (C.27) because the former is exact for normal populations.

EXAMPLE C.3	**Race Discrimination in Hiring**

The Urban Institute conducted a study in 1988 in Washington, D.C., to examine the extent of race discrimination in hiring. Five pairs of people interviewed for several jobs. In each pair, one person was black and the other person was white. They were given résumés indicating that they were virtually the same in terms of experience, education, and other factors that determine job qualification. The idea was to make individuals as similar as possible with the exception of race. Each person in a pair interviewed for the same job, and the researchers recorded which applicant received a job offer. This is an example of a *matched pairs analysis*, where each trial consists of data on two people (or two firms, two cities, and so on) that are thought to be similar in many respects but different in one important characteristic.

Let θ_B denote the probability that the black person is offered a job and let θ_W be the probability that the white person is offered a job. We are primarily interested in the difference, $\theta_B - \theta_W$. Let B_i denote a Bernoulli variable equal to one if the black person gets a job offer from employer i, and zero otherwise. Similarly, $W_i = 1$ if the white person gets a job offer from employer i, and zero otherwise. Pooling across the five pairs of people, there were a total of $n = 241$ trials (pairs of interviews with employers). Unbiased estimators of θ_B and θ_W are $\bar{B}$ and $\bar{W}$, the fractions of interviews for which blacks and whites were offered jobs, respectively.

To put this into the framework of computing a confidence interval for a population mean, define a new variable $Y_i = B_i - W_i$. Now, Y_i can take on three values: -1 if the black person did not get the job but the white person did, 0 if both people either did or did not get the job, and 1 if the black person got the job and the white person did not. Then, $\mu \equiv \text{E}(Y_i) = \text{E}(B_i) - \text{E}(W_i) = \theta_B - \theta_W$.

The distribution of Y_i is certainly not normal—it is discrete and takes on only three values. Nevertheless, an approximate confidence interval for $\theta_B - \theta_W$ can be obtained by using large sample methods.

The data from the Urban Institute audit study are in the file AUDIT. Using the 241 observed data points, $\bar{b} = .224$ and $\bar{w} = .357$, so $\bar{y} = .224 - .357 = -.133$. Thus, 22.4% of black applicants were offered jobs, while 35.7% of white applicants were offered jobs. This is *prima facie* evidence of discrimination against blacks, but we can learn much more by computing a confidence interval for μ. To compute an approximate 95% confidence interval, we need the sample standard deviation. This turns out to be $s = .482$ [using equation (C.21)]. Using (C.27), we obtain a 95% CI for $\mu = \theta_B - \theta_W$ as $-.133 \pm 1.96(.482/\sqrt{241}) = -.133 \pm .031 = [-.164, -.102]$. The approximate 99% CI is $-.133 \pm 2.58(.482/\sqrt{241}) = [-.213, -.053]$. Naturally, this contains a wider range of values than the 95% CI. But even the 99% CI does not contain the value zero. Thus, we are very confident that the population difference $\theta_B - \theta_W$ is not zero.

Before we turn to hypothesis testing, it is useful to review the various population and sample quantities that measure the spreads in the population distributions and the sampling distributions of the estimators. These quantities appear often in statistical analysis, and extensions of them are important for the regression analysis in the main text. The quantity σ is the (unknown) population standard deviation; it is a measure of the spread in the distribution of Y. When we divide σ by $\sqrt{n}$, we obtain the **sampling standard deviation** of $\overline{Y}$ (the sample average). While σ is a fixed feature of the population, $\text{sd}(\overline{Y}) = \sigma/\sqrt{n}$ shrinks to zero as $n \to \infty$: our estimator of μ gets more and more precise as the sample size grows.

The estimate of σ for a particular sample, s, is called the sample standard deviation because it is obtained from the sample. (We also call the underlying random variable, S, which changes across different samples, the sample standard deviation.) Like $\overline{y}$ as an estimate of μ, s is our "best guess" at σ given the sample at hand. The quantity $s/\sqrt{n}$ is what we call the standard error of $\overline{y}$, and it is our best estimate of $\sigma/\sqrt{n}$. Confidence intervals for the population parameter μ depend directly on $\text{se}(\overline{y}) = s/\sqrt{n}$. Because this standard error shrinks to zero as the sample size grows, a larger sample size generally means a smaller confidence interval. Thus, we see clearly that one benefit of more data is that they result in narrower confidence intervals. The notion of the standard error of an estimate, which in the vast majority of cases shrinks to zero at the rate $1/\sqrt{n}$, plays a fundamental role in hypothesis testing (as we will see in the next section) and for confidence intervals and testing in the context of multiple regression (as discussed in Chapter 4).

C.6 Hypothesis Testing

So far, we have reviewed how to evaluate point estimators, and we have seen—in the case of a population mean—how to construct and interpret confidence intervals. But sometimes the question we are interested in has a definite yes or no answer. Here are some examples: (1) Does a job training program effectively increase average worker productivity? (see Example C.2); (2) Are blacks discriminated against in hiring? (see Example C.3); (3) Do stiffer state drunk driving laws reduce the number of drunk driving arrests? Devising methods for answering such questions, using a sample of data, is known as hypothesis testing.

C.6a Fundamentals of Hypothesis Testing

To illustrate the issues involved with hypothesis testing, consider an election example. Suppose there are two candidates in an election, Candidates A and B. Candidate A is reported to have received 42% of the popular vote, while Candidate B received 58%. These are supposed to represent the true percentages in the voting population, and we treat them as such.

Candidate A is convinced that more people must have voted for him, so he would like to investigate whether the election was rigged. Knowing something about statistics, Candidate A hires a consulting agency to randomly sample 100 voters to record whether or not each person voted for him. Suppose that, for the sample collected, 53 people voted for Candidate A. This sample estimate of 53% clearly exceeds the reported population value of 42%. Should Candidate A conclude that the election was indeed a fraud?

While it appears that the votes for Candidate A were undercounted, we cannot be certain. Even if only 42% of the population voted for Candidate A, it is possible that, in a sample of 100, we observe 53 people who did vote for Candidate A. The question is: How *strong* is the sample evidence against the officially reported percentage of 42%?

One way to proceed is to set up a **hypothesis test**. Let θ denote the true proportion of the population voting for Candidate A. The hypothesis that the reported results are accurate can be stated as

$$H_0: \theta = .42 \qquad \text{[C.28]}$$

This is an example of a **null hypothesis**. We always denote the null hypothesis by H_0. In hypothesis testing, the null hypothesis plays a role similar to that of a defendant on trial in many judicial systems: just as a defendant is presumed to be innocent until proven guilty, the null hypothesis is presumed to be true until the data strongly suggest otherwise. In the current example, Candidate A must present fairly strong evidence against (C.28) in order to win a recount.

The **alternative hypothesis** in the election example is that the true proportion voting for Candidate A in the election is greater than .42:

$$H_1: \theta > .42. \qquad [\text{C.29}]$$

In order to conclude that H_0 is false and that H_1 is true, we must have evidence "beyond reasonable doubt" against H_0. How many votes out of 100 would be needed before we feel the evidence is strongly against H_0? Most would agree that observing 43 votes out of a sample of 100 is not enough to overturn the original election results; such an outcome is well within the expected sampling variation. On the other hand, we do not need to observe 100 votes for Candidate A to cast doubt on H_0. Whether 53 out of 100 is enough to reject H_0 is much less clear. The answer depends on how we quantify "beyond reasonable doubt."

Before we turn to the issue of quantifying uncertainty in hypothesis testing, we should head off some possible confusion. You may have noticed that the hypotheses in equations (C.28) and (C.29) do not exhaust all possibilities: it could be that θ is less than .42. For the application at hand, we are not particularly interested in that possibility; it has nothing to do with overturning the results of the election. Therefore, we can just state at the outset that we are ignoring alternatives θ with $\theta < .42$. Nevertheless, some authors prefer to state null and alternative hypotheses so that they are exhaustive, in which case our null hypothesis should be $H_0: \theta \leq .42$. Stated in this way, the null hypothesis is a *composite* null hypothesis because it allows for more than one value under H_0. [By contrast, equation (C.28) is an example of a *simple* null hypothesis.] For these kinds of examples, it does not matter whether we state the null as in (C.28) or as a composite null: the most difficult value to reject if $\theta \leq .42$ is $\theta = .42$. (That is, if we reject the value $\theta = .42$, against $\theta > .42$, then logically we must reject any value less than .42.) Therefore, our testing procedure based on (C.28) leads to the same test as if $H_0: \theta \leq .42$. In this text, we always state a null hypothesis as a simple null hypothesis.

In hypothesis testing, we can make two kinds of mistakes. First, we can reject the null hypothesis when it is in fact true. This is called a **Type I error**. In the election example, a Type I error occurs if we reject H_0 when the true proportion of people voting for Candidate A is in fact .42. The second kind of error is failing to reject H_0 when it is actually false. This is called a **Type II error**. In the election example, a Type II error occurs if $\theta > .42$ but we fail to reject H_0.

After we have made the decision of whether or not to reject the null hypothesis, we have either decided correctly or we have committed an error. We will never know with certainty whether an error was committed. However, we can compute the *probability* of making either a Type I or a Type II error. Hypothesis testing rules are constructed to make the probability of committing a Type I error fairly small. Generally, we define the **significance level** (or simply the *level*) of a test as the probability of a Type I error; it is typically denoted by α. Symbolically, we have

$$\alpha = P(\text{Reject } H_0 | H_0). \qquad [\text{C.30}]$$

The right-hand side is read as: "The probability of rejecting H_0 given that H_0 is true."

Classical hypothesis testing requires that we initially specify a significance level for a test. When we specify a value for α, we are essentially quantifying our tolerance for a Type I error. Common values for α are .10, .05, and .01. If $\alpha = .05$, then the researcher is willing to falsely reject H_0 5% of the time, in order to detect deviations from H_0.

Once we have chosen the significance level, we would then like to minimize the probability of a Type II error. Alternatively, we would like to maximize the **power of a test** against all relevant alternatives. The power of a test is just one minus the probability of a Type II error. Mathematically,

$$\pi(\theta) = P(\text{Reject } H_0 | \theta) = 1 - P(\text{Type II} | \theta),$$

where θ denotes the actual value of the parameter. Naturally, we would like the power to equal unity whenever the null hypothesis is false. But this is impossible to achieve while keeping the significance level small. Instead, we choose our tests to maximize the power for a given significance level.

C.6b Testing Hypotheses about the Mean in a Normal Population

In order to test a null hypothesis against an alternative, we need to choose a test statistic (or statistic, for short) and a critical value. The choices for the statistic and critical value are based on convenience and on the desire to maximize power given a significance level for the test. In this subsection, we review how to test hypotheses for the mean of a normal population.

A **test statistic**, denoted T, is some function of the random sample. When we compute the statistic for a particular outcome, we obtain an outcome of the test statistic, which we will denote by t.

Given a test statistic, we can define a rejection rule that determines when H_0 is rejected in favor of H_1. In this text, all rejection rules are based on comparing the value of a test statistic, t, to a **critical value**, c. The values of t that result in rejection of the null hypothesis are collectively known as the **rejection region**. To determine the critical value, we must first decide on a significance level of the test. Then, given α, the critical value associated with α is determined by the distribution of T, *assuming* that H_0 is true. We will write this critical value as c, suppressing the fact that it depends on α.

Testing hypotheses about the mean μ from a Normal(μ, σ^2) population is straightforward. The null hypothesis is stated as

$$H_0: \mu = \mu_0, \tag{C.31}$$

where μ_0 is a value that we specify. In the majority of applications, $\mu_0 = 0$, but the general case is no more difficult.

The rejection rule we choose depends on the nature of the alternative hypothesis. The three alternatives of interest are

$$H_1: \mu > \mu_0, \tag{C.32}$$

$$H_1: \mu < \mu_0, \tag{C.33}$$

and

$$H_1: \mu \neq \mu_0. \tag{C.34}$$

Equation (C.32) gives a **one-sided alternative**, as does (C.33). When the alternative hypothesis is (C.32), the null is effectively $H_0: \mu \leq \mu_0$, since we reject H_0 only when $\mu > \mu_0$. This is appropriate when we are interested in the value of μ only when μ is at least as large as μ_0. Equation (C.34) is a **two-sided alternative**. This is appropriate when we are interested in any departure from the null hypothesis.

Consider first the alternative in (C.32). Intuitively, we should reject H_0 in favor of H_1 when the value of the sample average, $\bar{y}$, is "sufficiently" greater than μ_0. But how should we determine when $\bar{y}$ is large enough for H_0 to be rejected at the chosen significance level? This requires knowing the probability of rejecting the null hypothesis when it is true. Rather than working directly with $\bar{y}$, we use its standardized version, where σ is replaced with the sample standard deviation, s:

$$t = \sqrt{n}(\bar{y} - \mu_0)/s = (\bar{y} - \mu_0)/se(\bar{y}), \tag{C.35}$$

where $se(\bar{y}) = s/\sqrt{n}$ is the standard error of $\bar{y}$. Given the sample of data, it is easy to obtain t. We work with t because, under the null hypothesis, the random variable

$$T = \sqrt{n}(\bar{Y} - \mu_0)/S$$

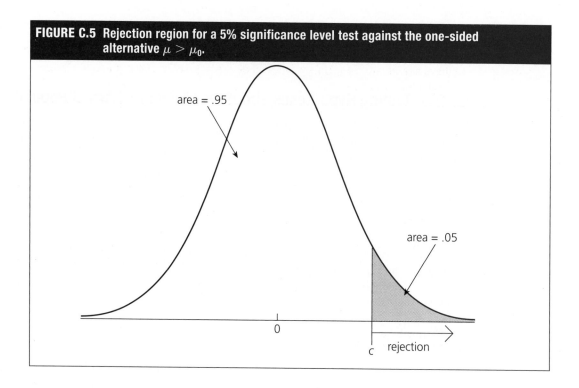

FIGURE C.5   Rejection region for a 5% significance level test against the one-sided alternative $\mu > \mu_0$.

has a t_{n-1} distribution. Now, suppose we have settled on a 5% significance level. Then, the critical value c is chosen so that $P(T > c|H_0) = .05$; that is, the probability of a Type I error is 5%. Once we have found c, the rejection rule is

$$t > c, \qquad\qquad\qquad [C.36]$$

where c is the $100(1 - \alpha)$ percentile in a t_{n-1} distribution; as a percent, the significance level is $100 \cdot \alpha\%$. This is an example of a **one-tailed test** because the rejection region is in one tail of the t distribution. For a 5% significance level, c is the 95th percentile in the t_{n-1} distribution; this is illustrated in Figure C.5. A different significance level leads to a different critical value.

The statistic in equation (C.35) is often called the t **statistic** for testing $H_0\colon \mu = \mu_0$. The t statistic measures the distance from $\bar{y}$ to μ_0 *relative* to the standard error of $\bar{y}$, $se(\bar{y})$.

EXAMPLE C.4   **Effect of Enterprise Zones on Business Investments**

In the population of cities granted enterprise zones in a particular state [see Papke (1994) for Indiana], let Y denote the percentage change in investment from the year before to the year after a city became an enterprise zone. Assume that Y has a Normal(μ, σ^2) distribution. The null hypothesis that enterprise zones have no effect on business investment is $H_0\colon \mu = 0$; the alternative that they have a positive effect is $H_1\colon \mu > 0$. (We assume that they do not have a negative effect.) Suppose that we wish to test H_0 at the 5% level. The test statistic in this case is

$$t = \frac{\bar{y}}{s/\sqrt{n}} = \frac{\bar{y}}{se(\bar{y})}. \qquad\qquad [C.37]$$

Suppose that we have a sample of 36 cities that are granted enterprise zones. Then, the critical value is $c = 1.69$ (see Table G.2), and we reject H_0 in favor of H_1 if $t > 1.69$. Suppose that the sample yields $\bar{y} = 8.2$ and $s = 23.9$. Then, $t \approx 2.06$, and H_0 is therefore rejected at the 5% level. Thus, we conclude that, at the 5% significance level, enterprise zones have an effect on average investment. The 1% critical value is 2.44, so H_0 is not rejected at the 1% level. The same caveat holds here as in Example C.2: we have not controlled for other factors that might affect investment in cities over time, so we cannot claim that the effect is causal.

The rejection rule is similar for the one-sided alternative (C.33). A test with a significance level of $100 \cdot \alpha\%$ rejects H_0 against (C.33) whenever

$$t < -c; \tag{C.38}$$

in other words, we are looking for negative values of the t statistic—which implies $\bar{y} < \mu_0$—that are sufficiently far from zero to reject H_0.

For two-sided alternatives, we must be careful to choose the critical value so that the significance level of the test is still α. If H_1 is given by H_1: $\mu \neq \mu_0$, then we reject H_0 if $\bar{y}$ is far from μ_0 in *absolute value*: a $\bar{y}$ much larger or much smaller than μ_0 provides evidence against H_0 in favor of H_1. A $100 \cdot \alpha\%$ level test is obtained from the rejection rule

$$|t| > c, \tag{C.39}$$

where $|t|$ is the absolute value of the t statistic in (C.35). This gives a **two-tailed test**. We must now be careful in choosing the critical value: c is the $100(1 - \alpha/2)$ percentile in the t_{n-1} distribution. For example, if $\alpha = .05$, then the critical value is the 97.5th percentile in the t_{n-1} distribution. This ensures that H_0 is rejected only 5% of the time when it is true (see Figure C.6). For example, if $n = 22$, then the critical value is $c = 2.08$, the 97.5th percentile in a t_{21} distribution (see Table G.2). The absolute value of the t statistic must exceed 2.08 in order to reject H_0 against H_1 at the 5% level.

It is important to know the proper language of hypothesis testing. Sometimes, the appropriate phrase "we fail to reject H_0 in favor of H_1 at the 5% significance level" is replaced with "we accept H_0 at the 5% significance level." The latter wording is incorrect. With the same set of data, there are

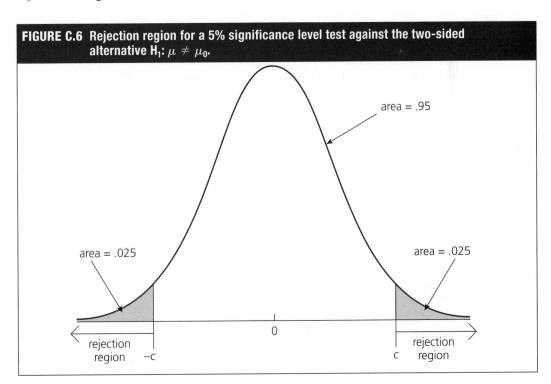

FIGURE C.6 Rejection region for a 5% significance level test against the two-sided alternative H_1: $\mu \neq \mu_0$.

usually many hypotheses that cannot be rejected. In the earlier election example, it would be logically inconsistent to say that $H_0: \theta = .42$ and $H_0: \theta = .43$ are both "accepted," since only one of these can be true. But it is entirely possible that neither of these hypotheses is rejected. For this reason, we always say "fail to reject H_0" rather than "accept H_0."

C.6c Asymptotic Tests for Nonnormal Populations

If the sample size is large enough to invoke the central limit theorem (see Section C-3), the mechanics of hypothesis testing for population means are the *same* whether or not the population distribution is normal. The theoretical justification comes from the fact that, under the null hypothesis,

$$T = \sqrt{n}(\overline{Y} - \mu_0)/S \overset{a}{\sim} \text{Normal}(0,1).$$

Therefore, with large n, we can compare the t statistic in (C.35) with the critical values from a standard normal distribution. Because the t_{n-1} distribution converges to the standard normal distribution as n gets large, the t and standard normal critical values will be very close for extremely large n. Because asymptotic theory is based on n increasing without bound, it cannot tell us whether the standard normal or t critical values are better. For moderate values of n, say, between 30 and 60, it is traditional to use the t distribution because we know this is correct for normal populations. For $n > 120$, the choice between the t and standard normal distributions is largely irrelevant because the critical values are practically the same.

Because the critical values chosen using either the standard normal or t distribution are only approximately valid for nonnormal populations, our chosen significance levels are also only approximate; thus, for nonnormal populations, our significance levels are really *asymptotic* significance levels. Thus, if we choose a 5% significance level, but our population is nonnormal, then the actual significance level will be larger or smaller than 5% (and we cannot know which is the case). When the sample size is large, the actual significance level will be very close to 5%. Practically speaking, the distinction is not important, so we will now drop the qualifier "asymptotic."

EXAMPLE C.5 **Race Discrimination in Hiring**

In the Urban Institute study of discrimination in hiring (see Example C.3) using the data in AUDIT, we are primarily interested in testing $H_0: \mu = 0$ against $H_1: \mu < 0$ where $\mu = \theta_B - \theta_W$ is the difference in probabilities that blacks and whites receive job offers. Recall that μ is the population mean of the variable $Y = B - W$, where B and W are binary indicators. Using the $n = 241$ paired comparisons in the data file AUDIT, we obtained $\overline{y} = -.133$ and $se(\overline{y}) = .482/\sqrt{241} \approx .031$. The t statistic for testing $H_0: \mu = 0$ is $t = -.133/.031 \approx -4.29$. You will remember from Appendix B that the standard normal distribution is, for practical purposes, indistinguishable from the t distribution with 240 degrees of freedom. The value -4.29 is so far out in the left tail of the distribution that we reject H_0 at any reasonable significance level. In fact, the .005 (one-half of a percent) critical value (for the one-sided test) is about -2.58. A t value of -4.29 is *very* strong evidence against H_0 in favor of H_1. Hence, we conclude that there is discrimination in hiring.

C.6d Computing and Using p-Values

The traditional requirement of choosing a significance level ahead of time means that different researchers, using the same data and same procedure to test the same hypothesis, could wind up with different conclusions. Reporting the significance level at which we are carrying out the test solves this problem to some degree, but it does not completely remove the problem.

To provide more information, we can ask the following question: What is the *largest* significance level at which we could carry out the test and still fail to reject the null hypothesis? This value is known as the **p-value** of a test (sometimes called the *prob-value*). Compared with choosing a significance level ahead of time and obtaining a critical value, computing a p-value is somewhat more difficult. But with the advent of quick and inexpensive computing, p-values are now fairly easy to obtain.

As an illustration, consider the problem of testing $H_0: \mu = 0$ in a Normal(μ, σ^2) population. Our test statistic in this case is $T = \sqrt{n} \cdot \bar{Y}/S$, and we assume that n is large enough to treat T as having a standard normal distribution under H_0. Suppose that the observed value of T for our sample is $t = 1.52$. (Note how we have skipped the step of choosing a significance level.) Now that we have seen the value t, we can find the largest significance level at which we would fail to reject H_0. This is the significance level associated with using t as our critical value. Because our test statistic T has a standard normal distribution under H_0, we have

$$p\text{-value} = P(T > 1.52|H_0) = 1 - \Phi(1.52) = .065, \qquad [\text{C.40}]$$

where $\Phi(\cdot)$ denotes the standard normal cdf. In other words, the p-value in this example is simply the area to the right of 1.52, the observed value of the test statistic, in a standard normal distribution. See Figure C.7 for illustration.

Because the p-value $= .065$, the largest significance level at which we can carry out this test and fail to reject is 6.5%. If we carry out the test at a level below 6.5% (such as at 5%), we fail to reject H_0. If we carry out the test at a level larger than 6.5% (such as 10%), we reject H_0. With the p-value at hand, we can carry out the test at any level.

The p-value in this example has another useful interpretation: it is the probability that we observe a value of T as large as 1.52 when the null hypothesis is true. If the null hypothesis is actually true, we would observe a value of T as large as 1.52 due to chance only 6.5% of the time. Whether this is small enough to reject H_0 depends on our tolerance for a Type I error. The p-value has a similar interpretation in all other cases, as we will see.

Generally, small p-values are evidence *against* H_0, since they indicate that the outcome of the data occurs with small probability if H_0 is true. In the previous example, if t had been a larger value, say, $t = 2.85$, then the p-value would be $1 - \Phi(2.85) \approx .002$. This means that, if the null hypothesis were true, we would observe a value of T as large as 2.85 with probability .002. How do we

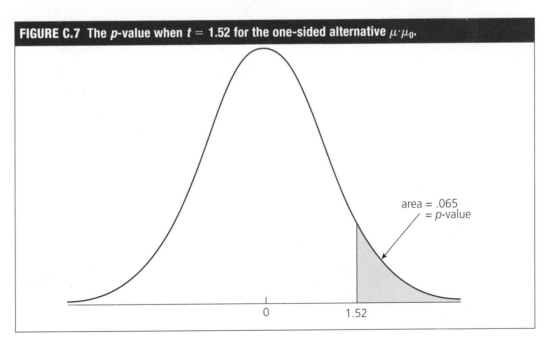

FIGURE C.7 The *p*-value when $t = 1.52$ for the one-sided alternative $\mu \cdot \mu_0$.

area = .065
= *p*-value

0   1.52

interpret this? Either we obtained a very unusual sample or the null hypothesis is false. Unless we have a *very* small tolerance for Type I error, we would reject the null hypothesis. On the other hand, a large *p*-value is weak evidence against H_0. If we had gotten $t = .47$ in the previous example, then the *p*-value $= 1 - \Phi(.47) = .32$. Observing a value of *T* larger than .47 happens with probability .32, even when H_0 is true; this is large enough so that there is insufficient doubt about H_0, unless we have a very high tolerance for Type I error.

For hypothesis testing about a population mean using the *t* distribution, we need detailed tables in order to compute *p*-values. Table G.2 only allows us to put bounds on *p*-values. Fortunately, many statistics and econometrics packages now compute *p*-values routinely, and they also provide calculation of cdfs for the *t* and other distributions used for computing *p*-values.

EXAMPLE C.6	**Effect of Job Training Grants on Worker Productivity**

Consider again the Holzer et al. (1993) data in Example C.2. From a policy perspective, there are two questions of interest. First, what is our best estimate of the mean change in scrap rates, μ? We have already obtained this for the sample of 20 firms listed in Table C.3: the sample average of the change in scrap rates is -1.15. Relative to the initial average scrap rate in 1987, this represents a fall in the scrap rate of about 26.3% ($-1.15/4.38 \approx -.263$), which is a nontrivial effect.

We would also like to know whether the sample provides strong evidence for an effect in the population of manufacturing firms that could have received grants. The null hypothesis is $H_0\colon \mu = 0$, and we test this against $H_1\colon \mu < 0$, where μ is the average change in scrap rates. Under the null, the job training grants have no effect on average scrap rates. The alternative states that there is an effect. We do not care about the alternative $\mu > 0$, so the null hypothesis is effectively $H_0\colon \mu \geq 0$.

Since $\bar{y} = -1.15$ and $\text{se}(\bar{y}) = .54$, $t = -1.15/.54 = -2.13$. This is below the 5% critical value of -1.73 (from a t_{19} distribution) but above the 1% critical value, -2.54. The *p*-value in this case is computed as

$$p\text{-value} = P(T_{19} < -2.13), \qquad [\text{C.41}]$$

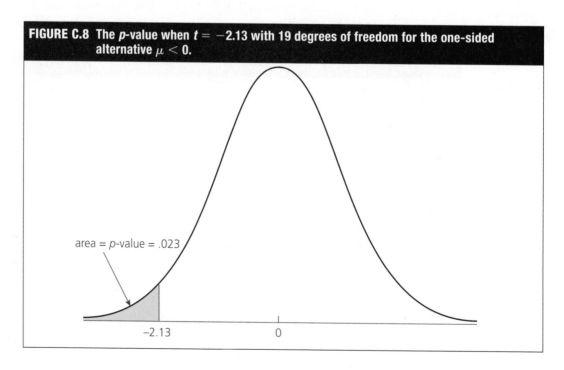

FIGURE C.8	The *p*-value when $t = -2.13$ with 19 degrees of freedom for the one-sided alternative $\mu < 0$.

area = *p*-value = .023

-2.13 0

where T_{19} represents a t distributed random variable with 19 degrees of freedom. The inequality is reversed from (C.40) because the alternative has the form in (C.33). The probability in (C.41) is the area to the left of -2.13 in a t_{19} distribution (see Figure C.8).

Using Table G.2, the most we can say is that the p-value is between .025 and .01, but it is closer to .025 (since the 97.5th percentile is about 2.09). Using a statistical package, such as Stata, we can compute the exact p-value. It turns out to be about .023, which is reasonable evidence against H_0. This is certainly enough evidence to reject the null hypothesis that the training grants had no effect at the 2.5% significance level (and therefore at the 5% level).

Computing a p-value for a two-sided test is similar, but we must account for the two-sided nature of the rejection rule. For t testing about population means, the p-value is computed as

$$P(|T_{n-1}| > |t|) = 2P(T_{n-1} > |t|), \qquad\qquad \text{[C.42]}$$

where t is the value of the test statistic and T_{n-1} is a t random variable. (For large n, replace T_{n-1} with a standard normal random variable.) Thus, compute the absolute value of the t statistic, find the area to the right of this value in a t_{n-1} distribution, and multiply the area by two.

For nonnormal populations, the exact p-value can be difficult to obtain. Nevertheless, we can find *asymptotic* p-values by using the same calculations. These p-values are valid for large sample sizes. For n larger than, say, 120, we might as well use the standard normal distribution. Table G.1 is detailed enough to get accurate p-values, but we can also use a statistics or econometrics program.

EXAMPLE C.7 **Race Discrimination in Hiring**

Using the matched pairs data from the Urban Institute in the AUDIT data file ($n = 241$), we obtained $t = -4.29$. If Z is a standard normal random variable, $P(Z < -4.29)$ is, for practical purposes, zero. In other words, the (asymptotic) p-value for this example is essentially zero. This is very strong evidence against H_0.

Summary of How to Use p-Values:

(i) Choose a test statistic T and decide on the nature of the alternative. This determines whether the rejection rule is $t > c$, $t < -c$, or $|t| > c$.

(ii) Use the observed value of the t statistic as the critical value and compute the corresponding significance level of the test. This is the p-value. If the rejection rule is of the form $t > c$, then p-value $= P(T > t)$. If the rejection rule is $t < -c$, then p-value $= P(T < t)$; if the rejection rule is $|t| > c$, then p-value $= P(|T| > |t|)$.

(iii) If a significance level α has been chosen, then we reject H_0 at the $100 \cdot \alpha\%$ level if p-value $< \alpha$. If p-value $\geq \alpha$, then we fail to reject H_0 at the $100 \cdot \alpha\%$ level. Therefore, it is a small p-value that leads to rejection of the null hypothesis.

C.6e The Relationship between Confidence Intervals and Hypothesis Testing

Because constructing confidence intervals and hypothesis tests both involve probability statements, it is natural to think that they are somehow linked. It turns out that they are. After a confidence interval has been constructed, we can carry out a variety of hypothesis tests.

The confidence intervals we have discussed are all two-sided by nature. (In this text, we will have no need to construct one-sided confidence intervals.) Thus, confidence intervals can be used to test against *two-sided* alternatives. In the case of a population mean, the null is given by (C.31), and the alternative is (C.34). Suppose we have constructed a 95% confidence interval for μ. Then, if the hypothesized value of μ under H_0, μ_0, is not in the confidence interval, then H_0: $\mu = \mu_0$ is rejected against H_1: $\mu \neq \mu_0$ at the 5% level. If μ_0 lies in this interval, then we fail to reject H_0 at the 5% level. Notice how any value for μ_0 can be tested once a confidence interval is constructed, and since a confidence interval contains more than one value, there are many null hypotheses that will not be rejected.

| EXAMPLE C.8 | **Training Grants and Worker Productivity** |

In the Holzer et al. example, we constructed a 95% confidence interval for the mean change in scrap rate μ as $[-2.28, -.02]$. Since zero is excluded from this interval, we reject H_0: $\mu = 0$ against H_1: $\mu \neq 0$ at the 5% level. This 95% confidence interval also means that we fail to reject H_0: $\mu = -2$ at the 5% level. In fact, there is a continuum of null hypotheses that are not rejected given this confidence interval.

C.6f Practical versus Statistical Significance

In the examples covered so far, we have produced three kinds of evidence concerning population parameters: point estimates, confidence intervals, and hypothesis tests. These tools for learning about population parameters are equally important. There is an understandable tendency for students to focus on confidence intervals and hypothesis tests because these are things to which we can attach confidence or significance levels. But in any study, we must also interpret the *magnitudes* of point estimates.

The sign and magnitude of $\bar{y}$ determine its **practical significance** and allow us to discuss the direction of an intervention or policy effect, and whether the estimated effect is "large" or "small." On the other hand, **statistical significance** of $\bar{y}$ depends on the magnitude of its t statistic. For testing H_0: $\mu = 0$, the t statistic is simply $t = \bar{y}/se(\bar{y})$. In other words, statistical significance depends on the ratio of $\bar{y}$ to its standard error. Consequently, a t statistic can be large because $\bar{y}$ is large or $se(\bar{y})$ is small. In applications, it is important to discuss both practical and statistical significance, being aware that an estimate can be statistically significant without being especially large in a practical sense. Whether an estimate is practically important depends on the context as well as on one's judgment, so there are no set rules for determining practical significance.

| EXAMPLE C.9 | **Effect of Freeway Width on Commute Time** |

Let Y denote the change in commute time, measured in minutes, for commuters in a metropolitan area from before a freeway was widened to after the freeway was widened. Assume that $Y \sim \text{Normal}(\mu, \sigma^2)$. The null hypothesis that the widening did not reduce average commute time is H_0: $\mu = 0$; the alternative that it reduced average commute time is H_1: $\mu < 0$. Suppose a random sample of commuters of size $n = 900$ is obtained to determine the effectiveness of the freeway project. The average change in commute time is computed to be $\bar{y} = -3.6$, and the sample standard deviation is $s = 32.7$; thus, $se(\bar{y}) = 32.7/\sqrt{900} = 1.09$. The t statistic is $t = -3.6/1.09 \approx -3.30$, which is very statistically significant; the p-value is about .0005. Thus, we conclude that the freeway widening had a statistically significant effect on average commute time.

If the outcome of the hypothesis test is all that were reported from the study, it would be misleading. Reporting only statistical significance masks the fact that the estimated reduction in average commute time, 3.6 minutes, seems pretty meager, although this depends to some extent on what the average commute time was prior to widening the freeway. To be up front, we should report the point estimate of -3.6, along with the significance test.

Finding point estimates that are statistically significant without being practically significant can occur when we are working with large samples. To discuss why this happens, it is useful to have the following definition.

Test Consistency. A **consistent test** rejects H_0 with probability approaching one as the sample size grows whenever H_1 is true.

Another way to say that a test is consistent is that, as the sample size tends to infinity, the power of the test gets closer and closer to unity whenever H_1 is true. All of the tests we cover in this text have this property. In the case of testing hypotheses about a population mean, test consistency follows because the variance of $\bar{Y}$ converges to zero as the sample size gets large. The t statistic for testing H_0: $\mu = 0$ is $T = \bar{Y}/(S/\sqrt{n})$. Since $\text{plim}(\bar{Y}) = \mu$ and $\text{plim}(S) = \sigma$, it follows that if, say, $\mu > 0$, then T gets larger and larger (with high probability) as $n \to \infty$. In other words, no matter how close m is to zero, we can be almost certain to reject H_0: $\mu = 0$ given a large enough sample size. This says nothing about whether μ is large in a practical sense.

C.7 Remarks on Notation

In our review of probability and statistics here and in Appendix B, we have been careful to use standard conventions to denote random variables, estimators, and test statistics. For example, we have used W to indicate an estimator (random variable) and w to denote a particular estimate (outcome of the random variable W). Distinguishing between an estimator and an estimate is important for understanding various concepts in estimation and hypothesis testing. However, making this distinction quickly becomes a burden in econometric analysis because the models are more complicated: many random variables and parameters will be involved, and being true to the usual conventions from probability and statistics requires many extra symbols.

In the main text, we use a simpler convention that is widely used in econometrics. If θ is a population parameter, the notation $\hat{\theta}$ ("theta hat") will be used to denote both an estimator and an estimate of θ. This notation is useful in that it provides a simple way of attaching an estimator to the population parameter it is supposed to be estimating. Thus, if the population parameter is β, then $\hat{\beta}$ denotes an estimator or estimate of β; if the parameter is σ^2, $\hat{\sigma}^2$ is an estimator or estimate of σ^2; and so on. Sometimes, we will discuss two estimators of the same parameter, in which case we will need a different notation, such as $\tilde{\theta}$ ("theta tilde").

Although dropping the conventions from probability and statistics to indicate estimators, random variables, and test statistics puts additional responsibility on you, it is not a big deal once the difference between an estimator and an estimate is understood. If we are discussing *statistical* properties of $\hat{\theta}$—such as deriving whether or not it is unbiased or consistent—then we are necessarily viewing $\hat{\theta}$ as an estimator. On the other hand, if we write something like $\hat{\theta} = 1.73$, then we are clearly denoting a point estimate from a given sample of data. The confusion that can arise by using $\hat{\theta}$ to denote both should be minimal once you have a good understanding of probability and statistics.

Summary

We have discussed topics from mathematical statistics that are heavily relied upon in econometric analysis. The notion of an estimator, which is simply a rule for combining data to estimate a population parameter, is fundamental. We have covered various properties of estimators. The most important small sample properties are unbiasedness and efficiency, the latter of which depends on comparing variances when estimators are unbiased. Large sample properties concern the sequence of estimators obtained as the sample size grows, and they are also depended upon in econometrics. Any useful estimator is consistent. The central limit theorem implies that, in large samples, the sampling distribution of most estimators is approximately normal.

The sampling distribution of an estimator can be used to construct confidence intervals. We saw this for estimating the mean from a normal distribution and for computing approximate confidence intervals in nonnormal cases. Classical hypothesis testing, which requires specifying a null hypothesis, an alternative hypothesis, and a significance level, is carried out by comparing a test statistic to a critical value. Alternatively, a p-value can be computed that allows us to carry out a test at any significance level.

Key Terms

Alternative Hypothesis	Mean Squared Error (MSE)	Sample Covariance
Asymptotic Normality	Method of Moments	Sample Standard Deviation
Bias	Minimum Variance Unbiased	Sample Variance
Biased Estimator	Estimator	Sampling Distribution
Central Limit Theorem (CLT)	Null Hypothesis	Sampling Standard
Confidence Interval	One-Sided Alternative	Deviation
Consistent Estimator	One-Tailed Test	Sampling Variance
Consistent Test	Population	Significance Level
Critical Value	Power of a Test	Standard Error
Estimate	Practical Significance	Statistical Significance
Estimator	Probability Limit	t Statistic
Hypothesis Test	p-Value	Test Statistic
Inconsistent	Random Sample	Two-Sided Alternative
Interval Estimator	Rejection Region	Two-Tailed Test
Law of Large Numbers (LLN)	Sample Average	Type I Error
Least Squares Estimator	Sample Correlation	Type II Error
Maximum Likelihood Estimator	Coefficient	Unbiased Estimator

Problems

1 Let Y_1, Y_2, Y_3, and Y_4 be independent, identically distributed random variables from a population with mean μ and variance σ^2. Let $\overline{Y} = \frac{1}{4}(Y_1 + Y_2 + Y_3 + Y_4)$ denote the average of these four random variables.

(i) What are the expected value and variance of $\overline{Y}$ in terms of μ and σ^2?

(ii) Now, consider a different estimator of μ:

$$W = \frac{1}{8}Y_1 + \frac{1}{8}Y_2 + \frac{1}{4}Y_3 + \frac{1}{2}Y_4.$$

This is an example of a *weighted* average of the Y_i. Show that W is also an unbiased estimator of μ. Find the variance of W.

(iii) Based on your answers to parts (i) and (ii), which estimator of m do you prefer, $\overline{Y}$ or W?

2 This is a more general version of Problem C.1. Let Y_1, Y_2, ..., Y_n be n pairwise uncorrelated random variables with common mean m and common variance σ^2. Let $\overline{Y}$ denote the sample average.

(i) Define the class of *linear estimators* of μ by

$$W_a = a_1Y_1 + a_2Y_2 + \ \ldots \ + a_nY_n,$$

where the a_i are constants. What restriction on the a_i is needed for W_a to be an unbiased estimator of μ?

(ii) Find $\text{Var}(W_a)$.

(iii) For any numbers $a_1, a_2, \ldots, a_n$, the following inequality holds:
$(a_1 + a_2 + \ldots + a_n)^2/n \le a_1^2 + a_2^2 + \ldots + a_n^2$. Use this, along with parts (i) and (ii), to show that $\text{Var}(W_a) \ge \text{Var}(\bar{Y})$ whenever W_a is unbiased, so that $\bar{Y}$ is the *best linear unbiased estimator*. [*Hint*: What does the inequality become when the a_i satisfy the restriction from part (i)?]

3 Let $\bar{Y}$ denote the sample average from a random sample with mean μ and variance σ^2. Consider two alternative estimators of μ: $W_1 = [(n-1)/n]\bar{Y}$ and $W_2 = \bar{Y}/2$.
(i)   Show that W_1 and W_2 are both biased estimators of μ and find the biases. What happens to the biases as $n \to \infty$? Comment on any important differences in bias for the two estimators as the sample size gets large.
(ii) Find the probability limits of W_1 and W_2. {*Hint*: Use Properties PLIM.1 and PLIM.2; for W_1, note that plim $[(n-1)/n] = 1$.} Which estimator is consistent?
(iii) Find $\text{Var}(W_1)$ and $\text{Var}(W_2)$.
(iv) Argue that W_1 is a better estimator than $\bar{Y}$ if μ is "close" to zero. (Consider both bias and variance.)

4 For positive random variables X and Y, suppose the expected value of Y given X is $\text{E}(Y|X) = \theta X$. The unknown parameter θ shows how the expected value of Y changes with X.
(i)   Define the random variable $Z = Y/X$. Show that $\text{E}(Z) = \theta$. [*Hint*: Use Property CE.2 along with the law of iterated expectations, Property CE.4. In particular, first show that $\text{E}(Z|X) = \theta$ and then use CE.4.]
(ii) Use part (i) to prove that the estimator $W_1 = n^{-1}\sum_{i=1}^{n}(Y_i/X_i)$ is unbiased for θ, where $\{(X_i, Y_i): i = 1, 2, \ldots, n\}$ is a random sample.
(iii) Explain why the estimator $W_2 = \bar{Y}/\bar{X}$, where the overbars denote sample averages, is not the same as W_1. Nevertheless, show that W_2 is also unbiased for θ.
(iv) The following table contains data on corn yields for several counties in Iowa. The USDA predicts the number of hectares of corn in each county based on satellite photos. Researchers count the number of "pixels" of corn in the satellite picture (as opposed to, for example, the number of pixels of soybeans or of uncultivated land) and use these to predict the actual number of hectares. To develop a prediction equation to be used for counties in general, the USDA surveyed farmers in selected counties to obtain corn yields in hectares. Let Y_i = corn yield in county i and let X_i = number of corn pixels in the satellite picture for county i. There are $n = 17$ observations for eight counties. Use this sample to compute the estimates of θ devised in parts (ii) and (iii). Are the estimates similar?

Plot	Corn Yield	Corn Pixels
1	165.76	374
2	96.32	209
3	76.08	253
4	185.35	432
5	116.43	367
6	162.08	361
7	152.04	288
8	161.75	369
9	92.88	206
10	149.94	316
11	64.75	145
12	127.07	355
13	133.55	295
14	77.70	223
15	206.39	459
16	108.33	290
17	118.17	307

5 Let Y denote a Bernoulli(θ) random variable with $0 < \theta < 1$. Suppose we are interested in estimating the *odds ratio*, $\gamma = \theta/(1 - \theta)$, which is the probability of success over the probability of failure. Given a random sample $\{Y_1, \ldots, Y_n\}$, we know that an unbiased and consistent estimator of θ is $\overline{Y}$, the proportion of successes in n trials. A natural estimator of γ is $G = \overline{Y}/(1 - \overline{Y})$, the proportion of successes over the proportion of failures in the sample.

(i) Why is G not an unbiased estimator of γ?

(ii) Use PLIM.2 (iii) to show that G is a consistent estimator of γ.

6 You are hired by the governor to study whether a tax on liquor has decreased average liquor consumption in your state. You are able to obtain, for a sample of individuals selected at random, the difference in liquor consumption (in ounces) for the years before and after the tax. For person i who is sampled randomly from the population, Y_i denotes the change in liquor consumption. Treat these as a random sample from a Normal(μ, σ^2) distribution.

(i) The null hypothesis is that there was no change in average liquor consumption. State this formally in terms of μ.

(ii) The alternative is that there was a decline in liquor consumption; state the alternative in terms of μ.

(iii) Now, suppose your sample size is $n = 900$ and you obtain the estimates $\overline{y} = -32.8$ and $s = 466.4$. Calculate the t statistic for testing H_0 against H_1; obtain the p-value for the test. (Because of the large sample size, just use the standard normal distribution tabulated in Table G.1.) Do you reject H_0 at the 5% level? At the 1% level?

(iv) Would you say that the estimated fall in consumption is large in magnitude? Comment on the practical versus statistical significance of this estimate.

(v) What has been implicitly assumed in your analysis about other determinants of liquor consumption over the two-year period in order to infer causality from the tax change to liquor consumption?

7 The new management at a bakery claims that workers are now more productive than they were under old management, which is why wages have "generally increased." Let W_i^b be Worker i's wage under the old management and let W_i^a be Worker i's wage after the change. The difference is $D_i \equiv W_i^a - W_i^b$. Assume that the D_i are a random sample from a Normal (μ, σ^2) distribution.

(i) Using the following data on 15 workers, construct an exact 95% confidence interval for μ.

(ii) Formally state the null hypothesis that there has been no change in average wages. In particular, what is $E(D_i)$ under H_0? If you are hired to examine the validity of the new management's claim, what is the relevant alternative hypothesis in terms of $\mu = E(D_i)$?

(iii) Test the null hypothesis from part (ii) against the stated alternative at the 5% and 1% levels.

(iv) Obtain the p-value for the test in part (iii).

Worker	Wage Before	Wage After
1	8.30	9.25
2	9.40	9.00
3	9.00	9.25
4	10.50	10.00
5	11.40	12.00
6	8.75	9.50
7	10.00	10.25
8	9.50	9.50
9	10.80	11.50
10	12.55	13.10
11	12.00	11.50
12	8.65	9.00
13	7.75	7.75
14	11.25	11.50
15	12.65	13.00

8 The *New York Times* (2/5/90) reported three-point shooting performance for the top 10 three-point shooters in the NBA. The following table summarizes these data:

Player	FGA-FGM
Mark Price	429-188
Trent Tucker	833-345
Dale Ellis	1,149-472
Craig Hodges	1,016-396
Danny Ainge	1,051-406
Byron Scott	676-260
Reggie Miller	416-159
Larry Bird	1,206-455
Jon Sundvold	440-166
Brian Taylor	417-157

Note: *FGA* = field goals attempted and *FGM* = field goals made.

For a given player, the outcome of a particular shot can be modeled as a Bernoulli (zero-one) variable: if Y_i is the outcome of shot i, then $Y_i = 1$ if the shot is made, and $Y_i = 0$ if the shot is missed. Let θ denote the probability of making any particular three-point shot attempt. The natural estimator of θ is $\bar{Y} = FGM/FGA$.
(i) Estimate θ for Mark Price.
(ii) Find the standard deviation of the estimator $\bar{Y}$ in terms of θ and the number of shot attempts, n.
(iii) The asymptotic distribution of $(\bar{Y} - \theta)/se(\bar{Y})$ is standard normal, where $se(\bar{Y}) = \sqrt{\bar{Y}(1 - \bar{Y})/n}$. Use this fact to test H_0: $\theta = .5$ against H_1: $\theta < .5$ for Mark Price. Use a 1% significance level.

9 Suppose that a military dictator in an unnamed country holds a plebiscite (a yes/no vote of confidence) and claims that he was supported by 65% of the voters. A human rights group suspects foul play and hires you to test the validity of the dictator's claim. You have a budget that allows you to randomly sample 200 voters from the country.
(i) Let X be the number of yes votes obtained from a random sample of 200 out of the entire voting population. What is the expected value of X if, in fact, 65% of all voters supported the dictator?
(ii) What is the standard deviation of X, again assuming that the true fraction voting yes in the plebiscite is .65?
(iii) Now, you collect your sample of 200, and you find that 115 people actually voted yes. Use the CLT to approximate the probability that you would find 115 or fewer yes votes from a random sample of 200 if, in fact, 65% of the entire population voted yes.
(iv) How would you explain the relevance of the number in part (iii) to someone who does not have training in statistics?

10 Before a strike prematurely ended the 1994 major league baseball season, Tony Gwynn of the San Diego Padres had 165 hits in 419 at bats, for a .394 batting average. There was discussion about whether Gwynn was a potential .400 hitter that year. This issue can be couched in terms of Gwynn's probability of getting a hit on a particular at bat, call it θ. Let Y_i be the Bernoulli(θ) indicator equal to unity if Gwynn gets a hit during his i^{th} at bat, and zero otherwise. Then, $Y_1, Y_2, \ldots, Y_n$ is a random sample from a Bernoulli(θ) distribution, where θ is the probability of success, and $n = 419$.

Our best point estimate of θ is Gwynn's batting average, which is just the proportion of successes: $\bar{y} = .394$. Using the fact that $se(\bar{y}) = \sqrt{\bar{y}(1 - \bar{y})/n}$, construct an approximate 95% confidence interval for θ, using the standard normal distribution. Would you say there is strong evidence against Gwynn's being a potential .400 hitter? Explain.

11 Suppose that between their first and second years in college, 400 students are randomly selected and given a university grant to purchase a new computer. For student i, y_i denotes the change in GPA from the first year to the second year. If the average change is $\bar{y} = .132$ with standard deviation $s = 1.27$, is the average change in GPAs statistically greater than zero?

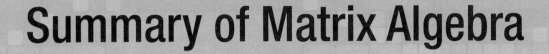

Appendix D

Summary of Matrix Algebra

This appendix summarizes the matrix algebra concepts, including the algebra of probability, needed for the study of multiple linear regression models using matrices in Appendix E. None of this material is used in the main text.

D-1 Basic Definitions

Definition D.1 (Matrix). A **matrix** is a rectangular array of numbers. More precisely, an $m \times n$ matrix has m rows and n columns. The positive integer m is called the *row dimension*, and n is called the *column dimension*.

We use uppercase boldface letters to denote matrices. We can write an $m \times n$ matrix generically as

$$\mathbf{A} = [a_{ij}] = \begin{bmatrix} a_{11} & a_{12} & a_{13} & \cdots & a_{1n} \\ a_{21} & a_{22} & a_{23} & \cdots & a_{2n} \\ \vdots & & & & \\ a_{m1} & a_{m2} & a_{m3} & \cdots & a_{mn} \end{bmatrix},$$

where a_{ij} represents the element in the ith row and the jth column. For example, a_{25} stands for the number in the second row and the fifth column of $\mathbf{A}$. A specific example of a 2×3 matrix is

$$\mathbf{A} = \begin{bmatrix} 2 & -1 & 7 \\ -4 & 5 & 0 \end{bmatrix}, \tag{D.1}$$

where $a_{13} = 7$. The shorthand $\mathbf{A} = [a_{ij}]$ is often used to define matrix operations.

Definition D.2 (Square Matrix). A **square matrix** has the same number of rows and columns. The dimension of a square matrix is its number of rows and columns.

Definition D.3 (Vectors)
(i) A $1 \times m$ matrix is called a **row vector** (of dimension m) and can be written as $\mathbf{x} \equiv (x_1, x_2, \ldots, x_m)$.

(ii) An $n \times 1$ matrix is called a **column vector** and can be written as

$$\mathbf{y} \equiv \begin{bmatrix} y_1 \\ y_2 \\ \vdots \\ y_n \end{bmatrix}.$$

Definition D.4 (Diagonal Matrix). A square matrix $\mathbf{A}$ is a **diagonal matrix** when all of its off-diagonal elements are zero, that is, $a_{ij} = 0$ for all $i \neq j$. We can always write a diagonal matrix as

$$\mathbf{A} = \begin{bmatrix} a_{11} & 0 & 0 & \dots & 0 \\ 0 & a_{22} & 0 & \dots & 0 \\ \vdots & & & & \\ 0 & 0 & 0 & \dots & a_{nn} \end{bmatrix}.$$

Definition D.5 (Identity and Zero Matrices)

(i) The $n \times n$ **identity matrix**, denoted $\mathbf{I}$, or sometimes $\mathbf{I}_n$ to emphasize its dimension, is the diagonal matrix with unity (one) in each diagonal position, and zero elsewhere:

$$\mathbf{I} \equiv \mathbf{I}_n \equiv \begin{bmatrix} 1 & 0 & 0 & \dots & 0 \\ 0 & 1 & 0 & \dots & 0 \\ \vdots & & & & \\ 0 & 0 & 0 & \dots & 1 \end{bmatrix}.$$

(ii) The $m \times n$ **zero matrix**, denoted $\mathbf{0}$, is the $m \times n$ matrix with zero for all entries. This need not be a square matrix.

D-2 Matrix Operations

D-2a Matrix Addition

Two matrices $\mathbf{A}$ and $\mathbf{B}$, each having dimension $m \times n$, can be added element by element: $\mathbf{A} + \mathbf{B} = [a_{ij} + b_{ij}]$. More precisely,

$$\mathbf{A} + \mathbf{B} = \begin{bmatrix} a_{11} + b_{11} & a_{12} + b_{12} & \dots & a_{1n} + b_{1n} \\ a_{21} + b_{21} & a_{22} + b_{22} & \dots & a_{2n} + b_{2n} \\ \vdots & & & \\ a_{m1} + b_{m1} & a_{m2} + b_{m2} & \dots & a_{mn} + b_{mn} \end{bmatrix}.$$

For example,

$$\begin{bmatrix} 2 & -1 & 7 \\ -4 & 5 & 0 \end{bmatrix} + \begin{bmatrix} 1 & 0 & -4 \\ 4 & 2 & 3 \end{bmatrix} = \begin{bmatrix} 3 & -1 & 3 \\ 0 & 7 & 3 \end{bmatrix}.$$

Matrices of different dimensions cannot be added.

D-2b Scalar Multiplication

Given any real number γ (often called a scalar), **scalar multiplication** is defined as $\gamma \mathbf{A} \equiv [\gamma a_{ij}]$, or

$$\gamma \mathbf{A} = \begin{bmatrix} \gamma a_{11} & \gamma a_{12} & \dots & \gamma a_{1n} \\ \gamma a_{21} & \gamma a_{22} & \dots & \gamma a_{2n} \\ \vdots & & & \\ \gamma a_{m1} & \gamma a_{m2} & \dots & \gamma a_{mn} \end{bmatrix}.$$

For example, if $\gamma = 2$ and **A** is the matrix in equation (D.1), then

$$\gamma \mathbf{A} = \begin{bmatrix} 4 & -2 & 14 \\ -8 & 10 & 0 \end{bmatrix}.$$

D-2c Matrix Multiplication

To multiply matrix **A** by matrix **B** to form the product **AB**, the *column* dimension of **A** must equal the *row* dimension of **B**. Therefore, let **A** be an $m \times n$ matrix and let **B** be an $n \times p$ matrix. Then, **matrix multiplication** is defined as

$$\mathbf{AB} = \left[\sum_{k=1}^{n} a_{ik} b_{kj} \right].$$

In other words, the $(i, j)^{\text{th}}$ element of the new matrix **AB** is obtained by multiplying each element in the ith row of **A** by the corresponding element in the jth column of **B** and adding these n products together. A schematic may help make this process more transparent:

$$i^{\text{th}} \text{ row} \rightarrow \begin{matrix} \mathbf{A} \\ \begin{bmatrix} & & & \\ a_{i1} a_{i2} a_{i3} \dots a_{in} & \\ & & & \end{bmatrix} \end{matrix} \begin{matrix} \mathbf{B} \\ \begin{bmatrix} b_{1j} \\ b_{2j} \\ b_{3j} \\ \vdots \\ b_{nj} \end{bmatrix} \end{matrix} = \begin{matrix} \mathbf{AB} \\ \begin{bmatrix} & & \\ & \sum_{k=1}^{n} a_{ik} b_{kj} & \\ & & \end{bmatrix} \end{matrix},$$

$$j^{\text{th}} \text{ column} \quad (i, j)^{\text{th}} \text{ element}$$

where, by the definition of the summation operator in Appendix A,

$$\sum_{k=1}^{n} a_{ik} b_{kj} = a_{i1} b_{1j} + a_{i2} b_{2j} + \dots + a_{in} b_{nj}.$$

For example,

$$\begin{bmatrix} 2 & -1 & 0 \\ -4 & 1 & 0 \end{bmatrix} \begin{bmatrix} 0 & 1 & 6 & 0 \\ -1 & 2 & 0 & 1 \\ 3 & 0 & 0 & 0 \end{bmatrix} = \begin{bmatrix} 1 & 0 & 12 & -1 \\ -1 & -2 & -24 & 1 \end{bmatrix}.$$

We can also multiply a matrix and a vector. If **A** is an $n \times m$ matrix and **y** is an $m \times 1$ vector, then **Ay** is an $n \times 1$ vector. If **x** is a $1 \times n$ vector, then **xA** is a $1 \times m$ vector.

Matrix addition, scalar multiplication, and matrix multiplication can be combined in various ways, and these operations satisfy several rules that are familiar from basic operations on numbers. In the following list of properties, **A**, **B**, and **C** are matrices with appropriate dimensions for applying each operation, and α and β are real numbers. Most of these properties are easy to illustrate from the definitions.

Properties of Matrix Operations. (1) $(\alpha + \beta)\mathbf{A} = \alpha\mathbf{A} + \beta\mathbf{A}$; (2) $\alpha(\mathbf{A} + \mathbf{B}) = \alpha\mathbf{A} + \alpha\mathbf{B}$; (3) $(\alpha\beta)\mathbf{A} = \alpha(\beta\mathbf{A})$; (4) $\alpha(\mathbf{AB}) = (\alpha\mathbf{A})\mathbf{B}$; (5) $\mathbf{A} + \mathbf{B} = \mathbf{B} + \mathbf{A}$; (6) $(\mathbf{A} + \mathbf{B}) + \mathbf{C} = \mathbf{A} + (\mathbf{B} + \mathbf{C})$; (7) $(\mathbf{AB})\mathbf{C} = \mathbf{A}(\mathbf{BC})$; (8) $\mathbf{A}(\mathbf{B} + \mathbf{C}) = \mathbf{AB} + \mathbf{AC}$; (9) $(\mathbf{A} + \mathbf{B})\mathbf{C} = \mathbf{AC} + \mathbf{BC}$; (10) $\mathbf{IA} = \mathbf{AI} = \mathbf{A}$; (11) $\mathbf{A} + \mathbf{0} = \mathbf{0} + \mathbf{A} = \mathbf{A}$; (12) $\mathbf{A} - \mathbf{A} = \mathbf{0}$; (13) $\mathbf{A0} = \mathbf{0A} = \mathbf{0}$; and (14) $\mathbf{AB} \neq \mathbf{BA}$, even when both products are defined.

The last property deserves further comment. If $\mathbf{A}$ is $n \times m$ and $\mathbf{B}$ is $m \times p$, then $\mathbf{AB}$ is defined, but $\mathbf{BA}$ is defined only if $n = p$ (the row dimension of $\mathbf{A}$ equals the column dimension of $\mathbf{B}$). If $\mathbf{A}$ is $m \times n$ and $\mathbf{B}$ is $n \times m$, then $\mathbf{AB}$ and $\mathbf{BA}$ are both defined, but they are not usually the same; in fact, they have different dimensions, unless $\mathbf{A}$ and $\mathbf{B}$ are both square matrices. Even when $\mathbf{A}$ and $\mathbf{B}$ are both square, $\mathbf{AB} \neq \mathbf{BA}$, except under special circumstances.

D-2d Transpose

Definition D.6 (Transpose). Let $\mathbf{A} = [a_{ij}]$ be an $m \times n$ matrix. The **transpose** of $\mathbf{A}$, denoted $\mathbf{A}'$ (called $\mathbf{A}$ *prime*), is the $n \times m$ matrix obtained by interchanging the rows and columns of $\mathbf{A}$. We can write this as $\mathbf{A}' \equiv [a_{ji}]$.

For example,

$$\mathbf{A} = \begin{bmatrix} 2 & -1 & 7 \\ -4 & 5 & 0 \end{bmatrix}, \quad \mathbf{A}' = \begin{bmatrix} 2 & -4 \\ -1 & 5 \\ 7 & 0 \end{bmatrix}.$$

Properties of Transpose. (1) $(\mathbf{A}')' = \mathbf{A}$; (2) $(\alpha\mathbf{A})' = \alpha\mathbf{A}'$ for any scalar α; (3) $(\mathbf{A} + \mathbf{B})' = \mathbf{A}' + \mathbf{B}'$; (4) $(\mathbf{AB})' = \mathbf{B}'\mathbf{A}'$, where $\mathbf{A}$ is $m \times n$ and $\mathbf{B}$ is $n \times k$; (5) $\mathbf{x}'\mathbf{x} = \sum_{i=1}^{n} x_i^2$, where $\mathbf{x}$ is an $n \times 1$ vector; and (6) If $\mathbf{A}$ is an $n \times k$ matrix with *rows* given by the $1 \times k$ vectors $\mathbf{a}_1, \mathbf{a}_2, \ldots, \mathbf{a}_n$, so that we can write

$$\mathbf{A} = \begin{bmatrix} \mathbf{a}_1 \\ \mathbf{a}_2 \\ \vdots \\ \mathbf{a}_n \end{bmatrix},$$

then $\mathbf{A}' = (\mathbf{a}_1' \, \mathbf{a}_2' \ldots \mathbf{a}_n')$.

Definition D.7 (Symmetric Matrix). A square matrix $\mathbf{A}$ is a **symmetric matrix** if, and only if, $\mathbf{A}' = \mathbf{A}$.

If $\mathbf{X}$ is any $n \times k$ matrix, then $\mathbf{X}'\mathbf{X}$ is always defined and is a symmetric matrix, as can be seen by applying the first and fourth transpose properties (see Problem 3).

D-2e Partitioned Matrix Multiplication

Let $\mathbf{A}$ be an $n \times k$ matrix with rows given by the $1 \times k$ vectors $\mathbf{a}_1, \mathbf{a}_2, \ldots, \mathbf{a}_n$, and let $\mathbf{B}$ be an $n \times m$ matrix with rows given by $1 \times m$ vectors $\mathbf{b}_1, \mathbf{b}_2, \ldots, \mathbf{b}_n$:

$$\mathbf{A} = \begin{bmatrix} \mathbf{a}_1 \\ \mathbf{a}_2 \\ \vdots \\ \mathbf{a}_n \end{bmatrix}, \quad \mathbf{B} = \begin{bmatrix} \mathbf{b}_1 \\ \mathbf{b}_2 \\ \vdots \\ \mathbf{b}_n \end{bmatrix}.$$

Then,

$$\mathbf{A}'\mathbf{B} = \sum_{i=1}^{n} \mathbf{a}_i' \mathbf{b}_i,$$

where for each i, $\mathbf{a}'_i \mathbf{b}_i$ is a $k \times m$ matrix. Therefore, $\mathbf{A}'\mathbf{B}$ can be written as the sum of n matrices, each of which is $k \times m$. As a special case, we have

$$\mathbf{A}'\mathbf{A} = \sum_{i=1}^{n} \mathbf{a}'_i \mathbf{a}_i,$$

where $\mathbf{a}'_i \mathbf{a}_i$ is a $k \times k$ matrix for all i.

A more general form of partitioned matrix multiplication holds when we have matrices $\mathbf{A}$ $(m \times n)$ and $\mathbf{B}$ $(n \times p)$ written as

$$\mathbf{A} = \begin{pmatrix} \mathbf{A}_{11} & \mathbf{A}_{12} \\ \mathbf{A}_{21} & \mathbf{A}_{22} \end{pmatrix}, \quad \mathbf{B} = \begin{pmatrix} \mathbf{B}_{11} & \mathbf{B}_{12} \\ \mathbf{B}_{21} & \mathbf{B}_{22} \end{pmatrix},$$

where $\mathbf{A}_{11}$ is $m_1 \times n_1$, $\mathbf{A}_{12}$ is $m_1 \times n_2$, $\mathbf{A}_{21}$ is $m_2 \times n_1$, $\mathbf{A}_{22}$ is $m_2 \times n_2$, $\mathbf{B}_{11}$ is $n_1 \times p_1$, $\mathbf{B}_{12}$ is $n_1 \times p_2$, $\mathbf{B}_{21}$ is $n_2 \times p_1$, and $\mathbf{B}_{22}$ is $n_2 \times p_2$. Naturally, $m_1 + m_2 = m$, $n_1 + n_2 = n$, and $p_1 + p_2 = p$.

When we form the product $\mathbf{AB}$, the expression looks just when the entries are scalars:

$$\mathbf{AB} = \begin{pmatrix} \mathbf{A}_{11}\mathbf{B}_{11} + \mathbf{A}_{12}\mathbf{B}_{21} & \mathbf{A}_{11}\mathbf{B}_{12} + \mathbf{A}_{12}\mathbf{B}_{22} \\ \mathbf{A}_{21}\mathbf{B}_{11} + \mathbf{A}_{22}\mathbf{B}_{21} & \mathbf{A}_{21}\mathbf{B}_{12} + \mathbf{A}_{22}\mathbf{B}_{22} \end{pmatrix}.$$

Note that each of the matrix multiplications that form the partition on the right is well defined because the column and row dimensions are compatible for multiplication.

D-2f Trace

The trace of a matrix is a very simple operation defined only for *square* matrices.

Definition D.8 (Trace). For any $n \times n$ matrix $\mathbf{A}$, the **trace of a matrix** $\mathbf{A}$, denoted $\text{tr}(\mathbf{A})$, is the sum of its diagonal elements. Mathematically,

$$\text{tr}(\mathbf{A}) = \sum_{i=1}^{n} a_{ii}.$$

Properties of Trace. (1) $\text{tr}(\mathbf{I}_n) = n$; (2) $\text{tr}(\mathbf{A}') = \text{tr}(\mathbf{A})$; (3) $\text{tr}(\mathbf{A} + \mathbf{B}) = \text{tr}(\mathbf{A}) + \text{tr}(\mathbf{B})$; (4) $\text{tr}(\alpha\mathbf{A}) = \alpha\text{tr}(\mathbf{A})$, for any scalar α; and (5) $\text{tr}(\mathbf{AB}) = \text{tr}(\mathbf{BA})$, where $\mathbf{A}$ is $m \times n$ and $\mathbf{B}$ is $n \times m$.

D-2g Inverse

The notion of a matrix inverse is very important for square matrices.

Definition D.9 (Inverse). An $n \times n$ matrix $\mathbf{A}$ has an **inverse**, denoted $\mathbf{A}^{-1}$, provided that $\mathbf{A}^{-1}\mathbf{A} = \mathbf{I}_n$ and $\mathbf{A}\mathbf{A}^{-1} = \mathbf{I}_n$. In this case, $\mathbf{A}$ is said to be *invertible* or *nonsingular*. Otherwise, it is said to be *noninvertible* or *singular*.

Properties of Inverse. (1) If an inverse exists, it is unique; (2) $(\alpha\mathbf{A})^{-1} = (1/\alpha)\mathbf{A}^{-1}$, if $\alpha \neq 0$ and $\mathbf{A}$ is invertible; (3) $(\mathbf{AB})^{-1} = \mathbf{B}^{-1}\mathbf{A}^{-1}$, if $\mathbf{A}$ and $\mathbf{B}$ are both $n \times n$ and invertible; and (4) $(\mathbf{A}')^{-1} = (\mathbf{A}^{-1})'$.

We will not be concerned with the mechanics of calculating the inverse of a matrix. Any matrix algebra text contains detailed examples of such calculations.

D-3 Linear Independence and Rank of a Matrix

For a set of vectors having the same dimension, it is important to know whether one vector can be expressed as a linear combination of the remaining vectors.

Definition D.10 (Linear Independence). Let $\{x_1, x_2, \ldots, x_r\}$ be a set of $n \times 1$ vectors. These are **linearly independent vectors** if, and only if,

$$\alpha_1 x_1 + \alpha_2 x_2 + \ldots + \alpha_r x_r = 0 \qquad \text{[D.2]}$$

implies that $\alpha_1 = \alpha_2 = \ldots = \alpha_r = 0$. If (D.2) holds for a set of scalars that are not all zero, then $\{x_1, x_2, \ldots, x_r\}$ is *linearly dependent*.

The statement that $\{x_1, x_2, \ldots, x_r\}$ is linearly dependent is equivalent to saying that at least one vector in this set can be written as a linear combination of the others.

Definition D.11 (Rank)

(i) Let A be an $n \times m$ matrix. The **rank of a matrix** A, denoted rank(A), is the maximum number of linearly independent columns of A.

(ii) If A is $n \times m$ and rank(A) $= m$, then A has *full column rank*.

If A is $n \times m$, its rank can be at most m. A matrix has full column rank if its columns form a linearly independent set. For example, the 3×2 matrix

$$\begin{bmatrix} 1 & 3 \\ 2 & 6 \\ 0 & 0 \end{bmatrix}$$

can have at most rank two. In fact, its rank is only one because the second column is three times the first column.

Properties of Rank. (1) rank(A') $=$ rank(A); (2) If A is $n \times k$, then rank(A) $\leq \min(n, k)$; and (3) If A is $k \times k$ and rank(A) $= k$, then A is invertible.

D-4 Quadratic Forms and Positive Definite Matrices

Definition D.12 (Quadratic Form). Let A be an $n \times n$ *symmetric* matrix. The **quadratic form** associated with the matrix A is the real-valued function defined for all $n \times 1$ vectors x:

$$f(x) = x'Ax = \sum_{i=1}^{n} a_{ii} x_i^2 + 2 \sum_{i=1}^{n} \sum_{j>i}^{n} a_{ij} x_i x_j.$$

Definition D.13 (Positive Definite and Positive Semi-Definite)

(i) A symmetric matrix A is said to be **positive definite (p.d.)** if

$$x'Ax > 0 \text{ for all } n \times 1 \text{ vectors } x \text{ except } x = 0.$$

(ii) A symmetric matrix A is **positive semi-definite (p.s.d.)** if

$$x'Ax \geq 0 \text{ for all } n \times 1 \text{ vectors.}$$

If a matrix is positive definite or positive semi-definite, it is automatically assumed to be symmetric.

Properties of Positive Definite and Positive Semi-Definite Matrices. (1) A p.d. matrix has diagonal elements that are strictly positive, while a p.s.d. matrix has nonnegative diagonal elements; (2) If $\mathbf{A}$ is p.d., then $\mathbf{A}^{-1}$ exists and is p.d.; (3) If $\mathbf{X}$ is $n \times k$, then $\mathbf{X}'\mathbf{X}$ and $\mathbf{X}\mathbf{X}'$ are p.s.d.; and (4) If $\mathbf{X}$ is $n \times k$ and rank$(\mathbf{X}) = k$, then $\mathbf{X}'\mathbf{X}$ is p.d. (and therefore nonsingular).

D-5 Idempotent Matrices

Definition D.14 (Idempotent Matrix). Let $\mathbf{A}$ be an $n \times n$ symmetric matrix. Then $\mathbf{A}$ is said to be an **idempotent matrix** if, and only if, $\mathbf{A}\mathbf{A} = \mathbf{A}$.

For example,

$$\begin{bmatrix} 1 & 0 & 0 \\ 0 & 0 & 0 \\ 0 & 0 & 1 \end{bmatrix}$$

is an idempotent matrix, as direct multiplication verifies.

Properties of Idempotent Matrices. Let $\mathbf{A}$ be an $n \times n$ idempotent matrix. (1) rank$(\mathbf{A}) = \text{tr}(\mathbf{A})$, and (2) $\mathbf{A}$ is positive semi-definite.

We can construct idempotent matrices very generally. Let $\mathbf{X}$ be an $n \times k$ matrix with rank$(\mathbf{X}) = k$. Define

$$\mathbf{P} \equiv \mathbf{X}(\mathbf{X}'\mathbf{X})^{-1}\mathbf{X}'$$
$$\mathbf{M} \equiv \mathbf{I}_n - \mathbf{X}(\mathbf{X}'\mathbf{X})^{-1}\mathbf{X}' = \mathbf{I}_n - \mathbf{P}.$$

Then $\mathbf{P}$ and $\mathbf{M}$ are symmetric, idempotent matrices with rank$(\mathbf{P}) = k$ and rank$(\mathbf{M}) = n - k$. The ranks are most easily obtained by using Property 1: tr$(\mathbf{P}) = \text{tr}[(\mathbf{X}'\mathbf{X})^{-1}\mathbf{X}'\mathbf{X}]$ (from Property 5 for trace) $= \text{tr}(\mathbf{I}_k) = k$ (by Property 1 for trace). It easily follows that tr$(\mathbf{M}) = \text{tr}(\mathbf{I}_n) - \text{tr}(\mathbf{P}) = n - k$.

D-6 Differentiation of Linear and Quadratic Forms

For a given $n \times 1$ vector $\mathbf{a}$, consider the linear function defined by

$$f(\mathbf{x}) = \mathbf{a}'\mathbf{x},$$

for all $n \times 1$ vectors $\mathbf{x}$. The derivative of f with respect to $\mathbf{x}$ is the $1 \times n$ vector of partial derivatives, which is simply

$$\partial f(\mathbf{x})/\partial \mathbf{x} = \mathbf{a}'.$$

For an $n \times n$ symmetric matrix $\mathbf{A}$, define the quadratic form

$$g(\mathbf{x}) = \mathbf{x}'\mathbf{A}\mathbf{x}.$$

Then,

$$\partial g(\mathbf{x})/\partial \mathbf{x} = 2\mathbf{x}'\mathbf{A},$$

which is a $1 \times n$ vector.

D-7 Moments and Distributions of Random Vectors

In order to derive the expected value and variance of the OLS estimators using matrices, we need to define the expected value and variance of a **random vector**. As its name suggests, a random vector is simply a vector of random variables. We also need to define the multivariate normal distribution. These concepts are simply extensions of those covered in Appendix B.

D-7a Expected Value

Definition D.15 (Expected Value)

(i) If $\mathbf{y}$ is an $n \times 1$ random vector, the **expected value** of $\mathbf{y}$, denoted $E(\mathbf{y})$, is the vector of expected values: $E(\mathbf{y}) = [E(y_1), E(y_2), \ldots, E(y_n)]'$.

(ii) If $\mathbf{Z}$ is an $n \times m$ random matrix, $E(\mathbf{Z})$ is the $n \times m$ matrix of expected values: $E(\mathbf{Z}) = [E(z_{ij})]$.

Properties of Expected Value. (1) If $\mathbf{A}$ is an $m \times n$ matrix and $\mathbf{b}$ is an $n \times 1$ vector, where both are nonrandom, then $E(\mathbf{A}\mathbf{y} + \mathbf{b}) = \mathbf{A}E(\mathbf{y}) + \mathbf{b}$; and (2) If $\mathbf{A}$ is $p \times n$ and $\mathbf{B}$ is $m \times k$, where both are nonrandom, then $E(\mathbf{A}\mathbf{Z}\mathbf{B}) = \mathbf{A}E(\mathbf{Z})\mathbf{B}$.

D-7b Variance-Covariance Matrix

Definition D.16 (Variance-Covariance Matrix). If $\mathbf{y}$ is an $n \times 1$ random vector, its **variance-covariance matrix**, denoted $\text{Var}(\mathbf{y})$, is defined as

$$
\text{Var}(\mathbf{y}) = \begin{bmatrix} \sigma_1^2 & \sigma_{12} & \cdots & \sigma_{1n} \\ \sigma_{21} & \sigma_2^2 & \cdots & \sigma_{2n} \\ \vdots & & & \\ \sigma_{n1} & \sigma_{n2} & \cdots & \sigma_n^2 \end{bmatrix},
$$

where $\sigma_j^2 = \text{Var}(y_j)$ and $\sigma_{ij} = \text{Cov}(y_i, y_j)$. In other words, the variance-covariance matrix has the variances of each element of $\mathbf{y}$ down its diagonal, with covariance terms in the off diagonals. Because $\text{Cov}(y_i, y_j) = \text{Cov}(y_j, y_i)$, it immediately follows that a variance-covariance matrix is symmetric.

Properties of Variance. (1) If $\mathbf{a}$ is an $n \times 1$ nonrandom vector, then $\text{Var}(\mathbf{a}'\mathbf{y}) = \mathbf{a}'[\text{Var}(\mathbf{y})\mathbf{a} \geq 0$; (2) If $\text{Var}(\mathbf{a}'\mathbf{y}) > 0$ for all $\mathbf{a} \neq \mathbf{0}$, $\text{Var}(\mathbf{y})$ is positive definite; (3) $\text{Var}(\mathbf{y}) = E[(\mathbf{y} - \boldsymbol{\mu})(\mathbf{y} - \boldsymbol{\mu})']$, where $\boldsymbol{\mu} = E(\mathbf{y})$; (4) If the elements of $\mathbf{y}$ are uncorrelated, $\text{Var}(\mathbf{y})$ is a diagonal matrix. If, in addition, $\text{Var}(y_j) = \sigma^2$ for $j = 1, 2, \ldots, n$, then $\text{Var}(\mathbf{y}) = \sigma^2\mathbf{I}_n$; and (5) If $\mathbf{A}$ is an $m \times n$ nonrandom matrix and $\mathbf{b}$ is an $n \times 1$ nonrandom vector, then $\text{Var}(\mathbf{A}\mathbf{y} + \mathbf{b}) = \mathbf{A}[\text{Var}(\mathbf{y})]\mathbf{A}'$.

D-7c Multivariate Normal Distribution

The normal distribution for a random variable was discussed at some length in Appendix B. We need to extend the normal distribution to random vectors. We will not provide an expression for the probability distribution function, as we do not need it. It is important to know that a multivariate normal random vector is completely characterized by its mean and its variance-covariance matrix. Therefore, if $\mathbf{y}$ is an $n \times 1$ multivariate normal random vector with mean $\boldsymbol{\mu}$ and variance-covariance matrix $\boldsymbol{\Sigma}$, we write $\mathbf{y} \sim \text{Normal}(\boldsymbol{\mu}, \boldsymbol{\Sigma})$. We now state several useful properties of the **multivariate normal distribution**.

Properties of the Multivariate Normal Distribution. (1) If $\mathbf{y} \sim \text{Normal}(\boldsymbol{\mu}, \boldsymbol{\Sigma})$, then each element of $\mathbf{y}$ is normally distributed; (2) If $\mathbf{y} \sim \text{Normal}(\boldsymbol{\mu}, \boldsymbol{\Sigma})$, then y_i and y_j, any two elements of $\mathbf{y}$, are independent if, and only if, they are uncorrelated, that is, $\sigma_{ij} = 0$; (3) If $\mathbf{y} \sim \text{Normal}(\boldsymbol{\mu}, \boldsymbol{\Sigma})$, then $\mathbf{A}\mathbf{y} + \mathbf{b} \sim \text{Normal}(\mathbf{A}\boldsymbol{\mu} + \mathbf{b}, \mathbf{A}\boldsymbol{\Sigma}\mathbf{A}')$, where $\mathbf{A}$ and $\mathbf{b}$ are nonrandom; (4) If $\mathbf{y} \sim \text{Normal}(\mathbf{0}, \boldsymbol{\Sigma})$, then, for nonrandom matrices $\mathbf{A}$ and $\mathbf{B}$, $\mathbf{A}\mathbf{y}$ and $\mathbf{B}\mathbf{y}$ are independent if, and only if, $\mathbf{A}\boldsymbol{\Sigma}\mathbf{B}' = \mathbf{0}$. In particular, if $\boldsymbol{\Sigma} = \sigma^2\mathbf{I}_n$, then $\mathbf{A}\mathbf{B}' = \mathbf{0}$ is necessary and sufficient for independence of $\mathbf{A}\mathbf{y}$ and $\mathbf{B}\mathbf{y}$; (5) If $\mathbf{y} \sim \text{Normal}(\mathbf{0}, \sigma^2\mathbf{I}_n)$, $\mathbf{A}$ is a $k \times n$ nonrandom matrix, and $\mathbf{B}$ is an $n \times n$ symmetric, idempotent matrix, then $\mathbf{A}\mathbf{y}$ and $\mathbf{y}'\mathbf{B}\mathbf{y}$ are independent if, and only if, $\mathbf{A}\mathbf{B} = \mathbf{0}$; and (6) If $\mathbf{y} \sim \text{Normal}(\mathbf{0}, \sigma^2\mathbf{I}_n)$ and $\mathbf{A}$ and $\mathbf{B}$ are nonrandom symmetric, idempotent matrices, then $\mathbf{y}'\mathbf{A}\mathbf{y}$ and $\mathbf{y}'\mathbf{B}\mathbf{y}$ are independent if, and only if, $\mathbf{A}\mathbf{B} = \mathbf{0}$.

D-7d Chi-Square Distribution

In Appendix B, we defined a **chi-square random variable** as the sum of *squared* independent standard normal random variables. In vector notation, if $\mathbf{u} \sim \text{Normal}(\mathbf{0}, \mathbf{I}_n)$, then $\mathbf{u}'\mathbf{u} \sim \chi^2_n$.

Properties of the Chi-Square Distribution. (1) If $\mathbf{u} \sim \text{Normal}(\mathbf{0}, \mathbf{I}_n)$ and $\mathbf{A}$ is an $n \times n$ symmetric, idempotent matrix with $\text{rank}(\mathbf{A}) = q$, then $\mathbf{u}'\mathbf{A}\mathbf{u} \sim \chi^2_q$; (2) If $\mathbf{u} \sim \text{Normal}(\mathbf{0}, \mathbf{I}_n)$ and $\mathbf{A}$ and $\mathbf{B}$ are $n \times n$ symmetric, idempotent matrices such that $\mathbf{A}\mathbf{B} = \mathbf{0}$, then $\mathbf{u}'\mathbf{A}\mathbf{u}$ and $\mathbf{u}'\mathbf{B}\mathbf{u}$ are independent, chi-square random variables; and (3) If $\mathbf{z} \sim \text{Normal}(\mathbf{0}, \mathbf{C})$, where $\mathbf{C}$ is an $m \times m$ nonsingular matrix, then $\mathbf{z}'\mathbf{C}^{-1}\mathbf{z} \sim \chi^2_m$.

D-7e *t* Distribution

We also defined the *t* **distribution** in Appendix B. Now we add an important property.

Property of the t Distribution. If $\mathbf{u} \sim \text{Normal}(\mathbf{0}, \mathbf{I}_n)$, $\mathbf{c}$ is an $n \times 1$ nonrandom vector, $\mathbf{A}$ is a nonrandom $n \times n$ symmetric, idempotent matrix with rank q, and $\mathbf{A}\mathbf{c} = \mathbf{0}$, then $\{\mathbf{c}'\mathbf{u}/(\mathbf{c}'\mathbf{c})^{1/2}\}/(\mathbf{u}'\mathbf{A}\mathbf{u}/q)^{1/2} \sim t_q$.

D-7f *F* Distribution

Recall that an *F* **random variable** is obtained by taking two *independent* chi-square random variables and finding the ratio of each, standardized by degrees of freedom.

Property of the F Distribution. If $\mathbf{u} \sim \text{Normal}(\mathbf{0}, \mathbf{I}_n)$ and $\mathbf{A}$ and $\mathbf{B}$ are $n \times n$ nonrandom symmetric, idempotent matrices with $\text{rank}(\mathbf{A}) = k_1$, $\text{rank}(\mathbf{B}) = k_2$, and $\mathbf{A}\mathbf{B} = \mathbf{0}$, then $(\mathbf{u}'\mathbf{A}\mathbf{u}/k_1)/(\mathbf{u}'\mathbf{B}\mathbf{u}/k_2) \sim F_{k_1, k_2}$.

Summary

This appendix contains a condensed form of the background information needed to study the classical linear model using matrices. Although the material here is self-contained, it is primarily intended as a review for readers who are familiar with matrix algebra and multivariate statistics, and it will be used extensively in Appendix E.

Key Terms

Chi-Square Random Variable	Idempotent Matrix	Matrix Multiplication
Column Vector	Identity Matrix	Multivariate Normal Distribution
Diagonal Matrix	Inverse	Positive Definite (p.d.)
Expected Value	Linearly Independent Vectors	Positive Semi-Definite (p.s.d.)
F Random Variable	Matrix	Quadratic Form

Random Vector   Square Matrix   Transpose
Rank of a Matrix   Symmetric Matrix   Variance-Covariance Matrix
Row Vector t Distribution   Zero Matrix
Scalar Multiplication   Trace of a Matrix

Problems

1 (i) Find the product $\mathbf{AB}$ using

$$\mathbf{A} = \begin{bmatrix} 2 & -1 & 7 \\ -4 & 5 & 0 \end{bmatrix}, \mathbf{B} = \begin{bmatrix} 0 & 1 & 6 \\ 1 & 8 & 0 \\ 3 & 0 & 0 \end{bmatrix}.$$

(ii) Does $\mathbf{BA}$ exist?

2 If $\mathbf{A}$ and $\mathbf{B}$ are $n \times n$ diagonal matrices, show that $\mathbf{AB} = \mathbf{BA}$.

3 Let $\mathbf{X}$ be any $n \times k$ matrix. Show that $\mathbf{X}'\mathbf{X}$ is a symmetric matrix.

4 (i) Use the properties of trace to argue that $\text{tr}(\mathbf{A}'\mathbf{A}) = \text{tr}(\mathbf{AA}')$ for any $n \times m$ matrix $\mathbf{A}$.

(ii) For $\mathbf{A} = \begin{bmatrix} 2 & 0 & -1 \\ 0 & 3 & 0 \end{bmatrix}$, verify that $\text{tr}(\mathbf{A}'\mathbf{A}) = \text{tr}(\mathbf{AA}')$.

5 (i) Use the definition of inverse to prove the following: if $\mathbf{A}$ and $\mathbf{B}$ are $n \times n$ nonsingular matrices, then $(\mathbf{AB})^{-1} = \mathbf{B}^{-1}\mathbf{A}^{-1}$.

(ii) If $\mathbf{A}$, $\mathbf{B}$, and $\mathbf{C}$ are all $n \times n$ nonsingular matrices, find $(\mathbf{ABC})^{-1}$ in terms of $\mathbf{A}^{-1}$, $\mathbf{B}^{-1}$, and $\mathbf{C}^{-1}$.

6 (i) Show that if $\mathbf{A}$ is an $n \times n$ symmetric, positive definite matrix, then $\mathbf{A}$ must have strictly positive diagonal elements.

(ii) Write down a 2×2 symmetric matrix with strictly positive diagonal elements that is *not* positive definite.

7 Let $\mathbf{A}$ be an $n \times n$ symmetric, positive definite matrix. Show that if $\mathbf{P}$ is any $n \times n$ nonsingular matrix, then $\mathbf{P}'\mathbf{AP}$ is positive definite.

8 Prove Property 5 of variances for vectors, using Property 3.

9 Let $\mathbf{a}$ be an $n \times 1$ nonrandom vector and let $\mathbf{u}$ be an $n \times 1$ random vector with $\text{E}(\mathbf{uu}') = \mathbf{I}_n$. Show that $\text{E}[\text{tr}(\mathbf{auu}'\mathbf{a}')] = \sum_{i=1}^{n} a_i^2$.

10 Take as given the properties of the chi-square distribution listed in the text. Show how those properties, along with the definition of an F random variable, imply the stated property of the F distribution (concerning ratios of quadratic forms).

11 Let $\mathbf{X}$ be an $n \times k$ matrix partitioned as

$$\mathbf{X} = (\mathbf{X}_1 \ \mathbf{X}_2),$$

where $\mathbf{X}_1$ is $n \times k_1$ and $\mathbf{X}_2$ is $n \times k_2$.

(i) Show that

$$\mathbf{X}'\mathbf{X} = \begin{pmatrix} \mathbf{X}_1'\mathbf{X}_1 & \mathbf{X}_1'\mathbf{X}_2 \\ \mathbf{X}_2'\mathbf{X}_1 & \mathbf{X}_2'\mathbf{X}_2 \end{pmatrix}.$$

What are the dimensions of each of the matrices?

(ii) Let **b** be a $k \times 1$ vector, partitioned as

$$\mathbf{b} = \begin{pmatrix} \mathbf{b}_1 \\ \mathbf{b}_2 \end{pmatrix},$$

where $\mathbf{b}_1$ is $k_1 \times 1$ and $\mathbf{b}_2$ is $k_2 \times 1$. Show that

$$(\mathbf{X}'\mathbf{X})\mathbf{b} = \begin{pmatrix} (\mathbf{X}_1'\mathbf{X}_1)\mathbf{b}_1 + (\mathbf{X}_1'\mathbf{X}_2)\mathbf{b}_2 \\ (\mathbf{X}_2'\mathbf{X}_1)\mathbf{b}_1 + (\mathbf{X}_2'\mathbf{X}_2)\mathbf{b}_2 \end{pmatrix}.$$

Appendix E

The Linear Regression Model in Matrix Form

This appendix derives various results for ordinary least squares estimation of the multiple linear regression model using matrix notation and matrix algebra (see Appendix D for a summary). The material presented here is much more advanced than that in the text.

E-1 The Model and Ordinary Least Squares Estimation

Throughout this appendix, we use the t subscript to index observations and an n to denote the sample size. It is useful to write the multiple linear regression model with k parameters as follows:

$$y_t = \beta_0 + \beta_1 x_{t1} + \beta_2 x_{t2} + \ldots + \beta_k x_{tk} + u_t, \quad t = 1, 2, \ldots, n, \qquad \text{[E.1]}$$

where y_t is the dependent variable for observation t and $x_{tj}, j = 1, 2, \ldots, k$, are the independent variables. As usual, β_0 is the intercept and $\beta_1, \ldots, \beta_k$ denote the slope parameters.

For each t, define a $1 \times (k + 1)$ vector, $\mathbf{x}_t = (1, x_{t1}, \ldots, x_{tk})$, and let $\boldsymbol{\beta} = (\beta_0, \beta_1, \ldots, \beta_k)'$ be the $(k + 1) \times 1$ vector of all parameters. Then, we can write (E.1) as

$$y_t = \mathbf{x}_t \boldsymbol{\beta} + u_t, \quad t = 1, 2, \ldots, n. \qquad \text{[E.2]}$$

[Some authors prefer to define $\mathbf{x}_t$ as a column vector, in which case $\mathbf{x}_t$ is replaced with $\mathbf{x}_t'$ in (E.2). Mathematically, it makes more sense to define it as a row vector.] We can write (E.2) in full matrix notation by appropriately defining data vectors and matrices. Let $\mathbf{y}$ denote the $n \times 1$ vector of observations on y: the tth element of $\mathbf{y}$ is y_t. Let $\mathbf{X}$ be the $n \times (k + 1)$ vector of observations on the explanatory variables. In other words, the tth row of $\mathbf{X}$ consists of the vector $\mathbf{x}_t$. Written out in detail,

$$\underset{n \times (k+1)}{\mathbf{X}} \equiv \begin{bmatrix} \mathbf{x}_1 \\ \mathbf{x}_2 \\ \vdots \\ \mathbf{x}_n \end{bmatrix} = \begin{bmatrix} 1 & x_{11} & x_{12} & \ldots & x_{1k} \\ 1 & x_{21} & x_{22} & \ldots & x_{2k} \\ \vdots & & & & \\ 1 & x_{n1} & x_{n2} & \ldots & x_{nk} \end{bmatrix}.$$

Finally, let **u** be the $n \times 1$ vector of unobservable errors or disturbances. Then, we can write (E.2) for all n observations in **matrix notation**:

$$\mathbf{y} = \mathbf{X}\boldsymbol{\beta} + \mathbf{u}. \qquad [\text{E.3}]$$

Remember, because **X** is $n \times (k + 1)$ and $\boldsymbol{\beta}$ is $(k + 1) \times 1$, $\mathbf{X}\boldsymbol{\beta}$ is $n \times 1$.

Estimation of $\boldsymbol{\beta}$ proceeds by minimizing the sum of squared residuals, as in Section 3-2. Define the sum of squared residuals function for any possible $(k + 1) \times 1$ parameter vector **b** as

$$\text{SSR}(\mathbf{b}) \equiv \sum_{t=1}^{n} (y_t - \mathbf{x}_t\mathbf{b})^2.$$

The $(k + 1) \times 1$ vector of ordinary least squares estimates, $\hat{\boldsymbol{\beta}} = (\hat{\beta}_0, \hat{\beta}_1, ..., \hat{\beta}_k)'$, minimizes SSR(**b**) over all possible $(k + 1) \times 1$ vectors **b**. This is a problem in multivariable calculus. For $\hat{\boldsymbol{\beta}}$ to minimize the sum of squared residuals, it must solve the **first order condition**

$$\partial \text{SSR}(\hat{\boldsymbol{\beta}})/\partial \mathbf{b} \equiv \mathbf{0}. \qquad [\text{E.4}]$$

Using the fact that the derivative of $(y_t - \mathbf{x}_t\mathbf{b})^2$ with respect to **b** is the $1 \times (k + 1)$ vector $-2(y_t - \mathbf{x}_t\mathbf{b})\mathbf{x}_t$, (E.4) is equivalent to

$$\sum_{t=1}^{n} \mathbf{x}_t'(y_t - \mathbf{x}_t\hat{\boldsymbol{\beta}}) \equiv \mathbf{0}. \qquad [\text{E.5}]$$

(We have divided by -2 and taken the transpose.) We can write this first order condition as

$$\sum_{t=1}^{n} (y_t - \hat{\beta}_0 - \hat{\beta}_1 x_{t1} - ... - \hat{\beta}_k x_{tk}) = 0$$

$$\sum_{t=1}^{n} x_{t1}(y_t - \hat{\beta}_0 - \hat{\beta}_1 x_{t1} - ... - \hat{\beta}_k x_{tk}) = 0$$

$$\vdots$$

$$\sum_{t=1}^{n} x_{tk}(y_t - \hat{\beta}_0 - \hat{\beta}_1 x_{t1} - ... - \hat{\beta}_k x_{tk}) = 0,$$

which is identical to the first order conditions in equation (3.13). We want to write these in matrix form to make them easier to manipulate. Using the formula for partitioned multiplication in Appendix D, we see that (E.5) is equivalent to

$$\mathbf{X}'(\mathbf{y} - \mathbf{X}\hat{\boldsymbol{\beta}}) = \mathbf{0} \qquad [\text{E.6}]$$

or

$$(\mathbf{X}'\mathbf{X})\hat{\boldsymbol{\beta}} = \mathbf{X}'\mathbf{y}. \qquad [\text{E.7}]$$

It can be shown that (E.7) always has at least one solution. Multiple solutions do not help us, as we are looking for a unique set of OLS estimates given our data set. Assuming that the $(k + 1) \times (k + 1)$ symmetric matrix $\mathbf{X}'\mathbf{X}$ is nonsingular, we can premultiply both sides of (E.7) by $(\mathbf{X}'\mathbf{X})^{-1}$ to solve for the OLS estimator $\hat{\boldsymbol{\beta}}$:

$$\hat{\boldsymbol{\beta}} = (\mathbf{X}'\mathbf{X})^{-1}\mathbf{X}'\mathbf{y}. \qquad [\text{E.8}]$$

This is the critical formula for matrix analysis of the multiple linear regression model. The assumption that $\mathbf{X}'\mathbf{X}$ is invertible is equivalent to the assumption that $\text{rank}(\mathbf{X}) = (k + 1)$, which means that the columns of **X** must be linearly independent. This is the matrix version of MLR.3 in Chapter 3.

Before we continue, (E.8) warrants a word of warning. It is tempting to simplify the formula for $\hat{\boldsymbol{\beta}}$ as follows:

$$\hat{\boldsymbol{\beta}} = (\mathbf{X}'\mathbf{X})^{-1}\mathbf{X}'\mathbf{y} = \mathbf{X}^{-1}(\mathbf{X}')^{-1}\mathbf{X}'\mathbf{y} = \mathbf{X}^{-1}\mathbf{y}.$$

The flaw in this reasoning is that $\mathbf{X}$ is usually not a square matrix, so it cannot be inverted. In other words, we cannot write $(\mathbf{X}'\mathbf{X})^{-1} = \mathbf{X}^{-1}(\mathbf{X}')^{-1}$ unless $n = (k + 1)$, a case that virtually never arises in practice.

The $n \times 1$ vectors of OLS fitted values and residuals are given by

$$\hat{\mathbf{y}} = \mathbf{X}\hat{\boldsymbol{\beta}}, \hat{\mathbf{u}} = \mathbf{y} - \hat{\mathbf{y}} = \mathbf{y} - \mathbf{X}\hat{\boldsymbol{\beta}}, \text{ respectively.}$$

From (E.6) and the definition of $\hat{\mathbf{u}}$, we can see that the first order condition for $\hat{\boldsymbol{\beta}}$ is the same as

$$\mathbf{X}'\hat{\mathbf{u}} = \mathbf{0}. \tag{E.9}$$

Because the first column of $\mathbf{X}$ consists entirely of ones, (E.9) implies that the OLS residuals always sum to zero when an intercept is included in the equation and that the sample covariance between each independent variable and the OLS residuals is zero. (We discussed both of these properties in Chapter 3.)

The sum of squared residuals can be written as

$$\text{SSR} = \sum_{t=1}^{n} \hat{u}_t^2 = \hat{\mathbf{u}}'\hat{\mathbf{u}} = (\mathbf{y} - \mathbf{X}\hat{\boldsymbol{\beta}})'(\mathbf{y} - \mathbf{X}\hat{\boldsymbol{\beta}}). \tag{E.10}$$

All of the algebraic properties from Chapter 3 can be derived using matrix algebra. For example, we can show that the total sum of squares is equal to the explained sum of squares plus the sum of squared residuals [see (3.27)]. The use of matrices does not provide a simpler proof than summation notation, so we do not provide another derivation.

The matrix approach to multiple regression can be used as the basis for a geometrical interpretation of regression. This involves mathematical concepts that are even more advanced than those we covered in Appendix D. [See Goldberger (1991) or Greene (1997).]

E-1a The Frisch-Waugh Theorem

In Section 3-2, we described a "partialling out" interpretation of the ordinary least squares estimates. We can establish the partialling out interpretation very generally using matrix notation. Partition the $n \times (k + 1)$ matrix $\mathbf{X}$ as

$$\mathbf{X} = (\mathbf{X}_1 | \mathbf{X}_2),$$

where $\mathbf{X}_1$ is $n \times (k_1 + 1)$ and includes the intercept—although that is not required for the result to hold—and $\mathbf{X}_2$ is $n \times k_2$. We still assume that $\mathbf{X}$ has rank $k + 1$, which means $\mathbf{X}_1$ has rank $k_1 + 1$ and $\mathbf{X}_2$ has rank k_2.

Consider the OLS estimates $\hat{\boldsymbol{\beta}}_1$ and $\hat{\boldsymbol{\beta}}_2$ from the (long) regression

$$\mathbf{y} \text{ on } \mathbf{X}_1, \mathbf{X}_2.$$

As we know, the multiple regression coefficients on $\mathbf{X}_2$, $\hat{\boldsymbol{\beta}}_2$, generally differs from $\tilde{\boldsymbol{\beta}}_2$ from the regression $\mathbf{y}$ on $\mathbf{X}_2$. One way to describe the difference is to understand that we can obtain $\hat{\boldsymbol{\beta}}_2$ from a shorter regression, but first we must "partial out" $\mathbf{X}_1$ from $\mathbf{X}_2$. Consider the following two-step method:

(i) Regress (each column of) $\mathbf{X}_2$ on $\mathbf{X}_1$ and obtain the matrix of residuals, say $\ddot{\mathbf{X}}_2$. We can write $\ddot{\mathbf{X}}_2$ as

$$\ddot{\mathbf{X}}_2 = [\mathbf{I}_n - \mathbf{X}_1(\mathbf{X}_1'\mathbf{X}_1)^{-1}\mathbf{X}_1']\mathbf{X}_2 = (\mathbf{I}_n - \mathbf{P}_1)\mathbf{X}_2 = \mathbf{M}_1\mathbf{X}_2,$$

where $\mathbf{P}_1 = \mathbf{X}_1(\mathbf{X}_1'\mathbf{X}_1)^{-1}\mathbf{X}_1'$ and $\mathbf{M}_1 = \mathbf{I}_n - \mathbf{P}_1$ are $n \times n$ symmetric, idempotent matrices.

(ii) Regress $\mathbf{y}$ on $\ddot{\mathbf{X}}_2$ and call the $k_2 \times 1$ vector of coefficient $\hat{\boldsymbol{\beta}}_2$.

The **Frisch-Waugh (FW) theorem** states that

$$\ddot{\beta}_2 = \hat{\beta}_2.$$

Importantly, the FW theorem generally says nothing about equality of the estimates from the long regression, $\hat{\beta}_2$, and those from the short regression, $\tilde{\beta}_2$. Usually $\hat{\beta}_2 \neq \tilde{\beta}_2$. However, if $\mathbf{X}_1'\mathbf{X}_2 = \mathbf{0}$ then $\ddot{\mathbf{X}}_2 = \mathbf{M}_1\mathbf{X}_2 = \mathbf{X}_2$, in which case $\hat{\beta}_2 = \tilde{\beta}_2$; then $\hat{\beta}_2 = \tilde{\beta}_2$ follows from FW. It is also worth noting that we obtain $\hat{\beta}_2$ if we also partial $\mathbf{X}_1$ out of $\mathbf{y}$. In other words, let $\ddot{\mathbf{y}}$ be the residuals from regressing $\mathbf{y}$ on $\mathbf{X}_1$, so that

$$\ddot{\mathbf{y}} = \mathbf{M}_1\mathbf{y}.$$

Then $\hat{\beta}_2$ is obtained from the regression $\ddot{\mathbf{y}}$ on $\ddot{\mathbf{X}}_2$. It is important to understand that it is not enough to only partial out $\mathbf{X}_1$ from $\mathbf{y}$. The important step is partialling out $\mathbf{X}_1$ from $\mathbf{X}_2$. Problem 6 at the end of this chapter asks you to derive the FW theorem and to investigate some related issues.

Another useful algebraic result is that when we regress $\ddot{\mathbf{y}}$ on $\ddot{\mathbf{X}}_2$ and save the residuals, say $\ddot{\mathbf{u}}$, these are identical to the OLS residuals from the original (long) regression:

$$\ddot{\mathbf{y}} = \ddot{\mathbf{X}}_2\hat{\beta}_2 = \ddot{\mathbf{u}} = \hat{\mathbf{u}} = \mathbf{y} - \mathbf{X}_1\hat{\beta}_1 - \mathbf{X}_2\hat{\beta}_2,$$

where we have used the FW result $\ddot{\beta}_2 = \hat{\beta}_2$. We do not obtain the original OLS residuals if we regress $\mathbf{y}$ on $\ddot{\mathbf{X}}_2$ (but we do obtain $\hat{\beta}_2$).

Before the advent of powerful computers, the Frisch-Waugh result was sometimes used as a computational device. Today, the result is more of theoretical interest, and it is very helpful in understanding the mechanics of OLS. For example, recall that in Chapter 10 we used the FW theorem to establish that adding a time trend to a multiple regression is algebraically equivalent to first linearly detrending all of the explanatory variables before running the regression. The FW theorem also can be used in Chapter 14 to establish that the fixed effects estimator, which we introduced as being obtained from OLS on time-demeaned data, can also be obtained from the (long) dummy variable regression.

E-2 Finite Sample Properties of OLS

Deriving the expected value and variance of the OLS estimator $\hat{\beta}$ is facilitated by matrix algebra, but we must show some care in stating the assumptions.

Assumption E.1   Linear in Parameters

The model can be written as in (E.3), where $\mathbf{y}$ is an observed $n \times 1$ vector, $\mathbf{X}$ is an $n \times (k + 1)$ observed matrix, and $\mathbf{u}$ is an $n \times 1$ vector of unobserved errors or disturbances.

Assumption E.2   No Perfect Collinearity

The matrix $\mathbf{X}$ has rank $(k + 1)$.

This is a careful statement of the assumption that rules out linear dependencies among the explanatory variables. Under Assumption E.2, $\mathbf{X}'\mathbf{X}$ is nonsingular, so $\hat{\beta}$ is unique and can be written as in (E.8).

Assumption E.3   Zero Conditional Mean

Conditional on the entire matrix $\mathbf{X}$, each error u_t has zero mean: $E(u_t|\mathbf{X}) = 0, t = 1, 2, ..., n$.

In vector form, Assumption E.3 can be written as

$$E(\mathbf{u}|\mathbf{X}) = \mathbf{0}.$$ [E.11]

This assumption is implied by MLR.4 under the random sampling assumption, MLR.2. In time series applications, Assumption E.3 imposes strict exogeneity on the explanatory variables, something discussed at length in Chapter 10. This rules out explanatory variables whose future values are correlated with u_t; in particular, it eliminates lagged dependent variables. Under Assumption E.3, we can condition on the x_{tj} when we compute the expected value of $\hat{\boldsymbol{\beta}}$.

THEOREM E.1

UNBIASEDNESS OF OLS

Under Assumptions E.1, E.2, and E.3, the OLS estimator $\hat{\boldsymbol{\beta}}$ is unbiased for $\boldsymbol{\beta}$.

PROOF: Use Assumptions E.1 and E.2 and simple algebra to write

$$\hat{\boldsymbol{\beta}} = (\mathbf{X}'\mathbf{X})^{-1}\mathbf{X}'\mathbf{y} = (\mathbf{X}'\mathbf{X})^{-1}\mathbf{X}'(\mathbf{X}\boldsymbol{\beta} + \mathbf{u})$$
$$= (\mathbf{X}'\mathbf{X})^{-1}(\mathbf{X}'\mathbf{X})\boldsymbol{\beta} + (\mathbf{X}'\mathbf{X})^{-1}\mathbf{X}'\mathbf{u} = \boldsymbol{\beta} + (\mathbf{X}'\mathbf{X})^{-1}\mathbf{X}'\mathbf{u},$$ [E.12]

where we use the fact that $(\mathbf{X}'\mathbf{X})^{-1}(\mathbf{X}'\mathbf{X}) = \mathbf{I}_{k+1}$. Taking the expectation conditional on $\mathbf{X}$ gives

$$E(\hat{\boldsymbol{\beta}}|\mathbf{X}) = \boldsymbol{\beta} + (\mathbf{X}'\mathbf{X})^{-1}\mathbf{X}'E(\mathbf{u}|\mathbf{X})$$
$$= \boldsymbol{\beta} + (\mathbf{X}'\mathbf{X})^{-1}\mathbf{X}'\mathbf{0} = \boldsymbol{\beta},$$

because $E(\mathbf{u}|\mathbf{X}) = \mathbf{0}$ under Assumption E.3. This argument clearly does not depend on the value of $\boldsymbol{\beta}$, so we have shown that $\hat{\boldsymbol{\beta}}$ is unbiased.

To obtain the simplest form of the variance-covariance matrix of $\hat{\boldsymbol{\beta}}$, we impose the assumptions of homoskedasticity and no serial correlation.

Assumption E.4   **Homoskedasticity and No Serial Correlation**

(i) $\text{Var}(u_t|\mathbf{X}) = \sigma^2$, $t = 1, 2, ..., n$. (ii) $\text{Cov}(u_t, u_s|\mathbf{X}) = 0$, for all $t \neq s$. In matrix form, we can write these two assumptions as

$$\text{Var}(\mathbf{u}|\mathbf{X}) = \sigma^2\mathbf{I}_n,$$ [E.13]

where $\mathbf{I}_n$ is the $n \times n$ identity matrix.

Part (i) of Assumption E.4 is the homoskedasticity assumption: the variance of u_t cannot depend on any element of $\mathbf{X}$, and the variance must be constant across observations, t. Part (ii) is the no serial correlation assumption: the errors cannot be correlated across observations. Under random sampling, and in any other cross-sectional sampling schemes with independent observations, part (ii) of Assumption E.4 automatically holds. For time series applications, part (ii) rules out correlation in the errors over time (both conditional on $\mathbf{X}$ and unconditionally).

Because of (E.13), we often say that $\mathbf{u}$ has a **scalar variance-covariance matrix** when Assumption E.4 holds. We can now derive the **variance-covariance matrix of the OLS estimator**.

THEOREM E.2

VARIANCE-COVARIANCE MATRIX OF THE OLS ESTIMATOR

Under Assumptions E.1 through E.4,

$$\text{Var}(\hat{\boldsymbol{\beta}}|\mathbf{X}) = \sigma^2(\mathbf{X}'\mathbf{X})^{-1}.$$ [E.14]

PROOF: From the last formula in equation (E.12), we have

$$\text{Var}(\hat{\boldsymbol{\beta}}|\mathbf{X}) = \text{Var}[(\mathbf{X}'\mathbf{X})^{-1}\mathbf{X}'\mathbf{u}|\mathbf{X}] = (\mathbf{X}'\mathbf{X})^{-1}\mathbf{X}'[\text{Var}(\mathbf{u}|\mathbf{X})]\mathbf{X}(\mathbf{X}'\mathbf{X})^{-1}.$$

Now, we use Assumption E.4 to get

$$\text{Var}(\hat{\boldsymbol{\beta}}|\mathbf{X}) = (\mathbf{X}'\mathbf{X})^{-1}\mathbf{X}'(\sigma^2\mathbf{I}_n)\mathbf{X}(\mathbf{X}'\mathbf{X})^{-1}$$
$$= \sigma^2(\mathbf{X}'\mathbf{X})^{-1}\mathbf{X}'\mathbf{X}(\mathbf{X}'\mathbf{X})^{-1} = \sigma^2(\mathbf{X}'\mathbf{X})^{-1}.$$

Formula (E.14) means that the variance of $\hat{\beta}_j$ (conditional on $\mathbf{X}$) is obtained by multiplying σ^2 by the jth diagonal element of $(\mathbf{X}'\mathbf{X})^{-1}$. For the slope coefficients, we gave an interpretable formula in equation (3.51). Equation (E.14) also tells us how to obtain the covariance between any two OLS estimates: multiply σ^2 by the appropriate off-diagonal element of $(\mathbf{X}'\mathbf{X})^{-1}$. In Chapter 4, we showed how to avoid explicitly finding covariances for obtaining confidence intervals and hypothesis tests by appropriately rewriting the model.

The Gauss-Markov Theorem, in its full generality, can be proven.

THEOREM E.3

GAUSS-MARKOV THEOREM

Under Assumptions E.1 through E.4, $\hat{\boldsymbol{\beta}}$ is the best linear unbiased estimator.

PROOF: Any other linear estimator of $\boldsymbol{\beta}$ can be written as

$$\tilde{\boldsymbol{\beta}} = \mathbf{A}'\mathbf{y}, \qquad\qquad\qquad \text{[E.15]}$$

where $\mathbf{A}$ is an $n \times (k + 1)$ matrix. In order for $\tilde{\boldsymbol{\beta}}$ to be unbiased conditional on $\mathbf{X}$, $\mathbf{A}$ can consist of nonrandom numbers and functions of $\mathbf{X}$. (For example, $\mathbf{A}$ cannot be a function of $\mathbf{y}$.) To see what further restrictions on $\mathbf{A}$ are needed, write

$$\tilde{\boldsymbol{\beta}} = \mathbf{A}'(\mathbf{X}\boldsymbol{\beta} + \mathbf{u}) = (\mathbf{A}'\mathbf{X})\boldsymbol{\beta} + \mathbf{A}'\mathbf{u}. \qquad\qquad \text{[E.16]}$$

Then,

$$E(\tilde{\boldsymbol{\beta}}|\mathbf{X}) = \mathbf{A}'\mathbf{X}\boldsymbol{\beta} + E(\mathbf{A}'\mathbf{u}|\mathbf{X})$$
$$= \mathbf{A}'\mathbf{X}\boldsymbol{\beta} + \mathbf{A}'E(\mathbf{u}|\mathbf{X}) \text{ because } \mathbf{A} \text{ is a function of } \mathbf{X}$$
$$= \mathbf{A}'\mathbf{X}\boldsymbol{\beta} \text{ because } E(\mathbf{u}|\mathbf{X}) = 0.$$

For $\tilde{\boldsymbol{\beta}}$ to be an unbiased estimator of $\boldsymbol{\beta}$, it must be true that $E(\tilde{\boldsymbol{\beta}}|\mathbf{X}) = \boldsymbol{\beta}$ for all $(k + 1) \times 1$ vectors $\boldsymbol{\beta}$, that is,

$$\mathbf{A}'\mathbf{X}\boldsymbol{\beta} = \boldsymbol{\beta} \text{ for all } (k + 1) \times 1 \text{ vectors } \boldsymbol{\beta}. \qquad\qquad \text{[E.17]}$$

Because $\mathbf{A}'\mathbf{X}$ is a $(k + 1) \times (k + 1)$ matrix, (E.17) holds if, and only if, $\mathbf{A}'\mathbf{X} = \mathbf{I}_{k+1}$. Equations (E.15) and (E.17) characterize the class of linear, unbiased estimators for $\boldsymbol{\beta}$.

Next, from (E.16), we have

$$\text{Var}(\tilde{\boldsymbol{\beta}}|\mathbf{X}) = \mathbf{A}'[\text{Var}(\mathbf{u}|\mathbf{X})]\mathbf{A} = \sigma^2\mathbf{A}'\mathbf{A},$$

by Assumption E.4. Therefore,

$$\text{Var}(\tilde{\boldsymbol{\beta}}|\mathbf{X}) - \text{Var}(\hat{\boldsymbol{\beta}}|\mathbf{X}) = \sigma^2[\mathbf{A}'\mathbf{A} - (\mathbf{X}'\mathbf{X})^{-1}]$$
$$= \sigma^2[\mathbf{A}'\mathbf{A} - \mathbf{A}'\mathbf{X}(\mathbf{X}'\mathbf{X})^{-1}\mathbf{X}'\mathbf{A}] \text{ because } \mathbf{A}'\mathbf{X} = \mathbf{I}_{k+1}$$
$$= \sigma^2\mathbf{A}'[\mathbf{I}_n - \mathbf{X}(\mathbf{X}'\mathbf{X})^{-1}\mathbf{X}']\mathbf{A}$$
$$\equiv \sigma^2\mathbf{A}'\mathbf{M}\mathbf{A},$$

where $\mathbf{M} \equiv \mathbf{I}_n - \mathbf{X}(\mathbf{X}'\mathbf{X})^{-1}\mathbf{X}'$. Because $\mathbf{M}$ is symmetric and idempotent, $\mathbf{A}'\mathbf{MA}$ is positive semi-definite for any $n \times (k+1)$ matrix $\mathbf{A}$. This establishes that the OLS estimator $\hat{\boldsymbol{\beta}}$ is BLUE. Why is this important? Let $\mathbf{c}$ be any $(k+1) \times 1$ vector and consider the linear combination $\mathbf{c}'\boldsymbol{\beta} = c_0\beta_0 + c_1\beta_1 + \ldots + c_k\beta_k$, which is a scalar. The unbiased estimators of $\mathbf{c}'\boldsymbol{\beta}$ are $\mathbf{c}'\hat{\boldsymbol{\beta}}$ and $\mathbf{c}'\tilde{\boldsymbol{\beta}}$. But

$$\mathrm{Var}(\mathbf{c}'\tilde{\boldsymbol{\beta}}|\mathbf{X}) - \mathrm{Var}(\mathbf{c}'\hat{\boldsymbol{\beta}}|\mathbf{X}) = \mathbf{c}'[\mathrm{Var}(\tilde{\boldsymbol{\beta}}|\mathbf{X}) - \mathrm{Var}(\hat{\boldsymbol{\beta}}|\mathbf{X})]\mathbf{c} \geq 0,$$

because $[\mathrm{Var}(\tilde{\boldsymbol{\beta}}|\mathbf{X}) - \mathrm{Var}(\hat{\boldsymbol{\beta}}|\mathbf{X})]$ is p.s.d. Therefore, when it is used for estimating any linear combination of $\boldsymbol{\beta}$, OLS yields the smallest variance. In particular, $\mathrm{Var}(\hat{\beta}_j|\mathbf{X}) \leq \mathrm{Var}(\tilde{\beta}_j|\mathbf{X})$ for any other linear, unbiased estimator of β_j.

The unbiased estimator of the error variance σ^2 can be written as

$$\hat{\sigma}^2 = \hat{\mathbf{u}}'\hat{\mathbf{u}}/(n - k - 1),$$

which is the same as equation (3.56).

THEOREM E.4

UNBIASEDNESS OF $\hat{\sigma}^2$

Under Assumptions E.1 through E.4, $\hat{\sigma}^2$ is unbiased for σ^2: $\mathrm{E}(\hat{\sigma}^2|\mathbf{X}) = \sigma^2$ for all $\sigma^2 > 0$.

PROOF: Write $\hat{\mathbf{u}} = \mathbf{y} - \mathbf{X}\hat{\boldsymbol{\beta}} = \mathbf{y} - \mathbf{X}(\mathbf{X}'\mathbf{X})^{-1}\mathbf{X}'\mathbf{y} = \mathbf{My} = \mathbf{Mu}$, where $\mathbf{M} = \mathbf{I}_n - \mathbf{X}(\mathbf{X}'\mathbf{X})^{-1}\mathbf{X}'$, and the last equality follows because $\mathbf{MX} = \mathbf{0}$. Because $\mathbf{M}$ is symmetric and idempotent,

$$\hat{\mathbf{u}}'\hat{\mathbf{u}} = \mathbf{u}'\mathbf{M}'\mathbf{Mu} = \mathbf{u}'\mathbf{Mu}.$$

Because $\mathbf{u}'\mathbf{Mu}$ is a scalar, it equals its trace. Therefore,

$$\begin{aligned}
\mathrm{E}(\mathbf{u}'\mathbf{Mu}|\mathbf{X}) &= \mathrm{E}[\mathrm{tr}(\mathbf{u}'\mathbf{Mu})|\mathbf{X}] = \mathrm{E}[\mathrm{tr}(\mathbf{Muu}')|\mathbf{X}] \\
&= \mathrm{tr}[\mathrm{E}(\mathbf{Muu}'|\mathbf{X})] = \mathrm{tr}[\mathbf{M}\mathrm{E}(\mathbf{uu}'|\mathbf{X})] \\
&= \mathrm{tr}(\mathbf{M}\sigma^2\mathbf{I}_n) = \sigma^2\mathrm{tr}(\mathbf{M}) = \sigma^2(n - k - 1).
\end{aligned}$$

The last equality follows from $\mathrm{tr}(\mathbf{M}) = \mathrm{tr}(\mathbf{I}_n) - \mathrm{tr}[\mathbf{X}(\mathbf{X}'\mathbf{X})^{-1}\mathbf{X}'] = n - \mathrm{tr}[(\mathbf{X}'\mathbf{X})^{-1}\mathbf{X}'\mathbf{X}] = n - \mathrm{tr}(\mathbf{I}_{k+1}) = n - (k+1) = n - k - 1$. Therefore,

$$\mathrm{E}(\hat{\sigma}^2|\mathbf{X}) = \mathrm{E}(\mathbf{u}'\mathbf{Mu}|\mathbf{X})/(n - k - 1) = \sigma^2.$$

E-3 Statistical Inference

When we add the final classical linear model assumption, $\hat{\boldsymbol{\beta}}$ has a multivariate normal distribution, which leads to the t and F distributions for the standard test statistics covered in Chapter 4.

Assumption E.5 **Normality of Errors**

Conditional on $\mathbf{X}$, the u_t are independent and identically distributed as Normal$(0,\sigma^2)$. Equivalently, $\mathbf{u}$ given $\mathbf{X}$ is distributed as multivariate normal with mean zero and variance-covariance matrix $\sigma^2\mathbf{I}_n$: $\mathbf{u} \sim \mathrm{Normal}(0,\sigma^2\mathbf{I}_n)$.

Under Assumption E.5, each u_t is independent of the explanatory variables for all t. In a time series setting, this is essentially the strict exogeneity assumption.

THEOREM E.5	**NORMALITY OF $\hat{\boldsymbol{\beta}}$**

Under the classical linear model Assumptions E.1 through E.5, $\hat{\boldsymbol{\beta}}$ conditional on **X** is distributed as multivariate normal with mean $\boldsymbol{\beta}$ and variance-covariance matrix $\sigma^2(\mathbf{X}'\mathbf{X})^{-1}$.

Theorem E.5 is the basis for statistical inference involving $\boldsymbol{\beta}$. In fact, along with the properties of the chi-square, t, and F distributions that we summarized in Appendix D, we can use Theorem E.5 to establish that t statistics have a t distribution under Assumptions E.1 through E.5 (under the null hypothesis) and likewise for F statistics. We illustrate with a proof for the t statistics.

THEOREM E.6	**DISTRIBUTION OF t STATISTIC**

Under Assumptions E.1 through E.5,

$$(\hat{\beta}_j - \beta_j)/\text{se}(\hat{\beta}_j) \sim t_{n-k-1}, j = 0, 1, \ldots, k.$$

PROOF : The proof requires several steps; the following statements are initially conditional on **X**. First, by Theorem E.5, $(\hat{\beta}_j - \beta_j)/\text{sd}(\hat{\beta}_j) \sim \text{Normal}(0,1)$, where $\text{sd}(\hat{\beta}_j) = \sigma\sqrt{C_{jj}}$, and c_{jj} is the jth diagonal element of $(\mathbf{X}'\mathbf{X})^{-1}$. Next, under Assumptions E.1 through E.5, conditional on **X**,

$$(n - k - 1)\hat{\sigma}^2/\sigma^2 \sim \chi^2_{n-k-1}. \qquad [\text{E.18}]$$

This follows because $(n - k - 1)\hat{\sigma}^2/\sigma^2 = (\mathbf{u}/\sigma)'\mathbf{M}(\mathbf{u}/\sigma)$, where **M** is the $n \times n$ symmetric, idempotent matrix defined in Theorem E.4. But $\mathbf{u}/\sigma \sim \text{Normal}(\mathbf{0}, \mathbf{I}_n)$ by Assumption E.5. It follows from Property 1 for the chi-square distribution in Appendix D that $(\mathbf{u}/\sigma)'\mathbf{M}(\mathbf{u}/\sigma) \sim \chi^2_{n-k-1}$ (because **M** has rank $n - k - 1$).

We also need to show that $\hat{\boldsymbol{\beta}}$ and $\hat{\sigma}^2$ are independent. But $\hat{\boldsymbol{\beta}} = \boldsymbol{\beta} + (\mathbf{X}'\mathbf{X})^{-1}\mathbf{X}'\mathbf{u}$, and $\hat{\sigma}^2 = \mathbf{u}'\mathbf{M}\mathbf{u}/(n - k - 1)$. Now, $[(\mathbf{X}'\mathbf{X})^{-1}\mathbf{X}']\mathbf{M} = \mathbf{0}$ because $\mathbf{X}'\mathbf{M} = \mathbf{0}$. It follows, from Property 5 of the multivariate normal distribution in Appendix D, that $\hat{\boldsymbol{\beta}}$ and **Mu** are independent. Because $\hat{\sigma}^2$ is a function of **Mu**, $\hat{\boldsymbol{\beta}}$ and $\hat{\sigma}^2$ are also independent.

$$(\hat{\beta}_j - \beta_j)/\text{se}(\hat{\beta}_j) = [(\hat{\beta}_j - \beta_j)/\text{sd}(\hat{\beta}_j)]/(\hat{\sigma}^2/\sigma^2)^{1/2},$$

which is the ratio of a standard normal random variable and the square root of a $\chi^2_{n-k-1}/(n - k - 1)$ random variable. We just showed that these are independent, so, by definition of a t random variable, $(\hat{\beta}_j - \beta_j)/\text{se}(\hat{\beta}_j)$ has the t_{n-k-1} distribution. Because this distribution does not depend on **X**, it is the unconditional distribution of $(\hat{\beta}_j - \beta_j)/\text{se}(\hat{\beta}_j)$ as well.

From this theorem, we can plug in any hypothesized value for β_j and use the t statistic for testing hypotheses, as usual.

Under Assumptions E.1 through E.5, we can compute what is known as the *Cramer-Rao* lower bound for the variance-covariance matrix of unbiased estimators of $\boldsymbol{\beta}$ (again conditional on **X**) [see Greene (1997, Chapter 4)]. This can be shown to be $\sigma^2(\mathbf{X}'\mathbf{X})^{-1}$, which is exactly the variance-covariance matrix of the OLS estimator. This implies that $\hat{\boldsymbol{\beta}}$ is the **minimum variance unbiased estimator** of $\boldsymbol{\beta}$ (conditional on **X**): $\text{Var}(\tilde{\boldsymbol{\beta}}|\mathbf{X}) - \text{Var}(\hat{\boldsymbol{\beta}}|\mathbf{X})$ is positive semi-definite for any other unbiased estimator $\tilde{\boldsymbol{\beta}}$; we no longer have to restrict our attention to estimators linear in **y**.

It is easy to show that the OLS estimator is in fact the maximum likelihood estimator of $\boldsymbol{\beta}$ under Assumption E.5. For each t, the distribution of y_t given **X** is $\text{Normal}(\mathbf{x}_t\boldsymbol{\beta}, \sigma^2)$. Because the y_t are independent conditional on **X**, the likelihood function for the sample is obtained from the product of the densities:

$$\prod_{t=1}^{n} (2\pi\sigma^2)^{-1/2} \exp[-(y_t - \mathbf{x}_t\boldsymbol{\beta})^2/(2\sigma^2)],$$

where Π denotes product. Maximizing this function with respect to $\boldsymbol{\beta}$ and σ^2 is the same as maximizing its natural logarithm:

$$\sum_{t=1}^{n} [-(1/2)\log(2\pi\sigma^2) - (y_t - \mathbf{x}_t\boldsymbol{\beta})^2/(2\sigma^2)].$$

For obtaining $\hat{\boldsymbol{\beta}}$, this is the same as minimizing $\sum_{t=1}^{n}(y_t - \mathbf{x}_t\boldsymbol{\beta})^2$—the division by $2\sigma^2$ does not affect the optimization—which is just the problem that OLS solves. The estimator of σ^2 that we have used, $SSR/(n-k)$, turns out not to be the MLE of σ^2; the MLE is SSR/n, which is a biased estimator. Because the unbiased estimator of σ^2 results in t and F statistics with exact t and F distributions under the null, it is always used instead of the MLE.

That the OLS estimator is the MLE under Assumption E.5 implies an interesting robustness property of the MLE based on the normal distribution. The reasoning is simple. We know that the OLS estimator is unbiased under Assumptions E.1 to E.3; normality of the errors is used nowhere in the proof, and neither is Assumption E.4. As the next section shows, the OLS estimator is also consistent without normality, provided the law of large numbers holds (as is widely true). These statistical properties of the OLS estimator imply that the MLE based on the normal log-likelihood function is robust to distributional specification: the distribution can be (almost) anything and yet we still obtain a consistent (and, under E.1 to E.3, unbiased) estimator. As discussed in Section 17-3, a maximum likelihood estimator obtained without assuming the distribution is correct is often called a **quasi-maximum likelihood estimator (QMLE)**.

Generally, consistency of the MLE relies on having a correct distribution in order to conclude that it is consistent for the parameters. We have just seen that the normal distribution is a notable exception. There are some other distributions that share this property, including the Poisson distribution—as discussed in Section 17-3. Wooldridge (2010, Chapter 18) discusses some other useful examples.

E-4 Some Asymptotic Analysis

The matrix approach to the multiple regression model can also make derivations of asymptotic properties more concise. In fact, we can give general proofs of the claims in Chapter 11.

We begin by proving the consistency result of Theorem 11.1. Recall that these assumptions contain, as a special case, the assumptions for cross-sectional analysis under random sampling.

Proof of Theorem 11.1. As in Problem E.1 and using Assumption TS.1′ we write the OLS estimator as

$$\hat{\boldsymbol{\beta}} = \left(\sum_{t=1}^{n} \mathbf{x}_t'\mathbf{x}_t \right)^{-1} \left(\sum_{t=1}^{n} \mathbf{x}_t'y_t \right) = \left(\sum_{t=1}^{n} \mathbf{x}_t'\mathbf{x}_t \right)^{-1} \left(\sum_{t=1}^{n} \mathbf{x}_t'(\mathbf{x}_t\boldsymbol{\beta} + u_t) \right)$$

$$= \boldsymbol{\beta} + \left(\sum_{t=1}^{n} \mathbf{x}_t'\mathbf{x}_t \right)^{-1} \left(\sum_{t=1}^{n} \mathbf{x}_t'u_t \right) \qquad\qquad \text{[E.19]}$$

$$= \boldsymbol{\beta} + \left(n^{-1}\sum_{t=1}^{n} \mathbf{x}_t'\mathbf{x}_t \right)^{-1} \left(n^{-1}\sum_{t=1}^{n} \mathbf{x}_t'u_t \right).$$

Now, by the law of large numbers,

$$n^{-1}\sum_{t=1}^{n}\mathbf{x}_t'\mathbf{x}_t \overset{p}{\to} \mathbf{A} \text{ and } n^{-1}\sum_{t=1}^{n}\mathbf{x}_t'u_t \overset{p}{\to} \mathbf{0}, \qquad \text{[E.20]}$$

where $\mathbf{A} = \mathrm{E}(\mathbf{x}_t'\mathbf{x}_t)$ is a $(k+1) \times (k+1)$ nonsingular matrix under Assumption TS.2′ and we have used the fact that $\mathrm{E}(\mathbf{x}_t'\mathbf{u}_t) = 0$ under Assumption TS.3′. Now, we must use a matrix version of Property PLIM.1 in Appendix C. Namely, because $\mathbf{A}$ is nonsingular,

$$\left(n^{-1}\sum_{t=1}^{n}\mathbf{x}_t'\mathbf{x}_t\right)^{-1} \overset{p}{\to} \mathbf{A}^{-1}. \qquad \text{[E.21]}$$

[Wooldridge (2010, Chapter 3) contains a discussion of these kinds of convergence results.] It now follows from (E.19), (E.20), and (E.21) that

$$\mathrm{plim}(\hat{\boldsymbol{\beta}}) = \boldsymbol{\beta} + \mathbf{A}^{-1} \cdot \mathbf{0} = \boldsymbol{\beta}.$$

This completes the proof.

Next, we sketch a proof of the asymptotic normality result in Theorem 11.2.

Proof of Theorem 11.2. From equation (E.19), we can write

$$\sqrt{n}(\hat{\boldsymbol{\beta}} - \boldsymbol{\beta}) = \left(n^{-1}\sum_{t=1}^{n}\mathbf{x}_t'\mathbf{x}_t\right)^{-1}\left(n^{-1/2}\sum_{t=1}^{n}\mathbf{x}_t'u_t\right)$$

$$= \mathbf{A}^{-1}\left(n^{-1/2}\sum_{t=1}^{n}\mathbf{x}_t'u_t\right) + o_p(1), \qquad \text{[E.22]}$$

where the term "$o_p(1)$" is a remainder term that converges in probability to zero. This term is equal to $[(n^{-1}\sum_{t=1}^{n}\mathbf{x}_t'\mathbf{x}_t)^{-1} - \mathbf{A}^{-1}](n^{-1/2}\sum_{t=1}^{n}\mathbf{x}_t'u_t)$. The term in brackets converges in probability to zero (by the same argument used in the proof of Theorem 11.1), while $(n^{-1/2}\sum_{t=1}^{n}\mathbf{x}_t'u_t)$ is bounded in probability because it converges to a multivariate normal distribution by the central limit theorem. A well-known result in asymptotic theory is that the product of such terms converges in probability to zero. Further, $\sqrt{n}(\hat{\boldsymbol{\beta}} - \boldsymbol{\beta})$ inherits its asymptotic distribution from $\mathbf{A}^{-1}(n^{-1/2}\sum_{t=1}^{n}\mathbf{x}_t'u_t)$. See Wooldridge (2010, Chapter 3) for more details on the convergence results used in this proof.

By the central limit theorem, $n^{-1/2}\sum_{t=1}^{n}\mathbf{x}_t'u_t$ has an asymptotic normal distribution with mean zero and, say, $(k+1) \times (k+1)$ variance-covariance matrix $\mathbf{B}$. Then, $\sqrt{n}(\hat{\boldsymbol{\beta}} - \boldsymbol{\beta})$ has an asymptotic multivariate normal distribution with mean zero and variance-covariance matrix $\mathbf{A}^{-1}\mathbf{B}\mathbf{A}^{-1}$. We now show that, under Assumptions TS.4′ and TS.5′, $\mathbf{B} = \sigma^2\mathbf{A}$. (The general expression is useful because it underlies heteroskedasticity-robust and serial correlation-robust standard errors for OLS, of the kind discussed in Chapter 12.) First, under Assumption TS.5′ $\mathbf{x}_t'u_t$ and $\mathbf{x}_s'u_s$ are uncorrelated for $t \neq s$. Why? Suppose $s < t$ for concreteness. Then, by the law of iterated expectations, $\mathrm{E}(\mathbf{x}_t'u_tu_s\mathbf{x}_s) = \mathrm{E}[\mathrm{E}(u_tu_s|\mathbf{x}_t'\mathbf{x}_s)\mathbf{x}_t'\mathbf{x}_s] = \mathrm{E}[\mathrm{E}(u_tu_s|\mathbf{x}_t'\mathbf{x}_s)\mathbf{x}_t'\mathbf{x}_s] = \mathrm{E}[0 \cdot \mathbf{x}_t'\mathbf{x}_s] = 0$. The zero covariances imply that the variance of the sum is the sum of the variances. But $\mathrm{Var}(\mathbf{x}_t'u_t) = \mathrm{E}(\mathbf{x}_t'u_tu_t\mathbf{x}_t) = \mathrm{E}(u_t^2\mathbf{x}_t'\mathbf{x}_t)$. By the law of iterated expectations, $\mathrm{E}(u_t^2\mathbf{x}_t'\mathbf{x}_t) = \mathrm{E}[\mathrm{E}(u_t^2\mathbf{x}_t'\mathbf{x}_t|\mathbf{x}_t)] = \mathrm{E}[\mathrm{E}(u_t^2|\mathbf{x}_t)\mathbf{x}_t'\mathbf{x}_t] = \mathrm{E}[\sigma^2\mathbf{x}_t'\mathbf{x}_t] = \sigma^2\mathrm{E}(\mathbf{x}_t'\mathbf{x}_t) = \sigma^2\mathbf{A}$, where we use $\mathrm{E}(u_t^2|\mathbf{x}_t) = \sigma^2$ under Assumptions TS.3′ and TS.4′. This shows that $\mathbf{B} = \sigma^2\mathbf{A}$, and so, under Assumptions TS.1′ to TS.5′, we have

$$\sqrt{n}(\hat{\boldsymbol{\beta}} - \boldsymbol{\beta}) \overset{a}{\sim} \mathrm{Normal}(\mathbf{0}, \sigma^2\mathbf{A}^{-1}). \qquad \text{[E.23]}$$

This completes the proof.

From equation (E.23), we treat $\hat{\boldsymbol{\beta}}$ as if it is approximately normally distributed with mean $\boldsymbol{\beta}$ and variance-covariance matrix $\sigma^2\mathbf{A}^{-1}/n$. The division by the sample size, n, is expected here: the approximation to the variance-covariance matrix of $\hat{\boldsymbol{\beta}}$ shrinks to zero at the rate $1/n$. When we replace

σ^2 with its consistent estimator, $\hat{\sigma}^2 = SSR/(n - k - 1)$, and replace A with its consistent estimator, $n^{-1}\sum_{t=1}^{n}\mathbf{x}_t'\mathbf{x}_t = \mathbf{X}'\mathbf{X}/n$, we obtain an estimator for the asymptotic variance of $\hat{\boldsymbol{\beta}}$:

$$\widehat{\mathrm{A}var(\hat{\boldsymbol{\beta}})} = \hat{\sigma}^2(\mathbf{X}'\mathbf{X})^{-1}. \tag{E.24}$$

Notice how the two divisions by n cancel, and the right-hand side of (E.24) is just the usual way we estimate the variance matrix of the OLS estimator under the Gauss-Markov assumptions. To summarize, we have shown that, under Assumptions TS.1' to TS.5'—which contain MLR.1 to MLR.5 as special cases—the usual standard errors and t statistics are asymptotically valid. It is perfectly legitimate to use the usual t distribution to obtain critical values and p-values for testing a single hypothesis. Interestingly, in the general setup of Chapter 11, assuming normality of the errors—say, u_t given $\mathbf{x}_t, u_{t-1}, \mathbf{x}_{t-1}, \ldots, u_1, \mathbf{x}_1$ is distributed as Normal$(0, \sigma^2)$—does not necessarily help, as the t statistics would not generally have exact t statistics under this kind of normality assumption. When we do not assume strict exogeneity of the explanatory variables, exact distributional results are difficult, if not impossible, to obtain.

If we modify the argument above, we can derive a heteroskedasticity-robust, variance-covariance matrix. The key is that we must estimate $\mathrm{E}(u_t^2\mathbf{x}_t'\mathbf{x}_t)$ separately because this matrix no longer equals $\sigma^2\mathrm{E}(\mathbf{x}_t'\mathbf{x}_t)$. But, if the $\hat{u}_t$ are the OLS residuals, a consistent estimator is

$$(n - k - 1)^{-1}\sum_{t=1}^{n}\hat{u}_t^2\mathbf{x}_t'\mathbf{x}_t, \tag{E.25}$$

where the division by $n - k - 1$ rather than n is a degrees of freedom adjustment that typically helps the finite sample properties of the estimator. When we use the expression in equation (E.25), we obtain

$$\widehat{\mathrm{A}var(\hat{\boldsymbol{\beta}})} = [n/(n - k - 1)](\mathbf{X}'\mathbf{X})^{-1}\left(\sum_{t=1}^{n}\hat{u}_t^2\mathbf{x}_t'\mathbf{x}_t\right)(\mathbf{X}'\mathbf{X})^{-1}. \tag{E.26}$$

The square roots of the diagonal elements of this matrix are the same heteroskedasticity-robust standard errors we obtained in Section 8-2 for the pure cross-sectional case. A matrix extension of the serial correlation- (and heteroskedasticity-) robust standard errors we obtained in Section 12-5 is also available, but the matrix that must replace (E.25) is complicated because of the serial correlation. See, for example, Hamilton (1994, Section 10-5).

E-4 Wald Statistics for Testing Multiple Hypotheses

Similar arguments can be used to obtain the asymptotic distribution of the **Wald statistic** for testing multiple hypotheses. Let $\mathbf{R}$ be a $q \times (k + 1)$ matrix, with $q \leq (k + 1)$. Assume that the q restrictions on the $(k + 1) \times 1$ vector of parameters, $\boldsymbol{\beta}$, can be expressed as $\mathrm{H}_0: \mathbf{R}\boldsymbol{\beta} = \mathbf{r}$, where $\mathbf{r}$ is a $q \times 1$ vector of known constants. Under Assumptions TS.1' to TS.5', it can be shown that, under H_0,

$$[\sqrt{n}(\mathbf{R}\hat{\boldsymbol{\beta}} - \mathbf{r})]'(\sigma^2\mathbf{R}\mathbf{A}^{-1}\mathbf{R}')^{-1}[\sqrt{n}(\mathbf{R}\hat{\boldsymbol{\beta}} - \mathbf{r})] \overset{a}{\sim} \chi_q^2, \tag{E.27}$$

where $\mathbf{A} = \mathrm{E}(\mathbf{x}_t'\mathbf{x}_t)$, as in the proofs of Theorems 11.1 and 11.2. The intuition behind equation (E.25) is simple. Because $\sqrt{n}(\hat{\boldsymbol{\beta}} - \boldsymbol{\beta})$ is roughly distributed as Normal$(\mathbf{0}, \sigma^2\mathbf{A}^{-1})$, $\mathbf{R}[\sqrt{n}(\hat{\boldsymbol{\beta}} - \boldsymbol{\beta})] = \sqrt{n}\mathbf{R}(\hat{\boldsymbol{\beta}} - \boldsymbol{\beta})$ is approximately Normal$(\mathbf{0}, \sigma^2\mathbf{R}\mathbf{A}^{-1}\mathbf{R}')$ by Property 3 of the multivariate normal distribution in Appendix D. Under H_0, $\mathbf{R}\boldsymbol{\beta} = \mathbf{r}$, so $\sqrt{n}(\mathbf{R}\hat{\boldsymbol{\beta}} - \mathbf{r}) \overset{a}{\sim}$ Normal$(\mathbf{0}, \sigma^2\mathbf{R}\mathbf{A}^{-1}\mathbf{R}')$ under H_0. By Property 3 of the chi-square distribution, $\mathbf{z}'(\sigma^2\mathbf{R}\mathbf{A}^{-1}\mathbf{R}')^{-1}\mathbf{z} \sim \chi_q^2$ if $\mathbf{z} \sim$ Normal$(\mathbf{0}, \sigma^2\mathbf{R}\mathbf{A}^{-1}\mathbf{R}')$. To obtain the final result formally, we need to use an asymptotic version of this property, which can be found in Wooldridge (2010, Chapter 3).

Given the result in (E.25), we obtain a computable statistic by replacing $\mathbf{A}$ and σ^2 with their consistent estimators; doing so does not change the asymptotic distribution. The result is the so-called Wald statistic, which, after canceling the sample sizes and doing a little algebra, can be written as

$$W = (\mathbf{R}\hat{\boldsymbol{\beta}} - \mathbf{r})'[\mathbf{R}(\mathbf{X}'\mathbf{X})^{-1}\mathbf{R}']^{-1}(\mathbf{R}\hat{\boldsymbol{\beta}} - \mathbf{r})/\hat{\sigma}^2. \tag{E.28}$$

Under H_0, $W \overset{a}{\sim} \chi_q^2$, where we recall that q is the number of restrictions being tested. If $\hat{\sigma}^2 = \text{SSR}/(n - k - 1)$, it can be shown that W/q is exactly the F statistic we obtained in Chapter 4 for testing multiple linear restrictions. [See, for example, Greene (1997, Chapter 7).] Therefore, under the classical linear model assumptions TS.1 to TS.6 in Chapter 10, W/q has an exact $F_{q, n-k-1}$ distribution. Under Assumptions TS.1' to TS.5', we only have the asymptotic result in (E.26). Nevertheless, it is appropriate, and common, to treat the usual F statistic as having an approximate $F_{q, n-k-1}$ distribution.

A Wald statistic that is robust to heteroskedasticity of unknown form is obtained by using the matrix in (E.26) in place of $\hat{\sigma}^2(\mathbf{X}'\mathbf{X})^{-1}$, and similarly for a test statistic robust to both heteroskedasticity and serial correlation. The robust versions of the test statistics cannot be computed via sums of squared residuals or R-squareds from the restricted and unrestricted regressions.

Summary

This appendix has provided a brief treatment of the linear regression model using matrix notation. This material is included for more advanced classes that use matrix algebra, but it is not needed to read the text. In effect, this appendix proves some of the results that we either stated without proof, proved only in special cases, or proved through a more cumbersome method of proof. Other topics—such as asymptotic properties, instrumental variables estimation, and panel data models—can be given concise treatments using matrices. Advanced texts in econometrics, including Davidson and MacKinnon (1993), Greene (1997), Hayashi (2000), and Wooldridge (2010), can be consulted for details.

Key Terms

First Order Condition
Frisch-Waugh (FW) theorem
Matrix Notation
Minimum Variance Unbiased
   Estimator

Scalar Variance-Covariance
   Matrix
Variance-Covariance Matrix
   of the OLS Estimator

Wald Statistic
Quasi-Maximum Likelihood
   Estimator (QMLE)

Problems

1 Let $\mathbf{x}_t$ be the $1 \times (k + 1)$ vector of explanatory variables for observation t. Show that the OLS estimator $\hat{\boldsymbol{\beta}}$ can be written as

$$\hat{\boldsymbol{\beta}} = \left(\sum_{t=1}^{n} \mathbf{x}_t'\mathbf{x}_t \right)^{-1} \left(\sum_{t=1}^{n} \mathbf{x}_t'y_t \right).$$

Dividing each summation by n shows that $\hat{\boldsymbol{\beta}}$ is a function of sample averages.

2 Let $\hat{\boldsymbol{\beta}}$ be the $(k + 1) \times 1$ vector of OLS estimates.
  (i) Show that for any $(k + 1) \times 1$ vector $\mathbf{b}$, we can write the sum of squared residuals as

$$\text{SSR}(\mathbf{b}) = \hat{\mathbf{u}}'\hat{\mathbf{u}} + (\hat{\boldsymbol{\beta}} - \mathbf{b})'\mathbf{X}'\mathbf{X}(\hat{\boldsymbol{\beta}} - \mathbf{b}).$$

{*Hint*: Write $(\mathbf{y} - \mathbf{Xb})'(\mathbf{y} - \mathbf{Xb}) = [\hat{\mathbf{u}} + \mathbf{X}(\hat{\boldsymbol{\beta}} - \mathbf{b})]'[\hat{\mathbf{u}} + \mathbf{X}(\hat{\boldsymbol{\beta}} - \mathbf{b})]$ and use the fact that $\mathbf{X}'\hat{\mathbf{u}} = \mathbf{0}$.}

(ii) Explain how the expression for SSR(**b**) in part (i) proves that $\hat{\boldsymbol{\beta}}$ uniquely minimizes SSR(**b**) over all possible values of **b**, assuming **X** has rank $k + 1$.

3 Let $\hat{\boldsymbol{\beta}}$ be the OLS estimate from the regression of **y** on **X**. Let **A** be a $(k + 1) \times (k + 1)$ nonsingular matrix and define $\mathbf{z}_t \equiv \mathbf{x}_t\mathbf{A}$, $t = 1, ..., n$. Therefore, $\mathbf{z}_t$ is $1 \times (k + 1)$ and is a nonsingular linear combination of $\mathbf{x}_t$. Let **Z** be the $n \times (k + 1)$ matrix with rows $\mathbf{z}_t$. Let $\tilde{\boldsymbol{\beta}}$ denote the OLS estimate from a regression of **y** on **Z**.

(i)   Show that $\tilde{\boldsymbol{\beta}} = \mathbf{A}^{-1}\hat{\boldsymbol{\beta}}$.

(ii) Let $\hat{y}_t$ be the fitted values from the original regression and let $\tilde{y}_t$ be the fitted values from regressing **y** on **Z**. Show that $\tilde{y}_t = \hat{y}_t$, for all $t = 1, 2, ..., n$. How do the residuals from the two regressions compare?

(iii) Show that the estimated variance matrix for $\tilde{\boldsymbol{\beta}}$ is $\hat{\sigma}^2\mathbf{A}^{-1}(\mathbf{X}'\mathbf{X})^{-1}\mathbf{A}^{-1'}$, where $\hat{\sigma}^2$ is the usual variance estimate from regressing **y** on **X**.

(iv) Let the $\hat{\beta}_j$ be the OLS estimates from regressing y_t on $1, x_{t1}, ..., x_{tk}$, and let the $\tilde{\beta}_j$ be the OLS estimates from the regression of y_t on $1, a_1x_{t1}, ..., a_kx_{tk}$, where $a_j \neq 0$, $j = 1, ..., k$. Use the results from part (i) to find the relationship between the $\tilde{\beta}_j$ and the $\hat{\beta}_j$.

(v)   Assuming the setup of part (iv), use part (iii) to show that $se(\tilde{\beta}_j) = se(\hat{\beta}_j)/|a_j|$.

(vi) Assuming the setup of part (iv), show that the absolute values of the t statistics for $\tilde{\beta}_j$ and $\hat{\beta}_j$ are identical.

4 Assume that the model $\mathbf{y} = \mathbf{X}\boldsymbol{\beta} + \mathbf{u}$ satisfies the Gauss-Markov assumptions, let **G** be a $(k + 1) \times (k + 1)$ nonsingular, nonrandom matrix, and define $\boldsymbol{\delta} = \mathbf{G}\boldsymbol{\beta}$, so that $\boldsymbol{\delta}$ is also a $(k + 1) \times 1$ vector. Let $\hat{\boldsymbol{\beta}}$ be the $(k + 1) \times 1$ vector of OLS estimators and define $\hat{\boldsymbol{\delta}} = \mathbf{G}\hat{\boldsymbol{\beta}}$ as the OLS estimator of $\boldsymbol{\delta}$.

(i)   Show that $\mathrm{E}(\hat{\boldsymbol{\delta}}|\mathbf{X}) = \boldsymbol{\delta}$.

(ii) Find Var $(\hat{\boldsymbol{\delta}}|\mathbf{X})$ in terms of σ^2, **X**, and **G**.

(iii) Use Problem E.3 to verify that $\hat{\boldsymbol{\delta}}$ and the appropriate estimate of $\mathrm{Var}(\hat{\boldsymbol{\delta}}|\mathbf{X})$ are obtained from the regression of **y** on $\mathbf{X}\mathbf{G}^{-1}$.

(iv) Now, let **c** be a $(k + 1) \times 1$ vector with at least one nonzero entry. For concreteness, assume that $c_k \neq 0$. Define $\theta = \mathbf{c}'\boldsymbol{\beta}$, so that θ is a scalar. Define $\delta_j = \beta_j, j = 0, 1, ..., k - 1$ and $\delta_k = \theta$. Show how to define a $(k + 1) \times (k + 1)$ nonsingular matrix **G** so that $\boldsymbol{\delta} = \mathbf{G}\boldsymbol{\beta}$. (*Hint*: Each of the first k rows of **G** should contain k zeros and a one. What is the last row?)

(v)   Show that for the choice of **G** in part (iv),

$$\mathbf{G}^{-1} = \begin{bmatrix} 1 & 0 & 0 & \cdot & \cdot & \cdot & 0 \\ 0 & 1 & 0 & \cdot & \cdot & \cdot & 0 \\ \cdot & & & & & & \\ \cdot & & & & & & \\ \cdot & & & & & & \\ 0 & 0 & \cdot & \cdot & \cdot & 1 & 0 \\ -c_0/c_k & -c_1/c_k & \cdot & \cdot & \cdot & -c_{k-1}/c_k & 1/c_k \end{bmatrix}$$

Use this expression for $\mathbf{G}^{-1}$ and part (iii) to conclude that $\hat{\theta}$ and its standard error are obtained as the coefficient on x_{tk}/c_k in the regression of

$$y_t \text{ on } [1 - (c_0/c_k)x_{tk}], [x_{t1} - (c_1/c_k)x_{tk}], ..., [x_{t,k-1} - (c_{k-1}/c_k)x_{tk}], x_{tk}/c_k, t = 1, ..., n.$$

This regression is exactly the one obtained by writing β_k in terms of θ and $\beta_0, \beta_1, ..., \beta_{k-1}$, plugging the result into the original model, and rearranging. Therefore, we can formally justify the trick we use throughout the text for obtaining the standard error of a linear combination of parameters.

5 Assume that the model $\mathbf{y} = \mathbf{X}\boldsymbol{\beta} + \mathbf{u}$ satisfies the Gauss-Markov assumptions and let $\hat{\boldsymbol{\beta}}$ be the OLS estimator of $\boldsymbol{\beta}$. Let $\mathbf{Z} = \mathbf{G}(\mathbf{X})$ be an $n \times (k + 1)$ matrix function of $\mathbf{X}$ and assume that $\mathbf{Z}'\mathbf{X}[\text{a } (k + 1) \times (k + 1) \text{ matrix}]$ is nonsingular. Define a new estimator of $\boldsymbol{\beta}$ by $\tilde{\boldsymbol{\beta}} = (\mathbf{Z}'\mathbf{X})^{-1}\mathbf{Z}'\mathbf{y}$.
  (i)   Show that $E(\tilde{\boldsymbol{\beta}}|\mathbf{X}) = \boldsymbol{\beta}$, so that $\tilde{\boldsymbol{\beta}}$ is also unbiased conditional on $\mathbf{X}$.
  (ii) Find $\text{Var}(\tilde{\boldsymbol{\beta}}|\mathbf{X})$. Make sure this is a symmetric, $(k + 1) \times (k + 1)$ matrix that depends on $\mathbf{Z}$, $\mathbf{X}$, and σ^2.
  (iii) Which estimator do you prefer, $\hat{\boldsymbol{\beta}}$ or $\tilde{\boldsymbol{\beta}}$? Explain.

6 Consider the setup of the Frisch-Waugh Theorem.
  (i)   Using partitioned matrices, show that the first order conditions $(\mathbf{X}'\mathbf{X})\hat{\boldsymbol{\beta}} = \mathbf{X}'\mathbf{y}$ can be written as

$$\mathbf{X}_1'\mathbf{X}_1\hat{\boldsymbol{\beta}}_1 + \mathbf{X}_1'\mathbf{X}_2\hat{\boldsymbol{\beta}}_2 = \mathbf{X}_1'\mathbf{y}$$
$$\mathbf{X}_2'\mathbf{X}_1\hat{\boldsymbol{\beta}}_1 + \mathbf{X}_2'\mathbf{X}_2\hat{\boldsymbol{\beta}}_2 = \mathbf{X}_2'\mathbf{y}.$$

  (ii) Multiply the first set of equations by $\mathbf{X}_2'\mathbf{X}_1(\mathbf{X}_1'\mathbf{X}_1)^{-1}$ and subtract the result from the second set of equations to show that

$$(\mathbf{X}_2'\mathbf{M}_1\mathbf{X}_2)\hat{\boldsymbol{\beta}}_2 = \mathbf{X}_2'\mathbf{M}_1\mathbf{y},$$

where $\mathbf{I}_n - \mathbf{X}_1(\mathbf{X}_1'\mathbf{X}_1)^{-1}\mathbf{X}_1'$. Conclude that

$$\hat{\boldsymbol{\beta}}_2 = (\ddot{\mathbf{X}}_2'\ddot{\mathbf{X}}_2)^{-1}\ddot{\mathbf{X}}_2'\mathbf{y}.$$

  (iii) Use part (ii) to show that

$$\hat{\boldsymbol{\beta}}_2 = (\ddot{\mathbf{X}}_2'\ddot{\mathbf{X}}_2)^{-1}\ddot{\mathbf{X}}_2'\,\ddot{\mathbf{y}}.$$

  (iv) Use the fact that $\mathbf{M}_1\mathbf{X}_1 = \mathbf{0}$ to show that the residuals $\ddot{\mathbf{u}}$ from the regression $\ddot{\mathbf{y}}$ on $\ddot{\mathbf{X}}_2$ are identical to the residuals $\hat{\mathbf{u}}$ from the regression $\mathbf{y}$ on $\mathbf{X}_1$, $\mathbf{X}_2$. [*Hint*: By definition and the FW theorem,

$$\ddot{\mathbf{u}} = \ddot{\mathbf{y}} - \ddot{\mathbf{X}}_2\hat{\boldsymbol{\beta}}_2 = \mathbf{M}_1(\mathbf{y} - \mathbf{X}_2\hat{\boldsymbol{\beta}}_2) = \mathbf{M}_1(\mathbf{y} - \mathbf{X}_1\hat{\boldsymbol{\beta}}_1 - \mathbf{X}_2\hat{\boldsymbol{\beta}}_2).$$

Now you do the rest.]

7 Suppose that the linear model, written in matrix notation,

$$\mathbf{y} = \mathbf{X}\boldsymbol{\beta} + \mathbf{u}$$

satisfies Assumptions E.1, E.2, and E.3. Partition the model as

$$\mathbf{y} = \mathbf{X}_1\boldsymbol{\beta}_1 + \mathbf{X}_2\boldsymbol{\beta}_2 + \mathbf{u},$$

where $\mathbf{X}_1$ is $n \times (k_1 + 1)$ and $\mathbf{X}_2$ is $n \times k_2$.
  (i)   Consider the following proposal for estimating $\boldsymbol{\beta}_2$. First, regress $\mathbf{y}$ on $\mathbf{X}_1$ and obtain the residuals, say, $\ddot{\mathbf{y}}$. Then, regress $\ddot{\mathbf{y}}$ on $\mathbf{X}_2$ to get $\check{\boldsymbol{\beta}}_2$. Show that $\check{\boldsymbol{\beta}}_2$ is generally biased and show what the bias is. [You should find $E(\check{\boldsymbol{\beta}}_2|\mathbf{X})$ in terms of $\boldsymbol{\beta}_2$, $\mathbf{X}_2$, and the residual-making matrix $\mathbf{M}_1$.]
  (ii) As a special case, write

$$\mathbf{y} = \mathbf{X}_1\boldsymbol{\beta}_1 + \beta_k\mathbf{X}_k + \mathbf{u},$$

where $\mathbf{X}_k$ is an $n \times 1$ vector on the variable x_{tk}. Show that

$$E(\tilde{\beta}_k|\mathbf{X}) = \left(\frac{\text{SSR}_k}{\sum_{t=1}^n x_{tk}^2}\right)\beta_k,$$

where SSR_k is the sum of squared residuals from regressing x_{tk} on $1, x_{t1}, x_{t2}, \ldots, x_{t,k-1}$. How come the factor multiplying β_k is never greater than one?
  (iii) Suppose you know $\boldsymbol{\beta}_1$. Show that the regression $\mathbf{y} - \mathbf{X}_1\boldsymbol{\beta}_1$ on $\mathbf{X}_2$ produces an unbiased estimator of $\boldsymbol{\beta}_2$ (conditional on $\mathbf{X}$).

Appendix F

Answers to Chapter Questions

Chapter 2

Question 2.1: When student ability, motivation, age, and other factors in u are not related to attendance, equation (2.6) would hold. This seems unlikely to be the case.

Question 2.2: About \$11.05. To see this, from the average wages measured in 1976 and 2003 dollars, we can get the CPI deflator as $19.06/5.90 \approx 3.23$. When we multiply 3.42 by 3.23, we obtain about 11.05.

Question 2.3: 54.65, as can be seen by plugging $shareA = 60$ into equation (2.28). This is not unreasonable: if Candidate A spends 60% of the total money spent, he or she is predicted to receive almost 55% of the vote.

Question 2.4: The equation will be $\widehat{salaryhun} = 9{,}631.91 + 185.01\, roe$, as is easily seen by multiplying equation (2.39) by 10.

Question 2.5: Equation (2.58) can be written as $\text{Var}(\hat{\beta}_0) = (\sigma^2 n^{-1})(\sum_{i=1}^{n} x_i^2)/(\sum_{i=1}^{n}(x_i - \bar{x})^2)$, where the term multiplying $\sigma^2 n^{-1}$ is greater than or equal to one, but it is equal to one if, and only if, $\bar{x} = 0$. In this case, the variance is as small as it can possibly be: $\text{Var}(\hat{\beta}_0) = \sigma^2/n$.

Chapter 3

Question 3.1: Just a few factors include age and gender distribution, size of the police force (or, more generally, resources devoted to crime fighting), population, and general historical factors. These factors certainly might be correlated with *prbconv* and *avgsen*, which means equation (3.5) would not hold. For example, size of the police force is possibly correlated with both *prbcon* and *avgsen*, as some cities put more effort into crime prevention and law enforcement. We should try to bring as many of these factors into the equation as possible.

Question 3.2: We use the third property of OLS concerning predicted values and residuals: when we plug the average values of all independent variables into the OLS regression line, we obtain the average value of the dependent variable. So $\overline{colGPA} = 1.29 + .453\,\overline{hsGPA} + .0094\,\overline{ACT} = 1.29 + .453(3.4) + .0094(24.2) \approx 3.06$. You can check the average of *colGPA* in GPA1 to verify this to the second decimal place.

Question 3.3: No. The variable *shareA* is not an exact linear function of *expendA* and *expendB*, even though it is an exact *nonlinear* function: $shareA = 100 \cdot [expendA/(expendA + expendB)]$. Therefore, it is legitimate to have *expendA*, *expendB*, and *shareA* as explanatory variables.

Question 3.4: As we discussed in Section 3.4, if we are interested in the effect of x_1 on y, correlation among the other explanatory variables (x_2, x_3, and so on) does not affect $\text{Var}(\hat{\beta}_1)$. These variables are included as controls, and we do not have to worry about collinearity among the control variables. Of course, we are controlling for them primarily because we think they are correlated with attendance, but this is necessary to perform a ceteris paribus analysis.

Chapter 4

Question 4.1: Under these assumptions, the Gauss-Markov assumptions are satisfied: u is independent of the explanatory variables, so $E(u|x_1, \ldots, x_k) = E(u)$, and $\text{Var}(u|x_1, \ldots, x_k) = \text{Var}(u)$. Further, it is easily seen that $E(u) = 0$. Therefore, MLR.4 and MLR.5 hold. The classical linear model assumptions are not satisfied because u is not normally distributed (which is a violation of MLR.6).

Question 4.2: $H_0\colon \beta_1 = 0, H_1\colon \beta_1 < 0$.

Question 4.3: Because $\hat{\beta}_1 = .56 > 0$ and we are testing against $H_1\colon \beta_1 > 0$, the one-sided p-value is one-half of the two-sided p-value, or .043.

Question 4.4: $H_0\colon \beta_5 = \beta_6 = \beta_7 = \beta_8 = 0$. $k = 8$ and $q = 4$. The restricted version of the model is

$$score = \beta_0 + \beta_1 classize + \beta_2 expend + \beta_3 tchcomp + \beta_4 enroll + u.$$

Question 4.5: The F statistic for testing exclusion of *ACT* is $[(.291 - .183)/(1 - .291)](680 - 3) \approx 103.13$. Therefore, the absolute value of the t statistic is about 10.16. The t statistic on *ACT* is negative, because $\hat{\beta}_{ACT}$ is negative, so $t_{ACT} = -10.16$.

Question 4.6: Not by much. The F test for joint significance of *droprate* and *gradrate* is easily computed from the R-squareds in the table: $F = [(.361 - .353)/(1 - .361)](402/2) \approx 2.52$. The 10% critical value is obtained from Table G.3a as 2.30, while the 5% critical value from Table G.3b is 3. The p-value is about .082. Thus, *droprate* and *gradrate* are jointly significant at the 10% level, but not at the 5% level. In any case, controlling for these variables has a minor effect on the *b/s* coefficient.

Chapter 5

Question 5.1: This requires some assumptions. It seems reasonable to assume that $\beta_2 > 0$ (*score* depends positively on *priGPA*) and $\text{Cov}(skipped, priGPA) < 0$ (*skipped* and *priGPA* are negatively correlated). This means that $\beta_2 \delta_1 < 0$, which means that $\text{plim}\ \tilde{\beta}_1 < \beta_1$. Because β_1 is thought to be negative (or at least nonpositive), a simple regression is likely to overestimate the importance of skipping classes.

Question 5.2: $\hat{\beta}_j \pm 1.96 se(\hat{\beta}_j)$ is the asymptotic 95% confidence interval. Or, we can replace 1.96 with 2.

Chapter 6

Question 6.1: Because *fincdol* = 1,000·*faminc*, the coefficient on *fincdol* will be the coefficient on *faminc* divided by 1,000, or .0927/1,000 = .0000927. The standard error also drops by a factor of 1,000, so the *t* statistic does not change, nor do any of the other OLS statistics. For readability, it is better to measure family income in thousands of dollars.

Question 6.2: We can do this generally. The equation is

$$\log(y) = \beta_0 + \beta_1 \log(x_1) + \beta_2 x_2 + \ldots,$$

where x_2 is a proportion rather than a percentage. Then, ceteris paribus, $\Delta \log(y) = \beta_2 \Delta x_2$, $100 \cdot \Delta \log(y) = \beta_2(100 \cdot \Delta x_2)$, or $\% \Delta y \approx \beta_2(100 \cdot \Delta x_2)$. Now, because Δx_2 is the change in the proportion, $100 \cdot \Delta x_2$ is a percentage point change. In particular, if $\Delta x_2 = .01$, then $100 \cdot \Delta x_2 = 1$, which corresponds to a one percentage point change. But then β_2 is the percentage change in y when $100 \cdot \Delta x_2 = 1$.

Question 6.3: The new model would be *stndfnl* = $\beta_0 + \beta_1$*atndrte* + β_2*priGPA* + β_3*ACT* + β_4*priGPA*^{2} + β_5*ACT*^{2} + β_6*priGPA·atndrte* + β_7*ACT·atndrte* + *u*. Therefore, the partial effect of *atndrte* on *stndfnl* is $\beta_1 + \beta_6$*priGPA* + β_7*ACT*. This is what we multiply by Δ*atndrte* to obtain the ceteris paribus change in *stndfnl*.

Question 6.4: From equation (6.21), $\bar{R}^2 = 1 - \hat{\sigma}^2/[\text{SST}/(n-1)]$. For a given sample and a given dependent variable, SST/($n-1$) is fixed. When we use different sets of explanatory variables, only $\hat{\sigma}^2$ changes. As $\hat{\sigma}^2$ decreases, $\bar{R}^2$ increases. If we make $\hat{\sigma}$, and therefore $\hat{\sigma}^2$, as small as possible, we are making $\bar{R}^2$ as large as possible.

Question 6.5: One possibility is to collect data on annual earnings for a sample of actors, along with profitability of the movies in which they each appeared. In a simple regression analysis, we could relate earnings to profitability. But we should probably control for other factors that may affect salary, such as age, gender, and the kinds of movies in which the actors performed. Methods for including qualitative factors in regression models are considered in Chapter 7.

Chapter 7

Question 7.1: No, because it would not be clear when *party* is one and when it is zero. A better name would be something like *Dem*, which is one for Democratic candidates and zero for Republicans. Or, *Rep*, which is one for Republicans and zero for Democrats.

Question 7.2: With *outfield* as the base group, we would include the dummy variables *frstbase*, *scndbase*, *thrdbase*, *shrtstop*, and *catcher*.

Question 7.3: The null in this case is H$_0$: $\delta_1 = \delta_2 = \delta_3 = \delta_4 = 0$, so that there are four restrictions. As usual, we would use an *F* test (where *q* = 4 and *k* depends on the number of other explanatory variables).

Question 7.4: Because *tenure* appears as a quadratic, we should allow separate quadratics for men and women. That is, we would add the explanatory variables *female·tenure* and *female · tenure*^{2}.

Question 7.5: We plug *pcnv* = 0, *avgsen* = 0, *tottime* = 0, *ptime86* = 0, *qemp86* = 4, *black* = 1, and *hispan* = 0 into equation (7.31): $\widehat{arr86}$ = .380 − .038(4) + .170 = .398, or almost .4. It is hard to know whether this is "reasonable." For someone with no prior convictions who was employed throughout the year, this estimate might seem high, but remember that the population consists of men who were already arrested at least once prior to 1986.

Chapter 8

Question 8.1: This statement is clearly false. For example, in equation (8.7), the usual standard error for *black* is .147, while the heteroskedasticity-robust standard error is .118.

Question 8.2: The F test would be obtained by regressing $\hat{u}^2$ on *marrmale*, *marrfem*, and *singfem* (*singmale* is the base group). With $n = 526$ and three independent variables in this regression, the *df* are 3 and 522.

Question 8.3: Certainly the outcome of the statistical test suggests some cause for concern. A t statistic of 2.96 is very significant, and it implies that there is heteroskedasticity in the wealth equation. As a practical matter, we know that the WLS standard error, .063, is substantially below the heteroskedasticity-robust standard error for OLS, .104, and so the heteroskedasticity seems to be practically important. (Plus, the nonrobust OLS standard error is .061, which is too optimistic. Therefore, even if we simply adjust the OLS standard error for heteroskedasticity of unknown form, there are nontrivial implications.)

Question 8.4: The 1% critical value in the F distribution with $(2, \infty)$ df is 4.61. An F statistic of 11.15 is well above the 1% critical value, and so we strongly reject the null hypothesis that the transformed errors, $u_i/\sqrt{h_i}$, are homoskedastic. (In fact, the p-value is less than .00002, which is obtained from the $F_{2,804}$ distribution.) This means that our model for $\text{Var}(u|\mathbf{x})$ is inadequate for fully eliminating the heteroskedasticity in u.

Chapter 9

Question 9.1: These are binary variables, and squaring them has no effect: $black^2 = black$, and $hispan^2 = hispan$.

Question 9.2: When $educ \cdot IQ$ is in the equation, the coefficient on *educ*, say, β_1, measures the effect of *educ* on $\log(wage)$ when $IQ = 0$. (The partial effect of education is $\beta_1 + \beta_9 IQ$.) There is no one in the population of interest with an IQ close to zero. At the average population IQ, which is 100, the estimated return to education from column (3) is $.018 + .00034(100) = .052$, which is almost what we obtain as the coefficient on *educ* in column (2).

Question 9.3: No. If $educ^*$ is an integer—which means someone has no education past the previous grade completed—the measurement error is zero. If $educ^*$ is not an integer, $educ < educ^*$, so the measurement error is negative. At a minimum, e_1 cannot have zero mean, and e_1 and $educ^*$ are probably correlated.

Question 9.4: An incumbent's decision not to run may be systematically related to how he or she expects to do in the election. Therefore, we may only have a sample of incumbents who are stronger, on average, than all possible incumbents who could run. This results in a sample selection problem if the population of interest includes all incumbents. If we are only interested in the effects of campaign expenditures on election outcomes for incumbents who seek reelection, there is no sample selection problem.

Chapter 10

Question 10.1: The impact propensity is .48, while the long-run propensity is $.48 - .15 + .32 = .65$.

Question 10.2: The explanatory variables are $x_{t1} = z_t$ and $x_{t2} = z_{t-1}$. The absence of perfect collinearity means that these cannot be constant, and there cannot be an exact linear relationship between them in the sample. This rules out the possibility that all the $z_1, \ldots, z_n$ take on the same value or that the $z_0, z_1, \ldots, z_{n-1}$ take on the same value. But it eliminates other patterns as well. For example, if $z_t = a + bt$ for constants a and b, then $z_{t-1} = a + b(t-1) = (a+bt) - b = z_t - b$, which is a perfect linear function of z_t.

Question 10.3: If $\{z_t\}$ is slowly moving over time—as is the case for the levels or logs of many economic time series—then z_t and z_{t-1} can be highly correlated. For example, the correlation between $unem_t$ and $unem_{t-1}$ in PHILLIPS is .75.

Question 10.4: No, because a linear time trend with $\alpha_1 < 0$ becomes more and more negative as t gets large. Since *gfr* cannot be negative, a linear time trend with a negative trend coefficient cannot represent *gfr* in all future time periods.

Question 10.5: The intercept for March is $\beta_0 + \delta_2$. Seasonal dummy variables are strictly exogenous because they follow a deterministic pattern. For example, the months do not change based upon whether either the explanatory variables or the dependent variables change.

Chapter 11

Question 11.1: (i) No, because $E(y_t) = \delta_0 + \delta_1 t$ depends on t. (ii) Yes, because $y_t - E(y_t) = e_t$ is an i.i.d. sequence.

Question 11.2: We plug $inf_t^e = (1/2)inf_{t-1} + (1/2)inf_{t-2}$ into $inf_t - inf_t^e = \beta_1(unem_t - \mu_0) + e_t$ and rearrange: $inf_t - (1/2)(inf_{t-1} + inf_{t-2}) = \beta_0 + \beta_1 unem_t + e_t$, where $\beta_0 = -\beta_1\mu_0$, as before. Therefore, we would regress y_t on $unem_t$, where $y_t = inf_t - (1/2)(inf_{t-1} + inf_{t-2})$. Note that we lose the first two observations in constructing y_t.

Question 11.3: No, because u_t and u_{t-1} are correlated. In particular, $\text{Cov}(u_t, u_{t-1}) = E[(e_t + \alpha_1 e_{t-1})(e_{t-1} + \alpha_1 e_{t-2})] = \alpha_1 E(e_{t-1}^2) = \alpha_1 \sigma_e^2 \neq 0$ if $\alpha_1 \neq 0$. If the errors are serially correlated, the model cannot be dynamically complete.

Chapter 12

Question 12.1: We use equation (12.4). Now, only adjacent terms are correlated. In particular, the covariance between $x_t u_t$ and $x_{t+1} u_{t+1}$ is $x_t x_{t+1} \text{Cov}(u_t, u_{t+1}) = x_t x_{t+1} \alpha \sigma_e^2$. Therefore, the formula is

$$\text{Var}(\hat{\beta}_1) = \text{SST}_x^{-2}\left(\sum_{t=1}^n x_t^2 \text{Var}(u_t) + 2\sum_{t=1}^{n-1} x_t x_{t+1} E(u_t u_{t+1})\right)$$

$$= \sigma^2/\text{SST}_x + (2/\text{SST}_x^2)\sum_{t=1}^{n-1}\alpha\sigma_e^2 x_t x_{t+1}$$

$$= \sigma^2/\text{SST}_x + \alpha\sigma_e^2(2/\text{SST}_x^2)\sum_{t=1}^{n-1} x_t x_{t+1},$$

where $\sigma^2 = \text{Var}(u_t) = \sigma_e^2 + \alpha_1^2\sigma_e^2 = \sigma_e^2(1 + \alpha_1^2)$. Unless x_t and x_{t+1} are uncorrelated in the sample, the second term is nonzero whenever $\alpha_1 \neq 0$. Notice that if x_t and x_{t+1} are positively correlated and $\alpha < 0$, the true variance is actually *smaller* than the usual variance. When the equation is in levels (as opposed to being differenced), the typical case is $\alpha > 0$, with positive correlation between x_t and x_{t+1}.

Question 12.2: $\hat{\rho} \pm 1.96\text{se}(\hat{\rho})$, where $\text{se}(\hat{\rho})$ is the standard error reported in the regression. Or, we could use the heteroskedasticity-robust standard error. Showing that this is asymptotically valid is complicated because the OLS residuals depend on $\hat{\beta}_j$, but it can be done.

Question 12.3: The model we have in mind is $u_t = \rho_1 u_{t-1} + \rho_4 u_{t-4} + e_t$, and we want to test H_0: $\rho_1 = 0$, $\rho_4 = 0$ against the alternative that H_0 is false. We would run the regression of $\hat{u}_t$ on $\hat{u}_{t-1}$ and $\hat{u}_{t-4}$ to obtain the usual F statistic for joint significance of the two lags. (We are testing two restrictions.)

Question 12.4: We would probably estimate the equation using first differences, as $\hat{\rho} = .92$ is close enough to 1 to raise questions about the levels regression. See Chapter 18 for more discussion.

Question 12.5: Because there is only one explanatory variable, the White test is easy to compute. Simply regress $\hat{u}_t^2$ on $return_{t-1}$ and $return_{t-1}^2$ (with an intercept, as always) and compute the F test for joint significance of $return_{t-1}$ and $return_{t-1}^2$. If these are jointly significant at a small enough significance level, we reject the null of homoskedasticity.

Chapter 13

Question 13.1: Yes, assuming that we have controlled for all relevant factors. The coefficient on *black* is 1.076, and, with a standard error of .174, it is not statistically different from 1. The 95% confidence interval is from about .735 to 1.417.

Question 13.2: The coefficient on *highearn* shows that, in the absence of any change in the earnings cap, high earners spend much more time—on the order of 29.2% on average [because $\exp(.256) - 1 \approx .292$]—on workers' compensation.

Question 13.3: First, $E(v_{i1}) = E(a_i + u_{i1}) = E(a_i) + E(v_{i1}) = 0$. Similarly, $E(v_{i2}) = 0$. Therefore, the covariance between v_{i1} and v_{i2} is simply $E(v_{i1}v_{i2}) = E[(a_i + u_{i1})(a_i + u_{i2})] = E(a_i^2) + E(a_iu_{i1}) + E(a_iu_{i2}) + E(u_{i1}u_{i2}) = E(a_i^2)$, because all of the covariance terms are zero by assumption. But $E(a_i^2) = Var(a_i)$, because $E(a_i) = 0$. This causes positive serial correlation across time in the errors within each i, which biases the usual OLS standard errors in a pooled OLS regression.

Question 13.4: Because $\Delta admn = admn_{90} - admn_{85}$ is the difference in binary indicators, it can be -1 if, and only if, $admn_{90} = 0$ and $admn_{85} = 1$. In other words, Washington state had an administrative per se law in 1985 but it was repealed by 1990.

Question 13.5: No, just as it does not cause bias and inconsistency in a time series regression with strictly exogenous explanatory variables. There are two reasons it is a concern. First, serial correlation in the errors in any equation generally biases the usual OLS standard errors and test statistics. Second, it means that pooled OLS is not as efficient as estimators that account for the serial correlation (as in Chapter 12).

Chapter 14

Question 14.1: Whether we use first differencing or the within transformation, we will have trouble estimating the coefficient on $kids_{it}$. For example, using the within transformation, if $kids_{it}$ does not vary for family i, then $\ddot{kids}_{it} = kids_{it} - \overline{kids}_i = 0$ for $t = 1,2,3$. As long as some families have variation in $kids_{it}$, then we can compute the fixed effects estimator, but the *kids* coefficient could be very imprecisely estimated. This is a form of multicollinearity in fixed effects estimation (or first-differencing estimation).

Question 14.2: If a firm did not receive a grant in the first year, it may or may not receive a grant in the second year. But if a firm did receive a grant in the first year, it could not get a grant in the second year. That is, if $grant_{-1} = 1$, then $grant = 0$. This induces a negative correlation between $grant$ and $grant_{-1}$. We can verify this by computing a regression of $grant$ on $grant_{-1}$, using the data in JTRAIN for 1989. Using all firms in the sample, we get

$$\widehat{grant} = .248 - .248\ grant_{-1}$$
$$(.035)\quad (.072)$$
$$n = 157,\ R^2 = .070.$$

The coefficient on $grant_{-1}$ must be the negative of the intercept because $\widehat{grant} = 0$ when $grant_{-1} = 1$.

Question 14.3: It suggests that the unobserved effect a_i is positively correlated with $union_{it}$. Remember, pooled OLS leaves a_i in the error term, while fixed effects removes a_i. By definition, a_i has a positive effect on log($wage$). By the standard omitted variables analysis (see Chapter 3), OLS has an upward bias when the explanatory variable ($union$) is positively correlated with the omitted variable (a_i). Thus, belonging to a union appears to be positively related to time-constant, unobserved factors that affect wage.

Question 14.4: Not if all sisters within a family have the same mother and father. Then, because the parents' race variables would not change by sister, they would be differenced away in equation (14.13).

Chapter 15

Question 15.1: Probably not. In the simple equation (15.18), years of education is part of the error term. If some men who were assigned low draft lottery numbers obtained additional schooling, then lottery number and education are negatively correlated, which violates the first requirement for an instrumental variable in equation (15.4).

Question 15.2: (i) For equation (15.27), we require that high school peer group effects carry over to college. Namely, for a given SAT score, a student who went to a high school where smoking marijuana was more popular would smoke more marijuana in college. Even if the identification condition equation (15.27) holds, the link might be weak.

(ii) We have to assume that percentage of students using marijuana at a student's high school is not correlated with unobserved factors that affect college grade point average. Although we are somewhat controlling for high school quality by including *SAT* in the equation, this might not be enough. Perhaps high schools that did a better job of preparing students for college also had fewer students smoking marijuana. Or marijuana usage could be correlated with average income levels. These are, of course, empirical questions that we may or may not be able to answer.

Question 15.3: Although prevalence of the NRA and subscribers to gun magazines are probably correlated with the presence of gun control legislation, it is not obvious that they are uncorrelated with unobserved factors that affect the violent crime rate. In fact, we might argue that a population interested in guns is a reflection of high crime rates, and controlling for economic and demographic variables is not sufficient to capture this. It would be hard to argue persuasively that these are truly exogenous in the violent crime equation.

Question 15.4: As usual, there are two requirements. First, it should be the case that growth in government spending is systematically related to the party of the president, after netting out the investment rate and growth in the labor force. In other words, the instrument must be partially correlated with the endogenous explanatory variable. While we might think that government spending grows more slowly under Republican presidents, this certainly has not always been true in the United States and would have to be tested using the t statistic on REP_{t-1} in the reduced form

$gGov_t = \pi_0 + \pi_1 REP_{t-1} + \pi_2 INVRAT_t + \pi_3 gLAB_t + v_t$. We must assume that the party of the president has no separate effect on $gGDP$. This would be violated if, for example, monetary policy differs systematically by presidential party and has a separate effect on GDP growth.

Chapter 16

Question 16.1: Probably not. It is because firms choose price and advertising expenditures jointly that we are not interested in the experiment where, say, advertising changes exogenously and we want to know the effect on price. Instead, we would model price and advertising each as a function of demand and cost variables. This is what falls out of the economic theory.

Question 16.2: We must assume two things. First, money supply growth should appear in equation (16.22), so that it is partially correlated with inf. Second, we must assume that money supply growth does not appear in equation (16.23). If we think we must include money supply growth in equation (16.23), then we are still short an instrument for inf. Of course, the assumption that money supply growth is exogenous can also be questioned.

Question 16.3: Use the Hausman test from Chapter 15. In particular, let $\hat{v}_2$ be the OLS residuals from the reduced form regression of $open$ on $\log(pcinc)$ and $\log(land)$. Then, use an OLS regression of inf on $open$, $\log(pcinc)$, and $\hat{v}_2$ and compute the t statistic for significance of $\hat{v}_2$. If $\hat{v}_2$ is significant, the 2SLS and OLS estimates are statistically different.

Question 16.4: The demand equation looks like

$$\log(fish_t) = \beta_0 + \beta_1\log(prcfish_t) + \beta_2\log(inc_t)$$
$$+ \beta_3\log(prcchick_t) + \beta_4\log(prcbeef_t) + u_{t1},$$

where logarithms are used so that all elasticities are constant. By assumption, the demand function contains no seasonality, so the equation does not contain monthly dummy variables (say, feb_t, mar_t, ..., dec_t, with January as the base month). Also, by assumption, the supply of fish is seasonal, which means that the supply function does depend on at least some of the monthly dummy variables. Even without solving the reduced form for $\log(prcfish)$, we conclude that it depends on the monthly dummy variables. Since these are exogenous, they can be used as instruments for $\log(prcfish)$ in the demand equation. Therefore, we can estimate the demand-for-fish equation using monthly dummies as the IVs for $\log(prcfish)$. Identification requires that at least one monthly dummy variable appears with a nonzero coefficient in the reduced form for $\log(prcfish)$.

Chapter 17

Question 17.1: $H_0: \beta_4 = \beta_5 = \beta_6 = 0$, so that there are three restrictions and therefore three df in the LR or Wald test.

Question 17.2: We need the partial derivative of $\Phi(\hat{\beta}_0 + \hat{\beta}_1 nwifeinc + \hat{\beta}_2 educ + \hat{\beta}_3 exper + \hat{\beta}_4 exper^2 + \cdots)$ with respect to $exper$, which is $\phi(\cdot)(\hat{\beta}_3 + 2\hat{\beta}_4 exper)$, where $\phi(\cdot)$ is evaluated at the given values and the initial level of experience. Therefore, we need to evaluate the standard normal probability density at $.270 - .012(20.13) + .131(12.3) + .123(10) - .0019(10^2) - .053(42.5) - .868(0) + .036(1) \approx .463$, where we plug in the initial level of experience (10). But $\phi(.463) = (2\pi)^{-1/2}\exp[-(.463^2)/2] \approx .358$. Next, we multiply this by $\hat{\beta}_3 + 2\hat{\beta}_4 exper$, which is evaluated at $exper = 10$. The partial effect using the calculus approximation is $.358[.123 - 2(.0019)(10)] \approx .030$. In other words, at the given values of the explanatory variables and starting at $exper = 10$, the next year of experience increases the probability of labor force participation by about .03.

Question 17.3: No. The number of extramarital affairs is a nonnegative integer, which presumably takes on zero or small numbers for a substantial fraction of the population. It is not realistic to use a Tobit model, which, while allowing a pileup at zero, treats y as being continuously distributed over positive values. Formally, assuming that $y = \max(0, y^*)$, where y^* is normally distributed, is at odds with the discreteness of the number of extramarital affairs when $y > 0$.

Question 17.4: The adjusted standard errors are the usual Poisson MLE standard errors multiplied by $\hat{\sigma} = \sqrt{2} \approx 1.41$, so the adjusted standard errors will be about 41% higher. The quasi-LR statistic is the usual LR statistic divided by $\hat{\sigma}^2$, so it will be one-half of the usual LR statistic.

Question 17.5: By assumption, $mvp_i = \beta_0 + \mathbf{x}_i\boldsymbol{\beta} + u_i$, where, as usual, $\mathbf{x}_i\boldsymbol{\beta}$ denotes a linear function of the exogenous variables. Now, observed wage is the largest of the minimum wage and the marginal value product, so $wage_i = \max(minwage_i, mvp_i)$, which is very similar to equation (17.34), except that the max operator has replaced the min operator.

Chapter 18

Question 18.1: We can plug these values directly into equation (18.1) and take expectations. First, because $z_s = 0$, for all $s < 0$, $y_{-1} = \alpha + u_{-1}$. Then, $z_0 = 1$, so $y_0 = \alpha + \delta_0 + u_0$. For $h \geq 1$, $y_h = \alpha + \delta_{h-1} + \delta_h + u_h$. Because the errors have zero expected values, $E(y_{-1}) = \alpha$, $E(y_0) = \alpha + \delta_0$, and $E(y_h) = \alpha + \delta_{h-1} + \delta$, for all $h \geq 1$. As $h \to \infty$, $\delta_h \to 0$. It follows that $E(y_h) \to \alpha$ as $h \to \infty$, that is, the expected value of y_h returns to the expected value before the increase in z, at time zero. This makes sense: although the increase in z lasted for two periods, it is still a temporary increase.

Question 18.2: Under the described setup, Δy_t and Δx_t are i.i.d. sequences that are independent of one another. In particular, Δy_t and Δx_t are uncorrelated. If $\hat{\gamma}_t$ is the slope coefficient from regressing Δy_t on Δx_t, $t = 1, 2, \ldots, n$, then plim $\hat{\gamma}_t = 0$. This is as it should be, as we are regressing one I(0) process on another I(0) process, and they are uncorrelated. We write the equation $\Delta y_t = \gamma_0 + \gamma_1\Delta x_t + e_t$, where $\gamma_0 = \gamma_1 = 0$. Because $\{e_t\}$ is independent of $\{\Delta x_t\}$, the strict exogeneity assumption holds. Moreover, $\{e_t\}$ is serially uncorrelated and homoskedastic. By Theorem 11.2 in Chapter 11, the t statistic for $\hat{\gamma}_t$ has an approximate standard normal distribution. If e_t is normally distributed, the classical linear model assumptions hold, and the t statistic has an exact t distribution.

Question 18.3: Write $x_t = x_{t-1} + a_t$, where $\{a_t\}$ is I(0). By assumption, there is a linear combination, say, $s_t = y_t - \beta x_t$, which is I(0). Now, $y_t - \beta x_{t-1} = y_t - \beta(x_t - a_t) = s_t + \beta a_t$. Because s_t and a_t are I(0) by assumption, so is $s_t + \beta a_t$.

Question 18.4: Just use the sum of squared residuals form of the F test and assume homoskedasticity. The restricted SSR is obtained by regressing $\Delta hy6_t - \Delta hy3_{t-1} + (hy6_{t-1} - hy3_{t-2})$ on a constant. Notice that a_0 is the only parameter to estimate in $\Delta hy6_t = \alpha_0 + \gamma_0\Delta hy3_{t-1} + \delta(hy6_{t-1} - hy3_{t-2})$ when the restrictions are imposed. The unrestricted sum of squared residuals is obtained from equation (18.39).

Question 18.5: We are fitting two equations: $\hat{y}_t = \hat{\alpha} + \hat{\beta}t$ and $\hat{y}_t = \hat{\gamma} + \hat{\delta}year_t$. We can obtain the relationship between the parameters by noting that $year_t = t + 49$. Plugging this into the second equation gives $\hat{y}_t = \hat{\gamma} + \hat{\delta}(t + 49) = (\hat{\gamma} + 49\hat{\delta}) + \hat{\delta}t$. Matching the slope and intercept with the first equation gives $\hat{\delta} = \hat{\beta}$—so that the slopes on t and $year_t$ are identical—and $\hat{\alpha} = \hat{\gamma} + 49\hat{\delta}$. Generally, when we use $year$ rather than t, the intercept will change, but the slope will not. (You can verify this by using one of the time series data sets, such as HSEINV or INVEN.) Whether we use t or some measure of $year$ does not change fitted values, and, naturally, it does not change forecasts of future values. The intercept simply adjusts appropriately to different ways of including a trend in the regression.

Appendix G

Statistical Tables

(continued)

TABLE G.1 Cumulative Areas under the Standard Normal Distribution									
z	0	1	2	3	4	5	6	7	8	9
−3.0	0.0013	0.0013	0.0013	0.0012	0.0012	0.0011	0.0011	0.0011	0.0010	0.0010
−2.9	0.0019	0.0018	0.0018	0.0017	0.0016	0.0016	0.0015	0.0015	0.0014	0.0014
−2.8	0.0026	0.0025	0.0024	0.0023	0.0023	0.0022	0.0021	0.0021	0.0020	0.0019
−2.7	0.0035	0.0034	0.0033	0.0032	0.0031	0.0030	0.0029	0.0028	0.0027	0.0026
−2.6	0.0047	0.0045	0.0044	0.0043	0.0041	0.0040	0.0039	0.0038	0.0037	0.0036
−2.5	0.0062	0.0060	0.0059	0.0057	0.0055	0.0054	0.0052	0.0051	0.0049	0.0048
−2.4	0.0082	0.0080	0.0078	0.0075	0.0073	0.0071	0.0069	0.0068	0.0066	0.0064
−2.3	0.0107	0.0104	0.0102	0.0099	0.0096	0.0094	0.0091	0.0089	0.0087	0.0084
−2.2	0.0139	0.0136	0.0132	0.0129	0.0125	0.0122	0.0119	0.0116	0.0113	0.0110
−2.1	0.0179	0.0174	0.0170	0.0166	0.0162	0.0158	0.0154	0.0150	0.0146	0.0143
−2.0	0.0228	0.0222	0.0217	0.0212	0.0207	0.0202	0.0197	0.0192	0.0188	0.0183
−1.9	0.0287	0.0281	0.0274	0.0268	0.0262	0.0256	0.0250	0.0244	0.0239	0.0233
−1.8	0.0359	0.0351	0.0344	0.0336	0.0329	0.0322	0.0314	0.0307	0.0301	0.0294
−1.7	0.0446	0.0436	0.0427	0.0418	0.0409	0.0401	0.0392	0.0384	0.0375	0.0367
−1.6	0.0548	0.0537	0.0526	0.0516	0.0505	0.0495	0.0485	0.0475	0.0465	0.0455
−1.5	0.0668	0.0655	0.0643	0.0630	0.0618	0.0606	0.0594	0.0582	0.0571	0.0559
−1.4	0.0808	0.0793	0.0778	0.0764	0.0749	0.0735	0.0721	0.0708	0.0694	0.0681
−1.3	0.0968	0.0951	0.0934	0.0918	0.0901	0.0885	0.0869	0.0853	0.0838	0.0823
−1.2	0.1151	0.1131	0.1112	0.1093	0.1075	0.1056	0.1038	0.1020	0.1003	0.0985
−1.1	0.1357	0.1335	0.1314	0.1292	0.1271	0.1251	0.1230	0.1210	0.1190	0.1170
−1.0	0.1587	0.1562	0.1539	0.1515	0.1492	0.1469	0.1446	0.1423	0.1401	0.1379
−0.9	0.1841	0.1814	0.1788	0.1762	0.1736	0.1711	0.1685	0.1660	0.1635	0.1611
−0.8	0.2119	0.2090	0.2061	0.2033	0.2005	0.1977	0.1949	0.1922	0.1894	0.1867
−0.7	0.2420	0.2389	0.2358	0.2327	0.2296	0.2266	0.2236	0.2206	0.2177	0.2148
−0.6	0.2743	0.2709	0.2676	0.2643	0.2611	0.2578	0.2546	0.2514	0.2483	0.2451
−0.5	0.3085	0.3050	0.3015	0.2981	0.2946	0.2912	0.2877	0.2843	0.2810	0.2776
−0.4	0.3446	0.3409	0.3372	0.3336	0.3300	0.3264	0.3228	0.3192	0.3156	0.3121

(continued)

TABLE G.1 (Continued)

z	0	1	2	3	4	5	6	7	8	9
−0.3	0.3821	0.3783	0.3745	0.3707	0.3669	0.3632	0.3594	0.3557	0.3520	0.3483
−0.2	0.4207	0.4168	0.4129	0.4090	0.4052	0.4013	0.3974	0.3936	0.3897	0.3859
−0.1	0.4602	0.4562	0.4522	0.4483	0.4443	0.4404	0.4364	0.4325	0.4286	0.4247
−0.0	0.5000	0.4960	0.4920	0.4880	0.4840	0.4801	0.4761	0.4721	0.4681	0.4641
0.0	0.5000	0.5040	0.5080	0.5120	0.5160	0.5199	0.5239	0.5279	0.5319	0.5359
0.1	0.5398	0.5438	0.5478	0.5517	0.5557	0.5596	0.5636	0.5675	0.5714	0.5753
0.2	0.5793	0.5832	0.5871	0.5910	0.5948	0.5987	0.6026	0.6064	0.6103	0.6141
0.3	0.6179	0.6217	0.6255	0.6293	0.6331	0.6368	0.6406	0.6443	0.6480	0.6517
0.4	0.6554	0.6591	0.6628	0.6664	0.6700	0.6736	0.6772	0.6808	0.6844	0.6879
0.5	0.6915	0.6950	0.6985	0.7019	0.7054	0.7088	0.7123	0.7157	0.7190	0.7224
0.6	0.7257	0.7291	0.7324	0.7357	0.7389	0.7422	0.7454	0.7486	0.7517	0.7549
0.7	0.7580	0.7611	0.7642	0.7673	0.7704	0.7734	0.7764	0.7794	0.7823	0.7852
0.8	0.7881	0.7910	0.7939	0.7967	0.7995	0.8023	0.8051	0.8078	0.8106	0.8133
0.9	0.8159	0.8186	0.8212	0.8238	0.8264	0.8289	0.8315	0.8340	0.8365	0.8389
1.0	0.8413	0.8438	0.8461	0.8485	0.8508	0.8531	0.8554	0.8577	0.8599	0.8621
1.1	0.8643	0.8665	0.8686	0.8708	0.8729	0.8749	0.8770	0.8790	0.8810	0.8830
1.2	0.8849	0.8869	0.8888	0.8907	0.8925	0.8944	0.8962	0.8980	0.8997	0.9015
1.3	0.9032	0.9049	0.9066	0.9082	0.9099	0.9115	0.9131	0.9147	0.9162	0.9177
1.4	0.9192	0.9207	0.9222	0.9236	0.9251	0.9265	0.9279	0.9292	0.9306	0.9319
1.5	0.9332	0.9345	0.9357	0.9370	0.9382	0.9394	0.9406	0.9418	0.9429	0.9441
1.6	0.9452	0.9463	0.9474	0.9484	0.9495	0.9505	0.9515	0.9525	0.9535	0.9545
1.7	0.9554	0.9564	0.9573	0.9582	0.9591	0.9599	0.9608	0.9616	0.9625	0.9633
1.8	0.9641	0.9649	0.9656	0.9664	0.9671	0.9678	0.9686	0.9693	0.9699	0.9706
1.9	0.9713	0.9719	0.9726	0.9732	0.9738	0.9744	0.9750	0.9756	0.9761	0.9767
2.0	0.9772	0.9778	0.9783	0.9788	0.9793	0.9798	0.9803	0.9808	0.9812	0.9817
2.1	0.9821	0.9826	0.9830	0.9834	0.9838	0.9842	0.9846	0.9850	0.9854	0.9857
2.2	0.9861	0.9864	0.9868	0.9871	0.9875	0.9878	0.9881	0.9884	0.9887	0.9890
2.3	0.9893	0.9896	0.9898	0.9901	0.9904	0.9906	0.9909	0.9911	0.9913	0.9916
2.4	0.9918	0.9920	0.9922	0.9925	0.9927	0.9929	0.9931	0.9932	0.9934	0.9936
2.5	0.9938	0.9940	0.9941	0.9943	0.9945	0.9946	0.9948	0.9949	0.9951	0.9952
2.6	0.9953	0.9955	0.9956	0.9957	0.9959	0.9960	0.9961	0.9962	0.9963	0.9964
2.7	0.9965	0.9966	0.9967	0.9968	0.9969	0.9970	0.9971	0.9972	0.9973	0.9974
2.8	0.9974	0.9975	0.9976	0.9977	0.9977	0.9978	0.9979	0.9979	0.9980	0.9981
2.9	0.9981	0.9982	0.9982	0.9983	0.9984	0.9984	0.9985	0.9985	0.9986	0.9986
3.0	0.9987	0.9987	0.9987	0.9988	0.9988	0.9989	0.9989	0.9989	0.9990	0.9990

Examples: If $Z \sim \text{Normal}(0, 1)$, then $P(Z \leq -1.32) = .0934$ and $P(Z \leq 1.84) = .9671$.

Source: This table was generated using the Stata® function normal.

TABLE G.2 Critical Values of the *t* Distribution

		Significance Level				
1-Tailed:		.10	.05	.025	.01	.005
2-Tailed:		.20	.10	.05	.02	.01
	1	3.078	6.314	12.706	31.821	63.657
	2	1.886	2.920	4.303	6.965	9.925
	3	1.638	2.353	3.182	4.541	5.841
	4	1.533	2.132	2.776	3.747	4.604
	5	1.476	2.015	2.571	3.365	4.032
	6	1.440	1.943	2.447	3.143	3.707
	7	1.415	1.895	2.365	2.998	3.499
	8	1.397	1.860	2.306	2.896	3.355
	9	1.383	1.833	2.262	2.821	3.250
	10	1.372	1.812	2.228	2.764	3.169
D	11	1.363	1.796	2.201	2.718	3.106
e	12	1.356	1.782	2.179	2.681	3.055
g	13	1.350	1.771	2.160	2.650	3.012
r	14	1.345	1.761	2.145	2.624	2.977
e	15	1.341	1.753	2.131	2.602	2.947
e	16	1.337	1.746	2.120	2.583	2.921
s	17	1.333	1.740	2.110	2.567	2.898
o	18	1.330	1.734	2.101	2.552	2.878
f	19	1.328	1.729	2.093	2.539	2.861
F	20	1.325	1.725	2.086	2.528	2.845
r	21	1.323	1.721	2.080	2.518	2.831
e	22	1.321	1.717	2.074	2.508	2.819
e	23	1.319	1.714	2.069	2.500	2.807
d	24	1.318	1.711	2.064	2.492	2.797
o	25	1.316	1.708	2.060	2.485	2.787
m	26	1.315	1.706	2.056	2.479	2.779
	27	1.314	1.703	2.052	2.473	2.771
	28	1.313	1.701	2.048	2.467	2.763
	29	1.311	1.699	2.045	2.462	2.756
	30	1.310	1.697	2.042	2.457	2.750
	40	1.303	1.684	2.021	2.423	2.704
	60	1.296	1.671	2.000	2.390	2.660
	90	1.291	1.662	1.987	2.368	2.632
	120	1.289	1.658	1.980	2.358	2.617
	∞	1.282	1.645	1.960	2.326	2.576

Examples: The 1% critical value for a one-tailed test with 25 *df* is 2.485. The 5% critical value for a two-tailed test with large (> 120) *df* is 1.96.

Source: This table was generated using the Stata® function invttail.

TABLE G.3a 10% Critical Values of the *F* Distribution

		\multicolumn{10}{c}{Numerator Degrees of Freedom}
		1	2	3	4	5	6	7	8	9	10
	10	3.29	2.92	2.73	2.61	2.52	2.46	2.41	2.38	2.35	2.32
D	11	3.23	2.86	2.66	2.54	2.45	2.39	2.34	2.30	2.27	2.25
e	12	3.18	2.81	2.61	2.48	2.39	2.33	2.28	2.24	2.21	2.19
n	13	3.14	2.76	2.56	2.43	2.35	2.28	2.23	2.20	2.16	2.14
o	14	3.10	2.73	2.52	2.39	2.31	2.24	2.19	2.15	2.12	2.10
m	15	3.07	2.70	2.49	2.36	2.27	2.21	2.16	2.12	2.09	2.06
i	16	3.05	2.67	2.46	2.33	2.24	2.18	2.13	2.09	2.06	2.03
n	17	3.03	2.64	2.44	2.31	2.22	2.15	2.10	2.06	2.03	2.00
a	18	3.01	2.62	2.42	2.29	2.20	2.13	2.08	2.04	2.00	1.98
t	19	2.99	2.61	2.40	2.27	2.18	2.11	2.06	2.02	1.98	1.96
o	20	2.97	2.59	2.38	2.25	2.16	2.09	2.04	2.00	1.96	1.94
r	21	2.96	2.57	2.36	2.23	2.14	2.08	2.02	1.98	1.95	1.92
D	22	2.95	2.56	2.35	2.22	2.13	2.06	2.01	1.97	1.93	1.90
e	23	2.94	2.55	2.34	2.21	2.11	2.05	1.99	1.95	1.92	1.89
g	24	2.93	2.54	2.33	2.19	2.10	2.04	1.98	1.94	1.91	1.88
r	25	2.92	2.53	2.32	2.18	2.09	2.02	1.97	1.93	1.89	1.87
e	26	2.91	2.52	2.31	2.17	2.08	2.01	1.96	1.92	1.88	1.86
e	27	2.90	2.51	2.30	2.17	2.07	2.00	1.95	1.91	1.87	1.85
s	28	2.89	2.50	2.29	2.16	2.06	2.00	1.94	1.90	1.87	1.84
o	29	2.89	2.50	2.28	2.15	2.06	1.99	1.93	1.89	1.86	1.83
f	30	2.88	2.49	2.28	2.14	2.05	1.98	1.93	1.88	1.85	1.82
F	40	2.84	2.44	2.23	2.09	2.00	1.93	1.87	1.83	1.79	1.76
r	60	2.79	2.39	2.18	2.04	1.95	1.87	1.82	1.77	1.74	1.71
e	90	2.76	2.36	2.15	2.01	1.91	1.84	1.78	1.74	1.70	1.67
e	120	2.75	2.35	2.13	1.99	1.90	1.82	1.77	1.72	1.68	1.65
d	∞	2.71	2.30	2.08	1.94	1.85	1.77	1.72	1.67	1.63	1.60

Example: The 10% critical value for numerator $df = 2$ and denominator $df = 40$ is 2.44.
Source: This table was generated using the Stata® function invFtail.

TABLE G.3b   5% Critical Values of the *F* Distribution

		Numerator Degrees of Freedom									
		1	2	3	4	5	6	7	8	9	10
D	10	4.96	4.10	3.71	3.48	3.33	3.22	3.14	3.07	3.02	2.98
e	11	4.84	3.98	3.59	3.36	3.20	3.09	3.01	2.95	2.90	2.85
n	12	4.75	3.89	3.49	3.26	3.11	3.00	2.91	2.85	2.80	2.75
o	13	4.67	3.81	3.41	3.18	3.03	2.92	2.83	2.77	2.71	2.67
m	14	4.60	3.74	3.34	3.11	2.96	2.85	2.76	2.70	2.65	2.60
i	15	4.54	3.68	3.29	3.06	2.90	2.79	2.71	2.64	2.59	2.54
n	16	4.49	3.63	3.24	3.01	2.85	2.74	2.66	2.59	2.54	2.49
a	17	4.45	3.59	3.20	2.96	2.81	2.70	2.61	2.55	2.49	2.45
t	18	4.41	3.55	3.16	2.93	2.77	2.66	2.58	2.51	2.46	2.41
o	19	4.38	3.52	3.13	2.90	2.74	2.63	2.54	2.48	2.42	2.38
r	20	4.35	3.49	3.10	2.87	2.71	2.60	2.51	2.45	2.39	2.35
D	21	4.32	3.47	3.07	2.84	2.68	2.57	2.49	2.42	2.37	2.32
e	22	4.30	3.44	3.05	2.82	2.66	2.55	2.46	2.40	2.34	2.30
g	23	4.28	3.42	3.03	2.80	2.64	2.53	2.44	2.37	2.32	2.27
r	24	4.26	3.40	3.01	2.78	2.62	2.51	2.42	2.36	2.30	2.25
e	25	4.24	3.39	2.99	2.76	2.60	2.49	2.40	2.34	2.28	2.24
e	26	4.23	3.37	2.98	2.74	2.59	2.47	2.39	2.32	2.27	2.22
s	27	4.21	3.35	2.96	2.73	2.57	2.46	2.37	2.31	2.25	2.20
o	28	4.20	3.34	2.95	2.71	2.56	2.45	2.36	2.29	2.24	2.19
f	29	4.18	3.33	2.93	2.70	2.55	2.43	2.35	2.28	2.22	2.18
F	30	4.17	3.32	2.92	2.69	2.53	2.42	2.33	2.27	2.21	2.16
r	40	4.08	3.23	2.84	2.61	2.45	2.34	2.25	2.18	2.12	2.08
e	60	4.00	3.15	2.76	2.53	2.37	2.25	2.17	2.10	2.04	1.99
e	90	3.95	3.10	2.71	2.47	2.32	2.20	2.11	2.04	1.99	1.94
d	120	3.92	3.07	2.68	2.45	2.29	2.17	2.09	2.02	1.96	1.91
o	∞	3.84	3.00	2.60	2.37	2.21	2.10	2.01	1.94	1.88	1.83

Example: The 5% critical value for numerator $df = 4$ and large denominator $df(\infty)$ is 2.37.

Source: This table was generated using the Stata® function invFtail.

TABLE G.3c 1% Critical Values of the *F* Distribution

		Numerator Degrees of Freedom									
		1	**2**	**3**	**4**	**5**	**6**	**7**	**8**	**9**	**10**
	10	10.04	7.56	6.55	5.99	5.64	5.39	5.20	5.06	4.94	4.85
D	11	9.65	7.21	6.22	5.67	5.32	5.07	4.89	4.74	4.63	4.54
e	12	9.33	6.93	5.95	5.41	5.06	4.82	4.64	4.50	4.39	4.30
n	13	9.07	6.70	5.74	5.21	4.86	4.62	4.44	4.30	4.19	4.10
o	14	8.86	6.51	5.56	5.04	4.69	4.46	4.28	4.14	4.03	3.94
m	15	8.68	6.36	5.42	4.89	4.56	4.32	4.14	4.00	3.89	3.80
i	16	8.53	6.23	5.29	4.77	4.44	4.20	4.03	3.89	3.78	3.69
n	17	8.40	6.11	5.18	4.67	4.34	4.10	3.93	3.79	3.68	3.59
a	18	8.29	6.01	5.09	4.58	4.25	4.01	3.84	3.71	3.60	3.51
t	19	8.18	5.93	5.01	4.50	4.17	3.94	3.77	3.63	3.52	3.43
o	20	8.10	5.85	4.94	4.43	4.10	3.87	3.70	3.56	3.46	3.37
r	21	8.02	5.78	4.87	4.37	4.04	3.81	3.64	3.51	3.40	3.31
	22	7.95	5.72	4.82	4.31	3.99	3.76	3.59	3.45	3.35	3.26
D	23	7.88	5.66	4.76	4.26	3.94	3.71	3.54	3.41	3.30	3.21
e	24	7.82	5.61	4.72	4.22	3.90	3.67	3.50	3.36	3.26	3.17
g	25	7.77	5.57	4.68	4.18	3.85	3.63	3.46	3.32	3.22	3.13
r	26	7.72	5.53	4.64	4.14	3.82	3.59	3.42	3.29	3.18	3.09
e	27	7.68	5.49	4.60	4.11	3.78	3.56	3.39	3.26	3.15	3.06
e	28	7.64	5.45	4.57	4.07	3.75	3.53	3.36	3.23	3.12	3.03
s	29	7.60	5.42	4.54	4.04	3.73	3.50	3.33	3.20	3.09	3.00
	30	7.56	5.39	4.51	4.02	3.70	3.47	3.30	3.17	3.07	2.98
o	40	7.31	5.18	4.31	3.83	3.51	3.29	3.12	2.99	2.89	2.80
f	60	7.08	4.98	4.13	3.65	3.34	3.12	2.95	2.82	2.72	2.63
F	90	6.93	4.85	4.01	3.54	3.23	3.01	2.84	2.72	2.61	2.52
r	120	6.85	4.79	3.95	3.48	3.17	2.96	2.79	2.66	2.56	2.47
e	∞	6.63	4.61	3.78	3.32	3.02	2.80	2.64	2.51	2.41	2.32

Example: The 1% critical value for numerator $df = 3$ and denominator $df = 60$ is 4.13.

Source: This table was generated using the Stata® function invFtail.

TABLE G.4 Critical Values of the Chi-Square Distribution

		Significance Level		
		.10	.05	.01
	1	2.71	3.84	6.63
	2	4.61	5.99	9.21
	3	6.25	7.81	11.34
	4	7.78	9.49	13.28
	5	9.24	11.07	15.09
	6	10.64	12.59	16.81
D	7	12.02	14.07	18.48
e	8	13.36	15.51	20.09
g	9	14.68	16.92	21.67
r	10	15.99	18.31	23.21
e	11	17.28	19.68	24.72
e	12	18.55	21.03	26.22
s	13	19.81	22.36	27.69
	14	21.06	23.68	29.14
o	15	22.31	25.00	30.58
f	16	23.54	26.30	32.00
F	17	24.77	27.59	33.41
r	18	25.99	28.87	34.81
e	19	27.20	30.14	36.19
e	20	28.41	31.41	37.57
d	21	29.62	32.67	38.93
o	22	30.81	33.92	40.29
m	23	32.01	35.17	41.64
	24	33.20	36.42	42.98
	25	34.38	37.65	44.31
	26	35.56	38.89	45.64
	27	36.74	40.11	46.96
	28	37.92	41.34	48.28
	29	39.09	42.56	49.59
	30	40.26	43.77	50.89

Example: The 5% critical value with $df = 8$ is 15.51.

Source: This table was generated using the Stata® function invchi2tail.

References

Angrist, J. D. (1990), "Lifetime Earnings and the Vietnam Era Draft Lottery: Evidence from Social Security Administrative Records," *American Economic Review* 80, 313–336.

Angrist, J. D., and A. B. Krueger (1991), "Does Compulsory School Attendance Affect Schooling and Earnings?" *Quarterly Journal of Economics* 106, 979–1014.

Ashenfelter, O., and A. B. Krueger (1994), "Estimates of the Economic Return to Schooling from a New Sample of Twins," *American Economic Review* 84, 1157–1173.

Averett, S., and S. Korenman (1996), "The Economic Reality of the Beauty Myth," *Journal of Human Resources* 31, 304–330.

Ayres, I., and S. D. Levitt (1998), "Measuring Positive Externalities from Unobservable Victim Precaution: An Empirical Analysis of Lojack," *Quarterly Journal of Economics* 108, 43–77.

Banerjee, A., J. Dolado, J. W. Galbraith, and D. F. Hendry (1993), *Co-Integration, Error-Correction, and the Econometric Analysis of Non-Stationary Data*. Oxford: Oxford University Press.

Bartik, T. J. (1991), "The Effects of Property Taxes and Other Local Public Policies on the Intrametropolitan Pattern of Business Location," in *Industry Location and Public Policy*, ed. H. W. Herzog and A. M. Schlottmann, 57–80. Knoxville: University of Tennessee Press.

Becker, G. S. (1968), "Crime and Punishment: An Economic Approach," *Journal of Political Economy* 76, 169–217.

Belsley, D., E. Kuh, and R. Welsch (1980), *Regression Diagnostics: Identifying Influential Data and Sources of Collinearity*. New York: Wiley.

Berk, R. A. (1990), "A Primer on Robust Regression," in *Modern Methods of Data Analysis*, ed. J. Fox and J. S. Long, 292–324. Newbury Park, CA: Sage Publications.

Betts, J. R. (1995), "Does School Quality Matter? Evidence from the National Longitudinal Survey of Youth," *Review of Economics and Statistics* 77, 231–250.

Biddle, J. E., and D. S. Hamermesh (1990), "Sleep and the Allocation of Time," *Journal of Political Economy* 98, 922–943.

Biddle, J. E., and D. S. Hamermesh (1998), "Beauty, Productivity, and Discrimination: Lawyers' Looks and Lucre," *Journal of Labor Economics* 16, 172–201.

Blackburn, M., and D. Neumark (1992), "Unobserved Ability, Efficiency Wages, and Interindustry Wage Differentials," *Quarterly Journal of Economics* 107, 1421–1436.

Blinder, A. S. and M. W. Watson (2014), "Presidents and the U.S. Economy: An Econometric Exploration," National Bureau of Economic Research Working Paper No. 20324.

Blomström, M., R. E. Lipsey, and M. Zejan (1996), "Is Fixed Investment the Key to Economic Growth?" *Quarterly Journal of Economics* 111, 269–276.

Blundell, R., A. Duncan, and K. Pendakur (1998), "Semiparametric Estimation and Consumer Demand," *Journal of Applied Econometrics* 13, 435–461.

Bollerslev, T., R. Y. Chou, and K. F. Kroner (1992), "ARCH Modeling in Finance: A Review of the Theory and Empirical Evidence," *Journal of Econometrics* 52, 5–59.

Bollerslev, T., R. F. Engle, and D. B. Nelson (1994), "ARCH Models," in *Handbook of Econometrics*, volume 4, chapter 49, ed. R. F. Engle and D. L. McFadden, 2959–3038. Amsterdam: North-Holland.

Bound, J., D. A. Jaeger, and R. M. Baker (1995), "Problems with Instrumental Variables Estimation When the Correlation between the Instruments and Endogenous Explanatory Variables Is Weak," *Journal of the American Statistical Association* 90, 443–450.

Breusch, T. S., and A. R. Pagan (1979), "A Simple Test for Heteroskedasticity and Random Coefficient Variation," *Econometrica* 47, 987–1007.

Cameron, A. C., and P. K. Trivedi (1998), *Regression Analysis of Count Data*. Cambridge: Cambridge University Press.

Campbell, J. Y., and N. G. Mankiw (1990), "Permanent Income, Current Income, and Consumption," *Journal of Business and Economic Statistics* 8, 265–279.

Card, D. (1995), "Using Geographic Variation in College Proximity to Estimate the Return to Schooling," in *Aspects of Labour Market Behavior: Essays in Honour of John Vanderkamp*, ed. L. N. Christophides, E. K. Grant, and R. Swidinsky, 201–222. Toronto: University of Toronto Press.

Card, D., and A. Krueger (1992), "Does School Quality Matter? Returns to Education and the Characteristics of Public Schools in the United States," *Journal of Political Economy* 100, 1–40.

Castillo-Freeman, A. J., and R. B. Freeman (1992), "When the Minimum Wage Really Bites: The Effect of the U.S.-Level Minimum on Puerto Rico," in *Immigration and the Work Force*, ed. G. J. Borjas and R. B. Freeman, 177–211. Chicago: University of Chicago Press.

Clark, K. B. (1984), "Unionization and Firm Performance: The Impact on Profits, Growth, and Productivity," *American Economic Review* 74, 893–919.

Cloninger, D. O. (1991), "Lethal Police Response as a Crime Deterrent: 57-City Study Suggests a Decrease in Certain Crimes," *American Journal of Economics and Sociology* 50, 59–69.

Cloninger, D. O., and L. C. Sartorius (1979), "Crime Rates, Clearance Rates and Enforcement Effort: The Case of Houston, Texas," *American Journal of Economics and Sociology* 38, 389–402.

Cochrane, J. H. (1997), "Where Is the Market Going? Uncertain Facts and Novel Theories," *Economic Perspectives* 21, Federal Reserve Bank of Chicago, 3–37.

Cornwell, C., and W. N. Trumbull (1994), "Estimating the Economic Model of Crime Using Panel Data," *Review of Economics and Statistics* 76, 360–366.

Craig, B. R., W. E. Jackson III, and J. B. Thomson (2007), "Small Firm Finance, Credit Rationing, and the Impact of SBA-Guaranteed Lending on Local Economic Growth," *Journal of Small Business Management* 45, 116–132.

Currie, J. (1995), *Welfare and the Well-Being of Children.* Chur, Switzerland: Harwood Academic Publishers.

Currie, J., and N. Cole (1993), "Welfare and Child Health: The Link between AFDC Participation and Birth Weight," *American Economic Review* 83, 971–983.

Currie, J., and D. Thomas (1995), "Does Head Start Make a Difference?" *American Economic Review* 85, 341–364.

Davidson, R., and J. G. MacKinnon (1981), "Several Tests of Model Specification in the Presence of Alternative Hypotheses," *Econometrica* 49, 781–793.

Davidson, R., and J. G. MacKinnon (1993), *Estimation and Inference in Econometrics.* New York: Oxford University Press.

De Long, J. B., and L. H. Summers (1991), "Equipment Investment and Economic Growth," *Quarterly Journal of Economics* 106, 445–502.

Dickey, D. A., and W. A. Fuller (1979), "Distributions of the Estimators for Autoregressive Time Series with a Unit Root," *Journal of the American Statistical Association* 74, 427–431.

Diebold, F. X. (2001), *Elements of Forecasting.* 2nd ed. Cincinnati: South-Western.

Downes, T. A., and S. M. Greenstein (1996), "Understanding the Supply Decisions of Nonprofits: Modeling the Location of Private Schools," *Rand Journal of Economics* 27, 365–390.

Draper, N., and H. Smith (1981), *Applied Regression Analysis.* 2nd ed. New York: Wiley.

Duan, N. (1983), "Smearing Estimate: A Nonparametric Retransformation Method," *Journal of the American Statistical Association* 78, 605–610.

Durbin, J. (1970), "Testing for Serial Correlation in Least Squares Regressions When Some of the Regressors Are Lagged Dependent Variables," *Econometrica* 38, 410–421.

Durbin, J., and G. S. Watson (1950), "Testing for Serial Correlation in Least Squares Regressions I," *Biometrika* 37, 409–428.

Eicker, F. (1967), "Limit Theorems for Regressions with Unequal and Dependent Errors," *Proceedings of the Fifth Berkeley Symposium on Mathematical Statistics and Probability* 1, 59–82. Berkeley: University of California Press.

Eide, E. (1994), *Economics of Crime: Deterrence and the Rational Offender.* Amsterdam: North-Holland.

Engle, R. F. (1982), "Autoregressive Conditional Heteroskedasticity with Estimates of the Variance of United Kingdom Inflation," *Econometrica* 50, 987–1007.

Engle, R. F., and C. W. J. Granger (1987), "Cointegration and Error Correction: Representation, Estimation, and Testing," *Econometrica* 55, 251–276.

Evans, W. N., and R. M. Schwab (1995), "Finishing High School and Starting College: Do Catholic Schools Make a Difference?" *Quarterly Journal of Economics* 110, 941–974.

Fair, R. C. (1996), "Econometrics and Presidential Elections," *Journal of Economic Perspectives* 10, 89–102.

Franses, P. H., and R. Paap (2001), *Quantitative Models in Marketing Research.* Cambridge: Cambridge University Press.

Freeman, D. G. (2007), "Drunk Driving Legislation and Traffic Fatalities: New Evidence on BAC 08 Laws," *Contemporary Economic Policy* 25, 293–308.

Friedman, B. M., and K. N. Kuttner (1992), "Money, Income, Prices, and Interest Rates," *American Economic Review* 82, 472–492.

Geronimus, A. T., and S. Korenman (1992), "The Socioeconomic Consequences of Teen Childbearing Reconsidered," *Quarterly Journal of Economics* 107, 1187–1214.

Goldberger, A. S. (1991), *A Course in Econometrics.* Cambridge, MA: Harvard University Press.

Graddy, K. (1995), "Testing for Imperfect Competition at the Fulton Fish Market," *Rand Journal of Economics* 26, 75–92.

Graddy, K. (1997), "Do Fast-Food Chains Price Discriminate on the Race and Income Characteristics of an Area?" *Journal of Business and Economic Statistics* 15, 391–401.

Granger, C. W. J., and P. Newbold (1974), "Spurious Regressions in Econometrics," *Journal of Econometrics* 2, 111–120.

Greene, W. (1997), *Econometric Analysis*. 3rd ed. New York: MacMillan.

Griliches, Z. (1957), "Specification Bias in Estimates of Production Functions," *Journal of Farm Economics* 39, 8–20.

Grogger, J. (1990), "The Deterrent Effect of Capital Punishment: An Analysis of Daily Homicide Counts," *Journal of the American Statistical Association* 410, 295–303.

Grogger, J. (1991), "Certainty vs. Severity of Punishment," *Economic Inquiry* 29, 297–309.

Hall, R. E. (1988), "The Relation between Price and Marginal Cost in U.S. Industry," *Journal of Political Economy* 96, 921–948.

Hamermesh, D. S., and J. E. Biddle (1994), "Beauty and the Labor Market," *American Economic Review* 84, 1174–1194.

Hamermesh, D. H., and A. Parker (2005), "Beauty in the Classroom: Instructors' Pulchritude and Putative Pedagogical Productivity," *Economics of Education Review* 24, 369–376.

Hamilton, J. D. (1994), *Time Series Analysis*. Princeton, NJ: Princeton University Press.

Hansen, C.B. (2007), "Asymptotic Properties of a Robust Variance Matrix Estimator for Panel Data When T Is Large," *Journal of Econometrics* 141, 597–620.

Hanushek, E. (1986), "The Economics of Schooling: Production and Efficiency in Public Schools," *Journal of Economic Literature* 24, 1141–1177.

Harvey, A. (1990), *The Econometric Analysis of Economic Time Series*. 2nd ed. Cambridge, MA: MIT Press.

Hausman, J. A. (1978), "Specification Tests in Econometrics," *Econometrica* 46, 1251–1271.

Hausman, J. A., and D. A. Wise (1977), "Social Experimentation, Truncated Distributions, and Efficient Estimation," *Econometrica* 45, 319–339.

Hayasyi, F. (2000), *Econometrics*. Princeton, NJ: Princeton University Press.

Heckman, J. J. (1976), "The Common Structure of Statistical Models of Truncation, Sample Selection, and Limited Dependent Variables and a Simple Estimator for Such Models," *Annals of Economic and Social Measurement* 5, 475–492.

Herrnstein, R. J., and C. Murray (1994), *The Bell Curve: Intelligence and Class Structure in American Life*. New York: Free Press.

Hersch, J., and L. S. Stratton (1997), "Housework, Fixed Effects, and Wages of Married Workers," *Journal of Human Resources* 32, 285–307.

Hines, J. R. (1996), "Altered States: Taxes and the Location of Foreign Direct Investment in America," *American Economic Review* 86, 1076–1094.

Holzer, H. (1991), "The Spatial Mismatch Hypothesis: What Has the Evidence Shown?" *Urban Studies* 28, 105–122.

Holzer, H., R. Block, M. Cheatham, and J. Knott (1993), "Are Training Subsidies Effective? The Michigan Experience," *Industrial and Labor Relations Review* 46, 625–636.

Horowitz, J. (2001), "The Bootstrap," in *Handbook of Econometrics*, volume 5, chapter 52, ed. E. Leamer and J. L. Heckman, 3159–3228. Amsterdam: North Holland.

Hoxby, C. M. (1994), "Do Private Schools Provide Competition for Public Schools?" National Bureau of Economic Research Working Paper Number 4978.

Huber, P. J. (1967), "The Behavior of Maximum Likelihood Estimates under Nonstandard Conditions," *Proceedings of the Fifth Berkeley Symposium on Mathematical Statistics and Probability* 1, 221–233. Berkeley: University of California Press.

Hunter, W. C., and M. B. Walker (1996), "The Cultural Affinity Hypothesis and Mortgage Lending Decisions," *Journal of Real Estate Finance and Economics* 13, 57–70.

Hylleberg, S. (1992), *Modelling Seasonality*. Oxford: Oxford University Press.

Kane, T. J., and C. E. Rouse (1995), "Labor-Market Returns to Two- and Four-Year Colleges," *American Economic Review* 85, 600–614.

Kiefer, N. M., and T. J. Vogelsang (2005), "A New Asymptotic Theory for Heteroskedasticity-Autocorrelation Robust Tests," *Econometric Theory* 21, 1130–1164.

Kiel, K. A., and K. T. McClain (1995), "House Prices during Siting Decision Stages: The Case of an Incinerator from Rumor through Operation," *Journal of Environmental Economics and Management* 28, 241–255.

Kleck, G., and E. B. Patterson (1993), "The Impact of Gun Control and Gun Ownership Levels on Violence Rates," *Journal of Quantitative Criminology* 9, 249–287.

Koenker, R. (1981), "A Note on Studentizing a Test for Heteroskedasticity," *Journal of Econometrics* 17, 107–112.

Koenker, R. (2005), *Quantile Regression*. Cambridge: Cambridge University Press.

Korenman, S., and D. Neumark (1991), "Does Marriage Really Make Men More Productive?" *Journal of Human Resources* 26, 282–307.

Korenman, S., and D. Neumark (1992), "Marriage, Motherhood, and Wages," *Journal of Human Resources* 27, 233–255.

Krueger, A. B. (1993), "How Computers Have Changed the Wage Structure: Evidence from Microdata, 1984–1989," *Quarterly Journal of Economics* 108, 33–60.

Krupp, C. M., and P. S. Pollard (1996), "Market Responses to Antidumping Laws: Some Evidence from the U.S. Chemical Industry," *Canadian Journal of Economics* 29, 199–227.

Kwiatkowski, D., P. C. B. Phillips, P. Schmidt, and Y. Shin (1992), "Testing the Null Hypothesis of Stationarity against the Alternative of a Unit Root: How Sure Are We That Economic Time Series Have a Unit Root?" *Journal of Econometrics* 54, 159–178.

Lalonde, R. J. (1986), "Evaluating the Econometric Evaluations of Training Programs with Experimental Data," *American Economic Review* 76, 604–620.

Larsen, R. J., and M. L. Marx (1986), *An Introduction to Mathematical Statistics and Its Applications*. 2nd ed. Englewood Cliffs, NJ: Prentice-Hall.

Leamer, E. E. (1983), "Let's Take the Con Out of Econometrics," *American Economic Review* 73, 31–43.

Levine, P. B., A. B. Trainor, and D. J. Zimmerman (1996), "The Effect of Medicaid Abortion Funding Restrictions on Abortions, Pregnancies, and Births," *Journal of Health Economics* 15, 555–578.

Levine, P. B., and D. J. Zimmerman (1995), "The Benefit of Additional High-School Math and Science Classes for Young Men and Women," *Journal of Business and Economics Statistics* 13, 137–149.

Levitt, S. D. (1994), "Using Repeat Challengers to Estimate the Effect of Campaign Spending on Election Outcomes in the U.S. House," *Journal of Political Economy* 102, 777–798.

Levitt, S. D. (1996), "The Effect of Prison Population Size on Crime Rates: Evidence from Prison Overcrowding Legislation," *Quarterly Journal of Economics* 111, 319–351.

Little, R. J. A. and D. B. Rubin (2002), *Statistical Analysis with Missing Data*. 2nd ed. Wiley: New York.

Low, S. A., and L. R. McPheters (1983), "Wage Differentials and the Risk of Death: An Empirical Analysis," *Economic Inquiry* 21, 271–280.

Lynch, L. M. (1992), "Private Sector Training and the Earnings of Young Workers," *American Economic Review* 82, 299–312.

MacKinnon, J. G., and H. White (1985), "Some Heteroskedasticity Consistent Covariance Matrix Estimators with Improved Finite Sample Properties," *Journal of Econometrics* 29, 305–325.

Maloney, M. T., and R. E. McCormick (1993), "An Examination of the Role that Intercollegiate Athletic Participation Plays in Academic Achievement: Athletes' Feats in the Classroom," *Journal of Human Resources* 28, 555–570.

Mankiw, N. G. (1994), *Macroeconomics*. 2nd ed. New York: Worth.

Mark, S. T., T. J. McGuire, and L. E. Papke (2000), "The Influence of Taxes on Employment and Population Growth: Evidence from the Washington, D.C. Metropolitan Area," *National Tax Journal* 53, 105–123.

McCarthy, P. S. (1994), "Relaxed Speed Limits and Highway Safety: New Evidence from California," *Economics Letters* 46, 173–179.

McClain, K. T., and J. M. Wooldridge (1995), "A Simple Test for the Consistency of Dynamic Linear Regression in Rational Distributed Lag Models," *Economics Letters* 48, 235–240.

McCormick, R. E., and M. Tinsley (1987), "Athletics versus Academics: Evidence from SAT Scores," *Journal of Political Economy* 95, 1103–1116.

McFadden, D. L. (1974), "Conditional Logit Analysis of Qualitative Choice Behavior," in *Frontiers in Econometrics*, ed. P. Zarembka, 105–142. New York: Academic Press.

Meyer, B. D. (1995), "Natural and Quasi-Experiments in Economics," *Journal of Business and Economic Statistics* 13, 151–161.

Meyer, B. D., W. K. Viscusi, and D. L. Durbin (1995), "Workers' Compensation and Injury Duration: Evidence from a Natural Experiment," *American Economic Review* 85, 322–340.

Mizon, G. E., and J. F. Richard (1986), "The Encompassing Principle and Its Application to Testing Nonnested Hypotheses," *Econometrica* 54, 657–678.

Mroz, T. A. (1987), "The Sensitivity of an Empirical Model of Married Women's Hours of Work to Economic and Statistical Assumptions," *Econometrica* 55, 765–799.

Mullahy, J., and P. R. Portney (1990), "Air Pollution, Cigarette Smoking, and the Production of Respiratory Health," *Journal of Health Economics* 9, 193–205.

Mullahy, J., and J. L. Sindelar (1994), "Do Drinkers Know When to Say When? An Empirical Analysis of Drunk Driving," *Economic Inquiry* 32, 383–394.

Netzer, D. (1992), "Differences in Reliance on User Charges by American State and Local Governments," *Public Finance Quarterly* 20, 499–511.

Neumark, D. (1996), "Sex Discrimination in Restaurant Hiring: An Audit Study," *Quarterly Journal of Economics* 111, 915–941.

Neumark, D., and W. Wascher (1995), "Minimum Wage Effects on Employment and School Enrollment," *Journal of Business and Economic Statistics* 13, 199–206.

Newey, W. K., and K. D. West (1987), "A Simple, Positive Semi-Definite Heteroskedasticity and Autocorrelation Consistent Covariance Matrix," *Econometrica* 55, 703–708.

Papke, L. E. (1987), "Subnational Taxation and Capital Mobility: Estimates of Tax-Price Elasticities," *National Tax Journal* 40, 191–203.

Papke, L. E. (1994), "Tax Policy and Urban Development: Evidence from the Indiana Enterprise Zone Program," *Journal of Public Economics* 54, 37–49.

Papke, L. E. (1995), "Participation in and Contributions to 401(k) Pension Plans: Evidence from Plan Data," *Journal of Human Resources* 30, 311–325.

Papke, L. E. (1999), "Are 401(k) Plans Replacing Other Employer-Provided Pensions? Evidence from Panel Data," *Journal of Human Resources*, 34, 346–368.

Papke, L. E. (2005), "The Effects of Spending on Test Pass Rates: Evidence from Michigan," *Journal of Public Economics* 89, 821–839.

Papke, L. E. and J. M. Wooldridge (1996), "Econometric Methods for Fractional Response Variables with an Application to 401(k) Plan Participation Rates," *Journal of Applied Econometrics* 11, 619–632.

Park, R. (1966), "Estimation with Heteroskedastic Error Terms," *Econometrica* 34, 888.

Peek, J. (1982), "Interest Rates, Income Taxes, and Anticipated Inflation," *American Economic Review* 72, 980–991.

Pindyck, R. S., and D. L. Rubinfeld (1992), *Microeconomics*. 2nd ed. New York: Macmillan.

Ram, R. (1986), "Government Size and Economic Growth: A New Framework and Some Evidence from Cross-Section and Time-Series Data," *American Economic Review* 76, 191–203.

Ramanathan, R. (1995), *Introductory Econometrics with Applications*. 3rd ed. Fort Worth: Dryden Press.

Ramey, V. (1991), "Nonconvex Costs and the Behavior of Inventories," *Journal of Political Economy* 99, 306–334.

Ramsey, J. B. (1969), "Tests for Specification Errors in Classical Linear Least-Squares Analysis," *Journal of the Royal Statistical Association*, Series B, 71, 350–371.

Romer, D. (1993), "Openness and Inflation: Theory and Evidence," *Quarterly Journal of Economics* 108, 869–903.

Rose, N. L. (1985), "The Incidence of Regulatory Rents in the Motor Carrier Industry," *Rand Journal of Economics* 16, 299–318.

Rose, N. L., and A. Shepard (1997), "Firm Diversification and CEO Compensation: Managerial Ability or Executive Entrenchment?" *Rand Journal of Economics* 28, 489–514.

Rouse, C. E. (1998), "Private School Vouchers and Student Achievement: An Evaluation of the Milwaukee Parental Choice Program," *Quarterly Journal of Economics* 113, 553–602.

Sander, W. (1992), "The Effect of Women's Schooling on Fertility," *Economic Letters* 40, 229–233.

Savin, N. E., and K. J. White (1977), "The Durbin-Watson Test for Serial Correlation with Extreme Sample Sizes or Many Regressors," *Econometrica* 45, 1989–1996.

Shea, J. (1993), "The Input-Output Approach to Instrument Selection," *Journal of Business and Economic Statistics* 11, 145–155.

Shughart, W. F., and R. D. Tollison (1984), "The Random Character of Merger Activity," *Rand Journal of Economics* 15, 500–509.

Solon, G. (1985), "The Minimum Wage and Teenage Employment: A Re-analysis with Attention to Serial Correlation and Seasonality," *Journal of Human Resources* 20, 292–297.

Staiger, D., and J. H. Stock (1997), "Instrumental Variables Regression with Weak Instruments," *Econometrica* 65, 557–586.

Stigler, S. M. (1986), *The History of Statistics*. Cambridge, MA: Harvard University Press.

Stock, J. H., and M. W. Watson (1989), "Interpreting the Evidence on Money-Income Causality," *Journal of Econometrics* 40, 161–181.

Stock, J. H., and M. W. Watson (1993), "A Simple Estimator of Cointegrating Vectors in Higher Order Integrated Systems," *Econometrica* 61, 783–820.

Stock, J. H. and M. Yogo (2005), "Asymptotic Distributions of Instrumental Variables Statistics with Many Instruments," in *Identification and Inference for Econometric Models: Essays in Honor of Thomas Rothenberg*, ed. D. W. K. Andrews and J. H. Stock, 109–120. Cambridge: Cambridge University Press.

Stock, J. W. and M. W. Watson (2008), "Heteroskedasticity-Robust Standard Errors for Fixed Effects Panel Data Regression," *Econometrica* 76, 155–174.

Sydsaeter, K., and P. J. Hammond (1995), *Mathematics for Economic Analysis*. Englewood Cliffs, NJ: Prentice Hall.

Terza, J. V. (2002), "Alcohol Abuse and Employment: A Second Look," *Journal of Applied Econometrics* 17, 393–404.

Tucker, I. B. (2004), "A Reexamination of the Effect of Big-time Football and Basketball Success on Graduation Rates and Alumni Giving Rates," *Economics of Education Review* 23, 655–661.

Vella, F., and M. Verbeek (1998), "Whose Wages Do Unions Raise? A Dynamic Model of Unionism and Wage Rate Determination for Young Men," *Journal of Applied Econometrics* 13, 163–183.

Wald, A. (1940), "The Fitting of Straight Lines If Both Variables Are Subject to Error," *Annals of Mathematical Statistics* 11, 284–300.

Wallis, K. F. (1972), "Testing for Fourth-Order Autocorrelation in Quarterly Regression Equations," *Econometrica* 40, 617–636.

White, H. (1980), "A Heteroskedasticity-Consistent Covariance Matrix Estimator and a Direct Test for Heteroskedasticity," *Econometrica* 48, 817–838.

White, H. (1984), *Asymptotic Theory for Econometricians*. Orlando: Academic Press.

White, M. J. (1986), "Property Taxes and Firm Location: Evidence from Proposition 13," in *Studies in State and Local Public Finance*, ed. H. S. Rosen, 83–112. Chicago: University of Chicago Press.

Whittington, L. A., J. Alm, and H. E. Peters (1990), "Fertility and the Personal Exemption: Implicit Pronatalist Policy in the United States," *American Economic Review* 80, 545–556.

Wooldridge, J. M. (1989), "A Computationally Simple Heteroskedasticity and Serial Correlation-Robust Standard Error for the Linear Regression Model," *Economics Letters* 31, 239–243.

Wooldridge, J. M. (1991a), "A Note on Computing R-Squared and Adjusted R-Squared for Trending and Seasonal Data," *Economics Letters* 36, 49–54.

Wooldridge, J. M. (1991b), "On the Application of Robust, Regression-Based Diagnostics to Models of Conditional Means and Conditional Variances," *Journal of Econometrics* 47, 5–46.

Wooldridge, J. M. (1994a), "A Simple Specification Test for the Predictive Ability of Transformation Models," *Review of Economics and Statistics* 76, 59–65.

Wooldridge, J. M. (1994b), "Estimation and Inference for Dependent Processes," in *Handbook of Econometrics*, volume 4, chapter 45, ed. R. F. Engle and D. L. McFadden, 2639–2738. Amsterdam: North-Holland.

Wooldridge, J. M. (1995), "Score Diagnostics for Linear Models Estimated by Two Stage Least Squares," in *Advances in Econometrics and Quantitative Economics*, ed. G. S. Maddala, P. C. B. Phillips, and T. N. Srinivasan, 66–87. Oxford: Blackwell.

Wooldridge, J.M. (2001), "Diagnostic Testing," in *Companion to Theoretical Econometrics*, ed. B. H. Baltagi, 180–200. Oxford: Blackwell.

Wooldridge, J. M. (2010), *Econometric Analysis of Cross Section and Panel Data*. 2nd ed. Cambridge, MA: MIT Press.

Glossary

A

Adjusted *R*-Squared: A goodness-of-fit measure in multiple regression analysis that penalizes additional explanatory variables by using a degrees of freedom adjustment in estimating the error variance.

Alternative Hypothesis: The hypothesis against which the null hypothesis is tested.

AR(1) Serial Correlation: The errors in a time series regression model follow an AR(1) model.

Asymptotic Bias: *See* inconsistency.

Asymptotic Confidence Interval: A confidence interval that is approximately valid in large sample sizes.

Asymptotic Normality: The sampling distribution of a properly normalized estimator converges to the standard normal distribution.

Asymptotic Properties: Properties of estimators and test statistics that apply when the sample size grows without bound.

Asymptotic Standard Error: A standard error that is valid in large samples.

Asymptotic *t* Statistic: A *t* statistic that has an approximate standard normal distribution in large samples.

Asymptotic Variance: The square of the value by which we must divide an estimator in order to obtain an asymptotic standard normal distribution.

Asymptotically Efficient: For consistent estimators with asymptotically normal distributions, the estimator with the smallest asymptotic variance.

Asymptotically Uncorrelated: A time series process in which the correlation between random variables at two points in time tends to zero as the time interval between them increases. (*See also* weakly dependent.)

Attenuation Bias: Bias in an estimator that is always toward zero; thus, the expected value of an estimator with attenuation bias is less in magnitude than the absolute value of the parameter.

Augmented Dickey-Fuller Test: A test for a unit root that includes lagged changes of the variable as regressors.

Autocorrelation: *See* serial correlation.

Autoregressive Conditional Heteroskedasticity (ARCH): A model of dynamic heteroskedasticity where the variance of the error term, given past information, depends linearly on the past squared errors.

Autoregressive Process of Order One [AR(1)]: A time series model whose current value depends linearly on its most recent value plus an unpredictable disturbance.

Auxiliary Regression: A regression used to compute a test statistic—such as the test statistics for heteroskedasticity and serial correlation—or any other regression that does not estimate the model of primary interest.

Average: The sum of *n* numbers divided by *n*.

Average Marginal Effect: *See* average partial effect.

Average Partial Effect: For nonconstant partial effects, the partial effect averaged across the specified population.

Average Treatment Effect: A treatment, or policy, effect averaged across the population.

B

Balanced Panel: A panel data set where all years (or periods) of data are available for all cross-sectional units.

Base Group: The group represented by the overall intercept in a multiple regression model that includes dummy explanatory variables.

Base Period: For index numbers, such as price or production indices, the period against which all other time periods are measured.

Base Value: The value assigned to the base period for constructing an index number; usually the base value is 1 or 100.

Benchmark Group: *See* base group.

Bernoulli (or Binary) Random Variable: A random variable that takes on the values zero or one.

Best Linear Unbiased Estimator (BLUE): Among all linear unbiased estimators, the one with the smallest variance. OLS is BLUE, conditional on the sample values of the explanatory variables, under the Gauss-Markov assumptions.

Beta Coefficients: *See* standardized coefficients.

Bias: The difference between the expected value of an estimator and the population value that the estimator is supposed to be estimating.

Biased Estimator: An estimator whose expectation, or sampling mean, is different from the population value it is supposed to be estimating.

Biased Towards Zero: A description of an estimator whose expectation in absolute value is less than the absolute value of the population parameter.

Binary Response Model: A model for a binary (dummy) dependent variable.

Binary Variable: *See* dummy variable.

Binomial Distribution: The probability distribution of the number of successes out of n independent Bernoulli trials, where each trial has the same probability of success.

Bivariate Regression Model: *See* simple linear regression model.

BLUE: *See* best linear unbiased estimator.

Bootstrap: A resampling method that draws random samples, with replacement, from the original data set.

Bootstrap Standard Error: A standard error obtained as the sample standard deviation of an estimate across all bootstrap samples.

Breusch-Godfrey Test: An asymptotically justified test for $AR(p)$ serial correlation, with $AR(1)$ being the most popular; the test allows for lagged dependent variables as well as other regressors that are not strictly exogenous.

Breusch-Pagan Test: A test for heteroskedasticity where the squared OLS residuals are regressed on the explanatory variables in the model.

C

Causal Effect: A ceteris paribus change in one variable that has an effect on another variable.

Censored Normal Regression Model: The special case of the censored regression model where the underlying population model satisfies the classical linear model assumptions.

Censored Regression Model: A multiple regression model where the dependent variable has been censored above or below some known threshold.

Central Limit Theorem (CLT): A key result from probability theory which implies that the sum of independent random variables, or even weakly dependent random variables, when standardized by its standard deviation, has a distribution that tends to standard normal as the sample size grows.

Ceteris Paribus: All other relevant factors are held fixed.

Chi-Square Distribution: A probability distribution obtained by adding the squares of independent standard normal random variables. The number of terms in the sum equals the degrees of freedom in the distribution.

Chi-Square Random Variable: A random variable with a chi-square distribution.

Chow Statistic: An F statistic for testing the equality of regression parameters across different groups (say, men and women) or time periods (say, before and after a policy change).

Classical Errors-in-Variables (CEV): A measurement error model where the observed measure equals the actual variable plus an independent, or at least an uncorrelated, measurement error.

Classical Linear Model: The multiple linear regression model under the full set of classical linear model assumptions.

Classical Linear Model (CLM) Assumptions: The ideal set of assumptions for multiple regression analysis: for cross-sectional analysis, Assumptions MLR.1 through MLR.6, and for time series analysis, Assumptions TS.1 through TS.6. The assumptions include linearity in the parameters, no perfect collinearity, the zero conditional mean assumption, homoskedasticity, no serial correlation, and normality of the errors.

Cluster Effect: An unobserved effect that is common to all units, usually people, in the cluster.

Cluster Sample: A sample of natural clusters or groups that usually consist of people.

Clustering: The act of computing standard errors and test statistics that are robust to cluster correlation, either due to cluster sampling or to time series correlation in panel data.

Cochrane-Orcutt (CO) Estimation: A method of estimating a multiple linear regression model with $AR(1)$ errors and strictly exogenous explanatory variables; unlike Prais-Winsten, Cochrane-Orcutt does not use the equation for the first time period.

Coefficient of Determination: *See* R-squared.

Cointegration: The notion that a linear combination of two series, each of which is integrated of order one, is integrated of order zero.

Column Vector: A vector of numbers arranged as a column.

Composite Error Term: In a panel data model, the sum of the time-constant unobserved effect and the idiosyncratic error.

Conditional Distribution: The probability distribution of one random variable, given the values of one or more other random variables.

Conditional Expectation: The expected or average value of one random variable, called the dependent or explained variable, that depends on the values of one or more other variables, called the independent or explanatory variables.

Conditional Forecast: A forecast that assumes the future values of some explanatory variables are known with certainty.

Conditional Median: The median of a response variable conditional on some explanatory variables.

Conditional Variance: The variance of one random variable, given one or more other random variables.

Confidence Interval (CI): A rule used to construct a random interval so that a certain percentage of all data sets, determined by the confidence level, yields an interval that contains the population value.

Confidence Level: The percentage of samples in which we want our confidence interval to contain the population value; 95% is the most common confidence level, but 90% and 99% are also used.

Consistency: An estimator converges in probability to the correct population value as the sample size grows.

Consistent Estimator: An estimator that converges in probability to the population parameter as the sample size grows without bound.

Consistent Test: A test where, under the alternative hypothesis, the probability of rejecting the null hypothesis converges to one as the sample size grows without bound.

Constant Elasticity Model: A model where the elasticity of the dependent variable, with respect to an explanatory variable, is constant; in multiple regression, both variables appear in logarithmic form.

Contemporaneously Homoskedastic: Describes a time series or panel data applications in which the variance of the error term, conditional on the regressors in the same time period, is constant.

Contemporaneously Exogenous: Describes a time series or panel data application in which a regressor is contemporaneously exogenous if it is uncorrelated with the error term in the same time period, although it may be correlated with the errors in other time periods.

Continuous Random Variable: A random variable that takes on any particular value with probability zero.

Control Group: In program evaluation, the group that does not participate in the program.

Control Variable: *See* explanatory variable.

Corner Solution Response: A nonnegative dependent variable that is roughly continuous over strictly positive values but takes on the value zero with some regularity.

Correlated Random Effects: An approach to panel data analysis where the correlation between the unobserved effect and the explanatory variables is modeled, usually as a linear relationship.

Correlation Coefficient: A measure of linear dependence between two random variables that does not depend on units of measurement and is bounded between −1 and 1.

Count Variable: A variable that takes on nonnegative integer values.

Covariance: A measure of linear dependence between two random variables.

Covariance Stationary: A time series process with constant mean and variance where the covariance between any two random variables in the sequence depends only on the distance between them.

Covariate: *See* explanatory variable.

Critical Value: In hypothesis testing, the value against which a test statistic is compared to determine whether or not the null hypothesis is rejected.

Cross-Sectional Data Set: A data set collected by sampling a population at a given point in time.

Cumulative Distribution Function (cdf): A function that gives the probability of a random variable being less than or equal to any specified real number.

Cumulative Effect: At any point in time, the change in a response variable after a permanent increase in an explanatory variable—usually in the context of distributed lag models.

D

Data Censoring: A situation that arises when we do not always observe the outcome on the dependent variable because at an upper (or lower) threshold we only know that the outcome was above (or below) the threshold. (*See also* censored regression model.)

Data Frequency: The interval at which time series data are collected. Yearly, quarterly, and monthly are the most common data frequencies.

Data Mining: The practice of using the same data set to estimate numerous models in a search to find the "best" model.

Davidson-MacKinnon Test: A test that is used for testing a model against a nonnested alternative; it can be implemented as a t test on the fitted values from the competing model.

Degrees of Freedom (*df*): In multiple regression analysis, the number of observations minus the number of estimated parameters.

Denominator Degrees of Freedom: In an F test, the degrees of freedom in the unrestricted model.

Dependent Variable: The variable to be explained in a multiple regression model (and a variety of other models).

Derivative: The slope of a smooth function, as defined using calculus.

Descriptive Statistic: A statistic used to summarize a set of numbers; the sample average, sample median, and sample standard deviation are the most common.

Deseasonalizing: The removing of the seasonal components from a monthly or quarterly time series.

Detrending: The practice of removing the trend from a time series.

Diagonal Matrix: A matrix with zeros for all off-diagonal entries.

Dickey-Fuller Distribution: The limiting distribution of the t statistic in testing the null hypothesis of a unit root.

Dickey-Fuller (DF) Test: A t test of the unit root null hypothesis in an AR(1) model. (*See also* augmented Dickey-Fuller test.)

Difference in Slopes: A description of a model where some slope parameters may differ by group or time period.

Difference-in-Differences Estimator: An estimator that arises in policy analysis with data for two time periods. One version of the estimator applies to independently pooled cross sections and another to panel data sets.

Difference-Stationary Process: A time series sequence that is I(0) in its first differences.

Diminishing Marginal Effect: The marginal effect of an explanatory variable becomes smaller as the value of the explanatory variable increases.

Discrete Random Variable: A random variable that takes on at most a finite or countably infinite number of values.

Distributed Lag Model: A time series model that relates the dependent variable to current and past values of an explanatory variable.

Disturbance: *See* error term.

Downward Bias: The expected value of an estimator is below the population value of the parameter.

Dummy Dependent Variable: *See* binary response model.

Dummy Variable: A variable that takes on the value zero or one.

Dummy Variable Regression: In a panel data setting, the regression that includes a dummy variable for each cross-sectional unit, along with the remaining explanatory variables. It produces the fixed effects estimator.

Dummy Variable Trap: The mistake of including too many dummy variables among the independent variables; it occurs when an overall intercept is in the model and a dummy variable is included for each group.

Duration Analysis: An application of the censored regression model where the dependent variable is time elapsed until a certain event occurs, such as the time before an unemployed person becomes reemployed.

Durbin-Watson (DW) Statistic: A statistic used to test for first order serial correlation in the errors of a time series regression model under the classical linear model assumptions.

Dynamically Complete Model: A time series model where no further lags of either the dependent variable or the explanatory variables help to explain the mean of the dependent variable.

E

Econometric Model: An equation relating the dependent variable to a set of explanatory variables and unobserved disturbances, where unknown population parameters determine the ceteris paribus effect of each explanatory variable.

Economic Model: A relationship derived from economic theory or less formal economic reasoning.

Economic Significance: *See* practical significance.

Elasticity: The percentage change in one variable given a 1% ceteris paribus increase in another variable.

Empirical Analysis: A study that uses data in a formal econometric analysis to test a theory, estimate a relationship, or determine the effectiveness of a policy.

Endogeneity: A term used to describe the presence of an endogenous explanatory variable.

Endogenous Explanatory Variable: An explanatory variable in a multiple regression model that is correlated with the error term, either because of an omitted variable, measurement error, or simultaneity.

Endogenous Sample Selection: Nonrandom sample selection where the selection is related to the dependent variable, either directly or through the error term in the equation.

Endogenous Variables: In simultaneous equations models, variables that are determined by the equations in the system.

Engle-Granger Test: A test of the null hypothesis that two time series are not cointegrated; the statistic is obtained as the Dickey-Fuller statistic using OLS residuals.

Engle-Granger Two-Step Procedure: A two-step method for estimating error correction models whereby the cointegrating parameter is estimated in the first stage, and the error correction parameters are estimated in the second.

Error Correction Model: A time series model in first differences that also contains an error correction term, which works to bring two I(1) series back into long-run equilibrium.

Error Term: The variable in a simple or multiple regression equation that contains unobserved factors which affect the dependent variable. The error term may also include measurement errors in the observed dependent or independent variables.

Error Variance: The variance of the error term in a multiple regression model.

Errors-in-Variables: A situation where either the dependent variable or some independent variables are measured with error.

Estimate: The numerical value taken on by an estimator for a particular sample of data.

Estimator: A rule for combining data to produce a numerical value for a population parameter; the form of the rule does not depend on the particular sample obtained.

Event Study: An econometric analysis of the effects of an event, such as a change in government regulation or economic policy, on an outcome variable.

Excluding a Relevant Variable: In multiple regression analysis, leaving out a variable that has a nonzero partial effect on the dependent variable.

Exclusion Restrictions: Restrictions which state that certain variables are excluded from the model (or have zero population coefficients).

Exogenous Explanatory Variable: An explanatory variable that is uncorrelated with the error term.

Exogenous Sample Selection: A sample selection that either depends on exogenous explanatory variables or is independent of the error term in the equation of interest.

Exogenous Variable: Any variable that is uncorrelated with the error term in the model of interest.

Expected Value: A measure of central tendency in the distribution of a random variable, including an estimator.

Experiment: In probability, a general term used to denote an event whose outcome is uncertain. In econometric analysis, it denotes a situation where data are collected by randomly assigning individuals to control and treatment groups.

Experimental Data: Data that have been obtained by running a controlled experiment.

Experimental Group: *See* treatment group.

Explained Sum of Squares (SSE): The total sample variation of the fitted values in a multiple regression model.

Explained Variable: *See* dependent variable.

Explanatory Variable: In regression analysis, a variable that is used to explain variation in the dependent variable.

Exponential Function: A mathematical function defined for all values that has an increasing slope but a constant proportionate change.

Exponential Smoothing: A simple method of forecasting a variable that involves a weighting of all previous outcomes on that variable.

Exponential Trend: A trend with a constant growth rate.

F

F **Distribution:** The probability distribution obtained by forming the ratio of two independent chi-square random variables, where each has been divided by its degrees of freedom.

F **Random Variable:** A random variable with an *F* distribution.

F **Statistic:** A statistic used to test multiple hypotheses about the parameters in a multiple regression model.

Feasible GLS (FGLS) Estimator: A GLS procedure where variance or correlation parameters are unknown and therefore must first be estimated. (*See also* generalized least squares estimator.)

Finite Distributed Lag (FDL) Model: A dynamic model where one or more explanatory variables are allowed to have lagged effects on the dependent variable.

First Difference: A transformation on a time series constructed by taking the difference of adjacent time periods, where the earlier time period is subtracted from the later time period.

First-Differenced (FD) Equation: In time series or panel data models, an equation where the dependent and independent variables have all been first differenced.

First-Differenced (FD) Estimator: In a panel data setting, the pooled OLS estimator applied to first differences of the data across time.

First Order Autocorrelation: For a time series process ordered chronologically, the correlation coefficient between pairs of adjacent observations.

First Order Conditions: The set of linear equations used to solve for the OLS estimates.

Fitted Values: The estimated values of the dependent variable when the values of the independent variables for each observation are plugged into the OLS regression line.

Fixed Effect: *See* unobserved effect.

Fixed Effects Estimator: For the unobserved effects panel data model, the estimator obtained by applying pooled OLS to a time-demeaned equation.

Fixed Effects Model: An unobserved effects panel data model where the unobserved effects are allowed to be arbitrarily correlated with the explanatory variables in each time period.

Fixed Effects Transformation: For panel data, the time-demeaned data.

Forecast Error: The difference between the actual outcome and the forecast of the outcome.

Forecast Interval: In forecasting, a confidence interval for a yet unrealized future value of a time series variable. (*See also* prediction interval.)

Frisch-Waugh Theorem: The general algebraic result that provides multiple regression analysis with its "partialling out" interpretation.

Functional Form Misspecification: A problem that occurs when a model has omitted functions of the explanatory variables (such as quadratics) or uses the wrong functions of either the dependent variable or some explanatory variables.

G

Gauss-Markov Assumptions: The set of assumptions (Assumptions MLR.1 through MLR.5 or TS.1 through TS.5) under which OLS is BLUE.

Gauss-Markov Theorem: The theorem that states that, under the five Gauss-Markov assumptions (for cross-sectional or time series models), the OLS estimator is BLUE (conditional on the sample values of the explanatory variables).

Generalized Least Squares (GLS) Estimator: An estimator that accounts for a known structure of the error variance (heteroskedasticity), serial correlation pattern in the errors, or both, via a transformation of the original model.

Geometric (or Koyck) Distributed Lag: An infinite distributed lag model where the lag coefficients decline at a geometric rate.

Goodness-of-Fit Measure: A statistic that summarizes how well a set of explanatory variables explains a dependent or response variable.

Granger Causality: A limited notion of causality where past values of one series (x_t) are useful for predicting future values of another series (y_t), after past values of y_t have been controlled for.

Growth Rate: The proportionate change in a time series from the previous period. It may be approximated as the difference in logs or reported in percentage form.

H

Heckit Method: An econometric procedure used to correct for sample selection bias due to incidental truncation or some other form of nonrandomly missing data.

Heterogeneity Bias: The bias in OLS due to omitted heterogeneity (or omitted variables).

Heteroskedasticity: The variance of the error term, given the explanatory variables, is not constant.

Heteroskedasticity of Unknown Form: Heteroskedasticity that may depend on the explanatory variables in an unknown, arbitrary fashion.

Heteroskedasticity-Robust *F* Statistic: An *F*-type statistic that is (asymptotically) robust to heteroskedasticity of unknown form.

Heteroskedasticity-Robust *LM* Statistic: An *LM* statistic that is robust to heteroskedasticity of unknown form.

Heteroskedasticity-Robust Standard Error: A standard error that is (asymptotically) robust to heteroskedasticity of unknown form.

Heteroskedasticity-Robust *t* Statistic: A *t* statistic that is (asymptotically) robust to heteroskedasticity of unknown form.

Highly Persistent: A time series process where outcomes in the distant future are highly correlated with current outcomes.

Homoskedasticity: The errors in a regression model have constant variance conditional on the explanatory variables.

Hypothesis Test: A statistical test of the null, or maintained, hypothesis against an alternative hypothesis.

I

Idempotent Matrix: A (square) matrix where multiplication of the matrix by itself equals itself.

Identification: A population parameter, or set of parameters, can be consistently estimated.

Identified Equation: An equation whose parameters can be consistently estimated, especially in models with endogenous explanatory variables.

Identity Matrix: A square matrix where all diagonal elements are one and all off-diagonal elements are zero.

Idiosyncratic Error: In panel data models, the error that changes over time as well as across units (say, individuals, firms, or cities).

Impact Elasticity: In a distributed lag model, the immediate percentage change in the dependent variable given a 1% increase in the independent variable.

Impact Multiplier: *See* impact propensity.

Impact Propensity: In a distributed lag model, the immediate change in the dependent variable given a one-unit increase in the independent variable.

Incidental Truncation: A sample selection problem whereby one variable, usually the dependent variable, is only observed for certain outcomes of another variable.

Inclusion of an Irrelevant Variable: The including of an explanatory variable in a regression model that has a zero population parameter in estimating an equation by OLS.

Inconsistency: The difference between the probability limit of an estimator and the parameter value.

Inconsistent: Describes an estimator that does not converge (in probability) to the correct population parameter as the sample size grows.

Independent Random Variables: Random variables whose joint distribution is the product of the marginal distributions.

Independent Variable: *See* explanatory variable.

Independently Pooled Cross Section: A data set obtained by pooling independent random samples from different points in time.

Index Number: A statistic that aggregates information on economic activity, such as production or prices.

Infinite Distributed Lag (IDL) Model: A distributed lag model where a change in the explanatory variable can have an impact on the dependent variable into the indefinite future.

Influential Observations: *See* outliers.

Information Set: In forecasting, the set of variables that we can observe prior to forming our forecast.

In-Sample Criteria: Criteria for choosing forecasting models that are based on goodness-of-fit within the sample used to obtain the parameter estimates.

Instrument: *See* instrumental variable.

Instrument Exogeneity: In instrumental variables estimation, the requirement that an instrumental variable is uncorrelated with the error term.

Instrument Relevance: In instrumental variables estimation, the requirement that an instrumental variable helps to partially explain variation in the endogenous explanatory variable.

Instrumental Variable (IV): In an equation with an endogenous explanatory variable, an IV is a variable that does not appear in the equation, is uncorrelated with the error in the equation, and is (partially) correlated with the endogenous explanatory variable.

Instrumental Variables (IV) Estimator: An estimator in a linear model used when instrumental variables are available for one or more endogenous explanatory variables.

Integrated of Order One [I(1)]: A time series process that needs to be first-differenced in order to produce an I(0) process.

Integrated of Order Zero [I(0)]: A stationary, weakly dependent time series process that, when used in regression analysis, satisfies the law of large numbers and the central limit theorem.

Interaction Effect: In multiple regression, the partial effect of one explanatory variable depends on the value of a different explanatory variable.

Interaction Term: An independent variable in a regression model that is the product of two explanatory variables.

Intercept: In the equation of a line, the value of the y variable when the x variable is zero.

Intercept Parameter: The parameter in a multiple linear regression model that gives the expected value of the dependent variable when all the independent variables equal zero.

Intercept Shift: The intercept in a regression model differs by group or time period.

Internet: A global computer network that can be used to access information and download databases.

Interval Estimator: A rule that uses data to obtain lower and upper bounds for a population parameter. (*See also* confidence interval.)

Inverse: For an $n \times n$ matrix, its inverse (if it exists) is the $n \times n$ matrix for which pre- and post-multiplication by the original matrix yields the identity matrix.

Inverse Mills Ratio: A term that can be added to a multiple regression model to remove sample selection bias.

J

Joint Distribution: The probability distribution determining the probabilities of outcomes involving two or more random variables.

Joint Hypotheses Test: A test involving more than one restriction on the parameters in a model.

Jointly Insignificant: Failure to reject, using an F test at a specified significance level, that all coefficients for a group of explanatory variables are zero.

Jointly Statistically Significant: The null hypothesis that two or more explanatory variables have zero population coefficients is rejected at the chosen significance level.

Just Identified Equation: For models with endogenous explanatory variables, an equation that is identified but would not be identified with one fewer instrumental variable.

K

Kurtosis: A measure of the thickness of the tails of a distribution based on the fourth moment of the standardized random variable; the measure is usually compared to the value for the standard normal distribution, which is three.

L

Lag Distribution: In a finite or infinite distributed lag model, the lag coefficients graphed as a function of the lag length.

Lagged Dependent Variable: An explanatory variable that is equal to the dependent variable from an earlier time period.

Lagged Endogenous Variable: In a simultaneous equations model, a lagged value of one of the endogenous variables.

Lagrange Multiplier (LM) Statistic: A test statistic with large-sample justification that can be used to test for omitted variables, heteroskedasticity, and serial correlation, among other model specification problems.

Large Sample Properties: *See* asymptotic properties.

Latent Variable Model: A model where the observed dependent variable is assumed to be a function of an underlying latent, or unobserved, variable.

Law of Iterated Expectations: A result from probability that relates unconditional and conditional expectations.

Law of Large Numbers (LLN): A theorem that says that the average from a random sample converges in probability to the population average; the LLN also holds for stationary and weakly dependent time series.

Leads and Lags Estimator: An estimator of a cointegrating parameter in a regression with I(1) variables, where the current, some past, and some future first differences in the explanatory variable are included as regressors.

Least Absolute Deviations (LAD): A method for estimating the parameters of a multiple regression model based on minimizing the sum of the absolute values of the residuals.

Least Squares Estimator: An estimator that minimizes a sum of squared residuals.

Level-Level Model: A regression model where the dependent variable and the independent variables are in level (or original) form.

Level-Log Model: A regression model where the dependent variable is in level form and (at least some of) the independent variables are in logarithmic form.

Likelihood Ratio Statistic: A statistic that can be used to test single or multiple hypotheses when the constrained and unconstrained models have been estimated by maximum likelihood. The statistic is twice the difference in the unconstrained and constrained log-likelihoods.

Limited Dependent Variable (LDV): A dependent or response variable whose range is restricted in some important way.

Linear Function: A function where the change in the dependent variable, given a one-unit change in an independent variable, is constant.

Linear Probability Model (LPM): A binary response model where the response probability is linear in its parameters.

Linear Time Trend: A trend that is a linear function of time.

Linear Unbiased Estimator: In multiple regression analysis, an unbiased estimator that is a linear function of the outcomes on the dependent variable.

Linearly Independent Vectors: A set of vectors such that no vector can be written as a linear combination of the others in the set.

Log Function: A mathematical function, defined only for strictly positive arguments, with a positive but decreasing slope.

Logarithmic Function: A mathematical function defined for positive arguments that has a positive, but diminishing, slope.

Logit Model: A model for binary response where the response probability is the logit function evaluated at a linear function of the explanatory variables.

Log-Level Model: A regression model where the dependent variable is in logarithmic form and the independent variables are in level (or original) form.

Log-Likelihood Function: The sum of the log-likelihoods, where the log-likelihood for each observation is the log of the density of the dependent variable given the explanatory variables; the log-likelihood function is viewed as a function of the parameters to be estimated.

Log-Log Model: A regression model where the dependent variable and (at least some of) the explanatory variables are in logarithmic form.

Longitudinal Data: *See* panel data.

Long-Run Elasticity: The long-run propensity in a distributed lag model with the dependent and independent variables in logarithmic form; thus, the long-run elasticity is the eventual percentage increase in the explained variable, given a permanent 1% increase in the explanatory variable.

Long-Run Multiplier: *See* long-run propensity.

Long-Run Propensity (LRP): In a distributed lag model, the eventual change in the dependent variable given a permanent, one-unit increase in the independent variable.

Loss Function: A function that measures the loss when a forecast differs from the actual outcome; the most common examples are absolute value loss and squared loss.

M

Marginal Effect: The effect on the dependent variable that results from changing an independent variable by a small amount.

Martingale: A time series process whose expected value, given all past outcomes on the series, simply equals the most recent value.

Martingale Difference Sequence: The first difference of a martingale. It is unpredictable (or has a zero mean), given past values of the sequence.

Matched Pair Sample: A sample where each observation is matched with another, as in a sample consisting of a husband and wife or a set of two siblings.

Matrix: An array of numbers.

Matrix Multiplication: An algorithm for multiplying together two conformable matrices.

Matrix Notation: A convenient mathematical notation, grounded in matrix algebra, for expressing and manipulating the multiple regression model.

Maximum Likelihood Estimation (MLE): A broadly applicable estimation method where the parameter estimates are chosen to maximize the log-likelihood function.

Maximum Likelihood Estimator: An estimator that maximizes the (log of the) likelihood function.

Mean: *See* expected value.

Mean Absolute Error (MAE): A performance measure in forecasting, computed as the average of the absolute values of the forecast errors.

Mean Independent: The key requirement in multiple regression analysis, which says the unobserved error has a mean that does not change across subsets of the population defined by different values of the explanatory variables.

Mean Squared Error (MSE): The expected squared distance that an estimator is from the population value; it equals the variance plus the square of any bias.

Measurement Error: The difference between an observed variable and the variable that belongs in a multiple regression equation.

Median: In a probability distribution, it is the value where there is a 50% chance of being below the value and a 50% chance of being above it. In a sample of numbers, it is the middle value after the numbers have been ordered.

Method of Moments Estimator: An estimator obtained by using the sample analog of population moments; ordinary least squares and two stage least squares are both method of moments estimators.

Micronumerosity: A term introduced by Arthur Goldberger to describe properties of econometric estimators with small sample sizes.

Minimum Variance Unbiased Estimator: An estimator with the smallest variance in the class of all unbiased estimators.

Missing at Random: In multiple regression analysis, a missing data mechanism where the reason data are missing may be correlated with the explanatory variables but is independent of the error term.

Missing Completely at Random (MCAR): In multiple regression analysis, a missing data mechanism where the reason data are missing is statistically independent of the values of the explanatory variables as well as the unobserved error.

Missing Data: A data problem that occurs when we do not observe values on some variables for certain observations (individuals, cities, time periods, and so on) in the sample.

Misspecification Analysis: The process of determining likely biases that can arise from omitted variables, measurement error, simultaneity, and other kinds of model misspecification.

Moving Average Process of Order One [MA(1)]: A time series process generated as a linear function of the current value and one lagged value of a zero-mean, constant variance, uncorrelated stochastic process.

Multicollinearity: A term that refers to correlation among the independent variables in a multiple regression model; it is usually invoked when some correlations are "large," but an actual magnitude is not well defined.

Multiple Hypotheses Test: A test of a null hypothesis involving more than one restriction on the parameters.

Multiple Linear Regression (MLR) Model: A model linear in its parameters, where the dependent variable is a function of independent variables plus an error term.

Multiple Regression Analysis: A type of analysis that is used to describe estimation of and inference in the multiple linear regression model.

Multiple Restrictions: More than one restriction on the parameters in an econometric model.

Multiple-Step-Ahead Forecast: A time series forecast of more than one period into the future.

Multiplicative Measurement Error: Measurement error where the observed variable is the product of the true unobserved variable and a positive measurement error.

Multivariate Normal Distribution: A distribution for multiple random variables where each linear combination of the random variables has a univariate (one-dimensional) normal distribution.

N

n-R-Squared Statistic: *See* Lagrange multiplier statistic.

Natural Experiment: A situation where the economic environment—sometimes summarized by an explanatory variable—exogenously changes, perhaps inadvertently, due to a policy or institutional change.

Natural Logarithm: *See* logarithmic function.

Nominal Variable: A variable measured in nominal or current dollars.

Nonexperimental Data: Data that have not been obtained through a controlled experiment.

Nonlinear Function: A function whose slope is not constant.

Nonnested Models: Two (or more) models where no model can be written as a special case of the other by imposing restrictions on the parameters.

Nonrandom Sample: A sample obtained other than by sampling randomly from the population of interest.

Nonstationary Process: A time series process whose joint distributions are not constant across different epochs.

Normal Distribution: A probability distribution commonly used in statistics and econometrics for modeling a population. Its probability distribution function has a bell shape.

Normality Assumption: The classical linear model assumption which states that the error (or dependent variable) has a normal distribution, conditional on the explanatory variables.

Null Hypothesis: In classical hypothesis testing, we take this hypothesis as true and require the data to provide substantial evidence against it.

Numerator Degrees of Freedom: In an *F* test, the number of restrictions being tested.

O

Observational Data: *See* nonexperimental data.

OLS: *See* ordinary least squares.

OLS Intercept Estimate: The intercept in an OLS regression line.

OLS Regression Line: The equation relating the predicted value of the dependent variable to the independent variables, where the parameter estimates have been obtained by OLS.

OLS Slope Estimate: A slope in an OLS regression line.

Omitted Variable Bias: The bias that arises in the OLS estimators when a relevant variable is omitted from the regression.

Omitted Variables: One or more variables, which we would like to control for, have been omitted in estimating a regression model.

One-Sided Alternative: An alternative hypothesis that states that the parameter is greater than (or less than) the value hypothesized under the null.

One-Step-Ahead Forecast: A time series forecast one period into the future.

One-Tailed Test: A hypothesis test against a one-sided alternative.

Online Databases: Databases that can be accessed via a computer network.

Online Search Services: Computer software that allows the Internet or databases on the Internet to be searched by topic, name, title, or keywords.

Order Condition: A necessary condition for identifying the parameters in a model with one or more endogenous explanatory variables: the total number of exogenous variables must be at least as great as the total number of explanatory variables.

Ordinal Variable: A variable where the ordering of the values conveys information but the magnitude of the values does not.

Ordinary Least Squares (OLS): A method for estimating the parameters of a multiple linear regression model. The ordinary least squares estimates are obtained by minimizing the sum of squared residuals.

Outliers: Observations in a data set that are substantially different from the bulk of the data, perhaps because of errors or because some data are generated by a different model than most of the other data.

Out-of-Sample Criteria: Criteria used for choosing forecasting models which are based on a part of the sample that was not used in obtaining parameter estimates.

Over Controlling: In a multiple regression model, including explanatory variables that should not be held fixed when studying the ceteris paribus effect of one or more other explanatory variables; this can occur when variables that are themselves outcomes of an intervention or a policy are included among the regressors.

Overall Significance of a Regression: A test of the joint significance of all explanatory variables appearing in a multiple regression equation.

Overdispersion: In modeling a count variable, the variance is larger than the mean.

Overidentified Equation: In models with endogenous explanatory variables, an equation where the number of instrumental variables is strictly greater than the number of endogenous explanatory variables.

Overidentifying Restrictions: The extra moment conditions that come from having more instrumental variables than endogenous explanatory variables in a linear model.

Overspecifying a Model: *See* inclusion of an irrelevant variable.

P

***p*-Value:** The smallest significance level at which the null hypothesis can be rejected. Equivalently, the largest significance level at which the null hypothesis cannot be rejected.

Pairwise Uncorrelated Random Variables: A set of two or more random variables where each pair is uncorrelated.

Panel Data: A data set constructed from repeated cross sections over time. With a *balanced* panel, the same units appear in each time period. With an *unbalanced* panel, some units do not appear in each time period, often due to attrition.

Parameter: An unknown value that describes a population relationship.

Parsimonious Model: A model with as few parameters as possible for capturing any desired features.

Partial Derivative: For a smooth function of more than one variable, the slope of the function in one direction.

Partial Effect: The effect of an explanatory variable on the dependent variable, holding other factors in the regression model fixed.

Partial Effect at the Average (PEA): In models with non-constant partial effects, the partial effect evaluated at the average values of the explanatory variables.

Percent Correctly Predicted: In a binary response model, the percentage of times the prediction of zero or one coincides with the actual outcome.

Percentage Change: The proportionate change in a variable, multiplied by 100.

Percentage Point Change: The change in a variable that is measured as a percentage.

Perfect Collinearity: In multiple regression, one independent variable is an exact linear function of one or more other independent variables.

Plug-In Solution to the Omitted Variables Problem: A proxy variable is substituted for an unobserved omitted variable in an OLS regression.

Point Forecast: The forecasted value of a future outcome.

Poisson Distribution: A probability distribution for count variables.

Poisson Regression Model: A model for a count dependent variable where the dependent variable, conditional on the explanatory variables, is nominally assumed to have a Poisson distribution.

Policy Analysis: An empirical analysis that uses econometric methods to evaluate the effects of a certain policy.

Pooled Cross Section: A data configuration where independent cross sections, usually collected at different points in time, are combined to produce a single data set.

Pooled OLS Estimation: OLS estimation with independently pooled cross sections, panel data, or cluster samples, where the observations are pooled across time (or group) as well as across the cross-sectional units.

Population: A well-defined group (of people, firms, cities, and so on) that is the focus of a statistical or econometric analysis.

Population Model: A model, especially a multiple linear regression model, that describes a population.

Population *R*-Squared: In the population, the fraction of the variation in the dependent variable that is explained by the explanatory variables.

Population Regression Function: *See* conditional expectation.

Positive Definite: A symmetric matrix such that all quadratic forms, except the trivial one that must be zero, are strictly positive.

Positive Semi-Definite: A symmetric matrix such that all quadratic forms are nonnegative.

Power of a Test: The probability of rejecting the null hypothesis when it is false; the power depends on the values of the population parameters under the alternative.

Practical Significance: The practical or economic importance of an estimate, which is measured by its sign and magnitude, as opposed to its statistical significance.

Prais-Winsten (PW) Estimation: A method of estimating a multiple linear regression model with AR(1) errors and strictly exogenous explanatory variables; unlike Cochrane-Orcutt, Prais-Winsten uses the equation for the first time period in estimation.

Predetermined Variable: In a simultaneous equations model, either a lagged endogenous variable or a lagged exogenous variable.

Predicted Variable: *See* dependent variable.

Prediction: The estimate of an outcome obtained by plugging specific values of the explanatory variables into an estimated model, usually a multiple regression model.

Prediction Error: The difference between the actual outcome and a prediction of that outcome.

Prediction Interval: A confidence interval for an unknown outcome on a dependent variable in a multiple regression model.

Predictor Variable: *See* explanatory variable.

Probability Density Function (pdf): A function that, for discrete random variables, gives the probability that the random variable takes on each value; for continuous random variables, the area under the pdf gives the probability of various events.

Probability Limit: The value to which an estimator converges as the sample size grows without bound.

Probit Model: A model for binary responses where the response probability is the standard normal cdf evaluated at a linear function of the explanatory variables.

Program Evaluation: An analysis of a particular private or public program using econometric methods to obtain the causal effect of the program.

Proportionate Change: The change in a variable relative to its initial value; mathematically, the change divided by the initial value.

Proxy Variable: An observed variable that is related but not identical to an unobserved explanatory variable in multiple regression analysis.

Pseudo *R*-Squared: Any number of goodness-of-fit measures for limited dependent variable models.

Q

Quadratic Form: A mathematical function where the vector argument both pre- and post-multiplies a square, symmetric matrix.

Quadratic Functions: Functions that contain squares of one or more explanatory variables; they capture diminishing or increasing effects on the dependent variable.

Qualitative Variable: A variable describing a nonquantitative feature of an individual, a firm, a city, and so on.

Quasi-Demeaned Data: In random effects estimation for panel data, it is the original data in each time period minus a fraction of the time average; these calculations are done for each cross-sectional observation.

Quasi-Differenced Data: In estimating a regression model with AR(1) serial correlation, it is the difference between the current time period and a multiple of the previous time period, where the multiple is the parameter in the AR(1) model.

Quasi-Experiment: *See* natural experiment.

Quasi-Likelihood Ratio Statistic: A modification of the likelihood ratio statistic that accounts for possible distributional misspecification, as in a Poisson regression model.

Quasi-Maximum Likelihood Estimation (QMLE): Maximum likelihood estimation where the log-likelihood function may not correspond to the actual conditional distribution of the dependent variable.

R

R-Bar Squared: *See* adjusted *R*-squared.

R-Squared: In a multiple regression model, the proportion of the total sample variation in the dependent variable that is explained by the independent variable.

R-Squared Form of the *F* Statistic: The *F* statistic for testing exclusion restrictions expressed in terms of the *R*-squareds from the restricted and unrestricted models.

Random Coefficient (Slope) Model: A multiple regression model where the slope parameters are allowed to depend on unobserved unit-specific variables.

Random Effects Estimator: A feasible GLS estimator in the unobserved effects model where the unobserved effect is assumed to be uncorrelated with the explanatory variables in each time period.

Random Effects Model: The unobserved effects panel data model where the unobserved effect is assumed to be uncorrelated with the explanatory variables in each time period.

Random Sample: A sample obtained by sampling randomly from the specified population.

Random Sampling: A sampling scheme whereby each observation is drawn at random from the population. In particular, no unit is more likely to be selected than any other unit, and each draw is independent of all other draws.

Random Variable: A variable whose outcome is uncertain.

Random Vector: A vector consisting of random variables.

Random Walk: A time series process where next period's value is obtained as this period's value, plus an independent (or at least an uncorrelated) error term.

Random Walk with Drift: A random walk that has a constant (or drift) added in each period.

Rank Condition: A sufficient condition for identification of a model with one or more endogenous explanatory variables.

Rank of a Matrix: The number of linearly independent columns in a matrix.

Rational Distributed Lag (RDL) Model: A type of infinite distributed lag model where the lag distribution depends on relatively few parameters.

Real Variable: A monetary value measured in terms of a base period.

Reduced Form Equation: A linear equation where an endogenous variable is a function of exogenous variables and unobserved errors.

Reduced Form Error: The error term appearing in a reduced form equation.

Reduced Form Parameters: The parameters appearing in a reduced form equation.

Regressand: *See* dependent variable.

Regression Specification Error Test (RESET): A general test for functional form in a multiple regression model; it is an *F* test of joint significance of the squares, cubes, and perhaps higher powers of the fitted values from the initial OLS estimation.

Regression through the Origin: Regression analysis where the intercept is set to zero; the slopes are obtained by minimizing the sum of squared residuals, as usual.

Regressor: *See* explanatory variable.

Rejection Region: The set of values of a test statistic that leads to rejecting the null hypothesis.

Rejection Rule: In hypothesis testing, the rule that determines when the null hypothesis is rejected in favor of the alternative hypothesis.

Relative Change: *See* proportionate change.

Resampling Method: A technique for approximating standard errors (and distributions of test statistics) whereby a series of samples are obtained from the original data set and estimates are computed for each subsample.

Residual: The difference between the actual value and the fitted (or predicted) value; there is a residual for each observation in the sample used to obtain an OLS regression line.

Residual Analysis: A type of analysis that studies the sign and size of residuals for particular observations after a multiple regression model has been estimated.

Residual Sum of Squares: *See* sum of squared residuals.

Response Probability: In a binary response model, the probability that the dependent variable takes on the value one, conditional on explanatory variables.

Response Variable: *See* dependent variable.

Restricted Model: In hypothesis testing, the model obtained after imposing all of the restrictions required under the null.

Retrospective Data: Data collected based on past, rather than current, information.

Root Mean Squared Error (RMSE): Another name for the standard error of the regression in multiple regression analysis.

Row Vector: A vector of numbers arranged as a row.

S

Sample Average: The sum of n numbers divided by n; a measure of central tendency.

Sample Correlation: For outcomes on two random variables, the sample covariance divided by the product of the sample standard deviations.

Sample Correlation Coefficient: An estimate of the (population) correlation coefficient from a sample of data.

Sample Covariance: An unbiased estimator of the population covariance between two random variables.

Sample Regression Function (SRF): *See* OLS regression line.

Sample Selection Bias: Bias in the OLS estimator which is induced by using data that arise from endogenous sample selection.

Sample Standard Deviation: A consistent estimator of the population standard deviation.

Sample Variance: An unbiased, consistent estimator of the population variance.

Sampling Distribution: The probability distribution of an estimator over all possible sample outcomes.

Sampling Standard Deviation: The standard deviation of an estimator, that is, the standard deviation of a sampling distribution.

Sampling Variance: The variance in the sampling distribution of an estimator; it measures the spread in the sampling distribution.

Scalar Multiplication: The algorithm for multiplying a scalar (number) by a vector or matrix.

Scalar Variance-Covariance Matrix: A variance-covariance matrix where all off-diagonal terms are zero and the diagonal terms are the same positive constant.

Score Statistic: *See* Lagrange multiplier statistic.

Seasonal Dummy Variables: A set of dummy variables used to denote the quarters or months of the year.

Seasonality: A feature of monthly or quarterly time series where the average value differs systematically by season of the year.

Seasonally Adjusted: Monthly or quarterly time series data where some statistical procedure—possibly regression on seasonal dummy variables—has been used to remove the seasonal component.

Selected Sample: A sample of data obtained not by random sampling but by selecting on the basis of some observed or unobserved characteristic.

Self-Selection: Deciding on an action based on the likely benefits, or costs, of taking that action.

Semi-Elasticity: The percentage change in the dependent variable given a one-unit increase in an independent variable.

Sensitivity Analysis: The process of checking whether the estimated effects and statistical significance of key explanatory variables are sensitive to inclusion of other explanatory variables, functional form, dropping of potentially outlying observations, or different methods of estimation.

Sequentially Exogenous: A feature of an explanatory variable in time series (or panel data) models where the error term in the current time period has a zero mean conditional on all current and past explanatory variables; a weaker version is stated in terms of zero correlations.

Serial Correlation: In a time series or panel data model, correlation between the errors in different time periods.

Serial Correlation-Robust Standard Error: A standard error for an estimator that is (asymptotically) valid whether or not the errors in the model are serially correlated.

Serially Uncorrelated: The errors in a time series or panel data model are pairwise uncorrelated across time.

Short-Run Elasticity: The impact propensity in a distributed lag model when the dependent and independent variables are in logarithmic form.

Significance Level: The probability of a Type I error in hypothesis testing.

Simple Linear Regression Model: A model where the dependent variable is a linear function of a single independent variable, plus an error term.

Simultaneity: A term that means at least one explanatory variable in a multiple linear regression model is determined jointly with the dependent variable.

Simultaneity Bias: The bias that arises from using OLS to estimate an equation in a simultaneous equations model.

Simultaneous Equations Model (SEM): A model that jointly determines two or more endogenous variables, where each endogenous variable can be a function of other endogenous variables as well as of exogenous variables and an error term.

Skewness: A measure of how far a distribution is from being symmetric, based on the third moment of the standardized random variable.

Slope: In the equation of a line, the change in the y variable when the x variable increases by one.

Slope Parameter: The coefficient on an independent variable in a multiple regression model.

Smearing Estimate: A retransformation method particularly useful for predicting the level of a response variable when a linear model has been estimated for the natural log of the response variable.

Spreadsheet: Computer software used for entering and manipulating data.

Spurious Correlation: A correlation between two variables that is not due to causality, but perhaps to the dependence of the two variables on another unobserved factor.

Spurious Regression Problem: A problem that arises when regression analysis indicates a relationship between two or more unrelated time series processes simply because each has a trend, is an integrated time series (such as a random walk), or both.

Square Matrix: A matrix with the same number of rows as columns.

Stable AR(1) Process: An AR(1) process where the parameter on the lag is less than one in absolute value. The correlation between two random variables in the sequence declines to zero at a geometric rate as the distance between the random variables increases, and so a stable AR(1) process is weakly dependent.

Standard Deviation: A common measure of spread in the distribution of a random variable.

Standard Deviation of $\hat{\beta}_j$: A common measure of spread in the sampling distribution of $\hat{\beta}_j$.

Standard Error: Generically, an estimate of the standard deviation of an estimator.

Standard Error of $\hat{\beta}_j$: An estimate of the standard deviation in the sampling distribution of $\hat{\beta}_j$.

Standard Error of the Estimate: *See* standard error of the regression.

Standard Error of the Regression (SER): In multiple regression analysis, the estimate of the standard deviation of the population error, obtained as the square root of the sum of squared residuals over the degrees of freedom.

Standard Normal Distribution: The normal distribution with mean zero and variance one.

Standardized Coefficients: Regression coefficients that measure the standard deviation change in the dependent variable given a one standard deviation increase in an independent variable.

Standardized Random Variable: A random variable transformed by subtracting off its expected value and dividing the result by its standard deviation; the new random variable has mean zero and standard deviation one.

Static Model: A time series model where only contemporaneous explanatory variables affect the dependent variable.

Stationary Process: A time series process where the marginal and all joint distributions are invariant across time.

Statistical Inference: The act of testing hypotheses about population parameters.

Statistical Significance: The importance of an estimate as measured by the size of a test statistic, usually a t statistic.

Statistically Different from Zero: *See* statistically significant.

Statistically Insignificant: Failure to reject the null hypothesis that a population parameter is equal to zero, at the chosen significance level.

Statistically Significant: Rejecting the null hypothesis that a parameter is equal to zero against the specified alternative, at the chosen significance level.

Stochastic Process: A sequence of random variables indexed by time.

Stratified Sampling: A nonrandom sampling scheme whereby the population is first divided into several non-overlapping, exhaustive strata, and then random samples are taken from within each stratum.

Strict Exogeneity: An assumption that holds in a time series or panel data model when the explanatory variables are strictly exogenous.

Strictly Exogenous: A feature of explanatory variables in a time series or panel data model where the error term at any time period has zero expectation, conditional on the explanatory variables in all time periods; a less restrictive version is stated in terms of zero correlations.

Strongly Dependent: *See* highly persistent.

Structural Equation: An equation derived from economic theory or from less formal economic reasoning.

Structural Error: The error term in a structural equation, which could be one equation in a simultaneous equations model.

Structural Parameters: The parameters appearing in a structural equation.

Studentized Residuals: The residuals computed by excluding each observation, in turn, from the estimation, divided by the estimated standard deviation of the error.

Sum of Squared Residuals (SSR): In multiple regression analysis, the sum of the squared OLS residuals across all observations.

Summation Operator: A notation, denoted by Σ, used to define the summing of a set of numbers.

Symmetric Distribution: A probability distribution characterized by a probability density function that is symmetric around its median value, which must also be the mean value (whenever the mean exists).

Symmetric Matrix: A (square) matrix that equals its transpose.

T

t **Distribution:** The distribution of the ratio of a standard normal random variable and the square root of an independent chi-square random variable, where the chi-square random variable is first divided by its *df*.

t **Ratio:** *See t* statistic.

t **Statistic:** The statistic used to test a single hypothesis about the parameters in an econometric model.

Test Statistic: A rule used for testing hypotheses where each sample outcome produces a numerical value.

Text Editor: Computer software that can be used to edit text files.

Text (ASCII) File: A universal file format that can be transported across numerous computer platforms.

Time-Demeaned Data: Panel data where, for each cross-sectional unit, the average over time is subtracted from the data in each time period.

Time Series Data: Data collected over time on one or more variables.

Time Series Process: *See* stochastic process.

Time Trend: A function of time that is the expected value of a trending time series process.

Tobit Model: A model for a dependent variable that takes on the value zero with positive probability but is roughly continuously distributed over strictly positive values. (*See also* corner solution response.)

Top Coding: A form of data censoring where the value of a variable is not reported when it is above a given threshold; we only know that it is at least as large as the threshold.

Total Sum of Squares (SST): The total sample variation in a dependent variable about its sample average.

Trace of a Matrix: For a square matrix, the sum of its diagonal elements.

Transpose: For any matrix, the new matrix obtained by interchanging its rows and columns.

Treatment Group: In program evaluation, the group that participates in the program.

Trending Process: A time series process whose expected value is an increasing or a decreasing function of time.

Trend-Stationary Process: A process that is stationary once a time trend has been removed; it is usually implicit that the detrended series is weakly dependent.

True Model: The actual population model relating the dependent variable to the relevant independent variables, plus a disturbance, where the zero conditional mean assumption holds.

Truncated Normal Regression Model: The special case of the truncated regression model where the underlying population model satisfies the classical linear model assumptions.

Truncated Regression Model: A linear regression model for cross-sectional data in which the sampling scheme entirely excludes, on the basis of outcomes on the dependent variable, part of the population.

Two-Sided Alternative: An alternative where the population parameter can be either less than or greater than the value stated under the null hypothesis.

Two Stage Least Squares (2SLS) Estimator: An instrumental variables estimator where the IV for an endogenous explanatory variable is obtained as the fitted value from regressing the endogenous explanatory variable on all exogenous variables.

Two-Tailed Test: A test against a two-sided alternative.

Type I Error: A rejection of the null hypothesis when it is true.

Type II Error: The failure to reject the null hypothesis when it is false.

U

Unbalanced Panel: A panel data set where certain years (or periods) of data are missing for some cross-sectional units.

Unbiased Estimator: An estimator whose expected value (or mean of its sampling distribution) equals the population value (regardless of the population value).

Uncentered *R***-squared:** The *R*-squared computed without subtracting the sample average of the dependent variable when obtaining the total sum of squares (SST).

Unconditional Forecast: A forecast that does not rely on knowing, or assuming values for, future explanatory variables.

Uncorrelated Random Variables: Random variables that are not linearly related.

Underspecifying a Model: *See* excluding a relevant variable.

Unidentified Equation: An equation with one or more endogenous explanatory variables where sufficient instrumental variables do not exist to identify the parameters.

Unit Root Process: A highly persistent time series process where the current value equals last period's value, plus a weakly dependent disturbance.

Unobserved Effect: In a panel data model, an unobserved variable in the error term that does not change over time. For cluster samples, an unobserved variable that is common to all units in the cluster.

Unobserved Effects Model: A model for panel data or cluster samples where the error term contains an unobserved effect.

Unobserved Heterogeneity: *See* unobserved effect.

Unrestricted Model: In hypothesis testing, the model that has no restrictions placed on its parameters.

Upward Bias: The expected value of an estimator is greater than the population parameter value.

V

Variance: A measure of spread in the distribution of a random variable.

Variance-Covariance Matrix: For a random vector, the positive semi-definite matrix defined by putting the variances down the diagonal and the covariances in the appropriate off-diagonal entries.

Variance-Covariance Matrix of the OLS Estimator: The matrix of sampling variances and covariances for the vector of OLS coefficients.

Variance Inflation Factor: In multiple regression analysis under the Gauss-Markov assumptions, the term in the sampling variance affected by correlation among the explanatory variables.

Variance of the Prediction Error: The variance in the error that arises when predicting a future value of the dependent variable based on an estimated multiple regression equation.

Vector Autoregressive (VAR) Model: A model for two or more time series where each variable is modeled as a linear function of past values of all variables, plus disturbances that have zero means given all past values of the observed variables.

W

Wald Statistic: A general test statistic for testing hypotheses in a variety of econometric settings; typically, the Wald statistic has an asymptotic chi-square distribution.

Weak Instruments: Instrumental variables that are only slightly correlated with the relevant endogenous explanatory variable or variables.

Weakly Dependent: A term that describes a time series process where some measure of dependence between random variables at two points in time—such as correlation—diminishes as the interval between the two points in time increases.

Weighted Least Squares (WLS) Estimator: An estimator used to adjust for a known form of heteroskedasticity, where each squared residual is weighted by the inverse of the (estimated) variance of the error.

White Test: A test for heteroskedasticity that involves regressing the squared OLS residuals on the OLS fitted values and on the squares of the fitted values; in its most general form, the squared OLS residuals are regressed on the explanatory variables, the squares of the explanatory variables, and all the nonredundant interactions of the explanatory variables.

Within Estimator: *See* fixed effects estimator.

Within Transformation: *See* fixed effects transformation.

Y

Year Dummy Variables: For data sets with a time series component, dummy (binary) variables equal to one in the relevant year and zero in all other years.

Z

Zero Conditional Mean Assumption: A key assumption used in multiple regression analysis that states that, given any values of the explanatory variables, the expected value of the error equals zero. (*See* Assumptions MLR.4, TS.3, and TS.3' in the text.)

Zero Matrix: A matrix where all entries are zero.

Zero-One Variable: *See* dummy variable.

Index

Numbers

A

U